GREAT BRITAIN AND THE
UNITED STATES

A History of
Anglo-American Relations
(1783–1952)

GREAT BRITAIN
AND THE
UNITED STATES

A History of
Anglo-American Relations
(1783–1952)

By H. C. ALLEN

ARCHON BOOKS
1969

First published 1954
Odhams Press, Limited
Reprinted 1969 with permission

SBN: 208 00758 X
Printed in the United States of America
Library of Congress Library Card Number: 69-11550

PREFACE TO 1969 EDITION

THIS book, first published in 1954 in Britain and 1955 in the United States, has now been out of print for some years on both sides of the Atlantic, and I am delighted at the opportunity to have it reprinted by Archon Books.

As this is a reprint rather than a full new edition, it is impossible to alter the actual text, so that I cannot take advantage of the passage of time and the appearance of new works of scholarship in the field to bring the volume up to date. It must stand as it was, warts and all.

But I have prepared a brief list of errata and addenda. This does not contain any substantial, let alone more refined, changes in interpretation, but rectifies a few misprints and a number of misstatements and factual errors. I have, however, been able to add a selective bibliography of the major books and articles on the subject which have been published in the last fifteen years, so that readers may, if they wish, themselves review the alterations and additions to our knowledge of the background of Anglo-American relations.

I hope that in this form the volume may still be of value to students of this rather special relationship, which, though long and frequently declared to be dead, obstinately refuses to lie down.

London University   H. C. ALLEN
Institute of United States Studies
July, 1968.

PREFACE

I HAVE not written this book purely as an academic study: I have written it because I believe in the necessity for cordial Anglo-American relations. That belief arises not only from a study of their history but also from a warm affection for the American people. Here, plainly, is a bias against which the reader should be warned, although he will doubtless become aware of it soon enough in any case. My object has been to tell the story of the Anglo-American relationship in the past in order that we may the better guide its course in the future.

I began serious work on the project in January, 1949, and I completed my first draft in December, 1952. I handed the final manuscript to my publishers in July, 1953. There are always risks in the writing of contemporary history: nevertheless, I decided that the political narrative should come forward to the end of 1952, which was, with the end of twenty years of Democratic rule, an obvious *terminus ad quem*. I resolved, however, that in the interval before publication I would not make any alterations of substance in the final chapter, and I have not done so. Furthermore, I have refrained from bringing the social and cultural analysis more up to date than the inter-war years, because it is not a satisfactory subject for contemporary treatment.

I have tried to write this history, despite its length, in such a way as to interest the general reader. It is not a work of original research based upon primary sources, for there is no need of such a book; excellent studies of many aspects of the subject are already in existence. My debt to the authors of these is correspondingly great. It is not possible to mention them all here, but I hope that a full recognition of my deep obligations to them is made in the footnotes and in the bibliography.

I would call the attention of the reader to the fact that, throughout the text, numerical footnotes are exclusively used for source references, so that the eye need not be distracted by them; explanatory footnotes, which have been reduced to a minimum, are indicated by some other symbol, such as the asterisk. For the most part I have used the orthodox typographical conventions, such as three dots for omissions, but I should mention that I have not used dots at the end or beginning of quotations, except for purposes of emphasis; omissions are there indicated by the position of punctuation points (either within or without the quotation marks) and by capitalization or otherwise (with or without the use of the square bracket). An alphabetical guide to abbreviations which are used very frequently in the footnotes is given, and also a list of the owners of copyright, for whose permission to publish I am most grateful.

I am very conscious that my limited experience as an historian does not really qualify me to attempt a work of such ambitious range, but I feel that the need for it is great enough to compensate for this. To the best of my knowledge, no full-scale history of Anglo-American relations has been published for almost thirty years, and no first-class one since W. A. Dunning's *The British Empire and the United States,* which was produced for the centenary of the Treaty of Ghent in 1914. Yet immense and fundamental changes have taken place in the relations of the two peoples since that date. There has been abundant work on American-Canadian relations, and one recent and brilliant overall study of this subject, J. B. Brebner's *North Atlantic Triangle* (1945), but this is primarily concerned with the interaction between the peoples of British North America and the United States, and leaves ample scope for a book on the transatlantic relationship.

I should like to make particular mention of certain of the books upon which I have leaned heavily. Among general works, I would acknowledge my debt especially to T. A. Bailey's stimulating *Diplomatic History of the American People*; S. F. Bemis's comprehensive *Diplomatic History of the United States*; Alan Nevin's invaluable *America Through British Eyes*; R. B. Mowat's *Americans in England*; and Beckles Willson's *America's Ambassadors to England* and *Friendly Relations.* Among detailed monographs I would particularly mention A. L. Burt's clear and cogent *The United States, Great Britain and British North America, 1783-1814*, E. D. Adams's classic *Great Britain and the American Civil War*, and Lionel M. Gelber's intensive study of *The Rise of Anglo-American Friendship.* To recent works, such as Robert E. Sherwood's *The White House Papers of Harry L. Hopkins*, and, above all, Sir Winston Churchill's *The Second World War*, my debt is peculiarly great, since they partake of the nature of both secondary and primary authorities.

In the course of the last part of the book I have—necessarily—discussed, and criticized where I felt it needful, the actions of many living persons. Of this I can only say, in the words of Burke, "I speak with the freedom of history and I hope without offence."

I should like to convey my thanks to the Warden of Rhodes House and to the Librarians of Rhodes House Library for their unfailing courtesy and help. I wish to express my gratitude to the Commonwealth Fund of New York, by whose generosity I was enabled to pay my first visit to the United States, and to the Rector and Fellows of my College, through whose tolerance of my administrative and tutorial short-comings during the past five years I have been able to find the time to write this book. I appreciate warmly the assistance of Dr. A. L. Rowse of All Souls' College, Oxford, and the help of Mr. G. C. Piper and other members of Odhams Press Book Department. I am grateful to Miss M. Andrews for her aid in the last stages of producing the work, and to Miss M. Welch for hers with part of the manuscript. I should like also to acknowledge my great debt to Mr. M. G. Price, who pain-stakingly checked all the references in the book.

I wish to thank the many friends in Australia who gave me the benefit of their advice and assistance, particularly Professor O. H. K. Spate, Mr. W. D. Borrie, Mr. J. Jennings, Miss K. Jupp, Mr. C. Kiernan, and, most especially, Professor R. M. Hartwell.

I am deeply beholden to my friend Max Beloff for his thorough, stimulating and most helpful criticism of my typescript, and I should like to express my gratitude to Professor D. W. Brogan for his kind encouragement. My most warm thanks are due also to my one-time tutor and ever-welcome mentor, R. B. McCallum; to my long-suffering neighbour and wise counsellor, Professor H. J. Habakkuk; to my colleague V. H. H. Green for his sage and helpful advice; to my old friend C. P. Hill for consenting to read through the proofs of the work and to give me his most useful comments; and to many others for their manifold forms of assistance.

They have enabled me to avoid many mistakes: those that I have made are all my own.

Above all, I owe thanks to my dear wife, who not only typed well over half a million of my frequently illegible words in less than twelve months, most of them while managing a household containing two small children, but also bore patiently through a number of years the heavy burden of my pre-occupation.

Canberra,   H. C. ALLEN
April, 1954.

ERRATA AND ADDENDA

page 35, line 18	*For* "the Great American Desert" *read* "the great desert between the Rockies and the Sierra Nevada"
page 40, line 9	*For* "Guadelupe" *read* "Guadalupe"
Page 41, line 15	*Under "Great Britain"* add "82%"
page 41, footnote†	*For* "Figure not yet available" *substitute* "England, Wales and Scotland."
page 56, line 22	*For* "a proportion . . . each case" *read* "being about a third, a quarter and a third respectively."
page 56, line 23	*For* "approximately one-third" *read* "a third to a quarter"
page 59, line 28	*For* "the latter's *read* "her total"
page 85, line 17	*For* "by which time" *read* "and by 1875"
page 90, line 20	*For* "Shay" *read* "Shays"
page 92, footnote	*Insert* "1"
page 102, line 22	*For* "Between 1891 . . . of all" *read* "Between 1841 and 1900 some seven-tenths of all"
page 109, line 14	*For* "travelled" *read* "went"
page 117, line 8	*For* "possible" *read* "likely"
page 183, line 5	*For* "negro" *read* "Negro"
page 314, line 16	*For* "1802" *read* "1800"
page 315, line 13	*For* "*Friends*" *read* "Frauds"
page 326, line 13	*For* "1809" *read* "1807"
page 327, line 2	*For* "1807" *read* "1809"
page 404, line 20	*After* "American people" *substitute a comma for the full stop and add* "although the 'Great American Desert', as the Great Plains were then called, was still thought to be a formidable natural barrier."
page 690. line 24	*For* "A. Russell Lowell" *read* "A. Lawrence Lowell"

CONTENTS

MAPS

ACKNOWLEDGMENTS

H. L. Stimson—Harper & Brothers; *Letters from America* by Alistair Cooke—Rupert Hart-Davis, Ltd.; *The United States and Britain* by C. Brinton, *The Monroe Doctrine* by D. Perkins—Harvard University Press; *The Life and Letters of Walter H. Page* by Burton J. Hendrick, *Midnight on the Desert* by J. B. Priestley, *Three Years with Eisenhower* by H. C. Butcher—William Heinemann, Ltd.; *Twenty-five Years* by Viscount Grey of Fallodon—Sir Cecil Graves, K.C.M.G., M.C., Hodder & Stoughton Ltd.; *The Memoirs of Cordell Hull*—Hodder & Stoughton, Ltd.: The Macmillan Co.; *A Letter from Grosvenor Square* by J. G. Winant— Hodder & Stoughton, Ltd.: Houghton Mifflin Co.; *A Diplomatic History of the United States* by S. F. Bemis, *American Social History as Recorded by British Travelers* by A. Nevins, *The Frontier in American History* by F. J. Turner—Henry Holt & Co., Inc.; *American Diplomacy During the World War* by C. Seymour, *The Rivalry of the U.S. and Great Britain over Latin America 1808-1830* by J. F. Rippy —The Johns Hopkins Press; *James Gillespie Blaine* by J. F. Stanwood— Houghton Mifflin Company; *The Migration of British Capital* by L. H. Jenks—Alfred A. Knopf, Inc.: Jonathan Cape, Ltd.; *The American Language* by H. L. Mencken—Alfred A. Knopf, Inc.: Routledge & Kegan Paul, Ltd.; *The Founding of the Second British Empire, 1763-1793* by V. T. Harlow—Longmans Green & Co., Ltd.; *From Sea to Sea and Other Sketches* by Rudyard Kipling—Mrs. George Bambridge: Macmillan & Co., Ltd.: Doubleday & Co., Inc.; *The Life of Neville Chamberlain* by Keith Feiling, *The Sterling Area* by A. R. Conan, *The Letters of Henry James* (selected and edited by Percy Lubbock)—Macmillan & Co., Ltd.; *America's Economic Supremacy* by Brooks Adams, *Woodrow Wilson and the Lost Peace* by T. A. Bailey, *Immigration, A World Movement and Its American Significance* by H. P. Fairchild—The Macmillan Co.; *The Commerce of the Nations* by C. F. Bastable—Methuen & Co., Ltd.; *America, Britain and Russia 1941-44* by W. H. McNeill— Oxford University Press and The Royal Institute of International Affairs; *Britain and the Independence of Latin America* by C. K. Webster, *Anglo-American Relations in the Atomic Age* by J. B. Conant— Oxford University Press; *The Growth of the American Republic* by S. E. Morison and H. S. Commager—Oxford University Press, Inc.; *Toward a New Order of Sea Power* by H. H. and M. Sprout, *The Anglo-American Trade Agreement* by C. Kreider, *Documents on American Foreign Relations* —Princeton University Press; *The Anglo-Saxon Century* by J. R. Dos Passos, *Blood, Sweat and Tears* by Winston S. Churchill—G. P. Putnam's Sons; *The Babbitt Warren* by C. E. M. Joad, *Midas or the Future of the United States* by C. H. Bretherton—Routledge & Kegan Paul, Ltd.; *American Diplomacy 1900-1950* by G. F. Kennan—Secker & Warburg; *American Policies Abroad: The United States and Great Britain. An Englishman's Point of View* by Sir Norman Angell—University of Chicago Press; *Anglo-American Relations* by the Earl of Halifax—University of

Leeds; *Propaganda for War* by H. C. Peterson—University of Oklahoma Press; *The American Impact on Great Britain 1898-1914* by R. H. Heindel —University of Pennsylvania Press; *British Criticisms of American Writings* by W. B. Cairns—University of Wisconsin Press; *The Road to Safety* by Sir Arthur Willert—Derek Verschoyle, Ltd.; *Eisenhower was my Boss* by Kay Summersby—T. Werner Laurie, Ltd.; *North Atlantic Triangle* by J. B. Brebner, *The Influence of International Trade upon British-American Relations* by J. M. Frankland, *The Colonial Background of the American Revolution* by G. M. Andrews, *American Neutrality 1914-17* by C. Seymour, *The Anti-Slavery Movement in England* by F. J. Klingberg, *The United States, Great Britain and British North America* by A. L. Burt, *The New Deal and World Affairs* by A. Nevins—Yale University Press.

Lack of space prevents me from listing here the many other books which I have consulted or from which I have quoted, but I gladly acknowledge the help that I have derived from the works of the various authors and editors concerned. Full acknowledgment will be found in the bibliography at the end of the book, and also in the footnotes. I have tried to locate the owners of all copyright property but if I have used any material for which permission has not been sought, or if any quotation has been incorrectly acknowledged I hope the persons concerned will accept my apologies.

ABBREVIATIONS

The following abbreviations have been used in the footnotes:

A.S.P.F.R.	*American State Papers, Foreign Relations,* Washington, 1832 *et seq.*
Bailey	T. A. Bailey, *A Diplomatic History of the American People,* New York, 1950.
Bemis	S. F. Bemis, *A Diplomatic History of the United States.* New York, 1942.
Brebner	J. B. Brebner, *North Atlantic Triangle,* New Haven, 1945.
E. D. A.	E. D. Adams, *Great Britain and the American Civil War* (2 vols.). London, 1925.
Messages and Papers	*A Compilation of the Messages and Papers of the Presidents.* New York, 1897.
Treaties	*Treaties and Other International Acts of the United States of America* (*ed.* Hunter Miller). Washington, 1931 *et seq.*
U.S.W.A.	*The United States in World Affairs* (Council on Foreign Relations). London, 1945-51.
W. A. A. E.	Beckles Willson, *America's Ambassadors to England 1785-1928.* London, 1928.
W. F. R.	Beckles Willson, *Friendly Relations, A Narrative of Britain's Ministers and Ambassadors to America, 1791-1930.* London, 1934.

Am.H.R., Can.H.R., and Eng.H.R. are used for the *American Historical Review, Canadian Historical Review* and *English Historical Review.*

PART I

THE RELATIONSHIP

CHAPTER ONE

INTRODUCTION

I

"THESE two great organizations of the English-speaking democracies, the British Empire and the United States, will have to
be somewhat mixed up together in some of their affairs for
mutual and general advantage. For my own part, looking out upon the
future, I do not view the process with any misgivings. I could not stop
it if I wished; no one can stop it. Like the Mississippi, it just keeps
rolling along. Let it roll. Let it roll on full flood, inexorable, irresistible,
benignant, to broader lands and better days."[1] Winston Churchill's
words of August, 1940, embody the confidence with which Americans
and Englishmen regarded the future of Anglo-American relations after
they fought together as allies in World War II. Indeed, Anglo-American
friendship until it was subjected, for the first time since 1940, to notable
strain by the China crisis which began in 1949, came almost to be
taken for granted on both sides of the Atlantic. This was, perhaps,
natural. The two peoples had always been conscious, even when serious
disagreements existed between them, of their peculiar relationship. In
1843, for example, Dickens heard England referred to as that "unnat'ral
old parent", and by 1900 in England, and soon thereafter in America,
the idea of war between the two countries had come to be almost
unthinkable.

But though it may have become natural by 1945 to take Anglo-
American friendship as read, things have not always been thus. Two
wars have been fought between the two nations, and, as late as the
Venezuela dispute of 1895, Anglo-American disagreements were
numerous and sometimes sharp. But by degrees, as the years passed,
friendship triumphed over these obstacles, though the triumph was not
one of sentiment alone, for only a wide complex of causes, political,
economic, social—the totality in fact of Anglo-American intercourse—
made it possible. Happily, the intimacy of Anglo-American relations
is by no means solely dependent upon the powerful but sometimes

[1] Winston S. Churchill, *War Speeches 1940-1945* (London, 1946), p. 35.

17

fickle bond of emotion; it has manifold links embedded deep in the lives of both peoples. To see what those links are, and how they came into being, is the object of this book. Part I traces the broad outline of the relationship. The remaining three Parts recount the history of Anglo-American diplomatic relations.

The term 'relations' is used in a wide sense. As one student of Anglo-American relations writes, "we talk and write glibly—as we must—about 'international relations'. . . . We are dealing with an immensely complicated web of interactions among human beings. There are relations between governments. . . . There are relations among travellers, students, business men, who have dealings abroad. There are all sorts of transactions conducted by correspondence. International relations are a constant flow of men, goods, and ideas across seas and frontiers."[1] The term 'Anglo-American' also may need precise definition. *American* refers to the United States alone. *Anglo* refers to Great Britain, and, more precisely, after 1921 to the United Kingdom of Great Britain and Northern Ireland.* Of course, the influence of other parts of the British Empire and Commonwealth, and particularly Canada, must be great, but it is primarily with Britain that I am concerned. My aim is the reverse of Brebner's in *North Atlantic Triangle,* for he wishes "to get at, and to set forth, the interplay between the United States and Canada—the Siamese Twins of North America who cannot separate and live. . . . The great obstacle to a simple account of this interplay was that . . . the United States and Canada could not eliminate Great Britain from their courses of action".[2] For us Canada is very much the *tertium quid,* and will therefore remain for the most part in the background; our concern is above all with the twofold relationship of Great Britain and the United States.

It is hardly necessary to stress the importance of this subject. How vital Anglo-American friendship is has been understood by the majority of Englishmen since the turn of the century and has become clear to most Americans at least since the entry of the United States into World War II. For a decade now it has been a commonplace of politicians—which has for all that some truth in it—that the future of democracy

---

[1] Crane Brinton, *The United States and Britain* (Cambridge, Mass., 1945), p. 121.

* I must confess to my Scottish and Welsh readers that I early abandoned any attempt to maintain a consistent distinction between the terms 'England' and 'Britain', and their derivatives. Nor have I endeavoured, because of its complexity, to enter into what is a matter of substance—the distinction between English and, for instance, Scottish influence in Anglo-American relations.

[2] J. B. Brebner, *North Atlantic Triangle* (New Haven, 1945), p. xi.

can only be safe in the hands of an Anglo-American alliance. In view of the tension between the two countries which began in 1949 over the policy to be pursued towards the People's Republic of China, the supreme importance of their friendship has suddenly become to Englishmen even more apparent than before, just because it has come to seem less certain, less safe. From his public utterances it is clear that at that time it remained uppermost, paramount, in the mind of Churchill, the greatest of England's living statesmen. It is significant of the danger of taking Anglo-American friendship for granted that the initial whisper of discord strikes the thinking Englishman like the first faint, but terrible, tremor of an earthquake. Of all historical subjects, it is possibly true that the history of Anglo-American relations is the most important, as well as the most relevant, to the future of Western civilization.

But no study of them will in the long run better Anglo-American relations unless it is an impartial one. Soft words which do not speak the whole truth in judgment will not turn away wrath; partisanship might merely increase danger. It has, therefore, been my aim to write a book for Americans and Englishmen indifferently. In the words of an Anglo-American master, Henry James, "I can't look at the English-American world, or feel about them, any more, save as a big Anglo-Saxon total, destined to such an amount of melting together that an insistence on their differences becomes more and more idle and pedantic. . . . I have not the least hesitation in saying that I aspire to write in such a way that it would be impossible to an outsider to say whether I am . . . an American writing about England or an Englishman writing about America".[1] I have striven to be, in this way, free from national prejudice, intensely difficult though that is. I have found in lecturing on Anglo-American relations in America, that neither I, nor those to whom I talked, were altogether immune from sudden gusts of emotion over contentious issues. But the blood may rush to the head of the best of us, and may as quickly run out again. Even more insidious is the unconscious predisposition which our lifelong habits give us to judge upon any question by our parochial, if well-intentioned standards. It may indeed be impossible for the historian to escape altogether from his environment into impartiality, and since national background constitutes a large part of environment for all of us, the risk of that form of bias is always with us.

[1] *The Letters of Henry James,* Selected and Edited by Percy Lubbock (London, 1920), I, p. 143.

It is worth while to spend a little time on this difficulty, for it still lies at the bottom of much international misunderstanding; certainly it must be a root cause of dissension between two nations who already have so much in common, both in history and principle, as Great Britain and the United States. Even the works of the best of academic historians can seldom wholly escape the taint of national bias, and examples of disagreement on national lines are plentiful among historians writing on Anglo-American relations. One striking example appears in the verdict of two first-class historians, one American, one English, on the Venezuela incident. S. F. Bemis writes in his *Diplomatic History of the United States*:

> A case had now arisen in which a first-class power still possessing colonies on one of the American continents, might, by advancing boundary claims and refusing to arbitrate them, arbitrarily expand its territory in violation . . . of the Monroe Doctrine. . . . Cleveland resolved not to take the rebuff. . . . The country as a whole—despite the chagrin of intellectuals—rallied behind the President.[1]

A glaring contrast is provided by R. C. K. Ensor in his *England, 1870-1914*, who writes of Cleveland's message to Congress on this question:

> This was certainly one of the most unexpected, least warranted, and least excusable steps ever taken in modern times by a Great Power. . . . The message evoked a frenzy of Jingoism throughout the United States; but a chastening influence was exerted by a catastrophic fall in American stocks. British opinion displayed restraint from the start. It became obvious that, while an Anglo-American war would still be the most popular of all wars in America, in England it was viewed as fratricidal.[2]

The effect of national preconceptions is sufficiently obvious.

Yet these books were written between the two world wars, at a time when most intelligent men, and these among them, tended to spurn chauvinist sentiments. Such divergences of judgment occur, of course, between the writers of all nations, but they are peculiarly apt to occur between Americans and Englishmen. Their very closeness, to say nothing of their common tongue, seems to make disagreements more frequent, or, at least, cause them to be noticed more often. We shall have occasion to revert frequently to this theme, the homely one, that

[1] S. F. Bemis, *A Diplomatic History of the United States* (London, 1936), pp. 416-9.

[2] R. C. K. Ensor, *England, 1870-1914* (Oxford, 1936), p. 230.

familiarity breeds family disagreements. Cecil Chesterton wrote in 1915, "what really produces trouble between peoples is when one is quite certain that it understands the other—and in fact doesn't. And I am perfectly certain that that has been from the first one of the primary causes of trouble between England and America."[1] The same analysis has been made and remade by acute observers of Anglo-American relations in this century. What is more, in any case where passions run high on either side, because of identity of language and similarity of ideas, no lack of knowledge of what is being said on the other shore of the Atlantic can long exist, for all is understood, and all is news; there is no veil of language or ignorance to obscure the beginnings of disputes. Thus they have all the bitterness—and happily some of the shortness—of family quarrels.

But not all the misrepresentations of one country by citizens of the other can be pardoned as the results of honest misjudgment or excessive frankness. On the wilder fringe of the literature of Anglo-American history are some authors who cannot be altogether acquitted of malice and all uncharitableness. The relations of no two other nations with so much in common have been so bedevilled by the writings of honest but mischievous publicists, and some brief consideration of a selection of them is, unfortunately, necessary. The harm they have done in the past has been very marked, and beside their misrepresentations the honest differences of academic historians shrink into insignificance. If the passages quoted above are a warning to us in our study of Anglo-American history, those quoted below are a warning to all mankind of how strong is the old Adam of spite within us.

The history of our subject offers us a rich and extensive, if malodorous, field of choice in this matter, but I propose to take my specimens from the inter-war years, when the consequences of irresponsibility might have been obvious to anyone on either side of the Atlantic. Probably examples from the early nineteenth century would be as striking, though it is questionable if they would be quite so obviously lacking in taste, but it is a happy indication of the changes wrought in the last decade that bad feeling of this intensity is hardly even conceivable today. Anti-Americanism and Anglophobia both exist indeed (as anyone who has recently resided in both countries will know), but in much more restrained and limited forms. I shall cite

---

[1] *Literary Digest* 19 June, 1915, p. 1,468: q. H. L. Mencken, *The American Language, An Inquiry into the development of English in the United States* (Fourth Edition, 1946), p. 44.

first some flagrant examples of misrepresentation of the United States by two Englishmen, whose attacks were made more deadly by the fact that they were men of ability who pretended to impartiality and proclaimed the best intentions.

The preface to the first work, if not indeed the very title—C. E. M. Joad's *The Babbitt Warren*—is quite enough to make the hackles of any good American rise: *

> These anecdotes have in every case been taken, usually verbatim, from paragraphs in the daily Press, which presupposes in English readers an inordinate interest in American extravagances. The author has not had the privilege of visiting the United States, and has no means, therefore, of judging of the accuracy of these reports. His acquaintance with Americans and those who have been to America forces him, however, to the conclusion that the stories given in the text, even if they are not in all respects literally true, possess at least the merit of the inventions of that distinguished author, Mr. Benjamin Trovato; that is to say, if they are not true they ought to be.[1]

The second author—C. H. Bretherton—had spent much time in America and so his preface to *Midas or The United States and the Future* cannot quite reach the level of Professor Joad's, but it is pretty good just the same, notwithstanding its lofty air of impartiality. It ends,

> Some time ago I read in a little volume of poems one by a lady called *Hates*. It recounted the various things the authoress disliked and contains the following lines:
>
> > '*I hate washing dirty plates.*
> > *I hate the United States.*'
>
> Those who hate the United States will get no satisfaction out of this volume. They will much prefer *Babbitt* and *Main Street*. Enthusiasts for the world's biggest republic will hardly be more satisfied but I do not know what antidote to recommend them unless it be the *Saturday Evening Post*.[2]

It is perhaps fair to note that both these books were published in 1926, in the high days of H. L. Mencken and Sinclair Lewis, but citizens of

---

* This passage was written some time before the death of the late Professor Joad, but, after very careful consideration, I have decided that it should stand.

[1] C. E. M. Joad, *The Babbitt Warren* (London, 1926), p. ix.

[2] C. H. Bretherton, *Midas or The United States and the Future* (London, 1926), pp. 7-8.

a country may say many things about it which will not easily, if ever, be forgiven to foreigners, even if they speak the same language. In those two passages of preface is epitomized what is, perhaps, most hateful to Americans in the English, their supercilious assumption of superiority.

But our authors do not content themselves with this. Bretherton proceeds to analyse the future of Midas with an appearance of distaste oddly combined with relish. He knows America and can hit where it hurts most. "The truth is that the modern American has no use for liberty and liberty plays no part in what he conceives to be democracy. He conspues the imaginary tyranny of kings and emperors but earnestly desires to replace them with the very real tyranny of the fifty-one per cent." For American culture, of course, he has nothing but contempt. "American poetry is vile. Nothing so readily reflects the temperament of a people as its poetry and the American passion for *vers libre* is simply a reflection of American superficiality."[1]

Bretherton, however, is a model of restraint beside Joad, who starts off well with a sidelight on American everyday life. "An American will go into raptures about his bath. It is the first thing he will show you when he takes you into his house." But he does not confine himself to light commentary on social habits: weightier topics are discussed, and he concludes an attack on the satisfaction of militarists at a rising population, by turning to America, whose population in 1926 was indeed still increasing, with the words, "Guns and babies, cannons and fodder, with America as usual in the van." It would be hard to imagine, let alone find, such another travesty of the truth about America at that time, but Joad manages it, as we shall see later. Meanwhile he passes to American materialism; perhaps he had some grounds for criticism on this score in 1926, but he did not indulge the British habit of understatement when he pronounced, "The power of money has so permeated every stratum of American society, that to the American no other object of desire seems conceivable."[2] "The rich American's table witnesses the same superfluity of expensive things, the same dearth of good ones, for he is no more of an epicure and no less of a glutton than Trimalchio; pointless jokes and imbecile anecdotes pass for humour, stale platitudes and threadbare clichés for conversation, purse-proud complacency and paunchy self-satisfaction for dignity, rough horseplay and inane catcalls for conviviality." This passage might seem to exceed all bounds of credibility, to say nothing of good taste, were it not for a final grim perversion of the

[1] Ibid, pp. 53, 76.　　[2] Joad, pp. 8, 24, 66.

truth: "When we read stories of lynchings in the Southern States, of thousands of cheap excursionists travelling by train to see a nigger's tongue torn out before he is burnt alive, Americans will, I feel sure, forgive us if we fail entirely to subscribe to the view that theories of social change necessarily, and in all cases, require combating in America."[1] On this note let us leave the opinions of these Englishmen on America, and turn to the opinion of one American about the English.

G. H. Payne published his *England: Her Treatment of America* in 1931, five years after Joad and Bretherton had put pen to paper. He, as they had done before him, started with high pretensions of profiting by the lessons of history: "This book is written not with an idea of antagonizing England nor of encouraging anti-English elements in America. It is written with a belief that some portion of the American public may read it with interest but not embitterment. It is written in the belief that it may be read by Englishmen who in all fairness will realize that it is the record of an attitude of mind that is more harmful to England than it is to America."[2] In fact, the Introduction by "George Higgins Moses, President Pro-tem of the U.S. Senate", seems to express the true aim of the book more accurately: "These are the days when the re-writing of history shares public honors with the Tom Thumb Golf Course and when the debunking of historic figures holds literary rank with the crossword puzzles. No one, however, has hitherto attempted the debunking of a nation. It is perhaps an exaggeration to say that this is Mr. Payne's thesis; *but** . . ."[3] The preface concludes in this manner:

> Among a great many Americans who have every desire to be fair and who have every wish that there should be friendship on an equal footing, there is a belief that certain basic factors not only act to make the British offensive to Americans but lead them to commit wrongs against our nation. Those factors are:
> 1. An apparent instinctive and unconscious assumption of superiority by Britons.
> 2. Their inability to co-operate on an equal basis.
> 3. Their assumption of propriety of British interests.
> 4. Their obviously highly organized widespread propaganda.
> 5. Their refusal to permit trade rivalry.
> 6. Their unethical and at times immoral diplomacy.[4]

[1] Ibid, pp. 63-4, 219.
[2] G. H. Payne, *England: Her Treatment of America* (New York, 1931), p. xii.
* Authors' italics.   [3] Ibid, p. xix.   [4] Ibid, pp. xiii-xiv.

Here is all the hyper-sensitivity of American opinion about Britain, with its belief in British conceit, egotism, deliberate propaganda, unscrupulousness in trade, and Machiavellianism in diplomacy.

The body of the work starts well, with a caption drawn from the remarks of that eminent movie character, Trader Horn: "No Englishman's ever a gentleman when it comes to taking what he wants from a foreign country." It continues in much the same vein, and I choose a number of the brighter passages. For a hundred and forty years the English followed "a policy toward America . . . of almost continuous insult."[1] It is "monstrous" that an Englishman, Dean Inge, should declare that in 1812 America was guilty of "stabbing England in the back,"[2] for the truth is that it is "the British opinion that in any war in which England is concerned there should be no neutrals . . . a position . . . that would never be countenanced in this country."[3] Of the Monroe Doctrine he writes, "For over a hundred years England's foreign policy with regards to the American has been a continuous effort to make the Monroe Doctrine inoperative."[4] More and more doubt as to the value of his pretensions to historical scholarship—"I know of only one way of judging of the future and that is by the past"[5]—penetrates the mind of the reader when he sees such statements as, "But recent researches have shown that . . . the Mexican War . . . was largely due to England's secret contempt for the Monroe Doctrine and her interference in Mexican and Texan affairs",[6] and when he refers to a non-existent eighteenth-century Englishman, Charles Henry Fox,[7] the doubt is confirmed.

In the same way that Joad attacks the Americanized Englishman, so Payne's own countrymen are not immune from criticism: "It is our misfortune that our representatives at the Court of St. James's are so frequently imbued with the English point of view that they forget their duty to their own country."[8] We shall see later something of the chequered history of Anglo-American relations over the project for an Isthmian Canal and shall observe that the English were not without fault in the matter, but Payne goes a good deal too far when he writes, "England has never been more clever than she has in the entire matter of the Panama Canal. Although this Canal was built with American money, made possible by American engineering and American sanitation, England so manipulated the diplomatic negotiations that a special treaty had to be made in order to get her permission to construct this important waterway."[9] More general reflections are also indulged:

[1] Ibid, pp. 1, 5.   [2] Ibid, p. 36.   [3] Ibid, pp. 36-7.   [4] Ibid, p. 50.   [5] Ibid, p. xiv.
[6] Ibid, p. 75.   [7] Ibid, p. 18.   [8] Ibid, pp. 144-5.   [9] Ibid, pp. 156-7.

"In international affairs the English are the leading humorists of the world. This pre-eminence does not arise from a willful desire to be light or trifling, but from a real appreciation of a good joke; especially if it is on others—as it usually is."[1] Yet even Payne is forced, albeit with obvious reluctance, to admit and comment upon the closeness of the Anglo-American relationship: "The average American has more a liking for England and the English people than he has a dislike."[2] It is in at least lip service to this relationship that his characteristic peroration closes, and on this note we may leave him:

> America and Great Britain, as they stand today, can dominate the world; but they must dominate the world for the benefit of the world and not for the benefit of the English ruling class. . . . The peace of the world may be insured by England and America, but only if England is rid of the carbuncles of two hundred and fifty years of selfishness. . . . Give the British people an opportunity to govern their own country and the prospect of war between America and England will forever vanish. . . . The hate that now smoulders in almost every corner of the earth will be replaced by a toast: "The British people—God bless them!"[3]

We have dwelt long enough in this nightmare world to make us wonder that Anglo-American friendship was ever able to survive such obfuscation and malignity at all, and certainly to put us on our guard against the false witness of some of our sources of information. But let us not, author and reader alike, forget the beam that may be in our own eye; let us be always on our guard against our instinctive partisanship. The responsibility in this respect is certainly more that of writer than reader, and so let me begin by outlining my thesis.

II

Two main themes dominate the history of Anglo-American relations. The first arises directly, and the second indirectly, from the peculiar relationship which has always existed between the two countries, both physically and psychologically. Connected as they are by the great North Atlantic waterway and by the agency of the ever-present British North America, and bound together by a common origin and by much common life and history, they have affinities altogether unusual among nations.

In a sense we can very well look upon them as father and son; at any

[1] Ibid, p. 153.   [2] Ibid, p. 284.   [3] Ibid, pp. 292-3.

rate the analogy has its uses. In infancy and adolescence, in the seventeenth and early eighteenth centuries, America is born and grows up under the protection of Great Britain. The political family is, if one may use the phrase, rather Victorian in its strictness, but the youth prospers none the less. By 1763, however, he has grown almost to manhood and finds life with father unduly restrictive, so that irritations and ill-will pile up on both sides. In 1776, America comes of age, and in one last glorious 'row' leaves home for ever. In the great world he finds friends to help him resist father's punitive efforts, and after an uncertain start he begins to form his own habits and live his own life. For a period in the first half of the nineteenth century relations remain bad between parent and offspring, with resentment on the one side and hatred on the other, and they even come to indecisive blows in 1812. But as the younger man fills out and makes his way in the world with astonishing rapidity and the older himself prospers as never before, so the mutual sense of filial soreness and aggrieved parental authority dies away. By the end of the century the mistrust has to a large extent subsided, and as the father becomes increasingly conscious of his past faults and his future dangers, and the son gains some of the restraint and confidence of maturity, so friendliness begins to take its place. The international developments of the twentieth century destroyed the isolation of the United States and strongly encouraged the process by which the two countries came to realize how much they had in common. Co-operation was born in World War I and alliance in World War II, and, despite the relapse of the inter-war years, cordiality increased steadily throughout the whole half-century. Between 1941 and 1945 there was a friendship and a unity between them certainly never surpassed since 1783, and hardly even before that date. The Communist China crisis of 1949 served to show that the danger of differences was not over, but, looking back over the whole course of Anglo-American relations from 1783 to the present day, we can see persistent, even steady, progress from mistrust to cordiality. This ripening of friendship is the first theme of this book.

It can be seen very clearly in the diplomatic sphere, but can be observed also in others. It appears in the growing similarity of political ideals and practices which accompanied the development of democracy in both countries, but particularly in Great Britain. It is obvious in social life generally, and the analogy, and indeed connexion, between the great reforming movements of the two nations throughout their history is unmistakable. In the economic sphere, though there is no relative increase in the extent of intercourse, there are manifold, sustained, and intimate contacts. In the subtle and complex emotional relationship of the two peoples there is perhaps most strongly perceptible an advance from the bitter literary battles, the hatred, of the early nineteenth century, to the often deep affection of the present.

The second main theme is concerned, not with the increasing amiability of the relationship, but with its nature, and with the shifting balance of power within it. Pre-eminently is one impressed by the fact that there is a remarkable reversal in the relative position of the two states between 1783 and 1952. In the beginning Great Britain was in every way the superior power: in the end America's strength exceeded hers by quite as large a margin. That this striking inversion might take place had long been apparent to percipient observers, even in the colonial period, because of the vast potentialities of the American continent. By the end of the Civil War it was clear that it was taking place, and by the end of World War I it was obvious that it had done so. In every branch of national life, political, social and economic, we are able to watch this transformation come over the relationship of the two powers.

Yet the change in the material balance of power was only relative: it did not mean any actual decline in the power of Great Britain. Indeed, in the nineteenth century she grew to a height of power far exceeding any in her history, and came to dominate the greatest empire the world has yet known. It was merely that the growth of the United States was even more astonishing; she had the vast vacuum of a virtually empty continent to fill, and she surged through it as if she abhorred the emptiness with an intensity that Nature herself might envy. This combination of unmatched natural resources with unparalleled vigour produced an economic and political development which overshadowed the really quite creditable performance of Great Britain. It is true that the advance of the latter has been checked in the twentieth century; the sceptic might even reflect that the colonial status of 1783 was not very far removed from that of the recipient of Marshall Aid in 1949. But it is to be hoped that the exhaustion of Britain after 1945 was only a temporary condition. She may be an ancient among the nations, but it does not necessarily follow that she is doomed inevitably to the weakness, and ultimately the decrepitude, of senility. There are, most decidedly, limits to the validity of the analogy between the old age of nations and that of individual human beings, and history furnishes many surprising examples of the longevity and resilience of states. So the decline of Great Britain, even in the twentieth century, may still be

28

considered only as relative to the growth of the United States. Although she grew rapidly in the nineteenth century, Britain was already a Great Power in 1783, and the pattern of her development in nearly all aspects of national life was foreshadowed, if not actually pre-determined, before that date. In her growth and actions after 1783, therefore, there can be detected a certain consistency: the main principles and interests upon which her policy was based were hardly to change in their broad outlines through the whole period.

The United States, on the other hand, was not a Great Power by 1783; she was in fact a respectable power, but there were those who were pessimistic of her future. Certainly all lay before her, but this future was as yet in the realm of possibility and not in the domain of fact. It follows from this that the whole nature of her progress was dynamic and ever-changing compared with that of Great Britain. Radical as were the alterations in the life of the latter, they pale almost into insignificance beside those which transformed that of the United States. This fact, though it is true of almost every aspect of existence, is perhaps most obvious in the international relations of the two states, for the foreign policy of Britain, as we shall see, followed general principles in 1783 very much the same as those it still pursued in 1951, whereas that of America was markedly different in 1812, in the mid-nineteenth century, and again (even more strikingly so) in 1952. To some extent, therefore, one may visualize the history of Anglo-American relations with Great Britain as a comparatively stable back-cloth, against which the United States moves off and on to the international stage, and it is convenient for the purposes of analysis to concentrate upon the changing policy of the United States and to tell the story from that point of view. We shall in this way watch the emancipation of America from the tutelage of Europe, her withdrawal into isolation during the opening up of the West, and her eventual return to active participation in world affairs as the greatest of the powers. The junior, if not the sleeping, partner in the First British Empire has become the senior partner in an alliance whose second, though not whose only other, member is Great Britain.

The increasing cordiality of the relationship and the increasing preponderance of the United States within it are, then, the two threads of which we shall be repeatedly aware as we follow the complicated pattern of the century and a half of what Franklin D. Roosevelt—even on so American an occasion as the commemoration in 1937 of the signing of the Declaration of Independence—could call "Anglo-American history."

CHAPTER TWO

THE TWO NATIONS

I

WHAT are and have been the basic determining factors in the development of these two nations? What are their main differences and what have they in common?

At first sight in mid-twentieth century their differences are striking. The area of the continental United States is 3,022,387 square miles; that of the United Kingdom of Great Britain and Northern Ireland 93,053 square miles. Within the former are to be found widely varying conditions of terrain and climate; within the latter there is a considerable physiographical uniformity. The population of the United States in 1950 was 150,697,361; that of the United Kingdom in 1951 50,210,472.* In 1950 and 1951 the average population densities of the two countries were 50 and (excluding Northern Ireland) 550 persons per square mile respectively. In agricultural and mineral resources the United States is very rich, even in proportion to her population, while Great Britain is less so. Thus the one is virtually self-sufficient in all the necessities of life, except for a few things such as uranium, chrome, tin, sugar, rubber and coffee, and in most luxuries, except tea, spices and tropical fruits; whereas the other is heavily dependent upon imports for her existence, having only two major raw materials in quantity, coal and iron, and importing, in 1950 for example, no less than 78 per cent of her wheat, 87 per cent of her oils and fats, and 94 per cent of her butter.

In social and political life there are differences nearly as great. The relative homogeneity of the population of Great Britain, which, despite internal racial differences, has remained comparatively unaltered in the composition of its basic constituents for nearly nine hundred years, contrasts strikingly with the racial diversity of the United States, which received within a hundred and twenty-five years, beginning in 1820, no less than 38,461,395 immigrants from many and various lands. Another difference is the lack in the past in America of a central capital like

* Preliminary figures of 1951 Census.

London. Equally vivid, perhaps, is the contrast between the long slow years of English development, stretching back, if not in unbroken continuity, at least with some genuine, though often unconscious, descent of political and social tradition, for more than a millennium, and the swift, and indeed fabulous, growth of the United States. America, founded three hundred years ago by a mere handful of men who clung for their livelihood to the edges of a vast and uncharted wilderness, emerged as a political community somewhat over a century later in a series of acts which were more nearly deliberate acts of political will than those which accompanied the birth of almost any other nation in the world. To these differences must be added the acquisition in the past by Great Britain, and to some extent her retention to this day, of a great colonial and maritime empire, which gave her a tradition markedly different from that of the United States, which has rarely, except at the end of the last century, sought overseas dominions. With this goes—to some extent it arises from it—the fact that Great Britain has been for many centuries heavily involved as a major power in the main current of international affairs, whereas the United States has until recently spent much of her independent existence in a vigorous and vocal isolationism. There must be noted, too, the difference between the republican written constitution of the one and the unwritten monarchical system of the other, and between the unitary compact government of Great Britain and the wide federal organization of the United States. Finally, one must mention, though not in this brief space attempt to define, the often-misleading but none the less significant contrast between the traditional social inequalities of English life and the proud egalitarianism of the American people.

Yet great as the contrasts at first appear, upon closer examination they shrink somewhat in significance, and similarities, some of them frequently overlooked, become more apparent. In the first place, many of these very differences are counteracted by others. Thus the existence of the great British Commonwealth and Empire makes the differences between the United Kingdom and the United States in area, population, terrain, climate and resources much less important than they otherwise would be. Though the population of the United States is three times that of the United Kingdom, that of the British Commonwealth as a whole—539,870,000—is much more than three times that of America, while the land area of the Commonwealth—14,435,060 square miles— is four times bigger and contains within it even greater diversity than America's. Similarly, the American admixture of Negro, Oriental and

31

Indian stocks is more than outweighed by the fact that only 70 of the 539 millions mentioned above are white men. In much the same way, Great Britain is to some extent able, either directly or indirectly, to make up for deficiencies in natural resources by the existence of the Commonwealth and Empire. So long as control of the sea is not gained by a hostile power, this situation gives her some of the advantages that accrue to the United States from her great internal resources.

There are also positive similarities between the two countries when they are gauged, which is the only possible way, by comparison with other nations or people. Both enjoy, relatively, a very high standard of living; though the average annual British income *per capita* in the years before World War II was estimated at $100 less than the American, which was $525, those of South America, India and China were all between $50 and $90 per head. Both are great industrial powers. Great Britain, of course, led the way in this, but the United States followed, and now stands head and shoulders above all the other nations of the world, producing in 1952 65 per cent of the world's manufactured goods and 52 per cent of its mechanical energy. Great Britain, however, still remains a very highly industrialized country. When the degree of her industrialization is compared even with that of Russia, whose strides in this respect are giant, she still makes quite a good showing. Her *per capita* consumption of steel and electricity, her *per capita* production of coal and pig-iron, and her *per capita* railroad-track mileage are all much less than those of the United States, but they were still, in 1952, greater than those of Russia, despite the rapidity of Soviet development. They are far greater than those of most of the other nations in the world. The nature of a country's armed forces is an interesting reflection of its state of industrialization, and those of Britain, almost alone, approach those of America in the degree of their mechanization.

There are positive, if not always very tangible, likenesses, too, between the two countries in other spheres than the economic. In their political life both are now democracies, a word which, despite slight differences of interpretation and emphasis, both use in sufficiently the same sense to understand one another with some clarity. To get the measure of this likeness it is sufficient to observe that the Russians use the word in an utterly different sense. In fact, the nineteenth and twentieth centuries witnessed a great growing together of the United States and Great Britain in this respect, and in their internal politics their differences became steadily less apparent than their similarities; the British monarchy, for example, seemed of less significance as a point of difference in a country ruled by a Labour government, and in the age of the New and Fair Deals the fact that the United States had a federal and rigid constitution seemed a less important divergence than it once had. In foreign affairs, too, the differences narrowed as America became irrevocably committed to active leadership of the democracies, and as she became aware, though she continued to shun colonial imperialism, of the need for strategic bases of the kind that Gibraltar had long been to Britain. In fact, the United States came more and more to play the part in the world that Great Britain had so long performed, but which she could no longer adequately execute alone. In 1945 the two peoples were much closer than they had been since 1776, and in some ways than they had been even before that date. But this political structure of alliance and friendship rested upon a broad social base, for, though the racial composition of the United States became increasingly divergent from that of Britain in the century 1820-1920, it remained true that the British was not only the largest single group, but also that those of British origin in the United States exceeded the total of all the rest. What is more, the history of Britain and the British people, at any rate before 1776, remained almost unconsciously a part of the American experience and background. What they did not acquire consciously by the reading of history they absorbed insensibly by their literature, because of the existence of their common tongue, a bond of great significance at any stage of human development but of literally inestimable importance in this age of swift communication, mass printing, telephone, radio, cinema, and almost universal literacy. It, more than any other single factor, has made possible the symbiosis.

These and other similarities, as well as differences, between the two nations will become apparent as the study proceeds. Indeed they constitute in some ways a third truth which emerges from the history of Anglo-American relations. One must add to their increasing cordiality, and to the reversal of the balance of power between them, which we have already noted, the fact that from their common heredity, environment, and will, there has developed an increasing similarity, and even sometimes identity, of opinion and action. It is not merely that they have grown together with the passage of time, but that they could not have done so without deep and prior similarities which in part determined the nature of their development. Again and again we shall be conscious of these likenesses. We shall see them in important things; in their common tongue; in their belief in a democracy which has its roots deep in English political thought and history; in their mutual high degree of industrialization; in the increasing identity of their inter-national roles. We shall see them in seemingly subtle and unimportant, but often notable and sometimes significant, things; in the slightly con-temptuous attitude of both Englishmen and Americans towards foreigners; in the corresponding sneers of those foreigners about nineteenth-century Englishmen and twentieth-century Americans, who cared only for the wealth they made in such abundance; in their vanity over such technological pre-eminences as that in plumbing; in the fact that the French still say of the American tourist what they first thought up to apply to his English predecessor; in the disheartening response which they both find greets a nation which steps out over the seas to rescue alien peoples from aggressive national dictatorships, the causes of whose existence it finds so hard to under-stand. In these and in many other things shall we be repeatedly reminded of the resemblance between the two peoples. But it arises from fundamental facts, chiefly of geography and history, and the chief purpose of this chapter is to examine, first, the geographical basis of Anglo-American relations, and, secondly, some of the effects of it.

II

IN the time-scale of human history, geography is a relatively stable component of man's environment, and in Anglo-American history the geographical background has been fairly constant. This is at least true of what may be called external geography, the geographical position that the nations occupy in the world and *vis à vis* one another, but it is less so of their internal geography, which may best be discussed first.

Within both lands the changes in geography wrought by the hand of man since 1783 are tremendous: the face of each has been transformed. In America the transformation is the more dramatic. In 1783 the United States consisted of a long and relatively narrow strip of popu-lated land stretching along the Atlantic coast from Massachusetts to Georgia, barely cresting the Appalachians except in the centre and seldom more than two to three hundred miles in width. Beyond lay the seemingly illimitable wilderness, whose western shores three thousand miles away had scarcely yet been charted, whose harsh forests, plains and mountains no white man had yet traversed, and in whose vast expanses the feared and hated savages moved and had their being.

There could hardly have been in the wildest imaginings of man a greater transformation than that which the last century and a half has effected. The change in Britain was much slower, but even here the hand of man has altered much, for from a country predominantly agricultural, and to some extent still hedgeless and unenclosed, it has become a land of immense industries and great cities. The industrialization of Britain does not match in rapidity or intensity of achievement the subduing of the vast American continent to the will of twentieth-century industry and agriculture, but in both lands internal geography has altered greatly.

Nevertheless, despite these changes, certain basic geographical factors remain the same in each country, and for the most part they tend to make for diversity in the one and uniformity in the other. The great continental United States—3,000 miles from east to west and 1,500 from north to south—is a land of geographical contrasts even greater than those of one part of Europe with another. Her mountains vary from 6,000 ft. in the Appalachians of the east to 14,000 ft. in the Cordillera region of the west; the Great American Desert, mostly at a height of over 4,000 ft., has no rival in Europe; the United States contains rivers greater than the greatest that Europe can show. These and many other geographical contrasts mean that America provides not one but several geographical environments for her people. Compared with this diversity, the homogeneity of the British Isles appears extreme. It is true that it consists of two parts, a mountainous north and west of hard rock and an eastern lowland plain of newer and softer rocks, so that the latter is traditionally more fertile and more abundant in easy communications, particularly by water, but its tiny island character binds it tightly together. Within it there are no mountains higher than 4,500 ft., no very large rivers, and certainly no deserts. Thus the uniformity of Britain's geographical environment is considerable compared with that of the United States.

When we look at the facts of climate, the comparison becomes even more notable. The mean annual temperature of the United States is 52 deg. F., varying between an average of 31 deg. in the coldest to one of 73 deg. in the warmest month, a range of 42 deg. F. The mean annual temperature of the United Kingdom is 49 deg. F., varying between 40 deg. and 61 deg., a range of 21 deg. F. The large land mass of the United States means wide extremes of climate, from the subtropical Gulf to the extremely cold North Dakota area, and of course a wide diversity of regional temperatures; the climate of the British Isles is much more uniform.

But once more the differences appear less if we measure them against a third country, or indeed against many of the countries of the world. The difference in average temperature, for example, is only 3 deg. F., while Ellsworth Huntington gives the most favourable span of temperature for the support of vigorous people as 40-70 deg., and both lands have their average temperatures at around 50 deg. The case of Russia again furnishes a contrast. The mean annual temperature of Russia in Europe is 40 deg. F. and of Russia in Asia 34 deg. The average coldest month temperature of the former is 16 deg., of the latter minus 1 deg.; warmest month temperatures are 65 deg. and 67 deg. respectively. This gives ranges of temperature as wide as 49 deg. and 68 deg., which constitutes a much wider diversity than exists even in America. Here again the contrast of both the United States and Great Britain with Russia is apparent, a contrast which would be even stronger with a largely tropical country like India.

Thus there are marked differences of internal geography between the two; in particular the political and social sectionalism of American life is very different from the compact homogeneity of the British political and social structure. But, though there are clearly great similarities in geography between Russia and America, their vast territory and their great variety of climate and terrain for instance, there are also material resemblances between Britain and America.

Even more manifestly is this true of external geography, where there is a most significant and positive likeness between Britain and America. One is vast and the other is tiny, but both are in their essence islands, and both have played the part of island powers in history. This has not escaped attention in the case of the British Isles, "anchored," as Emerson appreciated, "at the side of Europe and right in the heart of the modern world",[1] but in some respects Britain is much less an island than America, protected as she is by vast oceans, or their equivalent. This important fact, which has sometimes passed unobserved, was noted in 1893 by one well fitted to appreciate its significance, Admiral A. T. Mahan. He wrote in an article on "The Isthmus and Sea Power", "Fortunately, as regards other states, we are an island power, and can find our best precedents in the history of the people to whom the sea has been a nursing mother."[2] This

[1] R. B. Mowat, *Americans in England* (London), p. 132. [No date of publication given.]

[2] A. T. Mahan, *The Interest of America in Sea Power, Present and Future* (London, 1898), p. 104.

insularity is now beginning to break down for the United States, as it has already done for Great Britain, through the coming of air power, and it has disrupted her sense of security in much the same manner, except that the change appears much more startling and overwhelming to Americans. The extent of this insularity in the past is clearly reflected politically in the strength of isolationism in American history, but it can be plainly seen also in intrinsic geographical facts.

She is protected to east and west by the two largest oceans of the world, so that it is 4,521 miles from San Francisco to Yokohama and 3,043 from New York to Liverpool. In the south her protection is also formidable, with the barriers of the Caribbean and the Gulf of Mexico, for, while the Panama Canal gives her shipping access from coast to coast, the isthmus on which it is built is even yet hardly a serious means of north-south communication, and is in any case, because of its extreme narrowness, very easily defensible by the power controlling the sea on its flanks. Furthermore, it is worth while noting that it is farther by the direct route from New York to Rio de Janeiro than from New York to Moscow. None the less the barrier to the north is even more effective. The frozen waste lands of northern Canada, huge even if we make allowance for the deceptive effect of Mercator's Projection, and the icy expanse of the Polar Region form perhaps the last effective geographical barrier to man on the surface of the whole earth, and have in the past been a much more formidable obstacle than the ocean. The contacts of the United States with East and West, by the stepping stones of islands, are nearly all in the north where, through the curvature of the earth, the distances are shorter, but in the past this has been to a minor degree compensated by the bad weather and adverse winds of these latitudes.

In this age of the aircraft and the guided missile, the isolation of the island has gone, but it has been of immense significance in history, when it was emphasized by the weakness of her immediate neighbours. By 1783 the United States had, in reality, nothing to fear from her southern neighbour, Spain, and by 1820 the establishment of Mexican independence meant a permanently weak and inferior power upon her southern border. No power arose in Latin America to rival, let alone to threaten her. In the north, the situation has always been more complex, for though Canada was until recently a comparatively weak power, absolutely at first, and relative to the United States later, she was always sustained by the might of Great Britain. This is the reason for the incessant activity of Anglo-American diplomatic relations in the nineteenth century. Canada was a constant bond between the two powers, often a bond which appeared as a chain and chafed accordingly, but, whether pleasant or unpleasant, never absent. Historically this island position of the United States was effective from the beginning of her independent existence, for during the period of her weakness the great wilderness of the West formed as powerful a protection as the Pole or the oceans. If there was any doubt on this score it was removed by the Louisiana Purchase, and the point was made crystal clear after the Mexican War ended in 1848. It is indicated by the fact that in her early years and of late the United States has been a great maritime power. The first period of the Republic saw the great days of the American merchant marine and the Yankee Clipper Ship, but during the nineteenth century her maritime activities diminished in importance, because of the passing of the wooden ship, and, even more, her absorption in the West. With the closing of the frontier, however, and the attainment of the Pacific with its oriental trade, the United States became a two-ocean power, and not only constructed a two-ocean navy, but encouraged a revival in the strength of her merchant marine. This is essentially the story of an insular power, and that insularity goes far to explain the depth of the often unremarked similarity between the fundamental interests of the two peoples.

III

LET us follow this theme into some of the realms of national life arising from the geographical foundations, and discuss briefly what may perhaps, for want of a more elegant term, be described as certain geo-political factors; first population, then military potential, and finally diplomatic principles dictated directly by geographical considerations.

If we are to have an accurate picture in our minds of the changing relations between Great Britain and the United States during the last one hundred and seventy years, we must always be aware that those relations have in large part changed because each of the two nations itself has changed. This is perhaps most immediately illustrated by population figures.

England, Wales and Scotland		The United States	
		1790	3,929,214
1801	10,500,956	1800	5,308,483
1821	14,091,757	1820	9,638,453
1851	20,816,351	1850	23,191,876
1881	29,710,012	1880	50,155,783
1901	36,999,946	1900	75,994,575
1921	42,769,196	1920	105,710,620
—	—	1940	131,669,275
1951	48,840,893	1950	150,697,361

The figures show clearly, not only the startling rapidity of the American increase, but also the alteration in the relative power of the two states, for population is still an indispensable factor in political power. It is, of course, by no means the only factor, for in a world so highly developed technologically, industrial capacity is at least as important. China is certainly not three times as powerful as America, nor India six times as strong as Britain. But the factor of manpower cannot be ignored, and in any case, as between Great Britain and the United States, it is a fairly reliable gauge of their relative power because both are highly industrialized and technically skilled nations. America surpassed Britain in population in the early eighteen-forties, though it is doubtful whether she was her equal in political power until well after the Civil War, because of British industrial superiority.

It is noteworthy that the British increase (which was never greater or more rapid than it was in the first years of the nineteenth century) was comparatively gradual and steady, whereas that of the United States from the eighteen-forties onwards was extremely swift and frequently uneven; the relative flatness of the British curve contrasts with the steep rise of the American. This was because the British growth was due mainly to the increase in commerce and industry, which was comparatively regular, while to this process was added, in the case of the United States, not only the agricultural resources and immense incentives represented by the opening up of the West, but also the unprecedented immigration of the years 1820 to 1920. Of this admixture we shall see more when we discuss the intermingling of the two peoples. But the salient fact which emerges is that in 1783 Great Britain had more than three times the population of the United States, whereas in 1950 the United States had more than three times the population of Great Britain.

It is obvious, however, that throughout these years there has always been a great difference in the density of population in the two countries, that of the United States being, even today, incomparably sparser than that of Great Britain. But though the density of population in Britain has always been far higher than it has ever been in America, both have increased more or less steadily, except that there is a marked, if temporary, recession in the American figures in 1810 as a result of the Louisiana Purchase, and in 1850 as a result of the vast accession of territory from Mexico in the treaty of Guadelupe Hidalgo (1848). But once again the rate of increase in America has been even swifter than that of Britain. The population density of Great Britain, excluding Ireland, has increased about five-fold since 1801, that of the United States about tenfold since 1790. The figures (of persons per square mile) are as follows:

	United States	Great Britain		United States	Great Britain
1790	4·5	—	1880	16·9	337
1800/1*	6·1	119	1890	21·2	375
1810	4·3	136	1900	25·6	420
1820	5·5	160	1910	30·9	463
1830	7·3	184	1920	35·5	485
1840	9·7	210	1930	41·2	508
1850	7·9	236	1940	44·2	532†
1860	10·6	262	1950	50·7	550††
1870	13·4	296			

It is interesting to observe that the gap in this respect between the two has narrowed quite fast in the twentieth century, for whereas until about 1875 the density of the one was never less than twenty times that of the other, by 1950 it was only about eleven times as great. But these figures are mere averages. Quite obviously, the population density of the American South-west is utterly different from that of the American North-east and yet again from that of the South. Even in Great Britain, where there is more homogeneity, there are marked contrasts; for example, in 1801 the density of England and Wales was 152, but of Scotland 54, and in 1931 the figures were 685 compared with 163. But to the inhabitant of the megalopolis of the twentieth century it does not make much difference, from the point of view of

* U.S. Census in the even, G.B. in the odd years.
† Estimated.
†† Computed from preliminary Census figures for 1951.

cramped conditions, whether he lives in London or New York, and there is little to choose between the population densities of Birmingham and Chicago.

Firmer conclusions may possibly be drawn from figures of relative urbanization in the two countries. Once again we see a disparity between the two, though not quite as marked as before, and we see the United States rapidly overhauling Great Britain. The figures of urban as a percentage of the total population are as follows:

	United States	*Great Britain*
1800/1	6%	29%*
1850	15%	50%
1890	35%	72%
1910	46%	78%
1930	56%	80%
1950	59%	— †

In both countries there has been an increasing concentration in great cities, so that in 1930 in the United States there were 93 towns of more than 100,000 inhabitants, containing 29·6 per cent of the total population (in 1950 there were 107 containing 29·5 per cent), while in England and Wales 39·5 per cent of the population lived in such areas. Thus Great Britain is much more urbanized than the United States, but both are relatively rich in city dwellers. The essential difference between them today is the magnificently healthy balance between agriculture and industry which the United States is still able to maintain, and which is a vital element in her strength. But though their development here differs in degree, it does not do so as greatly as it does in the case of other lands. To take Russia once more as an example, neither the density of her population nor the number of her great cities compares with either Britain or the United States, while a recent estimate of her urbanization gives the figure of 33 per cent of the whole, one which was exceeded by Great Britain early in the nineteenth century, and which is not much more than one half of the American figure. Thus, in the extent of their urbanization, as elsewhere, the similarities between the two nations are perhaps as marked as their differences, and those similarities become more marked more rapidly as the twentieth century proceeds. From being in effect primarily a rural, one might almost say colonial, producer of raw materials in the early nineteenth century (which England had not really been since the sixteenth),

* Estimated.   † Figure not yet available.

America has, like Britain before her, become a great urban and industrial nation. It is not, perhaps, entirely coincidental that these later years have, as we shall see, also been the years of swiftly growing brotherhood, instead of traditional rivalry, between the two peoples.

IV

BUT in some ways even more illuminating than a study of population figures is that of what one may call, in a broad sense, military power. Of course, population and industrialization, as we have seen, are the crucial factors, excluding moral ones, in military potential: but in some ways a more satisfactory, because a more direct, way of assessing the power of a nation is by consideration of the history of its armed forces. A comparison of the history of the armaments of Great Britain and the United States produces, despite some contrasts, very interesting evidence of similarity. We can see the outstripping of the one by the other, with which we are already familiar, but we can also see that both naturally concentrate primarily upon maritime power for their defence. The naval power of Great Britain until World War I was more highly developed, largely because of her wide empire and extensive commerce, but as soon as America re-enters the international scene and ceases to be exclusively concerned with the development of the West, she creates a navy at first equal to and later far exceeding in power that of Great Britain. Both nations later concentrate heavily upon their air arms because they are a necessary complement to a great navy. The obverse also is true of both, that their armies were, if not neglected, at least the recipients of much less money and much less attention in time of peace than their other armed forces, though here again the imperial responsibilities of Britain make a difference; in 1848, for example, the United States War Department spent 5 million pounds, the British War Office 15 million pounds. Mahan wrote of the two countries in 1894:

> Partners each, in the great commonwealth of nations which share the blessings of European civilization, they alone, though in varying degrees, are so severed geographically from all existing rivals as to be exempt from the burden of great land armies; while at the same time they must depend upon the sea, in chief measure, for that intercourse with other members of the body upon which national well-being depends. How great an influence upon the history of Great Britain has been exerted by this geographical isolation is sufficiently understood. In her case the

42

natural tendency has been increased abnormally by the limited territorial extent of the British Islands, which has forced the energies of their inhabitants to seek fields for action outside their own borders; but ... the same tendency, arising from the same cause, does exist and is operative in the United States, despite the diversion arising from the immense internal domain not yet fully occupied, and the great body of home consumers which has been secured by the protective system. The geographical condition, in short, is the same in kind, though differing in degree, and must impel in the same direction.[1]

Largely effect of this, but partly cause, is the mistrust of standing armies in both peoples, a mistrust which has misled not a few other powers as to their efficiency as soldiers. It has also meant that there is a similarity between the inefficiency of the British and American armies at the beginning of every war which would be humorous if it were not so expensive in blood, for both have always inadequate immediate resources and are always, in the nature of things, slow in bringing their great military potential on to the actual field of battle. *The Economist* wrote on 24 June, 1899: "Since our own Crimean muddle there has been no worse instance of military mismanagement than that displayed by the American War Department in Cuba and the Philippines,"[2] while with the sort of defeat that the American armies suffered in the early weeks of the Korean war of 1950 the British have been only too familiar. Examination of a few statistics brings out this neglect of the army in favour of the navy and air force even more clearly.

Perhaps the best way to approach the problem is through the medium of expenditure on armaments as shown in the table on page 44.

What are the conclusions to be drawn from these figures? First, some obvious but none the less interesting facts. Though the population of the United States, as we have seen, overhauls that of Great Britain in the eighteen-forties, and though, as we shall see, her wealth and productivity do so about fifty years later, her total national expenditure does not exceed that of Britain until the nineteen-thirties, until the Depression and the New Deal, by which time her population and national wealth were nearly three times as great. More immediately relevant is the fact that the total annual expenditure on the American army does not surpass that on the British until just after 1910; on the

[1] Mahan, pp. 110-111.
[2] Article on "The American Political Situation," p. 899.

DEFENCE EXPENDITURE OF THE UNITED STATES AND GREAT BRITAIN

In Millions of Dollars* (To the Nearest 1 Million Dollars[1])

Date	Total National Expenditure		Expenditure on the Army		Expenditure on the Navy		Total Defence Expenditure		Naval as Percentage of Total Defence Expenditure		Population (in Millions) at nearest Census		Expenditure on Defence per head of population to nearest $		Ratio of Column O to Column N
A	B U.S.	C G.B.	D U.S.	E G.B.	F U.S.	G G.B.	H U.S.	I G.B.	J U.S.	K G.B.	L U.S.	M G.B.[2]	N U.S.	O G.B.	P
1789[3]	4	51	(·633)	11[4]	(·001)	10	(·634)	21	(·1)	48	4	11	(·2)	2	10
1821	16	226	4	45	3	28	8	73	38	38	10	14	(·8)	5	6¼
1841	27	203	9	44	6	34	15	78	40	44	17	19	(·9)	4	4½
1870	310	341	58	69	22	49	79	118	28	42	40	26	2	5	2½
1879	267	422	40	78	15	52	56	130	27	40	50	30	1	4	4
1890	318	380	45	88	22	71	67	158	33	45	63	33	1	5	5
1903	517	653	119	183	83	177	201	361	41	49	76	37	3	10	3⅓
1912	690	943	184	140	136	222	320	362	43	61	92	41	3	9	3
1923[5]	3,295	3,944	397	290[6]	333	320	730	610	46	52	106	43	7	14	2
1937	8,177	4,235	628	457	557	532	1,185	988	47	54	132	45	9	22	2½
1950	41,860	10,365	8,000[7]	1,232	6,268[7]	914	14,268	2,145	43	43	151	44	94	44	½

FOOTNOTE

* The problem of finding a satisfactory rule-of-thumb by means of which to convert dollar into sterling statistics throughout Anglo-American history is a formidable one. To follow the detailed fluctuations of the exchange markets is impossible, and some general rule must be found, inaccurate though it is bound to be. There are, however, four main phases in the sterling-dollar exchange rate. From 1783 to about 1830, despite violent fluctuations, the norm was something under $4.5 to the £; in Jay's Treaty, for example, the pound was reckoned at $4.44. During the century which followed the pound was normally worth between 4.8 and 4.9 dollars; the mint par of exchange when both were on gold was $4.86⅔ and treaties in 1848 and 1853 made the conversion at $4.84. During the third period, beginning in 1939, the British Government fixed a rate of $4.03, but in 1949 was forced to devalue to $2.80 to the £. Thus, in round figures, the following conversion table may serve our purpose.

1783-1830	$4.5 to the £	1939-1949	$4 to the £
1830-1939	$5 to the £	1949-1952	$3 to the £

NOTES TO THE TABLE

[American figures from *Historical Statistics of the United States, 1789-1945* (published by the United States Department of Commerce, 1949), pp. 299-301. British figures from *The Annual Register* (1789, p. 285; 1822, rp. 312, 319; 1841, pp. 377, 385; 1870, p. 234) and from *Whitaker's Almanack* (1881, p. 124; 1892, p. 183; 1905, pp. 186-7; 1914, p. 500; 1924, p. 490 and 1925, p. 494; 1938, p. 673 and 1939, p. 653; 1951, p. 590 and 1952, p. 577). American figures for 1950 from *Whitaker*, 1951, p. 821.]

[1] This produces some apparent discrepancies in columns H and I.
[2] Figures for England, Wales and Scotland.
[3] U.S. figures cover period 1789-91.
[4] Figures for 1789, 1821 and 1841 include Ordnance.
[5] Air Force expenditure for both countries divided between Army and Navy.
[6] British figures for 1923 and 1937 based on Estimates. British and American figures for 1950 based on Estimates.
[7] Approximate figures.

navy until World War I and the period immediately thereafter, when the Washington Conference recognized American and British naval parity; and on Defence as a whole until the same period. Before putting any great weight upon such figures one must appreciate, not only that exchange difficulties may make accurate comparison difficult, but, even more important, that differences of expenditure may to a considerable degree be accounted for by differences in national standards of living and costs of production. Where, as in the army, a substantial portion of the total expenditure goes in pay, the fact that American rates of pay are very much higher than British may explain much of the discrepancy and will not mean that the American army is as much more powerful than the British as army estimates might make it appear. The same argument applies to costs of production, particularly, for example, in naval expenditure, so much of which represents new capital construction. In other words, it is at least possible that in the nineteen-thirties the difference in defence expenditure between the two countries is partly to be explained by high American costs and rates of pay. Similarly, arguments depending on the proportion of total national expenditure spent on defence are very suspect because the total British national budget has usually been, throughout this century, relatively much greater than that of the United States. This is the result of many factors, particularly the heavy services of the vast British National Debt, the greater expenditure on social services, and the fact that in the United States much governmental expenditure is in fact made by state rather than federal authorities. But, even given these reservations, it is perfectly plain that Great Britain has until the inter-war years spent absolutely more on arms than the United States (Columns H and I), and, quite obviously, immensely more relatively. There could be no better illustration of the sense of security (and not merely the sense of it, but the thing itself), which the Americans derived from their insular position, which provided natural defences much better than the British Isles have ever enjoyed.

More conclusive still are the results of assessing the ratio of expenditure on defence to population figures. This is best seen in the form of a calculation of the expenditure annually per head of the population on defence, and the resulting figures are almost startling (Columns N and O). In 1789 the British expenditure was approximately $2 and the American approximately 20 cents; in 1879 $4 and $1 (the 1870 figures of $5 and $2 represent exceptional post-Civil War conditions); in 1912 $9 and $3; and in 1937 $22 and $9. Not until after World War II does the United States regularly spend more on defence per head of the population in peace time than Great Britain, as when in 1950, for example, she reckoned to spend $94 to Britain's $44. The ratio figures bring this out most clearly, and show, with some slight exceptions, a rough progression from ten times the expenditure on the part of Great Britain in 1789 to three and a third times in 1903, two and a half times in 1937, and twice on the part of the United States in 1950. It is abundantly clear from these figures—if proof were needed—how much greater the participation of Britain in world affairs has always been; indeed it is interesting how rapidly American expenditure upon armaments increases at just that crucial period in her history, at the end of the nineteenth century, when she re-enters international affairs as an active participant. It is also apparent how closely these facts in the political world conform to the geographical realities beneath them.

But this can perhaps be demonstrated most conclusively by a third set of facts, the proportion of the whole defence expenditure of the two states spent upon the navy (Columns J and K). Compared with the wide variations between the two in, for example, the proportion of total national expenditure taken by defence, the relative amounts they spend on their navies are not only very similar but very constant. Except for the first years after the formation of the national government in the United States, which were plainly exceptional, the proportion in the case of both is usually somewhat under 50 per cent, a figure to which Britain remains remarkably close through the whole of the century. In 1841, as a typical peace year, 40 per cent of the American defence budget went on the navy, 44 per cent of the British. In 1870 there was a drop in the American figure, which was not recovered till the turn of the century, owing principally in the first instance to the fairly large armies kept in being after the Civil War and later to the fact that this was the height of American isolation from Europe, the period when she felt most secure in her strength and her island position. By 1903, after the rise of American Imperialism, the proportion is back at 41 per cent, relatively close to the British 49 per cent, but shortly before this date Great Britain had begun to be affected by the beginning of the naval armaments race with Germany, and by 1912 was spending over 60 per cent of her defence budget on naval expansion. Her expenditure in the inter-war years continued to exceed 50 per cent. That of the United States increased much more gradually—43 per cent in 1912, 46 per cent in 1923, 47 per cent in 1937—and only in the post-World War II period did it just top that of Great Britain. But though there are discrepancies, the similarity between these figures is more notable than the variation, which is chiefly owing to the similarity between their fundamental positions in the world.

Mahan, as we have seen, pointed this out and, of course, actually formulated a policy for the United States based directly on his observations of the British tradition on the seas, but his influence was by no means confined to his own country; he had perhaps even more effect in England than at home. Lord Wolseley wrote: "Mahan's books have done the country, and the Navy for that matter too, a world of good. It is a sad reflection that it has taken a Yankee to wake up this generation of Englishmen to the meaning and importance of sea power."[1] Not only did his articles in the *Daily Mail* go far to arouse Britain to the German danger, but he even popularized the very term "sea power." He was in a sense the living symbol of the fundamental insularity of the two peoples, which found practical expression in the passage of technical knowledge between the two navies, particularly after the Spanish-American War, which taught, for instance, to both navies the use of electricity in ships and the need of distilling and repair vessels as adjuncts to the fleet. Other examples of this interchange were the American experiments with submarines, and the British introduction in 1902, partly on the American model, of a plan for the preliminary common training of all officers before specialization, in order to secure the interchangeable officer. Even the neglected national armies, small professional bodies of non-conscripts, had sufficient in common for Arthur Lee, one-time military attaché in Washington, to believe, according to Heindel, that "the American Army was the only one in the world which resembled the British Army to any degree."[2] These things arise at bottom from the insular position which the two countries occupy, and which creates a certain sympathy of outlook between them. Right-wing American talk in 1951 of a refusal to send troops to Europe, and the call of a Hoover or a Taft for American concentration on great naval and air strength causes alarm and utterly fails of comprehension on the continent of Europe, but in Britain it can only cause misgivings. She cannot but understand it well enough, since it has always been her own policy.

Once again, a glance at certain of these European powers serves to heighten the effect of similarity between Britain and America. As we have seen, the expenditure of these two on naval as opposed to land defences has normally averaged somewhat under 50 per cent, though

[1] R. H. Heindel, *The American Impact on Great Britain, 1898-1914* (Philadelphia, 1940), pp. 117-8.   [2] Ibid, pp. 123-4.

rising in the case of Britain to about 60 per cent in 1912. That of the Continental powers, as is to be expected, was always much less. In 1912, for instance, France spent only 32 per cent of her total defence budget on the navy, while Germany—it was the era of her greatest naval strength—spent only 27 per cent. In 1938 France spent only 24 per cent, and Germany probably less. Even now, in 1952, when Russia's is the second peace-time navy, it would seem doubtful if she spends more than a third of her defence outlay on it.

The same story appears from a cursory review of the relative size of armies, taking as the basis of calculation the number of fully trained reserves.

ARMY STRENGTHS
(In Thousands)

Year	U.S.	G.B.	France	Germany	Russia
1890	27	619[1]	2,000	1,492	2,151[2]
1912	212	730	3,120	3,800	2,700
1924	209[3]	517	3,300	100[4]	720
1938	263[3]	518	3,000[5]	2,500[5]	1,600
1948[6]	600	530	600	Nil	4,000

[Figures from *Whitaker's Almanack* (1891, pp. 215, 532, 536, 554, 565; 1913, pp. 105, 481; 1914, p. 694; 1925, pp. 243, 741, 785, 790, 824; 1939, pp. 427, 908, 1,015; 1949, p. 454).]

Even allowing for differences of population, the figures speak for themselves. The United States has always had the smallest of armies prepared for war, and, though Britain has had a larger army than her in peace-time, chiefly because of her imperial responsibilities, she has hardly been better prepared for large-scale war. Thus the latter only most reluctantly introduced peace-time conscription shortly before the outbreak of war in 1939, and the former only during the course of the war itself. The vast peace-conscripted armies of the Continental powers have always put them in a totally different category from the island powers protected by the seas, the oceans and the polar cold.

[1] All British figures include Indian troops.
[2] All Russian figures are unreliable, and those of later years almost certainly too small.
[3] Strength of National Guard estimated approximately at 80,000.
[4] Maximum under Versailles Treaty.
[5] Approximate figures; Germany certainly underestimated if para-military formations included.
[6] In 1946 the British Army had numbered 3 million, the American 8 million, and the Russian more than 10 million.

Thus over the century and three-quarters of their independent relationship, we can see clearly how the power of the United States, whether gauged in terms of population, of military potential or of actual armaments, has overhauled and overtaken that of Great Britain; we can observe that reversal in their relative positions of which we have already taken note. Great Britain is outstripped in potential strength by the end of the nineteenth century and decisively so in actual military strength in and after World War II, though, to prevent an exaggerated perspective in this matter, the present strength of the British Commonwealth of Nations as a whole must not be forgotten. We can see also, to a minor degree, in military affairs evidence of the growing co-operation of the two countries. But most clearly of all we see, what we shall often observe again in other spheres of life, the remarkable and fundamental similarities between the two lands, similarities by no means confined, as is so often assumed, to the possession of the same language and the fact that they are kindred stock, but arising from basic geographical situations surprisingly alike. We see their high degree of urbanization, of industrialization, of wealth; we see their preoccupation with naval, and later, air power; we see also the corollary of this, their neglect of peace-time armies. It is true, certainly, that there are many geographical factors which differentiate the two nations—size and variety of climate and resources, for instance —but they are not more influential than those which tend to identify them. The great land-mass of the continental United States, for example, has not prevented the Americans from being a great sea-faring people. In all these things the influence of geography is apparent.

V

But its influence is perhaps most obvious in the diplomatic sphere. It is thus the geographical proximity of Canada to the United States which was the fundamental cause of Anglo-American friction in the nineteenth century. Between these two extensive lands, inseparably conjoined, there were outstanding problems which could not but be a cause of irritation and which tended to counteract the powerful factors making for co-operation. Nearly all the diplomatic *causes célèbres* between the two states arose because of the existence of Canada, or of other indigenous British interests in the Western Hemisphere. The exception to this was the great dispute over the Freedom of the Seas, which arose directly from the fact that both were leading maritime powers:

the interests of the greatest of maritime neutrals and the greatest of maritime belligerents were perhaps bound to clash. Nearly all the Anglo-American issues centred in America or American waters; the western posts; the boundary disputes in Maine, the Great Lakes, Oregon and Alaska; the Caribbean disputes over Honduras and the canal; the perennial bickering over fisheries, seals and even the Navigation Acts themselves, the rub of which was chiefly in the West Indies.

Furthermore, because of this, the affairs always touched the Americans much more closely than the inhabitants of the British Isles, for they concerned issues remote from the interests of the bulk of the British people, interests which in the nineteenth century were scattered widely over the surface of the globe, and some of which, as was inevitable, were from time to time in dispute or jeopardy. Why should the Oregon question be of much deeper significance to the average Englishman than the acquisition of Hong Kong? The Canadians felt the full effect of this fact also, when Great Britain refused to support them in the dispute with the United States over the Alaska boundary, because Anglo-American friendship had become more vital to her in the rising tide of European tension than a Canadian border dispute. But Oregon was on the very doorstep of America, as Alaska was on that of Canada : it was important to her national development, and had it not been for the acquisition of California, would have been even more important. It followed naturally from this that the United States cared a great deal more about most Anglo-American disputes than did Great Britain, and, as Bryce justly observed, the American people were as a result much more bellicose and pugnacious, so that the desire for co-operation appeared somewhat earlier in Britain than in America. But though these irritants, arising from geographical proximity, frustrated for a period the operation of causes making for co-operation, they were not strong enough to do so for long, for there was no deep, inherent antagonism between the two peoples such as that which appeared to exist between France and Germany. There was no difficulty comparable to the "pressure of population on the Rhine" between Canada and the United States, because America had bountiful room for expansion to the west, the normal direction of her growth. The 'safety-valve' theory of the American frontier—that it provided an outlet for the social discontent of the East—may be no longer valid, but it is certainly true that the Westward Movement took the sting out of Canadian-American relations. In 1812 the United States was not strong enough to annex Canada, and in the eighteen sixties and seventies, when she was, it was not possible to arouse sufficient enthusiasm for the project among the American people, because there were still great unoccupied tracts of land in the United States itself. As E. L. Woodward writes, "The United States already held vast territories, and although the addition of certain areas might be desirable for strategic, economic, or sentimental reasons, there was nothing of the acute land-hunger or the desire to approach ice-free waters which affected the policies of European Powers."[1] There was thus no irreconcilable antagonism between Britain and the United States arising from North American geography, and by World War I all their disputes had been settled, in every case except the first by peaceable means. Indeed, the unfortified frontier between the two countries had become the ideal type of frontier in international relations. That this was so was not only the result of a growing cordiality between the peoples, but of the triumph of long-term similarities, arising partly from physiographic facts, over short-term differences arising from the same source.

Finally, geographical factors go far to explain, not simply the increasing warmth of Anglo-American relations in this particular aspect, but also the peculiar history of those relations in the broad theatre of world affairs. America's break from the mother country in the Revolution, her emancipation from Europe in the years up to 1814, her isolation in the nineteenth century, these were plainly influenced by her geographical position. The growth of America's Imperialism, and her slow, reluctant assumption of the leading role in world affairs in the twentieth century, were also forced upon her by the breakdown of her isolation in a world of rapidly developing technology. Geography explains equally clearly the persistent participation of Great Britain in the affairs of Europe and the world; there were periods when isolationism was powerful in Britain, and there were periods also when she was tempted to withdraw within the naval defences of her widespread Empire, but, despite these, she has played much the same part in the crises of world affairs since the sixteenth century. She has never been quite so isolated from the main currents of world affairs as has the United States, even in the age of sailing ships, for it is a mere twenty-two miles across the English Channel, and she has as a consequence been always of Europe, if not in it.

There have invariably been three main forces influential in the making of British policy: her tendency to isolation, her tendency to imperial development in colonies overseas, and her tendency to participate in European affairs. It was the dynamic resolution of these

[1] E. L. Woodward, *The Age of Reform, 1815-70* (Oxford, 1938), pp. 293-4.

51

forces which conditioned British political actions, and to them in the last fifty years has perhaps been added a fourth, the tendency to closer and closer co-operation with the United States. This last fact has become of increasing importance both to Great Britain and the United States, as well as to the rest of the world, since the surest hope, if not for peace, at least for the safety of the Western world lies still in Anglo-American friendship. This, too, derived much of its impetus from the facts of geography, and there is perhaps no more remarkable instance of it than the way in which the United States has come in the last decade increasingly to assume the role in international affairs which had in the past been played by Britain, but which she could no longer adequately perform. From her secure island base, strong on the sea and in the air over it, the United States has assumed the mantle of Britain and the indispensable task of holding together, as their principal protagonist, the nations of the free world, in their effort to ward off the aggressive domination of a single power entrenched firmly in the heart of the Eurasian continent.

CHAPTER THREE

ECONOMIC DEALINGS

IT IS not surprising to find that the economic relations of the United States with Britain have in general outline been analogous to their political relations. There has, in the first place, been a decisive swing-over in the balance of economic power from the one to the other, which is almost exactly paralleled by the similar change which we have observed in the political sphere. This steady increase in American strength has led to a reversal of the economic roles of the two countries, in the sense that the United States has had thrust upon her in the twentieth century the economic leadership of mankind which had been achieved by Great Britain in the nineteenth. As far as fundamental economic power was concerned, the scales had swung down decisively in America's favour by the turn of the century, though in finance it was not unmistakably clear until World War I.

In the second place, there has been throughout the history of the two countries since 1783, as obviously before that date, a great and remarkable intimacy of economic relations. It will be noted that this is not exactly analogous to the political or emotional development, which showed an increasing and broadening contact and friendliness as the years went by, for it does not seem that, considered relatively, the extent of economic relations grew at all during the latter half of the period; indeed, the reverse appears to be the case. It does not seem very probable that, taking into consideration such factors as national population and national income, Britain and the United States were more closely bound together economically in 1950 than they were in 1830, appearances to the contrary notwithstanding; the burgeoning of Anglo-American cordiality, from war in 1814 to close alliance in 1949, was essentially a political phenomenon. But the continuous economic intimacy from the beginning to the present is none the less of the greatest significance, although it has escaped popular attention. This has not been without unfortunate consequences in recent years, when the dollar gap and associated problems have all too often been thought of as arising from a new and, in some respects, unwelcome economic intercourse between the two countries in World War II. In fact, however new the dollar problem itself may appear, the powerful economic bonds have existed in one form or another since the American colonies were first founded, and their strength was remarkably little affected by the attainment of political independence in 1783; economic independence was much slower in coming. There can, indeed, be little doubt that the peculiar bitterness of certain aspects of Anglo-American relations in the early years and the important place occupied in those relations by commercial questions, and questions of international law concerning trade, owed much to the continued dependence of the American people for their economic development upon their political parent, and to their uneasy consciousness of it. It will be convenient, therefore, to discuss, first this intimacy of economic relations, and later the shift in the balance of economic power across the Atlantic.

I

THE extent of Anglo-American economic relations has always been remarkable. Brebner writes of the economic interplay of the North Atlantic Triangle, in the years 1815-50: "During that period much of what happened in Great Britain was almost as important in the lives of North Americans as what happened at home",[1] and in the period 1896-1940, "the economic triangle of buying and selling, investing and dividend-paying, migration and production, into which Great Britain, the United States, and Canada poured their efforts, became the mightiest thing of its kind on earth and seemed destined to remain so. ... Interestingly enough this economic co-operation persisted in spite of a curious procession of changes in the economic activity of the members."[2] In this triangle the hypotenuse was the Anglo-American trade, which remained greater than that of Canada and the United States until 1935, and as a result the "so-called world price for wheat, cotton, copper, beef, pork, cheese and wood products were pretty much the price which was set in the world's warehouse which was Great Britain, and if they read no other foreign news, the commodity brokers of Butte, Winnipeg, Chicago, Richmond and Houston never failed to look for certain prices quoted from Liverpool, Manchester, Bristol and London."[3] Goods were the life blood of this relationship. "Their movements, therefore, give the best idea of why the three countries remained locked in an interplay whose vitality could triumph over generations of economic isolationism, depressions, and wars."[4]

[1] Brebner, p. 109.   [2] Ibid, p. 225.   [3] Ibid, p. 240.   [4] Ibid, p. 239.

The flow of goods between the thirteen new-born states and the United Kingdom immediately after the end of the War of Independence showed very clearly that the political rupture was going to have little effect upon the volume of trade on the Atlantic. Though the plans of English liberals for free trade with the new republic failed, as we shall later see, the springs of commerce did not. In 1765, perhaps the last year of quite normal trade before the war, the United Kingdom had exported £1,944,114 of goods to the mainland colonies, and had received £1,151,698 of produce in return.[1] In 1784, the first full post-war year, the total exports from England and Scotland to the United States, including re-exports, had an 'official' value of £3,679,467, and the total imports therefrom of £749,329.* But it is apparent that the American market was positively deluged with British manufactured goods as soon as the War of Independence was over, and contemporary observers commented upon the tremendous flood of goods in these months.

It should be noted that this post-war situation made more pronounced the customarily adverse trade balance of America with Britain, which was also exaggerated by the slowness in the recovery of American exports, due no doubt to the disorganization resulting from the war and the shortage of credit. By 1786 British exports had sunk back to a much lower figure, £1,603,465, while imports from America had only risen to £843,119, largely owing to the severe American slump.

But what is perhaps most interesting to us is the proportion which British imports from and exports to the United States bore to the whole of Britain's import and export trade. In 1784 her total imports from all sources had an official value of £15,272,877 and in 1786 of £15,786,072; her total exports, of £15,101,491 and £16,300,730. Thus, whereas imports from the United States accounted for approximately

[1] David Macpherson, *Annals of Commerce* (London, 1805), III and IV, *passim*.

* All figures of trade in these early years must be treated with great caution, for they are unreliable and complicated by such factors as re-exports. Not until 1798 were re-exports distinguished from exports of home products, and until 1854 the values for imports and re-exports were largely 'official' ones. These were based on valuations made for the most part in the seventeenth century, and real values very greatly exceeded 'official' ones—perhaps by as much as fifty per cent on occasion. Not until precise government trade statistics become available after 1854— hitherto there had only been real, or declared, as opposed to 'official' values for *exports* in the years since 1798—can British estimates be relied on for more than quantitative comparisons.

one-twentieth of the whole in both years, exports thereto accounted for almost a quarter of our total exports in the exceptional year 1784 and almost one-tenth in the year 1786. Despite the altered flow of trade during the seven years of war, America had rapidly regained a place of great importance in Britain's economic life, particularly as an export market for British goods.

From the American point of view the importance of the British trade was already considerably greater. Once again the statistics must be treated with caution, but since they are all derived in this section from the same source they are a reasonably sure guide to proportion. The value of American exports to England, Scotland and Ireland in the years 1795, 1798 and 1801 was $6,324,066, $11,978,870 and $30,892,300; in the same years her total exports to all parts of the world amounted to $47,855,556, $61,527,097 and $93,020,513, so that her trade with Britain constituted somewhat under one-seventh, over one-sixth and about one-third of the whole in each of these years. This is an increasing ratio, which reflects America's growing productive capacity, chiefly in agriculture, but the ratio in imports is not only more constant, but very much larger. Total American imports from all sources in the same three years amounted to $69,756,258, $68,551,700 and $111,363,511, and those from Britain to $23,296,591, $17,275,161 and $39,398,620, a proportion of about one-third in each case. Thus already, approximately one-third of all America's imports, which chiefly consisted in manufactured goods, came from Britain, which is an impressive illustration of the importance of Anglo-American commercial relations. These years, too, set the course which trade was to follow until the American Civil War. It is, however, important to note, when comparing the very great dependence of the United States upon British imports with Britain's relatively (and only relatively) small dependence upon American produce and markets, that the people and economy of the United States as a whole were, and have been ever since, a great deal less dependent upon any kind of external trade than the British. America grew to economic greatness on the foundation of her own great internal free-trade area and her own vast resources; Britain upon the huge foreign trade which her industrial leadership in these early years made possible. Reductions in foreign trade were only of marginal importance in the lives of the American people; proportionate British reductions spread wide and serious misery. It must not, therefore, surprise us that America's dependence upon Britain seems at first sight so great: but though this effect is exaggerated, as it were by an optical illusion, it remains of great importance none the less.

The period of the Napoleonic wars, with its rapid development of economic warfare, makes generalization about Anglo-American trade difficult, particularly in view of the American embargo on British trade in the period prior to the outbreak of war in 1812 and of the actual war itself. Already the hostilities between Britain and Revolutionary France had had considerable effect on British economic life; the American imports from Britain in 1798, for example, which are quoted above, fell well below those given for 1795 when the war was still in its early stages, partly owing to an economic depression in both countries.[1] Now, during the second phase of the conflict such effects of war are even more marked. The combination of French economic measures with the American embargo, and subsequently the Non-Intercourse Act, reduced British exports to the United States from £11,846,513 in 1807 to £5,241,739 in 1808, and from £10,920,752 in 1810—a year when trade was freed to a great degree—to £1,841,253 in 1811.[2] In 1812, 1813 and 1814, during the course of the war, British exports to the United States, of course, virtually ceased, but in 1815 history repeated itself and there was a huge outpouring of British manufactured goods on to the American market, so that they attained in that year the unprecedented value of £13,255,374, which was not surpassed for over a quarter of a century. Again, as in 1784, this made up a quite exceptional proportion, more than a quarter, of our total exports during that year, and was to a great degree responsible for the beginning of American tariff protection in the following year, since the mass of British goods proved too much for many infant American industries which had been encouraged by the cutting off of British manufactures in the war. The tariff of 1816 was certainly one factor causing the sharp reduction in British exports to America in 1817, but that which occurred in 1819 was probably due to a severe depression in that year.

There was also a depression at this time in the United States—there had indeed been no real recovery since that which followed the war— and it is highly suggestive of the intimacy of Anglo-American economic relations that there has usually been a peculiarly sensitive interaction in this respect between the two economies. There is, of course, an international pattern in the trade cycle which becomes increasingly visible as industrialism spreads ever more widely over the surface of the earth, but, partly because one of the two has always been since 1783

[1] A. Achinstein, *Introduction to Business Cycles* (New York, 1950), pp. 168-9.
[2] G. R. Porter, *The Progress of the Nation* (Revised edition, London, 1912), p. 479.

the financial, and, in some respects, economic focus of the activities of mankind, there appears to have been a peculiarly long-standing and close coincidence between the troughs of the business cycle in America and Britain. This extends back to the birth of the United States, long before she developed her great industry, and is strong evidence for the closeness and significance of Anglo-American economic bonds. Later, in 1876, the American Minister, arriving in London, wrote: "I am not a little surprised to find the commercial depression in England, so exactly like our own in kind, varying only in degree. The two nations *surely sympathize in trade and finance if in nothing else.*"[1] There were other instances, besides those given below, of depressions in both countries, some of which were partly contemporary, but there were striking examples of correspondence in the beginnings of recessions in the following years: 1796 U.S., 1797 G.B.; 1802 U.S., 1803 G.B.; 1807 both; so too in 1815; 1825; 1828 U.S., 1829 G.B.; 1837; 1847; 1853 U.S., 1854 G.B.; 1857; 1865 U.S., 1866 G.B.; 1873; 1882 U.S., 1883 G.B.; 1890; 1900; 1907; 1913; 1918; 1920. The evidence is from our point of view most compelling in the early years, before the wide international character of the phenomenon was obvious.

Both countries had recovered from the post-war depression by 1821, and during the next thirty years a more stable situation prevailed. American figures for these years prove our contention of intimate economic intercourse most forcefully; they show the trade of the United States with the United Kingdom and all other countries, giving the percentage of it which was with Britain.[2]

The figures, shown in the table opposite, dispense with any further need to emphasize the dependence of the United States upon British trade in these years.

The British figures are still not to be relied upon for precise calculation, but they show clearly enough, as we have already seen to be the case in earlier years and as we should expect, that the proportion of her foreign trade which was with the United States was considerably less than that of the United States with her, though its importance to the national economy as a whole may not have been. Thus in 1825 18 per cent of all her exports went to the United States, and in 1840

---

[1] Pierrepont: q. *W.A.A.E.,* p. 368.

[2] Statistical Tables, H.R.Mis.Doc. 117, 52nd Congressional Session, 1893, x-xi: q. N. S. Buck, *The Development of the Organisation of Anglo-American Trade, 1800-1850* (New Haven, 1925), pp. 2-3.

Periods of Five Years	The United Kingdom	All Other Countries	Percentage from/to the United Kingdom
	IMPORTS FROM—		
	$	$	%
1821-5	151,346,561	217,885,821	40·39
1826-30	138,667,139	221,589,264	38·77
1831-5	219,976,517	317,452,362	40·93
1836-40	254,414,559	403,363,348	38·68
1841-5	178,359,348	298,895,659	37·37
1846-50	285,730,187	417,962,596	40·60
	EXPORTS TO—		
1821-5	122,154,837	221,828,068	35·51
1826-30	117,569,294	232,758,038	33·56
1831-5	188,287,249	270,533,755	41·04
1836-40	273,849,766	302,831,240	47·49
1841-5	221,175,606	285,131,492	43·68
1846-50	349,495,899	339,746,360	50·71

approximately 10 per cent, while in the same years she received approximately 13 per cent and 27 per cent of her imports thence.[1] One thing of importance should, however, be noted: it was during this period that the balance of trade between the two shifted finally and irrevocably into America's favour. Until probably the year 1829 British exports to the United States regularly exceeded her imports thence; during the eighteen-thirties the balance was in doubt, but by the beginning of the forties, probably by 1837, had swung down on the side of the United States, whose exports to Britain thereafter exceeded, later by great amounts, the latter's visible imports thence. From this time forward the dependence of America upon British trade diminished, while British dependence upon her American imports tended to increase and the proportion of her whole exports constituted by those going to America to decrease. This revolution was due to many things; fundamentally it was due to the increasing strength of the American economy; in later years it was to be due to the growth of free trade in Britain and of protection in the United States; it was also due latterly to the development of American industry and of Britain's need for

[1] John MacGregor, *Commercial Statistics: a digest of the productive resources, commercial legislation, customs tariffs, and etc. of all nations* (London, 1844-50), III.

American foodstuffs. But in this period it spelled the word cotton.

Since the end of the eighteenth century the Southern states had quite supplanted the West Indies as cotton-growers for the vast expansion of the British cotton industry, the first full fruit of her industrial revolution. This dual process of expanding industry in Britain and swiftly advancing the western frontier of the cotton area in the South soon locked the two countries in what appeared an unbreakable embrace, one indeed upon which the Confederacy based many of its hopes in the Civil War. By the five-year period 1846-50 the United States provided over 80 per cent of Britain's total cotton imports; in the five-year period 1850-4 over 70 per cent of her total cotton exports went to Britain; by 1860 cotton accounted for approximately three-quarters of her total exports of all commodities; and at the time of the Civil War the annual value of British cotton manufactures exceeded the total governmental revenue of the United Kingdom. Not merely was Britain very dependent upon imports of American cotton, but in these early years she exported a considerable quantity of cotton products to the United States. But, supremely important though the cotton link was, it was not the only one.

Americans, short of ready money still, as a frontier society always is, bought British goods, not merely because they were the cheapest, if not the only, ones available, but also because from Britain alone could they get such long terms of credit. The cut-throat competition between British merchants and manufacturers, particularly in the cotton industry, kept down prices, and the ready availability of capital for investment kept down rates of interest. These things applied in many other industries besides the textile; other characteristic British exports to the United States were Birmingham hardware, Sheffield cutlery and, in due course, iron rails. This vast flow of goods was facilitated by the fact that in these years both countries were extremely active in shipping across the Atlantic; they saw not merely the dominance of the American Clipper ship but the beginning of regular transatlantic routes, such as the Black Ball and Cunard lines, the latter being founded in 1840. Since 1814 this flow has never been stopped and only seriously checked, except through economic and natural causes, in the two world wars. Thus in these years the United States was the best of all Britain's customers, better than the colonies had been before the Revolution and better than any other country at the time; British exports to the United States far exceeded those to France and Germany combined, and the French and German trade of the United States amounted to less than half the British.

From the year 1854, when reliable and comprehensive government statistics are for the first time available, we can get a much more precise picture of the relative importance of American trade to Britain, and after 1880, when we have the British government version of American government statistics of American trade, of the comparative importance of the two.[1] The years following the repeal of the Corn Laws and the beginning of free trade in Britain saw, as we have remarked, a great increase in British imports, notably of foodstuffs but also of raw materials. Thus the official figure of £75,953,875 for imports from all sources in 1846 had risen by 1849 to £105,874,607, and though these are unreliable as an index of value, they give an idea of quantitative increase. By 1854 we are on solid ground, and in that year total imports into the United Kingdom amounted to £152 million, of which £30 million, or 19·7 per cent, came from the United States; the total from the whole of the British Empire in the same year amounted to £34 million, or 22·4 per cent, and the next largest single source was Germany, which sent £16 million, or 10·5 per cent of the total. Exports tell a similar tale. In 1854 total British exports amounted to £97 million, of which £21 million, or 21·6 per cent, went to the United States, £34 million, or 35·1 per cent, to the British Empire, and £9 million, or 9·3 per cent, to Germany, our next largest customer. One may already note here in passing the heavy adverse British trade balance in visible exports and imports, and the extent to which it was necessary for her to strike a balance by invisible exports, such as services and interest upon capital invested overseas.

The percentages of British imports from America and British exports to her, in five-yearly averages, until 1908 are set out below.

	Imports %	Exports %		Imports %	Exports %
1855-9	19·4	16·4	1885-9	22·5	12·2
1860-4	13·6	10·9	1890-4	23·4	11·0
1865-9	13·7	12·9	1895-9	24·4	8·6
1870-4	18·0	14·1	1900-4	24·3	7·4
1875-9	21·6	9·0	1905-8	20·9	7·0
1880-4	23·7	12·2			

Apart from such obvious incidental effects upon them as that of the Civil War and the Reconstruction period, with their shrinking of cotton

[1] *Statistical Tables and Charts relating to British and Foreign Trade and Industry (1854-1908)* (H.M.S.O., Cd. 4954, London, 1909), passim.

imports, the figures follow a fairly clear pattern—one of relative stability, though with a slight increase in the middle years as far as imports are concerned, and a gradual dwindling in exports as American industry develops and as competition increases from other industrial nations. In the last four-year period the annual average figures were as follows. Total imports, £603 million; total from the British Empire, £139 million, or 23·1 per cent; total from the next largest supplier, France, £52 million, or 8·6 per cent. Total exports, £368 million; total to the Empire, £123 million, or 33·4 per cent; total to Germany, the next biggest customer, £33 million, or 9·1 per cent.

The figures for the United States are, as they have been all along, more telling still. In the five-year period 1880-4 the annual average exports of the United States to all destinations were £165,429,000, less than a half of Britain's, which is what we should expect despite the already great disparity in population; of this total no less than 53·8 per cent, or £88,994,000, went to the United Kingdom. In the period 1905-8 the average total of exports from America was £359,281,000, of which £118,370,000, or 32·9 per cent, went to the United Kingdom. The intervening years show that this was a steady decline: 1885-9, 52·4 per cent; 1890-4, 50 per cent; 1895-9, 45·1 per cent; 1900-4, 39·1 per cent. That this process was primarily the result of the great growth of the American economy and of its search for new markets in fresh areas of the world is suggested by the fact that, as we have seen, this same flow of goods, seen as British imports, played a fairly constant part in Britain's total imports in the same period. With the closing of the frontier and the growth of American imperialism at the end of the century, there was a dramatic increase in American exports from a £213 million average per annum in 1895-9 to one of £292 million in 1900-4; this even produced some criticism of the protective system, under which this had been achieved, from men as internationally minded as Mahan, who wrote in 1898: "Our self-imposed isolation in the matter of markets, and the decline of our shipping interest in the last thirty years, have coincided singularly with an actual remoteness of this continent from the life of the rest of the world."[1] Great efforts were now put into the American export trade; aggressive American manufacturers replaced foreign—usually British—trading houses by their own export departments and it was to be symptomatic that monopoly agencies, for the export trade only, were to be specifically exempted from anti-trust legislation by the Webb-Pomerone Act of 1918. Whether or not the flag follows trade, American exports certainly

[1] Mahan, p. 19.

followed the Stars and Stripes at this time; in 1895 British exports to Puerto Rico and the Philippines totalled $1,995,854, and American (excluding Guam) $119,000, while by 1913 the respective figures were $4,718,000 and $25,360,000.

The impact of many new American commodities upon Britain was great; machine-made American boots were being worn by three-quarters of a million Britons by 1902, and in 1912 £415,468 worth of American cars were imported. This meant, too, increased competition for British exports, for between 1887-97 American exports to China increased 126 per cent and between 1895 and 1907 those to the British Empire itself increased at a faster rate than Britain's. The British reacted to this in specific ways, such as the defeat of an American effort to capture the retail tobacco trade by the formation of a trust on the American pattern (the Imperial Tobacco Company), and in a general way by supporting such powerful but abortive movements as those for tariff reform and imperial preference.

The pattern of American exports is clear, but reliable figures in terms of sterling for American imports from Britain are not to hand. They are, of course, the obverse of Britain's exports to America, but the latter figures can only be used as the roughest of guides; nevertheless, we can gain from this source an approximate impression of the ratio between her total imports and those from Britain. Thus in 1855-9 British exports to the United States seem to have averaged something like a third of America's total imports for home consumption, which does not disagree too violently with the established American figure, for the years 1846-50, of 40·6 per cent. Figures for later years seem to bear this out by showing the same decline as we have seen in the proportion of exports; in 1885-9 and 1905-8 they seem to have constituted roughly a fifth and a tenth of the whole. There is, therefore, an even more startling reduction in the proportion of the whole provided by Britain in the case of American imports, than in the case of American exports sent to the United Kingdom. This decline is explicable enough.

The great growth of American industry lay behind her increase in exports, and it was natural that these should seek an outlet in areas where they were not subjected, as in Britain, to fierce local industrial competition. Thus, as we have seen, the ratio of American to total imports into Britain remained remarkably constant in the sixty years before World War I, but the ratio of British to total exports from the United States declined, because the increasing flow of American exports was absorbed in other markets. But though Britain still needed

American imports, particularly of foodstuffs and raw materials, America had a decreasing need for Britain's chief exports, manufactured goods, in view of her own industrial development; this situation was exaggerated by the scale of American tariff protection, which was, after all, devised primarily for just this purpose of reducing British imports. There was, therefore, this sharp decline in imports from the United Kingdom. In practice this could be seen in such cases as that of Stanley Baldwin, who, according to G. M. Young, visited the United States in 1892, when a new and higher tariff was coming into operation; the effect of this was never forgotten by Baldwin, whose family business lost its best market within two years, first the cheap stuff, which could be made by anyone, and then the quality goods and specialities. In the case of Britain, as we have seen, this was reflected in an increasing dependence on invisible assets to right her balance of trade; she also tended to rely on types of triangular trade very similar to those by which the New Englanders had come to thrive in earlier days. Thus Britain began to utilize such methods as exports of raw materials, like tin, which America needed, from the British possessions overseas, which themselves had need of manufactured goods from the mother country, in order to pay for American commodities which she herself had to have. What, in the later day of the dollar gap, was to be a characteristic pattern of British trade was already perceptible.

In the case of the United States this situation was simply a reflection of her increasing economic stature, for, though her direct trade balance with Britain had been favourable by the beginning of the eighteen-forties, it was in these years that she had an export trade balance with the whole of the world for the first time, though she was to remain financially a debtor nation until World War I. Until 1873 she had been an immature debtor nation, with an import trade balance, but between 1874 and 1914 she became a mature debtor nation; in those years, except for 1875, 1888 and 1893, she had an export trade balance. In the years 1914-8 she was to become a creditor nation for the first time. It was this revolutionary economic development, which was to prove probably the most important happening in the economic history of mankind since the Industrial Revolution in Britain, that lay behind the great change which came over Anglo-American economic relations in these years.

World War I involved a gross distortion of world trade, and particularly of Anglo-American trade. Both before and, increasingly, after America's entry into the struggle, there was a great and growing flood of goods eastward, and a marked diminution of return traffic; the financial means which were found to make this possible, despite the drop in British exports, ranged from realization of British securities in America to outright American loans. The unprecedented extremity of Britain's economic dependence upon the United States during the war needs no further emphasis, but it is perhaps important to point out that the economic dependence of America upon Britain was decreased rather than augmented. In this respect the great crisis merely increased the swiftness of tendencies which we can see had been at work for a good many years, but this made it harder for Americans to adjust themselves to their new role, particularly towards Britain, who had for so long played that same part towards them. Whether they liked it or not, the United States had become by the end of the war the world's greatest creditor nation, a position which brought with it new economic responsibilities. This difficult adjustment was made even more painful by the fact that it occurred during, and was mixed up with, an upheaval which thrust her into an unwelcome political prominence in the affairs of the nations, and which emphasized her very important political obligations to Great Britain. These things complicated the American and British reactions, but they were never so crystal clear as they were to be in World War II. In 1940 it was becoming plain to Americans that Britain was defending the United States, and it seemed reasonable to repay that debt by unstinted economic aid; indeed this feeling carried enough weight after the war to contribute a good deal to the Anglo-American loan of 1946. In the aftermath of the first war, no such bargain could be struck, and this confusion, arising from America's sudden and bewildering position of economic dominance, combined with reluctance to accept corresponding political obligations, was merely worse confounded by the acrimonious war debts issue. But by the middle of the twenties some form of normality seemed to have returned to the economic affairs of mankind.

Certainly a very familiar pattern reappears in the commercial relations of Britain and America. The figures of relative exports and imports in both cases (see table on page 66) take up the story where we left it and speak for themselves.[1]

The figures show a continued decline in all categories in the twenties, but some sort of an equilibrium in the thirties. There is relatively little change in any category after 1931, but even in the two years before that there is not more than 3 per cent alteration anywhere; it is curious

[1] *League of Nations Memoranda on International Trade,* passim.

	UNITED KINGDOM		UNITED STATES	
	Percentage of whole constituted by :		Percentage of whole constituted by :	
Year	Imports from U.S.	Exports to U.S.	Imports from U.K.	Exports to U.K.
	(General Trade—Merchandise only)			
	%	%	%	%
1913	18·43	9·37	15·17	23·78
1923	19·22	9·67	10·66	21·17
1924	18·88	8·33	10·15	21·41
1926	18·47	9·49	8·65	20·22
1928	15·8	8·1	8·5	16·5
1929	16·1	7·4	7·5	16·2
1930	14·7	6·1	6·9	17·6
1931	12·1	5·8	6·5	18·8
1932	11·9	5·0	5·7	17·9
1933	11·2	6·3	7·7	18·6
1934	11·2	5·2	6·9	18·0
1936	11·0	7·4	8·3	17·9
1938	12·8	5·4	6·0	16·8

indeed to reflect that these apparently stable figures cover the greatest period of economic collapse in the history of industrial civilization. The total imports of Britain from America sank from £195,980,000 in 1929 to £82,100,000 in 1934 and her exports to America from £62,016,000 to £23,300,000. Anglo-American trade, in other words, was far more than halved in terms of money value, yet the relative dependence of the two peoples upon one another varied very little. In 1934 the United Kingdom was still America's best customer, and was only approached by Canada in this respect, for she still took more American exports than any other nation; on the other hand the United States imported more from Canada and a shade more from Japan than she did from the United Kingdom. Thus already the shape of the dollar gap looms more ominous on the horizon. Britain in the thirties has a consistently adverse balance of trade with the United States, though she is still able to continue the purchases she needs from there by indirect means of payment; thus it is significant that the United States had substantial adverse trade balances with Malaya and India. By such means as these Britain might have kept the wolf from the door for many years.

66

But World War II, like World War I, though to an even greater degree, speeded the processes already in operation, and by 1945 the wolf had pretty nearly effected an entry. With the details of this desperate situation for the British people and the efforts to remedy it, we shall deal at a later stage, for it had by then become a diplomatic and political matter; after World War II the economic relationship of the two countries thrust itself insistently and irresistibly on to the political plane. There had been a tendency in this direction over the war debts and reparations question in the inter-war years, particularly those of economic crisis, but now it was no mere question of the defalcation of Britain, but of her life and death. Yet, despite the new urgency of the situation and its extreme gravity, it was one with whose general outline we are already familiar. Once more the figures speak for themselves.[1]

| | UNITED KINGDOM | | UNITED STATES | |
| | Percentage of whole constituted by : | | Percentage of whole constituted by : | |
Year	Imports from U.S.	Exports to U.S. (including re-exports)	Imports from U.K.	Exports to U.K. (including re-exports)
Annual Average	%	%	%	%
1934-8	11·6	6·3	7·1	17·4
1943	58·7	7·3	3·1	34·8
1947	16·6	5·1	3·6	7·7
1948	8·8	4·3	4·1	5·1
1949	9·8	3·4	3·4	5·8
July, 1949, to June, 1950	8·8	4·1	3·4	5·4

The war year 1943, when Lend-Lease was approaching full flood, gives some idea of the vast dependence of Britain upon American economic resources, an ample reciprocation for the military dependence of the United States upon Britain in 1940; it also shows how seriously Britain's vital export trade to America dwindled owing to the exigencies of the struggle.

[1] J. M. Cassels (Editor), *The Sterling Area, An American Analysis* (London, 1951), passim.

Once more we see that while Britain needs to keep up her standard of living by maintaining her American imports, she has the greatest difficulty in keeping up her exports to the United States; she has, as always, a heavy adverse trade balance with America. Matters have not been improved by the decline in her invisible exports, and by her heavy indebtedness to the so-called Sterling Area, consisting chiefly of members of the British Commonwealth, upon some of whose dollar-earning capacity the mother country had long relied for her international solvency. Fundamentally, the whole problem arose from the change in the nature, as well as the strength, of the American economy; not only did she become a great creditor, but there was a continuous and marked decrease in the importance of her raw material exports relative to those of manufactures. In 1850 raw materials constituted three-fifths of the whole, but by 1940 they made up less than one-fifth, while finished manufactures rose from 12 per cent to 50 per cent; foodstuffs reached a peak in exports in the last quarter of the nineteenth century and then diminished. But, despite this change, so colossal was the expansion of the American economy that Britain, like the rest of the world, still showed an insatiable desire for American goods. The dollar problem, therefore, is not an entirely new one, but an old one writ exceedingly large by adverse circumstances which came to a head through World War II.

What then is the pattern of mutual Anglo-American commercial dependence during the century and three-quarters since independence? In the first place, naturally enough, it seemed as if British trade was throughout the nineteenth century more important to America than American trade to Britain, but this is an illusion produced by the relative unimportance of all foreign trade in the American economy. In the second place *it appears that it was in the second quarter of the nineteenth century that Britain's American exports were most important to her economy and that of the United States,* a conclusion which is broadly borne out by the financial history of that period which we shall consider later. British exports to the United States constituted approximately 10 per cent of her total exports in 1786. The curve rose to a height of just under 20 per cent between 1825 and 1850, after which a decline set in, and by 1949 they constituted, despite all the efforts to improve the position, only about 3 per cent of the whole. The obverse, American imports from Britain, which were approximately 33⅓ per cent of total American imports in 1795, rose to a plateau of around 40 per cent in the second quarter of the century, and then declined to a similar figure of 3 per cent of the total by 1949.

In the third place, however, *it seems to be in the second half of the century that America's exports to Britain were most important to the life of both countries.* In 1795 they constituted perhaps 14 per cent of her whole exports, had risen to about 50 per cent by 1850 and had remained at or near that level until the first half of the nineties, after which they sank to 5 per cent of the total by 1949. The importance of these goods to Britain, relative to her total imports, was greatest in the same period (though it began a little earlier and lasted a little later) while undergoing a slight decline in the sixties, no doubt a reflection of the significance of cotton, in the earlier, and grain, in the later years, as essential imports for the running of the British industrial machine. It is characteristic that Britain remained dependent upon American imports to a much greater degree until the present time, so that in 1949 they constituted 9 per cent of the total; the disparity between the 3 per cent of her exports and the 9 per cent of her imports is some indication of the dollar difficulty.

Thus it would plainly seem, as far as commercial relations are concerned, that the mutual dependence of the two countries was greatest between approximately 1825 and 1890; and that after this date a decline in the importance of the connexion set in, although it operated much less in the case of Britain, whose relative reliance upon America therefore increased as the years passed. It was during the years when American isolation was at its height and when the two countries were most remote from one another politically that their tangible economic bonds were strongest. It was perhaps a providential dispensation that, when the economic bonds were loosened, political ones, in some ways more powerful, were coming into existence to take their place.

But in some senses it is misleading to talk of a decline in the importance of mutual economic dependence in the twentieth century; certainly the period of the American Loan of 1946 and Marshall Aid seems to belie the very existence of such a decline. Partly, it is true, these things may be discounted as temporary expedients to meet a situation precipitated by World War II and motivated largely by political fears of Soviet Communism, but, even beneath these, there obviously lie economic ties of the greatest strength and sensitivity between the two nations. Perhaps the best analysis would be that the relationship has ceased, since the nineteenth century, to be the unique and exclusive thing it had been, but that it has lost little of its importance. In absolute terms of money value it has not declined at all except for the universal

69

shrinkage, though there has almost certainly been some decline in physical terms.[1]

	American Exports to Britain	American Imports from Britain	British Exports to United States	British Imports from United States
	$	$	£	£
1913	590,732,000	271,955,000	59,453,000	141,652,000
1929	848,000,000	330,000,000	62,016,000	195,980,000
1938	521,000,000	118,000,000	28,900,000	118,100,000
1948	644,000,000	290,000,000	70,900,000	183,200,000

Even given increases in population and national income, if we take triangular trade with the sterling area into account, this does not indicate a marked decline; the hard core of Anglo-American trade has not been too greatly affected in extent. But that is indeed what it has really become. In the nineteenth century it was more than a core, but by 1950 the stupendous growth of the American economy has simply meant that Anglo-American trade is a very similar core of a very much bigger fruit. In 1913 total American exports to all parts of the world were $2,484 million; in 1948 they were $12,653 million. Figures for the development of American national income show an even more remarkable increase. Thus the American domination of the world's economy has grown until it has greatly exceeded even that of Britain in the nineteenth century, and so complex and widespread has the web of that economy become, that changes at its heart can have the most far-reaching effects at its extremities. In this fashion Anglo-American trade has retained its significance. In general terms it remains the most important economic relationship of its kind on earth, one which is greatly enhanced if the Canadian and Commonwealth trade be reckoned in. America is the world's greatest producer, Britain its largest, most influential trader; and in the economic sphere each remains on the whole the best neighbour of the other. So the Anglo-American relationship has lost its peculiar and outstanding character, in that it can no longer be isolated from the broadening pattern of world economic development, but it has not lost its central and supreme position.

Thus our first point, the mutual economic dependence of the two peoples throughout their history, is amply proven. It cannot be described as a *growing* intimacy, parallel to the ripening cordiality in

[1] *League of Nations Memoranda* and *The Sterling Area*, passim.

the political sphere, since its unique and exclusive nineteenth-century basis was broadened in the succeeding years, but of its continuous existence and deep importance throughout the whole period from 1783 to the present there can be no question.

II

THUS the economic interdependence of the two peoples is incontrovertible, but it must not be imagined that this always meant an easy interchange of goods; except perhaps for one period, the channels of trade were indeed constantly blocked by obstacles raised by one or other of the two nations in the belief that it was in their interest to do so. In the event, the forces of nature triumphed over those difficulties, but the difficulties were none the less real. Brebner writes: "While it is rank heresy to say so to interested Americans, Britons or Canadians, the whole apparatus of tariffs, quotas and preferential duties . . . has been far less important than the irresistible floods of goods which have flowed through, by, or over those nationalistic locks, dams and weirs":[1] but though this is true, it would give a quite unreal picture of Anglo-American relations if one failed to depict the tariff history of the two countries. Frankland wrote in 1928: "In . . . raw-material resources . . . Britain and the United States mutually compensate one another's deficiencies. . . . Each is the other's greatest customer. The greatest damage either could suffer is to have the other's market shut to him. In international trade these two that one might expect to be rivals are drawn closer together by most compelling interests."[2] This is only true within strict limits—except in the first half of the nineteenth century when it was true almost without limit—and one of the difficulties of the twentieth century has been that it has become less and less true, except in so far as the British Commonwealth can be regarded as an economic unit; and even in that sense it seems possible that the science of synthetics may undermine America's need for raw materials from British possessions, such as rubber from Malaya. For the truth is that, whereas from 1783 to perhaps 1900 and even beyond, the United States was primarily a great raw material, and later food, exporter, from that time onwards she became increasingly an industrial nation exporting manufactured goods. Britain on the other hand was fast

[1] Brebner, p. 239.
[2] J. M. Frankland, *The Influence of International Trade upon British-American Relations* (New Haven, 1928), pp. 99-100.

71

becoming a great industrial power in 1783, and has remained such ever since, so that it was only in earlier years that the two economies were in a full sense complementary. Yet even then, the commercial policies of the two were not really in accord, except for the space of a very few years.

Let us consider first those of Britain. In 1783 Britain was still a mercantilist, economic-imperialist, and protectionist country, but two great documents published in 1776, the Declaration of Independence and *The Wealth of Nations,* had helped to cause or to symbolize the breakdown of this three-century-old system. Already by the coming of war in 1793, though the enlightenment of men like Pitt and the clamour of the new industrialists like Wedgewood had failed (in face of opposition from those, like Sheffield, imbued with a goodly measure of the old Adam) to implement the far-seeing plan proposed by extreme liberals like Shelburne for free trade with the erstwhile American colonies, it had produced moves in the direction of the freeing of trade, such as the Anglo-French commercial treaty of 1786. The twenty years of war suspended the process of change by encouraging concentration on economic nationalism as a means to victory, and by making the reduction of taxation impossible. Britain emerged from the war in 1815, as before, with a very high tariff wall, including duties, on manufactured goods ranging from 40 per cent to 180 per cent, and on such articles as tea of 100 per cent, while British West Indian sugar was charged 30 shillings per hundredweight and foreign sugar the colossal sum of 63 shillings per hundredweight.

But a revolutionary change was in prospect, for Britain's unrivalled industrial supremacy meant that she had a vast field of expansion if she could import the food and raw materials she needed and enable the producers thereof to buy her manufactured goods. The latter was by no means the less powerful motive; as a traveller of the period declared in a manner strikingly reminiscent of more recent travellers in the opposite direction, "If we persist in refusing to admit her corn into Great Britain, she must of necessity limit her importation of our manufactures; for her consumption is bounded by her means of payment, and by that alone."[1] The great free-trade movement was victorious in three stages, of which the second was the most important. The first included the reductions of duties and the removal of restrictions in the years 1824-7 which was chiefly the work of Huskisson,

[1] Q. J. L. Mesick, *The English Traveller in America, 1785-1835* (New York, 1922), p. 194.

though there were liberal measures after his death, such as the repeal of certain Orders-in-Council, restricting colonial trade with the United States, in 1830. The second, which was the work of Peel under the tremendous pressure of Cobden and Bright with the Anti-Corn Law League, began with great alterations in the protective system between 1842 and 1845, and culminated in the abandonment of the Corn Laws in 1846. The landed interest who supported these laws were the only very powerful political and economic force standing in the way of free trade, and when Peel in the face of Cobden's arguments crumpled up his piece of paper and left others to answer them, he not only broke his own party but symbolized the triumph of free trade. That triumph was finally celebrated by Gladstone, chiefly in 1853 and 1860. This system of virtually free trade, financed by regular income tax, monopolized the English scene for forty years and remained in operation for more than sixty; it became the gospel of the Liberal Party and was accepted by the Conservatives as the basis of the great national prosperity of this period, which indeed it was.

Yet, though it had not been inaugurated hastily, but over a period of at least thirty years, it was in a sense, as Mumford points out, a supreme act of faith. It is true that Britain could only attain greatness as well as wealth on the basis of a world-wide commerce, but the continued existence of that commerce, particularly in the form of free trade, and of the stable political conditions which made it possible, was, on any extensive view of history, problematical. Britain's difficulties in 1950 are more severe because her economic policy in 1850 was unrestrained by doubts, but one must also remember that her wealth and power in the intervening years can be traced to the same source. The voices of doubt began first to be raised in the economic depression of the eighties, but they did not become penetrating until conducted by Joseph Chamberlain in the tariff reform choir after 1903. The movement was precipitated by the agricultural depression produced by the competition of cheap overseas foodstuffs, by the growth of industrialism in other countries under the protection of tariffs, and by the wide revival of the imperialist spirit; it demanded protection of British manufactures, and also imperial preference in foodstuffs, because the latter alone appealed to the Empire as a whole, and this involved a tax on food. The effort failed, partly because of aversion from the idea of food taxes, and partly because it suffered, by association, from the disgrace of its forebear, the imperialism of the Boer War period, but in World War I the issue was kept alive by economic circumstances and by the close imperial association. The Coalition Government in 1920-1 took certain

73

tentative steps in continuation of the measures to protect "key" industries for strategic reasons which had been inaugurated during the war, but when the Conservatives, led by Baldwin, went to the country in 1923 on the full issues of protection and imperial preference, they were soundly defeated.

When they returned to power in 1924 they dared not do more than continue the "safeguarding experiment," as it was called after the Safeguarding of Industries Act of 1921, but the forces of nature were working on their side. The competition of the great new industrial nations was becoming ever more pressing, as the penetrating eye of Cobden had foreseen as early as 1835, after his visit to the United States, "Our only chance of national prosperity lies in the timely remodelling of our system, so as to put it as nearly as possible upon an equality with the improved management of the Americans."[1] The Great Depression made a return to protection almost inevitable; indeed it can be argued that an economic collapse on this scale will not only inevitably defeat any government in power, but almost inevitably reverse any economic policies then in operation. Certainly Great Britain abandoned free trade in 1931 in much the same way as America began to abandon unrelieved protection in 1933. The first importation duties in 1931 were followed in 1932 by the Ottawa Conference and the establishment of a system of imperial preference; there was also a marked tendency in British commercial policy towards conservative bi-lateral trade arrangements, which would ensure Britain a modicum of economic stability.

The Anglo-American Trade Agreement of 1938 ran counter, as we shall see, to this tendency, and was largely signed for political reasons, but World War II was to effect a change, and men even came to believe that they had already seen the light when they signed the agreement in 1938. Chamberlain was to say of it in 1940: "It was the very negation of that too prevalent system of bi-lateralism, of exclusive advantages, of discrimination carried to the pitch which clogs the wheels of commerce, and which promotes ill-feeling among the nations. . . . One of our foremost aims will be the restoration of international trade. . . . That is a policy that we have in mind when the time comes to turn once more from war to peace."[2] This repentance was in fact produced by the war, which is "the supreme destroyer of conventional modes of thought and habits of mind. Under its influence the

---

[1] Richard Cobden: q. Heindel, p. 153.
[2] Q. D. Abel, *A History of British Tariffs, 1923-1942* (London, 1945), p. 134.

outlook of many undergoes transformation. . . ."[1] Certainly during the war years Britain's leaders turned for the most part back towards forms of trade which were more free, partly perhaps in that warm feeling that all will, after victory, be well, which sustains men in time of war. So the new Lend-Lease Agreement of 1942 promised action "directed to the expansion . . . of production, . . . exchange and consumption of goods, which are the material foundations of the liberty and welfare of all peoples; to the elimination of all forms of discriminatory treatment in international commerce, and to the reduction of tariffs and other trade barriers. . . ."[2] Though, as we shall see, these intentions were not to prove easy of fulfilment, they were to remain the intentions of the British Government up to the present time.

The tariff history of the United States was very different; indeed it presents itself for the most part in terms of startling contrast. The first tariff of the Federal Government after its inauguration in 1789, though it was framed under the influence of Hamilton, was so low as to be little, if anything, more than a revenue tariff, but it was to be the foundation on which the later structure of American protectionism would be raised. The natural interests of the American republic, as a neo-colonial power and a prime producer of raw materials, were in free trade, but the fact that virtually the only source of manufactured goods was the hated mother country set up a conflict in the American mind between political mistrust and economic desire, which gave her a natural predisposition towards protection. The wartime blockade, the embargo and the Non-Intercourse Act, and above all the war of 1812 itself, all encouraged this predisposition as well as the domestic industries which alone would make it possible, except with the hardships which had been such a feature of the non-importation boycotts of the Revolutionary period. Thus, when in 1814 the flood of British goods threatened these infant industries, the tariff of 1816, the first truly protective American tariff, was imposed; its highest duties of a permanent nature were those of 20 per cent on textile manufactures and iron. The depression of 1818-19 strengthened protectionist sentiment and resulted in the tariff of 1824, which raised duties on cotton and woollen goods, among others, to 33⅓ per cent. In 1828 the protectionist interest succeeded in getting yet another tariff through Congress, which raised the duty on most textiles and iron to what was in effect 50 per cent; it doubled the duty on rum and left an average rate of duty, on all commodities taxed, of 41 per cent.

[1] Ibid, pp. 133-4.   [2] Article 7: q. Abel, p. 145.

But there had been a rising tide of protest against this policy, particularly in the South. Henry Clay's original "American policy" of tariffs and internal improvements had been intended to promote national unity, and had been supported even by John C. Calhoun of South Carolina, but this new "tariff of Abominations" threatened to disrupt the Union itself. The South, in the increasing grip of cotton culture, came to realize that excessive protection was directly contrary to its interest, which was in as free an exchange as possible of its raw material exports for the cheap manufactured goods of Britain; the demand for protection became increasingly a Northern and sectional one. South Carolina, which was suffering an economic decline, became the leader of opposition, and when it became clear from the passage of a new tariff in 1832, which, though it made some reductions, retained a considerable degree of protection (a 34 per cent average), that the Administration would not keep the protectionists in check, she precipitated the Nullification Crisis by refusing to accept this piece of legislation. The result was the "Compromise" tariff of 1833, which decisively reversed the protectionist trend. It provided for a gradual reduction of the high rates over the next nine years, which would result in the restoration of the 20 per cent level of the 1816 tariff by the year 1842. This policy was put into effect and was a measure of that influence of the South in the national government which was such a marked feature of this pre-Civil War period of Democratic ascendancy. But the economic crisis of 1837 and the accident of a Whig Administration enabled the protectionists to gain the passage of the measure of 1842, when the process of reduction was complete; this was, broadly speaking, a return to the rates of 1832 with some slight modifications, which produced an average rate of 30 per cent on dutiable articles. The return of the Democrats, however, led to the liberal Walker tariff of 1846, which, "though often described as a 'free-trade' measure . . . was really one of qualified protection, not much superior to the English system before Peel's reforms."[1] It completely reorganized the system, enlarging the "free list" and making eight schedules of goods each with a different rate; the duties varied from 5 per cent to 100 per cent and averaged about 25 per cent, with iron and wool at 30 per cent and cotton goods at 25 per cent. In 1857 there was a further relaxation which reduced the average rate to 20 per cent.

The triumph of the Republicans on a protectionist platform in 1860 and the secession of the chief opponents of a high tariff produced a

[1] C. F. Bastable, *The Commerce of Nations* (Ninth Edition (Revised), London, 1923), p. 75.

sharp change in American commercial policy, and this new trend was to remain dominant during what were in effect the next seventy years of Republican and Northern domination. It was under this régime of high protection that the giant of American industrialism was to be reared.

The first move made by the Senate, soon after the secession of the Southern Congressmen, was the Morrill tariff of 1861, which raised certain duties; it was followed by the Act of 1862, with an average rate of 37 per cent, and, in the flush of victory in 1864, by one with an average rate of 47 per cent. In 1867, in the post-war depression, wool was granted further protection, but by 1870 there was a mild reaction, and in 1872 this went as far as a general reduction of 10 per cent. A slump, however, began in 1874 and the 10 per cent was accordingly added again in 1875. The period until 1897 was complicated by differences as to the nature of reform demanded, and by changes in the structure of the tariff, and though efforts were made to effect reductions, particularly in 1883 and 1893-4 (the latter a serious attempt by the Democrat President Cleveland), they were obstructed in Congress and did not produce very decisive results. The legislation of 1883 was revised by the Republicans in 1890 and that of 1894 by the Dingley tariff of 1897, which was a distinct high-water mark in American protection to date; the average rate of the McKinley tariff of 1890 had been 49·5 per cent, and that of the Democratic tariff of 1894 39·9 per cent, but that of 1897 was 57 per cent. It was not altered for twelve years, after which President Taft obtained the passage of certain mild reductions, though against considerable opposition, by the Payne-Aldrich tariff, but it was not until the advent of Wilson and the Democrats to power in 1912 that any serious measure of reform was undertaken. This took shape as the Underwood tariff of 1913, which made certain reductions and which considerably enlarged the free list, but a great part of it consisted in the abolition or reduction of obsolete or nominal duties. It certainly left the United States a highly protectionist country compared with Great Britain, and a protectionist country by any standard.

But the return of the Republicans in 1921 on a surge of American isolationist nationalism resulted in an enthusiastic adoption of even more extreme protectionism than that of 1897. An emergency tariff in 1921 extended protection to agricultural produce and took strong measures against "dumping," which figure much in contemporary English legislation under the "safeguarding system." The Fordney-McCumber tariff of 1922 was the highest enacted to date, and not merely raised a number of basic duties, but gave the President discretionary powers of a wide order to raise these still further, in certain circumstances by as much as 50 per cent. The initial reaction of Congress to the economic collapse of 1929 was, contrary to the advice of economists, to pass the Hawley-Smoot tariff of 1930, which raised these unprecedented rates yet higher. But with the New Deal came an inevitable reaction; under the Trade Agreements Act of 1934 the President was authorized for three years to negotiate trade agreements with the consent of the Senate, and to raise or lower tariff rates by not more than 50 per cent, an interesting adaptation of the precedent of 1922, for there was certainly little idea now of *raising* them. The life of this Act was repeatedly extended throughout the next twenty years of Democratic rule, and until the end of that time America's face was set in the direction of the liberalizing of world trade. But the steps she was able, or willing, actually to take were by no means revolutionary. This was partly due to the occasional restiveness of Congress, and to the fact that all America's instincts were protective; even the Act of 1934 was in form an amendment to the Smoot-Hawley Act, which remained the basic tariff of the country. Furthermore, it should be noted that the continued pressure for the reduction of tariffs came primarily not from the Treasury or Commerce Departments, but from the State Department under Cordell Hull. This is perhaps significant, for it may indicate that the main desire in America was to induce other nations to lower their tariffs and thus facilitate American exports. The United States was willing to make reciprocal reductions and did so in the many trade treaties which she signed in the next twenty years, but she showed no ardent desire to lower drastically, let alone to abolish, her protective tariff walls. Between 1842 and 1860 Britain had gone the whole hog to free trade because her industrialists wished, not merely to gain markets by the economic and political inducements which a free-trade Britain offered to the exports of foreign lands, but also to gain tax-free food and raw materials. The situation in America, which had vast natural resources of her own, was different (though with the exhaustion of such American supplies as timber, petroleum and iron it was rapidly becoming less so), and she remained until 1952 a strongly protectionist country. One of the most critical questions at the close of 1952 was what the attitude of the new Republicans would be on this matter, for if they continued to move, however slowly, in the direction of free trade, there was a chance that Britain and America might, for almost the first time in their history, be facing the same way on tariff policy.

For the impressive fact which this résumé of Anglo-American tariff history reveals is that, except for the period of Southern ascendancy between 1832 and 1861 (discounting the years 1842-4) and for brief Democratic spells, such as those beginning in 1893 and 1913, the commercial policies of the two Governments have always, until World War II and the succeeding years, been moving in opposite directions. From 1783 to 1816 America's interest was in and her policy was in effect one of free trade, but Britain was still a highly protected imperial area on traditional mercantilist lines, whose severe restrictions on American trade with the colonies and the mother country undoubtedly made it more difficult for Americans to earn the money with which to pay for imports of British manufactured goods. In the twenties there began the trend in Britain towards free trade which was accomplished by 1860, but by the time her first reforms were inaugurated, the United States had embarked upon a policy of protection. In 1832, however, this policy was checked by the determined opposition of the South, and, broadly speaking, during the next eighteen years both countries moved in the direction of free trade; Britain virtually reached this goal by 1860, but America was still far from a free trade state even after the enactment in 1857 of her lowest tariff since serious protection had begun. It was one of the great ironies of the defeat of the Confederacy in the Civil War that it signified the weakening of the strongest single strand that has ever existed in the rope of Anglo-American economic relations, that woven of cotton. But there can be little doubt that this weakening was inevitable in any case; it was no more than a dream that, as Stephen Vincent Benet has it, the Civil War buried:

> *"And with these things, bury the purple dream*
> *Of the America we have not been*
>
> .   .   .   .
>
> *The pastoral rebellion of the earth*
> *Against machines, against the Age of Steam,*
> *The Hamiltonian extremes against the Franklin mean,*
> *The genius of the land*
> *Against the metal hand,*
> "[1]
>
> .   .   .   .

No one can doubt that America was destined to become a great industrial nation. Already, almost before the Southern supremacy had entered its prime, Cobden had published his first important work,

[1] S. V. Benet, *John Brown's Body* (New York, 1928), pp. 374-5.

which was on the subject of the United States. Supreme representative of the new industrial middle class, unhampered by Tory prejudices, he had prophesied the rise of American industrial might. But while the agricultural ascendancy of the South and West remained, it proved the perfect complement of the rising dominion of the British industrial interest; it was natural enough that there should follow a period of harmonious commercial policies.

But with the Civil War and the triumph of the Northern industrial section, there came the sharp change to severe protectionism which we have noted; restrained at first—for nearly forty years—by the agricultural interests which the North also contained, and by Britain's demand for grain, it reached new heights after 1897, while contemporary British tariff reform movements proved abortive. World War I twisted the effects of the Wilsonian reductions, and the Conservative move towards protection in the twenties, which might have put both countries on a protectionist basis, did not gain the support of the British electorate until the coming of the Great Depression. But by this time America's tariffs were higher than ever, and so in the great crash both countries sharply reversed their commercial policies and found themselves as a result facing once more in opposite directions. It is true that though they faced opposite ways they came gradually to stand closer together, since Britain was moving from free trade to moderate protectionism and America from extreme protectionism to the same stand, but this was counterbalanced by the contrast between America's new demand for the removal of restrictions upon trade and Britain's tendency to multiply them. The opposition between American protectionism and British free trade between 1860 and 1931 was, it must be remarked, natural enough; Britain was a developed industrial power dependent on the outside world for markets, food and raw material; the United States was a developing industrial power largely sufficient unto itself. But the policies of the thirties in both countries were overshadowed by what Churchill calls the "economic blizzard."

By 1945, however, the interests of the two nations were much more akin than they had perhaps been before; in the second quarter of the nineteenth century they had been complementary, but now they were very much alike. Both were highly urbanized industrial societies; both, though America to a less degree, needed export markets for their manufactures; both, though America to a less if increasing degree, needed imports of food and raw materials. Both, therefore, seemed to have a plain interest in the freeing of international trade and its consequent rapid expansion, and the realization of this appears to be reflected in their policies, for during and after World War II these were the causes to which they both paid at least lip service. Britain might still have balance of payments problems, America might still retain a high tariff, but both powers did at least seem, for the first time in nearly a hundred years, to be facing in the same direction on tariff policy.

III

THERE could no longer, however, in 1952 be any possible doubt whatever as to which was the paramount economic power; the United States had long since moved into that position. And this is our second thesis, that there is the same swing over in the mutual balance of power in the economic as in the analogous political field. This is apparent enough to anyone living in the nineteen-fifties; there is little need to emphasize it, and no need to prove it. What is not so often remembered is the long period during which the reverse was true, for it was only just before the end of the nineteenth century that supremacy passed unquestionably into American hands. It is true that her population passed that of the United Kingdom in the middle of the eighteen-forties, but it was not until the decade after 1890 that her total production of coal and pig-iron exceeded Britain's. The figures of industrial output make the acceleration in American development crystal clear. Indices of industrial output, from a base of 100 in 1860, when Britain's economy was already highly developed are as follows:[1]

	Great Britain	The United States	Germany
1860	100	100	100
1880	156	213	179
1900	232	675	464
1913	294	1,250	714

This surpassing of Britain by the United States had long been foreseen in America, with its boundless optimism and sense of power; Franklin had prophesied it, Lincoln had made an over-sanguine estimate of its rapidity. Henry Adams put his finger on it after the turn of the century with the uncanny accuracy of the Adamses; "The power of the railway system had enormously increased since 1870. Already the coal output of 160 million tons closely approached the 180 millions

[1] Howard S. Ellis, *The Economics of Freedom, The Progress and Future of Aid to Europe* (New York, 1950), p. 88.

of the British Empire, and one held one's breath at the nearness of what one had never expected to see, the crossing of courses, and the lead of American energies."[1] In England, too, the best heads had foreseen it. Gladstone wrote in 1879 in *Kin Beyond The Sea*:

> I do not speak of the vast contributions which from year to year, through the operations of a colossal trade, each makes to the comfort and wealth of the other, nor of the friendly controversy, which in its own place it might be right to raise between the leanings of America to Protectionism and the more daring reliance of the Old Country upon free and unrestricted intercourse with all the world, nor of the menace which in the prospective development of her resources America offers to the commercial supremacy of England. On this subject I will only say that it is she alone who, at a coming time, can and probably will wrest from us our commercial supremacy. . . . We have no more title against her than Venice or Genoa or Holland has had against us. . . .[2]

As much as twenty-eight years earlier *The Economist* had put it far more unequivocally: "The superiority of the United States to England is ultimately as certain as the next eclipse."[3]

Yet contemporaries, even when they perceived the revolution, were often slow to see its implications. Sir Norman Angell writes of the growth of the United States, "If, in 1910, a prophet had ventured to predict that there would take place in twenty years what has actually taken place, his forecast would have provoked contemptuous derision."[4] Brooks Adams saw much of what this entailed in the decline of Britain, and even what it might involve if the Anglo-American rapprochement of his day could be perpetuated:

> Friends and enemies now agree that an Anglo-Saxon alliance, directed to attain certain common ends, might substantially make its own terms; but how it would stand, if opposed by a power capable of massing troops at pleasure in the heart of China, is less clear. . . . Supposing . . . China to be closed, the centre of exchanges might move east from the Thames; and then London and New York could hardly fail to fall into geographical eccentricity. Before the discoveries of Vasco de Gama Venice and Florence were relatively more energetic and richer than they. On the

[1] H. B. Adams, *The Education of Henry Adams, An Autobiography* (London, 1919), p. 330.

[2] Q. J. D. Whelpley, *British-American Relations* (London, 1924), p. 166.

[3] 8 March, 1851: q. Heindel, p. 138.

[4] Norman Angell, "An Englishman's Point of View," in *American Policies Abroad, The United States and Great Britain* by Carl R. Fish and C. L. Hussey (Chicago, 1932), p. 85.

other hand, if an inference may be drawn from the past, Anglo-Saxons have little to fear in a trial of strength. . . . Exchanges would then move strongly westward. . . . Probably human society would then be absolutely dominated by a vast combination of peoples whose right wing would rest upon the British Isles, whose left would overhang the middle provinces of China.[1]

Neither of the future worlds glimpsed so starkly by this second seer of the Adams clan in 1900 has quite materialized, but the prophecy was pregnant enough.

Yet the change was perceived by many Englishmen at the crucial turning point of the end of the century, however much some of them may have desired to ignore it. As the historian of *The American Impact on Great Britain, 1898-1914* declares, "We helped to produce a fit of self-depreciation current in England at the turn of the century, a more receptive mentality, a desire to overhaul industry, and a blow to British complacency as effective as the German competition of the early nineties."[2] The impact is obvious to the historian. At the time of the Civil War, for example, there had been perhaps a dozen American enterprises in Britain; in 1900 there were about 75; and by 1929 there were to be 389. Again, American inventiveness, as gauged by patents, seems to have produced results equal to Britain's between 1876 and 1900, while between 1901 and 1908, they were three times as great; the first American industrial exhibition in Britain was held at Earl's Court in 1909. In many and various aspects of economic life, the impact of American methods and ideas was felt; American salesmanship and advertising methods were adopted by such men as Sir Thomas Lipton; Selfridge's was founded on the American model in 1909; Rotary, the mail order system, roll top desks, filing cabinets, and Westinghouse brakes, to take but random examples, were flourishing by 1914; and American influence was apparent in the development of engineering (particularly bridge building), steel production, the use of electrical power, automatic telephones, tramways, and all forms of standardization and specialization. What Britain's example had been to the world in the first phase of the Industrial Revolution, America's was now becoming. Not that there were no things in which Britain could make headway against the tide—though American insurance companies had eighty thousand policy holders in Britain in 1906, there were no less than eighty-three British companies operating in the United States by

[1] Brooks Adams, *America's Economic Supremacy* (New York, 1900), pp. 23-5.
[2] Heindel, pp. 138-9.

83

1934—but it was set irresistibly in an easterly direction. It was, however, one in which Britons could swim without too much difficulty; the economist Marshall wrote that "the Americans are the only great people whose industrial temper is at all like that of the English, and yet even theirs is not very like".[1] The American system with its freedom from certain forms of monopoly, whether in the form of restrictive land tenures or municipal and national corporativism, and its constant economic pressure upon, combined with its great incentives for, the individuals of society, had a freedom and yet a sometimes harsh immunity from governmental restraint, which came to be lacking in the British system; but the two remained very close in many ways. Yankee ingenuity, although it had impressed even early nineteenth-century observers, was merely a more uninhibited version of the spirit and skill which had been associated in Britain with the birth of industrialism. The parallel between America in 1900 and Britain in 1800 is very close; Arkwright and Ford were not so far apart, and the Englishmen of the earlier era demanded the same *laissez faire* as did the Americans later. One is repeatedly reminded in this respect of that other basic fact of which we have been aware, that the similarities between Britain and America are still, when all is said and done, more striking than the differences.

The swing over of economic leadership to the United States at the turn of the nineteenth century can be seen clearly in these evidences, but in none is it so compelling as in the financial history of the two countries. This topic requires some consideration because it brings out more clearly than anything else the importance of Britain's economic domination of America in the far off days of a century ago. While we consider it, however, we might also note that it illustrates, even more clearly than do trade and commerce, the intimacy of the economic relationship, whichever partner was dominant at the time. As Hacker writes, "English capital—poured into America with a generous hand . . .—helped to put the young republic on its feet. . . . This is one of the ties between the two countries American historians have been blind to. . . . British funds . . . made possible the expansion of the American foreign trade. . . . In effect, an English private revolving fund was set up which protected the American dollar. . . . (Need I mention the modern-day parallel?)"[2]

[1] Ibid, p. 201.
[2] L. M. Hacker, *England and America, the Ties that Bind* (Oxford, 1948), pp. 20-1.

America began life, as was natural in a colonial economy, as a debtor, and in the financial sphere this remained her status until World War I; her demand for capital was, indeed, insatiable, "The New World soaked up this flow of capital like blotting paper, for that was its oldest economic habit. . . ."[1] In the first years of the Republic it seems that nearly as much, if not more, of these funds came from Holland than from Britain, partly because of British mistrust of American investments after the confiscations of the war, but Britain's contribution was already great, and after 1814 began, slowly at first but later hugely, to exceed that of any other power. Even so, already by 1803, according to Hacker, total security issues came to $129,700,000, of which $59,250,000 was in foreign and $34,700,000 in British hands; of the bond issue of $11,250,000 for the Louisiana Purchase $9,250,000 came from Britain. "What was true" of "long-term requirements was even truer in the case of short-term financing."[2] British investment in the United States rose to a great crescendo in the second and third quarters of the century, by which time American domestic investment had expanded hugely, while America was replaced by other foreign fields for British capital, so that these middle years show the same intimacy in the financial as we have observed in the commercial sphere, which is no more than we should expect, for "Money, of course, was little more than the symbol of the . . . economic relationship."[3] By 1837, it has been estimated, there was $200 million of long-term foreign investment in the United States, mostly British; by 1914 $7,090 million, of which $4,250 million was British.

But already America had begun to prepare herself gradually, and for the most part unconsciously, for the change in her financial status from a debtor to a creditor country. After 1873 Americans began to replace the representatives of foreign banking houses in New York City by their own branches in foreign cities. By the turn of the century Americans were beginning to buy back their own railroad investments from foreigners on a large scale for the first time. It was the vast American expenditures in World War I and the corresponding need of the European powers for money which decisively turned the scale. Prior to the spring of 1917 Great Britain borrowed about £200 million in the United States and after that date the United States granted credits of over £1,400 million to the Allies, of which some £740 million went to Britain. Britain, of course, disposed also of a great many of her American investments. This change in the American situation is clearly illustrated in the figures of the balance of payments showing the inter-

[1] Brebner, pp. 109-10.   [2] Hacker, p. 20.   [3] Brebner, p. 239.

national investment position of the United States between 1843 and 1935; the sums are in billions of dollars.[1]

Year	Net Position Creditor + Debtor −	Total U.S. Investments Abroad	Total Foreign Investments in the U.S.
1843	− 0·20	negligible	0·20
1869	− 1·46	0·08	1·54
1897	− 2·71	0·69	3·40
1908	− 3·90	2·50	6·40
1914 (30 June)	− 3·70	3·50	7·20
1919	+ 3·70	7·00	3·30
1924	+ 7·00	10·90	3·90
1930	+ 8·80	17·20	8·40
1931	+12·10	15·90	3·80
1935	+ 7·10	13·50	6·40

This demonstrates clearly the nature of the change in America's investment position which took place in the first war.

By the onset of the Great Depression she was an exporter of capital on an enormous scale; this indeed, as is well known, contributed much to the dizzy heights of the boom which preceded it. In 1914 Europe had been virtually the only creditor of the United States; in 1918 Europe was both her principal debtor and her principal creditor. In this interesting relationship Britain was prominent. In 1928 Europe (chiefly Germany, but also others, including Britain) owed the United States 53 per cent of her credits abroad, while of her long-term debts abroad in 1927, of which 79 per cent were owed to Europe, Britain still owned 34 per cent. Great Britain probably also owned more of America's short-term capital liabilities than any other power except France. In 1914 British investments in the United States made up 20 per cent of her total foreign investments, as compared with 47 per cent in the British Empire; in 1935 the American constituted only 5·4 per cent, whereas the Imperial had risen to 58·7 per cent. On the other hand, in 1935 Britain still owned 19·9 per cent of the total foreign investment in the United States. The years of the depression saw a decline in American investment abroad and a relative increase in the figures of foreign capital moving to the United States; during the thirties, once the financial crisis of 1931 was over for Britain, her dependence upon

[1] *Historical Statistics of the United States, 1789-1945* (United States Department of Commerce, 1949), Series M, Columns 1, 4 and 9, p. 242.

the United States was not direct or obvious, as it had been in World War I.

But the second war and the years which followed it heavily emphasized that dependence once again. During the "cash and carry" period Britain pledged or actually sold her American holdings with alarming swiftness, and Lend-Lease, as we shall later see, came only just in time to save her, much as American loans in World War I had also done. The figures of Lend-Lease alone are eloquent testimony to the economic relationship in the war years. The United States between March 11, 1941, and September 30, 1946, disbursed $50,692,109,000 in Lend-Lease aid, and received only $7,819,322,000 in return, in the form of Reverse Lend-Lease; of the aid, no less than $31,392,361,000, or well over half, went to the British Empire, the United Kingdom getting by far the largest share. This dependence continued on into the years of peace. In 1946 the United States lent Britain $3¾ billion, plus a credit for outstanding Lend-Lease of 650 million; following the economic crisit of 1947, she had received, by the time she was able to suspend Marshall Aid, at the close of the better year 1950, a further $1,822,000,000; and the necessity for rearmament produced a further crisis in 1951, which was met by substantial American subsidies for military purposes. These transactions, though primarily economic in character, took place on the political level, thus contrasting with Britain's loans of a century before, for in the twentieth century governments had come to play a much greater part in the lives of nations. America, it is true, retained much of the spirit of free enterprise, even under the Democratic Administration, but individual Americans could not be easily induced to invest in European economies which were liable to socialization at any moment, and this forced governments to intervene to fill the $8 billion gap, which existed in 1948 between what the United States imported and what she exported. This gap in Britain's case a hundred years earlier had been largely filled by such private investment.

The persistence of the so-called dollar gap was partly due to the fact that the United States did not adopt after 1919 the international economic role played in the past by Britain. At the turn of the century Brooks Adams had warned that the focus of energy and wealth was shifting westward, and that "the United States must shortly bear the burden England has borne, must assume the responsibilities and perform the tasks which have within human memory fallen to the share of England, and must be equipped accordingly."[1] In the administrative

[1] B. Adams, *America's Economic Supremacy*, pp. 143-4.

87

sphere, she was not so equipped, for "Every progressive nation is superior to us in organization, since every such nation has been re-organized since we began."[1] As Brebner graphically puts it, "On grounds of analogy the United States might have been expected to take over a good many of Great Britain's traditional attributes after 1918."[2] She was now the world's greatest industrial producer and she possessed a unique 35 per cent of the world's visible gold supply; after 1815 Great Britain in similar circumstances had, by free trade and a free gold market, led the world, but the United States could not make so abrupt a break with her past. Even the ailing President Wilson saw the error of this when he said of the tariff of 1921: "If there ever was a time when America had anything to fear from foreign competition, that time has passed. If we wish to have Europe settle her debts . . . we must be prepared to buy from her".[3]

Whatever the differences, however, the analogy between Britain's financial dependence on America in mid-twentieth century and that of the United States upon the United Kingdom in mid-nineteenth, is too impressive and too important to be missed, and it would be well to examine it a little more closely. Upon the second we do not need to dwell any longer, for it is in the very air we breathe. But, though such contrasts are dangerous and unreliable, it could probably be maintained that the contribution made by British capital to American development then was relatively more important than the American contribution to Britain's survival now. Certainly it was on a lavish scale, for America offered much better conditions for investment than any other area in the world; British North America might offer more security but it offered much less opportunity for handsome returns, although it, too, had the same language and a kindred legal system. Investment suffered, however, severe setbacks as a result of the great American repudiations of debts accompanying the financial collapse of 1837 and the stoppage of interest payments on their debts in 1841-2 by a number of states. These defalcations aroused bitterness in the breasts of men like Charles Dickens and Sydney Smith, and Englishmen failed to understand the niceties of division of responsibility between the state and federal governments; even as late as the first decade of the twentieth century they were mystified by the effect on their investments of the Anti-Trust activities of Theodore Roosevelt. But the overwhelming pressures of

---

[1] Ibid, p. 48.   [2] Brebner, p. 275.
[3] President Wilson (1921): q. Brebner, p. 275.

commerce and finance bore down all such obstacles and overrode any such misgivings.

The commerce of the first half of the nineteenth century between the two countries was dominated by British wealth to such a degree that Talleyrand once declared: *"C'est donc réellement l'Angleterre qui fait le commerce de consommation de l'Amérique."*[1] In Buck's picture of its organization at this period Anglo-American trade is seen to be honeycombed with British credit. In the earlier post-war decades almost all goods were exported from Britain at the risk and on the account of the British merchant or manufacturer; nearly all American merchants operated on credit, and so keen was the competition between the British capitalists that it could be obtained for an average period of a year and often for as long as eighteen months. Anglo-American financial houses did not confine these arrangements to the direct trade, but served Americans engaged in commerce with other parts of the world, such as the Far East, where credit facilities of this kind replaced the old habit of shipping specie. A number of great English houses, such as Baring Brothers and Company, specialized in American business;* often they had American partners, such as Joshua Bates, or close connexions with the United States, such as those of Alexander Baring, Lord Ashburton, through his American wife. Another example of this type of connexion was the setting up, in 1860 by J. Pierpont Morgan, of a New York house, acting as agent for the London firm of Peabody and Company, of which his father was a partner. Nor were the activities of these houses confined to direct commercial operations of this kind; British trade came in fact to be partly supported by the willingness of British investors to buy American securities. "British exports settled the balances against the United States wherever they arose throughout the world; and to cover the large overdrafts which the luxurious tastes of Uncle Sam were continually running up, the merchant bankers took his stocks. Thus the bulk of the foreign trade of the United States came to depend

[1] Q. N. S. Buck, p. 113.

* The Barings dominated Anglo-American trade in its heyday, and between 1843 and 1867 were the sole financial agents of the Federal Government in London. From 1815 to 1828 they turned their main attention to the American scene, and by the latter date were the leading Anglo-American house; they retained their leadership till the middle of the century, for the crisis of 1837 strengthened rather than weakened their position. But in 1842, and even more in the fifties, they began shifting their principal activities to the Empire and Europe. By 1857 the American was no longer their predominant interest. This development was characteristic of that of the whole of Anglo-American economic relations. [R. W. Hidy, *The House of Baring in American Trade and Finance* (Harvard, 1949).]

upon a system of banking kept in motion by an increasing willingness of Englishmen to buy American securities."[1] Thin partitions, indeed, divide the bounds of commerce and long-term capital investment, and the export of capital from Britain to America took manifold forms. By far the largest proportion, however, went into the purchase of securities floated in the United States by state and municipal authorities and by private concerns, and nothing demonstrates more clearly than the history of these investments the dependence of the United States upon Britain at this period.

Some doubt is, indeed, expressed as to the exact importance of this outpouring of British capital; the author of *The International Financial Position of the United States,* for instance, points out that "not more than 5 per cent of the money value of the nation's economic wealth was ever represented by securities and other property titles held abroad."[2] While this is no doubt broadly true, it may be misleading, because what was needed for rapid American development was liquid capital and ready money. The importance of British investment was great because it was marginal, and the whole history of the debtor frontier, with its demand for specie, for paper currency and for inflationary monetary policies, from Shay to Bryan, witnesses to the extreme significance of British capital in American history. One has only to glance at the purposes for which it was employed to confirm this fact; though it had many and various uses, the large preponderance of it was employed in the swift opening up of the West. It went to finance a number of the states of the Middle West in the period of their greatest need for swift economic development, where it constructed or improved rivers and canals, roads and harbours, bridges and lighthouses, at a time when the Federal Government would care for none of these things; it went on a vast scale into the construction of railroads, such as the Baltimore and Ohio and the Illinois Central, which was actually controlled from abroad through its foreign stockholders; it went, finally, into private American enterprises of all kinds.

President Jackson estimated European holdings of State and corporation stocks and bonds in 1839 at $200 million, mostly British. The Erie Canal was financed by New York State bonds; between 1807 and 1825 over $7 million were raised, almost all of which passed at once into English hands. Before 1836 over $90 million had been invested

---

[1] L. H. Jenks, *The Migration of British Capital to 1875* (New York and London, 1927), p. 70.

[2] R. A. Young, *The International Financial Position of the United States* (Ph.D. Thesis, University of Pennsylvania, 1929), p. 29.

in Northern transportation facilities, most of it coming from Britain. In 1829 Barings made an issue of Louisiana securities to finance the Planter's Bank, one of the many which supported the development of the slave and plantation system in the South. Between 1860 and 1876, issues of private companies operating abroad made in London totalled £232 million, of which £70½ million were in American railways, while only about £19 million were in those of South America. There was much investment of an indirect kind, through State Banks, in the industrial revolution of the United States, as well as much of a direct nature. In 1800 no American securities were quoted on the London Stock Exchange; by 1825 nine issues of United States bonds, United States Bank shares and a number of city and State bonds were quoted. In 1869 Williamson estimates that the foreign indebtedness of the United States was $1,000 million, of which $243 million were payable in London to facilitate English investment; and by 1908 $9,000 million of American securities were quoted on the Stock Exchange. By the time that the American national debt was paid off in 1835, the categories of State and municipal bonds had enormously increased in number, and it is indicative of contemporaries' feeling of their financial dependence upon Britain that there was a widespread fear before it happened that the paying off of the debt would sweep away all specie, and that many states introduced legislation to enforce the holding of a majority of the stock in American banks by residents in the state.

But the best evidence of the strength of the economic bonds is still the sheer magnitude of the investments. The end of the Napoleonic Wars and government borrowing freed the abundant capital of the only great industrial power for export, and it went principally to Western Europe and the United States. Of perhaps £100 million raised in Britain in the years 1816-25 on account of foreign nations, about £9 million was for the United States.[1] With the development of the joint stock principle in Britain this process was facilitated, and in 1854 Jenks estimates that British overseas investments totalled between £195 million and £230 million, of which £50-60 million were in the United States. There followed in the third quarter of the century the greatest period of British export of capital, and between 1870 and 1880 the total market value of British overseas investments in Government bonds was approximately £458 million, of which £160 million were American, and in railway securities £175 million, of which £40 million were American. But already the amount flowing to the United States had been checked, first by the Civil War, after which there was a resurgence; then by the

[1] C. K. Hobson, *The Export of Capital* (London, 1914), p. 105.

crash of 1873, in which many railways defaulted; and then by the bimetallic controversy; above all, however, Britain was beginning to meet severe competition from America herself. The investments of the past half-century and more had had their effect, and the growing maturity of the American economy began to result in increasing domestic funds available for investment. She even began to export capital to Britain and the building of some of the London tube railways was partly financed with American capital. As a result more and more British capital began to flow to other parts of the world. In 1914, whereas 20 per cent of Britain's overseas investments were in the United States, approximately 47 per cent were in the British Empire. Nevertheless, in 1899 it is estimated that out of $3,100 million of European holdings in the United States, $2,500 million were British—more than ten times the holdings of the Dutch, the next greatest investors.

But the intimacy can best be felt, as opposed to seen, through the heated personal relationships which lay behind these financial transactions. Commerce is made for man, not man for commerce, and these close economic contacts between two peoples who had, not more than two generations before, violently severed their political connexion, were of a character to bring home at once that combination of intimacy and bitterness, of attraction and repulsion which we have seen to be peculiar and important to the Anglo-American relationship. The effect on government of the fact that the bulk of America's foreign debt had accumulated in British hands was considerable; as a contemporary declared at the height of one Anglo-American crisis in mid-century: "Railways, steamers, telegraphs and free trade are fast creating a diplomacy which will supersede notes and protocols. The ablest note of Lord Clarendon speaks with feeble force compared with a Stock Exchange List or Price Current, which tells people of a civilized country by breakfast time next morning that their property is depreciated 10 per cent because their Government has committed a folly overnight."[1] Economic incidents, however, did not always serve to promote goodwill by restraining the follies of governments; they could do the very reverse. Though the financial crises of the first half of the nineteenth century did not provoke serious Anglo-American disputes on the government level, they aroused the strongest private feelings, and these unquestionably kept alive the tradition of Anglo-American bitterness much beyond its normal term. (Such crises today, it may be observed, tend always to involve governments directly, which is far from an unmixed blessing.)

Samuel Laing, *The Times*, 20 October, 1856: q. Jenks, p. 286.

British investment in American securities, particularly American state issues, reached a dizzy height in the boom of 1836; it was estimated that in one trip in the late spring of that year Samuel Jaudon of the United States Bank carried $20 million of securities to London. When the crash came in 1837, Nicholas Biddle of the same bank was able to start a revival, owing to his intimate connexions with "the most eminent Bankers of London", all of whom were "inspired with the same confidence"[1] in him, but the British crop failure of 1838 brought nemesis, for Britain would no longer buy securities or cotton. In the end the United States Bank itself disappeared in the wreck. American finance could not support the structure of Anglo-American credit: not until the British Cabinet in 1931 waited to see if their economic measures would gain the approval of New York financiers was such another drama to be enacted. The results in Anglo-American relations were not happy. "Angered at the folly with which they had incurred indebtedness, American Commonwealths sought to vent their rage upon the obliging creditors. And . . . there arose a debacle of American credit as complete as the confidence which it had formerly elicited had been unquestioning. The tide of revulsion flowed anew in England against the foreign borrower. . . . What caused American stocks to join those of Portugal and Mexico and Greece in the ghettoes of finance was the failure of nine sovereign commonwealths to pay the interest upon their debts." That it was beyond the power of some of the states to pay; that in Louisiana a tax of $3 on every man, woman and child in the state would have been necessary to pay it, a tax which, if levied, would have resulted in a popular move to Mississippi; and that gullible investors in a free enterprise society must pay the price of their gullibility—these things did not affect the fact that for a decade after 1838 there was a virtual cessation of British lending to America. The circumstances gave Englishmen ample scope for that type of superior condemnation which above all other things Americans hated from them. Sydney Smith put it in its classical form in his *Humble Petition to the House of Congress at Washington,* which, of course—no doubt to its great delight—had no jurisdiction in the matter:

> Your petitioner lent to the State of Pennsylvania a sum of money for the purpose of some public improvements. . . . If their refusal to pay (from which a very large number of English families are suffering) had been the result of war . . . if it had arisen from civil discord . . . if it were the act of a poor State struggling against the barrenness of nature, every

[1] Jenks, p. 95.

friend of America would have been contented to wait for better times; but the fraud is committed in profound peace, by Pennsylvania, the richest State in the Union. . . . It is an act of bad faith which (all its circumstances considered) has no parallel and no excuse. . . . The Americans who boast to have improved the institutions of the Old World have at least equalled its crimes. A great nation, after trampling underfoot all earthly tyranny, has been guilty of a fraud as enormous as ever disgraced the worst king of the most degraded nation of Europe."[1]

But human economic need, or even human cupidity, overcomes the most serious apprehensions, and before long the banker merchant, and in due course the ordinary investor, began to pour into American railroads money as abundant as had once flooded into State securities. The panics of 1857, 1866 and 1873 administered further checks to the foreign loan mania in Britain, but by then her real work in America had been done.

This work had been to expedite American development. That development would have gone on in any case, but it would not have gone on nearly so fast; it owed most, of course, to American resources and to the genius of the American people and their economic system of free enterprise, but it owed much to British capital. Though the United States gained political independence by 1783 and economic emancipation by 1816, she did not cease to rely upon parental assistance—albeit profitable to the parent, too—until the fourth quarter of the century, no matter how much she disliked to admit it. The wheel had indeed come full circle when Britain held out her hands—though in an appeal as much political as commercial—for American aid in 1945 and 1947. Certainly the mutual economic dependence of the two throughout their history is plain in their financial dealings, and the political dangers which may arise from this peculiar economic relationship hardly less so. If that economic intimacy is to be maintained as between equals, it is clear that the British Commonwealth as a whole must be associated in it, and from the political point of view no consummation could be more devoutly to be wished.*

[1] Ibid, pp. 98-9, 104-5.
* The preliminary stages of research for this chapter were greatly assisted by the work of my friend M. H. Caine.

94

CHAPTER FOUR

SOCIAL AND POLITICAL CONTACTS

I

THOUGH there may be statistical difficulty in establishing the details of Anglo-American economic relations, there can be no doubt of their general pattern; but the interplay of certain social and political factors is considerably more nebulous, and more difficult to discern and trace with accuracy. There is, nevertheless, one important aspect of the relationship between the two peoples which is susceptible of a rudimentary quantitative assessment—the intermingling of the two national stocks, or what might be described as their racial relationship. The degree to which the two peoples have common origins is obviously of the first importance in the development of Anglo-American relations; among other things it accounts in part for the mutual sense of the peculiarity and uniqueness of those relations. This remains true despite the cloud under which the whole idea of 'race' has passed in the last twenty years. Because scientists cannot produce precise and all-embracing definitions of race, because racial edges are increasingly blurred by intermarriage, and because, in common political fact, races and nations are not capable of exact delineation, there has been an inclination to adopt an overall attitude of philosophic doubt on the matter. But biological inheritance of racial characteristics is plainly a fact, and there seems no clear proof that it does not also operate in the sphere of national character and even psychology. The fact of common Anglo-American racial origins has been of immense importance in their relationship. It has given them their greatest bond, the common language, which carries insensibly with it a hundred other ties, derived from common patterns of thought, and, though the direct importance of the common tongue is primarily cultural, it has also indirect effects.

And it is not only in public life that the persistence of national habits is important; it is far more so within the bosom of the family, where the main features of men's behaviour have in the past been developed. America has relied upon public opinion and a public educational

95

system to Americanize her legions of newcomers, but these things did not by any means completely destroy the basic, powerful and subtle influence of family life. In childhood the habits of generations past in different lands were insensibly renewed; it was indeed by processes such as this that, combined with wider cultural assimilations, America's membership of Western civilization has been assured. Samuel Lubell's whole book, *The Future of American Politics,* is in a sense evidence for the importance of the national origins of the American immigrants. He questions whether the "influence of ethnic and religious background on voting" can "ever really disappear", and asserts that one of the important factors responsible for American isolationism is "anti-British ethnic prejudices".[1] Because Frederick Jackson Turner said that the frontier took the European and made him into an American, it does not follow that his European origins were no longer of consequence; indeed, Turner stated his case so strongly partly because his immediate predecessors had greatly exaggerated the importance of American overseas origins. He was part of a reaction against the excessive emphasis on race which was characteristic of much thought in both Britain and America in the last years of the nineteenth century. Those years saw the luxuriant growth of the Anglo-Saxon legend, which burgeoned after 1880 and had a spectacular efflorescence in 1898. The legend had some substance in it, for as Rosebery said: "But whether you call it British or Anglo-Saxon, or whatever you call it, the fact is that the race is there and the sympathy of the race is there."[2] Senator Beveridge of Indiana put the same point with a boisterousness characteristic of the American plains: "God has not been preparing the English-speaking and Teutonic peoples for a thousand years for nothing. . . . No! He has made us master organizers of the world to establish system where chaos reigns."[3] In view of the phenomenon of 'Anglo-Saxonism' alone, the extent of the Anglo-American racial relationship demands some attention.

The study of that relationship rapidly resolves itself into a consideration of British emigration to the United States, for the vast bulk of the traffic was one way, east to west; indeed, in the nineteenth century the very ships which carried American goods to Britain carried emigrants back again to America. The total amount of immigration into Britain from all parts of the world has obviously been minute compared with that of immigration into the United States; between 1861 and 1931, for

[1] S. Lubell, *The Future of American Politics* (London, 1952), p. 132.

[2] Q. Heindel, p. 128.

[3] Q. M. Curti, *The Growth of American Thought* (New York, 1943), p. 675.

example, no decennial census in Great Britain showed a total of aliens and naturalized British subjects exceeding ·82 per cent of the whole population, the figure for 1911.[1] For vivid contrast it is only necessary to recollect that in 1910, 1920 and 1930 there were more than 13 million foreign-born in the United States, a figure of over 10 per cent of the whole population in the last year and very much more than that in the earlier ones. Indeed, from the middle of the nineteenth century onwards, and probably for a long time before that, Britain lost more migrants than she gained, despite the fact that a number of aliens in transit, particularly to the United States, in fact settled permanently in Britain.

American immigration into Britain, including, be it noted, returning emigrants, was on a very small scale. The rough figures for certain years before and after World War I are as follows; though they are not to be relied on as precisely accurate, they do give some idea of how limited it was compared with that in the reverse direction.

1913—16,619	1921—13,925	1925—8,045
1920—17,084	1923— 7,042	1927—6,765

In the thirties the numbers swelled markedly, in all probability owing to the increase in the number of emigrants forced to return home by the conditions created in America through the depression, but the number of native Americans emigrating to Britain was very small. This was even more true, no doubt, during the nineteenth century, but it is important to note that ever since the Revolution there has been a trickle of them, and that this trickle has had an influence out of proportion to its numbers, because it has contained a very high ratio of able and wealthy men. The main bulk of Britain's emigrants to the United States have been working people; many American expatriates to Britain have been of the leisured or professional classes. Some names, like those in literature of Henry James and T. S. Eliot, spring to mind, but there were many others, beginning with a number of prominent Loyalists immediately after the Revolution. One and all were castigated by Theodore Roosevelt as "that most undesirable class of citizens, the educated émigré."[2] Nevertheless, no degree of quality could outweigh the quantity of British emigration to America, and Whelpley is correct when he writes: "British influence upon American life is really far greater than that of American influence upon British life, but it does not lie so much in the obvious."[3] Only the statistics bring it home.

---

[1] *Chambers Encyclopedia* (New Edition, 1950), XI, pp. 81-7.

[2] Q. Whelpley, p. 204.   [3] Ibid, p. 192.

Conclusive evidence is provided by the fact that in 1851 the number of persons in the United States who were from the United Kingdom, excluding Ireland, was approximately six times as great as the total number of foreigners from all countries in Great Britain, which was then not far from equal in population to the United States. Though this proportion was to shrink and America's population to augment far more rapidly than Britain's, up to World War I there were never less than three times the number of British-born in America that there were foreign-born from all countries in Britain.

The statistics of British emigration to America are very impressive, but we must be cautious about them none the less. In the first place, the American figures prior to 1850 are not exact, since immigrants were not enumerated by country of origin, and prior to 1820 are little more than estimates, while the British figures of emigration did not distinguish before 1880 between British emigrants and emigrant foreigners shipping from Britain, though it is true that the former greatly exceeded the latter in the years prior to that date, as far as can be judged.

In the second place, it is very important to bear in mind the general background of American immigration. Beginning as a stream of some 250,000 persons in the whole period between 1776 and 1820, it swelled throughout the nineteenth century until it became a seething flood in the first years of the twentieth. Whereas in 1850 there were 2,244,602 foreign-born in the United States, in 1880 there were 6,679,943 and in 1910 13,515,886; in 1930 there were 14,204,149 and even as late as 1940 there were still 11,594,896. 1907 was the peak year of immigration with the fabulous total of 1,284,349 immigrants. One of the results of this phenomenon was the growth of anti-foreign or Nativist feeling in the United States; it sometimes took extreme forms, like Know-Nothingism or the Ku-Klux-Klan, but gradually, from 1850 onwards, increasingly tight checks were imposed upon immigration; first of undesirables, whether morally, physically or racially, and then, much later, by the quota system, of all immigrants by nationalities.

Amidst the isolationism of the nineteen-twenties Acts were passed in 1921, 1924 and 1927, which laid down that the total of persons to be admitted was "to be distributed among the various foreign countries in the same proportion that persons of the corresponding national origin were found in the general population of the United States. . . ."[1] But in fact the quota system operated—and deliberately so—in a very in-

---

[1] H. P. Fairchild, *Immigration, A World Movement and its American Significance* (New York, 1928), p. 461.

equitable manner, for the assessment of racial origins involved calculations of racial stocks at the time of the birth of the republic, and these gave a singular advantage to the British. They discriminated heavily against the "new immigrants" of the late nineteenth and early twentieth century, who were chiefly from southern and eastern Europe, such as Slavs and Italians, and in favour of the old immigrants of earlier years, chiefly British, German and Scandinavian. Thus the quota for Great Britain and Ireland in 1938 was 83,754, but only 3,347, or less than 5 per cent of that number, actually came; during the seven years ending in 1938 only a quarter of the immigrants allowed actually entered, and even the German quota, despite Hitler, was not filled, whereas the quotas of the "new immigrant" countries were filled to overflowing. It does not seem likely that the quota system will be substantially altered in the future; it was liberalized to some degree after World War II, but not fundamentally, and not without very strong opposition. A permanent restriction of this severity would seem to have riveted the fundamental British racial predominance into the American system, for it is difficult to conceive of circumstances in which it could now be destroyed.

But the third, and final, proviso we must make is best put in the form of a question: what figures give the fairest indication of the strength and importance of the racial bond in Anglo-American relations?* The figures of United Kingdom emigration might be the most straightforward, but they involve two difficulties. The first is that from the point of view of establishing Anglo-American bonds, they are not adequate, since they did not include the very substantial immigration to the United States from British North America which had nearly, if not quite, the same effect as that direct from the mother country. Thus it has been estimated that roughly 9 million people went to the United States from the British Isles between 1820 and 1919, but another 2 million or more from Canada and it is important that, as Brebner points out, people moved back and forth across the Canadian-American border, particularly in the first half of the nineteenth century, with remarkable freedom either from interference or from national self-

* That this question, because of its extreme complexity and its emotional implications, bristles with difficulties, is shown by A. B. Faust's *The German Element in the United States* (New York, 1909). He considered the German immigrants up to that period to have outnumbered those of any other group, but he not only separates Irish, and even Canadians, from British, but also (under the influence of the Nordic racial theory) includes both Swiss and Dutch in his German figures; furthermore, he takes little account of the serious political and religious divisions between Germans in the years prior to 1870.

consciousness. It might, therefore, serve our purpose much better to take the figures of English-speaking immigrants, were it not for the very serious problem of the Irish, who constituted more than half the total emigration from the British Isles between 1820 and 1945, and who exceeded somewhat the total of immigrants to the United States from British North America in the same period. To what extent can the Irish-Americans, who were thus so numerous, be reckoned an agent of co-operation between Britain and America? Not in the very least, it would seem at first sight, but rather the reverse. It may, however, be found on closer examination that they have constituted a kind of bond, like that which binds together relatives whose temperaments are plainly incompatible.

The Irish have always played a very influential part in American history. Though the talk of the "Scotch-Irish" in America in the eighteenth century has perhaps been exaggerated, it must be borne in mind that there is a strain, albeit a highly recessive one, of orange in the green of the Irishmen of America; William Jennings Bryan, for example, at one time favoured special treatment of Ulster because of its staunch Protestantism. This remains true despite the immense influence of the Irish in the Catholic Church in America, a tribute to the importance of the common tongue as well as to Irish organizing experience. It must also be remembered that Irishmen in America often felt, or appeared to feel, even more strongly about British activities in Ireland than did Irishmen who remained there; Abel and Klingberg can write of Daniel O'Connell, the great Irish leader, that his "hatred of America was so intense because of what he regarded as her gross hypocrisy"[1] on the slavery question. It can be maintained that the solution of the Irish problem was made considerably more difficult by Irish-American interference. For all in all, American Irishry was vociferously anti-British, and had an influence quite proportionate to its numbers, which were very great. Irish historians, according to one of them,[2] have claimed that one-third of the population of the thirteen colonies was Irish and that fifty per cent of Washington's soldiers were Irish; though both are gross distortions, the latter may be more nearly true than the former. At least Washington accepted membership of the Friendly Sons of St. Patrick as "a Society distinguished for the firm adherence of its members to the glorious cause in which we are embarked."[3] Nevertheless, in early days, the incoming Irish often "had

[1] A. H. Abel and F. J. Klingberg, *A Side-Light on Anglo-American Relations, 1839-1858* (Lancaster, Pa., 1927), p. 31.

[2] E. F. Roberts, *Ireland in America* (London, 1931).   [3] Q. Ibid, p. 30.

to face the fact that public opinion in their new home invariably was shaped and directed by men who had inherited many of the prejudices and antipathies of their English oppressors."

They made their mark, however, from the beginning, in walks of life as diverse as those of Andrew Jackson and Robert Fulton, and during the years after 1828 began to become indissolubly associated with the Democratic party, particularly in the big cities whose political machines owed much to "the peculiar genius of the Irish for political organiza- tion",[1] particularly covert organization, and this they had certainly learned at the hands of the English. This skill, like their language, they carried with them, and it was a sort of bond with Britain whether they liked it or not. They had captured Boston, Philadelphia, and New York City, including Tammany, by 1820, and in 1899 John Hay wrote to Henry White in London that all the State conventions of the Democrats "put the anti-English plank in their platform to curry favour with the Irish (whom they want to keep) and the Germans (whom they want to seduce). It is too disgusting to have to deal with such sordid liars."[2] It is probable that the Irish group had more influence upon American foreign policy than any other body of opinion, and that influence was usually anti-British; its effect was frequently specific, whereas the anti- Irish feeling which kept it in check—its power was shown in the defeat of Al Smith in 1928—was more generalized and thus less efficacious in practice. It is significant that journalism was a favourite Irish pro- fession (something which once again they owed to the common tongue) and also that they were as prominent in the organization of the trades unions as they had been in the political machines, which was yet another thing they owed to their British experience. The persistence of the Irish problem in the British Isles kept American anti-British feeling alive, and it was not until after the settlement following World War I that it began to die away.

This curious dichotomy made the Irish free of the British tradition, but at the same time made them hate it; gave them the invaluable asset of the English language and British experience, and thus made them England's most formidable critics; and made them unwilling instru- ments of the perpetuation of some forms of British influence in the United States. It is very nicely illustrated in one of the sayings of Mr. Dooley. Of the remarkably similar waves of imperialist feeling, which swept Britain and America in the last years of the nineteenth century, he said, in a curiously mixed vein of irony and reluctant understanding:

[1] Ibid, pp. 76, 124.

[2] Q. R. B. Mowat, *The American Entente* (London, 1939), p. 131.

"I tell ye, Hinnissy, ye can't do th' English-speakin' people. . . . Th' Anglo-Saxon race meetin's now goin' on in th' Ph'lippeens an' South Africa ought to convince annywan that, give us a fair start an' we can bate th' wurruld to a tillygraft office." He went on to comment on the volte-face of the hitherto anti-British Senator "Hinnery Cabin Lodge", who relied so much on the Boston Irish vote: "Now where's Hinnery? Where's the bould Fenian? . . . Faith, he's changed his chune, an' 'tis 'Sthrangers wanst, but brothers now,' with him, an' 'Hands acrost th' sea an' into some wan's pocket'." Very soon, Mr. Dooley predicted, the time might come when "th' subjick races" would rebel against the Sahibs "beloved iv Gawd an' Kipling".[1] Mr. Dooley and his countrymen can hardly be accounted agents for the promotion of Anglo-American goodwill, but neither can they be disregarded altogether as carriers of the germs of British culture and institutions. We must therefore give the figures, as far as possible, of Irish emigration, but must distinguish them whenever we can from the rest. With these things in mind we can turn to a brief examination of British emigration to America.

Brebner estimates that, of those who left Britain between 1815 and 1940 for English-speaking societies, "about 58 per cent went to the United States, and 18 per cent to Canada, about 10·5 per cent to Australasia, about 6 per cent to South Africa, and about 7 per cent to all other regions."[2] Between 1891 and 1900 about 72 per cent of all British emigrants went to the United States; before 1840 more had gone to British North America than to the United States, but after that the balance altered decisively. The scale of this movement was very remarkable, and it was largely a free movement unassisted by the public authorities. It was true that there were inducements to emigration to America; plenty of land, freedom from taxes and tithes, lack of actual want, social and political equality, and good prospects for the children. But there were also serious deterrents; fear of the Indians, lack of employment for mechanics, extremes of climate, fierce competition in everything but subsistence farming, lack of comforts and pleasures, and the deep human fear of the unknown. But the stream bore down all obstacles in its path.

British emigration to North America rose to three peaks, one between 1846 and 1854, one between 1869 and 1873, and one in the years before World War I.[3] It was much affected by conditions both

[1] Q. Brebner, p. 252.   [2] Ibid, p. 109, note.

[3] S. C. Johnson, *Emigration from the U.K. to North America, 1763-1912* (London, 1913), passim.

at home and in the new continent; thus in the Hungry Forties men were pressed out of the British Isles, and after 1849 were attracted by the California Gold Rush; they were encouraged to emigrate by British unemployment in the nineteen-twenties, and repelled by the even worse conditions in America in the thirties. The following table gives figures which clearly show the relative importance of emigration from Britain to the United States and to other parts of the British Commonwealth during the pre-World War I period.[1]

Date	Emigrants to British North America	Emigrants to the United States	Emigrants to Australia and New Zealand
1821–30	139,269	99,801	8,935
1831–40	322,485	308,247	67,882
1841–50	429,044	1,094,556	127,124
1851-60	235,285	1,495,243	506,802
1861–70	195,250	1,424,466	270,499
1871–80	232,213	1,531,851	311,946
1881–90	395,160	2,546,018	383,729
1891–1900	328,411	1,814,293	131,629
1901–10	1,142,550	2,714,188	235,852
	3,419,667	13,028,663	2,044,398

Nearly four times as many British emigrants went to the United States as went to British North America in these years, and six times as many as went to Australasia.

After World War I the numbers fell off substantially, particularly in the thirties, a process which continued after World War II. In 1947 there were 18,555 emigrants from Britain to the United States, 22,960 to British North America, 13,012 to Australia, and 5,918 to New Zealand.[2] Although in the pre-1914 figures the Irish are, of course, included, and although it has been estimated that a very large number of nineteenth-century emigrants to America returned home, the scale of emigration is obviously such as to constitute a very powerful bond between the two societies.

This is borne out by the figures at the receiving end, although they are considerably more complicated to evaluate. A comprehensive table is perhaps the clearest way of doing so, but reliable figures do not exist prior to 1820, and precisely accurate ones not till 1850. Official esti-

[1] Ibid, Appendix I, Tables 1 and 2.
[2] *The Statesman's Year Book, 1949*, p. 57.

mates have been made, however, of the racial composition of the American population at the end of the colonial period, which prove some sort of guide, if not a close one; they show 82·1 per cent English, 7 per cent Scotch, 1·9 per cent Irish, a total of 91 per cent. In the next forty years most of the immigrants came from Britain and Germany, and the figures take up the tale more lucidly from 1820 onwards. They show that between 1820 and 1945 English-speaking immigration into the United States accounted for just under one-third of the total from all countries, and English-speaking minus Irish for just under one-fifth of the whole. In more detail, they show that between 1820 and 1849 the English-speaking was well over one-half of all immigration, and English-speaking less Irish over one-sixth; that between 1850 and 1879 the proportions were over one-half and just over one-quarter; that between 1880 and 1909 they had sunk to just over one-fifth and just over one-eighth, owing to the rush of the new immigrants; and that from 1910 to 1945, under the influence of the wars and the quota system, they rose to just over and just under one-quarter. These are all, even those for 1880-1909, very substantial ratios.

A closer examination demonstrates that the English-speaking contribution to the American population was by far the biggest of all the national and racial groups. The next largest groups after the British are Germany, Italy and Russia; their figures are as follows.

Period	Germany	Italy	U.S.S.R. and Baltic States
1820-49	515,913	4,131	886
1850-79	2,451,575	64,792	37,270
1880-1909	2,352,975	2,801,896	2,134,100
1910-45	708,324	1,849,939	1,206,849
	6,028,787	4,720,158	3,379,105

Thus the lead of the English-speaking group is proportionately greatest in the earliest years, so that, given the high rate of natural American increase, the number of Americans of British stock has always exceeded all other groups; this lead has never been lost, and, with the coming of the quota system, is unlikely ever to be lost.* This remains broadly true, though to a less degree, of the English-speaking group without the Irish. It is, of course, somewhat misleading to talk of this

* Faust estimated that in 1900, 20,400,000 Americans were of English stock, 13,900,000 of Scots and Irish stock, and 18,400,000 of German stock. The total white population of the United States in 1900 was 66,990,000.

TOTALS OF IMMIGRATION INTO THE UNITED STATES[1]

Period	All Countries	Great Britain excluding Ireland	Ireland	Canada and Newfoundland*	Australia and New Zealand	Total English Speaking Immigrants, less the Irish	Total English Speaking Immigrants
1820-49	2,094,220	319,258	878,434	48,457	8,969	367,715	1,246,149
1850-79	7,637,952	1,556,725	1,879,169	506,459	21,687	2,072,153	3,951,322
1880-1909	17,145,250	1,609,177	1,424,711	619,030	21,687	2,249,894	3,674,605
1910-45	11,583,973	783,885	410,853	1,885,288	26,512	2,695,685	3,106,538
Total	38,461,395	4,269,045	4,593,167	3,059,234	57,168	7,385,447	11,978,614

[1] Based on *Historical Statistics of the U.S.*, pp. 33-4.

* Canadian figures subject to reservations in that they include some Irish and French Canadians, as well as other foreign strains.

group as a group at all; as the years passed the stock became more and more native and Americanized and would increasingly have resented any suggestion that it was British. On the other hand, they were very frequently—witness such areas as the South—very proud of their British ancestry and by no means uninfluenced by the fact in their political judgments, let alone their private habits. It is probably no coincidence that every American President, except Van Buren, Eisenhower, and the Roosevelts, has been of almost entirely British stock.

Thus in every year before about 1892 except 1854 (when the Germans were more numerous) the British immigrants, from all sources, outnumbered the largest other single group, but by the end of the century they were regularly outnumbered in the "new immigration." After 1921, with the operation of the quota system, the British group becomes again the largest, and remains so, except for 1939 and 1940, when it was exceeded by the German. This supremacy is partly due to the fact that there are three great internal waves of predominance within the British group. Between 1820 and 1879 the Irish form the largest element; in the later of these years they do so, if at all, by slight margins. From 1880 to 1909 the element from the rest of Great Britain takes the lead, again by a narrow margin. After that date the Canadians and Newfoundlanders take a very substantial lead, with the Irish still running somewhat behind the rest from the British Isles. But it is unnecessary to labour further the strength of the racial bond between the British and the American peoples. One might echo the words of Emerson, exaggerated though they are, that "the American is only the continuation of the English genius into new conditions".[1]

One further point should perhaps be made. It was pointed out of American expatriates to Britain that their strength was in their quality, while that of the British emigrants to America was in their numbers. This would be misleading if it gave the impression that the British immigrants were relatively of poor quality; in fact nothing could be farther from the truth when they are compared with the immigrants coming from other lands. Despite the fact that in 1825 the inquiries of a committee into British emigration to America revealed that the main argument in its favour from the labouring classes was good wages and good food, "three meat meals a day",[2] and despite the fact that the

[1] Q. Mowat, *Americans in England*, p. 133.

[2] E. D. Adams, *Great Britain and the American Civil War* (London, 1925), I, p. 24.

steerage fare from England to the United States was still only about six pounds just before 1914, Henry B. Fearon, sent to America to prospect for English emigrants, wrote correctly in 1817: "It was no longer merely the poor, the idle, the profligate, or the worldly speculative, who were proposing to quit their native country; but men also of capital, of industry, of sober habits and regular pursuits".[1]

This conclusion is decisively borne out by the analysis of immigrants by occupations made by John R. Commons in his *Races and Immigrants in America,* which is based on the year 1906. In that year there were 1,100,735 immigrants, of whom 285,460 declared that they had "no occupation", these being chiefly women and children. The table speaks for itself:

People	Total (100%)	Occupation (Per Cent)			
		Professional	*Commercial*	*Skilled*	*Unskilled*
English	28,249	10·8	13·5	51·3	24·4
Irish	35,387	1·7	2·9	15·1	80·3
Scotch	11,207	5·7	9·9	62·8	21·6
Welsh	1,639	4·9	6·7	62·4	26·0
Polish	77,437	0·2	0·2	7·7	91·9
Scandinavian	47,352	1·8	1·6	23·5	73·1
German	55,095	4·3	6·7	29·7	59·3
Magyar	34,559	0·6	0·5	9·3	89·6
Total (for all countries	815,275	1·8	3·1	21·7	73·4

Thus, with the exception of the Irish, who were inferior in this respect to all the nations cited save the Magyars and the Poles, the British very easily led all others in the quality of their immigrants; they sent a far higher proportion of professional, commercial and skilled workers than any other country, and a far smaller proportion of unskilled workers. This fact augmented the already greatly superior strength and influence in the United States of those of British origin. That influence has often been underestimated because the group was far less homogeneous than some, but it is a paradoxical fact that there has never been a "British" vote or "English" lobby, except the Irish one, largely because the ethnic group has been too large to function as a whole and has been so readily absorbed. But it is, none the less, of great residual strength and of corresponding importance in the history of Anglo-American relations.

[1] A. Nevins, *American Social History as Recorded by British Travellers* (New York, 1923), p. 77.

It remains only to note that these facts throw considerable light on our major theses. Though it was virtually one way, except for a substantial number of returned emigrants to Britain (placed at 207,683 between 1908 to 1937), this racial intercourse helps notably to explain the progress of Anglo-American cordiality. In the early years the shock of the breach was great, but by 1814 the emancipation of the United States from British political tutelage was complete. During approximately the next quarter century the British contribution of well over half America's immigrants was predominantly Irish; far more than two-thirds of them, in fact. Driven out by poverty and economic oppression, they carried with them much hatred of England, but some knowledge of her political methods. This has unquestionably much to do with that curious and paradoxical mixture of intimacy and dislike which is characteristic of Anglo-American feelings in the middle years of the century; it illuminates the fact which we have noted—which also applies in this realm of immigration—that economic bonds were strongest when affection was weakest. In the third quarter of the century those of British stock still constituted more than a half of total American immigration, but Ireland provided only a few more than the remainder of the United Kingdom; and it was a period in the political arena when old habits persisted but were losing their strength. By the years between 1880 and 1909 Ireland's portion of total British immigration had sunk somewhat, and she sent less than the remainder of the United Kingdom, while between 1910 and 1945, with the vast inflow of Canadians, her contribution was less than one-sixth of the whole, and she sent little more than half the number who came from the United Kingdom. It is true that between 1880-1909 the British flow was swamped by the flood of new immigrants, but it regained its impetus between the wars, and in any case its work had already been done. As to the Irish, the new preponderance of the rest of the British, in the years at the turn of the century, began to drown out their persistent brogue, and must have contributed much to the fact that, as we shall see, these were the crucial years in the rise of Anglo-American friendship. Developments after World War I did nothing but strengthen this trend. Less changeable than the channels of commerce, where America's growth is spreading her influence farther and farther afield from the exclusive Anglo-America waterway, the course of America's racial history, particularly in view of the quota system, seems predetermined; it should remain a constant factor in Anglo-American amity.

II

W E have seen that the racial intermingling was, broadly speaking, one way only; more casual social contacts were certainly not. In 1922 approximately 20,000 Americans were resident in Great Britain. The number of Americans who visited Britain between 1910 and 1914, excluding those who came from Europe, was nearly 320,000, while American tourist expenditure in Britain pre-1914 averaged between 15 and 20 million dollars annually; in 1927 the figure was 40 million dollars and in 1933 18 million dollars. Nor is it true that the only British arrivals in America were emigrants. Between 1898 and 1914, for example, over one million British nationals entered the United Kingdom after embarking from the United States; between 1900 and 1903 approximately 22,500 non-immigrant aliens arrived in America from England, Scotland and Wales, and between 1921 and 1936 about 250,000 Britons travelled to the United States. The balance of this non-immigrant traffic is increasingly in American favour, for whereas in 1920 over 200,000 Americans came to England, only 50,000 Britons went to the United States. The obvious fact is that, with the coming of steam and other increasingly rapid and efficient means of communication by the middle of the nineteenth century, the extent of Anglo-American social intercourse entered a period of swift expansion which has not ended today. Manifold further examples of this could be quoted. One might note at hazard that Henry Irving became the first great Anglo-American stage figure after his visit to the United States in 1883; and that in 1908 the cheap Anglo-American postal rate was introduced, and inaugurated a persistent growth in postal traffic. Nor was intercourse unsupported by deliberate encouragement, for the Rhodes Scholarships, which began early in the century, were reciprocated in 1925 by the Commonwealth Fund Fellowships, also for student residence across the Atlantic, and these were but the outstanding organizations of the kind. The increase in intimacy was perhaps first symbolized by the visit of the Prince of Wales, later Edward VII, to America in 1860, and it is characteristic of its continued development that that of his grandson eighty years later should have been an equal success, and of its consistent character that it should have actually followed very much the same geographical route.

These other forms of social contact—and one can do no more than scratch the surface of this subject by quoting a random miscellany of examples—which began to blossom so swiftly from the latter years of

109

the nineteenth century onwards are a conclusive illustration of the shift
of the balance of Anglo-American power across the Atlantic, which we
have seen so distinctly in the economic sphere. As Brooks Adams
forecast between 1898 and 1900, in Britain's heyday, "In inventions,
in industries, in political institutions, in scientific theories, even in social
fashions, all Europe has taken her as a model. Americans, in particular,
have relied on her to police the globe and keep distant markets open,
allowing them to sit at home and reap the advantage without cost and
without danger. . . . All signs now point to the approaching supremacy
of the United States. . . ."[1] Britain's domination over American life in
the colonial period was near to absolute; it was weakened but by no
means destroyed by the Revolution; and it remained important
throughout the nineteenth century. As America grew stronger, however,
she began to turn the tables, and by the last years of the century she
was, as in so many other things, beginning to take the lead in social
influence. Though these historical processes are seldom, if ever, abrupt,
the American people seemed to move into a position of power, socially
as well as politically, with dramatic suddenness in these years of the
closing of the frontier. It was as if the rest of the world, like she herself,
became suddenly conscious of the strength of this new giant in its
midst. From this time forward the pressure of the American society
upon the British is progressively heavier than its counterpart. Upon
this phenomenon of shifting power we can only dwell momentarily, and
it is unnecessary in any case for us to do more, since it has been vividly
depicted by R. H. Heindel in a book with the pregnant title, *America's
Impact on Great Britain 1898-1914.* To quote but a few of his facts
will amply demonstrate our contention.

American influence upon the British Press was very marked, ranging
between the introduction of *The Times'* Supplements by Robert P.
Porter after his American experience, and Northcliffe's sensationalism
in the *Daily Mail,* for which he hired Pomeroy Burton of Hearst's
Evening Journal. Though British coverage of America remained
markedly inferior to American coverage of Britain till after World War
II (in 1939 there were eighty-five American pressmen from daily newspapers in Britain and only about ten British journalists in America),
and though this was a constant cause of complaint by Americans,
Lodge saying once to Balfour, "Until very lately your newspapers gave
us less space than to Belgium and Holland",[2] it did improve gradually;
Northcliffe's interest in America, for instance, was reflected in his good
American coverage. American magazines like *Harper's,* which started

[1] *America's Economic Supremacy,* pp. 190-2.   [2] Q. Heindel, p. 15.

an English edition in 1880, began to circulate and have a great influence. *Country Life* was made possible by American developments in fine printing, and American companies began to push linotype in England about 1889. Even British trade journals became notably more breezy under American competition. Similarly, the American influence on English education was considerable, particularly in the technical sphere; America's economic progress was increasingly ascribed to her concentration in education on practical preparation for life rather than on culture. The development of research degrees, as well as of co-education, owed much to American experience, and her example became more widely appreciated with the growth of the study of American history and institutions led by men like James Bryce and G. O. Trevelyan.

The same growing impact can be seen in many aspects of British social life. Intermarriage increased apace, sometimes in the form of alliances between British gentility and American wealth, and sometimes for more romantic reasons, a phenomenon which provoked a spate of British novels on the subject. By 1903 over seventy Americans had married titled Englishmen, by 1914 over a hundred and thirty; among famous American matches were those of Joseph Chamberlain, Rudyard Kipling and Lord Randolph Churchill. In 1901, for the first time, the volume of letters sent from the United States to Great Britain exceeded that in the other direction; between 1894 and 1920 the volume of American letters to Britain doubled; and—for those who like fantastic statistics—the letters and postcards which passed from the United States to Britain between 1920 and 1936 would make a pile 276 miles high. American charitable endowments, like those of Peabody and Carnegie, became very lavish. American religious influence became significant in the case of new religions like Christian Science and Mormonism, and very important in the case of Nonconformity and Revivalism, through media such as Moody and Sankey, and later, exotics like Aimée Semple MacPherson. As W. T. Stead wrote, "To those who have been brought up in the sectarian seclusion of the Anglican cult, it is difficult to realize the extent to which American books, American preachers, American hymnody, mould the lives of the Free Churchmen of this country."[1] *Per contra,* America was responsible for a certain loosening of social conventions and an increasing emphasis on domestic comfort and labour-saving devices; light kitchen utensils and the ice habit (even including iced champagne) came from America, as did the chapter of Dr. Charles Knowlton's *Fruits of*

[1] Q. Heindel, p. 364.

111

Philosophy on birth control, which was reprinted in 1876 by Charles Bradlaugh and Annie Besant, who were prosecuted for the action, as a result of which the publication ran through 200,000 copies in a week. The impact of American science was illustrated by the increase after 1889 of "foreign" American members of the Royal Society. American dentistry long led the way to British, and (with its bad as well as good results) American capacity to sell proprietary and patent medicines. There was much British admiration for American surgery and for medical schools like Johns Hopkins, while many influential improvements came from America in spheres like hospital planning, sanitation and such aspects of public health as milk control.

But it was, as perhaps befitted a democracy, in the pleasures and pursuits of the people that the American influence was probably most radical. Americans began to gain sporting triumphs in such fields as golf and athletics; they won Olympic victories in 1908 and 1912. On the stage *The Belle of New York* inaugurated a formidable rival to the English music hall, even though it appealed to somewhat different audiences, and by 1902 Americans controlled eight London theatres. "Nigger minstrels" had long been a popular item, and Buffalo Bill and Western plays prepared the way, as it were, for the coming of the films. In popular music the arrival of rag-time and modern dance steps was immensely important; by 1912 250,000 copies of "Alexander's Rag Time Band" had been sold in England, and between 1919 and 1933 eleven of the sixteen most popular songs in England were of American origin. As with the Press, radio was slowly beginning to transmit more programmes eastward across the Atlantic, but the demand was not notable till after World War II; in 1930 there were a hundred westward to two eastward broadcasts, in 1936 a hundred to thirty-one—British provincialism and conservatism was hard to break down in some spheres. But the cinema was not one of them, and it is here that the most spectacular American impression was made. An investigation in 1936 showed that for British children aged 13-16 the cinema was the most important source of ideas about America, and six times as important as the next source, the Press. Between 1908 and 1914 it is estimated that 60 to 75 per cent of the films shown in Britain were American, and in 1917, with British loss of production in the war, 90 per cent, while the weekly English cinema audience in 1914 was already about seven million. With the coming of the talkies the influence increased, because it became aural as well as visual, and in 1933, 330 out of 476 important films shown in Britain were American.

Such was the sort of impact which America had upon Britain during this crucial period in the shift of the balance of power. Naturally it did not go unobserved or unopposed. There was strong criticism of many of its aspects. Englishmen deplored the excessive commercialism of Americans and their lack of social and aesthetic taste; they disliked the high American divorce rate; they pointed to such social scandals as those depicted in *The Jungle* of Upton Sinclair; they never missed a lynching; above all, they still displayed a Dickensian mistrust of what they regarded as the extreme American worship of the Golden Calf. Though some of these criticisms were perhaps justified, Englishmen, because of their likenesses to their American cousins, were in a poor position to cast the first stone. But whatever their feelings—and, sometimes insensibly, sometimes reluctantly, sometimes approvingly, they accepted, as the new century wore on, a vast number of American innovations—the American social pressure was continuous and increasingly strong, and it would remain so into the foreseeable future. The destiny of America had indeed been fulfilled since there landed on the Virginia shore in 1607,

"*. . . on the twenty-sixth day of April,*
Just over four months from London,

.   .   .   .

A handful of men in hot, heavy, English gear,
With clumsy muskets, sweating but light at heart".[1]

III

IN THE political, or, perhaps one might describe it as constitutional, sphere, there is at once apparent the same drawing together as in social life, and it is much more sustained in later years than the economic intimacy. It reflects—indeed, is partly responsible for—the gradual affiliation which is the keynote of the diplomatic history. Its great theme is the development of democratic government, which is the supreme contribution of the English-speaking peoples to the civilization of mankind, that combination, as Mahan said, common to both peoples, of individual freedom with subjection to law. Webster had put it more fully in 1843: "I find at work everywhere, on both sides of the Atlantic . . . the great principle of *the freedom of human thought, and the respectability of individual character. I find, everywhere, an elevation . . . of the individual as a component part of society. I find

[1] S. V. Benet, *Western Star* (New York, 1943), pp. 49-50.

113

everywhere a rebuke of the idea, that . . . government is anything but an *agency* of mankind."[1] When the Anglo-American *rapprochement* was nearing completion in World War II, Churchill was able more succinctly to convey the same idea in the phrase "the English-speaking democracies." After it Lord Halifax declared, "that 'life, liberty and the pursuit of happiness' is our common aim; and that from it flows the sap which determines and invigorates our policy . . . [I]t is this kinship of thought and purpose that will weight the scales . . . [F]orces are at work stronger than any event or any human opinion; forces invisible but irresistible, holding the two peoples together. . . ."[2]

With this immense subject we cannot grapple here, but no study of Anglo-American relations could be right which did not lay great emphasis upon it, as one of the integral factors in the maturing of Anglo-American friendship. Broadly speaking, the story can be understood in terms of the development of British democracy, for one of the main difficulties in the way of co-operation and understanding in early days was the persistence of that aristocratic tradition in Britain which was so suspect to Americans; for a century the difficulty was a serious one, but its effects have not, even yet, ceased to ruffle the surface of the relationship, notably in the social sphere. Yet this generalization must be accepted with reserve; no idea of a United States, democratic since 1783, dragging a reluctant Britain into the democratic fold can be substantiated. American democracy has been of enormous importance as a pioneer in whose footsteps other nations could follow, and with the huge growth in her power during the nineteenth century her influence upon Britain greatly increased; the Civil War was in a sense, as Lincoln claimed, a war to test whether any nation conceived in liberty and dedicated to the proposition that all men are created equal, could long endure, and its vindication of democracy was instrumental in the advancement of the cause in Britain. Some historians have, as we shall see, exaggerated the importance of this, since the seeds of democratic development were latent in the whole of British political development; indeed, it was to their English forebears that the Americans in the American Revolution looked for inspiration, and Emerson wrote in 1847-8: "The tendency in England towards social and political institutions like those of America, is inevitable".[3] More than that, any idea that the United States in 1789 was a fully democratic country would

[1] Q. J. R. Dos Passos, *The Anglo-Saxon Century* (New York, 1903), pp. 63-4.

[2] Lord Halifax, *Anglo-American Relations* (Fifth Montague Burton Lecture on International Relations, Leeds University, 1947), p. 12.

[3] *The Works of Ralph Waldo Emerson* (London, 1888), p. 116.

be mistaken; a glance at the electoral laws of, for instance, South Carolina, will effectively dispose of it. America was more democratic than Britain, but then Britain was much more democratic than almost all the other powers in Europe. It was not until Jeffersonian and Jacksonian Democracy had done their work that the United States really began to be a democracy in the full sense of the word. At the other end of the scale, Britain in the years of Liberal rule before 1914 and in the Labour years 1945-50 was, if the word democracy be not interpreted in a strictly and exclusively political, as opposed to economic, sense, far ahead of the United States. This fact was succinctly expressed by H. W. Nevinson in his farewell to America in 1922: "Goodbye to the land where Liberals are thought dangerous and Radicals show red! Where Mr. Gompers is called a Socialist, and Mr. Asquith would seem advanced."[1] Later, Harry Hopkins noted that even Conservatives in Britain were far ahead of America in such matters as social security and public housing; in fact, "the British statute book was raided on a wholesale scale" by the New Deal.[2]

But, with such reservations as these, one can accept the picture of the years 1783-1952 as ones of common progress towards democratic government and popular economic policies; the United States attains political democracy so much more swiftly than Britain that the latter's slowness is for a period a formidable obstacle to understanding, while in movement towards the welfare state Britain later went much faster than did America. But this growing and persistent similarity of object and methods, of ends and means, has been of inestimable importance in the development of fraternity, and particularly so in the twentieth century when, amidst a world of conflicting and often anti-democratic ideologies, the Anglo-American political affinity has become ever more marked and significant. It is perhaps the most powerful evidence for one of our main theses, that the likenesses of America and Britain are at bottom greater than their contrasts.

This, of course, is only relatively so, and there are many instances to the contrary. The constitutional systems of the two countries broadly illustrate both similarities and differences. The American constitution has undergone less apparent change than the British since 1789, but it is possible that the alterations made, by convention rather than law and indirectly rather than directly, are not much less important than the revolutionary ones made in the British system of government. But, though both have endured radical changes, they have retained their

[1] Q. Nevins, p. 554.   [2] Brebner, p. 307.

115

basic structure from the eighteenth century to the present day; the American constitution, after all, was closely modelled on what its makers thought the then British constitution ought to be. About a hundred years later Gladstone was able to say that, "as the British constitution is the most subtle organism which has proceeded from progressive history, so the American constitution is the most wonderful work ever struck off at a given time by the brain and purpose of man."[1]

Nor did the only important contrasts between the constitutions lie in the methods of their birth; the separation of the powers in the American, and legislative sovereignty in the British, the fissure between President and Congress in the one and the Cabinet's indissoluble bonds with the House of Commons in the other, have been significant motifs from the beginning. In Anglo-American relations this difference has taken awkward shape in the Senate's treaty-making powers, which have tended on occasion to produce diplomatic crises. As early as 1824, when the Senate altered a convention between the two countries in the course of ratification, Canning wrote to the American Minister:

> The knowledge that the Constitution of the United States renders all their diplomatic compacts liable to this sort of revision undoubtedly precludes the possibility of taking exception at any particular instance in which that revision is exercised; but the repetition of such instances does not serve to reconcile to the practice the feelings of the other contracting party whose solemn ratification is thus rendered of no avail, and whose concessions in negotiation having been made . . . conditionally, are thus accepted as positive and absolute, while what may have been the stipulated price of those concessions is withdrawn.[2]

But, as John Quincy Adams, who was quite a match for Canning, replied, other powers were not under any obligation to ratify before they heard of the actions of the Senate, while they were quite willing to refuse to ratify treaties themselves when their agents exceeded their instructions, a particular dig at Canning, as we shall see. But until the study of American institutions became more popular towards the end of the century, Englishmen tended to share the bewilderment of the Prince Regent related by Adams: "He seemed not to comprehend how it was possible to manage a Government where the members of the executive Government could not sit as members of the Legislature".[3]

[1] Q. Dos Passos, p. 133.

[2] *American State Papers, Foreign Relations,* 1818-1826, V. p. 365.

[3] Beckles Willson, *America's Ambassadors to England,* 1785-1928 (London, 1928), p. 137.

(Initially Americans, with their experience and historical knowledge of British political life, were at an advantage in knowledge of one another's institutions, though later the advantage was lost, since far more was written about the American than about the British constitution.) American officials, like Secretary of State Hay, were long to bemoan the actions, though not always the powers, of the Senate, and even to envy, like Secretary of Defence Forrestal, the Canadian system of unified government control, but no radical alteration was possible in a nation which genuinely looked to public opinion for support and even guidance of executive policies.

The constitutional problem could, however, usually be evaded by tact and goodwill, of which Canning had so much less in diplomacy than Castlereagh, who had advised Canning's cousin when he went to Washington as Minister in 1819: "The first precept which I will recommend is to transact your business with *the American Government as far as possible by personal intercourse with the Secretary of State rather than by writing notes,* thereby avoiding diplomatic controversy. The tendency of the American Government is rather to contentious discussion. Their official notes are generally seasoned to the temper of their people, being more frequently communicated to their Legislative bodies than the papers of other States usually are."[1] This tendency to greater publicity in American foreign policy was to persist; it took formal shape after a century in Wilson's demands for open covenants openly arrived at, but later American diplomats, like George F. Kennan, spoke up in criticism of a system which tended to place policy at the mercy of every gust of popular passion. The truth is that, though British public opinion had by the end of the nineteenth century fully asserted its control over the Government's policy, the long tradition of governmental leadership, and the power of custom in an ancient and compact community, made it less immediately effective; this gave a stability to British policies which, at first sight paradoxically, was lacking in the apparently more rigid American system.

The institutional contrast is very interestingly elaborated by Max Beloff in his article, *Is there an Anglo-American Political Tradition?*[2] He emphasizes the differences more than the similarities, but it would appear that these only stand out in the mind of the student if the Anglo-American relationship is considered *in vacuo*; if it is compared with that between other powers, the likenesses become instantly predominant. Nor, perhaps, is sufficient account taken of the democratiza-

[1] Beckles Willson, *Friendly Relations* (London, 1934), pp. 109-10.
[2] History, XXXVI, 1951, pp. 73-91.

117

tion of Britain or the growth of political and economic centralism in the United States. This contrast between British authoritarian habits and American egalitarian instincts was at first very marked; in the preamble to Jay's Treaty there is a notable antithesis in the references to "His Majesty" on the one hand, and the "people" of the United States on the other. It was to become less marked as time went on—indeed in the twentieth century the power of judicial review often came to seem highly undemocratic to Englishmen—but it never died away entirely. John G. Winant, after his Ambassadorship in London in World War II, wrote: "With us there is a tacit assumption that sovereignty is lodged in the people. . . . This is quite a different plan of government from the British. . . . The Acts of Parliament . . . are not subject to judicial review. . . . In Great Britain loyalty is owed to the Crown; with us it is an idea symbolized by the flag." He records that the refusal of Churchill to hold press conferences for American journalists in Britain caused some heart-burning, since it was not appreciated that Parliament was the Prime Minister's principal forum. But once more tact was able to do much to smooth out such difficulties.

Nor can one say that one method of government is better than the other. To Englishmen the separation of the powers seems inefficient, while to Americans there seems something morally wrong about anything which prevents an extension of popular control over government. The British system of centralized control often seemed to the American to produce delay and inefficiency in war; as Winant wrote, "The clear authority delegated under the constitution . . . to the Executive, which included war powers, allowed wide discretion of action within the administrative field. . . . This . . . often gave us a time advantage in dealing with the British Ministers. . . . It is outside usual British practice to delegate political authority to the military."[1] By contrast, it seems dangerous to Britons that Congress alone can declare war, a fact which can only with difficulty be reconciled with explicit military alliances. But the pragmatic character of the two peoples has made the necessary compromises possible. Thus, when there was much criticism in Britain at one period of World War II of Churchill's dual role as Defence and Prime Minister, it was to some extent undermined by the American Ambassador's public reminder that it greatly facilitated his dealings with the President, who is also Commander-in-Chief.

In general, though the offices of President and Prime Minister are

[1] J. G. Winant, *A Letter from Grosvenor Square* (London, 1947), pp. 70-1, 78-9.

clearly distinguished by the fact that the former is a Head of State, their responsibilities in the field of foreign affairs are very similar; in the case of strong personalities they tend to assert control, but in other circumstances they leave more in the hands of the Secretary of State and the Secretary of State for Foreign Affairs. These two officials have almost exactly analogous functions, and preside over departments which are very, and always have been quite, alike. The office of Foreign Secretary as we know it was established in 1782, only seven years before the State Department was created; it then threw off the encumbrance of domestic duties, a few of which the Secretary of State fulfilled until well into the nineteenth century. Neither Foreign Office nor State Department was adequately staffed or very efficient; the Foreign Office, an Under-Secretary recorded in 1789, kept no note or index of the despatches from foreign governments, so that it was necessary to rummage over a whole year's accumulation to find a particular one, and in its early years the State Department had sometimes to send original papers to the Senate for want of copyists. Neither was assisted by the fact that there tended to be a sharp distinction between what in England was called the Diplomatic Service, and the members of the Ministry or Department at home. In America, it is true, there was a very efficient period of foreign representation in the first years of the Republic, but in the eighteen-twenties, with the Democratic inauguration of the spoils system, there began a long, and on the whole baneful, tradition of political appointments, which was matched in a milder form in Britain by the appointment of members of the Diplomatic Service through family influence.

Nevertheless, broadly parallel reforms were gradually instituted in both countries. In the eighteen thirties the State Department was reorganized, and in 1856 Britain took the first step in the direction of appointment to the Foreign Service by merit, with Clarendon's establishment of qualifying examinations; a Congressional reform of a similar nature in 1855, however, proved ineffective, and it was not until the re-emergence of the United States upon the international scene at the turn of the century that the merit system began to make serious headway in Washington. In 1870 the State Department was organized for the first time on a basis of geographical sections, which example was followed by the Foreign Office in 1881. As a result of the sudden strain placed upon the inadequate American machinery in World War I— the average output of letters multiplied tenfold almost overnight—an Act of Congress in 1924 reorganized the whole of it, combining the diplomatic and consular services in one Foreign Service, selection for which was by competitive examination. The examination system had now prevailed for a considerable time in Whitehall, but during World War II the British Foreign Service was unified in a similar manner, so that the two Foreign Services are now on much the same basis. This provides an interesting example, if not of political interaction, at least of similar reactions to similar circumstances on the part of the two societies.

IV

IT IS indeed a problem throughout their history to determine whether common or analogous courses of action in the two countries are due to direct influence of the one upon the other, or to similar responses to similar stimuli. There are certainly many examples of both. Because of the common language and increasing intercourse, men moved freely from one land to the other, preaching the causes they had at heart; because of their remarkably similar political reactions and of the many problems they had in common, the same arguments often tended to convince. Upon the diverse manifestations of this political interplay, we have no time to dwell; some have been investigated by historians, many more have not. But even to the casual glance there are broad parallels in the two histories which cannot possibly be ascribed merely to coincidence. The surging tide of Jeffersonian Democracy in the first years of the nineteenth century had a counterpart in the New Whiggism of Charles James Fox, but this was stunted in its growth by the overwhelming reaction of British middle-class opinion against the Jacobin menace; in the end, however, it was to save English democracy by leading the movement which passed the Great Reform Bill of 1832. The Federalist reaction in America was but an echo of the Tory voices in England led by Burke, because France was far away and because Tom Paine's arguments appealed more to Americans than to Englishmen, but it spoke the same language; the conservative elements in American society had done their great work in 1787 and 1788 when, as Brogan has pointed out, they ensured, by the formation of the Federal Constitution, that the American Revolution stopped where they intended it to stop. Truly they were fitting descendants of the Englishmen of 1688.

The long French wars distorted English history for a period, and there was no American counterpart to Peterloo and the Six Acts, but once the broad highroad of the nineteenth century had opened up before the two peoples, it began to become apparent that they were both moving towards very much the same goal. In this way, though they naturally differed in character and in immediate objectives, the reform movement, which sprang spectacularly to life in Britain around 1830, and Jacksonian Democracy, with its sudden-seeming triumph in 1828, were plainly comparable. They inaugurated, too, the final stage in the movement of both peoples towards democracy. Full American democracy came much quicker than that of Britain (which grew more steadily) and, partly perhaps as a result, suffered certain setbacks after the Civil War through the materialism of the Gilded Age, but the contacts between the reforming movements in the two countries were, as Brebner writes, "close and persistent. The visit in 1833 of Garrison, the Abolitionist, to Wilberforce, the dying Emancipator, was typical of the transatlantic to-and-fro of practicing Utopians like the Owens, or the close communion between Emerson and Carlyle."[1] He goes on to point out the parallel between the movements against the established Churches in the two countries (the free Churches, old and new, Methodism and the Salvation Army, were always a powerful bond), between the secularizing tendencies in education which produced the University of London and the Universities of North Carolina and Michigan, and between the outburst of mechanics' institutes, libraries and lecture programmes on both sides of the water. A direct link was the enthusiastic American adoption of the English Young Men's Christian Association of 1844, and there were parallel temperance movements among the two peoples, the United Kingdom Alliance of 1853 being partly inspired by the Maine Liquor Laws. In the years 1837-70 nearly a hundred thousand Britons were converted to Mormonism, and over thirty thousand of the converts emigrated to the United States.[2] Rowland Hill inspired the American movement for cheap postal services, and even in the establishment of the popular press America owed much to British mass production of print. Frances Wright, the bold champion of feminism, was a Scotswoman who took up residence in America in 1824, and Chartist emissaries crossed the Atlantic from London. Brebner writes :

> The transatlantic interplay stands out again in the beginnings of trade unionism. The same British statute . . . in 1824 and 1825 . . . legalized trade unions and permitted the export of British machinery. The two crossed the Atlantic together, for the factory system which grew up in New England and the Middle States was never out of touch with the

[1] Brebner, p. 136.

[2] M. Hamlin Cannon, "Migration of English Mormons to America" (*Am.H.R.*, LII, 1947).

parent system in Great Britain. Thus the famous mill girls of Lowell . . . reflect Owen's New Lanark in Scotland; and the Workingmen's Association which was founded in 1828 at Philadelphia was the counterpart of the new British unions.[1]

So important an Englishman as Jeremy Bentham could go so far as to describe himself to Andrew Jackson as more of a United States man than an Englishman.

A specific example of co-operation was the development of British and American peace movements, which were strong at this period. It is interesting that, as in other spheres, Britain's leadership was vigorous; Phelps writes that London was the "radiating centre" for philanthropic enterprises.[2] There was a great similarity between the London Peace Society, founded in 1815, and the American Peace Society of 1828, while their officials made great efforts to keep in close touch; not only was there a good deal of personal contact and much correspondence, but also a mutual exchange of publications. They co-operated in what proved—interestingly enough from our point of view—the very uphill work of promoting Continental peace societies. Nor was their work merely academic; in the Anglo-American crisis of 1837-41 both societies were very active in endeavouring to assuage the war fever in the two countries. It is illuminating that in such cases the Americans relied chiefly on appeals to the public, the British on petitions to the government. The chief British names were Joseph Sturge and Henry Richard; the American, William Ladd and Elihu Burritt, of whom it was written that he "not only attended" but "actually organized on European soil, popular congresses for the promotion of humanitarian crusades."[3]

But the most fascinating and best documented of the common humanitarian movements is that of the anti-slavery agitators. Once again the importance of the British impulse is recognized; Abel and Klingberg write: "In the forward movements of the nineteenth century, British humanitarianism was one of the strongest forces . . . [W]hile the scope of the American was limited, that of the British covered a wider field". "If a religious or a benevolent society originated in the United Kingdom, its counterpart soon appeared in the United States."[4] The parallel between the two is striking: "And, across the Atlantic, en-

[1] Brebner, pp. 137-8.

[2] C. Phelps, *The Anglo-American Peace Movement in the Mid-Nineteenth-Century* (New York, 1930), p. 26.

[3] Curti, p. 400.   [4] Abel and Klingberg, pp. 1, 11.

thusiasts like the Tappan brothers and Jay and Leavitt and Goodall were to America what Clarkson, Wilberforce, Buxton and many another were or had been to England."[1] The British and Foreign Anti-Slavery Society was formed in 1839, and in 1840 the first World Anti-Slavery Convention was held in London and attended by a strong American delegation. In 1841 active co-operation began with the mission of Joseph Sturge and John Candler to the United States, and was followed up by a second Convention in 1843 and a further mission. There can be no doubt that "the English anti-slavery contest gave a powerful stimulus to that of the United States. Some Englishmen came to this country to propagate their views but much more important was the vast outpouring of British anti-slavery literature into America. . . . Such leaders as Garrison, Sumner and Mrs. Stowe drew inspiration from the success of the English effort. Brougham repeatedly stated the 'higher law' doctrine before it was taken up by Americans."[2] Abel and Klingberg go so far as to write that "the British of those years, at least the philanthropists, manifested an interest in and knowledge of American life and politics such as has . . . if equalled, assuredly never been surpassed."[3] *Uncle Tom's Cabin,* for instance, which was supposed to have been read three times by Palmerston, ran to a sale of 150,000 copies in its first year in America and over a million in Britain,[4] while Mrs. Stowe made triumphal tours of Great Britain in 1853, 1856 and 1859.[5] But the main traffic was in the other direction, so that in corre-spondence there "appears an amazing dependence upon British help and sympathy and an almost abnormal sensitiveness to British opinion."[6] Not only did a certain amount of money pass from Britain, but an immense mass of letters; apart from the Tappan and Leavitt letters which abound in political detail, one group of English philan-thropists corresponded regularly with the Society of Friends, another with the American Colonization Society, and yet another with Garrison's rival American Anti-Slavery Society. George Thompson, during his visit to the United States in 1834-5, collected 2,400 publica-tions on American slavery. Perhaps one of the best tributes to the extent of the British influence on American opinion over the slavery question comes from one not very well disposed towards it; Buchanan said to Clarendon in 1853: "Congress had no . . . power to . . . abolish

[1] Ibid, p. 10.

[2] F. J. Klingberg, *The Anti-Slavery Movement in England* (London, 1926), pp. 305-6.   [3] Abel and Klingberg, p. 24.   [4] Klingberg, p. 306.

[5] F. J. Klingberg, "Harriet Beecher Stowe and Social Reform in England", (*Am.H.R.,* XLIII, 1938), p. 547.   [6] Abel and Klingberg, p. 369.

. . . slavery . . . yet ever since the establishment of the British Anti-Slavery Society and their associated societies in America they had kept up an incessant war on this subject. These fanatics ought to know that they were defeating their own ends".[1]

But it was going to need more than the protests of "Old Buck" to check the spate of Anglo-American political intercourse, just as it needed more than his words to stop the avalanche of Civil War. With the coming of that war and the triumph of the Northern cause, a pronounced fillip was given to the cause of democracy in Britain; the Reform Bill of 1867 owed much to American influence. In the late nineteenth and early twentieth centuries the general parallel between British and American political developments becomes very marked indeed. Britain's tendency to isolationism chimed in well with the familiar notes of American withdrawal behind the screen of the Monroe Doctrine. Their irruption once more upon the international scene came under the impulse of an imperialism which they both experienced and which was very remarkable in the case of the United States. In the second quarter of the nineteenth century British imperialism had been greatly weakened; the salutary lesson of the American Revolution had sunk deep home, and Englishmen tended to believe that their colonies would drop off the parent tree like ripe fruit when they came to maturity, a political doctrine which did not seem economically alarming in the heyday of free trade and British industrial supremacy. This was a tribute to American influence, and the United States was at the same time demonstrating, under her much more rigid constitutional system, how new territories could be equitably absorbed in the body politic; as Mahan pointed out, Britain had learned from her American mistakes: "Since she lost what is now the United States, Great Britain has become benevolent and beneficent to her colonies."[2] Now there came a revival of British imperialism, but it was only partly owing to the economic causes which have caught the eye of historians; these operated very little in America, but she felt the same impulse. It was to some extent inspired by racial ideas, which began to assume lunatic shape in the writings of Houston Stewart Chamberlain, but which, in a milder version, emphasized the superiority of the Anglo-Saxon race over "lesser breeds without the law," and its consequent responsibilities. This was the era of the *cri du*

[1] Q. W.A.A.E., p. 280.

[2] A. T. Mahan, *Lessons of War with Spain, and other Articles* (London, 1900), p. 243.

coeur for unity between the two great Anglo-Saxon peoples, when Britons took to their hearts, as the typical American, "Teddy" Roosevelt, the advocate of *The Strenuous Life.*

This aspect of America did not, of course, appeal to all of them, any more than did their own Empire to the pro-Boers and Little Englanders, and almost more remarkable than the correspondence between British and American Imperialism is that between the reactions which followed in both countries. There were many contacts, such as the influence of Bellamy on the English Socialists and of Henry George on the Fabians, but the main comparison between Wilsonian Democracy and Asquithian Liberalism is so inescapable as hardly to need elaboration; and it went to the roots of popular feeling, for, as no less a person than Joseph Chamberlain chided the Webbs, who were inclined to be anti-American, "Cultured persons complain that the society there is vulgar. . . . But it is infinitely preferable to the ordinary worker."[1] Though men in Britain deplored the corruption of American politics, the American democratic example was quoted constantly in the great struggles over Home Rule and the powers of the Lords. If more specific indications of the similarity are needed, they can be found in full measure in Colonel House's remarks to Asquith on the Democrats and Liberals in 1914: "I felt very much at home in London now, for the reason that his Government was being abused in exactly the same terms and by the same sort of people as were abusing the Wilson Administration in the United States. This amused him. I thought the purposes of the Liberal Government and of the Democratic Party were quite similar; that we were striving for the same end. . . . He agreed to this."[2]

World War I saw the two peoples to a great degree united in the objectives for which they fought their first war in alliance; Wilson became the supreme spokesman for many British radicals and the *bête noir* of many British Conservatives, so that he split British opinion almost as sharply as he did that of his own country. The day was not far distant now when Winston Churchill could address himself without offence or ambiguity to both peoples at once, but before it came there was a period of drifting apart in the twenties. In the thirties it was gradually reversed, partly because of the ultimate internationalism of Roosevelt and the Democrats, and partly because the New Deal tended to look back with approbation to some early British social and economic legislation; as Morison and Commager write, "Indeed, much that seemed revolutionary to Americans in the nineteen thirties had

[1] Q. Heindel, p. 242.
[2] *The Intimate Papers of Colonel House* (London, 1926), I, p. 275.

been accepted by conservative Englishmen . . . for a generation."[1] With the advent of the Labour Government in Britain in 1945 she moved once more farther and faster than America was prepared to go, even under the Fair Deal, but the two governments were certainly still facing in the same direction. With a moderate Toryism in control in Britain in 1952 and a liberal Republican Administration coming to power in 1953, it was possible to hope that the ideological sympathy of the two governments would still to some extent be maintained.

Whether it would ever be more than an ideological union, whether it would ever be less than two governments, is merely a question for conjecture. Ever since the closing years of the nineteenth century men have talked of Anglo-American unity. Nearly all have agreed with Whelpley that, "It is the logical destiny of the British Empire and the United States to draw ever closer together in the discharge of their international activities and responsibilities."[2] In 1890 Mahan had written: "In conclusion, while Great Britain is undoubtedly the most formidable of our possible enemies . . . it must be added that a cordial understanding with that country is one of the first of our external interests. . . . Formal alliance between the two is out of the question, but a cordial recognition of the similarity of character and ideas will give birth to sympathy, which in turn will facilitate a co-operation beneficial to both; for if sentimentality is weak, sentiment is strong."[3] In 1894 he felt able to write an article entitled *Possibilities of an Anglo-American Reunion,* and in 1898 Joseph Chamberlain made his famous plea for an alliance of the Stars and Stripes and the Union Jack. In 1897 Professor A. V. Dicey had, in an article warmly commended by Bryce, proposed, "That England and the United States should, by concurrent and appropriate legislation, create . . . a common citizenship, or, to put the matter in a more concrete and therefore in a more intelligible form, that an act of the Imperial Parliament should make every citizen of the United States, during the continuance of peace between England and America, a British subject, and that simultaneously an Act of Congress should make every British subject, during the continuance of such peace, a citizen of the United States." He was careful to point out that "Common citizenship . . . has no necessary connexion whatever with national or political unity", and added that

[1] S. E. Morison and H. S. Commager, *The Growth of the American Republic* (New York, 1942), II, p. 591.

[2] Whelpley, p. 327.

[3] *The Interest of America in Sea Power,* p. 27.

"It would be not only an absurdity, but almost an act of lunacy, to devise or defend a scheme for turning England and America into one state."[1] Despite his caution Dicey's suggestion fell absolutely flat, but the coming of the Spanish-American War in the very next year kindled the issue—and even more startling ones—into flames which have never quite died down.

In 1903 John R. Dos Passos could write a book proposing an Anglo-American union; he envisaged Canada entering the United States, a common British citizenship, free trade within the union, interchangeable coinage of the same value, and an arbitration tribunal to decide all questions in dispute. Others gave voice to similar hopes and projects. Andrew Carnegie, as became the great steel master, was splendidly confident: "Let men say what they will, I say that as surely as the sun in the heavens once shone upon Britain and America united, so surely it is one morning to rise, shine upon, and greet again the Reunited States—the British-American Union."[2] Such high flights of fancy lost their touch with reality, and such projects struck no roots. Despite the co-operation of World War I, the United States rejected even the League of Nations; perhaps one should not use the word "even", for it is possible that by demanding all, Wilson lost the opportunity to get anything, that a limited alliance might have proved more acceptable to the Senate than the "all or nothing" of the League. But the ideas sown at the turn of the century still fermented in the minds of men, and, under the pressure of events before and during World War II, they reappeared in new but kindred forms. Clarence K. Streit in *Union Now* struck a note reminiscent of the schemes of Dos Passos and many others. No less a person than Winston Churchill espoused the cause of a common Anglo-American citizenship, and the unprecedented intimacy of the Anglo-American relationship opened up rosy vistas of Anglo-American co-operation.

These were not, in the cool days of peace, fully realized, nor would the sober observer expect otherwise, but much was achieved; not only did America become a founder member of the United Nations, but, under pressure of the Russian menace, the North Atlantic Treaty Organization came into existence. Here were bonds of a positive kind, going beyond those of the purely conventional type of alliance by their establishment of a permanent organization headed by the North Atlantic Council and a Supreme Military Commander. Furthermore, the Berlin airlift, the stationing of American atom bombers in Britain,

[1] Q. Dos Passos, p. 212.

[2] *The Autobiography of Andrew Carnegie* (London, 1920), p. 282.

127

and the Korean War showed that the unique Anglo-American relationship was capable of swift revival when needed for special purposes. And there were new and exciting, strange and almost unheard of, intrusions of the ideal into the real world under the penetrating rays of Russian activity; at urgent American behest men actually began to try and put into effect the vision of European unity. It seemed unlikely that Britain would willingly play an integral part in this movement, and probable that her desire would be for closer relations within the whole North Atlantic basin; there were, indeed, those in Britain, and even in America, who desired above all else closer and more institutionalized relations between the British Commonwealth and the United States. There were grave practical obstacles in the way of such an achievement, but in a world where France and Germany were being forced in the direction of military union, little seemed impossible. It was, after all, a much farther cry to the days of Charlemagne than to those of Chatham. Certainly in the year 1952 it was by no means beyond the range of possibility that the deed of 1776 might in some sense be undone.

CHAPTER FIVE

THE CULTURAL TIE

I

THE cultural has probably been the most important of all the ties binding Great Britain to the United States, although its strength is very difficult to assess in any practical manner. Since the proportion of a people which can travel abroad must, even in this age, remain small, it is through the vehicle of culture that knowledge of one nation by another must be acquired. And that mutual knowledge is the only sure way to tolerance: an increase of international knowledge is an essential element in any increase in international understanding. In Anglo-American relations—it is another cliché of profound importance—the common language has made the process of reciprocal comprehension very much easier. We forget all too often how effective a barrier politically lack of a common tongue may be; nations can, like Switzerland, be solidly constructed without a single shared language, but the task is immensely more difficult, because language is the most cohesive national force. It is true that the English language may seem at first, as G. B. Shaw—that addict of the paradox—put it, to separate and not unite the two great peoples; that little of the savour of mutual comment is lost in crossing the Atlantic; and that superficially this makes always for dispute and has in the past made for immense Anglo-American bitterness. More subtly, it may, as Max Beloff has recently pointed out, lead to assumptions that there is an understanding more precise and complete than actually exists. But these are better than the deepest ignorance, and relatively—which is the only valid basis of comparison—the two peoples understand one another much better than peoples which do not possess a common tongue. Unless one takes a deeply gloomy view of human nature, one must believe that in the end he that increaseth knowledge does not increase sorrow; that, in most human relationships, beyond initial mistrust there lies understanding. Certainly the history of Anglo-American relations, with their persistent development of warmth and cordiality as reciprocal information multiplied, appear to be a triumph-

ant vindication of this idea. The instruments of that swelling trans-
mission of knowledge have necessarily been cultural.

Yet a realistic evaluation of the cultural tie is exceedingly hard. Any
discussion of "culture"—the very word is suspect—must be conducted
with infinite caution, even if it is not primarily concerned with cultural
values. There can be no doubt, however, that the culture of the two
peoples has, until quite recently, been dominated by England; it is
indeed the sphere where the predominance of the British in earlier
years was most overwhelming and where it was longest sustained. The
air of the United States in the first half of the nineteenth century was
filled with lamentations that Americans were

> intellectually the slaves of Britain. The longing for English praise, the
> submission to English literary judgment, the fear of English censure, and
> the base humility with which it was received, was dwelt on incessantly
> in magazines, in newspapers, in addresses, in recollections of distinguished
> men, and in the prefaces to books. . . . When we examine an American
> literary production, said the reviewer of a wretched book written in
> imitation of English models, the first thing we do is to determine whether
> the author has or has not adopted an English fashionable model. . . .
> The inevitable consequence . . . is a state of colonization of intellect,
> of subserviency to the critical opinion of the once mother country.[1]

This dominance was, of course, partly the result of historical events.
Though the United States proclaimed her political independence in
1776, she could not assert her cultural independence at once, for the
weight of the English tradition was too great and the American lack
of it too absolute. Because in 1776 she had in effect no cultural history,
America made the previous centuries of English culture her own, as
indeed they already were, and with the voices of Chaucer, Shakespeare,
Milton and the rest speaking from over the sea, it is small wonder that
America long remained culturally subservient to Britain.

This she would doubtless have been in any case, but it was made
doubly sure by the facts of her life. She was in 1783, and was to remain
for many years, a frontier society; with prospects of immense riches
before them, and only wealthy in the present through the sweat of their
brows, Americans were more heavily engaged in pioneering in the
wilderness than in the field of letters. When Gouverneur Morris said in
1787 that "The busy haunts of men, not the remote wilderness, was the

---

[1] J. B. McMaster, *A History of the People of the United States, from the
Revolution to the Civil War* (New York, 1903), V, p. 287.

proper school of political talents",[1] he was on dangerous ground, but if he had applied his aphorism to culture, he would not have been. There is unquestionably, however difficult it may be to define precisely, a relationship between wealth and culture in society; culture can perhaps only bloom fully after a large economic surplus is attained. As Jefferson said in 1813: "We have no distinct class of literati in this country. Every man is engaged in some industrious pursuit".[2] Not, of course, as the very remark of Morris implies, that America was exclusively a frontier society or that she produced no literature or art. Within half a century of independence a genuine American literature had begun to make its appearance, and Melville, Hawthorne, Emerson and Longfellow could be matched against much that England could show. But their voices were not the voices of America; indeed to some extent they were voices crying not so much in as to the wilderness, for the function of New England in American life was largely educative. In a curious way she was to the rest of the United States, and particularly the Great West, what England was to her: just as her schoolmarms spread enlightenment towards the frontier, so "The true Bostonian always knelt in self-abasement before the majesty of English standards; far from concealing it as a weakness, he was proud of it as his strength."[3] But in due time, America's wealth and cultural confidence developed, and the cultural ascendancy of Britain tended to diminish.

But it was considerably slower to disappear than any of her other ascendancies, such as those in commerce and in political power, which we have already seen to be over and done with before World War I. In fact, it may be open to question whether it has yet disappeared entirely. Certainly if educated Englishmen are asked to point to any aspect of life where they are not yet outweighted by their American rivals and friends, they would be inclined to point to literature, and possibly music and the arts; equally certainly this is a claim which would be bitterly rebutted by many Americans. It is one which it is obviously peculiarly difficult for an Englishman to evaluate justly, while, partisanship apart, questions of this kind have an intrinsic complexity and nebulosity, which make generalization highly dangerous. It does seem possible that cultural bloom tends to follow rather than to precede, or even to accompany, economic maturity—though each of these terms in succession defies exact analysis—and that American native springs of talent have

[1] S. E. Morison, *Sources and Documents Illustrating the American Revolution, 1764-1788* (Oxford, 1923), p. 270.

[2] Q. Mencken, *The American Language*, p. 17.

[3] *Education of Henry Adams*, p. 19.

yet to develop their full strength. Indications that English culture can still hold up its head in the presence of American, that it still equals if it no longer surpasses it, are not entirely lacking. Admittedly, the hey-day of the American intellectual emigré is over; there will be few more Jameses and Eliots, at least until Britain's economic position becomes a good deal better than it is, and there were, after all, Huxleys moving in the reverse direction, even when England was still, in the nineteen-thirties, quite well off. There are, naturally, many more now. But England can still produce practitioners in the arts to rival any nurtured by America, and it is not without significance that in 1951 Britain, with only a third of the population, produced eighteen thousand book titles to America's ten thousand. She is still in some degree a cultural Mecca, not merely to the English-speaking peoples of the Commonwealth, but to Americans also.

If this is so, how is it to be explained? It is at least arguable that it is owing to Britain's aristocratic tradition; that it is not only because of the existence of the American frontier, but also of the democracy which it helped to foster. There are some grounds for believing that, in the initial stages of a society's growth, democracy is not the most fertile of soils for the seeds of culture; indeed it remains to be distinctly proven that democracy is ever positively good for the arts. This is obviously a question that bristles with difficulties, and in which it is more than doubtful if proof can ever be forthcoming, but it is a suggestive basis for the analysis of the Anglo-American cultural connexion. No one who has seen Mount Vernon, or Monticello, or even Lee's home at Arling-ton, can doubt the cultural value of early America's contribution. But those years were in many senses aristocratic years; after them there came, with the triumph of the North in the Civil War, the decadence of the Gilded Age. But a similar decadence can be seen in the archi-tecture, and some of the associated arts, of the Victorian era in the Old World. (Notice in passing as evidence of the strength of the cultural connexion the common American use of the term Victorian.) And this Old World vulgarity may also be due to the strength of a new social class, if, indeed, it is not simply a product of industrialism. But the effects of this revolution were perhaps less marked in Britain, where tradition dies hard; taste depends in a high degree upon the acceptance of social and artistic authority, and this came more naturally to Britain than the United States. What K. B. Smellie writes of the development of the English Civil Service may be very aptly applied to the realm of taste: "It may be said that it was the very slowness with which in

England democratic government was substituted for aristocratic privilege that made possible the success of our Civil Service. It was rescued from private patronage without becoming public spoils."[1]

It may be that this persistence of aristocratic traditions in social life accounts for a division among the English in their reception of American culture, which has been more readily accepted by the common people, and more frequently rejected by the upper classes. It is through the media of mass culture that the power of America has been chiefly exercised, such as the press, popular music, and the cinema. English influence on America remains greatest in the more esoteric cultural realms, for, as Tocqueville would have it, the "permanent inequality" of Europe led men to "the arrogant and sterile researches of abstract truths, whilst the social conditions and institutions of democracy prepare them to seek immediate and useful practical results of the sciences."[2] Pessimistic observers see in this fact a gloomy fulfilment of the destiny of the West hinted at by Toynbee, in which, because the springs of culture remain pure and vigorous and undefiled only in the immediate area of its central wells, the massive powers on the peripheries of civilizations inevitably experience the debasement of culture at the hands of a powerful proletariat. It is from this point of view that criticisms of American materialism become most to the point and most alarming.

For such criticisms reasonable grounds can be found, but they can also be found with nearly equal reason for similar criticisms of the developing pattern of British life. If American culture has points of inferiority to English, they are merely matters of degree; if the Americans are, as Oliver Wendell Holmes said in 1858, "the Romans of the modern world—the great assimilating people",[3] the English are only to an exceedingly limited degree its Greeks. They are tarred too much with the same brush, of pragmatism, democracy, industrialism and materialism, for deep cleavage. Even America is not wholly democratic culturally; there are remarkable enclaves of aristocratic culture in the cosmopolitan and tradition-bound society of the eastern seaboard, whose members look east towards Europe far more than they look west towards the heartland of Americanism. If any doubts are still felt on the score of America's cultural vigour, a glance at Soviet Russia, whose whole life, including its culture, is in the iron grip of an inflexible materialist dogma, will rapidly dispel them; for the present situation of all her arts, save those most remote from politics, show clearly the effect of the dead hand of Communism.

[1] Q. Brebner, p. 139.   [2] Q. Curti, p. 338.   [3] Q. ibid, p. 233.

But judgments of American culture are more dangerous than even these things suggest, because they are essentially judgments of value. Who shall dare to weigh quality against quantity with infallible certainty? English university teachers are well aware of the fact that the average academic standard of the American student of university age is below that of his English counterpart, and this fact is often loudly proclaimed as a general criticism of the American educational system. The criticism has some validity, but the English superiority is gained at a price; how many of the critics are aware of the *magnitude* of the American educational effort compared with the British? Average American schoolchildren are educated considerably longer than their British counterparts, and a far higher proportion of them (almost certainly much more than twice as many) go to a college than proceed in Britain to university or technical college or their equivalent. There are some qualitative advantages in Britain to offset these facts, but a great deal of English quality is needed to make up for this tremendous American superiority in quantity. Particularly is this so when one of the primary reasons for the economic failure of Britain today is the lack of that abundance of skilled technicians which American universities do so much to produce. Critical Britons might well be reminded that those who live in such a precarious and draughty glass-house are singularly ill-equipped to cast the first stone at the super-heated dwellings of their American friends.

II

IF WE turn to examine the common language as an index of the extent of Anglo-American cultural intercourse, we are, although not immune from the infection of value judgments, in a much healthier atmosphere, for it provides a fascinating and relatively concrete guide. To explore it fully the reader has only to turn to H. L. Mencken's monumental but absorbing work, *The American Language*. In the first place, however, one must consider to what extent one can truly talk of the common language. It seems that one can more justifiably do so in mid-twentieth century than one could do at any time in the preceding two hundred years, for very soon after the formation of the colonies, the new environment began to produce swift changes in the language of the inhabitants; though, as in other spheres, they were not able to throw off the domination of the mother tongue till after the War of 1812, they did so then with a vengeance. During the succeeding years the flow of language eastward increased steadily in volume until, despite a sustained British resistance up to World War I, it had virtually conquered by the middle of the twentieth century. This history provides a remarkable illustration of the course of the whole Anglo-American relationship. It not only shows the gradual but insistent restoration of an intimacy unmatched since 1776, despite the ill-feeling of the early nineteenth century, but also the assumption by America of the dominant role in the partnership; the main difference is that America's insensible effort to dominate the language began much earlier than her efforts in other spheres, for the tide of language had begun to turn by the second quarter of the nineteenth century. This swift reaction was due primarily to the stimulating effect of a new environment—the settlers simply had to invent new words to describe new things—and to the tremendous racial admixtures in the new state, but there can be no doubting also the American genius for improvisation, in this as in other branches of human activity, and its swift growth in the climate of freedom, and liberation from tradition, which America offered.

American innovations had begun as early as 1621, with such words as *maize* and *canoe,* and they increased steadily in number. They were derived not only from the Indian, as with *caribou, hickory* and *war-path,* but also direct from the Spanish, as well as from Spanish adaptations of the Indian, as in the case of *tobacco, tomato* and *hammock*; some came from the French, such as *portage* and *bogus*; and yet others from the Dutch, such as *dope* and *waffle.* As well as making new words out of old English material, as with *stumped, locate* and *oppose,* they altered the meaning of old ones, such as to *squat,* and revived English archaisms, such as the *fall, cross purposes, din* and *offal.* Above all they invented new terms, such as those of politics, to *endorse, affiliate, let slide, high falutin, filibuster* and *lobbying.*

According to Sir William Craigie, writing in 1927, the tide began to turn about 1820, in the surge of nationalism after the War of 1812, which finally severed America's English moorings. "For some two centuries . . . the passage of new words or senses across the Atlantic was regularly westward; practically the only exceptions were terms which denoted articles or products peculiar to the new country. With the nineteenth century, however, the contrary current begins to set in. . . ."[1] Then, indeed, the swelling flood begins. John Pickering's *Vocabulary or Collection of Words and Phrases which have been supposed to be peculiar to the United States of America,* published in 1816, contained some five hundred terms; a similar glossary by John

[1] *The American Language,* Supplement One, p. 440.

Russell Bartlett in 1848 contained 412 pages, and another edition of the same work, in 1877, 813 pages. Richard Harwood Thornton's *American Glossary* of 1912 listed 3,700 terms; the University of Chicago's *Dictionary of American English on Historical Principles* of 1944, edited by Sir William Craigie, contained 2,552 large double-columned pages and listed 26,000 terms. Indeed, as one picks at random in this mighty cataract, one is amazed at the words which are in fact Americanisms; *reliable, influential, lengthy, to phone, editorial, filing cabinet, worth-while, make good, fall for, stand for, placate, antagonize, donate, presidential*—the list could be indefinitely extended. As Alastair Cooke said in 1935: "Every Englishman listening to me now uses thirty or forty Americanisms a day."[1]

Some had a longer struggle for acceptance than others, such as *caucus* and *bunkum* (until it was instantly received as *bunk*); others had a special send-off, such as the *"Indian Summer" of a Forsyte* by Galsworthy, and *shyster* in R. L. Stevenson's *The Wrecker*; but mostly they came flooding in, not silently but often unnoticed. Noah Webster was certainly wise when he said in 1827: "[I]t is quite impossible to stop the progress of language—it is like the course of the Mississippi, the motion of which, at times, is scarcely perceptible; yet even then it possesses a momentum quite irresistible."[2] In the twentieth century, with the coming of such instruments of culture for the masses as the cinema, the flood got almost beyond measurement, as the succession of new editions of Mencken's work nicely illustrates, for it was primarily, as Tocqueville had seen a century earlier, in the spoken word that the American impact was felt.

The growth of American power in later years is glaringly illustrated by the paucity of the westward flow of language, for though a few terms like *browned off, good show* and possibly *char*, may make a very precarious lodgement in the spoken vocabulary of some Americans, most English expressions, such as *shop, maid, nursing home, rotter*, which are for the most part "society" terms, undoubtedly have for Americans—and it is perhaps significant—"a somewhat pansy cast."[3] It is not surprising that the influence of America is so overpowering; as Brogan pointed out in 1943, "If American could influence English a century ago, when the predominance of the Mother Country . . . was secure, and when most educated Americans were reverentially colonial in their attitude to English Culture, how can it be prevented from influencing English to-day . . . ? . . .Of the 200 million people speaking

[1] Q. Mencken, p. 232.   [2] Q. Nevins, p. 156.
[3] J. M. Cain: q. Mencken, p. 264.

English, nearly seven-tenths live in the United States. . . . As an international language, it is American that the world increasingly learns. . . ."[1] Certainly it is not artifacts like Basic English, which, as Roosevelt once pointed out, could do no better "with five famous words" than "blood, work, eye water and face water".[2] As an Englishman wrote as early as 1926, "It is chiefly in America—let us frankly recognize the fact—that the evolution of our languge will now proceed."[3]

This frank recognition has been but reluctantly extorted. Ever since in 1735 Francis Moore set the tone of English criticism with the words "the bank of the River (which they in barbarous English call a bluff)",[4] the English have fought a strong delaying action, sometimes, as in the case of John Witherspoon, who invented the term Americanism in 1781, and Richard Grant White after the Civil War, aided and abetted by culture-conscious Americans. The reactions of the main body of the American people have been very different. A committee of Congress as early as 1778 set the tone by talking of "the language of the United States"; but it was Noah Webster, with his *"American" Dictionary of the English Language* of 1828, who was perhaps the most important single opponent of subservience to Britain's fiat, declaring that "As an independent nation, our honor requires us to have a system of our own, in language as well as government."[5] During the period of the great literary battles of the nineteenth century, which were exacerbated by the comments of British travellers and the waspishness of certain English periodicals, a ferocious struggle ensued over language; it caused particular bitterness because it took the form which has always infuriated Americans most, lofty and contemptuous British denunciation. The English assumption of superiority which it implied was resented all the more because it seemed to extend far beyond the cultural sphere and to involve a denigration of democracy; this attack upon the ark of the American covenant still further added to American political rancour against Britain, and fortified the American belief in the fundamental iniquity of the Old World habits and aristocratic institutions of the mother country.

In 1787 a London review of Jefferson's *Notes on the State of Virginia* read: "*Belittle!* What an expression! . . . For shame, Mr. Jefferson!

[1] Ibid, Supp. One, pp. 75-6.

[2] Elliott Roosevelt (Editor), *F. D. R., His Personal Letters* (New York, 1950), II, p. 1514.

[3] Q. Mencken, p. 611.   [4] Q. ibid, p. 3.   [5] Q. ibid, pp. 4, 9-10.

Why, after trampling upon the honour of our Country, and representing it as little better than a land of barbarism—why, we say, perpetually trample also upon the very grammar of our language, and make that appear as Gothic as, from your description, our manners are rude?" Even more difficult for Americans to take than this forthright sort of attack was the process of damning with faint praise, and assenting with civil leer, which is to be found in such comments as those in 1804 on John Quincy Adams's *Letters on Silesia*: "The style of Mr. Adams is in general very tolerable English; which, for an American composition, is no moderate praise."[1] The apogee of English sarcasm was reached in the works of the—from this point of view—terrible twins, Charles Dickens and Mrs. Trollope. It is necessary only to quote the former's comments on the American use of the word *fix*:

> I asked Mr. Q . . . if breakfast be nearly ready, and he tells me . . . the steward was *fixing* the tables. . . . When we have been writing and I beg him . . . to collect our papers, he answers that he'll *fix* 'em presently. So when a man's dressing he's *fixing* himself, and when you put yourself under a doctor he *fixes* you in no time. T'other night . . . when I had ordered a bottle of mulled claret . . . the landlord . . . fear'd it wasn't properly *fixed*. And here, on Saturday morning, a Western man . . . at breakfast inquired if he wouldn't take some of "these *fixings*" with his meat.[2]

Henry James was later, it is not surprising to note, to agree with his predecessor, for when his niece said to him: "Uncle Henry, if you will tell me how you like your tea, I will *fix* it for you", he replied, "Pray, my dear young lady, what will you *fix* it with and what will you *fix* it to?"

But if British resentment began to subside in the closing years of the nineteenth century, American counter-resentment did not; indeed it rose to new heights as American power and confidence grew, and only finally died with the passing of the English contempt for Americanisms which had given it birth. Edward Everett carried the battle to the enemy by declaring that "there is no part of America in which the corruption of language has gone so far as in the heart of the English counties", and Walt Whitman proclaimed his wonted faith in the future of America with the words: "The Americans are going to be the most fluent and melodious voiced people in the world—and the most perfect users of words."[3] As the Middle West was the home of isolation-

[1] Q. ibid, p. 14.   [2] Q. ibid. p. 26.   [3] Q. ibid, pp. 67, 68, 73.

ism, so it "has always been the chief centre of linguistic chauvinism",[1] and it was there that, in the era of Mayor Thompson of Chicago, a bill was moved in the Illinois Legislature—and passed in a modified form in 1923—in these terms: "*Whereas*, since the creation of the American Republic there have been certain Tory elements in our country who have never become reconciled to our republican institutions and have ever clung to the tradition of King and Empire . . . the . . . official language of the State of Illinois shall be known hereafter as the 'American' language, and not as the 'English' language."[2] Perhaps the official issue to British and American soldiers twenty years later of what were, in fact, little Anglo-American dictionaries, may be deemed to have closed this chapter of Anglo-American history.

For, however loud the British protests, they were steadily drowned out. Take the word *talented* as an instance. In 1832 Coleridge called it "that vile and barbarous vocable"; in 1842 Macaulay designated it a word which it is "proper to avoid",[3] but in that same year Pusey used it without comment; and fifteen years later it received the imprimatur of Gladstone. The American humorists, such as Petroleum V. Nasby and Artemus Ward, who actually moved to London at the end of his life, did much to break down the barrier, and in 1899, perhaps for the first time, a decided English voice, that of William Archer, was raised in favour of the American influence: "Let the purists who sneer at 'Americanisms' think for one moment how much poorer the English language would be today if North America had become a French or Spanish instead of an English Continent."[4] Soon others were heard, such as Robert Bridges, Wyndham Lewis and Edward Shanks; and Virginia Woolf wrote: "The Americans are doing what the Elizabethans did—they are coining new words. . . . In England, save for the impetus given by the war, the word-coining power has lapsed. . . . All the expressive, ugly, vigorous slang which creeps into use among us first in talk, later in writing, comes from across the Atlantic."[5] So, as the years passed, the clamour died, until *The Times* could write in 1943: "There is urgent need for surmounting what someone has called the almost insuperable barrier of a common language. It would never do for Great Britain and America to think they understand, yet miss, the point of each other's remarks just now. Both versions of the common language must be correctly understood by both peoples."[6] In fact that great journal was, after a fashion not unknown to it, pontifically shutting the stable door after the horse had escaped, for, broadly

[1] Ibid, p. 81 [2] Q. ibid; pp. 82-3. [3] Q. ibid, p. 223.
[4] Q. Nevins, p. 446. [5] Q. Mencken, p. 47. [6] Q. ibid, Supp. One, p. 76.

speaking, the common people had then been talking American prose all their lives without being aware of it. As Mencken claims, amongst the younger generation the languages are almost approaching assimilation. There are still many traps, differences and obstacles; as Churchill points out, for example, the phrase "tabling a motion" has exactly opposite meanings in the political life of the two countries. But there is a greater linguistic intimacy, something nearer to a truly common language, than there has been since early colonial days.

III

IN THE wider cultural sphere America was very much slower to make her influence upon the mother country felt. There is no need to emphasize the "unique legacy of the English-speaking Colonial Americans"[1] to the culture of the United States; they were in 1776 even more dominant in letters, the law, political ideas, scientific knowledge, economic theories and social practices than they were in race. What requires, perhaps, more attention is the continued English ascendancy in culture after the attainment of political independence. It is true that other influences began to play a part; French influence, in the democratic movement led by Jefferson, who, although he revered the England of the seventeenth century, despised what he considered its eighteenth century decadence; German influence, particularly in education; and even Italian, Spanish and South American influence, as a reaction from dependence on Britain. It is true also that America began to try hard to stand on her own feet, and that the popularization of knowledge began to develop apace, spurred on by the mistrust of what were believed to be the Anglophile tendencies of the patrician leaders of culture. Thus already Americans were displaying the tendency to spread what knowledge they had much more widely than the British, and by 1815 the United States produced annually three million more copies of newspapers than did Britain, which had a very much larger population, while American popular education was very much more advanced. But the most important factor in American culture was still the English supremacy, and nothing shows it so clearly as American resentment of the fact. An American wrote in 1816: "Dependence, whether literary or political, is a state of degradation, fraught with disgrace; and to be dependent on a foreign mind, for what we can ourselves produce, is to add to the crime of indolence, the weakness of

[1] Curti, p. 3.

140

stupidity."[1] As Henry Cabot Lodge remarked at the end of the century, "The first step of an American entering upon a literary career was to pretend to be an Englishman in order that he might win the approval, not of Englishmen, but of his own countrymen."[2] This habit of looking up to England as the fountain head of fashion in every aspect of social life was not entirely due to lack of American models or natural subserviency, for, as McMaster writes, "Their preference was not subserviency, but sound literary judgment. Never in the course of two centuries had Great Britain produced at one time such a goodly company of men of letters."[3] But the subserviency remained real none the less.

Partly it did so for purely practical reasons, arising from a natural course of events, closely analogous to those producing the dependence which we have observed in the economic sphere:

> Much the same condition prevailed, another critic remarked, in the literary as in the industrial world. In the manufacture of coarse fabrics we distanced Great Britain. In the manufacture of fine goods we could not approach her. The great literary staple of our country was the newspaper, on which the very best talent was spent and wasted. Next must be placed pamphlets, magazines, and periodicals, which, with a few books of travel and some popular histories, generally succeeded and were widely read.[4]

At the time of the Revolution colonial printing presses had been very poor; the first foundry for casting type had been established only in 1772. Such presses as did exist were occupied chiefly with the journals, so that most books were imported from Britain; 80 per cent of the total still in 1820, and 70 per cent in 1830.

Partly it was that colonial pride in the glories of English letters died very hard—indeed did not really die at all—in the years after the Revolution; a great deal of space was still given to English *belles lettres* in American newspapers. There was a persistent flow of teachers and intellectual leaders, including men like Longfellow, Legaré, Ticknor and Cogswell, to Europe and back again. An institution like the University of Virginia drew liberally for its staff upon British universities. American artists had a pronounced tendency to become expatriates; in these early years they included J. S. Copley, Benjamin West and John Turnbull, who set the example for Abbey, Sargent and Whistler later.

[1] Q. Curti, p. 233. [2] Q. Mencken, pp. 20-21.
[3] McMaster, V., p. 290. [4] Ibid, p. 287

Partly it was that the conservative reaction of the Federalists against the Enlightenment drew greatly upon Britain for its inspiration; against the figure of Jefferson must be matched that of Hamilton, to whom it seemed that "To create in America an English system of finance, and an English system of industrialism"[1] was the surest way to achieve the kind of American society he desired. Nor was his admiration of Britain confined to the economic sphere, for Jefferson reported him as saying of the English political system: "purge it of its corruption" and "give to its popular branch equality of representation, and it would become an *impracticable* government; as it stands at present, with all its supposed defects, it is the most perfect government which ever existed."[2] Nor could this Federalist warmth towards Britain, which was enhanced during the French Revolution, be regarded as Tory and pro-British in the old sense, and thus expelled or eradicated, for, though Hamilton, who was born in the West Indies, might be suspect, no one could seriously regard George Washington or John Adams as traitors to the American Revolution. This conservative force, despite the triumph of Jefferson in 1800, had gained an important victory by the establishment of the Federal Constitution.

The English influence varied very much in intensity from section to section. It was always far weakest in the West, where the European most rapidly became American. It was strongest in the East, except for the Middle States, largely because of the cosmopolitanism of parts of Pennsylvania and New York. Yet even here one finds Washington Irving, perhaps the most Anglicized of early American writers, and James Fenimore Cooper, of whom Parrington writes not only that he was "an English squire of the old school turned republican, who did not quite like the company he found himself in", but also that "No other American was so unsettled by contact with European civilization", whose "dignified and generous culture . . . was a challenge to his Americanism."[3] The English influence upon the Mind of the South is indisputable, for since the mid-eighteenth century, when, as Wertenbaker points out, the seventeenth-century Virginia merchant-class gave way to one which modelled itself upon the Cavaliers, the South had aspired "to realize the ideal of the English country gentleman."[4] When the English Romantic movement reached the plantations in the eighteen-twenties, the Southern social system was transmuted into a legendary ideal, which was petrified in golden colours by its passing,

[1] V. L. Parrington, *Main Currents in American Thought* (New York, 1927), I, p. 396.
[2] Q. ibid, p. 302. [3] Ibid, II, pp. 223, 226. [4] Curti, p. 28.

in the War between the States. Yet the English squirearchy which Southerners admired was one which they supposed to have existed in an earlier age, and, as Owsley points out, the South was in fact more influenced by the England of the eighteenth century than of the nineteenth. The English romanticism which they made their own was pre-eminently that of Scott, rather than of Shelley. There were, of course, more recent contacts, such as the familiarity of Legaré and Grayson with Bentham and J. S. Mill, but the flavour was pre-dominantly "old world." Nevertheless, of the strength of the English influence upon the South there can be no question. Legaré wrote of Charleston: "We are decidedly more English than any other city of the United States",[1] and Robert Toombs "quite frankly preferred the English system to the American."[2]

But it was in New England that direct admiration for contemporary Britain was most pronounced. Producing the best of American native literature, New Englanders were steeped in English culture, past and present. The Transcendentalists had many sources of inspiration, but important among them was Coleridge and "the English intuitionalists".[3] "All through life", wrote Henry Adams, "one had seen the American on his literary knees to the European",[4] and what he said of Charles Sumner was true of most of the Boston Brahmins: "He, too, adored English standards. . . . He was rarely without a pocketful of letters from duchesses or noblemen in England".[5] Lothrop Motley early said to Adams that "the London dinner and the English country house were the perfection of human society." By the time that Adams himself left London after the Civil War, it "had become his vice . . . he had become English to the extent of sharing their petty social divisions . . . he took England no longer with the awe of American youth, but with the habit of an old and rather worn suit of English clothes."[6] Imitation is, indeed, the sincerest form of flattery, and it is significant that Parrington can write of that New Englander of New Englanders, Daniel Webster: "No Englishman was ever more English than he"; with his estate, his farm, and his good living, he was "an English country squire". He was equally English in his political views, for "He was of the distinguished line of political realists, from Harrington through Locke and Burke, to Hamilton, Madison and John Adams".[7] Emerson said of him, "In Massachusetts, in 1776, he would, beyond all question, have been a refugee."[8] The fact that New England was the first American area to

[1] Q. Parrington, II, p. 109.   [2] Q. ibid, p. 86.   [3] Curti, pp. 303-4.
[4] *Education of Henry Adams*, pp. 319-20.
[5] Ibid, p. 30.   [6] Ibid, pp. 200, 236.   [7] Parrington, II, p. 304.   [8] Ibid, p. 315.

follow in the industrial footsteps of Old England—almost exactly in them what is more—constituted another powerful contemporary bond. As Henry Adams remarked: "The Paris of Louis Philippe, Guizot and De Tocqueville, as well as the London of Robert Peel, Macaulay, and John Stuart Mill, were but varieties of the same upper-class bourgeoisie that felt instinctive cousinship with the Boston of Ticknor, Prescott and Motley. . . . England's middle-class government was the ideal of human progress."[1]

In the first half of the nineteenth century, the cultural domination of America by Britain still seemed complete. This resulted in one of the most interesting phenomena in the whole history of Anglo-American relations, the outburst of mutual criticism and ill will which centred around the so-called Battle of the Quarterlies. The two torrents of abuse, flowing at the literary, or at least the literate, level, were certainly unequalled at any other period, except perhaps that of the American Revolution itself, and the interesting thing is that they suddenly burst into flood in the years after the War of 1812. Before that event they had flowed in the same way but with nothing like the strength they acquired later, and one is more and more driven to the conclusion that that disastrous episode set back by half a century the cause of Anglo-American friendship. After 1783 British interest in American thought and writing had been considerable, and "The great majority of English readers were disposed to be fair, though they were unable to restrain the expression of their own feeling of superiority, and were likely to adopt a paternal, if not a patronizing manner."[2] The English periodicals began to align themselves on the American issue, for and against, but "In general . . . British utterances regarding the intellectual state of America show a strange combination of bewildered curiosity, ignorance of exact conditions, prejudice, and more or less condescending goodwill."[3] The feverishness with which the early American writers worked is evidence of their extreme sensitivity to the charge that America had no literature, but the impression with which we are left before 1812 is of two nations of the same race and language, "both sore as a result of a bitter war, watching each other rather better satisfied to be offended than to be pleased, yet both honest enough in the determination to be true to the best in literature wherever they saw it."[4] But, after the second, and in some ways more

[1] *Education of Henry Adams*, p. 33.
[2] W. B. Cairns, *British Criticisms of American Writings, 1783-1833* (Madison, 1918), Part I, p. 93.   [3] Ibid, p. 37.   [4] Ibid, p. 62.

galling, war, much of this honest determination was blown to the winds.

Some of it had, indeed, been lost in the difficult years of embargo and Non-Intercourse; as commercial rivalry grew, so did American resentment of her cultural, as well as her economic, dependence upon Britain. *Niles's Weekly Register* in 1812 contained the accusation, later to become familiar: "It cannot for a moment be doubted that such men as Smyth and Moore, Ashe and Parkinson, have been well paid by the ministry for their tours and travels through the United States. A government under whose benign influence all are happy, all are equal, must be an eternal reproach to the tyrants of Europe."[1] For this accusation of conspiracy, which took detailed shape in charges that the British attacks were for motives of revenge, or to stave off parliamentary reform, or to check emigration, or to protect British markets against American enterprise, there was no vestige of evidence, but there is no doubt that the attacks on American life and culture in English publications increased sharply in volume and bitterness. The attacks were based, as Nevins has shown, not only on American literary productions, but on the published accounts of the increasing number of English travellers in the New World searching for new experiences and fresh literary material. When their comments on American life were published, names like those of Captain Marryatt, Basil Hall, Mrs. Trollope and Charles Dickens made headlines in both countries, but for purposes chiefly of execration in the United States. We shall see the effect of their utterances upon broader national feelings in the next chapter, but they added, because some of them were considerable literary figures, highly combustible fuel to the flames of the literary battle. The struggle had already been rendered more confusing, but no less embittered, by the peculiar effect of the war, which was, in the words of Cairns, "almost unique in the fact that so many citizens of both contending countries opposed it. Even during the period of hostilities the American cause was warmly supported in British periodicals. At the same time, no real Briton could have escaped a feeling of satisfaction when his nation won a victory, or a feeling of chagrin when she suffered a naval defeat. This conflict between intellectual judgment and patriotic emotions continued after the war."[2]

British periodicals fell into three main groups; the *Quarterly Review,* the *Edinburgh Review,* and the *Literary Gazette* were strongly anti-American; *Blackwood's* and the *Athenaeum* were mildly patronizing, though not notably hostile; and—a very much longer list—the *Monthly*

[1] Q. McMaster, V, p. 308.   [2] Cairns, Part II, p. 295.

145

Review, the *Gentleman's Magazine,* the *Eclectic Review,* the *Westminster Review,* the *London Magazine* and the *Literary Chronicle and Weekly Review* were sympathetic. But the first group's accusations, abetted by books and pamphlets, accusing the Americans (apart from slave-flogging, moral grossness, political corruption, and demagogism) of lack of true religious feeling, materialism, bad taste, vulgarity, bigotry, ignorance and vanity, were the ones most frequently apprehended on the other side of the Atlantic; Americans were, naturally enough, primarily conscious that a number of Englishmen despised them, as, in the words of McMaster, "[A] whittling, spitting, guessing, reckoning, gambling, slave-beating, dram drinking people".[1]

The worst outburst of trouble began with a highly critical article about the Americans, which was in the form of a book review, in the *Quarterly Review* of January, 1814, rumoured to have been written by the Poet Laureate, Southey. Timothy Dwight and James Kirke Paulding took up arms in defence of their countrymen, the former beginning, however, by expressing his great "regret that two peoples which ought to be firm friends were rapidly becoming implacable enemies";[2] they not only rebutted each charge against America by pointing to similar British failings, but attacked such characteristic English vices as exploitation of the people by the decadent remnants of a feudal aristocracy. But the anti-American periodicals in Britain were now in full cry, with such characteristic criticisms as: "The North American Republicans are the most vain, egotistical, insolent, rodomontade sort of people that are anywhere to be found", and "The greater number of States declare it to be unconstitutional to refer to the providence of God in any of their public acts."[3] Men, like Robert Walsh Jr., Alexander H. Everett, Christopher Gore, and Joshua E. White, and periodicals, like the *North American Review,* now counterattacked violently; White, a Southerner, denounced the blot of the British factory system, and Walsh, in a comprehensive onslaught, attacked British mercantilism, the English origins of the slave trade, Britain's treatment of Catholics, paupers and imprisoned persons, her brutal love of prize and cock fighting, and the corruption of her courts and legislature. He also emphasized the proper American defence against charges of lack of civilization, that the hands of the American people were all too full for cultural activities, in their conquest of the wilderness, which was a task of whose magnitude and difficulty Englishmen had no conception.

[1] McMaster, V, pp. 313-14.   [2] Ibid, p. 313.
[3] *Quarterly Review:* Q. ibid, pp. 315-6

It was when the battle was at its height that, at the hands of Sydney Smith, the chorus of denunciation enjoyed its only moments of artistic immortality. In the *Edinburgh Review* for the quarter beginning December, 1818, he had reviewed four books of travel in America—the usual source of misunderstanding, be it noted—and had begun with genuine praise for America's achievements of expansion and democratization. He had proceeded, however, to point out that, apart from a few small pieces, "Native literature the Americans have none. It is all imported. . . . But why should the Americans write books when a six weeks' passage brings them in their own tongue our sense, science and genius in bales and hogsheads? Prairies, steamboats, grist-mills, are their natural objects for centuries to come. By and by, when they have got to the Pacific Ocean, they may have epic poems, plays, pleasures of memory, and all the elegant gratifications proper to an ancient people who have tamed the wild earth and sat down to amuse themselves."[1] This, McMaster writes, was "galling enough": why was it so? It had an appearance of truth, and was couched in characteristic Sydney Smith terms, but it grossly under-emphasized the speed of America's conquest of the continent (although it was early days yet), and it emphasized to an uncomfortable degree the truth of America's cultural dependence upon the erstwhile mother country. Possibly these things might have been forgiven, but the attack on slavery which followed was not. "What is freedom where all are not free? . . . Let the world judge which is the more liable to censure, we who in the midst of our rottenness, have torn off the manacles of the slaves all over the world, or they who, with their idle purity and useless perfection, have remained mute and careless while groans echoed and whips cracked around the very walls of their spotless Congress". This cut a great deal too near the bone not to damage American self-esteem seriously, and it seemed to his readers in the United States that Smith was guilty of an extreme complacency, considering that slavery was not abolished in the British Colonies until 1833.

But the portly cleric—who was not only a wit but accounted a liberal in his own land—had not yet hurled his last shaft. In the first quarter of 1820 appeared the most famous of his attacks upon America. Beginning with a résumé of the material and political achievements of the United States, he declared:

Such is the land of Jonathan, and thus has it been governed. In his honest endeavours to better his condition and in his manly purpose of

[1] Q. McMaster, V, p. 318.

147

resisting injury and insult we most cordially sympathize. Thus far we are friends and admirers of Jonathan. But he must not grow vain and ambitious, or allow himself to be dazzled by that galaxy of epithets by which his orators and newspaper scribblers endeavour to persuade their supporters that they are the greatest, the most refined, the most enlightened, and the most moral people upon earth. The effect of this is unspeakably ludicrous on this side of the Atlantic. . . . During the thirty or forty years of their independence they have done absolutely nothing for the sciences, for the arts, for literature, or even for the statesmanlike studies of politics or political economy. . . . In the four quarters of the globe, who reads an American book? or goes to an American play? or looks at an American picture or statue? What does the world yet owe to American physicians or surgeons? What new substances have their chemists discovered, or what old ones have they analysed? What new constellations have been discovered by the telescopes of Americans? What have they done in the mathematics? Who drinks out of American glasses? or eats from American plates? or wears American coats or gowns? or sleeps in American blankets? Finally, under which of the old tyrannical governments of Europe is every sixth man a slave whom his fellow-creatures may buy and sell and torture?[1]

One American might write in 1819: "We attach too much consequence to these attacks. They cannot do us any essential injury. . . . We have but to live on, and every day we live a whole volume of refutation",[2] but one can sympathize with the bitter resentment of the majority of his countrymen. Even when the English were being restrained, according to their own standards, they could not avoid the appearance of lofty condescension which Americans detested even more than outright abuse. Thus later numbers of the *Edinburgh Review* tried to smooth things down, but did so in such a patronizing manner as merely to add to the offence. Characteristic of this softer, yet no less irritating, approach was an article in *The New Monthly Magazine and Literary Journal* of February, 1821, which was obviously intended to be friendly:

> Now, the generality of Englishmen know of their own knowledge that in this country America is not the object of hatred and contempt. On the contrary, we take a very anxious interest in all that relates to her. We feel the endearing influence of consanguinity in all its force. . . . Many generations must pass away and great changes in our common sentiments and relations mark the close of each before a contest between America and Great Britain can be anything else than what the late one was—an

[1] Q. McMaster, V, pp. 328-30.

[2] Q. J. L. Mesick, *The English Traveller in America* (New York, 1922), p. 285.

unnatural civil war. We cannot but feel that the character of the principles and institutions that most attach us to our own country is vitally connected with the moral and political destiny of the United States; that, in spite of the violent separations . . . the Americans of future times will be regarded by the world as a race either of improved or degenerate Englishmen.

Thus there came a sting in the tail, but that was not the end of it.

"Other nations boast of what they are or have been, but the true citizen of the United States exalts his head to the skies in the contemplation of what the grandeur of his country is going to be." Though Americans are not prone to understatement of their own virtues (or of anything) what else should they do? "Others appeal to history; an American appeals to prophecy"—and very accurate the prophecy in many respects—"and with Malthus in one hand and a map of the back country in the other he boldly defies us to a comparison with America as she is to be and chuckles in delight over the splendors the geometrical ratio is to shed over her story. . . . If an English traveller complains of their inns and hints his dislike to sleeping four in a bed he is first denounced as a calumniator and then told to wait a hundred years and see the superiority of American inns to the British." And very superior they are in 1952. "If Shakespeare, Milton, Newton, are named, he is again told to 'wait till we have cleared our land, till we have idle time to attend to other things; wait till 1900, and then see how much nobler our poets and profounder our astronomers and longer our telescopes than any that decrepit old hemisphere of yours will produce'." It is true that T. S. Eliot moved to England, but there remains Palomar. "The American propensity to look forward with confidence to the future greatness of their country may be natural and laudable. But when they go further and refer to the wished-for period as one in which the glory of England shall be extinguished forever, their hopes become absurdities. . . . Let us suppose the time arrived when American fleets shall cover every sea and ride in every harbor for purposes of commerce, of chastisement, or protection; when the land shall be the seat of freedom, learning, taste, morals, all that is most admirable in the eyes of man, and when England, sinking under the weight of years and the manifold casualties by which the pride of empires is levelled in the dust, shall have fallen from her high estate." An uncomfortably true vision, albeit a distorted one, of the mid-twentieth century reality. "In that day of her extremity . . . might an Englishman . . . not truly say: America has reason to be proud; but let her not forget whence came the original stock of glory she has laid out to such good account. . . . America can achieve no glory in which England has not a share."[1]

Here indeed was the rub. Independent though the two nations now were politically, they were indissolubly joined by their common history, traditions and culture; as members of the same family the common effects of their childhood could never be eradicated, and constituted a peculiar and powerful bond between them. These were the fundamental facts. To them was added the English vexation, albeit concealed to some extent, at the original loss of the United States and at their surprising subsequent successes; this was increased by the exaggerated American claims to cultural equality, and fanned by the mischief-making reports of many of Britain's travellers. The British attitude was, therefore, a mixture of reluctant admiration, some envy of America's future, and an unwise emphasis on Britain's power over the lives even of independent Americans. These things rubbed the people of the United States on the raw. Conscious also of the common bonds, they were highly sensitive to their extreme cultural and economic dependence upon a mother country from whom it was their greatest pride to be politically independent. Knowing deep in their bones the tremendous future that was in their grasp and believing that Englishmen, in their ignorance, hugely underestimated their achievements, Americans resented their cultural subservience, while at the same time forced in honesty to continue it till they produced work as good. Psychologically men always tend to resent dependence, particularly when the person depended upon is not slow to point out its existence. Into this explosive atmosphere came the spark of war in 1812, the most inconclusive and one of the least bloody of wars; the national passions were not, happily, purged by victory or defeat or exhaustion, and when the peace came they found vent in the storm of ill-feeling which we have described.

In time the storm died down. America began to stand on her own feet and to obtain recognition of the fact in Britain. The works of Irving and Cooper appeared, and were successful on both sides of the Atlantic; Emerson gained the respect of other Britons besides Carlyle; the full flowering of New England literature began. In other spheres, such as political economy, America, with the beginning of protectionism, began to show its intellectual independence; in the works of men like Henry Carey, for instance, whose "inherited dislike of England led him to fear its industrial pre-eminence".[2] Symptomatic was the fact that in 1816 Congress actually imposed a tariff on foreign books. Between

[1] Q. McMaster, V, pp. 332-4.   [2] Parrington, III, p. 106.

1841 and 1846 at least 386 American books were reprinted in England, although many of them were for export to the United States. From this time forward the predominant factor in the betterment of feeling between English and American men of letters was the growth of America's contribution to the common culture.

But the improvement was very slow. The warning of the *North American Review* in 1824, that if the campaign of abuse went on it would "turn into bitterness the last drops of good-will toward England that exist in the United States,"[1] had been heeded none too soon. The literary travellers kept the skies dark, at least, according to Nevins, until 1845, and their task was made easier by the American financial crisis of the second quarter of the century. Nor did the vexed question of copyright improve English literary tempers, for pirated editions of English novels made their appearance in their cheap thousands within a matter of hours of the arrival of the first editions in America; this situation became so intolerable that in 1836 fifty-six English authors vainly petitioned Congress for copyright legislation. This financial loss, combined with that from repudiated investments, proved too much for Dickens, whose *American Notes* of his visit in 1842 gave free rein to his opinions of America, which also found expression in *Martin Chuzzlewit*. Though his reputation across the Atlantic was eventually restored before his last visit, the copyright question was not settled till after his death, by a Congressional law of 1891. The lack of it before that date was, as G. S. Gordon points out,[2] not only maddening to English authors, but highly detrimental to Americans who had to compete with English works sold at cut-throat prices. As an Englishman said to Emerson: "As long as you do not grant us Copyright we shall have the teaching of you."[3]

By the thirties, however, "England seemed settling into the attitude of distrust and slight disdain which characterized her views of America for so much of the nineteenth century. . . . Most reviewers gave to American writings all the praise they deserved, but they so mixed with this a modicum of censure that the flavor of the whole mass was tainted."[4] This legacy of the great literary battle has only ceased to be of importance, if indeed it has ceased to be so, after the passage of fully a century. That it was such an unconscionable long time a-dying was partly due to the facts of the situation, to the relatively high quality and quantity of British output, to the continued slowness of American

---

[1] Q. Mencken, p. 23.

[2] *Anglo-American Literary Relations* (Oxford, 1942), pp. 82-98.

[3] Works, II, p. 16.   [4] Cairns, Part II, p. 57.

cultural development, and to her continued sense of British cultural leadership—and partly to an obstinate British determination to cling to almost the only form of pre-eminence left to her in the face of American competition.

But steadily the ill will did abate, and the puffs and squalls of anger and resentment became fewer and weaker. America's intellectual maturity approached; Walt Whitman and Mark Twain were fully and truly American, the latter in particular, with "everything European fallen away, the last shred of feudal culture gone, local and western yet continental."[1] But not all the dependence upon Europe, and Britain especially, disappeared; this was very true of the East, for there were two reactions among intellectuals to the Gilded Age, one to demand reform, the other to revive the tradition of deference to the Old World. Henry Cabot Lodge wrote: "Our literary standards, our standards of statesmanship, our modes of thought . . . were as English as the trivial customs of the dinner table and the ballroom",[2] and in some American intellectuals, notably Henry James, the reaction took the form of a desire to escape, which was naturally resented by many of their countrymen. William Archer could write as late as 1900: "I am much mistaken if there is a single club in London where American periodicals are so well represented on the reading-room table as are English periodicals in every club in New York."[3] But English influence came to be less irritating in proportion as America was able to reciprocate. Men like E. L. Godkin, who went to America in 1856 at the age of 25, might be equipped, as he was, with the complete social philosophy of J. S. Mill, but they remained in the United States to make their life, which was balm to Americans' wounded pride. Equally satisfying was the work of such a man as James Bryce, with the publication in 1888 of his great and friendly masterpiece, *The American Commonwealth*. But most satisfying of all, as the century closed, was the knowledge of a growing galaxy of American stars whose light shines too in Britain, like John Dewey, William James, Oliver Wendell Holmes, Thorstein Veblen, Frederick Jackson Turner, William Dean Howells and Marion Crawford. This was reflected in the fact that by 1903 at least ten firms of English publishers were importing American books on a substantial and ever-increasing scale. From this time forward there was a steadily growing intimacy between the two peoples in art and letters. As H. W. Nevinson declaimed in 1922, "Goodbye Americans! I am going to a land very much like yours. I am going to your spiritual home."[4]

[1] Parrington, III, p. 86.   [2] Curti, p. 522.
[3] Q. Heindel, pp. 22-3.   [4] Q. Nevins, p. 555.

CHAPTER SIX

EMOTIONAL BONDS

Hard as certain of the other aspects of Anglo-American relations are to assess with accuracy, the emotional is much the most difficult to describe and to evaluate. Not only must the predilections of the writer hinder balanced judgment, but there are immense obstacles in the way of accurate generalizations about human emotions, even in the case of individuals, let alone of whole nations. This is true of a nation like Great Britain, which is homogeneous and unified in a high degree, but it is doubly so of one which, like the United States, is bewildering in the variety of its origins, surroundings and circumstances. J. F. Muirhead in his *Land of Contrasts,* published in 1898, wisely wrote that the object of his book would be "achieved, if it convinces a few Britons of the futility of generalizing on the complex organism of American society from inductions that would not justify an opinion about the habits of a piece of protoplasm."[1] From time to time glaring examples of the disregard of this salutary advice thrust themselves upon the attention; Geoffrey Gorer's *The Americans* is a supreme instance of the nemesis which overtakes even observant and perspicuous men who rush into complex social problems and emerge hastily with simple 'scientific' solutions. The many notes of interest which he strikes are utterly vitiated by the fact that he raises upon the precarious pinpoint apex of a neo-Freudian theory of universal American "father rejection" a vast inverted pyramid of unsubstantiated conclusions. The writer may, therefore, be pardoned if he approaches such questions with the utmost caution.

Yet approached they must be, for human actions are very frequently emotional; this is true of national as well as of individual decisions— no one who witnessed the career of Adolf Hitler can have any doubt of that—and we must therefore hazard some generalizations about national emotions, for in international affairs we have, to some extent, to live by such conclusions. It is peculiarly necessary to do so in the case of peoples who have advanced to democracy for, as Mahan pointed out in the germinating years of Anglo-American friendship, in nations

[1] Q. Nevins, p. 531.

153

"of more complex organization . . . the wills of the citizens have to be brought not to submission merely, but to accord."[1] It has been a commonplace, at least since 1820 when Castlereagh spoke the words, that "there are no two states whose friendly relations are of more practical value to each other and whose hostility so inevitably and so immediately entails upon both the most serious mischiefs [than] . . . the British and American nations".[2] With the development of full-blown democracy and the re-entry of America into world affairs, the feelings of the two peoples towards one another have become of crucial importance to the destiny of mankind, and it behoves us to venture some discussion of them. Nor is the way unlighted nor all the precedents discouraging; whatever the obstacles, men like Bryce and Brogan have brilliantly overcome them, and may help us to do so. But we cannot hope in the space of a brief chapter even to hint at all the important facts in a subject which has filled many books and could fill many more. We shall try merely to indicate in what ways the predominant cast of Anglo-American feeling has altered since 1783, and to show how complex, unstable, and often transient, are the movements lying behind these general changes.

I

THE writer is emboldened to generalization by the undoubted fact of common national reactions to the phenomena of other lands. Shortly after returning from his first visit to the United States in 1946, he read J. B. Priestley's *Midnight on the Desert,* and was powerfully struck by the identical impressions made upon him and upon Priestley by a multitude of things American both great and small, despite the passage, since the book was published, of a decade which altered much in life on both sides of the Atlantic. These impressions were not merely of things physical—the contrast, for instance, between the overwhelming antiquity of the western deserts and the neoterism of humanity; or the fabulous nature of the Grand Canyon. Nor yet only of the works of men—the ubiquity of the advertisement in American life, the shoddy untidiness of much of the countryside, the superb magnificence of Boulder Dam, or "that long dissonant, mournful cry of American trains, that sound which seems to light up for a second the immense

[1] Q. Forrest Davis, *The Atlantic System* (New York, 1941), p. 27.

[2] W.F.R., title page.

distances and loneliness of that country."[1] They were impressions also of the American people themselves—the combination of individual kindness and mass heartlessness in American life, the lack of a feeling of security, the sense of harsh realities not far beneath the surface of things, the emphasis on individualism and yet the lack of individuality, the extent of anti-Semitism in America, or the bizarre culture of Southern California, where a neon sign "Psychologist," recalled by Priestley, matched one recalled by the writer, "Jesus Saves." Some changes were visible even in ten years—a growth in appreciation of art and music, for example, and a diversification of the economy of Southern California—but a surprising amount remained the same.

Similarly, one can take courage from the correspondence of so many American views of Britain; a multitude of Americans have been impressed by the sort of things that are recorded, for instance, by Margaret Halsey in *With Malice Toward Some,* published in 1938. The smallness of English trains and the diminutive scale of the patchwork countryside (Robert Benchley once said that the British "take pleasure in such tiny, tiny things"[2]); the splendour of English flowers; the Stygian gloom of the English Sunday; the waitress who, when asked by adults for a glass of milk, shakes her head and says, "You Americans!" (the writer once blurted out that Englishmen never drink milk after they have "grown up"); the English "blend of shabbiness and imperturbable good nature"[3] (Emerson noted a century earlier that the English were "good-natured",[4] and that an English lord "dresses a little worse than a commoner"[5]); the wonder constituted by polite English children; the courtesy of English railway porters, and the horror of English railway stations (an appalled American of the writer's acquaintance habitually referred to Euston as the Hall of Death); the rural English refusal to recognize the existence of English industrialism; the constant English criticism and jealousy of America: "They have just one big blanket indictment of America. It isn't England"; the masculine dominion in English society; the lack of high pressure salesmanship in British stores; and the placidity of English life compared with American, where there is so much more violence, "a good deal in England makes the blood boil, but there is not nearly so much occasion as there is in America for blood to run cold."[6] Here again, the war has wrought

[1] J. B. Priestley, *Midnight on the Desert* (London, 1937), p. 2.

[2] Q. Alistair Cooke, *Letters from America* (London, 1951), p. 113.

[3] Margaret Halsey, *With Malice Toward Some* (London, 1938), p. 53.

[4] Mowat, *Americans in England,* p. 134.

[5] Works, II, p. 57. [6] Halsey, pp. 201, 239.

changes—the courtesy of porters is not now so marked and placidity has almost degenerated into inertia—but much remains unaltered.

Nor are such generalizations as these altogether invalid over longer stretches of time. Some English comments upon America run like a recurrent theme through almost the whole history of the two peoples. The wooden houses of Americans have been remarked upon by travellers from Cobbett to the present day; their rocking chairs and their abundant use of ice for almost as long a period; the wonders of the New England fall make a universal impression ("Lord Bryce, not a reticent man about American vices, couldn't trust his English reserve to speak properly about its virtues. Lloyd George confessed after his only trip to America that no matter how inconclusive his political mission he would at least go home remembering the overwhelming experience of the fall. A hundred years ago, Mrs. Trollope, who liked very little about these United States, broke down and wrote that at this season of the year 'the whole country goes to glory'."); the lack of privacy which was bemoaned by Basil Hall on the river steamboats is regretted by J. F. Muirhead in railroad sleeping-cars; the power of the Press and the persistence of its reporters is noted from Dickens to Priestley; the heat of the houses is constantly the subject of comment by Englishmen, so that even Henry James installed central heating in his English home, and could report, "my poor little house is now really warm—even hot"[2]; their headlong hurry is almost universally decried from the earliest times, even before Thackeray wrote: "There is some electric influence in the air and sun here which we don't experience on our side of the globe; people can't sit still, people can't ruminate over their dinners, dawdle in their studies, they must keep moving"[3]; there is even more universal praise for their "crushing hospitality"; the allegedly high rate of dyspepsia among them frequently calls forth amateur diagnoses and no doubt equally erroneous suggestions for cure; but the one persistent trait for which there is never any sympathy is the chewing and spitting habits of the land dubbed by Rupert Brooke, "El Cuspidorado".[4]

There are also constant strains in the comments of Americans about England during the last century and three-quarters. Gouverneur Morris commented on the stiffness of English manners, and Fenimore Cooper on their proneness to silence, but both found friendship beneath the somewhat forbidding exterior; Morris lamented English cooking, and

---

[1] Cooke, p. 151.   [2] Q. Mowat, p. 225.

[3] *The Virginians* (London, 1899), p. xvii.

[4] Rupert Brooke, *Letters from America* (London, 1916), p. 4.

more than a century later that great Anglophile W. H. Page wrote, "they have only three vegetables and two of them are cabbages"; Cooper's complaints about the English weather found a similar echo in Page: "In this aquarium in which we live . . . it rains every day"'; the London fog comes in for almost as much condemnation as the English rain, although G. H. Putnam spoke of the rush of reminiscence produced by "a whiff of that wonderful compound of soot, fog and roast mutton that go to the making of the atmosphere of London"[2]; Cooper experienced, upon seeing the White Cliffs of Dover for the first time, a common American feeling of being "home"; Hawthorne also struck a familiar, but more unpleasant, note, when he said: "These people think so loftily of themselves and so contemptuously of everybody else, that it requires more generosity than I possess to keep always in perfectly good humour with them"; he also found the deadweight of English rural tradition, where "Life is . . . fossilized in its greenest leaf", very distasteful, and declared that it was better to endure the ceaseless changes of the New World than this "monotony of sluggish ages"[3]; yet, as Emerson admired the orderliness of English life, so Hawthorne loved its scenery, which presented a "perfect balance between man and nature"[4]; almost as many Americans have commented adversely upon the dirt of English barbers' shops, as (from Emerson to Santayana) favourably upon the domesticity of the English; and there has been continuous and universal contempt for the "abject"[5] servility involved in the English social system.

II

SOME generalizations about the mutual feelings of the British and American peoples are, then, possible. In the formation of those feelings their attitude to one another's institutions and ideas is clearly of primary importance, and those attitudes have been conditioned by the quantity and quality of the information upon which they were based. Walter Page could still write during his ambassadorship, after many years of mutual indoctrination by such bodies as the Anglo-American Association (1871), the Anglo-American League (1898), and The Pilgrims (1901): "The longer I live here the more astonished I become at the fundamental ignorance of the British about us and at our funda-

[1] Q. Burton J. Hendrick, *The Life and Letters of Walter H. Page* (London, 1923), I, p. 158. [2] Q. Mowat, p. 203.
[3] Q. ibid. pp. 162, 171. [4] Q. ibid, p. 169. [5] Page, p. 155.

mental ignorance about them."[1] The position has improved since then, but to one who has specialized to any extent in Anglo-American history new examples are repeatedly forthcoming. Another Anglo-American Ambassador, Lord Halifax, pointed to one deficiency as late as 1947: "The teaching of American history in British schools too often ends at Yorktown, as the teaching of American history in American schools too often begins with Bunker Hill. . . . It might be said . . . that Anglo-American history was for Englishmen to learn and for Americans to rewrite."[2] Nevertheless, it remains true that American knowledge of Britain has always far exceeded her knowledge of any other country, and that British knowledge of America has improved out of all recognition in this century, and is now, perhaps, with the advent of the mass media of information, approaching its counterpart in quantity.

There are two main sources of such knowledge; direct, through travel and reports thereof, and indirect, through culture. In the case of direct knowledge the two peoples have perhaps been on an equal footing; in the case of indirect, the Americans were at first at an unquestionable advantage, though in recent years the English have probably been able to reverse this situation and learn more about the United States. But in any case the common language has always made mutual knowledge far easier than it normally is between different nations. It was no isolated instance when Nathaniel Hawthorne, steeped in English literature, wrote: "Almost always, in visiting such scenes as I have been attempting to describe, I had a singular sense of having been there before"[3]; familiarity with England through the reading of English literature is a factor of the utmost importance in American understanding of Britain. Not that it is always without disadvantages; it often renders information out of date and misleading. To Henry Adams on his first visit to London, "Aristocracy was real. So was the England of Dickens. Oliver Twist and Little Nell lurked in every churchyard shadow. . . . In November, 1858, . . . it was the London of the eighteenth century that an American felt and hated."[4] Frequently, too, as we have seen, Americans reacted against this cultural bondage, as witness the oration of an American schoolboy heard by Captain Basil Hall in 1827-8: "Gratitude! Gratitude to England! What does America owe to her? . . . We owe her nothing! For eighteen hundred years the world had slumbered in ignorance of liberty. . . . At length, America arose in all her glory, to give the world the long-desired lesson."[5]

[1] Q. W.A.A.E., ix.   [2] *Anglo-American Relations*, pp. 6-7.
[3] Q. Mowat, pp. 159-160.
[4] *Education of Henry Adams*, pp. 72-3.   [5] Q. Nevins, p. 119.

But in the end the balance of true knowledge outweighed the distortions and the emotional rejections.

Perhaps the most reliable gauge of Anglo-American feeling is to be found among the travellers between the two lands, and here the historian of Anglo-American relations is fortunate enough to find two monographs on the subject ready to his hand. Allan Nevins in his excellent analysis and anthology, *America through British Eyes*, gives a most comprehensive account of American social history as seen by British travellers, which throws much light on the emotional relationship between the two peoples. He sees the subject as falling into five main periods, each in its turn broadly reflecting, with one exception, that ripening of friendship over the years, which we know to be one of the main features of Anglo-American relations. The first period, from 1783 to about 1825, he characterizes as one of utilitarian enquiry, which marked a distinct improvement after the hatred of the Revolutionary period; the tone of reports was on the whole factual and just. Men like Henry Wansey, interested in American woollen manufacture, Henry B. Fearon, investigating for the settlement of twenty English families, George Glover, who laid out a number of English settlements in Illinois, John Woods, one of those Illinois settlers, and William Cobbett, best known to American readers as *Peter Porcupine,* set the tone of commentary, and drowned out the ill-natured accounts of unreliables, like Thomas Ashe and Isaac Weld, and simpletons, like William Faux.

Unfortunately, in the second period, from about 1825 to 1845, the hyper-critical and malicious voices gained the mastery, and the result was a distinct deterioration in Anglo-American feeling. The outburst of mutual ill-will, which we have seen in the cultural sphere after the War of 1812, was both reflected and caused by the new type of traveller; "instead of seekers after a living, there came seekers after new sights and experiences."[1] Political passions also played their part, for men like Captain Marryat, Captain Thomas Hamilton and Godfrey T. Vigne, while admitting the necessity of democracy in America, bitterly opposed its extension to Britain; their criticisms were made more telling by the fact that, with the advent of Jacksonian Democracy, the tone of American political life had deteriorated in comparison with that of patrician days. Furthermore, the visitors tended to penetrate farther west, where conditions were worst; it was the western experiences of *Martin Chuzzlewit* that were the most unpleasant, and it was Dickens's description of them that Americans found it hardest to forgive, because,

[1] Nevins, p. 111.

although they contained much that was true to life, they were at once the most characteristically American and yet—however unpleasant—the most indispensable for the development of the country. Above all, because the new travellers included so many authors in search of literary material, American weaknesses were exposed with merciless and often consummate skill. Dickens was not mealy-mouthed at home, and, though his *American Notes* were not so very harsh, they seemed immensely so, because of his popularity in America, and because, with unerring instinct, he put his finger on the tenderest spots in American life, such as slavery. Dickens had, in fact, a number of very appreciative things to say, as did others like Hamilton, Marryat, Thackeray and Charles Augustus Murray, while Harriet Martineau, after careful and searching investigation, was full of praise for many aspects of American society. Unfortunately, men are prone to remember criticism and to forget praise, and Americans in particular, conscious of the newness of their nation, have always been acutely sensitive to criticism—much more so throughout their history than the smug British, long inured to abuse—and never more so than in these formative years of what Tocqueville called "irritable patriotism", when English criticism was most virulent and supercilious.

The tone of it was unhappily set by critics like Basil Hall, and above all, Mrs. Trollope, whom Nevins justly describes as a "censorious harridan."[1] Her son, who made amends for his mother's bitterness in his own account of America later, described her *Domestic Manners of the Americans* as "somewhat unjust . . . to our cousins over the water", and as one of those works which have "created laughter on one side of the Atlantic, and soreness on the other."[2] Her pen was veritably dipped in gall: "I do not like their principles, I do not like their manners, I do not like their opinions". Her supercilious assumption of English superiority struck Americans, as always, on the raw; religious "[p]ersecution exists [in America] to a degree unknown, I believe, in our well-ordered land since the days of Cromwell": it would be hard to pack more, calculated to pain Americans, into a single short sentence. Her absolute want of sympathy may be explained by her personal difficulties; it may even be pardoned to her for the gallant struggle she made to support and bring up her family, but it cannot be forgotten. Her ill-humoured comment on American lawlessness contrasts too painfully with the later good humour of, for example, G. K. Chesterton. She wrote: "In England the laws are acted upon, in America they are

Ibid, pp. 3, 114.

[2] Evan John, *Atlantic Impact, 1861* (London, 1952), p. 12.

not"'; his words were: "The Americans may go mad when they make laws, but they recover their reason when they disobey them."[2]

But before the tolerance of Chesterton could replace the contumely of Mrs. Trollope a respite was needed. This was provided by the years from approximately 1845 to 1870, a period of narration and description, or what Nevins calls unbiased portraiture. Akin in tone to the first years of the relationship, its accounts are less practical in object and wider in scope, but the "incorrect and caricatured"[3] reports, as William E. Baxter called them, fall into disrepute. There are still some hostile voices, such as Edward Sullivan, Hugh Seymour Tremenheere, and Nassau William Senior, but they are once more drowned out by those of juster critics, such as Sir Charles Lyall, Lord Carlisle, Colonel Arthur Cunynghame, Lady Emmeline Stuart Wortley and Mrs. Houston. Most significant were the serious and encyclopedic works of James Silk Buckingham, and, above all, Alexander Mackay. Despite the differences of opinion in the Civil War between such men as W. H. Russell, who believed the Union could never be restored, and Edward Dicey, who was much more favourable to the North, nearly all Englishmen tended to be well disposed towards the United States as a whole. This was very true of such representatives of the British working class as James D. Burn in his book, *The Working Classes in the United States.* Without doubt this was to a considerable extent due to the growing English realization of the potential power of America. As Eliot Warburton wrote in 1846: "Most of the present generation among us have been brought up and lived in the idea that England is supreme in the Congress of Nations . . . but . . . this giant son will soon tread on his parent's heels."[4]

By 1870 Britain was almost overtaken, and there began the first period of serious and comprehensive analysis, of the quality as well as the scale of which the mere list of the leading names gives ample proof: Rudyard Kipling, James Bryce, H. G. Wells, Matthew Arnold, Herbert Spencer, E. A. Freeman, Frederic Harrison, Arnold Bennett, and G. K. Chesterton. In this era a second Mrs. Trollope, Sir Lepel Griffin, was a curious anomaly, whose name is lost to all but the specialist. Not that the British were no longer critical. Bryce himself, the greatest figure of them all in Anglo-American relations, made plain his dislike of corruption in politics. Arnold, as might be expected, found plenty of the same Philistinism that he denounced at home. Spencer and

[1] Q. Nevins, p. 116.
[2] *What I Saw in America* (New York, 1922), p. 254.
[3] Q. Nevins, p. 283.   [4] Q. Nevins, p. 290.

Kipling echo the criticism of political corruption. Wells spoke out against the extreme manifestations of capitalism which were equally his target in Britain. But the criticisms were based on sound information and were much more just and balanced as a result; what is more, almost all the signs of offensive superciliousness have disappeared, and an increasing warmth of appreciation pervades the whole. Bryce's massive work is instinct with admiration for the United States. Bennett's account was acute and friendly, and Chesterton's amiable despite the wildness of his paradoxes—"this land had really been an asylum; even if recent legislation . . . had made" some people "think it a lunatic asylum."[1] Wells paid tribute to the "enormous scale of this American destiny."[2] Some works by lesser figures were important because of their thoroughness, such as James F. Muirhead's *America the Land of Contrasts,* or their enthusiasm, such as William Archer's *America To-day* and W. T. Stead's *Americanization of the World,* all three published between 1898 and 1902. Even Kipling, who did not mince matters—he characterized the American spittoon as "of infinite capacity and generous gape"[3] and remarked of an American boom town: "The papers tell their readers in language fitted to their comprehension that the snarling together of telegraph wires, the heaving up of houses, and the making of money, is progress"[4]—declared:

> Let there be no misunderstanding about the matter. I love this People, and if any contemptuous criticism has to be done, I will do it myself . . . I admit everything. Their Government's provisional; their law's the notion of the moment . . . and most of their good luck lives in their woods and mines and rivers and not in their brains; but for all that, they be the biggest, finest, and best people on the surface of the globe! Just you wait a hundred years. . . . There is nothing known to man that he will not be, and his country will sway the world with one foot as a man tilts a see-saw plank![5]

To such criticism Americans did not find it too hard to reconcile themselves.

The fifth and final period continued this process of amelioration; from World War I onwards, and particularly during World War II, good feeling grew apace under the influence of the increasing likenesses between the two societies. There were still discordant cries, but a new

[1] *What I Saw in America,* p. 48.
[2] Nevins, p. 451.   [3] Q. ibid, p. 447.
[4] Kipling, *From Sea to Sea and Other Sketches* (London, 1900), II, p. 154.
[5] Ibid, pp. 130-1.

note of respect and admiration for many aspects of American life tends to be dominant. As Priestley, who was by no means unreserved in his praise, put it in 1936: "America is definitely in front. She hardly knows she is leading us, but she is. Russia can turn the old economic and political system upside down, but no sooner has she done so than she takes a long look at America. One country after another follows suit."[1] As the number of travellers increased, so did the flow of books, many of them ephemeral. But there was a residue of works of permanent value, pre-eminent among them *The American Political System* of D. W. Brogan, who worthily continued the work of Bryce. Others were those of J. A. Spender, who almost erred on the side of charity to the Americans in *The America of Today* (1928); of L. P. Jacks, *My American Friends* (1933), who displays that insight which is so characteristic of his other works; and of Graham Hutton, *Midwest at Noon* (1946), who depicts the Middle West in a fascinating period of change from isolationism to something nearer to an active will to participate in international affairs. Most English commentators were impressed by the fact that the New Deal brought the two countries into much closer accord, but the dominant impression, particularly after 1940, is of the growing strength and increasing warmth of Anglo-American friendship.

The picture painted by R. B. Mowat of American travellers' views of Britain, *Americans in England,* is much less comprehensive than that of Nevins. Nevertheless, it makes it obvious that the attitude of American travellers has changed very much less over the years. In the first place, because American travellers to Britain were of the wealthier classes, they tended to be sympathetic to the English for cultural reasons; indeed, "background" was what they were usually seeking. Because so much American business was in British hands, there were relatively few American business men in England in earlier days, and these might have constituted the most critical section of the well-to-do American public. This meant that there was never a very bad period in American opinion of Britain comparable with British opinion of America in the second quarter of the nineteenth century. The mere list of early American travellers, who left a mark, indicates their sympathetic attitude; Gouverneur Morris, the Federalist, who described the "madness" of war in 1812 as the work of men, "who for more than twenty years have lavished on Britain the bitterest vulgarity of Billingsgate because she impressed her seamen for self-defence"; the cosmo-

[1] *Midnight in the Desert,* p. 88.

politan and Anglophile Washington Irving, who painted so romantic a picture of English society; Fenimore Cooper, who, though less sympathetic, seemed to be won over despite himself to something like respect, and even wrote on one occasion that "the English gentleman stands at the head of his class in Christendom"; Emerson, who retained many close British friendships, such as that with Carlyle, for over forty years; and Nathaniel Hawthorne, who said: "I seldom came into personal relations with an Englishman without beginning to like him, and feeling my favourable impression wax stronger with the progress of the acquaintance. I never stood in an English crowd without being conscious of hereditary sympathies."[1] These men found many things in Britain to condemn, and did so freely, but they were altogether more restrained in their criticism or more sympathetic in their approach—showed, not to put too fine a point on it, better manners—than their opposite numbers. Though the correspondent of the *New York Observer* who wrote in 1831, "England to an American is not foreign", exaggerated, Henry Adams spoke for his countrymen who visited England when he wrote later: "Considering that I lose all patience with the English about fifteen times a day . . . I get on with them beautifully and love them well."[2] With the great development of friendly contacts which began in the last years of the century, the broadly sympathetic attitude of American travellers did not change materially, but simply fitted in better with the growing warmth of British views of America.

But it is a sign of the unreliability of the views of travellers as a complete guide to Anglo-American feelings, that the nineteenth century appears from them as a period of American goodwill to Britain, when in truth Anglophobia was at its height. The fact is that, though American travellers, who were few, tended to be sympathetic, the mass of the American people at home tended to be hostile; the factors which made for American hatred went deep into her history, and it was only exaggerated by her continued economic and cultural dependence on Britain. It had been born in the Revolutionary period, and had waxed under the impact of the War of 1812 and the literary battle which came afterwards; it remained a powerful influence until the middle years of the century, and a significant, though declining one, for nearly a hundred years more. Only after World War II did the slumbering animosity really seem to be sinking into the grave. There is no doubt that it had been kept alive and active by British abuse in the second quarter of the century, but that the advocacy of American travellers and Anglophiles generally had done much to hasten its demise. As

[1] Q. Mowat, pp. 70, 116, 161.   [2] Q. ibid, pp. 104, 223.

Mowat justly remarks: "[T]he American was more generous in his appreciation, and the Englishman less sensitive in his reaction."[1] Mencken puts it in a different way: "There is in the United States . . . a formidable sect of Anglomaniacs . . . but the corresponding sects of British Americophils is small and feeble though it shows a few respectable names."[2] Though this contains some truth—that Anglophiles in America were vigorous and outspoken, partly because of the challenge of widespread and violent Anglophobia—it is not correct to deny the importance of English Americophils, for one of the characteristics of Anglo-American history is that there has always been a group in each country strongly advocating the cause of co-operation with the other. Successors to the English Whigs and the American Tories of the Revolution have never been lacking, although for many decades they tended to be small minorities amongst their own people. The progress of Anglo-American friendship has in fact consisted in turning those minorities into majorities; majorities were achieved somewhere near the end of the nineteenth century, and by the middle of the twentieth, they had become overwhelming.

The course of this development was not the same in England as in America. The pro-American elements had, until the coming of democracy in the last half of the nineteenth century, been a radical and progressive minority, instead of, as in America, a conservative one. Though the American Anglophile group was predominantly wealthy, there were among the pro-American British radicals a number of great Whig aristocrats, like the first Lord Lansdowne, "full of love and kindness for America".[3] Nor was the mass of the British people ever anti-American, in the way that the mass of the American people was anti-British; truth to tell, the impact of America upon Britain was much less than that of Britain upon America until the last quarter of the century. Britons had other interests in plenty, and were never anything like as conscious of American shafts as were Americans of British barbs. The vast majority of Englishmen were indifferent to America until the close of the nineteenth century, all the more so because of their relative political ignorance and immaturity; in America where democracy and literacy were far ahead, the feeling against Britain was genuinely popular. It follows that the anti-American feeling of the British was largely confined to a dominant Tory minority, and that it owed its violence in considerable degree to their consciousness that the great threat to the aristocratic system they represented came from

[1] Ibid, p. 162.   [2] *The American Language*, p. 28.
[3] Gouverneur Morris: q. Mowat, p. 62.

the example of American democracy. In America it was a case of an Anglophile minority and an Anglophobe majority; in Britain of anti-American and pro-American minorities, and an indifferent majority. But as the cause of democracy triumphed, so did popular awareness of America and her increasing power grow, and so did the hold of the anti-American upper classes diminish. It was on the basis of a common democracy that Anglo-American friendship was finally built.

This much is clear. The hurricane of 1776 left the waters of Anglo-American relations vastly troubled; when it looked like blowing itself out, the turbulence was renewed by the storm of 1812 and its aftermath; after that had, by the middle of the century, died away, a calm began, slowly but steadily, to settle upon the rough waters; by 1914 only a surface swell remained, while by 1945 there was something approaching stillness; and in 1952, despite the drop in pressure in 1950, the barometer seemed to be set fair yet. But further than these generalities it is perilous to go. If we try to survey the unruly seas more closely and more accurately, the chart becomes so complex as to diminish rather than increase our understanding. The breezes and eddies, the winds and currents of Anglo-American emotions and attitudes are so disconcerting, variegated and uncertain, that they defy investigation in the short space at our disposal. To examine one only of the main cross currents of Anglo-American feeling is to become convinced that further elaboration of such a study merely adds confusion, but it is salutary to make the examination in order that we may become fully aware of how dangerous it is for Englishmen and Americans to sit in judgment upon one another.

III

LET us take, as our one example of the hazards of this subject, the familiar accusation, which buzzes insistently through Anglo-American history, of the "materialism" and "vulgarity" of the United States. The indictment was most fully drawn by Henry James: "There is but one word to use in regard to them—vulgar, vulgar, vulgar. Their ignorance—their stingy, defiant, grudging attitude towards everything European—their perpetual reference of all things to some American standard or precedent which exists only in their own unscrupulous wind-bags . . . these things glare at you hideously". But James is a just man, and, his predilections apart, sees the other point of view: "On the other hand we seem a people of *character*, we seem to have energy, capacity and intellectual stuff in ample measure. What I have pointed at as our vices are the elements of the modern man with *culture* quite left out. It's the absolute and incredible lack of *culture* that strikes you in common travelling Americans."[1] Arnold Bennett, interestingly enough, gives him a lesson in tolerance of his country-men: "But it ought to be remembered by us Europeans (and in sack-cloth!) that the mass of us with money to spend on pleasure are utterly indifferent to history and art. . . . I imagine that the American horde 'hustling for culture' . . . will compare pretty favourably with the European horde in such spots as Lucerne."[2]

Nevertheless, James not only saw the other point of view, but the reason for it; in *The American* Newman says, "The fact is I have never had time to 'feel' things so very beautifully. I've had to *do* them, had to make myself felt."[3] More than that, standing as James did on the threshold of American greatness, he was aware of the part America would play, and anxious that it should be a worthy one. His appre-hension comes out in the words of Mrs. Tristram to Newman: "You're the great Western Barbarian, stepping forth in his innocence and might, gazing a while at this poor corrupt old world and then swooping down on it."[4] The mutual feeling of discomfort in this period of cultural adjustment is epitomized in Newman's relationship with the Marquis, who "struck his guest as precautionary, as apprehensive; his manner seemed to indicate a fine nervous dread that something disagreeable might happen if the atmosphere were not kept clear of stray currents from windows opened at hazard. 'What under the sun is he afraid of?' Newman asked himself. 'Does he think I'm going to offer to swap jack-knives with him?' "[5] The lingering flavour of aristocracy, often sweet to Englishmen but unpalatable to Americans, is seldom absent from this question; as E. A. Freeman wrote, "the reading class . . . of those who . . . read enough and know enough to be worth talking to . . . form a larger proportion of mankind than they do in England. On the other hand, the class of those who read really deeply . . . is certainly much smaller."[6] James's predilections, however, would not be gainsayed; he became, as he said, a "cockney *convaincu*",[7] and, after moving finally to England in 1876, wrote to his brother William: "I . . . am turning English all over. I desire only to feed on English life and the contact of English minds. . . ."[8] He occasionally felt uneasy about this expatriate urge; as Roderick Hudson said: "It's a wretched

[1] *The Letters of Henry James*, I, pp. 22-3.   [2] Q. Nevins, p. 458.
[3] Henry James, *The American* (London), p. 37.   [4] Ibid, p. 38.
[5] Ibid, p. 185.   [6] Q. Nevins, p. 431.   [7] *Letters*, I, p. 74.   [8] Ibid, p. 54.

business . . . this virtual quarrel of ours with our own country, this ever-lasting impatience that so many of us feel to get out of it",[1] and it should be noted that Roderick succumbs to the temptations of the Old World, if in a less lurid way than Harry Warrington before him. But James was fundamentally unrepentant; in 1877 he wrote that he felt more at home now in London than anywhere else in the world, and his acceptance, at his life's end, of British citizenship at the height of World War I bore fitting witness to that fact.

But James was not alone in observing, and being fascinated by, this problem. Some saw it like him very much from the European point of view. Curiously, perhaps, Kipling was one of them, the Kipling of *Puck of Pook's Hill* and not the Kipling of *The Night Mail*, and in *An Habitation Enforced* the English countryman says: "Nah—there's no gentry in America, no matter how long you're there. It's against their law. There's only rich and poor allowed."[2] Others, like Mrs. Humphrey Ward in *Eleanor*, though seeing all round the subject, laid more emphasis on the contribution which a young, a fresh, even a naïve America might make to the progress of mankind. But even if it be accepted that some distinction of this kind exists between the two societies, to define the American attitude precisely bristles with new and complex difficulties. Supercilious Englishmen may talk of the Almighty Dollar, but the question is not as simple as that. As James makes Newman say, "I cared for money-making, but I never cared so very terribly for the money. There was nothing else to do".[3] Chesterton pointed out that the Englishman's ideal was leisure not labour, the American's labour not dollars, and—acutely—that the American, quite apart from any love of money, has a great love of measurement. It might even be said that the snobbery of Americans is size, and the snobbery of Englishmen antiquity. The cast of mind is in some respects utterly different; as Henry Adams put it:

The English mind was one-sided, eccentric, systematically un-systematic, and logically illogical. . . . From the old-world point of view, the American had no mind; he had an economic thinking-machine which could work only on a fixed line. The American mind exasperated the European as a buzz-saw might exasperate a pine forest. . . . The American mind was . . . a mere cutting instrument, practical, economical, sharp and direct. . . . Americans needed and used their whole energy, and applied it with close economy; but English society was eccentric by law

[1] Henry James, *Roderick Hudson* (London), p. 30.
[2] Rudyard Kipling, *Actions and Reactions* (London, 1919), p. 37.
[3] *The American*, pp. 222-3.

and for the sake of the eccentricity itself. . . . Often this eccentricity bore all the marks of strength.[1]

This was not the kind of strength that America could afford: the great melting pot had to be strongly and rigidly constructed, and a ruthless pressure of public opinion—"a prairie fire"[2] Chesterton once called it—was needed to create a strong and patriotic American nation.

And the advantages were by no means all on the European side. Rowland might be able to say in *Roderick Hudson*, "But I have the misfortune to be rather an idle man, and in Europe both the burden and the obloquy of idleness are less heavy than here",[3] and reckon it in his heart of hearts a blessing for civilization that it was so; but Dickens saw another truth when he wrote: "By the way, whenever an Englishman would cry 'All right!' an American cries 'Go ahead!' which is somewhat expressive of the national character of the two countries."[4] If America owes much culturally to Britain, Britain's economic predicament at the present time can only be cured by a vigorous transfusion of the American spirit. America may be obsessed with technical progress, but technical progress is still highly necessary; as L. P. Jacks reminded his English readers as early as 1933, "standardization is a condition absolutely essential to all forms of human originality."[5] English lethargy and hidebound tradition are as suspect to Americans as American materialism is to Britons. As J. F. Muirhead wrote in 1898, "It is not easy for a European to the manner born to realize the sort of extravagant, nightmare effect that many of our social customs have in the eyes of our untutored American cousins. . . . The idea of an insignificant boy peer taking precedence of Mr. John Morley! [T]he necessity of backing out of the royal presence!"[6] And, as Henry James pointed out, the English did not take to satire against themselves quite as naturally as a duck to water: "It is an entirely new sensation for them . . . to be (at all delicately) *ironised* or satirised, from the American point of view, and they don't at all relish it. Their conception of the normal in such a relation is that the satire should be all on their side against the Americans".[7] Finally, be it noted, these differences are always rendered sharper by the fact of American overstatement and English understatement; Chesterton does not exaggerate when he writes, "But the

---

[1] *Education of Henry Adams*, pp. 180-1.

[2] *What I Saw in America*, p. 162.

[3] p. 66.   [4] Q. Nevins, p. 126.

[5] Q. Nevins, *America Through British Eyes* (Oxford, 1948), p. 414.

[6] Q. Nevins, *American Social History*, p. 440.   [7] *Letters*, I, p. 68.

real cross-purposes come from the contrary direction of the two exaggerations, the American making life more wild and impossible than it is, and the Englishman making it more flat and farcical than it is."[1]

Thus the complications, the reservations, the explanations, which are involved in such generalizations as this one concerning American materialism and English culture, become readily apparent. And this is not all. When such generalizations are extended in time, they become even more unreliable, and may prove simply untrue. It is not merely that in the eighteenth century an Englishman might appear overdressed in New York, and in the twentieth an American overdressed in London, nor that Fenimore Cooper in the eighteen-twenties found that his London comforts cost him a third of what they would have done in America, while Nathaniel Hawthorne in the fifties found living more expensive in London than at home. Nor is it only that, with the passage of time, the crude material basis of society becomes encrusted with the delicate evasions of civilization, so that Margaret Halsey could write with justice in 1938, "The English have refined upon our naïve American way of judging people by how much money they happen to have at the moment. The subtler English criterion is how much expensive, upper-class education they have been able to afford."[2] It is not these things alone: it may be that the whole national character has changed over the years. There are certainly, it is true, remarkable instances of continuity. It is quite fascinating, for example, to see Kipling in 1900 forestalling Aldous Huxley and Evelyn Waugh in his comments on the materialism of America's attitude to death. When he was talking to an American mortician on the subject of embalming, the undertaker said: "And I wish I could live a few generations just to see how my people keep. But I'm sure it's all right. Nothing can touch 'em after I've embalmed 'em". Kipling concludes, "Bury me cased in canvas . . . in the deep sea; burn me on a back-water of the Hughli . . . or whelm me in the sludge of a broken river dam; but may I never go down to the Pit grinning out of a plate-glass window, in a backless dress-coat, and the front half of a black stuff dressing-gown; not though I were 'held' against the ravage of the grave for ever and ever".[3] But, apart from the instances of continuity, there are also radical transformations. The America of 1929, the United States of H. L. Mencken and Sinclair Lewis, was in many ways unrecognizable to the visitor of 1946; the

[1] Q. Nevins, p. 461.   [2] *With Malice Toward Some*, p. 184.
[3] *From Sea to Sea*, II, p. 150.

development of the cultural maturity of the American people in the intervening years was phenomenal, for nothing chastens like a dose of adversity. There are many such instances, but there is in Anglo-American history one supreme example of this kind of change.

We have often had occasion to note the similarities between the two peoples, and, in particular, the way in which America has tended to assume the role played earlier by Britain. Before we accept generalizations about the materialism of the United States and our own high culture too freely, we should look at the impact made by Britain upon the rest of the world in the first half of the nineteenth century. It was not for their culture that the British were then primarily admired. George Santayana puts the matter well:

Admiration for England, of a certain sort, was instilled into me in my youth. My father (who read the language with ease although he did not speak it) had a profound respect for British polity and British power. In this admiration there was no touch of sentiment nor even of sympathy; behind it lay something like an ulterior contempt, such as we feel for the strong exhibiting at a fair. The performance may be astonishing, but the achievement is mean. So in the middle of the nineteenth century an intelligent foreigner, the native of a country materially impoverished, could look to England for a model of that irresistible energy and public discipline which afterwards were even more conspicuous ... in the United States. It was admiration for material progress, for wealth, for the inimitable gift of success.[1]

Even more striking evidence of the dominance of materialism in the Britain of the Industrial Revolution is provided by the comments of Emerson during his visit to England in 1847-8. We have but to shut our inner eyes for a moment, as the remarks follow one after another, to be convinced in extraordinary fashion that they are spoken in judgment not of nineteenth-century England, but of America a century later. "The culture of the day, the thoughts and aims of men, are English thoughts and aims. A nation ... has ... obtained the ascendant, and stamped the knowledge, activity, and power of mankind with its impress. Those who resist it do not feel it or obey it less. The Russian in his snows is aiming to be English. The Turk and Chinese also are making awkward efforts to be English. The practical common-sense of modern society, the utilitarian direction which labour, laws, opinion, religion take, is the natural genius of the British mind." "Certain

[1] G. Santayana, *Soliloquies in England, and Later Soliloquies* (London, 1922), pp. 2-3.

171

circumstances of English life are not less effective; as, personal liberty, plenty of food; . . . open market, or good wages for every kind of labour; . . . readiness of combination among themselves for politics or for business strikes; and sense of superiority founded on habit of victory in labour and in war; and the appetite for superiority grows by feeding." "The bias of the nation is a passion for utility. . . . Now, their toys are steam and galvanism. They are heavy at the fine arts, but adroit at the coarse; . . . the best iron-masters, colliers, wool-combers, and tanners, in Europe." "Steam is almost an Englishman."[1] "Machinery has been applied to all work, and carried to such perfection, that little is left for the men but to mind the engines and feed the furnaces. But the machines require punctual service, and, as they never tire, they prove too much for their tenders." "What influence the English have is by brute force of wealth and power".[2]

Even in the broader effects of all this, in everything from the seeing of sights to the smoking of marijuana, the similarity is amazing. "The young men have a rude health which runs into peccant humours. They drink brandy like water. . . . They chew hasheesh . . . they saw a hole into the head of the 'winking Virgin', to know why she winks; . . . measure with an English footrule every cell of the Inquisition, . . . every Holy of holies. . . . There are multitudes of rude young English . . . who have made the English traveller a proverb for uncomfortable and offensive manners." "But the English stand for liberty. The conservative, money-loving English are yet liberty-loving; and so freedom is safe. . . . But the calm, sound . . . Briton shrinks from public life, as charlatanism." "There is no country in which so absolute a homage is paid to wealth. . . . An Englishman . . . labours three times as many hours in the course of a year, as any other European. . . . He works fast. Everything in England is at a quick pace. They have reinforced their own productivity by the creation of that marvellous machinery."[3] It is needless to pursue the analogy further. The counter to the present-day accusation of American materialism, that in the early nineteenth century England was equally materialist, can, of course, be modified by reference to the contemporary English cultural outburst and explained as the effect of a new and ill-understood industrialism upon a country where the aristocratic cultural tradition was yet able to survive. But we should have proceeded far enough to convince ourselves of the danger of further generalization: any effort here to make our outline chart of the ocean of Anglo-American emotions more detailed must be

[1] *Works,* II, pp. 15-16, 21, 37, 42.
[2] Ibid, pp. 46, 56.   [3] Ibid, pp. 59, 63, 68, 70.

doomed to failure. We must rest content with the conclusion that, apart from a distinct deterioration in the first half of the last century, there has been a persistent ripening of Anglo-American cordiality. It is indeed the most important theme of our story.

It justly gives ground for confidence in the future of Anglo-American friendship. There may be differences as to how best to promote that future. Many would agree with Hawthorne, that it would not "contribute in the least to our mutual advantage and comfort if we were to besmear one another all over with butter and honey."[1] Some would not, however, agree with Chesterton, that "the very worst way of helping Anglo-American friendship is to be an Anglo-American."[2] Most would agree with Lord Halifax, that the friendship which now exists between the two peoples "often demands more . . . than a treaty which is negotiated in a few weeks and signed in a day. Matrimony is a more exacting affair for both parties than a commercial contract." Others, advocates of Atlantic union, might not altogether agree with him when he writes that, "There is no magic formula which, when applied to Anglo-American relations, will place and keep them for all time upon a satisfactory footing"; they could point out that part at least of his prophecy, uttered in 1947,—"So, as I see it, in the case of the United States, more substantial than any treaty of alliance, *which we are unlikely to achieve*,* is an association of friendship and understanding",[3] —had already been falsified by 1949 when N.A.T.O. was born. All would agree that there may be grave Anglo-American differences in the future. But it is certain that greater efforts have never been made by two sovereign and independent nations to create the conditions in which such differences can be prevented from doing harm. And these positive efforts are supported by the long traditions of Anglo-American history, by the common language, by a kindred democracy, and by the strong emotional bonds of mutual friendship and dependence forged in the one hundred and forty years of Anglo-American peace.

---

[1] Q. Mowat, p. 162.   [2] *What I Saw in America*, p. 243.
* Author's italics.   [3] *Anglo-American Relations*, pp. 5-6.

CHAPTER SEVEN

THE DIPLOMATIC RELATIONSHIP

BEFORE we plunge into the protracted and detailed story of Anglo-American diplomatic relations in the three remaining Parts of the book, it would be wise to consider the general character of those relations; so often in diplomatic history the general shape of things, which alone is of cardinal importance, is lost to view in the confusion of manifold events. It is the plan of this chapter, therefore, to consider first, very briefly, the role of Canada in Anglo-American diplomatic history; then to analyse the essential constituent elements in British and American foreign policy in the last century and three-quarters; and finally to trace swiftly the salient features of Anglo-American diplomatic relations since 1783, so that the reader may not be so easily lost afterwards in the great mass of detail.

I

"THE behaviour of nations", writes Brebner in *North Atlantic Triangle*, "bears close analogies to the emotional surges, the anomalies, and the self-defeating actions of individuals",[1] and though it is most dangerous in the historian, as in the political scientist, to press the analogy between the nation and the individual too far, it certainly has its uses. Indeed, as we have already observed, one can hardly refrain from regarding the Anglo-American relationship as a family one; the simile thrusts itself forward at every turn. As early as 1823, in reference to the parallel course pursued by the two countries in the events leading up to the declaration of the Monroe Doctrine, Canning remarked that "the force of blood again prevails", and that "the mother and the daughter stand together against the world".[2] The analogy is put in its extreme form by Geoffrey Gorer in *The Americans*: "Most Americans feel towards England as though it were a father—authoritarian, wicked, past its

[1] p. 242.
[2] Q. R. W. Seton-Watson, *Britain in Europe, 1789-1914* (Cambridge, 1945), p. 85.

prime, old-fashioned, passed and left behind, but still a father; they can never be indifferent to Britain as they can to the rest of the world. They are more sensitive towards Britain . . . just as one is more sensitive to the public behaviour of relations than to that of strangers."[1] There is some truth in this in a psychological sense, for most of the difficulties between the two arose, as between parent and child, from the existence of bonds of intimate physical contact in the beginning, and of necessary association later. The colonies were founded very largely by men and women from Britain, and there remained a very intimate relationship until the Revolution, a relationship of which their common tongue, common history and common literature still and continually remind both parties. Throughout the nineteenth century British interests in the American continent, and particularly the existence of a common frontier between Canada and the United States, forced the two nations, even after America had attained independence, to live in close contact, so that, until they were finally cleared out of the way, causes of friction were never lacking. An American can write, "The United States has had more diplomatic controversies, and more serious ones, with Great Britain than with any other nation."[2] Yet in fact there was no fundamental clash of interest between them, and though the controversies themselves were serious, the causes of them were all capable of amicable adjustment. They gained their bitterness, and they were so frequent, largely because there was much misunderstanding and much psychological tension between the United States and the mother country.

But, largely because it was, in a sense, a family relationship, it survived the period of bitterness and animosity following upon the Revolution. It even survived the War of 1812, and indeed did so partly because it was so "futile and unnecessary" a conflict.[3] The nineteenth century accomplished the task of applying soothing balm to the resentment of the United States and the injured pride of Britain: "Great Britain had to learn to accept the United States as an equal for the first time. . . . The United States had to go through a period of blustering behaviour and international irresponsibility before she could adapt herself to the power and weight in the world with which her enormous growth had endowed her." Slowly but with some sureness the mellowing process continued. Perhaps the Civil War, as John Morley claimed, was the turning point; certainly Brebner rightly asserts, "The somewhat reluctant respect for the United States which Great Britain acquired

---

[1] London, 1948, p. 191.   [2] Bemis, p. 405.

[3] Morison and Commager, I, p. 431.

175

between 1861 and 1871 was almost bound to persist, in spite of all kinds of friction, misunderstanding, and chauvinistic altercations. Its strength for survival lay, on the one hand, in recognition of the growing weight in the world of the American Republic, and, on the other, in a dim but increasing understanding of the complementary roles which the two countries might play in the Atlantic region and in the world as a whole."[1] By the turn of the century—in 1894—Mahan could write that "a common tongue and common descent are making themselves felt, and are breaking down the barrier of estrangement which have separated too long men of the same blood. There is seen here the working of kinship—a wholly normal result of a common origin, the natural affection of children of the same descent, who have quarrelled and have been alienated with the proverbial bitterness of civil strife, but who all along have realized—or at least have been dimly conscious—that such a state of things is wrong and harmful."[2] Diplomatic relations were by then on a fairly satisfactory basis, but the apprehension of these facts was still—it is the operative word in both passages—'dim'.

By the middle of the twentieth century realization of them was complete and explicit. During the nineteenth century the way had been prepared by that "remarkable series of arbitrations which successively narrowed and finally dissipated the subjects of controversy." Common interests and sentiments prevailed over diplomatic difficulties and divergent national policies, for all the diplomatic controversies between them since 1815 have been "peaceably settled. . . . Such common sense rests on the pervading fact that it has been well for these nations to put aside their own quarrels in the face of greater menaces."[3] Because the menaces became real and apparent to Britain first, and because the causes of dissension were much closer and more important to the Americans than to her people, the will for good relations grew more rapidly in Britain than in the United States. But in due time America reciprocated, and it became so close a *rapprochement* that it had more the air of a family reunion than an *entente cordiale* between two foreign powers; and in fact by 1949 a very special relationship existed between them, much broader and yet closer than any formal alliance, such as the North Atlantic Pact, would make it appear. It is not perhaps without a certain symbolic significance that in 1912 *Whitaker's Almanack* for the first time did not include its information about the United States under "Foreign Countries", but gave it a separate heading of its own, coming immediately after the British Commonwealth. This peculiar relation-

[1] Brebner, pp. 242-3, 244.

[2] *The Interest of America in Sea Power*, pp. 108-9.   [3] Bemis, p. 405.

ship is a very real, if indefinable, thing, and, as the British Ambassador in Washington pointed out early in 1951, the very fact that the divergence of British and American policy over the recognition of Communist China caused so much alarm was a measure of the closeness of it. The restoration of the sense of brotherhood between America and Britain is one of the most important facts in twentieth century history.

Certainly it is the most significant theme in the history of the Anglo-American relationship, and in its development the part played by Canada, "the coupling-pin of Anglo-American relations",[1] is of unique importance. She was in the beginning a counterweight to the thirteen colonies within the First British Empire, then a bone of contention between Britain and the United States, then a hostage in American hands for British good behaviour which balanced British command of the seas, and finally, as she herself grew in power, the most powerful catalytic agent in, and occasionally even, by a strange paradox, the chief victim of, Anglo-American friendship. The Quebec Act of 1774, which helped to alienate the thirteen colonies from the mother country, also helped to prevent the participation of Canada in the revolt, and the reorganization of 1791, combined with the interests of the Montreal fur traders, enabled her to gain strength and to preserve her territory and independence in the War of 1812. It was virtually certain from 1814 onwards that only force could have united her with her great neighbour: "In general, traditional dependence on the Mother Country and traditional fear and dislike of the United States, combined with a disinclination to change and an unwillingness or inability to shed familiar cultural garments, were quite naturally so strong that it would have required a profound cataclysm to have projected the colonists into the American Union."[2] It was in Quebec that this "curious but understandable culture complex" was strongest, but it affected Canadians everywhere. "As a highly intelligent people, surpassed by no nation anywhere, Canadians resented the greater force of American culture coming from mere power of territory, natural resources and infinitely greater population."[3]

This Canadian national sentiment was fostered by the firm inauguration of Canadian self-government in 1847, and exacerbated by the growth of outspoken American annexationist designs in the sixties and seventies. Canadians in this era of Little Englandism could not but contrast the enlightened readiness of the mother country to loosen her

[1] Ibid, p. 791.   [2] Brebner, p. 179.   [3] Bemis, p. 801.

bonds, with the anxiety of the United States to enmesh her in new ones, and even the adverse effects of British free trade upon the Canadian economy did little to lessen her mistrust of her southern neighbour, who had alleviated those effects by making the Reciprocity Treaty of 1854, but, under the rule of protectionist Republicans, refused to renew it in 1866. It was ironical that the post-Civil War period, which saw a distinct betterment of Anglo-American relations, also saw American-Canadian relations at their nadir, but it was a reflection of the fact that, as Canadian independence grew, so did direct British interest in disputes between Canada and the United States lessen.

> During the early days of the Dominion, a good many thoughtful Canadians were justified in doubting whether Great Britain rated Canadian rights above Anglo-American understanding. These Canadian misgivings had a long ancestry, beginning with the surrender of the mid-continent to the new United States in 1783, and coming down through other territorial and fisheries settlements to the unexpected loss of territory north of the Columbia River in the Oregon settlement of 1846. Canadian political leaders knew that British leaders like Gladstone, Granville, Cobden and Bright expected the New Dominion to become part of the United States.[1]

Their answer to this fear was the formation of the Canadian federation of 1867, which was the immediate product of mistrust of the United States, combined with the pressure of particular Canadian economic (chiefly railroad) interests.

From this time, as Canada's strength grew and as it became clear that annexationism lacked wide support among the American public, American-Canadian relations improved as fast as Anglo-American relations. The extraordinarily intimate association of the Canadian and American peoples began to bear fruit in understanding, though some elements of mistrust remained, and the kinship of Canadians and Americans became very much closer and more marked even than that of Americans and Englishmen: "So unrestricted and so natural have been the freedom of movement and interplay of populations, that Canadians and Americans do not think of themselves as foreign to each other; rather they consider themselves independent of each other."[2] It still remained true, as late as the Alaskan boundary dispute of 1903, that Canadian interests were sometimes ground between the upper and nether millstones of American power and of the now eager British desire for the friendship of the United States; Canada was a "puny third

[1] Brebner, p. 182.   [2] Bemis, p. 791.

party to a grand settlement between two Great Powers". But it was better that a minor Canadian interest should suffer from the amity of the two powers, than that she herself should be utterly crushed by their enmity; and, beginning with Macdonald, Canadian statesmen adjusted themselves admirably to the new dispensation, and made a very good best of it. He and his successors "saw clearly that Anglo-American understanding must be the basic objective of any realistic Canadian foreign policy."[1] Though from time to time she showed her independence, as in her rejection of the Taft Reciprocity Treaty of 1911 and her support of Britain rather than the United States over the Korean crisis of 1950-2, Canada has done all in her power for the last three-quarters of a century to promote Anglo-American friendship. And she has been in an increasingly strong position to do this owing to the rapid growth of her power in the twentieth century and to the coming of Dominion Status. She showed the extent of her influence very plainly in World War II, for Roosevelt's clear guarantee of Canadian integrity in 1938 did but make explicit what had been implicitly recognized by Canadians since the beginning of the century; as early as 1902 Laurier had remarked that the Monroe Doctrine protected Canada against enemy aggression.[2] After the actual outbreak of hostilities, she formed an admirable bridge between neutral America and belligerent Britain, making easier, and even possible, such early forms of united effort as the American-Canadian Joint Defence Board, the naval co-operation in the Atlantic, and the smooth working of Lend-Lease.

Bemis sums it up:

> Canada . . . has always been in effect a hostage for the benevolent conduct of the British toward the United States and the Monroe Doctrine. At no time during the nineteenth century could the United States have withstood a challenge of the British navy on the seas; but at no time since, say 1850, certainly since 1866, could Great Britain have defended Canada against an overland movement by the United States on the long exposed flank of her Empire. . . . Canada has always been instinctively conscious of this position of hostage for the good conduct of Great Britain toward the United States. . . . If only for this reason—among many other pleasanter ones—she has become the natural link of friendship, geographically, politically, economically, and culturally, between the two great English-speaking powers.[3]

One of the most remarkable phenomena of Anglo-American history, as we have suggested earlier, is the way in which the United

---

[1] Brebner, pp. 183, 191.   [2] Ibid, p. 271.   [3] Bemis, pp. 793-4.

States in the twentieth century has gradually assumed the role in international affairs which Britain so long performed. She has taken up, with misgivings and reluctance, the burden of leading the independent nations against the threat of domination by any single aggressive and dictatorial power. We can, and shall, see many other likenesses in diplomatic policy between the two countries, but none is so startling as this.

We can see, for instance, how both powers, at different periods, suffered a revulsion from the Atlas-burden of prime responsibility for the freedom of mankind. In this respect the isolationism of Britain after the Napoleonic wars resembles closely that of the United States almost exactly a century later.

> The policy which the United States pursued toward Europe after the separate peace with Germany, Austria, and Hungary, following the rejection of the League of Nations, may be compared to that of Great Britain after the Napoleonic wars and the peace settlement of 1815. Great Britain refused to make of the Quadruple Alliance . . . a pediment for the Holy Alliance. . . . Unchallenged in her absolute control of the sea, and thus safe behind the English Channel, she preferred to stand aloof from the issues of continental politics as long as no one upset the balance of power. Similarly a century later the United States, safe behind the Atlantic, rejected Woodrow Wilson's ideal of internationalism and stepped back from Europe to its own continent after the defeat of Germany.[1]

Equally interesting is the similarity between Britain's acceptance of the League of Nations in 1919 and America's acceptance of the United Nations in 1945. As the Swiss historian Rappard once pointed out, the very term 'United Nations' is a tribute to the 'United States', and the same might possibly be said of the terms 'League of Nations' and 'British Commonwealth of Nations'. Certainly the analogy illustrates nicely the way in which the United States has tended to assume the diplomatic role of Great Britain during the middle years of the twentieth century. Partly because, in her insular position, she has, like Britain, few direct quarrels with other nations; partly because, her land-hunger having been sated by the acquisition of her continental territories, as had that of Britain by that of her colonial empire, she has no aggressive intentions; partly because, owing to her way of life and form of government, she desires peace rather than war, as Britain has done at most periods of her history—America has, again like Britain before her, assumed her new diplomatic functions with distaste.

[1] Ibid, p. 712.

The emotional reaction of English Tories against the British participation in the War of the Spanish Succession at the beginning of the eighteenth century is almost ludicrously like the attitude of American Republican isolationists in modern times, while the parallel between the Little Englanders of the Boer War, and the American opponents of Republican policy in the Philippines at the same period, could hardly be more exact. But, though taken up with reluctance, the burden has never been put down by either power until the day was over and the struggle won, though, alas, neither has yet been able to cross the Delectable Mountains and lead the nations into the Promised Land.

But, having this general picture in our mind's eye,—a picture in which the United States swiftly outgrows Great Britain and comes more and more to take her leading place in the council of the free nations, a picture in which Canada is at once an agent and a symbol of the ever-deepening and widening cordiality of Anglo-American friendship—let us examine a little more closely, before we proceed with our story, the pattern which emerges from the history of Anglo-American relations.

II

WE CAN most readily discern this pattern if we first appreciate that Great Britain had reached a certain political maturity by 1783. This was most especially true of her foreign policy; she was old, even then, in the ways and vicissitudes, the alarums and excursions of national diplomacy, and she had for many years past picked her path, not without success, through the tangled thickets of international affairs. But it was also true to some extent of other aspects of her national life. There were, certainly, radical changes to come in the next one hundred and fifty years: she was in the nineteenth century to fulfil the promise of the seventeenth, and become a democratic state; she was to overhaul her whole governmental machine and to pass through a period of *laissez-faire* economic policies; she was to acquire a vast new African empire; she was to become one of the most highly urbanized and industrialized communities in the world. But the main lines of her national development were already clearly determined by 1783.

She was already one of the dominating European powers, and was moving into a position almost of supremacy; indeed, French historians describe the eighteenth century itself as the period of the *"préponder-*

ance Anglaise", and she was to remain a Great Power, in so far as that vague classification has any meaning, well into the twentieth century. She was already unquestionably the greatest of colonial powers, and she remains so today, even after the liquidation of large portions of her empire. She was already the paramount naval power, having faced, without absolute disaster, in the last stages of the War of American Independence the combined maritime strength of France, Spain, Russia, America and Holland; and she remains today a formidable naval power, even though she has relinquished her naval supremacy to the United States. She had by 1783 comfortably taken the lead over Holland, her nearest rival, in the extent and importance of her commerce; her foreign trade is still vast, and she still is more dependent on it than any other nation in the world. Her population was to increase fivefold before 1950, but already the curve of her population graph had turned decisively upwards by 1783, and a swift movement of population from country to town had already begun. Finally, economic developments were already irresistibly under way which were to make her in the nineteenth century pre-eminently the greatest of industrial powers, the unique pioneer of industrialism on the national scale, and which were to keep her in some respects, even in mid-twentieth century, an industrial power of the greatest importance. The differences between the land ruled by the Younger Pitt and that ruled by Clement Attlee (and between the ways in which they ruled it) are very great, but they are not so great as those which separate Pitt from Cardinal Wolsey. Her peaceful, almost regular, growth after 1832 contrasts vividly with the turbulence of her development in the seventeenth century. In 1783 Englishmen looked back as far to Shakespeare as we look back to Dr. Johnson, and already, in Shakespeare's day, the English government could claim an older and more continuous and effective tradition than any other European institution, except perhaps the Papacy. By the final breach with the United States in that year Great Britain was already in many ways a mature political power, and the main lines of her development were already determined.

Nothing could be less true of the United States. As we have seen, her population was to increase between forty- and fifty-fold, and, from a mere coastal strip of inhabited territory, she was to become a great continental power bordering on the two main oceans of the world. From a people living by agriculture, shipping and commerce, they were to become the greatest industrial community the world has ever seen, producing by any reckoning far more manufactured products than

182

all the rest of mankind put together. Though she has always been in some senses a democratic nation, she too had to undergo a serious process of democratization in the early nineteenth century, and she had, above all, in a supreme struggle, to throw off the dead hand of negro slavery. Her constitution has in theory remained virtually unchanged since its foundation in 1789, but in practice it has altered enormously. Her history since 1783 equals in length and hugely exceeds in importance the absolute total of her history before that date. From a colony of Britain she has become unquestionably the most powerful state on earth, and one accused by her enemies of an imperialism more dangerous than any which has preceded it. The foreign policy of the United States has responded, and has adapted itself to these revolutionary changes in her life, in the same way that that of Britain has remained singularly unchanged just because her life has changed, comparatively, so little. This continuity of British policy between 1783 and the present day, and its contrast with the fundamental transformation of American policy in the same period, is the main fact in the history of Anglo-American diplomatic relations.

One would like to use the word 'consistency' to describe British policy over the years, except that it carries with it certain undesirable overtones; in particular, it implies the use of the word 'inconsistency' to describe the policy of the United States, a term which is not fitting, both because it has an air of denigration and because it is not altogether accurate. But if it is clear that the word is not used in the sense of what one might call day-to-day consistency—the changeless prosecution of a policy which never alters to meet new circumstances—but of the pursuit of policies which do not in fact change much because the interests on which they are based do not alter radically, it is perhaps an illuminating description. It is true that on the surface Great Britain could be very inconsistent on occasion, as for instance in the way in which she swung in the nineteenth century between the poles of isolation from and participation in European affairs, whereas the United States during the same period pursued a policy of avoiding entangling alliances with the utmost consistency. But, taking the full stretch of the years, and having some regard for the traditions which Britain had already established before 1783, it is clear that British foreign policy was, throughout, consistent in its pursuit of certain fundamental objectives, and in the way it was guided by certain principles, whereas that of the United States completely altered in its objectives, its character and even its principles, between the Farewell Address of Washington and Roosevelt's Fourth Inaugural. Let us first consider British policy.

183

III

WITHIN ten years of the Treaty of Versailles of 1783 Great Britain entered the war against Revolutionary France. This struggle, in which the Younger Pitt became so reluctantly involved, and which, merging as it did into that against Napoleon, lasted with only one short break for more than twenty years, was the greatest struggle in the history of mankind to date. Improved cannon, better firearms, increased productive power, the coming of universal military service, all these things rendered it more destructive than any of its predecessors. It changed its character to some extent during its course since it ceased to be a war against a *soi-disant* democracy and became one against the increasingly tyrannical régime of Napoleon: but, in both its phases, it was from the British point of view essentially a war to prevent the conquest of Europe by France, a war to prevent the domination of the European continent by a single power. In this sense it was nothing new; it was just another war of a type which was traditional in British policy. It can certainly be asserted that the tradition began in the late sixteenth century, when England joined the Netherlands in their struggle to gain independence from Catholic Spain, and thus to prevent Philip II from moving closer to the establishment of an effective European hegemony, a design which was dramatically, or at least symbolically, frustrated by the defeat of the Armada. During the early seventeenth century England was largely preoccupied with her internal troubles, but after 1688 she is to be found, once more in collaboration with the Dutch, opposing the schemes of Louis XIV for the domination of Europe. After the accession of William III to the English throne, and even more after his death, effective leadership of the anti-French coalition passed into the hands of Britain, and it was largely the work of Marlborough that made possible in 1713 a reasonably successful conclusion to the War of the Spanish Succession, which checked French designs, if it did not render them impossible, for the future. During the eighteenth century Britain was involved in two major wars, both against France, the War of the Austrian Succession and the Seven Years' War, and was able in the latter to add greatly to her colonial empire.

In 1793 came the long French wars against what Pitt described as "a danger the greatest that ever threatened the world . . . a danger which has been resisted by all the nations of Europe, and resisted by none with so much success as by this nation, because by none has it been resisted so uniformly and with so much energy."[1] The nineteenth century saw only one major war in which Great Britain was involved, the Crimean, for she stood apart from the Franco-Prussian war between her traditional enemy and her traditional ally. But she was soon to find that old friend would become new enemy, and therefore old enemy new friend, so that in 1914 she was once again involved in fighting a war to prevent the conquest of Europe by a single power, in this case, Germany. This was a war beside whose bloodshed that of all previous wars paled into insignificance, but yet we find that by 1939 Great Britain is once more fighting for her life, and for that of Europe, if not of the world, against a revivified Germany more mighty in arms than ever before. Once more, though by a narrow margin, she was able, with the aid of her giant allies, who were forced into the struggle at a later stage by the direct and lunatic attacks of the enemy, to carry the war to a successful conclusion. Only she among the United Nations entered the war at the beginning and remained in it until the end, and from her shores alone was the great reconquest of Europe possible; in this sense, she was once more the foundation stone of the coalition which eventually frustrated the ambitions of Germany, Italy and Japan. Such a policy as this has now been pursued with remarkable consistency by Britain for four hundred years, and though the power whose supremacy she opposed has been different, her primary objectives have not changed. What have those objectives been?

The first and fundamental object of British policy, as of the policy of every nation, was, of course, national survival, and her very existence as a nation was threatened by Hitler, and probably by Napoleon, both of whom contemplated and planned, though they never attempted, actual invasions. At other times, though her life itself may not have been in quite such jeopardy, her existence as a great and independent power certainly was. In the midst of the protracted conflict with France, on 17 February, 1800, Pitt was asked in the House of Commons what were his war aims, and he replied, "In one word . . . it is *Security*".[2] On 13 May, 1940, Churchill, when asked the same question in the same place, echoed this reply, though in a characteristically pugnacious form, "You ask, What is our aim? I can answer in one word: *Victory*".[3] But whatever its precise form, the fundamental objective was continued existence as an independent power.

[1] Q. *Britain in Europe*, p. 17.   [2] Q. ibid, p. 17.

[3] Winston S. Churchill, *The Second World War*, II, (London, 1949), p. 24. Author's italics.

The second objective was a less fundamental, but none the less very important, modification of this, a modulation, one might call it, in a minor key, the well known and much abused policy of the balance of power. This phrase, which is so apt to arouse the ire of liberals and idealists, merely embodied the intention of preventing excessive power from falling into the hands of any single state, because this threatened the independence of the other states, Great Britain among them. This policy has been criticized, partly as unconstructive, and partly because it seemed to some an effort on the part of Great Britain to assure her own preponderant influence, by encouraging an even balance between the greatest powers or groups of powers; it has been held to result merely in the construction of two great blocs of mistrustful nations, whose very existence inevitably precipitates war. In fact the policy has no such object and has had no such result, for it is apparent that, in nearly all the great wars of the last three hundred years in which Britain has played a leading role, the major cause of conflict has been the desire of some great power or group of powers to establish their own supremacy. Britain's balance of power policy is in reality her "instinctive opposition to any bid for world power, from whatever quarter, and her no less marked preference for a certain equilibrium of forces on the European continent."[1] Britain's balance of power policy had certain specific manifestations, certain particular objects in view, the most important being a determination to prevent the Low Countries from falling wholly into the hands of a hostile, or even of any, Great Power; this object British governments have pursued with unswerving consistency from the Revolt of the Netherlands in the sixteenth century to the invasion of Belgium in 1914. It was here, where the pistol pointed to her heart, that she was most sensitive to any threat to the balance of power.

The third principle of British policy was that she sought no territorial gains in Europe; after the loss of Calais by Queen Mary, Britain never sought, even under the Hanoverian Kings, to make continental acquisitions, with the occasional exception of strategic bases such as Gibraltar. Indeed she instinctively avoided for many years even alliances or definite commitments to action there. When she entered wars, her traditional policy was to pursue for the most part colonial gains overseas. This meant that she tended to try and fight her battles in the colonies, where, through her pre-eminence at sea, she could most effectively bring her weight to bear. The Tory party in the Spanish Succession War first made this demand vocal, in their opposition to

[1] *Britain in Europe* p. 35.

Marlborough's later policy, and it was classically expounded and triumphantly vindicated by Chatham in the Seven Years' War; it was the policy which so struck the imagination of Macaulay when he wrote of Frederick the Great's attack upon Maria Theresa: "[I]n order that he might rob a neighbour whom he had promised to defend, black men fought on the coast of Coromandel, and red men scalped each other by the Great Lakes of North America."[1] The Younger Pitt has always been criticized by historians because he frittered away his forces in futile military ventures, but he certainly swept all the available French colonies into his net. Even in World War I Allenby's Palestine campaign was an effort in the same direction, while in World War II it was in North Africa that the "hinge of fate" turned.

But Great Britain has never been able in the course of these life and death struggles to neglect the European theatre altogether, for in World War I she made her main effort there, and the Peninsular War and the D-day campaign were both decisive in their day. Nevertheless she has always kept her actual contribution of armed forces as small as possible; Marlborough's British troops formed a surprisingly small part of his command, Wellington's army was by no means wholly British, and in 1944 Eisenhower's forces became increasingly American as the months passed. Whenever she could, Britain has preferred to fight her European battles, as opposed to those in the colonies and at sea, by the use of her political and financial power, by building up coalitions against the enemy, by subsidizing the armies of her allies. Upon the solid base of her island position she has attempted to build, and when they collapsed to build again, a succession of common fronts against the common enemy. The masterly diplomacy of Marlborough, the almost superhuman patience of Pitt and his successors in erecting successive European alliances against a triumphant France, Churchill's revival, even to the very phrase, of his ancestor's Grand Alliance; this has been the British path to victory. It has been by no means popular with other nations, for until World War II Britain herself remained immune from the worst ravages of war, and the taunt that she would fight to the last drop of blood of the last Frenchman came sometimes from deep in the European heart. But there can be no doubt that it was the best way to win, if indeed it was not the only way, for her population was never as great as that of her opponents, so that she could never match man for man, while her riches were often much greater and, combined with her island position, gave her her trump card—staying power.

Her fourth objective was always to retain effective control of the seas,

[1] Macaulay, *Critical and Historical Essays* (London, 1852), p. 780.

or at least to prevent control of them falling into the hands of another power. Not until the opening years of the twentieth century did she give up her effort to retain a navy equal to that of any two other powers; and only after World War I did she come to admit the equality, and in World War II the supremacy, of the United States Navy. To other powers, particularly the United States, the term Freedom of the Seas has had a quite different meaning, and Britain's traditional diplomatic role has brought her into frequent collision with America, the greatest of the neutral powers; the interest of the former was obviously in time of war to restrict as far as possible neutral commerce with the enemy, for economic warfare was her most potent weapon, whereas the interest of the latter was naturally the very reverse. To Britain, Freedom of the Seas meant freedom for the shipping of all countries to trade without restriction, except with Britain's enemies in time of war; to America, it tended to mean absolute freedom for the shipping of all nations in war as well as in peace. This question, which had been serious enough to be chiefly responsible for the outbreak of the War of 1812, became less important as the United States became less and less primarily a maritime power, and as in world affairs her interests became more and more allied to those of Britain. It is interesting, for instance, that in the Civil War the North advanced many traditional British arguments to support her blockade of the South, while in World War I America was content to acquiesce in practices after 1917 which she had condemned —at least in theory—before that date.

To Britain this maritime policy was absolutely vital. It was essential to the maintenance of her commerce, which was never during the years with which we are concerned, as it was to America, a comparative luxury. Already, by the time of the American Revolution, she had ceased to export grain, and during the Revolutionary and Napoleonic wars she became increasingly dependent on imports, not only of raw materials for industry, but, even more vital, of food. In every great war this problem of ensuring her flow of imports increased in severity, until in 1941 it assumed its most acute form; without question it was in both World Wars the most dangerous weapon which Germany could use against her. Strategically this means that Great Britain has always been, has always considered herself, and has always been considered by others, as primarily a naval power; she was so long before 1783 and, with the necessary addition of an air force, she is still so today. This has made her policy of building up coalitions against menacing powers —rather than fighting them, except at intervals, single-handed—even more obviously the right policy; her power of blockade and her capacity to continue her own indispensable commerce have again and again been the foundation of her victories.

Finally, though it is a difficult concept to express in words which will be equally accurate in 1783 and 1952, Great Britain has always stood in greater or less degree in her foreign policy for what may be called 'constitutional' government. One can perhaps say of the United States that she has always, since the formation of the Constitution, been a 'democratic' state, though, as we have pointed out, considerable qualifications must be made in the use of the term in the Federalist era. But one certainly cannot say so of Britain until the late nineteenth century, for Castlereagh and most of his contemporaries in the ruling class shuddered at such a notion. It is clear that during the war against Revolutionary France, Britain was not fighting for democracy as Jefferson knew it, since he would more probably have awarded that palm to the French themselves; yet even here the question is complex, for there is not so very much to choose between the repressive policy of Pitt and that of Washington in this era, particularly if it be remembered that England was less than thirty miles from France and America three thousand. But on the other hand, Great Britain certainly did stand for opposition to tyrannical and arbitrary, as well as aggressive, governments. It is possible at least to make out a case for the idea, as Churchill has done in his biography, that Marlborough's chief motive in the War of the Spanish Succession was to prevent future French aggressions, by imposing some sort of internal constitutional check on the power of the French monarchy. It is true that the democratic lustre of seventeenth century England became somewhat tarnished in the Britain of the Hanoverians, and that the governing class increasingly forgot that Locke had defended the Revolution of 1688 because it was popular, and remembered only that he had done so because it protected the sacred right of property: but it is also true that the English constitution in the eighteenth century was the cynosure of European (if not American) eyes, and that Englishmen still looked back, if without any intention of repeating the performance, to the Revolution of 1688 as the foundation of their liberties.

Certainly, in her everyday policy Britain has never refused to deal with absolute or arbitrary governments just because they were absolute or arbitrary. In 1936 Anthony Eden, in what Seton-Watson describes as "the true tradition of all his predecessors since Castlereagh and Canning,"[1] declared that it was "neither necessary nor desirable that our likes or dislikes for foreign forms of government should prejudice

[1] R. W. Seton-Watson, *Britain and the Dictators* (Cambridge, 1938), p. 266.

our international friendships or influence the course of our foreign policy."[1] This certainly echoes what Canning said in Parliament in 1823: "The general acquisition of free institutions is not necessarily a security for general peace", and Britain should retain an "essentially neutral" attitude, "not only between contending nations, *but between conflicting principles*."[2] As Seton-Watson sums it up, "This country has never insisted upon identity of political outlook as a basis of alliance and friendship".

"But", he goes on to say, ". . . it is quite clear that political affinities render co-operation easier."[3] Canning, for instance, prefaced the words quoted above with another sentiment: "No man can witness with more delight than I do, the widening diffusion of political liberty. . . . I would not prohibit other nations from kindling their flame at the torch of British freedom".[4] Others, such as Palmerston and Russell, would have gone a good deal further, and Gladstone declared in the famous Midlothian campaign that British foreign policy

> should always be inspired by love of freedom. . . . In the foreign policy of this country the names of Canning, of Russell and of Palmerston, will ever be honoured by those who recollect the erection of the Kingdom of Belgium and the union of the disjointed provinces of Italy. It is that sympathy—not with disorder, but on the contrary founded on the deepest and most profound love of order—which ought in my opinion to be the very atmosphere in which the Foreign Secretary of England ought to live and move.[5]

In the early nineteenth century Britain's hesitance to declare unrestricted support for liberal causes in time of peace was reflected in those mysterious and equivocal words which chase one another through the diplomatic records of the period, 'intervention' and 'non-intervention' in the affairs of Europe. The Concert of Europe after the Napoleonic Wars demanded intervention against democratic causes in certain countries, and Britain refused to intervene, but Palmerston and Russell tried to turn the tables on their opponents by fostering subsequent liberal movements, while still talking of non-intervention—a situation which was characteristically summed up by Talleyrand in his definition of 'non-intervention' as *"un mot métaphysique et moral qui signifie à peu près la même chose qu'intervention"*. In normal times the policy of Great Britain, whether calling for intervention or opposing it, could fairly be described in Granville's words as a policy by which the government would try to cultivate especially intimate relations "with

[1] Q. ibid, p. 266.   [2] Q. ibid, p. 371.   [3] *Britain in Europe*, p. 650.
[4] Q. *Britain and the Dictators*, p. 371.   [5] Q. *Britain in Europe*, pp. 547-8.

the countries which have adopted institutions similar in liberality to our own."[1]

But the hesitancy disappeared altogether in time of war, when Britain was prepared to support any country, or movement in a country, which would further the cause. In 1808, for example, Sheridan in the Commons urged support for Spain against Napoleon, and Canning at once declared, "we shall proceed upon the principle that any nation of Europe which starts up with a determination to oppose a Power which is the common enemy of the nations, becomes instantly our essential ally."[2] Naturally, too, a preference was given to popular movements, and this became increasingly clear as the century progressed; by World War I she could wholeheartedly associate herself with Wilson's desire to make the world safe for democracy, and in World War II could readily participate in the framing of the Atlantic Charter. So strongly had she come, by 1939, to pursue this objective, that while in the throes of war with Germany she ran the temerous risk of becoming involved at the same time with Russia, by threatening to give way to the popular British demand to send unrestricted aid to Finland when she was attacked by the Soviet Union. This principle of supporting 'constitutional' forms of government, though it became stronger as she herself became increasingly democratic, has always been a part of British foreign policy from the eighteenth century onwards. Primarily Britain opposed France and Germany because they had aggressive designs, but she opposed them also because they were ruled by what she believed were despotic governments dangerous to liberty.

Great Britain, then, traditionally pursued five main objectives: her national survival, the balance of power, control of the seas, an overseas empire, and free government. She has pursued them, in some sort at least, since the sixteenth century, and throughout that time has been persistently active in European affairs. There were, it is true, periods of so-called isolation in her policy: an important one, for example, in the seventeenth century, a less notable one under Walpole in the early eighteenth, and another important one in the nineteenth. These phases were a natural reflection of her geographical position; as an island power, at once in and out of Europe, she alternated between "the wish for isolation and an extreme policy of interference," and these "apparent hesitations and half-measures . . . foreign observers have sometimes sought to explain . . . by farsighted and calculated policy."[3]

[1] Q. *Britain in Europe*, pp. 293-4.   [2] Q. ibid, p. 25.
[3] *Britain and the Dictators*, p. 7.

This tendency to withdraw into her own shell, particularly after a crisis in which she had participated, confused foreigners, and gained for her the reputation embodied in the term "Perfidious Albion"; and her refusal to enter into binding commitments in time of peace merely added to this effect. Only by slow degrees did she accept the idea of permanent participation in any form of European political organization.

Castlereagh at first accepted the system of the European Concert of Powers, and wrote of it in 1817: "I am quite convinced that past habits, common glory and these occasional meetings, displays and repledges are among the best securities Europe now has for a durable peace", but within two or three years he found it necessary to protest against some of the doings of the reactionary European rulers, while Canning had already declared that regular conferences "with the great despotic monarchs . . . would really amount to a combination of governments against liberty." Later, when he had succeeded Castlereagh in power, he withdrew altogether from the Concert, arguing that the system of periodical meetings was "new and of very questionable policy, and that it will necessarily involve us deeply in all the politics of the Continent, whereas our true policy has always been not to interfere except in great emergencies and then with commanding force."[1] He put it more theatrically in the form, "Every nation for itself and God for us all."[2]

This participation in, followed by withdrawal from, European events was characteristic of nineteenth-century English policy. As Russell said, the "traditionary policy of this country is not to bind the Crown and country by engagements, unless upon special cause shown arising out of the special circumstances of the day".[3] Palmerston in particular tended always to follow his own path, agreeing with Russell that "it is very difficult to lay down any principles from which deviations may not frequently be made", or, as he put it in his more belligerent mood, "I hold with respect to alliances that England is a Power sufficiently strong, sufficiently powerful to steer her own course. . . . I hold that the real policy of England—apart from questions which involve her own particular interests, political or commercial—is to be the champion of justice and right, . . . giving the weight of her moral sanction and support wherever she thinks that justice is".[4] A return to isolation after the

---

[1] Q. *Britain in Europe*, pp. 52-3.

[2] Q. E. Halévy, *History of the English People, 1815-30* (London, 1926), p. 168.

[3] Q. *Britain in Europe*, p. 293.

[4] Q. P. Guedalla, *Palmerston* (London, 1926), pp. 280-1.

Crimean War was partly checked by Disraeli, who expressed the view in one of his last great speeches that, "If . . . one of the most extensive and wealthiest empires in the world, . . . from a perverse interpretation of its insular geographical position, turns an indifferent ear to the feelings and fortunes of continental Europe, such a course would, I believe, only end in its becoming an object of general plunder. *So long as the power and advice of England are felt in the councils of Europe, peace, I believe, will be maintained, and for a long period.* Without their presence war . . . seems to me inevitable."[1] There followed in the last two decades of the century, nevertheless, a period of marked isolationism under the leadership of Salisbury; indeed, with the exception of the Crimea, which, as a Near Eastern question, affected the Empire more than the mother country, the mid and late nineteenth century saw the high water mark of Britain's "splendid" isolation. This was largely because during much of this time she was without peer in Europe.

France had passed the peak of her relative strength, and Italy and Germany were only just coming into existence, while no European power had yet felt the full impact of the Industrial Revolution as Britain had, and therefore none could equal her in economic strength. Comparative figures of population, too, show that during these years she was stronger, relative to the other nations, than at any previous or subsequent period.

Population Figures in Millions

	1815-21	1870-2	1880-1	1890-1	1900-1	1910-1
France	30.4	36.1	37.6	38.3	38.9	39.6
Germany	(21)	41	45.2	49.4	56.3	64.9
U.K.	20.8	31.8	35.2	38.1	41.9	45.3
U.S.A.	9.6	38.5	50.1	62.6	75.9	91.7
Italy	—	—	28.4	30.3	32.4	34.6

[Figures are from R. C. K. Ensor, *England, 1870-1914*, pp. 102-3, 269, 498. They are based on census returns within the years indicated.]

In fact, between about 1830 and 1880 Britain was nearer to being the paramount power in the world than at any other era in her history.

But with the rapid growth of the German menace she became conscious of her isolation as an unhappy condition, so that, in the difficult years leading up to World War I, she set about the task of seeking friends, and, in the years after it, considered herself as very nearly irretrievably committed to European affairs. Thus, though it

[1] Q. *Britain in Europe*, p. 544.

might appear at first sight true to say of Britain's policy since 1783, "The desire for isolation, the knowledge that it is impossible—these are the two poles between which the needle of the British compass continues to waver",[1] in reality the periodic revulsions from participation in European affairs only serve, on a broader view, to emphasize the persistence of her habit of intervention whenever a crisis arose.

On the whole Britain remained remarkably constant to her tradition and her basic principles, and this applies as much to the years after World War I when her power had declined relative to that of the new rising nations, such as the United States, as it does to the earlier years. One is repeatedly reminded of this by the analogies which strike the eye between one period and another. Seton-Watson rightly claims that in 1914 the main lines of British policy showed "surprisingly little change since the days of Napoleon",[2] while the similarity between her situation in 1914 and in 1939 was, for the inhabitants of the country, too obvious to need emphasis.

Even more remarkable in some ways is the likeness between the part she played in the Napoleonic Wars and in World War II. In both she was, as an island power, the essential foundation of ultimate victory; in both, her determination to persist to the end made that victory possible. In both, she entered, although reluctantly, upon the struggle because she feared the overweening ambition of the enemy and because she desired security from aggression, and in both she found in the end that only the destruction of the personal dictatorships of her enemies could give her any hope of that security. In both, she was able to retain control of the seas and keep her own life lines open, though nearly the whole coastline of Europe fell under enemy influence, and though the enemy replied to blockade with counter-blockade. In both, she suffered early and frequent military disasters, and saw her allies destroyed with depressing swiftness. In both, she was able to watch the enemy make his first uneasy and temporary terms with Russia, while he conquered virtually the rest of Europe; to observe how he was forced to abandon his plans for a direct assault on England because he lacked control of the sea; to gaze fascinated as each dictator in turn—whether impelled by a similar megalomania, or by a remorseless but mysterious logic, which forces the master of a great national army in time of war to turn it to use on land when baulked by the sea—hurled himself in desperate and fatal folly upon that "cloud of power in the north". Well might the British have murmured in both cases, "*Quos Deus vult perdere prius dementat*". Finally, in both cases, in conjunction—co-

[1] Ibid, p. 37.   [2] Ibid, p. 646.

operation would be perhaps too cordial a word—with a Russia advancing in massive numbers from the east, she was able to gain a foothold on one of the Mediterranean peninsulas, which sapped the strength of the enemy, and, eventually, with her allies to achieve a final victory. This particular parallel is merely the most impressive of many which illustrate the continuity and comparative changelessness of British policy between 1783 and the present day.

IV

THE policy of the United States, on the other hand, changed much in this time, for it underwent at least two fundamental transformations. At first, after the Revolution, the United States was primarily concerned with cutting the remaining political bonds which tied her to Europe, and particularly to Britain, but after the end of the War of 1812 her emancipation was complete, and, in increasingly self-conscious isolation, she devoted herself to the problems of expansion across her own continent. At the same time, the Monroe Doctrine, and, even more, the mid-century gloss upon it, which virtually prohibited any further European intervention in the Americas, consolidated this continental isolation and made it secure. But by the end of the century, with the closing of the frontier and the vast development of American wealth and power, she began to be conscious of her own strength, and, along with other things, her trade upon the two great oceans of the world began to break down this traditional isolation, first in Asia and then in Europe. The first clear sign of it was in the outburst of so-called American Imperialism in the Spanish-American War, but this was followed by the eventual and reluctant American intervention in World War I, and, after a period of renewed isolationism, in World War II. The latter seemed clearly to signify that the United States had entered world affairs to stay.

Thus American policy has undergone two radical changes; first a retirement from the political affairs of Europe, and then a return to them, or rather to the broader ones of the world as a whole. Both have been perfectly natural developments. It was obviously to be expected that, after establishing her independence in name, she should do so in fact, particularly with the whole world of the West to conquer, and with that powerful element present in the American people which tended to regard the political life of Europe as a sink of iniquity. It was equally obvious that, as the earth contracted under the influence of modern technology, and as the United States expanded, so she should come to play a leading part in international affairs. Furthermore, in a broad sense, it is apparent that the policies of the United States could not follow traditional lines, because no such lines existed; most of the objectives of American foreign policy which were established by 1900, as they are recounted by its historian, were in the very nature of things new objectives which had to be hammered out to deal with new situations.

> It was in the eighteenth and nineteenth centuries that the essentials of American foreign policy were clearly defined and successfully achieved in the teeth of a hostile world: the winning and preservation of independence; the redemption of the territorial integrity of the United States within the boundaries laid down in the treaty of peace and independence; the westward expansion across North America to form a Continental Republic—the supreme achievement of American nationalism; the Freedom of the Seas; the Monroe Doctrine; commercial reciprocity accompanied by the conditional most-favored-nation formula; the breakdown of the commercial monopoly of the European colonies in the New World; wide-open occidental immigration, accompanied by the doctrine of the right of expatriation; voluntary arbitration. Only two of these fundamental policies remained challenged at the end of the nineteenth century; the right of expatriation and the Freedom of the Seas.[1]

With the cessation of large-scale immigration the former ceased to be of such importance as it had been, and after American participation in World War I little more was heard of the latter. Once her own position was securely established in this way, America began to become involved in the wider affairs of the world, where many of the problems followed the old lines, though some indeed were new; these wider problems required a change in American policy, but this change was in many ways a return to those very European entanglements, against which Washington and Jefferson had so strongly and, for a while, so successfully warned.

This process of withdrawal and return—it is in many ways a classic example of Toynbee's thesis—contrasts in marked fashion with the continuity of British policy. It means that the foreign policy of the United States can conveniently be considered under three main headings, emancipation from Europe, isolation, and emergence as a world power. Before considering this history in detail, in Parts II, III, and IV,

[1] Bemis, p. 877.

let us glance swiftly at the general pattern of Anglo-American relations between 1783 and 1952.

The first period, that of American emancipation from Europe and especially from Britain, begins with the Revolution and can (in so far as precise dates mean anything in such a context) justly be said to end with the Treaty of Ghent in 1814, for by that time the United States had fairly well shrugged off the garments of European influence. The Revolution, which broke the back of the attachment, had swiftly become a possibility in the period following the end of the Seven Years' War in 1763, and had burst into reality in 1776: but when the flood subsided with the recognition of American independence by the Treaty of Versailles in 1783, it was found that many of the familiar landmarks of European association, though weakened, were still standing, and even that new European threats to the infant republic had come into existence. During the next thirty years they were very largely removed.

The avoidance by Washington of an entanglement of a permanent nature with France, by his proclamation in 1793 of the neutrality of the United States in the war between France and Britain, inaugurated the American tradition of neutrality in European struggles. Jay's Treaty of 1794 solved the major and immediate problems of Anglo-American relations which had been left unsettled in the Treaty of 1783, and made a living thing of the formal diplomatic intercourse which had been established between the two countries. Under President Adams, Federalist influence over the government continued to gain strength, and its conservative mistrust of French Jacobinism led not merely to increasing feeling against France, but to the beginnings of a better feeling towards Great Britain. In 1799 the United States found herself on the brink of actual hostilities with France, but Adams held back until he was succeeded in 1801 by Jefferson, who, as leader of the Republicans, was pro-French in sympathy. During his presidency a determined effort was made to apply the theory of American neutrality consistently, even if the embargo policy, which implemented it, proved materially harmful to America. This was a logical attempt to throw off impartially all the bonds of Europe, though it was sanguine in its idealism, but the complications arising from the great maritime interests of the eastern seaboard of the United States made its operation difficult. Though the Louisiana Purchase opened up the West to America during Jefferson's Administration, Republican enthusiasm for France waned as Napoleon's pretensions to democratic government became transparently false. But this did not mean much increase in pro-British feeling (Tocqueville still said in 1830 that he could conceive of no hatred more poisonous than that which the Americans then felt for England); rather it gave strength to American isolationist sentiments. Actual war broke out between Britain and the United States in 1812, partly through rivalry in the West but largely because of the clash of maritime interests. Paradoxically, however, it did not embitter relations further, but seemed to have the ultimate effect of clearing the air. It ended in military stalemate, was terminated by a peace which ignored all the main issues between the two nations, and resulted in a vague realization on both sides that little was to be gained and much to be lost by active hostility. After this date there was never war between them again, and there was a slow but steady improvement in relations. The United States decisively turned her back upon Europe, in the way which Tocqueville so brilliantly illustrated by pointing out that in mid-eighteenth century an American meant by the phrase 'back-country' the wilderness of the West, because he was oriented to Europe, while by mid-nineteenth century he meant the eastern regions of the American continent, because he now faced instinctively West.

The second period, that of American isolation from the non-American world, lasted nearly as long as the century, and throughout it the American people were primarily occupied, as the Mexican War showed, in the tremendous task of opening up the Great West. This was the era of most significant growth in the internal life of the United States, which naturally left little time or energy for international affairs, particularly during the middle years of the century, when even interest in the West was for a while overlaid by intense absorption in the Civil War. It began appropriately with the inauguration of the Monroe Doctrine, which was from a continental point of view a public declaration of isolationism; and for the future of Anglo-American relations this act of fundamental agreement, though not co-operation, was a good augury. The two most serious border disputes between the two nations, in Maine and Oregon, which might have involved a struggle between them despite American isolation, were happily settled in the eighteen-forties. The Civil War raised serious problems in Anglo-American relations, which came to a head in the *Trent* and *Alabama* disputes, for the natural difficulties arising from the cleavage in the United States were made worse by an acute division of English sympathies and interests. The well-intended, if sometimes inefficient, British policy of neutrality did enable the obstacles to be surmounted, as was their aftermath, the *Alabama* claims. The settlement of these brought into salutary prominence the use of arbitration for the settlement of disputes between the two governments. As the years passed, the mistrust of the earlier period between the nations began to evaporate, and to be replaced, at first by indifference, and later by something approaching warmth. The Venezuela incident of 1895 showed how strong anti-British feeling in the United States could still be, though anti-American feeling in Britain was very much weaker, but it was perhaps the last severe flurry in the blizzard of Anglo-American misunderstanding. It was a fortunate thing—partly cause, partly coincidence—that this fruition of comradeship began just at the time of what Mahan described as the American "projection" of "our physical power . . . beyond the waters that gird our shores."[1] The same decade which saw the closing of the frontier, the symbol of American maturity, ended with the Spanish-American War, the symbol of the new American Imperialism, which was merely one manifestation, though an important one, of the emergence of America as a world power. This was what Mahan meant when he wrote in 1894, "Whether they will or no, Americans must now begin to look outward. The growing production of the country demands it. An increasing volume of public sentiment demands it."[2] These things meant the end of American isolationism as a permanent policy.

But it is not possible to put a date to the beginning of the third period, that of America's appearance as a world power, for not only were there times in the twentieth century when she reacted vigorously from it into isolationism, but there had already been signs of it well before 1898. The increased participation of the United States in world affairs had two phases or aspects; first, American Imperialism, and second, her assumption of a leading role among the Great Powers. But these both sprang from a common source, her great and increasing strength, and her recognition, albeit reluctant, of the power which it carried with it. This was appreciated in some quarters in England even sooner than in the United States, for as early as 1872 Disraeli pointed out that the New World was "throwing lengthening shades over the Atlantic" and creating "vast and novel elements in the distribution of power."[3] The first manifestation of this was in the imperial sphere; already, by the end of the Reconstruction period, America had begun to show a marked interest in the Pacific islands, and, even before the Civil War, her interest in such Caribbean territories as Cuba had been

---

[1] *The Interest of America in Sea Power*, p. 98.
[2] Ibid, pp. 21-2.   [3] Q. *Britain in Europe*, p. 502.

intense. This imperialism had a meteoric career, with the Spanish-American War and the acquisition of the Philippines, and partly inspired the building of the Panama Canal and the two-ocean navy, but the coming of Wilsonian Democracy led to a gradual reversal of the imperialist policy, and to its ultimate abandonment in the years between the world wars. These years, however, did not see any significant American withdrawal from international affairs, but rather the reverse, for under Wilson she became involved in the even broader issues of World War I. (In any case, irrespective of American internal politics, there was a tendency for wars, heretofore regarded as 'colonial' or 'imperial', to become increasingly interlocked with world events as a whole, so that the sequence of Spanish-American, Boer, Russo-Japanese and World Wars was not a surprising one. Thus an imperialist America probably could not long have avoided a major war.) The technical reason for her entry into World War I was the traditional American doctrine of the Freedom of the Seas, but behind this, though largely unrecognized, lay her fear of a disastrous disturbance of the balance of power in case of a German victory and her accompanying fear for the future of democratic government in such an event.

In 1919, at the height of victory and with a prestige and power in the world that she had never previously attained, she underwent in an especially severe form the disillusion with war, even successful war, which affected all the nations. She had not, it is true, suffered as severely as her allies, but she felt even more acutely that the suffering had not been worth while, and many of her people repudiated Wilson's League of Nations, in the belief that American re-entry into world affairs had been a grave error. After the Presidential election of 1920, isolationism became for a period the professed policy of a majority of the American people. In the long run, however, events proved that, even for the United States, no such policy was possible in a world of national and ideological rivalries. It came to pass in the end as Mahan had prophesied, "In this same pregnant strife the United States doubtless will be led, by undeniable interests and aroused national sympathies, to play a part, to cast aside the policy of isolation which befitted her infancy, and to recognize that, whereas once to avoid European entanglement was essential to the development of her individuality, now to take her share of the travail of Europe is but to assume an inevitable task, an appointed lot, in the work of upholding the common interests of civilization."[1]

[1] *The Interest of America in Sea Power*, p. 123.

It was not, in fact, in Europe that the first strain came, but in the Pacific, where America was by habit perhaps more sensitive and certainly less inhibited—between China and Japan; nevertheless, whether or not the United States would have taken firm action there, Britain would not, so that the political calamities which successively befell Europe in the nineteen-thirties were at first met in America by the uncompromising isolationist policy which reached its high-water mark in the neutrality legislation of 1937. This, in its efforts utterly to withdraw from contacts which might involve risk of war, harped back to Jefferson's embargo policy, and was as little able to stand the test of action, for, under the dynamic leadership of Roosevelt, American influence began once more to make itself felt in the world, and by the outbreak of World War II had become a potent moral and economic factor in the balance of power. The Cash and Carry law of November, 1939, frustrated in large part the practice of the neutrality legislation, and America's response to the overwhelming continental victories of Hitler in 1940, the Lease-Lend plan and "shoot at sight" orders to the U.S. Navy, utterly destroyed it. Pearl Harbour put full-scale American participation in the war beyond all doubt, and with it the part which the United States was in the future to play in world affairs. After she had pushed the war, along with her companion nations, to overwhelming victory in 1945, she became the corner-stone of the United Nations, and in 1949 entered wholeheartedly into the North Atlantic Treaty Organization. Her powerful and noble intervention in Korea in 1950 put the seal upon her leadership of the free peoples against a new enemy; after this, despite the minor resurgence in the persons of Taft and Hoover in 1951 of isolationist sentiment, there could be no serious doubt that America was in world affairs to stay.

The half-century which had seen this transformation had also witnessed the final blossoming of Anglo-American friendship; the great arbitrations of the late nineteenth century had prepared the way for a working-together in relatively minor matters in the early years of the twentieth, so that the foundations were laid for close co-operation in the world wars. Though in the inter-war years there were emotional and contentious problems, such as that of the war debts, at issue between the two countries, the peoples maintained an unprecedented and unprecedentedly cordial intercourse at all levels, so that, as Roosevelt indicated in 1939, the Americans could never in such a war be "neutral in thought." As it proceeded in fact, Anglo-American unity, as personified not only in the close friendship of Roosevelt and Churchill but even more in the single personality of an Eisenhower, attained a completeness never before equalled between two sovereign allies. The rumblings of disagreement after 1949 only served to throw the fundamentals of agreement into more intense relief.

V

THUS indeed has the wheel turned full circle. The United States, from an erstwhile dependency of Great Britain in 1783, had become by 1947 the dispenser of Marshall Aid to an ailing parent. Throughout this period of transformation, British policy remained comparatively unchanged, while that of the United States effected a complete revolution, from eighteenth-century participation in European affairs, through a studied isolation, to renewed participation in world events, only now in the role of a principal, though a principal perhaps closer emotionally to her partner than she had ever been before, even in colonial days.

But it is not surprising that America should so largely have assumed the role which Britain had played in the past, for despite the radical alterations in American diplomacy, the policies of the two countries have always had much in common at the roots. We have already seen how important is the geographical basis of these similarities, and certain political affinities arise more or less directly from them. The insular position of both, in fact, is the basis of their diplomacy; the differences are largely matters of degree. We have seen, for instance, that both have a marked tendency towards an isolationist policy; that Britain in the nineteenth century showed, though to a lesser degree, the same reluctance as America to become embroiled in European affairs. It was merely that physical isolation was not so possible for her, and, in the same way, as the oceans narrowed in the twentieth century, so did the United States find herself less and less able physically to stand apart. In fact, the contrast between the policy of America in 1850 and in 1950 was not due to a change in her motives, but to a change in her circumstances; she was greater and the world was smaller, so that new policies were forced upon her if she was to maintain her traditional aims.

In reality, the success, and indeed the feasibility, of American isolationism had always depended in the nineteenth century upon the existence of a suitable balance of power in Europe, and, because Great Britain made a similar balance the prime objective of her foreign policy, this meant in practice that American isolationism was made possible only by the supremacy of the British navy. As Bemis points out, the great successes of American diplomacy before 1898 "were due to taking advantage, without much deliberate calculation, of the wars, rivalries and distresses of Europe, in other words, to the balance of power in the Old World".[1] This unconscious dependence of the United States upon British preservation of the balance of power in Europe he more epigrammatically describes by writing, "Manifest Destiny might much better be described as Manifest Opportunity."[2] To the historian it is clear that this dependence of American isolation upon the British navy already existed at the time that the Monroe Doctrine was first enunciated, for, though Monroe's declaration was a unilateral one, it could never have had any reality had it not been known that the general aims of British and American policy were similar, for the United States had not yet the power to stop Britain from actions she might wish to take in the Western hemisphere. To the politically enlightened and realistic American, this fact became clear as the twentieth century progressed; thus, "The intervention of the United States in the First World War in 1917 preserved the balance of power in Europe in favor of Great Britain and behind Great Britain in favor of the United States, which could always balance the exposed position of Canada against British seapower: the preservation of that balance was the real victory of the United States."[3] In 1940 the proposition, now a practical rather than a theoretical one, was crystal clear to the majority of Americans; if Britain had fallen, America might have been, at least for a time, without adequate defence against Germany, and this fact was epitomized in the exchange of the fifty American destroyers for the British bases for hemispheric defence. The balance of power was in fact shown to be what it always had been, as vital an objective of American policy as of British—only she was protected from the necessity of positive action before the twentieth century by the combination of her geographical isolation and British sea power.

Another basic similarity in the diplomacy of the two nations is a difficult and contentious one to elucidate. Both have been, as nations go, peace-loving in their policy. Bellicose leaders have held sway in their time in both states—Palmerston in the one and Theodore Roosevelt in the other—as have men ardently ready for war when war appeared inevitable—Winston Churchill in the one and Jackson in the other—but in neither has militarism, nor the desire for war as

[1] Bemis, p. 877.   [2] Ibid, p. 216.   [3] Ibid, pp. 878-9.

such, held sway for long. The record of both has been occasionally questionable—in some of the Indian wars of the United States and some of the colonial wars of Great Britain for example. Indeed, the cynic, or the embittered European, may well suggest that it is just because their reputation in such spheres is doubtful, that their reputation elsewhere is good; they were fortunate to be so situated that their national desire for expansion could be satisfied in the empty lands of the American West, or of Africa and Australasia.

But the fact remains that in international affairs the record of Britain, and even more of the United States, is relatively good, partly because they expanded under the impulse of a vigorous nationalism in places where not much disturbance was caused to the balance of power and way of life of the civilized nations of the Western world. Seton-Watson writes:

> British policy may be said to have thrown its weight from time to time into the European scales in order to secure virtual immunity for her overseas designs. . . . What . . . has scarcely ever varied is the importance attached to naval power, both as a bulwark against invasion, as a protection to British carrying trade, and as a screen behind which colonial expansion could be conducted. . . . From this it follows that certain strategic routes of empire have always been specially in the mind of British statesmen . . . and . . . for two centuries and a half Mediterranean interests have also bulked very largely . . . in British calculations.[1]

This imperial preoccupation canalized British chauvinism in channels where it did less harm than that of France or Germany. Similarly, Bemis writes of America that, after 1823,

> The remaining years of the nineteenth century were to witness throughout the vacant western reaches of this continent a process of self-sustained expansion destined to make the United States a world power fronting on the two great oceans of civilization and ready to control a waterway between them. . . . Expansion expressed the pent-up forces of the developing national spirit in the United States. It has remained its principal and most successful manifestation.[2]

Such a power had little time for aggressive designs elsewhere while she was expanding in America, and not much desire to expand further when she had completed her continental development.

But important though these facts are in explaining the peaceful

[1] *Britain in Europe*, pp. 36-7.   [2] Bemis, p. 215.

intention of these 'sated' powers, they are not adequate to the effect, for satiety alone does not seem to induce pacifism in nations. In trying to explain the peaceful policies of the two powers, it is hard to avoid the conclusion that their desire for peace is not unconnected with a democratic form of government, that political liberty and popular control of government tend on the whole to promote pacific policies. It is possible certainly to throw doubt on such a conclusion; to point, for instance, to the Mexican War, in the inauguration of which popular opinion in the United States played a powerful part. But, though there may be exceptions to the rule, it is, broadly speaking, true that the common people desire peace, for they are the ones who suffer most in war. They do not desire it at any price, and with their backs to the wall they will fight with valour, pertinacity and desperation; but their first instincts are pacific, and, in countries where they have some measure of control over their governments, there is a tendency to seek peace and ensue it.

But, whatever its cause, it is substantially true that the policies of Britain and the United States since 1783 have been for the most part peaceful. In truth the record of no other great power can match that of the United States in its honourable desire for peace; Bemis truly writes, "Manifest Destiny . . . was not based on militarism. . . . American expansion across a practically empty continent despoiled no nation unjustly, and . . . there is no American today who would want to see that expansion undone."[1] The record of Britain, too, is on the whole creditable; though perhaps more prepared for war when necessary than the United States, at least until very recent times, she has pursued a peaceful policy in more difficult circumstances with commendable perseverance, and though subject—with decreasing frequency—to fits of jingoism, the original sentiment remained true in its entirety *"We don't want to fight, but by Jingo if we do!"* "For if there is one fact which emerges from the speeches and actions of successive Foreign Secretaries from Pitt to Grey, it is the paramount importance which they attached to Peace as the foremost British interest."[2] In their desire for peace, then, the policies of the two nations have had much in common, and have had it in common in an increasing degree as the years passed, for in the twentieth century the knowledge that both peoples desired peace above almost all else has constituted an ever more powerful bond between them.

In other ways also their policies have more in common than has

[1] Bemis, pp. 215-6.   [2] *Britain in Europe*, p. 647.

always been realized. It has been usual, particularly—as was natural—among Anglophobe Americans, to contrast the iniquitous imperialism of Britain with the egalitarian idealism of the United States, rather in the same way that certain English liberals have been wont to point the finger of scorn at American policy towards the Negroes, who constitute a problem of which the average Englishman has neither knowledge nor experience. But even here the differences have been exaggerated at the expense of the similarities. We have seen how very alike the waves of late nineteenth-century imperialism in the two lands were, but Americans, seeing these things always through the eyes of Jefferson, have until very recently placed too little credence in the expressed intention of Britain to guide all her colonial dependencies towards complete self-government, and have insufficiently understood the nature and importance of the development of the Second British Empire as a free association of equal and independent member nations. In what may be called 'strategic imperialism' there has, in the last hundred years, been little to choose between them, and now there is nothing at all. Britain, at least since her acquisition of Gibraltar in 1704, and the United States, at least since an abortive effort by Secretary Marcy in 1854 to annex Hawaii, have both sought and obtained strategic bases for national defence, which are in a different category from colonial conquests. Britain was earlier off the mark in this pursuit, and, chiefly because of her extensive trade and empire, spread her network of national defence much wider, but before long it had become clear to the United States that such bases were also indispensable to her.

As powers slow to take up arms, they have both been equally slow to lay them down; unwilling to precipitate war, they have usually been ill prepared for it except in the basic strength of their position. They have, however, been seldom equalled and never surpassed in their ultimate capacity to win victories, for, relying upon their wealth and staying-power rather than upon their numbers, neither has ever been beaten in a great modern war, except Britain in the War of American Independence itself. In these respects also, their policies have been closely akin.

Both, finally, have usually had the cause of human liberty at heart. Both were, or came to be, democracies, and both have sought to promote constitutional or democratic systems of government, for their own sake and because they thought them more conducive to the peace of the world. In this they have grown ever closer together, particularly as it became apparent that the ascendancy which liberal ideas had established in the nineteenth century was not necessarily or automatically to be perpetuated in the twentieth. The totalitarian systems of Fascism and Communism drove the two greatest democracies into parallel courses of action; indeed, even in their weaknesses in the face of the enemy they were alike, for in a sense the appeasement policy of Chamberlain (and even more the isolationism of Beaverbrook and the *Daily Express*) was but the isolationist policy of Harding, Coolidge and Hoover writ small. The rejection by the United States of the American guarantee of French integrity, incorporated in Wilson's Versailles Treaty, led directly to the similar repudiation by Britain, since the guarantee of the latter had been made conditional on that of the former.

It is, then, by no means surprising that the United States should so largely have assumed Britain's role in international affairs; it is in fact natural that the cloak of Elijah should thus have fallen upon Elisha, that America in her power should have become the leader of the free nations. Of the five main objectives of traditional British policy, only that of imperialism is not equally now a major motive in American diplomacy, and even this has been in the past, and is still, in a strategic sense, not without its influence upon United States policy. All the others—national survival, the balance of power, control of the seas and free government—are important, indeed pre-eminently the most important, principles upon which America bases her actions in international affairs. Never perhaps before in history, has there been such correspondence, almost identity, of fundamental interests and intentions between two sovereign nations.

Thus the twentieth-century cordiality of Anglo-American relations is solidly based on a foundation of similar, even common, policies, and we may be conscious of this as we relate the history of Anglo-American diplomatic relations. But, because the changes in policy have been chiefly on the American side, it is more convenient to let our story follow the contours of American rather than British diplomacy. In other words, we can attain the best and clearest view of the history of Anglo-American relations by seeing it from the standpoint of American history. It is this which has determined the structure of the chapters which follow.

PART II

EMANCIPATION

CHAPTER EIGHT

PROLOGUE—THE AMERICAN REVOLUTION

THE diplomatic relationship of Great Britain and the United States, as sovereign and independent powers, had an unusual inauguration in the violence of the American Revolution. The emancipation of Latin America is analogous, but by no means so significant, for, though its peoples retained a cultural affinity with Spain, their political relations were of less international consequence. The United States and Britain not merely maintained their cultural links after their separation, but their political relationship had become, within a century of independence, more important than it had ever been.

Yet the bitter struggle inevitably left its mark upon both of them, and particularly upon the younger and thus more impressionable; indeed, the trauma inflicted by it has not even now ceased to affect America's conduct, and for many years remained the mainspring of her political actions. Such a simile, of course, must grossly over-simplify the facts; the War of American Independence was not fought between two united peoples, as the attitude of the United Empire Loyalists in America and the Opposition Whigs in Britain plainly showed, but the relentless pressure of events, culminating in the convulsion of actual war, did impose a certain unity upon both sides. This process was greatly facilitated by the actions of determined and inflexible individuals, who seized every opportunity to promote the cause in which they believed. Samuel Adams said truly that the American radicals could not have made the American Revolution by themselves, but they contributed to it by knowing what they wanted, and by exploiting every tactical situation to obtain it. In this sense it is true that deliberate volition in the American people made the Revolution and in a similar sense it is true that deliberate and intelligent volition to avert it was lacking in those who controlled the British Government: but in both cases many underlying causes, reaching far back into history and deep into the nature of things, tended to predispose men to the decisions they in fact made.

The truth is that in the late eighteenth century some kind of crisis in the relationship of the mother country with the American colonies was inevitable. Complete independence could only have been avoided by diverting the stream of events into another path, the stream itself could not have been stopped: a great river cannot be halted suddenly in its course, but can be turned with skill into another channel. There were theoretical alternatives to separation, such as a federal imperial organization, or a gradual development of self-government in the colonies, or even, it must not be forgotten, an effective despotism imposed by force of arms, but, though possible in theory, given the circumstances of the time one may doubt how much chance they had of success in practice. Certainly one cannot doubt that a glance at these fundamental predisposing causes of the Revolution is necessary to an understanding of the Anglo-American relationship, for the process, slow in the beginning, rapid in the end, by which the two peoples grew away from one another, affected the whole subsequent development of Anglo-American relations.

I

THE most fundamental of these causes was plainly and simply geographical, and it was natural that this should be so in the technological circumstances of the eighteenth century. Burke put it in his matchless fashion when he said in the House of Commons that it was "laid deep in the natural constitution of things. Three thousand miles of ocean lie between you and them. No contrivance can prevent the effect of this distance in weakening Government. Seas roll, and months pass, between the order and the execution. . . . In large bodies, the circulation of power must be less vigorous at the extremities. Nature has said it. . . . This is the immutable condition, the eternal law, of extensive and detached empire."[1] Thus the direct effect of distance was to loosen the bonds which tied the colonies to the mother country in the years prior to the Revolution, when their need of her protection was declining, and in the war itself to make the victory of the United States probable.

The indirect effect of geography was almost as important, for it resulted in the transformation of the habits and outlook of the American colonists. The Europeans who had first peopled America

[1] *The Works of The Right Honourable Edmund Burke* (London, 1864), I, pp. 468-9.

were very different from the Americans of 1776, who had not only mastered their American environment, but had been powerfully influenced by it. This was the first phase in the great process classically expounded by Frederick Jackson Turner, the effect of the frontier upon American society. As he wrote, "The frontier is the line of the most rapid and effective Americanization,"[1] and in the seventeenth century all of America, and in the eighteenth century much of it, was frontier. As the American environment steadily produced its effect, so Americans became less and less European and less and less patient of European ways. This subtle and slow yet cumulatively vast and incalculably important change, spread as it was over the first two centuries of American history, both produced an American nation and laid the foundations of the American Revolution, for, as John Adams said in his old age, "the Revolution was effected before the war commenced. The Revolution was in the minds and hearts of the people."[2] This mastering of the wilderness was symbolic as well as influential; as Parrington writes, the years before the Revolution "were engaged in clearing away encumbrances more significant than the great oaks and maples of the virgin wilderness: they were uprooting ancient habits of thought, destroying social customs that had grown old and dignified in class-ridden Europe. A new psychology was being created by the wide spaces that was to be enormously significant when it came to self-consciousness."[3]

After the geographical came the other fundamental causes: in the seed bed of physiography sprang the social, the economic, the constitutional and the political origins of revolution. The differences which had developed by 1776 between the society of America and that of Europe, and in particular Britain, were very marked. The first roots of colonial development lay in seventeenth-century English settlement, the prototypes being the Puritan settlements of New England and the commercial settlements of the South, but we should note that, from the first, the emigrant is one who regards his mother country with mixed feelings. He has had difficulties there—perhaps in the free exercise of his religion, perhaps in the cramping of his sense of economic enterprise—and he has reason to cleave to the land of his adoption. He may perhaps plan one day to return to his native hearth; unless he is deeply embittered, the soothing imperfections of human memory will imperceptibly sweeten his recollections of it; he will, as a member of his

---

[1] *The Frontier in American History* (New York, 1937), pp. 3-4.
[2] Q. Parrington, I, p. 179.   [3] Ibid, p. 31.

community if not as an individual, be long dependent upon the mother country for many of the necessities and most of the luxuries of life; but he will be a European no longer, and he will pride himself upon it. In course of time he will be an American.

And from the point of view of the peculiar relationship of Great Britain with her colonies, there were other factors making for estrangement. Already between the English colonies of North and South lay the more cosmopolitan areas of the middle colonies. New Amsterdam was easily rechristened New York, but the Dutch influence therein was not so easily altered. Pennsylvania's policy of toleration attracted from the first many who were not British, and even more who were not English, at a time when neither Scots nor Irish rested contentedly under what many of the latter at least regarded as the English yoke. As the eighteenth century moved on, the number of non-English immigrants increased, and even as early as 1736 it has been estimated that two-fifths of the white population of the colonies were of other than English extraction. The German, the Scots-Irish, and, on a lesser scale, the French Huguenot, currents in contemporary immigration have been singled out as the most significant, but the stream, though it had not yet become the flood it was to be in the nineteenth century, grew rapidly in volume and variety. The rate of natural increase of the population was certainly swift, but could not alone have accounted for the startling overall growth. In 1713, it is reckoned, there were nearly 360,000 inhabitants in the twelve colonies; by 1760 the figure was 1,600,000, and by 1776 2,500,000, of whom certainly 2,000,000 were whites.

But it was not merely that the cousins became more and more distant in each generation, that they had fewer and fewer hereditary characteristics in common, but also that the different environments at home and overseas produced marked changes in the social attitudes of the two peoples, and particularly of the colonists. It is not surprising that it should be so, for we should expect a contrast between the inhabitants of a great virgin continent, isolated, rich in resources as well as hardships, and with great diversities of climate and terrain, and the inhabitants of a small compact group of islands, of uniform climate and fairly homogeneous terrain, located close to the European mainland. By 1783 this contrast had become very marked, though it is necessary always to remember that it was even more striking between the colonies and the rest of Europe. The contrast was heightened by the declining importance of social contacts between the two in the eighteenth century, for there came to be, relative to total population, less and less return of individual mainland colonists to Britain. Once again, this was natural enough, for in the beginning all of America had been sea-board and in constant reach of British influence, but as the frontier moved steadily westwards, an increasing proportion of the population shifted out of her gravitational field; as the centre of gravity of American life moved towards the Appalachians, so did British influence diminish.

What was the nature of the society in Great Britain upon which the United States was to turn its back? For her, the culmination of the turbulent civil wars of the seventeenth century had been the so-called Glorious Revolution of 1688, which was increasingly regarded in succeeding years as having finally rid the country of tyranny and brought the political system to near-perfection; it seemed indeed the supreme event towards which all English history had moved. After it, the readiness to resort to violence to achieve political or religious aims, and even the very desire for change, died away. 'Enthusiasm' in religion, and undue zeal in any branch of life came to be regarded with mistrust, being succeeded by common sense as the chief guide of conduct. The social system, as well as the political, was regarded with complacency. This spirit was clearly illustrated by Burke, its great prophet, when he said, "England . . . is a nation, which still, I hope respects, and formerly adored, her freedom".[1] Ardent adoration had been replaced by respectable respect. This complacency extended to what Americans have always tended to regard as the great faults of the system, its inequalities and its domination by the landed aristocracy, the gentry and the established Church. These were to many Englishmen a source of positive pride, and the overtones of that pride have lingered long in English life; they were best suggested, perhaps, by Bagehot in the nineteenth century when he wrote that the most marked of British traits was "a deferential character". The aristocratic nature of English society must not be over-emphasized, for by European standards the rise of the commercial classes witnessed to the great flexibility of the British social system. But the desire of the merchants was to raise themselves to a higher rank and not to pull others down to theirs; they had no wish to equalize the classes of society. It was still very true that every Englishman loved a lord.

This static idea of society led to a growing conservatism, which was often hardly distinguishable from sloth, and this in turn led to a growing readiness to accept corruption and inefficiency in society. We do not have necessarily to look to the eighteenth century for instances

[1] Works, I, p. 464.

of corruption, for we know today how easily it can be ingrafted into an institution by force of habit, but then it was part of the all-pervading attitude of social lethargy, of the readiness to accept what exists, without much alteration, lest worse befall. The toleration of corruption and inefficiency was made more widespread and acceptable by the great complexity of traditional institutions, so that aristocratic, and even royal, influence over Parliamentary representation was, within limits, considered necessary. Parliamentary 'influence', indeed, became considered as a kind of property, assumed by prescriptive right, and reflecting the wider emphasis on the sacrosanct nature of hereditary property rights. Primogeniture and other ancient practices governed the inheritance and transfer of land, and the great estates still dominated the country, as the aristocracy and gentry dominated social and political life. The whole national scene was conditioned still by the long tradition of a thousand years of national life, and it would be hard to exaggerate the significance of this cloud of precedent and custom overhanging eighteenth-century English life. Its chambers were in truth still haunted by "the grim spectres of departed tyrants—the Saxon, the Norman and the Dane; the stern Edwards and fierce Henries".[1]

This tradition produced a governing class better than any that Europe could show, but it was still essentially that of a small, if important, group of islands on the north-west extremity of Europe; and, although its horizons were being rapidly widened by commercial and imperial responsibilities, its outlook remained in many respects narrow and confined. "But it may be truly said, that men too much conversant in office are rarely minds of remarkable enlargement. . . . [They] do admirably well as long as things go on in their common order; but when the high roads are broken up, and the waters out, when a new and troubled scene is opened, and the file affords no precedent, then it is that a greater knowledge of mankind, and a far more extensive comprehension of things, is requisite".[2] Perhaps the most salutary lesson in their education for world influence was the loss of the American colonies itself, but in part at least they brought this upon themselves by their own actions. Yet those actions sprang naturally from the limitations of their outlook, and from their habits and character. Between these conservative and lethargic, narrow and proud, wealthy and powerful people, steeped in the consciousness of their long ancestry, successful tradition, and superiority to the rest of Europe; and the new American people whom they had fathered, but of whose strength,

[1] Burke, II, p. 83.   [2] Burke, I, p. 407.

216

character, and maturity they were for the most part woefully ignorant, there was an increasing likelihood of fundamental cleavage.

The contrast which the colonial scene presented in mid-eighteenth century was dramatic, for there the wild wind of the frontier blew, "strong, resistless, the wind of the western star".[1] The stimulus of the American environment differed according to climate and terrain, so that the structure of Southern society was markedly different from that of the North, but something it had of the same effect everywhere in the new land, something which was at its most typical in the West, where men were most directly in contact with the hardness as well as the potential bounty of nature, something which has been named the frontier spirit. There were conservative elements in American society, to be sure, but in the course of the Revolution they became submerged in the triumphant tide of radicalism:

> A middle-class America was to rise on the ruins of the colonial aristocracy. . . . The disruption of colonial society resulting from the expulsion of the Loyalists was far graver than we commonly assumed. . . . The change of temper that came over American society with the loss of the Loyalists, was immense and far-reaching. . . . Dignity and culture henceforth were to count for less and assertiveness for more. . . . A franker evaluation of success in terms of money began to obscure the older personal and family distinction.[2]

This change had begun long before the Revolution; in fact, the aristocracy of which Parrington writes was already very different from its English counterpart; it was simpler in its manners, closer to commerce, and easier of entry. The hero of *The Virginians*, and the story of his fall among noble English thieves is a not unfair illustration of the corruption of English society and manners in the eighteenth century, compared with those of even aristocratic colonial circles. Franklin, though he had, as he said, grown up in respect for England and veneration for English tradition, complained bitterly of "the extreme corruption prevalent among all orders of men in this rotten old state. . . . I wish all the friends of liberty and of man would quit that sink of corruption and leave it to its fate."[3] In 1775 he went even further and declared that for America to remain in the British Empire was like "coupling and binding together the dead and the living."[4]

Burke claimed that, as between the North and the South, the spirit of

[1] Benet, *Western Star*, p. 181.   [2] Parrington, I, pp. 192-3.   [3] Ibid, p. 169.
[4] Q. J. C. Miller, *Origins of the American Revolution* (London, 1945), p. 301.

liberty was even higher and haughtier in the South than elsewhere, because the possession of slaves encouraged a very heavy emphasis on the right of freedom in the master, but social bonds were certainly looser in the North. As he also claimed, "the religion most prevalent in our northern colonies is a refinement on the principle of resistance; it is the dissidence of dissent, and the Protestantism of the Protestant religion. This religion, under a variety of denominations agreeing in nothing but in the communion of the spirit of liberty, is predominant in most of the Northern provinces."[1] It was in this area and for this reason that the provisions of the Quebec Act of 1774, very reasonably extending religious toleration to the almost universal Roman Catholicism of Canada, were greeted with such fear, hatred and vituperation, and that Protestant intolerance became an important cause of the Revolution. In the North the commercial and legal classes were the professed leaders of American society, and, as the activity of lawyers was far less circumscribed by tradition than in the mother country, so the business men were already famous for their vigorous and successful enterprise. What Burke said of the New England whale fishery can be applied to much of America:

> And pray, Sir, what in the world is equal to it? . . . No sea but what is vexed by their fisheries. No climate that is not witness to their toils. Neither the perseverance of Holland, nor the activity of France, nor the dexterous and firm sagacity of English enterprise, ever carried this most perilous mode of hardy industry to the extent to which it has been pushed by this recent people; a people who are still, as it were, but in the gristle, and not yet hardened into the bone of manhood. When I contemplate these things . . . I pardon something to the spirit of liberty.[2]

But this spirit was at its most intense in the frontier areas. They were already, as they long remained, the chief source of American radicalism, because in them the springs of American vitality and of the American impulse to exploit the Great West gushed most urgently. This majestic and seemingly irresistible surge to the west is one of the most impressive and powerful movements in American history. To interfere with it has always been to court a disastrous American reaction, to galvanize popular feeling by touching, as it were, an exposed nerve of the body politic. Yet, whatever its motives, the imperial government did just this in the critical years before the Revolution. Alarmed by Pontiac's rising in 1763, desirous of protecting both the Americans and the Indians by controlling the disorderly sprawling

[1] Works, I, p. 466.   [2] Ibid. p. 462.

growth of society to the west, and not without some hope of checking smartly the turbulence of the unruly colonials, the Government in London issued in 1763 an ordinance, declaring in effect that no British subject should settle or buy land west of a line corresponding roughly with the crest of the Alleghanies. It was, in fact, designed as a temporary measure, to be followed by orderly arrangements for the protection of the Indians (which might have slowed down although they could not have halted the westward movement), but its authors were swept away in the current of events, and it remained the law of the land for eleven years, though, of course, as a dead letter. It had no effect whatever, except to infuriate Eastern land-speculators and Western frontiersmen alike. It was, therefore, one of the most potent causes of discontent in the *ante bellum* years, and when, with remarkable obtuseness though again with some good intentions, the government made the Quebec Act of 1774 seem to try to resuscitate it, by placing the whole territory north and west of the Ohio under Canadian rule, it became one of the prime factors precipitating open conflict. By this time, even those British actions designed for the betterment of colonial conditions irritated rather than soothed, because American ideas as to what was for their own good differed very widely from those of the mother country. The American environment had done its work well in the production of a frontier spirit which was vigorous, self-assertive, ebullient and very sensitive to outside interference.

Though there were, of course, large exceptions to it, this pioneer spirit of a new society, this rising democracy and radicalism, pervaded the whole of American life and became more and more its dominating characteristic. It is perhaps best expressed by a Frenchman, Crèvecoeur, in his letters:

A European, when he first arrives, seems limited in his intentions, as well as in his views: but he very suddenly alters his scale. . . . [H]e no sooner breathes our air than he forms new schemes, and embarks in designs he never would have thought of in his own country. . . . He begins to feel the effects of a sort of resurrection; hitherto he had not lived, but simply vegetated; he now feels himself a man, because he is treated as such; the laws of his own country had overlooked him in his insignificancy; the laws of this cover him with their mantle. Judge what an alteration there must arise in the mind and thoughts of this man; he begins to forget his former servitude and dependence, his heart involuntarily swells and glows; this first swell inspires him with those new thoughts which constitute an American. . . . From nothing to start into being, to become a freeman, invested with lands, to which every municipal blessing is annexed! What a change indeed! It is in consequence of that change that he becomes an American.[1]

II

THIS rising spirit of American nationalism was based upon an increasing economic strength. The growing population of the colonies is an unmistakable sign of their rapid economic development, for only a startlingly swift exploitation of the great natural resources of the land could have rendered such an increase in numbers possible. But, unreliable though they may be, estimates of the extent of commerce during the period show the development equally clearly. Annual average figures of the total volume of trade (that is the sum of exports *plus* imports) of the American mainland colonies with England are as follows: for the years 1701-10, £556,000; for the years 1731-40, £1,313,000; and for the years 1761-70, £2,843,000. Economically as well as socially, America was growing up and growing up fast.

But this might not in itself necessarily have meant a desire for absolute political independence, except that, in the eighteenth century, the whole concept of colonial status was, in the eyes of nearly all the inhabitants of the mother country, bound up with the question of trade. The notions of what history has called Mercantilism had been attacked by a few theoreticians and were shortly to be subjected to a sweeping onslaught by Adam Smith in the *Wealth of Nations*, but they still held undisputed sway over all European governments, including the British. The British Mercantile system was, it is true, more liberal than that of most other powers, but, such as it was, it had still in 1776 an overwhelming hold on the minds of the British governing class; it was, indeed, a mental assumption, a pre-conception, so fundamental as to be almost unconscious. It is highly significant that the term 'empire' itself, as applied to the colonies, only began at the very end of this period to have anything more than a purely commercial meaning; hitherto the empire had been an empire of trade, and the word had carried few territorial or ideological implications. It was because the growing economic expansion of the colonies conflicted with this deep and powerful Mercantilist conviction at home that it became so serious a cause of discontent.

This Mercantile outlook had roots deep in the history of Europe.

[1] Q. Parrington, I, p. 143.

In origin it was closely connected with the rise of the nation state and the accompanying development of commerce and a money economy, and it was apt to consider all economic questions in terms of national power. It was a form of economic nationalism, which found expression in national trade rivalries, and its main economic objective was a favourable balance of external trade, expressed in terms of bullion. As a result of these doctrines, to which there seemed no alternative in European experience, the British Government tended to emphasize the inferior and subordinate position which its colonies ought to occupy, and thus to exacerbate its difficulties with them. The notion of a fixed pool of trade, and of consequent competition with, for instance, France, reinforced this instinct to extract as much as possible from them; the bullionist theory discouraged the export of precious metals from Great Britain, and thus increased the severity of the perennial shortage of coin in her colonies; consideration of economic problems in terms of power led to a natural fear of losing the colonies to the French, and therefore to so-called 'firm' policies for their control. More than this, Mercantilism accepted as a veritable article of faith the essential subordination of colonial interests to those of the mother country. International rivalries strengthened this belief, but basically it was a selfish economic concept, and the obstinacy with which it was held was due largely to this fact, and to the inherent narrowness of vision of most of the British governing classes, even as to their own true interest. Few were able, like Burke, to see that to force the American colonies out of the Empire for a revenue which would inevitably be lost was the height of folly: "But what (says the financier) is peace to us without money? Your plan gives us no revenue. . . . It does not indeed vote you £152,750 11s. 2¾d., nor any other paltry limited sum.—But it gives the strong box itself, the fund, the bank from whence only revenues can arise amongst a people sensible of freedom".[1] In the end, it needed fifty years of corrosion by the logic of enlightened self-interest to achieve the destruction of the British Mercantile system; in the eighteenth century the commercial classes clung still to Mercantilism, and with it to a belief in the essential need for the subordination of colonies to the mother country.

This attitude may seem narrow, but it was not unnatural. Many of the colonies had been in origin purely trading ventures, in which great losses had often been sustained in early days, and all the colonies contained elements which represented vast financial investments to the mother country. Since so much British capital had been sunk in the

[1] Works, I, p. 506.

colonies, it appeared only natural to the owners of the capital that they should insist on conditions which made it secure. This point of view found contemporary expression in the fact that in the first half of the eighteenth century the West Indian, or 'sugar', colonies remained in the eyes of the British the ideal type of colonial enterprise, since they were in essence simply excellent commercial investments. This situation was (or seemed to be) perpetuated by the fact, as Adam Smith pointed out, that all the commercial and most of the colonial thinking of the governing classes was controlled by the merchants themselves, who played a large part in the support of eighteenth-century British governments. The merchants were not always strict or pedantic in their interpretation of this subordinate colonial status; they were largely responsible for the repeal of the Stamp Act, because they had no great interest in the proceeds of such a direct tax and because they feared the independence of the American colonies, which would involve, as they thought and as the Non-Importation agreements of the Americans were designed to make them think, the loss of their trade. But in the end they were caught in the toils of their own desires, for when, after the Townshend Acts, the American protest extended from direct to indirect taxation, from the Stamp Act to the Navigation Laws themselves, they felt their own interests formidably threatened. Since they were the chief beneficiaries of the Mercantile system as it was applied to America, they felt that they could consent neither to its abrogation nor to her independence. Incapable of the intellectual effort required to see in Adam Smith's talisman of Free Trade an answer to their dilemma, they lost control of the situation to those at home who believed that the issue was a political and financial one, to which the application of force was now the only answer.

Certain changes did occur in mid-century which might have altered this attitude on the part of the commercial classes. With the growth of industry in England, the old paramount need for raw materials from the colonies was augmented by a need for markets in the colonies for manufactured goods. As a result, commerce and industry began to lose their exclusive regard for the West Indian and Southern colonies, and to look with more favour on those hitherto rather despised and neglected godchildren, the Northern colonies, which, though they produced little that did not compete with the produce of the mother country, might provide a better market for manufactured goods. This change, however, came too late to affect the American issue. Too late, also, came the change from the idea of a purely commercial imperialism to an emotional and territorial one, associated first with the spirit and career of Chatham. The British attitude remained fundamentally the very myopic one of protecting a limited economic profit at the risk of huge ultimate loss. Reading Burke's magnificent appeals to a greater and nobler self-interest, and reflecting upon the huge majorities by which his wise motions for conciliation were voted down, one has a real sense of the measure of this stupidity, which still has the power to infuriate after nearly two centuries.

The actual manner in which the Navigation Acts cabinned, cribbed, and confined the growth of the American economy, has been clearly demonstrated by historians of the American Revolution. The main features of the Old Colonial System were five in number. The first was the protection of British shipping, both in order to maintain her commercial strength and in order to provide a solid basis for her naval supremacy, through a monopoly of the colonial carrying trade by British manned and built ships. The second was the restriction of the export to England alone (though they could be re-exported thence) of certain 'enumerated' commodities, produced in the colonies, with the object of establishing English control over them for commercial and fiscal purposes and of encouraging their growth in the colonies. In effect, after the beginning of the eighteenth century, colonial trade outside the Empire was forbidden, except to Europe south of Cape Finisterre in certain commodities. The Corn Laws of the mother country prohibited the import of colonial cereals, while, by what seems to us a remarkable peculiarity, there was a substantial English customs tariff on colonial products. The third was an effort to monopolize colonial imports for the British merchant and manufacturer, by a very high tariff in the colonies on all goods except those imported through England in British manned and built ships, which enabled taxes to be levied in England on all goods imported for re-export to the colonies and encouraged the purchase by the colonies of goods manufactured in England. The fourth was the prohibition to the colonies of all trades and industries which might compete with those of the mother country. The fifth, which was only in small degree due to specific legislation, and much more to the existence of a far wider economic problem, the shortage of currency in any frontier or debtor society, was the restriction of the export of coin to the colonies and the prohibition of colonial minting of coins or issuing of paper money.

All of these restrictions, as well as a number of others, proved in some degree irksome to many Americans. The grievances of the different sections were not the same; many Southern planters, for instance, naturally disliked a system which left them perpetually in debt to British merchants (in 1760 it is estimated that Southern planters owed them more than £2 million), while the active merchants of the North bitterly resented the restrictions upon the expansion of trade and industry. But there were very few Americans without a grievance of some kind against the system.

In fact, however, its effects were by no means always harmful to American interests, or, at least, were seldom without some compensation. The monopoly of British shipping led to a flourishing ship-building industry in the colonies because costs were distinctly cheaper there than at home, while Yankee seafaring men became renowned for their skill and daring. The restrictions upon the export of the enumerated articles were very irksome, but even here there were ameliorations, for certain of these commodities, such as tobacco, were given an absolute monopoly of the home market, others were highly protected there against foreign competition, and export bounties were paid upon yet others, such as naval stores. In addition, it is fair to point out that very large quantities of these goods (four-fifths of all tobacco imported into Britain, for example) were successfully re-exported and sold; that a great many articles, such as fish and grain, were not enumerated and were exported direct to other countries; and that in the then state of colonial development it was, in fact, economically sound to encourage the primary development of the extractive industries.

The complementary effort, to give British manufacturers a monopoly on exports to the colonies, seemed obviously harsh on the surface, but the burden of these taxes upon the colonies was relieved by the system of 'drawbacks', or repayments of customs duties paid on articles re-exported to the colonies from England, so that, for instance, even after additional shipping costs, German linen sold cheaper in New York than in London. Furthermore, the economic burden was largely theoretical, since British manufactures were on the whole better and cheaper than those of any other country, as their retention of the American market after 1783 clearly shows, and since, though there were price-fixing agreements among British merchants, mutual competition for the most part seemed to keep prices down. The prohibition of colonial industries, which might compete with those of the mother country, was likewise hard, but had its compensations; production of articles for local use was not forbidden, importations from England were frequently cheaper than the local product would have been for some years, and there was considerable legitimate industry for export in the colonies, particularly New England. Finally, the currency problem, though it did a great deal to worsen relations with the mother country, was primarily the result of the adverse trade balance of the colonies, which was in itself a measure of their dependence upon the capital of Great Britain and hence of the benefits the colonies enjoyed from British investment. In any case, these regulations were in all cases so inefficiently applied that they were much less of a burden than they might have been.

There was thus something of a silver lining to the dark cloud of British economic domination, but it remained a dark cloud none the less. It hampered and restricted colonial development in ways of which Americans were always being reminded. If a New England sea captain wished to extend his traffic direct with Europe, he was severely hindered. If a Pennsylvania iron merchant wished to broaden his activities from the mining of pig iron to the processing of it, by sinking capital in a plating mill, he was forbidden to do so. If a Southern planter wished to sell his tobacco crop in Germany, he could only do so through England, and usually through an English merchant. If a Westerner wished to supply himself with certain tools or household goods, he virtually had to have ones made in the mother country, and, though rich in land and resources, he might well be without the specie which the English merchant would demand in payment, unless he were lucky enough to obtain a suitable bill of exchange on a reputable firm. These were cramping restrictions, but yet they were overcome; the very wealth and growth of the colonies, unsurpassed perhaps in the history of man, are ample proof of that. They would seem to have been irritants rather than ruinous prohibitions, and it is indeed the case that they were annoying to the colonist chiefly because he was becoming more self-dependent and more self-conscious, rather than because of their inherent vice. Only as his economy prospered, and as he felt able to expand into spheres which hitherto circumstances had compelled him to ignore, did he begin to feel the full weight of the irksome Mercantile regulations.

Yet, even this does not suffice to explain the economic aspect of the Revolution; it might explain discontent, protest, even sporadic disorder, but the American War of Independence is another matter. The colonists had after all suffered the Navigation Acts since the beginning, and might well have continued to do so. As Burke said:

> Sir, they who are friends to the schemes of American revenue say, that the commercial restraint is full as hard a law for America to live

under. . . . But America bore it from the fundamental act of navigation until 1764. Why? because men do bear the inevitable constitution of their original nature with all its infirmities. The act of navigation attended the colonies from their infancy, grew with their growth, and strengthened with their strength. They were confirmed in obedience to it, even more by usage than by law. They scarcely had remembered a time when they were not subject to such restraint.[1]

Such a situation might have endured even longer than it did, had it not been for the peculiar development of the American commercial system and its relationship to the financial policy of the British Government.

We have seen how phenomenal was the growth of America between 1714 and 1760, a period which was one of drowsy inactivity in English political life, particularly towards colonial affairs. During this period of "salutary neglect" of the colonies, their growth continued apace. As Burke wrote,

> [T]he trade of America had increased far beyond the speculations of the most sanguine imaginations. It swelled out on every side. It filled all its proper channels to the brim. It overflowed with a rich redundance, and breaking its banks on the right and on the left, it spread out upon some places where it was indeed improper, upon others where it was only irregular. It is the nature of all greatness not to be exact; and great trade will always be attended with considerable abuses. The contraband will always keep pace in some measure with the fair trade.[2]

Smuggling existed, in fact, upon a gigantic scale. It was bad enough in England, where it has been estimated that as much as one-third of all commodities imported were smuggled, but it was far worse in the colonies, which were so much wilder and more extensive and so much farther from the seat of the central government. It has been computed, for instance, that the rum distillers of Rhode Island imported less than one-sixth of their molasses from British sources; in other words that five-sixths was smuggled. Another estimate asserts that at least £700,000 of merchandise annually was smuggled into the colonies in the years prior to the Revolution, a figure amounting to perhaps half the total imports of the mainland colonies from Great Britain. Some of the smuggled goods came from, or went to, Europe, but far more to and from the West Indies. The connivance of the customs officials at all this was notorious. So difficult was the problem, that, at the end

[1] Works, 1, p. 403.　　[2] Ibid, I, pp. 407-8.

of the Seven Years War, the collection of £2,000 of revenue was costing the government £7,000.

The result of this huge illicit trade, growing up over a half a century, was that a very large proportion of the new American population was actually dependent on smuggling for its prosperity, particularly in the Northern and Middle colonies. It was not merely a matter of a few cheap luxuries, but of the very means of livelihood, so that when a serious effort was made by the home government to stop smuggling, the standard of living of these elements in society was endangered; indeed, a number of them were faced with something amounting to economic extinction. The sudden change of government policy, towards a pursuit which had become not only common but respectable, had a disastrous effect.

The history of the problem is epitomized in that of sugar. In 1733, under pressure of the West Indian sugar interests, Parliament passed the Molasses Act, which put a duty of 6d. a gallon on foreign molasses imported into the colonies. This molasses was peculiarly important in the economy of the Middle and New England colonies because, when distilled there into rum, it became the basis of one of the famous triangular trades, between Europe and Africa and the West Indies, by which the great commercial interests of the colonies survived. Rum, for instance, was carried to Africa in return for slaves, which were carried to the West Indies, where molasses was picked up for distillation in America. Because of the neglect by the home government, and the persistence of smuggling, for thirty halcyon years the Act was not enforced, and the trade, based on French, Dutch and Spanish sugar, continued to grow, and with it a large class dependent upon it for their living. During the Seven Years War this illegal trade, with what were now enemies, continued and even increased, which brought the fact of its existence forcibly home to the British public. Pitt made efforts to enforce the law, which resulted in a doubling of the revenue, and when peace came Pitt's successors continued to try and extract the duty. This was serious enough, even though it merely nibbled at the edge of the vast smuggling problem. But worse was to come, for in 1764 Grenville, a thorough financier with comprehensive, if not imaginative, views on imperial relations, passed the Sugar Act, which had the object not only of enforcing the collection of the duties for reasons of efficiency, but also that—specifically stated—of raising a revenue in America. This revenue was to be used to help pay off the national debt, which had been largely increased in the recent war, to open up the West under proper governmental control, and to reform the whole

227

colonial administration, including, of course, the customs. The last step would thus complete a circle, which, however admirable from the point of view of the British Government, could not but appear vicious to the American trader. The gravity of the problem is illustrated by nothing better than the fact that the Act *reduced* the tax from 6d. to 3d. a gallon, but proposed to collect it for the first time with some pretence at efficiency: seldom, if ever, in history can the reduction of a tax have contributed so directly to the onset of a revolution.

This was the economic background against which the taxation controversy arose, and the fact that America seemed to have got off lightly in fiscal matters did not appear to the American people as the crux of the matter. It might be true, as North estimated in 1775, that the average annual taxation paid by Englishmen was 25s., while that paid by Americans was 6d., or that in 1763 the *per capita* public debt of the colonies amounted to 18s., and that of Great Britain to £18, but from the American point of view there always lay in the background the fear of taxes over whose formulation they had no control. Whether the Stamp Act or the Townshend duties were specifically in question, there was always in the American mind dread of a tax, like that embodied in the Sugar Act, which, though seeming reasonable on the surface, was ruinous to an established interest. Of course, the discrepancy between English and American levels of taxation was not as great as it seemed to some Englishmen, for the indirect contributions of the colonists through trade were considerable; Pitt estimated, for instance, that colonial commerce brought an annual profit of over £2 million to British merchants. But the difference was none the less substantial, and appeared even greater to the country gentry in the British Parliament, who, through the importance of the Land Tax in the English fiscal system, bore the brunt of taxation, and constituted an extremely important element in British governmental opinion. Similarly on the American side, a particular economic group was most hard hit by the effects of the Sugar Act, but it was an important sectional interest, and fear of exorbitant exactions in the future extended to all classes of the community. Other aspects of the Navigation Acts likewise alarmed or irritated other sections and interests, and the Stamp Act had a similar effect, arousing fears, for instance, that it would make the problem of shortage of specie worse. No people ever likes any form of taxation; where the power to resist it exists, and where fear of the ruinous effects of it has already been aroused, as in the colonies after 1763, only far greater wisdom than that which then animated the

British governing class can prevent conflict. Most of the rulers of Britain signally failed, at first, to realize that, though questions of principle were not being raised, they inevitably would be before long, and that, once this had happened, disastrous political results would be bound to ensue.

Taxation is the point where the economic sphere impinges most directly upon the political, and it remained, almost till the end, the heart of the American problem. The economic situation forced the whole political question of the imperial relationship into inescapable prominence. Economic factors in Britain caused the application of the new taxation: economic factors in America caused its repudiation. Thus was inevitably propounded the problem as to where lay the power to tax, which is an essential inherent power of sovereignty. Once this was done, the matter passed beyond the economic sphere into the political; passions were aroused on both sides; and any but a violent solution became virtually impossible.

III

BUT it would be wrong to suppose that the economic causes of the Revolution were the only significant ones; the constitutional causes had an importance ultimately as great. They followed the same broad pattern—a clash between an America growing into maturity and independence, and a Britain, not merely conservative and tradition-bound, but also corrupt and therefore temporarily weak. This constitutional conflict had both a practical and a theoretical aspect, the latter being, as it were, the ultimate refinement of the former, the distillation of all the other causes of conflict, the realm in which, finally, the momentous decision of independence had to be taken and justified.

The practical constitutional difficulties arose naturally from the social and economic background in the two countries. Symptomatic of this was the fact that Britain was ruled by a composite legal sovereign, known to constitutional law as the King in Parliament; this system, if such it can be called, had never been clearly formulated in theory, and its component parts worked together, as yet, far from harmoniously in practice; but the queer amalgam of King, Lords and Commons, with the latter playing increasingly the dominant part, was accepted as the sole source of sovereign power. The struggle of these three agents within the constitution, however, was of great consequence in the history of the American Revolution. The links between Lords and Commons, forged by a governing class which controlled both, were strong, and before the accession of George III, partly owing to the German interests of his two predecessors, the royal political power was to some extent in abeyance; the magnates, lawyers, and merchants, who controlled Parliament, in effect ruled the country. The new King, however, became determined to reassert royal influence, though through Parliament, and not against it as had been attempted in the previous century.

This influence could be formidable largely because of the corrupt and unrepresentative nature of the House of Commons, which had come, in the last hundred years, to be elected by a few thousand voters, a mere handful of the whole population. Many of the borough constituencies, the so-called rotten boroughs, were under governmental or aristocratic control, and, even more serious, all the Members of Parliament, once elected, were subject to governmental influence through the grant of actual and potential favours. It has been estimated, for example, that in the Parliament of 1761 something approaching one-third of the members of the House of Commons had actual government employments, while many others, of course, lived in hope. In the Parliament of 1768 the figures were even higher. The King's assertion of his personal control over the governmental machine which had been built up in the first half of the century, enabled him in the last resort to control the policy of the government during most of the time of the American troubles. This English acceptance of corruption in political institutions was very alarming to the Americans; not that corruption was unknown in America—gerrymandering in favour of the seaboard against the West, for example—but it was comparatively rare, particularly on the frontier. Americans criticized freely, not merely the extension of these practices to the colonies, but also their existence in the mother country. James Otis exclaimed that if great new cities like Birmingham and Manchester were not represented in Parliament, they ought to be, and he expressed the instinctive sentiments of many Americans. Calls for reform, led by Chatham, were also to be heard in England, but they were as yet weak, whereas in America there was a wide, though by no means universal, demand for a nearer approach to manhood suffrage. As in social manners, so in politics, the fresh winds from the West tended to blow away the cobwebs which had accumulated over centuries of English life and institutions, and which seemed to breed the narrowness and inefficiency that, by sheer maladministration alone, nearly lost the War of American Independence for Britain.

The actual inefficiency of the system of imperial government was not calculated to endear it to a people who had already developed their ready aptitude for the efficient conquest of natural hazards and obstacles. There had, in fact, been no serious changes in the methods of colonial administration since the beginning of the century, when the attempt under William and Mary to establish a uniform system of government in the colonies lapsed owing to the increasing spirit of political lethargy. This reluctance to change made it virtually impossible for the creaking and antiquated political system to adjust itself to the rapidly changing framework of economic and social life even in Britain, and the results in the colonies, where change was far swifter and where the system had never in any case been very well suited to its circumstances, were very much more grave.

Just one symptom of the malady was the fact that no one, either in England or the colonies, really knew where to look for proper authority, whether to the King, to the Privy Council, to the Secretary of State, or to the Board of Trade, between all of whom responsibility was divided. A practical example of the bewildering confusion arising from the complexity of this traditional mode of governing was the variety of forms in which instructions could be issued to royal Governors of the colonies. They could be issued in the form of Letters Patent under the Great Seal of England (either as charters or commissions), or in the form of other instruments under lesser seals (such as writs or letters of Privy Seal, Instructions to Governors, Royal Proclamations, Commissions under Signet or Sign Manual, Royal Warrants or Royal Letters); they could be issued in the form of Orders-in-Council, or of Commissions under the Great Seal of Admiralty; and they could be issued in the correspondence of manifold officials and departments, such as the Secretary of State, the Board of Trade, and the Commissioners of the Treasury and the Admiralty.[1] It is small wonder that men, whose society had been conditioned by the untrammelled life of the American frontier, and whose initial concept of federal government was to have the simplicity and elegance of the American constitution, should soon have lost patience with English eighteenth-century methods, which were dominated by the sentiment that, "when it is not necessary to change, it is necessary not to change".

Thus the impact of the imperial government upon colonial affairs

[1] L. W. Labaree, *Royal Government in America* (London, 1930), pp. 6-7.

was by no means dynamic, and it is indisputable that those organs of government in America which were under the control of, and gained their impetus from, the local inhabitants, had much more vigour and efficiency. Graft and inefficiency probably increased the nearer one got to the Royal Governor, the immediate representative of the central government; this was natural enough, not only because he and his entourage might more readily acquire the taint of English manners, but also because he remained, as the executive arm of the administration, the fountain head from which nearly all appointments and favours still proceeded. Thus there became evident, during the pre-Revolution period, an increasing tension within the colonial governments themselves. The usual system, in so far as one can generalize about it, was patterned upon that at home: the government was headed by a Governor, appointed from England; he was advised by a Council, of perhaps a dozen members, which was frequently under his influence, if not actually appointed or controlled by him; and there was a local elected Assembly, the right to which had been clearly established by the colonies during the course of the eighteenth century. The analogy of this system to that of King, Lords and Commons is obvious to us, as indeed to American, though by no means always to British, contemporaries; and tensions arose within it very similar to those which had reft the British constitution in the previous century, though this was again obscured for many Englishmen by the confusing fact that the royal Governor represented not the King, but the British Parliament, which had in 1688 become the effective sovereign of the country, thus establishing once and for all a constitutional, if not a popular, system of government. That Parliament had become decreasingly representative of the British people, and that it had never been in any sense representative of the colonies was a fact which largely escaped British attention, or failed to gain British interest. But this was by no means the case with the Americans, who tended to regard the Governor as a royal appointee (which technically he still was), and to identify his position with that of the early Stuart kings and their own with that of the Stuarts' opponents in Parliament. It was not unnatural that they should do so, particularly as they were fully aware of the extent to which, by 1770, George III exercised an effective control over Parliament.

Thus there developed a constant and irritating friction between the Governor, acting in the interests and under the instructions of the imperial government, and the assembly, representing local interests, in each colony. The assemblies were by no means always democratic—in all of the colonies there was a property qualification for the franchise, sometimes a very high one—but there was freedom of discussion and public knowledge of debates, and there was probably no colonial legislature so unrepresentative, or at least so anomalous in its representative character, as the British Parliament. The divergence of character and interests between colonies and mother country came to a head, in the sphere of practical politics, in the tension between governors and assemblies, a tension which began early in the century as irritating friction, and ended, by the Revolution, in the complete collapse of government.

Thus the Anglo-American conflict was not at first a direct or overt one, nor was it clear and simple in its outlines, for the discord between the English and American ways of life was matched by another, albeit less powerful, dissonance within the colonies themselves. This, the disagreement between the East and the West, the frontier and the seaboard, which had long existed and was long to dominate the politics of the United States, was in a sense a muted variation on the major theme. The distaste of the radical frontiersman for the conservative Easterner was sometimes swallowed up in his hatred of Britain, which seemed to him to have all the failings of the eastern seaboard in an exaggerated form. Perhaps it would not be too much to say that the conservative elements in American life, centred in the East, concurred reluctantly in the Revolution under pressure from the radicals, though the most audible of these were also in the East; their views on domestic as well as international issues were nearly triumphant at the height of the conflict, but the conservatives reasserted their control in some measure at the formation of the Constitution. In an unmistakable fashion the new federal government assumed over the states the same sort of control that the old imperial government had exercised over the colonies, while the permanent tension between the executive and legislative arms of government in a sense merely continued the old tradition.

The struggle before the Revolution hinged, as constitutional conflicts in British history have so often done, upon finance. The British Government, particularly after the increase of its national debt in the wars of the century, did not wish to pay the colonial governors or their officials, and considered it only fair that the colonies should do so. On the other hand, the colonial assemblies were reluctant to vote money for these, as for most other, purposes, though, paradoxically, they were almost equally reluctant that royal officials should be paid by the British, since this merely reinforced their dependence upon the imperial government. They therefore followed a policy of making grants for the payment of officials which were quite inadequate or strictly conditional, thus hoping to establish, as Pym and Hampden had hoped before them, an effective control over the executive branch of government. The ideal of the imperial government was exactly the reverse; a permanent regular revenue, paid by the colonists but not subject to the day to day control of the local assemblies, which would meet the expenses of colonial government and yet be administered from London. This the colonial assemblies feared most of all, regarding it, with justice, as the negation of self-government, and seeing all too clearly in Britain the effects of a royal influence established, as they believed, partly through the existence of a permanent royal revenue.

But, though the assemblies in great degree held the purse strings, the central government fought back vigorously with all the weapons at its disposal, particularly the veto powers of the governors as well as of the central government itself. The previous consent of the crown was, for instance, made necessary for certain whole categories of legislation, while any law was subject to veto in Westminster. Furthermore, instructions were issued to governors before their assumption of office, ordering them automatically to veto certain types of legislation; these prohibited acts were very numerous, and mostly of a financial or economic character. This use of the veto is most interesting as an illustration of the complexity of the whole constitutional relationship, for the veto proper, exercised by the English Monarchy, had in England been in desuetude throughout the eighteenth century, and was in fact only exercised in the colonies, where it appeared as grossly inequitable. In fact, of course, this colonial veto was used, not by the Monarch, but by the Government, supported by Parliament; at a time, however, when George III in the last resort controlled his ministers and to a large degree his Parliament, this appeared to the colonists a distinction without a difference.

IV

But this friction between governors and members was not only symptomatic of a practical divergence between the British and American governments, but it also raised in an acute form the whole question of the proper constitutional relationship between the colonies and the mother country. The process was, of course, gradual; no one at first questioned the imperial relationship as such, since, as Andrews writes, "Colonial subordination to the authority of the mother country was no legal fiction, for the vast majority of the colonists accepted it as the normal condition of their lives."[1] In 1764 most men agreed with Governor Pownall: "I do not believe that there ever was an instance when the principle of the supreme legislature's power to raise monies by taxes throughout the realm of Great Britain was ever called in question, either in the assemblies or in the courts of the colonies; nor did I ever hear of any book, treatise or even newspaper essay that ever until this moment even moved it as a question of right."[2]

The colonies (and even the mother country) were developing fast in the eighteenth century, and no one knew for certain what in the colonies was the law, and what was not. On this subject opinions ranged between that of the Governors of Connecticut, that English statute law had no validity unless adopted by the colony itself, and that of Daniel Dulaney, that all English law, common and statute, had a place in America. In this state of uncertainty, a very crucial, yet almost unnoticed, step had been taken during the course of the century, without any serious colonial opposition or even protest, when Parliament had assumed, as of right, functions hitherto exercised by the Privy Council, thus conforming to English constitutional development, but sowing the seed of later confusion in the colonial relationship. Even as early as 1754 Franklin's Albany plan for a colonial federation under imperial auspices was rejected because, as he wrote, the colonial assemblies "thought there was too much *prerogative* in it" while "in England it was judged to have too much of the *democratic*."[3] As events unfolded after 1763, the veils concealing the central constitutional issue, the *arcanum imperii,* were dragged aside one after another until it became quite clear that the colonial system of government, patterned on that of King, Lords and Commons, was regarded quite differently on opposite sides of the Atlantic. To the colonists it seemed that it was a genuine representative system in which their assemblies should act in exactly the same capacity as the House of Commons, but to the British a colony remained essentially a subordinate, or, as the term went, a municipal institution, subject to the absolute sovereignty of the imperial Parliament.

As is to be expected, there was at no time a precisely formulated and universally accepted theory on either side of the Atlantic. Some individuals propounded a point of view and adhered to it consistently; others changed their views as events developed, very many of them

[1] C. M. Andrews, *The Colonial Background of the American Revolution* (London, 1924), p. 26.   [2] Q. ibid, p. 61.   [3] Q. Brebner, p. 35.

more than once. In the mother country, for example, Chatham, Johnson, and, on the whole, Burke, were consistent; in the colonies consistency was more difficult, since the pressure of events and opinions was stronger, but Dickinson struggled hard to maintain it. In England, quite obviously, a number of members of the House of Commons changed their views as the years passed, and in America the same was true of many men of affairs as eminent as Franklin. And the danger of over-simplification does not end here, for not all the theories themselves were clear cut or original. But one can perhaps discern, without straining the facts unduly, six main points of view.

On the right was the Tory and ultra-legalist English view, expressed by Dr. Johnson in his work, *Taxation No Tyranny*, that sovereignty was an indivisible authority reposing inalienably in the Westminster Parliament, and that in sovereignty there are no gradations:

> There may be limited royalty, there may be limited consulship, but there can be no limited government. There must in every society be some power or other from which there is no appeal, which admits no restrictions, which pervades the whole mass of the community, regulates and adjusts all subordination, enacts laws or repeals them, erects or annuls judicatures, extends or contracts privileges, exempt itself from question or control, and bounded only by physical necessity. . . . It is not infallible, for it may do wrong; but it is irresistible, for it can be resisted only by rebellion, by an act which makes it questionable what shall be thenceforward the supreme power.[1]

The adherents of this view held that legally a colony was "an inferior and subordinate corporate body, similar in type to the gilds, boroughs, and trading companies of England, all of which exercised self-governing powers but within certain defined limits",[2] and that the sovereignty of Parliament essentially contained the right to tax: "America must forever hereafter be considered as a separate kingdom, if our parliament cannot tax that country. A country which we cannot tax is a country not subject to us."[3] This point of view had at least the merit of simplicity, and, perhaps because it was so easily grasped, it was widely and stubbornly held in Britain.

Less simple were the intermediate theories of those who endeavoured to maintain positions between the extremes of absolute sovereignty and independence. Perhaps the most interesting of these was that of an

[1] *Taxation No Tyranny* (London, 1775), pp. 24-5.
[2] Andrews, p. 31.　　[3] Q. Miller, p. 157.

imperial federation, with American representation at Westminster, put forward by persons as diverse as Adam Smith in the *Wealth of Nations* and Francis Maseres in a pamphlet of 1770 entitled, *Considerations on the Expediency of Admitting Representatives from the American Colonies into the British House of Commons.* Some prominent figures, such as Thomas Pownall, strongly advocated it; others such as James Otis inclined towards it; and yet others, such as Franklin, toyed with it for a while and then abandoned it. But it had no wide appeal, particularly in view of the fundamental difficulty which Burke expressed when he said, "The ocean remains. You cannot pump it dry."[1]

A more pragmatic and therefore hopeful version of the federal idea was that advocated by Chatham. He, in common with such influential men as Camden, Barré and Shelburne in England, and Galloway, Nicholas and Pendleton in America, believed, in effect, that sovereignty was divisible, and that in the crucial financial question there was a clear distinction between an external tax, or customs regulation, and an internal tax for revenue, the former being within and the latter not within the competence of the imperial Parliament to levy. As Chatham declared in one of the most famous of his speeches,

> It is my opinion that this kingdom has no right to lay a tax upon the colonies. At the same time, I assert the authority of this kingdom over the colonies to be sovereign and supreme, in every circumstance of government and legislation whatsoever. . . . The Americans . . . cannot be bound to pay taxes without their consent. In everything you may bind them except that of taking their money out of their pockets without their consent. . . . I rejoice that America has resisted. . . . If the gentleman cannot understand the difference between internal and external taxes, I cannot help it. But there is a plain distinction between taxes levied for the purpose of raising revenue and duties imposed for the regulation of trade . . . although in consequence some revenue may accidentally arise from the latter. . . . [W]e may bind their trade, confine their manufacturers and exercise every power whatsoever . . . except that of taking their money out of their pockets without their consent.[2]

This view retained legislative sovereignty, while preventing taxation without representation, and had perhaps the best practical chance of success in staving off the conflict, but it was less popular in England than in America, so that the illness of Chatham put an end to all hope of its acceptance.

[1] Works, I, p. 475.

[2] Basil Williams, *William Pitt* (London, 1913), II, pp. 190-5.

Another intermediate point of view, not strictly federal in essence, was the one which ultimately became the inspiration of the British Commonwealth of Nations, that of a free association of equal member states under the Crown. This view was not at first widely held on either side of the ocean, but it did come to be accepted by a very large number of people in America when all other resources had failed. The idea was, with the pardonable over-simplification of hindsight, best expressed by James Madison: "The fundamental principle of the Revolution was that the colonies were co-ordinate members with each other, and with Great Britain, of an empire united by a common executive sovereign, but not united by any common legislative sovereign."[1] The examples of the Channel Islands, and of England and Scotland between 1603 and 1707, were cited by its advocates, such as Richard Bland in the colonies and John Almon in London. Once again, it is noteworthy that Franklin held this view for a short while after 1769.

There were certain other intermediate view-points; one was Galloway's scheme for a Grand Council for the colonies, reciprocal and co-equal with Parliament, which had little prospect of success; another was the idea of the 'virtual representation' of the colonies in the House of Commons, as great cities like Manchester were 'virtually' if not actually represented there, which was little more than an argument for retaining the convenient and corrupt *status quo* in Britain, and which was swept aside by Chatham and the Americans with a contempt best expressed in the words of the former: "The idea of a virtual representation of America in this House is the most contemptible idea that ever entered the head of man: it does not deserve a serious refutation."[2] But these and other kindred ideas do not need to delay us long, for they were not of major importance.

Only one other compromise position had a real chance of success, because it might have tided over the crisis and because it had a substantial group of supporters in Britain; it was that supported by the Rockingham Whigs and best expressed by Burke. This was a common-sense proposal, or series of proposals, and it cut directly across legalistic constitutional opinions. In theory—and, of course, it was never tested in practice—it is one of the supreme examples of largeness of mind and nobility of sentiment in the history of politics, even though it concentrated exclusively upon the question of whether it was *expedient* to tax the colonies. But never was expediency dignified with such exalta-

[1] Q. R. G. Adams, *Political Ideas of the American Revolution* (Pennsylvania, 1922), p. 42.   [2] Q. Basil Williams, II, p. 191.

tion of language, nor pressed to the service of a cause less narrow and pedantic. "Sir, I think you must perceive, that I am resolved this day to have nothing at all to do with the question of the right of taxation. Some gentlemen startle—but it is true; I put it totally out of the question. . . . [M]y consideration is narrow, confined, and wholly limited to the policy of the question." At the heart of his thinking was the unassailable truth that the retention of America was worth far more to the mother country, economically, politically, and even morally, than any sum which might be raised by taxation, and even than any principle, so-called, of the Constitution. "The question with me is, not whether you have a right to render your people miserable, but whether it is not your interest to make them happy. It is not, what a lawyer tells me I *may* do; but what humanity, reason, and justice tell me I ought to do." This policy involved, not the assertion of British rights at the expense of those of the colonies, but the very reverse:

> Let the colonies always keep the idea of their civil rights associated with your government;—they will cling and grapple to you; and no force under heaven would be of power to tear them from their allegiance. But let it be once understood, that your government may be one thing, and their privileges another . . . and everything hastens to decay and dissolution. . . . Slavery they can have anywhere. It is a weed that grows in every soil. They may have it from Spain, they may have it from Prussia. But, until you become lost to all feeling of your true interest and your natural dignity, freedom they can have from none but you. This is the commodity of price, of which you have the monopoly. This is the true act of navigation which binds to you the commerce of the colonies, and through them secures to you the wealth of the world.[1]

This specific, of complying with the American spirit as necessary, might conceivably have led gradually, step by step, and without violent rupture, to the establishment of a British Commonwealth of Nations including America. Certainly it was the kind of solution most acceptable to the English political temperament, a cautious, evolutionary, pragmatic solution, uncomplicated by high-sounding abstractions. On the other hand, it suited the more vigorous, definite and radical, though equally pragmatic, American temperament rather less, perhaps, than the rigid and plain solution propounded by Chatham, which aroused far more support in America. In any case, though it had the initial support of the British merchants, there was insufficient magnanimity in the little minds of those who controlled the actions of the British Government to give Burke's policy a fair trial, and it remains merely

[1] Works, I, pp. 479, 508.

a grievous illustration of how seldom the political wisdom of men is sufficient to make them in truth the masters of their own fate.

Ultimately, the great majority of Americans, and even a number of Englishmen, accepted the sixth point of view, the necessity for a final severance of all constitutional links between the two countries, and welcomed the propositions so splendidly expressed in the Declaration of Independence. There had been considerable reluctance to accept this irrevocable solution in America, and an even greater reluctance to do so in Britain. It is true that a few Britons, like Adam Smith after the failure of his plan of imperial federation, came to the conclusion that by their parting good friends, the natural affection of Americans for the mother country would quickly revive; but only one man of any note, Dean Tucker of Gloucester, had from the beginning favoured allowing the wayward sisters to depart in peace, on the ground that a political and military alliance between two independent countries would be far more productive of good than an attempt to suppress the smothered rebellion.

Thus by 1776 the issue had become plain; it was a contest between a majority of Americans, believing in the necessity of independence, and a majority of Englishmen, believing in the necessity for enforcing the subordination of the colonies. There were still exceptions on both sides. John Adams in 1813 estimated that the American Loyalists, in the Revolutionary period, constituted one-third of the whole population, and the United Empire Loyalists who actually left the United States for Canada numbered well over fifty thousand; on the other hand, many Whigs in England always considered it as a civil war, heeding Chatham's warning that slaves in America would be fit instruments to make slaves at home. But even before 1776, beneath the confusion of opinions and the welter of events, it is perhaps possible to detect two incompatible views of the nature of the imperial relationship. Under pressure of facts, this *bona fide* constitutional issue, as MacIlwain describes it, became constantly clearer. As Governor Bernard had indicated, "it is my opinion that all the political evils in America arise from want of ascertaining the relations between Great Britain and the American Colonies".[1] As Van Tyne argued, in England "no taxation without representation" meant "no taxation without Parliament," and between this and the American view there was a great gulf fixed. Bernard again puts the matter succinctly, "In Britain the American Governments are considered as Corporations . . . existing only during

[1] Q. R. G. Adams, p. 49.

the Pleasure of Parliament. . . . In America they claim to be perfect States, no otherwise dependent upon Great Britain than by having the same King."[1]

The American view of empire was rooted solidly in the past, for, as in other spheres of life, so even in the rarified atmosphere of ideas, there developed, after the seventeenth-century foundations, a divergence between the notions of the colonies and those of the mother country. Interestingly, it was in this respect in Britain that the chief change occurred. As Burke pointed out, the colonies took their political bias from the period in English history when ideas of freedom were at their strongest, and they remained imbued with them, in some of their incidentals as well as their main features. In the seventeenth century the idea of Natural Law dominated European political thought, and it was held not only to be the chief guarantee of liberty, but to play a real and fundamental part in government. James Harrington's *Oceana* of 1656, in its advocacy of a democratic form of government, expressed the prevalent belief that, "Government is the Empire of Laws, and not of Men", a sentiment embodied specifically in the Constitution of Massachusetts. There was possibly some flavour of this in the words of Cromwell when he said that, "In every government there must be somewhat fundamental, somewhat like a Magna Carta, that should be standing and be unalterable."[2] This idea of Natural Law as the firm and final basis of the rights and government of the people remained fixed in American minds, and it was accompanied by a belief that these rights were also assured by the charters of the colonies and by the British Constitution. The first Continental Congress resolved in 1774 "That the inhabitants of the English Colonies in North America, by the immutable laws of nature, the principles of the English constitution, and the several charters or compacts, have the following rights".[3] Defendants of colonial claims tended to move back from one to the other of these grounds as each proved untenable, until they reached their last stand, that of rights guaranteed to them by Natural Law, at which point the American struggle became a revolution of world significance, because it was thenceforth irrevocably based upon universal abstract rights possessed by all men everywhere. But charter rights and rights under the British Constitution, as indeed all laws, had to be in accord-

[1] Q. C. H. Van Tyne, *The Causes of the War of Independence* (London, 1928), pp. 217-8.

[2] Q. *Cambridge History of the British Empire* (1929), I, pp. 607, 611.

[3] H. S. Commager, *Documents of American History* (New York, 1948), I, p. 83.

241

ance with Natural Law if they were to have validity; thus Tom Paine insisted that a constitution was a thing antecedent to government, and that the government was only the creature of the constitution, which, it is interesting to note, is still exactly true of the American Constitution.

This belief carried the further implication, accepted by many American constitutional lawyers such as John Adams, that the executive should reject any law contrary to the constitution; as James Otis expressed it, "An act against the Constitution is void."[1] The connexion between this and the idea of judicial review by the Supreme Court is clear, as also is its connexion with Chatham's idea of a distinction between internal and external taxation, the former being, by its very nature, invalid in the colonies. From another angle, the idea went back to the belief of some English seventeenth-century common lawyers, expressed by Hobart in a judgment of 1614, that "an Act of Parliament made against natural equity is void in itself,"[2] and American lawyers continued to draw a distinction between private and constitutional law. At the time of the Revolution, for instance, James Wilson placed great emphasis on the importance of law, and believed that the Americans were defeating Parliament to preserve law (a proposition incomprehensible to most contemporary English lawyers), because law was not properly, as the English believed, the 'command of a superior', but the expression of the will of the people. The whole American position was perhaps best expressed by a solitary English lawyer of eminence, Lord Camden, who still took the English seventeenth-century view-point. He said of the Declaratory Act, which accompanied the repeal of the Stamp Act, "In my opinion, the legislature has no right to make this law.... [T]he omnipotence of the legislature is a favourite doctrine, but there are some things which you cannot do. You cannot enact anything against divine law. You cannot take away any man's private property without making him compensation. You have no right to condemn any man by bill of attainder without hearing him." On another occasion he added, the "bill . . . is illegal, absolutely illegal, contrary to the fundamental laws of nature, contrary to the fundamental laws of the Constitution".[3]

By the late eighteenth century, the orthodox English view of the Constitution was quite different, not only from that of the Americans, but also from that of the previous century. The idea of Natural Law had been much weakened in England, and practical lawyers mistrusted

[1] Q. R. G. Adams, pp. 128-9.

[2] Q. Sir Ernest Barker, *Traditions of Civility* (Cambridge, 1948), p. 284.

[3] Q. R. G. Adams, p. 92.

it. Paley wrote that the terms 'constitutional' and 'unconstitutional' meant 'legal' and 'illegal' and nothing else; and no distinction was drawn by most Englishmen between private and public law, so that there could be in their eyes no *legal* right of resistance to a bad law. There could only be a revolutionary right of resistance, which, though still recognized in theory, was almost universally deplored in practice. The Whig Bishop Watson, for example, agreed that the people might in theory exercise the right of resuming the reins of government, but held that in practice it was quite another question: "It was exercised at the Revolution; and we trust that there will never, in this country, be occasion to exercise it again; for we hope, and are persuaded that the wisdom of the House of Hanover will keep at an awful distance from the throne men professing principles which have levelled with the dust the House of Stuart."[1] To these men, who were accustomed to regard the Constitution, admired as it was by liberal Europeans like Montesquieu and Voltaire, with the veneration of Blackstone,—"Of a Constitution, so wisely contrived, so strongly raised, and so highly finished, it is hard to speak with that praise, which is just and severely its due—the thorough and attentive contemplation of it will furnish its best panegyric"[2]—to these men, the popular right of revolution had become impossible to contemplate. The upshot of all this was that the legislative authority came to be regarded during the century as absolutely sovereign; this supreme power of the King in Parliament, wrote Paley, "may be termed absolute, omnipotent, uncontrollable, arbitrary, despotic", for "as a series of appeals must be finite, there necessarily exists in every government a power from which the Constitution has provided no appeal".[3]

This position was later to find its classical expression in the Austinian definition of sovereignty, which laid down that a political sovereign is a determinate human superior, not in the habit of obedience to a like superior, receiving habitual obedience from the bulk of a given society. This purely practical and factual definition owed nothing to an immutable Natural Law, belief in which had largely disappeared through the corrosive effect of the works of thinkers like Hobbes, Hume and the forerunners of Bentham, who had little influence on the development of political thought in the colonies. Later English constitutional theorists, like Dicey, might evolve a distinction between political and legal sovereignty, which restored effective popular control of this unrestricted sovereign power, but to this day, legally, there is nothing in

[1] Q. V. H. H. Green, *The Hanoverians* (London, 1948), p. 32.
[2] Q. Green, p. 29.   [3] Barker, p. 246.

243

Britain that the King in Parliament cannot do, as the saying goes, except make a man into a woman. This still remains an important and characteristic difference between the written American and the unwritten British Constitution, despite the increase of popular control in the latter and the decrease in the rigidity of obstacles to the effective power of the Federal Government in the former, and in the eighteenth century it was of immense significance. The stability and security, and indeed freedom, which, compared with most Europeans, the English enjoyed, they ascribed to the Parliamentary Revolution of 1688 and identified with the supremacy of Parliament; this supremacy even John Locke appeared within limits to have supported in his advocacy of the supreme power of the legislature. That Parliament (and particularly the House of Commons) must, as it had largely done in 1688, represent, and indeed be chosen by, the people was a fact that became obscured in practice by the corruption and lethargy of English political life. As a result, more and more veneration and more and more power were bestowed upon it as the eighteenth century progressed, yet this change, for change it was, was embodied in no legislation and supported by little theory; it appeared as a development in the practice rather than the content of the Constitution, and was little noticed in the colonies, where Parliament played in any case a comparatively small part in the life of the community, which looked primarily for guidance to its own officials and organs of government.

The control of colonial affairs was thus divided between the local governments and the imperial government in Westminster, plainly foreshadowing the epoch-making division of sovereignty embodied in the American Federal Constitution. Such a division of sovereignty was incomprehensible to the British constitutional lawyer, born and bred in a compact and unitary state. In the same way, the idea of absolute power, even in the hands of a representative assembly, was repugnant to Americans. There was significance, too, in the fact that the British Constitution was altering and developing, for, paradoxically again, it was the conservative side which, by its changes, precipitated the conflict of theories. The American view of constitutional law at this period was essentially static, whereas that of Great Britain was groping after the idea of the organic growth of institutions, with all that that implied for the doctrine of human progress. On the one hand, Mansfield wrote that the Constitution "has always been in a moving state, either gaining or losing something"; on the other hand, Samuel Adams wrote, "In all free states the Constitution is fixed".[1] Here is the focus of the conflict,

---

[1] Q. *Cambridge History of British Empire*, I, p. 632.

the point of theory at which the final jarring clash of the two societies took place. But both peoples had something of value to contribute to the future development of political theory and practice, the one the idea of national sovereignty and the evolution of human institutions, the other a vital emphasis on the importance of effective popular control of government and of the people as the true source of law.

V

THE development of events precipitated and protracted the struggle of ideas. "When the controversy with Great Britain began in 1764, the preconceptions of the Natural Rights philosophy lay quiescent in Colonial minds, ready to be drawn upon in case of need, but never yet having been called forth in the service of any concrete issue."[1] Prior to 1764 there was practical friction in the working of the governmental system, but no clear-cut constitutional issue. The Sugar Act of 1764 first raised the question of taxation for revenue by the Parliament of Great Britain through external or customs duties, which had always in their regulative capacity been an integral part of the imperial system. The Stamp Act of 1765 widened the problem by imposing a virtually unprecedented internal tax purely for revenue, and, swallowing up the opposition to the Sugar Act as it did so, united North and South against the imperial government. On the whole, the majority of Englishmen accepted from the beginning the orthodox Tory belief in the right of Parliament to tax the colonies, and English opinion hardened obstinately until war was accepted, and then pursued to disaster.

In America, on the other hand, there was a development of ideas, a great change in majority opinion over more than a decade. The mass of the public accepted the legality of the Sugar Act, though many detested its contents and had grave fears of what exactions might follow it in the future. When the Stamp Act was passed, common American opinion accepted the view of those who denounced it as an illegal internal tax, though the legality of external taxes was not seriously challenged. With the passage of the Townshend duties, however, which were entirely external in their application and professedly for revenue only, public opinion took a step backward by claiming that, just as internal taxes for revenue were unconstitutional, so the *intention* of the government to raise a revenue or not by an external tax, governed its legality. This was followed by yet another step, denying all power of

[1] Carl Becker, *The Declaration of Independence* (New York, 1922), p. 80.

taxation to Parliament. From this it was but a short step again to the total denial of Parliamentary legislative sovereignty, and to the idea that the Crown alone was the real bond between the co-equal partners, Great Britain and the colonies, which came later to be called the 'dominion status' theory; this was a widespread belief of many in the period immediately before the Declaration of Independence, as the fact that this document was exclusively directed against the King clearly shows. But by now men were tired of these theoretical arguments, for as Franklin said, "[N]o middle ground can be maintained; I mean not clearly with intelligible arguments,"[1] and so, when the coercive or 'abominable' Acts were passed in 1774, public opinion in America moved rapidly to belief in the necessity of independence, that same public opinion which had but twelve years before accepted, almost without question or even thought, the theory, if not the practice, of colonial subordination. Thus there came to pass that which Burke had prophesied when he wrote, "When you drive him hard, the boar will surely turn upon the hunters. If that sovereignty and their freedom cannot be reconciled, which will they take? They will cast your sovereignty in your face."[2]

The political events which led to this consummation were to a great extent symptoms of the malaise in the imperial relationship; they do not call for lengthy discussion here, since they are well known, and since they are but the prologue to the main thread of our history, which starts from the final establishment of America's independent nationhood, with the recognition of her sovereign status by Great Britain in 1783. It is well known that the British conquest of Canada in the Seven Years War removed one of the most potent bonds between Great Britain and the colonies, the latter's fear of France, and it is also well known that the divisions of the colonies were not in the end strong enough to prevent a common front being presented by them to the mother country. It is an old story, and one that we have already touched upon, how the English landed gentry, who paid the bulk of British taxation, demanded that a revenue be raised from the colonies in order that their own burdens might be reduced, a proposal which seemed to them not unreasonable considering the benefits that America enjoyed under British protection, and considering that it was proposed to spend much of the revenue so raised in the colonies themselves, above all in colonial defence. It is an old story, too, how the British Government set about this task; first, by reforming the customs and endeavouring to enforce

[1] Q. R. G. Adams, p. 81.   [2] Works, I, p. 433.

such duties as those levied under the Sugar Act of 1764, and then, by imposing the Stamp Act of 1765. Even more familiar is the tale of subsequent events: the clamour against the Stamp Act, the convening of the Stamp Act Congress, and the success, through their effect upon the British merchants, of the Non-Importation agreements—the colonial economic self-denying ordinances—in inducing the repeal of the Stamp Act in 1766. The calm which succeeded the repeal, despite the passage of the Declaratory Act, was broken by the passage of the Townshend duties in 1767, an ill-advised response to continued English pressure for a reduction in domestic taxation and to American assertions that they objected to the Stamp Act solely on the ground that it was an internal tax. There followed the renewed American measures of opposition and the repeal of all the duties except that on tea in 1770. Finally came the widening of the gap between the two peoples, even during the comparative calm of the years 1770-1773, owing to the continued obstinacy of men like George III in Britain, and the incessant activity and increasing power of radicals like Samuel Adams in America, working through the committees of correspondence. And so, with all the remorselessness and pathos of classical tragedy, the drama moves swiftly to its close, through the Tea Act of 1773, the Boston Tea Party, the coercive Acts of 1774, and, finally, the fatal shots at Lexington and Concord. We, in the latter-day atmosphere of Anglo-American cordiality, are sometimes wont to under-estimate the passions aroused in these days of crisis, and in the bitter struggle which followed them, particularly because the sentiments were different in the two countries. In Britain there was obstinate traditional patriotism, but, even outside the minority who opposed the war, there was a feeling that such a sentiment, in this most unsuccessful, indeed disastrous and calamitous, of all British wars, was somehow tarnished and even debased. But for the Americans it was a noble, a vigorous, a life-giving passion which found its expression in the Declaration of Independence.

These, then, were some of the causes of the American Revolution. What was its effect upon the future of Anglo-American relations? Briefly, because of the violence of the rupture, it gave to the relationship between the two peoples its unusual and peculiar quality. Their common origin, their common tongue, their kindred institutions, and their very strong mutual interests still remained. These provided a basis for political and social friendship almost unprecedented between two independent nations, and on this basis there was in the end built what, it is to be hoped, will be a permanent and unshakable union. The foundations of this union always remained, but the tide of emotion by which they were overlaid in the bitter struggle for independence took many years to subside, leaving the foundations still solid and clearly to be observed, though even yet washed by many a wave of ill-feeling. For at least a half a century suspicion became the most apparent characteristic of Anglo-American relations, suspicion which once again burst into the flame of war in 1812. The British, whose pride had received a severe blow in 1783, took refuge in an even more marked and freely expressed contempt for Americans than existed for other 'colonials'; most British criticism took the form of supercilious derision of American society and an openly expressed belief—and hope—that the American democratic and republican experiment would fail. Only with the coming of political and social reform, and of a new doctrine of colonial relationships in Britain itself, did this attitude begin to disappear. The Americans reacted even more strongly. All their hatred of arbitrary government, all their dislike of aristocratic inequalities, all their animosity towards the ways of the Old World, became centred in their revulsion from everything British. Anti-British sentiments became almost a *sine qua non* of American political success, and this spirit died even harder in America than did anti-Americanism in Britain.

Yet, despite all this, the basis of common interest remained and in some ways grew more solid. Geographically, though America might seek to draw in her garments from European contamination, she could not do so; as David Hartley wrote in 1783, "Great Britain and the United States must still be inseparable, either as Friends or Foes. This is an awful and important truth."[1] Technical developments, following hard upon the heels of the Revolution, forced the two peoples into closer and closer proximity, for within twenty-five years of the Peace of Paris a steamship was plying upon American waters, and even before that date improvements in the design of vessels had ushered in the era of the swift Clipper ship. Socially and culturally this meant an ever-increasing measure of contact between the two peoples, and the more contact there was the harder it became to ignore the amount they had in common. Small wonder that the British and American minds were torn between feelings for and against each other. Anglo-American feeling has indeed something of the schizophrenic in it. It is remarkable, for instance, how little their emotions bore any relation to the gravity of particular issues; trivial questions like the Sackville-West letter of

[1] Q. V. T. Harlow, *The Founding of the Second British Empire, 1763-1793* (London, 1952), p. 471.

1888 and General Butler's New Orleans order in the Civil War were to arouse more fury than many of the grave border disputes. Their common interests bound them indissolubly together, however much their surface sentiments might pull them apart. Of this peculiar relationship Canada remained a remarkable symbol; geographically and economically inseparable from the United States, she yet retained her political and cultural relationship with Britain. She remained at once a hostage for, and an agent of, Anglo-American understanding.

Once independence had been achieved, it was in its effect upon the psychology, or the outlook of the two peoples that the Revolution was most important. In Britain, though there was suspicion on the surface, there was below that a marked increase of respect. She was not, after all, accustomed to disastrous defeats in war such as she suffered in 1783; it was comforting to reflect that, though faced towards the end of the war by the most formidable array of European enemies ever ranged against her in her whole history, it was not really by them that she had been beaten, but by the Americans, who were her own flesh and blood. When all was said and done, it took a man of British stock to beat an Englishman. This grudging respect for America has in some senses always remained the characteristic English feeling towards her. It took time to work to the surface, but when, ultimately, it did so, it was accompanied by, and to some extent effected, a great revolution in English political thinking. No doubt the success of the American experiment did something to forward the cause of domestic democratic reform in England in mid-nineteenth century, but the grim and salutary lesson of the American Revolution directly revolutionized, though with a delayed action, the British concept of Empire. The idea of the free association of equal members of the British Commonwealth, which arose out of the movement in the eighteen-thirties and forties symbolized in the Durham Report, owed its inspiration to the English realization that any other course must ultimately lead to a repetition of the American disaster, as well as to a growing clarity of democratic purpose, which was to some extent derived from the American example operating either directly or through France and her history. In a different way, the Revolution reinforced a lesson which England had already begun to learn, the lesson that the only way to avoid revolution is to promote evolution. The march of the British Dominions towards independent and equal membership of the Commonwealth was effected by gradual changes, by steps spread over a century of history. Thus, paradoxically as it might seem, the sudden breach effected by the Revolution produced in Britain a strengthening of that characteristically English belief, in the adaptation of existing institutions to new purposes, in preserving in order to reform.

The effect upon America was different, for it is not perhaps fanciful to claim that the clean break which the Revolution made exaggerated a tendency, which was already strong in the American people, to like fresh beginnings and radical solutions to political and social problems. It is easy for an Englishman to under-estimate the effect of the Revolution upon American history. It was to the Americans much more than just one event in a long history: it was the very birth of their nation. Englishmen see it as one almost inevitable step in the long development of the colonies, but, rather naturally, Americans are not so very conscious of its relationship to imperial history. Myths have their importance, even when they have little basis in reality, and the importance of the Revolution in American legend has obscured in the American mind the fact that the United States did not, in a kind of spontaneous political generation, spring fully armed and adult from the head of the mother country. When Lincoln talked of a new birth of freedom, he gave voice unmistakably to this American preconception, and he signified a very important fact about it, that it marked for them not only the birth of their country, but the birth of liberty also. For Americans the United States was from its inception inextricably involved in the human search for freedom; America and liberty were indeed born as twins and were nurtured in the same cradle. This effect of the Revolution was burned into the American soul by the fact that the fighting was done on their native soil. Both in adversity and in success, the war was the crucible in whose white-heat American patriotism was born: on the anvil of Valley Forge the steel of Americanism was tempered.

But the steel was tempered, too, in the waters of success, for confidence followed upon triumph in the war; the gaining of the Mississippi boundary, for instance, when Congress would at a pinch have accepted one along the crest of the Appalachians, pointed forward to the American conquest of their continental domain. Even in the dangerous disillusion of peace, the critical years were terminated by the remarkable and unprecedented, yet solid, success of the formation of the Federal Constitution. These achievements gave to the development of the American attitude to the world its characteristic flavour. It gave it at home its belief in republicanism, in political democracy, and to some extent, radicalism; it gave it, in its policy towards the rest of the world, that revulsion from all things European, and most particularly at first, all things English, which was to find expression in the powerful forces of American isolationism. This went hand in hand with a great absorption of national effort in rapid exploitation of the West, and the brushing aside of all obstacles thereto; Manifest Destiny in the West implied a maximum withdrawal from the affairs of Europe. Yet, oddly combined with this, was the strenuously idealistic tone of American foreign policy, which found expression, not only in impractical notions as far apart as Jefferson's embargo policy and the Kellogg Peace Pact, but also in great international ventures like the League of Nations and the United Nations. The desire for isolation was accompanied, often thwarted, and in the end, it seems, overlaid, by an almost Messianic sense of mission, a powerful urge to democratize the affairs of men. This development is clearly reflected in the history of Anglo-American relations. The deep-seated mistrust of Britain which followed the Revolution was, though very slowly, replaced by an appreciation of their common outlook and interests.

In this way the American Revolution set the tone of Anglo-American relations for many years. There was an inevitable bitterness and mistrust on both sides, though it was stronger and lasted longer in America. At the same time, it could not indefinitely obscure the wide basis of potential agreement between them, and there developed in the twentieth century an increasing measure of co-operation, which must remain a source of satisfaction, if only because it is a source of strength, to both parties. Yet, emotionally tinged as human thoughts are, Englishmen and Americans cannot be expected to regard the American Revolution in the same light. To the Englishman, conscious of the later free development of the other British colonies, it must seem, at best regrettable and at worst lamentable, that the folly of his ancestors was so great, or at least that their wisdom was so small, that they were unable to avoid the disruption of the First British Empire. He cannot but reflect how useful it might have been in this century to have constituted part of a great commonwealth of which the United States would have been a full, and, by this time, the dominating member. The American must see the matter differently; to him the Revolution is too important, too integral, too glorious a part—the very foundation indeed—of his national history, for him to wish that it had never happened. And perhaps he is right, for even the Briton, when he reflects upon the fruitfulness of American independence, and the benefits which have arisen, and may yet arise, from free and friendly rivalry and competition between the two peoples, may doubt the wisdom of his regrets. Perhaps Nathaniel Hawthorne was right when he wrote, "If England had been wise enough to twine our new vigour round her ancient strength, her

CHAPTER NINE

INDEPENDENCE (1783-94)

THE disastrous surrender at Yorktown on 19 October, 1781, was the heaviest blow in the destruction of Great Britain's will to win the war, which had now lasted for six years. The American failure to conquer or win over Canada in its initial stages had been more than outweighed by the failure at Saratoga of the British plan to sever New England from Virginia; furthermore, though British maritime control was not deeply endangered by the United States and her allies, and, though Britain could hold New York and conduct successful military operations in the Middle and Southern colonies, she had shown herself quite unable effectively to subdue the country. This was partly due to the success of Washington in keeping an American army in being and in maintaining the American will to fight; partly to the strength of the American position, her size, her distance from Europe, and her increasing power and resources; partly to the inefficiency and even half-heartedness of the British war direction; and partly to the alliance of the United States with France and Spain.

From the British point of view the last consideration came increasingly to outweigh all others, for the entry of France and Spain into the war, in 1778 and 1779 respectively, found Britain virtually without a friend in Europe. Indeed, the irritation caused by the British blockade, skilfully exacerbated by French diplomacy, resulted in 1780 in the formation of the so-called Armed Neutrality, a league consisting of Russia, Sweden, Denmark and Holland, and pledged to the principle that free ships make free goods. A Russian fleet appeared in the English Channel, and Britain declared war upon Holland when it became known that the latter was engaged in negotiations with the United States. Seldom in her history had the international situation appeared so dangerous to Britain, and in the midst of a deepening gloom, where men prophesied freely the utter and final eclipse of her greatness, this grave military defeat of Yorktown, made possible by an even more ominous, if less irremediable, loss of control of the western seas, convinced public opinion, and eventually even the Government and the King, that losses must be cut somewhere. Late in February, 1782, a motion to renounce all further efforts to subjugate the thirteen colonies was passed by the House of Commons, and, before his resignation in March, Lord North despatched an emissary to contact Benjamin Franklin, the representative of the United States in Paris.

I

THE proceedings thus begun issued in British recognition of American independence before the end of 1783, but the political future of the United States was not in fact assured until Jay's Treaty in 1794. Certain problems of vital concern to her, partly arising from the provisions and omissions of the initial treaty, were only disposed of—and then largely through the personal determination of Washington—eleven years later. The negotiations for the Treaty of Versailles, often called the Peace of Paris, began in earnest after the fall of North and the establishment of a Whig government, under the leadership of Rockingham, Shelburne, and Fox, all of whom had in greater or lesser degree opposed the American War. Because of the relative proximity of the negotiations in France, the Cabinet in London exercised a close control over them, and the British commissioners, the most notable being James Oswald, were left comparatively little latitude. Two important changes in the composition of the government exerted some, though not a decisive, influence upon the course of the negotiations; the first was the succession of Shelburne to the Prime Ministership on Rockingham's death in July, 1782, and the second the replacement of his government by the Fox-North coalition in April, 1783, largely on the ground that the preliminaries of peace were grossly favourable to the Americans, particularly in the matter of the Canadian boundary. Through geographical necessity and because of the loose nature of the American governmental structure, the American commissioners, Benjamin Franklin, John Jay, and John Adams, had a much greater freedom of action, being bound only in a general way by the terms of reference laid down in Congressional resolutions.

Two serious preliminary problems to the negotiation of a peace treaty existed; first, British reluctance to commit herself to an irrevocable and explicit recognition of American independence, and the American demand that this should precede the opening of negotiations; second, the American obligation, by her treaty of 1778 with France, not to make a separate peace.

The first difficulty was obvious: Oswald was empowered to discuss peace terms with commissioners representing, not the 'United States', but the 'colonies'. The one and only *sine qua non* of the latest instructions of Congress to its commissioners in 1781 was the recognition of independence, and Franklin and Jay, particularly the latter, were adamant in their refusal to negotiate until the British agreed to a preamble, as well as a first Article, recognizing the United States. The second difficulty seemed at first, however, a more formidable one, but "with a mature realism which surprised European statesmen"[1] the American commissioners, when enjoined by their British counterparts to beware of the French—whom Britain believed, with some justice, to be prepared to play a double game themselves—went ahead upon separate negotiations. The preamble to the Preliminary Articles of Peace between Britain and the United States, however, stated that they were "To be inserted in, and to constitute the Treaty of Peace proposed to be concluded, between the Crown of Great Britain, and the said United States; but which Treaty is not to be concluded, until Terms of a Peace shall be agreed upon, between Great Britain and France; and his Britannic Majesty shall be ready to conclude such Treaty accordingly."[2] Franklin, in his affection for France, had been somewhat more reluctant than the other commissioners to consent to separate negotiations, but once he had done so was more than a match for any European diplomat. The practice of playing off doubtful friends against open enemies was not new to diplomacy, and it was one which all the parties at this time were willing to play, but the British and the Americans were able to play it much the best, for they started with the considerable advantage of long association. Despite the bitterness between them (which John Adams expressed when he said that "The pride and vanity of that nation is a disease, it is a delirium; it has been flattered and inflamed so long by themselves and by others that it perverts everything"[3]) this basis for co-operation still existed beneath the surface. Indeed Shelburne, in the words of Harlow, "hated the idea of separation", only accepting it reluctantly and hoping against hope for some form of federal union; when he did accept it, he "endeavoured to establish interim conditions that would facilitate and not impede the process of reconciliation", in order that the connexion between the two lands might be revived before all those having links with Britain had disappeared from the scene. These foundations of co-operation,

---

[1] Brebner, p. 57.

[2] Hunter Miller (Editor), *Treaties and Other International Acts of the United States of America* (Washington, 1931), II, p. 96.

[3] Q. J. C. Miller *The Triumph of Freedom, 1775-1783* (Boston, 1948), p. 632.

though they were overlaid in the next century, became once more of great importance in the twentieth, when "the greatness of Shelburne's conception impresses itself upon the mind."[1]

Recognition of this common interest was at this time, and for a long time to come, much more agreeable to British than to American diplomats, largely because they had much more to gain from it. Even George III could say to the House of Lords on 5 December, 1782, "Religion, language, interests and affection may, and I hope will, yet prove a bond of permanent union between the two countries",[2] and other Englishmen could be far more enthusiastic. Though the Americans were on the whole less impressed with this possibility than the English, Vergennes concluded, after the somewhat embarrassing interview in which Franklin broke the news of the separate peace preliminaries with England, that "there was a fatal predilection in Americans for Englishmen—no matter how badly they were treated, these republicans always came back for more. No foreigner, however honest or worthy, could long come between them."[3] Already there was apparent to the Frenchman the unusual character of the Anglo-American relationship. Thus, though there was hard Anglo-American bargaining in the negotiations and though Englishmen were not without vindictive feelings towards the rebels, traditional fear of France and the fact that the peace was made by Whig "friends of America" served to rivet English attention on the serious European situation and to induce her to use her diplomatic strength (which was augmented in the course of negotiation by the raising of the siege of Gibraltar and by Rodney's victory over De Grasse in the West Indies) against her old European enemies rather than against the Americans. This was not without its effect upon the future of Anglo-American relations.

Peace was made in three distinct stages. Preliminary Articles of Peace were signed between America and Britain on 30 November, 1782, and were ratified by them on 15 April and 6 August, 1783, respectively, but fighting continued until Britain signed separate preliminaries of peace with France and Spain on 20 January, 1783, on which date an armistice between the British and Americans was also declared. The definitive peace between them, as between all the other parties, was signed at Paris on 3 September, 1783, and ratified by them early in 1784. In fact there were no changes, except of form, between the Anglo-American preliminaries and the definitive peace. There were intensive negotiations, particularly on commercial reciprocity, in the interim period, conducted

[1] Harlow, I, pp. 310-11.
[2] Q. Mowat, *Americans in England*, p. 54. [3] Q. Miller, p. 642.

by David Hartley, for Fox, who was now Secretary of State, was even more liberal in his views of the American relationship than Shelburne, but he eventually accepted the latter's preliminaries, in their entirety, as the definitive terms of peace, intending that they should be followed by a sweeping commercial treaty which he did not believe should be negotiated under the eye of France. For the future he was very sanguine, and predicted that through an Anglo-American alliance "the sun of Britain might rise again, and shine forth with dazzling lustre."[1]

The final treaty consisted of a preamble and ten Articles. The former expressed the desire "to forget all past Misunderstandings and Differences that have unhappily interrupted the good Correspondence and Friendship which they mutually wish to restore; and to establish such a beneficial and satisfactory intercourse between the two Countries upon the Ground of reciprocal Advantages and mutual Commerce as may promote and secure to both perpetual Peace and Harmony",[2] which had a more genuine ring than many diplomatic pretensions to friendship. The first Article recognized the United States to be "free sovereign and Independent States", thus severing all formal political ties between Britain and her erstwhile colonies and recognizing their absolute independence. The second Article began, "And that all Disputes which might arise in future on the Subject of the Boundaries of the said United States, may be prevented, it is hereby agreed and declared that the following are and shall be their Boundaries", a faint and very sanguine hope in view of the fact that boundary disputes between the two nations continued until the twentieth century and that the article had already been the subject of much hard negotiation. Future border difficulties were to be of two kinds: first and more serious, demands on both sides, but particularly the American, for radical alterations, such as the incorporation of Canada in the United States; second, interpretative disputes, promoted no doubt by interested groups, but arising in essence from the loose phraseology of this Article of the treaty, which was more due to lack of geographical knowledge than to the linguistic evasions of diplomacy.

The chief diplomatic prize in the negotiations had been the land north-west of the Ohio and east of the Mississippi,* land long bound to Canada by political, economic and geographical ties, and long dominated by the Montreal fur traders; this territory, which was easier of access from the St. Lawrence than from the Atlantic sea-board of the United States, had actually been placed under the control of Canada

---

[1] Q. ibid, p. 625. [2] Treaties, II, p. 151 *et seq.* * See Map I.

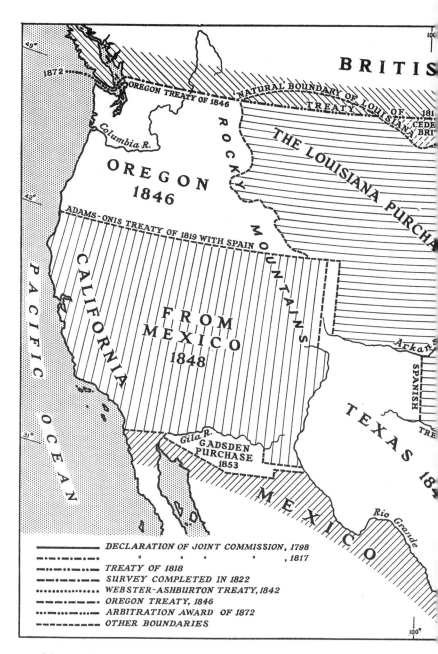

Map 1. *Development of the United States and its Boundaries. (For a consecutive account of the definition and delineation of the boundaries of the United States, see Edward M. Douglas, "Boundaries, Areas,*

Geographic Centers and Altitudes of the United States and the Several States", U.S. Department of the Interior, Geological Survey Bulletin 817, Washington, 1930. For further details see Maps 2, 3 and 4.)

by the ill-fated Quebec Act of 1774. Canadian economic interests, seeing the continental hinterland upon which their trade depended threatened by American independence, demanded the Ohio boundary. Franklin, on the other hand, setting a pattern of behaviour for successors as different as Henry Clay and Charles Sumner, put forward a demand for the whole of Canada; or, when he saw that this could not be achieved, for the so-called Lake Nipissing line, running almost entirely north of the Great Lakes and incorporating most of the present Province of Ontario in the United States, a line associated with the British Proclamation of 1763, when the primary concern of the imperial government had been the protection of the Indians. Its replacement by the more southerly line of the Ohio in the Quebec Act had little influence on the negotiations in 1783 because of the extreme unpopularity of that Act as a whole. In the event, however, a compromise line between that of Nipissing and that of the Ohio was agreed upon. Britain was at one moment prepared to grant not only independence but the Nipissing line also, and the only difficulty was the form of the recognition of independence. The American delegates, and particularly Jay, intent upon this—for them—indispensable and primary requirement, insisted on a change in Oswald's form of commission. The delay which this occasioned allowed time for Lord Howe to raise the siege of Gibraltar, so that the British hand was strengthened, which no doubt contributed to the fact that they felt able to demand a better boundary for Canada. They could perhaps have obtained the Ohio line, or even more, by perseverance, but the revulsion of British feeling against the war, particularly in its purely American aspect, made this impossible, despite the fact that indications had not been lacking in America that important interests would be prepared to accept a far worse boundary than that which eventuated, for there was even talk of the line of the Appalachians as the American frontier with Louisiana. These indications had, without doubt, not been lost upon the American delegates, and when they quite rightly began to suspect a Franco-Spanish plot to deny them the Mississippi boundary, they were not afraid to accept the compromise northern boundary in order to expedite the still secret Anglo-American negotiations.

But even when a compromise had been reached on the major issue, there remained the detailed delineation of the boundary, which involved some arduous negotiation, and resulted, through lack of exact cartography, in a number of decisions which were to be productive of difficulty in the future. There were three areas of subsequent uncertainty in the boundary, one in the north-west, and two in the north-east. The first section, which was to be uncertain, was defined as running from

"Lake Superior northward of the Isles Royal and Phelipeaux" through Lake of the Woods due westward to the Mississippi, but since the source of the river was in fact, as was later discovered, almost due south of the lake, and since the line from Lake Superior to Lake of the Woods was very obscurely and mistakenly defined, this problem remained to vex Anglo-American relations until the Webster-Ashburton Treaty of 1842. The second uncertainty also was not settled until that treaty; here, in the east, the boundary was defined as beginning at the mouth of the St. Croix river, proceeding up that river to its source, then on a line due north to the watershed of the St. Lawrence and Atlantic river-systems, then south-west down those highlands to the "Northwestern-most Head" of the Connecticut river. Two difficulties arose from this: the vagueness of the highland watershed line from its beginning to its end, and the fact that Mitchell's map, on which the line was based, marked the course of the St. Croix quite wrongly even though quite clearly. Thus the way was prepared for the later dispute between Maine and New Brunswick. The third uncertainty arose from the way in which ownership of the islands in the Bay of Fundy was defined. Islands within twenty leagues of the United States, between lines drawn due east from the two ends of the boundary, the mouths of the St. Croix and St. Mary rivers, were to belong to the United States, "excepting such islands as now are or heretofore have been within the Limits of the said Province of Nova Scotia". The difficulties arising from the imprecision of this last phrase were not finally solved until 1910.

The remainder of the boundary was clear, running down the Connecticut river to the 45th parallel, thence west to the St. Lawrence, and through the centre of the Great Lakes to Lake Superior. When picked up again at the source of the Mississippi, it followed that river south to the 31st parallel, thence due east to the Chattahoochee, and along its course to the junction with the Flint river; thereafter it pursued a straight line to the head of St. Mary's river, and followed the course of the latter into the Atlantic. The last part of this boundary, that with East and West Florida, later acquired by the United States, provides a good illustration of the difficulties arising from inaccurate contemporary cartography, for the maps used at the time indicated that a line due east from the junction of the Mississippi and the 31st parallel would strike the Chattahoochee south of its junction with the Flint river, whereas in fact it strikes it north of the junction. It also serves to illustrate the anti-Spanish sentiments of the American delegates and the reality of their improving feelings towards Britain, for in the Anglo-American preliminaries appeared a separate and secret article, which was not in the event ratified, agreeing that in case Great Britain at the end of the war should be in possession of, or secure, West Florida from the Spanish, its boundary in the north with the United States should be a line drawn from the mouth of the Yassous river, where it unites with the Mississippi, due east to the Apalachicola river, a line considerably north of the boundary the United States was to accept from Spain.

The third Article of the treaty concerned the fisheries, which were not only important to Canadians and Englishmen, but also, at this period when the United States was in many ways predominantly a maritime power, to the Americans. The basic complication was that the best fisheries were off Canadian shores, but a minor one was that the French also, as the masters of Canada till 1763, were interested in them, and had certain rights and privileges which they were by no means willing to risk losing by encouraging American participation therein; they had even induced the United States in 1778 to accept provisions in the Treaty of Alliance which implied a restriction of American fishing rights. The American delegates, particularly Jay, harboured deep suspicions that the French were preparing to try and oust the Americans from the fisheries, which they were, and this made the three Americans much readier to conclude an agreement with the British, who in their turn were quite willing to do all in their power to break up what they considered the unnatural alliance of the United States with France. In the subsequent arguments with the British on the point, the vigour, and bluntness, of John Adams, who as a New Englander was most intimately concerned, did much to gain American desires; the English, not being so vitally affected, were not in fact prepared to take as strong a line as Canadian fishing interests might have wished. Englishmen were, it is true, much affected by their belief, as good disciples of Adam Smith, that in the future era of reciprocity and free trade, economic interests would not suffer if they did not have political protection, but it is also possible to discover, in this readiness to hold out against the extreme demands of Canadian fur and fishing interests, germs of the later tendency of England to sacrifice immediate Canadian needs to the overriding necessity for Anglo-American accord. The actual terms of the Article on the fisheries granted to the people of the United States the "right" to fish in the open sea off the Canadian coast in the manner they had heretofore done, and the "liberty" to fish on the coasts themselves and to dry and cure their fish anywhere except Newfoundland, subject to the prior consent of the inhabitants where such existed. The distinction between a right and a liberty was definitely and deliberately drawn, but, none the less, John Adams did well by his countrymen, for whom these were generous terms.

On the boundary and the fisheries Great Britain had been able to concede a great deal, but on the subjects embodied in the next three Articles, the payment of debts and the position of the Loyalists, she had to stand firm. As it was, Shelburne's terms were considered extremely favourable to the Americans, but without these clauses the treaty would have had no hope of acceptance by Parliament. Article 4 agreed that creditors on either side should "meet with no lawful Impediment to the Recovery of the full Value in Sterling Money of all bona fide Debts heretofore contracted". Because of the persistently adverse balance of trade of the colonies, American creditors were almost non-existent so that this provision was for the particular benefit of the English merchants, and the reference to sterling reflected their very justifiable fear of depreciated American currencies. Franklin had opposed even this clause, asserting American counterclaims for damage done by the British in the war, but had been over-ruled by Jay and Adams; in any case, as the word "lawful" might almost seem to have implied, it remained quite impossible of fulfilment in the United States, and very few debts were in fact settled. Article 5 showed explicitly the weakness that Article 4 had demonstrated tacitly, for it agreed "that the Congress shall earnestly recommend to the Legislatures of the respective States" such action as would effect the restoration of the property of Loyalists, which had been confiscated during the Revolution, and such legislation concerning the Loyalists themselves as would promote the spirit of reconciliation proper to the return of peace. The American commissioners were here very ready to plead the constitutional inability of the Congress to do more than recommend these measures and leave it at that, but in Article 6 (which stated that "there shall be no future Confiscations . . . nor . . . Prosecutions" and that those "who may be in Confinement" as a result of the war "shall be immediately set at liberty"), not even this subterfuge was used, though in fact this was constitutionally almost as difficult to ensure as the provisions of Article 5. All these three Articles were largely disregarded by the states, which was perhaps explicable, given both the emotional and constitutional situation of the American people, and became as a result one of the immediate and important causes of post-war difficulties with Britain.

Article 7 dealt with the cessation of hostilities, the freeing of prisoners of war, and the withdrawal of British forces, leaving American artillery in any fortifications where it existed, and refraining from destroying or carrying away "any Negroes or other Property of the American In-habitants". Of the last point more will be heard later, for British viola-tion of it provided the United States with a useful counter to Britain's complaints about American failure to implement the three previous clauses. Finally, Article 8 stated that "The Navigation of the River Mississippi, from its source to the Ocean shall for ever remain free and open to the Subjects of Great Britain and the Citizens of the United States", obviously reflecting the expectation and even hope of both parties that West Florida at its mouth would end the war in British hands. In fact it remained Spanish, and not till the Treaty of San Lorenzo between Spain and the United States in 1795 did this right become a reality even for the Americans. This one short article was all that was actually left in the treaty of what had, in earlier draft proposals, been a grandiose liberal project for the future of Anglo-American commerce. Partly in order to win over Shelburne, at a time when they feared that Britain might be induced to make a separate peace with France by French offers of gains in the interior at American expense, Jay and Franklin put forward a proposal for free navigation, not only of the Mississippi, but also of other British and American waters, and for free trade between the United States and the British Empire. Such comprehensive ideas were common at the time on both sides of the Atlantic, for all advanced economic and political thought tended to accept the free trade doctrines expressed by Adam Smith; Oswald, though a very old man, shared them with the young Shelburne who had commissioned him. But conservative doubts in London as to the advantage to be gained by admitting America into the imperial trade network resulted in the removal of everything except the Missis-sippi provision, though Oswald was definitely instructed to say that the King wished subsequently to conclude a separate commercial treaty. After Fox and North had replaced Shelburne, the first-named continued to be an ardent advocate of a commercial treaty. This treaty never eventuated, except—an exceedingly pale reflection of the idea of 1782—as a few clauses in the treaty of 1794, but it had an important effect upon the framing of the Treaty of Versailles itself. The British delegates and ministers in particular, convinced that within a short time free trade would come between the two countries and that ever closer social and political contacts must inevitably follow, as the night follows the day, were very much readier than they might otherwise have been to make generous concessions; as Shelburne emphatically declared, *"we prefer trade to dominion."*[1] But the omission of the trade issue and

[1] Q. Harlow, I, p. 436.

the failure to negotiate the expected commercial treaty was one of the great weaknesses of the settlement of 1783. Britain had cause later to regret her fault in this, not only because it might have avoided the War of 1812, but also because it prevented the two economies from continuing to grow in quite such intimate union as they might otherwise have done. The dream of a great rural West directly dependent upon British manufactures was never anything like as fully realized as men like Shelburne had hoped, nor did it form the basis of a rapid political *rapprochement*.

But the Treaty of Versailles, though it contained obscurities, did not in the event make too unsatisfactory a foundation for Anglo-American relations. There is no doubt that, of all the powers who made peace in 1783, the United States profited most, largely through the concessions made by Britain, and that France fared the worst. Britain not only avoided the disasters which her gloomy position in the face of her European enemies had threatened, but retained Gibraltar and a reasonable Canadian boundary. America also owed much to her delegates, who proved amply worthy of the wide powers with which they were entrusted; indeed, as two American historians have written, "This Peace of Paris certainly gives the lie to the epigram that 'America never lost a war, or won a peace conference'."[1] Liberal gains by the Americans, at the expense of the British, made in fact the best basis for the future; as it was, the terms of the agreement left a sufficiency of difficult problems to be encountered later.

Feelings were already warmer among the English responsible for the treaty, old-line Whigs as they were, than among the Americans; of the general public, those in Britain who had opposed the war remained friendly to the United States, while the Tories continued suspicious. In America, too, ardent republicans remained very hostile to Britain, but, which was much more surprising, there was soon formed an influential body of opinion, largely centring in the more conservative elements in society, who were strongly in favour of closer and more cordial relations with the erstwhile mother country. Soon these parties were to congeal around the opposing figures of Jefferson and Hamilton. The former declared that the British nation and, above all others, the King and his ministers hated America: the latter that he could not foresee any solid grounds of difference between the two countries. The diplomats who actually negotiated the treaty parted in mutual respect, warming in some cases into cordiality. David Hartley wrote to the

[1] Morison and Commager, I, p. 227.

265

Foreign Office after the final signature, expressing his sense of the "fairness, personal character and equitable conduct" of the American plenipotentiaries,[1] and added, even more strongly, "Upon this argument I always make my stand—that we may proceed to open an intercourse between our two countries, as nearly as possible, to the point of *as we were*."[2] Even one of the Americans, Jay, could remark on the question of federal union with Britain, "as for regaining the affections of America, time . . . would be required . . . but in a few years things would become right probably for some wise association or other, because common interests would generate it."[3] After the signature of the Preliminary Articles on 30 November, 1782, at Oswald's lodgings in Paris, all the commissioners, British and American, went out to dine with Franklin at Passy. In such an atmosphere there was some hope for the future.

II

TWENTY months elapsed between the signing of the definitive peace and the presentation of his credentials by the first American Minister to Britain, which opened formal diplomatic relations between the two states, but Britain's first representative was not to reach the United States until six years later. In sending the honest, outspoken and sometimes irritable, John Adams, the Congress may not have chosen the most diplomatic of men, but did show the importance it attached to relations with the one-time mother country, since he was among the most distinguished American leaders, a future President and one of those omitted in 1777 from the list of rebels that George III had announced his willingness to pardon. His first interview with the King was rather tense, but he got off to an excellent start by saying, "I shall esteem myself the happiest of men if I can be instrumental in recommending my country more and more to your Majesty's royal benevolence and . . . restoring . . . the old good-nature and the old good-humour between people who, though separated by an ocean and under different governments, have the same language, a similar religion and kindred blood." George, according to Adams, replied with obvious emotion:

> Sir, the circumstances of this audience are so extraordinary, the language you have now held is so extremely proper and the feelings

[1] Q. R. B. Mowat, *The Diplomatic Relations of Great Britain and the United States* (London, 1925), p. 13.

[2] Mowat, *Diplomatic Relations*, p. v.   [3] Q. Miller, p. 645.

you have discovered so justly adapted to the occasion that I must say that I not only receive with pleasure the assurance of the friendly dispositions of the United States, but that I am very glad the choice has fallen upon you to be their Minister. . . . I will be very frank with you. I was the last man in the Kingdom to consent to the separation; but the separation having been made and having become inevitable, I have always said, as I say now, that I would be the first to meet the friendship of the United States as an independent Power.

But Adams's mission did not develop on quite the comfortable lines that this suggested. Socially he and his wife lived an active life, particularly amongst the Whigs, but many English people, especially those influenced by the bitter exiled Loyalists, remained deeply hostile. C. F. Adams, Adams's grandson, wrote in his *Memoir of His Grandfather*: "Of civility, cold and formal, such as only the English know how in perfection to make offensive, there was enough. No marked offence, but supercilious indifference." His situation was not made easier by the critical state of relations between the thirteen states at home in these years prior to the adoption of the new Constitution: "To an indifferent observer looking from the English point of view, Mr. Adams soon ceased to appear as representing anything but disorder. . . . In Great Britain, especially, this spectacle was witnessed with a mixed feeling of disgust and exultation. No disposition to palliate faults or to overlook errors. The observation of them served rather as a relief to wounded pride."[1] But, uncomfortable as the position of any diplomatic representative of Congress anywhere was at this time, it was primarily Great Britain's refusal to send a representative to America which made it impossible for Adams to achieve the object of his mission by clearing up the outstanding difficulties between the two countries. His position became in time so humiliating that the King was said to have snubbed him severely when he was presenting Jefferson at Court, an action, incidentally, which was hardly likely to modify Jefferson's dislike of all things British. When taxed with their failure to appoint a Minister, the British Government stated that they were awaiting the inauguration of the new Constitution, a polite way of indicating their mistrust of the chaotic situation arising from the lack of an effective central government in America; later, when the Constitution was put into effect they fell back upon the argument, in which there was probably some truth, that it was difficult to get a suitable envoy for a post so far away and in such an uncongenial environment. Fundamentally, however, there can be little doubt that the British reluctance was con-

[1] Q. W.A.A.E., pp. 9-10, 13, 14.

nected with her refusal to implement the Treaty of Paris until, as she considered, the United States had done so. It was small wonder, in this situation, that Adams shortly tired of brazening out his difficult position, and arranged his recall in 1788.

The United States very understandably refused to send a successor to Adams until the British sent their first Minister, but Gouverneur Morris, a Federalist sympathetic to Britain and close to the President, who was in France on business, was in 1790 sent to London in a semi-official capacity, which was a sign of the anxiety of Washington and the Federalists to promote good relations with the British. Morris, even in his semi-official role, was able to achieve more than Adams, for he was well suited to the task and his contacts were very much better, largely because his brother, General Staats Morris, who had married the Duchess of Gordon, was living in London at the time. Though his relations with Fox and the Opposition Whigs were the more cordial, he got on well with Pitt and with Leeds, the Foreign Secretary, and was careful to make the best of his position by ostentatiously remaining in some degree on intimate terms with the French Embassy. In an interview with Pitt and Leeds in 1790 he raised, among other matters, the question of a British Minister in the United States. When asked in return by the Prime Minister about an American representative in Britain, he replied that the United States would almost certainly make an appointment if England did so. After a considerable delay, he prevailed upon Leeds' successor, Grenville, to appoint a British Minister Plenipotentiary to the "Court of President Washington".[1]

As a result of this decision, George Hammond, a young English diplomat of only twenty-eight, was appointed, and reached America in 1791, but would not present his credentials until an American Minister to London had been nominated. The British authorities had picked a staunch and obstinate Tory, and, though he married an American wife, Hammond was not a success. Partly through the difficulty of his position, partly through his mistrust of democratic tendencies in America particularly after the outbreak of the French Revolution, and partly through his character and opinions, he acquired a reputation for coldness and became extremely unpopular at the time of Jay's Treaty, so that he was by no means sorry to be recalled in 1795. His opposite number in London, Thomas Pinckney, took up his appointment towards the end of 1792, and, though he was much more successful than Hammond, did not achieve as much as might have been expected from the fact that he and his brother, like many other Southerners, had

[1] Q. ibid, p. 35.

been educated at Westminster and the Middle Temple. Respectable and amiable, he lacked driving power, and though, as usual, he received kindness from the Whigs, he was, according to Morris, looked at rather askance in Court circles. He had not the advantage of being of the inner Federalist group, and so, after the deterioration of the situation consequent upon the outbreak of war between Britain and France in 1793, he had to accept virtual supersession by Washington's special envoy, John Jay. He was somewhat mollified, no doubt, by being sent on a mission to Spain, in which he was successful, but soon after his return to England he asked for leave to return home, which he did in July, 1796.

The content as well as the form of these newly inaugurated diplomatic relations was not too auspicious, for difficulties at once became apparent. In the years before the signing of the Treaty of London of 1794, commonly known as Jay's Treaty, four main questions occupied the attention of the two governments, three of them rising out of the Treaty of Versailles. The first was that of the commercial relationship of the two countries; the second and third, which rapidly became bound up together, were the evacuation of the western posts by Britain, and the fulfilment of her obligations to British creditors and Loyalists by the United States. A fourth and formidable question arose out of the war which broke out in 1793 between Britain and Revolutionary France, that of neutral rights.

When Hartley said to the American commissioners in 1783, "Our respective territories are in vicinity, and, therefore, we must be inseparable. Great Britain, with the British power in America, is the only nation with whom, by absolute necessity, you must have the most intimate concerns", he was giving expression to the feeling, which had been strong in the liberal minds responsible for the Treaty, that it must —and would—be followed by a very high degree of commercial reciprocity between the two nations. But, unfortunately, all English minds—as the war itself had shown clearly enough—were not liberal, and there had already been great uneasiness in commercial circles about the preliminaries of peace laid before Parliament on 27 January, 1783. These did not clarify the commercial situation at all, so that the legislation, prohibiting all trade with the American colonies which had been passed on the outbreak of war, remained in operation; this gave the matter great urgency, while, in any case, the Navigation Acts would remain even if the prohibition was lifted. On 3 March Pitt, still acting temporarily as Chancellor of the Exchequer after the fall of Shelburne's ministry, consequent on the vote of censure by the House of Commons on the peace preliminaries, introduced a comprehensive and radical measure designed to settle the basis of the whole American trade. The bill opened with a repeal of the prohibitory legislation, and continued with an expression of intention to establish trade "on the most enlarged principles of reciprocal benefit to both countries".[1] It admitted American goods in American ships to the ports of Great Britain and her possessions in the New World, on the same terms as British goods in British ships; it continued the same drawbacks, exemptions and bounties on exports from Britain to the United States as in colonial days, and gave equal rights to American with British ships in the export of goods from British ports in America to the United States. This in effect admitted Americans freely to that part of British trade upon which they had in colonial days overwhelmingly concentrated their efforts.

Opposition to the measure developed as the debate proceeded, and soon came to be led very effectively by Lord Sheffield, many of whose arguments were, in the narrow sense of immediate British economic interest, powerful and cogently presented. He pointed out particularly that Britain could have all the trade she needed with America without the necessity of granting such generous terms; she alone had the industrial products and the capital which America had to have, and, under the terms of the bill, America was making no reciprocal contribution to outweigh this dominant consideration. "By clinging to her navigational laws, under which she had grown great, Britain could make the Americans pay for their own political independence."[2] To this powerful economic consideration was undoubtedly added a Tory willingness to re-establish Britain in her own esteem at the expense of those who had disrupted the old Empire, a sentiment fiercely encouraged by Loyalist exiles living in England such as Deane, Galloway and Oliver, who even fostered hopes that this economic weapon might bring New England back into the fold, a contingency which might not have been inconceivably remote in 1814. Thus opinion hardened against the measure, and it was shelved. Hartley, Fox's emissary in the American negotiations, fought fiercely for some kind of commercial treaty, though he was handicapped by the American insistence on absolute reciprocity in any intercourse, but the opposition of the

[1] Q. A. L. Burt, *The United States, Great Britain and British North America, From the Revolution to the Establishment of Peace after the War of 1812* (London, 1940), pp. 55-56.　　[2] Ibid, p. 58.

mercantile interests and the country's very deep (and not altogether unfounded) fear for its maritime supremacy proved too strong, and Fox lost the battle to the more conservative elements in the coalition led by North.

Fox did, however, later secure, first, the repeal of the prohibitory legislation, and second, governmental power for six months to regulate trade by Order-in-Council. An order of 2 July drafted by William Knox, an arch-Tory who believed it better *"to have no Colonies at all, than not to have them subservient to the maritime strength and commercial interests of Great Britain"*,[1] reopened a limited trade between the United States and the West Indies, but, since it excluded American fish and meat, two of the most important exports, and confined it to British subjects in British bottoms, it was a great blow to American hopes. The Act empowering regulation by Order-in-Council was renewed annually until 1788, when it was made permanent; at the same time some rights of trade between America and Britain proper, as well as the West Indies, were granted, but the barrier against American trade with the British North American provinces was just as high as that against the trade of other foreigners. Gradually the idea of reciprocity faded. When Pitt succeeded Fox he was at first working on too narrow a margin of support to live up to his own original designs, and by the time he was firmly in power his desire to do so had cooled. On 2 May, 1790, Gouverneur Morris wrote to Washington that he inclined to think that the administration "consider a treaty of commerce with America as being absolutely unnecessary and that they are persuaded they shall derive all benefit from our trade without treaty."[2]

The hopes of those who thought, with Sheffield, that the Maritime Provinces would be able to take over the American trade with the West Indies in provisions and lumber, were disappointed by the low output of these things in the Provinces, for they even had to be imported thereto for domestic consumption under regulations suspending the full rigour of the Navigation Acts. These gaps in the wall between the Maritime Provinces and the United States were never closed, and were even extended in 1793, despite the fact that great quantities of the goods imported from the United States were re-exported to the West Indies. Furthermore, the illicit trade in many commodities must have attained vast proportions, for the broken coast line, on which American rights to fish were guaranteed, was a smuggler's paradise. At the Caribbean end, the legal—to say nothing of the illegal—gaps in the protective

[1] Q. Harlow, I, p. 479.   [2] Q. W.A.A.E., p. 26.

wall were far more extensive; indeed, so great was the need of American lumber and provisions, and so numerous and sweeping were the resultant *ad hoc* proclamations of the local authorities suspending parts of the restrictions, that these became more honoured in the breach than the observance.[1]

To the West, though there were no legal gaps in the wall between the United States and Canada proper, in so far as commerce by sea and down the St. Lawrence was concerned, the long inland frontier presented a new kind of problem to the British Government, who answered it in the end by delegating the decision to the local authority, which in effect meant opening up by 1786 virtually unlimited trade in this area between the two peoples. There thus emerged quite clearly "the dual aspects of British policy toward North America which were to persist for at least another twenty years, that is to say, the oceanic and the continental. Any matter which affected tidewater, the great semicircle from Newfoundland to the West Indies, or world markets, was bound to receive closer attention and more deliberate regulation than what happened in the interior of the North American continent."[2] Thus the sluices in the dykes of the Mercantile system were few, and were as carefully controlled as possible on the seaboard, whereas on the inland frontier the flow of goods was virtually uncontrolled; already it was suggested that Upper Canada could most easily draw its imports from Europe through the geographically more convenient United States rather than down the St. Lawrence. This little measure of interchange in the West was almost all that was left of the high hopes of reciprocity which had flourished in 1782, and it owed more to the lack of interest of the British Government in this wild and undeveloped area than to any conversion of the English ruling class as a whole to liberal trade policies. In any case, it affected only the inland provinces and not even the whole of British North America, let alone the English homeland. Free trade was still a very distant dream.

Article 7 of the Treaty of Versailles had laid down that "his Britannic Majesty shall with all convenient speed . . . withdraw all his Armies, Garrisons and Fleets from the said United States". This was not done in the case of a number of Western posts now on American territory, notably Ogdensburg, Oswego, Niagara, Erie, Sandusky, Detroit and Michilimackinac,* which gave to those who garrisoned

---

[1] Alice B. Keith, "Relaxations in the British Restrictions on the American trade with the British West Indies, 1783-1802" (in *Journal of Modern History*, XX, 1948.)

[2] Brebner, p. 71. * See Map 1.

them effective control over a vast tract of the United States. The withdrawal of these British troops became the first object of American diplomacy, though one not attained for more than a decade. Adams, Morris and Pinckney all failed to obtain it, and it was only achieved by Jay at the cost of terms which involved him in immense unpopularity.

When Adams asked Pitt when the posts would be handed over, he replied "that it was the intention of His Majesty's Ministers to comply with the treaty, in its fullest extent, whenever the courts of law in the United States were open to British creditors."[1] Very soon the American refusal, for the most part, to fulfil the obligations undertaken by them to restore the rights and properties of the Loyalists, was added to this as a reason for British retention of the forts. The Americans, for their part, explained their remissness on the accurate, if highly convenient, constitutional ground that Congress had no power whatever to compel the thirteen sovereign states to honour the obligations it had assumed on their behalf, a fact of which the American commissioners had never made any secret, but which had been winked at by the British in their desire for peace, just as the Americans, for the same reason, had turned a blind eye to the very real possibility that Britain might not give up the posts when the time came. The Americans also complained that the British had violated the treaty, by carrying away with their armies Negroes who had been slaves; this they had done largely because the idea of returning captured slaves, whom they had freed, to their masters was distasteful to them. The American Government argued, too, that the British retention of the posts had deprived the American people of a trade which would have gone a long way towards paying their debts to their British creditors. But none of these reasons was the fundamental one which caused the retention of the forts, nor as A. L. Burt has conclusively shown, was it due primarily to Canadian desire to keep the fur trade. Montreal interests certainly wanted to keep it, and at first this fact weighed with the British Government, but it soon ceased to do so since the cost of keeping up the garrisons far exceeded the profits derived from the trade. For a brief period Britain nursed the vain hope that American Westerners of the type of Aaron Burr might, in their fear of Spain with her control of the mouth of the Mississippi and the stranglehold it gave her over the commerce of its valley, return to the British fold in return for military aid against the Spaniards, but this was a mere passing phase and no more the chief British motive than was her desire for pelts. What then was that motive?

As far back as 1763 the British Government, assuming the French

[1] Q. Mowat, *Diplomatic Relations*, p. 18.

tradition of retaining good relations with the Indians in order to continue the Canadian trade, had tried to protect them by preventing any except a controlled westward expansion of the American colonies beyond the Appalachians. The policy of the Americans, intent upon settlement and not only upon trade, had been, and was to be, very different and much more ruthless. The frontier settler was understandably feared and hated by the Indian, and the Indian warrior equally understandably feared and hated by the settler. Even when wise and moderate heads in the American central government realized the need for a balanced and orderly Indian policy on the frontier, they could effect little against the opposition of the frontier society. Once again, after, as during the Revolution, it became clear that the urge for westward expansion, probably the most deep-seated in American life, could not be challenged with impunity. The British Government had long been pledged to the Indians of the West to protect them, and now they had pledged themselves to do just the reverse, by handing over the Indian lands to the Americans whom the Indians hated. It appeared that they had to break their word to somebody. First to those on the spot, who felt the difficulty most acutely, and then to the Government in London, there occurred the idea of retaining the western posts indefinitely, or at least until such time as they could restore British prestige with the Indians, who were as important to the future of Canada as to that of the United States, and induce them to come to terms with the Americans. To this end they held on to the forts, while, in Canada, Governor Haldimand, and later Lord Dorchester, endeavoured without success to convince the Americans of the necessity of making a satisfactory treaty direct with the Indians and the Indians of the necessity of coming to terms with the victors of the late war. Actual efforts at mediation failed completely, and only the initial weakness of the central government of the United States prevented the Americans from taking matters into their own hands. When they tried to do so by sending a force against the Indians under General St. Clair in 1790, and again in 1791, he was, on both occasions, utterly defeated.

The position in the West became increasingly difficult, for the British, being the allies of the Indians, not only protected them in effect by holding the forts, but also traded with them in supplies and arms which they used against the Americans, who could hardly be blamed for believing, even more ardently than they already did, in the villainy of British designs against the United States. Britain, on the other hand, was increasingly apprehensive of a surprise attack on the forts by the Americans, under the guise of an expedition against the Indians, and as a result it was rashly decided by the Canadian authorities, on purely military grounds, to build a new fort at Miami on the vital Maumee river. The United States had always taken a strong line in theory about the posts, but her weakness internationally and in the West had hitherto prevented her from getting her way. In 1791 her fortunes seemed at their nadir, and the British Government was even toying with the quite unrealistic idea of a great neutral Indian buffer state, or zone, between Canada and the United States, under joint guarantee, but entirely carved out of American territory. But the hand of the United States Government was now steadily strengthened as Washington's first administration gained power and confidence. In the West her position improved fast under General Wayne, who in 1794 decisively defeated the Indians in the Battle of Fallen Timbers, within earshot and almost within sight of Fort Miami under its British commander, Major Campbell. Considering the fact that a small number of Canadian militiamen, acting as individuals, actually fought with the Indians, it is hardly surprising that the situation between British and Americans became so tense that in the course of the battle a match was actually lit in the fort to fire a gun on a group of the latter when, after a few breathless seconds, they suddenly and providentially wheeled away out of range. The marvel is that no actual hostilities broke out, but before long the danger was over, for in Europe a new situation had arisen which drastically altered British policy.

Jay had already left for Britain to negotiate a treaty by the time of this moment of suspense. Signs of British weakening on the question of the posts had already appeared as early as 1790, when the Nootka Sound dispute between Britain and Spain, over an incident off the disputed territory of California, threatened war between the two countries, a war in which Britain would prize highly the friendship, or at least the neutrality, of the United States. This had come to nothing, for the Spaniards were unable to make a stand without the assistance of the navy of France, and in Paris the Revolution had already begun which nullified the Family Compact with Spain, so that the British attitude over the frontier posts stiffened once again. In 1793, however, actual war broke out between Britain and France, that war which was to last, with only one intermission, for over twenty years, and which was to change the face, not only of Anglo-American relations but also of the whole world. Already it had raised the first of those many Anglo-American disputes concerning neutral rights, which arose naturally from the conflicting interests of the greatest belligerent and the greatest neutral maritime power. The British Government, therefore, extended a

275

warm welcome to Washington's special envoy on his arrival in England, and early showed a willingness absolutely to vacate the western posts in return for what were by now considered more tangible advantages. The Treaty of Greenville, signed between the United States and the Indians in 1795 as a sequel to Wayne's victory, salved what prickings of conscience they still had over the redskin question, since the Americans now assumed the old British guarantee to the Indians, and the Indians accepted—they had little choice—the exclusive protection of the United States. For the way that protection was exercised in the future the British felt that they had no responsibility, a view with which, in practice at least, there can be no disagreement. In any case, in time of war blunt national self-interest comes to the fore, and in this war, which was to become one for Britain's national survival, self-interest clearly dictated to the British Government the early settlement of a problem so remote from the heart of Britain's interests.

III

ALL these questions, indeed, had come to seem unimportant to Britain, compared with those arising from the war itself, which were to dominate Anglo-American relations for the next twenty years and finally to involve the two nations in open war. They did not, alone, produce the War of 1812, but it is very hard not to accept the thesis that they, rather than westward expansion in the United States, were the principal cause of it. The question, which can be broadly described as that of the 'freedom of the seas', was, because it took the form of a series of doubtful points in a very uncertain body of international law, complex in its particulars but simple in its general outline. In time of war it is the vital interest of belligerents to weaken their enemies by reducing their trade with the outside world to a minimum. This is particularly so in the case of Great Britain who, because of her island position and her reliance upon her trade and colonial empire for her strength, had in 1793 long been pre-eminently a naval power, increasingly wont to bring pressure to bear upon her enemies by means of blockades, enforced by her paramount navy. In the Seven Years War this had been a powerful weapon in her hands, and in the War of Independence had so aroused neutral ire that she had been faced with the Armed Neutrality. For, and this is the crux of the matter, while it is the interest of belligerents to reduce all branches of the enemy's trade as much as possible, it is plainly the interest of neutrals to increase theirs as much as they are able, particularly since, as America discovered, war provides them with excellent opportunities of doing so at the expense of those nations which are at war.

As Adam Smith pointed out in the *Wealth of Nations,* in the conditions of land transportation of this period, the vast bulk of mankind's trade was carried on by sea, which means that it was among maritime powers that the weapon of blockade had by far its greatest effect. Furthermore, though blockade by land is possible, as Napoleon showed, it is a simple and clear-cut business and limited in its effect. Land frontiers are, on the whole, precise, and there were few limitations, even in the eighteenth century, to the absolute sovereignty of neutrals in their own territory. Only by open war, or the threat of it, could a belligerent having a common frontier with a neutral prevent that neutral from carrying on trade with the enemy over another of its land frontiers. At sea the case was very different. There were no serious disputes between naval powers involving their respective territorial waters, but between those narrow ribbons of sea there flowed the vast expanses of the ocean, where no sovereignty existed and few unchallenged writs ran. But this area of grave legal uncertainty had not escaped the attention of previous generations, who had endeavoured to avoid some of the vexatious and dangerous disputes arising in time of war by trying to create a system of international law, which no doubt served many useful purposes, but hardly that of simplifying the issues; an outright balance of crude force would have had this merit at least—it would have been more generally and easily understood. There are, of course, those today who believe that law of any kind is a mere cloak for the interplay of fundamental forces, and certainly in the realm of international law this appears to be more nearly so than in any other sphere of jurisprudence, but many in the eighteenth century, as perhaps today, genuinely believed in the international law that they expounded. We, however, shall not understand the situation which brought Britain and the United States to war, unless we apprehend the forces of self-interest which were at work below the surface technicalities of law.

And those technicalities are even more difficult to grasp than those of lawyers usually are because of their great uncertainty, which arose partly from the novelty of the whole concept of international law in the eighteenth century and partly from the fact that it was itself changing under pressure of events. Many historians and many lawyers in the twentieth century have come to recognize that any body of law tends to grow and alter as its circumstances change (and many would

277

say that this must be so if the law is to live and to serve its purpose), but very few, if any, of those concerned in the eighteenth century accepted this element of change, so that in its adjustment to new conditions the machinery of international law creaked and groaned, and created almost as much irritation as it allayed. Confusion was worse confounded by the fact that it was not changing from one known condition to another, but altering by means of the many differences of opinion already—indeed almost since its birth—apparent among its authorities. The opinions of Vattel differed from those of Grotius, as did the views of Britain from those of the United States, while many nations signed in practice treaties and conventions, which either rendered their theoretical view null by contradicting it, or made exceptions to it which proved the rule—one can take one's choice.

But beneath the confused triangular situation in these years, involving the two principal belligerents and the chief neutral, Britain, France and the United States, there lay a comparatively simple conflict of interest. The situation was particularly ominous for Anglo-American relations because it was unprecedented, in the sense that until 1776 America had been part of, and had contributed largely to, the maritime greatness of belligerent Britain, and because the sea-going trade of the United States, far from shrinking after Independence, grew so swiftly, especially during the war itself, that her tonnage was soon second only to that of Britain in size and importance. Her shipping in foreign trade rose from 123,893 tons in 1789 to 981,017 tons in 1810. Thus she became the greatest of the neutrals, and the one on whose shoulders the chief responsibility for defending the rights of neutrals, as she understood them, must fall. Indeed in the event, though there were some abortive attempts at reviving the Armed Neutrality, she stood virtually alone in this position, since the successes of the French and the increasing bitterness of the struggle with Britain made a long maintenance of neutrality by any important European power virtually impossible. Thus did those very maritime interests of the two powers, which had been their strongest bond in colonial days, thrust them into conflict. Only after the catharsis of 1812 and the decline of Mercantilism did the importance of the neutral rights issue fade. It lingered through the nineteenth century, but its importance was undermined by the fact that in the American Civil War the victorious North was forced, by her unusual role as the belligerent blockading power, to revise previous attitudes and to adopt in many respects the British viewpoint. When in 1914 she became once more the greatest of neutrals, her case carried, even to herself, rather less conviction than it had once done, while after she became a belligerent in 1917, it carried less still, for it ran directly contrary to her new interest. As always, interpretations of international law tended to respond to such changes in circumstance, and by the time the United States became a belligerent in World War II, there was no discernable difference between the ideas of the two nations.

But it was not the British and the Americans alone who took issue on grounds of international law, for the difficulties which arose between the United States and France were in theory no less formidable, and in practice brought them to the very brink of war in 1799. But after the renewal of European war in 1803 not only was a Republican and therefore instinctively anti-British administration in power in the United States, but, far more important, the British were triumphant at sea and even more determined to carry the struggle through to a successful conclusion. After the victory of Trafalgar in 1805 their naval supremacy was unchallenged, and French maritime commerce was virtually at a standstill, which meant that there were even greater opportunities of French trade for the Americans, and an even greater possibility of clashes with a Britain determined to prevent advantage being taken of them. Napoleon was well aware of this fact and played upon it to the utmost of his ability—with ultimate success in 1812. But by that date the whole level of the quarrel had altered, with the coming of Napoleon's Continental System and Britain's counter-blockade, since neither side any longer pretended that they were acting in accordance with even their own interpretations of international law, but merely maintained that they were effecting reprisals for the illegal actions of the enemy, which they would only cease when their opponent mended his ways. In fact, all pretence of legality fell away. Furthermore, another cause of Anglo-American friction, and one existing between these two alone, had been added to the Freedom of the Seas as a major issue, the impressment of seamen. Equally defended by the British and denounced by the Americans on grounds of international law, it had been a bone of contention since the beginning of the first war, but had become increasingly prominent as the strain of the long struggle told upon British maritime strength. Never as important to the United States materially as the commercial issue, it became emotionally on the American side perhaps the prime cause of war, for it concerned lives not money, to the former of which—as if to give the lie to the legend of the Almighty Dollar—American diplomacy has always been particularly sensitive.

What, then, were the legal issues apparently at stake between belligerent Britain and the neutral United States? Weaker neutral states had long and unsuccessfully endeavoured to build up a body of international law opposed to that put forward by Britain, the predominant naval power, but some small measure of agreement, of common ground, did exist between the two schools of thought. It was agreed by all parties that a belligerent could seize and condemn in a prize-court any neutral vessel sailing with contraband of war to an enemy port, that 'contraband' included arms and accoutrements of war; and that a belligerent could prohibit any neutral vessel, whatever her cargo, from entering or leaving a port which was effectively blockaded. Beyond this there was disagreement.

Successful maritime belligerents, particularly Britain, extended the definition of contraband to cover almost everything that could be used by enemy forces, whereas neutrals, particularly the United States (and incidentally belligerents unsuccessful at sea like the French) wished to interpret it in a much narrower sense. Britain wished as loose a definition of the term 'effective blockade', and the United States as strict a one, as possible. Britain held that, arising from the right to capture enemy vessels and goods at sea, she had a right also to seize enemy goods other than contraband from neutral ships, while the United States proclaimed the doctrine of 'free ships, free goods', that is to say that a neutral flag effectively protected enemy goods other than contraband. On the disputed question as to whether a belligerent had the right to prevent a neutral from entering a trade with the enemy which had been forbidden to that neutral in peace time (a step which France took by opening much of her trade to Americans once her own ships had been driven from the seas), there was no agreement at all between Britain and the United States, either as to the colonial or the coastal trade of the enemy. To prevent France getting succour in this way in the Seven Years War, British prize courts had proclaimed the new "Rule of the War of 1756". When pressed by the United States in 1794 to do so, Britain restricted the operation of this rule—in the case of the United States only, and without renouncing her full theoretical rights—to the direct trade by American vessels from the French West Indies to France, relying on the normal customs duties and costs of unloading and reloading to prevent excessive trans-shipment of goods via the United States to France. But later, Congress relaxed such taxes, and the American authorities winked at evasion, by which ships did not unload at all, but proceeded with their West Indian goods virtually direct to Europe, so that a great deal of commerce slipped through the British net into France. Thus between 1803 and 1805 the British courts re-established the doctrine of "continuous voyage", preventing indirect as well as direct passage of prohibited categories of goods, and in 1807 forbade all commerce of neutrals between ports under Napoleon's control, though by this time the various legal issues had been swallowed up in reprisals for the Berlin Decrees. In other words, undisguised self-interest had come to overshadow legal pretexts, and there was increasing bitterness on both sides of the Atlantic.

It is important to realize that, despite the beginning of free trade ideas before the war, notions of Mercantilism still dominated at least the British and French Governments, and they saw the measures of economic war not merely as adjuncts of military policy, but as a means of draining the enemy's commercial life-blood, at the same time as enriching oneself at his expense. One man's loss was still thought of as very much another's gain, and neutrals were by no means regarded as exempt from the operation of this law. Britain suspected that America was cheating her out of her rights and profiting at her expense, and she was confirmed in this view by observing how vastly American commerce had increased since 1789. These feelings were reciprocated in full measure. It was by no means difficult for Americans, with their memories of the Navigation Acts and of the British refusal after Independence, despite one-time promises of virtual reciprocity, very substantially to relax them, to believe that Britain was using the war as a means to an old familiar end, that of crushing the commerce of her rivals, of whom America was by now much the greatest. This suspicion alone might have produced the atmosphere necessary for war, but to it was added the burning issue of impressment, which was even more heavily charged with emotion.

The heart of the matter of impressment was as simple as that of Freedom of the Seas in commerce, perhaps simpler; the basic fact was that, in the harsh and difficult circumstances of contemporary service in the British Navy; it was a great and natural temptation to the sailor on a British naval vessel to desert to the British merchant navy, where conditions were much easier, or—far, far better—to the American merchant marine, where they were better still, and where, best of all, he was not liable to be 'pressed' once more into naval service. This temptation was very understandable in a service largely recruited by that highly inequitable system of conscription, the press gang, either on shore in port or actually from merchantmen at sea; and as a result of it many thousands of British naval seamen in the course of the long

281

war deserted to American ships. The British Navy, therefore, claimed the right to search all American vessels on the high seas, except those of the United States Navy, and to remove British deserters from them, and this right they exercised repeatedly. They impressed their nationals from their own merchant ships, whether they were deserters or not, and in practice they tended to do so from the ships of neutrals also. This the United States strongly resisted, agreeing with the words of Gouverneur Morris to the Duke of Leeds, "I believe, my Lord, this is the only instance in which we are not treated as aliens."[1] Once again, of course, this situation was a new one, for in previous wars America had been either friend or foe, and it was unique to Anglo-American relations not only because of the size of the American merchant marine, hungry in its expansion for recruits, but also because it was virtually impossible to tell a fugitive Briton from an American, so that unlimited possibilities of confusion and deception existed.

The question was not at the beginning of the war very serious, but as the years passed, despite some improvement in British naval conditions following the mutinies at the Nore and Spithead, the strain on the British Navy became increasingly severe, while with the decline of her merchant marine, replacement of deserters became much more difficult. So grave was the situation that Albert Gallatin, one of the American delegation who negotiated the Treaty of Ghent, estimated that by 1807 the British were losing annually at least 2,500 men to American ships; as a result the British depredations upon the crews of American vessels became more frequent and more ruthless.

The British Government, however, did not base its right of search upon force alone, but upon its sovereign rights over its nationals, at least in places where they were not subject to the territorial jurisdiction of another power. The common view of the nations at this period was that nationality was inalienable, and the British Government held that no British subject could throw off his obligations to the British Crown. The United States has, ever since an Act of Congress of 1790, for the obvious reason that her immigration was on so stupendous and unprecedented a scale, taken the opposite point of view, and insisted on the right of expatriation; in due time she was to bring many states, including Britain, largely round to her point of view. But in this instance the United States did not raise the naturalization issue, and merely denied the British right to search their ships for deserters, though the later history of the naturalization controversy has perhaps made American historians even less patient of the British case than they

[1] Q. W.A.A.E., p. 26.

might otherwise have been. In fact, it was the abuses of the practice which caused most of the trouble. An American captain, his vessel boarded under threat of force and faced with the removal of a sizable portion of his crew, was not likely to co-operate in a process of sorting out impostors from genuine Americans, in the legality of which he did not in any case believe, while the British naval officer who conducted the search and who had desperate need of seamen, was not likely to distinguish very carefully the British deserter from the American sailor, when, as it always was, the armed strength was on his side. Abuses thus arose all too easily. In an effort to prevent them the American Government began to issue, through their officials, certificates of American citizenship, but since these rapidly multiplied and could readily be purchased for very small sums, they only made matters worse by inflaming ill-feeling. Thus, as the war went on, the number of British deserters in the American marine was probably matched by the number of Americans pressed into service in the British Navy, and an intense hatred burned in America of a system which Britain believed had become virtually indispensable to her if she was to defeat Napoleon.

IV

BUT in the few months between the outbreak of the war in 1793 and the signing of Jay's Treaty, these troubles existed only in embryo; it was not until the later years of the great war that they brought about open hostilities between Britain and the United States. Not but that considerable tension, and even the danger of actual war, existed between them in 1793. As we have seen, the British Navigation Acts provided a nagging background of discontent, and events in the West were moving rapidly to a crisis when France declared war on Britain on 1 February, 1793. The issue was further complicated by the growing division between the nascent Republican and Federalist parties in the United States. At first Washington was able to get a sufficient measure of agreement between the two factions to allow the Administration to function; Jefferson and Hamilton were agreed, for instance, on the President's Proclamation of what amounted to neutrality in the European war, which was signed on 22 April, 1793. But as Federalist disinclination to take issue with Britain and mistrust of Revolutionary France became apparent and even increased, more and more open discord developed.

Hammond, the British envoy, was misled by his Tory prejudices when he suggested that the new Constitution lacked stability, but he was soon able (as had been his unofficial predecessor, the British agent Beckwith) to appreciate, and to cause his government at home to appreciate, that there was a strong party in America desirous of good relations with Britain. In fact Hamilton encouraged the British representatives to have recourse to him as Secretary of the Treasury when they could not get what they wanted from Secretary of State Jefferson, and this certainly contributed to the latter's resignation on 31 December, 1793. We must note that during his term of office Anglo-American relations had deteriorated markedly, even though it was by no means entirely his doing. His sympathizers in Congress in 1791 brought forward legislation designed as retaliation against the hated British Navigation Acts, but the Federalists were able to stop it in the Senate, and, after the appointment of the British Minister in America, a report Jefferson had prepared on the subject was pigeon-holed. It is possible that this threat of economic retaliation expedited the appointment of Hammond but, until the outbreak of war, the attitude of Jefferson was probably not widely different from that expressed by Morris to Pitt on the subject of the frontier posts in 1790, "[T]he conduct you have pursued naturally excites resentment in every American bosom. We do not think it worth while to go to war with you for these posts, but *we know our rights, and will avail ourselves of them when time and circumstances may suit.*"[1]

Circumstances began to look more as if they did suit after it became apparent, from the British Order-in-Council of 8 June, 1793, that she was determined to try and prevent the French from profiting by their action on the outbreak of war in opening up colonial trades, hitherto forbidden, to the United States. This Order authorized the enforced purchase of food cargoes on neutral ships bound for French ports, but was succeeded on 6 November by another, much more severe, which ordered the detention of "all ships laden with goods the produce of any colony belonging to France, or carrying provisions or other supplies for the use of any such colony".[2] It did not improve matters that the first information even Hammond received of the Order was accompanied by news of the actual seizure of some three hundred American ships from among those trading with the French islands. To cap all this, intelligence was soon afterwards received of an unwise, if supposedly secret, speech made to an important gathering of Indians

[1] Q. W.A.A.E., p. 28.
[2] S. F. Bemis, *Jay's Treaty* (New York, 1923), p. 158.

in the West by Lord Dorchester, virtually prophesying an Anglo-American war and adjuring them to take the British side. Amidst all this, Jefferson's pigeon-holed report on the Navigation Acts, which recommended vigorous retaliatory measures, was presented to Congress early in December, and, despite his resignation in the interim, an Act was passed in April placing an embargo for one month, and later for two, on all shipping in American harbours, in the hope of shutting off the food supplies of the British West Indies. The two countries at the turn of the year were obviously on the verge of war, and even the Federalists supported measures to. strengthen the defences of the United States.

But already a rift had appeared in the clouds, for the British Government realized that it had overstepped the mark by the Order-in-Council of 6 November, which exceeded even the strictest interpretation of the Rule of 1756, since a limited trade with the French West Indies in ships of small burthen had been allowed to the Americans before the war. By a new Order-in-Council of 8 January, 1794, which was a practical compromise with the United States—alone among neutrals—Britain receded even beyond the Rule of 1756, and contented herself with the seizure of vessels laden in the French West Indies with produce of those islands and sailing thence for Europe, though she also naturally continued to insist on her own interpretations of international law in other spheres. Furthermore, on 6 August another Order-in-Council waived certain restrictions on legal appeals in prize cases, which was important to the Americans because colonial Vice-Admiralty courts were notoriously partial. A yet more conciliatory Order twelve days later, which stopped the enforced purchases, was in fact prompted more by a good harvest in Britain than by tactful diplomacy, and the practice was begun again in the spring of 1795 when the price of wheat rose substantially. The August Orders did not stop the passage of the American embargo but they did encourage the Federalist leaders to make a great effort for peace by sending a special mission to London. Hamilton wisely abandoned any idea of going himself, owing to his unpopularity, and advised Washington to send Jay. His appointment was confirmed by the Senate, which also defeated, though only by the casting vote of John Adams, a measure passed by the House providing for the suspension of all commercial intercourse with Britain until American grievances, including the evacuation of the posts, were satisfied. Jay had said that the passage of this bill would make his task impossible. On 12 May he embarked for England.

By the time that negotiations were well begun, even the tension in the West had abated, and Dorchester had been reprimanded by the British Government for his part in raising it. Though American opinion remained inflamed, the immediate threat of war was ended. But the task that faced Jay was a formidable one, for it was doubtful whether the British Government would—or, on the neutral rights issue, could— concede anything like enough to satisfy popular demand in the United States. As he himself said before he heard of his appointment, "Such were the prejudices of the American people that no man could form a treaty with Great Britain, however advantageous it might be to the country, who would not by his agency render himself so unpopular and odious as to blast all hope of political preferment." As Chief Justice of the United States he might be considered beyond the need of such preferment, and his past career as Secretary of State and one of the peace commissioners in 1783 seemed to render him, as Hamilton wrote, "the only man in whose qualifications for success there would be perfect confidence"; but he was opposed by the Republicans as a Federalist sympathizer. Even though he was not of British but of Huguenot descent, he was considered as very English in manner and too pro-British. His health was not good and his difficulties were increased by the fact that he had to go out of his way to mollify Minister Pinckney's sensibilities by emphasizing the dignity and solemnity of his special mission to the British Government. He was also instructed to keep before that government "the strong agitations excited in the people of the United States, by the disturbed condition of things between them and Great Britain".[1] This was hardly necessary, since with his ship came a large backlog of letters from Hammond to Grenville, making quite clear the gravity of the situation, of which the British had so far been unaware, and this inclined them, with one war on their hands already, to respond warmly to Jay's overtures. In fact Jay felt that he was received with nothing but friendliness, even the King going out of his way to be conciliatory. Though, or perhaps because, Grenville received a report on Jay which read, "He can bear any opposition to what he advances, provided that regard is shown to his abilities. . . . On the whole they could not have made a better choice, as he certainly has good sense and judgment, both of which must have been mellowed since I saw him; but almost every man has a weak and assailable quarter and Mr. Jay's weak side is *Mr. Jay*",[2] they got on very well together, proceeding by conversation and without correspondence or secretaries. Jay had a full sense of the importance of his

[1] Q. W.A.A.E., pp. 41, 43.　　[2] Q. Mowat, *Diplomatic Relations*, p. 23.

mission and wrote that it was not to be "a trial of diplomatic fencing, but a solemn question of peace or war between two peoples, in whose veins flowed the blood of a common ancestry, and on whose continued good understanding might perhaps depend the future freedom and happiness of the human race."[1]

Both parties desired peace, and they wisely ceased recriminations as to who had first violated the Treaty of Versailles, while agreeing to maintain the *status quo* on the Canadian-American frontier during the course of the negotiations, a situation which they did not attempt to define too precisely. On the two major questions facing them, it soon became clear that Britain was quite ready to evacuate the posts, but that she would not yield any of the principles regarding neutral rights and impressment, thus demonstrating her primary preoccupation with maritime rather than Canadian affairs, particularly when engaged in a general war. It was Jay's realization that she would not, or could not, concede more, and his acceptance of the fact that made a treaty possible at all, whatever might be its reception in America. The Treaty "of Amity, Commerce and Navigation"[2] was signed in London on 19 November, 1794, the first Article promising "a firm inviolable and universal Peace, and a true and sincere Friendship" between the two peoples.

The second Article promised the evacuation of the posts, which was fully effected by the British in 1796, as soon as American forces arrived to take them over. The third Article, harking back to an abortive proposal of Jay himself at the time of the Treaty of Versailles, which was then designed to protect the Canadian and Indian rights to trade south of the border, and was now made reciprocal on Jay's suggestion, guaranteed to Americans, British and Indians, subject to reasonable limitations on the goods to be carried and subject to the payment of normal duties without national discrimination, the right "freely to pass and repass by Land, or Inland Navigation, into the respective Territories and Countries of the two Parties on the Continent of America . . . and freely to carry on trade and commerce with each other." The land of the Hudson's Bay Company was excepted, since it was forbidden even to British traders, and it was specifically confirmed that no exception was made by this article to the full application of the Navigation Acts on the seaboard. The origin of the article in the minds of the Montreal fur traders is clearly shown by the special provision that no "Duty of Entry" should ever be levied by either party on peltry

[1] Q. W.A.A.E., p. 45.   [2] Treaties, II, p. 245 *et seq.*

brought overland, as also by the clause which stated that the British right to free navigation of the Mississippi, guaranteed in "the Treaty of Peace", should be confirmed. A proposal by Jay, which echoed a prophetic demand by John Adams in 1783, for that demilitarization of the Canadian-American border, which was later to be the particular pride of the two countries, came to nothing, and no immediate solution proved possible of the problem of the boundary in the north-west, between the Lake of the Woods and the Mississippi.* Jay could not accept either of the British proposals for a new definition, since these involved a cession of territory claimed by the United States, nor would he agree with Grenville's contention that it was the obvious intention of the original treaty so to have drawn the boundary, that British subjects would have had easy access to that navigation of the Mississippi which was guaranteed to them. Grenville would not accept the idea of a joint commission to settle it unless the latter point was included in its terms of reference. All that could be decided was, on Jay's very sensible suggestion, to carry out a joint survey, which would be followed by "amicable negotiation", and this provision formed the content of Article 4. That part of the confusion in the north-eastern boundary due to the error concerning the St. Croix river line was much easier of settlement, and, in Article 5, a most fruitful and most important precedent in Anglo-American relations was set, by the decision, which was easily reached, to appoint a commission of three to decide the matter, one to be appointed by each party and the third by agreement between them or, if that did not materialize, by lot. The commissioners were to decide "what River is the River St. Croix intended by the Treaty", and when they had done so "both parties agree to consider such decision final and conclusive, so as that the same shall never thereafter be called into question, or made the subject of dispute or difference between them". The other ambiguities in the north-eastern boundary, both inland and in Passamaquoddy Bay and the Bay of Fundy, were not mentioned in the treaty.†

The method of joint commission was also applied to the awkward question of the recovery of British debts, on which Grenville absolutely insisted as a condition of the treaty. Two commissions of five, each appointed in a similar way to the commission of three described above, were to be set up, the first to decide upon a just settlement of the debts claimed by British merchants and others against American citizens and still outstanding from before the peace, the second to act in the same way with regard to the claims of Americans against the British Govern-

*† See p. 261 above.

ment and of Britons against the American Government, for damage done to them by illegal or irregular action during the war then in progress. In all three instances the governments promised to make full payment in specie. The establishment of the first commission represented a very considerable concession by the Government of the United States, which thus assumed responsibility for the debts of its individual citizens at a time when the newly opened Federal Courts were in fact beginning to adjudicate in these long-standing cases. A further article was designed to avoid recurrence of the original difficulty by its stipulation that private debts and money properties of individuals should never be sequestered or confiscated by either government in the event of national differences, "it being unjust and impolitick that Debts and Engagements contracted and made by Individuals having confidence in each other, and in their respective Governments, should ever be destroyed or impaired by national authority, on account of national Differences and Discontents". Yet another article protected the real property of the citizens of the two countries by laying down that it might be held and disposed of "in like manner as if they were Natives", which was an effort to prevent future discrimination similar to that against the Loyalists in the Revolution. These ten articles concluded the first and political portion of the treaty, the remainder of which was commercial and maritime in character; the two parts were distinguished by the fact that the first ten articles were to be permanent, while the remainder were to be of limited duration.

Of the potentially loose-ends left by these ten articles, only one was satisfactorily tied up in the immediate future, when on 25 October, 1798, the joint commission of three signed a unanimous award accepting the Schoodic (the St. Croix of Mitchell's map) as the true boundary between Maine and Nova Scotia in that area,* a decision unfavourable to American interests, even though very minor adjustments were made in their favour in the upper reaches. Though this was the only immediately successful arbitration arising from the treaty, it was peculiarly significant that its third member, chosen by agreement and not by lot, was an American, which made its decision against the American claim a very happy augury for the future of Anglo-American relations.

The other uncertainties in the north-eastern boundary, though a number were broached by this commission, remained unsettled, and, for some reason unknown, the joint survey of the Mississippi, a very wise preliminary to any solution of the north-west boundary problem,

*See Map 3.

was not carried out. The other two commissions, those on the debts and the claims, proved less successful. That on the British pre-war debts, which sat in Philadelphia, broke down in 1799, and that on mutual claims for spoliations suspended its operations in London when the British Government withdrew its commissioners in retaliation for the withdrawal of the American commissioners in Philadelphia. In 1802 a compromise convention was signed in London, which abrogated the article of Jay's Treaty setting up the former commission and agreed that the United States should pay £600,000 to Great Britain, "in the Money of the said United States"—a tribute to the effect of Hamilton's work in establishing the financial credit of the new government. The government of the United States never recovered, nor tried to recover, this sum from its own citizens whose private debts it thus settled. The convention directed the London commission to meet again, which it did, and in 1804 concluded its work with awards of £2,330,000 to American claimants and $143,428 to British claimants. Subtracting debt settlements from spoliation settlements left a balance of $7,641,572 in favour of the United States. The last had now been heard of these particular questions, which had haunted Anglo-American relations since the Treaty of Versailles, but unhappily they were not to be the last of their kind.

The commercial provisions of the treaty were for the most part embodied in the next six articles, which, even in their totality, were a veritable mouse compared with the mountain for which believers in reciprocity had once hoped. The extent of the concessions, indeed, belied the grandiose words of Article 11 which began, "It is agreed between His Majesty and the United States of America, that there shall be a reciprocal and entirely perfect Liberty of Navigation and Commerce, between their respective People," for it ended, "in the manner, under the Limitations, and on the Conditions specified in the following Articles". Yet a considerable measure of reciprocity was achieved, which one is inclined to underestimate by failing to appreciate fully the comprehensiveness, the rigidity and, above all, the complexity of the British Mercantile system, from the benefits as well as the disadvantages of which Americans had been excluded almost entirely since 1776. Because in later days reciprocity has come to be thought of primarily as a curtailment of tariffs and customs dues, it must be borne in mind that the British system contained a much more serious hindrance to foreign commerce than the financial—nothing less than the absolute exclusion of all foreign, including American, merchants, ships, and (virtually) crews, from all participation in her colonial trade. The trade of the

United Kingdom, as opposed to the empire as a whole, was not absolutely prohibited to foreigners, but they were subjected to severe hindrances; the coastal trade was forbidden to any vessel of which part-owner or master were alien, foreign ships were forbidden to import goods from any country but their own, and even those they could import were subjected to aliens' duties, while the long-standing prejudice against foreigners and the multifarious and sometimes effective, if fading, local regulations against them, made their position exceedingly difficult. On top of this, there might, of course, be a tariff on foreign goods carried in British vessels. Further complications might be introduced, even if the former prohibition was abolished, by the levying of port and harbour fees on foreign vessels, or by the raising of discriminatory tariffs against a particular nation. Broadly speaking, the commercial articles of the Treaty endeavoured to remove the barrier against American ships and merchants, and to prevent discriminatory fees or tariffs, but it was not designed to achieve immediately a lowering of tariff barriers; the free trade idea, which had seemed so compelling in Britain in the first flush of enthusiasm after 1776, had been there driven on to the defensive by the natural conservatism of the merchant class and by the long war with France.

The first detailed commercial Article, the twelfth, had an unfortunate history, for, despite the fact that the major portion of it was designed to satisfy the chief American commercial desire, freedom to trade with the West Indies, the right was granted subject to such stringent conditions and limitations that the Senate, very understandably, refused to ratify the whole of that part of it, a procedure to which Great Britain agreed in an additional article negotiated before ratification. This abortive section opened the West Indian trade to American merchants in ships of less than seventy tons (which were the chief type of ship engaged in the trade, but which could not compete with British ships by making the long haul to Europe), subject only to the same limitations, duties and charges as were imposed upon British merchants; but it insisted that their goods should be carried only to the United States, to prevent competition with British shipping elsewhere, and—a far more doubtful demand—that as long as this arrangement continued, the United States should prohibit the carriage by American vessels from the United States to any other part of the world whatsoever of all the great staple crops of the West Indies, molasses, sugar, coffee, cocoa, or cotton. Furthermore, British ships during the same period were to have the same right to export and import between the United States and the West Indies as Americans, at the time of the

291

signing of the treaty, enjoyed. The British object was to prevent American competition by the re-export of the produce of the West Indies from the United States, but they seriously over-reached themselves, since molasses, sugar and cotton were also important products of the United States, and since they insisted on equal participation in American trade with the West Indies while appearing to refuse to reciprocate, except in certain parts of their own possessions. The former consideration was quite sufficient to ensure rejection by the Senate, and it is hard to see how Jay ever hoped for acceptance of this provision. The part of the twelfth Article which was not suspended in effect pledged the two governments to reopen negotiations on its expiry, which was to take place two years after the termination of the Anglo-French war, in order to examine the West Indian trade with a view to its extension, and to consider a further definition of disputed questions of maritime rights. The justification for the rejection of the part of Article 12 by the Senate, and for the American belief that Britain was getting too much and giving too little in the Treaty, was greatly weakened by its remaining commercial articles which granted substantial concessions to the United States.

The fourteenth Article established between "all the Dominions of His Majesty in Europe, and the Territories of the United States, a reciprocal and perfect liberty of Commerce and Navigation", which was more than an empty phrase since it formally abandoned, as far as Americans were concerned, that tradition in British economic life which discouraged, as much as possible, foreign merchants from participation even in British homeland trade. It is true that it was reciprocal, and that British merchants gained the right to trade in the United States, and were, because of their superior capital resources, the better able to dominate Anglo-American commerce for many years, but it is also worth remembering that, because of the imperative American need of British goods, it is unlikely that the United States could for many years effectively have excluded the British from their trade. The thirteenth Article granted Americans certain rights of trade with the British East Indies; they were given, subject to certain safeguards, which for the most part applied equally to British merchants, the right to carry on commerce between those islands and the United States in vessels of any size and at no higher charges than those payable by British vessels entering the ports of the United States, provided that they did not enter the coastal trade of the British territories, and provided that their trade was bona fide trade with their own country and not a concealed carrying trade. Here the British showed the same concern for their carrying trade, and for their shipping which depended on it, as in the provisions concerning the West Indian trade embodied in Article 12, but this should not blind us to the extent of the concessions granted by Britain to America. This provision gave to Americans, as far as trade with the United States was concerned, a right denied to all British merchants except those few who were actually members of the East India Company, which had a British monopoly of the East India trade. In effect, Articles 12 and 13 together admitted the Americans in a limited degree to the trade of virtually the whole British Empire, and a comparison of these terms with those of the Anglo-French commercial treaty of 1786, which confined itself largely to a reduction of customs duties on certain commodities, will readily demonstrate their sweeping nature.

The penultimate commercial Article guaranteed mutual 'most favoured nation' treatment, prohibiting any discrimination against each other's trade which was not equally applied to all other nations, and endeavouring to equalize and stabilize tonnage duties payable in the ports of both countries. Most important from the British point of view, it was "agreed, that the United States will not . . . increase the now subsisting difference between the Duties payable on the importation of any articles in British or in American Vessels," though in fact such action was unlikely, in view of the American demand for British goods, and of the fact that her tariff at this period was primarily for revenue purposes only. The final commercial Article granted mutual recognition of consuls for trade protection and of their special rights, a concession which Britain had sought for some time and which the United States had hitherto refused, partly out of mistrust and partly as an answer to the long British delay in appointing a Minister to Washington. General negotiations for the more exact equalization of duties on navigation were to be undertaken at the end of the war, along with the other regotiations arranged for that time. As has been seen, the Senate refused to ratify the article granting the right to trade with the West Indies in small vessels to the Americans, but in fact the islands were so dependent upon North America for provisions, and the Maritime Provinces were able to supply them with so little, that the British Government had, almost at once, to open just such a limited trade by Order-in-Council, and in effect to keep it open until the outbreak of war in 1812, after the end of which the matter was taken up again. As this implies, the negotiations, which were, according to the treaty, to have been undertaken two years after the termination of hostilities, never came to anything because the Peace of Amiens proved abortive and war broke out once again between Britain and France. The deterioration in Anglo-American relations which followed frustrated all hopes of a new treaty. In effect, however, the American merchant continued to trade with the British West Indian, illegally no doubt where not legally, to their mutual benefit, though Britain lost the excessive safeguards she had sought.

The remainder of the Treaty dealt with perhaps the most difficult question of all, and the one on which most criticism has been levelled at Jay, that of neutral rights. Because he knew that no treaty was possible unless he did so, he acquiesced, silently and temporarily, in British practices at sea. Article 7 provided compensation for American citizens who had been affected by the Orders-in-Council recently withdrawn, but there was virtually no mention in the treaty of any principle of maritime law which was seriously in dispute. There was, expressed in passages of considerable length, an effort to lay down rules which would avoid friction in the operation of those parts of the law on which there was substantial agreement between the parties, but the great area of dispute was left untouched. Reading through this part of the treaty, it is hard to avoid the conclusion that words were deliberately being multiplied in the largely unnecessary elucidation of agreed or minor matters, in order to obscure the fact that no one of the really momentous issues was being settled.

Thus, the procedure for seizing contraband was laid down, and contraband was defined (rather more in the British than in the American sense, since the list was a fairly comprehensive one which included naval stores), but the definition was not exclusive, so that Britain could claim that articles not mentioned were also contraband. Because of the "difficulty of agreeing on the precise Cases in which alone Provisions and other articles not generally contraband may be regarded as such" it was agreed that in these cases the articles should be purchased and not seized, which in fact left things exactly as, in practice, they were. Thus, too, regulations were laid down about ships entering blockaded ports, but no definition of "blockade" was attempted, so that the dispute about effective and paper blockades remained. Thus, administrative and disciplinary provisions were included concerning commissioning and restraining of privateers, but no exact regulations to avoid friction during visitation and search were made. Thus, in fact, much time was spent on relatively unimportant details, such as a prohibition of assistance to pirates by either party, a ban on the recruitment or commissioning of privateers in either country by the enemies of the other, reception of ships of war of each in the ports of the other, an agreement to make no reprisals before claims had duly been laid before the other government and unreasonably denied, refusal of assistance to privateers of states at war with the other country, and denial of the right to allow seizure of ships and goods of the one country by its enemies within the territorial waters of the other; all this while grave conflicts of principle like that over the British Rule of 1756 and over the American claim to Freedom of the Seas were passed over in silence. Nor was any mention made of impressment, which is perhaps surprising, even though it had not yet become the emotional issue in the United States that it was later to be, nor the naval necessity it appeared, subsequently, to the British, under stress of the long war with Napoleon. Jay's instructions said nothing on the matter and neither did the treaty. It was, of course, hoped by Jay that all these matters could be settled in a better atmosphere when peace came, in the negotiations provided for in Article 12.

Two small items of interest were included in Articles 26 and 27; the former pledged the governments, in case "at any Time a Rupture should take place (which God forbid)" between them, to give law-abiding citizens of each country at least a year for the removal of their persons and property from the other country if such removal were considered necessary, which was an obvious effort to avoid the difficulties that had arisen from the Revolutionary War, and the latter, in a rather modern vein, granted mutual extradition rights against those accused of murder and forgery. Finally, in an effort to square the provisions of the treaty with those of the Franco-American Treaty of 1778, and to placate the already very suspicious French Government, it was agreed in Article 25 that "Nothing in this Treaty contained shall however be construed or operate contrary to former and existing Public Treaties with other Sovereigns or States. But the Two parties agree, that while they continue in amity neither of them will in future make any Treaty that shall be inconsistent with this or the preceding article", which concerned the agreements affecting foreign privateers. Though nothing in the treaty explicitly contradicted any provisions of the Treaty of 1778, the two documents were not too easy to reconcile in spirit, since the French convention had clearly enunciated the principle of free ships, free goods.

As has been seen, the first ten articles of the treaty were permanent, but the remainder expired two years after the making of peace between France and England, that is to say in the autumn of 1803. The very last words of the treaty were: "And Whereas it will be expedient in order the better to facilitate Intercourse and obviate Difficulties that other Articles be proposed and added to this Treaty, which Articles from want of time and other circumstances cannot now be perfected; It is agreed that the said Parties will from Time to Time readily treat of and concerning such Articles, and will sincerely endeavour so to form them, as that they may conduce to mutual convenience, and tend to promote mutual Satisfaction and Friendship; and that the said Articles after having been duly ratified, shall be added to, and make a part of this Treaty." Though these good intentions were swallowed up in the events leading to the War of 1812, they were able to survive that upheaval, and to come to fruition in the years that followed it.

After the signature of the Treaty on 19 November, 1794, the two principals parted in high mutual regard. On that day Grenville wrote to Jay, "I cannot conclude this letter without repeating to you the very great satisfaction I have derived from the open and candid manner in which you have conducted, on your part, the whole of the difficult negotiation which we have now brought to so successful an issue, and from the disposition which you have uniformly manifested to promote the objects of justice, conciliation, and lasting friendship, between our two countries." On the same day Jay reported to his government, "I do not know how the negotiation could have been conducted, on their part, with more delicacy, friendliness, and propriety, than it has been from first to last."[1]

Nevertheless, Jay had harboured no illusions as to the probable reception of the treaty in America. But the storm of opposition which it aroused when it finally arrived, after the original copies had been lost at sea, surpassed even his expectations, and he was faced with violent unpopularity. So great was fear of the hostility which might arise when the provisions were known, that the Senate, by a narrow majority, decided to consider the treaty in secret, and, after a bitter debate spread over more than two weeks, it was adopted by only 20 votes to 10, exactly the two-thirds majority needed under the Constitution. Despite the renewed Senate order for secrecy, one of the minority published its terms, and an awesome wave of popular criticism swept the Union. But Washington was convinced of the necessity of approving the Treaty, and he had never lacked courage to resist ill-advised popular clamour, so, ignoring a flood of addresses against it, he affixed his signature. Ratifications were exchanged on 28 October, 1795, despite the Senate's rejection of Article 12, an unprecedented action arising from the new constitutional requirement of Senate ratification,

[1] Burt, p. 156.

which threw some doubt upon the proper procedure in such a case, for it was the first treaty signed by the United States since the inauguration of the Constitution. This requirement was to be heard of again in the history of Anglo-American relations. This was not true of another danger which threatened the treaty even after its ratification, for the Republican opposition, which was stronger in the House of Representatives than in the Senate, made a final effort to overthrow it in 1796, first claiming that a treaty requiring an appropriation of money or regulating commerce needed the consent of the House as well as the Senate, a claim which was refused by Washington, and then trying to defeat the appropriation for the joint commissions. This attempt failed by a mere three votes but, along with Washington's firmness, set a sound and healthy precedent.

Few international acts of the United States have been so heavily criticized both by American contemporaries and American historians as Jay's Treaty. S. F. Bemis in his *Jay's Treaty* has been among those critics who claim that Jay could have obtained much more than he did; he has elsewhere laid down the principle that the successes of American diplomacy have in large part been due "to taking advantage of the wars, rivalries and distresses of Europe",[1] to the principle that the divisions of Europe were the opportunties of America. Yet when this principle operates in reverse, he does not see its strength; in the case of the Anglo-French wars of 1793-1815, the divisions of Europe were the loss of the United States. As long as she was locked in a death struggle with France, Britain would certainly give up all non-essentials, chiefly concerning the distant American continent, to the United States, but could never surrender any claim which directly affected her chances of victory in the war, which necessarily dominated all other considerations in the mind of the British Government. Jay grasped this fact, and was supported by his Federalist colleagues; their Republican successors were less prescient. But Jay had achieved much before they came to power; and in particular had prevented a war with Britain at a time when the new Federal government was in its infancy, and when the French war had not taken up nearly as much of Britain's strength as it had done by 1812.

The positive achievements of the Treaty, too, were by no means negligible. In the matter of maritime rights the United States, it is true, gained almost nothing, for, though she gave up very little explicitly, she surrendered some of her principles by implication, and she

[1] *A Diplomatic History of the United States,* p. 802.

297

acquiesced, by default of opposition, in British practices. The best that Jay could have obtained, and he knew it, was the agreement to discuss the whole question when the great war was over. But as against this, he made a gain which was important above all others to the future of the United States, the surrender of the British frontier posts and all that that implied. Hemmed in as the United States still was by Spanish lands in the south-west, had Britain not given up her effective control over the whole north-west, the glittering prize of the Louisiana territory, which was so shortly and so unexpectedly to descend into the laps of those who opposed Jay's Treaty so fiercely, might well have proved worthless, or at least uncertain. No objective of American diplomacy at this time can have been of remotely comparable importance with the opening up of the West, and Jay's Treaty, in conjunction with the Treaty of San Lorenzo, which granted the Americans free and effective access for their persons and goods to the Mississippi through New Orleans, accomplished just this. To have made possible the development of the Great West was the supreme achievement of Washington's Administration.

But the United States made other gains of some moment. In commerce, in particular, she acquired important rights in Britain, on the Canadian frontier, in the East Indies and, in effect though not through the treaty, in the West Indies. Britain, on the other hand, though most of the actual concessions were hers, had no real cause for dissatisfaction, even if the treaty was so far from popular that Lord Sheffield, many years later, welcomed the War of 1812 because it enabled Great Britain to annul the treaty in which Grenville had been "duped by Jay the American." But she had arranged for the settlement of the vexing question of the Revolutionary debts, and the American envoy had demanded no impossible concessions on maritime rights: in the midst of a war she could have expected no better terms. Pinckney, who had no personal reason to like it, approved of the treaty, and Jay's own view that it was the best possible under the circumstances, though by no means quite satisfactory, was the realistic one. Grenville believed that no "just objection can be stated to the great work which we jointly accomplished, except on the part of those who believe the interests of Great Britain and the United States to be in contradiction with each other or who wish to make them so",[1] among whom one is forced to number the Jeffersonian Republicans in the United States.

But in a broader sense Jay and the treaty deserve even higher praise. What might have been a very difficult new diplomatic relationship had

[1] Q. W.A.A.E., pp. 52-3.

begun with the Treaty of Versailles, and in this basic instrument, to which Anglo-American diplomacy continued to revert for many years, there were inevitably many defects and obscurities. The spirit of the earlier negotiations had been surprisingly good, and in this same spirit Jay—who had been one of the original peace-makers—took up his task in 1794; he set the tone for a continuity of objectives, and even of personalities, which was to be notable in the future of Anglo-American relations. With the unhappy exception of the War of 1812, and largely owing to the geographical isolation of America, the interruptions of Anglo-American relations by the accidents and catastrophic storms of international diplomacy were few and mostly unimportant. Indeed, the sixty years of diplomacy following the Treaty of Versailles can for the most part be regarded as a steady process of clarifying and settling the problems left unsettled in the original agreement, a period which merged gradually into one concerned with the settlement of new problems arising chiefly from the internal history and westward expansion of the United States. To the remarkable success of this process Jay made a singular and important contribution, befitting a Chief Justice of the United States, the inauguration of the tradition of judicial procedure in international affairs—what was later, in effect, the principle of arbitration, which was to dominate Anglo-American history and to have an influence far beyond this sphere. It was his personal achievement, following upon what he had earlier advocated as President of Congress in 1779 and Secretary of State in 1785, to induce Grenville to accept the joint commission method for the settlement of differences, and though only two of the three commissions were ultimately successful, this alone was a momentous achievement, and would fully justify W. G. Summer's judgment in his life of Jay: "Jay's Treaty was a masterpiece of diplomacy, considering the time and the circumstances of this country."[1]

---

[1] Q. ibid, p. 52.

CHAPTER TEN

TENSION, WAR AND PEACE
(1794-1821)

DESPITE its unpopularity and the fact that it left many problems unsettled, Jay's Treaty was followed by an immediate, if only a temporary, improvement in Anglo-American relations. Indeed, it was succeeded by such a deterioration in the relations of America with France, that for a brief period the United States virtually went to war with Britain's enemy; but a settlement between them was reached in 1800, and made secure by the signing of the Peace of Amiens between Britain and France in the next year. With the renewal of the war in 1803 tension between the United States and both belligerents mounted steadily, for neutrality in the great struggle became steadily harder to maintain, even for so distant and increasingly powerful a country as the United States. Because of the very success of the British at sea, as well as because of the propinquity of British North America and the United States, the friction between these two became more and more severe. War eventually broke out in 1812. The inconclusive struggle was ended by the Treaty of Ghent in 1814, though the agreements supplementary to the treaty were not concluded until 1821. The period thus falls into five main sections; tension with France, tension with Britain, the war, the peace, and its aftermath.

I

IN THE United States these years begin with the final consolidation of the new constitutional arrangements, and continue with the rapid development of the party system. The election of John Adams as President in 1797 was a Federalist triumph, but his defeat in 1801 by Jefferson inaugurated a long period of Republican rule, and it was by no means entirely a coincidence that a deterioration in Anglo-American relations, over and above that produced by the renewal of war, began a year or so after this date. During the Federalist period

300

full rein had been given to conservative fear of French Jacobinism, culminating in the repressive Alien and Sedition Acts of 1798, which are remarkably similar to the legislation passed in England a few years earlier during the Tory reaction against the radicalism of the Revolution. But though the Republicans were pro-French by instinct they were a good deal disillusioned by the excesses of the French Revolution before Jefferson came to power in 1801, and very soon after that date were increasingly hostile to the dictatorial methods of Napoleon. Indeed, under the unbroken twenty-four year rule of the 'Virginia' dynasty of Presidents Jefferson, Madison and Monroe, their increasing conservatism ushered in the so-called Era of Good Feelings.

In Britain the impact of the French Revolution strengthened the hold of Pitt and the Tories upon the country, but drove all thought of reform out of their heads; only Charles James Fox, with a very few Whig followers, continued to maintain a more liberal attitude. The death of Pitt in 1806, followed very shortly by that of Fox after a brief spell of office, deprived the country of its outstanding political leaders, but it was as determined as ever to defeat Napoleon, being now convinced that it was engaged in a fight to the finish, not merely for national liberty, but for national survival. It is impossible to understand the British attitude to the United States in these years, if this exclusive preoccupation with the supreme struggle against Napoleon is not fully apprehended; to Britain nothing else could compare with it in importance, nothing else could rid the country of the consciousness of its shadow. For her, friction with the Americans was an unhappy complication, but not more, in the supreme struggle, and only the apparent termination of that struggle in 1814 enabled her to devote much of her energies to the War of 1812. This is the reason why the latter left so little impression on the British mind compared with the American; it was a distant episode in a great history, and one which was distasteful because it seemed almost like a stab in the back from erstwhile friends, who talked much of liberty but seemed incapable of appreciating that Britain, as she had done before and was to do again later, was at that time strenuously defending the liberty of mankind against the very real menace of Napoleonic tyranny. This attitude is one which Americans are today better able to comprehend than they were then.

When it became clear that the American Administration was determined strictly to enforce Washington's proclamation of neutrality of 1793, French relations with the Federalists steadily deteriorated. Even the very pro-French Ambassador in Paris, Monroe, could not make Jay's Treaty agreeable to the French National Convention; indeed, he could only try to do so by attacking Washington to the French behind the President's back, and was, as a result, withdrawn from his post. At the same time in America, the French Minister, Genêt, and his successor, Adet, attempted unsuccessfully to appeal over the heads of the Federalist Administration to the people, with some of whom the French cause was still very popular, and to use the United States as a base for stirring up trouble in British North America, particularly among the French Canadians. When it became clear that nothing could be expected of the Federalists, and even more when their hopes of a Republican victory in the Presidential election of 1797 were frustrated, the French Government began, in so far as they were able, to follow the British example, and, by repudiating their agreement of 1778 with the United States that free ships make free goods, to bring the utmost pressure to bear upon American shipping. A 'retaliatory' decree of 1798, issued by the Directory, even foreshadowed Napoleon's Continental System. The Americans struck back, in theory by the abrogation in 1798 of all previous agreements with France, and in practice by such vigorous measures that there were 14 American men-of-war and 200 merchant vessels armed with letters of marque at sea in that year. Thus the two countries moved nearer and nearer to open war, for which the Federalist extremists were by no means unwilling. Washington consented, in such an event, to take command of the Army if Hamilton were made second-in-command.

But both Talleyrand, who was French Foreign Minister, and President Adams drew back from the brink, and the latter, despite the failure of a similar American attempt to stop the rot in 1797, sent a peace commission to France in 1800. The negotiations were slow, and in the end only a commercial agreement was signed, but on the insistence of the French the old maritime provisions of the treaty of 1778, which were unfavourable to Britain, were once more included. Though Napoleon made peace with Britain very shortly—which automatically ended the Franco-American tension—he intended it only to be a truce, and was looking forward already to the day when he might turn the weapon of blockade against the British themselves. It was for this reason that Grenville said to the American Minister in London that, though he thought the Franco-American treaty not inconsistent with Jay's Treaty, some points in it had "somewhat of a less friendly appearance than could be wished."[1]

But this was in 1800, six years after Jay's Treaty and almost at the

[1] Q. W.A.A.E., p. 72.

end of the Federalist tenure of office, and those six years had in fact seen a growing improvement in Anglo-American relations; indeed, there was something approaching a ripening of friendship between the two governments, due in part to the friendly sentiments of the Federalists and the increasing British realization, in the midst of a European war, that American friendship was worth having, but also to the improved character of their mutual representation. Pinckney was succeeded in London in 1796 by Rufus King, an ardent Federalist and a close friend of Hamilton, who was very unpopular with Republicans like Monroe. This unpopularity with his political opponents was not lessened by the fact that he was very intimate with men in public positions in England, and came, as did so many of his successors, to see the English point of view too forcibly to please his own countrymen. He early grasped the crucial factor in the situation, for he wrote to the Secretary of State on 16 October, 1796:

> But as they [the British] believe that their national safety depends essentially upon their marine, they feel unusual caution relative to a stipulation that by mere possibility can deprive their navy of a single seaman, who is a real British subject, or that may even diminish the chance of obtaining the services of those who are not British subjects, but who by various pretences are detained in service as such. Hence . . . they desire to postpone a convention with us on this subject till the return of peace. . . . I believe that the administration, together with the nation throughout, desire to live with us in friendship, and I do not think they would for a slight cause disagree with us. But their colony trade and marine are topics intimately and exclusively connected with their prosperity and security and more deeply with their prejudices. If we cannot agree, we may still remain friends.[1]

The effect of King's period as Minister was wholly beneficial, so much so that even when Jefferson came to power he was not withdrawn; but he felt it fitting to resign his appointment on 5 August, 1802.

His counterpart in Washington, Robert Liston, who took over the Legation in May, 1796, saw the situation equally clearly, and was equally desirous of promoting Anglo-American friendship, but though an experienced diplomat, he was not quite so universally successful as King. For one thing, his task was more difficult, owing to the sensitivity of American public opinion; for another, though he got on very well personally with Adams and with Pickering, the Secretary of State, he acquired considerable unpopularity when he rather unwisely became

[1] Q. W.A.A.E., pp. 59-60.

involved, though in a purely passive role, in a wild American plot to seize New Orleans from the Spanish. But he was a great improvement, even in American eyes, on his predecessor, Hammond, and, like King, he firmly grasped the essentials of the situation. He wrote privately to Grenville on 7 May, 1800:

> The advantages to be ultimately reaped from perseverance in the line of conduct which Great Britain had adopted for the last four years appear to my mind to be infallible and of infinite magnitude; the profitable consequences of a state of hostility, small and uncertain. I have been pleasing my imagination with looking forward to the distant spectacle of all the northern continent of America covered with friendly though not subject, States, consuming our manufactures, speaking our language, proud of their parent State, attached to her prosperity. War must bring with it extensive damage to our prosperity, our navigation, the probable loss of Canada, and the *world* behind it and the propagation of enmity and prejudices which it may be impossible to eradicate. ... The rulers are certainly in earnest in wishing to be well with us and it appears to me possible to arrange our differences.[1]

It was probably not unconnected with the fact that in 1800 the government moved to an incomplete, expensive and uncomfortable Washington, that in this year Liston took leave of absence, and left Edward Thornton, his Secretary of Legation, as Chargé d'Affaires, a position which he occupied with zeal and distinction until a successor to Liston was appointed in 1803.

The early years of this period tended to be dominated by Federalist fear of Jacobinism, which was so strong as to illustrate forcibly how close were the bonds which still tied the United States to Europe, and this steadily brought the United States and Britain closer together. The Republican reaction to this was powerful, and the presidential election of 1796 was the first of many in which the bogey of John Bull was summoned, in this case by the Jeffersonians, to alarm the American electorate. Federalist feelings were clearly expressed by Senator Cabot: "If England will persevere, she will save Europe and save us; but if she yields, all will be lost. She is now the only barrier between us and the deathly embraces of our dear Allies—between universal irreligion, immorality and plunder, and what order, probity, virtue and religion is left."[2] As the United States moved closer and closer to war with France, all the mutual manifestations of an Anglo-American alliance

[1] Q. W.F.R., p. 26.   [2] Q. Morison and Commager, I, pp. 371-2.

began to make their appearance. There was talk of a British approach to the United States for common action in the Spanish colonies if France conquered Spain. There were British offers to convoy American ships, though they were refused on the ground that such action would be incompatible with the dignity of the United States. There was even, as Brebner points out, a rudimentary sort of Lend-Lease, when a number of 24-pounders at Halifax were loaned by the British Government to the United States (who were very short of ordnance) and none reclaimed, "thus terminating" in the words of the British Minister "a transaction which, while it discovers on the part of my Sovereign a perfect confidence in the sentiments of the American Government, cannot but tend to consolidate the connexion so happily subsisting between the two countries."[1] In London there was great enthusiasm about the news of American preparations for war with France, and King himself wrote, advising war and assuring the administration that, in the event of hostilities, "we shall instantly receive a part of what they possess and that the supply shall be continued." Americans may naturally incline to consider these small events as the first of many British efforts to lure the United States into the tangled web of European interests, but Englishmen cannot refrain from reflecting how different might have been the history of both countries, and perhaps of mankind, if war with France had come and had resulted in a firm Anglo-American alliance. Not only would the War of 1812 have been avoided, but a tradition of American internationalism might possibly have been created more than a century before it was, with all that that could have implied for the future of peace and liberty.

But such was not to be. Adams avoided open war with France, and the tone of Anglo-American relations changed noticeably as a result. King wrote some months later, "For some time past . . . I have observed here a coldness towards the United States . . . and in my ordinary intercourse with the Government I have met with more difficulties than I had before been accustomed to experience."[2] But the change of opinion was not yet fundamental; the death of Washington was the occasion of much respectful comment in the British Press, and, with the coming of peace in 1801, the issues which bulked largest between the two countries fell into abeyance. Even the coming to power in 1801 of Jefferson and the Republicans was by no means an insuperable obstacle to good relations, for, though by instinct anti-British, he was primarily concerned with American interests; he said to Thornton at the time, that "he had been represented as hostile to Great Britain; but this

[1] Q. Brebner, p. 73. [2] Q. W.A.A.E., pp. 67, 70.

had been done only for electioneering purposes [in a fashion not to be unfamiliar in Anglo-American relations in later years], and he hoped henceforward that such language would be used no longer." After his inauguration he declared, "For Republican France he might have felt more interest; but that was long over and he had no partiality to it", and went even further and denounced "Bonaparte's usurpation, the arbitrary nature and spirit of his government and his love of flattery and vain pomp". Henry Adams in his History of the United States goes so far as to say that he was "rapidly becoming the friend and confidant of England".[1]

But his pre-eminent concern was, of course, the future of the United States, and he was peculiarly sensitive to the importance of Louisiana, which he believed, quite rightly, was the key to the future destiny of the country. After the retrocession of Louisiana by Spain to France in 1800, the French were toying with ideas of reasserting their once great position in North America on this foundation, and Jefferson not merely regarded it as a certain cause of future war between France and the United States, but made no secret of the fact that if they could not oust the French alone, they would have to seek the assistance of Great Britain in doing so. Once more the possibility of Anglo-American alliance became apparent, for the British Government displayed willingness to see Louisiana pass into the hands of the United States, but once more the possibility was frustrated, and this time in a way which was in the end to be decisive. Knowing that war with England would shortly be renewed and that Louisiana would then certainly be lost to France, Napoleon suddenly executed a volte-face and in April, 1803, proposed the outright sale of the whole vast Louisiana territory to the United States, a proposal which the latter accepted with alacrity. The treaty was signed on 30 April, and on 15 May, as he had foreseen, Great Britain declared war upon France. Jefferson's mind now reverted to its normal mistrust of Britain, at the very moment when war brought the old issues between the two countries to the surface in a form which was to be far more dangerous than any they had hitherto assumed. (Unhappily King had recently failed to reach an agreement on impressment, owing to the last-minute decision of Lord St. Vincent to insist on retaining the right in the Narrow Seas.) The British Chargé d'Affaires in Washington wrote of this diplomatic revolution:

I can scarcely credit the testimony of my own senses in examining the turn which affairs have taken and the manifest ill-will discovered towards

[1] Q. W.F.R., pp. 31, 33, 36.

us by the Government at the present moment. . . . I believe that the simple truth of the case is, after all, the circumstances that a real change has taken place in the views of the Government, which may be dated from the first arrival of the intelligence of the Louisiana purchase, and which has since derived additional force and acrimony from the opinion that Great Britain cannot resist under her present pressure, the new claims of the United States. . . . A hostile disposition towards us is their best recommendation to the favour of France. The cession of Louisiana has lifted Jefferson, beyond imagination, in his own opinion.[1]

For the next eleven years, Anglo-American relations, which had recently promised so well, deteriorated steadily, until they ended in the second, if last, of the wars between the two peoples.

II

THIS disastrous deterioration was by no means entirely due to a great impersonal clash of interests; this was present indeed, but might readily have been controlled if both governments at the same time had shown a reasonable desire for accommodation. Personal pride, ill will, and folly, at all levels on both sides of the Atlantic, must take a great deal of blame. Among the Republicans, Jefferson and, to a lesser degree, Madison were the dominating figures, and in that proportion must they accept responsibility at the bar of history. Among the Tories, no less opposed to American democracy now that they were fighting a dicta-torial rather than a Jacobin France, the guilt is very largely that of George Canning. Of the British it may be said that their pride blinded them to the understandable sentiments of the Americans; of the Americans it may be said that their bitterness blinded them to the true nature of the British struggle with Napoleon. Even the Ministers in London and Washington must accept a share of the blame for they, like all else, seemed to go badly to seed in this period. Either in ability or in good will, one and all of them fell below the high level set by King and Liston.

In July, 1803, almost a year after King's resignation, James Monroe arrived to take up his post as Minister to the Court of St. James. He was an ardent Republican and a close friend of both Jefferson and Madison, the Secretary of State, and he came directly from negotiating the Louisiana purchase with Talleyrand, so that he was in a position

---

[1] Q. ibid, p. 48.

accurately to represent the Republican view to the British. Things were not improved by the fact that, in a laudable desire to live in republican simplicity, he dispensed with even the services of a Secretary of Legation in London and dwelt in increasing isolation, for, as Gore, an American friend of King still in London on the claims commission, wrote: "[Y]ou know they [the English] do not press their knowledge, no more than their civility, on any man." Monroe was, however, sensitive, and, particularly after the arrival of news of the social difficulties of the new British Minister in Washington, was, along with Mrs. Monroe, subjected to frequent snubs, which caused him pain. So rapid was the mutual dissipation of confidence that commonsense seemed to desert the British Government. For several years they refused to allow the American, Robert Fulton, to order two steamboats from Boulton and Watt for use on the Hudson River, despite the efforts of Monroe, on the ground that they were "diving machines that are to blow up the British Navy, the dockyard, etc., at Portsmouth, of which they have some apprehension."[1] Monroe was thought, even by Jefferson, to be getting out of his depth, but, though anxious to leave England, he refused the governorship of Louisiana on the ground that it was not a post of sufficient importance; this did not improve his relations with the President, while the Secretary of State was not anxious that Monroe should cut too fine a figure, since he was a rival, although a friendly one, for the succession to the Presidency. Needless to say, as a Virginia Republican, he was firmly opposed at home by certain New England interests, while in old England men longed for a return of the good old days of the Federalists, William Wilberforce writing, for instance, to Rufus King that he wished he was still Minister in London. However, after the death of Pitt, Monroe's relations with the Government improved; according to Lord Holland, one of its members, he had overcome some of his Anglophobia and Francophilia, which was perhaps an instance of the insidious effect of the English environment upon even so staunch a democrat as Monroe. He was replaced, discredited, as a result of the negotiation of an abortive treaty on 29 October, 1807, thus earning the unenviable diplomatic epitaph of Henry Adams: "In many respects Monroe's career was unparalleled, but he was singular above all in the experience of being disowned by two Presidents as strongly opposed to each other as Washington and Jefferson, and of being sacrificed by two Secretaries as widely different as Timothy Pickering and James Madison."

He was succeeded by William Pinckney, who had shared with him

[1] Q. W.A.A.E., pp. 77-8.

the task, though apparently not the odium, of negotiating the ill-fated treaty. He was an equally good Republican, and wrote of the Orders-in-Council: "The time when they were issued—the arrogant claims of Maritime dominion which they support and execute—and the contempt which they manifest, in the face of the world, for the rights and powers of our country, make them altogether the most offensive act that can be laid to the charge of any Government. The least appearance of a disposition to submit to such an attempt will encourage to further aggressions, until our national spirit will be lost in an habitual sense of humiliation".[1] But he did not have the angularity and lack of judgment which Monroe displayed at this time, and was liked and socially respected in England; indeed there is a touching instance of the humanity underlying political differences in the offer of Lord Holland to look after his son in the holidays, if he wished to leave the lad at school in England in case of war between the two countries. Thus, despite his firmness, he did his utmost to reach an agreement with the British, and was able to carry on his task during the most difficult period to date in the history of the two states. But his efforts had made him unpopular with the fire-eaters at home, and he was not unwilling to accede to the clamour for his recall owing to the great costs of maintaining his position. As he wrote, "The compensation (as it is called) allotted by the Government to the maintenance of its representatives abroad, is a pittance which no economy, however rigid, or even mean, can render adequate"—a complaint which we shall hear frequently in the future. In January, 1811, he informed the Foreign Secretary that he was to be withdrawn, since there was still no British Minister in Washington, and Jonathan Russell, one of the earliest and ablest of American career diplomats, who became Chargé d'Affaires, was unable, despite energetic efforts, to check the tendency of the two countries to drift apart.

British representation in Washington followed a surprisingly similar pattern of tactlessness, manifest ill will, and incompetent good will. There was considerable delay in the appointment of a successor to Liston, largely due to the notorious lack of amenities in the new capital city, but in November, 1803, Anthony Merry arrived with his wife to take up the position, an event no doubt accelerated by the renewal of war with France. The tone for the period was set when the President received Merry, who was in full dress, in his old morning clothes, and there followed a determined effort by Jefferson to democratize diplomatic life, which was regarded with horror by the whole diplomatic

[1] Q. ibid, pp. 92, 96.

corps, and even more by their wives. But there were graver troubles in Anglo-American relations than the chaos which resulted at diplomatic dinners from the abolition of precedence; apart from the serious difficulties already in existence, Merry, like his predecessor Liston, became at least theoretically involved in a plot concerning the future of the Mississippi valley, this time that of Aaron Burr. Before the latter was actually brought to trial, however, Fox had come to power in Britain, and had replaced Merry on the score of an ill-health of which, though it was real enough, he had never complained. His ministry had done no fundamental harm, and he saw to the root of the present trouble when he reported, "But while it is my duty to do justice to Mr. Madison's temperate and conciliatory language, I must not omit to observe that it indicated strongly a design on the part of this Government to avail themselves of the present conjuncture by persisting steadily in their demands of redress of their pretended grievances, in the hope of obtaining a greater respect to their flag, and of establishing a more convenient system of neutral navigation than the interests of the British Empire have hitherto allowed His Majesty to concur in." But there was a marked difference in tone between his period and that of Liston, even though he was not entirely to blame for it.

His successor, David Montague Erskine, the son of the Lord Chancellor, was, as the appointee of Fox whom Jefferson greatly admired, *persona gratissima* to the Republicans, and it early became apparent that his views were often closer to those of Jefferson than to those of Fox's successor, Canning. To some extent no doubt he fell under the influence of powerful American personalities, but he was by no means without a grasp of the situation, as is shown by his early remark that, "Mr. Jefferson has always pursued a temporising line of conduct against all foreign nations, *except* Great Britain". He probably saw the inevitable end to which the intransigence of both parties was tending, and was anxious to avert the calamity by British concessions. Certainly, from the beginning, he pressed upon Canning the repeal of the disputed Orders-in-Council and tried to bring home to him how intolerable a grievance the Americans appeared to find impressment. Canning's despatch of George Henry Rose as an Envoy Extraordinary, to deal with the Chesapeake question, implied, he said, no mistrust of the Minister, but when Erskine later, after Rose's mission had proved abortive, outran what Canning considered the letter of his instructions and negotiated an unacceptable agreement with Madison, it was repudiated instantly. Part of the trouble was that Erskine accepted a note from Jefferson stating that certain British actions would not "*best comport with what is due from His Britannick Majesty to his own honour"*, which Canning regarded as an expression "offensive to His Majesty's dignity, such as no Minister of His Majesty ought to have submitted to receive and to transmit to his Government"; a crushing rebuke was administered to Erskine, and he was at once replaced by Francis James Jackson. Erskine had established the best relationship yet of a British Minister with an American administration (and that a Republican one), and, what is more, attacks on him in the anti-British press had ceased. Here was yet another possible basis of agreement between the two countries, and the responsibility for refusing it was Canning's alone: perhaps at no other period in the history of Anglo-American relations has British arrogance shown to such ill-effect. This incident, which Canning passed off by describing Erskine as that "damned Scotch flunkey", gives one more sympathy for some of the contemporary mistrust of Canning. Certainly Erskine did not deserve the censure of his successor, that he was "really a greater fool than I could have thought it possible to be";[1] indeed, if the coming of war between the two countries in 1812 was the useless act of folly it appears to the historian, Jackson himself more properly deserves the appelation.

He was a dyed-in-the-wool Tory, and for that reason eminently unsuited to the post, but that was not the only ground of unsuitability. He was described by Rufus King as "positive, vain and intolerant" and was in fact an opinionated and supercilious Englishman, expressing from the first a determination to "stand no nonsense" from the Americans. His mere appointment must be ground for further indictment of Canning. From his browbeating of the Danes in an earlier mission to Denmark he had acquired the nickname of "Copenhagen Jackson", and he endeavoured to employ the same methods in Washington. He arrived in 1809 with a coach and liveried servants, and refused all explanation of the British rejection of the Erskine treaty, except that given to the American Minister in London. So insufferable was his manner that Secretary Smith shortly refused to communicate with him except in writing, at which unprecedented action Jackson was highly indignant. When he went so far as to insinuate that the President and Secretary had entered into agreement with Erskine, knowing it to be contrary to his instructions, Smith informed His Britannic Majesty's representative that all diplomatic relations between him and the American Government were at an end, and released the correspondence to the Press. Jackson retired to New York until in 1810 he was sum-

[1] Q. W.F.R., pp. 42-3, 55, 62-4.

311

moned home, remarkable as it may seem, with honour, but the fate
of Erskine had been avenged. Jackson was utterly lacking in tact or
finesse, and he was the kind of Englishman most detested—and
properly—by Americans; it is impossible to imagine a more disastrous
British representative in the United States.

There was no hurry to replace him and no one eagerly desired the
post, but in March, 1811, when Secretary Smith quarrelled with
Madison and was dismissed, Augustus Foster, who had been Secretary
of Legation under Merry, was appointed. He was an able man, a Whig
of good will, as well as of knowledge, but things had gone too far for
anyone in his position to improve them. As he wrote, "Your lordship
will see that unless we change our system, this country is disposed to go
to war with us notwithstanding they have few resources. . . . Yet even
if we made a small concession I am in doubt if our enemies . . . would
be satisfied."[1] These enemies were increasingly vocal, and in 1812 the
atmosphere in Washington became so difficult for Foster that he
applied for leave, and left for Halifax. Yet he remained conciliatory,
and pressed repeal of the Orders-in-Council on Castlereagh, pointing
out the fundamental fact that times were more auspicious for agreement now that so many of the old veterans of the Revolution had disappeared. Even more remarkable, there remained strong Federalist
opposition to the anti-British administration; it centred, of course, in
the North-east and was to endure through the war itself. One of the
Federalists wrote of the Republicans, "That party is the most implacable and persevering enemy Great Britain can have."[2] Even the impossible Jackson had found defenders, quite ardent ones, among the
ranks of these American opponents of the Jeffersonians and friends of
Britain. But on the subject of the British Ministers in Washington in
these years before the war it is hard not to agree with the member of
Congress from Kentucky who said: "Mr. Rose was sent here to gull us,
Mr. Erskine did us some justice for which he was disgraced; Mr. Jackson was sent to bully us and Mr. Foster as an opiate to lull us to sleep."[3]

That the Administration's change of attitude to Britain in 1803 had
been primarily due to the Louisiana purchase was now clearly demonstrated. When the negotiated settlement (arising from Jay's Treaty) of
the claims question was in sight in 1802, Madison as Secretary of State
raised with the British Government the question of the boundary
disputes in the North-east and in the North-west. It was natural enough
that this initiative should come from the United States, whose interests

[1] Q. ibid, pp. 38, 81.   [2] Q. ibid, p. 86.   [3] Q. ibid, p. 81.

were, as always, more directly engaged in the matter than those of Britain. Negotiations began and were carried to a conclusion which was acceptable to both sides, but particularly to the Americans, whose suggestion of a north-west boundary, which ran from the nearest source of the Mississippi direct to the north-west corner of the Lake of the Woods, was the basis of agreement. The signature of the actual convention was largely due to the energy of Rufus King in London, but unfortunately, in the period between its completion and its presentation to the Senate, the Louisiana treaty was signed, and accepted by that body. The geographical situation in the area affected by the British treaty was still somewhat obscure, and certain members of the Senate feared that it would lop off a section of the territory so suddenly and unexpectedly acquired from France; in fact this fear was unfounded, as became apparent later, but in passing the treaty in February, 1804, the Senate excluded the fifth article, in which this agreement was embodied, by 22 votes to 9. As a result, though for reasons which are not clear, the British Government refused to ratify the rest, and the whole convention lapsed.

Meanwhile, of course, the Anglo-French war had broken out again, and Monroe had started his unhappy career in London. Even before Monroe's arrival, the American Administration had shown itself anxious to conclude an agreement on neutral rights; as Madison wrote, "The essential objects are the suppression of impressments, and the definition of blockade. Next to these in importance are the reduction of the list of contraband, and the enlargement of our neutral trade with hostile Colonies."[1] The return of Pitt to power in 1804,. with Lord Harrowby as Foreign Secretary, did not produce any change, for the latter in effect said that he was too busy with matters arising from the war to occupy himself for long in negotiations with the United States. Already there was becoming apparent considerable irritation in British Government circles at Republican failure to understand the true nature of their struggle against Napoleon, which Federalists appreciated. As Sir Francis Benny wrote to Rufus King at the time: "My opinion is, as it always has been, that Britain was the bulwark to America and that the downfall of one would be followed by the destruction of the other. Indeed, I cannot discover in what manner universal empire is to be prevented if the power of France remains intact, for its impulse is irresistible."[2] [Substitute *Germany* for *France* and the words might apply exactly to 1941.] At first, Monroe was not deeply concerned at his failure to make progress, and in October, 1804, was sent to assist

[1] Q. Burt, p. 227.   [2] Q. W.A.A.E., p. 83.

the American Minister in Madrid, William Pinckney, in negotiating a Spanish treaty; he did not return until July, 1805, by which time the situation had given rise to an increasing number of grievances on the part of the Americans against the British maritime system, while the British could not see what in the world the American Government was complaining about, since American commerce continued to increase by leaps and bounds.

The British noticed particularly that American re-exports, since the renewal of war, had grown so fast as to exceed their exports, developing from $13,590,000 in 1803 to $53,180,000 in 1805, which meant that, in fact, the Rule of 1756 was being undermined in its effect by American carriage of goods to French territories via the United States. An Order-in-Council of 24 June, 1803, had put neutral commerce substantially on the same basis as it was before the Treaty of Amiens, but had recognized the doctrine of broken voyage, which had been decided upon during the peace, in 1802, in the *Polly* case, and had relied on American tariffs, and the inconveniences of unloading goods there, to prevent excessive re-exports to enemy territory. It now became apparent that these obstacles were by no means effective, and in the very month that Monroe returned to London the Prize Appeal Court of the Privy Council, influenced no doubt by popular opinion, gave judgement in the *Essex* case, which in effect imposed the doctrine of continuous voyage by deciding that only a bona fide import duty, not subject to rebate or remission on re-export from the neutral country concerned, could neutralize goods. Furthermore, other irritations at sea, particularly impressments, were having a grave effect on relations between the two countries. As Steel has pointed out,[1] hitherto impressment had been a relatively minor issue—far more than twice the number of impressments made between 1792 and 1802 were made in the succeeding decade —on which the British Government had tended to be conciliatory. But, with the increasing severity of the struggle, its opinion hardened, while in America the Administration's indignation was allowed increasing play when the *Essex* case made strong diplomatic bargaining counters essential if the trade of the United States was to be protected by its government. Furthermore, the issue began to acquire a distinct emotional force in the American mind, and Congress passed a law to punish British officers committing trespass on American vessels.

[1] Anthony Steel, "Anthony Merry and the Anglo-American Dispute about Impressment, 1803-6" (in the *Cambridge Historical Journal*, 1949); and "Impressment in the Monroe-Pinckney Negotiations, 1806-7" (in *Am.H.R.*, LVII, 1952).

Monroe was obviously alarmed, immediately on his return, at the situation he found. He began to press harder for an agreement, since he was coming to believe that the British Government were procrastinating deliberately: "I am inclined to think that the delay which has been so studiously sought, in all these concerns, is the part of a system, and that it is intended, as circumstances favor, to subject our commerce at present and hereafter to every restraint in their power. It is certain that the greatest jealousy is entertained of our present and increasing prosperity, and I am satisfied that nothing which is likely to succeed will be left untried to impair it."[1] It was natural that he should think so, for such was the predominant Mercantilist idea of warfare, while public opinion, inflamed by such pamphlets as James Stephen's *War in Disguise, or the Friends of the Neutral Flags* was shouting the idea from the rooftops; but actually the chief motive of the British for delay was the fact that in any negotiations with the United States, Britain must be the one to give up something, for she was at war and America was not. If these issues seemed vital to an America whose commerce was flourishing as never before, they appeared much more so to a people locked in mortal combat, and even in 1806, after the *Essex* case, American re-exports continued to increase, reaching $60,280,000 in that year. To make matters worse, there was still a feeling in Britain that the American Government was, by the very nature of its Constitution, unable to take a vigorous line in foreign policy; certainly heretofore she had always drawn back from the brink of war. There seemed to be a good chance that she would do so again, and the hope therefore persisted among Britons that they might both have their cake and eat it. It was only too natural in these circumstances that Britain should procrastinate in the hope that ultimately something would turn up, which would alter the situation in her favour.

But Congress would not wait, and in April, 1806, reacting to the widespread British seizures following the *Essex* case, passed a measure, inspired by the example of the Revolutionary Non-Importation agreements and pregnant with significance for the future. In order to coerce Britain, it excluded a list of important British manufactures from the United States, but suspended the operation of the measure until 15 November. This non-importation act was thus a threat, but it was accompanied by the despatch of an olive branch, in the form of William Pinckney, who was to constitute with Monroe a special commission for negotiations with Britain. By the time Pinckney reached London in May, 1806, the hopes of the Americans had been greatly raised by the

[1] Q. Burt, p. 230.

315

succession of Fox to power on the death of Pitt. That the sympathetic bond of the Tories and the Federalists was not the only possible one in Anglo-American relations is shown by the attendance of an Englishman, John Melish, at a military dinner at Louisville, Georgia, on 4 July, 1806, at which, naturally, patriotic toasts were drunk; he, when it came to his turn, proposed, "Mr. Fox and the independent Whigs of Britain, May their joint endeavors with the Government of the United States be the means of reconciling the differences between the two countries; and to the latest prosperity may Americans and Britons hail one another as brothers and friends",[1] a toast which was cordially received. But, as events were to show, even the Whigs in a Britain at war with France could make only limited concessions to the United States, while in any case Fox was all too soon to be succeeded by the Tory Canning.

Just at the time when serious negotiations were about to begin, however, the whole commercial question was undergoing a transformation; it was developing from a situation where there were disputes as to the interpretation of international law, to one where neither belligerent any longer pretended that what it was doing was legal, but merely that it was a necessary reprisal for an illegal action of the enemy. The first step in this transformation was claimed by the British as quite legal, but they declared that it was imposed as a consequence of the extraordinary measures taken by Napoleon to distress British commerce; it was the imposition in May, 1806, of a British blockade of the whole coast of Europe from Brest to the Elbe, though it was to be absolute only from the Seine to Ostend. The idea of a blockade of a whole coast, instead of a number of specific ports, was a revolutionary one, but neither the way the blockade would work, nor its implications, were apparent for some time, so that the negotiations continued, after Fox's death in September, with his nephew, Lord Holland, and with Lord Auckland, formerly William Eden, both of whom were apparently chosen for their friendly feelings towards America. Fox's ill health had hitherto prevented progress, which was now rapid.

The crux of the negotiations was impressment, for the American Administration insisted on the explicit abandonment of the practice, while the British came round to the view that they could not surrender it if they were to win the war with France. The position of the American delegates was very difficult; they later suggested, perhaps rightly, that neither Jefferson nor Madison really desired a treaty, and certainly not one without the abandonment of impressment, which Madison was obstinate in pursuing and which Jefferson thought of as a diplomatic

[1] Q. Nevins, *America Through British Eyes,* p. 49.

316

means of maintaining pressure on Britain. The two Americans in England, however, saw much more clearly, because they were on the spot, both that no treaty would be possible if they insisted on the British renunciation of impressment, and that a war was very probable if they did not get a treaty. After considerable hesitation they accepted a solemn diplomatic note from the British Government declaring that it had given and enforced, and would continue to do so, orders that in the impressment of British seamen the greatest care would be taken to preserve Americans from molestation and injury, and that they would give immediate and prompt redress on any complaint. The treaty itself did not mention impressment, but this note embodied a not unimportant practical concession by the British; once this matter was out of the way, the remaining questions were swiftly settled, and the final draft was signed on 31 December. Monroe, who realized in essence that it was in the interest of the United States to make the best of a bad job, declared that the treaty was an honourable and advantageous adjustment with England, but when it reached Washington on 3 March, 1807, it was rejected outright by the Administration, on the ground that it did not contain a British repudiation of the right of impressment. Jefferson informed a Joint Committee of Congress that very evening that he would not even call on the Senate to consider it, and his later expression, through his plenipotentiaries, of his desire to continue the negotiations had no outcome, since the Whigs had fallen from power. With the treaty disappeared plans for a convention to replace the abortive boundary agreement of 1803 and certain of the articles of Jay's Treaty, which had lapsed in that year. Britain had been prepared to make concessions to avoid practical difficulties, while shelving the principle, and Jefferson's must be the chief blame for spurning this hopeful instrument for quieting Anglo-American strife.

Now, each month that passed made reconciliation more difficult, for the causes of dissension piled up on one another as the war increased in ferocity. Even before these negotiations ended, Napoleon took the transformation of the commercial struggle a stage further, by his publication on 21 November, 1806, of his Berlin Decree. This brought into the open his design to use his military control of Europe and its coastline, which was now practically absolute, as a counter-weapon to Britain's naval blockade; it proposed to strangle the latter commercially by depriving her of her essential European trade, and to this end it declared a blockade of the British Isles, condemned all British manufactures and colonial produce as lawful prize, and prohibited any ship

317

which had even called at a British port from entering a European harbour. It was declared to be a reprisal for the British blockade of May, 1806, which Napoleon claimed to be illegal. The effect of this on the United States was unfortunate, for now, far more acutely than before, she began to feel herself squeezed on both sides; France as well as Britain began to give twists to the vice in which all the neutrals were caught. The Administration was increasingly to be faced with a situation in which, if it was to try and insist on its rights, it had to do so against both of the chief belligerents; America might even find herself fighting both of them at once. Of this possible predicament, one American remarked:

> As to war with Great Britain and France, I should wish to delay that till I could understand how it was with two nations at war with each other, I should like first to make some enquiry on the subject. I wish to know if any gentleman of military talents has drawn up any system of fighting three armies together. One against two on the same side, is no new thing, sir, but three against each other is a perfect novelty. I really do not know how they should draw up their troops in order of battle, supposing three enemies to meet. They could not be drawn up in parallel lines, for each army must be opposed to two others. It is a sort of *prismatic or triangular thing*.[1]

But in fact the pressure of the two belligerents was not equal; in theory perhaps it might have been, and in lack of scruple it was worse on the French side, but in practice, because it controlled the oceans, the British system weighed most heavily upon the Americans. After their victory at Trafalgar in 1805, their mastery of the seas was undisputed, so that Napoleonic pressure on land could not affect American ships and goods until they had already passed through the British net at sea. More than this, the British could never afford, if they were to beat Napoleon, to make as many concessions to the United States as he could. He could satisfy the American Government simply by exempting American vessels from the Continental System, but Britain could not accept this as obligating her to cease her reprisal system, for the restrictions on other neutral vessels still remained. She had, therefore, to insist that the United States demand of Napoleon the abolition of the whole Continental System, for anything less would be of little value to her. In her own view, and in fact, Britain's life, with her increasing urban and industrial population, depended on her freedom to export, if necessary in neutral ships, to European markets. Without this freedom,

[1] Q. Burt, p. 268.

or at least some way of achieving the same object, she must, it seemed, infallibly perish, whereas the interruption of Napoleon's designs caused by exempting American ships from the operation of the Continental System would be negligible. Napoleon knew this; it was the basis of his whole system of economic attack. Britain's system was not merely one of attack, but of defence, even of self-preservation. Over and above this, if Napoleon had merely refrained from applying his decrees beyond the territorial waters under his control (and he could do little more in fact, in face of British command of the seas), he could have preserved his system, and yet the United States could have had no right of complaint, concerning such "municipal regulations" of a state within its own borders.[1] And on top of these things, which made the friction between Britain and the United States much more severe than between France and the United States, there began to pile up other difficulties, unsettled and passion-charged disputes arising out of impressment as well as the commercial issues. Thus the countries began to slide more rapidly down the path to war.

Already, within a week of the signing of the abortive Pinckney-Monroe treaty, the commercial war had taken another step by the issue on 7 January, 1807, of an Order-in-Council, which outlawed all neutral trade between any ports under the control of Napoleon; Britain had warned the American negotiators of the possibility of such a reprisal for the Berlin Decree of the previous November, in a note, delivered before the signature of the treaty. But the most grievous, and in some ways the most characteristic, of the events of this time was an incident highly charged with emotion, the famous *Chesapeake* affair, which showed all too clearly how trouble could arise from the impressment issue. A number of seamen deserted from the British ship-of-war *Melampus* when it was in Chesapeake Bay, and were actually known to have enlisted in the American naval service; the request of the British, through diplomatic channels, for their surrender was refused, and they became members of the crew of the American naval vessel, the *Chesapeake,* whose commander was aware that they were deserters, though he believed that they were American citizens. The British knew that they were there, knew that the American commander knew it, but did not know that he thought they were Americans. Admiral Berkeley, the British Commander-in-Chief in American waters, believing himself faced with a national incident, misguidedly and rashly gave the order to remove them from the *Chesapeake* at

[1] Ibid, p. 294.

sea. This was done by force on 22 June, 1807, by the British ship, *Leopard,* at the cost of about twenty serious casualties on the American vessel, which certainly amounted to an overt attack upon the United States. The action of Berkeley can perhaps be explained, but it cannot be excused : it was, indeed, the height of folly, for Britain had never at any time claimed the right of impressment from any but American merchant vessels. Naturally, American public opinion was enraged, and it was united in its fury against Britain as never again; indeed, to all appearances the two countries were much nearer to war emotionally and in fact, than they seemed to be when war actually came in 1812. But Jefferson had never wanted war, and kept his head in the crisis. He issued a proclamation on 2 July, expelling all British armed vessels from American waters, which satisfied public opinion as a vigorous measure, and at the same time went far to avoid further incidents. His demands for satisfaction from Britain included an insistence upon British renunciation of the right of impressment, and from this time it became the burning issue on which no Administration could hope to control popular feeling. Britain, despite some belligerent voices which clamoured that it served America right, was anxious to conciliate; she disavowed the action, and the principle on which it was based, and she recalled Berkeley, but she refused to renounce impressment from merchant vessels. This determination to keep the weapon for use against Napoleon rendered futile the mission of her special envoy, Rose, and the question remained as a serious aggravation of Anglo-American relations.

Other aggravations were not lacking, for the apparent imminence of war unsettled the American West; tension between the Americans and the Indians was already high, and though the British had let their close relations with the latter lapse since 1794, they were forced, by fear that they might be forestalled by the Americans, to resurrect the old Indian alliance. This came near to being effected during 1808, though things relaxed again in the next year, when it became clear that the United States was not going to declare war yet. Meanwhile, in 1807, Napoleon at Tilsit had persuaded Alexander of Russia, whom he had just defeated, to apply the Continental System in his dominions, and its increasing ruthlessness and effectiveness drove Britain on 11 November to issue the most famous of her Orders-in-Council in retaliation.

These declared a blockade of all countries in Napoleon's control, as well as their colonies, and condemned all their produce as lawful prize, which was in effect what the Continental System had done to Britain.

There was however a difference, for whereas Napoleon wanted to strangle Britain by stopping all her trade, and did not so much care about French commerce, Britain wanted not merely to prevent French trade but to maintain her own. This gave her policy a somewhat more humane appearance than Napoleon's and a greater air of legality (as did her policy in World War I look better than the unrestricted German submarine warfare), but it did not make matters easier between Britain and the United States, just because Napoleon was powerless at sea to enforce his rules, whereas Britain could do so almost to the letter. In this spirit, however, Britain allowed neutral vessels through the blockade if they were cleared from or bound for a port in Britain, even relaxing her Navigation Laws to do so, and also allowed direct neutral trade with enemy colonies, since they were effectively cut off from France by the navy. But shipping taking advantage of a Napoleonic system, by which French agents abroad certified that they contained no goods of British origin, was automatically to be confiscated. Napoleon's answer to these Orders-in-Council was the Milan Decree of 17 December, 1807, which really marked the last stage in the development of the economic war. It tightened up the Berlin Decree by warning that any neutral ship which even consented to be searched by the British became lawful prize owing to that remote contact with Britain. Thus the extremity of strain and stress had been reached and the scene was finally set; any alteration in it must be caused by the success of one or other of the belligerents, or by the action of the neutrals. Of these neutrals America was by now much the most influential commercially. What action, if any, would she take?

She took a course of action designed to achieve its object without recourse to war; it failed in this, but it is of the greatest interest, because it was a unique and in many ways a characteristically American and Jeffersonian contribution to methods of international diplomacy. As Burt puts it, "Both Jefferson and Madison, as well as other Americans, had long cherished a comfortable belief that Nature had placed in the armoury of the United States a most effective weapon that might be produced at any time to coerce an offending power such as Britain and France."[1] This weapon was what in the twentieth century came to be called "economic sanctions", but it was then a relatively new concept, finding its origin in the Revolutionary period. Thus the Administration thought that a little economic pressure would soon bring a Britain deeply dependent on American markets and raw materials

[1] Q. Burt, p. 255.

to her knees without the ugly necessity for the use of military force, and this was pleasing to them since they had—and they deserve credit for it—a deep dislike of war. This notion of economic warfare, unaccompanied by other forms of hostility, bears distinctly the hall mark of Jeffersonianism; it typified that strain of idealism in American foreign policy which has given it some of its strength and much of its weakness. The naïve idealism, which produced the Neutrality Law of the nineteen-thirties is dangerous except in moderation, and there is more than a hint of it in Republican policy at this period. Its effects were dangerous for two reasons; first, because they not only involved the United States in difficulties with both the chief belligerents—Madison himself admitted at one stage that war might equally come with either Britain or France—but also because they put her in a position from which it became increasingly difficult to extricate herself, without a war which could do her little good; second, because in their exalted faith in the economic weapon, the Administration persistently neglected to put the defences of the country, which had not been at war for a quarter of a century, into order, though in fact that very policy of which they were at first so proud led them steadily towards war. American failure to achieve even a small proportion of the successes which might have been expected of her in 1812 can in part be ascribed to this weakness.

The 'sanctions' had been inaugurated some time previously by the Non-Importation Act of April, 1806, excluding certain British manufactures, but its operation had been continually suspended for diplomatic reasons. In view of the events of 1807, it was finally allowed to take effect on 14 December of that year. Just at this moment news arrived that Napoleon was violently seizing American shipping, contrary to the Franco-American treaty of 1800, and it became clear that both France and Britain were going to persist in their policies. It was felt that not a moment should be lost, and, on the recommendation of the Administration, Congress in three days passed the Embargo Act which has been called "a self-blockade of the purest water".[1] Its object was to bring economic pressure to bear on both the belligerents (which in practice meant Britain almost exclusively, so that it had to the British an air of supplementing Napoleon's efforts), even at the cost of hardship at home. It was modified in a number of later measures, but, broadly speaking, it prohibited the sailing of any vessel, American or foreign, from any American to any foreign port, except foreign ships in ballast or foreign armed public ships; coastal trade was allowed to American vessels under very heavy sureties. In the spring of the next

[1] Q. Bemis, p. 151.

year the President was authorized to lift it from whichever belligerent removed her restrictions on American commerce. This "singular act," as *The Times* put it, was "little short of an absolute secession from the rest of the civilized world. The sweeping impartiality of the proceeding will, it may be conceived, leave Great Britain little subject of complaint; yet it must be observed that though the prohibition of intercourse is general, its effects will be most forcibly felt by that Power which partook in the greatest degree in the communications which are now interdicted. . . ."[1]

But very soon it became apparent that the system, made up of the Embargo Act and the Non-importation Act, was a failure. It was evaded at every turn by the American people, particularly those of New England, whose geographical position and fishing rights off the coasts of British North America gave them magnificent opportunities for smuggling, and whose mercantile interests bitterly opposed the whole policy of the Republicans. Only an Administration, reliant on other areas than New England for its support, could have contemplated such a policy for a moment, and it is one of the ironies of American history that this system of economic warfare, whose chief ostensible purpose was to preserve the trade of America, was opposed tooth and nail by virtually all her traders, on whom the hardships caused by the embargo fell with incomparably greater severity than those caused by the trade restrictions imposed by the belligerents. This factor soon entered the constitutional sphere, and the Federalists of the North found themselves taking their stand upon those States Rights, which had hitherto been the pride of their Southern and Western opponents, while the Republicans had to use the power of the Federal Government to its utmost against those who had always been its advocates. So strongly did the New Englanders feel, and so hard were they pressed commercially, that many American ships and sailors who were abroad sailed the seas under the British flag. But even the planters of the South, where the Republicans enjoyed perhaps their greatest strength, soon began to feel the pinch, since they were unable to export their great staple crops; and, though, as an agricultural people living directly on the land, they did not suffer so soon or so much as the merchants of the North, their discontent grew. The whole country suffered in some degree, and soon it could be written by an observer, that "the grass had begun to grow upon the wharfs. . . . In short, the scene was so gloomy and so forlorn that . . . I should verily have thought that a malignant fever was raging in the place; so desolating were the effects of the

[1] 27 January, 1808: q. Mowat, *Diplomatic Relations*, pp. 47-8.

embargo, which, in the short space of five months, had deprived the first commercial city in the States of all its life, bustle, and activity; caused above one hundred and twenty bankruptcies; and completely annihilated its foreign commerce!"[1]

Meanwhile, the Administration's hopes of coercing either, let alone both, of the belligerents into ceasing their activities against neutral commerce were being rapidly proven quite without foundation. Napoleon refused to budge (even, by the Bayonne Decree, confiscating all American ships, on the ground that they must either be in fact British, or merely evading the embargo which he could thus assist Jefferson to enforce), and so did Britain, the latter's attitude being epitomized in Canning's earlier reply to Erskine's assurance of the conciliatory disposition of the Administration, that he "could not discover this conciliatory diposition in their acts or in the debates of Congress."[2] Yet neither side contemplated war on the commercial issue, for Erskine reported that, if the *Chesapeake* affair was settled, "Congress would never dare to consider them [the offending Orders-in-Council] as justifying hostilities",[3] while Pinckney wrote to Madison from London, "They will not go to war if they can help it . . . they will be content to have things as they are, and to trust to the influence of events, and a hope will perhaps be indulged that we cannot persevere in the Embargo".[4] The fact that the British Government did nourish this hope and that, largely due to the development of new British markets in South America, the effect of the measures on her economy was slight, is shown by Canning's ironic remark to the American Minister, that he would gladly have facilitated the removal of the embargo as a measure of inconvenient restriction on the American people. It is clear from this that Canning had the measure of Jefferson's unrealistic policy; the economic weapon had proved even less useful on this occasion than the weapon of King Cotton was to be in the hands of the South in the Civil War. Economic sanctions alone, without a willingness to support them by force, have yet to win a war. By the time that Congress met in November, 1808, Jefferson was caught in a cleft stick: the embargo was a failure, and yet national prestige had become so involved that he could not recommend its repeal. The only escape seemed to be by war, from which he shrank in genuine horror, though he was not entirely unmoved by the Southern feeling that a war with Britain could benefit only the Northern states, by a conquest of British North America. Indeed, as was President Buchanan to do much later, he yearned for March

[1] Lambert: q. Mesick, *The English Traveller in America*, pp. 186-7.
[2] Q. W.F.R., p. 59.   [3] Burt, p. 263.   [4] Q. W.A.A.E., p. 98.

and the Inauguration of his successor, hoping only that peace might be vouchsafed that long.

In fact, a temporary solution was found by Congress, against the apparent wishes of the Administration, which saved national face by altering the character of the economic sanctions, and at the same time removed the impossibilities of the embargo system, thus preventing an open and final breach with New England. Both the general embargo, and the original Non-Importation Act, which had been directed against Britain alone, were to end on 4 March, except in so far as they both applied to countries in possession of the two major belligerents. In their place was passed the Non-Intercourse Act, which was directed against these two great powers. It excluded all their vessels, public and private, from the United States and its territorial waters, while the remnants of the Embargo and Non-Importation Acts prohibited all trade in American vessels with either of them. Thus American trade was opened with neutral nations, though these were relatively few and far between in 1809, but still forbidden with the belligerents. These measures have an even more striking resemblance than their predecessors to the neutrality legislation of the nineteen-thirties. The President was once again given the power to suspend their operation against either belligerent should repentance show itself. This was the moment at which Jefferson was succeeded by Madison; the situation was better than that under the embargo, but at bottom it was much the same. As Erskine wrote, "The project of engaging in hostilities with both powers seems so chimerical, and so little likely to be attended with any advantages, as the commerce of the United States would be thereby excluded from the whole world as much as by an embargo, and the evils of war added to it, that it has caused the greatest embarrassments to determine what course ought to be pursued."[1]

New hands were at the helm in both countries; Canning had become Foreign Secretary some time before, and Robert Smith was now Secretary of State. Erskine, who was intimate with the Republicans, was, most properly, anxious for a settlement which would avoid adding America to the list of Britain's enemies, relieve her commerce, and perhaps even embroil the United States with Napoleon, for Madison frequently assured him that America would have "no hesitation about fighting Napoleon if he should not recall his Decree".[2] He saw an excellent opportunity to effect this when he received instructions to open negotiations for a *Chesapeake* settlement, and a subsequent agreement

[1] Q. Burt; p. 268.   [2] Q. W.F.R., p. 60.

325

on the vexed question of the Orders-in-Council, and he plunged in forth-with. He was easily able to conclude an agreement, which Pinckney and Canning had proved quite unable to do in London in the previous year, largely because there was less mistrust in Washington, and because the new Administration seemed much more fully aware than its predecessor of the difficulties attendant upon its present policy. Early in 1809 Pinckney had still reported back the traditional Republican view of the British Orders-in-Council, which, "As a belligerent system ... were nothing. They were a trick of trade—a huckstering contrivance to enrich Great Britain and drive other nations from the seas",[1] though he commented in this letter on the better air of a new Order-in-Council of 26 April, 1809, issued during the work of, but unknown to, the negotiators in Washington, which revoked that of 11 November, 1809, but declared that the ports of Holland, France, and Italy were to be blockaded. This was probably, on the whole, a relaxation of the British system, but when news of it reached America after the completion of Erskine's agreement, it threw doubt upon British intentions, an instance of the difficulties in diplomacy attendant upon the slowness of com-munications. Yet another example of this was that Canning's orders to Erskine to negotiate reached him on 7 April, 1807, so that while he knew of the Non-Intercourse Act, Canning did not when he framed his instructions. It was largely because of this and of the haste made necessary by the impending assemblage of a Congress which might override the conciliatory disposition of the Administration, that Erskine determined to exceed the letter of his instructions during the negotiations, by not insisting on an explicit recognition of the right of the British navy to enforce the Non-Intercourse Act against France and an explicit American recognition of the Rule of 1756, being satisfied that in fact the objects of these stipulations would be effectively achieved by the agreement.

It may be that he was more influenced by the arguments of Smith, to the effect that the agreement fulfilled the spirit of his instructions, than he was by their letter, but he saw the greatness of the opportunity and also its fleeting character, and there can be little doubt that, in the eyes of posterity, his convention met all the essential needs of Britain, and opened up, as had Jay's Treaty and the abortive Monroe treaty before it, a prospect, glittering from the ultimate British point of view, of cordial Anglo-American co-operation. It should further be noted that Madison was now prepared quietly to drop the American demand, on account of which Jefferson had rejected the Monroe treaty, that

[1] Q. W.A.A.E., pp. 103-4.

the British should explicitly renounce the right of impressment. The agreement was signed on 18 April, 1807, and in an exchange of notes it was proclaimed that on 10 June the Orders-in-Council would be withdrawn by Britain, and that on the same day the President would suspend the operation of the Non-Intercourse Act against Britain. A *Chesapeake* settlement was to be made, and a special British envoy despatched, as Canning had suggested, to complete the formalities. The effect of the publication of these notes in America was splendid; even the deliberate shooting, in a case of mistaken identity, of an innocent Canadian schoolmaster seized by American soldiers on Canadian soil at Brockville on 1 May, 1809—an incident in a smaller way as serious as that of the *Chesapeake*—cast no shadow. Congress, when it met a few days later, felt as if a great cloud had been lifted from the land. Its course was now clear, for a war with France, which had no naval power and no lands adjoining those of the United States, held little terror, while any ideological sympathy the Republicans had once had for the generation of the Revolution had long since disappeared; they renewed the Non-Intercourse Act largely unaltered, knowing that it would now apply only to France. On 10 June, the day appointed, in a manner worthy of the people who invented the gold rush, six hundred American vessels sailed fully laden for British ports: even New England was satisfied.

Doubly shattering, therefore, after this false dawn, was the news that Canning had absolutely repudiated the agreement, recalled Erskine, and refused to send a special envoy, though magnanimously allowing those ships which had already sailed to proceed with their cargoes, largely of raw materials, to the British ports which were hungry for them! When Jackson was named as Erskine's successor, it became clear that all hope of a present agreement was at an end, and that the chances of future good relations, as long as the war lasted, were remote. Of all the decisive acts worsening Anglo-American relations since the American Revolution, this was the worst; Canning's responsibility was far more grave than that of Jefferson two years earlier, for the situation had deteriorated badly and the strain of the war on Britain was much more severe, so that the prize of American friendship was so much the more desirable. The reasons for Canning's action are, as Burt says, hard, if not impossible, to understand; those he advanced sound like mere pretexts, yet Canning's was one of the ablest minds of his day. It is possible that he over-estimated the importance to Britain's victory of the letter of the maritime system as it affected America, and probable that he under-estimated the strength of the United States and the determination of its Government; certainly he had more than his share of that obstinacy and pride which was so characteristic of the British at this period. In truth, Canning's failings were predominently of personality rather than intellect, and perhaps there is an explanation of his conduct in an antipathy to the Scotch Erskine, appointed by his Whig predecessor Fox—whom Canning had disliked in proportion as he had admired his opponent Pitt, "the pilot who weathered the storm"— or, even more likely, in those growing personal tensions in the British Cabinet which shortly ended in its disruption and his duel with Castlereagh, whose future ascendancy was largely responsible for his opponent's long period in the political wilderness. Suffice it to say here that his action brought war with the United States very much nearer.

The activities of Jackson, the new British envoy, led, as we have seen, to a partial suspension of diplomatic relations, and, emotionally, the American people were ready for war, though the absolute unpreparedness of the armed services rendered it inconceivable; indeed, the effect of the economic measures upon national revenue had been such that Congress was actually forced to cut down military appropriations, for there were, with a hostile New England, virtually no other sources of money than the Customs. On 9 August, Madison proclaimed the restoration of the Non-Intercourse Act against Britain, and confusion reigned, while it became increasingly apparent that it, like its predecessor the Embargo, would have to go, since its economic effects were almost as serious, in view of the vast importance of Anglo-American trade. Eventually, on 1 May, 1810, just before adjournment, Congress passed Macon's Bill No. 2, which "was substantially the old measure turned inside out."[1] It reopened American trade with all the world, but forbade British and French armed vessels to enter American waters; in a queer inverted form it maintained the economic sanction, for it empowered the President, should either France or Britain repent of its commercial edicts, and should the other one refuse to do likewise within three months, to put the old Non-Intercourse Act back into operation against the recalcitrant one. In a sense, the negative American inducement had been replaced by a positive American threat, which had the great advantage of letting American trade continue, although subject to belligerent restrictions. In fact, the measure was a defeat for the United States, whose prestige suffered accordingly, for it virtually restored the British-controlled *status quo,* which the whole economic policy had been devised to alter.

[1] Burt, p. 278.

But curiously enough, it seemed to inaugurate an easier period of relations. New England had less cause for dissatisfaction, and the replacement of Canning by Lord Bathurst led Pinckney to write in March, 1810, "that a more friendly disposition towards the United States exists in this country at present than for a long time past."[1] When Bathurst himself was succeeded by Lord Wellesley, efforts, though in the event futile, were even made to negotiate an agreement in London. But the calm was a delusive one, for it depended upon American national humiliation, by her acceptance of the British point of view; there was a rush of American shipping to trade under the protection of the Union Jack, and New England rejoiced in what began to look almost like a trend back towards the control of the British Empire. Beneath the surface of American opinion, however, there was building up a renewed and powerful animosity towards Britain. It was not merely that positive hopes of cordiality were frustrated, but that there was a definite deterioration of feeling; bitterness in America in this period, culminating in the War of 1812, grew to be at least as strong as it had been at the time of the Revolution, and the growth of Anglo-American friendship was correspondingly retarded.

Furthermore, Napoleon did not accept this situation lying down, and his reprisals against American shipping became so severe that Madison in June, 1810, had to make specific and particular, though useless, threats against him rather than Britain. The Emperor, however, was not the man to let matters rest here; he saw an opportunity, which was too good to be missed, to embroil America with Britain by trickery. On 5 August, 1810, his Foreign Minister wrote to the American Minister in Paris that, non-intercourse having ceased against France, "the decrees of Berlin and Milan are revoked, and that after the 1st of November they will cease to have effect; it being understood that, in consequence of this declaration, the English shall revoke their Orde.s in Council, and renounce the new principles of blockade . . . or that the United States . . . shall cause their rights to be respected by the English."[2] This equivocal note was in fact a trap, as John Quincy Adams warned Madison, for Napoleon had not repealed and never did repeal the Decrees. Whether the President really believed in their repeal, or whether he was merely anxious to seize any pretext to re-assert American honour and prestige, he proclaimed on 2 November, 1810, that the Non-Intercourse Act would go into effect against Great Britain on 2 February, 1811, unless in the interim she repealed the Orders-in-Council. Britain refused to accept Napoleon's note as proper

[1] Q. W.A.A.E., p. 105.   [2] Bemis, p. 154.

evidence of repeal, and when, after 2 February, it became increasingly apparent that the Decrees were still in force and that American shipping was still being molested by the French, Federalist and New England opposition broke out again with redoubled fury, though it had no legal redress since the Republicans still had control of Congress, which confirmed the Non-Intercourse Act against Britain on 1 March, 1811.

But even now, no effective measures were taken to prepare the country for war, which, as Foster, the new British Minister, wrote, many wished "from mere amusement, their puerile imagination supposing it would be but an agreeable march to take possession of Canada"[1]—this in despite of the increased danger of war arising from Madison's orders, at the end of October, 1810, for the occupation of Spanish West Florida, which he claimed belonged to the United States under the Louisiana Purchase agreement, a claim which Britain might well dispute by force of arms. But Britain was still determined to play a waiting game, and in February, 1811, decided to send a Minister to the United States to try and improve relations. He was faced with an impossible task, for by the time he reached Washington at the end of June, the fight between the American frigate *President* and the British corvette *Little Belt* had taken place. This arose indirectly out of the impressment issue, but the Americans were as much in the wrong over it as the British had been in the *Chesapeake* affair; it inflicted even heavier casualties, and added yet another to the array of obstacles to Anglo-American accord.

But, fundamentally, the most serious problem was the increasing feeling, among the Republican majority of the American people, against Britain. Quantitatively the causes of war piled up, but qualitatively no worse cause was to ensue; there is no logical reason why a particular straw should break the back of the camel, but in the end public patience was at an end, and this was what in reality precipitated the final breach. When Congress met in 1811, Foster reported that the tone, particularly of its Irish members, was exceedingly hostile to Britain, though it "had changed and . . . now her great power and energy are as much descanted on as were formerly her internal weakness and certainty of a national bankruptcy."[2] As war came nearer it appeared to Americans less and less likely to be easy. As a result, however, of this rising spirit in the United States, the American price for peace was raised by Madison, who now added to the demand for the repeal of the Orders-in-Council a further demand for a British repudiation of Fox's blockade of 1806. When the support of Congress for Madison's proclamation enforcing the Non-Intercourse Act against

[1] Q. W.F.R., p. 81.   [2] Q. ibid, p. 80.

Britain became apparent, the relaxation of seizures of American ships, which Wellesley, in his hope for a settlement, had ordered, was stopped, and the letter of the British claim was once more enforced. All that Foster was able to achieve in this deadlock was a settlement of the *Chesapeake* affair on 1 November, 1811, but the impressment issue which gave rise to it remained, a running sore which increasingly poisoned the attitude of the American people towards Britain.

It is true that the Federalists still bitterly opposed the Republicans, and that feeling against the French ran almost as high in the nation as against the British—so much so indeed that when war was actually declared by Congress a proposal made in the Senate to include France in it only failed to pass by two votes—but during 1811 even the Federalist attitude underwent a change. To some extent they felt that British demands went too far, but they professed to an even greater fear of yet stricter economic sanctions imposed by the Administration; they thought defeat, though not destruction, probable in case of war, and this would at any rate, they hoped, have the effect of getting rid of the Republicans and returning them to power. Even to Foster they expressed a wish to have a good war and be done with it, so that they might be better friends afterwards, and, in the event, the War of 1812 did purge public opinion on both sides of the Atlantic of much of the perilous stuff that weighed upon it. If such an attitude as this of the Federalists seems to the modern eye extreme to the point of treason, it is important to remember how close, in fact, New England was to come to actual secession in three or four years time. In any case they thought better of it, and opposed the war when it actually became imminent. In the diplomatic sphere there was no hope of improvement so long as Monroe, who had now become Secretary of State, persisted in the pretence (there is now little doubt that this was what it was) that Napoleon had really repealed the Decrees, and so long as he refused, as a consequence, to consider declaring war on Napoleon if the Orders-in-Council were rescinded.

Meanwhile, a quite distinct, though not separate, train of events in the West brought war even nearer. The causal relationship between these and the maritime factors has been the subject of much historical controversy. The conclusion of Bemis, based on that of Julius W. Pratt, that "without the peculiar grievances and ambitions of the West there would have been no war",[1] is denied by Burt, who believes that the questions of neutral rights were the primary cause of the war. There seems no doubt that this is correct, but there can be little doubt that,

[1] J. W. Pratt, *Expansionists of 1812* (New York, 1925), p. 14.

though secondary, the Western was an effective cause, as is clearly shown by a geographical analysis of the voting for and against the declaration of war in the House of Representatives. In so far as generalization is possible, the West voted solidly for war, with the significant exception of upstate New York and part of Vermont. The Deep South also voted for it, though the Upper South was less solid, while most of New England and the Northern maritime states voted against it. The West was more positive and united than any other section. This may have been partly, as Burt points out, because they would be less affected by war and therefore were prepared to be more sensitive to national honour; the South and West certainly felt that the North-east was too ready to sell its birthright for a mess of pottage, and considered it was their duty to check the Anglophilia of the Federalists by asserting American dignity against British outrage. Furthermore, they had positive reasons to cause them to support a war, though probably not powerful enough to cause them to initiate one.

The first and most urgent of these was the renewal of war between the Indians, inspired by Tecumseh, and the Americans, under the leadership of General Harrison, at Tippecanoe in November, 1811. Whether it was precipitated by the deliberately provocative actions of Harrison, or by the long-mounting and passionate discontent of the Indians who were certainly bent on war in the end, is of little consequence; it was neither the first nor the last of the Indian wars, which, given the fundamental attitude of the two parties, must be regarded as inevitable. What is important from our point of view is that the natural American suspicion, that the war was deliberately precipitated by the British, was unfounded. When Indian feelings rose again in 1810, the Canadian authorities did all they could to restrain them from war, and, when it appeared that the Indians were about to cease listening to their counsels of moderation, ensured that the Administration were warned of the fact. But the red men could not have been in ignorance of the mounting Anglo-American tensions, and, though the Canadians abhorred the initiation of an Indian war, they could not have been entirely displeased, given the disparity between their resources and those of the United States, at the thought that if war did come they were assured of the aid of the Indians and their enemies deprived of it. But in any case, the Western American belief that the Indian war was fomented by the British, whether justified or not, led to a Western readiness for war, a war with the object of capturing Canada, including its fur trade, and thus ending for good and all the dangerous rivalry of Britain in the

West. This ambition, however, did not derive primarily from Tecumseh's war; it was an ambition as old as the Revolution, one which was to last at least into the final quarter of the nineteenth century, and which was perfectly natural in the American people, particularly in the age of Manifest Destiny. It was very natural, too, in the period when the emigration of Americans into the two Canadas, and particularly Upper Canada, was going on on such a great scale, that in 1812 two-thirds of the members of the Upper Canadian legislature were United States born. It was a latent desire which any other grievance against Britain inevitably tended to bring to the surface; it added strength to the maritime causes, but it is doubtful if, even joined to suspicion that Britain started the Indian war in 1811, it could have replaced them.

A fortiori is this true of the second of the Western causes adduced by Pratt, that the Southern ambition to attain East Florida, because of the already existent rift between the Northern and Southern sections, could only be fulfilled if the North was able to gain Canada as a sop, and that to this end the South supported the British war. It is true that Madison and Monroe, their appetite whetted by the acquisition of West Florida in 1810, ardently desired to acquire the remainder, and it is also true that their one territorial gain during the war period was in fact an extension of West Florida, but before war broke out they had to disavow the actions of their General Matthews in East Florida; furthermore, even if Britain had been in alliance with Spain since 1808, it does not seem that going to war with her was the best way of acquiring the Spanish territory which they coveted, particularly since it was fairly obvious that in such a war Britain was likely to assert herself very strongly in the New Orleans area. Such a thesis pre-dates so intense a North–South rivalry. If the plain facts of the maritime contest do not explain the War of 1812, and in particular the South's support for it, the great slump in the value of agricultural produce in these years helps to do so, for the planters of the South, particularly in the case of tobacco, the value of which had sunk almost to zero, constituted "the one section of the country that was vitally dependent upon the markets controlled by Napoleon",[1] and thus for obvious reasons hoped to crush the British blockade by war.

But the most convincing argument for the primary, though not the exclusive, importance of the maritime causes is the fact that they were put forward by the Administration as pre-eminent, and that, though Madison was dependent upon Congress, where after the elections of

[1] Burt, p. 308.

333

1810-1 the War Hawks of the West were strong, the initiative for war came from him in the end. Though Mahan later judged that the war had become inevitable by 1811, the Administration held back for another year, hoping against hope for a softening of the British attitude, but the President's temper was not improved by the fact that it now became perfectly clear that he had been duped by Napoleon. The publication in March, 1812, of the correspondence of an Irish adventurer, John Henry, which seemed—wrongly—to show at first reading that the British Government had been intriguing with treasonable Federalists, looked as if it might precipitate the conflict at once, but again caution prevailed. When Congress met, Madison requested belated war preparations, and on 27 or 28 May Foster communicated to the Administration the contents of a note from Castlereagh, which seemed to end all hope of a repeal of the Orders-in-Council as long as the Napoleonic Decrees remained in effect, which they obviously were going to do. This appears to have been the decisive moment, for on 1 June Madison presented a war message to Congress. It dwelt at length on impressment and the commercial grievances, and made a reference, consisting of only two sentences, to the Indian war, but it showed the old difficulty quite plainly in a final paragraph, which postponed any recommendation on the subject of France's "violence and retrospective orders" for the seizure of American property, and "other outrages," until the receipt of news of discussions then proceeding in Paris.[1] A bill declaring war was finally signed by the President, and became law on 18 June, 1812. Thus did the United States, avoiding open hostilities with France at the same moment, slide into war with Britain, who was still heavily engaged in the great life and death struggle with Napoleon.

It has always been held as one of the great ironies of history that on 23 June, the day on which Foster, after a last effort to obtain a suspension of hostilities until the declaration of war could reach England, took formal leave of the American Government, the Orders-in-Council were repealed in London. They were, however, only repealed conditionally, and had knowledge of this fact of repeal been available in Washington (by electric telegraph for instance), it might have led to a postponement of the American declaration though it it is by no means certain that it would have prevented war altogether, particularly because impressment was probably as important as commercial rights in the minds of Americans and because almost Castlereagh's last words to the American Chargé d'Affaires were that "no administration could

[1] *A Compilation of the Messages and Papers of the Presidents* (New York), p. 490.

expect to remain in power that should consent to renounce the right of impressment, or to suspend the practice".[1] This must remain one of the insoluble "might-have-beens" of history.

Suffice it to say that Britain had opened the door for negotiations, and might have done so earlier but for the assassination of the Prime Minister, Perceval. Public opinion in Britain had for some time been turning against the Orders-in-Council, and Castlereagh took advantage of yet another Napoleonic diplomatic deception—a claim that the Decrees had ceased to apply to the United States for over a year already—to repeal the orders, subject to American repeal of the Non-Intercourse provisions, and to do so without, as he had previously insisted, reviving the blockade of 1806 or any other blockade, which was a substantial concession to the American point of view. This change in the British attitude was brought about largely by the situation in Europe. Napoleon had invaded Russia; the Continental System was at its zenith; there was a glut of manufactured goods in Britain; and a bad harvest had completed her difficulties. It was natural she should be reluctant to add another to the list of her enemies, but even now she did not feel able to sacrifice a right—impressment—which might weaken her supreme weapon against Napoleon, the Royal Navy. Thus, when Madison rejected a last appeal for an armistice from Foster at Halifax, impressment remained the residual cause of war.

It is very hard to assess its true importance to Britain. American official estimates were that perhaps 10,000 impressments of seamen with some colour of American citizenship were made in the two decades of war: Castlereagh later said that "three thousand five hundred seamen in the British Navy claimed their discharge as American citizens, of whom one thousand seven hundred were probably entitled to it."[2] These do not seem very large figures, in view of the fact that the total number of seamen in the navy in 1812, the peak year of the war, was 113,600, but they are marginal, and could be important when ships of the line were chronically undermanned; even more significant is the fact that a relaxation of the right would almost certainly have meant a much increased rate of desertion, which already amounted, according to Albert Gallatin in 1807, to 2,500 men a year.

Analogous to the impressment issue was the action of the British Government in threatening to ship to England, and try for treason, twenty-three men captured at the battle of Queenston and alleged to be British subjects, a privilege the British claimed could never be surrendered, which was a contention clearly contrary to American

[1] Q. Burt, p. 315.   [2] Q. W.A.A.E., p. 56.

theory and practice.[1] This notion of unchangeable allegiance did not in fact enter into the actual governmental controversy over impressment, since it was never raised by a British Government content to get back only seamen who were still British subjects even in American eyes, but it always lurked in the background. Britons inclined to feel that British subjects had no right to become American citizens, even if their Government refrained from saying so, and Americans harboured corresponding resentment against what they felt was the underlying British desire to prevent the swift growth of the United States by denying the right of her nationals to alter their allegiance.

The American attitude on impressment itself is easily understood and appreciated; it is best expressed in the words of an American seaman, serving under impressment in the British Navy, in a letter to Pinckney, much of whose time was spent on this sort of case, on 9 August, 1795: "the treatment on board an English man-of-war is so different from what we might expect as American subjects, as being at such a distance from our families and uncertainty of their situation, makes us very uneasy. . . . Consider, Sir, after an absence of two years and upward from a wife and five helpless children what my situation must be, and what theirs is, to lose a husband and a father and be in the service of another country against inclination, unable to afford them any relief or comfort—such is the situation of me. . . . John Pridy."[2] It is not hard to understand the bitterness of American Anglophobia.

Of such stuff were the causes of the War of 1812. Commercial and maritime rivalry, impressment, Western ambition and Anglophobia— no one of them was, on the surface, a sufficient cause of war. But all were exaggerated and intensified by the poison of mistrust, and so the nations slithered into war.

III

BUT whatever the objects of the struggle, they were not achieved, for it ended in a stalemate which, since such ambitions as there were had been on the American side, constituted a kind of defeat for the United States; certainly it was a disappointment for the War Hawks and expansionists of the West, who hoped for a swift conquest of Canada and a merry one. It is true that, if either side had won outright, it would have been a worse disaster than it was, since it would probably have em-

[1] Ralph Robinson, "Retaliation for the Treatment of Prisoners in the War of 1812" (in *Am.H.R.*, XLIX, 1943).   [2] Q. W.A.A.E., p. 56.

bittered the defeated one so seriously as to frustrate all future attempts at the settlement of outstanding issues, instead of leaving them both with at least a healthy respect for the power of the other. But Morison and Commager do well to call it "a futile and unnecessary war, which might have been prevented by a little more imagination on the one side, and a broader vision on the other. . . . Anglophobia became a tradition in the United States, when, by a happier combination of events, it might have been exorcized."[1]

The Administration, conscious of the disastrous lack of preparedness of the country, probably hoped for an early peace, but the West wanted victory in Canada first, and, since the population of Canada was about half a million, mostly French, and that of the United States over seven millions, their wish seemed not unlikely of fulfilment. But America was to be singularly unsuccessful in the war. Fundamentally this was due to the fact that, even in the West and South, the mass of the people were not prepared to make sacrifices for victory; enlistments in the armed forces remained so disappointing that conscription was considered. This general lethargy was made far worse in its effects by the bitter opposition of the North-east to the whole idea of the war; there it was believed that the real issue facing America was whether the military despotism of Napoleon would conquer Britain and the world. To Federalists the Republican war appeared both unwise and immoral, although, as the neighbours of Canada whose conquest was its primary strategic objective, and as the great traders of the country whose commerce was one of its main issues, New Englanders might have been expected to support it. But even those among them who did not care much about Napoleon had long been alienated by the commercial policy of the Administration. The British played upon this feeling by exempting northern New England from their blockade until 1814, so that its trade with Canada and the outside world continued virtually uninterrupted; to such lengths was this carried that Congress actually voted an embargo on American commerce, which merely supplemented the British blockade, to last from December, 1813, to April, 1814, when the fall of Napoleon opened up profitable European markets. Not only did the North-east continue to draw off the national supply of specie and other monies by its continued trade, thus making the war harder to finance, but it actually helped the enemy by investing freely in British Treasury notes, as well as keeping the British armies, to a considerable extent, provided with meat and other supplies. Its State Governments refused to meet the President's requisitions for militia, and discouraged

[1] Morison and Commager, I, p. 431.

337

enlistments; it flew its flags at half-mast when the war broke out and celebrated allied victories in Europe during its course. When in 1814 the blockade was eventually extended to Massachusetts, and much of Maine was captured by the British, the legislature of the former summoned a New England convention at Hartford, with the avowed object of considering amendments to the Federal Constitution, and the possible one of recommending secession from the Union.

It met in secret session at the end of December, but the moderate Federalists gained control, and the report it issued on 5 January, 1815, after the Treaty of Ghent had been signed but before information of it reached America, was moderate, ruling out secession and a separate peace, and proposing a few constitutional amendments. No more was heard of these when the news of peace had arrived, and, when the doctrine of States rights was again enunciated, it was to be once more from the lips of its originators to the South. Feeling between the North-east and the West was allayed temporarily, though it was to surge irresistibly to the surface again with the triumph of Jacksonian Democracy in 1828. The coming of peace in 1814, however, gave new life to the Administration, which tended to make New England its scapegoat; certainly the North-east had carried its commercial and sectional Anglophilia to an extreme, and the Federalists never lived down their so-called lack of patriotism in this period. It was one of the reasons for their disappearance as a party, though perhaps a more significant one was that, through the war of which she so disapproved, New England's economy began to diversify itself industrially, so that, after a lapse when the war-time blockade was lifted, her transformation from a commercial into an industrial community proceeded swiftly. In the end this was to make her a competitor of Britain rather than a dependent, while she, like the rest of the country, began to turn her eyes slowly away from the sea to the West, which became the principal market for her goods.

But the antipathy of New England and the apathy of the rest of the country were not the only reasons for American lack of success in the war. Her apparent advantages did not have much weight at its outset, when Canada had about 12,000 effectives (a third regular soldiers, a third Canadian regulars, and a third Indian auxiliaries), whereas the regular army of the United States numbered less than 7,000, while very few of the 400,000 state militia called into service ever went into effective action. What is more, at the time when America's potential advantages might have tended to come into play, Britain was able very substantially to re-inforce her armies owing to the ending of the European war; indeed, this ability of the British Government to turn their attention seriously to what had hitherto been an outlying struggle in a remote part of the Empire, really divides the war into two parts. Nothing in Anglo-American history better illustrates the important truth, that Americans have remained much more sensitive to the causes of Anglo-American discord and to the disagreements resulting—for the very good reason that they nearly all affected them more closely—than the British, who have felt them less at the time and forgotten them more easily afterwards. Nathaniel Hawthorne wrote during his period in England in the middle years of the century, "I was mystified to find that the younger ones had never heard of the battle of New Orleans, and that the elders had either forgotten it altogether, or contrived to misremember, and twist it wrong end foremost into something like an English victory. They have caught from the old Roman . . . this excellent method of keeping the national glory intact, by sweeping all humiliations and defeats clean out of their memory."[1] There was no doubt much of this happy amnesia, but there was also a sense of the remoteness of the struggle, and to this day many educated Englishmen have never heard of the burning of Washington, even if they do not all respond to the information like the one who said, "Oh! I always thought he died peaceably in his bed." It is not unnatural that the sounds of the battle of Plattsburg should to English ears be lost in the thunder of Waterloo.

Thus the release of British forces and energies for the American war made United States chances of conquering Canada, their only worthwhile objective, distinctly less promising. That it had not been achieved already was largely explained by one grave American strategical error and by ineptitude in her war direction; instead of mustering all their strength for a decisive attack upon Montreal, the trunk of the Canadian tree, the American forces dissipated their energies in lopping off its branches in Upper Canada, while the Republicans were not natural war leaders and produced no first class American commander except Jackson, who was in the South. Though, for these reasons, the United States made poor use of its opportunities, the British, because they remained strictly on the defensive, did almost as badly at the strategical level, contributing nothing but the naval blockade, which was ineffective on the whole against those parts of the country which favoured the war, and which failed, though perhaps by a narrow margin, to disrupt the Union.

[1] Q. Mowat, *Americans in England*, p. 163.

Tactically, too, the honours were very even, and it was this that made possible the redeeming feature of the war, its inconclusiveness. At sea, according to Mahan, American privateers captured no less than 1,344 prizes, though an effective British convoy system prevented worse losses; the few American men-of-war had some sharp successes in individual combats, which were as unexpected in England as they were pleasing in the United States, though they could not, of course—it had never been dreamed that they would—challenge British command of the seas. On land, British successes in the North were balanced by American victories on and around Lakes Erie and Champlain, while in the South the burning and fleeting occupation of Washington, which had prestige value only, was more than outweighed by Jackson's invasion of Florida and disastrous defeat of a strong British expeditionary force at New Orleans, even though the latter engagement was fought after the Treaty of Ghent was signed. Thus the military situation could only support a compromise or a non-committal treaty: persistence in the war by one side or the other alone could decisively alter this fact. When a deadlock was reached in negotiations in November, 1814, the Prime Minister, Lord Liverpool, wrote to Wellington in Paris suggesting that Britain might continue hostilities, with the Duke taking command in America "with full powers to make peace, or to continue the war . . . with renewed vigour."[1] But he declined to accept the responsibility because he saw no means of acquiring the indispensable naval superiority on the lakes, bluntly advising, in effect, a peace on the basis of the *status quo ante bellum*: "Why stipulate for the *uti possidetis*? You can get no territory; indeed, the state of your military operations, however creditable, does not entitle you to demand any."[2] Such in the end was the nature of the treaty, but the negotiations leading to it were long and complex.

IV

INDEED, they extended over the whole length of the war. Pre-occupied with the European campaigns, the British Government were at first anxious for a swift peace, and Admiral Warren was sent to the American theatre of war bearing armistice proposals. But public opinion was outraged by what it considered an unpardonable American stab in the back, and, after the abdication of Napoleon in April, 1814, the Government began to see the American struggle in a different light.

[1] Q. Morison and Commager, I, p. 430.   [2] Q. Burt, p. 362.

It prepared to reinforce its operations there and to go over to the offensive, in the expectation of teaching the United States a lesson and strengthening the position of Canada. The Administration in Washington was also, at first, anxious for peace on its own terms, and in March, 1813, in an effort to solve the impressment difficulty Madison signed an Act forbidding the service of any foreigner in any private or public vessel of the United States. Since American expectations of spectacular victories were not fulfilled, this desire for peace did not diminish as the war continued, and the Chargé d'Affaires in London, Russell, remained in contact with Castlereagh throughout its course. But, despite these facts, it took a long time for the two parties to get around to actual negotiations, for the British refused an offer of mediation by the Czar, although American commissioners, appointed on the assumption that Britain would accept, cooled their heels for some months in St. Petersburg. Eventually, direct negotiations were decided upon, and began at Ghent on 8 August, 1814. Conducting them, however, proved almost as slow as arranging them, and it was not until Christmas Eve, 1814, that, after repeated delays and frequent deadlocks in which hope was almost abandoned, and even after procrastinations caused by differences between the American delegates themselves, that the Treaty was signed.

The basic reason for the long diplomatic wrangle lay in the attitude of mind of the two parties which was dramatically illustrated by their original instructions, intentions and demands, for both started out with expectations, or at least hopes, which were not only wildly, even absurdly, optimistic, but which were in some respects so out of touch with reality that most of them failed even of mention in the final treaty. The negotiations in fact consisted of disillusionments and concessions on both sides, produced by a growing realization that the only way of getting a treaty at all was by postponing, shelving, or even ignoring most of the vital issues. The attitude of the British Government was less unrealistic than that of the American, since there was the possibility of decisive military successes in America now that her hands were free in Europe, but her pretensions were worn down by the fact that her new role was that of a would-be conqueror in America, and, though the British public had no love of the United States, they had had their fill of war in any form but that of the strictest self-defence. If the peace had not been already made, the disaster at New Orleans and the escape of Napoleon from Elba would undoubtedly have ensured it.

The attitude of the American Administration was fantastically out of touch with reality, and indeed there is no more convincing proof of

341

the effect of distance in isolating the United States from world affairs than the extent to which Madison was at first unaffected even by the vital fact of the ending of the European war. He had instructed the American commissioners to break off negotiations unless the right of impressment was renounced, and had high hopes that the Northern powers, even including Britain's new ally Russia, would support his demand for a wide definition of neutral rights in the American sense. The American commissioners who were actually in Europe very soon realized that America had not a friend in the Old World, and at once abandoned all expectation of a British renunciation of the rights she had claimed in the war; in fact, this was no longer necessary because of the return of peace, for until a large scale European war broke out again the question was an academic one. But even though the commissioners jettisoned these exaggerated hopes, they still had a long hill to climb, for Britain was now at the pinnacle of her power in the world; neither before nor since has her influence in international affairs been so great or so unchallenged. On the other hand, they realized all too well that the war had revealed a grave weakness in their own country, a sectional split which even had its echoes in the differences between two of their own number, Clay, the Westerner, and Adams, the New Englander. They might indeed have given up more than they did, but for their belief that, if, in the last resort, negotiations broke down and the war continued, it would be a war for national survival in which sectional differences might be healed and the American people might fight as they had never fought before. The objectives would be near and dear to them, but distant and detached to the English, without whose support Canada could not triumph.

The three British delegates at Ghent, Lord Gambier, Henry Goulburn and William Adams, were, as their predecessors at Paris had been thirty years before, undistinguished as statesmen and under the immediate and comprehensive control of the authorities in London. The American commissioners, on the other hand, were, as their predecessors had been also, men of renown, with wide discretionary powers in practice; Henry Clay of Kentucky, a powerful political personality conscious of the expanding strength of the American people; John Quincy Adams of Massachusetts, untainted personally by New England secessionism and the son of one of the delegates of 1783, but sensitive to Northern maritime interests; Albert Gallatin of Virginia, a Swiss born diplomat who was by nature as well as by geographical situation the peacemaker between Clay and Adams. With them came James A. Bayard and Jonathan Russell. This somewhat unwieldy commission was able in the event to resolve its differences, and, on the whole, by the nature of the peace they made the commissioners justified the wide trust placed in them by their Government and countrymen.

The Treaty of Ghent opened with an article promising, in almost the very phrase of Jay's Treaty, "a firm and universal Peace"[1], which was to come into effect as soon as both parties had ratified the treaty; this ratification was to be of the full treaty, "without alteration by either" party and within four months of the date of signature. In fact, ratifications were exchanged on 17 February, 1815, the Senate having—contrary to British fears—accepted it, rapidly and unanimously, on the previous day. Its basis was simply that of the *status quo ante bellum*. Arrangements were made in the first three articles for the cessation of hostilities, the restoration of all captured territory and property, and the exchange of all prisoners-of-war, a cartel concerning whom the two governments had—in an action unusual in that age but not insignificant in the history of Anglo-American diplomacy—signed during the course of the war. Out of these first three articles there was to arise once again an American claim for compensation for slaves carried off by the British but not returned, which had eventually to be settled by arbitration in 1822 and further negotiation in 1826. Such a claim might seem to assort oddly with Article 10 of the treaty which laid down that, "Whereas the Traffic in Slaves is irreconcilable with the principles of humanity and Justice . . . it is hereby agreed that both the contracting parties shall use their best endeavours to accomplish" its entire abolition. This article was inserted at the request of Britain as part of her great diplomatic campaign, which was inaugurated in this period and pursued throughout the nineteenth century, almost as an implied responsibility arising from her naval supremacy, for the abolition and effective prevention of the slave trade.

Of the six remaining articles of the treaty, five followed that vital and fertile example of international judicial procedure, inaugurated at the suggestion of Jay in the Treaty of 1794, the joint commission.* But, at the suggestion of the British, this procedure was improved upon, in an effort to end deadlocks such as had marred the work of some of the previous commissions; instead of commissions of three, there were to be commissions of two, and if they failed to agree, a final decision was to be made by referring the matter to the arbitration of a friendly sovereign or state, whose judgment was to be "final and conclusive." Though some of the questions tackled in this manner were not

[1] Treaties, II, p. 574 *et seq.*   * See p. 288 above.

settled, the addition of specific arbitration to the joint commission was a highly significant step forward, and, in the particular circumstances of the long but tense negotiations at Ghent, it had the added advantage of postponing difficult questions and still making peace, the effect of which in its turn would be to make these difficult questions easier to settle. There were three such commissions appointed to decide the most con- troversial boundary questions still pressing upon the attention of both governments;* the first was to ascertain the ownership of the disputed islands in the Passamaquoddy Bay area; the second to survey and determine the north-eastern boundary between the St. Croix source and the junction of the 45 deg. line and the St. Lawrence; the third to survey and define the water boundary from the St. Lawrence through the Great Lakes, as far as the western end of Lake Huron, and also from that point to the north-west corner of the Lake of the Woods.†

The only article now left undiscussed is the ninth, which, innocuously enough as it appears on the surface, agreed that both parties would make peace with the Indians against whom they were respectively fighting, granting to them such conditions as they had enjoyed in 1811, provided that the Indians themselves desisted from hostilities. But in fact the negotiations probably came nearer to breaking down on this issue than on any other, for they started with a demand from the British which symbolized the wide hopes they at first entertained of turning back the clock in North America. It was to be the last serious diplomatic appearance of the old Canadian claim to protect the redskin against the American, for though this had been genuinely in abeyance before the war, it had naturally come to the fore with the renewed Indian alliance, which once more had aroused Indian hopes of British protection in the treaty. The British negotiators revived the old project of a mutually guaranteed Indian buffer state, but since this was to be carved exclusively out of United States territory, since it would have affected many white men already settled in the area, and since it would, above all, have recognized a British right to interfere in the domestic affairs of a sovereign United States, it was quite unrealistic and absolutely unacceptable to the American delegation. Step by step, therefore, the British retreated, until all that was left was this inoffensive mutual obligation of the ninth article, and never again did Britain interfere on behalf of the Indians against the westward surge of the American people.

Such were the terms of the Treaty of Ghent, but in truth its stipula-

* See p. 288 above. † See Map 1.

tions are less striking than its omissions, for none of the primary causes of the war even received a mention in it. Basically this was because the military and political stalemate put neither side in the position of victor, but other factors also played their part. Impressment the British Government refused to renounce, and, even in the years of amicable negotiations which followed the peace, Castlereagh still was unable to do so. Thus the matter remained unsettled, yet curiously enough it never appeared again in history, for by the time of the next great war the whole procedure was quite out of date. The question of maritime rights, on the contrary, was to have a long history, though not quite the one that might at this time have been expected; in this treaty, however, it made no appearance, for the American delegation saw that, whatever their Government might have wished, the opportunity provided by the coming of peace to let this whole question, as well as that of impressment, drop, must, in view of the British attitude, be accepted with a good grace.

These two things were not even discussed, but the other two striking omissions from the treaty occurred for the opposite reason, that they were considered at very great length but could not be agreed upon, so that there was no possibility except that of ignoring them; they were, first the question of the fishing privileges of the Americans in British North America, which had been granted in the treaty of 1783 but which had lapsed in the war, and second that of the British right to free navigation of the Mississippi, along with the implied right of access to it, also guaranteed in the Treaty of Paris. (This implied right claimed by the British led to the disappearance of an agreement reached on the boundary from the Lake of the Woods to the Rocky Mountains, a frontier line over which there was to be further difficulty in the future as a result of this postponement.) These two substantive questions early became linked together, and it was soon clear that both or neither must be accepted, but this very bond nearly wrecked the treaty by splitting the American delegation. Clay refused to consider the inclusion of the Mississippi clause, claiming, quite rightly, that the whole nature of the problem was altered by the fact that the river was no longer an international boundary but flowed almost exclusively—and soon it would be quite exclusively—through the sovereign territory of the United States, but Adams, whose father had, almost single-handed, acquired the fishing privilege for New England, could not readily consent to its omission, though in the end he was to do so, partly owing to the pressure of his colleagues and partly to the fact that the American claim was a weak one in view of the distinction, carefully drawn in the original

Treaty of Paris, between their 'right' to fish on the high seas and their 'liberty' to do so inshore. Thus neither the Mississippi nor the fisheries questions were mentioned. In much the same way, no mention was made of the vexed question as to whether, as specified under Article 3 of Jay's Treaty, the British right to trade with the Indian tribes on American soil was to be continued.

On all these points the negotiators knew what they were doing in their omissions, but of the significance of one minor issue on which they made no decision they were probably not aware. Astoria, a fur trading post at the mouth of the Columbia River, which the British North-West Company had purchased from the American John Jacob Astor, but which was occupied shortly afterwards by a British sloop, did not appear in the treaty. It was handed over by Britain as the restitution of a conquest made from the United States, partly to avoid suspicion of ill faith but partly because she did not believe the United States had any just claim to territory in that area, a belief the exact reverse of which was cherished by the Government of the United States. That the British claim was not laid down in writing by Bagot when the arrangements for the hand-over were made in 1818, was probably a serious diplomatic error, since the issue was one of which much would be heard later, for it was, in the form of the Oregon question, to be the last really grave territorial dispute between Britain and America.

Thus the treaty was essentially a negative one; as Burt writes, its "only definitive achievement . . . was the termination of hostilities. Both sides were deeply disappointed at the result, but the stalemate was fortunate. The treaty did nothing that had to be undone, which is more than can be said for many treaties of peace".[1] But strangely enough it marked as decisive a turning point as can be found in the history of Anglo-American relations. Partly this was due to the fact that it was supplemented during the next seven years by a number of accepted arbitrations and successful agreements. Partly it was due to the fact that the swift acceleration of the westward march of the United States meant that, by 1821, the end of the Anglo-American partition of North America was in sight, for what had not been actually achieved had been foreshadowed in discussion and negotiation. Partly it was due to the very intensity of the American absorption in her own affairs, which had its obverse in the increasing and deliberate political isolation of the United States from Europe; she had thrown off the leading strings of the Old World, and, once her destiny in the West was apparent, was content to spend the nineteenth century seizing it with both hands,

[1] Burt, p. 371.

and though complications with Canada might ensue, the fact that she had turned her back on Europe meant a steady lessening of tension with England. Partly it was due to the change in the economy and political outlook of Britain, for she began shortly to abandon the ways of Mercantile imperialism and to follow the paths of free trade, which gave her every economic as well as political incentive to improve relations with the United States, while at the same time her progress towards full democracy, inaugurated by the Great Reform Bill of 1832, gave the British people a steadily broadening basis for political understanding of the United States.

Yet even these things do not complete the tale, for the Treaty of Ghent decisively checked the deterioration in Anglo-American relations which had begun with Jefferson's rejection of the Monroe-Pinckney treaty. It is important to see this decade of dispute and war in its proper perspective; to remember that Anglo-American relations were fairer in the last years of the eighteenth century than they were again to be until the last years of the nineteenth. With the advent of the Republicans in 1801 there came a danger of deterioration, and it might be argued that their mere accession to power indicated that Federalist Anglophilia had produced a false dawn in the relations of the two nations, which was not solidly rooted in American public opinion, were it not for the fact that for a brief spell before the Louisiana purchase, Jefferson himself could hardly have been warmer towards the British. With the establishment of the arbitrary rule of Napoleon there was nothing further to tie even a Republican Administration ideologically to France, and other bonds were much stronger with Britain. But this happy growth of cordiality in Anglo-American relations was not to be, and mistaken policies, begun in Washington but continued in London, particularly by Canning, led to conflict and to war; one can sympathize with Metternich's description of him as a "malevolent meteor" flashing through Europe.[1] These years must be seen as constituting a definite, unhappy lapse in the relations of the two nations; this was so serious a retrograde step as to postpone, perhaps for half a century, the growth of Anglo-American friendship, and should serve as a warning to statesmen in both lands that perpetual vigilance is the price of friendship, as well as of liberty.

This much, however, should be said: the issue might yet have been worse than it was. The stalemate war left no permanent scars and gave the two nations a fresh respect for one another's strength. Both now checked any tendency to further deterioration, partly because they

[1] H. Temperley, *The Foreign Policy of Canning* (London, 1925), p. 456.

took, as it were, a renewed grip on themselves, and partly because all the basic factors making for agreement arose once more from the waves of violence and bitterness. "Great Britain now recognized more clearly than ever the intrinsic strength of the United States and the vulnerability of the Canadas, but on the other hand the United States had been awakened both to the awful threat of her own domestic schism and to the overwhelming power of the British Navy. Both nations were aware of their mutual dependence in trade."[1] These things were in the minds of the Governments on both sides of the ocean, even if they had not yet sunk very deep into the popular consciousness, particularly in America. This seed-bed proved, however, to be sufficiently deep and fertile to nourish anew, with the increasing care now concentrated upon it, the damaged and as yet, in some respects, fragile plant of Anglo-American understanding.

V

ONLY the epilogue to this chapter of our story remains, and it can equally be considered as the prologue to the next chapter, for the years until 1821 can be regarded either as completing and tidying up the unfinished work begun at Ghent, or as opening up the long, and, largely happy, series of Anglo-American diplomatic and judicial adjustments which were to continue until the twentieth century. The new harmony of contacts at the governmental level early became apparent; the peace commissioners themselves set the tone by reversing the situation of 1783 (when the English had dined with Franklin at Passy after signing the treaty) by dining together, in British-occupied Ghent, as the guests of the English plenipotentiaries, on the day after the signature of the peace. It being Christmas Day, they ate roast beef and plum pudding brought from England. On 5 January, when both parties were entertained by the government in the Hotel de Ville, a band continued to play "Hail, Columbia" and "God Save the King" alternately, until—a good sign this—both sides agreed that it was tiresome enough to be stopped.

The same change is reflected in the person of the new British Minister in Washington, for there were happily to be no more Jacksons. Charles Bagot was not only a very competent diplomat, but was also determined to foster Anglo-American goodwill, and, as a result, he and his wife enjoyed a quite unprecedented popularity, which was shown not merely by the negative fact that he aroused no enmity or trouble between the time he arrived in 1816 and the time he departed owing to ill-health in

[1] Brebner, p. 88.

1819, but also by the positive action of Washington society in giving in his honour before his departure the so-called Bagot Ball. Here began the practice, now happily commonplace, of having on the tables "little flags of the two countries united", and here once again music played its part in soothing the savage breasts of English and Americans, for, in Bagot's words, "Upon drinking our healths, the band, to my infinite surprise and somewhat to my apprehension for the effect, played 'God Save the King', which the company heard standing. As this was a *pierre de touche*, I hinted to one of the managers to tell the band to play 'Yankee Doodle' the moment 'God Save the King' was finished, in order that it might be understood as a union of the two national airs, which I believe it was, for not a murmur was heard."[1] Bagot, obviously a born diplomat, was equally skilful in more immediately important diplomatic affairs.

His opposite number in London, John Quincy Adams, who took up his appointment in 1815, was a very experienced statesman, though he was hardly a good diplomatist by nature, for he inclined to stiffness of manners and was apt to lose his temper; neither was tact a strong point with him, as he showed, for example, by knowingly keeping Castlereagh, on one occasion, over an hour late for a Cabinet Meeting. He experienced some social difficulties, in his resentment at the scale of diplomatic 'tipping' demanded by London custom, and his accompanying feeling that he had to refuse under the Constitution the compensatory gift made by the British authorities to returning ambassadors (King and Monroe had accepted £500 apiece), but these only matched the problems set to the Bagots by Washington etiquette, particularly after Monroe's tendency to renewed magnificence in the Presidency became apparent; he had, indeed, changed in more ways than one since his early days of Republican simplicity in Paris and London. Nevertheless, Adams lived an active social life, though he found it very wearisome, and was determined in his own way to do his best for Anglo-American understanding, as his many speeches show; he expressed in one typical passage his heartfelt wish "that the harmony between Great Britain and the United States may be as lasting as the language and the principles common to both."[2] He believed, probably rightly, that such harmony was not to be best founded on lack of American self-assertion, for the English had certainly not yet outlived their arrogance, and he showed his belief in many ways, as, for instance, in the small but not unimportant question of precedence in the signature of treaties; the Treaty of Ghent had been signed first by the British commissioners,

[1] Q. Burt, p. 426.   [2] Q. W.A.A.E., p. 128.

contrary to precedent and normal diplomatic procedure, and he insisted that the commercial convention which he negotiated should be signed with reversed precedence in each alternate draft. When he left in 1817 to take up the post of Secretary of State in Monroe's Cabinet, he was replaced by a good friend, Richard Rush, who had himself for some months been acting Secretary of State; this is another indication of the importance attached throughout Anglo-American history to the post of American Minister in London, which has always been considered the leading American diplomatic office. It is an interesting commentary on the European orientation of British diplomacy that only comparatively recently has Britain's Ambassador in Washington become more important than her Ambassador in Paris.

The first development arising from the Treaty of Ghent, however, was not in the hands of the Minister in London *qua* Minister but of Adams, Gallatin and Clay, as a commission authorized to negotiate a commercial convention, to replace that embodied in Jay's Treaty which had expired before the war and not been replaced. The treaty, which was signed in July, 1815, was a disappointment to Americans, for it did not include any provisions concerning neutral rights and did not enlarge upon Jay's Treaty, but in effect merely renewed its main commercial provisions for a term of four years; it was, however, accepted by the Senate. It renewed the reciprocal liberty of commerce between the United States and Britain's territories in Europe; it renewed the American right to trade with the British possessions in the East; it renewed most favoured nation treatment, and prohibited discriminatory duties by either party against the other, which was very important to Britain since America was her best foreign customer. But it maintained the Mercantile exclusion of Americans from trade with British possessions in America, though certain practical concessions by Order-in-Council were continued, despite a great increase during the war in the productivity of the British Maritime Provinces in those commodities most needed by the West Indies. Finally, American efforts to include in the treaty provision for unrestricted commerce on the international waterways between the two states failed, because the British insisted that it should not apply to waterways "where the middle is not the boundary",[1] thus excluding the St. Lawrence, and because the Americans refused to allow a reopening of British trade with Indians living in the United States, which was finally and specifically prohibited by Congress in 1816, thus bringing to an end the ancient fur trade of

[1] Q. Burt, p. 396.

Montreal, though in fact this had long since shifted its centre of gravity to areas much farther west. Smuggling continued, of course, both in the Maritimes and on the rest of the border, but with the American tariff born of the war, the United States began to use retaliatory weapons against Britain to prize open the trade with her North American possessions, the most notable step being the American Navigation Act of 1818, which excluded from American harbours foreign vessels coming from ports shut against American ships. More will be heard of this when the convention of 1818 is discussed; for the moment commercial relations rested on this treaty of 1815.

The second achievement of these years was the allaying of friction and tension on the Great Lakes border, where incidents were all too common in the months after the war, before ill feeling had quite died away. This was done by a sensible approach to the incidents as they arose, by a determination in London and Washington not to let local animosities rupture relations at the centre, and by the final laying of the American bogey of British ambitions in this area. It received practical embodiment in a proposal actually put forward, for the first time, by the Americans in 1815—though it had been in American minds as far back as 1783—for the disarmament of the two powers upon the Great Lakes. The war had shown the crucial importance of maritime supremacy there, and although she was at first surprised at the proposal, it was obviously to the interest of Britain to accept it, since she could never hope in future to compete successfully with the superior local resources of the United States in a naval armaments race on the Lakes. Though Burt somewhat denigrates the agreement as being the result of peculiar conditions and not of peculiar virtue, and though both powers paid considerable attention to the defence of this border in the ensuing years,[1] the American Administration, and particularly Monroe, are to be commended for their conception, which was to lead in due course to the great unfortified Canadian-American boundary. The agreement confined forces on the Lakes to those necessary to act as revenue cutters, and was effected by an exchange of notes in 1817, subsequently ratified, in the manner of a treaty, by the Senate. Though it could be repudiated at six months notice by either side, it has remained uninterruptedly in force to this day, and was only once—in 1865—in serious danger of such repudiation; it has remained one of the major symptoms, and to some extent one of the causes, of growing Anglo-American friendship.

[1] C. P. Stacey, "An American Plan for a Canadian Campaign" (in *Am.H.R.*, XLVI, 1941).

While these arrangements were being made, the three boundary commissions were having but slow and mixed success.* The first of them was successful, for in 1817 the two commissioners agreed on a compromise which divided the islands in the Passamaquoddy Bay area between the two powers, though the division was slightly in favour of Britain;† except for a small treaty which was necessary, as late as 1910, to remove uncertainties, this was a definitive and creditable settlement. The second commission did not complete its survey of the North-eastern boundary until 1820, and even when this was done it was unable to overcome difficulties of the kind that had prevented the solution of the problem during the actual negotiations for the Ghent Treaty, for the British claim involved the sacrifice of a large area of what the Americans considered American soil; the commission, therefore, became deadlocked in 1822. In 1827, in accordance with the Treaty, the case was submitted for arbitration to the King of the Netherlands. Largely on the ground that he lacked information to decide on the merits of the actual points in dispute, the arbitrator proposed in 1831 a compromise, which divided the territory into two roughly equal parts. Both parties realized that the King had exceeded his authority, and that they need not accept the decision, but London, and at first Washington, were prepared to agree to the compromise as such. When, however, the politically important state of Maine objected, Jackson asked the Senate for advice, and they gave it against acceptance of the proposed line. There the matter rested. The third commission, though it was also long delayed by the making of the surveys, agreed by 1822 on the Great Lakes boundary, from the St. Lawrence as far west as the western end of Lake Huron.‡ They were unable to agree, even after surveys lasting till 1826, on the boundary from the western end of Lake Huron westward to the north-west corner of Lake of the Woods. This deadlock, like that in the North-east, was not resolved until the Webster-Ashburton Treaty of 1842.§

Two other serious difficulties left over from the Treaty of Ghent caused trouble in the relations of the two countries in the years immediately after the war; the first, that of the fisheries, and the second, that of determining the boundary from the north-west corner of Lake of the Woods to the far West, it being assumed that all the remainder of the boundary would be settled by the commissioners investigating it. The first was one of great consequence to the Americans, particularly those on the north-east seaboard, and Monroe was most anxious to heal

* For the terms of reference of these commissions see p. 344 above.

† See Map 3.   ‡ See Map 1.   § See Map 2.

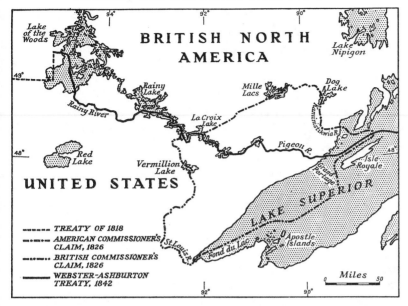

Map 2. *Boundary from Lake Superior to Lake of the Woods*

the sectional cleavage which had appeared in the war by showing himself peculiarly careful of New England interests; this policy was ensured
by his appointment of J. Q. Adams as his Secretary of State after the
latter's return from London. The British Government was anxious to
avoid any rupture with the United States, but it could not accept
Adams's contention that what was specifically described as a "liberty"
in the Treaty of 1783 was in fact an inalienable American right. The
American case may have been weak in theory, but their practical position was strong, since Britain, in order to avoid a breach, pursued a
vacillating policy, which in effect gave the Americans the fishing they
wanted, while she pressed for a settlement. It was obviously in the
American interest, therefore, to delay any agreement as long as possible,
for they were already enjoying the fruits of it, by fishing inshore and
drying and curing their catches on British soil. But Britain used her
navy from time to time to put the screw on, and there was always the
possibility of an ugly incident and an explosion.

The same became increasingly true of the other major difficulty, the
north-west boundary, as the westward movement continued and as
settlement on the Pacific coast began. In fact, only the swift actions of
Bagot and the willingness of Castlereagh to behave with moderation

prevented just such an incident over an ill-advised surprise American effort to take possession of Astoria, the disputed post at the mouth of the Columbia river, in 1818; Canning's later criticism of these actions of Castlereagh and Bagot was far from justified in view of the broad issues involved. As a result of this danger signal, Castlereagh proposed a settlement by commissioners, before further complications arose from the occupation of more land by westward moving settlers. It was symptomatic of the change in the tone of relations that Monroe not merely accepted the proposal with alacrity, but improved upon it, by suggesting a general negotiation covering the fisheries dispute and any other item that either government might wish to add. As Adams wrote of the President, "He had seen with peculiar satisfaction the rapid decline of that animosity which had formerly subsisted" and earnestly desired "to cherish and improve this state of public sentiment."[1]

Rush and Gallatin, who was the American representative in Paris, were appointed plenipotentiaries, and negotiations were soon begun in London with Goulburn and Robinson, the Treasurer of the Navy. They were conducted in a cordial spirit, but it soon became apparent that yet again a number of questions would have to be left unsettled, though agreement of a kind was obtained on the most important ones. Once more there was no meeting of minds on impressment and maritime rights, though there was more nearly one than there had been previously. Another English effort to couple a boundary settlement with their old right of access to and navigation on the Mississippi was absolutely refused by the Americans, and thus made its final exit from the diplomatic scene. Finally, an American proposal to widen the scope of the commercial agreement of 1815, by opening up the colonial trade to their people, failed, for the American Navigation Act had been a damp squib, and did not worry the British Government, whose primary concern was for the export of manufactured goods from Britain to the United States direct, a traffic which was not affected by the Act. It is appropriate, however, to note here, that in 1822, with the beginning of the great British move towards free trade, some substantial relaxation of the British colonial restrictions was made, by a statute which named certain free ports in the West Indies and British North America to which provisions, timber and naval stores could be carried in either British or American vessels. Neither this, nor other commercial and fishing concessions, which in effect allowed the Americans to enter the charmed circle of the Navigation Acts, were pleasing to the British in North America, and one can already hear that Canadian complaint,

[1] Q. Burt, p. 415.

so frequent later, that her immediate interests were being sacrificed by the imperial government on the altar of Anglo-American friendship. But as the idea of free trade came more and more to dominate British policy, this opening of commerce to the Americans continued, and it certainly removed one of the main causes of dissension between Britain and the United States.

Thus all that was done was to renew the provisions of the commercial convention of 1815 for a period of ten years from 1818; and in 1827 they were once again renewed, this time for an indefinite period. Agreement was also reached on the fisheries question. The American right to fish on the high seas, of course, needed no mention, and Article 1 granted to the United States "for ever" the "liberty" to fish, "dry and cure"[1] in two main areas, the southern coast of Newfoundland and the coast of Labrador and northwards therefrom, subject to the prior consent of the inhabitants where such existed; it also granted the liberty, subject to certain safeguards, to fish only and not to dry and cure, on the west coast of Newfoundland and the shores of the Magdalen Islands. In return, the United States renounced "for ever" any liberty to fish, dry or cure anywhere else in British territory or territorial waters. Though this might seem a thorough and comprehensive settlement, and was more liberal than the American delegates had expected, the fisheries were to continue as a bone of contention in Anglo-American diplomacy for many years.

The only two remaining articles of consequence concerned the Western boundary. Article 2 agreed a line "drawn from the most North-Western Point of the Lake of the Woods, along the forty-ninth Parallel of North Latitude", or, if this was not possible, a line "drawn from the said Point due North or South as the case may be, until the said line shall intersect the said Parallel", and thence westward to "the Stony Mountains".* Thus a simple and certain boundary had now been drawn over the prairies, though there were still grave uncertainties to the East, but no such clear-cut decision was possible from the Rockies westward to the Pacific coast. The American delegates had been willing to continue the 49th parallel to the sea and even to loop a little south of it, but the British were unwilling to surrender their claims to the land south of this line. Both parties were, however, aware that, whatever they might agree, the claims of both Spain and Russia in this area would still have to be reckoned with, and made mention of the fact in the compromise solution which they eventually reached, than which nothing could better illustrate the more hopeful tone of the relationship.

[1] Treaties, II, p. 658 *et seq.*   * See Map 1.

Acting on a British suggestion, Article 3 agreed "that any Country that may be claimed by either Party" west of the Rockies should, for a period of ten years, "be free and open" to the "Vessels, Citizens, and Subjects of the Two Powers", thus establishing a kind of unorganized condominium. This arrangement was extended indefinitely, subject to the right of either party to annul after a year's notice, in 1827, and the question of ownership was not finally settled until the Oregon Treaty nearly twenty years later.

In this happy fashion did these years of friendly and fruitful diplomacy open up a century of fairly steady progress in Anglo-American relations. Most of the residual difficulties left from the partition of the First British Empire had been, or were to be, solved. After signing the commercial treaty of 1815, Goulburn said to Adams, referring to the Ghent Treaty, "Well, this is the second good job we have done together." "Yes", replied Adams, "and I only hope we may do a third, going on from better to better."[1] These words were prophetic of the development of the relations of Britain and the United States throughout the nineteenth century. There were to be disappointments and difficulties in plenty, but, with America, for many years to come, turning her eyes steadfastly to the West, and with Britain entering the greatest period of peace and prosperity in her history, "truly," as Burt says, "a new era had begun."[2]

[1] Q. Mowat, *Dip. Relations of Britain and the U.S.,* p. 72.

[2] Burt, p. 426.

PART III

ISOLATION

CHAPTER ELEVEN

THE MONROE DOCTRINE
(1821-3)

I

THE determination of the United States to isolate herself from European affairs and to devote her resources to the opening up of the Great West, which is the key to her nineteenth-century foreign policy, was the subject, in effect, of a remarkable affirmation with the enunciation in 1823 of the Monroe Doctrine, for this solemn declaration of policy by the executive branch of the Federal Government postulated that the wars of Europe were no concern of the United States, and, conversely, warned the powers of Europe against interference in American affairs. But it was much more than an isolationist platform, for within the withdrawal there was an advance, within the limitation of interest there was an extension, and an important extension, in that the doctrine threw the mantle of the Republic's power and protection over the whole American continent, South as well as North. It was from the first a hemispheric concept.

But its long and influential history must not lead us to exaggerate the immediate importance of the Monroe Doctrine. The United States was as yet relatively weak, and it is doubtful if she could have made good her intentions had they been put to an actual test, and quite certain that she could not have done so against the will and the naval might of Great Britain. Indeed, the very enunciation of the doctrine was only possible because it was already known to the members of the Administration that the attitude of the British Government was not too far removed from their own. As was much emphasized later, in the great debate of 1940, the long and successful maintenance of this policy by the United States depended in practice, at least until after World War I, on the acquiescence of Britain; the British Navy was in this way America's first line of defence, for distance was only an effective barrier against foreign interference if control of the seas remained in friendly hands. In the twentieth century the United States was to build a navy large enough to protect herself effectively, but even then only on the assumption, at first tacit and later explicit, that it would not in the foreseeable future be opposed by that of Britain. A proof of this American inability in early years to implement the doctrine fully by herself can perhaps be found in the fact that it was largely forgotten, or at least ignored, in what Dexter Perkins—its historian—calls the period of quiescence after its first publication, until its formal revival by President Polk in a message to Congress on, curiously enough, exactly its twenty-second anniversary (2 December, 1845) and that even then it remained for some years almost a partisan dogma. But quite soon it became accepted as a fully national policy, and was strongly maintained for almost a century, even being for a period extended, under the so-called corollary of Theodore Roosevelt, until it asserted a positive American duty to interfere when necessary for the general international good in the internal affairs of the states of Latin America.

Thus President Monroe's famous message was of great ultimate importance, but it was also, in the particular field of Anglo-American relations, of immediate interest and significance, because by its implicit assumptions it set their tone for the rest of the century, and because it was yet another missed opportunity for an explicit Anglo-American *rapprochement*. It is perhaps not without significance that Canning and Jefferson, neither far from the grave, who had been the chief obstructors of Anglo-American agreement heretofore, were agreed in a desire to promote by common action, in this instance, what would virtually have been an alliance between Britain and the United States, and it is certainly not without irony that their wishes were not fulfilled.

In this crisis personal factors did play a considerable part. Though Castlereagh was on much better terms with the Americans than his successor and more conciliatory by disposition, it is questionable if the explicit proposal of co-operation would have occurred to him, not only because of his temperamental aversion from the dramatic in politics, but also because he was more inclined to compromise with Spain. How cordial he was to the United States is emphasized by Sir Charles Webster: "Castlereagh was a Tory, but he was the first British statesman to recognize that the friendship of the United States was a major asset to Britain, and to use in his relations with her a language that was neither superior nor intimidating."[1] Rush wrote after Castlereagh's suicide, "Let those who doubt . . . point out the British statesman, of any class or party, who . . . made more advances or did more . . .

[1] C. K. Webster, *Britain and the Independence of Latin America, 1812-1830* (London, 1938), I, p. 42.

towards placing their relations upon an amicable footing."[1] This was in no small measure due to Rush himself, who, apart from being a statesman and a charming personality, was distinctly Anglophile, avowing that the idea of England had stirred him from his earliest years:

> Her fame is constantly before him. . . . In the nursery he learns her ballads. Her poets train his imagination. Her language is his with its whole intellectual riches, past and for ever newly flowing; a tie, to use Burke's figure, light as air and unseen, but stronger than links of iron. "Is it not fit," he reflected, "that two such nations should be friends? Let us hope so. . . . If, nevertheless, rivalry is in the nature of things, at least let it be on fair principles. Let it be generous, never paltry, never malignant."[2]

But he kept his enthusiasm within the bounds befitting a representative of the United States, and so satisfied the Administration in the negotiations of 1823 that he was told he could not have behaved more wisely if he had had the whole American Cabinet at his right hand. He was never able to get as close to Canning as to Castlereagh, which was not surprising, since Canning's desire for an American *entente* arose from his perception of its practical advantage to Britain and by no means from any love of America; in this sense the leopard had not changed his spots, and his words to Bagot on his appointment to Washington contrasted very vividly with those of Castlereagh to Bagot's successor quoted below: "[T]he hardest lesson which a British Minister has to learn in America is not what to do, but what to bear."[3] Certainly, however, American representation during the vital years from Rush's appointment in 1817 until he returned to take up a Cabinet post in 1825, could not have been in better hands.

English representation in Washington, after the departure of Bagot in 1819, was in the equally distinguished, but not quite such warmly cordial, care of Stratford Canning, cousin of Castlereagh's successor. He was a brilliant diplomat and conscientiously fulfilled Castlereagh's wise and characteristic instructions:

> You will make it your constant duty to cultivate a good understanding with the Government. . . . The ancient relation of the British and American nations and the jealousies as yet imperfectly allayed inclines the Government of the United States to maintain their pretensions in discussion with us in a tone of greater harshness than towards any other

[1] Q. W.A.A.E., p. 153. [2] Q. ibid, pp. 138-9.

[3] Q. W. A. Dunning, *The British Empire and the United States* (New York, 1914), p. 19.

Government whatever. The American people are more easily excited against us and more disposed to strengthen the hands of their Ministers against us than against any other State. Time has done a good deal to soften these dispositions. The more we can permit them to subside by avoiding angry discussions the less will the American Government be capable of contesting unreasonably these various points which the reciprocal interests of the two countries may present themselves for adjustment.[1]

Thus Stratford Canning, though a powerful rather than an ingratiating diplomat, went out of his way to avoid giving offence, and must have regretted that he quitted Washington on account of ill health in August, 1823, three months before the crisis began, leaving the Legation for the next two years in the competent, but necessarily weaker, hands of the Chargé d'Affaires, Henry Addington. Stratford Canning thought the President amiable, upright and pacific, and it is true that, as the author of the abortive Monroe-Pinckney treaty he was probably inherently less hostile to Britain than Jefferson and Madison, who, though both out of office, remained important because of their closeness to Monroe; but time had mellowed all three of them, and, taking counsel together upon their Virginia hilltops, they were inclined to accept Canning's offer of co-operation. The Cabinet, however, was divided, and John Quincy Adams steadily hardened in his opposition to the project. He, too, is already familiar to us, as a determined statesman; his determination, indeed, was not far from obstinacy, and his middle age did not seem to lessen the unevenness of his temper. His experience as commissioner at Ghent and as Minister at the Court of St. James had encouraged in him the conviction, which came naturally enough in any case, that a forthrightness which on occasions approached bullying, and even mere bluster, was necessary in diplomatic dealings with Englishmen. Stratford Canning himself said in later years that "Under much waywardness on the surface there lay a fund of kindly and beneficent intentions",[2] in Adams, but he was the man who, for reasons which appeared sufficient to him, and in the end to his colleagues, laid most emphasis on independent (though not opposed), rather than concerted, action on the part of the two governments.

II

THE Monroe Doctrine was primarily the American answer to questions arising from the revolutions which overthrew the dominion of Spain

---

[1] Q. W.F.R., pp. 109-10.   [2] Q. W.F.R., p. 117.

in her Latin-American colonies during and after the Napoleonic Wars. It was also her answer to the claims of Russia (advanced in a not unfriendly fashion in a decree of September, 1821) that her Alaskan jurisdiction extended down to the 51st parallel, well south of the northern boundary for Oregon claimed both by the United States and Britain, but this Russian aspect was secondary, even though it led to the declaration of the 'non-colonizing' principle, which was to be important in the future relations of the United States with Britain. The dispute between Russia and America was amicably settled by a treaty signed in 1824, fixing the line 54 deg. 40 min. as the southern limit of Russian territory, which was virtually all that the American Government desired, and in 1867 the decision was put beyond cavil by the American purchase of Alaska. Canning had proposed joint negotiations on this issue to Adams, parallel with the proposal for joint action in Latin America, and, on the rejection of the latter and the subsequent receipt of information of the Russo-American treaty, he came to a separate agreement with the Russians on similar lines early in 1825, leaving the disagreement between Britain and the United States to be settled finally in the Oregon Treaty of 1846.

The substantive issue, that of the future of the Spanish American colonies, was more complex, as well as more important for Anglo-American relations, for it was of considerable consequence to Britain and of supreme consequence to the United States. It is vital to recollect that, until it was settled, the future not merely of most of South America, but of Mexico, of Spanish territories stretching to an undefined northern point on the Pacific coast, and also of East and West Florida, was in doubt, and with it the whole future of the United States. The first part of the problem to be settled, as it was the most immediate, was that of the Floridas; and it was potentially the most explosive in Anglo-American relations, just because it arose in an acute form during the course of the Napoleonic Wars, when Britain was not only in alliance with the legitimate Government of Spain against Napoleon and his puppet Madrid régime, but also conducting military operations against the United States in the region of the Floridas. The dispute continued after the wars were over, and the English sentiment of friendship for Spain died slowly, while in the United States, to which the Floridas were contiguous in territory and vital in importance, hostility to both Britain and Spain remained powerful. America had desired to obtain Florida from the beginning of her history, and in 1810 a revolt of Americans in Baton Rouge, and European preoccupation with Napoleon, allowed President Madison to annex part of West Florida, the rest being added in the course of the War of 1812. British protests, at the time and during the negotiations at Ghent, had no effect on these accomplished facts, though they probably helped to prevent much of East Florida from going the same way for the present.

After it was over, the military agents, recognized or unrecognized, of both powers were still meddling in the confused affairs of Florida, largely through Indian agencies, and both governments suspected the intentions of the other, though the United States had less justification for doing so than Britain. Adams, in an interview with Castlereagh in London, said that the United States had

> received strong and confident intimations from various quarters that there had been a cession of Florida by Spain to Great Britain. "There is not and never has been the slightest foundation for it whatsoever," said Castlereagh. "It never has been even mentioned." "Your lordship knows that such rumours have been long in circulation, and that the fact has been positively and very circumstantially asserted in your own public journals", remarked Adams. "Yes, but our public journals are *so* addicted to *lying*," replied Castlereagh. "We have no desire to add an inch of ground to our territories in any part of the world. . . . Military positions may have been taken by us during the war of places which you had taken from Spain, but we never intended to keep them. Do you only observe the same moderation. If we should find you hereafter pursuing a system of encroachment upon your neighbours, what we might do *defensively* is another consideration.[1]

The disorder on the Florida border grew steadily worse, and in 1818 General Jackson, in an effort to check it finally, not only invaded Florida and captured Pensacola, but hanged two Englishmen captured there on a charge of inciting the Indians to war. The outcry in England was such that Castlereagh declared that war would have come "if the Ministry had but held up a finger",[2] but he refused to intervene on behalf of British subjects engaged in such nefarious activities, and wrote to Bagot that "The avowed and true policy of Great Britain . . . in the existing state of the world" was "to appease Controversy, and to secure, if possible, for all states a long interval of Repose."[3] Monroe returned the Spanish posts, and, though he did not discipline Jackson, in view of the great popularity of the Florida exploit, the danger of war

[1] Q. J. F. Rippy, *Rivalry of the United States and Great Britain over Latin America, 1808-1830* (London, 1929), pp. 58-9.

[2] Q. W.A.A.E., p. 143.   [3] Q. Rippy, p. 66.

with Britain subsided, while Spain was now convinced of the necessity
of yielding gracefully, since it had become clear that Britain would not
support her and that the United States would not accept British mediation in the dispute. On 22 February, 1819, the Adams-Onis Treaty,
signed at Washington, in effect sold the Floridas to America for
£5 million and at the same time defined the western boundary of the
Louisiana purchase in such a way as to surrender any Spanish claim to
the Pacific coast north of 42 deg., so that Spain was not involved later
in the complications of the Russian-British-American dispute over
Oregon, for her rights descended to the United States by virtue of the
Louisiana purchase. British public opinion denounced the treaty, which
caused Rush to write, "The English papers raise a clamour, charging
ambition and rapacity upon the United States. They say nothing of the
acquisitions which England has been making in all parts of the globe,
by her arms or policy, since the days of Elizabeth and Cromwell."[1]
This shows well enough that, even in an Anglophile, the common
language and a knowledge of English history do not necessarily produce
only Anglophile arguments. Castlereagh did not pretend to like the
agreement, but accepted it on behalf of the British Government with a
refreshingly good grace.

Thus the future of one Spanish dominion was settled and one complication in Anglo-American relations removed, in such a fashion that
British sympathy for Spain continued to fade rapidly, while American
mistrust of British intentions grew no more marked than it already was;
furthermore, the immediate territorial ambitions of the United States
were satisfied, since, despite the fact that ratification of the Spanish
treaty was delayed for two years by the Senate, owing to their reluctance
to relinquish the American claim to Texas by the new boundary definition, the undisputed areas of the Louisiana territory offered for the
present ample scope for settlement and growth. But the political future
of the vast bulk of the Spanish Empire in America remained to be
decided. In the later years of the Napoleonic Wars rebellions had broken
out in the Spanish colonies, so that the beginnings of the problem had
appeared in 1810 when Monroe was Secretary of State, but in 1814-5
it had seemed quite possible that, with the restoration of Ferdinand VII
to the Spanish throne, Spanish commanders in America would be able
to restore effective Spanish control. In 1817, however, the situation
changed with the coming of much more serious and successful revolutions—that in La Plata was virtually triumphant by the end of the year

[1] Q. W.A.A.E., p. 148.

—and the problem was fairly laid in the laps of the diplomats and statesmen. During the next six years it became steadily more obvious that some radical solution was going to be necessary, and that, the longer it was delayed, the more radical it would have to be.

Adams, who was at the State Department, never seriously altered his opinion: "That the final issue of their present struggle would be their entire independence of Spain, I had never doubted. That it was our true policy and duty to take no part in the contest . . . was equally clear." There was unquestionably a great deal of enthusiasm in the United States for the cause of South American republicanism; it was strongly voiced by Henry Clay, and shared in considerable degree by Monroe himself, the ardent emotions of whose youth no doubt stirred once more within him. Adams, however, though convinced that they would, and rightly, gain their independence, did not have great hopes for the future of democracy in the infant states, and wrote, with little trace of idealistic emotion: "I wished well to their cause; but I had seen and yet see no prospect that they would establish free or liberal institutions of government. . . . Arbitrary power, military and ecclesiastical, was stamped upon their habits, and upon all their institutions. Civil dissension was infused into all their seminal principles. . . . I had little expectation of any beneficial result to this country from any future connection with them, political or commercial."[1] He foresaw clearly enough the future of the republics in the next century, described so vividly by Martin Decoud in Conrad's *Nostromo*: "There is a curse of futility upon our character: Don Quixote and Sancho Panza, chivalry and materialism, high-sounding sentiments and a supine morality, violent efforts for an idea and a sullen acquiescence in every form of corruption. We convulsed a continent for our independence only to become the passive prey of a democratic parody, the helpless victims of scoundrels and cut-throats, our institutions a mockery, our laws a farce".[2] Thus Adams regarded the new states with reserve, almost coldness, and pursued a course of strict neutrality towards them, which did in fact terminate in recognition of their independence, although this consummation came far too slowly for many of the American public. But, cautious though he was, independence remained the only acceptable solution to Adams as to all Americans.

The attitude of Britain was necessarily different; she had but recently been an ally of Spain and the principal agent in the restoration of the Spanish royal house to its European dominions. Furthermore, Castle-

[1] Q. Morison and Commager, I, p. 453.

[2] Joseph Conrad. *Nostromo, A Tale of the Seaboard* (London, 1918), p. 146.

reagh, in the years immediately following the Treaty of Vienna, pursued a policy of co-operation with the other powers constituting the so-called Concert of Europe, and these, particularly Austria and later Russia, regarded revolutions of the Spanish-American type with horror, a horror which increased with the sudden outcrop of revolutions in Europe itself in 1820-1. To this must be added the fact that Britain was, after all, a monarchy, even though by now a monarchy of a very unusual kind. But even Castlereagh, who was regarded by English radical opinion as the archetype of the reactionary, had never seen exactly eye to eye with the European despots, and Britain had in 1815 ostentatiously refused to be associated with that piece of "sublime mysticism and nonsense", the Holy Alliance. For this refusal British public opinion was profoundly thankful when it became clear that the Alliance was merely to be an instrument for the suppression of all liberty of expression and all constitutional government in Europe. The attitude even of the extreme English Tory was quite distinct from that of the continental reactionary; England had fought the long war against France at least partially in defence of constitutionalism, and however much Castlereagh might mistrust public opinion and tremble at the word democracy, he could not and would not flout the former altogether. It has, indeed, been clearly established that he had begun before his death that process of breaking away from European reaction which historians so long attributed exclusively to Canning. The attitude of the British public to the Spanish-American revolutions, therefore, varied between two extremes, that of a few radicals who were filled with enthusiasm for them, and that of the most conservative elements, such as George IV himself, who regarded any kind of rebellion with distaste; most effective opinion was moderate and sought a middle course.

For such a course Castlereagh hoped, and his proposed solution was characteristically English, a combination of the monarchical and liberal principles in the form of a constitutional monarchy. He favoured, therefore, efforts to restore the Spanish monarchy in the colonies, subject to certain restrictions, by persuasion, but not by force; by the time of his death, however, changing circumstances were rendering this impossible. In 1818, at the Congress of Aix-la-Chapelle, Spain had already refused to listen to his appeals for a reconciliation with the colonists, and he himself had interdicted the ominous Franco-Russian proposal for intervention; in the ensuing three years the rebels in America went on from success to success, and in 1821 revolution also broke out in Spain itself, King Ferdinand being forced by the successful revolutionaries to accept a liberal constitution, to the great dismay of the other absolute monarchs of Europe, who were obviously likely to intervene. At this juncture, in August, 1822, Castlereagh died and was succeeded by his long-time rival, Canning.

Canning personally favoured independence as the solution of the colonial problem, but was unable to make this the avowed policy of the Government, owing to the resistance of his more conservative colleagues; he did not propose to promote a reconciliation between Spain and her colonies, because on the whole he considered it most unlikely to succeed, but he would not have intervened to prevent it. At the Congress of Verona in the autumn of 1822 Wellington, as Britain's delegate, put out, in the interests of British commerce, feelers towards a *de facto* recognition of the new governments, but when France took the side of the Continental powers in demanding intervention, Wellington made it clear that, "come what may",[1] England would not participate in any form of intervention, diplomatic or otherwise. This made explicit the breach with the Holy Alliance which had been implicit at Aix four years before, and, combined with subsequent events, it made a great impression on American public opinion.

Adams had refused an earlier offer to the United States to join the Holy Alliance, even when it was thought of as a kind of League of Nations, in words which foreshadowed the Monroe Doctrine itself: "To stand in firm and cautious independence of all entanglements in the European system has been a cardinal point of their policy under every administration of their government from the peace of 1783 to this day. . . . As a general declaration of principles . . . the United States . . . give their hearty assent to the articles of the Holy Alliance. . . . But . . . for the repose of Europe as well as of America the European and American political systems should be kept as separate and distinct from each other as possible."[2] When the wolf appeared beneath the sheep's clothing the Holy Alliance became regarded with the hatred that might have been expected in the land of the free. "The Holy Alliance and the Devil", ran a contemporary American toast, "May the friends of liberty check their career, and compel them to dissolve partnership";[3] in 1821 the Russian Minister, in a gesture strangely reminiscent of the nineteen-fifties, refused to attend a Fourth of July banquet on the ground that some one would be sure to attack the policy of his country. Britain's course of action, Stratford Canning wrote to his cousin, "has had the effect of making the English almost popular in

---

[1] Halévy, p. 168.

[2] Q. Morison and Commager, I, pp. 454-5. [3] Q. Bailey, p. 179.

the United States. The improved tone of public feeling is very perceptible, and even Adams has caught a something of the soft infection.
... On the whole, I question whether for a long time there has been so favourable an opportunity—as far as general disposition and good will are concerned—to bring the two countries nearer together. . . . It may possibly be worth your while to give this a turn in your thoughts."[1] Here was, indeed, a glittering opportunity for Canning to try to undo the harm he had done to Anglo-American relations in an earlier age.

But it came to naught, for much still divided the two countries, and mistrust was still a powerful corrosive of co-operation. Each strongly suspected the intentions of the other. Britain was still fearful of American ambitions in Latin America, particularly Cuba and Texas, and ultimately there is no doubt that the United States desired these and other Spanish lands, though her immediate intentions were honourable. Britain dreaded the rise of a great American maritime empire based on the Caribbean, the very vision which was to haunt the imagination of the South for the next forty years, but the American desire for expansion was not at this time "imperative."[2] Likewise, American opinion was more than half convinced that Britain wished to seize some at least of the Spanish colonies; this conviction was unjustified, for in fact England was entering a period of deep mistrust of colonial ventures and never contemplated any armed intervention, except possibly in Cuba and there for the sole purpose of preventing an American annexation. Canning, for instance, wrote to Wellington in 1822, "I hope I may not have to tell you, before your return, that the Yankees have occupied Cuba; a blow which I do not know how we can prevent, but which as a government I hardly know how we should survive."[3] Adams saw it a little differently, and declared, in 1823, that if the Holy Alliance subdued Spanish America,

> Great Britain, as her last resort, if she could not resist the course of things, would at least take the island of Cuba for her share of the scramble. . . . Suppose the Holy Allies should attack South America, and Great Britain should resist them alone and without our co-operation. I thought this not an improbable contingency, I believed in such a struggle the allies would be defeated and Great Britain would be victorious by her command of the sea. But, as the independence of the South Americans would then be only protected by the guarantee of Great Britain, it would throw them completely into her arms, and in the result make them her Colonies instead of those of Spain."[4]

[1] Q. Dexter Perkins, *The Monroe Doctrine, 1823-26* (London, 1927), p. 60.
[2] Rippy, p. 71.   [3] Q. Perkins, p. 62.   [4] Q. Rippy, pp. 117-8.

Political mistrust was much reinforced and complicated by commercial rivalry. Such a rivalry had sprung up as soon as the collapse of the exclusive Spanish mercantile system had made it possible, and it was to continue, and to increase in severity, until the present day; on the whole, after a beginning in which the Americans had a head start, Britain dominated the field during the nineteenth century, before the fruition of the American economy, but this trend was decisively reversed in the twentieth. Lively contests between local representatives of the two powers in the years during and after the Napoleonic Wars reflected the growth of this competition, and already by 1808 Britain's trade with the Spanish colonies was approaching $25 million in annual value, for with the restriction of her exports to Europe through the Continental System she found in this trade, until recently virtually prohibited to her by Spanish control, a much needed outlet. The annual Spanish American trade of the United States, whose merchants had long been able to conduct it on a considerable scale in small ships, was nearly $30 million in 1808. In 1822 the figures were $30 million for Britain, and under $14 million for the United States; in 1825 $60 million and $24 million; and in 1830 $32 million and $20 million. Here was another cause of antagonism, but, once again, the actual cause was in fact much less formidable than it appeared when seen through the old fog of mistrust and misconception.

It must be remembered that the connexion between political and commercial developments in this period was still much more intimate and immediate than it became later in the nineteenth century. The United States had, from the first moment of independence, set her face against the European policy of commercial exclusion and monopoly in the colonies, and her whole commercial diplomacy had been directed to forcing her way into the closed system of the British Navigation Acts. In this she had already enjoyed some small measure of success. The policy arose directly from her national economic interests and was not based in any great degree upon theoretical principles, except in so far as it was motivated by a mistrust of colonialism natural in the heirs of the American Revolution. "The word *colony* brought to American minds a train of unpleasant associations. To them it signified the old colonial system instituted by Spain and Portugal and followed in large measure by all the colonizing nations. Certain American statesmen feared that the English Government . . . might attempt to apply the old exclusive principles to Hispanic America, and they felt that this must be vigorously opposed."[1] Thus commercial rivalry fed on

[1] Rippy, p. 111.

fear of colonialism and mistrust of political intentions on desire for trade.

In the event, as we shall see, America's battle with Britain on this colonial-commercial issue was almost won by 1830, and in 1849 the Navigation Acts were to be finally and completely repealed. But it is ironical that in fact this was due hardly at all to American diplomacy and very largely to the rise of free trade doctrines in Britain, supported by a new and powerful class of manufacturers. With this decline of Mercantilism in Britain went a growing mistrust, not only of colonial enterprises, but even of colonies already possessed, which showed itself, first, in the avowed expectation of "Little Englanders"* that the colonies would quite soon secure their independence, and, later, in the policy of colonial development towards freedom and self-government. This English trend in some of its aspects was reversed towards the end of the century, but in its middle years it was virtually unchallenged. It is true that in 1820 it was not yet dominant in Britain, and that the sentiments of many of the governing class lagged behind those of bolder thinkers. Lord Liverpool, for instance, who was Prime Minister from 1812 to 1827, wrote as late as 1824, "The great and favourite object of the policy" of Britain

> for more than four centuries has been to foster and encourage our navigation, as the sure basis of our maritime power. In this branch of national industry the people of the United States are become more formidable rivals to us than any nation which has ever yet existed. . . . The views and policy of the North Americans seem mainly directed toward supplanting us in navigation in every quarter of the globe, but more particularly in the seas contiguous to America. Let us recollect that as their commercial marine is augmented, their military marine must proportionately increase. And it cannot be doubted that, if we provoke the new states of America to give a decided preference in their ports to the people of the United States over ourselves, the navigation of these extensive dominions will be lost to us, and it will, in great measure, be transferred to our rivals.[1]

Liverpool took the rivalry of the United States very seriously, and in some ways there could hardly be a better statement of the old Mercantilist viewpoint, but there is more emphasis on naval power than on commerce, and in any case the dawn was at hand, for the ideas of Britain were already changing fast.

* Though this term is not strictly applicable until later in the century, I have followed the increasingly common practice of using it anachronistically.

[1] Q. ibid, pp. 109-10.

Furthermore, though commercial rivalry and fear of each other's ultimate intentions existed and were important, these things did not prevent commercial interests in the two countries from supporting the same immediate policy of independence for the rebellious colonies. Restoration of Spanish control would almost certainly have meant a renewal of the policy of commercial exclusion, and to the British merchants in particular this was highly undesirable. At the outset this was a much more powerful motive than fear of an American rivalry which was as yet very much in embryo, and it was one of great importance in the making of Canning's policy, for he was very sensitive to the wishes of commercial interests. Their pressure for recognition of the states of Latin America, against the opposition of the extreme Tories, was continuous and strong. But though commercial pressure was powerful in England, there is little, if any, evidence of it in the United States, where the decisions of the Administration appear to have been taken on the political grounds of antagonism to despotism. By 1860 the old identification of commercial and colonial power had, at least for the moment, disappeared from British policy, and it is a pity that in the eighteen-twenties this outworn formula remained strong enough seriously to exacerbate Anglo-American differences in Latin America, by making both parties suspect the intention of the other to annex, or at least to dominate, the erstwhile Spanish colonies.

III

BUT the harm done was not irreparable; indeed, it lay chiefly in the prevention of positive co-operation, rather than in any actual deterioration of relations, for each power acted for the first time in its history with considerable sensitivity towards the opinion of the other. The attitude of the United States towards the rebellious colonies had been, largely owing to the coolness of Adams, studiously correct, and it was not until March, 1822, when it was quite clear that their independence was in fact assured, that Monroe sent a message to Congress, recommending the recognition of the new states, which was approved within two months. This action was taken quite independently of Europe, but in obvious opposition to the views of the Holy Alliance; it was, however, the actions of a European power which precipitated the crisis. Following the breach with Britain at Verona in 1822, the *Ultras* in France gained control of policy, and in April, 1823, a French army invaded Spain, and, in one rapid campaign, released King Ferdinand from the bonds of the liberal constitution which had been imposed upon him. He immediately inaugurated a revengeful policy of absolutist reaction. Canning himself had for some time favoured recognition of the South American states, though he could not even yet carry the Cabinet with him, but the French action utterly transformed the situation; it filled him with alarm, and led him "in the direction of an understanding with the only power which, in this important question, could be trusted to see, to some extent at least, eye to eye with Great Britain,"[1] for there was now raised the spectre of interference in Latin America by the Holy Alliance (or by one of its members—a France ambitious of reviving her colonial greatness), avowedly on behalf of Spain.

On 16 August, 1823, Canning proposed to Rush an Anglo-American understanding, and a common policy on the question of the Spanish colonies. Though Canning deserves credit for this firm offer, it was not a sudden inspiration on his part, for the attitude of the two countries to the Holy Alliance had been similar for some time past. As early as 1815, Monroe, as Secretary of State, had made tentative advances to Britain for a concert of action, and in May, 1818, as President, he had "suggested to his Cabinet the possibility of a concert of action with Great Britain to promote the independence of the new states, and . . . renewed the proposal to Adams two months later"; he gained the strong support of Calhoun for this policy. In December of that year Adams directly suggested to Bagot, the British Minister, concerted action for the recognition of La Plata, so that "by the summer of 1823 . . . Canning might logically have assumed that any overtures on his part for common action in the South American question would meet with success", and even the opportunity of opening the subject was provided by Rush, who in the course of a conference, "transiently asked him" about recent events on the Continent, saying that he assumed Britain would not "remain impassive"[2] if France endeavoured to acquire territories in America from Spain. In reply Canning suggested a common understanding, and asked what Rush thought the Administration would say to such co-operation, affirming that in his opinion mere knowledge of their agreement would restrain the French, because of "the large share of the maritime power of the world which Great Britain and the United States held, and the consequent influence which the knowledge of their common policy, on a question involving such important maritime interests, present and future, could not fail to produce everywhere."[3] But Rush, with commendably swift insight, realized that the situation had changed radically since 1818, because the United States had

[1] Perkins, p. 59.   [2] Ibid, pp. 49, 61, 63.   [3] Q. ibid, p. 63.

373

already recognized the republics, and hinted at this very first interview that co-operation would have to depend on a British recognition, which Canning could not yet prevail upon his colleagues to give. Upon this rock in the end co-operation was to founder, for without it Rush could not possibly pledge his country to common measures save by instructions from his government, however hard he was pressed—and he was pressed very hard—by Canning, who declared that "there has seldom in the history of the world occurred an opportunity when so small an effort of two friendly Governments might produce so unequivocal a good and prevent such extensive calamities." It seems probable that Canning was so anxious for this co-operation that, when he had failed with Rush, he made approaches in Washington through Addington; but in any case it is clear that the Administration knew early in October of Canning's desire for common action.

News of the British proposal reached Washington almost as soon as the full implications of the French invasion of Spain became clear, and from the first the President and Calhoun were convinced of the real and urgent danger of the successful intervention of the Holy Alliance in Latin America, the President being, according to Adams, "alarmed far beyond anything that I could have conceived possible", and Calhoun "perfectly moonstruck". Adams himself refused to believe that it was a serious possibility—"I no more believe that the Holy Allies will restore the Spanish dominion upon the American continent than that the Chimborazo will sink beneath the ocean"[1]—and subsequent events went far to prove him right. It was natural, however, that Monroe's first reaction should have been to accept the offer of co-operation, and this was strengthened by the urgent and agreed advice of Jefferson and Madison to this effect. Jefferson's well-known argument upon this question, "the most momentous ... since that of Independence",[2] is well worth quoting at length:

> Our first and fundamental maxim should be, never to entangle ourselves in the broils of Europe. Our second, never to suffer Europe to intermeddle with cis-Atlantic affairs. America, North and South, has a set of interests distinct from those of Europe, and peculiarly her own. She should therefore have a system of her own, separate and apart from that of Europe. . . . Great Britain is the nation which can do us the most harm of any one, or all on earth; and with her on our side we need not fear the whole world. With her, then, we should the most sedulously cherish a cordial friendship, and nothing would tend more to knit our affections than to be fighting once more side by side, in the same cause.

[1] Q. ibid, pp. 64-5, 72-3.   [2] Morison and Commager, I, p. 458.

Not that I would purchase even her amity at the price of taking part in her wars. But the war in which the present proposition might engage us, should that be its consequence, is not her war, but ours. Its object is to introduce and establish the American system, of keeping out of our land all foreign powers, of never permitting those of Europe to interfere with the affairs of our nation. It is to maintain our principle, not to depart from it."[1]

One motive against co-operation weighed with Monroe, that it might particularly alienate Russia, against whom in some part the eventual message was directed, since she "dreads a connexion between the United States and Great Britain."[2] Adams, however, seems from the first to have had very grave doubts about co-operation, and was to declare later that such a policy would be a revival of that of the United States during the last thirty years of convulsions in European affairs, and that it would hasten or even provoke an open breach with the powers of Europe. He argued strongly that "it would be more candid as well as more dignified, to avow our principles explicitly to Russia and France, than to come in as a cock-boat in the wake of the British man-of-war,"[3] and that "The ground that I wish to take is that of earnest remonstrance against the interference of the European powers by force with South America, but to disclaim all interference on our part with Europe; *to make an American cause, and adhere inflexibly to that.*"[4]

After earnest consideration his cautious approach prevailed, though the idea and form of the message to Congress on 2 December, 1823, were very much the President's own. There are grounds, however, for the view that the message was thought of as a stop-gap, and that it was hoped that co-operation with Britain might still be possible afterwards. This, in the event, proved impossible because Canning quickly cooled off when it became clear that the United States would continue to demand immediate recognition of the Latin American states. That the President's chief motive, unlike that of Adams, was a feeling for what he hoped was the cause of freedom in Latin America is suggested by the inclusion in the message of a paragraph, expressing ardent sympathy with the revolutionary party in Greece, which hardly accorded with those isolationist affirmations in the same message, which later interpreters of the Monroe Doctrine conceived to be its essential core and purpose, any more than did the appearance before long in the Aegean of an American naval squadron.

[1] Q. Perkins, p. 91.　[2] Q. ibid, p. 75.
[3] Q. ibid, p. 74.　[4] Q. Bailey, p. 185.

The message contained four main propositions. First, "The citizens of the United States cherish sentiments the most friendly in favor of the liberty and happiness of their fellow men on that [the European] side of the Atlantic."[1] Second, "In the wars of the European powers in matters relating to themselves we have never taken any part, nor does it comport with our policy so to do. It is only when our rights are invaded or seriously menaced that we resent injuries or make preparation for our defence." Third, "With the movements in this hemisphere we are, of necessity, more immediately connected, and by causes which must be obvious to all enlightened and impartial observers. The political system of the allied powers is essentially different in this respect from that of America. . . . We owe it, therefore, to candor and to the amicable relations existing between the United States and those powers, to declare that we should consider any attempt on their part to extend their system to any portion of this hemisphere as dangerous to our peace and safety." Fourth, "With the existing colonies or dependencies of any European power we have not interfered and shall not interfere." Such were the main points of the Monroe Doctrine. What was its effect upon Anglo-American relations?

Its actual and immediate effect was small. Already, after Rush's refusal of early joint action, Canning had independently obtained from France, in the Polignac Memorandum of 9 October, 1823, a formal and decisive disclaimer of any intention on her part to intervene in Spanish America, so that not only was Adams proved right in his assessment of the danger, but the cause of the crisis had almost disappeared before Monroe's message was sent. It was accepted, for the most part, with enthusiasm in America and with satisfaction by English liberal opinion. In Canning, who dominated British policy still, it evoked very mixed feelings, for, though it helped to accomplish the object he had in mind, it was a distinct rebuff to his proposal of concerted action, in that it was a quite independent American gesture; indeed Webster calls it a "severe diplomatic defeat".[2] This was necessarily distasteful to a man of his character, and, more important, the message contained some principles which Britain could not accept, and which were absolutely anathema to his more conservative colleagues.

The first proposition was the crux of the matter, for it was clearly a democratic one, which could not be unreservedly pleasing to all Englishmen at this period. Britain's refusal to recognize the independence of the new states at once was the real reason why America would

[1] A.S.P.F.R., V, p. 250.   [2] Webster, I, p. 49.

not co-operate with her. In the Cabinet, Canning and Huskisson favoured it; Wellington, Liverpool and others opposed it. Yet recognition was in fact accorded by the British Government in 1824; so small a lapse of time prevented a possible Anglo-American alliance, and it did so, once more, because of mutual mistrust.

The Americans suspected Canning's motives, even Rush writing, "I am bound to own, that I shall not be able to avoid, at bottom, some distrust of the motives of all such advances to me . . . by this government, at this particular juncture of the world. . . . [W]e are not as yet likely to witness any very material changes in the part which Britain has acted in the world for the past fifty years, when the cause of freedom has been at stake; the part which she acted in 1774 in America, which she has since acted in Europe, and is now acting in Ireland."[1] American historians—Perkins for example—have echoed these misgivings, and the character of Canning and many of his policies give strength to them; yet they have not done justice to Britain's attitude in these years, largely because of the overpowering American sense of the folly and wickedness of her actions in 1776. Jefferson, for example, characteristically wrote of the "bastard liberty"[2] of the British with their aristocracy and inequalities. It has never been appreciated in America that Britain could and did mistrust democracy, and yet favour liberty; that this was as much natural to her as was outright support of both to most Americans. Gradual constitutional progress, political evolution, was fast becoming the overt and characteristic English dogma in politics; American pragmatism operates in a different fashion. Americans might say that the British adjust themselves to hard facts by compromising and degrading their principles; Britons might say that the Americans achieve the same end by maintaining their principles in theory and ignoring or evading them in practice. The "iniquitous" slowness of English political development towards democracy in the nineteenth century can be regarded as the counterpart of the "disgraceful" corruption of American institutions in the same period. Rush was wrong to see British policy in the Napoleonic wars as inimical to freedom just because Castlereagh detested democracy. It has perhaps been an enduring weakness, as well as a great strength, of American diplomacy that it has tended to see issues either as black or white, seldom as grey, and that the essential compromises of diplomacy are irksome to the American people, who have been, until recently, remarkably insulated

[1] Q. Perkins, p. 82 note.
[2] Q. F. Merk, *Albert Gallatin and the Oregon Problem, A Study in Anglo-American Diplomacy* (Harvard, 1950), p. 21.

against international pressures. To the normal jostlings and tensions of international diplomacy, Great Britain had already in 1823 been long inured, and Canning expressed a very real truth when he said that British policy should "hold the balance between the conflicting principles of democracy and despotism".[1] Yet the gap between this view and the American was sufficiently wide to prevent co-operation.

But there were other grounds for British disagreement with certain parts of the Monroe Doctrine. The second principle, American isolation from European affairs, was in itself unexceptionable, though it did on this occasion embody the rebuff to Canning's proposal of co-operation. The third was not so straightforward, for while its direct rebuke to any possibility of intervention by the Holy Alliance in Latin America pleased Canning and was in accord with the general lines on which British foreign policy was developing, it contained two unacceptable implications. First came the implication that there was a special United States sphere of interest which extended throughout the whole American continent, and which might one day amount almost to a hegemony: to this Britain, with her own interests, colonial and commercial, in the area, could never consent. The determination of Canning to prevent such a hegemony showed itself clearly in his efforts, which were not altogether unsuccessful, to foster enmity between the Latin American republics and the United States at the Panama Congress in 1826, and was best expressed in his instructions to the British representative attending it: "Any project for putting the United States of North America at the head of an American Confederation as against Europe would be highly displeasing to your Government."[2] He continued to be fearful of a consolidation of the New World against the Old, under the leadership of the United States—"a division of the world into European and American, Republican and Monarchical; a league of worn-out Gov[ernmen]ts on the one hand, and of youthful, and stirring Nations, with the United States at their head, on the other"[3]—and wished "to mediate between the two hemispheres and to bring the New World (*pace* Monroe) into connexion with the Old."[4] But his fears were unfounded, for, despite popular clamour in favour of the new republics, there was no serious American intention of establishing such a system at this time, and the only thing which might have produced it, pressure from the opposing system of the Holy Alliance, no longer existed.

[1] Q. Temperley, p. 471.   [2] Q. Perkins, p. 252.
[3] Q. Temperley, pp. 158-9.   [4] Ibid, p. 471.

The second implication of the principle was that, as it was bluntly put by Henry Clay in 1825: "[T]he American continents are not hence-forth to be considered as subjects for future colonization by any European powers."[1] Though this was, of course, qualified by the fourth principle, that there would be no interference with colonies already existing in America, Britain could not yet accept it, although she was moving into the era of Little Englandism, for the interests of her colonies, which were now beginning to take on independent life, were too heavily involved. As Canning said, "How could America be closed to future British colonization, when America's geographical limits were actually unknown?" In fact the enunciation of this non-coloniza-tion principle was probably directed primarily at Russia, though it affected Britain far more, and Canning summed up what was to remain the British attitude in a conversation with Rush: "If we were to be repelled from the shores of America, it would not matter to us whether that repulsion was effected by the ukase of Russia excluding us from the sea, or by the New Doctrine of the President excluding us from the land. But we cannot yield obedience to either."

Canning's attempt, in famous words, to gain credit in Europe for having called forth the Presidential pronunciamento—"I called the New World into existence to redress the balance of the Old"[2]—was in reality a boast to conceal the diplomatic loss of face he had suffered through the rejection of his proposal for co-operation and America's independent action. Yet it was not without some elements of truth, for Monroe acted in the knowledge of Britain's attitude and could never have maintained his position had Britain seriously opposed it; Seton-Watson goes so far as to say, "it is hardly too much to assert that Canning's attitude rather than the Monroe Doctrine, was the decisive factor in 'creating the New World' ".[3] But here lies the seed of the future growth of the Monroe Doctrine as a factor in the history of Anglo-American relations. Britain never accepted the Doctrine—never has formally accepted it—but until the *rapprochement* between the two countries in the twentieth century, which was contemporaneous with the greatest burgeoning of American strength, she acquiesced in it in practice, and this alone made its effective maintenance possible.

In fact little was heard of it till mid-century once its immediate effects had died down. These showed themselves both in an increase in Anglo-American political and commercial rivalry in Latin America, par-ticularly Mexico, which had, because of its common frontier and its

[1] Q. Perkins, pp. 198-9.　　[2] Q. Mowat, *Diplomatic Relations*, pp. 94, 96.
[3] Seton-Watson, *Britain in Europe*, p. 88.

possession of the western lands, most to fear from the United States, and also in Canning's efforts in the years following 1823, to promote settlements between Spain and her one-time colonies on the basis of totally independent Latin American monarchies, possibly ruled by members of the Spanish royal house, on the pattern of the new Brazilian Empire with its autonomous Portuguese monarch. They showed themselves most decisively in his great success in convincing his conservative colleagues in the Cabinet that British recognition of the republics was necessary. In truth, he persisted during the next few years in making good the loss of influence in Latin America which Britain had suffered by Monroe's message; the strength of his feelings is shown in a letter to Grenville, the British Ambassador in Paris, "The deed is done. . . . Spanish America is free, and if we do not mismanage our affairs sadly, she is English. The Yankees will shout in triumph, but it is they who lose most by our decision."[1] What Canning meant was that he had prevented the new states from falling under the domination of the United States, as well as France, and he had in mind mere British influence, which was largely commercial, and not her colonial aggrandisement. But it is small wonder that Americans were mistrustful of his intentions.

But the facts of power remain, and even after Polk's revival of the Doctrine and its acceptance in the United States as a fundamental maxim of American foreign policy, it was only effective in so far as American power could make it so. When Lord Clarendon said in the fifties to the American Minister in London, "The Monroe Doctrine is merely the dictum of its distinguished author",[2] he was indicating politely that Britain had never accepted it, and that in practice its effectiveness depended upon the acquiescence of the power which still controlled the seas. In fact that power did acquiesce, and continued to do so until the relationship between the two was so cordial that she actively welcomed it, by which time the strength of the United States was so great that she might well have made it effective even against British opposition. That yet another opportunity for Anglo-American co-operation had been lost was not on this occasion the fault of Canning; if it was the fault of any man—and it was rather the fault of circumstances—that man was John Quincy Adams, strong willed, penetrating and forceful diplomat, who mistrusted sentiment and was an individualist and a realist in politics; he, more than anyone else, was responsible for the emergence of a practical, distinctive, American

[1] *Cambridge History of British Foreign Policy,* II, p. 74.
[2] Q. Bailey, p. 191.

policy. He determined, if any man did, that the course of Anglo-American relations for nearly a century to come was to be one in which, if much less overt ill feeling began to prevail than heretofore, the two powers followed separate and independent paths. Many matters were settled between them, but not until the turn of the century did a continuous Anglo-American co-operation enter once more into the realms of possibility.

CHAPTER TWELVE

BORDER DISPUTES (1823-60)

URING the years between 1823 and the outbreak of the Civil
War in 1861 the story of Anglo-American relations seems to
lose that unity which to some extent it has manifested since
1783, a unity derived from the cohesive effect of the basic instrument in
Anglo-American diplomacy, the Treaty of Paris of that year. Now,
however, with the vast extension of the power and territories of the
United States and the swift changes in the structure of the British
Empire, new problems, arising in widely different areas, come to match
the old familiar ones in importance. Yet the old disagreements still
remain, and the settlement of a number of them is the main achievement of the period. The chief stages in the process were: the settlement of the long-standing question of commercial relations between
the United States and the British colonies, particularly the West Indies,
which was virtually complete by 1830; the settlement of the Maine
boundary dispute, and certain other matters, by the Webster-Ashburton
Treaty of 1842; and the settlement of the Oregon question, and further
problems arising from the westward expansion of the United States,
notably in Texas, before the end of the Mexican War in 1848. To these
three must be added a novel one, the Isthmian problem, the first of the
two main stages in whose long and difficult development was reached
by 1860. These were not the only important developments in Anglo-
American relations, but they were the principal ones, and beside them
runs a continuous theme, the increasing importance of British North
America, which was clearly marked by the rebellion of 1837 and the
Durham Report which followed it, and which was further demonstrated
in the Reciprocity Act of 1854.

I

ALL these problems show that the ups and downs of Anglo-American
diplomacy were by no means at an end, and these fluctuations were
caused not only by intractable diplomatic disputes but also by personal

factors. Sentiment at governmental level was very variable. During the first period, Adams in the United States, until 1829, and Canning in England, until his death in 1827, remained mutually mistrustful, but afterwards, Jackson and Van Buren showed themselves much more cordial. Van Buren, indeed, was rebuffed by the Senate for his pro-British policy as Secretary of State, which may have made him less amenable during his term as President. Jackson's advances were met half way by the government of Wellington and the conciliatory Aberdeen between 1828 and 1830, and also by Aberdeen's successor, Palmerston, who appreciated the President's "natural frankness of character"[1] and who at this time "showed himself a good friend"[2] of the United States, partly because his manly approach had not yet acquired a hectoring tone. In the second period there was at first a deterioration, but things had improved by the third, when not even the pro-slavery views of Calhoun, as Secretary of State (1844-5), could tempt the anti-slavery Aberdeen into trouble over Texas. A little later the mollifying influence of Secretary of State Buchanan helped to prevent what might have been a serious conflict between the belligerent personalities of Palmerston and Polk. The Whigs, Clayton and Webster, who followed them, were firm advocates of Anglo-American friendship, and the return of the more obstreperous Democrats under Pierce in 1853 did no fundamental harm. Indeed, despite his and his successor Buchanan's efforts to extract Cuba from an unwilling Spain during the fifties, Anglo-American relations remained relatively cordial throughout the decade, as was demonstrated in a positive way by the American-Canadian Reciprocity Treaty of 1854, and in a negative way by the calmness with which the rising American demand for the island was received in Britain, as compared with the alarm which the mere hint of such an idea had aroused in the breast of Canning thirty years earlier. This change is the best measure of the improvement of Anglo-American relations, for, despite the fluctuations in temperature, they unquestionably underwent a solid and remarkable, if unspectacular, development throughout the period. It is too early to speak of cordiality, but there are persistent efforts to solve outstanding problems by negotiation, there is an increasing respect and tolerance at the governmental level, and there are on occasions signs of warmth, which in the later years of the century were to flourish and increase until the great thaw of popular animosity and prejudice on both sides of the Atlantic began.

From the enunciation of the Monroe Doctrine to the resurgence of

[1] Q. C. K. Webster, "British Mediation Between France and the United States, 1834-6 (in *Eng. H. R.*, XLII, 1927), p. 70.   [2] Ibid, p. 59.

the Maine conflict in 1837, British representation in Washington showed unmistakable signs of this warmth, for Charles Richard Vaughan, the successor of Stratford Canning in August, 1825, was a charming and experienced diplomat, who, despite ill health, travelled widely in the United States and was very acceptable to the Americans. So much was this the case that he retained this most difficult of posts for the unprecedentedly long period of ten years. He reported, "I have observed everywhere an expression of friendly feeling towards Great Britain with which I had not expected to meet",[1] and he found even Adams talking anew of Anglo-American friendship. America's representation in London was more disturbed, but hardly less amicable. The veteran Federalist, Rufus King, who had been Minister in London many years before, was sent over in 1825 by Adams to conclude a new treaty of commerce and was hailed by Canning as his "dear old friend",[2] but he was unable to make any headway and sailed for home after only just a year. He was succeeded by another elder statesman, Gallatin, who was also appointed with the specific object of concluding a treaty on outstanding questions, particularly that of West Indian trade; he was accordingly appointed for one year only. He had been Minister in Paris for some time after being a commissioner at Ghent, and he wrote to Adams towards the end of 1826, "it is impossible for me not to see and feel the temper that prevails here towards us. It is ... quite changed from what it was in 1815-21; nearly as bad as before the last war, *only they hate more and despise less,* though they still affect to conceal hatred under the appearance of contempt." This unfortunate change he ascribed chiefly to Canning's succession to Castlereagh. Gallatin's son, James, has left a lively account of their full and agreeable social life, in which the only painful incident was at Brighton : "We were bid to sup with the Royal circle. I could see that father could hardly dissemble his disgust. The conversation was boisterous and indecent. . . . The only remark he made was, 'And that is a King.' " Gallatin's mission, too, failed in its primary object, and Adams appointed James Barbour of Virginia, Secretary of War, to follow him in 1828, but in 1829 Jackson, after his defeat of Adams, replaced him by the suave and able Senator Louis McClane of Maryland, whose hand was greatly strengthened by having Washington Irving, with his invaluable local knowledge, as his Secretary of Legation. The Minister was fully able to take advantage of Jackson's pro-British policy and the increasing friendliness of the British Government. The death of George IV had a notably beneficial effect on the position of the American Minister at

[1] Q. W.F.R., p. 130. [2] Q. W.A.A.E., p. 160.

Court, where he "was formerly," according to Irving, "received with coldness and reserve".

When McClane was forced by the ill health of his wife to leave in July, 1831, the Secretary reigned most successfully in his stead until the arrival, in September, of the new Minister, Martin Van Buren, who came direct from the Secretaryship of State. His "amiable and ingratiating" manners made, according to Irving, a very good impression, and William IV said to him on the presentation of his credentials: "As to the particular country from which I came" (Van Buren reported to Secretary of State Livingston), "he had always been anxious for the preservation of the very best relations between it and Great Britain, that not only did their common interest point to that course, but their common origin and the kindred relations subsisting between them should stimulate both nations to practise forbearance towards each other."[1] Just when things appeared to be going well, however, news arrived that the Senate had refused to ratify Van Buren's appointment, on the ground that he had been too subservient to British interests when Secretary of State, and he returned to America amidst general English sympathy. Jackson refused for a time to nominate a successor, lest he should suffer the same indignity, and when he did so in 1834 the nomination was again rejected, so that for four years Aaron Vail, a devoted and talented diplomat *de carrière*, acted as Chargé d'Affaires, getting on very well with both opposition and government, including Palmerston. It was perhaps typical of a professional diplomat that he thoroughly reorganized the Legation and its methods, and he implemented the welcome arrangements made by Van Buren for the establishment of consulates in the chief British manufacturing towns. His efforts were reinforced by the fact that Jackson began, in his quarrels with Congress and the Supreme Court, to correspond more directly with his representatives abroad during his second term, writing characteristically to Vail that in future the inscription of missives from foreign governments, which had hitherto run "to the President and Congress of the United States . . . should be to 'the President of the United States of America' without any other addition in such communications as *pass from one Sovereign to another*." Jackson's interest in English affairs helped to make the long absence of a Minister unimportant, for he enjoyed the respect of William IV, corresponded with the young Victoria and exchanged portraits with her, and, after his retirement, followed the arrangements for the coronation of his "little good friend"[2] with intense interest. But in the meantime he had, in

[1] Q. ibid, pp. 175, 188, 194-5.   [2] Q. ibid, pp. 205-6, 208.

1836, at last gained Senatorial approval of the appointment of Andrew Stevenson, as Minister to London, and he took up his post in June of that year. But the period without a Minister had done no harm to Anglo-American relations, which were better from 1830 to 1836 than they were immediately before or immediately after those dates.

As long as Canning and Adams held the reins, the course of Anglo-American diplomacy remained far from smooth, and mutual mistrust, which was by no means allayed by the Monroe Doctrine and the events which led up to it, persisted. Adams called Canning an "implacable and rancorous enemy"[1] of America, and Stratford Canning called Adams's hatred of the British "ravenous."[2] Canning's words to Vaughan in 1826 run true to form:

> The general maxim that our interest and those of the United States are essentially the same, etc., etc., is one that cannot be too readily admitted, when put forward by the United States. But we must not be the dupes of this conventional language of courtesy. The avowed pretension of the United States to put themselves at the head of the confederacy of all the Americas, and to sway that confederacy against Europe (Great Britain included), is *not* a pretension identified with our interests, or one that we can countenance as tolerable. It is however a pretension that there is no use in contesting in the abstract; but we must not say anything that seems to admit the principle.[3]

Things were not improved by the failure of the Senate to ratify without crippling amendments a treaty for the suppression of the slave trade signed in 1824*, but the real source of trouble in these years was the question of American commerce with the British colonies, particularly in the West Indies.

The United States had been endeavouring since 1783 to break into the exclusive British Mercantile system, and was in fact near to success in so doing, but the process was made difficult and painful by suspicion on both sides and by the unwise diplomacy of Adams. He had long felt very keenly on this question, and followed his usual habit of never mincing matters with John Bull, so that he almost went so far as to claim that freedom to trade with the British American colonies, and even to navigate the St. Lawrence, was a natural right of American citizens. This met the kind of reaction that might have been expected

---

[1] Q. S. F. Bemis, *John Quincy Adams and the Foundations of American Foreign Policy* (New York, 1949), p. 445.

[2] Q. Merk, p. 21.   [3] Q. Dunning, p. 56.   * See p. 400 below.

from Canning as long as he was in control, and he told Gallatin in blistering terms that what Britain did about the trade of her colonies was very much her own affair, so that the growing sympathy of certain English interests for free trade was temporarily checked as far as America was concerned. But the fault was not entirely Adams's; we have seen already how great was Canning's fear of the United States, and, even more interesting, Huskisson, who was the real inspiration of Britain's new free trade policies, was much less liberal towards the United States than towards any other power, apprehending perhaps already, as the representative of the new industrial class, the potential economic rivalry of the United States. But the ease with which this question was settled, when goodwill became apparent on both sides, indicates clearly that the blame for delay must lie primarily at the door of Adams.

The American campaign—so reminiscent of the methods of the embargo of earlier years—had begun with retaliatory economic legislation in the years between 1817 and 1820, which had gone so far by the latter date as to refuse entry to all British ships coming from British ports in the New World and to prohibit the importation of their products unless coming directly from the colony of origin; the most important single measure was the American Navigation Act of 1818. This policy revived the old sectional cleavage of the War of 1812, though this time it was the commercial interests who were in power and who alienated the agrarian interests. However, in 1822, Parliament, her moves in that direction accelerated by these economic sanctions, opened a limited colonial trade to American ships,* on condition of reciprocity. This the British Government claimed was not fully granted by the Act of Congress, which was passed for the purpose, on Adams's advice, in 1823, since it made the removal of American alien duties on British products, among those of other nations, dependent on the British removal of preferences given to her own imports from her own colonies in British ships. In effect, it made conditions of British domestic imperial trade dependent upon conditions of American international trade, which was a fundamentally untenable position, and this accounted for the failure of both King and Gallatin, Adams's very experienced envoys, to obtain in London the settlement that an increasingly voluble section of American opinion desired; failure on this issue also meant failure on others, such as the Maine and Oregon boundaries. In 1825 Parliament made certain further concessions, but would not, naturally enough, accept America's right to interfere in the

* See p. 354 above.

domestic economic affairs of the Empire; Adams, however, still refused to consent to the removal of the alien duties, which would establish the reciprocity required by the British.

As a result, opinion in Britain, led by a no doubt none too reluctant Canning, hardened swiftly, and in July, 1826, while Gallatin was actually on the way to London, an Order-in-Council closed West Indian ports absolutely to American ships, while on Gallatin's arrival Canning flatly declined to discuss the issue. Neither Adams nor Canning was now prepared to yield, and not until 1828, well after the latter's death, did the former, under the shadow of the Presidential election in which the failure of his commercial policy was a very important issue, authorize Clay, his Secretary of State, to concede the abolition of the alien duties without insisting on the removal of preferential duties in British inter-colonial trade. But the concession came too late—even if it could ever have done so—to save Adams and his Administration from disastrous defeat at the hands of Jackson and the Democrats. That the broader deadlock in Anglo-American negotiations, however, was by no means altogether Adams's responsibility is shown by the fact that all that could be achieved was the indefinite renewal of the joint occupation of Oregon and the commercial treaty of 1815— and even this when Canning was already a dying man—while after his death on 8 August, 1827, the atmosphere began to improve so swiftly that on 29 September a convention, albeit ultimately unsuccessful in its object, was signed arranging the arbitration of the north-eastern boundary dispute.

This welcome change in the British attitude was reciprocated and fortified by the rather unexpected, yet quite characteristic, friendliness of Jackson towards his old enemy, Britain, after his accession to the Presidency in 1829. Barbour in London had already reported that the Foreign Secretary of the new administration, Aberdeen, was well disposed to the United States, while in later years Vail was not only to notice the likeness between Wellington, who was now Prime Minister, and Jackson, but also to report that the former was particularly anxious for friendship with the United States. In his first address to Congress Jackson declared:

> With Great Britain, alike distinguished in peace and war, we may look forward to years of peaceful, honorable, and elevated competition. Everything in the condition and history of the two nations is calculated to inspire sentiments of mutual respect and to carry conviction to the minds of both that it is their policy to preserve the most cordial relations. . . . Although neither time nor opportunity has been afforded for

a full development of the policy which the present cabinet of Great Britain designs to pursue towards this country, I indulge the hope that it will be of a just and pacific character.[1]

When shortly afterwards a new and much more tactful approach than that of Adams was made to Britain—splendid lesson from the blunt soldier to the opinionated diplomat—on the subject of the West Indies trade, suggesting a restoration of commerce on the basis of the Act of Parliament of 1825, the British Government agreed, after some negotiation, to do so as soon as Congress had made good Jackson's proposals by positive legislation. This was done in 1830, and on 29 May of that year a British Order-in-Council reopened the West Indian ports to American vessels, in return for the reopening of American ports to British vessels by Presidential proclamation. This "honourable understanding" opened only a limited trade, but it was the crucial step, and, with the rapid advance of British free trade policies in succeeding years, the long-standing American desire for unrestricted commerce with the British colonies was soon achieved.

The new warmth, which had crept into the relationship, did not decline with the coming of the Whig government in Britain in 1830, for Palmerston, its Foreign Secretary, was in his mildest mood, and felt himself on so sound a footing with the United States that he was even able to do something to smooth out the disagreement which existed from 1830 to 1835 between France and America; indeed, the warmth endured until the end of Jackson's tenure of office in 1837. More significant in the long run than any superficial or individual cause of concord was the fact that this Whig ministry passed the Great Reform Bill of 1832 and a number of other major reforms, thus setting Great Britain, for the first time since 1776, firmly on that high road towards fully democratic institutions which the United States had already begun to tread. No disturbance of the relationship—and there were still to be plenty—was as influential in the end as this general and highly important trend.

II

THE crisis which arose in 1837, and which lasted until the abatement of public feeling after the signing of the Webster-Ashburton Treaty in 1842 was much more serious than that of 1824-7, but much less due to the misguided actions of those concerned. Certainly it was not

[1] *Messages and Papers,* p. 1006.

exacerbated by the British Minister in Washington, Henry Stephen Fox, who was a nephew of Charles James Fox and not unlike him in character; he was a gay bachelor of great social popularity, who managed, after his supersession, to continue in America his merry and, as it turned out, short life, despite the persistent attentions of his creditors. He obtained the post in 1836 because he was a member of a great Whig family, having started his diplomatic career as soon as the Whigs returned to office from the political wilderness in 1830, and even now Whigs, particularly those having any associations with the great Fox, started at an advantage in the American democracy. In fact he was not particularly conciliatory to the Americans, though he kept his opinions as much as possible away from the public. He wrote strongly of the *Caroline* border incident, which we shall discuss shortly, "If the Americans either cannot or will not guard the integrity of their own soil or prevent it becoming an arsenal of outlaws and assassins . . . they have no right to expect that the soil of the United States will be respected by the destined victims of such un-heard of violence", and he held that the only remedy was a British army of occupation in Canada to protect the border, a considerably more radical solution than that of Durham. But his eighteenth-century manner of life assorted ill with his position, and he was recalled in 1844; as Aberdeen said, "I have nothing against Mr. Fox, except that I do not think he carries the moral and intellectual weight that the present situation demands."[1]

Andrew Stevenson, a henchman of Jackson's from the South, took up his post as Minister in London in 1836; he was politically rather more of "a stormy petrel on the diplomatic ocean"[2] than his counterpart in Washington, though he was equally unable to satisfy his masters at home, for, though he was tough and a firm supporter of Jackson's policy even on such difficult matters as slavery, he was more than once reprimanded for not being sufficiently assertive of American rights. He was also accused of alarmism at the time of the *Caroline* affair, while Jackson would not allow him to try and handle the Maine boundary question on the ground that it was very much in America's interest to deal with the matter in Washington. On the other hand, he departed in 1841 on a characteristic note, protesting violently to the new Peel government against the right of search for slaves (on which Palmerston had been so insistent as to endanger the peace), while he had succeeded earlier in the far from easy task of extracting from the Foreign Secretary and the British Parliament compensation, at $479 per head, for a number of American slaves freed from an American ship, the *Comet*,

[1] Q. W.F.R., pp. 147, 149. [2] W.A.A.E., p. 226.

in Nassau in 1834. His personal relations in London were, on the whole, good, and he had a much more difficult task than his successor, the New Englander, Edward Everett, who served Daniel Webster at the State Department and was faced with the more complaisant Peel-Aberdeen Ministry.

As a matter of fact, however, Everett was much better fitted for his task; he had been Professor of Greek at Harvard, and lived a very full and happy social life in London, being friendly with Englishmen of many types, including Hallam, Peel, Disraeli, Wellington, Carlyle, Monckton Milnes and even Sydney Smith, who was particularly outspoken against Americans but who wrote to the *Morning Chronicle* about Everett, "[W]e thought him (a character which the English always receive with affectionate regard) an amiable American republican without rudeness, and accomplished without ostentation. . . . In diplomacy, a far more important object than falsehood is, to keep two nations in friendship. In this point, no nation has ever been better served than America has been served by Mr. Everett."[1] He established a very cordial relationship with Aberdeen, with whom he saw eye to eye in many things, finding, for instance, as a humane Northerner, constant American claims for freed slaves distasteful, and receiving as a result a certain amount of criticism from home. Thurlow Weed, for whose company he no doubt showed little relish, strongly criticized his alleged ostentation of dress on formal occasions—a perennial problem to American diplomats—which was symptomatic of the extreme suspicion to which almost all really successful (and some unsuccessful) American Ministers in London have been subjected. That it was an unjust suspicion in the case of Everett is indicated by his words many years later, "John Bull is very amiable in private life, and many of my best friends inhabit the 'fast anchored Isle'; but in his foreign politics he is selfish and grasping, and where he dares, insolent."[2] By the time his successor arrived, in August, 1845, there had been a marked drop in the heat of these Anglo-American ill-feelings.

Their temperature had begun to rise in 1837, and the fever reached its climax in 1841; the causes of the malady were complex, but centred largely in Canadian-American relations. They were exacerbated by ill feeling over such things as slavery and American debt repudiations, as well as the literary battles of the period, but, fortunately, the basic economic bonds between the two peoples had the opposite effect. Really, however, the differences were political, for the doctrine of

[1] Q. ibid, p. 233.   [2] Q. ibid, p. 241.

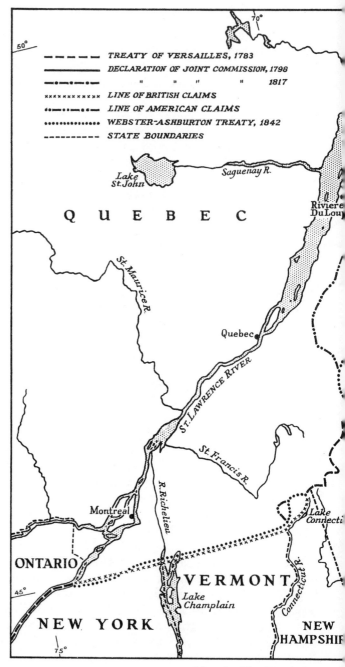

Map 3. *The North-Eastern*

Boundary Dispute

Manifest Destiny not unnaturally had a disturbing effect upon the relations between the two nations. Unquestionably the most important causes of tension were the boundary disputes, particularly that in the north-east, and the problems arising from the Canadian rebellion of 1837.

The most significant part of the north-eastern dispute concerned the Maine boundary,* the proposed settlement of which in 1831 the opposition of that State had prevented, and it became progressively more threatening in the years following this failure, as both Americans and Canadians pressed into the disputed area of the St. John River, so that the danger of local incidents increased. Two other north-eastern disagreements, one over the exact location of the north-westernmost head of the Connecticut River, and the other over the actual line that the 45 deg. boundary was to follow on the ground, made the problem more intractable, while much farther to the west the frontier line between the western end of Lake Huron and the north-west corner of Lake of the Woods was still undetermined.† These uncertainties†† were bound to cause trouble in view of the increasing flow of Canadian-American trade across the long inland boundary; this commerce, despite the prohibition of British trade with the American Indians in 1816 and the lack of formal treaty arrangements, grew apace under the auspices of domestic legislation on both sides of the boundary, particularly between the establishment of West Indian reciprocity in 1830 and the full development of the American railroad system. In Upper Canada especially, where economic relations were closest, this was a contributory factor to the armed Canadian rebellion of December, 1837. Precipitated by the economic crisis of 1837, it had complex political causes; partly the result of anti-British feeling, partly of French-Canadian independence of spirit, and partly of democratic sentiment, which was inspired in some degree by the American example and which tended towards annexation by the United States, the revolt, though swiftly and easily suppressed, made the boundary disputes far more serious. On the British side, the freezing of the St. Lawrence hindered troop movements to put down the risings, which made a military road from the Canadas to the Maritimes seem imperatively necessary; and the only practical route ran through the disputed area of the Maine salient. On the American side, there was, understandably, a good deal of feeling in favour of the rebels, not unconnected with a revival of the old dream of the annexation of British North America—a dream of much the same kind as that which was being realized in Texas.

* See Map 3.   † See Map 2.   †† See p. 352 above.

The Canada vision, however, was based on a serious over-estimate of the Canadian desire for independence from Britain, which was in the event swiftly swallowed up in resentment at the unneutral activities during the rebellion of certain American citizens along the international boundary; these men, many of them rendered idle by the depression of 1837, by no means represented sound American opinion which steadily developed against the rebels, but the grave and numerous incidents arising from their activities—the foundation, for instance, of secret societies, like the Hunters' Lodges "to emancipate the British Colonies from British Thraldom",[1]—gravely imperilled the peace. Things were not improved when the defeated leader of the revolt in Upper Canada, William L. Mackenzie, fled over the border to Buffalo and established his headquarters at the Eagle Tavern. The most serious border incident occurred on the Niagara River on 29 December, 1837, when a party of Canadian volunteers crossed to American territory and, killing an American in the process, destroyed the *Caroline*, an American vessel which was being used to ferry supplies across to a small Canadian island, where Mackenzie had established himself with American help. Blame for the incident attached in some measure to both parties, though more largely to the Canadians, but, whatever its rights and wrongs, it aroused violent feeling along the border. The Secretary of State protested strongly to the British Minister, but the British Government, on the advice of Palmerston, took as little action as the United States had done when Andrew Jackson had invaded Florida two decades before. Heads on the whole remained cool at the summit of affairs; Van Buren, whose hands were tied by the "penal, not preventive"[2] nature of the American neutrality law, issued a proclamation appealing for its careful observance, and sent General Winfield Scott to the border, where he succeeded admirably in the difficult task of allaying strife. Lord Durham, after his arrival in May, 1838, studiously and very successfully cultivated the good will of the Americans. Earlier in the year the President had obtained from a reluctant Congress an Act, strengthening—though to a very limited extent—the neutrality legislation of 1794, 1817 and 1818, action which, it is interesting to note, Mexico had not been able to obtain at the time of the Texan Revolution a few years earlier. Fox wrote from Washington that the Neutrality Bill is "a proceeding of national honesty, from a sincere desire to avert a war with Great Britain. Some Senators

[1] Q. Bailey, p. 207.
[2] A. B. Corey, *The Crisis of 1830-1842 in Canadian-American Relations* (London, 1941), p. 44.

oppose the bill. . . . They cannot yet bring themselves to believe . . . that the British population when invited to an alliance with the licentious democracy of the United States should have rejected that alliance with scorn, indignation and abhorrence. . . . [I]t is humiliating to the pride of the American people and to their cherished notions of supreme political perfection." He added that the devotion of the Canadians is "no less gratifying to Englishmen and lovers of English constitutional liberty".[1]

But in England, the hand of distance, as so often in Anglo-American disputes in the nineteenth century, was already at work, and the incident aroused little attention. This was just as well, for more was to come. In May, 1838, a Canadian vessel, the *Sir Robert Peel*, was destroyed, as a reprisal, while in American waters on the St. Lawrence; and yet other incidents followed. But Van Buren continued to do his duty—to an extent, indeed, which contributed to his defeat in the election of 1840— and an open rupture was averted. Even the McLeod case in 1840-1, which aroused the ire of Palmerston, did not quite undo this good work. One Alexander McLeod, it was alleged, was rash enough to boast, while in New York State, that he had participated in the *Caroline* incident and killed a man, presumably Amos Durfee the American; and he was consequently arrested and tried for murder. Palmerston formally demanded his release, and declared that he could not be held guilty because he was participating in a military operation; thus in a sense the British Government assumed responsibility for the *Caroline* affair which now began, three years after the event, to contribute to the dangerously high feeling about McLeod in Britain. Palmerston went so far as to say unofficially that the execution of McLeod would produce war, and the hands of the Federal Government were tied by the fact that the State of New York refused to surrender him for trial in a Federal Court, though Governor Seward intimated that his execution would in the last resort be prevented by a pardon, while Webster, who had now become Secretary of State, took all precautions to ensure an orderly and fair trial. Fortunately, McLeod produced a convincing alibi to prove that he was some miles away from the scene of the raid at the time it took place and was rapidly acquitted. The McLeod issue was dead, though not that of the *Caroline*, but it resulted in the passage of a law by Congress in 1842, providing for the discharge or removal to Federal jurisdiction of any person accused of an unlawful act proved to have been committed under the orders of a foreign sovereign.

In the meantime, however, the border situation in Maine seemed

[1] Q. W.F.R., p. 147.

about to burst into flame. In 1839 Canadian lumberjacks began operations on the Aroostook River, a tributary of the St. John in the disputed area, and an equally tough American party entered the fray singing:

> *Britannia shall not rule the Maine,*
> *Nor shall she rule the water;*
> *They've sung that song full long enough,*
> *Much longer than they oughter.*[1]

Maine and New Brunswick called out their militia forces, and the Nova Scotia legislature voted war credits amid singing of "God Save the Queen", to which Congress replied with an appropriation of $10,000,000. Happily, however, Winfield Scott was able to repeat his performance as a pacificator, and the Aroostook "War" remained in the realm of the might have been. Even more happily, the entry of Aberdeen into office in September, 1841, opened the way to the immediate acceptance of Webster's offer to negotiate a conventional line in the boundary dispute. For this purpose the British took the somewhat unusual, but excellent, step of sending, as their plenipotentiary to Washington, Lord Ashburton, a business man rather than a diplomat, and one whose personal, as well as public, sentiments—he had an American wife—were very cordial towards the United States which he had first visited in 1795; he had specialized in American commerce, and in 1808 he had written an excellent pamphlet urging that the prosperity of the United States ought to be welcomed in Britain, economically as well as politically. The spirit of goodwill which this indicated was reciprocated by Webster, who had in 1839 paid a very happy visit to England, where he had been remarkably lionized. On becoming Secretary of State he declared outright, "No difference shall be permitted seriously to endanger the maintenance of peace with England."[2] Negotiations began in April, 1842, and on Ashburton's suggestion proceeded by informal personal discussion; they provided a warming example of what can be done between diplomats with a common tongue, a kindred background and a determination to reach a mutually acceptable agreement, which was clearly illustrated by Ashburton's remark, "For my own part what seems most important is that there should be a settlement of some sort, and I do not attach all the importance which some do to the precise terms."[3]

The final treaty, which was signed on 9 August, 1842, dealt with two main topics, the boundary dispute in the North-east and on Lake

[1] Q. Bailey, p. 214.   [2] Q. W.F.R., p. 149.   [3] Q. Crey, p. 166.

Superior, and the suppression of the slave trade. In addition, in Article 10, the extradition agreement of Jay's Treaty, which had expired early in the century, was renewed and very much broadened in scope so as to include virtually all serious crimes; though crimes of a political nature were not included, this did something to prevent future difficulties on the border. Although Ashburton was authorized to discuss Oregon, neither the Englishman nor the New Englander was very interested in the Pacific Coast, and it was not discussed. The treaty was accompanied by an exchange of notes, which was held to dispose satisfactorily of the *Caroline* affair; Ashburton's note was not an actual apology, but went far enough in that direction to enable Webster to claim, with a reasonable appearance of justice, that it was. Agreement was easily reached on the boundary between the western end of Lake Huron and the north-west corner of Lake of the Woods since there was no problem of settlement to complicate the issue, and a line, somewhat favourable to the United States, was laid down in Article 2.* Between the two negotiators themselves, because they were both ready to compromise, agreement was also reached without too much difficulty in the north-east on a line which settled all the outstanding problems; the difference was split. Britain got the best of the bargain on the main issue, and was able to construct her military road, while the United States obtained somewhat more favourable terms than her rival over the 45 deg. line and at the head of the Connecticut River. The consent of Maine and Massachusetts, however, was less easily obtained, while the necessity —to which Ashburton reluctantly consented—of its inclusion not only in the negotiations but in the actual terms of the treaty as well, greatly slowed down proceedings, and, as Ashburton wryly complained to Webster, kept the negotiators an unduly long time in the heat of a Washington summer. It was, however, very necessary; as Webster declared, "the grand stroke was to get the previous consent of Maine and Massachusetts",[1] of which no one had thought before. Eventually agreement was reached on the payment of a very substantial sum to the two States, found almost entirely by the United States, and very acceptable to Maine, which was in a grave fiscal situation; further clauses protected the rights of property holders in the territory in question, and guaranteed mutual free navigation of the St. John River, as also of certain channels in the St. Lawrence and the Great Lakes system. It was of fundamental importance that Maine had recently

* See Map 2.
[1] Q. T. Le Duc, "The Maine Frontier and the North-Eastern Boundary Controversy" (in *Am.H.R.*, LIII, No. 1, 1947), p. 40.

come to realize that the land which she gained was richer in resources than that which she gave up, but on the technical level of finesse in diplomatic negotiation her consent to the compromise was gained primarily in the first comic bout of what came to be called the "Battle of the Maps", for Webster had, unknown to Ashburton and the British, a copy of a map recently discovered by an American in the French archives, which seemed to substantiate the British claims to Maine territory, and it was Webster's secret use of this, both on the representatives of Maine and on the Senate, which finally clinched the treaty. The humour of the situation lay in the fact that the British Foreign Office, unknown to Webster and the Americans, was in possession of another map which seemed to substantiate the American claim, and this map was used by Aberdeen with great effect when Palmerston, now in opposition, violently attacked the treaty. Twentieth-century research has in fact confirmed the American claim, but it cannot be doubted that agreement was better for either country than diplomatic victory, for the treaty settled, once and for all, every serious disagreement about the long boundary from the Atlantic Coast to the Rocky Mountains.

The remaining two articles treated of the vexed question of the suppression of the slave trade, which had been increasingly an issue between the two governments since Great Britain began her long diplomatic campaign for its universal suppression during the negotiations at Vienna in 1814-5, and which was not to be settled—though then it was settled absolutely—until 1862. This date is, of course, significant, for, though the sensitivity of American public opinion to any suggestion of an agreement to give the British Navy the right to visit American ships to determine if they were 'slavers' (a right too reminiscent of the "right of search") was a serious obstacle to settlement of the problem, the real issue was the Southern attachment to the slavery system. That this was indeed the fundamental difficulty is shown by the fact that the persistent efforts of the British to reach an agreement had been almost rewarded at their very outset by the signature of a convention on the subject in 1824, when J. Q. Adams was Secretary of State, and when positive pro-slavery sentiment in the South had hardly begun to take solid shape. A series of acts had been passed by Congress in 1818, 1819 and 1820, stiffening the penalties against the slave trade —except the authorized coastal slave trade—and declaring it piracy and a capital offence. Between 1822 and 1824 the concession of the reciprocal right of search was recommended by both Houses of Congress, but was at first rejected by Monroe; in the latter year, however, the Administration, having changed its mind, successfully negotiated a convention with Britain on the subject. But the Senate now decided to ratify the treaty subject only to certain conditions, the principal one being the exclusion of the coast of America from the seas where the reciprocal right of capture was permitted. The British Government stated that it believed this was an unfair exception, and in fact probably believed, in view of the continued existence of slavery and the local slave trade in the Southern States, that it was an exception which would utterly vitiate the rule; it refused to agree to the amended version. This proved to be the last opportunity for many years of settling the slave trade issue to the satisfaction of both parties.

After this, any settlement was rendered more and more unlikely by the association in the Southern mind of restrictions upon the slave trade with the rising power of the hated Abolitionists in the Northern States. This fact made English humanitarian opinion, strengthened by its victory over slavery in the British colonies in 1833, increasingly suspicious of American intentions. On the other hand, many Americans believed that Britain demanded the right to search ships of other nations, which were suspected of carrying slaves, merely in order to retain her maritime supremacy, and it was perhaps the case that the sort of Tories who were later to be Confederate sympathizers in fact cared little about the slavery issue. Yet the British efforts to attack the slave trade by diplomacy continued, and, indeed, extended beyond the trade to slavery itself; British policy in Texas, for instance, was very largely inspired by the hope of preventing slavery from taking permanent root there, a motive with which the South naturally failed to sympathize, since it was convinced of the positive goodness of the slavery system. After the rejection of the 1824 convention, Britain continued, particularly during Palmerston's long period at the Foreign Office between 1830 and 1841, to press for the reciprocal right of search with vessels of the United States as part of an ever broadening scheme of agreements with other powers. Van Buren's reply to a feeler of Palmerston's in 1831 was expressive of the American point of view, even that of Northerners who disliked slavery; he thought the idea impossible owing to the fact that it "was so repugnant to the feelings of our people". The result was that, increasingly, illicit slave traders flew the flag of the United States, since this rendered their detection much more difficult. Britain could not maintain the right of searching American vessels without their agreement, but in order to prevent this evasion she modified her demands and asked only the right to "visit", without stopping and without search, in order to find out if the ship in question was in fact entitled to the American flag. Everett reported that at his first meeting with Aberdeen in 1841 the latter "disclaimed all right of search, detention or interference with American vessels in African waters. All he claimed was the right to board vessels 'strongly suspected of being those of other nations unwarrantably assuming the American flag.' If a mistake was made, full and ample reparation should follow."

Britain felt so strongly on this that she for some time ran the risk of visiting such ships even without the consent of the American Government; as Aberdeen told Everett, it was "impossible for Her Majesty's Government to make the slightest compromise on the subject of slavery." It must not be assumed from the foregoing that the United States made no efforts to check the slave trade, for in October, 1819, Congress empowered the President to employ the American Navy for the seizure of American slavers, and appropriated $100,000 for the purpose. Sums appropriated sank to $50,000 in 1823, to $5,000 in 1834, and thereafter to nothing until 1842, so that American search cruisers were sent on anti-slave trade patrol but sporadically. After the election of Van Buren to the Presidency, Minister Stevenson in London was informed that in future the United States would have a naval force in African waters, but in view of past performances Palmerston remained not merely sceptical but belligerent on the issue of the right of search, so that this fact added further to the tension on the eve of Palmerston's resignation in 1841. It was increased even more by the fact that the refusal of the French to ratify a Quintuple Treaty, negotiated in 1841 between France, Austria, Prussia, Russia and Britain, and guaranteeing reciprocal rights of search, was in part produced by the vigorous diplomatic representations of General Cass, the American Minister in Paris, against it. Even after this, the affair of the *Creole* in November of that year—perhaps the most serious of a number of incidents of a similar kind—served to make the matter more intractable. A hundred and thirty-five slaves, being carried on this American brig from Hampton Roads to New Orleans, mutinied, seized control of the ship at the expense of casualties among the few passengers and crew, and took the vessel into the British port of Nassau in the Bahamas. Though arresting the slaves involved in the actual mutiny, the local authorities forcibly freed the rest. The rage of the South was not tempered by the exultant joy of the Northern Abolitionists, nor by Aberdeen's flat statement "that when slaves were found within British jurisdiction, by whatever means, or from whatever quarters, they were *ipso facto* free."[1]

[1] Q. W.A.A.E., pp. 197, 230, 237.

Webster and Ashburton grappled with this problem in the negotiations and made as good an agreement as was possible, given the increasing vehemence of the slave interest in the United States; certain representatives of this interest were to begin, during the next decade, to moot the idea of the actual reopening of the trade, although this was a demand uttered by few responsible Southerners even in the immediate pre-Civil War years. An exchange of notes supplementary to the treaty made it clear that the United States would not accept the right of search or even of visit, while Britain would equally not repudiate the old right of impressment which Aberdeen considered would be "tantamount to an absolute and entire renunciation of the indefeasible right inherent in the British Crown to command the allegiance and services of its subjects, wherever found."[1] But in Article 8 both parties agreed to maintain on the coast of Africa a naval force of not less than eighty guns for the suppression of the slave trade, each to be independent but to co-operate with one another. Article 9 agreed that both parties would endeavour to strike at the root of the problem by representations to any power where markets for the purchase of African negroes existed, a policy which became increasingly disagreeable to the American Government during the succeeding years of Southern dominance. These clauses of the treaty were also attacked from the opposite camp by a radical minority in England, as a betrayal of the anti-slavery cause, which could only in their view be advanced by the assertion of the full right of search. The American obligation was in theory honoured, though for many years very little actual time was spent by their vessels on the coast itself, owing to the necessity of obtaining supplies from distant ports, which arose because the American Government set its face against the establishment of a base in Africa. Towards the end of the period a more vigorous effort was made, and in 1860 President Buchanan obtained an appropriation of $40,000 which resulted in a number of captures off the Congo, but on the whole American efforts languished, and it was largely owing to a revival of the British practice of visiting American vessels, after the end of the Crimean War, that Buchanan made this effort to instil vigour into American anti-slavery operations. The languor was not surprising, for by this time the United States was by far the largest importer of slaves in the world, despite the illegality of the trade, and in 1863 the British Consul at New York estimated that of 170 slaving expeditions fitted out between 1857 and 1861, 117 were known or believed to have sailed from American ports, 74 of them from New York.

[1] Q. Bemis, pp. 265-6.

By 1839 Britain had largely succeeded in stopping all the holes in the net except those made under illicit cover of the American flag, which meant that this device was more and more popular with the slavers. Britain's success was attained by her persistent policy of coercion, even though this was under heavy attack at home by men like Bright and Gladstone, particularly when in 1857 the revival of the British practice of visiting suspected slavers flying the flag of the United States was met by powerful opposition from Secretary of State Cass, and by a unanimous resolution of the Senate in 1858 declaring that the "immunity of their merchant vessels upon the high seas will be steadily maintained by the United States under all circumstances as an attribute of their sovereignty never to be abandoned".[1] The incoming Tory government, with Malmesbury as Foreign Secretary, not merely declined to maintain this Palmerstonian position, but, in a note of 8 June, 1858, formally disclaimed any pretension to a right of search in peace time. The result was a marked increase in the trade in 1859. But in all other fields of the slave trade the success achieved by 1861 was remarkable, and with the coming of the Civil War even that which had flourished under the illegal use of the American flag was doomed irrevocably. In 1862 the first slave trader to meet such a fate in the United States was hanged, and, following the withdrawal of the American vessels from Africa to participate in the war, Secretary Seward, not unmindful of its effect upon European opinion as well as firmly believing in its rectitude, signed in April, 1862, a convention with Great Britain, granting the reciprocal right of search in the most important sea areas and setting up mixed courts to try offenders. The treaty was unanimously ratified by the Senate, now shorn of its Southern members, and the arrangements worked very smoothly towards the rapid extinction of the trade, which thus ceased to be an issue in Anglo-American relations. As Bemis writes, "It is clear enough that once the slave power was removed from national politics all opposition disappeared to co-operation against the atrocious trans-Atlantic traffic in black human beings."[2]

The Webster-Ashburton Treaty was accepted by the big Senate majority of 39 votes to 9, which was due largely to Webster's skilful handling of public opinion. It owed its chief intrinsic importance to its settlement of the two boundary disputes, particularly that in Maine, but there is no doubt that it was of at least equal consequence because it brought to an end the ugliest Anglo-American crisis for many years

[1] Q. W.F.R., p. 199.   [2] Bemis, p. 333.

and one rendered the more formidable by the bitterness of feeling between the two peoples in other spheres than the diplomatic. The oil which was thus so beneficially applied to troubled waters did not, however, meet with universal contemporary approbation. There was some discontent in America, though perhaps for the first time since 1783 a treaty with Britain was more popular in the United States than in England, where, indeed, it was attacked as a capitulation. This view cannot be maintained; the treaty was, on the contrary, a vital step in the improvement of Anglo-American relations, one which cleared away "the poisonous atmosphere that had enshrouded"[1] them and which made possible the settlement of other outstanding, and in many ways more serious, problems.

III

THESE new problems arose principally from the fact that America was on the immediate threshold of the greatest period of expansion in her history; she was in the full flood of belief in, and accomplishment of, her Manifest Destiny. The school of "limitationists" deriving from Jefferson, who believed that the Rockies might be a natural and permanent western boundary and that all that could be hoped for beyond them were friendly sister-republics, was now quite dead, with the coming of steam and the rise of nationalism in the American people. In 1844 the area of the United States was 1,792,223 square miles: in the next four years the staggering total of 1,204,896 square miles was added to this, some of it being land in dispute with Britain. It was fortunate indeed for the two countries that the treaty of 1842 had cleared the air before these cataclysmic events took place; it was fortunate, too, that the Conservatives remained in power in England, with the conciliatory Aberdeen as their Foreign Secretary, until the direct controversy over the Oregon boundary was settled, although Palmerston, who succeeded him, was careful enough not to become embroiled in the war between Mexico and the United States, which ended in the Treaty of Guadalupe Hidalgo of 1848.

Britain's legation in Washington until 1847 was in the hands of a lean Anglo-Irish aristocrat, Sir Richard Pakenham, who succeeded Fox in 1844 and who was capable, as we shall see, of at least one major diplomatic blunder; and thereafter until 1850 in those of a Chargé d'Affaires, John Crampton, who was capable of another. Polk was

[1] Bailey, p. 227.

determined to have as American Minister in Britain at this crucial period an experienced diplomat, and one moreover whose Americanism was proof against the subtle social flattery of London, so Louis McClane returned to his old post in August, 1845. The policy of Polk naturally aroused suspicion in Britain, even though this was lessened by the greater moderation of James Buchanan, his Secretary of State, and McClane was very early and sensibly affected by what he felt to be the deep hostility of English public opinion, which made his mission very different from that in 1829-31, so that he shortly asked for his recall. He was succeeded by the historian George Bancroft, who, as the prophet of American democracy, was also reckoned by Polk proof against English flattery. This reckoning was on the whole correct, for he wrote, rejoicing in the neutrality of the British during the Mexican War, "The English people are already well aware of the rapid strides of America towards equality in commerce, manufacturing skill and wealth. They therefore look with dread on any series of events which tend to enlarge the sphere of American industry and possessions." "They do not love us; but they are *compelled to respect us*."[1] Mrs. Bancroft, however, was a mollifying influence for, as her published letters show, she liked "the English extremely".[2] He achieved a notable little diplomatic success when the Postal Treaty he negotiated was ratified by the Senate in January, 1849, a treaty which, with its successor convention between the two Post Offices in 1867, went far towards cheapening the transit of mail of all kinds between the two peoples, and which opened the way for the ever increasing intercommunication around the turn of the century. But when, later in the year, desirous of a parting stroke, he began without proper authority to negotiate a commercial treaty affecting American coastwise trade, he fell foul not only of Webster and New England opinion, but also of the new Whig administration, which recalled him shortly afterwards. He professed to be glad to return to his historical studies, but Mrs. Bancroft was very sorry to go.

The first problem in Anglo-American relations arising from the westward expansion of the United States, that of Texas, had been in existence since that state established its independence of Mexico in 1836. Dominated by American immigrants and assisted to independence by American funds and volunteers, the new Lone Star Republic hoped for annexation to the United States, but the existence of slavery within its borders produced Northern opposition quite strong enough

[1] Q. W.A.A.E., p. 252.   [2] Q. ibid, p. 251.

to prevent all but the recognition of her independence in 1837; the Texans withdrew their annexation offer in 1838, and began to make the best of their independent position. The possibility of reconquest of their 70,000 inhabitants by Mexico's 7 million forced them to look for diplomatic and commercial support elsewhere, particularly to England. The latter's motives, though subject to suspicion in the United States, which found it hard to believe that English colonial aspirations really were no more, certainly did not include any desire to establish British hegemony in Texas. She did desire to maintain an independent Texas as an alternative source of cotton supply for her mills, and she was certainly not averse, particularly while Palmerston was at the Foreign Office, to the idea of a buffer against increasingly aggressive American designs to the west: but there was also present, particularly in the mind of Aberdeen, the idea of gaining the abolition of slavery in Texas and using her thereafter as a lever against slavery and slavery expansion in the United States. In 1840 Palmerston signed with Texas treaties concerning commerce and the abolition of the slave trade, and their ratification was completed by Aberdeen, whose idea of joint action in the matter with France and the United States was uncompromisingly refused by the latter.

The course of Aberdeen's policy after this date is obscure, but it is clear that the local situation might well have got out of hand but for the skill with which the Texans played Britain off against the United States. Britain's agent in Texas, Charles Elliott, gave Pakenham in Washington, who constantly urged caution on Downing Street, some anxious moments by allowing his zeal to outrun his discretion, though he was quite outclassed in fervour by Calhoun's agent, 'General' Green. Aberdeen, however, remained cautious and did not wander far from the policy he had laid down to Pakenham: "Great Britain desires, and is constantly exerting herself to procure the general abolition of slavery throughout the world" in an open fashion, and would rejoice to see it abolished in Texas as part of the recognition of her independence by Mexico, but she does not seek a dominant influence in Texas, nor has she any intention of acting "directly or indirectly in a political sense on the United States through Texas."[1] Britain's efforts to mediate between Mexico (which had not yet faced up to the *fait accompli* of independence) and Texas were frustrated by the procrastination of Mexico, despite a second failure in the United States to accept a Texan offer of annexation in 1844, largely through the unexpected accession to the office of Secretary of State at the crucial moment of John C. Calhoun,

[1] Q. Bemis, pp. 228-9.

who read Aberdeen a public lecture on the merits of slavery, and gave the impression to the North that the chief object of the annexation of Texas was to prevent the abolition of slavery there and to provide a new area for slave expansion; as a result of this the proposal was heavily defeated by Northern voters in the Senate. The American antagonism to Britain, which was strongest in the aggressive Democratic party, found vent in the Presidential election of 1844, and Polk's victory on an expansionist platform, though it was not overwhelming, convinced a majority in Congress that the annexation of Texas was necessary. But a two-thirds majority was not possible, and it had to be accomplished by a joint resolution, which was signed by the outgoing President on 1 March, 1845. Though there was a strong minority opinion against the constitutionality of this step, the defeat of Clay had confirmed Pakenham's warning against arousing further Anglophobia in the United States, and by the time, in May, 1845, that Britain at last induced Mexico to recognize Texan independence, the American offer had been made. Texas shortly accepted it with enthusiasm, for it was the solution which most Texans had always desired.

Partly arising out of the annexation came war between the United States and Mexico in May, 1846, and, after a rapid campaign, the cession of an area, comprising the present states of California, Nevada, Utah, and part of New Mexico, Arizona, Wyoming and Colorado, to the United States. In the period leading up to and during the war the same spectre of British interference haunted American opinion as in the case of Texas, and there was just as little substance in it, for Britain never envisaged the establishment of her power in California. It is true that British local representatives, and even Admiral Seymour commanding the Pacific squadron of the Royal Navy, advocated more vigorous action in that direction, but they were consistently held back by their Government; it is true that Pakenham himself had in 1841, urged by Barron and Forbes who were consular officials in the area, pressed on Palmerston the desirability of obtaining Upper California as a repayment of certain British holders of Mexican bonds, but the idea had been sharply and decisively rejected by Aberdeen, on the ground that Britain desired no colonial ventures, and it was not heard of again; it is true that when, in 1846, Mexico became really frightened, she did endeavour to embroil Britain by making a definite offer to sell the territory to her, but the proposal was immediately refused by Palmerston, particularly since the land was by then virtually in the hands of the United States. In fact, the policy of the British Government at no time went farther than to let it be known in California, where a revolt against Mexico was

407

long thought to be possible, that, if she established her independence, "Great Britain would view with much dissatisfaction the establishment of a protectoral power over California by any other foreign state."[1] Even this attitude was not long or strongly maintained, but was a result of the disillusion of Aberdeen with the obduracy of Mexico over the Texan question, for as long as he hoped to remain in amity with the Mexican Government and to get something from it, he could not even by implication support a rebellion against it in its own territories. Here was a difference from the case of Texas, for her independence was already firmly established, and at no time did British policy in California do more than consider promising to help her maintain her independence if she achieved it, rather than letting her fall into the waiting hands of the United States. But even this proved impossible, and she only gained her independence under the immediate shadow of the American Union, a contingency which was met with calm acceptance even by Palmerston.

But as was so often the case in Anglo-American relations, the situation was made, by mutual mistrust, to appear much worse than it was. As long as the Oregon affair remained unsettled, Mexico was inclined to think wishfully of an Anglo-American war to solve her problems for her, a delusion in which the belligerence of the English Press encouraged her, *The Times* writing, for instance, on 15 April, 1845, "The invasion and conquest of a vast region by a State which is without an army and without credit, is a novelty in the history of nations. . . ."[2] On the other hand, the American Press tended to take the line indicated by the words of the New York *Courier*, "This idea that England is desirous to possess herself of the Californias seems as great a bugbear with the American people as the designs of Russia on India are with the English."[3] But, whereas the British Government did not endorse but restrained public opinion, the American Administration took a strong and popular line, for the very material reason that the United States had vital interests and large ambitions in erstwhile Mexican territories, and Britain had not. It was in respect of these territories that Polk in his message to Congress on 2 December, 1845, reaffirmed for the first time in twenty years the two main principles of the Monroe Doctrine, which now slowly began to assume the position of an accepted axiom of American foreign policy. He declared, for Great Britain's benefit, that there must be no interference by European powers "with

[1] E. D. Adams, "English Interest in the Annexation of California" (in *Am.H.R.*, XIV, 1909), p. 752.
[2] Q. Bailey, p. 272.   [3] Q. ibid, p. 266.

the independent action of the nations on this continent" and that "no future European colony or dominion shall with our consent be planted or established on any part of the North American continent."[1] Britain had, of course, never accepted Monroe's doctrine, but Polk's interpretation of it, as keeping non-American intruders out of areas which the United States might herself seek, went a good deal farther than the original pronouncement. Happily, by his day, Britain had ceased to desire new colonies, and, although she had not yet come to the position of actively welcoming increases in American power, was not prepared to go to war to prevent them. Thus it is certainly the case, that once the Oregon question was settled, any serious danger of hostilities between the two powers on this sort of issue was at an end.

The Oregon question* was, indeed, the most serious of those which came to a head between Polk's election and that of his successor, since it alone involved a direct clash between a British and an American claim. Yet it was not, perhaps, as formidable as others which had gone before it, since reasonable grounds for a compromise solution satisfactory to both parties obviously existed, and since the so-called joint occupation† of the disputed area had on the whole caused so little friction. The decisive fact leading to settlement, however, was the embroilment of the United States with Mexico; Aberdeen, though desirous of a good bargain, was always inclined towards a reasonable settlement, and the Mexican dispute ensured that Polk, who was a Southerner, should see reason in the north-west, for even the most aggressive of Democratic administrations, in the full fervour of Manifest Destiny, could not for long contemplate a war on two fronts, that on the north flank being against the strongest power in the world, and for a cause on which a perfectly satisfactory compromise was possible. An agreement was made essential and urgent by the opening up of the area, and by the realization that it would very shortly be the scene of substantial settlement.

Compromise of some kind had been in the air ever since the problem had come into existence. In the negotiations of 1818 the Americans had been prepared to make a deviation southward from the 49th parallel, in order to secure the rich substantive prize of the Oregon territory. In those of 1824-6 Adams had refused to offer this concession, but had authorized the extension of the 49 deg. boundary straight to the Pacific and the granting of free navigation of the Columbia from south of that

[1] *Messages and Papers*, pp. 2248-9.
* See Map 4.　† See pp. 355-6 above.

line; Canning had even been prepared for some sort of concession, though not to give up the British claim to the line of the Columbia River. Only a relatively narrow margin thus separated two such obstinate negotiators, and others might have settled the matter then and there. After the *modus vivendi* had been renewed in 1827, the question lay dormant until the Webster-Ashburton negotiations, by which time increased American emigration to the far West, though almost none of it was north of the Columbia, had made the matter one of increasing importance in American public opinion and had alarmed the Hudson's Bay Company. As early as 1841 a bill, which had failed to pass the House of Representatives, had provided for the erection of forts along the route to Oregon, and had been greeted by Palmerston in the House of Commons with the statement that, if it passed, it would be a declaration of war. In the cordial atmosphere following the Treaty of 1842, Tyler and Webster put forward a tentative but interesting project, for a tripartite agreement between the United States, Britain and Mexico, whereby Mexico would cede California north of 36 deg. to the United States for a substantial price, out of which British and American creditors of Mexico could be paid, while America would cede to Britain a considerable portion of the territory north of the Columbia; but the project came to nothing after Webster's resignation in 1843. America's loud claim to a boundary at 54 deg. 40 min. was weaker than Britain's claim to the Columbia line, but she had good prospects of obtaining the 49 deg. boundary, to which, on all other occasions than this and the very first in 1818, she adhered as her minimum claim; this suggested concession, proposed by Webster with the understandable object of obtaining a large part of California without war, no doubt made an impression on the British Government. After 1842 both countries reverted to their usual claims, to the 49 deg. line and the Columbia line respectively, but, realizing, as did Calhoun while Secretary of State, that time was on their side, the Americans always refused to arbitrate the question.

Feeling had been increased during 1844 by a brief flurry over Great Lakes armaments, but the situation was brought to the boil by the election of Polk, whose platform declared that "our title to the whole of the Territory of Oregon is clear and unquestionable; that no portion of the same ought to be ceded to England or any other power, and that the re-occupation of Oregon and the re-annexation of Texas at the earliest practicable period are great American measures, which this Convention recommends to the cordial support of the Democracy of the Union." In his Inaugural, however, the President omitted the vital word

Map 4. *The Oregon Boundary*

411

"whole" when laying claim to the Oregon country, and his Secretary of State, Buchanan, put forward to Pakenham a proposal to divide the territory along the 49th parallel, with free ports for Britain in Vancouver Island south of that line. In England, in the meantime, the Press had been denouncing what they regarded as Yankee bluster, and even Aberdeen had declared in the Lords with regard to the demand for 54 deg. 40 min.: "We possess rights which, in our opinion, are clear and unquestionable; and, by the blessing of God, and with your support, those rights we are fully prepared to maintain."[1] There were "extensive and indeed formidable"[2] increases in British naval preparations, according to McClane in London, even though these were primarily directed at the menacing situation in Europe. No doubt misled by these things Pakenham committed a major diplomatic blunder by rejecting the offer without even referring it home. As a result, Buchanan, on Polk's insistence, withdrew it, though with reluctance, and the President, who felt that he had made a reasonable suggestion, only to have it rejected out of hand, now demanded—not unnaturally—54 deg. 40 min., confiding to his diary his words to a Congressman at the time, "that the only way to treat John Bull was to look him straight in the eye; that I considered a bold and firm course on our part the pacific one; that if Congress faultered (sic) or hesitated in their course, John Bull would immediately become arrogant and more grasping in his demands".[3] In his first Annual Message he not only asserted the American title "to the whole Oregon Territory,"[4] but recommended to Congress the passage of legislation terminating, after the due year's notice, the joint occupation; this was eventually passed. What is more, in the same document he immediately followed his discussion of the Oregon question by his general pronouncement reviving the Monroe Doctrine, so that it seemed applicable to this dispute as well as to that over California, and recommended the establishment of protective forts on the Oregon trail, the prospect of which had so enraged Palmerston four years before. Nevertheless, Oregon still took second place to California in his message as well as in his mind, and Buchanan remained a moderating influence, saying, when the President talked of leaving the matter of Oregon to God and the people, that he did not think God was much to be relied upon north of 49 deg. Furthermore, American commercial interests ardently desired a compromise, which would give them Pacific ports but would not damage their trade by war.

In Britain, too, moderate counsels were prevailing. Pakenham's rejec-

[1] Q. Bailey, pp. 233, 236.   [2] Q. W.A.A.E., p. 242.
[3] Q. Bailey, p. 238.   [4] *Messages and Papers*, p. 2245.

412

tion of Buchanan's offer was swiftly disavowed by Aberdeen, who had long felt that the 49 deg. boundary might be acceptable, and who now began to prepare public opinion in Britain for concessions, notably through *The Times*. His hand was strengthened by the support of the industrial and commercial interests, and even Palmerston's attacks were silenced by the determination of Lord John Russell not to allow his party to be damaged by the sort of violence which had done it so much harm at the time of Palmerston's opposition to the Webster-Ashburton Treaty. After the humiliating failure of Russell to form a ministry in December, 1845, when Peel resigned, the Tories returned to office in February with assurances from the Whigs that they would cease their attacks on the Oregon policy of the Government. These things, combined with the rising strength of anti-colonialism, produced a strong reaction; this was epitomized in the attitude of *The Times*, which effected what was really a *volte-face*. Indeed, the pacific editorial which it published on 3 January, 1846, might lay claim to constitute the most important turning point in the history of Anglo-American relations:

> That there are men in America who long for war with Great Britain is, we fear, no less true than that there are men in this country to whom a war with the United States would be by no means unwelcome. But . . . in both countries, the real strength of public opinion is arrayed against a belligerent policy. The relations of commerce—the affections of kindred—identity of origin, of language, and laws—the common pursuit of similar objects, the common prevalence of similar sentiments, and the common deference to the same principles of moral action—bind the two nations together by ties which it would be atrocious to sever by the sword. We are two people, but we are of one family. We have fought, but we have been reconciled.[1]

So we find a chastened Pakenham going so far to the other extreme as to confide to Buchanan that "the British Government would be glad to get clear of the question on almost any terms, that they did not care if the arbitrator should award the whole territory to us (the United States)."[2] But Polk was in a strong position and rejected two British offers of arbitration in rapid succession; he then refused to put forward the offer of 49 deg. again, as Pakenham now suggested, and recommended military preparations to Congress. His formal notification of the termination of the joint occupation followed, though it was couched

---

[1] Q. F. Merk, "British Government Propaganda and the Oregon Treaty" (in *Am.H.R.* XL, No. 1, 1934), pp. 55-6.   [2] Q. Bailey, p. 241.

in courteous terms. On 6 June, 1846, however, Pakenham put forward to Buchanan a compromise offer of the 49th parallel as far as the Straits of Fuca, with free navigation of the Columbia River for the Hudson's Bay Company, whose rights were also to be guaranteed. Polk declared that he wished to reject the offer, but his Cabinet voted to submit it to the Senate for consideration *before* it was signed, a very unusual procedure, which was probably adopted only because previous soundings among Senators had made its acceptance seem likely. Thus the President's reluctance was probably a face-saving matter; certainly it is hard to believe that the arrival of an honourable offer of compromise from Britain so shortly after the outbreak of war with Mexico could have been altogether displeasing to him. The Senate advised acceptance by a substantial majority, and the treaty was accordingly signed on 15 June, 1846, and later ratified, word for word, exactly as it had been framed in the Foreign Office.

This hasty acceptance of the British formula, that the boundary, after leaving the 49th parallel at "the middle of the channel which separates the continent from Vancouver's Island", followed "through the middle of the said channel, and of Fuca's Straits" southward to the Pacific Ocean, was a cause of future difficulty, for it left uncertain whether the channel was that of the Haro Strait to the westward or the Rosario Strait to the eastward, the former being territorially and strategically beneficial to the United States, and vice versa. In 1856 a mixed commission of two, appointed to determine the proper channel, disagreed, and it was not until the Treaty of Washington of 1871 that the so-called San Juan dispute was referred to arbitration, that of the German Emperor, for two years earlier the Senate had refused to ratify a convention with Great Britain which would have permitted a compromise. The arbitrator, forced to decide which channel was actually intended, decided in favour of the claim of the United States. A short time previously, in 1869, another cause of difficulty had been eliminated by the purchase of the navigation rights of the Hudson's Bay Company on the Columbia River by the United States. In this way, by 1872, the settlement of the Oregon dispute, which had been made in the treaty of 1846, was finally rounded off in all its details. This settlement formed the counterpart of the Webster-Ashburton agreement on the north-eastern boundary, for in the west the United States fared better than its claim warranted, and in the east so did Great Britain; but essentially they both appeared to contemporary opinion as compromise measures, and as such they can still fairly be regarded. The settlement in this fashion of the last fundamental border dispute between the two countries was of signal importance in the history of Anglo-American relations, for, although afterwards the accidents of international events did make an Anglo-American conflict on occasions a possibility, that possibility became gradually more remote.

IV

Nor that new causes of difficulty did not appear—that concerning the Isthmus of Panama very soon shows itself to prove the contrary—but they showed themselves less and less intransigent and more and more amenable to settlement by friendly diplomacy; the period 1849-60, for instance, saw two more treaties of major significance between the two countries, the Clayton-Bulwer Treaty of 1850 and the Reciprocity Treaty of 1854. The year 1849-53 saw a return of the Whigs to power in the United States, which meant, with responsible and experienced men such as Clayton, Webster and Everett as Secretaries of State, a cordial period in American feelings towards Britain. The ruling combinations, from 1853-7 and 1857-61, of the Democrats Pierce and Marcy, and Buchanan and Cass, meant somewhat more difficulty, though not of the gravest kind. In Britain, Palmerston dominated the scene from 1846-51 as Foreign Secretary, and from 1855-8 as Prime Minister, which meant some unease, though in the former period he was restrained by Prime Minister Russell, whom the then American Minister in London considered "more alive to the importance of preserving the most friendly feelings with us";[1] but happily Aberdeen was Prime Minister from 1852-5, during the years of Pierce's presidency, when the strain was greatest. After a year of Lord Derby as Prime Minister from 1858-9, Palmerston returned once more to power in the latter year.

In London Bancroft was succeeded in 1849 by a typical Whig appointee, a quiet but efficient cotton manufacturer from Massachusetts, Abbot Lawrence, who not only appreciated from personal experience the importance of the economic bonds between the two countries, but probably did much in an unobtrusive way to prepare the way for the Clayton-Bulwer Treaty, writing to Palmerston shortly after his arrival in 1849, "A ship canal connecting the two oceans will do more to perpetuate peace between Great Britain and the United States, and in fact the whole world, than any other work yet achieved." Like his Secretaries of State, Clayton and Webster, he placed the value of Anglo-

[1] Q. W.A.A.E., p. 253.

American friendship high, and was pleased to note in 1851 a great increase in the intercourse between the two peoples, "first, because the English people are beginning to regard American affairs with a greater interest, and second a greater number of Americans are visiting Europe."[1] Striking evidence for the latter point is the number of passports issued by the American Minister, which rose from 170 in 1831 to 1,145 in only six months of 1851. In his last despatch before his departure in 1852 he wrote: "I can say with truth . . . that the relations between the United States and Great Britain have never in my judgment been so cordial". Their cordiality was shown by his signature in 1850 of a little treaty with Palmerston ceding Horseshoe Reef in the Niagara River to the United States, so that the latter could build and maintain a lighthouse upon it. After a brief tenure by another Whig, J. R. Ingersoll, who wrote characteristically, "There is certainly a tendency to cultivate good feelings with our country, which is worth cultivating in return",[2] James Buchanan arrived in August, 1853, as the new Democratic nominee.

He displayed some of the sensitivity of his party from the first by complaining, unjustifiably according to his biographer, that he was only able to enter the best English society because of his official position; he showed even more of it by what cannot now be regarded as other than the comedy of the Court clothes. Yet this question, which has been heard of before but which reached its head in this decade, was by no means without interest, for it was indicative of a marked difference in national outlook. Americans tended to regard elaborate Court dress as iniquitous flummery, while the British were inclined to consider refusal to wear it as an insult to the Queen. Secretary of State Marcy at this time sent a circular to American diplomats instructing them to appear at Courts whenever possible "in the simple dress of an American citizen." A resultant conversation between Buchanan and an English Court official ended, according to Buchanan, in this not uncharacteristic fashion:

> He grew warm by talking, and said that, whilst the Queen herself would make no objections to my appearance at Court in any dress I thought proper, yet the people of England would consider it *presumption*. I became somewhat indignant in my turn, and said that while I entertained the highest respect for her Majesty, and desired to treat her with the deference which was eminently her due, yet it would not make the slightest difference to me, individually, whether I ever appeared at Court.

[1] Q. ibid, pp, 262-3.   [2] Q. ibid, pp. 269-70, 273.

The *Morning Chronicle* delivered itself of the opinion, "There is not the least reason why her Majesty . . . should be troubled to receive the gentleman in the black coat from Yankee-land. He can say his say at the Foreign Office, dine at a chop-house in King Street, sleep at the Old Hummums, and be off as he came, per liner, when his business is done." But things sorted themselves out in the end, and Buchanan was able to report:

> The dress question, after much difficulty, has been finally and satisfactorily settled. I appeared at the levée on Wednesday last in just such a dress as I have worn at the President's one hundred times. A black coat, white waistcoat and cravat and black pantaloons and dress boots, with the addition of a very plain black-handled and black-hilted dress sword. This is to gratify those who have yielded so much, and to distinguish me from the Upper Court servants. I knew that I would be received in any dress I might wear; but could not have anticipated that I should be received in so kind and distinguished a manner. Having yielded, they did not do things by halves.[1]

Thus was Buchanan reconciled to his lot in London, but his successor, George Mifflin Dallas, as ardent a Democrat as one might expect of Polk's Vice-President, ran into further difficulties soon after his arrival in March, 1856, for he declined to attend a levée to which an American companion, although dressed in his official uniform as a Professor of Engineering at West Point, was refused admittance. There were other troubles also, arising largely from his determination to follow Polk's example in looking John Bull straight in the eye, which appeared to the English as arrogance; he disclaimed any belief in "all the balderdash about mother country, kindred and so forth",[2] and was able to make little headway as long as Palmerston was in power, but he was much more successful during Malmesbury's brief tenure of the Foreign Office. He had, however, another two years of "Pam" to endure before he was succeeded in May, 1861, by Charles Francis Adams.

Yet the faults in Anglo-American relations were by no means all on Palmerston's side, for this was "a feverish period in American history . . . unparalleled for restlessness and lawlessness",[3] which in itself made difficulties, as the British representatives in Washington discovered. Palmerston put his finger on a vital fact when he said in 1848, "It is very probable that half the calumnies which from time to time are circulated in the United States against Great Britain owe their

[1] Q. W.A.A.E., pp. 282, 283, 284-5.
[2] Q. ibid, p. 296.   [3] W.F.R., p. 176.

origin to mistakes and ignorance, as much as to malice or interested motives," and indeed he thought it would be a "good thing to keep the Washington Legation very fully informed as to European transactions and so enable the Minister to explain to any fair-minded and candid man the reasons and facts of any course of policy on the part of Great Britain which may have attracted attention in the United States". His sentiments can be compared with Webster's earlier complaints of the ignorance of the English Press about America.

Sir Henry Lytton Bulwer, who took over from John Crampton, the British Chargé d'Affaires in Washington, early in 1850, fully appreciated Palmerston's point, and inaugurated the tradition of speechmaking by British Ministers in the United States, stating that he "wished to get at the heart of the American people and to cure this anti-English disease at its source."[1] This policy was approved by Palmerston, who, in the tradition of Canning, utilized public opinion to the utmost as a weapon and support of diplomacy, and was a master of the art of directing it; from this time forward Britain came increasingly to rely on a policy of making the truth about the British point of view known to the American people. With the growth of belief in democracy there came the faith that the true facts in any case were the best guarantee of agreement between the two peoples. Bulwer himself was renowned for his sang-froid, for a sort of "studied high-bred negligence," but he showed an acute understanding of the American situation in this uneasy period, at once aftermath of Manifest Destiny and prelude to Civil War. He wrote before leaving, "The position of this people and Government is peculiar. The United States Government is honourable, just and prudent; it is not likely to originate wars of an ambitious or aggressive character, but the people who live under this Government are of a wild, adventurous and conquering character".[2]

On his resignation in 1851, John Crampton once more became Chargé d'Affaires, and in 1852 was appointed Minister in his own right. He was a diplomat of ability and commanding presence, and was very popular in Washington, but he became the centre of one of the diplomatic *causes célèbres* of Anglo-American relations. Under stress of the losses suffered in the Crimean War, which began in 1854, the British Government commenced to enlist foreigners in the British Army, and the Washington Legation was pressed to organize recruiting in the United States. Crampton took legal advice, and thought that a loophole had been found in the American Neutrality legislation which would make this possible; he exercised caution throughout these activities, declaring

[1] Q. ibid, pp. 167, 174.   [2] Q. ibid, pp. 168, 178.

that only British subjects (whose citizenship was considered indefeasible by the British Government) were wanted, enjoining (though often with little effect) caution upon his agents, such as Joseph Howe, and ensuring that the actual enlistments were only made on Canadian soil. But there is little doubt that illegalities were committed as a result of the urgent orders of the British Government, and American opinion, habitually anti-British and in some respects pro-Russian, reacted violently.

Secretary of State Marcy protested to Crampton, and, when his protestations proved unavailing, demanded the Minister's recall. In the meanwhile a number of British consular agents had been indicted, and the British Government gave orders to cease recruitment, but refused to withdraw Crampton. Pierce, now in the final throes of seeking the Democratic nomination for the Presidency, was anxious to take strong action, and was unquestionably irritated by Crampton's pertinacious protests against American filibustering in Central America and, in particular, against the President's unwarrantable recognition of the rebel government of William Walker in Nicaragua. On 28 May, 1856, therefore, he summarily dismissed the British Minister and three British Consuls. There was strong talk in the British Press, but once again pacific sentiments and economic ties prevailed. As a result, the American Minister in London was not even dismissed (though Crampton was knighted on his return home, and no successor was appointed until the end of the Pierce administration ten months later) while Pierce's actions were unpopular with many Americans. It is interesting to note that many soldiers for the Northern armies in the Civil War were quietly recruited in Europe.

When the British Government did appoint a new Minister to Washington, they sent one who was already, at thirty-eight years of age, an experienced, and was reckoned to be a brilliant, diplomat—Francis, Baron Napier, who was Americophile enough for Palmerston to write, "I think Napier should . . . remember that he has not become a Naturalized Citizen of the Union."[1] Though his period as Minister was a troubled one, Buchanan as President was anxious to preserve British friendship, writing in 1859 to Clarendon, "No two countries have ever existed on the face of the earth which could do each other so much good *or* so much harm. Perhaps I attribute too much importance to the cultivation of friendly relations . . . but I think you do not estimate this as highly as it deserves. Your mission here ought always to be

[1] Q. R. W. Van Alstyne, "Anglo-American Relations, 1853-7" (in *Am.H.R.*, XLII, No. 3, 1937), p. 499.

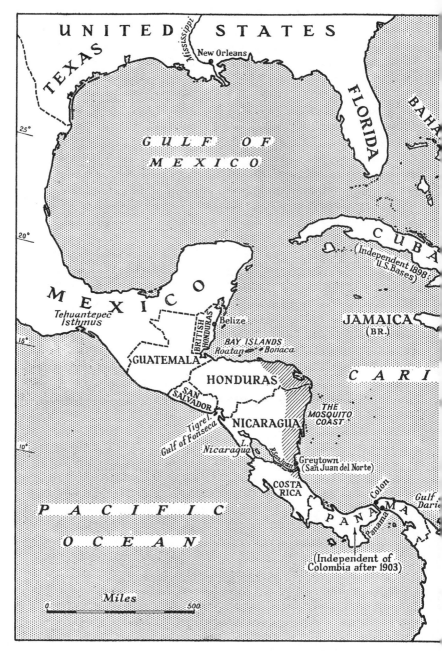

Map 5. *The Caribbean*

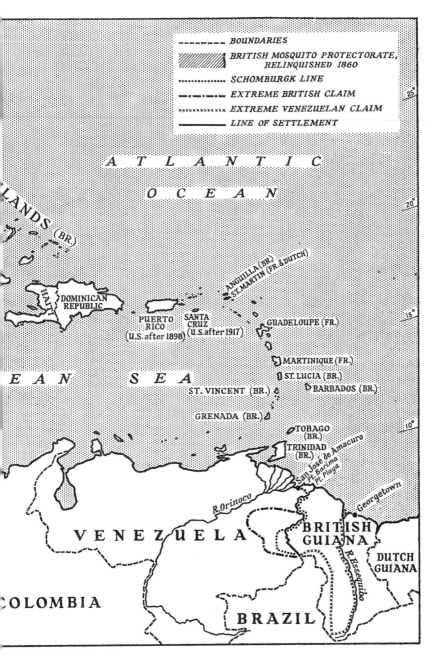

LEGEND:

- - - - - - - BOUNDARIES
▨▨▨▨▨ BRITISH MOSQUITO PROTECTORATE, RELINQUISHED 1860
················ SCHOMBURGK LINE
—··—··—··— EXTREME BRITISH CLAIM
xxxxxxxxxxxx EXTREME VENEZUELAN CLAIM
————— LINE OF SETTLEMENT

Controversies

421

filled by a first rate man whose character is known in this country and whose acts and opinions will command respect and influence in England." Though Napier was not, as this implies, a complete success in this post, Lytton called him "the only man of genius in the diplomatic service of his time";[1] perhaps men of genius fit less easily into Washington's Legation than men of great talents like Napier's successor, Lord Lyons.

Now that the main border disputes had been amicably settled, tension in Anglo-American relations shifted primarily, in the years between 1847 and 1861, to the Central American Isthmus* and the potentially explosive question of a canal there, to join the Atlantic and the Pacific. This shift was important because it clearly reflected the extension of American power and interests; it was an obvious sequel to the doctrine of Manifest Destiny, which had placed over a thousand miles of Pacific Coast in American hands, and it was precipitated by the discovery of gold in newly acquired California in 1849. As yet, it should be observed, this desire, particularly of the Democratic party, to spread the eagle's wings wider still, was largely confined to the Americas, and took cover beneath the Monroe Doctrine; it is true that the first tentative American moves into the far Pacific were made in these years, but they were as yet portents no bigger than a man's hand. The real cloud of American might began to concentrate over Central America, and there, by evoking the Monroe Doctrine's exclusion of other powers from the Western hemisphere and trying to make it a reality, America continued to emphasize the detached nature of her policy: the expansion of American power was disguised in a garb of isolationism. It was in this garb that most Americans liked to see the policy, though some were more outspoken. The New York *Herald*, for instance, proclaimed on 11 October, 1852: "National glory—national greatness—the spread of political liberty on this continent, must be the thought and action by day, and the throbbing dream by night, of the whole American people, or they will sink into oblivion",[2] yet the words "on this continent" remained a saving grace for American consciences. Thus did the United States take the first important step towards the Roosevelt corollary of the Monroe Doctrine, comforted by the illusion of isolationism, in much the same way as the second Roosevelt, in laying the groundwork of the United Nations in World War II, declared that the need for the old and odious spheres of influence and regional arrangements was at an end, but did not reckon the Pan-American Union as one of those arrangements.

[1] Q. W.F.R., p. 202.   * See Map 5.   [2] Q. Bailey, p. 281.

To other peoples, particularly the British of the mid-nineteenth century, the sacrosanctity and uniqueness of the western hemisphere made little appeal; as Palmerston said in 1857, "These Yankees are most disagreeable Fellows to have to do with about any American Question; They are on the Spot, strong, deeply interested in the matter, totally unscrupulous and dishonest and determined somehow or other to carry their Point." He went on, in words worth quoting at length, because they illustrate not only his attitude but also that of the British people, which was by no means identical:

> We are far away, weak from Distance, controlled by the Indifference of the Nation . . . and by its Strong commercial Interest in maintaining Peace with the United States. The result of this State of Things has been that we have given away Step by Step to the North Americans on almost every disputed matter, and I fear that we shall have more or less to do so upon almost every other Question except the maintenance of our own Provinces and of our West Indian Islands—I have long felt inwardly convinced that the Anglo-Saxon Race will in Process of Time become Masters of the whole American Continent North and South, by Reason of their superior Qualities as compared with the degenerate Spanish and Portuguese Americans; But whatever may be the Effects of such a Result upon the interests of England, it is not for us to assist such a Consummation, but on the Contrary we ought to delay it as long as possible.[1]

Though the difficulties arising from the extension of American power in Central America gravitated around the Canal question, they were by no means confined to it, for this was the age of Southern imperialism, of "the tropic empire, seeking the warm sea".[2] Strong in the conviction of the rectitude of the cotton-slavery system, faced with the exhaustion of actual and potential cotton lands in the United States, fearful of losing the predominance in the national government that it had for many years enjoyed, the South dreamed dreams of a great slave empire based upon the Caribbean, and during the Southern-influenced administrations of Pierce and Buchanan, particularly the former, strove to give the dreams actuality. The Cuban question was the embodiment of this spirit, for here the longstanding American desire for annexation was strengthened by the eagerness of the South to gain ready-made material for more slave states, but the wish was frustrated by the opposition of Britain and France, the former of which the American people had long—though largely erroneously—suspected of cherishing designs against the island on its own account. Polk's efforts to purchase

[1] Q. R. W. Van Alstyne, p. 500.   [2] Benet, *John Brown's Body*, p. 374.

it failed, and between 1849 and 1851 three attempts by American fili-busterers to seize it by fostering internal insurrection brought matters to a head; only Webster's tact—he was back for a brief spell at the State Department—averted a war with Spain. In 1852 the British and French Governments proposed a tripartite declaration with the United States, guaranteeing Cuba to Spain. Webster favoured the scheme but his successor rejected it, and when the Democrats returned to power the question of annexation was once more raised, as might have been expected under a President whose Inaugural Address contained the words, "the policy of my Administration will not be controlled by any timid forebodings of evil from expansion."[1] There followed in 1854 the so-called Ostend Manifesto—a misnomer for a private despatch from the American Ministers in Spain, France and England, recommending the use of any means to gain Cuba from Spain—which was one of the strangest manifestations of American expansionist desires in this period.

The remarkable thing is that this aggressive spirit was checked as effectively as it was, that the United States did not press her claims in this area and back them by force, thus precipitating a fatal breach in Anglo-American relations. That she did not is due to a number of factors, including the British Navy, but pre-eminently to the increas-ingly bitter national cleavage in the United States itself; even had she had the physical force, she had not the united will, for her mind was, until the internal slavery question was settled, irrevocably split. At the height of the Cuban crisis in 1851, *The Times* wrote, "If the Southern States are allowed to incorporate Cuba . . . the North will turn in self-defence upon the nearest territory which it may seize to restore the balance of power, and that territory is our own."[2] This fear for Canada seemed very justified by the pattern of only too recent events in California and Oregon, which had been to some extent based on a bargain between North and South, yet in fact it proved to be without real foundation, for it failed to take account of the violent change coming over Northern sentiment, which now plainly was beginning to dread the extension of slavery more than it desired the expansion of the United States. The very reverse of what *The Times* feared actually occurred, for the increasing sectional tension, far from precipitating aggression against Canada, in reality gave her a respite from annexa-tionist demands, and it was only after the Civil War that they again became vociferous; it also checked most effectively Southern desires for expansion in the Caribbean area. Not only is this shown by the

[1] *Messages and Papers*, p. 2731.   [2] Q. Bailey, p. 309.

failure of Democratic designs upon Cuba, but also by the fact that the heavily criticized Clayton-Bulwer Treaty was signed at the very height of the sectional conflict, and that it was the work of the Whigs, who were primarily responsible for the Compromise of 1850, which temporarily allayed the internal tension. Nor were the restraining factors in Central America all on the American side, for it was in the middle of the decade 1850-60 that the dissatisfaction of the Americans with that treaty was at its height, and it was in these crucial years, from 1854-6, that Britain was embroiled in the Crimea, the only major war she fought between 1815 and 1914 and one in which, despite her strength and that of her allies, she suffered grievous military disasters. At such a time it was natural for her to show restraint in her Central American policy.

But the change in her attitude towards the United States went deeper than that, and was of more lasting effect. Mere involvement in a European war after nearly forty years of peace and twenty-five years of virtually isolationist policies was a shock to English sensibilities, and she began to consider the expansionist activities of such a potentially dangerous enemy as the United States with much less animosity. A notable transformation came over her attitude to America, even though one less clearly cut and strongly marked than that which took place in very similar circumstances at the turn of the century, when, in the course of the Boer War, Britain became suddenly conscious of her isolation and her vulnerability, of the enmity of her rivals and her lack of allies, or even friends. Then she was to turn decisively, with open arms, to seek American friendship; now, in the eighteen-fifties, she by no means went so far as that, but she did take a step in the same direction. During the American expansion of the previous decade, she had adopted an attitude of disapproval, and had endeavoured by diplomatic means to check it, though she had recoiled from open conflict and as a result had failed to affect the issue; this lesson was not entirely lost on her, and she began to appreciate that if America was going to be powerful whether she approved or not, it was better that she should be amicable than hostile. Furthermore, in the particular case of Central America, the idea suggested itself that the order which the United States might bring would be more beneficial to the trade of Britain than the existing disorder in that area. In any case the vast trade of the United States herself with Britain, particularly that in cotton, was a powerful argument for friendship. Other reasons also existed, such as the relative decline in strength, and therefore potential rivalry, of the American merchant marine, the laying of the Atlantic cable in 1858 (even though it went out of action for a considerable time shortly afterwards), and the decline of the literary animosity between the two English-speaking peoples. Thus in 1856 *The Times* even went so far as to "look with great resignation and even pleasure" on the prospect of American domination of Central America, while the *Economist* declared, "We could not hinder the ultimate absorption by the Anglo-Saxon republics of the whole of Central America if we would;—and we are by no means certain that we would if we could".[1] This was indeed a change from the days of Canning, and it foreshadowed further developments in the future.

Ever since the Spanish treasure had crossed the Isthmus of Panama on its way to Spain in the sixteenth century, there had been notions of a canal across Central America, and ever since Drake had attacked a Spanish treasure train there, England had been interested in this vital trade route.* With the great growth of her international trade, the project of such a canal became more and more important to her, just at the time that American expansion produced the same interest in the idea in the United States; the resulting rivalry had already been vigorously fanned by the local representatives of the two governments, and the discovery of gold in California made it seem an urgent question. Britain had, since her rivalry with Spain in the eighteenth century, maintained certain claims in the area, centring in Belize, or British Honduras, where there was a substantial British settlement; its local inhabitants pressed repeatedly for full colonial status, but the British Government, as for instance under Aberdeen in 1840, had been reluctant to grant it in view of America's awakening interest in the area. Meanwhile, the British steadily established their claim also to the Bay Islands, and to a protectorate over the Indians of the Mosquito Coast. These areas gave her an important measure of potential control over the two most likely canal routes, that from the north-west corner of Honduras to the Gulf of Fonseca, and that through the San Juan River and Lake Nicaragua, also to the Gulf of Fonseca. The Tehuantepec and Panama routes were less favoured at this period, even though in December, 1846, the American Minister in Bogota signed a treaty with the Government of New Granada (Colombia) granting to the United States, in return for protection (which Britain and France had previously declined to give in the form of a guarantee of Colombia's sovereignty and neutrality) far-reaching transit rights over the Isthmus of Panama; an American canal through Mexican territory was rendered almost

[1] Q. ibid, p. 300.   * See Map 5.

impossible by the bitterness which naturally arose from the Mexican War.

During the last year of the war, violent clashes took place at Greytown or San Juan (which commanded the mouth of the river of that name) between the British, who claimed that their protectorate over the Mosquitos included this possible canal terminus, and the Nicaraguans, who would, if they admitted this British right, be excluded, not only from control of the eastern end of the canal, but from all access to the Atlantic. In February, 1848, Palmerston extended the claim to a line well south of the port, and the Nicaraguans had no recourse, owing to American preoccupation in Mexico, save to come to terms with the local British commander. But American suspicions of British intentions were once more aroused, this time perhaps with more justice than in Texas or California, and an American emissary who reached Nicaragua in the last months of Polk's administration signed, on 21 June, 1849, an unauthorized treaty granting to the American Government, in perpetuity, the right of way for transit purposes across Nicaragua, and permitting the fortification of such a route, while already, some months earlier, an American company had begun to prepare for the construction of a canal. Great Britain, however, now had effective control of the east coast, and a rival British Canal Company had been formed, so that local tension increased, particularly when the British representative on the spot, Chatfield, committed in 1849 the quite unauthorized indiscretion of getting possession of Tigre Island, which commanded the Gulf of Fonseca, even though he did so nominally as temporary security for unpaid debts to Britain of the government of Honduras, and even though the action was at once repudiated by the British authorities.

Meanwhile, however, the new Whig administration in Washington had replaced Polk's emissary by another, named Squier, who had concluded a somewhat more moderate treaty with Nicaragua, recognizing her "rights of sovereignty and property" in the canal route and guaranteeing its neutrality "as long as it should be controlled by American citizens", but opening the rights and privileges "given by the treaty . . . to any other nation willing to enter into an agreement with Nicaragua for the protection of the contemplated canal."[1] This reflected the deliberate policy of Secretary of State Clayton, who hoped to settle the Isthmian question in such a way that neither side claimed exclusive control of any canal, for the naturally pacific interests of the Whigs were reinforced by the growing threat of sectional cleavage, and he was

[1] M. W. Williams, *Anglo-American Isthmian Diplomacy, 1815-1915* (London, 1916), p. 63.

alarmed at the prospect of a serious Anglo-American rupture; as he wrote, "We are deeply anxious to avoid any collision with the British Government in relation to this matter; but that collision will become inevitable if great prudence be not exercised on both sides." There is little doubt, too, that the change of government in the United States had determined Palmerston, whose chief motive for obduracy had been the great fear of Democratic expansion into the Isthmus, that the time was ripe for a settlement, on just such lines as Clayton suggested, for when the matter was broached he declared that Britain already had more colonies than she could manage and *"that, as to any idea of their holding exclusive possession of the mouth of the San Juan as the Key of the contemplated communication between the Atlantic and the Pacific, nothing could be further from their minds."*[1]

Thus a political basis for agreement now existed, and there were strong economic forces working in the same direction, since wealthy Whigs tended to see eye to eye with British capitalists, while even the London financiers were unlikely to be able to raise by themselves the capital needed for such a titanic project. It was typical that the new American Minister, Lawrence, should write to Palmerston, "In order to give full confidence to the capitalists of Europe and America neither the United States nor Great Britain should exercise any power over the Indians or any of the States of Central America."[2] Furthermore, public opinion in Britain would not have supported a policy of rigid opposition to American expansion. As G. F. Hickson writes, "Palmerston was not alone amongst British statesmen in declining to accept the principles of the Monroe Doctrine as held in the United States. But others . . . adopted a more generous view of the expansion of the United States on the American continent and that public opinion was not prepared to risk the severance of commercial relations for the sake of a dispute concerning obscure and distant parts of Central America."[3]

Despite this, however, negotiations were long, and at times difficult, and, as we shall see, the finished treaty was no sooner made than it was questioned in the United States. What is more, the whole Isthmian question remained a source of trouble and misunderstanding in Anglo-American relations for the next fifty years. Judgments on the treaty varied between that of one American, "Thus, after almost unparalleled difficulties, was completed the Clayton Treaty, probably the most persistently unpopular agreement ever made by the United States with a

[1] Q. ibid, pp. 75, 78.   [2] Q. W.A.A.E., p. 262.

[3] G. F. Hickson, "Palmerston and the Clayton-Bulwer Treaty" (in *Cambridge Historical Journal*, III, 1931), p. 303.

foreign government", and that of another, Seward, that it was a land-mark in diplomacy, "an international agreement with aims not primarily selfish."[1] That the difficulties arose in the first place was very largely due to the Mosquito question, for in order to prevent antici-pated American aggression, or exclusive control of potential canal routes, the British Government had proclaimed the Indians' right to the San Juan river-mouth, as well as its own protectorate over them, and from this position, which really prevented the building of a truly international waterway, they found it exceedingly difficult to withdraw. Matters were made worse by the very comprehensible, though in fact unjustified, American suspicion that the British intended to enlarge their colonial empire in the area. It was symptomatic that negotiations were transferred from London to Washington because of Lawrence's insistence on discussing the Mosquito question, as well as because the British Government hoped that Bulwer might get better terms from Clayton than they could from the American Minister, owing to the Secretary of State's anxiety to settle the matter before the rising temper of American public opinion got out of hand.

The Clayton-Bulwer Treaty did eventually emerge from the complex negotiations which preceded it because both parties concentrated upon the points of agreement between them, in order to make sure of a settlement, and endeavoured by a subtle use of words to gloss over the fissures of disagreement in the manner beloved of the skilful diplo-matist; Cobden spoke, in reference to this, of "the unfortunate pro-pensity of diplomatists to involve their sentences in phraseology which becomes unintelligible not only to others but to themselves."[2] The obscurity, however, was deliberate; the treaty was in fact a compromise, which prevented any exclusive control over the possible canal route, and which not only left other matters as they were, but also enabled the Americans to believe that the British had made very substantial con-cessions in practice, though not specifically in so many words. This, Bulwer had made sure, they had not in fact done; as *The Times* put it, the negotiations in fact became a battle of verbal dexterity, a struggle "for generalship in the use of terms".[3] The difficulties, which arose from the treaty, did so almost exclusively from the ambiguity of the first article, for the other parts were quite straightforward; they provided in detail for the possible construction of the canal and its neutralization in that event; for the establishment, if it could be done, of a free port at each end of the waterway; for the inclusion in these arrangements of any other power agreeable to its conditions; and, finally, for the estab-

[1] Q. W.F.R., pp. 172, 173.   [2] Q. Hickson, p. 298.   [3] Q. Williams, p. 92.

lishment of "a general principle", extending the protection of the two powers "to any other practicable communications, whether by Canal or railway, across the Isthmus which connects North and South America . . . especially . . . by the way of Tehuantepec, or Panama."[1]

In contrast with the clarity of these provisions, the first article stated that neither party "will ever obtain or maintain for itself any exclusive control over the said Ship Canal",[2] which was plain enough, but continued,

> agreeing, that neither will ever erect or maintain any fortifications commanding the same, or in the vicinity thereof, or occupy, or fortify, or colonize, or assume, or exercise any dominion over Nicaragua, Costa Rica, the Mosquito Coast, or any part of Central America; nor will either make use of any protection which either affords or may afford, or any alliance which either has or may have, to or with any State or People for the purpose of erecting or maintaining any such fortifications, or of occupying, fortifying, or colonizing Nicaragua, Costa Rica, the Mosquito Coast or any part of Central America, or of assuming or exercising dominion over the same. . . .

Herein lay the obscurity, and even before the treaty was signed and ratified, each party was having second thoughts.

First, the British expressed fear of American designs against the Bay Islands of Roatan and Bonaca, and these were only quieted by a note from Clayton to Bulwer stating that "this Government has never desired to occupy, fortify or settle either of those Islands; that I have no knowledge or information or belief that Americans desire to establish themselves in those islands."[3] Next, a suspicion arose in Palmerston's mind that the treaty was intended by the Americans to apply to Belize and the Bay Islands, and he instructed Bulwer to deliver to Clayton prior to the actual exchange of ratifications a declaration that "Her Majesty does not understand the engagements of that Convention to apply to Her Majesty's settlement at Honduras or to its Dependencies."[4] The Americans thereupon suspected that this was a British attempt to obtain definite recognition of their claims to Honduras and the Bay Islands, and in order to avoid giving it, proceeded by a counter-declaration, handed to and accepted by Bulwer at the exchange of ratifications, which stated that "the treaty . . . was not intended . . . to apply" to them, and that the "Chairman of the Committee on Foreign Relations of the Senate . . . informs me that 'the Senate perfectly understood that the treaty did not include British Honduras'."[5]

[1] Treaties, V, p. 675.　　[2] Ibid, pp. 671-2.　　[3] Ibid, p. 773.
[4] Ibid, p. 681.　　[5] Ibid, pp. 682-3.

And the complications only begin here, for there was subsequently revealed in the State Department archives a counter-counter-declaration by Bulwer, dated 4 July, 1850, to the Secretary of State, which ran :

> I understand the purport of your answer [the counter-declaration] . . . to be, that you do not deem yourself called upon to mark out at this time the exact limits of her Majesty's settlement at Honduras, nor of the different Central American States, nor to define what are or what are not the dependencies of the said Settlement; but that you fully recognize that it was not the intention of our negotiation to embrace in the Treaty of 19th April whatever is her Majesty's Settlement at Honduras, nor whatever are the dependencies of that settlement; and that her Majesty's title thereto subsequent to the said Treaty will remain just as it was prior to that Treaty, without undergoing any alteration whatever in consequence thereof. . . .[1]

This was obviously the result of Bulwer's desire to prevent the evasion of the issue by Clayton, but the difficulty is that Clayton later declared, when this document was published in a British Blue Book in 1856, that he had never seen it. Ratifications had actually been exchanged, in the cold light of a dawn following a night of comings and goings, on 5 July : President Taylor had died on 9 July, and Clayton had immediately resigned. His successor, Webster, was much less interested in Central America, and the question arises whether Bulwer took advantage of the confusion in the State Department to have the final document inserted fraudulently. It is impossible to know, but his previous diplomatic reputation does not belie such a possibility, nor does his whole attitude over these negotiations.

But, whatever the truth, the fundamental disagreement remained, and the instrument was open to the divergent interpretations of both parties, a situation which was made more serious by the fact that the existence of the clarifying statements was not generally known to members of the Senate. On the one hand, the Americans believed that the wording of the first article had rendered the British protectorate over the Mosquito Indians null; it was solely on account of this belief that the treaty passed the Senate by a large majority, and Clayton himself wrote while it was before that body, "I trust that means will speedily be adopted by Great Britain to extinguish the Indian title . . . within what we consider to be the limits of Nicaragua. . . . Her protectorate will be reduced to a shadow . . . for she can neither occupy, fortify, colonize or

---

[1] Q. J. D. Ward, "Sir Henry Bulwer and the United States Archives" (in *Cambridge Historical Journal*, III, 1931), pp. 305-6.

431

exercize dominion or control in any part of the Mosquito Coast or Central America."[1] On the other hand, though the British Government realized that their "relations with the Indians had been decidedly weakened",[2] the treaty clearly did not explicitly renounce the protectorate, and Bulwer affirmed the central fact, which he had deliberately engineered, in a personal memorandum of the negotiations: "The treaty, indeed, was intended to apply to future and not to present possessions in Central America; so that . . . H.M's settlement in Honduras and its dependencies are not included in the said treaty."[3] Almost immediately after ratification it became apparent that this divergence of view existed.

At first, however, the divergence appeared to be less formidable than it was later to become, and, indeed, was so, for the British Government remained conciliatory and did not push its claims as far as Bulwer had shown that it could; Palmerston wrote to Bulwer that the Government

feel that the present state of things in regard to the Mosquito Territory, and especially with regard to the Port of Greytown, is in many respects inconvenient, and not entirely in conformity with the true spirit and meaning of the Convention just concluded between Great Britain and the United States. The British Government is bound in honour to protect the Mosquitos, but Her Majesty's Government are of the opinion that the protection of Great Britain might be afforded to that nation as effectively in a different way, and without any direct interference of any agent of the British Government in the internal affairs of that country.[4]

As a result, after Webster became Secretary of State, determined efforts were made to reach a compromise settlement which would enable Britain to withdraw gracefully, but these failed in the end because of the determined refusal of the Nicaraguan Government to agree to the terms suggested by the great powers. While a settlement was thus being sought at the top level, tension mounted on the spot, due at first to the continued hostility of the local agents, Chatfield and Squier; the American followed up the British disavowal of the former's seizure of Tigre Island by seizing it himself in the name of the United States. He was recalled in the autumn of 1850, but returned to Central America in a private capacity to work against the British; Chatfield was not withdrawn till 1852. Other incidents, however, arose spontaneously from the American dislike of the British protectorate, and only tact on

[1] Q. Williams, p. 107.   [2] Ibid, p. 109.
[3] Q. ibid, p. 108, footnote.   [4] Q. ibid, 111.

the part of the Governments prevented serious trouble when the naval representatives of both sides became involved. As a result of these ominous signs, however, the British Consul at Greytown withdrew from active participation in the affairs of the city, which became in effect a free and semi-autonomous port; and Britain and America recognized its government *de facto* and sent identical instructions to their naval commanders in the area that they should reach a satisfactory agreement, which for a while allayed the increasing difficulties arising from the flow of Americans through Central America *en route* for California.

But a more difficult period was ushered in by the issue of a royal proclamation constituting Roatan, Bonaca and four neighbouring islands the "colony of the Bay Islands" on 20 March, 1852, for this action forced both governments to adopt extreme views. Though the British Government had discouraged British settlement upon the islands, it no doubt hoped by retaining them that they might one day, when the canal was built, become a very important commercial station, while the Clayton declaration and the subsequent disinterest of the Whig administration had led it to believe that the United States might not object to its retention of them, though in fact the Americans had never understood the term, the "dependencies" of British Honduras, to apply to the islands in question. Violent suspicion was now aroused among the Democrats, whose Senators assaulted the Whig administration on the ground that the plain terms of the treaty engaged Great Britain to withdraw from the whole of Central America, and when they heard—for the first time in most cases—of the declaration that Belize was not included in the treaty, affirmed that they never would have voted for it if they had known of its existence. The foundation of the new colonial government was, therefore, in their view, a plain violation of the Clayton-Bulwer Treaty, but the British, in full knowledge of this opinion, made a last unsuccessful effort to settle the Mosquito question before the Fillmore Administration ended. After this failure, however, Clarendon's attitude stiffened; this is probably explained in a letter he received from Aberdeen in November, 1854:

> I looked into this subject five and twenty years ago, and I never could discern on what pretext we made San Juan [Greytown] . . . a part of the Mosquito territory. As for the Bay Islands, our title is little better than manifest usurpation. . . . Still, this is not the moment to abandon these claims; for it is very clear that the concession is made to Russia and not to the United States alone. . . . I should think the people of the United States were not actually desirous of quarrelling with us; and I would carefully avoid quarrelling with them. But I would contrive to hang up

all matters in dispute by means of civil negotiations for some indefinite period.[1]

Buchanan was at this juncture appointed Minister in London, with full power to negotiate a direct agreement. As the Crimean War was impending when he arrived, he could at first make little progress, but when he was able to press Clarendon into a discussion of the Bay Islands question, the British Government advanced the view that Bulwer had held from the beginning (but which they had not hitherto espoused because they hoped for a reasonable settlement) that the treaty was entirely prospective in its operation and had no effect upon the British possessions which already existed in the area. Against this the American Government's view was now, emphatically, that the treaty was retrospective in its operation and implied British withdrawal from Central America altogether. The incompatibility of these views Buchanan later made quite plain when he wrote to Clarendon: "That unfortunate Clayton and Bulwer Treaty must be put out of the way. What else should be done with a treaty on which directly opposite constructions have been placed by the two nations? ... It will be a bone of contention and a root of bitterness between the two Governments as long as it exists."[2] Thus the main issue was plainly joined between them, and the subsidiary question of the Mosquitos also remained unresolved, the British holding that the protectorate was certainly not affected by the treaty, the Americans that the British were in honour bound to relinquish it. In these differences of opinion lay ample opportunity for violent disagreement in the future. This, indeed, seemed imminent when the inauguration of a more bellicose American Administration was followed by a yet more dangerous local tension than had hitherto existed. The trouble on the spot was in part produced by the activities of Borland, an American representative in Central America, who was striving hard to restore the confidence of governments there in the United States, for this had been seriously undermined by the Mexican War in all the Latin-American states except Honduras, which was an exception because its interests seemed so directly threatened by the British Mosquito protectorate.

Disputes in the area, between the American Transit Company and the Greytown authorities, built up into a situation in which disorder broke out, in the course of which Borland was cut in the face by a broken bottle; partly as a result of Borland's advice, tendered in person in Washington, the Administration decided to send the American

[1] Q. Van Alstyne, p. 498. [2] Q. W.F.R., p. 195.

sloop-of-war *Cyane* to the scene, with instructions to the officer in charge to teach these people "that the United States will not tolerate these outrages, and that they have the power and the determination to check them. It is, however, very much to be hoped that you can effect the purposes of your visit without a resort to violence and destruction of property and loss of life. . . . The department [of the Navy] reposes much in your prudence and good sense." In the event, perhaps, too much, for it is hard to believe that the Administration, though they undoubtedly authorized by implication the use of force, and though they probably wanted to test the strength of the British protectorate, envisaged the bombardment and total destruction of the town which was in fact carried out, despite the solemn protest of a British Lieutenant in command of a naval schooner, who was present but powerless to prevent what Clarendon later described to Crampton as this outrage "without a parallel in the annals of modern times".[1]

The Administration were taken aback by the violence of the *Cyane's* action, and by the resultant outcry in the United States even among Democrats, the best elements of whom felt that they could not defend the deed, but after a long delay of some five months replied to the British protest by a passage in the President's second Annual Message of 4 December, 1854, which concluded, "It certainly would have been most satisfactory to me if the objects of the *Cyane's* mission could have been consummated without any act of public force, but the arrogant contumacy of the offenders rendered it impossible to avoid the alternative either to break up their establishment or to leave them impressed with the idea that they might persevere with impunity in a career of insolence and plunder."[2] Thus the American Government assumed official responsibility for the bombardment of a British protectorate, and had it not been for the fact that the British Government's hands were tied by the Crimean War, it is possible that a grave situation might have arisen—possible, but not probable, for Aberdeen was still Prime Minister and he was not the man for forceful action against the United States—while British public opinion agreed on the whole with the assertion of the London *Globe*, that if cause for war with the United States were wanted, the very positive grounds necessary for a quarrel with kinsfolk "should not be mixed up with the assertion of anything quite so aboriginal as the ill-defined rights, titles, and dominions of the tawny (sic)—and to confess the truth,—somewhat trumpery majesty of Mosquito."[3] The Government, therefore, allowed itself to be

[1] Q. Williams, pp. 175-6, 180.   [2] *Messages and Papers*, p. 2817.

[3] Q. Williams, p. 185, footnote.

mollified by the loud denunciations of the bombardments in the American Press, and contented itself with the protest it had already made; not even a possible claim for damages to British subjects was pressed any further.

But the difficulties were not yet at an end, for the increasing activity of American filibusterers, who hoped, by promoting domestic disorders in the Central American communities, to advance the interests of the United States there, were already causing growing alarm in London by the time of Pierce's Message, and during 1855 the success of one of these, William Walker, in Nicaragua brought matters to a head. Pierce's efforts to enforce the neutrality laws of the United States against filibustering expeditions—admittedly sometimes a difficult task—were patently feeble, despite the persistent protests of Crampton, the British Minister, whose own position was becoming increasingly awkward owing to the rising American indignation over Crimean recruitment. Indeed, the two questions were, as we have seen, politically and emotionally linked, for, as Crampton wrote, "If I had proved more complacent with regard to Nicaragua and the filibusters, they might have forgiven me my recruiting for the Crimea."[1] But he received very little encouragement from the Government at home for his protests, since it was already displaying an unwillingness at such a time to challenge what looked like a deliberate and calculated American policy over Central America. Initiative in any negotiations had, therefore, to be American. This initiative Buchanan took in 1855, with the result that by the end of the year both Governments had merely reaffirmed their antagonistic interpretations of the Clayton-Bulwer Treaty, Pierce doing so publicly in his third Annual Message.

There was, however, a significant difference between the situation in Britain and that in the United States, for American public opinion, as shown in the speeches of the Senate, was now virtually united behind the American claims, which was in marked contrast with the situation three years before, whereas there was a distinct cleavage in that of Britain, where a strong party favoured moderation. Derby declared in the speech in answer to the Queen's Address at the opening of Parliament in January, 1856, that there was no other nation on earth with which war would be so mutually suicidal as the United States, and Cobden reiterated that a hostile collision with America would be a most horrible calamity. As a result, the Government chose to emphasize the more friendly aspect of its American policy, and

[1] Q. W.F.R., p. 191.

Clarendon drew attention to his verbal offer to Buchanan (repeated to Crampton for Marcy's ears but overlooked by the former), to refer the whole question to the arbitration of a third person; the offer, which was now considered for the first time by the Administration, had a beneficial effect on American public opinion, but the Crimean recruitment deadlock remained, while the British had reinforced their West Indies squadron and Congress had voted a special military appropriation. The United States then, in their turn, increased their naval forces in the Gulf of Mexico, and Britain sold two thousand muskets to Costa Rica to facilitate hostilities against Walker's newly established Nicaraguan Government. Dallas in London and Marcy and Pierce in Washington all believed that Britain wished to dispose of the Isthmian Treaty and bring Central America under her control, while the British were equally suspicious that Manifest Destiny was about to find a further fulfilment there.

Colour was given to the American belief by Britain's imperial history and by the inflated nature of her claims in this instance, despite her actual Little Englandism, and there is no doubt that Palmerston desired to slow down the pace of American expansion; as he wrote on 4 July, 1857,

> [A]s to propitiating the Yankees by countenancing their schemes of annexation it would be like propitiating an animal of Prey by giving him one of one's travelling companions. It would increase his Desire for similar Food and spur him on to obtain it. . . . There can be little doubt that in the course of Time the Anglo-Saxon race will spread far to the South in America, but it is for our Interest that this should not happen until the Swarms are prepared to separate from the Parent Hive.[1]

It is also true that the immediate past of the American people gave no cause for confidence to Britons as to their intentions in Central America. As Palmerston wrote six months later, "The Clayton-Bulwer Treaty opposes a barrier to . . . the Yankees . . . and therefore they . . . detest the Treaty. . . . If we were quite sure that . . . it would be honestly observed I should be inclined to . . . the Sacrifice of those Points of difference as to its Interpretation on which the United States insist. But the Yankees are such . . . ingenious Rogues that it . . . would . . . be . . . Texas over again."[2]

Matters came to a head in May, 1856, when Pierce first of all recognized Walker's Government in Nicaragua, and then discontinued diplomatic relations with Crampton. Immediately, it became clear that

[1] Q. Van Alstyne, p. 499.   [2] Q. ibid, p. 500.

437

American fears of British intentions were unfounded, for neither Press nor Government (Clarendon was still Foreign Secretary although Palmerston had succeeded Aberdeen as Prime Minister) thought either action an occasion for war, and a soothing tone was adopted by the British in face of the possibility of a breach. Clarendon welcomed conciliatory letters, which Marcy thereupon despatched to him on both subjects, that on Central America stating that though the United States could not accept arbitration on the meaning of the Clayton-Bulwer Treaty, they would not object to arbitration on some questions of fact connected with it; Palmerston himself gave an assurance that Dallas would not be dismissed as a reprisal for the dismissal of Crampton, going to the—for him—surprising length of saying in Parliament, "It would be lamentable in the extreme if two countries which have so many interests in common should, through the perverseness of any man, be brought into a state of hostility with each other."[1]

Thus the atmosphere of Anglo-American relations suddenly and distinctly improved, owing largely to Marcy's two conciliatory messages, whose despatch was probably not unconnected with the sudden ending of the Crimean War. But in fact, only some rash American act could have precipitated a conflict, for Britain was conscious of the weakness of her position and of her claims both on the Mosquito Coast and in the Bay Islands, and even more conscious of the enormous and increasing extent of her trade with the United States, which amounted, according to the *Examiner* to £29,795,590 of imports and £21,410,369 of exports in 1854. It was no accident that Cobden, representing Manchester, and Roebuck, representing Sheffield, were the moving spirits of the peace party; this economic influence in Anglo-American relations, as we have seen already, played a large part in the establishment in Britain of a new and more friendly attitude towards the United States in these middle years of the century. A minor symptom of the change was the establishment in 1853 of a joint claims commission to decide upon the mutual claims of citizens of each country against the other since 1814, which awarded $277,102 to British claimants and $329,734 to American claimants. This change became very obvious with the sudden clearing of the ominous clouds which had begun to collect over the Isthmian question in 1856.

This clearance of the atmosphere made possible early negotiations in London, though lingering suspicions on the part of both principals, and mistrust, obduracy and political uncertainty in the Central

[1] Q. Williams, pp. 217-8.

American states delayed for four years the making of a final and satis-factory agreement. At first, however, it seemed that a rapid settlement was possible for a direct treaty between Britain and Honduras, making the Bay Islands a free state under the sovereignty of Honduras, was soon followed by a convention between the United States and Britain, negotiated by Clarendon and Dallas, which was later to be offered by the great powers jointly to Nicaragua and Costa Rica for their agree-ment. This convention recognized the British withdrawal from the Bay Islands and the Mosquito Coast, subject to certain guarantees to British colonists in the former and to the Indians in the latter; it settled the boundary of Belize with Guatemala on the lines of the British claim; and it made proposals for the settlement of the most serious boundary disputes between the Central American States. President Pierce, having failed to obtain the Democratic nomination for a second term, was taking a much less chauvinistic line in foreign affairs, and sent the convention to the Senate with his approval. There it was amended to replace the Bay Islands article, which had been carefully based upon the British-Honduras treaty, by a simple article binding both parties to recognize them as under the sovereignty of Honduras, but even with this and other amendments it passed by only one vote. In its amended form, however, it was unacceptable to Clarendon, since there was no guarantee to British settlers in the Islands, and it now became apparent that a deadlock was in the offing; when it became known that the Honduran assembly had in any case refused to ratify the original treaty with Britain, the impasse seemed complete.

American moves in the direction of outright abrogation of the Clayton-Bulwer Treaty, which then gained strength, especially in the Senate, were met by Britain with a statement of her determination, in case of a mutually agreed abrogation—to which she did not object, though she would not submit to a unilateral abrogation by Congress—to retain the Bay Islands, unless the United States would reaffirm the neutrality of the Isthmus; she made it plain that she must have either its neutralization or her possessions. Though Buchanan, who was now President, ardently desired abrogation of the offensive treaty, he wanted Britain to clear out of Central America even more, and so the proposal was dropped. A repetition of the British offer of arbitration was met by a repetition of the American refusal of it, and a new, if temporary, difficulty arose from disorders on an American railroad, opened in 1855 across the Isthmus at Panama. But Britain was still most anxious to avoid a rupture with the United States, and Buchanan and his Secretary of State, Cass, were heavily involved in the Kansas

439

struggle at home. Buchanan at any rate was also fundamentally desirous of cordial relations with Britain, having declared that "The English and American people owe it to their own dearest principles and interests to cultivate the most friendly relations with each other". He now realized that he must accept the retention of the Clayton-Bulwer Treaty, if he could obtain British agreement to interpret it substantially in the American sense. This was wise and statesmanlike, particularly in view of the fact that, as Napier wrote, "The treaty is obnoxious to the people of America and there is unfortunately in this country an impatience of international engagements and a surprising heedlessness in regard to the questions of political relations involving the claims of foreign nations."[1] The way out of the difficulty had been suggested earlier by Napier, who constantly urged the necessity of rapid and vigorous diplomatic measures by Britain to forestall any rash American Congressional action; he proposed an independent British mission to Central America, which should conclude agreements with the states in the broad sense of the American interpretation of the Clayton-Bulwer Treaty. This would give the United States her way, but would save Britain's face, since the settlement would be an independent one. After long delays in 1858 and 1859, owing to local difficulties and the incompetence of the first British representative, Ouseley, his successor, Wyke, was able to bring his mission to a successful conclusion in 1860.

During this trying period a British policy of absolute frankness was reciprocated by the Administration, and Buchanan's Annual Message in 1859 stated that he confidently expected a final adjustment of the difficulty in the near future, which allayed Congressional discontent, while that of 1860 announced the belief that it had been finally effected, in the words, "Our relations with Great Britain are of the most friendly character. . . . The discordant constructions of the Clayton and Bulwer treaty between the two Governments, which at different periods of the discussion bore a threatening aspect, have resulted in a final settlement entirely satisfactory to this government." It was embodied in treaties, duly ratified, between Britain and the states of Honduras and Nicaragua, the contents of which were notified to Cass by Russell, who was now Foreign Secretary, in 1860, with the words, "These Treaties . . . provide for the relinquishment of the Protectorate of the Mosquito Indians by Great Britain, and for the cession of the Bay Islands to Honduras; and thus, it may be hoped, finally set at rest the questions respecting the interpretation of the Clayton-Bulwer Treaty which have been the subject of so much controversy between this country and the

[1] Q. W.F.R., pp. 195-6, 198.

United States."[1] Suitable guarantees were included for the British settlers and the Indians, and Greytown was made a free port. The only respect in which the maximum American demands were not met was that the boundaries of Belize, which Britain retained, were left as Britain had claimed them to be, and were not restricted as America had at one time wished, while the Clayton-Bulwer Treaty remained intact in its neutralization of the Isthmus, as Britain desired. This solution was a compromise of their most extreme claims on the part of both nations, though much the more substantial concessions were made by Britain; in a sense this was just, since her interpretation of the original treaty was less warranted by its content than the American, and since that interpretation had probably been more extreme than the convictions of a substantial portion of her people.

But this happy issue out of their afflictions was no mere diplomatic solution; it reflected a deep and basic change in the relationship of the two powers and in the attitude of certainly one of them. In some senses this decade, which left Anglo-American relations in a better condition than any perhaps since 1783, is the most important turning point in their whole history; it saw possibly the most distinct movement in British opinion away from contempt towards cordiality. The growth of friendship at the end of the century and the coming of permanent alliance in World War II are more spectacular, but they would have been impossible without the fundamental readjustment of British opinion in these middle years. That it was a fundamental national readjustment is indicated by the small effect, compared with previous times, which the frequent changes of government in England had upon the development of British policy, for it was not merely that they all tended, owing to the peculiarly fragmentary nature of British party alignments at this period, to seek a middle course, but that they were forced to do so by a moderate public opinion. It was in these years that Britain first began to see clearly that America was destined to be a great power whether she liked it or not, and to apprehend dimly, yet with increasing force, that it was very much better to be her friend than her enemy. At the same time, with the settlement of the chief border disputes, she began, for the first time, to appreciate that at bottom the two nations had much in common, and relatively little to divide them. The growth of democratic tendencies in British domestic politics gave a great and accelerating impulse to mutual understanding, which was reflected in the decline of literary warfare and the welcoming of some

[1] Q. Williams, p. 266.

441

American literature in Britain, while the increase in the speed and efficiency of communications emphasized more than ever before the international intimacy which could result from a common tongue.

This new attitude found its most notable political expression in the British acceptance, with equanimity, if not with actual pleasure, of the possibility of American expansion in Central America. During the full flood of Manifest Destiny in the forties Britain had attempted, though without success, to check it by diplomatic means; in 1850 she had still remained suspicious, though prepared to settle for a mutual self-denying ordinance; by 1860 she was virtually prepared for outright American annexation, in the fullness of time, of Central American territories, whereas her own interests had become more and more exclusively commercial. In the middle of the decade Russell declared, "There is room for us both on the globe",[1] and in 1858 Malmesbury, then British Foreign Secretary, said to Dallas, "that he was one of that class of statesmen who believed that all the southern part of North America must ultimately come under the government of the United States: that he had no objection to what seemed the inevitable course of things: that on the contrary, he thought it would be beneficial as well to the population occupying the countries referred to as to the United States, and the rest of the world."[2] There could hardly be a more striking statement of the case, and, as it implies, this was also a great turning point in the other major theme of Anglo-American relations, the reversal of their respective international roles, for it marked, tentatively yet distinctly, the beginnings of the expansion of American power beyond her own borders. Her Manifest Destiny had been accomplished: the United States faced the oceans to the east and to the west. She was likely now to overleap them or to turn elsewhere. It is highly significant that it was in this same decade that her first uncertain efforts were made to extend her influence in the distant Pacific, but it is even more so that she seemed to turn decisively south, and that she did so with the acquiescence of Britain, who could not but regard this trend with pleasure since it constituted a kind of protection for Canada.

V

SUCH, then, was the state of Anglo-American relations in 1860, a state surprisingly satisfactory, despite the fact that the United States was to be much slower to change her attitude of suspicion than Britain had

[1] Q. Hickson, p. 302. [2] Williams, p. 269, footnote.

been. A remarkable illustration of the new harmony is to be found in the successful visit of the Prince of Wales, later Edward VII, to the United States in the autumn of 1860. *The Times* wrote that he was sent to do a work "beyond the power of either soldier or diplomatist"; he was to bridge "the bloody chasm which for near a century has gaped" between the two nations; he was to assuage the American "triumph of success" and the British "sneers of disappointed dominion." He succeeded in his object of showing British friendship to this "great cognate nation", than which, the article continued, there is "none in which we are all so interested, none the successes and glories of which we all hear of with such unmixed satisfaction."[1] It was good that the state of relations was so satisfactory, for they were suddenly in the near future to be subjected to a strain of a novel and very dangerous kind.

The rising sectional conflict in the United States had come increasingly to dominate the minds of Americans in this decade, and was indeed influential in determining Buchanan to pursue a moderate policy towards Britain, since Pierce's idea of uniting the American sections behind a policy of national expansion, involving perhaps a conflict with Britain, had failed decisively, largely because the North had regarded it as a pretext for the expansion of Southern influence. This was indicative of the nature of the problem soon to arise in Anglo-American relations, for the recent agreements had been reached with a Democratic Administration under Southern domination, and American motives for Central American expansion were in truth largely Southern. Further, the great economic bond of which Britain had become so conscious of late, was also largely Southern in character, for of the £29,795,590 of British imports from the United States in 1854, which so largely determined Britain's pacific policy, no less than £17,274,671 was raw cotton from the South. It remained to be seen, in the event of civil war, how much the new foundations of Anglo-American friendship depended upon Southern strength in the American body politic, but when the war did come it shifted the focus of attention from Central America, because the exertions of combat, as well as the inherent difficulties involved in the project, made an Isthmian Canal seem for the moment less and less practicable; after the war had been lost by the South, the added motive of Southern slave expansion existed no more, and so, for almost twenty years, the Central American question remained in the background. During the war, the struggle itself raised unprecedented and dangerous questions which fully absorbed the attention of the British Government, but when it was over the spot-

[1] Q. Mowat, *Diplomatic Relations*, pp. 166-7.

light in Anglo-American relations shifted far to the North, and was centred once more upon Canada.

But here, too, the years before the Civil War had marked a turning point, not merely because one of the most significant actions of the Pierce administration was the signing of a great commercial reciprocity treaty with Canada, but even more because the era saw the decisive beginnings of responsible government in British North America, which now took the first steps along the road that was to give Canada, in the Statute of Westminster of 1931, absolute control over her own affairs. The development is of great consequence in our history of Anglo-American relations, which is primarily concerned with the interplay of Great Britain and the United States, and only secondarily with that between Canada and America. Hitherto, this distinction has been a fine one, because the responsibility for the government, as well as the defence, of British North America has rested upon the imperial government in Westminster. Canada, though acquiring strength and an independent existence, has had as yet, in the nature of things, no independent policy, and the most that her great interests have been able to do has been to bring pressure to bear upon the central government and its agents. With the coming of responsible government this begins to alter, and after the achievement of confederation in 1867 it alters very swiftly.

At first, however, the process was a slow one, and to a considerable degree the responsibility and control of the mother country remained; the constitutional position was in fact a compromise, on the part of Englishmen like Durham, Grey and Elgin, and Canadians like Robert Baldwin, Louis H. Lafontaine and Joseph Howe, between the extremes of Tory reaction and radical demands for absolute independence. It is clearly illustrated by the mechanics of the treaty of 1854, which was negotiated, on the British side by Lord Elgin, the Governor-General of Canada, appointed as Plenipotentiary by the Government in London, and on the American by Secretary of State Marcy, but which had to receive the concurrent approval not only of the Senate, but also of the imperial Parliament at Westminster, and, under the new idea of responsible government, of the legislatures of the British North American provinces affected. The great change in the status of this group of British colonies was of immense significance for the future, because it was the foundation stone upon which the free association of peoples, which is now called the British Commonwealth of Nations, was built.

That it was possible at all was due to the growing liberalism of

English political life, which found expression in the so-called Great Age of Reform; though the concept of colonial self-government was almost entirely developed by the Whigs, in this, as in other spheres, the Tories, either moved by the new spirit of the age or driven by the actions of their opponents, accepted some of the liberal doctrines. In colonial matters this was an age of Little Englandism in all parties, and Disraeli and Peel, as well as Gladstone and Russell, looked forward with equanimity to the coming of colonial self-government, and indeed independence. Until its revival later in the century in a different form, British Imperialism was virtually non-existent. It was this revolution in British policy, which was so difficult for American statesmen, bred in the anti-colonial tradition and well knowing the history of the mother country, to appreciate, and which made American suspicions of British policy in, for instance, Central America, so unjustified although so understandable. Because there was in later years a vigorous revival of Imperialism in Britain, there was long a tendency among Americans to discount, if not to disbelieve, the very existence of the anti-colonialism of this era, which was in fact a very real thing.

It was so real because it owed its existence as much, if not more, to economic than to political considerations, and it is significant that Cobden, the apostle of free trade, was perhaps its most ardent exponent. It is very far from a coincidence that the ideas of free trade and of colonial self-government went hand in hand, for the old British Empire was identified, to a degree which it is hard for us to remember or imagine, with the old Mercantile commercial system; the Empire was almost exclusively a commercial one, and its bonds were the ties of protection and trade. When men became determined enemies of trade restriction, their belief in imperial government of any kind was inevitably weakened. The gradual dissolution of the British Empire, which many envisaged, might well have followed, had not a determined group of men, regarded as radicals at home but as moderates in British North America, realized and insisted upon the fact that, as Burke had pointed out long ago, there were bonds of sentiment, emotion and enlightened political self-interest which would hold an empire together much better than the plenty of commerce or the power of government; it was, as he might be said to have prophesied, the association of their freedom and their rights with the imperial connexion which was to bind the peoples of the British Commonwealth together. The point came out clearly in Joseph Howe's statement, in an open letter to Lord John Russell, that it was absurd to think that a citizen of Liverpool was any less an Englishman because he had self-government, than he would

445

have been if governed direct from Westminster, and that this applied quite as much to an Englishman in Canada as in Liverpool. This was the foundation of the new imperial system, and it took American opinion many decades to grasp the fact of its existence, just as, in the rebellion of 1837, Americans had found it very hard to believe that the mass of Canadians did not desire independence of Britain, and almost as hard to credit that they would not ultimately prefer annexation by the United States to independence itself. In fact, however, much of the animosity in these troubles in Canada had been directed to internal privilege rather than to the imperial tie.

Yet the easy suppression of the 1837 revolt was followed by the despatch of a Commission of Inquiry under Lord Durham, the result of which was the profoundly influential Durham Report, recommending colonial self-government and the uniting of French Lower and British Upper Canada into one province; the first being a splendidly wise recommendation, the second, in many ways, a mistake, even though it did point forward to ultimate confederation. Unfortunately, the second was effected without the first, and the policy pursued after the Whigs went out of power in 1841, by the Tory Governors-General, who were opposed to the idea of accepting the guidance of their colonial legislatures, made matters worse. Not until the appointment of Lord Elgin, the son-in-law of Lord Durham, as Governor-General of Canada, in 1847, can it be said that the idea of colonial self-government in internal matters and of the responsibility of the Crown's officials to the provincial legislatures was firmly and finally accepted in British North America.

It was accomplished only just in time, for in the year 1849 there was more serious trouble in Canada than there had been since 1837, though this time from the extreme right instead of the extreme left. The unrest was primarily the result of economic conditions, which were peculiarly bad in Canada in the late forties. There was a severe depression in 1846-7, beginning with the collapse of the railway boom in Britain, and it was made worse by an increase in the American tariff in 1846, which resulted in a great emigration of Canadians to the United States. In addition, the gradual acceptance of free-trade policies by Peel, beginning in 1842 and reaching a crisis in the repeal of the Corn Laws in 1846, soon destroyed the privileged position of Canadian interests (including, later, that of timber) in the British market; this policy was to culminate in the repeal of the Navigation Acts in 1849, and it administered a rude shock to the economy of British North America. The repeal of the Corn Laws, though its effect upon Canada has been exaggerated, seemed a peculiarly bitter blow because in 1843 Peel had passed an Act giving Canadian wheat preferential treatment in the British home market. Some Canadians might welcome responsible government, but many others, typified by the Tory commercial interests of Montreal, were very far from relishing the loss of imperial economic protection and the privilege which was its result. In April, 1849, these elements tried, by violence, to force the hand of Elgin, who was supporting, and supported by, Liberal Ministers commanding a majority in the Assembly. He stood firm, however, and the disorder fizzled out.

But it was followed by a potentially more dangerous situation, when, in October of that year, the discontented parties, chiefly "treasonable Tories" in Montreal, issued the so-called Annexation Manifesto. The expression of the document was temperate, but it claimed that the only remedy for Canada's ills was "a friendly and peaceful separation from British connexion, and a union upon equitable terms with the great North American confederacy of sovereign states." Contrasts between Canadian dependence and American independence lost much of their effect in a province enjoying ministerial responsibility, and the most important of the arguments, the economic one that Canada essentially needed admission to American markets and access to American products, lost some of its power owing to the general realization that its exponents, the erstwhile ultra-loyal Tories, had flatly reversed their political beliefs for purely financial reasons, and even more of it owing to an economic revival in 1850. The divisions between the Tory and extreme radical signatories of the Manifesto further weakened its appeal. Most important of all, the movement attracted very little attention in a United States at the height of the worst sectional conflict to date, and moving towards a period of Southern domination in which the accession of a large expanse of free territory would have been far from welcome. Ten years earlier or twenty years later the story might have been a very different one; it was fortunate for the independent future of Canada that annexationism was strongest among her people when it was weakest in her great neighbour, for British opposition to annexation was at this time unlikely to have been very bitter or prolonged. It was even more fortunate that men from Britain, like Elgin, and Canadians, like his ministers and supporters, were determined to cleave to a middle path between the tyranny of Westminster and the annexation to the United States which might so easily follow absolute independence.

It was happy, too, for the future of Anglo-American relations. The Manifesto had prophesied gloomily that "Disagreement between the

447

United States and her chief, if not only, rival among nations [Britain] would make the soil of Canada the sanguinary area for their disputes".[1] Canadians never lost sight of this vital fact, but, as their independence grew, they gained the power to do something about it; they remained hostages for the good conduct of the great powers, but they were active and successful in their efforts to prevent serious conflict, and the greater their power became, the more success they had. As Joseph Howe was to say in the course of the Civil War, "The Northern States are our immediate neighbors, and next to the mother country, ought to be our fast friends and firm allies. We claim a common origin, our populations are almost homogeneous . . . our commerce is enormous . . . our people intermarry, and socially intermix all along the frontier. . . . All these neutral ties and intimate relations are securities for the preservation of peace."[2] Indeed, so successful were they that, on occasion, they were the chief victims, not of Anglo-American enmity, but of Anglo-American friendship, for Britain came to think Anglo-American amity more important than Canada's special interests. In the long run, the wisdom of Canadian statesmen convinced them of the truth of this fact as well. Thus Canadian independence has been a powerful historical instrument for the promotion of Anglo-American friendship.

But, though the Canadian annexationist movement faded out in the early fifties, it had performed the useful service of calling vigorous attention to the Canadian need for some measure of commercial reciprocity with the United States, and this kept alive proposals for an agreement, which had actually been in negotiation in Washington since 1846, but which had failed to make progress in Congress. British efforts to reopen negotiations in 1849 were discouraged by the Whig administration as contrary to their financial policy, and, despite all the efforts of the British, egged on by the Canadians, who tried every expedient to obtain their desires—including the extremes of unilateral concessions to American commerce and retaliatory measures against it—nothing was achieved during the next four years, partly because the Canadians seemed to have too little of value to offer in exchange for commercial concessions by the United States. During these years, however, a Canadian-American dispute of very long standing came to a head, and seemed to offer just such a *quid pro quo*.

In the commercial convention of 1818 the United States had renounced "for ever" the liberty of taking fish "within three marine Miles of any of the Coasts, Bays, Creeks or Harbours"[3] of most of the

[1] Q. Dunning, p. 179.   [2] Q. Brebner, p. 161.   [3] Treaties, II, p. 659.

coasts of British North America, which the British thought had conclusively settled this particular problem. That it did not, is a measure of the extent to which diplomacy can find excuses for what nations want or do not want, for American fishermen desired to extend their fisheries as far as possible inshore, and the Canadians to restrict them as much as possible. During the succeeding years friction continued, indeed increased, and the Canadian Provinces began to take action against intruders. Meanwhile, the technical issue was rendered down to this, that the United States claimed that their people could fish anywhere, except within a line drawn parallel to the coast, three miles away from it and exactly following its every indentation, while Britain claimed that this line should be three miles from another line, drawn, not exactly parallel to the coast, but joining headland to headland. In other words, the Americans claimed the right to fish in so-called "open bays," and the Canadians repudiated it.

In 1852 both governments sent naval vessels to enforce their rights, and a difficult situation arose, so that President Fillmore mooted tentatively the idea of exchanging reciprocity for fishing rights. His successor, the Democrat Pierce, took up the idea more vigorously, for, though he himself was a protectionist, Democrats were more likely to be prepared for tariff concessions than Whigs, particularly when traffic concessions on Canadian waterways, which appealed to men like Douglas from the West, were added to the bargain, while as a New Englander he was in a position to appreciate that desire for fisheries might outweigh desire for protection in the northern political balance. Thus Marcy, his Secretary of State, pressed on preliminary negotiations with Crampton, and took precautions to avoid a clash in the fisheries, impressing the while on the British Government the seriousness with which America viewed the question; he wrote to Buchanan, "If the negotiation falls through and England insists on excluding us from the open bays, there will be trouble."[1] The British Government under Aberdeen, entangled in a tense European situation, were most anxious to settle the disputes, and appointed Elgin as a special commissioner. He arrived in Washington on 26 May, 1854. The negotiations resembled those for the Webster-Ashburton Treaty in that other parties than the two principals were involved; in the end their consent was obtained, that of British North America partly by the efforts, persuasive and financial, of the American lobbyist, Andrews, and that of Congress partly by Elgin's lavish hospitality, of which his young secretary could

---

[1] J. M. Callahan, *American Foreign Policy in Canadian Relations* (New York, 1937), p. 255.

write, "It was the height of the season when we were at Washington, and our arrival imparted a new impetus to the festivities, and gave rise to the taunt, after the treaty was concluded . . . that 'it had been floated through on champagne'."[1] Certainly, in the hands of the skilful, that beverage is not without diplomatic value.

Marcy and Elgin signed the treaty on 5 June, only ten days after the latter's arrival. It granted to American fishermen an unrestricted liberty to fish on the coasts of British North America at any distance from the shore and a virtually unrestricted permission to land for the purposes of curing their catch, and to British fishermen exactly reciprocal rights on the coast of the United States north of the 36th parallel; it provided for automatic arbitration in case of disputes. The American sea-board States thus got what they wanted. In return, the Canadians were granted the right to export an extensive list of raw materials, not manufactured goods, to the United States free of duty, reciprocal rights being of course granted to the Americans. A further bargain, designed to gain Western support for the treaty, gave to Canadians the right freely to navigate Lake Michigan, and to Americans the right freely to navigate the St. Lawrence. It was to last for at least ten years, and after that until one year after either side should give notice of a wish to terminate it. Though manufactured goods were excluded, free trade Americans hoped that Canada would follow a progressively more liberal policy in commerce, and begin to admit American manufactures; and the Federal Government agreed to urge on the States the granting of rights of navigation to the Canadians on State canals, for, with the astonishing development of communications in the United States, the inhabitants of the British provinces began to feel their own backwardness in this respect. On 2 August, the treaty was submitted to the Senate and approved by 32 votes to 11. Among such a substantial majority, so soon after the bitter discords over the Kansas-Nebraska Act, motives were necessarily mixed, and, apart from particular economic motives, it is probable that many supported it for directly opposite reasons, Northerners in the hope that it might be a step towards the annexation of Canada, Southerners in the hope that reciprocity would allay the Canadian desire for that step. Within a year it was accepted by Canada, Prince Edward Island, and Nova Scotia, and shortly afterwards by Newfoundland.

It was immediately successful in stimulating Canadian-American trade, which rose from $35,000,000 in 1854 to $57,000,000 in 1856—an increase much greater than normal—but gradually, with the growth of

[1] Q. Bailey, pp. 296-7.

American industry, it became more favourable to Canada than to the United States. This tendency was greatly exaggerated when, beginning in 1859, Canada, partly through the financial requirements of a government policy of internal development and partly through pressure of the commercial interests of the Lower St. Lawrence, adopted a high tariff policy. From this time onwards, feeling in the United States against the treaty grew steadily, and was strengthened by the friction engendered by the Civil War, until in 1865 the American Government gave notice of its desire for abrogation. It is significant of the extent to which this had become a problem not of Anglo-American, but of Canadian-American relations, that when the British attempted in 1859 to prevent Canadian tariffs, which were in conflict with the spirit of the treaty, Canada affirmed its right to regulate its own tariffs without interference. In this case the increasing independence of Canada had adverse effects for the United States, but on the whole she welcomed it, not only on ideological grounds, but also, on occasion, in the hope that it would be the means to annexation. It was symptomatic that in 1856 the United States Attorney-General actually applied direct to the Governor-General of Canada for the extradition of an American fugitive, which, the British Secretary of Legation in Washington wrote, had "somewhat the appearance of a desire to establish a precedent of treating with Canada independently of the British Government."[1] This was not to be possible for many years yet, but it illustrated the marked trend in that direction, a trend which was to be strengthened greatly by the Canadian confederation of 1867. These things are a measure of the extent to which the relations of Canada with the United States have, by 1860, become a side-track from the main road of our history, an important track, no doubt, but one which we can less and less afford to follow.

But even in the relations of the two North American neighbours, these incipient disagreements were in 1860 mere distant rumblings, and for the moment all was quiet and calm, while Anglo-American relations proper had never seemed so auspicious. With the main traditional causes of disagreement for the most part settled, and with a greater mutual tolerance and respect than had hitherto been possible, it seemed, despite much residual ill-feeling in the United States, as if Anglo-American friendship might, henceforth, go broadening steadily down from precedent to precedent. This happy vision was shortly, however, to be dispelled by the gunfire in Charleston harbour which, in April, 1861, marked the beginning of the American Civil War.

[1] Q. W.F.R., p. 194.

451

CHAPTER THIRTEEN

THE CIVIL WAR (1860-72)

FOR the smooth development of Anglo-American relations the Civil War was something approaching a disaster, because it placed the British people and the British Government in that most invidious position, neutrality in the civil struggles of a friendly power. Though as between nation and nation the North was overwhelmingly stronger than the South in every respect except military aptitude, as between a firmly united group of rebellious provinces and a not-too-powerful central government the South was perhaps stronger than any dissident political movement in history has been, which ultimately failed to obtain the independence it sought. The South sought only that independence; the North was forced, when all hope of compromise was passed, to seek nothing less than the conquest, the subjugation, of the South, for that was the only road to reunion. The diplomatic corollary was that the Confederacy, while hoping for active intervention on its behalf by one or more foreign powers, ostensibly asked only for recognition of its independent existence, whereas the North maintained that no form of recognition whatever should be extended to an authority which it regarded solely as a conspiracy between rebellious subjects. Yet this claim of the North appeared little more than a fiction as long as she was struggling in ruthless combat with an adversary who for at least two years appeared to give quite as good blows as she received.

Here was the fundamental dilemma of British policy—how to recognize the fact of a great international war without permanently alienating a South which might become a great nation, or a North which already was one. To recognize the Confederacy would not have achieved this object, for it would have fanned to a new white-heat the latent embers of Northern anti-British feeling, as the effects of this kind, which followed the moderate policy she in fact adopted, clearly show; yet anything less was bitterly disappointing to the South. The only answer to the question lay in the military situation, and this underlines for the historian the real danger in British policy, the inability of her leaders to credit that the reconquest of the South was a military possibility. Over and over again the temptation to depart from her strict and cautious neutrality arose from the conviction that the South would not be subjugated by the military power of the North, and over and over again the government in London was restrained from precipitate action by news from the battlefield. To the paramount importance of military developments, the despatches of Confederate representatives in Europe, urging the truth of this contention, bear frequent witness; in the grave contemporary uncertainty as to what the future held, the military situation was the only really reliable guide. Doubt as to the outcome of this terrible war was, indeed, rife in America, let alone in distant Britain. The path the British Government had to tread was a narrow and precarious one.

In fact, it succeeded in preventing any open and irreparable breach, even of sentiment, though the events of the war left a considerable legacy of mistrust and even hatred of Britain in the North, and of dis-illusion and bitterness towards her in the South, although the latter were overshadowed by anti-Northern sentiments. These things could hardly have been avoided. But that no actual rupture occurred was due, not to the natural course of events, but to statesmanship on both sides, which was on the whole wise in most difficult circumstances. The burden of responsibility throughout the whole war fell on four pairs of shoulders, those of Lincoln, Palmerston, Seward and Russell. Of the four, neither Palmerston nor Seward had past histories which seemed to augur well for the preservation of good Anglo-American relations at a time of acute tension : Palmerston's belligerence had waxed rather than waned with the passing years, and he was always suspected by such men as Bright of sharing "upper class hostility"[1] to the North, while Secretary of State Seward was chiefly known in Britain for his alleged remark to the Duke of Newcastle, during the Prince of Wales's visit to the United States in 1860, that if he became a member of the next administration it would become his duty to insult England, and that he meant to do so. At first, though he frequently denied having made such a remark, even in jest, he gave some grounds for believing that he might pursue a reckless policy, but, as the war progressed, his attitude appeared to alter, and his handling of the State Department's affairs became increasingly skilful. Palmerston on the whole behaved with sensible caution throughout this, his last, premiership, when "fear of war with one or more European powers was the dominant anxiety" in his mind.[2] Foreign Secretary Russell displayed the same caution, except

[1] Q. G. M. Trevelyan, *The Life of John Bright* (London, 1925), p. 310.
[2] Max Beloff, "Great Britain and the American Civil War" (In *History*, XXXVII, 1952), p. 42.

for one major aberration towards a proposal for mediation in the conflict. In much the same way, Lincoln can be said to have justified his words to Lyons when the latter was leaving on a visit to England in 1862, "I suppose my position makes people in England think a great deal more of me than I deserve, pray tell 'em I mean 'em no harm."[1] In both countries it can perhaps be considered a measure of the value of free institutions that responsibility was divided, so that it happened that each minister could restrain the other in the inevitable periods of personal irritation and despondency. Thus, on occasion, one happily blew cold when the other blew hot: Lincoln restrained Seward in his early chauvinistic efforts to save the Union by precipitating a foreign war, while Seward restrained Lincoln and his colleagues in the *Trent* affair.

But much credit was also due to the two representatives in the two capitals, who held their posts throughout virtually the whole period; indeed, it is doubtful if any other two Ministers in Washington and London have ever been so admirably suited to their posts, or have exercised such a decisive influence, not only over their governments but also over events. Richard Bickerton Pemell, second Lord Lyons, who took up his post in Washington in April, 1859, was ideally suited to the times; not a diplomat of the overbearing kind, he had a brilliant career in front of him. Sensible, far sighted, honest, of prodigious industry and great devotion to his country, he was fixed in his determination to do all in his power to prevent difficulties between Britain and the United States, and he was soon very much *persona grata* with the Americans. Throughout the war he showed a balance of judgment and furnished a flow of sound advice, the value of which became rapidly very apparent when, in 1862, he took leave on account of ill health, and left the Legation temporarily in the hands of a Chargé d'Affaires, who took an unrealistically sanguine view of the prospects of the South. He resigned his position in 1864, once more owing to ill-health, and its tenure by his successor, Sir Frederick Bruce, was cut short by his sudden death in 1867.

But, important as was the Washington post and able as was Lyons, the responsibilities of the American Minister in London were heavier, and they were even. more superbly discharged by Charles Francis Adams, who was sent by the new Republican administration to replace Dallas. Son and grandson of Presidents of the United States, both of whom had been Ministers in London, but neither of whom had been

[1] Q. E. D. Adams, *Great Britain and the American Civil War*, I, p. 301.

notable for pro-British feeling, his own son could write, he "naturally looked on all British Ministers as enemies; the only public occupation of all Adamses for a hundred and fifty years at least . . . had been to quarrel with Downing Street".[1] In fact, however, as he himself stated in his first interview with Russell, he had come to England with the idea "of preserving the relations actually existing between the two nations from the risk of being unfavourably affected by the unfortunate domestic disturbances prevailing in my own country",[2] and he was singularly well adapted to this difficult task of preventing "so far as I can do it honestly . . . the mutual irritation from coming to a downright quarrel."[3]

A lawyer by training and a statesman by nature, he had the coolness of judgment, the patience and the wisdom indispensable to success, in what he could not help regarding as the purgatorial task which lay before him; happily, he outlasted the crisis and enjoyed the rewarding pleasures of the immediate aftermath. Even before the end of the war his success had been complete and unique. "Little by little, in private, society took the habit of accepting him, not so much as a diplomat, but rather as a member of opposition, or an eminent counsel retained for a foreign Government. . . . This . . . gave the Minister every possible advantage over a European diplomat. Barriers of race, language, birth, habit, ceased to exist." In the end "he could afford to drop the character of diplomatist, and assume . . . the character of a kind of American Peer of the Realm . . . a kind of leader of Her Majesty's American Opposition. . . . The years of struggle were over, and Minister Adams rapidly gained a position which would have caused his father or grandfather to stare with incredulous envy."[4] He was an individual symbol, as well as an agent, of that Anglo-American *rapprochement* which had gone far by 1860 and which was able to triumph even over the difficulties arising from the War between the States.

II

THERE can be no doubt that the fundamental British motive in the period just before the Civil War was truly expressed in the Speech from the Throne on 5 February, 1861:

> Serious differences have arisen among the States of the North American Union. It is impossible for me not to look with great concern

[1] *The Education of Henry Adams*, p. 116.   [2] E.D.A., I, p. 98.
[3] Q. Mowat, *Diplomatic Relations*, p. 172.
[4] *Education of Henry Adams*, pp. 123, 194.

455

upon any events which can affect the happiness and welfare of a people nearly allied to my subjects by descent and closely connected with them by the most intimate and friendly relations. . . . The interest which I take in the well-being of the people of the United States cannot but be increased by the kind and cordial reception given by them to the Prince of Wales during his recent visit to the Continent of America.[1]

As yet American affairs did not loom large in the public mind, which had many other things to worry it, but the main lines of public opinion were becoming faintly visible. They were by no means simple.

In January, 1860, the Russian Minister in Washington wrote that Britain was about to experience one of those "strokes of fortune"[2] which happen but rarely in the history of nations, in the approaching dissolution of the American Union, for she alone, of all the nations of the world, would benefit by it through the expansion of her power, hitherto blocked by the might of the United States. To the professional diplomat, these motives of *realpolitik* seemed clear and inevitable, yet they were far from the only effective ones. That there were people in Britain who thought on these lines is true; that they had until 1860, and particularly in the eighteen-twenties, been the dominant voice in British policy towards America is also true; but by that year the decisive change which we have already noted in the British attitude to the future of the United States had taken place. There were, of course, individuals, and individuals in very high places, who retained this view, but for the most part they kept their feelings under control; as Gladstone wrote much later, "Lord Palmerston desired the severance as a diminution of a dangerous power, but prudently held his tongue."[3] Much more characteristic and mixed, however, were the feelings of Gladstone himself and of Russell, who were far more active at one critical moment in proposing recognition of the South than the realistic Palmerston, but who both tended to favour the cause of Union, though believing it impossible of re-establishment. British feelings towards a disrupted United States were further complicated by ignorance of conditions and circumstances; on only one issue was there a general and decided opinion, that of slavery.

On this the long British anti-slavery tradition, pressed since her Emancipation Act of 1833 in all quarters of the globe (particularly, be it said, by Palmerston), made even apologies for the Southern institution very difficult, and this proved the most influential factor in deter-

[1] Q. W.A.A.E., p. 308.   [2] Q. E.D.A., II, p. 269.
[3] John Morley, *The Life of William Ewart Gladstone* (London, 1908), I, p. 535.

mining, in the interval between secession and Sumter, a public opinion in England favourable to the North. Herbert Spencer wrote on 15 May, 1862: "As far as I had the means of judging, the feeling here was at first *very decidedly* on the side of the North",[1] and on this, public opinion, as seen in the press, was virtually united; even *The Times* led the way, in a forthright approval of Lincoln's election on the "no extension of slavery" platform, and predicted a quick suppression of any unwise resistance by force on the part of the South. But the degree of Southern opposition to the new Administration, culminating in the secession of the whole of the Deep South, showed that the expectation of a rapid assertion of Federal authority was unlikely to be fulfilled, so that a greater respect for the power of the South began to take hold of British opinion, even though disapproval of its peculiar institution was hardly weakened.

True, there did begin in 1861 tentative airings in the Tory Reviews of the theory, which later gained much strength, that the Southern planter (at a distance of 3,000 miles) bore "a resemblance to the English country gentleman which led to a feeling of kinship and sympathy with him on the part of those in England who represented the old traditions of landed gentility."[2] Yet even in its later stages it is questionable how powerful this sentiment was. Doubtless there was an appeal of one agricultural landed oligarchy to another, but it is significant that what might seem the most powerful of all bonds between Britain and the South, the economic, bound the planter to the *enemy* of the English landowner, the great free trade industrialist. That Cobden and Bright, the great apostles of free trade, could rise superior to that economic interest was remarkable; Cobden was more reluctant to do so at first, writing, "In your case we observe a mighty quarrel: on one side protectionists, on the other slave owners. The protectionists say they do not seek to put down slavery. The slave owners say they want Free Trade. Need you wonder at the confusion in John Bull's poor head? He gives it up!"[3] But before he died in 1864 he had cast all reservations aside. This attitude was, on the whole, typical. There was a school which sympathized with the Confederacy (which prohibited any tariff except for revenue) because of its desire for free trade, and it was naturally strengthened by the Republican Party's advocacy of a protectionist policy in the North, put into effect by the Morrill tariff of 1861, but it was surprisingly weak, and chiefly confined to those with direct interests

---

[1] Q. E.D.A., I, p. 38. [2] Duffus, *English Opinion*: q. E.D.A., I, p. 48.
[3] Q. F. J. Klingberg, "Harriet Beecher Stowe and Social Reform in England," (In *Am. H.R.*, XLIII, 1938), p. 543.

in commerce with the South. Where the economic motive prevailed, it more often took the short view and enjoyed the continuance of war profits; Bright always dismissed its advocates, one of whom had written to Cobden in that vein, with contempt, declaring on this occasion, "Your friend is either a fool, or he takes you and me to be fools when he objects to my statement that . . . the whole question is one of slavery".[1]

Furthermore, it is difficult to find a great deal of positive evidence of specific aristocratic fellow feeling for the upper classes of the South. Even Sheldon Van Auken, in his study of English feeling for the Confederacy,[2] which shows distinct Southern sympathies, is not able to lay very much emphasis on this aspect. He lays more on English mistrust of the "mongrel" and corrupt civilization of the North, their deep admiration for such soldiers as the gallant Stonewall Jackson and the saintly Lee, and above all, their instinctive warmth towards a people engaged in a valorous struggle for freedom against a powerful foe. It is not possible to accept his conclusions, or those of Owsley, as to the extent of English sympathy for the Confederacy, despite their researches, for they greatly underestimate the simplicity of an "accurate estimate"[3] of public opinion. It is doubtful if their assessment of the power of the so-called "educated million" is accurate; it is certain that the English lower classes were more than the "politically apathetic, sodden, ignorant, and docile" proletariat, that Owsley describes,[4] in mid-nineteenth century. In the words of an American who had lived in England, quoted by Randall, men talk in America "of the Governing Classes as being all against us as if there was no People as a power there";[5] or, as Macaulay had written to Palmerston as early as 1845, "It may be an evil that a man of your eminent capacity for the conduct of great affairs should be under the necessity of consulting the prejudices of people who do not know the difference between the Texas question and the Oregon question, and who confound Doost Mahommed with Mehemet Ali. But this is the price which we pay for the advantages of representative government."[6]

[1] Q. Trevelyan, p. 302-3.
[2] S. Van Auken, "English Sympathy for the Southern Confederacy" (thesis read in manuscript).
[3] F. L. Owsley, King Cotton Diplomacy (Chicago, 1931), p. 196.
[4] Ibid, p. 565.
[5] J. G. Randall, Lincoln the Liberal Statesman (London, 1947), p. 139.
[6] Q. F. Merk, "British Party Politics and the Oregon Treaty" (in Am. H.R., XXXVII, 1932), p. 667.

In fact there are other and better explanations of the British attitude than universal sympathy or aristocratic fellow feeling for the Confederacy. As the crisis approached and an appreciation of Southern strength developed, there began a vital process by which the North sank in English esteem; it was not so much that the South became purer, but rather that the North's motives became less laudable to Englishmen, and as the one came to seem darker, the other began to appear lighter in British eyes. This great change was due to an increasing perplexity as to the real nature of the struggle, for though Lincoln was determined not to allow the extension of slavery into the territories, he was also anxious to commit no unconstitutional act, lest it give a greater appearance of rectitude to the actions of the South in breaking up the Union. He declared in his Inaugural Address: "I have no purpose, directly or indirectly to interfere with the institution of slavery in the States where it exists. I believe I have no lawful right to do so, and I have no inclination to do so."[1] Again and again this point was to be re-iterated by Lincoln, both because he believed it, and because it was tactically indispensable if he was to prevent the secession of the Upper South before Sumter and if he was to retain the allegiance of the vitally important Border States once hostilities had broken out. The cause of the war when it came, therefore, appeared to the British increasingly constitutional and decreasingly concerned with slavery; slavery in fact continued to exist within the borders of the Union and to be protected by its government, while not for well over a year after Sumter was there any sign of a determination on the part of the Administration to attack the institution directly. The result was a rapid decline in pro-Northern sentiment in Britain, for the niceties of American constitutional law were hard for Englishmen to follow, and both sides seemed to present constitutional arguments of great plausibility.

But though this reaction savoured something of the cry, "a plague o' both your houses", it did mean an effort at impartiality; Russell promptly instructed Lyons, who had personal ties with the leaders of both factions, to be careful not to seem to favour one party rather than the other, and not to express opinions or give advice, unless asked for, in which case the advice should be against all violent action as tending towards civil war. This policy was scrupulously pursued, and there is little overt sign in British governmental circles, either of desire to interfere with, or of pleasure at the weakening of, her great rival. It is impossible to see what other or better course could have been followed by

[1] Q. E.D.A., I, p. 50.

459

Britain, yet already the seeds of dissension with the North were being sown, for the very proof of British beneficence towards the whole of America, her hope that the break up of the Union would not be followed by a bloody civil war, was at once held up in Republican circles in the North as a proof of her cold-hearted desire to weaken the United States by encouraging the rebellion. Already the implications of the Northern position were becoming plainer, namely, that she could be satisfied with nothing less than the restoration of the Union, and the recognition by foreign powers of the maintenance of the theoretical *status quo*. The South, on the other hand, sought only recognition of what seemed already amply to exist, her independence, and from the first she sought it primarily from Britain. The lengths to which Southerners were prepared to go to attain this end were shown by the expressions of regret, now said to be often heard in the South, at the events of 1776, and of a wistful hope that her allegiance to the mother country might perhaps be restored as an alternative preferable to Yankee tyranny; one of the leading Confederate statesmen, Judah P. Benjamin, himself British born, was even accused—he vigorously denied it—of writing a letter to this effect to the British Consul at New York in August, 1860.

Thus, as secession became an accomplished fact, British opinion as to the possibility of reversing it hardened, so that Russell in January, 1861, wrote to Lyons, expressing the prevalent British view: "I do not see how the United States can be cobbled together again by any compromise. . . . The best thing *now* would be that the right to secede should be acknowledged. . . . But above all I hope no force will be used". Already the long tug-of-war between North and South for the mind and body of Britain had begun. By 12 March the *volte-face* in much of the press had been signalized by *The Times*, in an article on the North and South which declared:

> Their internal institutions are their own affair; their financial and political arrangements are emphatically ours. . . . If the Northern Confederacy of America evinces a determination to act in a narrow, exclusive, and unsocial spirit, while its Southern competitor extends the hand of good fellowship to all mankind, with the exception of its own bondsmen, we must not be surprised to see the North, in spite of the goodness of its cause and the great negative merit of the absence of Slavery, sink into a secondary position, and lose the sympathy and regard of mankind.[1]

Thus strength of feeling for the North evaporated and prepared the

[1] Q. E.D.A., I, pp. 52-3, 56-7.

way for more definite sympathy with the South, but whatever opinions they held as to the respective merits of the two parties, Englishmen were united in deploring a resort to violence; that is to say, in fact, in accepting the break up of the Union as final. This was not unconnected with an increasing British apprehension as to the effect upon her trade with the Southern States of a war possibly accompanied by a Northern blockade of Southern ports; of this possibility Russell and Lyons were uncomfortably aware, and, after the inauguration of the new Administration, did their best to prevent it.

This and other diplomatic tasks facing Lyons were not made easier by the apprehension which was felt as to Seward's intentions as Secretary of State, in view of his presumed Anglophobia; and indeed the apprehension was justified by his proposals to Lincoln during this period, even though the details of them were not publicly known. It was on 1 April that he presented to the President "Some Thoughts" for his consideration, which contained a section suggesting that a foreign policy should be inaugurated, which would, by rousing "a vigorous continental spirit of independence on this continent against European intervention"[1] in its affairs, reunite the Union against the common foe. Lincoln quietly rejected the idea, by pointing out that it would be contrary to the instructions already despatched to Ministers abroad, drawn in terms recalling to foreign powers their long traditions of friendly relations with the United States, and showed clearly for the first time that he, and not Seward, was to be master in the Cabinet. Nevertheless, the attitude of Seward was of great importance, since he was to continue as Secretary of State until 1867, and it requires some explanation. He was, and remained, an ardent American expansionist, but in so far as his reputed hatred of Britain had existed, or existed at this time, it became less and less evident as the months went by; he, who began his Secretaryship of State with this wild scheme, became before long the exponent of caution in foreign affairs and one of the best of American Secretaries of State. It is true that this nostrum to cure disunion was in accord with one of the classical precepts for dealing with domestic political discontent, and that it must have appeared less than absurd to the generation which had seen the heyday of Manifest Destiny, but it was irresponsible and chimerical none the less. It can only be explained in terms of his inexperience in international affairs, which are very different from New York domestic politics, and of the understandable discontent and chagrin of a naturally ebullient man of warm patriotism, who had been recently disappointed in his ambition for the highest

[1] Q. ibid, I, p. 119.

461

office in the land, during a most trying period of inaction before the outbreak of the impending and calamitous civil war. These seem the most likely explanations of his aberration; but, whatever its cause, it was short lived.

He endeavoured to re-assert it against Britain in the famous "Despatch No. 10", of 21 May, to Adams, protesting against the British recognition of Southern belligerency, but the whole tone of the document was softened by certain alterations made by Lincoln, and in its final form it began, as the President wished, by stating that the United States "neither means to menace Great Britain nor to wound the sensibilities of that or any other European nation". It contained instructions that it was not to be read or shown to the British Secretary of State, which Seward had wished, and that none of "its positions" were "to be prematurely, unnecessarily, or indiscreetly made known. But its spirit" was to be Adams's "guide."[1] There were, during May and June, one or two more outbursts of decreasing significance, but by the middle of July Seward was writing to Adams in London almost apologetically:

> I may add, also, for myself, that however otherwise I may at any time have been understood, it has been in earnest and profound solicitude to avert from foreign war; that alone has prompted the emphatic and sometimes, perhaps, impassioned remonstrances I have hitherto made against any form or measure of recognition of the insurgents by the government of Great Britain. I write in the same spirit now; and I invoke on the part of the British Government, as I propose to exercise on my own, the calmness which all counsellors ought to practice in debates which involve the peace and happiness of mankind.[2]

But this earlier belligerence of Seward probably had, on balance, a salutary effect upon Anglo-American relations, because of the sobering influence it exerted upon the British Government, who became, as a result of it, more than ever determined to step warily in the difficult circumstances arising from the American war.

III

THIS caution had already been presaged by many things, including Russell's refusal to commit himself in any way to Dallas about the diplomatic status of the South, but became pronounced after the actual outbreak of hostilities, news of which reached England on 27 April.

[1] Q. ibid, I, p. 126.   [2] Q. ibid, pp. 134-5.

This was shortly followed by information that Davis had approved a proclamation offering to issue letters of marque, and that Lincoln had proclaimed the Northern intention to treat privateers operating under such letters as pirates, and, more important, to institute in due course a blockade of Southern ports. On 29 April two accredited agents of the Confederacy reached London, and Russell saw them unofficially, while keeping officially in contact with Dallas, though he suspended a good deal of Northern business pending the arrival, in a fortnight's time, of Adams with his fuller knowledge and instructions.

Meanwhile, under pressure of events, British policy was maturing in the only direction possible if serious entanglement was to be avoided; it was expressed forcibly by Russell in the Commons when he said, with very general approval from the House and the country: "We have not been involved in any way in that contest by any act . . . and, for God's sake, let us if possible keep out of it." The complications likely, as it seemed, to arise out of the war at sea gave urgency to the situation, and on 13 May a Proclamation of Neutrality was issued. It recognized the existence of a *Justum Bellum*—anything less would not have been in accord with the facts—and hence of the belligerency, but no more, of the Confederacy—anything more would have recognized the independence of the South, which was most carefully avoided. It thus chose a very precise course between recognition of Southern independence on the one hand, and failure to recognize the existence of a major war on the other; the first would mortally have offended the North, and the second would have caused serious risk of maritime friction with her, while mortally offending the South. The same spirit of caution inspired the rest of the proclamation, which referred only to "states styling themselves the Confederate States of America".[1] It was issued in agreement with France; it was addressed only to British subjects and its existence was never formally notified to Seward; it enjoined a strict neutrality on Britons and warned them that failure to comply with it rendered forfeit their right to the protection of their government; it regretfully acknowledged the Southern right to send out privateers, and recognized any effective blockade which might be established by the North, though such was thought, mistakenly as it turned out, to be utterly impossible in the case of a three thousand mile coast line. The proclamation as a whole was almost unanimously welcomed by British opinion.

Such was the situation which greeted Adams when he reached England, on the very day the proclamation was issued. That the British

[1] Q. ibid, pp. 90, 94.

action was not going to be pleasing to the North is clearly shown by his son's description of his own feelings: "He [Henry Adams] thought on May 12 that he was going to a friendly Government and people, true to . . . anti-slavery principles. . . . On May 13, he met the official announcement that England recognized the belligerency of the Confederacy. . . . [T] his shock . . . produced only a dullness of comprehension—a sort of hazy inability to . . . realize the blow."[1] The outcry in the North was bitter, the Administration taking strong exception to the British action on two grounds; first, that it was exceedingly premature, because the South had not yet shown herself capable of sustained war, and second—a much broader ground which was never entirely relinquished—that the rebels were and remained mere individuals in treasonable rebellion against their country. This latter concept was not without domestic importance to the Administration, since the right of the Federal government to coerce individuals was plain, while that to coerce States was not. The North, it was now clear, had expected from Britain much more than a "cold neutrality"; it had expected her to ignore the very existence of the war on the pretext that it was a mere local internal rebellion. Such an expectation was doomed in the nature of things to disappointment, for the maritime complications, arising from the great war which was shortly to develop, themselves condemned it. In answer to Adams's protests Russell reiterated that the only British motive for issuing the proclamation had been a desire not to interfere in any way, while a crisis threatened by Adams's instructions from Seward to cease all relations with the British Government as long as it was in official or unofficial communication with the Southern agents, was averted by Russell's statement that "he had no expectation of seeing them any more."[2]

Meanwhile, British opinion showed itself more and more determined, in the words of *The Times*, to take "the utmost care . . . to avoid giving offence to either of the two incensed belligerents. . . . Neutrality—strict neutrality—is all that the United States Government can claim."[3] How difficult this could be is shown by the fact that the Southern Commissioners, who had good reason to be pleased with events thus far, since the Proclamation recognized their belligerency if not their independence, only just refrained from protesting to Russell that his statement to Adams that he had no expectation of seeing them again was a breach of the neutrality which Britain had recently proclaimed. Adams and his entourage did not believe that her "Majesty's Government were

[1] *The Education of Henry Adams,* pp. 114-5.
[2] Q. E.D.A., I, p. 106. [3] Q. ibid, 103-4.

really animated by a desire to favour the rebellion", but Northern opinion never fully accepted this view. This prejudice is understandable, for Henry Adams himself could never quite throw off, in the first three years of war, the suspicion that Russell had lied and deceived from the beginning. This suspicion varied in emotional intensity according to the ups-and-downs of the diplomatic situation; in September, 1861, he wrote: "Lately, England has behaved very well. Lord Russell was very open and confidential towards the Chief",[1] but in 1862 he "wanted nothing so much as to wipe England off the earth. Never could any good come from that besotted race!"[2] Though he later saw that the suspicion was unfounded, others, less perceptive and farther from the sources of information, did not, and there built up in some Northern quarters during the war a great depth of bitterness against Britain. Similarly, a progressive disillusion with the North was displaying itself in the British Press, of which the opinion of *The Times* on 30 May, 1861, was not unrepresentative:

> We have been told, in fact, by Northern politicians, that it does not become us to be indifferent, and by Southern leaders that they are half inclined to become British once more. Both sides are bidding for us, and both sides have their partisans over here. On such perilous ground we cannot walk too warily.... The real motives of the belligerents ... appear to be ... essentially selfish ... that it to say, they are based upon speculations of national power, territorial aggrandizement, political advantage, and commercial gain. Neither side can claim any superiority of principle, or any peculiar purity of patriotism. . . .[3]

Though some opinion might yet swing much further in favour of the South, the war, certainly, was no longer in English eyes a noble struggle of the North against slavery. In such circumstances the impartial course the British Government chose was the only possible one.

Yet the difficulties in the maintenance even of neutrality were grave, particularly those arising from the war at sea. Maritime law had had, as we know, a long and chequered history in Anglo-American relations, but its incidence in the Civil War is of a new, indeed a quite opposite, kind from that of the past, for, whereas in the Napoleonic Wars the United States had occupied her accustomed position of the great neutral, and Great Britain hers of major belligerent, now these roles were exactly reversed: the North was the belligerent whose interest it

[1] Q. W.A.A.E., pp. 315, 319.
[2] *Education of Henry Adams*, p. 128.   [3] Q. E.D.A., I, p. 97.

was to enforce blockade as fully as possible, and Britain the neutral who desired to protect her trade as much as she could. Each side in fact was now a biter well and truly bit, and they might gladly have exchanged their opposed and arduously elaborated interpretations of international law. Russell had apprehended this fact as early as 9 March when he wrote to Lyons: "If he blockades the Southern ports we shall be in a difficulty. But according to all American doctrine it must be an actual blockade kept up by an efficient force."[1] In fact, however, Britain was loath to push this argument to an extreme, since she realized that to do so might imperil her future use of this, her own most powerful weapon, naval blockade. On the other hand, the North's need was to reduce, in view of her naval weakness for the purpose, the amount of actual force required before her blockade should be accepted as effective by neutral powers. It was this desire to obtain foreign recognition of her blockade that determined her, against her first inclination, to grant belligerent rights to the Confederacy, and to declare a blockade, rather than merely to try and enforce a closure of Southern ports. That it was wise to do so was shown by the uproar in Britain against the alleged, and allegedly barbarous, plan of the North (which in fact came to nothing) to block Charleston and other Southern harbours by sinking vessels across their entrances; British protests affirmed that it would permanently impair the commercial facilities of the area, but British feeling was in reality a reaction to the explicit American proposal at the time, which was never put, and probably never intended to be put, into effect, to close the Southern ports by what amounted to a 'paper' blockade. Even more striking, in view of past history, was the Northern maintenance of the doctrine of continuous voyage, to prevent transhipment of vast loads of Confederate war material at Nassau in the Bahamas, and her seizure of certain types of non-contraband; both of these things the British Government accepted gracefully, with one eye on the future, though sometimes objecting strongly to the methods used. She was to make full use of these precedents in the first years of World War I.

But the complicating effect of past history upon maritime rights did not stop here, for it was no mere Anglo-American question just like that of 1812; other powers and later developments were involved. During the course of the Crimean War, the first large scale European conflict since Waterloo, and one, moreover, in which Britain's enemy had relatively little maritime commerce, the Allies had relaxed the strict letter of the international law affecting neutral trade. This action was naturally acceptable to powers which had in the past felt the weight

[1] Q. ibid, p. 62.

of Britain's naval blockade, such as France and the neutrals; its acceptance by Britain, against whose whole naval tradition it was, no doubt derived from a softening of the rigidity of her old ideas in nearly forty years of peace, from the necessity of co-operation with her allies, and, as Palmerston later declared, from a fear of alienating the United States, and even of driving her into the arms of Russia. That the latter was by no means an absolute impossibility was shown by the history of the War of 1812, by the signs of Americo-Russian *rapprochement* during the Crimean War, and by the feeling for Russia engendered in some quarters of the United States by the appearance of part of her fleet in American ports, in the course of the Civil War itself, at a time when it appeared possible that an offer of mediation from Britain might lead to a British entry into the war on the Southern side. Russian policy, much affected still by her recent defeat in the Crimea at the hands of Britain and France, was deliberately friendly to the United States throughout the war, a fact which does something to explain her sale of Alaska to America in 1867.

But the British Government did not stop at practical concessions in the Crimean struggle; it agreed, in the Declaration of Paris, which was signed by Prussia, Russia, Austria, France, Sardinia and Turkey in 1856, to four far-reaching principles which, taken as a whole, were in future to govern maritime warfare. The Declaration was strongly attacked by the Opposition in Britain, on the ground that it blunted her chief weapon, but it was accepted none the less. The stipulations were as follows:

1. Privateering is, and remains, abolished.
2. The neutral flag covers enemy's goods, with the exception of contraband of war.
3. Neutral goods, with the exception of contraband of war, are not liable to capture under enemy's flag.
4. Blockades, in order to be binding, must be effective; that is to say, maintained by a force sufficient really to prevent access to the coast of the enemy.[1]

Within a short time, virtually all the maritime powers save the United States had accepted it; she refused to do so unless it were widened to protect privately-owned, non-contraband enemy goods under the enemy's flag—the most extreme extension of neutral rights ever proposed by a great power—and this Britain refused to contemplate. The real reason for the American demand was a desire to retain privateer-

[1] Q. ibid, p. 140.

ing, which had in the past served her so well, and the matter therefore lapsed until 1861.

Very soon after the outbreak of hostilities, Seward proposed to Britain to accede to the four points of the Declaration of Paris, and negotiations were well on the way to success when the British Government realized that Article 1 might be used as a lever by the United States, which had not recognized Southern belligerency, to force other powers to treat the privateers, which the South had already declared its intention of using, as pirates. In fact, Seward's object had probably become, in the course of negotiation, a desire to force the European powers, and particularly Britain, into a withdrawal of their recognition of Southern belligerency, but, once Russell's suspicions were aroused, he refused to accept anything but a full American acceptance of all four points and an explicit denial of their retrospective operation. Seward's refusal in his turn to make an exception of the very case for which alone he desired to alter the past American rule in favour of privateers brought the negotiations to an end. They had achieved nothing except to render Russell more suspicious of American intentions and less convinced that the neutrality policy could be maintained under any circumstances. But the studious correctness of the British attitude to the blockade on the seas themselves prevented, throughout the war, much friction which might have arisen from disputes about maritime rights.

With their defeat at Bull Run in the first serious engagement of the war, it became apparent that the North would not be speedily triumphant, and English opinion became more and more doubtful whether the conquest of the South would ever in fact be possible. At the same time, opinion became increasingly divided as to the merits of the two parties. Pressure by Northern and Southern propaganda was intensified, that of the Confederacy under the able leadership of Henry Hotze, and led to a battle of opinions only to be equalled in intensity by that between German and Allied information agencies amongst the American people in World War I. The Press began to form permanent alignments. Some journals were by now convinced that the separation was permanent and should be accepted as such; this formed the basis of pro-Southern feeling in such publications as the violent and influential *Index,* which was shortly to be founded by Confederate agents, and *The Times,* whose partisanship became increasingly pronounced. On the other hand, the *Spectator* and the *Daily News* remained firm advocates of the Northern cause. Yet other journals, such as the *Economist,* tried to preserve their neutrality, and, like the public who read them, changed their opinions in accordance with events.

The Government's adherence to strict neutrality was still generally approved, however, and the policy continued despite the revocation by Seward of the *exequatur* of the British Consul in Charleston, on the ground that he had exceeded his rights in the course of conducting his Government's business with the Confederacy. The incident appeared for a time to be grave, but as he had not conducted himself tactfully and had probably exceeded his instructions, his departure was accepted by the British Government. The question was of importance because it showed that, though Britain claimed the right to contact the South in case of need, she did not press it when the North reacted strongly. During the same period certain Frenchmen, led by Mercier, the French Minister in Washington, showed themselves for the first time ready to go very much farther than mere contact with the South, and to recognize the Confederacy, provided Britain would do so too. This was an effort to break the blockade, whose effect upon European economic life was becoming marked, but the British Government, with the strong approval of Lyons, declined to change its policy.

But the seizure, on the high seas on 8 November, from the British ship *Trent*, by Captain Wilkes of the United States Navy, commanding the *San Jacinto*, of two "Special Commissioners of the Confederate States of America", James M. Mason and John Slidell, destined to Britain and France respectively, not only endangered that policy, but precipitated perhaps the most tense of the many incidents in the war. How very tense is shown by Slidell's exultant conviction that his own capture would inevitably achieve the chief object of Confederate diplomacy, recognition of the South by Britain. The danger lay in the wild enthusiasm with which Wilkes's rash action was greeted in the United States, an enthusiasm difficult even for Americans to understand in retrospect, but due, in all probability, to a Northern craving for exciting successes in view of their initial lack of them, to the great national reputation that Mason and Slidell enjoyed, and to American delight in being able to turn the odious British claim to a right of search against Britain herself.

The British Government had been apprehensive of some such incident, and, when it actually happened, thought at first that it was a deliberate act authorized by the American Government as the culmination of Seward's chauvinistic policy. Their lawyers had advised them that, while they could not prevent the ship being seized as a prize, the seizure of the two men was illegal, and on 30 November they instructed

Lyons to demand the restoration of the prisoners with an apology, on the grounds that their capture was a breach of international law. The first draft of these instructions was materially softened by the Prince Consort in what was probably his last political action, particularly by the insertion of an expression of hope that the action of Wilkes was unauthorized, but it was still a document very cold, though correct, in tone. Lyons was, however, given discretion to authorize a delay of seven days if needed, and, in a private letter from Russell, was told to abstain from menace, but at the same time the fleet was put in readiness and preparations begun to send troops to Canada. British public feeling ran high, and Henry Adams wrote: "How in the name of all that's conceivable could you suppose England would sit quiet under such an insult? *We* should have jumped out of our boots at such a one."[1] If Seward's mood had been the same as that of six months before, it is hard to see how war could have been avoided, but, as we have seen, it had mellowed. Furthermore, in the three blessed weeks of delay, which the slowness of transportation provided, Americans had begun to ponder the legality of the action, and even to wonder in some cases why they had been so wildly enthusiastic in the first place; on the other hand, America's pristine enthusiasm so astonished the British public that after a first belligerent reaction, British utterances in their turn began to display a note of caution and to dwell increasingly on the vulnerability of Canada and the calamity which a war with the North would constitute.

But it was in the American Cabinet that the crucial decision had to be made—whether or not to return Slidell and Mason. While this decision was awaited, Adams was able on 19 December to assure Russell officially that the action of Wilkes was unauthorized, and Lyons pushed his discretionary power to the limit in the wise realization that the longer the delay the cooler the decision would be, so that he notified Seward unofficially of his instructions five days before he presented them formally, since it was from the latter date that the seven-day time limit would be reckoned. Some of the American Cabinet opposed release, even including Lincoln (who had apparently thought better of his first opinion that the two prisoners might be "a couple of white elephants"[2]), but Seward had realized from the first that America was in an impossible position. Christmas Day and the day following were occupied in lengthy Cabinet debate, but by the second evening Seward was able to convince all his colleagues, and on the 27th this was announced by him to Lyons. Seward claimed that Mason and Slidell were contra-

¹ Q. W.A.A.E., p. 322.   ² Evan John, *Atlantic Impact*, p. 262.

band of war which could justly be captured, but stated that Wilkes had done wrong not to bring the *Trent* into port for trial by an American prize court; his statement contained no apology, but was accepted by Lyons, in view of the return of the prisoners, as complying substantially with the British demands. Though not accepting Seward's arguments, the British Government was well satisfied with this closure of the incident, while they were even more cautious than they otherwise would have been not to extend any measure whatever of official recognition to the two commissioners either *en route* or on arrival. This reaction was almost universal in England; as Henry Adams wrote, "The first effect of the surrender . . . has been extraordinary. The current which ran against us with such extreme violence six weeks ago now seems to be going with equal fury in our favour." This owed much to British uneasiness that a war with the North would mean alliance with a slave power, as well as to the feeling expressed by Trollope, then in America, that it would be a fratricidal struggle, "an unloosing of hell upon all that is best upon the world's surface."[1] Thus the determination to preserve neutrality was strengthened rather than weakened.

In the North, on the other hand, the reaction was not so salutary. Very great credit is due to Seward whose work the settlement was; he displayed here for the first time the great statesmanship of which he was capable, even in the face of a hostile public opinion, though the fact that his view prevailed may not have been unconnected with the fact that his previous actions made it hard for his colleagues to believe him capable of unnecessary moderation. What is more, he bore no later grudge for the event, whereas the American people as a whole resented the British attitude strongly; it was a dramatic affirmation of that cold British neutrality which was such a disappointment to them. As Lowell wrote:

> *It don't seem hardly right, John,*
> *When both my hands was full,*
> *To stump me to a fight, John—*
> *You cousin, tu, John Bull!*[2]

Plain hints were uttered by others as to how serious its ultimate effect might be: "The feeling against Great Britain is of intense hatred and the conclusion of the whole matter is, that we must give up the traitors, put down the rebellion, increase our navy, perfect the discipline of 600,000 men in the field, and then fight Great Britain."[3] This was not to

[1] Q. E.D.A., I, pp. 238-9.   [2] Q. ibid, p. 236.
[3] Bigelow's *Retrospections*: q. ibid.

471

be the outcome, largely because Seward's control as Secretary of State became increasingly firm, but much of the trouble arising from anti-British feeling in America after the war can be traced to just such pent-up feelings of bitterness. Lincoln summed up its effect in a characteristic parable. "This was an elaborate story about a man who, believing that he was dying, allowed himself to be persuaded to make a most affecting peace with his worst enemy. Then, when his weeping, departing visitor had almost reached the door, the sick man rose up on his elbow and said, 'But see here, Brown, if I should happen to get well, mind, that old grudge stands.' "[1]

IV

THE next six months were relatively calm, but saw a steady development in the effectiveness of the Northern blockade, so that it became apparent to the British that they had been too sanguine in believing that it could never be effective. Owsley's elaborate analysis of the effectiveness of it shows that it was slow in coming into operation, and also shows that it was never successful in stopping even a great majority of ships, but his calculations seem to be a little wide of their target, for it is exceedingly doubtful whether *any* power interpreted the term "effective" to mean one hundred per cent or anything approaching it. British blockades of France in the Napoleonic wars had never been of this degree of effectiveness. Certainly from this time on the blockade looms steadily larger as the cause of difficulty in Anglo-American relations. Edge was given to the realization of this increase in American naval power by the engagement between the Southern iron-clad ram, *Virginia*, previously called the *Merrimac*, and the Northern iron-clad gunboat *Monitor*, for this indicated clearly that the day of the wooden ship was done. There was no serious long-term British fear that she could not, as the leading industrial nation, outbuild any rival power in iron vessels—she already had one launched and a number more on the stocks—but there were some transient misgivings lest, as Russell wrote, the Yankees should turn upon Britain before she could transform her navy and "renew the triumphs they achieved in 1812-3 by means of superior size and weight of metal",[2] and a very real temporary fear of France, which was actually ahead of Britain in ironclad design and construction. It did mean, as Adams said, "the commencement of a new era in warfare, and that Great Britain must consent to begin over again",[3] but

[1] Q. Brebner, p. 164.   [2] Q. E.D.A., I, p. 277.   [3] Q. ibid, p. 276.

very soon this was accepted, and the *Monitor* remained important chiefly as an indication of a new Northern energy in the prosecution of the war at sea. The main effort of Commissioner Mason in the beginning was directed to inducing Britain to terminate the blockade on account of its ineffectiveness and, therefore, illegality; but, though all reports agree that it was not fully effective, in late November Lyons had reported: "I suppose the ships which run it successfully both in and out are more numerous than those which are intercepted. On the other hand it is very far from being a mere Paper Blockade. A great many vessels are captured; it is a most serious interruption to Trade; and if it were as ineffective as Mr. Jefferson Davis says . . . he would not be so very anxious to get rid of it."[1] France, too, felt the pinch, and joint protestations by the two European powers in the summer restrained the Administration from the imposition, by a proposed article in the "Southern Ports" Proclamation authorized by Congress, of a purely paper blockade on the whole South.

Joint action between the two, reinforced by Spain but not by the United States, despite an invitation, was also the basis of a military expedition sent to Mexico late in 1861 to enforce the payment of some long outstanding debts; when such a plan had been envisaged in 1860 Buchanan had issued a warning against any territorial ambitions on the part of foreign powers, and the three governments pledged themselves not to seek any such gains and not to interfere in the internal affairs of Mexico. As soon as it became apparent that Napoleon had in fact far-reaching designs on the American continent, Britain, along with Spain, withdrew her troops and dissociated herself completely from French actions there. France was obviously taking advantage of American weakness in order to challenge the Monroe Doctrine, by establishing the ill-fated Hapsburg Empire in Mexico, and it is a measure of changed British feelings both towards America and towards colonial adventures that she so swiftly withdrew her forces. Had she not done so, Anglo-American relations might not have stood the strain after the war, which the Mexican adventure in fact placed upon those between the United States and France.

France at this time was more forward in relations with the North than Britain, for though in the last resort he would not act without British support, it is probable that Napoleon, desiring to cut a striking figure, in this as in other fields of international affairs, was anxious to press the British Government to a joint offer of mediation, or even of recognition of the South. Both of these ideas were naturally anathema

[1] Q. ibid, p. 254.

473

to the North, but recent Federal successes in the war had convinced many Frenchmen (notably Mercier, who had recently visited Richmond, though not Thouvenel, the Foreign Minister) that the struggle was likely to be protracted, with disastrous results to European trade; as reconquest of the South seemed impossible, Napoleon was prepared to risk Northern antagonism by an effort to bring the struggle to an end on the basis of Southern independence. But the prospect of a long war did not produce the same effect in England, for the Government showed themselves more than ever determined to cleave to neutrality and to induce the French to do likewise, although they did not absolutely exclude a change of policy and an offer of mediation, if a very strong desire for peace became apparent in the North. Even the Opposition could not be persuaded to bring pressure to bear on the Government, either by Southern or French influences, and a proposed motion in the Commons in June calling for mediation or recognition of the South never even came to a debate.

What is more, a debate on the economic effects of the blockade, initiated by the Government some months earlier, although bringing out clearly the increasing seriousness of the situation, gravely affected the strength of the South's supporters, who appeared at a disadvantage, and who showed their weakness by withdrawing their motion, urging the Government to declare the blockade ineffective, without pressing it to a division. This proved a deep disappointment to the South, since it became clear that Napoleon would not move without the British, and it was upon foreign intervention that the Confederate Secretary of State, Benjamin, had built his highest hopes. Indeed, the South was at a later date, in its search for European aid, to go so far as to make it clear that it was favourably disposed towards Napoleon's protégé in Mexico. Lee, almost alone of Southern leaders, made up his mind to the fact that, "We must . . . fight our battles and win our independence alone. No one will help us."[1]

The refusal of the British in 1862 to budge from their neutrality was the first and perhaps the worst of many similiar Southern disappointments, and shortly afterwards Confederate hopes were temporarily raised once again by a contretemps between Palmerston and Adams; this arose from a letter written by the former to the latter on the publication of General Butler's famous order in New Orleans, authorizing his Federal soldiers to treat as "women of the town" those Southern women who publicly insulted Northern troops. British opinion regarded this as an incitement to atrocities, and Palmerston wrote that " it is difficult

[1] Q. John, p. 250.

if not impossible to express adequately the disgust which must be excited in the mind of every honourable man by the general order of General Butler".[1] Whatever may be thought of Butler—and though he may be defended in the North, he is "Beast" Butler in the South to this day—there is no doubt that Palmerston's letter was a grave error. Though he obviously thought his feelings did him credit, they should not have been gratuitously intruded upon the international stage, while even if they were private in character, Adams, at least, did not regard a man of Palmerston's way of life as particularly well fitted to make such a protest. For a time the situation looked ugly, since Adams was personally very aggrieved and suspected that this apparently irrational act was a mere excuse for a change in British policy towards the war. This was not the case, however, and Russell showed Palmerston pretty plainly that he disapproved of this intervention in his department, and Russell's position vis à vis his chief was much stronger than that of a Foreign Secretary usually is, for their roles had in a previous ministry been reversed. Adams, as always, kept his head superbly well. His first action was a note asking Palmerston whether the letter was official or purely "a private expression of sentiment between gentlemen", and though Palmerston prevaricated and wriggled for over a week, and never actually apologized, it was on the basis of his acknowledgement, that the "Secretary of State for Foreign Affairs is the regular official organ for communications",[2] and his expressed gratification that Lincoln had curtailed Butler's authority, that the matter was allowed by Adams to rest, on the assumption that Palmerston's "offensive imputations" had been withdrawn.

Thus once again a surface calm descended on the relations of Britain with the North, but below the surface the economic situation was becoming sufficiently serious to give new hope to the South and her friends. The Confederacy had always been convinced that their virtual monopoly of the world cotton market was a decisive weapon in their hands. So strongly had they believed that shortage of cotton would force Britain to break the blockade by one means or another that at the beginning of the war they had encouraged a voluntary embargo on its export and had burnt two and a half million bales lest they ease the foreign shortage, thus voluntarily doing the work of their enemies' blockade before it had time to become effective. Indeed, classic expression had been given to this cardinal article in the Southern faith—for it was more than a reasonable hope—even before the war began, by

[1] Q. E.D.A., I, p. 302. [2] Q. ibid, pp. 303, 305.

Senator Hammond of South Carolina, who said in 1858: "What would happen if no cotton were furnished for three years? I will not stop to depict what everyone can imagine, but this is certain: England would topple headlong and carry the whole civilized world with her save the South. No, you dare not make war on cotton. No power on earth dares make war on it. Cotton *is* King."[1] As might be expected, after hostilities had begun this belief took an even firmer hold on the South; the *Charleston Mercury* wrote on 4 June, 1861: "The cards are in our hands! And we intend to play them out to the bankruptcy of every cotton factory in Great Britain and France for the acknowledgement of our independence."

When the war broke out, one fifth of the population of England lived directly or indirectly by the cotton industry, and the South provided about 80 per cent of the raw material, so that the Southern illusion as to the strength of King Cotton was not without foundation, though it was an illusion none the less. By the summer of 1862 the situation appeared grim, for in the first six months of the year only 11,500 bales were received in England, which was less than 1 per cent of the amount for the same six months of the previous year, while, in the distressed districts of Lancashire, where 48,000 people received poor relief in normal times, 113,000 received it in March, 1862, and 284,418 in December, which was, however, the peak month. Why in the face of these figures did the King Cotton theory fail? Primarily for a reason which the cotton manufacturers had good cause to conceal from contemporary opinion—that when Sumter fell there was a 50 per cent oversupply of raw cotton in England as well as an excess of manufactured cotton products. In fact the cotton interests were actually saved from a very serious slump by the coming of the war, for instead of continuing to shut down mills and lower prices as they were doing early in 1861, the severe restriction in the supply of cotton enabled them to make most handsome profits on their enormous stocks and to cushion the effects upon the mills. Furthermore, during the course of the war perhaps a million and a half bales of cotton—three-quarters of a normal year's supply—got through the blockade. By the time these temporary palliatives had ceased to be effective new sources of supply were beginning to become available in India, Egypt and elsewhere, while the Northern Administration did all it could to foster cotton exports from the reconquered areas of the South.

These facts explain well enough why the cotton manufacturers, even in 1862, brought very little pressure to bear on the Government

[1] Q. ibid, II, p. 2.

to change the neutrality policy, but they do not explain away the very serious figures of unemployment and distress in the cotton area. In December, 1862, apart from those on public relief, private charity, organized on a national scale, was given to 236,000 persons, so that in a working population of between 500,000 and 600,000 perhaps 400,000 were receiving aid of some kind. There was dire distress, but no starvation, for, as Bright wrote, the people were "kept alive by the contributions of the country."[1] And the difficulties, though severe, were essentially localized, for in other ways and in other parts of the country industry was booming as a result of the war; steel, munitions and shipbuilding flourished, as did the linen and woollen industries, which had so long struggled against competition from cotton. Paradoxically, despite the Lancashire situation, the total of unemployed in the country seems, in so far as it can be estimated, to have been about normal. Finally, the diplomatic strength of Southern cotton was to some extent counterbalanced by increasing English purchases of cereals from the North, which went far to pay for British exports of munitions. Though the actual importance of this King Wheat theory, early propounded by Karl Marx, has been minimized by some critics on the ground that the food could have been bought elsewhere for a somewhat higher price, the fact remains that a great trade in cereals did spring up between Britain and the North. In addition, North American philanthropists sent several shiploads of food to the distressed areas, and Northern propaganda made the most of these welcome contributions. Thus as *The Times* declared: "We are as busy, as rich, and as fortunate in our trade as if the American war had never broken out, and our trade with the States had never been disturbed. Cotton was no King, notwithstanding the prerogatives which had been loudly claimed for him."[2] These economic facts were primarily responsible for softening the blow of unemployment upon the body of the nation in 1862, and in the next year, as we shall see, there began to operate also a powerful political motive for the endurance of their distress by many of the workers. Their voices might in any case not have been raised very loud in a country whose franchise was still oligarchical, had it not been for the fact that the North in its struggle against the South became the inspiration for an increasingly powerful democratic movement in England directed towards Parliamentary reform; the new democracy made its voice heard in no uncertain fashion, but it could not, whatever its economic distress, raise that voice against the land which was in its eyes the very heart land of popular government. Finally, the working

[1] Q. ibid, p. 13.   [2] Q. Bailey, p. 362.

477

classes, like their middle-class masters, became more and more aware during 1863 that the war was indeed, as they had at first suspected, a war against slavery, which made an alliance with the South increasingly distasteful.

But these things were in the future in August, 1862, when Parliament adjourned for the summer, and the British Government was acutely aware not only of the distress in Britain, but also of the failure of the military projects of the North (though not of her resolution), of the continued desire of Napoleon for action, and of the activity of pro-Southern Britons like Lindsay, Beresford-Hope, Gregory and Spence, whose book, *American Union,* had put the Southern point of view with great success. The Government had, on 18 July, forced the withdrawal of Lindsay's motion in the House demanding consideration of "the propriety of offering mediation with the view of terminating hostilities", and had declared its intention to maintain the policy of neutrality for the moment, but some of its members, notably Gladstone, had come to the conclusion privately that "it is . . . much to be desired that this bloody and purposeless conflict should cease." The secret was well kept, but there was a definite movement towards mediation, and on 6 August Russell could write to Palmerston, "Mercier's notion that we should make some move in October agrees very well with yours. I shall be back in England before October, and we could then have a Cabinet upon it. Of course the war may flag before that. I quite agree with you that a proposal for an armistice should be the first step; but we must be prepared to answer the question on what basis are we to negotiate?"[1]

Adams suspected that a change might be afoot, for he had noted the fact that Palmerston's chief argument against mediation was that the time was not yet ripe, and he was very perturbed at the Government's failure to respond to his appeals to prevent the sailing of the famous *Alabama* from Liverpool for the South, a failure which was to cost the British Government dear and the cause of Anglo-American relations even dearer. Adams informed Seward of his fears, and, as this, the gravest crisis of the whole war in the relations of Britain with the North, approached, he received from Washington an instruction outlining the exact steps he should take if the apprehended change in British policy took place. If he were approached with propositions implying a purpose "To dictate, or to mediate, or to advise, or even to solicit or persuade, you will answer that you are forbidden to debate, to hear, or in any way receive, entertain or transmit, any communication of the kind. . . ." If the South were "acknowledged", he was immediately to suspend his

[1] Q. E.D.A., II, pp. 18, 26, 32.

function. From this it is clear that the Administration were determined to resist any European intervention if this became necessary; in face of such calm resolution it is probable that any British or European move would have resulted in war. "You will perceive", said Seward, "that we have approached the contemplation of that crisis with the caution which great reluctance has inspired. But I trust that you will also have perceived that the crisis has not appalled us."[1] This fixed American resolution meant that in the next few weeks Anglo-American peace hung by a thread.

What was the nature of that thread? Its nature on the British side was predetermined by the fact that British opinion was still virtually united in believing that the South could never be reconquered; hardly anyone believed seriously that the eventual peace could be on any other basis than some form of separation. Some went so far as to suggest that the falling away of the South was a kind of fulfilment of 1776, a process analogous to that by which Britain now fully expected in due time to lose all her colonies; even Russell stated that the North were contending for "empire" and the South for "independence".[2] This meant that the question Englishmen always put to themselves was whether they could help to end now on some such basis a war which in due course was bound to end in that fashion anyway. In essence the whole argument was merely as to whether the time was ripe, and the conditions determining this were, in the last resort, military; other factors no doubt influenced the decision but fundamentally it was made on the battlefields in America. The protracted nature of the war and the Southern successes in the summer of 1862 made Russell feel, despite his personal leaning towards the North, that he should make some move to try and end hostilities and reopen trade with the South; lack of Southern success in the autumn moved Palmerston, though more inclined than Russell to be irritated by the North, to restrain his Foreign Secretary before it was too late. In Anglo-American relations, as indeed in the whole history of the Civil War, the fateful battle of Antietam seems more and more the vital turning point. When Lee gave up his Maryland campaign and retreated, two days after the great battle, it caused not merely the British Government to hold its hand, but Lincoln to issue the Emancipation Proclamation, which, though it had at first a most unfavourable reception in England, was ultimately to prove the main factor in ensuring that intervention was never again seriously contemplated by the British Government.

Russell's determination to take action hardened early in September,

[1] Q. ibid, pp. 35-6.   [2] Q. Van Auken.

and at first Palmerston, with whom he kept in close contact, agreed; but the Foreign Secretary was dangerously vague as to what exact action he envisaged. Sometimes he thought in terms of proposing an armistice, sometimes in terms of mediation, and sometimes even of recognizing the South or raising the blockade; he always professed that he contemplated making it quite clear "that we shall take no part in the war unless attacked ourselves",[1] but it is more than doubtful if such ingenuous protestations would have availed to preserve peaceful relations with a furious North. His first move was to approach the French on 13 September, and, because the moderate Thouvenel was still in charge of foreign affairs, he received a surprisingly cool response; furthermore, Palmerston, his eye always on realities, was already beginning to show signs of caution, and insisted on the inclusion of Russia with France in the invitation to action, although "she might probably decline." He said at the time to Russell: "It is evident that a great conflict is taking place to the north-west of Washington, and its issue must have a great effect on the state of affairs. If the Federals sustain a great defeat, they may be at once ready for mediation, and the iron should be struck while it is hot. If, on the other hand, they should have the best of it, we may wait awhile and see what may follow."[2] Opinion in the Cabinet was divided; Cornewall Lewis and Granville, who was in attendance on the Queen abroad and probably consulted her, were strongly averse to action, and Gladstone strongly favoured it.

On 7 October Gladstone, in a speech which he later in his life admitted to be a mistake of "incredible grossness",[3] thrust the whole matter into the open by uttering in famous words what appeared to be a demand for some form of recognition:

> We know quite well that the people of the Northern States have not yet drunk of the cup—they are still trying to hold it far from their lips—
> —which all the rest of the world see they nevertheless must drink of. We may have our own opinions about slavery; we may be for or against the South; but there is no doubt that Jefferson Davis and other leaders of the South have made an army; they are making, it appears, a navy; and they have made what is more than either, they have made a nation.[4]...
> We may anticipate with certainty the success of the Southern States so far as regards their separation from the North.[5]

There seems little doubt that he spoke simply as an individual and because he could not restrain his feelings against the continuance of so

[1] Q. E.D.A., II, p. 46.   [2] Q. ibid, pp. 40-1.   [3] Morley, I, p. 535.
[4] Ibid, p. 533.   [5] Q. Bailey, p. 364.

much bloodshed abroad and distress at home; he was duly reprimanded for his indiscretion by Russell, but the public naturally
thought his words inspired. The situation became clearer to them when
a fellow cabinet member, Cornewall Lewis, answered Gladstone powerfully in another speech. Russell pressed on his proposals, but Palmerston consulted Derby, the leader of the Opposition, indirectly, and
found that he was strongly opposed to recognition or mediation on the
ground that "recognition would merely irritate the North without
advancing the cause of the South or procuring a single bale of cotton,
and that mediation in the present temper of the Belligerents *must* be
rejected". Lyons, who was in England on sick leave, was pressing
Russell to make no move, and the latter accepted the prospect of
further delay by acknowledging that "we ought not to move *at present*
without Russia." The matter was for the moment clinched by Palmerston who wrote to Russell on 22 October:

> [A]ll that we could possibly do without injury to our position would
> be to ask the two Parties not whether they would agree to an armistice but
> whether they might not turn their thoughts towards an arrangement
> between themselves. But the answer of each might be written by us
> beforehand. The Northerns would say that the only condition of arrange-
> ment would be the restoration of the Union; the South would say their
> only condition would be an acknowledgement by the North of Southern
> Independence—we should not be more advanced and should only have
> pledged each party more strongly to the object for which they are fighting.
> I am therefore inclined to change the opinion on which I wrote to you
> when the Confederates seemed to be carrying all before them, and I am
> very much come back to our original view of the matter, that we must
> continue merely to be lookers-on till the war shall have taken a more
> decided turn.[1]

The matter never came before a formal Cabinet meeting, but on
23 October Adams sought information from Russell, and was told that
the Government was not inclined at present to change its policy, but
could make no promises for the future.

But Russell, perhaps made more obstinate by the rebuff he had
received, seemed more determined than ever to propose an armistice,
although he now declared that not less than five European powers were
needed to participate, where he had originally contemplated only the
need for France and Britain. The debate therefore continued between
the members of the Government, until, with the fall of Thouvenel,
Napoleon's long-held desire for intervention found expression in a

[1] Q. E.D.A., II, pp. 51, 54-5.

renewed appeal from France to the British Government that England and Russia should with her propose an armistice of six months, including a suspension of the blockade. A Cabinet meeting on 11 and 12 November discussed the proposal at length. Russell pronounced in favour of it, and Palmerston gave it, according to Gladstone "a feeble and half-hearted support";[1] this he did, as it appeared to Cornewall Lewis, because his "principal motive was a wish to seem to support" Russell. Gladstone alone supported Russell strongly, and there seems little doubt that Palmerston was in his heart of hearts very glad that the feeling of the Cabinet was so averse from the idea that it was decisively rejected. France was told that it seemed best to postpone any overture until there was "a greater prospect than now exists of its being accepted". Public opinion in Britain was, on the whole, strongly in favour of the decision, agreeing with *The Times* when it wrote, "We are convinced that the present is not the moment for these strong measures."[2] This opinion was strengthened as time passed and it became clear that the North was determined to press on energetically with the war, and that no one of account in the Northern States had favoured foreign mediation. Indeed, Napoleon III became even more unpopular there than he already was, because he seemed to the public to have initiated the proposal. In the South, on the other hand, there was now a very strong anti-British trend; Bunch wrote from Charleston of the "Constitutional hatred and jealousy of England, which are as strongly developed here as at the North. Indeed, our known antipathy to Slavery adds another element to Southern dislike."[3]

Thus passed potentially the most serious, though not the most obvious or sharpest, crisis of the war. Minister Adams had not had to carry out his reserve instructions, and, though this was not yet absolutely clear, he was not to have to do so in the future. Seward was right when he wrote, "We are no longer to be disturbed by Secession intrigues in Europe. They have had their day. We propose to forget them." Lyons was now back in Washington and, with his usual calm and penetrating judgment, was flatly contradicting the recent pro-Southern arguments of his excited Chargé d'Affaires, Stuart; he was firmly opposed to mediation unless a radical change in circumstances occurred. When France made a proposal for mediation on her own in February, 1863, Great Britain did not object, but the move undoubtedly marked a serious weakening of the hitherto united Anglo-French front over the Civil War. In the same month Parliament showed itself strongly in favour of the Government's policy of maintaining neutrality,

[1] Q. ibid, p. 65.　　[2] Q. ibid, pp. 64-6, 67.　　[3] Q. ibid, p. 71, footnote 2.

and in the course of the debate Russell declared for the first time that a complete Northern victory now seemed possible, emphasizing that recognition of the South could with justice be regarded as an "unfriendly act"[1] by the North. Undoubtedly the continued Northern energy in the prosecution of the war and the possibility, now for the first time opening up, of a complete Northern reconquest of the South was the most important positive factor in reinforcing Britain's policy of neutrality in 1863, as the fact that the economic distress caused by the Northern blockade had about reached its peak by the end of 1862 was the most important negative one.

There was, however, another and increasingly formidable obstacle to any British intervention which might aid the South, even indirectly, —the slavery question. As we have seen, the British had instinctively, at the very opening of the Secession controversy, favoured the North in the belief that slavery was the fundamental issue. As late as May, 1861, Yancey and Mann had written to Secretary Toombs that, "we are satisfied . . . the public mind here is entirely opposed on the question of slavery, and that the sincerity and universality of this feeling embarrasses the Government in dealing with the question of our recognition."[2] But as the South survived, and as the North continued to maintain that slavery was not the *casus belli* and, what was more, took no action against it, this sentiment died away, and Benjamin was with some justice informed from Paris in September, 1862, that the slavery question had been dropped in England. In fact, this month marked the turning of the tide, for it was the period when Britain came closest to recognition of the South, and it was an interesting thing that the closer she came to assisting the great slave power the less she liked it; the idea that she might end up as an ally of the last great stronghold of slavery was, at bottom, still very repugnant to her people. As Argyll wrote in December, 1861, if England and America became enemies "we necessarily become virtually the *Allies* of the *Scoundrelism* of the South."[3]

These were natural developments of thought and feeling, though they were in the long run to be vigorously stimulated by Lincoln's emancipation policy, but this was not the immediate effect of the preliminary Emancipation Proclamation, which was issued on 22 September. The reasons which had so long restrained Lincoln from this momentous step were still influential, but his persistent efforts, to achieve compensated

[1] Q. ibid, pp. 71, 78.
[2] Q. R. D. Meade, *Judah P. Benjamin* (New York, 1943), p. 263.
[3] Q. E.D.A., I, p. 238.

emancipation and to promote the emigration of slaves who had been freed, had met with little favour in America compared with Congress's Confiscation Bill, which included punitive emancipation clauses. Seward, for the first time, in 1862, instructed Adams and other Northern representatives in Europe to include the suppression of slavery in their statements of the objects of the war, and at the same time Northern supporters in Britain began to call attention to the Slave Trade agreement which had been signed in April, in fact at Britain's suggestion, but, as Seward wished, ostensibly at America's. But this new line of argument was accompanied by another, that, if foreign nations interfered in the struggle, the North would be bound to resort to the horrors of a servile war. So impressed was British opinion with this argument, so disillusioned had it become after eighteen months of near inaction on the slavery question by the Administration, and so bemused was it by the complexities of Lincoln's reasons (most of which could not be stated explicitly) for issuing the proclamation in the peculiar form he did, that its initial reaction to the move was distinctly unfavourable.

Despite the clear appeal which it contained to the freed negroes to avoid violence, it was considered as an incitement to what Russell described as the "terrible"[1] expedient of a servile insurrection, and was vehemently attacked as such by supporters of the South. Britons were peculiarly susceptible to fears of race war at this time owing to the yet green memories of the Indian Mutiny. *The Times* reported in October, 1862: "Mr. Peacock, M.P. for North Essex, said at Colchester that the Emancipation Proclamation, even if it had been in the interests of the negro, would have been a political crime; but ... it was merely a vindictive measure of spite and retaliation upon nine millions of whites struggling for their independence, it was one of the most devilish acts of fiendish malignity which the wickedness of man could ever have conceived."[2] These attacks were peculiarly virulent because the ablest among the Southern supporters realized that the proclamation was potentially the most serious hindrance yet raised to their recognition and victory; so much was this so that the far-seeing Benjamin had probably admitted to himself by this time that emancipation of the slaves by the South offered the best hope of survival, though he knew that to propose it would be political suicide.

As Seward had feared, therefore, Britons, in the beginning, suspected or denounced the Proclamation; and it did at first sight appear as anomalous or worse that in fact it freed no single slave at the moment of its issue, since it applied only to areas in arms against the Union

[1] E.D.A., II, p. 49.   [2] Q. W.A.A.E., p. 328.

(that is, not yet reconquered) on the operative date, 1 January, 1863. Yet the reasons for this were cogent, if not unanswerable; Lincoln had still no constitutional power to interfere with slavery in the Union, and it would in any case have been politically and militarily disastrous to attempt to abolish it, without local consent, in the vital Border States; furthermore, the whole object, though it proved unavailing, of having a preliminary proclamation was to induce seceded states to return to the Union at the price of keeping their slaves, at least for the moment. Lincoln took a strong moral line against slavery, but never against slaveholders: at bottom he had always wished for gradual emancipation. His only power was the war power, and this he believed he could justly use against the main economic prop of the Southern system, and, indeed, that militarily it was his duty to do so; only by dealing the South this mortal blow and by arming the blacks could the war be shortened and possibly even won. Yet although these were his reasons, he was also very well aware that he was signing the ultimate death warrant of slavery, for, as the armies of the North penetrated the South, increasing numbers of negroes would be freed, in practice as well as in theory, and when the war was won this step could never be retraced; slavery in the Confederacy would inevitably be doomed by Northern victory, and how long would Border State slavery be able to survive it? In many ways, the Proclamation showed Lincoln's peculiar combination of moral strength, political moderation and practical astuteness better than any other single act of his career. It is highly significant that though he had long been under violent pressure from the extreme radical wing of the Republican party to free the slaves, the Proclamation was attacked by most of them either as a half-measure or as an outright betrayal; small wonder that it was not at first understood in Britain.

But, though there is little evidence that Lincoln had its effect upon the foreign situation much in mind when he issued it, and no doubt that he was concerned primarily with the situation in America, it is hard to believe that he was not aware of the advantages which the North would gain abroad by identifying itself with the great anti-slavery cause. Certainly Adams in London had for some time been convinced of the great value of such a move in winning over English opinion, and, after the first widespread outburst of derision and contempt which greeted it, he proved to be right, though Seward was amply justified in having obtained the postponement of the Proclamation until after Antietam, since before that success the first outcry might just have turned the scales of British opinion in favour of mediation. It was significant that

Mason, the Confederate Agent in London, wrote home that it was generally believed the proclamation was issued "as the means of warding off recognition. . . . It was seen through at once and condemned accordingly."[1] But by the end of 1862 a great change was apparent in British opinion. The servile war had not eventuated, and the true worth of the Proclamation had begun to be apparent; Jefferson Davis's order that all slaves captured, even in the regular Northern army, should be handed over to their State authorities, that is to say in all probability to their death, enhanced rather than detracted from the new feeling towards the Proclamation. During 1863, urged on by anti-slavery meetings, speeches and publications, opinion mounted in favour of the North, particularly, according to Adams, among the ranks of the religious Dissenters and the working classes. This trend continued despite the fact that Southern sympathizers put forward their greatest propaganda efforts at this time. Even amongst the hitherto reputedly cool upper classes, pamphlets like Cairnes's *Slave Power*, a refutation of Spence's *American Union*, began to have a greater appeal, and even in the distressed areas, groups like the Manchester Working Men could send resolutions of support to Lincoln, such as that which obtained from him the reply, "I cannot but regard your decisive utterances upon the question as an instance of sublime Christian heroism which has not been surpassed in any age or country."[2] In the face of this rise in the temperature of public feeling all fear of British mediation or interference seemed at an end, yet Lyons was right to be apprehensive lest a strong American reaction should result from some failure of the British Government to fulfil its whole duty as a neutral, or even to fulfil the new American expectations of a more favourable attitude to their cause. The two nations, indeed, were not yet out of the wood, for just such a British failure in American eyes was in the making.

V

WE have seen how perturbed was Adams at the failure of the Government to prevent the sailing of the war-steamer 290 from Liverpool at the end of July, to a rendezvous with a British ship on the high seas, there to collect her armament and war material, and thence to a long and successful career of depredations against Northern shipping under her name of *Alabama*. This was not the first of the natural Southern

[1] Q. E.D.A., II, p. 104.   [2] Q. E.D.A., II, pp. 108-9.

efforts to supply themselves with some form of maritime force from British shipyards, though it was the most serious to date; nor was it to be the last, though it had the effect of calling attention to this problem of neutrality in no uncertain terms, owing to the understandable outburst of rage with which it was greeted in the North. What made it so peculiarly dangerous for Anglo-American relations was that the *Alabama* was not merely built in England and supplied from England, but had a crew largely consisting of British volunteers enlisted in the Confederate Navy. The root of the trouble, nevertheless, lay in the questionable legitimacy of constructing war vessels for belligerents in the ports of a neutral power, for however disastrous her subsequent career was to be, nothing more could now be done about the *Alabama*; it was clear, however, that others would soon be abuilding to follow her.

It is fair to note that the whole question was, in international law, in a very confused and uncertain state at this period, there being, in particular, no clear ruling as to the duties of neutrals with regard to the construction of belligerent warships. In the broad sphere of neutral duties the United States had already had severe problems to face in the Canadian rebellion of 1837 and the Crimean War. In the former case the American Administration had taken reasonable steps to enforce the existent law, and Congress had gone even farther by amending it in March, 1838, to give Federal officials power to act upon mere suspicion in order to prevent unneutral acts. The British Foreign Enlistment Act of 1819 forbade British subjects to "be concerned in the equipping, furnishing, fitting out, or arming, of any ship or vessel, with intent or in order that such ship or vessel shall be employed in the service" of a belligerent, but did no more than provide for preventive action or subsequent punishment on due proof of the offence. Yet in fact proof was extremely difficult, if not impossible, to obtain before the damage was done, while the South thought that they had found a loophole in the Act, which seemed to apply only to ships both constructed and equipped in the country. But even if international law, as is argued by Professor Owsley, allowed the construction of ships, and there were technical means of evading the British law, there is no doubt that the Foreign Enlistment Act was intended to prevent just such incidents as that of the *Alabama*. She had in effect slipped away while Adams was vainly trying to convince Russell and his advisers that the requisite evidence for a seizure existed; partly owing to bad luck, partly to dilatory methods and partly to unwise hesitations, by the time the Government had sent telegrams to stop the vessel it was clear of Liverpool. Russell might write, "I confess the proceedings of that vessel

487

are enough to rile a more temperate nation",[1] but he did not take steps to alter the situation, so that this pedantic insistence on the idea that offenders are innocent until they are proven guilty, in a sphere—international affairs—where it is not altogether applicable, became a source of grave difficulty in Anglo-American relations. Henry Adams believed at the time, and most of his countrymen long continued to believe, that the actions of the British Government were those of deliberate policy, when in fact they were the result of lethargy and inefficiency; it is indeed a nice instance of the proneness of the rest of mankind to see deep cunning in the policies of Perfidious Albion where in fact mere incompetence and stupidity all too often prevail.

The *Alabama* was the first serious mistake of its kind, and the British Government could perhaps be forgiven that, but when they subsequently took no effective steps to prevent its recurrence until the eleventh hour, there can be little excuse for them. Seward, too, contrived by imaginative diplomacy to bring home to them the gravity of the situation without precipitating a breach, for he hung over their heads as a threat a Congressional proposal to authorize privateering, against the use of which the United States was not pledged. Officially it was to be authorized against vessels of the type of the *Alabama*, but, as appeared likely to the British Government, in practice it might have been employed as a supplement to the blockade, which would have been most efficient and very damaging to British commerce. This threat without doubt had some effect upon British public opinion, which now began to think that the ministry had been unduly lax over the *Alabama*, for merchants, who had originally supported the ship-building interest in the matter, began to see that the *Alabama* was being all too successful against Northern ships engaged among other things in British trade; but it may also have encouraged a misguided obstinacy in members of the British Government who resented the American diplomatic pressure. That the supporters of the North, like Bright, chose this time to intensify their attacks upon the privileged classes and in favour of Parliamentary reform did not improve ministerial tempers. Meanwhile, it became common knowledge that Lairds, the shipbuilding firm, had in construction two formidable ironclad ships of war, equipped with rams for use against wooden vessels, which might, in Southern hands, have gone far to break the Northern blockade; though the Confederate agent for their purchase, Bullock, concealed their true destination, it was naturally suspected that they were for the South. It was this that gave peculiar point to the reply of Laird in a Commons debate on the

[1] Q. ibid, pp. 116, 121.

Alabama to Bright: "I would rather be handed down to posterity as the builder of a dozen *Alabamas* than as a man who applies himself deliberately to set class against class, and to cry up the institutions of another country which, when they come to be tested, are of no value whatever, and which reduce the very name of liberty to an utter absurdity." As a result of the debate Government opinion seemed to harden, and Palmerston not only defended its actions in the *Alabama* case, but avoided any kind of pledge as to the future.

Nevertheless, fear of American reprisals by privateering, and desire to avoid trouble with the North still proved the paramount concern of the Foreign Secretary, and a few days later the *Alexandra*, which was shortly to have joined the *Alabama*, was seized by the Government in Liverpool, in order that the law might be tested and, if possible, the danger averted. At this time, before news of the British action reached Washington, Lyons was showing himself extremely apprehensive as to the explosive nature of the situation, and was clearly of the opinion that steps simply had to be taken to prevent the escape of the vessel, and the evidence indicates that the seizure of the *Alexandra* resulted in a great change in Seward's attitude, for the privateering proposal was dropped, and he became more and more publicly cordial towards Lyons. He was justified in this, if not by the British Government's withdrawal from its position of insistence on clear proof to one of satisfaction with "apparent" intention,[1] at least by the growing feeling in Britain against Southern shipbuilding; but he remained vigilant none the less, which proved wise when judgment in the *Alexandra* case went against the Government in June. It was immediately appealed, and Seward seemed confident that the Government would find some way out of the impasse now that its intentions were satisfactory. He had been Governor of New York during the McLeod affair, and, like all American statesmen, he was familiar with the difficulties arising out of disagreement between the legislative and executive arms of government.

But these difficulties cannot be cited in exoneration of the British ministers, for they have in reality little importance under a unitary and sovereign central government; this whole problem in its purely legal aspect could have been settled, at any time, once and for all, by legislative action, and it is very hard to understand why it was not until long after the crisis that the Government announced its intention suitably to modify the Foreign Enlistment Act. Since the intention of the 1819 Act was reasonably clear, such action could hardly with

[1] Q. ibid, pp. 134, 136.

justice have been described as unneutral by the South. It is very difficult to agree with the argument of Maine that the amendment of the Foreign Enlistment Act in this sense in 1870 was reactionary, or of other jurists that it created a new offence—that of building a ship—which was not forbidden by the law of nations or by other municipal laws, for the object of the half-century-old legislation seems plain. During this period of delay the *Alexandra* case was twice appealed, and the Government twice defeated, which clearly demonstrated the ineffectiveness of the Act as it stood, after which the vessel proceeded to Nassau in the Bahamas, where it was again delayed by litigation, so that it took no part in hostilities against the North.

The reluctance of the Government to act seems particularly regrettable when it is remembered that effectiveness of action against the rams appeared to hinge exclusively upon the *Alexandra* precedent, for from 11 July, when Adams began to bombard Russell with affidavits as to their purpose and destination, public attention was increasingly focused on these vessels, which were so much more dangerous than the *Alexandra*, or indeed the *Alabama*, although the latter was, with some assistance from other commerce raiders, to destroy or incapacitate more than 250 Northern ships in the course of the war. The delay, necessitated by Russell's desire for enough evidence to convict, did not reflect any weakening in the Government's determination to seize the vessels in the end, but it was dangerous because it alarmed Adams, who was not kept fully informed. It was in fact two days after positive instructions to detain them had been given by Russell, on 3 September, that Adams presented to him his famous protest containing the ominous, if carefully and ambiguously phrased sentence, "It would be superfluous in me to point out to your Lordship that this is war." Happily, once the danger of escape was at an end, an ever warmer tone began to prevail in the State Department, for Seward's confidence had been justified. To avoid further risk from legal torpedoes, the rams were finally purchased by the British Government, partly perhaps because it did not wish to push its case to a legal conclusion in view of the likelihood of Northern claims against Britain for the damage done by the *Alabama*. Significant, also, of the new sympathy was a Foreign Office communication sent at this time to the Confederate Secretary of State, calling upon the South to "forbear from all acts tending to affect injuriously Her Majesty's position"[1] in this matter of getting warships built in British ports. This air of resolution undoubtedly owed much to the realization in Britain of the grave dangers with which she herself

[1] Q. ibid, pp. 144, 148.

might be faced in future wars, if enemies without maritime resources could furnish themselves with a navy from any neutral state that could provide it.

Equally significant is the fact that the message was not sent through Mason, the Confederate Agent, probably because this would have come too near to an appearance of recognition, for it shows in some measure how very strong was the pro-Northern tide now running in Britain. Indeed, by the middle of 1863 it can fairly be maintained that all serious danger of conflict between the North and Great Britain was at an end. Yet, perhaps because of their increasing weakness at home and abroad, the Southerners and their friends and supporters seem to have been at this period more active in Britain than at any time previously, when they abounded in confidence, or later, when the hand of defeat was heavy on them. They took full advantage of the conviction, which was still retained by most Englishmen, and expressed by Trollope, in late 1862, after an actual tour of the North, that "The North and South are virtually separated," to which he even added, "and the day will come in which the West also will secede."[1] In 1863 Freeman published the first volume of his uncompleted work, bearing the significant title, *History of Federal Government from the Foundation of the Achaean League to the Disruption of the United States.* The activities of friends of the South, in organizing public meetings and other forms of propaganda, were redoubled, and one of their most influential agencies, the Southern Independence Association, came into existence at this time.

The Confederate Government was beginning to run seriously short of European funds, and, in an endeavour to rectify this and to create a powerful European vested interest in favour of the South, the French firm of Erlanger and Company was persuaded to float, in March, 1863, the "Seven per cent: Cotton Loan of the Confederate States of America for 3 Millions Sterling at 90 per cent", most of which was subscribed in Britain. Sufficiently good terms were offered to make it appear less of a wild speculation than it was to turn out, but it realized much less than was hoped for the Confederacy, and became a source of political weakness rather than strength. Most of the $12 million of bonds left outstanding at the end of the war were in the hands of British investors, but these people bought them, not out of sympathy for the South so much as out of that desire for investments bearing a high rate of interest which had already cost so many Englishmen dear in the American market.

[1] Q. ibid, p. 113.

Shortly after the launching of the loan, the pro-Southern Roebuck, on 30 June, moved his famous motion in the House of Commons requesting the Queen to enter into negotiations with foreign powers for joint action in recognition of the Confederacy, but it turned out as disappointing to the Southern cause as the loan had been, since he had to withdraw it, in the certainty that it would be overwhelmingly defeated by Government forces, supported by most of the Tories, whose attitude he had seriously misunderstood. This grave blow to the Southern cause in England—Owsley calls the whole business a "farce"[1]—was quickly followed by the arrival of news of the Northern victories at Gettysburg and Vicksburg; and the disappearance of Southern hopes of English interference to their benefit was shown, not merely in the decline of pro-Southern activity and feeling, but in Benjamin's withdrawal of Mason on 4 August on the ground that "your continued residence in London is neither conducive to the interests nor consistent with the dignity of this Government."[2] Public opinion in the South rose correspondingly against Britain, and by the end of the year diplomatic relations had been finally severed by the expulsion from the Confederacy of all her remaining consuls.[3] Despite periodic difficulties, occasioned by such things as a wild notion of Russell's (perhaps precipitated by Seward's irritating insistence that the war was nothing but the crushing of a rebellion) of withdrawing Northern belligerent rights unless those of the South were conceded by the Administration, which was happily and effectively discouraged by Lyons, and also by such things as the sometimes tactless efforts of Northerners to recruit soldiers in Ireland, the Foreign Secretary gave a fair indication of the state of relations when he wrote to Lyons at this time: "I hope you continue to go on quietly with Seward. I think this is better than any violent demonstrations of friendship which might turn sour like beer if there should be a thunderstorm. But I am more and more persuaded that amongst the Powers with whose Ministers I pass my time there is none with whom our relations ought to be so frank and cordial as the United States."[4]

Hopes cherished by Lindsay and Spence, and other Southern friends, during the first part of 1864, that Palmerston and Russell were prepared to execute a volte-face in favour of Southern recognition, can be explained by the wishful thinking, to which they were still prone following the continuation of Southern resistance after the defeats of the previous year, and by the cunning political manipulations by means of

[1] Owsley, p. 450.   [2] Q. E.D.A., II, p. 179.

[3] Milledge L. Bonham, *The British Consuls in the Confederacy* (New York 1911), p. 233.   [4] Q. E.D.A., II, pp. 183-4.

which the two old politicians hoped to get all the Parliamentary support they could for their Schleswig-Holstein policy, which was under such heavy fire at the time. By this date the British Government certainly had no intention whatever of departing from the neutrality policy. Disappointment in Britain at the long and obstinate continuance of the war, and the feelings of sympathy for the South in their long, remarkable and gallant struggle against a much more powerful opponent, were more than outweighed by the now dominating conviction that the war was in truth a war against "the foul blot" of slavery.

So overwhelming was the anti-slavery sentiment that even the most pro-Southern organs, such as the *Index*, never dared to defend the institution as such, but merely to point out that in the South it was not what it appeared; and even this was going almost too far for safety. Most able Southern supporters, such as Spence, held out the promise of Southern emancipation in due time, and this idea at length began to permeate even the Southern Administration itself. Benjamin, the ablest and most realistic of its members, had long been moving in this direction, and by the end of 1864 had not merely come to see the necessity for the arming of the slaves, with emancipation as the reward for service, but had persuaded Davis to send an emissary to Europe with an offer of emancipation in return for recognition. This was, indeed, as the South had said of Lincoln's Emancipation Proclamation, a last despairing hope, but it came too late to be of any use : the cause was too hopeless and public opinion in Britain too overwhelmingly against the system by which the South had lived, as was shown clearly by the cessation of Southern public meetings, and, paradoxically, by the drop in the number of pro-Northern meetings, which showed that people needed no more convincing. Yet, even now, much of the Press, such as *The Times*, was slow to realize or admit that complete Northern victory was in sight; the re-election of Lincoln, though generally welcomed, did not convince them; Sherman's capture of Atlanta hardly did it; only with the news of Appomattox did some of them seem to realize at last that Northern reconquest of the South, final and absolute, had been achieved.

VI

How is this obduracy in some circles in Britain to be explained? Partly, no doubt, by the incompetence of men like Delane, the editor of *The Times*, as military critics; and partly by such things as the rapidity of the final collapse, the vast distances involved, the daring of Sherman's march to the sea through Georgia, and the short-sighted obsession of observers with the Virginia front. But the real explanation must go much deeper. These were mere excuses for failing to see the truth: the real reason lies at the very heart of the matter, in the claim of the Lincoln Administration and its supporters everywhere, that the war was fundamentally a war for democracy. This claim, its rebuttal by the South, and its effect in Britain, make a fascinating subject of study, which helps to explain much that otherwise appears mysterious in British actions and thoughts. In other respects the attitude of most Britons was fairly clear; all, even Palmerston, long a powerful fighter against the slave trade, disliked the peculiar institution of the South; some among the commercial interests favoured the South in their desire for free trade; some held essentially to the need for a neutrality which would keep us out of the war; some favoured the restoration of the Union, lest a frustrated North turn and rend Canada; others, like Palmerston again, were not unwilling to see a powerful rival weakened by dismemberment. But all were affected in their judgment by their view of the United States as the stronghold, and now the great testing ground, of free and democratic institutions. Lincoln had from the very first maintained what he was to express so wonderfully later, that the war was to test whether the American nation or any other nation "conceived in liberty, and dedicated to the proposition that all men are created equal . . . can long endure": the North was resolved to ensure "that government of the people, by the people, for the people, shall not perish from the earth."[1] In his first message to Congress in special session on 4 July, 1861, he declared: "[T]his issue embraces more than the fate of these United States. It presents to the whole family of man the question whether a constitutional republic or democracy—a government of the people by the same people—can or cannot maintain its territorial integrity against its own domestic foes."[2] "This is essentially a people's contest."[3] It was not merely that slavery was undemocratic—here the issue was clouded by Lincoln's moderate view that the negroes were not then fitted for political rights—but that the whole democratic method was on trial before the world.

This was vehemently denied by the South, on grounds that are not without interest. Jefferson Davis, steeped, like his Southern contemporaries, as Owsley points out, in the social contract and natural law theories of eighteenth-century rationalism, maintained that liberty

---

[1] Abraham Lincoln, *Complete Works, Comprising His Speeches, Letters, State Papers, and Miscellaneous Writings,* Ed. John G. Nicolay and John Hay (New York, 1920), II, p. 439.   [2] Ibid, pp. 57-8.   [3] Ibid, p. 64.

consisted in the preservation of certain natural rights against the encroachments of the central government, that in the United States these liberties were protected by a fixed constitution and by the powers of the States, and that Lincoln's doctrine would convert it into a government of the mass, which was the very antithesis of democracy because it left a minority powerless in the hands of the majority. Our feeling about this argument is hopelessly biased by our knowledge that the chief right the South desired to protect was that of keeping its negroes enslaved, but it should not be allowed to blind us to the fact that enlightened liberal opinion was beginning to move in the nineteenth century towards just this Southern view of liberty. When tyrants had ruled, the claim that the people should govern themselves was sufficient unto itself, but with the establishment of free governments, the spectre of the tyranny of the majority began to raise its head; it was this problem of controlling the overweening majority which exercised, above all others, the mind of John Stuart Mill, greatest of nineteenth-century English liberal thinkers, in his *Essay on Liberty* published in 1859. Lord Acton strongly sympathized with the South for this reason. He wrote to Lee in 1866:

> I saw in State Rights the only availing check upon the absolutism of the sovereign will, and secession filled me with hope, not as the destruction but as the redemption of Democracy. The institutions of your Republic have not exercised on the old world the salutary and liberating influence which ought to have belonged to them, by reason of those defects and abuses of principle which the Confederate Constitution was expressly and wisely calculated to remedy. I believed that the example of that great Reform would have blessed all the races of mankind by establishing true freedom purged of the native dangers and disorders of Republics. Therefore I deemed that you were fighting the battles of our liberty, our progress, and our civilization; and I mourn for the stake which was lost at Richmond more deeply than I rejoice over that which was saved at Waterloo.[1]

This must give us pause, and make us consider carefully before we accept out of hand the assertions of the North that theirs was the cause of democracy, although in the end we must agree with Lincoln that the doctrine of secession is the essence of anarchy.

But this whole question adds greatly to the complexity of the already complicated British reactions to the Civil War, for it made strange bedfellows. Gladstone, who, although he had not yet entirely thrown

[1] Q. D. S. Freeman, *R. E. Lee* (New York, 1935), IV, pp. 516-7.

off the conservatism of his early years, was able to make in 1864 the vital pronouncement which so alarmed some of his colleagues—"I venture to say that every man who is not presumably incapacitated by some consideration of personal unfitness or of political danger is morally entitled to come within the pale of the constitution"[1]—and who was already gaining popularity by his feeling for the rights of common men, yet could not but feel sympathy for the Confederacy, not merely because its fight was heroic but because it was a struggle on the part of a weaker body against the overpowering forces of a stronger: were it not for the strong "counter-current"[2] of feeling which arose in his mind because of the South's connexion with slavery, he would, like his friend Acton, have regarded the issue purely as that of a nation "rightly struggling to be free."[3] He and, for the matter of that, Russell, who were apostles of Italian and to some extent Polish freedom, could not be insensible to this aspect of the Confederate cause, and he was later to say of the slavery of the South that it was their calamity rather than their crime. It is an interesting paradox that those favouring recognition of the South could come almost as well from the liberal as from the reactionary camps; both extremes could agree upon this policy. But these complications must not be allowed to obscure the main fact, that the cause of the North came increasingly to be recognized for what it was, the cause of democracy, for this was of the greatest moment, since feeling for the North and joy at Northern triumphs became more and more associated with the movement for Parliamentary reform in Britain, and its future became closely bound up with the outcome of the Civil War. There is no doubt that the Northern victory greatly facilitated the passage of the Reform Bill of 1867.

Some American historians have, like E. D. Adams, thrown this American influence into perhaps too high relief, by exaggerating the impact it made upon the mind and actions of a Britain still powerful, and in many ways insular and complacent. It is true that she was still, in some respects, an aristocratic country; she boasted an Earl of Shrewsbury who could declare: "I see in America the trial of Democracy and its failure. I believe that the dissolution of the Union is inevitable, and that men now before me will live to see an aristocracy established in America."[4] But England was also in many ways a middle-class state; the economic policies of the previous two decades had not been those favoured by the landed great. And these middle classes were

[1] Morley, I, p. 569.   [2] Ibid, p. 538.
[3] Q. Van Auken.   [4] Q. E.D.A., II, p. 282.

very far from obstinate in their retention of political power, for hardly more than a blast of the trumpet was to be necessary before the walls of privilege fell. The truth is that there had been no great demand for reform, for which there had been a number of proposals in recent years; Russell had put forward bills in 1852 and 1854, Disraeli in 1859, and Russell again in 1860. Similarly, C. F. Adams was probably going too far when he wrote to Seward in 1864: "There is no longer any sort of disguise maintained as to the wishes of the privileged classes. Very little genuine sympathy is entertained for the rebels. The true motive is apparent enough. It is the fear of the spread of democratic feeling at home in the event of success."[1]

The generalization was far too sweeping, but there were undoubtedly many who had long felt a lingering regard for the "Aristocracy" of the South, and who became obsessed as the war proceeded with the fear of reform at home. In a mild degree Palmerston was one, for in many ways he himself constituted the principal obstacle to a widening of the franchise, and he had never concealed his personal lack of enthusiasm for the North; yet it is not certain to what extent the two were connected in his mind. The Civil War ended and Palmerston died in the same year, and it is not necessarily the case that the former was more influential in promoting reform than the latter, since the possibility of reform, indeed the trend towards it, plainly were already in existence in English life. But though the argument may be carried too far, there is without question substantial truth in it. There were those in Britain who hated democracy, and hated the North for that reason, and they said so in no uncertain fashion; there were many more of those who loved democracy, and loved the Northern cause for that reason, and they said so with equal if not greater vigour. But the specific identification of reform with Northern victory, from the end of 1861 onwards, was almost exclusively the work, and the deliberate work, of the latter.

Indeed, almost to the extent that one man, Palmerston, was responsible for holding up reform, one man, John Bright, was responsible for its association with the Northern cause, and for its ultimate success. He was constantly in touch with Sumner, Chairman of the Senate Foreign Relations Committee, and through him with Lincoln, whom he resembled in some ways, and he sometimes gave a salutary reminder to the Administration of the existence of powerful opposition in Britain to a number of the acts of her government, which were distasteful to the North. He also made a significant contribution by tendering on

[1] Q. ibid, p. 300.

occasion calm advice to the Northern leaders, as when, in the *Trent* affair, his letters to Sumner were actually read aloud in Lincoln's Cabinet. But his greatest work was the succession of masterly speeches which he made up and down the country between the beginning of 1862 and the end of 1864 and which so aroused public feeling in favour of the North and reform; at these meetings he from time to time presented resolutions actually framed by Lincoln himself. The most famous and influential of these was that at a Trades Union Meeting in London on 26 March, 1863, in which he said :

> Privilege thinks it has a great interest in this contest, and every morning, with blatant voice, it comes into your streets and curses the American Republic. Privilege has beheld an afflicting spectacle for many years past. It has beheld thirty millions of men, happy and prosperous, without emperor, without king, without the surroundings of a court, without nobles, except such as are made by eminence, in intellect and virtue, without State bishops and State priests . . . without great armies and great navies, without great debt and without great taxes. Privilege has shuddered at what might happen to old Europe if this grand experiment should succeed. . . . I speak . . . to you, the working men of London, the representatives, as you are here tonight, of . . . the millions who cannot hear my voice. . . . Dynasties may fall, aristocracies may perish, privilege will vanish into the dim past; but you, your children, and your children's children, will remain. . . . You wish the freedom of your country. You wish it for yourselves. You strive for it in many ways. Do not then give the hand of fellowship to the worst foes of freedom that the world has ever seen. . . .[1]

These attacks may often have done more immediate harm than good to the cause of the North by hardening the hearts of some of those in power, and by causing in indefinable ways those delays and hesitations in governmental policy, of which we have seen so many, for, as Henry Adams wrote of this speech, "An ingenious man, with an inventive mind, might have managed, in the same number of lines, to offend more Englishmen than Bright struck in this sentence; but he must have betrayed artifice and hurt his oratory. The audience cheered furiously, and the private secretary [Adams] felt peace in his much troubled mind, for he knew how careful the Ministry would be, once they saw Bright talk republican principles before Trades Unions".[2] His father's outward attitude was characteristically more cautious, for, as he wrote to Seward, this particular meeting, as well as others of the kind, had verged

[1] Q. Trevelyan, pp. 307-8.   [2] *Education of Henry Adams*, pp. 189-90.

498

much too closely upon the minatory in the domestic politics of this Kingdom to make it easy to recognize or sympathize with by Foreign Governments. . . . I am not sure that some parties here would not now be willing even to take the risk of war in order the more effectually to turn the scale against us, and thus, as they think, to crush the rising spirit of their own population. That this is only a feeling at present and has not yet risen to the dignity of a policy may be true enough; but that does not the less impose upon the Government at home a duty so to shape its actions as, if possible, to defeat all such calculations and dissipate such hopes. . . . We owe this duty not less to the great body of those who in this kingdom are friends to us and our institutions, than to ourselves.

This policy Adams very properly followed, yet in fact he probably exaggerated the strength of privilege; the feeling never became more than a feeling, and he had spoken very wisely earlier when he said: "Hence it seems to me of the greatest consequence that the treatment of all present questions between the two nations should be regulated by a provident forecast of what may follow it [the political struggle in England] hereafter."[1] What followed after the death of Palmerston, and an abortive bill proposed in 1866 by Russell and Gladstone, was the Bill of 1867, a measure for which the demand was now so strong, that it was passed by a minority Tory ministry in a House of Commons elected under the influence of Palmerston, and that it was characterized by the Prime Minister of the government that proposed it, as "a leap in the dark."[2] Thus the future was democracy's, and it is perhaps not too much to claim that it was inevitably so even before the Civil War hastened the process; less competent as a diplomatic prophet of the immediate future than his father, Henry Adams with one of those flashes of deep insight which were later so characteristic of his historical writing saw the real trend of things when he concluded his judgment on this great occasion: "Everyone called Bright 'un-English'. . . but to an American he seemed more English than any of his critics."[3] In this way, as the war moved to its close, the British public, with Dissenting and working-class opinion increasingly vociferous on foreign and domestic issues, swept along on a mounting tide of enthusiasm for the North.

This tide became irresistible and universal when peace was

[1] Q. E.D.A., II, p. 294.
[2] R. Muir, *A Short History of the British Commonwealth* (4th Edition, London, 1927), II, p. 512.   [3] *Education of Henry Adams,* p. 190.

immediately followed by the assassination of Lincoln. Bright might be expected to write to Sumner, "For fifty years, I think, no other event has created such a sensation in this country. . . . The whole people positively mourn, and it would seem as if again we were one nation with you, so universal is the grief, and the horror of the deed";[1] but it was a measure of the revolution in British feeling that *The Times* could write: "If anything could mitigate the distress of the American people in their present affliction, it might surely be the sympathy which is expressed by the people of this country. We are not using the language of hyperbole in describing the manifestation of feeling as unexampled. Nothing like it has been witnessed in our generation." It was Disraeli, with his characteristic mastery of sentiment, who struck the best note in the Parliamentary debate:

> There are rare instances when the sympathy of a nation approaches those tenderer feelings that generally speaking, are supposed to be peculiar to the individual, and to form the happy privilege of private life; and this is one. . . . [I]n the character of the victim, and even in the accessories of his last moments there is something so homely and so innocent that it takes as it were the subject out of all the pomp of history and the ceremonial of diplomacy; it touches the heart of nations, and appeals to the domestic sentiment of mankind. . . . Nor is it possible for the people of England, at such a moment, to forget that he sprang from the same fatherland, and spoke the same mother tongue.[2]

Not until the death, eighty years later, of another American President at the end of another great war, though a foreign one and one in which Britain and America stood side by side as allies, was the British public to be so moved by the passing of a great American statesman. The power of the legend which has surrounded Lincoln's name was certainly augmented, if it was not created, by his death, but the grip of that legend upon the imagination of the British people, almost as tenacious as upon that of the Americans, has been a measure of and a factor in the growth of Anglo-American friendship.

VII

FOR by 1865 the relations of the two peoples were once more upon a sound footing, and with the advent of political reform in Britain it really was for the first time becoming a broad relationship between

[1] Q. Trevelyan, p. 326.   [2] Q. E.D.A., II, pp. 260-1, 263-4.

peoples. Yet the auspices were not quite as favourable as they had been in 1860, for the war had thrown up in its course new disputes, which remained to be settled, and had also re-opened ancient sores; more than that, it had revived the old deep feelings of hatred and ill will in the United States towards Britain. Henry Cabot Lodge said that, "The North was left with a bitter sense of wrong and outrage, and the South with a conviction that they had been uselessly deceived and betrayed."[1] Seward had once instructed Adams that the conduct of Great Britain during the war must be regarded "as a national wrong and injury to the United States,"[2] and though his opinion might have altered, that of the American public as a whole had not; neither now, nor for many years to come, could most Northerners, as a natural result of the long and agonizing war, see the British attitude of neutrality as an inevitable result of circumstances, any more than they could welcome the South back into the fold in the superhumanly charitable fashion that Lincoln had wished. To them it remained true that "he who is not for me is against me", and "For nearly half a century after the . . . [w]ar the natural sentiments of friendship, based upon ties of blood and a common heritage of literature and history and law, were distorted by bitter and exaggerated memories."[3] This spirit was not, on the whole, reciprocated in Britain, for the power of the class which had in the past been foremost in hatred of American democracy was permanently weakened by the Reform Bill of 1867, but in the months after the war ended, when the Union still had vast armies in being, it rose to a high pitch amongst the American people; for they were very conscious of the fact that with their victory had come, not only a short-term military might of unprecedented strength, but a long-term political power far greater than they had ever possessed before in their history. This strength was amply illustrated by the hasty way in which Napoleon withdrew his interfering hands from Mexico, on Seward's prompt reassertion of the principles of the Monroe Doctrine, and this American diplomatic triumph had the effect, in some degree, of diverting immediate American attention from Britain, and above all from British North America.

This was fortunate, for the last years of the war had witnessed difficulties in plenty between the United States and her northern neighbour, upon whom a large proportion of America's animosity against Britain was concentrated. The gravest of the difficulties, most of which arose from those peculiar problems of neutrality on a long

[1] Q. R. B. Mowat, *Americans in England*, p. 186.
[2] Q. Dunning, p. 244.   [3] E.D.A., II, p. 305.

frontier which we have seen to exist also in earlier years, resulted from the activities of accredited agents of the Confederacy in Canada, who fomented a series of border incidents, culminating in a raid by twenty-five Confederates on St. Albans, Vermont, in October, 1864, which inflicted casualties and caused much damage; though not in uniform, the men claimed with truth to be acting under the direct orders of the Confederate Government. Opinions vary as to the degree of blame to be attached to the Canadian authorities, but they seem to have been at least as blameworthy as the United States Government was to be over the Fenian raids of 1866 which we shall discuss shortly; certainly there was from the first a strong spirit of reprobation amongst Canadians of the failure of their own government to prevent such incidents, and it is probably true that they took more effective steps to prevent any recurrence of them than the Administration was then to do, but there were unfortunate hitches and delays in bringing the captured members of the band to justice, owing to the confusion in law as to the responsibility of agents acting directly under the orders of a foreign power.

There were no further incidents of this degree of seriousness, but tension had risen so high on the American side of the border that before the end of October Seward gave notice, in accordance with the terms of the Rush-Bagot agreement, that "at the expiration of six months . . . the United States will deem themselves at liberty to increase the Naval Armament upon the Lakes, if, in their judgment, the condition of affairs in that quarter shall then require it."[1] This was ratified by Congress, and in December severe passport restrictions were introduced by the United States on their northern border. Furthermore, opinion hostile to the Reciprocity Act had long been gathering strength in the United States. Though there was a strong protectionist interest in favour of abrogation, there were also those in favour of retaining the purely economic aspects of reciprocity, but, since it had been on balance more advantageous to Canada, and since there was less opposition to it there, irritated American opinion tended to unite against it for political reasons. After long consideration the Congress passed in January, 1865, a joint resolution, authorizing the President to give notice of the termination of the Reciprocity Treaty in 1866, which was accordingly done. This meant that the pleasure with which Seward's withdrawal, both of the passport restrictions and the notice of abrogation of the Rush-Bagot agreement (which he had always claimed would be temporary), in March, 1865, was greeted in Canada,

[1] Q. L. B. Shippee, *Canadian American Relations, 1849-1874* (New Haven, 1939), p. 133.

was considerably lessened, and other occasions of disagreement rapidly appeared.

But all these difficulties derived their malignity from the whole attitude of the United States in 1865; had it been benign, they could have been easily overcome, but it was not—it was "truculent and expansionist." "I know", cried Seward, who was much more cordial to Britain now than the radical Republicans, "that Nature designs that this whole continent, not merely these thirty-six states, shall be sooner or later, within the magic circle of the American Union."[1] He was in 1867 to take a step towards the attainment of Nature's aim by the purchase of Alaska from Russia. Annexationist agitation in the United States had died away in the fifties under the influence of the Reciprocity Treaty, but during the course of the Civil War, and even more in the years immediately following, it rose to a new intensity of enthusiasm in the ranks of the dominant majority of the Republicans, and men who were prepared to impeach a President, elected Vice-President by their own party, might very well not hesitate to employ force for a popular cause such as the absorption of Canada into the Union. Typical were the words of the New York *Herald* during the war: "When the termination of our civil conflicts shall have arrived, it may be the turn of our foreign enemies. . . . Four hundred thousand thoroughly disciplined troops will ask no better occupation than to destroy the last vestiges of British rule on the American Continent, and annex Canada to the United States."[2]

It was not surprising that British North America was apprehensive of American intentions, for there was by this time little support for annexation north of the border; the greater the American pressure, the greater was the Canadian irritation and the stronger seemed to her the ties binding her to the mother country. But these ties were now weaker on the English side than ever before, for with free trade Little Englandism had continued to gain strength, and Bury's "natural law of colonial independence"[3] was widely accepted; a change was in fact not so very distant, but Disraeli, who was to be one of the chief agents of that new imperialism, could still exclaim now, "An army maintained in a country which does not permit us even to govern it! What an anomaly!"[4] Even Queen Victoria wrote in her diary on 12 February, 1865: "Talked of America and the danger, which seems approaching, of our having a war with her as soon as she makes peace; of the impossibility of our being able to hold Canada, but we must struggle for it;

[1] Q. Brebner, p. 165.   [2] Q. Shippee, p. 185.
[3] Brebner, p. 172.   [4] Q. ibid. p. 173.

and far the best would be to let it go as an independent kingdom under an English prince."[1] Thus in the separate provinces of British North America, to fear of the United States was added an uncomfortable sense of isolation from Britain, as well as from one another; the British Minister in Washington impressed upon the mother country the need for her "to support by all the force at her command her colonies as long as they are loyal and to resent injustice towards them as an injustice to herself",[2] but at the same time he made it clear—almost uncomfortably clear from the Canadian point of view—that she would be happy at any time to grant British North America its freedom. The result was a great increase in the strength of the movement towards Confederation in the provinces, particularly Canada, where centred the chief special interests, railroad and financial, in favour of the union; to these particular incentives were added the obvious advantages, in strategy and in communications with the Far East, to be derived from Confederation.

Though in fact American pressure began to weaken slowly after the coming of peace, this was not immediately apparent in Canada, which saw, for example, with some misgivings, a bill introduced into the House of Representatives in 1866 to admit her to the Union. Furthermore, early in the same year, the Fenian question began to assume formidable proportions. The Fenian Brotherhood became prominent after the recent troubles in Ireland, and was pledged ultimately to the establishment of Irish independence, but its immediate objectives included anything which would weaken or annoy Britain. Since, after the full flood of Irish emigration to the United States, it was primarily financed and inspired by Irishmen in America and never was able to obtain the undivided support of the native Irish peasantry, Canada was an obvious point of attack. Pressure could here, in their eyes, be brought to bear upon Britain to relieve Ireland, and there were even wilder ultimate notions of a conquest of Canada. The American Press gave some support to them, American politicians did not like to run the risk of losing the Irish vote, and there were those in the United States who were not averse from giving Canadians a dose of their own St. Albans medicine; so that considerable strain was placed upon Canadian resources in preparing to meet the threat. On 31 May, 1866, some hundreds of Irishmen crossed the border at Buffalo, by night, in boats, but were easily dispersed the next morning by Canadian forces; this was, however, the most serious of all the border troubles of this kind to date and the least defensible. What is more, the American Government made no real effort to prevent the preparations for the invasion

[1] Q. Bemis, p. 381.   [2] Q. Shippee, p. 194.

before it actually took place, and, though they took very prompt measures after it had begun and seized no less than seven hundred prisoners themselves (so that they were even congratulated by the British), they proclaimed rather too rapidly afterwards that all danger was at an end, for there were sporadic alarums and excursions until a last futile raid in 1870. Meanwhile, the Canadian prisoners eventually received long terms of imprisonment, as did some captured on the American side of the border, and the public excitement died away.

But it had been enough in 1866 to win over Canadian waverers to the cause of Confederation, and by the British North America Act of 1867, the Dominion of Canada came into existence on 1 July of that year. It had a Federal system of government, owing as much to the American as to the British example, and consisted in the first instance of the provinces of Ontario, Quebec, New Brunswick and Novia Scotia; it was joined in 1870 by Manitoba, in 1871 by British Columbia and in 1873 by Prince Edward Island, while Newfoundland remained aloof. It was a revolutionary step in the development of the British Commonwealth of Nations, and fulfilled the prophecy of Henry Adams when he wrote, "For England there is still greatness and safety, if she will draw her colonies around her, and turn her hegemony into a confederation of British nations."[1] Most important of all, it gave Canada the strength for independent political, and ultimately economic, existence, and, though it was not at once apparent, it ended all possibility of realizing, unless by force, the American dream of annexation, which was as old as the United States itself. The irony of the situation was that in this very American ambition lay the chief reason for its own failure, for Confederation was primarily made a political possibility by fear of the United States. In some quarters of the great Republic the news was unwelcome. In March, 1867, the House of Representatives had actually passed a resolution deploring the formation of the Dominion as a step in the direction of strengthening the institution of monarchy, and even the legislature of the State of Maine went on record against Canadian Union;[2] in 1869, before British Columbia joined Canada, much was heard of the desire of that gateway to Alaska for annexation to the United States, while in the same year Sumner was to show that extremists of the Republican party had one final arrow in their quiver with which to try and slay the dragon of British power in North America.

[1] Q. W.A.A.E., p. 323.
[2] Alice R. Stewart, "The State of Maine and Canadian Confederation" (in *Can.H.R.* XXXIII, June, 1952), pp. 148-164.

For, despite the restoration of sound relations between the British Government and the American Administration by the end of the war, the anti-British feeling in many sections of the American public still gathered like a storm around the highly charged question of the *Alabama* claims. For a time the dying anti-Northern interests in Britain had believed that the United States intended, in the words of Delane, the editor of *The Times*, "to finish off the dreadful Civil War with another war with us scarcely less horrible",[1] while even Dickens wrote: "If the Americans don't embroil us in war before long it will not be their fault. What with their swagger and bombast, what with their claims for indemnification, what with Ireland and Fenianism, and what with Canada, I have strong apprehensions."[2] In fact, however, the Administration in Washington, for four years acted as a buffer to Britain against the extremists in its own party, as indeed did its American representatives in London, for C. F. Adams, rich in honour and with a great part yet to play in Anglo-American friendship, was succeeded in 1868 by the veteran lawyer, Reverdy Johnson of Maryland, who wrote to Seward soon after arrival, "I continue to receive the strongest evidence from other members of the Government, as well as Lord Stanley and from the English public generally, of the friendly feeling entertained by them all for the Government and citizens of the United States."[3] But he was a convivial figure, as well as a garrulous and pompous one, and enjoyed himself so well as to justify his soubriquet of Junketing Reverdy Johnson; his speeches wooing the British were so effusive that they caused a smile even among those at whom they were aimed, but his *faux pas* in cordially shaking by the hand Laird, the builder of the *Alabama*, aroused more than smiles in the United States. Congress was at loggerheads with the Administration at the time, and an Act of Congress in 1867, enjoining the wearing of simple evening dress by American diplomats at formal ceremonies abroad, was characteristic of its belligerent democracy in these years. Johnson negotiated the ill-fated Johnson-Clarendon Convention on the instructions of his Government, but was promptly recalled by the new Grant Administration, which seemed, at first, likely to take a much stronger line over the *Alabama* claims than its predecessor.

Fortunately, given his own limitations, Grant had appointed the wealthy Hamilton Fish of New York Secretary of State, and this capable man was in due time to help make possible a comprehensive settlement of the differences with Britain. He did unwisely, however, to submit to the pressure of the Chairman of the powerful Senate Committee on

[1] Q. E.D.A., II, p. 254.　　[2] Q. Bailey, p. 406.　　[3] Q. W.A.A.E., pp. 337-8.

Foreign Relations, in appointing as Minister in London Sumner's friend J. L. Motley, the historian, for this high-spirited and able, but opinionated and, as he had proved while Minister at Vienna, tactless, man, very soon outran the precise and careful instructions Fish had given him on the *Alabama* claims, and began to press upon Clarendon, not the ideas of the Administration, but the extreme demands of Sumner. Though Grant wished to punish this disloyalty by instant dismissal, Fish prevailed on him to hold his hand in order not to alienate the influential Senator, but when relations between Grant and Sumner deteriorated hopelessly, owing to Sumner's refusal to support Grant's ambitions in Santo Domingo, which Fish encouraged as a screen behind which to pursue a settlement with Britain, nothing could save Motley. He was dismissed, after refusing to resign, in July, 1870, just a year after his arrival, the only withdrawal to date of an American Minister to Britain by the same President who appointed him, but by no means the "monstrous injustice"[1] Motley considered it, for he had imperilled good relations at a most critical stage in the *Alabama* dispute. Adams remarked that he evidently expected to represent two powers abroad, Mr. Sumner and the United States, and it is written that no man can serve two masters. Yet his fault was not so much lack of good will to Britain as an overweening ambition to bring off a great diplomatic *coup de main*, for he recorded a most enlightening conversation with Clarendon, the British Foreign Secretary, in which Clarendon, deeply moved, declared that "He could contemplate the possibility of war between Great Britain and any other foreign Power, but war with America inspired him with abhorrence. He regarded it as a *crimen non nominandum inter Christianos*. He never could bring himself to look upon Americans as foreigners". Motley, for his part "confessed to a despondent feeling sometimes as to the possibility of the two nations *ever* understanding each other—of the difficulty at this present moment of their looking into each other's hearts." "Yes," replied Clarendon, "[W]e both have the same Saxon stubbornness and absolute confidence in ourselves and each in our own cause. When we quarrel, it is Greek meeting Greek."[2]

It is comforting that such despondents as Motley have been elbowed aside in the forward march of Anglo-American history, and happily, Britain's Minister in Washington for the long period of thirteen years after his arrival in February, 1868, was no such despondent; able and very popular with the Americans, Sir Edward Thornton stayed long enough to see a marked change in the tone of the American Press and

[1] Q. W.A.A.E., p. 356.   [2] Q. ibid, p. 348.

public towards Britain, following the decline of the animosity of the immediate post-war period. To this waning of bitter anti-British feeling he contributed much himself, not least in the negotiating of the great Treaty of Washington, which laid the basis for settlement of the *Alabama* dispute and re-affirmed the tradition of Anglo-American arbitrations which had been established in the years before the Civil War.

Although Russell was later to admit, in his *Recollections*, that the delay which prevented the detention of the *Alabama* was "my fault as Secretary of State for Foreign Affairs",[1] he and Palmerston had brusquely refused in 1865 to consider claims arising from actions of the *Alabama*, since they were incompatible with the dignity of the British Crown, because "England would be disgraced for ever if a foreign government were left to arbitrate whether an English secretary of state had been diligent or negligent in his duties".[2] Seward, much more justifiably and equally brusquely, refused to agree to a joint commission to consider all mutual claims except those arising from the actions of the armed cruisers. In view of the belligerent mood of many Americans, things began to look grave, but public opinion in Britain did not support this Russell-Palmerston stand, for it saw the dangers it involved for the supreme naval power in future wars, particularly when, in 1866, the House of Representatives unanimously amended the Neutrality Act of 1818 to permit the sale of naval vessels to belligerents in time of war. Irishmen, indeed, were already seeing visions of a republic of Ireland fighting Britain with hosts of American-constructed *Alabamas*. With the change to a Tory government in 1866 Stanley stated a willingness, therefore, to arbitrate the *Alabama* question, but firmly refused Seward's demand to include consideration of whether the recognition of the belligerency of the Confederacy on 13 May, 1861, was justifiable; the matter therefore dropped.

In the next two years, though the Canadian Dominion came into existence and anti-British feelings began to die away in America, there still existed pressing difficulties, some of them new. Americans realized that the abrogation of Reciprocity had not, as they had some of them hoped, encouraged annexationism in Canada, but Confederation, and were correspondingly disillusioned; indeed Canada, coming to realize that the Americans would not again agree to large-scale reciprocal arrangements, began to move steadily in the direction of estab-

[1] *The Cambridge History of British Foreign Policy* (Cambridge, 1923), III, p. 59.   [2] Q. Morley, II, p. 4.

lishing her own protective system, which she in due course did. Meanwhile, a crisis arose from the fact that fishery interests in the Northeastern United States claimed to be very badly hit by the withdrawal of the fishing rights off the Canadian coasts which had been granted in the Reciprocity Treaty, although the Canadian authorities showed themselves reasonable, and desirous of an agreement, by instituting a licensing system which allowed Americans to fish for a nominal fee. Finally, the San Juan water boundary, later to be a Canadian matter, but still now, before the entry of British Columbia into the Confederation, one for the imperial government, was becoming increasingly irksome. Uneasiness at these difficulties on the part of the British Government, and Seward's desire to set the final seal on his long period of public service by an agreement with Britain, were sufficient to overcome the obstacles, and on 14 January, 1869, there was signed in London with the new Gladstone ministry, during Seward's last weeks as Secretary of State, the Johnson-Clarendon Convention.

This did not deal with any of the questions specifically, but consisted of general provisions for the arbitration, either by a mixed commission, or, if that failed, an arbitrator, of all claims upon either government arising since 1853. This agreement tacitly allowed of judgment upon every aspect of the American claims, including even the British recognition of the belligerency of the Confederacy, which she had hitherto refused to consider, so that it might have permitted a much more comprehensive settlement than was eventually achieved. But it did not strike Congress that way, for it merely made possible a mutual settlement of claims, and contained no particular mention of, let alone apology for, the *Alabama* incident. There is no doubt that it was widely unpopular, for Americans, even those as sane as C. F. Adams, had become obsessed with the idea that Canada might still be annexed as a kind of recompense for damage inflicted by the *Alabama*, a *quid pro quo* in settlement of American claims. This idea was, of course, encouraged by misunderstanding of England's readiness to let Canada go if she wished to do so; indeed, Thornton was quite unpopular in Canada for his emphasis on this fact, and had to make it very clear to Fish that "Great Britain is quite willing to part with Canada when the latter requests it, but will not cede it, in any negotiations, as a satisfaction for any claim, nor until Canada herself unequivocally expresses her wish for separation."[1] But that Britain was, in her own eyes, bound in honour in this way was not yet apparent in the United States, and on 13 April, 1869, the Senate rejected the convention by the vast majority

[1] Q. Shippee, p. 205.

of 54 to 1. This was a foregone conclusion, but the extreme form in which American claims were put in the debate by Sumner, who was beginning to show that lack of moderation which was soon to amount to near-insanity, was a severe shock to British public opinion. He not merely assessed the damage done directly by the *Alabama* at $15 million, and added $110 million for national losses arising from destruction of the American marine, but put forward a claim for indirect damages due to the prolongation of the war through Britain's moral and material support of the Confederacy; this he asserted had doubled the length of the war, which had cost $4,000 million and, as he said, "Everybody can make the calculation."[1] He did not say that the United States would take Canada instead of cash, but everyone knew that he meant it, for even he did not expect Britain to meet this staggering bill. As Senator Chandler aptly expressed it, he "put on file a mortgage upon the British North American Provinces for the whole amount."[2]

But Sumner had gone too far; as Henry Adams put it, "If war was his object and Canada were worth it, Sumner's scheme showed genius . . . but if he thought he could obtain Canada from England as a voluntary set-off to the *Alabama* Claims, he drivelled."[3] The reaction in England was such as might have been expected, and there is no doubt that Britain would have fought rather than submit to such claims as those suggested by the Chairman of the Senate Committee. This fact began to sink into the mind of Fish, partly through his close friendship with Thornton, and through his into the mind of the President, particularly as his relations with the increasingly violent Sumner got worse; though the Administration would, like other Americans, have been happy to acquire Canada, they had never been as sanguine or unrealistic as Sumner, who, when he persisted in demanding the withdrawal of the British flag from North America as a mere preliminary to negotiations, was forced out of his chairmanship in the same way that his disciple Motley had been from his ministry. Sometime in 1870, probably in September, Fish determined to take advantage of the informal negotiations which had been going on in Washington since 1869, partly through Sir John Rose, the Canadian Minister of Finance, and partly through Thornton, and to grant such concessions as were necessary to make full scale negotiations possible; under the influence of Gladstone and Clarendon, both of whom were perturbed by the uneasy international situation elsewhere, the British showed themselves prepared to meet him half way.

[1] Q. Bailey, p. 411.   [2] Q. Brebner, p. 171.
[3] *Education of Henry Adams*, p. 275.

510

A Joint High Commission to negotiate a settlement met in Washington on 27 February, 1871, consisting of five British representatives (including Thornton, the Earl of Ripon from Gladstone's Cabinet, Sir Stafford Northcote of the Conservative Opposition who was Governor of the Hudson's Bay Company, and, very significantly, Sir John Macdonald, Prime Minister of Canada), and five American representatives (including Fish and General Schenck, the Minister-Designate to London). On 8 May, after long and difficult negotiations, not unrelieved by some of the social festivities of which Elgin had showed the use in 1854, there came forth the Treaty of Washington. This was a magnificent, indeed monumental, diplomatic triumph, consisting of no less than forty-three articles on many and diverse subjects, and negotiated in effect, through the presence of Canada's representative, by three parties with different interests, knowing that it had finally to receive the approval of the Senate of the United States, the British Parliament, the Canadian Parliament, and the legislatures of Prince Edward Island and Newfoundland. That it did receive approval was particularly the achievement of Macdonald, for it was in Canada that it encountered the strongest opposition; already she was beginning to feel the weakness as well as the strength of her new position of virtual autonomy, in that her interests were likely to be sacrificed to the cause of Anglo-American concord. Thus in the negotiations Macdonald was, as he put it, the "nigger on the fence"[1], but he played his cards in masterly fashion, making the utmost use of every Canadian grievance, so that he gained as much as was humanly possible for his country. The crucial issue at bottom, however, was that of the *Alabama* claims between Britain and America, and when this was settled Canada was steadily edged into line by the mother country.

The last article of the treaty dealt with ratification formalities, and, the nine articles before that with arbitration of the San Juan dispute, which has already been discussed.* Articles 26 to 32 dealt with such questions as the mutual navigation of waterways, and the mutual conveyance of merchandise under bond. Articles 18 to 25 dealt with the vexed question of the fisheries, granting to the United States fishing liberties similar to those of the 1854 treaty, in return for more restricted rights granted to Canadians off the American coast. As well as imposing this limitation on mutual fishing rights the Americans refused to incorporate any reciprocity provisions in the treaty, except in the case of fish and fish oil, although these had been the basis of the original

[1] Q. Shippee, p. 364.   * See p. 414 above.

bargain with Canada seventeen years before. To compensate Canada, the American Government agreed to pay in cash a sum to be determined by arbitration, which was eventually fixed at $5,500,000 for the period of the treaty, a sum considered quite excessive by Americans. This, by Article 23, was to be for ten years, and then until two years after either party should give notice of termination, except for the provisions of a permanent nature, such as those dealing with the international law governing the *Alabama* incident.

These articles affecting Canada, even despite the monetary compensation provided, were most unpopular in the Dominion, because of their one-sidedness and their lack of reciprocity arrangements, and only the masterly political management of Macdonald made possible the acceptance of the treaty by a large majority of the Canadian Parliament. He had grasped already, and was able to bring home to Canadians, the three most important truths in Canadian political life; that Canada was a political hostage in the hands of America for the good conduct of Britain, that Canada's role should be that of peacemaker, and that, above all, friendly Anglo-American relations were more important to Canada even than they were to Britain and the United States themselves.

> Let Canada be severed from England—let England not be responsible to us, and for us, and what could the United States do to England? . . . England has got the supremacy on the sea—she is impregnable in every point but one, and that point is Canada; and if England does call upon us to make a financial sacrifice . . . for the good of the Empire . . . I say that we would be unworthy of our proud position if we were not prepared to do so. I hope to live to see the day, and if I do not that my son may be spared to see Canada the right arm of England, to see Canada a powerful auxiliary to the Empire, and not a cause of anxiety and a source of danger.[1]

The Canadians did not press their claims for the damages arising from Fenian activities, on the understanding that Britain would make them some form of financial compensation, an illustration of the extent to which the final treaty was pressed on Canada by Britain for the general good of relations between the mother country and the United States.

Another illustration of this British policy of conciliation, also linked closely with the Irish question, was a separate Anglo-American treaty signed in 1870 which had been set on foot under Seward, and which had, indeed, been given diplomatic priority by him in

[1] Q. Shippee, p. 414.

512

his dealings with Britain. This finally settled the vexed question of mutual naturalization in accordance with American wishes; in fact, it was a minor American diplomatic triumph, for Britain at last gave up her old shibboleth, "once an Englishman always an Englishman" (which she had still applied quite recently to Irish-born naturalized Americans who got into trouble in Canada), thus admitting the full right of naturalization and expatriation for which the United States had long contended. In a last group of articles, which only partially affected Canada (12-17), a joint commission was set up to arbitrate the claims of the citizens of each country against the other during the period between 13 April, 1861, and 9 April, 1865, excepting only the *Alabama* claims. This commission eventually disallowed all the American claims, and awarded the sum of $1,929,815 to Great Britain.

Finally, the heart of the matter, the situation "growing out of the Acts committed by the several vessels which have given rise to the claims generally known as the *Alabama* Claims",[1] was dealt with in the first eleven articles. These opened with one containing words which the American Government accepted as a British apology: "Her Britannic Majesty has authorized her High Commissioners . . . to express in a friendly spirit, the regret felt by Her Majesty's Government for the escape, under whatever circumstances, of the *Alabama* and other vessels from British ports, and for the depredations committed by those vessels". An arbitration tribunal, to consist of appointees of the United States, Britain, Italy, Switzerland and Brazil, was set up to meet in Geneva as soon as possible "to examine and decide all questions that shall be laid before them" by either government, all questions to be finally decided by majority vote. But the terms of reference went much farther than this, and indeed than was usual in such cases, by laying down three rules to govern the arbitrators, which defined the duties of neutral governments as to the furnishing or assisting of belligerent war vessels in very strict terms. The salient rule ran:

> A neutral government is bound . . . to use due diligence to prevent the getting out, arming or equipping, within its jurisdiction, of any vessel which if has reasonable ground to believe is intended to cruise or to carry on war against a Power with which it is at peace; and also to use like diligence to prevent the departure from its jurisdiction of any vessel intended to cruise or carry on war as above, such vessel having been

[1] *Treaties and Agreements in Force affecting Canada between His Majesty and the United States of America* (Ottawa, 1927), p. 38 *et seq.*

specially adapted, in whole or in part, within such jurisdiction, to warlike use.

Both parties agreed "to observe these rules as between themselves in future, and to bring them to the knowledge of other maritime Powers and to invite them to accede to them." This agreement was of the greatest consequence to Britain, for it pledged the two leading maritime powers to accept, and to try and get others to accept, a very strict interpretation of neutral duty, and thus erected a formidable barrier against practices which might have been disastrous to the greatest of maritime powers in any struggle yet to come : it banished the nightmare of a horde of anti-British *Alabamas* in future wars.

But it was accompanied by another proviso, that Her Majesty's Government

> cannot assent to the foregoing rules as a statement of principles of international law which were in force at the time when the claims mentioned in Article 1 arose, but that Her Majesty's Government, in order to evince its desire of strengthening the friendly relations between the two countries and of making satisfactory provision for the future, agrees that, in deciding the questions between the two countries arising out of those claims, the Arbitrators should assume that Her Majesty's Government had undertaken to act upon the principles set forth in these rules.

This meant two things, the first quite simply being that Britain, for the selfish reason noted above, and from her genuine desire for good relations with the United States, was content to be judged by the strict law laid down; this was no mean concession, but was in fact the *sine qua non* of a treaty, and it meant that, at least over the *Alabama,* if not the other cruisers, she had virtually admitted her guilt before the tribunal met. But it meant also that, in order to save face, to preserve her honour, she did not admit that this had in fact been the law at the time; she accepted the strict rule as an act of grace and not the concession of a right. Thus, by a remarkable piece of diplomatic sophistry, Russell's point was heeded and judgment was not passed on a British Foreign Secretary directly; by diplomatic legerdemain worthy of a Gladstone ministry, Britain contrived both to have her cake and eat it. It is one of the instances—and they are in fact few—when Americans might have complained with justice of the wiles of old Albion, were it not that they themselves looked after their interests in like fashion on this occasion.

The United States also made a concession in agreeing to these terms, for the claims based on the allegedly premature recognition of the belligerency of the Confederacy by Britain were quietly dropped and not heard of again; this was wise, as well as politic, of the American representatives, for here their case was very weak. But one pitfall was left in the treaty, for no mention was made specifically of the indirect, as opposed to the direct, claims arising out of the activities of the *Alabama.* The British certainly believed that they had been dropped, too, and the Americans certainly believed that they could not have been specifically excluded in the terms of the treaty if it was to pass the Senate. In this exclusion there was, though at first not foreseen, a very serious potential cause of future difficulty. But it was still in the future, and the Treaty of Washington was from the first greeted, both in America and Britain, for the excellent and successful piece of diplomacy that it was; the press in both countries was on the whole favourable, although it was recognized even in America that, as the New York *World* put it, "nearly all of the concessions were made on the British side."[1] It was ratified by the Senate within sixteen days of its conclusion, by a majority of 50 to 12, even Sumner voting in its favour.

All the auguries now appeared favourable, but when on 19 December, 1871, the tribunal received the printed arguments, it became known that the American case unexpectedly included a claim for the indirect damages, which the British had believed to be dropped. Whether the Americans had intended to include this claim all along, or whether they changed their minds after the signing of the treaty, it appears likely that Fish included them at this stage lest Congress should refuse to execute the treaty which the Senate had ratified, and lest they should re-appear to bedevil the relations of the two countries in later years. The second of these motives was justified in the event, for as things turned out the claims were actually ruled out once and for all, whereas an omission of them might have caused trouble at a later date. That it was Fish's object to raise the claims merely in order to have them disallowed is demonstrated by the closeness with which the American arbitrator, C. F. Adams, worked with the American Government's representatives at Geneva in the eventual solution of the problem. But this was not seen in Britain, where all the old fears of annexationism were revived, and where more extreme elements did not scruple to charge the Americans with bad faith. The Government and Opposition leaders did not go so far, but were very incensed and alarmed. Gladstone calculated that Britain might conceivably be liable for the

[1] Q. Bailey, p. 419.

colossal sum of $8,000 million, eight times the reparations Germany had recently exacted from France, and, when Disraeli said that the claims were preposterous and wild, declared that this was an understatement, for "we must be insane to accede to demands which no nation with a spark of honour or spirit left could submit to even at the point of death."[1] Five months of delay, filled with diplomatic and public dispute, now intervened, and it looked as if Britain might renounce the treaty and refuse to go to arbitration, but in the end it was decided to go to the opening meeting of the tribunal on 15 June, but to ask for an adjournment for eight months because the two governments did not agree on the scope of arbitration.

Meanwhile, however, in America, public opinion, which had favoured the treaty, began to realize that Britain was in earnest and that it might be lost altogether; one English magazine pictured John Bull telling Brother Jonathan, "Look here my young friend! If you don't stop that howling about indirect damages, I'll give you some direct damages to howl for!"[2], while a financial panic resulting from fear of war was proving more costly to the United States than any failure to get indirect damages would be. America therefore greeted almost as gladly as did Britain the way out of the impasse devised by C. F. Adams on his own responsibility, though in consultation with the Americans at Geneva; it was a brave and noble act, not the less so for this support from his countrymen, and formed a fitting culmination to his role in the history of Anglo-American relations. He induced his colleagues, the other arbitrators, to precede their work by a spontaneous declaration that, according to the principles of international law, the indirect claims ought to be excluded from their consideration; this was made on 19 June, 1872, and was accepted by both parties. Adams justly said: "I should be assuming a heavy responsibilty; but I should do so, not as an arbitrator representing my country, but as representing all nations."[3]

On 14 September, the arbitrators gave their award; the highly-strung British arbitrator, Sir Alexander Cockburn, violently dissented in a manner hardly reflecting credit on British sportsmanship, but, though some sections of the public still remained disgruntled, the decision was accepted with a tolerably good grace by the British Government. The sum awarded to the United States on account of Britain's lack of "due diligence" was the fairly large one of $15,500,000, which was accordingly paid; this was done by means of a cheque, which, when cancelled, was framed and hung upon the wall of the Foreign Secretary's room in the Foreign Office, in proud memory of the greatest of Anglo-

[1] Q. Morley, II, p. 11.　　[2] Q. Bailey, p. 420.　　[3] Q. Morley, II, p. 15.

American arbitrations. It is customary in assessing the terms of the Treaty of Washington to balance this sum against the other two sums paid by the United States for claims and fishing rights, pointing out that the British Empire thus actually paid out only $8,070,181. This gives a false picture, for it ignores the new independence and importance of Canada, which received not only $5,500,000 for the fisheries, and no doubt some of the $1,929,812 claims money, but also a British loan, at a very low rate of interest, in return for the abandonment of the Fenian claims. Canada had to find no money, but paid the price by giving up fishing rights and foregoing hopes of reciprocal trade. The United States had to find $7,429,812, a larger sum than she liked but which she paid in time. Great Britain had to find 15\frac{1}{2}$ million outright, and guaranteed a loan of 12\frac{1}{2}$ million, which was no mean sum for a nation whose annual average exports to the United States between 1875 and 1879 amounted to $90 million.

But the results achieved were well worth the price. Few arbitrations are of much value unless their awards are in some degree painful to both parties, and the Treaty of Washington banished once more the fear of fratricidal war, at a time when in every other respect the prospects for amity were fast improving. It was a triumph for the policy of concession and conciliation, which alone has worked well between these two peoples; it confounded the pessimists, as for example Judah P. Benjamin, by then practising at the English Bar, who wrote: "I have long been of opinion that war is inevitable between the countries, and that our (*sic*) main cause of the calamity will be the inexplicable and inconceivable folly of the English in supposing that it is to be averted by concessions and indications of dread of results, instead of by a firmness of attitude and a manifestation of resolution to repel aggression."[1] Inconceivable folly in fact turned out to be the beginning of wisdom. But not only did the Treaty avert the immediate possibility of war; it also strengthened the tradition of negotiating and arbitrating even the most serious disputes between the two states, until it became eventually unbreakable. However bitter American feeling might be in the last great active crisis of Anglo-American relations —that over Venezuela later in the century—it is not to be believed that war was a serious possibility. This, indeed, is a measure of the progress in Anglo-American friendship since 1814.

[1] Q. Meade, p. 347.

CHAPTER FOURTEEN

THE QUIET YEARS (1872-98)

COMPARED with the years which preceded and followed them
the last years of the nineteenth century in Anglo-American relations were lacking in violent incident, but in international affairs
it is pre-eminently true that no news is good news. This period of relative
inaction served a most useful purpose in stabilizing the relationship of
the two countries and giving depth to the now still water running
between them. If we take 1898 as an approximate end to it, twenty-five
years have elapsed since the *Alabama* award, and, though not encom-
passing a complete political generation, a quarter of a century is a long
time; it is a span in which many old patterns of behaviour can drop out
and many new habits be formed. If, then, our treatment of these years
is brief, let their importance not be underestimated, for they allowed of
a vital change in the relations of the two peoples. Their quietude affords
a lull between two periods of activity, but the new activity of the twentieth century will be of a different type from that of the nineteenth, for
it is in this period that the balance of strength passed decisively from
Britain to America: the great republic was, by the end of it, greater
in population, stronger economically, and potentially more formidable
politically than Britain. Henry Adams rightly wrote of the year 1867,
"The revolution since 1861 was nearly complete, and for the first time in
history the American felt himself almost as strong as an Englishman.
He had thirty years to wait before he should feel himself stronger."[1]
The result of this change was in the end that emergence of the United
States as a world power of the first magnitude, which will be the theme
of the final Part of this work, and it was a good thing for Britain that the
basis of her friendship with the United States was by this time well and
truly laid.

Up to the end of the Civil War and its aftermath, their relations had
been much troubled, and concerned very largely with the solution of
the difficult problems outstanding between them: with defining
beyond dispute, as it were, their spheres of habitation and of influence.
After the Quiet Years they were to be concerned, broadly speaking, with

[1] Q. W.A.A.E., p. 334.

518

the ripening of cordiality and with laying the groundwork for actual international co-operation. These two developments, moreover, occurred against very different backgrounds in world affairs; their problems in the nineteenth century were on the whole peculiarly Anglo-American problems, developing, if not in a vacuum, at least in an atmosphere which owed little to the actions of other powers; those of the twentieth were by no means peculiar to the two Western nations, but rose more and more directly from wider world events, which could not be ignored, and over which the United States and Britain had at best but a limited control. Amidst the tumult and darkness which bade fair in these later years to engulf mankind, the knowledge of fundamental agreement and friendship between them was an increasing solace and comfort to both, though most particularly to Britain, whose weakness, relative to America, was becoming steadily more apparent. But such developments were, as yet, in the future, and these must be regarded as halcyon days, in which the history of Anglo-American relations pursued an unwontedly even course.

It is characteristic of the period that the diplomatic representatives of the two powers were, for the most part, quiet men who worked steadily but effectively at the task of tying more tightly their bonds of friendship. Of the American Ministers in the seventies, only the name of General Robert Schenck sticks in the British memory, and that because of his enforced resignation, owing to a connexion with one of the unsavoury financial transactions of the Grant period, but with the appointment of James Russell Lowell, the author and scholar, in 1880, all traces of the influence of the Gilded Age disappeared from American representation in London. Lowell was inclined to be sensitive to criticism of his country, and was indeed the author of an essay, "On a certain Condescension in Foreigners", but he strove to be fair to Britain and became exceedingly popular there. He also became very happy, declaring that he liked London beyond measure, and, more surprisingly, that *"The climate also suits me better than any I ever lived in."*[1] But his rectitude and impartiality over the difficult Irish question made him as unpopular in certain sections at home as he was popular in Britain, so that he was on one occasion denounced for his "sickening sycophancy to English influence".[2] His views on Ireland were, indeed, too blunt and realistic for lovers of the shamrock among his own countrymen : "The true office of the Irish Washington would be to head a rebellion against thriftlessness, superstition and dirt. The sooner the barri-

[1] Q. W.A.A.E., p. 383.   [2] Q. ibid, p. 382.

519

cades are thrown up against these the better."[1] Henry James wrote his political epitaph for him in 1885 : "Don't forget that you have produced a relation between England and the U.S. which is really a gain to civilization."[2]

His successors, Edmund J. Phelps (1885-9) and Robert Todd Lincoln (1889-93) carried out their duties with efficiency but without ostentation, the latter indeed with all the simplicity of his father, which to some extent counteracted the flamboyance of his Secretary of State, Blaine. Lincoln was certainly appointed partly because of the need felt in America to have a representative clearly proof against the insidious wiles of English men and society. To succeed him, in 1893, came a man of great ability and distinction, an eloquent diplomat with a good measure of that chivalry appropriate to one of his name, Thomas Francis Bayard. It was indeed fortunate that he occupied this vital post during the most serious of the diplomatic contretemps of the period, that over Venezuela, and also that his voice was powerful in Administration circles, since he had been Cleveland's own Secretary of State in his previous Administration. He acted throughout as a restraining influence, and found his situation one of great stress and difficulty, owing to the clash between his personal convictions in the matter and his loyalty to the President. He, like many of his predecessors and successors, though perhaps to an even greater degree, was denounced as an Anglophile; one newspaper declared, "Thomas Francis Bayard is the most popular Englishman ever born in the United States", and even John Hay objected to his "slobbering over the British."[3] He resigned in 1896 upon the defeat of the Democrats in the Presidential election of that year.

In Washington during these years only three British representatives held sway; Thornton continued his good work until 1881, when he was succeeded by Sir Lionel Sackville-West, later Lord Sackville, who remained until the disaster of 1888, after which he was replaced by Sir Julian Pauncefote, who not only moved up from the rank of Minister to that of Ambassador in 1893, but continued to hold that post for a further nine years. The creation of it was, he wrote to the Secretary of State, "intended as a fresh proof of the desire of the Queen and her Government still further to cement the bond of blood, sympathy and friendship which should ever unite the two great nations that speak the English tongue".[4] Though both Sackville-West and Pauncefote were able men, the latter quiet and the former positively reserved, it would

[1] Q. ibid, p. 377.   [2] *Letters*, p. 119.
[3] Q. Bailey, p. 483.   [4] Q. W.F.R., p. 265.

be impossible to conceive of careers in Washington more startlingly contrasted from beginning to end. Sackville-West arrived in honour, remained through a period of difficulty, and departed in dishonour; Pauncefote arrived in the unpopularity created by his predecessor, lived through a long period of maturing Anglo-American friendship, and died at his post, amidst widespread grief, in 1902. Sackville-West was sociable and even-tempered, a safe man with a distinguished diplomatic career behind him, but the Presidential election of 1888 was to be his undoing.

On his first arrival Blaine, the Secretary of State, had taken the unusual step of going to meet him, and had signalized the good feeling existing between the two countries by speaking in admiration of Queen Victoria as, "the first ruler of England that has been popular and beloved throughout the whole realm of Anglo-Saxon people." But a rising tide of anti-British feeling of considerable vehemence made itself felt during the decade, chiefly owing to the Irish troubles; Sackville-West attributed "the whole anti-British spirit in America . . . almost wholly to the Irish".[1] In the course of the election campaign, Cleveland had, no doubt partly for political motives, suddenly developed a line of policy of considerable vigour towards Canada; how much foreign affairs were at this time the servants of domestic vote-catching is shown by the fact that, because of the intense Anglophobia, Joseph Chamberlain's engagement to the daughter of a member of the Cleveland Administration was kept carefully secret until after the election. On 12 September, Sackville-West received a letter, purporting to come from a naturalized Briton, asking for advice on how to vote in the election. Though normally a poor letter writer, he sat down next day, having nothing better to do on a rainy afternoon, and replied, advising his correspondent to vote for Cleveland. Though he marked the letter "Private," he had made a fatal error, which his Mexican opposite number, who was similarly approached, avoided. A few days before the election the Republican newspapers published the story; one New York journal printed a full-page facsimile of the letter under the headline, "The British Lion's Paw Thrust Into American Politics to Help Cleveland." Having made the initial mistake, Sackville-West made it worse by failing to apologize at once, and by talking to the Press, saying to one reporter, "But now that it is published, I don't care."[2] Cleveland instructed the American Minister in London to ask for the recall of Sackville-West, but Salisbury considered that a low deception had been practised upon Her Majesty's Minister, and set a

[1] Q. W.F.R., p. 247.   [2] Mowat, *Diplomatic Relations*, p. 244.

521

deliberate process of Foreign Office inquiry in motion. With the election imminent, Cleveland could not wait, and was in any case angered at Sackville-West's action; on 31 October, nine days after the publication of the letter, Secretary of State Bayard sent him his passports. This abrupt action angered Salisbury, who refused to send a successor until the Cleveland Administration had left office, an attitude which gained wide support in Britain. But neither the original action of its representative, nor the subsequent actions of the British Government can be excused; they may have lost Cleveland the election, and they certainly fanned anti-British feelings once more into a flame which was to make the Venezuela incident in the next decade much more serious.

Such was the atmosphere just before Pauncefote arrived; he had been Under-Secretary of State at the Foreign Office, and there was some criticism of his appointment owing to his lack of diplomatic experience, but he proved to be one of the best of Britain's American ambassadors. Despite the fierce Anglophobia, sober elements in the country were thinking in the same way as Theodore Roosevelt, who wrote at the time, "a good deal of feeling against England—mind you none whatever against an Englishman—still foolishly exists in certain quarters of our purely American communities."[1] The process of restoring amiability made some progress, but it was not until after the Venezuela incident, with the coming of a Republican administration and of the Spanish-American and Boer wars, that really spectacular advances were made. Then the warmth grew so swiftly that Henry Adams wrote—and as an intimate friend of Hay he knew—"without Pauncefote's quiet, powerful help, Hay could not have carried on his work. . . . For the moment Hay had no ally, abroad or at home, except Pauncefote, and Pauncefote alone pulled him through."[2] Small wonder that Roosevelt called him "a damn good fellow", that the flag of the White House flew at half mast when he died in his sleep on 24 May, 1902, and that it was in the United States battleship *Brooklyn* that his remains were taken back to Britain.

At the governmental level it is doubtful whether the two countries, and, it is fair to say, the United States in particular, were as well served as they were at the diplomatic. In Anglo-American relations Britain was better served in the first years by Gladstone and Disraeli, than by Salisbury later. Disraeli, with that deep insight which so impressed Bismarck, was very sensitive to the strength of America, which, he said in 1872, was "throwing lengthening shades over the Atlantic" and creating

[1] Q. W.F.R., p. 263.   [2] Q. W.F.R., pp. 274-5.

"vast and novel elements in the distribution of power",[1] and from 1874-8 his Foreign Secretary, Lord Derby (previously Lord Stanley), was assiduous in the cultivation of good relations with the United States. Gladstone, who dominated the scene between 1880 and 1886, became increasingly popular in the United States as his devotion to liberal causes became recognized, so that the Reform Bill of 1884 set the seal on the attitude of Americans to him; he personally had also the great advantage that his Irish policy made him much less disliked by the American-Irish than most English statesmen, but after the defeat of Home Rule in 1886 and the inauguration of a long period of Tory government, Ireland became an increasing cause of British unpopularity in America. Salisbury, who ruled the country from 1886-1902, with the exception of the years 1892-5, was a most accomplished diplomat and master of foreign affairs, but he was very much the aristocrat and had some of the inclination of the old Tory aristocracy to despise all things American; this tended to be exaggerated in its effects because he combined the offices of Prime Minister and Foreign Secretary during most of the time. This was particularly serious when, as in the Venezuela crisis, he was faced with a President as determined as Cleveland and a Secretary of State as stiff-necked as Olney.

The period is one of considerable mediocrity among American Presidents and, for the most part, Secretaries of State. Between 1877 and 1893 virtually none of the former and only one of the latter had had any previous diplomatic experience. Among the Secretaries of State, we have seen something of Bayard, who held office during Cleveland's first term, 1885-9, when his diplomatic policy was generally criticized in America as weak, and the only other figure worth considerable attention was James G. Blaine, who was a man of great strength of personality and some breadth of imaginative vision, but who was too much of a journalistic orator to become a good diplomat in the conventional sense and who was made very self-assertive by a long series of frustrations in his ambition for high office. During his only substantial term at the State Department, 1889-92, he was tired, and closely controlled by a jealous President, Harrison, so that his main contribution to American foreign policy was to lay down a number of lines for future advance. In all this time, perhaps the most important fact about that foreign policy was its relative unimportance in the eyes of its people, compared with domestic issues. Thus foreign nations had to accustom themselves to outbursts of jingoism at such times as Presidential elections.

But both the United States and Britain were democracies by 1884,

[1] Q. Seton-Watson, *Britain in Europe*, p. 502.

and the feelings of their peoples were a vital, if not the vital, factor in the formation of policy. In the United States, particularly in the late eighties and early nineties, Anglophobia was a force to be reckoned with. It owed something to long and hallowed tradition, and a good deal to the fact that, in their comfortable isolation, Americans had no foreign bogey other than Britain to denounce; as Kipling put it, France has Germany, Britain has Russia, and America has us, "And, indeed, when you come to think of it, there is no other country for the American public speaker to trample upon."[1] It was fanned by a number of other causes, particularly the hatred of England among the Irish, who were so peculiarly important in the political machinery of the United States. The importance and pervasiveness of American-Irish Anglophobia is shown by the fact that in 1886 the Senate refused to include the crime of "dynamiting" in the extradition treaty, which was finally concluded with Britain in 1889 and added greatly to the list of extraditable crimes, because of the number of Irish efforts to blow up British buildings in the United States. A more curious form of Anglophobia arose among the fanatical advocates of "free silver", which was so violent a political issue in America in the last years of the century, because Britain was chief pillar of the gold standard. Senator Chandler of New Hampshire was reported as advocating "a war with England, with or without cause, in the interests of silver."[2] *Per contra*—and it shows the curious illogicality of the situation—Democratic advocates of a lowering of the tariff were in earlier years attacked violently as the tools of British free-trade interests. This passion against Britain rose to its height in the Venezuela crisis.

Yet one cannot help feeling that, if by no means sound and fury signifying nothing, it was perhaps less fearsome and deep-seated than it seemed. The American system of government, as is inevitable in a sectional continental democracy, is based fundamentally upon the tension of opposed opinions; policy results from a resolution of these forces, and this inevitably means that there is a tendency to shout as loud as you can in order to get your way. Understatement, too, has never been an American habit, and this makes public expressions of opinion, whether of praise or blame, sound more emphatic than they are; Kipling, himself no exponent of the refined understatement, was vastly impressed with this aspect of America: "What amazed me was the calm with which these folks gathered together and commenced to belaud their noble selves, their country, and their 'institootions' and everything else that was theirs. . . . An archangel, selling town-lots on

[1] *From Sea to Sea,* II, p. 14.   [2] Q. Bailey, p. 477.

524

the Glassy Sea, would have blushed to the tips of his wings to describe his property in similar terms."[1] Finally, in the superb and unexampled American achievement of making out of the heterogeneous elements of nineteenth-century immigration a nation, second to none in love of country, a premium was necessarily and naturally placed upon outspoken patriotism; in difficult moments every good American spoke strongly out for Columbia. These things meant that Anglophobia was vociferous and swift in any crisis, but that moderation later tended to prevail. It is very noteworthy that, in the Venezuela affair, immediate national uproar followed Cleveland's message and lasted three days, but that after that wiser counsels began to prevail. If the Anglophobia had gone so very deep, would the settlement have been followed so shortly by an effort to establish a universal arbitration treaty which had at least some chance of success? Intense movement on the surface should not blind us to the many factors making for friendship, factors ranging from British sympathy in the assassination of Garfield to the publication in 1888 of Bryce's *American Commonwealth*, from the growth of transatlantic travel to the passage of a new copyright law by Congress in 1891, which was very pleasing to English authors.

American public opinion may well at this time have displayed a bark much worse than its bite, but English popular reactions to the United States were ceasing to show either. Anti-Americanism, traditionally associated with a disappearing social order, had long been on the wane, and now, as a policy of isolation began to result in a sense of loneliness in the face of the old fear of Russia and the new fear of Germany, it was being rapidly replaced by a strong desire for American friendship. Thus in all the tensions of the period, and particularly in the Venezuela dispute, the most important influence for amity and peace was the new English democracy.

II

T HE first mild tension arose out of Isthmian diplomacy, and was occasioned by the news that de Lesseps, fresh from the construction of the Suez Canal, which was opened in 1869, had in 1878 secured a concession from Colombia to build a canal across Panama. This at once brought back to life American interest in an inter-oceanic canal which had, owing to the defeat of the South in the Civil War and the establishment of trans-continental railroads in the United States as well as Panama, been quiescent since 1860. It straightway became plain that,

[1] *From Sea to Sea*, II, p. 76.

because American strength had so vastly increased in the last two decades, despite the Civil War, and because her development in the far West had been so swift, her interest in the question was now hardly to be satisfied by less than exclusive control over any such waterway. This was quite in accord with the realities of American power, except for the extent of British trade in the area and the overwhelming supremacy of the British Navy, and it was a natural development of the Monroe Doctrine, premonitions of which had not been lacking in the utterances of American Secretaries of State since 1865.

But an obstacle lay in the path of any project for a purely American canal, the hardly remembered but once unpopular Clayton-Bulwer Treaty with Britain, which guaranteed mutual, or international, protection of any such waterway in Central America. In a special message to Congress on 8 March, 1880, which was enthusiastically received, President Hayes raised the whole question anew by saying,

> The policy of this country is a canal under American control. . . . If existing treaties between the United States and other nations or if the rights of sovereignty or property of other nations stand in the way of this policy—a contingency which is not apprehended—suitable steps should be taken by just and liberal negotiations to promote and establish the American policy on this subject consistently with the rights of the nations to be affected by it.[1]

A strong movement towards the abrogation of the treaty had, therefore, already taken shape when Blaine became Secretary of State a few weeks later, and he was not the man to let the grass grow under his feet, for he "was different from every Secretary of State who preceded him. . . . He entered upon his duties with a distinct and definite purpose", to enforce "the logic of the Monroe Doctrine . . . by the adoption of an American Continental system."[2] His Pan-Americanism, which aimed at the economic and political consolidation of the Western hemisphere, as well as his natural ebullience, led him to leap into action on the Isthmian issue with a letter to America's European Ministers, stating that by a treaty of 1846 between the United States and Colombia the former alone had the right to guarantee the proposed Panama Canal; he made no mention of the Clayton-Bulwer Treaty. Britain's Foreign Secretary, Granville, in reply, merely called attention to the treaty and expressed Britain's confident reliance upon American observance of its engagements, but Blaine had already despatched another note to

[1] Q. Williams, p. 275.

[2] E. Stanwood, *James Gillespie Blaine* (New York, 1905), pp. 241-3.

Britain claiming in effect that the complete change in circumstances since 1850 made a readjustment of the treaty's terms essential and inevitable, and expressing the hope that it might be made in a spirit of amity and concord. He later reiterated his main points, demanding that the United States be freed from her inequitable obligations to Britain "under the vague and, as yet, unperfected compact of 1850",[1] but Granville stood pat on Britain's rights under the treaty, which, he declared, she desired to maintain.

Blaine's successor, Frelinghuysen, tried at first a more technical mode of diplomatic argument, but when he could not move Britain, took an independent line by negotiating a singular Nicaraguan canal treaty, which ignored the Clayton-Bulwer agreement altogether. With the entry into office in 1885 of Cleveland, who held strong views on the honouring of such obligations, the treaty was withdrawn from the consideration of the Senate, and the United States reverted to the policy of a neutralized canal under international guarantee, although powerful interests, which were in the end to prevail, continued to work for an exclusively American enterprise. Despite some Anglo-American difficulty prior to the final absorption of the Mosquito Indians in the Nicaraguan state in 1894 (to the satisfaction of both Britain and the United States), the Isthmian question thus fell out of the public eye once more until after the Venezuela crisis. Though, apparently, nothing had been achieved by Blaine's initiative, there is little doubt that Britain began to readjust her ideas, with ultimately beneficial results; as the *Daily Telegraph* opined in 1884, Britain would do well not to oppose the United States "over the long forgotten Clayton-Bulwer Treaty, to which few Englishmen attach very great importance."[2]

But though Cleveland's policy allayed tension in one direction, it soon sprang up in two others, one being almost entirely, and the other primarily, Canadian in character. The first was one of hoary antiquity in Canadian-American relations, the everlasting fisheries question. Partly owing to the large fisheries arbitration award under the Treaty of Washington, which had been very unpopular in the United States, partly to the opposition to the Treaty of American fish-packing interests, and partly to an American manufacturers' desire to force a lowering of the Canadian tariff, which was now strongly established, the Republican administration gave due notice for the termination of the relevant clauses of the Treaty of Washington, which accordingly expired at the end of June, 1885. The Canadians, largely in a final attempt to obtain a

[1] Q. Williams, p. 279.   [2] Q. Bailey, p. 434.

renewal of some form of commercial reciprocity of a broader kind with the United States, then proceeded to enforce the letter of their interpretation of the old international fisheries law, as laid down in the Treaty of 1818; serious incidents began to occur, particularly in 1886, and Congress passed a retaliatory law—which was never put into effect —authorizing the President to exclude all Canadian ships and goods from American waters in case of further ill treatment of American fishermen. These events had a sobering effect, and a practical system of licences and other expedients to avoid trouble was put into operation.

Meanwhile, Cleveland who, though by no stretch of imagination a free-trader, favoured some measure of tariff reform to ease the flow of international trade, and who was very prepared to try and settle this annoying question, agreed to a Joint Commission which met in Washington in 1887. Though Joseph Chamberlain represented Britain very effectively, Canada in fact called the tune, as indeed she had done all along in this matter, and Bayard was the first American statesman fully to grasp the fact that the United States must deal with her henceforth as an autonomous nation. Largely owing to the efforts of the Secretary of State, whose unhappy if noble lot it was to struggle for Anglo-American friendship under most unauspicious circumstances, a treaty was signed in 1888, which gave very reasonable terms to the United States, and which might have gone far to solve the problem permanently. Unfortunately, in the bitter state of party warfare—Cleveland was the first Democratic President since Buchanan—it had really no hope of passing the Senate, which had a small Republican majority, and was defeated by 30 votes to 27, really on grounds of sheer Anglophobia. However, Cleveland considered that the Senate, having refused to accept a compromise with Canada, should logically be prepared for a strong policy, and he turned the tables on his opponents by sending a message to Congress recommending legislation to give him power to retaliate against the Dominion by suspending the passage of all bonded goods to Canada, whereupon he was flooded with congratulations from the country on taking a firm line against Britain. The Senate, hoist with their own petard, took no action, but Cleveland did not forget what manifestations of support could still be produced by "twisting the lion's tail." The whole incident illustrates very well the notable subserviency of American foreign to domestic politics, but fortunately the defeat of the treaty did not mean an immediate breakdown in Canadian-American relations, and the *modus vivendi* continued from year to year, until, eventually, 1909. Doubtless there would have been much more trouble over this issue than there was, in the intervening years, had it not been for the great general improvement in Anglo-American relations at the turn of the century.

No sooner, however, was this first maritime alarm temporarily allayed, than a second and quite novel one arose to perplex Anglo-American diplomacy. Though the Province of British Columbia was most intimately concerned, the question was one affecting Great Britain and other powers as well, that of "sealing" in the waters near the main breeding grounds of the seals in the Bering Sea, the Pribilof Islands, which had passed into American ownership with Alaska. Virtually all other seal-herds in the oceans had been exterminated by what is known as pelagic sealing, that is to say killing seals in the open sea, which involves a high rate of loss and virtually exclusive destruction of females, who range the ocean for food while the males bask in the breeding grounds. Since 1867 an American company had enjoyed a monopoly of sealing on the teeming islands, subject to stringent conditions designed to preserve the herds, but an alarming diminution took place owing to the unrestrained pelagic sealing of foreigners. In 1886 American revenue cutters began to seize Canadian sealers outside the three mile limit, to which their jurisdiction was technically limited, and Canada was incensed. Yet in response to Bayard's first approaches Salisbury appeared to be inclined to come to some agreement, since he plainly saw the force of the American moral case against the wiping out of the herds, and was perhaps conscious of the interests of the English fur-curing industry; the Canadian Government, however, was adamant, and Salisbury felt it incumbent on him to support them. In this case, as in that of the fisheries, it is interesting to note, Canadian interests were by no means sacrificed to Anglo-American friendship. In March, 1889, Congress, under continuous pressure from the Alaska seal lobby, authorized the President to seize vessels trespassing upon American rights in the Bering Sea, and as soon as Blaine once more became Secretary of State a few weeks later, he opened a long diplomatic argument with Salisbury defending the American position. The details of the contentions need not concern us, save that he seemed to argue, though denying that he did so very stoutly, that the Bering Sea was *mare clausum,* and that pelagic sealing is *contra bonos mores* and should be treated in the manner of piracy, which was an ingenious case and put with considerable oratorical vehemence, but which was, despite his search for precedents during the period of Russian ownership, a very weak one. Salisbury, no doubt quite reconciled to supporting the Canadians by the strength of his legal case, had no difficulty in demolishing that of his opponent in a series of calm and collected notes,

529

one of which in 1890 affirmed that "Her Britannic Majesty's Government must hold the Government of the United States responsible for the consequences that may ensue from acts which are contrary to the established principles of international law."[1] There was, inevitably, loose talk of war, but the situation never looked really serious; temporary arrangements were patched up to regulate the seasons of 1891 and 1892, and in the latter year a convention was signed referring the matter to arbitration. It was typical of the case that one of the two British commissioners and the British agent were both distinguished Canadians.

The award was unfavourable to the Americans on every point, and it was hardly to be expected that a case put forward by the United States, of all nations, which in effect flatly contradicted the doctrine of Freedom of the Seas, would gain much credence. Following a supplementary arbitration arranged four years later, the United States had to pay $473,151 damages for the seizure of the Canadian schooners. As the commentators have pointed out, the arbitration was a triumph for all parties except the United States and the seals. The arbitrators endeavoured to correct this by laying down regulations to protect the herds, which were put into force by both governments, but they proved largely ineffective because the pelagic sealers of other nations continued their activities. However, the Anglo-American example led, in 1911, to a quadruple convention with Japan and Russia, which had a marked effect in increasing numbers in the herds. Thus the seals disappear from our story, leaving arbitration very unpopular for a time in the United States; but in fact they had made little impact even upon a public still, in 1889, violently anti-British as a result of the Sackville-West incident of the previous year. In 1892 Blaine disappears also, leaving, as his one substantial legacy, the basis of the Pan-American Union, along with his hopes of goodwill and reciprocity between the American nations; this legacy is only of significance to us because of the resurgence in Canada, under the leadership of men like Goldwin-Smith, of a movement for economic union with the United States, which owed something to the kindred ideas which were in the air concerning Latin America. It was balanced in Canada, however, by the move for British Imperial Federation, so that in fact neither Annexationists nor Federalists gained the day, but those, like the Conservative Macdonald, whose desire was to retain a British connexion of the old type. The Democratic victory of 1892 alone saved Canada, for four further years only, from a tariff war *à outrance* with the United States, but, before the

[1] Q. Bailey, p. 448.

Dingley tariff of 1897 began the battle, the Venezuela dispute had brought Great Britain and the United States for the last time within measurable distance of war.

III

THE incident is one of the most curious in the history of Anglo-American relations, coming as it did at the end of two decades in which the actual concrete causes of disagreement between the two countries were far fewer and on a far smaller scale than in any previous period of comparable extent. To add to this there is the fact that, though America's interests were affected by what happened in Venezuela almost as much as were Britain's, for example, by what happened in the Low Countries (as Salisbury himself admitted), they were in no direct or immediate sense threatened. Pulitzer, the editor of the New York *World,* went so far in his opposition to the policy of the Administration as to say, "There is no menace in the boundary line, it is not our frontier, it is none of our business." To Britons—no one man in ten of whose Members of Parliament, as Bryce later told Roosevelt, "even knew there was such a thing as a Venezuelan question"[1]—the boundary of British Guiana, a far-distant and insalubrious colony, was a question of the utmost insignificance, and certainly not in their wildest imaginings worth a war with the United States. The whole thunderstorm, arising out of an apparently sunny sky, was a shocking surprise to Britons, and in fact its genesis must be sought in the public opinion of the United States.

Anglophobia had been particularly strong during the preceding decade, and had centred, as always, largely upon the Irish question; the main practical difficulty had been the effect of British coercive legislation upon naturalized American-Irish, who, in the words of Minister Lowell, have "gone back to Ireland with the hope, and sometimes, I am justified in saying, with the deliberate intention of disturbing friendly relations between the U.S. and England." Though the legislation was regarded by Americans as "exceptional and arbitrary ... contrary to the spirit and foundation principles of both English and American jurisprudence", most non-Irish Americans might have been forced to agree with Lowell that, since it was the law of the land, "it is manifestly futile to claim that naturalized citizens of the United States should be exempted from its operations."[2] But as long as trouble pre-

[1] Q. ibid, p. 487. [2] Q. W.A.A.E., p. 380.

vailed in Ireland, so long were Anglo-American relations liable to be poisoned by it; only with the decline of Irish immigration in the twentieth century did the poison begin to lose its virulence. It is characteristic that at the height of the Venezuela crisis Redmond wrote to Pulitzer: "You ask for an expression of opinion from me, on the war crisis, as a representative of British thought. In this, as in all other matters, I can speak only as a representative of Irish opinion. If war results from the reassertion of the Monroe Doctrine, Irish national sentiment will be solid on the side of America. With Home Rule rejected, Ireland can have no feeling of friendliness for Great Britain."[1] The anti-British feeling was apparent at every turn, yet it could find no satisfactory outlet, and it built up steadily until the charge was released in the cloudburst of 1895. In a way, it was precisely because the years were diplomatically so quiet that they ended with such an explosion of feeling, and to the particular emotion engendered by hatred of Britain in certain sections of American society must be added the general American ebullience resulting from her increasing consciousness of her own strength. The Venezuelan fury was as much the first serious symptom of American Imperialism as the last symptom of Anglo-American discord and dissension. Most happily, it served, as summer storms often do, to clear the air for the future, and American belligerence was henceforth directed into other and, from Britain's point of view, less harmful channels.

The frontier between Venezuela and British Guiana had never been properly determined.* In 1840 the British had arranged a survey by Sir Robert Schomburgk, and in 1844 Aberdeen had offered to Venezuela as a boundary the so-called Schomburgk line (but excluding Point Barima, which dominated the Orinoco River from British territory) in return for a rectification in the interior in Britain's favour; when by 1850 no reply to the British note had been received, Britain withdrew the offer. She made other proposals, though this was the most favourable to Venezuela, but repeated revolutions there rendered any negotiations impossible before 1876. Matters were in this vague and undefined state when prospectors discovered gold in the disputed section of the interior. At this stage Britain extended her claims westwards, to include this now important area, and Venezuela reciprocated by putting forward extravagant pretensions to a large part of Guiana, which was wealthy in mineral resources and already occupied by

[1] Q. R. McElroy, *Grover Cleveland, The Man and the Statesman* (New York, 1923), II, pp. 197-8.   * See Map 5.

British settlers. In 1876 the Venezuelans had tried to enlist the good offices of the United States, without any tangible result, thus inaugurating the policy of endeavouring to get their great neighbour to fight, on their behalf, a battle which they were too weak to fight themselves. In 1884 they offered Aberdeen's line, but it was refused by Britain; in 1885 the hope of a mutually agreed treaty between Venezuela and Britain, providing for arbitration if negotiation failed, disappeared with a note from Salisbury rejecting the offer. This refusal of arbitration was largely due to the fact that arbitrators have a habit of splitting the difference, which, in view of their wild claims, would serve the Venezuelans all too well, and to a refusal to hand over British citizens of long standing to the disorders and dangers of Venezuelan rule, as well as to fear of what such a precedent might mean to Britain's colonial frontiers all over the world. In 1887 Venezuela suspended diplomatic relations with Britain, and redoubled her efforts to involve the United States, by continuing to represent Britain in Washington as an aggressor, and by invoking there the name of the "immortal Monroe".[1] These efforts were to some extent rewarded when Secretary Bayard in 1888 showed mild sympathy by calling attention to the fact that Britain had enlarged her boundary claims since the beginning of the dispute. Britain, to whom the squabble seemed undignified and relatively unimportant, did not press her point of view in Washington, but in 1890 Salisbury offered to arbitrate all the territory in dispute beyond the Schomburgk line, though none behind it, an offer which the astonished, and no doubt chagrined, Venezuelans would not take up. There the matter rested when Cleveland became President in 1893.

He had, in his previous Administration, shown a marked tendency towards a mild American policy overseas, and had been bitterly attacked for it, but he had also shown a pronounced sympathy for the underdog, for the small power against the greater, which was just the impression of their case the Venezuelan authorities had long been trying to create in Washington. Furthermore, Cleveland had never forgotten either the Sackville-West tiff with Salisbury, or the enthusiasm aroused among the public when he had taken an anti-British line. Though there is no strong evidence that the actions of the Administration were motivated by a desire to play to the gallery for reasons of party popularity, the tradition of recent years in American political life certainly suggests it, while there are distinct signs of Cleveland being moved by an irritation at Britain's attitude, which was exacerbated by her action in sending troops in April, 1895, to collect claims for

[1] Bailey, p. 480.

damages against Nicaragua, by seizing temporarily the customs house at Corinto. To these motives must be added the rising tide of American self-assertion, which was making itself heard very loudly outside the Administration and which made men believe that strong language was necessary to make Britain pay attention to the American point of view; as Olney wrote many years later, "In English eyes the United States was then so completely a negligible quantity that it was believed only words the equivalent of blows would be really effective."[1]

As far as the mass of English opinion was concerned, this was not so, for they had become steadily more conscious of American power, but it is unfortunately true that Salisbury, though he was too wise a statesman fundamentally to underestimate the strength of the United States, created an initial impression of doing just that. It is true that the belligerent tones of Olney and Cleveland grated on this accomplished diplomat, proud descendant of Burleigh and Cecil, but the tone of his replies, that of a cross between a bored aristocrat and a precise pedagogue, grated just as badly upon American ears. Fortunately, no two men were better fitted to smooth this situation over than Pauncefote and Bayard, although the latter in negative fashion contributed to its onset by writing soon after his arrival in London in 1893, "Great Britain has just now her hands very full in other quarters of the globe. The United States is the last nation on earth with whom the British people or their rulers desire to quarrel, and of this I have new proofs every day in my intercourse with them. The other European nations áre watching each other like pugilists in the ring." Such sentiments were an invitation to American action.

In 1894 Secretary of State Gresham's questions to the British Government on the subject of arbitration were met with a willingness to arbitrate only the area west of the Schomburgk line, and so his more belligerent successor, Olney, resolved to demand an unambiguous answer to the question as to whether Britain would go to arbitration or not. Though Cleveland softened a little the resulting note of 20 July, 1895, it was still remarkably blunt and remarkably sweeping for a diplomatic document, and the President dubbed it "Olney's twenty-inch gun".[2] It claimed that

> the Government of the United States has made it clear to Great Britain and to the world that the controversy is one in which both its honor and its interests are involved and the continuance of which it cannot regard with indifference. . . . That America is in no part open to colonization, though the proposition was not universally admitted at the time of its

[1] Q. ibid, p. 477. [2] Q. McElroy, II, pp. 178, 181.

first enunciation, has long been universally conceded. We are now concerned, therefore, only with that other practical application of the Monroe Doctrine the disregard of which by an European power is to be deemed an act of unfriendliness towards the United States. . . . The rule in question has but a single purpose and object. It is that no European power or combination of European powers shall forcibly deprive an American state of the right and power of self-government and of shaping for itself its own political fortunes and destinies.

This, he went on to claim, Great Britain was in effect doing, by advancing her boundary line against a weaker power and then refusing to arbitrate it, which was thus a violation of the Monroe Doctrine and might lead to its breakdown and to a scramble for territory in South America such as was then going on in Africa. The note ended by voicing a thinly veiled threat:

Today the United States is practically sovereign on this continent, and its fiat is law upon subjects to which it confines its interposition. Why? It is not because of the pure friendship or good will felt for it. It is not simply by reason of its high character as a civilized state, nor because wisdom and justice and equity are the invariable characteristics of the dealings of the United States. It is because, in addition to all other grounds, its infinite resources combined with its isolated position render it master of the situation and practically invulnerable as against any or all other powers.[1]

This was a strained interpretation of the Monroe Doctrine and it was certainly not couched in diplomatic terms, no doubt partly in the expectation of startling Britain into a prompt reply, but in fact four months ensued before Salisbury's answer was received; this delay was occasioned by the serious and lengthy nature of the subject, by pressing British problems elsewhere, and by some inefficiency in the Foreign Office. Such a delay is often salutary in times of crisis, but now it merely had the effect of increasing the irritation of the Administration with Britain's apparently casual treatment of problems concerning America, and of giving the public tension time to mount. When Salisbury's answering lectures did arrive they simply added fuel to the flames, for in terms more urbane than Olney's, but equally forceful, they rejected arbitration and, in effect, American interference. He wrote that, as far as he was aware, the Monroe Doctrine

---

[1] R. J. Bartlett (Editor) *The Record of American Diplomacy* (New York, 1947), pp. 343-5.

has never been before advanced on behalf of the United States in any written communication addressed to the Government of another nation; but it has been generally adopted and assumed as true by many eminent writers and politicians in the United States. . . . It must always be mentioned with respect, on account of the distinguished statesman to whom it is due, and the great nation who have generally adopted it. But international law is founded on the general consent of nations; and no statesman, however eminent, and no nation, however powerful, are competent to insert into the code of international law a novel principle which was never recognized before, and which has not since been accepted by the Government of any other country.

On the specific issue he declared:

> The disputed frontier of Venezuela has nothing to do with any of the questions dealt with by President Monroe. . . . It is not a question of the imposition upon the communities of South America of any system of government devised in Europe. It is simply the determination of the frontier of a British possession which belonged to the Throne of England long before the Republic of Venezuela came into existence.[1]

If the initial step of Olney had been a mistake, this was one almost as bad, for it left no way open to either side to retreat or compromise: a flat demand had been met with a flat rejection. It is unquestionable that Salisbury did not appreciate the explosive nature of the situation, in which he may have been misled by Bayard, but was inclined to ascribe it to pre-election bluster which would collapse in face of a firm response.

The very reverse in fact occurred, for Cleveland was incensed and gave free rein to his feelings, though as he said: "I am fully alive to the responsibility incurred, and keenly realize all the consequences that may follow."[2] Yet even now, things did not appear too bad to Bayard in London, for it was only the fantastic fervour which greeted the President's next step which transformed the look of the thing; Bayard wrote:

> The replies of Lord Salisbury to your Venezuelan instructions are in good temper and moderate in tone. Our difficulty lies in the wholly unreliable character of the Venezuelan rulers and people, and results in an almost undefinable, and therefore dangerous, responsibility for the conduct by them of their own affairs. I believe, however, that your interpretation of this boundary dispute will check efficiently the tendency to 'land grabbing' in South America, which is rather an Anglo-Saxon disposition everywhere.[3]

[1] Q. Bartlett, pp. 346-7.   [2] Q. ibid, p. 351.   [3] Q. McElroy, II, p. 188.

On 17 December, the President sent his famous message to Congress, stating that the time had now come when the United States itself must "take measures to determine with sufficient certainty for its justification what is the true divisional line between the Republic of Venezuela and British Guiana. The inquiry to that end should of course be conducted carefully and judicially and due weight should be given to all available evidence, records and facts in support of the claims of both parties." Congress should therefore make appropriation for the expenses of a Commission for this purpose which should report without delay. "When such report is made and accepted it will in my opinion be the duty of the United States to resist by every means in its power as a wilful aggression upon its rights and interests the appropriation by Great Britain of any lands or the exercise of governmental jurisdiction over any territory which after investigation we have determined of right belongs to Venezuela."[1] This amounted in fact to an enforced arbitration by the United States.

Cleveland's relations with his Congresses had not always been easy, but, coming no doubt as somewhat of a surprise from one often accused of excessive moderation in foreign affairs, his strong language swept Congress and the country off its feet. The House cheered; even the sedate Senate applauded; and both Houses unanimously appropriated $100,000 for the commission. "A wave of jingoism swept over the entire country with the speed of a prairie fire. Public men in all walks of life applauded. Twenty-six of twenty-eight governors who were approached pledged their support. Civil War veterans offered their services. The Irish National Alliance pledged 100,000 volunteers. . . . The New York *Sun* carried the headline, 'WAR IF NECESSARY'."[2] For about three days chauvinism held the field, and then the frenzy began to subside.

Already moderating voices had been raised. Bassett Moore, a Cleveland supporter and a leading exponent of the arbitration method, wrote to a member of the Administration: "The whole system of arbitration presupposes that nations will be reasonable in their claims. The claim of Venezuela to all territory west of the Essequibo is not a scrupulous claim. . . . For twenty years Venezuela, instead of settling her boundary dispute, has in various ways, some of them obviously dishonest, been trying to drag the United States into the dispute." He concluded with the hope that the President would "not be willing to launch his country on a career as mad and as fatal as that on which France was started by Louis XIV." In every branch of national life, churches, universities, and the intellectual press, voices were raised for moderation; financial

[1] Q. Bartlett, p. 351.　　[2] Bailey, p. 486.

interests were seriously alarmed by a catastrophic fall in American stocks. From Bayard in London came a warning voice; he wrote to the President, "with this note I send you *The Times* of this morning—in order that you may perceive the tone of *average British comment.* . . . I am not able to shake off a grave sense of apprehension in allowing the interests and welfare of our Country to be imperilled or complicated by such a government and people as those of Venezuela."[1]

The first reaction of the British public was amazement and incredulity that so serious an issue could have appeared so swiftly out of a clear sky. Some High Tory voices, singing still the same old tune, were raised in favour of giving Uncle Sam a drubbing; after all, the United States had but two second-class battleships and twelve cruisers to Britain's forty-four battleships and forty-one first-class cruisers afloat. But they were now voices crying in the wilderness; though, no doubt, the mass of the people would not have been prepared to submit to too much at the hands of the United States, a very powerful opinion developed against a war which "would be a crime against the laws of God and man; and would cause unspeakable misery to the peoples of both countries."[2] This spirit was not confined to the common people; 354 Members of Parliament signed a memorial asking for arbitration and sent it to the President and Congress, while in the Government itself, Chamberlain, who was in a strong position, was vigorously pro-American. These sentiments rapidly became apparent, and would in any case have prevailed, but their victory was made absolutely certain by the despatch on 3 January, 1896, of the Kaiser's famous telegram of congratulation to Kruger, President of the Boer Republic, on his success in having repelled the British raider, Jameson, and his band "without appealing to the help of friendly powers",[3] that is, Germany. This not only so enraged public opinion in Britain as to banish all thought of Venezuela, but put the border dispute in its proper perspective; when "Yankee Doodle" was cheered and "Die Wacht am Rhein" hissed in London, it demonstrated clearly how utterly different was popular feeling towards the two countries. Most important of all, and perhaps most influential at the summit of affairs, it called unmistakable attention to that isolation of Britain in the world, which no longer seemed splendid so much as dangerous, and apprehension of which was to be the key to British diplomacy in the years to come.

The anguish of a convinced Anglo-American was expressed by Henry James; "The American outbreak has darkened all my sky—and made

[1] Q. McElroy, II, pp. 184-6, 190-1.
[2] Q. Bailey, p. 488.   [3] Q. Bemis, p. 420.

me feel, among many other things, how long I have lived away from my native land, how long I *shall* (D.V.!) live away from it, and little I understand it today. The explosion of jingoism there is the result of . . . domestic . . . conditions—. . . a split almost between the West and the East."[1] The pacific public opinion of the British became known in the United States and strengthened the hands of the moderates. Pulitzer, in his campaign to make his countrymen realize that "to raise the spectre of war over a false sentiment and a false conception is something more than a grave blunder. If persisted in, it will be a colossal crime",[2] obtained and published the views of prominent Englishmen; even the Prince of Wales broke the powerful convention of royal silence to reply that I "earnestly trust, and cannot but believe, that the present crisis will be arranged in a manner satisfactory to both countries, and will be succeeded by the same warm feeling of friendship which has existed between them for so many years."[3] Chamberlain made perhaps the most influential contribution in a great speech which included the words:

> War between the two nations would be an absurdity as well as a crime. . . . The two nations are allied and more closely allied in sentiment and in interest than any other nations on the face of the earth. While I should look with horror upon anything in the nature of a fratricidal strife, I should look forward with pleasure to the possibility of the Stars and Stripes and the Union Jack floating together in defence of a common cause sanctioned by humanity and justice.[4]

Thus was the way prepared for compromise, but it was still not easy to attain it because things had gone so far. Fortunately, Cleveland had left the door slightly ajar by demanding a careful inquiry before action, and the British Government expressed its willingness to give to the American commission "all the information we are able to give at the earliest possible moment."[5] Salisbury expressed publicly his appreciation of the naturalness and propriety of American interest in Venezuela under the Monroe Doctrine, and suggested informally a conference of those countries having colonies in the American hemisphere with the United States "to proclaim the Monroe Doctrine—that European Powers having interests in America, should not seem to extend their influence in that Hemisphere." This suggestion was refused, but after a good deal of diplomacy, including a visit to America by Chamberlain, a solution was found for arbitration on lines proposed in the same letter. In Olney's words, there was to be unrestricted arbitration, "provided it

[1] *Letters* (I), pp. 249-50.   [2] Q. Bailey, p. 487.   [3] Q. McElroy, II, p. 197.
[4] Q. Bemis, p. 421.   [5] Q. McElroy, II, p. 200.

were made the rule of the arbitration that territory which had been in the exclusive, notorious, and actual use and occupation of either party for sixty years should be held to belong to such party";[1] this in fact gave Britain all that she wanted, a guarantee of retaining her own long established settlers. Any idea of picking up any extra gold fields, if it had existed in the recent past at all, had certainly been completely banished by the emotional purge of the crisis. Britain appointed two arbitrators, the United States appointed two on behalf of Venezuela, and these four chose a fifth; when the decision was issued in 1899, public interest in it was practically dead. The award[*] was virtually that of the Aberdeen proposal, except that Venezuela made a quite substantial gain at the southern end of the line, and, ironically enough, Olney had practically to coerce the Venezuelan authorities into accepting it.

Thus terminated the Venezuela affair. In the end it cleared from the soul of the American public much of the perilous stuff of Anglophobia which weighed upon it, and it brought home to Britons the essential need of assiduously cultivating friendly relations with their great neighbour across the Atlantic. While it lasted, it showed the danger of letting the activities of unimportant third parties inveigle the two great principals into courses of action tending towards war with one another; when either nation faced up squarely to the issue of fratricidal war it drew back decisively, but both had, by vigilant and foreseeing diplomacy, to ensure that they never advanced in argument too far to withdraw. It was an affirmation on the part of the United States of something approaching the Roosevelt Corollary to the Monroe Doctrine, which Britain was to learn to regard with equanimity and even approval; it was a symptom of the imperialist spirit which was seizing the American mind. It was a further lesson to Englishmen to expect violent, but often unfulfilled, expressions of American intentions from the American public and even American statesmen. In the end it strengthened the belief of the two countries in arbitration, but it only just did so, for it had been a close call. Most important and most salutary of all, it was a triumph for democratic public opinion, and particularly for that of the new democracy of Britain, which was the chief peacemaker; the British public never looked like accepting war, the American public after the first fine careless rapture drew back from the prospect of making it. On the whole it has proven true amongst peoples speaking the English tongue and sharing the tradition of British free institutions, and in

[1] Q. ibid, pp. 199, 201.   [*] See Map 5.

particular between the British and American nations, that, since the advent of democracy in both lands, and perhaps because of it, war has come to be little less than unthinkable.

IV

THIS spirit had an immediate manifestation in the abortive Arbitration Treaty of 1897. There had long been an influential movement in Britain and America in favour of the arbitration of international disputes. In 1849 Cobden, its most powerful advocate, had moved in the House of Commons, "That an humble Address be presented to Her Majesty, praying that She will be graciously pleased to direct Her principal Secretary of State for Foreign Affairs to enter into communication with Foreign Powers, inviting them to concur in Treaties, binding the respective parties, in the event of any future misunderstanding, which cannot be arranged by amicable negotiation, to refer the matter in dispute to the decision of Arbitrators."[1] It had been defeated by 176 votes to 79, but in 1873 an even wider motion of Henry Richard, calling for a permanent system of general arbitration, was accepted by the House, and Congress followed suit in the next year. In 1890 Congress unanimously passed a resolution calling for the negotiation of arbitration treaties with all civilized powers, and in 1893 the House of Commons unanimously reciprocated.

The alarm caused by the Venezuela crisis gave a powerful impetus to this movement in Britain and the United States, where support for arbitration suddenly became vociferous and widespread. Olney and Salisbury both favoured some general arrangement of the kind, and, arising out of a suggestion of the former made as early as 17 December, 1895, he and Pauncefote negotiated a convention of general arbitration which was signed on 11 January, 1897. It provided for two pecuniary tribunals, one to deal with small and the other with large claims, and for a mixed tribunal of three American and three British judges to deal with any territorial question; the decision of the majority was to be final in the first two cases, and of a majority of five to one in the third case. If on a territorial claim either power was dissatisfied with the award of a majority of less than five to one, the award was of no validity, but "there shall be no recourse to hostile measures of any description until the mediation of one or more friendly Powers has been

[1] Q. C. Phelps, *The Anglo-American Peace Movement in the Mid-Nineteenth Century* (New York, 1930), p. 153.

invited".[1] The treaty was accepted by Parliament, and there seemed to be a greater measure of popular support for it in the United States than for any subsequent measure of the kind; *The Times* made bold to predict that the Senate would not defeat "a policy that has obtained a decided and unusual degree of approval among the American people."

But the Senate seemed little affected by this largely spontaneous enthusiasm. Partly out of bitterness on the part of Republicans against Cleveland, the treaty was held over into the next Administration, though this also supported it strongly. The Senate then emasculated it by a number of amendments which would have defeated its object, but, to make assurance doubly sure, failed by three votes to give it the necessary two-thirds majority. Thus yet another was added to the Senate's long list of refusals to ratify treaties important to Anglo-American relations. The retired and embittered Olney turned his powerful dialectic against the Senate's decision in these words: "Before the treaty came to a final vote, the Senate brand had been put upon every part of it, and the original instrument had been mutilated and distorted beyond all possibility of recognition. The object of the Senate in dealing with the treaty—the assertion of its own predominance—was thus successfully accomplished and would have been even if the treaty as amended had been ratified."[2] The remnants of general Anglophobia no doubt played their part in the rejection, but study of the subsequent course of events makes it plain that the real obstacle to it was the cautious realism, or, according to the point of view, obstinate bigotry, of the Senate. The main amendments proposed had exempted certain questions from arbitration, had required a two-thirds vote of the Senate before the submission of all cases, and had demanded a special agreement for the submission of any difference, "which in the judgment of either power materially affects its honor or its domestic or foreign policy",[3] a provision designed to safeguard the Monroe Doctrine. These are the sort of reservations which continue, for many years to come, to vitiate similar proposals; the same instinct fifty years later was to make the Senate, as well as Russia, insist upon the Great Power veto in the Security Council of the United Nations.

The defeat of the treaty of 1897 was a grave disappointment to its supporters in both countries, but they by no means gave up the struggle. Two years later, under the influence of John Hay as Secretary of State,

[1] Q. Bartlett, p. 337.   [2] Q. McElroy, II, pp. 243, 245.
[3] Q. Dunning, p. 320.

the United States, along with many other powers including Britain, signed a treaty setting up permanent arbitration machinery in the form of the Hague Permanent Court of Arbitration. This was a step in the direction of general arbitration, but no more than a step, for it began with the ominous words: "With a view to obviating, *as far as possible,** recourse to force in the relations between States. . . ." In fact it only bound signatories to have recourse to the Court if they volunteered to do so; furthermore, the convention called for a special *compromis* or agreement between disputants, before they appealed to the tribunal, defining specifically the scope of the dispute and the extent of the powers of the arbitrators. Not content with these safeguards, the Senate ratified the treaty subject to the reservation: "Nothing contained in this convention shall be so construed as to require the United States of America to depart from its traditional policy of not . . . entangling itself in the political questions of policy . . . of any foreign state; nor shall anything contained in the said convention be construed to imply a relinquishment by the United States of America of its traditional attitude toward purely American questions."[1]

Nevertheless Hay was not yet disheartened, for this constituted an advance, however minute, over 1897, and in the far more cordial atmosphere prevailing five years later with Britain, he negotiated with her in 1904 another general treaty of arbitration, which was to be the model for similar treaties with other nations. It agreed to arbitrate all differences not settled by diplomacy, which were "of a legal nature or relating to the interpretation of treaties," except questions affecting the "vital interests", the "honor", the "independence" of either party, or "the interests of third powers."[2] Once again the Senate proved dissatisfied with even such stringent limitations as these, since they did not protect its legislative rights, and amended the treaty to ensure that the *compromis* required in each case must obtain their preliminary consent. President Roosevelt considered that this nullified the treaty and refused to proceed with it; Hay was utterly downcast by this waste of many months of painstaking labour, and declared that it was useless to try any more in the then temper of the Senate. When he died in 1905, to some extent as a result of the burden of his duties, his successor, Elihu Root, prevailed upon Roosevelt to accept the Senate's proviso, which was accordingly incorporated in the body of the treaty, while Britain reserved to herself similar "freedom of action"[3] prior to the exchange of ratifications, in an annex to the treaty, which accordingly

---

* Author's italics.   [1] *Treaties Between U.S. and H.M.,* pp. 109, 118, note.
[2] Q. Bemis, p. 428.   [3] *Treaties Between U.S. and H.M.,* p. 298.

went into effect on 4 June, 1908. It did perhaps once more represent a minuscule advance in that it accepted general arbitration, though in such a restricted form as to render it virtually useless as a preventative of war.

But even now the struggle continued, for President Taft was more enthusiastic for arbitration than Roosevelt, and, Britain being still willing, a really effective treaty was signed with her, and also France, on 3 August, 1911, which was once again to serve as a model for others. It provided for the arbitration of all questions "justiciable in their nature",[1] before the Hague Court, and laid down a joint commission procedure to determine in case of disagreement whether disputes were justiciable; these procedures were mandatory, but the assent of the Senate was required for every *compromis*. The instrument would undoubtedly have been an effective treaty of general arbitration, but the Senate, led once more by Henry Cabot Lodge who disliked "mushy philanthropists",[2] went to work with a will; its amendments substituted voluntary for mandatory arbitration, and ensured that no questions should be arbitrated which concerned the admission of aliens, State debts, the "territorial integrity of . . . the United States . . . or . . . the maintenance of the traditional attitude of the United States concerning American questions, commonly described as the Monroe Doctrine, or other purely governmental policy."[3] Taft felt very strongly on the issue and took it to the country. Bailey claims, "There can be little doubt that public opinion was strongly behind him",[4] but the Senate ratified only the rump of the treaty, by 76 to 3, and Taft did not proceed with ratification. In view of his defeat in the election of 1912 and the strength of Senate opposition, it seems questionable how far public opinion really did favour the treaty, for over a period of nearly eighteen years the voters, though admittedly not concerned primarily with foreign affairs, had continued to send back to the Senate men unfavourable to genuine arbitration.

Happily, it is clear that these treaties of arbitration were defeated because they were arbitration treaties, not because they were Anglo-American agreements. It is nevertheless significant that all three were primarily, in fact, treaties with Britain, for after the solution of the Venezuela problem we are on the threshold of the first great period of positive Anglo-American agreement. This was in part due to deep-seated movements in the structure of international society and the balance of its power, which were beyond the control of either country,

[1] Q. Bartlett, p. 338.   [2] Bailey, p. 590.
[3] Q. Bartlett, p. 338.   [4] Bailey, p. 590.

but it was also due to the fact that most of the disputes which had vexed Anglo-American history since 1776 had been finally settled, and that there had developed a very different feeling between the two great democratic peoples. In this process the twenty-four Quiet Years—for quiet they were in proportion to their length, even given the near-explosion with which they ended—had been invaluable.

PART IV

WORLD POWER

CHAPTER FIFTEEN

AMERICAN IMPERIALISM (1898-1912)

THE first steps of the United States on to the world stage at the end of the nineteenth century took the form of what has been called "the great aberration" of American imperialism; they were impelled more by internal pressures upon the formation of her foreign policy than by those external pressures upon her from the outside world, which were to become dominant in the period of World War I. Both, however, are at bottom manifestations of the same process, that emergence of the United States as a world power, which Henry Adams noted when, in 1904, he reached Washington, "where the contrast of atmosphere astonished him, for he had never before seen his country think as a world-power."[1] Because this is so, the phenomenon of American imperialism is of greater relevance than might at first appear to the history of Anglo-American relations, for these years were of incalculable importance in that story, since they saw not merely the growth of American power, but a simultaneous growth among the British people, for the first time for a century, of a sense of insecurity amidst world affairs. These two facts led to the formation of an Anglo-American understanding far more positive than any which had preceded it, or had even appeared possible since the Monroe Doctrine was first enunciated, although the understanding hardly reached the stage of positive co-operation, let alone of actual alliance. With America's awakened interest in the outside world, there were far more points of contact between the two nations, but this in fact led to a greater rather than a less degree of understanding, partly because British imperialism at the turn of the century had an instinctive feeling of sympathy towards the novel American brand, but very much more because Britain was increasingly anxious to secure her rear by friendship with her great neighbour.

Now, for the first time, the British people and their governments gave full rein to those kinder sentiments towards the United States which had long been developing, had been very apparent at the time of the Clayton-Bulwer Treaty, and had recently regained strength after the

[1] *Education of Henry Adams,* p. 463.

delay imposed by the Civil War; they came to welcome, as the Hay-Pauncefote Canal Treaty was to show, the extension of American power in the Western hemisphere, and even far beyond it, as was demonstrated with equal clarity by their sympathy towards the United States in the Spanish-American War and their positive pressure on her to annex the Philippines after it was over. Happily, American Republican imperialism coincided in office with British Conservative imperialism in the critical years from 1897 to 1905, which contained both the Spanish-American and Boer wars, and happily, too, American imperialism was short-lived, as was the late nineteenth-century phase of it in Britain, for, by 1905 in the latter and at least by 1912 in the former, liberal governments had repudiated the creed. Yet while it lasted, American imperialism was a very real thing; as Brebner writes, "a host of domestic and external circumstances had launched the United States on an almost uncontrollable international rampage. . . . Mr. Dooley's favourite image for Roosevelt after the Spanish-American War was as the ebullient motorman of a runaway trolley car."[1] Though it had roots in the past, it was an apparently swift growth, for in 1889 Henry Cabot Lodge wrote: "our relations with foreign nations today fill but a slight place in American politics, and excite generally only a languid interest",[2] and declared that American separation from the affairs of other peoples was so complete as to make it difficult to realize how large a part they had occupied when the American government was originally founded.

The causes of the phenomenon were, as such causes always are, complex and difficult to isolate, but brief mention may be made of some of them. Certainly the growth of American wealth was one; as Bryce, who disapproved of American, as of British, imperialism, wrote: "In this age, more than any preceding, wealth means power, offensive power in war as well as financial power in peace. . . . The Republic is as wealthy as any two of the greatest European nations, and is capable, if she chooses, of quickly calling into being a vast fleet and a vast army. Her wealth and power has in it something almost alarming."[3] The desire of American industry for foreign markets was one manifestation of this, and in 1898 Senator Beveridge of Indiana declared: "American factories are making more than the American people can use; American soil is producing more than they can consume. Fate has written our policy for us; the trade of the world must and shall be ours. . . . And we will get it as our mother England has told us how."[4] From this it

---

[1] Brebner, p. 254.   [2] Q. Morison and Commager, II, p. 314.
[3] Q. Nevins, p. 539.   [4] Q. Curti, p. 668.

was but a small step to colonialism. With this wealth there came a consciousness of the strength it brought; colonialism, and indeed the mere effect of a world diminishing in size, implied the need for strategic bases to defend a decreasingly secure United States, and there is a powerful strategic element in American imperialism which goes far to explain its brief duration. Even finance could come to contemplate the risks of overseas investment, and see them as a contribution to an ultimate national destiny; as the American financial titan in Conrad's *Nostromo* expressed it:

> Of course, some day we shall step in. We are bound to. But there's no hurry. Time itself has got to wait on the greatest country in the whole of God's Universe. We shall be giving the word for everything; Industry, trade, law, journalism, art, politics, and religion, from Cape Horn clear over to Smith's Sound, and beyond too, if anything worth taking turns up at the North Pole. And then we shall have leisure to take in hand the outlying islands and continents of the earth. We shall run the world's business whether the world likes it or not. The world can't help it—and neither can we, I guess.[1]

America's isolationism in the nineteenth century had been greatly encouraged by her absorption in the opening up of the West; when this form of Manifest Destiny was fulfilled and Americans lined the Pacific coast, it was only natural that their eyes and ambitions should turn outward in a new form of the old idea. It was no coincidence that the closing of the frontier was followed almost immediately by the Spanish-American War; materially and psychologically, American strength had to find an outlet. As Frank Norris put it, with the licence of the novelist, "On the 1st of May, 1898, a gun was fired in the bay of Manila and, in response, the skirmish line crossed the Pacific, still pushing the frontier before it."[2] Thus journalists and politicians took up the cry in a manner worthy of the days of Manifest Destiny itself, though the new expansionism found its chief supporters not among Democrats, but among Republicans. Their spokesman, Lodge, declared in an article in one of the popular magazines, entitled "Our Blundering Foreign Policy":

> From the Rio Grande to the Arctic Ocean there should be but one flag and one country. . . . In the interests of our commerce . . . we should build the Nicaragua canal, and for the protection of that canal and for the sake of our commercial supremacy in the Pacific, we should control the Hawaiian islands and maintain our influence in Samoa. . . . [T]he island of Cuba . . . will become a necessity. . . . The tendency of modern times is toward consolidation. . . . The great

[1] Conrad, *Nostromo*, p. 65.   [2] Q. Davis, *The Atlantic System*, p. 68.

nations are rapidly absorbing for their future expansion and their present defence all the waste places of the earth. It is a movement which makes for civilization and the advancement of the race. As one of the great nations of the world the United States must not fall out of the line of march.[1]

It might have been ominous that he also said, "England has studded the West Indies with strong places which are a standing menace to our Atlantic seaboard. We should have among those islands at least one strong naval station". But the foundations of Anglo-American friendship, as we shall see, were now too firmly laid, the British people and their governments were too determined to acquire American goodwill, and the tide of the next years was running too strongly towards this amity for incidental rivalries to disrupt these developments.

Though America surged forward with apparently startling swiftness into the possession of an imperial domain in the years following the outbreak of the Spanish-American War in 1898, it would be a grave distortion of the truth to see the movement as altogether a sudden one; the beginnings of American imperialism must be sought long before these years. Delayed primarily by the more urgent desire to open up the continental United States, and secondarily by strong political inhibitions against any form of foreign entanglement, it came to fruition when these obstacles gave way, with seeming suddenness, at the turn of the century. In the Caribbean, American ambitions had only failed to rise to a climax in the years before the Civil War because they were primarily Southern, and therefore increasingly suspect in the North. They had then shown themselves in the Isthmian and Cuban questions, but, despite the unsuccessful projects of Seward to acquire Caribbean footholds for the United States, had suffered a marked eclipse as a result of the Northern victory in the Civil War. Only with the revival of interest in the Canal project in the nineties, and with the Cuban revolution and the war against Spain, did they reassume their former importance.

In the vast area of the Pacific, however, there was no such recession, but rather a steady growth of American influence and desires, which accelerated naturally with the opening up of California and the Oregon territory, with the coming of the steamship and with the completion of a number of trans-continental railroads after 1869. American trade in the era of the Clipper ship grew swiftly in the Pacific, and in 1844 Caleb Cushing signed the first American commercial treaty with China; in

[1] Q. Morison and Commager, II, p. 323.

552

this treaty China made a noose for her own neck by insisting on keeping open the door of commercial opportunity equally for all foreign powers —a noose because all the nations, by the operation of most favoured nation clauses, were able to keep pace with the concessions extracted by the most unscrupulous among their number. Even earlier in the century, in 1833 the Jackson administration had made certain minor treaties of trade, such as that with Siam, which was patterned on the British treaty of 1826. In Japan the United States took the initiative in extracting concessions, largely through the vision and forceful diplomacy of Commodore Perry in his expedition of 1853 and in the treaty which resulted in the next year. Here Britain shortly followed suit with a treaty of her own, but neither power had any inkling of the revolution they had wrought in the world by turning the Japanese so swiftly towards that staggeringly swift self-modernization which was to make them a great power in a generation.

Perry saw Japan as part of a larger picture, for he wrote: "It is self-evident that the course of coming events will ere long make it necessary for the United States to extend its jurisdiction beyond the limits of the Western continent, and I assume the responsibility of urging the expediency of establishing a foothold in this quarter of the globe as a measure of positive necessity to the establishment of our maritime rights in the east."[1] For many years, American trade in the Far East had been second only to that of Britain, which was however considerably greater, and, in common with other powers, the United States continued throughout the century to extend her influence and her special rights in the area, particularly in China and Japan, although she was much more scrupulous than others in refusing territorial concessions. This led to her early popularity in China, though she was not averse from taking advantage of the pressure of others to extract, as a friendly power, what she herself wanted. However, it was not in these parts of Asia, but in Samoa and Hawaii, bastions of the southern and northern Pacific, that she had made the most decisive advances before the Spanish-American War, for, with the growing speed of communications, outer defences in this area became more and more desirable for her. This was particularly true after the purchase of Alaska had vastly extended her territory to the west, and had made Hawaii an even more vital possession for the United States than heretofore.

American interest in Samoa did not become really marked until a coaling station became indispensable there after the Civil War, when a similar awakening of British and German interest led to the first of

[1] Q. Morison and Commager, II, p. 315.

553

those triangular situations of tension between the three powers which were to be a feature of this period. An American treaty of 1872 with the local chieftain, granting the United States exclusive rights to a naval base at Pago-Pago in return for her protection, was not accepted by the Senate, and even the British deportation thence in a cruiser of a special agent of Grant in 1873 did not cause any trouble owing to mistrust in Congress of the President's interference in such far-off places. In 1878, however, a more limited treaty granting some naval rights, but establishing no protectorate, was ratified by the Senate. The British and German Governments followed with similar treaties in the next year, and local friction between the three groups of nationals, led by three none too tactful consuls, became steadily worse. Secretary of State Bayard arranged a tripartite conference in Washington in 1887, but found himself faced with a prior Anglo-German agreement—part of a wider colonial deal between the two powers, made by Britain owing to her need for German acquiescence in her Near Eastern policy —to press for a system of control by the commercially dominant power in the islands, Germany. Bayard refused to countenance this plan, and even let it be known that the United States would not participate in a joint protectorate, so that the conference broke up without achieving anything, and the local situation went from bad to worse.

By 1889, one British, three German, and three American warships were assembled in Apia harbour; the proportionate strength is interesting, for, though the new British imperialism was under way, she was, as a power rich in Far Eastern possessions, less interested in Samoa than a United States concerned for her maritime strength in the Pacific, and a Germany conscious of her tardy arrival in the field of colonial expansion. The ugly situation at Apia was ended in March, 1889, by an appalling hurricane in which all six American and German ships were lost, but it is characteristic of the new feelings between Britain and America that the Americans on one of the doomed vessels raised a cheer as the British *Calliope* struggled painfully toward the open sea and safety. The chastening effect of the hurricane led to a better frame of mind when a second Samoan conference was held in Berlin in the same year, and agreement was reached on a tripartite protectorate. The United States accepted it, partly to avoid a German one, and partly because the new Republican administration, which took office in that year, was less disinclined to an entangling commitment than that of Cleveland had been, or was to be when he came to office again in 1893; during this second term he still disapproved of the protectorate, and his Secretary of State, Gresham, deplored it as "the first departure from our traditional and well established policy of avoiding entangling alliances with foreign powers in relation to objects remote from this hemisphere."[1] The arrangement certainly proved unworkable in practice, and friction with Germany in the area became almost as serious as it had been before the establishment of the system, but the solution was not found in the Democratic suggestion of terminating the protectorate. With the coming of the McKinley administration and the new attitude of the United States to overseas possessions, the joint protectorate came to be regarded as an unsatisfactory stepping stone to an even more extreme entanglement, outright possession, and in 1899 the Samoan islands were, after matters came to a head in a nasty incident at Apia which the British and Americans agreed in blaming upon the German consul, divided between Germany and the United States, Great Britain receiving compensation elsewhere.

The new possession, however, was not the first which the United States acquired, for she had annexed Hawaii two years before, after a number of slow and tentative steps in that direction; it was fitting that it should be so, for it is, of all Pacific island groups, the most important to the defence of the United States, being nearer to the American mainland than to the dominions of any other power. As early as 1826, a form of treaty had been made with the native king for the friendly reception of American ships, and increasing commercial and missionary activity led to the early establishment of a paramount American influence. By 1842 five-sixths of all shipping visiting Hawaii was American, and even the anti-expansionist Webster, when Secretary of State, could declare that, though the United States had no intention of acquiring Hawaii, they could not view with equanimity any attempt by a foreign power to do so. In 1843 a rash British naval officer seized it, but happily his action was promptly repudiated by Aberdeen, who procured an Anglo-French agreement to respect the independence of the islands, which was very pleasing to the Administration in Washington, although America declined to enter such an entanglement herself.

After a number of abortive attempts to bring the islands into a more formal association with America, a comprehensive reciprocity agreement was finally ratified between Hawaii and the United States in 1875, followed by an amplification, in 1887, giving the United States exclusive right to the wonderful naval base of Pearl Harbour. The resident Americans, who were politically dominant there, strove by every means to promote annexation, particularly after 1890 when Congress discriminated against Hawaiian şugar, but were for some time frustrated by

[1] Q. ibid, p. 318.

American inhibitions against colonization (which were very strong in President Cleveland) and by native opposition, so that even the Harrison administration's connivance at the use of force did not suffice to achieve its object. Only with the wave of imperialism accompanying the Spanish-American War, and the feeling that Admiral Dewey must be supported by a firm base in his rear after his triumphant victory over the Spanish navy at Manila, was a resolution of annexation passed by both Houses of Congress in July, 1898. Japan protested, but Britain actually went so far as to bring unofficial pressure to bear upon the Administration to annex the islands quickly, for advice from Spring-Rice, then a very anti-German attaché at the British embassy in Berlin, direct to Ambassador Hay, caused the latter to advise his government to act "before war closes as otherwise Germany might seek to complicate the question with Samoa or Philippine Islands."[1] This was but one of many symptoms of the deliberately and warmly cordial attitude of the British Government to American expansion in the era of American imperialism.

II

THIS new Anglo-American understanding must, as L. M. Gelber writes, "take first rank" among "the decisive events of modern history".[2] These critical years were ones of apparent perplexity, but beneath the choppy waters of Anglo-American diplomacy the tide ran strongly and swiftly towards agreement. In both countries, emerging from a traditional isolation which, of course, went much deeper in the United States than in Britain, long-term political, social and sentimental trends worked towards it, and in both, sharp, immediate difficulties placed a premium on mutual friendship. The United States, venturing suddenly on a decisive scale into imperialist enterprise, was surprised, even shocked, by the hostility of the great powers of Europe, and correspondingly fortified by the friendliness of Britain, which not only took the form of a benevolent neutrality very vexing to most of Europe, but extended to a widespread sympathy for the kindred colonial adventures of the other 'Anglo-Saxon' nation. As Hay wrote to Lodge from London even before the war had broken out: "I do not know whether you especially value the friendship and sympathy of this country. I think it important and desirable in the present state of things, as it is the only European country

[1] L. M. Gelber, *The Rise of Anglo-American Friendship* (Oxford, 1938), p. 27.   [2] Ibid, p. 1.

where sympathies are not openly against us. . . . If we wanted it—which of course we do not—we could have the practical assistance of the British Navy—on the *do ut des* principle, naturally."[1] Britain was less surprised by the hostility of the other powers a year later, in the remarkably similar circumstances of the Boer War, but she was even more grateful for the resolute sympathy of the American Government because she was more conscious of the danger of her isolated position in the world. Indeed, the chief initiative, the primary impulse, towards an Anglo-American *entente* unquestionably came from Britain, and this was largely so because of her uneasiness at the international situation in which she found herself. Salisbury had been a leading exponent of Britain's isolation, and though he never quite overcame a reluctance to sacrifice her independence of action, he was forced to accede, before he gave up the Foreign Office in 1900, to the necessity for a quest for allies; after that date the search accelerated rapidly under the leadership of Lansdowne, the new Foreign Secretary, and above all of the dominating Chamberlain.

British misgivings arose not merely from the vague but ominous sense of being faced with more powerful rivals in the world, but also from the specific circumstances of international affairs. Russia had long been the British bogey and France the traditional enemy, and relations with both were strained. Germany was not a traditional foe, but now that the restraining hand of Bismarck had been removed, the British people began to be increasingly apprehensive of the aims of an Empire ruled by the flamboyant Kaiser Wilhelm II. Yet, in the aftermath of the Venezuela incident, the attitude of the United States remained aloof, and it was in any event most unlikely that she could be tempted into anything as decisive as an alliance. At first, therefore, Britain looked elsewhere for support. In the Far East, after the United States had refused to respond to overtures for positive co-operation, she was successful in finding the aid she sought in Japan, with whom she signed a specific alliance—her first hard and fast international commitment in this era—in 1902.

In Europe efforts were made to explore the possibilities of an alliance with Germany; tentative feelers had been put out as early as 1895 by Salisbury, and rejected by the Kaiser. Despite this rebuff, Chamberlain in 1898 began, in the absence of Salisbury in the South of France, and continued after his return, a campaign for an Anglo-German alliance, even offering to join the Triple Alliance, which was already dividing Europe into two armed camps; but he accompanied it

[1] Q. Mowat, *Diplomatic Relations*, p. 280.

by an equally ardent expression of his desire for a wide understanding with the United States, and this was certainly his prior wish, his first love. "He is extremely desirous of a close alliance with us," wrote Hay after a conversation with him on 3 April, "or if that is prevented by our traditions, of an assurance of common action on important questions." He even went so far as to say, "I should rejoice in an occasion in which we could fight side by side. The good effect of it would last for generations."[1] What he envisaged at this time was a threefold combination of Britain, the United States and Germany, but, though his desire to find friends led him to make a public approach to Germany in his famous speech of 13 May, he showed clearly where his heart really lay by his references to America on the same occasion :

> I don't know what the future has in store for us; I don't know what arrangements may be possible with us; but this I do know and feel, that the closer, the more cordial, the fuller, and the more definite these arrangements are, with the consent of both peoples, the better it will be for both and for the world—and I go even so far as to say that, terrible as war may be, even war itself would be cheaply purchased if, in a great and noble cause, the Stars and Stripes and the Union Jack should wave together over an Anglo-Saxon alliance.[2]

The American Administration did not object to British efforts to win over Germany from her hostility to the American attack upon Spain, though Hay wrote, "Of course I give no encouragement to any suggestion of an alliance, which seems to me impracticable",[3] but in another speech eighteen months later on 30 November, 1899, Chamberlain declared, "If the Union between England and America is a powerful factor in the cause of peace, a new Triple Alliance between the Teutonic race and the two great branches of the Anglo-Saxon race will be a still more potent influence in the future of the world." This utterance, which impertinently tweaked the noses of Russia and France in the most difficult days of the Boer War and which came only two days after the termination of a most unpopular visit to England by the Kaiser himself, outraged opinion in all three countries addressed, as well as in the rest of Europe. Not only did Grey say that Chamberlain must be kept out of foreign politics "or he will make everything impossible, even friendship with America",[4] but American public opinion, now that the Spanish-American War was over, displayed a marked lack of enthusiasm for the proposal, although the Administration were not unsympathetic towards it, at least in theory. Happily, however, for Anglo-

[1] Gelber, p. 21.   [2] Q. Mowat, *Diplomatic Relations*, p. 280.
[3] Q. Gelber, p. 22.   [4] Q. ibid, p. 70.

American relations, though not for Anglo-German friendship, German public opinion was even more bitterly averse from it, and in face of the storm of Anglophobia which blew up, Von Bulow not merely avoided any reference in the Reichstag to Chamberlain's proposal, but chose the moment to ask support for a new programme of naval building. Hope of an Anglo-German alliance did not expire yet, though it was dying fast in the face of German hostility and the swift growth of anti-German feeling in Britain. In 1901 a last official Anglo-German exploration of the possibilities took place under the aegis of Lord Lansdowne, but came to nothing, owing to the mutual mistrust of the two powers. One of the five clauses in the British draft for a treaty stipulated, "It is agreed that this Convention shall not apply to questions on the American Continent, nor bind either High Contracting Party to join in hostilities against the United States of America", but, even despite that fact, the failure of the negotiations seems to have been ascribed by Lansdowne primarily to "[t]he risk of entangling ourselves in a policy which might be hostile to America. With our knowledge of the German Emperor's views in regard to the United States, this is to my mind a formidable obstacle."[1]

Fundamentally it was fear of Germany which drove Britain to turn elsewhere, and to seek—among other things—for any practicable form of association with the United States, in order to effect a reinsurance which would protect her rear in the west should she be engaged in battle to the east. As Henry Adams put it,

> [I]n London, in 1898, the scene was singularly interesting to the last survivor of the Legation of 1861. He thought himself perhaps the only person living who could get full enjoyment of the drama. He carried every scene of it, in a century and a half since the Stamp Act, quite alive in his mind. . . . [E]very step . . . had the object of bringing England into an American system . . . and suddenly, by pure chance, the blessing fell on Hay. After two hundred years of stupid and greedy blundering . . . the people of England learned their lesson. . . . [T]he sudden appearance of Germany is the grizzly terror which in twenty years effected what Adamses had tried for two hundred years in vain—frightened England into America's arms.[2]

And America welcomed her, after her own fashion, for despite sporadic efforts by the German Government to win her friendship, she was almost as convinced as Britain of the danger of Germany's aspirations.

German hostility during the Spanish-American War made plain what sustained differences over such issues as that of Samoa had long indi-

[1] Q. ibid, pp. 89, 92. [2] *Education of Henry Adams*, pp. 362-3.

cated, and Admiral Dewey could declare outright in 1899 that America's next war would be with Germany, while American suspicion grew that Germany had rash designs in the Western hemisphere. This suspicion, though perhaps unfounded, was very real, and was not lessened by Germany's part in the coercion of Venezuela in 1902-3, when the British Ambassador could write from Washington that "suspicion of the German Emperor's designs in the Caribbean Sea is shared by the Administration, the Press, and the public alike."[1] Nor was it reduced by the persistent efforts of the German Government, once they became alive to its seriousness, to woo the Americans, and thus break up the Anglo-American *entente*, for these attempts patently did not come from the heart. The difficulties in German economic life, precipitated by the high American tariffs of the nineties, bred German hatred for the United States, and this economic envy was accompanied by a profound jealousy of the strength and position of this great rival newcomer among the powers. Even before the Spanish-American War Roosevelt had been suspicious of German intentions, and he and many other influential Americans hardened in this conviction as the years went by. In 1898 Hay wrote to Lodge that "the jealousy and animosity felt toward us in Germany is something which can scarcely be exaggerated. . . . The Vaterland is all on fire with greed and terror of us."[2] According to Mark Sullivan in *Our Times* fear of Germany was a principal American motive in the *rapprochement* with Britain, for Germany had now become "the dark and dreadful enemy to be feared and guarded against",[3] which, according to Kipling, England had still been, even as late as 1896.

This great change owed much to the influence of Admiral Mahan, for his long mission to convince not only the whole Anglo-Saxon world of the identity of its fundamental interests, but also to teach the American part of it the supreme importance of sea power, had far-reaching effects upon the diplomatic and international developments of these years. It reinforced Britain's determination to look to her moat; it taught the Americans to build a great navy; it made axiomatic the British and American beliefs that their navies could only be complementary and never hostile; and it caused both to fear any potential rival's nautical strength, at the same time as it convinced such rivals of the necessity or desirability of acquiring it. The masters of Germany had themselves devoured Mahan's works; as the Kaiser said, "I am trying to learn it by heart. It is a first-class work and classical in all

[1] Q. Gelber, p. 119.   [2] Q. Davis, p. 97.

[3] Q. Mowat, *American Entente*, p. 143.

parts". Presciently did he pencil alongside the Admiral's name, in the list of delegates to the First Hague Conference, the words, "Our greatest and most dangerous foe."[1] It has long been appreciated that the naval question, as Halévy wrote, was "beyond all doubt the decisive factor which determined the breach between"[2] Britain and Germany, and that it was the great 1901 naval law of Germany (which had possessed only a third-class navy in 1895), proclaiming her intention of providing herself with a fleet inferior only to the British and capable even of meeting that on equal terms in the North Sea, which precipitated the long and deadly rivalry. It is not so commonly realized that this naval rivalry was also a potent factor in arousing American mistrust of Germany, for although the rise of the two into the first rank of naval powers coincided almost exactly, the growth of American naval armaments had not attracted so much attention as that of Germany.

This development in the policy of the United States was a natural manifestation of the new American power, and one advocated by Mahan and his disciples. These were naturally strong in the Policy Board of the Navy, which recommended in 1890 raising the number of American battleships from none to thirty-eight; to so remarkable an American ambition the Kaiser felt impelled to call Queen Victoria's attention. In the event, the Secretary of the Navy only asked for twenty, and Congress only authorized three, but these were a beginning in a swift and formidable growth, and by 1905 the strength of the navy in battleships, built or building, was twenty-eight. In 1913 the General Board of the Navy, first created in 1900, called for forty-eight battleships; perhaps more significant, Senator Lodge had in 1904 launched a campaign for a navy second only to Great Britain's, and in 1906 *Jane's Fighting Ships* for the first time actually placed the U.S. Navy second to the British. Congressional debates made it very clear that this new force was directed primarily at Germany, which now ran a close third, even though some American alarm was being felt at the rising power of Japan. The opening of the Panama Canal in 1914 put the seal on the strength of the two-ocean navy of the United States, three years before she had occasion to use it against Germany.

Thus an increasing sense of insecurity on the part of both powers, and particularly their fear of Germany, drove them towards agreement. But the process was not only the result of negative, and to a great extent impersonal, causes. Germany was not feared simply because she was powerful, but because of British and American mistrust of what she

---

[1] Q. Davis, pp. 25-6.   [2] *England 1895-1905*, p. 126.

would do with her power. It was because such fears no longer divided the British Empire and the United States that the three thousand mile Canadian frontier remained undefended and that it was not merely presumed, but accepted as the fundamental basis of all defensive calculations in both lands, that their two navies would never be turned against one another. Anglo-American co-operation and British and American sea power were indissolubly linked together, not only in the thought of Mahan, but by the remorseless logic of facts. Their swift realization of this was greatly to the credit of both peoples, and they reaped their reward in mutual friendship, but it served also to stimulate crusaders in the good cause to greater exertions. Efforts made to achieve amity were more strenuous in the case of Britain because her need was more urgent and much greater. The Atlantic was still a most formidable barrier when protected by a great fleet: the English Channel was less daunting to a potential foe. The American isolationist spirit and American inhibitions against international entanglements went very deep: those of Britain less so. It was no accident that Anglo-American friendship grew in strength almost exactly in proportion as American world interests expanded. Mahan had written in 1897, with that prophetic sense which has made Englishmen accept his main judgements as axioms of international life:

> The same tendency is shown in the undeniable disposition of the British people and of British statesmen to cultivate the good-will of the United States, and to draw closer the relations between the two countries. For the disposition underlying such a tendency Mr. Balfour has used an expression, "race patriotism",—a phrase which finds its first approximation, doubtless, in the English-speaking family, but which may well extend its embrace, in a time yet distant, to all those who have drawn their present civilization from the same remote sources. . . . That there is a lukewarm response in the United States is due to that narrow conception which grew up with the middle of the century, whose analogue in Great Britain is the Little England party, and which in our own country would turn all eyes inward, and see no duty save to ourselves. How shall two walk together except they be agreed? How shall there be true sympathy between a nation whose political activities are world-wide, and one that eats out its heart in merely internal political strife? When we begin really to look abroad, and to busy ourselves with our duties to the world at large in our generation—and not before—we shall stretch out our hands to Great Britain, realizing that in unity of heart among the English-speaking races lies the best hope of humanity in the doubtful days ahead.[1]

[1] *The Interest of America in Sea Power*, pp. 257-9.

From this he went on to point out how the Atlantic binds rather than divides the nations living upon its shores; and it was, indeed, in the North Atlantic alliance of the mid-twentieth century that his prophecy finally found its fulfilment. But though it was many years before the majority of his countrymen came to agree with Mahan, his perception of Britain's desire to cultivate American friendship in his time was exceedingly accurate.

This desire can come as no surprise to us, who have observed that, for many years, warm feelings in Britain towards America had always been far more pronounced than had reciprocal sentiments in the United States, but it is still something of an effort to bring home to our minds and imaginations the extent to which Britons deliberately, persistently, energetically and even with a sense of urgency, set out to win the friendship of the United States at this time. As Henry James put it in 1898, "It's strange, the consciousness possible to an American here today, of being in a country in which the drift of desire . . . is that we shall swell and swell, and acquire and *require*, to the top of our opportunity."[1] Britain veritably laid siege to the citadel of American confidence, and of this wholehearted procedure their positive assault upon Mahan himself may serve as a good example. In his first published work in 1890 he had avowed a "cordial understanding with Britain" to be "one of the first of our external interests," and he remained always the apostle of Anglo-American friendship. His motives for this belief were not sentimental, for he was "unemotional as a gun turret"[2] and declared that "both nations . . . properly seek their own interest",[3] but his opinions were none the less influential or solid for that. They were not merely welcomed in Britain more enthusiastically than in the United States, because they embodied a policy of sea power which Britain had followed instinctively for more than two centuries, but also because of the power over Englishmen at this time of his appeal for Anglo-American co-operation.

Seldom has any man been lionized in English society as he was on his first visit to Britain in 1894, two years before the Venezuela incident; and few Americans, if any, have exercised a comparable influence over English minds. The Prince of Wales summoned him specially for a second audience in order to continue their discussion of sea power; he talked with Kitchener and Roberts, with the First Lord of the Admiralty and Admiral Beresford; he received degrees from both Oxford and Cambridge in one week; Oxford seriously considered providing him with a chair of history; and the Prime Minister, Lord

[1] *Letters of Henry James* (I), p. 316.   [2] Davis, p. 19.   [3] Q. ibid, p. 19.

Rosebery, was reduced to writing to him "in the forlorn hope of being able to persuade you to dine with me quietly . . . [w]hen we might have a conversation less interrupted than was possible the other night; but I know it is a forlorn hope." Though his influence at home, where he was not preaching to an audience already converted, was slower of growth, it was great and sure, while he early threw under his spell figures as diverse and as influential as Cabot Lodge, Theodore Roosevelt, John Hay, Henry White, Walter Hines Page and even, in his last months, Franklin D. Roosevelt.

It was typical of the extremes to which many Englishmen at this time were prepared to go in the hope of an American alliance that Lord George Hamilton, once before, and again later, First Lord of the Admiralty, proposed as a toast at the great banquet in Mahan's honour towards the end of his tour, "England and the United States are not two nations, but one; for they are bound together by Heaven's act of Parliament and the everlasting law of nature and fact."[1] Mahan himself gave serious consideration to *Possibilities of Anglo-American Reunion*, in 1894, and Cecil Rhodes expressed the feelings of the advocates of Anglo-American unity succinctly when he said: "What an awful thought it was that if we had not lost America . . . the peace of the world would have been secured for all Eternity."[2] Britons, who were toying with the idea of English Speaking Union at the turn of the century, numbered in their midst men as different as H. G. Wells, Bertrand Russell, Sidney Webb, Lord Haldane, Sir Charles Dilke, Alfred Austin, Francis Thompson, Rudyard Kipling and W. E. Henley. Austin, the Poet Laureate, put it in perhaps its most famous form:

> *Yes, this voice on the bluff March gale,*
> *We severed too long have been:*
> *But now we have done with a worn-out tale,*
> *The tale of an ancient wrong,*
> *And our friendship shall last long as love doth last*
> *And be stronger than death is strong.*[3]

On 13 July, 1898, the Anglo-American League was formed in London, and fourteen days later its Anglo-American Committee in New York, for it was in these months that the most sudden and vocal outburst of British friendliness towards America took place. The publication of James Bryce's *American Commonwealth* in the previous decade had heralded the new British attitude, and it was exemplified in such

[1] Q. ibid, pp. 22-3.　　[2] Q. Heindel, p. 130.
[3] Q. Davis, pp. 94-5.

small things as the restoration in 1897 to the United States of the manuscript of the *Log of the Mayflower*, through the good offices of the Queen and the Archbishop of Canterbury, which, according to Senator George F. Hoar, "did more to cement the bonds of friendship between the people of the two countries than forty canal treaties."[1] But though these sentiments were reciprocated by some Americans like Professor G. B. Adams and Carl Schurz, many remained indifferent and even hostile; as Andrew Carnegie conceded at the beginning of the decade, there was a general ill will in America towards Britain, whereas "the masses of the English people cordially loved and admired America." During the period with which we are concerned, opinion in America underwent a rapid change in the face of a British display of affection, which it was hard to resist when common interests pulled in the same direction, but the time-lag did not pass unobserved in Britain. As the *Telegraph* put it, "American diplomacy still seems to be affected with a curious dislike of England, while any Englishman now feels a kind of family pride in the strength of America."[2]

English statesmen took a lead in seeking American friendship, and in some cases seemed to outrun public opinion, as displayed in the Press, in doing so. All the important figures of these years, with the possible exception of Salisbury, went repeatedly on record in favour of co-operation with America, and even the old Marquess, in his realistic fashion, saw the implications of America's new position and rapidly learnt the lesson, which English public opinion taught him, in the Venezuela affair. Balfour, who succeeded him as Prime Minister, said in later years to Ambassador Page: "I have now lived a long life . . . but if I have been fortunate enough to contribute, even in the smallest degree, to drawing closer the bonds that unite our two countries, I shall have done something compared with which all else that I may have attempted counts in my eyes as nothing."[3] The Liberal Opposition, led by Campbell-Bannerman, Asquith and Grey, were even more strongly drawn to the United States because they had a far deeper mistrust of militaristic Germany.

But head and shoulders above all other exponents of Anglo-American friendship in these years rose Joseph Chamberlain. Married to an American wife, strong emotions prompted him to this course; a self-made Birmingham business man and Dissenter, he had in some ways more in common with Americans than with such colleagues as

[1] Q. B. A. Reuter, *Anglo-American Relations during the Spanish-American War* (New York, 1924), p. 56.

[2] Q. Davis, pp. 12, 17.   [3] Q. *Life and Letters of W. H. Page*, II, p. 250.

the aristocratic Salisbury and the aloof Balfour; the foremost English opponent of the old isolationism, he sought instinctively and primarily a *rapprochement* with the United States. Throughout this decade of Conservative and Unionist power, stretching between his visit to Washington during the Venezuela crisis and his determination to solve the Alaskan dispute in 1903 by negotiation, all his influence in international affairs was thrown in favour of as full an Anglo-American understanding as could be achieved. He, and most of his countrymen, would have gone any distance in this pursuit, but he and they early realized, and to a large extent appreciated the reason for it, that they could expect only limited tangible gains from it.

This attitude was very clearly expressed in an article written by Chamberlain himself in *Scribner's* in December, 1898:

> So far as the United Kingdom is concerned, it may be taken as a fact that the British nation would welcome any approach to this conclusion, *that there is hardly any length to which they would not go in response to American advances,* and that they would not shrink even from an alliance *contra mundum,* if the need should ever arise, in defence of the ideals of the Anglo-Saxon race—of humanity, justice, freedom, and equality of opportunity.
>
> It must not be supposed, however, that in accepting an alliance as a possible and welcome contingency, *anything in the nature of a permanent or general alliance is either desirable or practicable.*
>
> Any attempt to pledge the two nations beforehand to combine defensive and offensive action in all circumstances must inevitably break down and be a source of danger instead of strength. All therefore that the most sanguine advocate of an alliance can contemplate is *that the United States and Great Britain should keep in close touch with each other, and that whenever their policy and their interests are identical they should be prepared to concert together the necessary measures for their defence.* It is to such a course of action that Washington seems to point when he says:
>
> "Taking care always to keep ourselves, by suitable establishments, in a respectable defensive posture, we may safely trust to temporary alliances for extraordinary emergencies."[1]

It can be seen that the British case was not advanced altogether without skill, and enemies of the Anglo-American *entente*, like Germany, might well have maintained here that the Devil could quote Scripture to his own purpose, for recognition of the limitations imposed upon the action of every American administration, by a long tradition of isolation firmly embedded in a democratic public opinion, was perhaps the

[1] Q. Dos Passos, pp. 213-4.

first pre-requisite of any form of co-operation. Bulow might write, in his *Memoirs*, with something like contempt, "England will stand far more from America than from any other Power, and even in purely diplomatic issues it is more difficult to make England take sides against America than to make any other Power do so",[1] but to that amenability she in large degree owed American participation in inflicting the two disastrous defeats which Bulow's countrymen were to suffer in the next half-century. This essential self-denying ordinance did mean that in the crisis of 1914 Britain had to wait three years, and in that of 1939 two years, for full American support, but without it, particularly in the former case, none might have been forthcoming at all.

Even the American statesman who was most ardent in his support of an Anglo-American *rapprochement*, and who dominated American foreign policy during most of McKinley's Presidency and influenced it even during Roosevelt's, John Hay, always accepted the practical limitations upon what he desired as axiomatic and unalterable: "As long as I stay here no action shall be taken contrary to my conviction that the one indispensable feature of our foreign policy should be a friendly understanding with England. But an alliance must remain, in the present state of things, an unattainable dream."[2] In fact, Hay, in his desire for British friendship and his gratitude for her benevolence during the Spanish-American War not only felt uncomfortable in this situation, but failed to realize as clearly as some members of the Senate he so much despised the distance that Britain would go for American good will, as the history of the Hay-Pauncefote Treaty was to show. But by 1901 the tune of American foreign policy had begun to be called by the other figure who dominated it during these years, Theodore Roosevelt, and he was to demonstrate even more clearly, in the Alaskan boundary dispute, how much America could get her way with Britain if she was determined to do so. Yet, though Roosevelt was not so Anglophile as Hay, and prided himself on the sturdy independence of United States policy during his Presidency, his basic feelings seem to have been expressed when he wrote in 1898, "I am glad there seems to be so friendly a feeling between the two countries, though I don't believe that we ought to have an alliance",[3] and when he wrote five years later to Mahan, whom he so much admired, "The settlement of the Alaskan boundary settled the last serious trouble between the British Empire and ourselves. . . . I feel very differently towards England from the way I feel towards Germany."[4]

[1] Q. Gelber, p. 55.   [2] Q. Mowat, *Diplomatic Relations*, p. 284.
[3] Q. Gelber, p. 18.   [4] Q. Bemis, p. 428.

Thus, though many Americans hung back, powerful personalities and groups in the United States in these years reacted cordially, though within limits, to British advances, or rather to what seemed to them the necessities of the situation. This found expression in some quarters which seem at first surprising, as when Richard Olney, only two years after the Venezuela outburst in which he played so prominent a part, wrote in the *Atlantic Monthly*:

> Nothing can be more obvious, therefore, than that the conditions for which Washington made his rule [of isolation] no longer exist. . . . There is a patriotism of race as well as of country—and the Anglo-American is as little likely to be indifferent to the one as to the other. Family quarrels there have been heretofore and doubtless there will be again, and the two peoples, at a safe distance which the broad Atlantic interposes, take with each other liberties of speech which only the fondest and dearest relatives indulge in. Nevertheless, that they would be found standing together against any alien foe by whom either was menaced with destruction or irreparable calamity, it is not permissible to doubt. Nothing less could be expected of the close community between them in origin, speech, thought, literature, institutions, ideals and in the kind and degree of the civilization enjoyed by both.[1]

The truth is that the flowering of Anglo-American friendship in these years, which are in many respects the vital ones in our story, was not due solely to American emergence as a world power, nor to Britain's increasing sense of insecurity, nor even to the actions of those in both countries who actively sought it, but also to the increasing similarities of predilection, interest and outlook between the two peoples. This symbiosis was to continue and to gain strength, but it was already obvious in these years. The dominance, during this decade, of conservative and imperialistic policies in both countries is most striking; the similarities of principle are plain and the sympathies of personality are almost equally so. Whether or not they had intimate personal contacts, the leading figures in both lands were well fitted to understand one another, for they talked — in the broadest sense — the same language; there were indeed some remarkable parallels. There was much in common between Theodore Roosevelt and Joseph Chamberlain; John Hay was well equipped to understand Lord Lansdowne; though the first was never really a political figure, it would be hard to find two men more alike in fundamental outlook than Henry Adams and Arthur Balfour. What is more, the sympathy between the Liberal

[1] Q. Dos Passos, pp. 226-7.

and Democratic Oppositions grew steadily, and was to provide an even stronger instance of cordiality in the next period. Parallels exist even between the careers of such significant figures for the future as Eugene Debs and Keir Hardie, Samuel Gompers and John Burns; those between such figures as Bret Harte and Rudyard Kipling need no emphasis.

It was no coincidence that in September, 1895, William Randolph Hearst purchased the New York *Journal*, and that in May, 1896, Alfred Charles William Harmsworth, later Lord Northcliffe, started the London *Daily Mail*; their methods, to some extent their policies, and the type of reader to which they appealed, were the same. There was a growing likeness between the two peoples which Grey pointed out to Roosevelt in 1906 in the words, "I should say that some generations of freedom on both sides have evolved a type of man and mind that looks at things from a kindred point of view."[1] This found recognition, in however imperfect and inaccurate a fashion, in the new vogue of "Anglo-Saxonism", for, as Heindel writes, "the strength of this racial concept was that . . . it picked up helpful additions wherever possible, the community of language, ideals, tradition, institutions, morals, morale, ethos, righteous ethics, tolerant justice, humanitarianism, and even political aims."[2] These multifarious points of contact made infinitely easier and much more enduring the *rapprochement* which the national self-interest and political ideals of the two peoples seemed increasingly to dictate.

III

CONGRESSIONAL creation of American ambassadorships in 1893, in the conviction that ministerial rank was no longer commensurate with the dignity of the United States, was not only symptomatic of America's new position in the world, but seemed also to have inaugurated the heyday of Anglo-American diplomatic representation; perhaps the only exception to an able run of diplomats on both sides was Sir Mortimer Durand, who replaced Pauncefote's successor, Herbert, when the latter died suddenly in September, 1903, quite soon after his appointment. Durand had more of the instincts of the administrator—he had been an Indian Civil Servant—than the diplomat, which largely accounted for his great admiration for Theodore Roosevelt, but which put him at a considerable disadvantage as Ambassador despite his undoubted

[1] Q. Heindel, p. 129.   [2] Ibid, p. 126.

ability. This admiration was not reciprocated by the President who found him "hard to know",[1] partly because Roosevelt had set his heart on getting, as British Ambassador, Cecil Spring-Rice, a relatively junior English diplomat who had kept bachelor quarters with Roosevelt in Washington one summer many years before and had even been best man at his wedding. Durand felt, too, that the influential Senator Lodge, though not Secretary of State Hay, mistrusted him. Despite all this, he was very warmly disposed towards the Americans, although he could write: "I do not believe concession pays in dealing with this country, any more than newspaper gush. It is a country where all the leading men are lawyers or men of business, and they negotiate on business lines with a tendency to sharp practice, if cornered."

But though his knowledge of the United States was in some respects superficial, he did perceive the new importance of Canada and said: "[T]he Canadians understand dealing with Americans better than we do, besides knowing the facts, so far as Canadian issues are concerned." "I believe that by using and directing the force of the Canadians in such matters, we shall do better than by trying to fight the case ourselves." In 1906 he was removed as a result of tactful pressure by the Americans.

Though Roosevelt did not get Spring-Rice as his successor, he did get an Ambassador who could certainly not be criticized for superficial knowledge of the United States—James Bryce, renowned and lifelong student and lover of the Americans. He set out from the moment of his arrival in March, 1907, as Lowell said, "to charm a people", and he tried to go direct, as his successors were increasingly to do, to the true source of American political power, the people. Though he was never, in fact, exuberantly popular with the masses or the Press, he was often treated rather as a distinguished American than as a stranger. He got on well with Secretary of State Root, but it is significant of the closeness of certain groups and attitudes in the two countries that he was, as an ardent Liberal, regarded by Roosevelt as "a dreamer of dreams,"[2] much as the Canadian Reciprocity Treaty which he negotiated was considered by the young bloods of the Tariff Reform Party in the British Parliament "as Bryce's plot".[3] Even more than his predecessor he made energetic efforts to keep a close contact with Canada. His old friend, Lord Grey, the Governor-General, wrote to him on one occasion: "The idea that Canada has been sacrificed again and again by John Bull in his desire to cultivate the friendship of Uncle Sam is rooted so deep in the conviction of Canadians that nothing that I can say, nothing that you can say, nothing that any Englishman can say, can uproot it". But later, he

[1] W.F.R., p. 286. [2] Q. ibid, pp. 290, 295, 307. [3] Q. ibid, p. 305.

could modify his opinion to the extent of saying, "You have dissipated, I hope for ever, the fear that the British Ambassador at Washington will not jealously protect the rights and interests of Canada."[1] The measure of the progress of Anglo-American understanding during previous years is shown by his comment, soon after his arrival, that he detected "a great change for the better since his earlier travels in the States, in American feeling towards Great Britain", and in the "tone of respect"[2] with which Canada was now mentioned; and both these improvements were certainly enhanced by his six-year period as Ambassador.

John Hay became Ambassador to the Court of St. James in 1897, during the aftermath of the Venezuela crisis; he was already well known in England and was one of the foremost American statesmen of his age. He wrote in 1898, "It is hardly too much to say that the interests of civilization are bound up in the direction the relations of England and America are to take in the next few months", and it was soon apparent that this direction was to be what he considered the right one, for he was a most important witness to the warmth of British feeling towards the United States during the Spanish-American War, at which time he wrote, "The commonest phrase here is: 'I wish you would take Cuba at once. *We* wouldn't have stood it this long.'"[3] Of his potentialities as Ambassador, his good friend Henry Adams correctly wrote, "In the long list of famous American Ministers in London, none could have given the work quite the completeness, the harmony, the perfect ease of Hay". When he left to take up the Secretaryship of State, only just a year after his arrival, he was succeeded by a man equally well disposed to the English, though not of such outstanding ability, Joseph Hodges Choate, a distinguished New York lawyer, who was popular in America except with the Irish; a leading Irish-American journal wrote: "In appointing Joseph Choate to be Ambassador to England Mr. McKinley has virtually spat into the face of every man and woman of Irish birth or blood in the United States". His popularity in Britain was evidenced by the rare honour of unanimous election as a Bencher of the Middle Temple, and by the great number of public speeches demanded from him, in one of which he made the happy observation that Downing Street was named after a native American, Sir George Downing, so that "We feel entirely at home in it."

In 1905 he was replaced by Hay's old friend Whitelaw Reid, who, as a man of great wealth, had been a Special Ambassador alongside Hay at the Diamond Jubilee of Queen Victoria, in order, as Hay said, that

[1] Q. ibid, p. 301.   [2] Q. ibid, p. 298.   [3] Q. W.A.A.E., p. 416.

he could administer to the pomps and vanities of this world which the expensive occasion demanded. It had long been the ambition of this editor and owner of the New York *Tribune* and close friend of Roosevelt to be appointed to the London Embassy. He made many warm friendships in England, from the King downwards, and declared, "There is no mistaking the absolute determination of the British Government and the Royal Family to embrace every opportunity to show their marked friendship for the United States."[1] That he reciprocated these sentiments and realized their full importance is shown by his quotation of words he heard forty years earlier from the lips of Dickens: "It would be better for this globe to be riven by an earthquake, fired by a comet, overrun by an iceberg and abandoned to the Arctic fox and bear, than that it should present the spectacle of those two great nations, each of whom has in its own way and hour striven so hard and so successfully for freedom, ever again being arrayed the one against the other."[2] He died at his post in Britain, the first American Ambassador to do so, in 1912, amidst widespread sorrow. His remains were sent back to America in the armoured cruiser *Natal,* and the King sent a heartfelt message of sympathy to President Taft, to which the latter replied very justly, "His intimate knowledge of both countries, his profound respect and love for England, entirely consistent with the highest loyalty on his part to this country, gave him peculiar influence for good in his great station."[3]

IV

IN the increasingly swift development of Anglo-American friendship the outbreak of the Spanish-American War in 1898 marked a first decisive acceleration. The Cuban rebellion of February, 1895, was the last and gravest revolt in a series stretching back through the nineteenth century, and it coincided with a more powerful disposition in the United States to interfere than had existed since the years of Southern expansionism before the Civil War. It found, too, a United States with the undisputed strength to do so, except possibly in the case of opposition from the still paramount naval power, which had on more than one occasion in earlier years prevented American annexation of Cuba. But Great Britain, it very soon became clear, no longer had any objection to American intervention, and events were to show that the United

[1] Q. ibid, pp. 418, 421, 427, 431.　　[2] Q. W.A.A.E., pp. 439-40.
[3] Q. ibid, p. 440.

States had no overwhelming disposition to annex this particular island. American action, indeed, was motivated partly by a deep and genuine humanitarianism, which became more influential as the civil war was protracted by the ruthless measures of the Spanish commander, General, or as he was commonly called in the American Press, "Butcher" Weyler, as well as by a desire to protect American lives and property. Economic expansionism, and the instinct to strengthen her strategic position also played their part.

As the situation grew more serious, the British Government began to make plain where its sympathies lay, and in October, 1897, Lord Salisbury informed Hay that British interests in Cuba were purely commercial and that she would look with favour on any policy which might restore tranquillity there. In the early months of 1898, despite half-hearted Spanish concessions to the Cubans, rumours of war multiplied, and on 9 February the Cuban rebels published a highly indiscreet private letter written to a friend by De Lôme, the Spanish Minister in Washington, which contained the assertion that Great Britain's policy was to encourage a war between Spain and America in order to cripple the economic expansion of the latter, which was becoming so threatening to Britain. This was not only a characteristic Spanish overestimate of the harm which a war with Spain might do the already mighty United States, but completely misunderstood British intentions. In fact, the publication of the letter did Anglo-American relations far more good than harm, since it also contained a most unflattering series of remarks about President McKinley, and, as the London correspondent of the New York *Tribune* wrote: "English comments on the Spanish Minister's breach of international etiquette have been inspired by a sense of justice and a spirit of good-will toward the United States. Nearly every journal describes the letter as an unpardonable outrage."[1]

But if they were at all in danger then, Anglo-American relations were shortly to be put to a much sharper test, for on 15 February the United States battleship, *Maine*, was sunk in Havana harbour by a mysterious and terrible explosion, with the loss of more than 250 American lives; and, despite Spanish attempts to avert the wrath to come which were now undoubtedly genuine, it became clear that outraged American feelings must produce war. Relations amply stood the strain. On the 16th Pauncefote called on the President to express British regret at the disaster, and British messages of sympathy flowed in, beginning with ones from the Queen and Prince of Wales. Despite a poignant appeal from the Spanish Queen-Regent to Queen Victoria and some traditional

[1] Q. Reuter, p. 68.

British feelings of friendliness towards Spain, Salisbury made it perfectly clear to his monarch that Britain would not intervene in the cause of peace, a determination which was strengthened by the "firmness, caution, and pacific circumspection"[1] of McKinley's policy during the next two months, which lasted until public opinion forced him to send his war message to Congress on 11 April, 1898. On 20 April he signed the joint resolution of intervention, and war was shortly declared to have existed since 21 April. During March close contact was maintained between the British and American Governments and there were constant rumours of an Anglo-American alliance; though this did not exist, the British Government created an impression which justified the American belief, as *The Times* reported, "that she has England's moral support in the policy of which she accepts the President as exponent."[2]

But on 7 April Pauncefote had participated, with the other major European representatives in Washington, in the presentation of a joint note expressing a hope that in the interests of humanity peace would be preserved. There was nothing improper in the tendering of such friendly offices, and the action was not badly received by American public opinion; indeed, there is some evidence that Pauncefote, who, as *doyen* of the diplomatic corps, presented and probably drafted the note, actually submitted the proposed form of it to Secretary of State Day before it was presented, and it is certain that, on instructions from London, he ascertained beforehand that such a note would be acceptable to the President.

Rather different was the proposal, which followed a week later, for a second joint note; but even this would never have seen the light of day, if the German Government had not later published what was almost certainly a biased account of the affair, in order to embarrass Anglo-American relations during the Boer War. It seems probable, though the affair is somewhat mysterious, that Pauncefote, as was proper in the senior ambassador, summoned, at the request of his colleagues, a further meeting at the British Embassy; he then proceeded, himself to draft a further note for presentation to the State Department, which was not wise, though his motive was, perhaps, to phrase it more moderately than might otherwise have been done. The French Ambassador was then permitted to make one or two very small alterations, which, however, changed the whole spirit of the note; Pauncefote failed to observe their effect and signed it, but it was fortunately referred back to the various governments before despatch. Not only Britain, but also Germany, refused to send it, which gave the latter the

[1] *The Times,* 8 March: q. ibid, p. 71.   [2] Q. ibid, p. 70.

opportunity to imply later that she had been the principal agent in preventing European intervention, rather than Britain. This later effort to promote Anglo-American misunderstanding, though it distressed Pauncefote's last weeks of life, did not achieve its object, for the Ambassador's reputation in the United States was far too solid to be upset by a doubtful German *canard*, even if his own Government felt bound to say that his actions had been "personal to himself and not in pursuance of any instructions from Her Majesty's Government."[1] President Roosevelt paid a special visit to the British Embassy to assure Pauncefote of his complete confidence, and is reported to have said,

> Not only do I not believe this Berlin story, but I know it is false. . . . I know Lord Pauncefote to be incapable of an act unfriendly to this country. Since he has been Ambassador he has striven with all his heart to promote good-will between England and us. If he had said and done what Germany accuses him of, it would have been disloyal to himself and treacherous to us. He is incapable of that. He is incapable of anything but true and honourable conduct.[2]

Nevertheless, only good luck and the good sense of the British Government, presided over, in the absence of Salisbury in the South of France, by Balfour, prevented what might have been an untoward incident in Anglo-American relations, for whatever Germany's motives in refusing to participate in the second note, they were not those of a power much more sympathetic towards the United States than the rest of the European Great Powers, which were strongly pro-Spanish. But everything depended upon Britain, for as long as she controlled the seas, no amount of anti-American feeling in Europe could have the least effect if she did not share it, and so far was this from being the case that Hay could write even before the war began that, so far as any hostile European coalition was concerned, the United States already enjoyed "the practical assistance of the British Navy".[3] From the very beginning, Balfour, powerfully supported by Chamberlain, easily carried the Government with him in a declaration to Hay on 6 April that, "Neither here nor in Washington did the British Government propose to take any steps which would not be acceptable to the United States."[4] To this policy of benevolent neutrality the Government adhered without faltering throughout the course of the war, and there is no question that they in time enjoyed the wholehearted and often enthusiastic support

---

[1] Hansard: q. R. B. Mowat, *The Life of Lord Pauncefote* (London, 1929), p. 220.   [2] Q. ibid.   [3] Q. Gelber, p. 23.   [4] Q. Gelber, p. 19.

of the British people. There is some doubt as to the swiftness of this hardening of British opinion. Gelber writes, "From the outset, and almost unanimously, British public opinion swung to the side of the United States",[1] but Heindel, writing two years after Gelber, warns us that, "The reaction was not so blindly enthusiastic as legend has embalmed. . . . Our tariff policies, the threat to the gold standard, the Bering Sea controversy and especially Cleveland's warlike message of 1895 about the Venezuela boundary, had not been forgotten."[2] There were perhaps signs of caution in the Press at first, and some organs such as the *Saturday Review* remained anti-American throughout, but the words of this journal themselves, as Reuter points out, give a very suggestive indication of where the truth lies: "When we find the bulk of the English newspapers calling on us to admire the attitude of the United States and accord our moral support to the Washington Government, it is time to protest."[3]

Government policy certainly ran ahead of popular opinion in seeking American friendship, though it observed a strict technical neutrality, but there can be no doubt of the widespread support for this attitude. It showed itself practically in the British assumption of diplomatic responsibility for American interests in Spain and her colonies, and many of the populace in the former found it hard to distinguish between the neutral British and those whose interests they represented, so that they encountered considerable hostility. It was as true of the Spaniards then, as of the Mexicans later, that, as Spring-Rice was to write in 1913, they "can no more distinguish between a Britisher and an American than between a crocodile and an alligator."[4] In the Spanish colonies, and particularly Cuba, the British consuls not only did varied and painstaking work in the American interest, but far outran necessity in their zealous efforts to alleviate the sufferings, not only of the Americans, but also of the Cubans on behalf of the Americans, who were most anxious to ameliorate the condition of the native population they were liberating. The exertions of F. W. Ramsden, the British Consul at Santiago, for instance, were so great that he contracted a fatal illness from exhaustion and died on 10 August; General Wood, the American commander, ordered all flags to be flown at half-mast in tribute, and a formal note of appreciation was forwarded from Washington to the British Government.

In this Atlantic battle area was focused the chief attention of the

[1] Gelber, p. 17.   [2] Heindel, p. 51.   [3] Q. Reuter, p. 82.

[4] Stephen Gwynn (Editor), *The Letters and Friendships of Sir Cecil Spring-Rice* (London, 1929), II, p. 191.

United States blockade, in which, as in the American Civil War, her interest was that of a blockading power anxious to assert maximum rights against neutrals. But even less than in those days was Britain likely strongly to assert the contrary position. The United States had, in any case, early gained British approval in the war at sea, by declaring, which she had undertaken no previous obligation to do, that she would discountenance privateering, the great British naval bogey of the nineteenth century; and Britain firmly preserved her policy of strict but friendly neutrality when minor irritations arose at sea following the rapid establishment of a rigid American blockade in the West Indies. The United States, furthermore, behaved in a moderate manner towards British shipping, for out of a total of ten British prizes captured by the North Atlantic Fleet only four seem to have been condemned.

In the Pacific theatre, principally through the foresight of Theodore Roosevelt as Under-Secretary of the Navy, the forceful Admiral Dewey, in command of the Asiatic squadron, was able to defeat the Spanish fleet in the very harbour of Manila on 1 May, 1898. That his squadron had been able to coal before the war began was very largely due to the warm assistance of the British at Hong Kong, and, though, after the actual outbreak of war, neutrality was carefully observed, it is symptomatic that, even if the soldiers and sailors on the British warships, who watched the Americans sail out thence for the Philippines on 25 April, were not allowed to cheer, those on a hospital hulk moored nearby did so lustily. In Dewey's anxious weeks of waiting off Manila for troops from the United States which would enable the capture of the city, the situation in the Bay became increasingly tense, owing to the presence there, along with three other neutral forces, of a German fleet of five vessels, which was considerably stronger than Dewey's whole squadron. The reason for a fleet so disproportionate to the value of German interests was unquestionably Germany's hope by this means to stake a diplomatic claim to the possession of all or part of the Philippines after the war; uncertainty as to the future of the islands was encouraged by the reluctance of much of American public opinion to contemplate their retention, and it is unlikely that Germany had any actively hostile intentions against the United States. But this was by no means clear to the Administration, which certainly did not favour Germany as a residuary legatee of lands she had won by force of arms, for the last phase of the long Samoan dispute was beginning and German officials at all levels were behaving with a lack of tact which was becoming recognized as endemic in them, and which was irritating to a United States herself conscious of her new-found strength. In Berlin to the

Germans, and in London to his friend Hay, and no doubt the Foreign Office, the warning voice of Spring-Rice made itself heard, while the plain probabilities, in case of trouble between Germany and the United States, were evidenced by an increasing display of cordiality between British and American statesmen, and by increasing rumours in Europe of the negotiation of an Anglo-American alliance.

This further drawing together of the English-speaking naval powers was even more dramatically illustrated in the Pacific theatre of operations, where Vice-Admiral von Diederichs behaved with all the suspicious sensitiveness and effrontery of his superiors in Berlin. A series of incidents arose with Dewey, the gravest concerning the heaving-to of a German cruiser by an American ship, and feeling ran so high that he told Von Diederichs that "if Germany wants war, all right, we are ready."[1] In four of these incidents the senior British Officer, Captain Chichester, made positive decisions in favour of the American interpretation of international law, and on one occasion refused to join the Germans in a protest with the words, "This American admiral is so deadly right in all that he has done and all that he proposes to do, that, if we protest, we will surely show that we do not understand the law."[2] He had made it clear at the outset that his Government's orders were to comply with even more severe restrictions than those to which the German commander took exception. Furthermore, Dewey and Chichester were firm personal friends, spending a good deal of time together, and as the American vessels sailed into the bombardment of the city on 13 August, Chichester's guard was paraded on his ship, the *Immortalité*, and her band played a favourite tune of Dewey's, "Under the Double Eagle", while on receipt of official notification the next day that the port was open, he alone among the foreign officers acknowledged it by the national salute of twenty-one guns fired with the American ensign at the main. The moral of all this was perfectly plain, but the movement of the British ships on the 13th to a position from which they could better observe the effects of the bombardment, and which brought them between the American and German forces, resulted in a picturesque legend of silent service by the British to the American Navy which gave it even more striking point.

Events on the other side of the world at Gibraltar, where the Spanish Government's fears of an Anglo-American alliance caused the construction of fortifications menacing the fortress and brought down on its head so tart an assertion of Britain's neutrality that work on the fortifications promptly ceased, showed just the same blend of actual

[1] Q. Bailey, p. 515.　　[2] Q. Reuter, p. 146.

British neutrality with warm British sympathy for the United States, a combination which, in view of British sea power and the ease with which her friend could handle the actual war, suited America's book much better than British belligerency, which might have had to be bought for a high price payable in the future.

In the first flush of realization, on both sides of the Atlantic, of the extent of the outburst of Anglo-American goodwill over the Spanish-American War, there had been much talk of an actual alliance, which had been well received in both countries but particularly in Britain. In the United States, however, as it became certain that there would be no European intervention and that victory would be swift and easy, reservations as to so cast-iron an entanglement multiplied. Typical are the reactions to Chamberlain's outright proposal in his 13 May speech. The Chicago *Tribune* wrote on 14 May: "There may never be such an alliance in formal written terms. And there may be. But . . . the two great branches of the Anglo-Saxon race are drawing nearer and nearer together for co-operation in peace, and, in logical sequence, in war as well." But the next day it added that, though the two nations "should live on terms of amity, so that if it is best at any time that they should act together there will be no existing bad feeling to make it more difficult for them to do so," an Anglo-Saxon alliance was not "likely".[1]

There is little doubt that British support for an alliance would have been forthcoming, for Chamberlain's ex-colleagues of the Liberal party, in Opposition, were so enthusiastic for Anglo-American co-operation that Hay advised Chamberlain, to whom he was very close, "not to let the Opposition have a monopoly of expressions of goodwill to America."[2] But when it became apparent that no such fixed arrangement was possible, Britain understood—to some extent sympathized with—the American viewpoint, and remained ardent for her friendship. Chamberlain made this very clear when he defended his policy in the Commons in June, predicting the dangers of British isolation in the face of a European coalition. He agreed that the Americans did not then desire an alliance: "They do not ask for our assistance and we do not want theirs." But who could say "that the occasion may not arise, foreseen as it has been by some American statesmen, who have said that there is a possibility in the future that Anglo-Saxon liberty and Anglo-Saxon interests may hereafter be menaced by a great combination of other Powers? Yes, Sir, I think that such a thing is possible, and, in that case, whether it be America or whether it

[1] Q. Reuter, pp. 155-6. [2] Q. ibid, p. 152.

be England that is menaced, I hope that blood will be found to be thicker than water."[1] There were few things that Britain would not have done for American friendship; there was hardly any form of it, however limited, that she would not accept. To milder forms of American imperialism she had long been accustomed; in its present vigorous form she welcomed it with open arms—indeed it stimulated her in her turn. "America had acted as a much needed tonic. America's example . . . gave renewed life to her belief in manifest destiny. . . . Acquiescence in our new imperialism struck the British as being the best bid for Anglo-American friendship."[2]

Thus both British public opinion and the British Government began to press the United States to retain the Philippines after the war; only in the last resort would Britain herself try to obtain them in order to prevent any other power from doing so. In July, 1898, Hay cabled to the Secretary of State that the "British Government prefer to have us retain Philippine Islands, or failing that, insist on option in case of future sale."[3] Even the anti-imperialist James Bryce declared that Great Britain would regard the entrance of the United States into the Philippines "with nothing but satisfaction." Though there was to be some disillusion later when things went wrong in the Philippines, and though their attitude was not untouched by the condescension of an elder brother, this British enthusiasm for American expansion extended as far as a belief in Yankee capacity for colonial government; as the *Quarterly Review* wrote, "We have no doubt whatever of the capacity of our kinsmen to grapple effectively with all the difficulties and dangers which they may encounter in the Philippines. We believe that they share the British secret of governing inferior races at a distance with justice and firmness, and with the smallest possible exercise of military power."[4] This is what Kipling put in the form of a challenge,

Take up the White Man's burden—
Ye dare not stoop to less—
Nor call too loud on Freedom
To cloke your weariness.

Or, as a Nebraska editor wryly remarked, "In other words, Mr. Kipling would have Uncle Sam take up John Bull's burden."[5] In the same way Britain was shortly to urge that intervention in Latin America, later known as the Roosevelt Corollary to the Monroe Doctrine, which was a feature of American policy in these expansive years, and this she did

[1] Q. Gelber, p. 26.   [2] Heindel, p. 73.
[3] Q. Gelber, p. 31.   [4] Q. Reuter, pp. 164, 179.   [5] Q. Brebner, p. 246.

not merely in order that she might thus have assurance of the recovery of her own debts, but also because it marked an effective extension of American power.

Britain was not unaware of the instability of American public opinion, and of the resultant risk of subsequent American refusals to participate in European crises, but this made no difference to her pursuit of American friendship; by it she had everything to gain, while unthinkable disaster faced her if she brought down American hostility upon her head. With a sensitiveness to international trends born of long experience, she realized first among the nations of Europe the true extent of American power; from this time forward she never ceased to be aware of the writing on the wall and to do her best to ensure that American enmity should never be directed at her, but, if possible, against her enemies. Thus early was the tone of Anglo-American relations for the next half century set, a tone of general agreement on broad principles, allowing for specific arrangements on particular questions, but avoiding always unilateral and entangling alliances.

It is this broad agreement of principle which accounts for the remarkably platitudinous nature of much public speaking and writing about Anglo-American friendship, but it accounts also for the unprecedented success of the relationship, despite blunders on both sides. John Hay—very fittingly, since none was more the architect of the relationship than he—was striking exactly this note when he declared at the Lord Mayor's banquet on 21 April, 1898 : "The good understanding between us is based on something deeper than mere expediency. All who think cannot but see there is a sanction like that of religion which binds us in partnership in the serious work of the world. . . . We are joint ministers in the same sacred missions of freedom and progress, charged with duties we cannot evade by the imposition of irresistible hands."[1]

Thus with the terms of the Spanish-American peace treaty signed on 10 December, 1898, the British were very well pleased, for it constituted a decisive extension of American power, and a weakening, albeit temporary, of American inhibitions against imperialism, and even against some participation in world affairs. By it, Spain gave up sovereignty in Cuba, and the United States established what was in effect a form of protectorate over it; Puerto Rico was ceded outright to the United States, whose position in the Caribbean was thus greatly strengthened. But her most spectacular expansion was in the Pacific, as befitted an administration of Republicans whose foreign policy had

[1] Q. Reuter, p. 151.

581

had a Pacific bias, as Walter Lippman points out, ever since the days of Seward. In that area the United States gained Guam and the Philippines, the latter for a payment of $20 million. In this same year she had annexed Hawaii; in 1899 she also acquired American Samoa; in the next year she took final possession of unclaimed Wake Island; in 1925 she was to do so of Swain's Island, which had been inhabited by Americans as early as 1856. She had already taken possession of the Midway Islands in 1867. To Johnston's Island and the Palmyra Islands, which she and Britain both claimed, the British Government in due course relinquished its claim—specifically in the case of the former, by default of possession in the case of the latter. Thus both in the Caribbean and the Pacific, but particularly the Pacific, the Spanish-American War marked a revolution in the balance of power, for despite violent opposition to this abandonment, as it appeared to some, of traditional American policies of isolation, the Treaty of Paris passed the Senate by 57 votes to 27, on 6 February, 1899. As Henry Adams wrote, "America had made so vast a stride to empire that the world of 1860 stood already on a distant horizon somewhere on the same plane with the republic of Brutus and Cato".[1]

The increase in American power in the Caribbean was very largely, and in the Pacific to a considerable extent, at the expense of Britain, yet the loser cheerfully urged the winner on, happy in the new dispensation. No enunciation of the new American creed was too strong for British opinion, since it seemed but an echo of, and not a jarring counter-blast to, many of her own voices; even such words as those of Albert J. Beveridge, which would have sounded so starkly ominous from Berlin, were not unacceptable:

> But did the opposition say that, unlike the other lands, these lands of Spain are not contiguous? The ocean does not separate us from the lands of our duty and desire—the ocean joins us. . . . Steam joins us, electricity joins us—the very elements are in league with our destiny. Cuba not contiguous? Porto Rico not contiguous? The Philippines not contiguous? Our navy will make them contiguous![2]

They were acceptable words because they came from the same source as others which were comforting and even flattering:

> If England can govern foreign lands, so can America. If it can supervise protectorates, so can America. . . . Never forget that we are

[1] *Education of Henry Adams*, p. 367.

[2] Q. C. G. Bowers, *Beveridge and the Progressive Era* (Cambridge, 1932), pp. 75-6.

Anglo-Saxon at heart. . . . We are of the blood which furnishes the world with its Daniel Boones, its Francis Drakes, its Cecil Rhodes.[1]

If it means Anglo-Saxon solidarity . . . if it means . . . an English-speaking people's league of God for the permanent peace of this war-worn world, the stars in their courses will fight for us, and countless centuries will applaud.[2]

Even those in Britain who opposed American, just as they opposed British, imperialism had the comforting knowledge that a band of brothers in the United States were just as vigorous in their opposition.

But sentiment, even the sentiment of patriotism, is not enough to explain British friendliness; conditions of self-interest had to dictate that the two patriotisms said mutually compatible things. The truth was that, as Henry Adams said, the Spanish-American War brought "England into an American system," which seemed to him for the first time in his life some evidence of a "possible purpose working itself out in history." But, though this might be the ultimate logic of the new situation, it meant equally that America was fulfilling certain British purposes. Both in the Caribbean and the Pacific the emergence of American power not only blocked some of the possible designs of Britain's potential enemies, but in due time actually released British forces and attention for concentration in other and more vital danger-areas. We shall see this process in the west with the settlement of the Isthmian question, to which British enthusiasm for the new dispensation in Cuba and Puerto Rico already pointed the way. More obvious now, and more immediately important to the British, was its effect in the Far East, and, indeed, for the United States the same was in a sense true, for the China and Panama questions were closely linked, in that American power policies in the Pacific dictated the necessity for a naval canal, as the voyage of the battleship *Oregon* round the Horn in the recent war dramatically illustrated. Henry Adams saw both things and drew his own conclusions:

He knew that Porto Rico must be taken, but he would have been glad to escape the Philippines. Apart from too intimate an acquaintance with the value of islands in the South Seas, he knew the West Indies well enough to be assured that, whatever the American people might think or say about it, they would sooner or later have to police those islands, not against Europe, but for Europe and America too. Education on the outskirts of civilized life teaches not very much, but it taught this; and one felt no call to shoulder the load of archipelagoes

[1] Q. ibid, pp. 74, 77.   [2] Q. ibid, p. 69.

in the antipodes when one was trying painfully to pluck up courage to face the labor of shouldering archipelagoes at home.

But "[t]he country decided otherwise"; and in any case, of Britain's paramount and immediate concern at this time there could be no doubt, for "in London, the balance of power in the East came alone into discussion".[1]

V

F OR though, in the long run and in Europe, it was to be fear of Germany which most influenced the Anglo-American relationship, at this juncture the Far East loomed perhaps larger in British minds, and the Caribbean alone exceeded the Orient in importance in the eyes of Americans. There the defeat of China by Japan in the Korean War of 1894-5 was the signal for a series of European depredations, for Russia, France and Germany intervened to check the advance of Japan upon the mainland and to reward themselves at the expense of China; Russia by the concession to build the Manchurian railway, France by a sphere of influence in Kuang-Chow-Wan, and Germany by Kaio-Chau, which she seized in November, 1897, whereupon Russia also took Port Arthur. This alignment of the Continental powers seemed politically most ominous to the British Empire, as well as threatening to her trade with China, which exceeded £32 million a year and was more than 70 per cent of China's total foreign trade.

The generally accepted British policy was that of the Open Door, designed to protect her trading interests, which Balfour described in a speech on 10 January, 1898; this declared that its sole object was to insist that the policy of the Chinese Government "shall not be directed towards the discouragement of foreign trade."[2] Britain had no desire to carve accessions of territory out of the Chinese Empire, and she was not opposed to the extension there of the legitimate commercial interests of other nations. This attitude coincided closely with that of the United States, whose trade with China was second only to Britain's, and who had close contacts with China in the mission field. Needless to say, a Japan whose spoils of war had been seized by other powers was likely to sympathize with any Anglo-American move to assert these principles in China.

When an effort to make a direct agreement with Russia failed, the British Government, under the impulse of a Chamberlain already

[1] *Education of Henry Adams*, pp. 363-4.   [2] Q. Reuter, p. 116.

584

anxious for Anglo-American co-operation in every possible sphere, approached the Administration in Washington on 8 March to enquire, as the Secretary of State reported, whether it

> could count on the co-operation of the United States in opposing action by foreign Powers which may tend to restrict freedom of commerce of all nations in China. . . . British Ambassador has been answered . . . saying that the President is in sympathy with the policy which shall maintain open trade in China, that all his advices . . . indicate no foreign occupation which interferes with that trade . . . , and that he does not see any present reason for the departure of the United States from our traditional policy of respecting (*sic*) foreign alliances and so far as practicable avoiding interference or connection with European complications.[1]

This decision was natural enough in view of the imminence of the Spanish War, and in any case, though Sherman was not a far-sighted Secretary of State, and though there was some American desire, as expressed in the New York *Times* for instance, to support the British Open Door policy, there is little doubt that the American public would have endorsed McKinley's decision had they known of it. Indeed, when the proposal was renewed on 8 January, 1899, three months after Hay had left London to become Secretary of State, it was again rejected, and, as we shall see, even Roosevelt did not in actual fact go so very much farther. Already the actions of the United States were showing their gravest early twentieth-century weakness, the inability of advocates of a bold foreign policy to obtain public consent to the use of force in the world for purposes which they believed to be ultimately essential to American interests. Yet this was to some extent a failing of democracy, rather than of American democracy, for in 1931 Washington was to receive an analogous reply from London to what seemed in some respects a similar request for co-operation in the Far East; it was a failing, however, to which the United States was to be peculiarly prone for the first forty years of the century.

Its immediate result in this case was to make Britain turn elsewhere, with perhaps incalculable consequences for the future of the East, for in 1902 she finally signed the alliance with Japan by means of which the latter sprang so swiftly into the ranks of the Great Powers. But before that date, Britain felt compelled, by the American reluctance to participate, to play her own hand in the European game, by the occupation of Weihawei, by the enlargement of the Hong Kong area, and by extracting substantial railway concessions from the Chinese—all in the course of

[1] Q. Gelber, p. 13.

1898. In the next year she recognized Russia's sphere of influence north of the Great Wall in return for recognition of her own in the Yangtze valley. Thus when America in due course turned to Britain for Far Eastern support, the latter's hands were no longer free, as they had been in March, 1898. But it is to be observed that there is already apparent here the willingness of Britain to accept diplomatic rebuffs from the United States without undue resentment; the American cold shoulder did not in the least affect the growth of her friendliness. This determination to humour America was really put to the test—and triumphed—when it became apparent that the United States might erect a high tariff in the Philippines, for to many it seemed that protection and the Open Door were incompatible. But the British Press and British public opinion soon convinced themselves, as the *Statist* put it, that, "High duties are not inconsistent with the 'open door'. What the open door means is that traders of all nationalities shall have equal opportunities, not that there shall be absolute freedom of trade."[1] Even the free trade interests of the greatest international trading nation could not now prevail against her supreme desire for Anglo-American understanding.

The outbreak of the Boer War in 1899, which in some ways, as *The Times* wrote, bore so curious a resemblance to the situation in the Philippines (whose inhabitants rose in revolt against their new masters on 4 February, 1899, and fought them for two years under the leadership of Emilio Aguinaldo), did nothing, as we shall see, but reinforce this British attitude of mind, though it revived much latent anti-British feeling in America.

But Secretary of State Hay did not share, indeed despised, this "mad-dog hatred of England,"[2] and he resented a state of affairs, as he was to say later, which "compelled this Government to refuse the assistance of the greatest power . . . in carrying out our own policies because all Irishmen are Democrats and some Germans are fools."[3] His Far Eastern policy, indeed, was to some extent directly influenced by Lord Charles Beresford, an Englishman, who advocated to him an Anglo-American commercial alliance in the Far East and some form of co-operation to rescue China from the clutches of Russia and France. Hay and his American expert on China, W. W. Rockhill, were also advised by another Englishman, Alfred E. Hippisley, a former member of the Chinese Customs service, who suggested that America should take the lead in the Open Door policy, which Britain would then follow, thus enabling the Administration to achieve its object by what was in effect

[1] Q. Reuter, p. 180.   [2] Q. Davis, p. 137.   [3] Q. ibid, p. 136.

co-operation, while avoiding, by her independence of action, the full blast of American Anglophobia.

The new programme, which began to take shape in Hay's mind in the summer of 1899, was based on a memorandum drawn up by Hippisley, and on 6 September Hay sent the first of his Open Door Notes, couched in identical terms, to Britain, Germany and Russia, and later to Tokyo, Rome and Paris. He asked for assurances that within its sphere of influence no power would interfere with any treaty port or vested interest, that the Chinese tariff should be universally applied and the duties collected by the Chinese Government, and that no power would discriminate there in favour of its own nationals over harbour dues and transport charges. As Hay was all too aware, this verbal intervention fell far short of the earlier British proposal to co-operate in preserving the territorial integrity of China (which Hay at this stage ignored), but it marked a distinct step forward by America.

Coming on the very eve of the Boer War, it was welcomed in Britain, though she was forced to make a conditional acceptance owing to the steps she had taken since her own earlier overture to the United States had been rejected; Salisbury replied that Britain would be prepared to make a declaration in the sense desired, provided that the other powers also agreed to do so. Others made further conditions and Russia virtually refused, but Hay decided to go ahead none the less, and declared on 20 March, 1900, that all the powers had acceded to the principles contained in the note, a *fait accompli* which none of them could very well dispute. In theory, the Open Door was, as H. Hale Bellot calls it, a kind of "application in the Far East of the principles of the Monroe Doctrine",[1] but it was one which other powers would hardly feel bound to respect, given the circumstances of its birth, and which America had not got the will—and perhaps as yet not the power—to enforce. In fact, it recognized the establishment of spheres of influence, and did not preserve the territorial integrity of China, while the range of trade it protected was very limited, since it did not mention such activities as mining and the building of railroads.

Yet it was a dramatic innovation in American policy to take the lead in seeking from the nations a binding multilateral agreement in the Far East, or indeed in any part of the world, and the fact that it had ostensibly a purely commercial object must not blind us to this important fact. Hay's motives are obscure, but—apart from a desire to assert, in however small a way, American influence in the Orient (in the

[1] H. Hale Bellot, *American History and American Historians* (London, 1952), p. 260.

manner that Roosevelt was to do much more forcefully, though still tentatively, in the Russo-Japanese War)—it is at least possible that the one-time Ambassador in London wished to do some little thing to demonstrate an Anglo-American solidarity which could never assume formal diplomatic shape. Certainly his political opponents tended to regard it in this light, for the Democrats in the election of 1900 attacked the "ill-concealed Republican Alliance with England";[1] certainly, too, crumb though it might be, Britons tended to seize on it as a sign, not only of American agreement, but also of American movement into the international arena, than which they desired nothing more ardently.

The 1899 Note was regarded in some quarters as a stop-gap, and the events of the next year in China were to witness a more dramatic and more practical American invitation in the Far East. Henry Adams, from his vantage point in the other half of the double mansion in Lafayette Square occupied by his friend Hay, relished, and indeed perhaps exaggerated, the significance of it, when he declared that Hay's diplomacy had "broken history in half."[2] The Boxer rebellion, in which violent anti-foreign revolt in China resulted in the siege of the foreign legations in Pekin, broke out in the spring of 1900, and it was largely through Hay's establishment of telegraphic communication with the American Minister in the Chinese capital, and the unusual participation of American soldiers and vessels in the international relief force, that the besieged were rescued, for the other powers could hardly overcome their mutual mistrust for long enough to co-operate, while Britain was reduced to offering to repay Japan's expenses if she contributed 30,000 troops to balance the large Russian forces. But the hand of the United States was also a restraining one, for her Asiatic squadron refused to participate in what it believed to be an unnecessary international shelling of forts near Tientsin, and Hay improved the shining hour by a dramatic American diplomatic initiative. On 3 July, while the siege continued, and fearing that the Boxer revolt might give the Powers an excuse to dismember China altogether, Hay issued his second Open Door Note. This took the form of a statement of American policy, and needed no acknowledgement, but Salisbury hastened to endorse it to Ambassador Choate; at home, however, Hay was careful to point out to critics that no previous consultation had taken place with Britain.

The American policy was to seek "a solution which may bring about permanent safety and peace to China, preserve Chinese territorial and administrative entity, protect all rights guaranteed to friendly powers by treaty and international law, and safeguard for the world the prin-

[1] Q. Davis, p. 135. [2] Q. Davis, p. 129.

ciple of equal and impartial trade with all parts of the Chinese empire."[1] It will be seen that this went very much farther than the mere Open Door, for it sought to preserve the Chinese Empire and not merely equal foreign rights of trade in the Chinese area. Of Hay's action Henry Adams wrote, "Nothing so meteoric had ever been done in American diplomacy. . . . For a moment, indeed, the world had been struck dumb at seeing Hay put Europe aside and set the Washington Government at the head of civilization so quietly that civilization submitted, by mere instinct of docility, to receive and obey his orders".[2] Though this is perhaps overstating the case, and though Hay himself could not have had too high an idea of the value of his purely diplomatic efforts, since only six months later he authorized the Navy Department secretly to obtain a base at Samsah Bay, his second Note undoubtedly had an immediate effect in discouraging the partition of China at the moment in history when it was perhaps most likely.

The American Samsah initiative, which was quietly and ironically brought to nought by Japan, was unknown to Whitehall, the failure of whose agreement with Germany to preserve the Open Door in China was, by contrast, well known and pleasing to Hay, who said he would rather have been "the dupe of China, than the chum of the Kaiser";[3] but it would not have affected Britain's attitude to America even if it had been. Nor had Hay really resented the Anglo-German agreement to maintain an American policy in China, though he was not sorry to see the *entente* collapse shortly afterwards, and though he was at pains to point out to Downing Street that "We have steadily withstood every overture—and there have been many—on the part of Russia and Germany for a more intimate understanding to the disadvantage of Great Britain."[4] In truth, Hay knew that America could never effectively, in face of her own public opinion, maintain her doctrines in the Far East, though she pretended to do so for many years. The Samsah affair had been a mere aberration, and when in 1901 Japan asked what the United States would do to check brazen Russian aggression in Manchuria, which was as alarming to Hay as to Britain, he replied that she would take no positive action. Thus it became increasingly clear to Britain that it was no use looking for concrete assistance in the Far East to the United States, and so she turned to Japan. But the basis of Anglo-American understanding remained unimpaired, for in the Far East the two peoples looked at things in approximately the same way, while elsewhere more positive agreements were being formulated.

[1] Q. Davis, p. 135.   [2] *Education of Henry Adams,* p. 392.
[3] Q. Gelber, p. 83.   [4] Q. ibid, p. 82.

VI

THAT this was so was, on the American side, very largely Hay's doing, for the coming of the Boer War in October, 1899, and its continuance for nearly three years placed some strain on Anglo-American relations. The conflict early revealed a British isolation and a European animosity towards her, which exceeded even those from which the United States had suffered in the Spanish-American War, but, much more serious from our point of view, it resulted in a revival of Anglophobia amongst many sections of the American people. This was, after all, a colonial war, and the attitude of good Americans to such wars had been decided irrevocably in 1776. The Democratic platform of 1900 contained the following plank:

> Believing in the principles of self-government and rejecting, as did our forefathers, the claims of monarchy, we view with indignation the purpose of England to overwhelm with force the South African Republics. Speaking, as we believe, for the entire American Nation, except its Republican office holders, and for all free men everywhere, we extend our sympathy to the heroic burghers in their unequal struggle to maintain their liberty and independence.[1]

There is little doubt that the bulk of the people were sympathetic to the Boers, and Hay wrote that "We had great difficulty to prevent" even the Republican Convention "from declaring in favor of the Boers".[2] Henry Adams, bred in the anti-colonialism of Bright and Cobden, as well as born in that of the Founding Fathers, was outraged by the war, despite his closeness to Hay, and wrote of himself: "He had been taught from childhood, even in England, that his forbears and their associates in 1776 had settled, once for all, the liberties of the British free colonies, and he very strongly objected to being thrown on the defensive again".[3] It is probably true that the majority of the Senate were opposed to Britain's policy but, by rigid party discipline, the Republican members were persuaded to follow the official line, and took no action embarrassing to the Administration. The Boers, however, with great assiduity and considerable skill, played upon this public feeling by propaganda and appeals for recognition and intervention, and the State Department and the President were thus subjected to extremely vocal and powerful pro-Boer pressure.

That this was unsuccessful even at the time of the Presidential elec-

[1] Q. J. H. Ferguson, *American Diplomacy and the Boer War* (Philadelphia, 1939), p. 197.
[2] Q. ibid, p. 195.   [3] *Education of Henry Adams*, p. 372.

tion was undoubtedly the work of Hay, who was absolutely determined to maintain good relations with Britain, and to repay her for
the friendship which she had shown to the United States in the analogous circumstances of the Spanish War. He was openly and bluntly
anti-Boer; he wrote to Henry White in the Embassy in London just
before the war began, "I hope, if it comes to blows, that England will
make quick work of Uncle Paul. Sooner or later, her influence must
be dominant there, and the sooner the better"[1]; and when things went
wrong for Britain he did not alter his tone, indeed he strengthened it.
He wrote to Henry Adams:

> What do you think now of our poor dear British? Was there ever
> seen anything like it. . . ? I have the greatest admiration for the Boers'
> smartness, but it is their bravery that our idiotic public is snivelling
> over. If they were only as brave as they are slim, the war would have
> ended long ago by their extermination. We do occasionally kill a
> Filipino, but what man has ever yet seen a dead Boer? . . . The serious
> thing is the discovery . . . that the British have lost all skill in
> fighting. . . . It is a portentous fact, altogether deplorable, in my
> opinion; for their influence on the whole makes for peace and
> civilization. If Russia and Germany arrange things, the balance is lost
> for ages.[2]

His contempt for his domestic opponents was almost as deep, for, he
went on, "Your friend Bryan, ass that he is, says that the Boer War is
an issue in our campaign—I suppose because the British are 16 to 1."
His friendly feelings towards Britain were at the heart of his policy, and
at the height of her humiliation, he said, amid Russian and German
plans for intervention, that she could count on the friendship of the
United States in every circumstance arising from the war. Had Anglophobe feeling in America got control at this critical juncture in the
development of Anglo-American relations incalculable harm might
have been done, and that it did not do so is Hay's unique personal
contribution to their future.

Yet he did not stand quite alone, and certain influences fought on his
side. For one thing, the growth of American imperialism and, above all,
the acquisition of the Philippines had bred a powerful group less
unfavourable than Americans had been in the past to the British
Empire as such, and recent events made it difficult to oppose Britain as
self-righteously as had previously been possible. Mahan wrote of the
war to an Englishman: "I am satisfied of the right and duty of great
Powers, where occasion offers, to put an end to gross evils at their doors,

[1] Q. Ferguson, p. 123.   [2] Q. ibid. pp. 124-5.

and while I can see two sides to the present question, I think upon the whole your interference justified, nay, imperative—upon grounds much the same as ours in Cuba."[1] Even Bryan himself said:

> While I think this Government should use its good offices to prevent war between England and the Boers, yet I do not care to join in a petition to the President on this or any other subject. Our refusal to recognize the rights of the Filipinos to self-government will embarrass us if we express sympathy with those in other lands who are struggling to follow the doctrines set forth in the Declaration of Independence. Suppose we send our sympathy to the Boers? In an hour England would send back, "what about the Filipinos?"[2]

There did exist, too, in Britain, an extremely vocal minority in the Liberal party—the Pro-Boers—who opposed the whole imperialist enterprise, so that even men in America who thought like Bryan were always being reminded that their animus was not against the British people as a whole but merely against a no doubt transient majority of them. For another thing, powerful American instincts militated against intervention, which was the only way in which the United States could substantially assist the Boers; this, after all, would be an entanglement with a vengeance, and opposition to such a participation in a non-American struggle was strongest, by a strange paradox, in those very hearts which beat warmest for the Boers. Mahan pointed out, no doubt not without relish, that the Monroe Doctrine would forbid any such "interference of the United States in matters of purely European concern."[3] Thus from beginning to end the policy of the Administration followed the same course of benevolent neutrality towards Britain that the British Government had followed towards the United States in the Spanish War.

Anxious on the first outbreak of war to try and enlist the sympathy of the most powerful European nation, Britain asked Germany to represent her interests in the Boer Republics, but she was refused; she thereupon turned to Washington, which readily consented to repay British help in the Spanish War. Hay even agreed to the appointment of his eldest son as Consul at Pretoria, whither he travelled via Britain, a procedure hardly calculated to please either the Boers or the Democrats. Vociferous demands by Boer sympathizers were answered by McKinley in an announcement of 12 October, which stated that he had

[1] Q. W. D. Puleston, *The Life and Work of Captain Alfred Thayer Mahan, U.S.N.* (London, 1939), p. 214.

[2] Q. Ferguson, p. 183.   [3] Q. Puleston, p. 215.

received petitions asking him to offer mediation, but also contrary petitions "desiring him to make common cause with Great Britain", especially on account of the wrongs alleged to be suffered by American citizens in the Transvaal. "As to taking sides with either party to the dispute, it is not to be thought of. As regards mediation, the President has received no intimation from the countries and in the absence of such intimations from both parties there is nothing in international rules or usages to justify an offer of mediation in the present circumstances."[1] With the arrival, however, of a formal request from the Boers, the President and Hay felt it advisable, in view of the aroused state of American opinion, to forward it to London in March, 1900, "with an expression of the President's platonic desire for peace."[2] This action went no further than Britain had gone in the joint note of the British and other ambassadors to McKinley in 1898, and the nature of the message was well appreciated by Salisbury, who thanked "the President for the friendly interest shown by him, and added that Her Majesty's Government cannot accept the intervention of any other power." The prompt publication of this reply by Hay very effectively quashed a Russian proposal of mediation made to the neutral Powers at almost the same time, and it was fully understood in Britain to have been a domestic political manoeuvre. Even earlier, Hay had been authorized by the President to refuse a Russian proposal for joint representations against the actions of British naval forces in Delagoa Bay, and without American participation there could be no effective interference by others on behalf of the Boers, who were thus bound in the end to be defeated by the vastly stronger British Empire, which rallied round in strong support of the mother country.

Hay dismissed in an almost peremptory manner the arguments of three official envoys of the Boer Republics, who reached Washington on 18 May, 1900, in search of American mediation, stating that the President felt that he had gone as far as possible and that "no course is open to him except to persist in the policy of impartial neutrality. To deviate from this would be contrary to all our traditions, and our natural interests, and would lead to consequences which neither the President nor the people of the United States would regard with favor." Britain rejoiced, and Ambassador Choate said that the Prince of Wales and the Duke of Cambridge had expressed to him their "great admiration for your speech to the Transvaal delegates and of your dignified treatment of that business."[3] This policy McKinley endorsed, despite

[1] Q. Ferguson, p. 136.   [2] Hay: q. Ferguson, p. 139.
[3] Q. ibid, pp. 139, 150, 156.

the triumphal reception accorded to the Boers by many of the public, and as the war dragged its slow length along it was firmly maintained.

This was true even after the assassination of McKinley in September, 1901, when Roosevelt's entry into office deprived Hay of some of his domination over American foreign policy, though not of his influence over it. Roosevelt was at this time inclined to be pro-Boer, though it is extremely doubtful if he ever contemplated any overt action in the matter; his bounce always tempted him into extreme positions. At first he had said of the war that it "had to come", and that the Boers "are battling on the wrong side in the fight of civilization and will have to go under." He also believed that the United States could not stand aloof if the European Powers threatened Britain, telling the British Military Attaché that, "if the powers of continental Europe menace your people," he "certainly hoped" that the United States would "promptly give them notice of 'hands off'."[1] But as the war continued and this danger did not arise, and as his sympathy was aroused by the gallant struggle of the outnumbered Boers and his contempt by the military incompetence of the British, he underwent a change of heart. Yet when he became President, and the pro-Boers began to put intense pressure upon him, culminating in another visit by two Boer envoys, it was clear that, despite his sympathy, there would be no change of policy. Hay was still a power and still at the State Department.

Even protests over the concentration camps of the British, where Boer refugees were herded after the destruction of their homes, which caused the Administration grave embarrassment, did not deter Hay from what he believed to be the best course for America and for mankind. He wrote to Lodge: "The Boer women and children are in the Concentration Camps simply because their husbands and brothers want them there, and as to the war with all its hideous incidents and barbarities, it will stop the instant Botha and De Wet wish it to stop". In a letter to the associate editor of the *Indianapolis Journal* he was even more forceful, if more subtle:

> As to the general subjects of these concentration camps. I have never said a word in public, and do not propose to. I am not the attorney of the British Government to defend their acts. There is, of course, great suffering and loss of life, but it ought to be remembered that when Lord Kitchener and General Botha met some time ago to discuss terms of surrender, Lord Kitchener appealed to General Botha to spare the farms and houses of surrendered Boers, and promised on his part not to disturb the families and farms of Boers

[1] Q. ibid, pp. 208-9.

fighting against them. This, General Botha refused to agree to. . . . But, as I said before, we are neutral in this fight, and have nothing to say on either side.[1]

Happily for Anglo-American relations, Britain wanted no more than that the United States should continue to say nothing; what she wanted and what Hay gave her was benevolent neutrality. In this the situation resembled that of the Spanish War, but not the American Civil War, when the North had desired more than mere cold neutrality from Britain, though the position of the Boers *vis à vis* the United States was almost exactly that of the South *vis à vis* Britain in 1861, since they could win only by exhausting the resolution of the enemy or by American or other intervention. There were other resemblances with the Civil War, in that Britain, like the North before her, in claiming suzerainty over the Boers, refused to regard the war as anything more than a domestic rebellion, and thus refused to consider mediation. Difficulties which arose over such awkward questions of neutrality as the purchase in the United States of horses, mules and accoutrements by British officers in uniform, have also a familiar ring about them.

But the really close parallel is with World War I. The Boers, for instance, were virtually cut off from American economic resources by British control of the seas, while there was a rapid expansion of Anglo-American trade, chiefly in supplies used directly by the British armies; annual average exports from the United States to the United Kingdom and British South Africa rose from $464, 676, 489 for the period 1895-8, to $577,043,635 for the years 1899-1902. In the same way, the Boers were able to sell very few securities in the United States owing to the speculative nature of such an investment, whereas the British raised large sums, the biggest flotation being $50 million of Consols in April, 1901, which were heavily oversubscribed; this might have given some inkling of the financial interests which Americans would acquire in Britain in World War I. Thus the Boers took the traditional American viewpoint, that as broad a definition of neutral commercial rights as possible should be asserted, but America could not support this stand with her old vigour in view of the claims made by her when she, not Britain, was the dominant belligerent at sea, in the Civil and Spanish Wars. Nevertheless, the events of 1914-17 once more cast their shadows before them. But none of these things was permitted by Hay to interfere with the progress of Anglo-American goodwill in this or other spheres. Typical of their new relationship was the British payment to the United States, in respect of claims by her citizens for damages

[1] Q. Ferguson, pp. 174-5.

done during the war, of a sum which averaged out at roughly $2,000 per claimant, as compared with sums to other nations which approximated to $316 per head. By 1902 the two peoples were truly entering that period in which their relations were, in many and subtle ways, of a different order from those between other sovereign states. But the most important positive steps in this direction remain yet to be discussed.

VII

OF these, the most significant by far was the settlement of the Isthmian question. Since the repudiation by Cleveland in 1885 of the Republican policy of trying to force amendment of the unpopular Clayton-Bulwer Treaty, and the failure of De Lesseps in 1889 to construct a trans-Isthmian canal, the question had ceased to attract much public attention, though powerful interests had continued to press for an American canal under American control. The new American attitude typified in the Spanish-American War, however, combined with her new strength and her new Pacific possessions, thrust it urgently to the fore. Now acutely conscious of the importance of sea power, she realized that she must either have two navies, each strong enough for the needs of its own ocean, or, which was obviously much more satisfactory, a canal joining the Atlantic to the Pacific. Even before the treaty with Spain was signed, President McKinley in his message to Congress on 5 December, 1898, said of the Canal in words very reminiscent of those of President Hayes in 1880: that "our national policy now more imperatively than ever calls for its control by this Government" is a proposition "which I doubt not the Congress will duly appreciate and wisely act upon."[1] Yet the treaty of 1850 prohibited an all-American canal and there was always the danger that Britain would once more stand upon her rights under that instrument; this might produce an ominous situation, since American public opinion was becoming vociferous in its demands for a canal under the exclusive control of the United States.

It is true that there was now little likelihood of Britain refusing to alter the treaty, in view of the warmth of her new attitude towards the United States; indeed, there was relatively little indignation in the British Press against McKinley's clear indication of the possibility of unilateral American action. Furthermore, Henry White was able to assure Salisbury, during a week-end at Hatfield, that the President did

[1] *Messages and Papers*, p. 6327

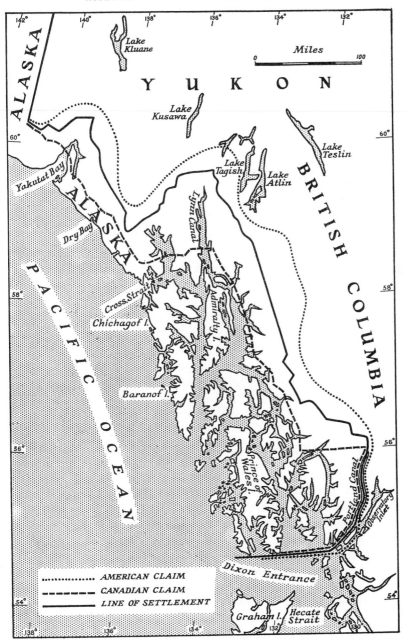

Map 6. *The Alaska Boundary Dispute*

597

not intend to repudiate the treaty, and Salisbury assured him that Britain would not object to an American canal now that the Suez Canal fulfilled her major needs, though he sought an assurance, which White felt able to give, that it would, like its counterpart, be unfortified, and also neutralized in time of war. But Britain was not altogether a free agent in the matter, for a formidable external obstacle to agreement existed, in the shape of the Canadian dispute with the United States over the Alaskan boundary, and other and lesser questions. There were, however, good hopes of agreement, for in May, 1898, as it happened, a treaty had been signed in Washington, under impulse no doubt of the new Anglo-American amity, setting up a Joint High Commission to settle outstanding Canadian-American differences. The Commission contained British, American and Canadian representatives, the last including Sir Wilfred Laurier, the Prime Minister of Canada, and was to consider among other things such familiar topics as the fisheries, seals, and reciprocity, but as soon as it met it became clear that the rock on which the vessel was to founder was the boundary question.

The five hundred mile long coastal panhandle of Alaska,* consisting of an archipelago of islands and peninsulas, lay between the Yukon and the open sea; this was inconvenient to Canada owing to the lack of internal transportation facilities, but was not a matter of life and death to her continental existence now that she had firm roots on the coast-line of British Columbia. But all North American states have been strongly sensitive to barriers against uninterrupted lateral access to the west coast, as the history of the United States and California clearly shows, and Canada was no exception to this rule. The terms of the Russo-British Treaty of 1825, upon which the boundary was based, were the origin of disagreement; they stated obscurely that it ran along the summit of a range of mountains, parallel to the ocean but impossible to identify with certainty, unless these ran farther back than thirty marine leagues from the coast, in which case it was to run at that distance from the sea. There was also some dispute as to the possesion of the Portland Canal, but the chief disagreement lay in practice in a Canadian claim that the line should be drawn across the mouths of the numerous fiords and inlets, which would give their shipping direct access to the sea, and the American counterclaim that it should follow the sinuosities of the coastline, thus in effect barring such Canadian access. This conflict of views was analogous to the fisheries dispute on the Atlantic coast, in which similar claims as to the extent of coastal

* See Map 6.

598

territorial waters were put forward by both sides. Feeling ran so high on the Alaskan question because it appeared to the Americans that the Canadians were trying to prevent direct communication between Alaska in the north and its panhandle in the south, while to the Canadians it seemed that the Americans were trying to bar them from access to the sea. The question was rendered really acute by the discovery of gold in the Klondike in 1896, for this not only made the Canadian need of communications more pressing, but also greatly increased the possibility of border incidents in the frenzied atmosphere of a gold rush.

But the Canadian Government, whether or not their case was prompted by the needs of the situation, could not afford to take too narrow a ground or too strong an attitude in the matter, for there was a grave practical weakness to their case, since it seemed that the American interpretation had long been accepted in practice, for on British as well as Russian and American maps the boundary was shown as running round the heads of the inlets. The Canadian Government, therefore, urged on the British a general settlement of a kind which appealed to Salisbury, by which in return for the great British concession on the Isthmian question, America should make a similar concession in Alaska. Such a diplomatic arrangement was not without attractions to Hay, even though he considered the full Canadian claim "a ridiculous and preposterous boundary line"; accordingly, in January, 1899, the American commissioners offered Canada access to the sea and a port under Canadian jurisdiction, but subsequently withdrew the proposal, under pressure of Western commercial interests, which was very effective in view of the fact that McKinley was shortly to run again for President. Nevertheless, in the next month Britain replied to this abrupt action by a concession, offering to arbitrate the Alaskan question, and making it clear that she would amend the Clayton-Bulwer Treaty as soon as this was agreed to by the Commission. As Hay himself wrote, "After we had put forth our entire force and compelled—there is no other word for it—England to accept arbitration in the Venezuela matter, we cannot feel entirely easy in refusing an arbitration in this", but none the less America had to reckon with "the fatal tendency of all arbitrators to compromise",[1] and she accordingly refused. Hay's counter-proposal of a tribunal of six jurists, three from each side, without an impartial chairman and with a majority vote necessary for a final decision, really meant that, as subsequent events showed, America could not lose, though she might win. This was not, in its political context, an impartial arbitration at all, and it was

[1] Q. Gelber, pp. 42, 47.

rejected by Canada amidst rising tempers in Ottawa and Washington. The Commission adjourned in February without achieving anything, but agreement was reached in an exchange of notes in October for a temporary *modus vivendi* in Alaska.

Deadlock in the Caribbean as well as on the Pacific coast had now been reached, and a trial of wills was in fact going on, in which the United States had shown clearly that she was prepared to cede nothing substantial in either place in return for the great concession which she demanded of Britain over the canal. In 1900 a Bill was introduced into the House of Representatives empowering the American Government to undertake the construction of a canal alone. Though deprecating the nature of the threat, Hay used it most effectively to break the deadlock; he appealed to Salisbury to sign the Isthmian convention, which had already been drafted, without any reference to the Alaskan question, in order to overcome the danger to Anglo-American friendship, even hinting that failure to do so might result in his own resignation, and his replacement by a much less conciliatory Secretary of State. He reiterated to the British sentiments already made unmistakable by Lodge: "the American people mean to have the canal and they mean to control it. . . . England does not care enough about it to go to war . . . and it would be ruinous [for her] if she did make war on us."[1]

Britain was, at this crisis of the Boer War, unusually dependent on the goodwill of Canada, which made it necessary to consult her, but Chamberlain from the Colonial Office did so with unmistakable meaning, saying to the Canadian Ministry that refusal by Britain to sign "would be regarded as an affront to the United States Government, and would tend to shake the position of the President, whose friendly attitude is in the present condition of public affairs of great importance."[2] The dilemma was now presented to Laurier; for him to agree to the separate treaty meant in effect, as events were to confirm, abandonment of any real hope of getting the Canadian way in Alaska by a diplomatic bargain, but to refuse to do so might seriously endanger that Anglo-American friendship upon which the very existence of Canada must depend. He made the only choice open to a Canadian statesman and agreed, only asking the British Government to press the Canadian case vigorously in Washington. The signs and portents were unmistakable; for the future neither Canadian nor any other subordinate interests would in the last resort be allowed by the British Government to stand in the way of Anglo-American concord.

[1] Q. Davis, p. 109.   [2] Q. Gelber, p. 50.

Yet the auguries were to be made even clearer before long. On 5 February, 1900, the Isthmian treaty was signed by Hay and Pauncefote, authorizing the United States to construct, regulate and manage a canal across the isthmus, but stipulating that it should be open in peace and war on equal terms to the naval as well as commercial vessels of every nation, without discriminating charges or conditions, and that it should never be blockaded or be the scene of belligerent acts. In these reservations it not only followed the pattern of the Suez canal convention, but was in fact merely a modified form of the Clayton-Bulwer Treaty, which it did not abrogate or supersede. This meant that other powers could adhere to the treaty and become its joint guarantors, and that the United States was specifically debarred from fortifying the canal or its adjacent waters, though they could keep on it such military police as were necessary to maintain law and order.

The outcry in America was loud and immediate, and was led by Theodore Roosevelt, who was so soon to be Hay's master; his strong views, expressed to the Secretary of State at this time, were not without their effect even upon a relationship so close as theirs was to be, for they left a faint tinge of acrimony. Roosevelt asserted that the possible participation of other guarantors would be a violation of the Monroe Doctrine, and that the neutrality of the canal would be a grave handicap to the effective strength of the American Navy in time of war. The Rooseveltian outlook assumed the necessity of entire American self-dependence, whereas that of Hay, and even Mahan and Dewey, emphasized the *rapprochement* with Britain and the continued supremacy of the British Navy; Roosevelt was in fact, when in office, to pursue policies for the most part agreeable to the British Government, but he did not openly make her friendship the principal motive in his actions as did Hay. Britain had conceded everything that the Secretary of State asked, and he felt that he could not demand more without offering some compensation; as he wrote, "All I have ever done with England is to have wrung great concessions out of her with no compensation."[1] "[A]nd yet these idiots say that I am not an American because I don't say 'to hell with the Queen'."[2]

But Hay's judgment as to what could be extracted from Britain was wrong, no doubt because of his Anglophilia as well as his reluctance to countenance the form of blackmail to which Congress was ready to resort, but at first it seemed that he might be right. The opposition forces in the Senate, led by Lodge, ratified the treaty, but only subject

[1] Q. ibid, p. 55.   [2] Davis, p. 112.

601

to far-reaching amendments, which declared the Clayton-Bulwer Treaty superseded, arranged that the neutralization clauses should not apply to American defensive measures in the canal, and omitted the article providing for the adhesion of other Powers. McKinley's position, now that the election was over, was much stronger, and he asked Hay to remain as Secretary of State, but the Government in Britain was similarly invigorated by the election of 1900, and new hands, those of Lord Lansdowne, were at the Foreign Office. Great Britain courteously refused to ratify the treaty, though leaving the door open to further discussion, and it seemed as if Hay's fears were to be realized, for in March, 1901, the month when Lansdowne's note reached Hay, Anglo-German conversations on a possible alliance began.

But these were, as we have seen, abortive, while the British need of American friendship waxed rather than waned; it remained in this case, as in the successful negotiation of the Anglo-Japanese Treaty in the next year, the essential postulate of British foreign policy. American friendship was more necessary to Britain than British friendship was to America, and of this fact the perpetual threat of the Senate's willingness, if necessary, to denounce the Clayton-Bulwer Treaty without British consent, was ample and unambiguous evidence. To countenancing the extension of American power Britain was already committed, and she shortly reverted to an overt acceptance of the fact by negotiating a new canal treaty, the initiative for which came from Hay, who now properly perceived that his chief function must be to effect by agreement what the Senate might otherwise achieve unilaterally. Britain, it was becoming clear, would have to accept the *fait accompli* in the long run, even though her navy was still immensely the more powerful, because of her commitments elsewhere and because of America's growing might, but she could do so with a much better grace and with much more beneficial effects upon the future of Anglo-American relations if common ground could be found by diplomacy between the viewpoints of the British Government and the Senate. In his efforts to find it Hay was ably abetted by Pauncefote, who had advised his government against the refusal to ratify the original treaty, and in whose hands the negotiations once again were, for he apprehended clearly that Britain's true interest lay in cultivating American friendship at almost any cost.

Britain once again conceded every major American demand, and enabled Hay to obtain all that the Senate desired; thus Henry Adams wrote, "For the moment, things were going fairly well, and Hay's unruly team were less fidgety, but Pauncefote still pulled the whole load and turned the dangerous corners safely".[1] To that team, in the midst of the negotiations, was added President Roosevelt, the vital embodiment of the new American imperialism, and it was doubly fortunate that Britain was prepared to grant everything demanded, since Hay would never have succeeded in restraining Roosevelt in the event of British obduracy. The Hay-Pauncefote Treaty, which was signed in Washington, on 18 November, 1901, superseded the Clayton-Bulwer Treaty; agreed to American construction and control of the canal, subject to freedom of use, and equitability and "entire equality" of tolls, for all ships of whatever nationality; and laid down that no political changes in Central America should affect the operation of the treaty. British face was saved only by the form of the clause which was recognized as giving the United States the right to fortify and defend the canal; it read: "The canal shall never be blockaded, nor shall any right of war be exercised nor any act of hostility be commited within it. The United States, however, shall be at liberty to maintain such military police along the canal as may be necessary to protect it against lawlessness and disorder."[2] The treaty passed the Senate by the overwhelming majority of 72 votes to 6. Great Britain had, after some hesitation, granted every significant demand of the United States, and neither she nor Canada had received a single concrete gain in exchange. Yet it was, perhaps, in the long run as great a victory for Britain as it was for the United States, because it was an essential foundation of the American friendship which was indispensable to her very existence in the modern world.

VIII

FOR the present the Alaskan issue lapsed, but further evidence was shortly forthcoming of the acute anxiety of the British Government, as well as people, to base their policy more and more upon friendship with the United States. Cipriano Castro, dictator of Venezuela, had for some time past given increasing cause for complaint to foreign governments by the damage done in civil disturbances to the property of their citizens, and by his government's refusal to meet payments on its external debts; Great Britain and Germany felt their interests to be the most weighty among those of the powers. In fact, Britain's amounted to $20 million, but Germany's to only $2 million, so that the former had far the most cause for intervention, although it was

[1] *Education of Henry Adams*, p. 393.
[2] *Treaties Between U.S. and H.M.*, p. 148.

the latter who first proposed action when matters came to a head in 1902, after repeated protests to Venezuela had produced no effect. Germany's motives for proposing strong measures caused the gravest suspicion in the United States, for her violence seemed disproportionate to her financial stakes, while her actions in the Spanish War had not been forgotten. There is little doubt that she had no immediate ambitions in America, and that she was not prepared to risk the full wrath of the United States for the attainment of her objectives, but there is none at all that she was not averse from cutting a striking figure on the international stage, particularly if Britain, by consenting to act as her stalking-horse, gave her the chance to weaken the Anglo-American *entente*.

That the British Government consented to put itself in this invidious position was partly due to the removal of Salisbury's guiding hand in favour of the less experienced and perhaps less decisive grip of Balfour and Lansdowne, and partly to a very serious misunderstanding by the Conservative and Unionist leaders of the trend of British public opinion towards Germany. This was much better grasped by the Liberal Opposition; as John Morley was to write, "Balfour has a thousand gifts, but he is not really a sound man to be the chief ruler of this country."[1] Though Anglo-German negotiations for an alliance had broken down by the end of 1901, and though the German Government were, in February, 1902, to make (as we have seen) the Pauncefote disclosures in Washington, the British Government were still prepared, during the Kaiser's English visit in November, 1902, to overlook his attitude during the Boer War, his Naval Programme and the Anglophobia of many of his people. Public opinion was not so ready to forgive, and certain elements in it were deeply apprehensive of a policy which seemed to threaten the new found understanding with the United States.

The Monroe Doctrine, now that America bade fair to enforce it vigorously, did from time to time present problems like this of Venezuela by acting as a shield for the misdeeds to which Latin American governments were, alas, all too prone. Of this President Roosevelt himself was not unconscious, and he himself, by a gratuitous piece of characteristic outspokenness, did contribute something to the onset of the Castro incident, for he stated as a general principle in his Annual Message of December, 1901, "We do not guarantee any state against punishment if it misconducts itself, provided that punishment does not take the form of the acquisition of territory by any non-American

[1] Q. Davis, p. 162.

power."[1] But the British Government did not rely on general pronouncements; when, in November, Anglo-German coercion appeared
inevitable if Castro was to be brought to reason, Sir Michael Herbert
informed the Secretary of State, who, hamstrung by Roosevelt's
declaration, replied that he regretted the use of force, but could not
protest against it. Formalities justified the British Government, but
they should have been warned, by the tone of Hay's reply and of
Herbert's report, of the dangers they were running.

These very soon became apparent when Venezuela's four gunboats
were seized, her ports blockaded, and some of her forts bombarded,
for, though Castro saw reason very quickly and proposed, almost at
once, through American diplomatic channels the arbitration of a
portion, albeit only an inadequate portion, of the Anglo-German
claims, the outcry in both America and Britain was swift and vociferous. Indeed, the kindred and spontaneous reactions of the two
peoples to the situation is one of the most striking evidences of the
growing similarity of their outlook in these years; in both countries,
fear of Germany and a marked distaste for the spectacle of British co-
operation with her, predominated. In Britain Campbell-Bannerman
called it "a blunder with the seed of war in it",[2] and he set the tone for
the uproar in the Liberal press, which was always highly sensitive to
any threat to American friendship. But there was indignation also
amongst the elements in society who were normally more inclined to
belligerence; even Kipling talked of "the Goth and the shameless
Hun", and wrote in *The Times* on 22 December,

> *'Neath all the flags of all mankind*
> *That use upon the seas,*
> *Was there no other fleet to find*
> *That ye strike hands with these?*[3]

Morley forwarded to Balfour a message from Andrew Carnegie expressing grave perturbation, and White cabled Hay that opinion was
coalescing rapidly against the Government.

If their initial steps had ignored public opinion, Britain's rulers now
reacted to its demands with an admirable and nervous promptitude.
In both Houses conciliatory statements were made, pointing out that
no territory would be occupied, and strict restraining orders were issued
to the naval forces. Balfour hastily wrote to Carnegie of his desire to
"preserve the warmest and most friendly feelings" between Britain and

---

[1] *Messages and Papers*, p. 6665.
[2] Q. Gelber, p. 115. [3] Q. Bailey, p. 553.

the United States and declared that he had "not the smallest objection (rather the reverse!)"[1] to the Monroe Doctrine; his letter was placed in the hands of the President and the Secretary of State. Most significant of all, the Cabinet decided to accept the arbitration proposal within four days of its receipt, and put pressure on Germany to follow suit. Whether or not, as he later claimed, Roosevelt brought even more direct and blunter pressure to bear on her by threatening the German Ambassador with the despatch of Dewey's fleet to the scene of action, there is no doubt that American fleet movements during the crisis, as well as an interview of Hay with the German Chargé d'Affaires on 18 December, left the German Government with no illusions as to the American attitude of hostility.[2] On the very day after they were informed of the British Government's attitude, they followed her example in accepting arbitration. British and American public opinion had caused the British Government to back water furiously, and Germany had done the same rather than lose her shield against American ire by becoming separated from Britain.

But the trouble was not yet at an end, for until suitable terms could be reached with Castro, whose intentions the British and German Governments, with some reason, still mistrusted, a pacific form of blockade was maintained. The British, now fully alive to the danger to Anglo-American relations, endeavoured to extricate themselves as rapidly as possible from their embarrassing association with Germany, for as time went on and British opinion fell over itself in its efforts to reassure the United States, American feeling against Germany continued to rise, as that against Britain ebbed, particularly because the Germans continued the blockade in an unnecessarily truculent manner. Herbert was able to write to Lansdowne on 29 December, 1902: "The Administration has been most friendly throughout, and, if the dispute be referred without delay to arbitration . . . it will be almost safe to affirm that the friendly relations between Great Britain and the United States, instead of being impaired, have, if anything, been strengthened by the Venezuelan incident."

As Germany continued to drag out the affair, however, this began to seem optimistic, and Herbert wrote again, on 7 February, 1903, to Lansdowne: "I feel myself bound to warn your Lordship that a great change has taken place in the feeling of this country towards us since . . . December . . . last, and that our good relations with this country

[1] Q. Davis, p. 162.

[2] Seward W. Livermore, "Theodore Roosevelt, The American Navy, and the Venezuelan Crisis of 1902-3" (in *Am. H.R.,* LI, 1946).

will be seriously impaired if this Alliance with Germany continues much longer. The time has almost come, in American opinion, for us to make the choice between the friendship of the United States and that of Germany."[1] Of course, this choice had sometime since been irremediably made, but the unwise diplomacy of the British Government had obscured the fact. Now seriously alarmed, Lansdowne redoubled his pressure upon Germany to end the "wretched mess",[2] and within six days of the receipt of Herbert's missive, Venezuela and the Powers signed a protocol referring the claims to the adjudication of the Hague Tribunal. At the same time Balfour declared in a speech at Liverpool that the Monroe Doctrine had "no enemies in this country that I know of. . . . We welcome any increase of influence of the United States . . . upon the Great Western Hemisphere. We desire no colonization. We desire no alteration in the balance of power. We desire no acquisition of territory. We have not the slightest intention of interfering with the government of any portion of that Continent."[3] So fundamental a principle had the desire for American friendship already become in British foreign policy, that the mere word of danger to it from Washington now sufficed to stop a British diplomatic campaign, to recover her just debts, dead in its tracks.

Even more remarkable proof of this was shortly to follow, not in the superficial course of day to day diplomacy, but in the basic disposition of Britain's most vital guarantee of continued existence, her naval power. Conscious of the impossibility, in a world containing an increasing number of Great Powers, of maintaining either her diplomatic isolation or her absolute naval supremacy, Britain had signed the Japanese alliance of 1902, and was to institute the Anglo-French *Entente Cordiale* in 1904; the essential complement of these, though it could take no such formal shape, was her policy of friendship with America. Perhaps less immediately productive of positive political and military benefits to her, it was fundamentally of far greater significance, for as the First Lord of the Admiralty pointed out, the whole naval strategic situation had undergone a revolution with the birth of the American Navy, and that navy was to go on increasing in the future in order to keep pace with the continuing development of American strength. Britain welcomed this new American power because she was conscious of the many ties between the two peoples, but she had no real alternative; Roosevelt put the case too strongly when he remarked, "If we quit building our fleet, England's friendship

[1] Q. Gelber, pp. 119, 124.   [2] Davis, p. 162.   [3] Q. Davis, p. 167.

would immediately cool,"[1] but it was true that Britain could never henceforward face the prospect of a prolonged naval rivalry with the United States, and hence, since her life depended upon her sea communications, any serious clash with her. She might possibly have faced her for a few years to come, at the head of a coalition of other powers, but American friendship seemed in every way a more satisfactory solution to her international problems. This was particularly true in view of her ever more absorbing fear of Germany; happily it was a fear in which the Americans also shared. The paramount naval fact, as far as both powers were concerned in these years, was the irrepressible German determination to construct a large fleet, and the instinctive reaction of the United States, as well as Britain, was to strengthen her own.

The correspondence, indeed the intermingling, of British with American naval thought, and even affairs, at this period is striking. The General Board of the U.S. Navy in 1906 reported, with its eye on Germany: "The welfare of the United States and its immunity from entanglements with other Powers is greatly strengthened by strong ties of friendship and by unanimity of action with Great Britain."[2] In the case of Britain, it was the nautical doctrine of concentration, taught by Mahan, which inspired the great naval reorganization undertaken by Sir John Fisher in 1904; this took the form of a concentration of British naval forces in home waters, made possible not only by the Japanese alliance but also by the new Anglo-American understanding in the Caribbean and the North Atlantic. In the course of it Britain withdrew naval forces both from the Far East and from the west. In the Orient she relied primarily upon Japanese strength to replace them, particularly after Japanese victories in the Russian war, but secondarily on the assumed complaisance of the United States Pacific forces; in the West Indies her new friendship with France played a small part, but she felt able to withdraw her ships primarily because she relied upon the United States, strong in her new navy and shortly in her new canal, to assume control of these waters.

That America, or at least some Americans, were quite prepared for this was demonstrated by an announcement of American policy arising out of Roosevelt's reflections upon the impotence of the United States to allay the dangers of the Venezuela incident, the famous Roosevelt Corollary to the Monroe Doctrine. By this, in effect, the American Government undertook to police the whole of the Western hemisphere in case of need: "Chronic wrongdoing . . . may in America, as else-

[1] Q. Brebner, p. 262.   [2] Q. Gelber, p. 135.

where, ultimately require intervention by some civilized nation, and in the Western Hemisphere the adherence of the United States to the Monroe Doctrine may force the United States, however reluctantly, in flagrant cases of such wrong doing or impotence, to the exercise of an international police power."[1] The doctrine had a certain logic, but it was to be the cause of a great deal of friction between the United States and her southern neighbours. It fittingly accompanied, however, the virtual withdrawal of British military power from the Caribbean, and British acceptance (with pleasure in the result, if occasional raised-eyebrows at the method) of the American domination, and, indeed, fabrication, of the new state of Panama. Heindel goes as far as to say, "Once the Panama Canal was . . . on the way to completion, opinion held that our control over Central America was inevitable."[2]

The reduction in British strength was dramatic in its air of permanence, for not only did she drastically reduce her naval forces in the West Indies, but her land establishments steadily declined in importance, while in Canada she soon handed over responsibility for defence to the Canadian Government. These changes point forward already to the leasing of British bases in America to the United States in the 1940 crisis, which marked in effect the handing over of defence of British lands in the Western hemisphere entirely to America. Even more clearly did debates in Parliament in this first decade of the twentieth century point forward to the explicit recognition in later years of the fact that the whole of British naval policy (and thus the existence of Britain) must be based on the premise that she could never go to war with the United States, for there was a persistent refusal of Ministers and others to estimate their naval requirements by the size of the American fleet. The British Two-Power standard—the traditional British superiority in capital ships over the pooled strength of the next two largest navies —was never reckoned to take account of the United States Navy, and by the time the American fleet stepped into second place in the world, it had been abandoned altogether in favour of a mere policy of maintaining an adequate lead over Germany.

IX

THE Alaskan issue, which was virtually the last territorial dispute between the British Empire and the United States, still remained un-

[1] Q. Bailey, p. 558.   [2] Heindel, p. 108.

settled, and its solution was not to be altogether easy; Canadian feelings in the matter were strong yet, and Roosevelt was in no conciliatory mood, writing that "The English behaved badly in Venezuela, despite the fact that we had behaved with scrupulous impartiality during the Boer War. I don't intend that they shall do any shuffling now."[1] As the affair developed, he made it obvious that he was determined to get his way, and that no compromise worthy of the name would be acceptable to him; in this he carried an ageing and ailing Hay with him, for increasingly he dominated America's foreign as well as domestic policy, which was for the next six years to bear the unmistakable imprint of his character. His was not a diplomatic temper; he talked of speaking softly and carrying a big stick, but, though he made full use of his stick, his words were seldom as he advised they should be, for he did not err on the side of under-emphasis. It was perhaps a good thing for Anglo-American relations that he only came to power when he did, for, by 1902, when he had assumed full control, the work of Hay had already been done; his determination to preserve his intimate understanding with Britain had carried the two peoples through possibly the most important crisis in their relationship and into the relatively calm waters beyond, where Presidential ebullience would not have deeply serious consequences. Yet Roosevelt, though he might from time to time decry his feeling for Britain and declare, "I do not at all believe in being over-effusive",[2] was "emotionally pro-English",[3] and he came near to the truth about himself when he wrote to Spring-Rice: "I feel so perfectly healthy myself and the Americans and Englishmen for whom I care . . . seem so healthy, so vigorous and on the whole so decent that I rather incline to the view of my beloved friend, Lieutenant Parker . . . whom I overheard telling the Russian naval attaché at Santiago that the two branches of Anglo-Saxons had come together, and 'together, we can whip the world, Prince'."[4] Thus, in Davis's words, "Although Roosevelt's utterances imply that he saw himself as a wholly independent ruler . . . in reality he conducted this country's foreign affairs as if guided by an Anglo-American entente. By some polar attraction, he inevitably pursued in both Asia and Europe the line of British interest."[5] He had many and influential British friends and he acquired many more, for, from King Edward downwards, they courted him with enthusiasm and determination; their zeal was rewarded in the long run, and if in the short run he sometimes proved obstreperous, they ascribed it to his fine mettle; the

[1] Q. Gelber, p. 126. [2] Q. Davis, p. 147. [3] Ibid, p. 149.
[4] Q. ibid, p. 147. [5] Ibid, p. 148.

affectionate comment of Henry Adams to a mutual friend well expressed their thoughts: "The twelfth century still rages wildly here in the shape of a fiend with tusks and eye-glasses across the way. The wild boar of Cuba (sic) I love him. He is almost sane beside his German and Russian cousins. . . . What is man that he should have tusks and grin?"[1]

During the Alaskan affair the tusks were much in evidence, but they could do little harm, for the conclusion was predestined. Canada's case was not a strong one at the outset; the only substantial British bargaining counter had been cast upon the waters with the signing of the Hay-Pauncefote Treaty. Britain's support of Canada was naturally weak, since she had now no direct interest in the boundary question, except to see that it did not prove dangerous to Anglo-American relations; and her primary, overpowering motive, as well as, at bottom, Canada's pre-eminent interest, lay in the preservation of American friendship whatever it might cost. The price of the loss of her Alaskan claims to Canada would be a passing pang, but no more; to Britain it would merely be the discomfort of seeing Canada pained. Even so, Hay expressed his belief that the British Government "deferred too much to Canada."[2]

The *modus vivendi* in Alaska arranged in 1899 did not work well, and in May, 1901, Hay repeated his earlier proposal for an arbitration tribunal of jurists, three from each side; but the Canadians would only accept it if two of the members were neutral commissioners, which was unacceptable to the Americans, and so once more the matter rested. Roosevelt did not press the issue during the Boer War, but early in 1902 quietly despatched additional troops to southern Alaska, eight hundred cavalrymen compared with the forty police that Canada had sent to establish her claim in 1898. The upshot could be in no doubt; as Roosevelt said, "if trouble comes . . . it would not be pleasant for us, but it would be death for them." After final unavailing efforts on the part of Canada to obtain a genuine arbitration, either by a neutral commission or at the Hague, she and Britain accepted, in a treaty of 24 January, 1903, Hay's plan for a joint tribunal of six members. America had won another and an easy diplomatic victory, though even Hay thought the Canadian case so hopeless that he deemed it a friendly act to have given the British a dignified means of extricating themselves from an "untenable position."

The tribunal, which, it was stipulated, was to give a judicial, and not an arbitral, decision by majority vote, was to "consist of six impartial

[1] Q. ibid, p. 149.   [2] Q. W.A.A.E., p. 414.

611

jurists of repute".[1] Such a procedure, though it represented once more a triumph for peaceful methods of diplomacy between Britain and America, was in reality perhaps a retrograde step from the long established Anglo-American tradition of arbitration, but this would not have been so noticeable had Roosevelt's choice of the American delegates not been so flagrantly unjudicial. It can be argued in his favour that, had this not been the case, and been known to be so in the Senate beforehand, that body might not have passed the initial instrument; but it is not to be forgotten either, that the Senate was no doubt reinforced in its obduracy by that of the President, whose views were well known. After inviting Justices of the Supreme Court to sit on the tribunal in the obvious expectation that they would decline, which they did, he appointed Elihu Root, who was a good jurist, but also Secretary of War; Senator Turner, who may have been a jurist, but came from the most intensely affected section of the United States; and Senator Lodge, who was no jurist and was also notoriously *parti pris*. Even Chamberlain privately protested to Henry White that the very strength of the American case ought to have made it easier for Roosevelt to make more judicious appointments. Canada wished to protest, but even a sympathetic Colonial Office replied, "His Majesty's Government are . . . virtually in the position of having to choose between breaking off the negotiations altogether or of accepting the American nominations."[2] The Canadian burden was a heavy one to bear, but to their great credit they refused Whitehall's proposal that their appointments should be political also, and named two Canadian jurists of repute, while Britain appointed the Lord Chief Justice, Lord Alverstone.

But it was plain from now on that the process was to be neither arbitral nor judicial, but political; and it is to the President's credit, at least relatively, that he made no secret of this fact, nor of his fixed determination to have his way. On 25 July, 1903, he wrote to Mr. Justice Holmes a letter which he was to show to Chamberlain, stating bluntly that if the tribunal failed to agree he would "request Congress to make an appropriation which will enable me to run the boundary on my own hook . . . without any further regard to the attitude of England and Canada. If I paid attention to mere abstract right, that is the position I ought to take anyhow. I have not taken it because I wish to exhaust every effort to have the affair settled peacefully and with due regard to England's dignity."[3] This thrust a heavy political burden upon the shoulders of Alverstone; it may be disputed whether he was right judicially to take the course he did, but there is no doubt that he

[1] Q. Gelber, pp. 139, 143.   [2] Q. ibid, p. 146.   [3] Q. ibid, p. 150.

did the only possible thing politically. In fact, Roosevelt was roughly right when he declared later that the British Government had "tipped the wink" to the Chief Justice, for undoubted and heavy pressure was brought to bear on him during the hearings. Purists may denounce this defiling of the legal process, but for the historian it is often hard to see the difference between legal and political decisions in international matters, and impossible to draw a precise line between international law and international policy. For the Lord Chief Justice to have taken the Canadian point of view might well have spelled disaster for Canada, as well as Britain; that he took the American, caused pain and vexation for a time, but reinforced in the end the fundamental Anglo-American concord upon which Canada's life depends.

Negotiations, for that in fact was now the real nature of the proceedings, began on 3 September, 1903, with the two Canadian commissioners unaware of much that was happening behind the scenes; when they became fully alive to the way the wind was blowing and the force it had reached, they wanted to withdraw, but Sir Wilfred Laurier instructed them to remain and put up a bitter fight for the Portland Canal, thus himself recognizing the fundamentally political character of the proceedings. The American commissioners pressed their advantage even farther than Roosevelt, and eventually Alverstone reached conclusions agreeable to them, which were embodied in an award signed on 20 October, 1903. This granted to the Americans their main contention that the boundary ran round the heads of the inlets, but it went further and gave them, which did less than justice to the Canadian claim, very nearly the thirty marine mile strip along the coast which they demanded, as well as two of the four Portland Canal islands. The remaining two islands and the Portland Canal itself were Canada's share, one deemed so inadequate by the Canadians that their two commissioners refused to sign the award on the grounds that it was not properly judicial in character.

The award met with the reception which might have been expected in Canada; as Brebner writes, "To President Roosevelt, the Award was 'the greatest diplomatic victory during the present generation.' In Canadian eyes, the rights of the Dominion had been sacrificed again, this time dishonorably, to Anglo-American understanding."[1] On the surface it appeared that Canada had once more paid the price of Anglo-American friendship, yet Laurier went too far when he said, "It is one of those concessions which have made British diplomacy odious to Canadian people, and it will have the most lamentable effect."[2] It was,

[1] Brebner, p. 261.   [2] Q. Gelber, p. 160.

indeed, responsible for much ill feeling in Canada, and for the failure in all probability of the Reciprocity Treaty eight years later, while it hastened Canada's desire to control her own foreign affairs; but the bitterness passed and the three thousand miles of undefended frontier, which an Alaskan war might have rendered impossible, remained. Characteristic was the signature in 1908 of a treaty defining once and for all the whole Canadian-American boundary from the Atlantic to the Pacific. Canada had no alternative but to accept the ironical axiom of her political existence, that though she might pay the highest price for Anglo-American friendship, she was also its greatest beneficiary.

X

WITH the settlement of the Alaskan boundary dispute, there becomes increasingly apparent that tendency, which we have already noted, for Anglo-American relations to become primarily concerned with problems arising out of their dealings with third parties, with problems stemming directly from the broad stream of international affairs. This tendency is exaggerated by the fact that, of all American Presidents prior to his great namesake, Roosevelt perhaps was the one most ready to play a large part in the drama of world events, and most successful in gauging how much support in doing so he could gain from his countrymen. Thus Anglo-American relations, for the remainder of his term of office, constitute merely a part in the events leading to Roosevelt's arbitration in the Russo-Japanese War and to his participation in the Algeciras conference; but the new friendship of the English-speaking peoples was an indispensable factor in determining the policy of each country and in ensuring that their paths ran on the whole parallel. German efforts in both cases to disrupt their understanding proved unavailing, and the British change of government in 1905 served only to reinforce it, since the Liberals were more strongly pro-American even than their predecessors. The end of the Boer War ushered in a more tranquil period in the popular relationship, for Anglophobia receded into the background. Roosevelt said on one occasion: "The cheapest thing for a politician to do, the easiest and too often politically one of the most remunerative, [as his friend Lodge found] is to make some yell about England",[1] but he was happy that in the election of 1904 he was able to avoid any such resort. What he had written to Spring-Rice when Governor of New York was in fact now coming true:

[1] Q. W.F.R., p. 308.

"Americans who are Anglo-Saxon by adoption are . . . quite as strong about the unity of the two peoples as any others. . . . The Navy is a unit in wanting to smash Germany. . . . The professional Irishman is losing his grip and the bulk of the Irish are becoming American. . . . The feeling of hostility to England is continually softening."[1]

When the Russo-Japanese war broke out on 8 Feburary, 1904, the Anglo-American concert showed at once the high state of its development, for both powers were agreed in their attitude to it, and took pains to see that they remained in agreement. The United States, mistrusting Russian actions in Manchuria, had approved of the Anglo-Japanese alliance, and in April, 1903, Lansdowne had assured Washington that Britain was "prepared to follow the United States step by step up to any point that may be necessary for the protection of our common interests in China."[2] Britain was not reluctant to see her new ally check her traditional foe in an area where her trading interests were vast, and Roosevelt, in the Open Door tradition, declared that "Japan is playing our game." He was prepared, indeed, to go very much farther than Hay alone had felt able to do in the original Open Door Notes, and, according to his own statement to Spring-Rice:

> As soon as this war broke out . . . I notified Germany and France in the most polite and discreet fashion that in the event of a combination against Japan to try to do what Russia, Germany and France did to her in 1894, I should promptly side with Japan and proceed to whatever length was necessary on her behalf. I, of course, knew that your Government would act in the same way, and thought it best that I should have no consultation with your people before announcing my own purpose.[3]

The technique of action on parallel lines, with America somewhat in the lead, was the same as that employed in the Far East by Hay, but the British this time were prepared for it and welcomed it, all the more so because Roosevelt—it was one of the fixed and declared principles of his diplomacy—was ready to back up his policy by force. Britain would willingly have reverted to her 1898 proposal for a binding alliance in the Far East, but her rulers were now wiser, and did not expect such a consummation; as Balfour declared for Roosevelt's benefit:

> If America and ourselves were to enter into a treaty, binding us jointly to resist . . . aggression, it would never, I believe, be attempted. Together we are too strong for any combination of powers to fight

[1] Q. Davis, p. 149.   [2] Q. Gelber, p. 167.   [3] Q. ibid, p. 170.

us. I believe there would be no difficulty on this side of the Atlantic. The difficulty, I imagine, would be rather with the United States, whose traditions and whose Constitution conspire to make such arrangements hard to conclude.[1]

This caution was justified, but co-operation was none the less close, despite Germany's effort to split the two nations by suggesting that Britain was privy to a general European plan to despoil China, for in response to an official query from the United States she and all the other powers concerned replied that they were in favour of the Open Door and the territorial integrity of China. More than that, Britain consented to send Spring-Rice on a private though semi-official visit to Washington, where he stayed with "Uncle Henry" Adams; this visit, despite the embarrassment it caused to the technically adequate Ambassador in Washington, Durand, resulted in an Anglo-American understanding which was at the basis of the Far Eastern settlement. Spring-Rice's account of his return to England speaks for itself:

> In England, of course, as Chamberlain told me very earnestly, every thinking man is convinced of the absolute necessity for England of a good understanding with America—but they know, most of them— that they had better not say so. . . . The King was (as you know) anxious and more than anxious to do everything in his power, and in fact his enthusiasm had to be damped by constitutional reminders. I should think you could be certain that we will follow your lead and that you will find us ready and anxious to take any action which you suggest beforehand.

Roosevelt's own view was expressed in his letter of thanks to the King for the gift of a miniature of John Hampden on his Inauguration in 1905, accompanying a return gift of a copy of some of his studies on the American West: "I absolutely agree with you as to the importance, not only to ourselves but to all the free peoples of the civilized world, of a constantly growing friendship and understanding between the English-speaking peoples. One of the gratifying things in what has occurred during the last decade has been the growth in this feeling of good will."[2]

Yet there were practical difficulties still ahead, for Roosevelt envisaged, with his penchant for *realpolitik*, a balance of power in the Far East, and became increasingly apprehensive, as the overwhelming nature of Japan's victory over Russia became clear, of an over-mighty Japan. Already there is visible here the first sign of that increasing

[1] Q. Davis, p. 156.   [2] Q. Gelber, pp. 180, 185.

mistrust between the United States and Japan which was to culminate in Pearl Harbour, but which, long before that distant date, was to provide yet another instance of the primacy of American friendship among the aims of British policy, in Britain's abandonment, at American behest in the early twenties, of the Anglo-Japanese alliance. But this cleavage was merely hinted at now, and the Anglo-American divergence of opinion was one as to means only, and not as to ends, for Britain, as Lansdowne repeatedly affirmed, was just as desirous of peace in the Far East as America, and welcomed Roosevelt's efforts to bring it about. The difficulty arose out of the President's desire that Britain should bring pressure to bear upon Japan to moderate what he feared, even in the light of Japan's mounting list of victories, were her excessive terms. This the British did not feel that they could in honour do, for they were pledged allies and not mere neutrals, though the terms of their alliance did not call for intervention in a war of Japan against a single opponent. When the tension temporarily showed signs of mounting between the White House and the Foreign Office— Roosevelt was now in full control of foreign policy, for Hay, long sick, died on 1 July—Spring-Rice was once more called in to advise the British Government and to allay Presidential discontent; in this he succeeded to some extent, despite the efforts of Berlin and St. Petersburg to prevent it, though he did so at the cost, which was probably necessary, of further undermining Durand's position in Washington.

The American demands that pressure be brought to bear upon Japan were peculiarly embarrassing to the British Government at this time, since they were secretly engaged in negotiating a revision of the Anglo-Japanese treaty, which the war had rendered necessary. At the end of May the Japanese had requested Roosevelt to come forward and propose mediation, and for the period up to the beginning of the Peace Conference at Portsmouth, New Hampshire, on 10 August, the British Government maintained an attitude of aloofness; as Durand rightly surmised in June, it would probably "be reluctant to take any step which could embarrass Japanese." During the actual negotiations however, Lansdowne forwarded to Tokyo, without comment, Durand's report of a conversation with Roosevelt, in which the latter urged Britain to press Japan to moderate her demands for a large indemnity and the whole of the island of Sakhalin; and this gesture was probably not without its effect. Perhaps more important was the serious financial situation in which Japan now found herself, and the informal intimation she received, that the American and British financial houses upon which she so largely depended would be unlikely to continue to extend their facilities to her if she persisted in her demands. Most important of all was probably the signing of the new Anglo-Japanese alliance, two days after the Conference began, for it recognized Japanese hegemony in Korea and gave her confidence in the future, so that she moderated her demands and consented to sign the Treaty of Portsmouth on 5 September, 1905. Curiously enough, the new Anglo-Japanese alliance was also a principal means of healing the slight strain in Anglo-American relations, for throughout its negotiation Britain made quite transparent her profound concern for American friendship. In the discussion of certain abortive clauses, specifying Anglo-Japanese naval and military commitments in the Far East, the British Government stipulated that each party should maintain a force superior in strength, not to that of any other power, but to that of any *European* power in those seas. This, as Lansdowne explained to the Japanese Minister, "was done in order that we might not be compelled to level our fleets up to the strength of the naval force maintained by the U(nited) S(tates) in or near the Far East." In the course of negotiations over Korea Lansdowne cabled the British Minister in Tokyo, "all we desire is that we should not be compelled to go to war say with the U(nited) S(tates) in the event of a violation of established Treaty rights by Japan."[1]

In fact, the turning point in the Anglo-Japanese negotiations was Roosevelt's assurance to the Japanese through Taft, his Secretary of War, who was visiting Tokyo, that, since Japan asseverated that she desired only peace in the Far East and had no designs whatever on the Philippines, he had no objection to Japanese suzerainty in Korea. His association with the Anglo-Japanese alliance was thus as close as he dared to make it, in view of the still powerful isolationist traditions of his country. It is probable, indeed, that he recommended a revision of the Anglo-Japanese alliance in the first place; and at the outset of the negotiations the Japanese Minister in London actually inquired of Lansdowne whether there was any chance of the United States becoming a party to the alliance, to which the Englishman, wise in the ways of American foreign policy even under a Roosevelt, replied:

> I said . . . that I had had frequent discussions with the United States
> Government with regard to affairs in the Far East, and that I had
> good reasons for knowing that their policy was eminently friendly
> to Japan, and I thought I might say identical with ours. There was
> therefore every reason for anticipating that American influence would
> be exerted upon the same lines as ours. The United States Government

[1] Q. ibid, pp. 208, 221, 225.

were however notoriously opposed to the idea of entangling themselves in foreign alliances, and although I should expect to find them
moving upon parallel lines with us, I doubted whether they were likely
to do more.

At the critical stage of the negotiations, three days after the President's confirmation of the Taft-Katsura agreement, Lansdowne consulted Roosevelt as to the actual terms of the treaty, a courtesy certainly
not shown to any other power, and as Durand reported, "He accepted
it at once without demur."[1] Consideration by Britain towards America
could hardly have gone farther; American intervention in the Far East
had in the end strengthened the Anglo-American accord. The Japanese
public was at first violently incensed against Roosevelt for depriving
them of what they believed to be possible gains, but this extreme bitterness was allayed in due time, partly perhaps by the world cruise in
1907 of the United States fleet, which visited not only such outposts of
the English-speaking world as Australia and New Zealand, but also
Japan. This formidable Armada, the British Ambassador in Tokyo
wrote to London, "has had all the effect our *allies** wanted it to and has
put an end to all nonsensical war talk"; as Davis aptly puts it, "The
British Ambassador seems to have forgotten with which country
Britain was allied."[2] But, as was clearly to be shown in the coming
years, when relations between America and Japan did not entirely lose
the bitterness they had now acquired in the matter of priority of British
friendships, the Ambassador had got hold very firmly of the right end
of the stick.

Since America's annexation of the Philippines, her intervention in
Far Eastern affairs could not come altogether as a surprise, but during
the last stages of the Russo-Japanese War there occurred a European
crisis in which Roosevelt, exceeding the diplomatic dreams even of the
departed Hay, played a notable part. Germany's precipitation of the
Moroccan incident on 31 March, 1905, was a direct reaction to the
Anglo-French Mediterranean agreement of the previous April, and
in this effort to break up the Anglo-French combination, the Kaiser
hoped to enlist the assistance of Roosevelt, thus equally breaking up the
Anglo-American accord. But the British Government were able to convince the President without too much difficulty of the unreliability of
the German Emperor, and of the danger inherent in his request for
American mediation.

Nevertheless, the tension grew and Roosevelt became convinced of

[1] Q. ibid, pp. 219-220, 231.   * Author's italics.   [2] Q. Davis, pp. 155-6.

the imminence of war. Wishing to keep a balance in Europe such as he also desired in the Orient, and fearing a war between France and Germany which would widen until it became "literally a world conflagration",[1] he prevailed upon Germany, with the consent of the French, to accept a European conference, which America as well as Britain attended. Germany, which had turned to the United States at the height of the crisis, was satisfied with what appeared to her a diplomatic victory, but when the conference assembled at Algeciras on 16 January, 1906, it soon became clear that it was with France, Britain's friend, and not with Germany, that Roosevelt's sympathies lay. In the meantime, increasing Anglo-German tension over naval building contrasted vividly with the great reception accorded in the autumn to a British cruiser division which paid a courtesy visit to the United States, while the incoming Liberal government of Campbell-Bannerman, with Grey at the Foreign Office, announced that the cardinal and immutable principle of its foreign policy was "the growing friendship and good feeling between ourselves and the United States, a matter of common ground and common congratulation to all parties in this country."[2] The feelings of the new Secretary of State, Elihu Root, were also friendly, and the only technical difficulty in promoting concord lay in the mistrust between Durand and Roosevelt; the measure of its gravity was the ignorance of the British Government as to the extent of the President's influence at Algeciras, and, though unfortunate, the Ambassador's removal in October, 1906, was an undoubted necessity.

It was partly through this lack of liaison that a difference between the two governments as to the best means of attaining their common aim was allowed to appear during the course of the Conference, and even that some suspicion grew in Britain that Roosevelt was 'falling for' the "Emperor's assiduous efforts to cultivate the most intimate relations" with him. As Whitelaw Reid wrote to him, "a common comment upon it is that the Emperor overdoes his love-making as he does his diplomacy, with a certain German confidence in the value of brute vigor in either pursuit!"[3] This was far from being the case, for the President was quite equal to the Kaiser, having extracted at the very beginning of negotiations, in return for persuading the British and French to consent to a conference, an undertaking from Wilhelm that he would "in every case be ready to back up the decision which you [Roosevelt] consider to be most fair and most practicable."[4] In fact it was Roosevelt who screwed French courage to the sticking place, when

[1] Q. ibid, p. 185.   [2] Q. Gelber, p. 252.
[3] Q. ibid, p. 270.   [4] Q. Davis, p. 184.

they and the British were inclined to accept an Austrian compromise solution, which might have given Germany an indirect foothold, however tenuous, in the port of Casablanca, and he who got a full pound of flesh from the Kaiser by insisting on the acceptance of an American plan carefully concocted in the French interest. His influence was considerable and he was perhaps justified in writing to Reid: "In this Algeciras matter you will notice that while I was most suave and pleasant with the Emperor, yet when it became necessary at the end I stood him on his head with great decision".[1] Thus the balance was for the present restored in Europe, and Germany's power checked; even within, or almost within, the confines of the American diplomatic tradition, the President had been able to achieve peaceful settlements in East and West.

Though it has its ironical side that the belligerent Rough Rider should be awarded the Nobel Peace Prize for these achievements, it was by no means as comical as it has appeared to some writers, nor as absurd as dubbing Neville Chamberlain a peacemaker on the strength of the Munich Agreement of 1938; the world of the subsequent nineteen-forties was to come strongly to the belief that weakness and lack of readiness to use force in a just cause is a supreme incitement to war, and of this Theodore Roosevelt was never guilty. Henry Adams saw to the heart of the matter: "We have got," he wrote to a friend in late January, 1906, "to support France against Germany and fortify the Atlantic system beyond attack; for if Germany breaks down England and France, she becomes the center of a military world, and we are lost."

XI

BUT even in a more idealistic sense, Roosevelt was not without claims as a contributor to the cause of international peace, and some have seen in his acceptance speech for the Nobel Prize, with its call for a "league of peace",[2] the origin of the League of Nations. This is no doubt going too far, but the period of fifteen years before World War I, of which his Presidency forms the hard core, were singularly rich in efforts to achieve peaceful and humanitarian aims in international affairs. The list of international agreements of this kind to which Great Britain and the United States were both parties is impressive, even though so many of them were conclusively to demonstrate their impotence in the chaos of World War I; between 1899 and 1912, excluding broad inter-

[1] Q. Gelber, p. 270.   [2] Q. Davis, pp. 197, 201.

national agreements such as those made at the Hague, they signed thirty-six conventions, covering a wide variety of topics, beginning with a minor one on the disposal of real and personal property, and ending with a major one respecting the North Atlantic fisheries. This tendency to international agreement owed its strength, it is true, chiefly to the prevailing spirit of the age, and one cannot but remark, in the contrast between the world's overt desire for peace and the way in fact that it rushed headlong to destruction, a pattern which is epitomized in the contrast of Roosevelt's own character. His attitude to the arbitration treaties, which we have already discussed, was characteristic; supporting them at first, perhaps without great enthusiasm, he was prepared when the Senate emasculated them to throw in the sponge, and only the determination of Root, his Secretary of State, and the greater enthusiasm of his successor led to persistence in the almost futile struggle.

A similar contrast appears in the policy of the Roosevelt Administration to the Second Hague Conference. The First, which had met in 1899, had started badly, owing to the failure of specific proposals for disarmament or for an armaments holiday, through the opposition of Britain and Germany, the chief naval and military powers respectively, and also of the United States. Little real progress was made with plans to humanize warfare, because of the differences of opinion between the experts of the various countries; from Britain's point of view the most significant proposal was that sponsored by the American and other delegations to exempt private property from capture at sea. Here American policy harked straight back to Secretary of State Marcy's refusal to accept the Declaration of Paris of 1856, on the ground that it did not go nearly far enough in the protection of private property at sea; and the British, under the imperially minded government of 1899, also ran true to form by refusing even to discuss the matter. The only substantial step that was taken, as we have seen, was the establishment of the permanent Arbitration Tribunal at The Hague for the voluntary arbitration of international disputes; in pressing for this, the two English-speaking powers, who had set so high a standard in the matter in their own recent disagreements, were virtually at one.

The problems before the Second Hague Conference in 1907 were very much the same, though some modifications in the attitudes of the Powers were apparent. Britain, now under a more idealistic Liberal Government, pressed for a discussion of disarmament, against the wishes of the Central European Powers, and was supported by the United States, but it came to nothing. Much more interesting was the attitude of the two Governments to the renewed proposal for the immunity of private property on the high seas, for Germany chiefly defended her claim to a large navy on the grounds that her commerce had to be protected in time of war, so that the protection of private property might in theory lead to an acceptance of naval disarmament. That it was in theory only was shown by the failure of any power to press for an equal protection of private property in land as in sea warfare, and by the essentially aggressive use of German naval power in World War I. Yet it was a measure of the effect of the change of Government that the British delegates were permitted to discuss the question, and even to leave a hope that, if general disarmament ever took place, they might consider it again; nevertheless, their stand was essentially the same as in 1899 and it defeated the project. Similar, too, was the stand of the United States delegation in favour of it, but it was a measure also of their changing circumstances that they did so against the wishes of their own naval advisers, and even of their Secretary of State.

This overruling of the Navy Board was Roosevelt's, and it marked a complete disagreement with Mahan. The Admiral based all his assumptions on the fundamental axiom of American self-interest as he saw it, that is to say, agreement with Great Britain; to him, therefore, it followed that America should reverse her traditional attitude and welcome any policy which added to the strength of the British Navy. "The United States has certainty of a very high order that the British Empire will stand substantially on the same lines of world privileges as ourselves; that its strength will be our strength, and the weakening it injury to us." More than that, Britain stood squarely between Germany and her colonial and commercial aspirations in Central and South America; exempt her carrying trade from the power of Britain, "and you remove the strongest hook in the jaw of Germany that the English-speaking people have—a principal gage for peace."[1] He pointed to the American interest in 1861 and 1898, and called for a reversal of the earlier and traditional American attitude to Freedom of the Seas. With him the General Board of the Navy agreed: "Should private property at sea be immune in time of war, this great advantage would be lost to Great Britain, as well as to the United States, and the immense assistance we might expect to receive from Great Britain would be tremendously decreased."[2] Whether because he was reluctant to commit America so wholeheartedly to one camp, thus losing his independence of action; whether relishing his new-found role of peacemaker; or

[1] Q. Gelber, p. 134.   [2] Q. Davis, p. 199.

whether moved by the sort of humanitarian sentiments he so often declared that he despised, the President disagreed, and his delegation pressed for the immunity of private property at sea. As the pressure was fruitless, it was perhaps of little importance except that it is conceivable, though not much more, that a reversal of the traditional American policy in 1907 would, even under a later Democratic administration, have alleviated some of the Anglo-American tension in the first phase of World War I.

But if this might possibly have made a difference, it is probable that British action in other aspects of the same question in 1907 might have done so very decisively. Some progress was made in the humanization and regularization of war, particularly at sea, and agreement was reached for the conditional abolition of the use of force in the recovery of international debts; but, from Britain's point of view, much the most interesting outcome of the Second Hague Conference was the signature of a convention for the establishment of an International Prize Court. The sequel to this was a conference to which the British Government invited the powers at London in 1908, for the purpose of codifying "the acknowledged principles of international law",[1] so that the Court might come into existence and begin to function smoothly. With their long history of disagreement on this topic, such a discussion might obviously place a strain on the new Anglo-American relationship. Little theoretical change had taken place in the views of the powers since the United States declined to accept the Declaration of Paris in 1856, but as the division between naval and administration opinion in the United States had recently shown, America's changing interests and the effects of the Civil and Spanish wars had produced some possibility of a shift in her position. A half century without a major international war had also produced a softening of the British attitude, particularly with governmental power in the hands of the Liberal party; they had shown signs of this weakening by their acceptance, with modifications, of the German proposal for the Prize Court, and even in suggestions, which they sponsored, for the restriction of the free use of floating mines, they managed to combine some measures of humanitarianism with obvious self-interest.

Thus it was no surprise when the Declaration of London, issued by the Conference, embodied some substantial concessions by both Britain and the United States. The saving grace of the Declaration of Paris from Britain's point of view, had been that, though it protected neutral goods under the enemy flag and enemy goods under a neutral flag,

[1] Encyclopedia Britannica, XVIII, p. 528.

contraband was excepted in both cases and no definition of contraband was reached. The Declaration of 1909 included three definitive lists; one of objects unconditionally contraband, one of objects which might be declared contraband, and one of objects which could under no circumstances be regarded as contraband. This marked a considerable British concession, for, as a belligerent, though her food and raw material supplies might be protected by such a definition, it was much safer for her to rely on her naval power to achieve this. As to the possibility of Britain being a neutral in the next great war, who could believe this possible in the midst of the great Anglo-German naval rivalry which was then in full swing? The Declaration of London also refined the doctrine of continuous voyage, by validating in effect the American Civil War practice, which marked an American recession from her strict traditional position.

But in the event, the Prize Court was not established and the Declaration was not ratified by Britain or the United States. In Britain the whole arrangement was regarded with grave suspicion by a large body of public opinion, just as its predecessor, the Declaration of Paris, had been, but in this case the opposition, led by the Conservatives, were in a position to prevent ratification. Under the British constitutional system, ratification of treaties was a royal prerogative, not needing specific Parliamentary sanction, but the Government had agreed not to ratify the Declaration without Parliamentary approval. In the Commons the issue was shelved, but after much procrastination the House of Lords, in the summer of 1911, at the very height of the struggle between the Houses over the Parliament Act, refused consent to the Declaration, which therefore lapsed as far as Britain was concerned. The Senate had ratified it some time before, but on receipt of this news the President withheld ratification. Thus at the outbreak of the war in 1914, neither Britain nor the United States had ratified the Declaration of London, and there is no doubt that from the point of view of the former this was a most happy fact, for observance of it would have crippled her war effort against Germany, while an actual breach of a ratified treaty might have been disastrous for Anglo-American relations. Even as it was, though the Declaration was not ratified by either power, we have not yet heard the last of it.

Roosevelt not only contributed something to the Hague Conference and the peace movement it represented, but submitted the first case for arbitration to the new Arbitration Tribunal; this was the long-standing Newfoundland fisheries question. In so doing he reverted, after the deviation of the Alaska case, to the path of genuine arbitration of Anglo-American disputes, but that this issue was so successfully arbitrated was primarily owing to his Secretary of State, Elihu Root. A great lawyer and close friend of Bryce, the British Ambassador, he had been responsible for the arbitration treaty with Britain, which was signed, in common with many others, in 1908, and he had actually visited Newfoundland in 1905, just before taking up his duties at the State Department, to see the problem at first hand. It was not only, as his biographer claims, his greatest diplomatic triumph, but it was the one in which he was least overshadowed by his vigorous President, perhaps because so mundane a subject had little appeal to the more flamboyant Roosevelt; certainly it was a substantial contribution to Anglo-American friendship finally to lay to rest this very irritating and malicious spectre, which had so long haunted the relations of the two countries. The situation had never been finally stabilized since the abortive treaty of 1888, and at the beginning of the century it became once more a cause of great discontent to New Englanders, owing to the vexatious and discriminatory regulations imposed by the Newfoundlanders; temporary arrangements were once more made, but were followed this time, in January, 1909, by a convention submitting the case to the Hague Court. After relinquishing the State Department, Root argued the case before the Court, which handed down what was in fact a compromise decision, in 1910; it safeguarded New England fishermen, but supported the Newfoundland claim to local jurisdiction, while its award put into effect the provisions of the 1888 Bayard-Chamberlain agreement, specifying some of the bays as exclusively British, and for others laying down that a territorial bay must be less than ten miles across from head to head. Not only did the Court rule in detail on all disputed points, but in 1912 an Anglo-American treaty set up a permanent body to deal with future problems as they arose. For this final agreement, the Taft administration was responsible, and it forms a useful link between the administrations of Roosevelt and his successor.

Taft, who was a jurist by inclination and was later to be Chief Justice of the Supreme Court, had, indeed, much more in common with Root than with Roosevelt, and his period of office saw a pronounced effort to continue the internationalist arrangements begun in the time of his predecessor. There was in America a widespread peace movement in these years, against which only cool realists like the venerable Mahan stood out, and into it Taft entered wholeheartedly amidst the plaudits of English Liberals. In Anglo-American relations his most striking initiative was the general treaty of arbitration of 1911, which was impressive in its scope; into it Bryce and his masters at Westminster plunged with zeal, too, so that its failure to gain sufficient support from Americans and their Senate, despite all Taft's efforts, was to the British Ambassador "the keenest disappointment of his diplomatic career."[1]

Abortive though it was, however, it gave yet another instance of the readiness of British statesmen to subordinate all other considerations to American friendship, for it materially affected the terms on which the Anglo-Japanese alliance was renewed in 1911, four weeks before the arbitration treaty was signed. American-Japanese relations had never returned to their original friendliness after the victory of Japan in the Russo-Japanese War. The Japanese indignation at Roosevelt's peace-making had hardly abated when violent public feeling was aroused there by acts of anti-Oriental discrimination by the state of California. The tabloid Press of the West Coast gave tongue in reply, and for some time the situation even looked as if it might lead to war. Roosevelt handled the crisis well, and when denunciation of the Californian authorities did no good, modified his attitude, and granted them what they really wanted, termination of the influx of Japanese into the United States. This he managed to achieve by the so-called Gentleman's Agreement of 1907-8, by which the Japanese Government agreed to refuse passports to Japanese labourers bound direct to the United States, while the San Francisco Board of Education was induced to repeal the regulation which had been the occasion of difficulty. The Root-Takahira agreement of 30 November, 1908, consolidated the situation by a mutual recognition of each other's possessions, of the *status quo* in the Pacific, and of the Open Door in, and territorial integrity of, China. But, though formal good relations were thus restored, Britain was all too uneasily conscious of the change which had come over the relations of her ally with her indispensable friend, and when the Anglo-Japanese negotiations to renew the alliance took place, the British Government insisted on the insertion of a clause providing that neither power should be obliged to go to war with a nation with which it had a general treaty of arbitration. This was, and was known to be, specifically designed to remove any danger of conflict between Britain and America, and it was a clear sign to the Japanese, as to the Americans, of where the primary allegiance of Britain lay.

That allegiance was not subjected for the present to any strain, and Grey in his memoirs could think of no question in Anglo-American relations between 1906 and 1912 which was even worthy of mention.

[1] Q. W.F.R., p. 307.

This reflected not only the calm waters into which the two countries had sailed, but also the extent to which Canadian interests had come to be thought of as separate from those of the mother country, for the last serious tiff between the United States and Canada took place in these years. The wish of many Canadian Liberals for increased reciprocity with the United States, cherished ever since the expiry of the treaty of 1854, was fulfilled by Taft's negotiation of a sweeping legislative reciprocity agreement in 1911, designed to prevent a tariff war arising from the American tariff of 1909 and to satisfy domestic critics of the Administration's high tariff policy. Taft was only just able to force the measure through Congress, and in the course of supporting it, a number of rash American statements, including one from the President himself, raised once more the bogey of annexation, which had always bedevilled reciprocity negotiations; the Speaker of the House of Representatives went so far as to say that he supported the measure, "because I hope to see the day when the American flag will float over every square foot of British North American possessions clear to the North Pole."[1] The Conservatives in Canada, partly from economic and partly from patriotic motives, opposed the agreement, and it became the main issue of a general election in 1911. There is no doubt that Canadian resentment at American treatment of the Alaskan boundary question loomed large in the defeat of Sir Wilfred Laurier and the Liberals, and the consequent failure to ratify the reciprocity agreement. From our point of view it is significant that this disturbance, though technically negotiations had originally been initiated through the British Ambassador, caused scarcely a ripple in the calm pool of Anglo-American relations proper; indeed, Canada was shortly to signalize her new-found strength and independence of action, in practice if not in theory, by a rebuff to Britain in matters of imperial defence almost as significant as, though less abrupt than, her rejection of American reciprocity. From this time the thread of Canadian-American is clearly distinct from that of Anglo-American relations.

Of the latter there is little more to be said before the election of Wilson in 1912. The so-called "dollar diplomacy" of Taft's Secretary of State, Philander C. Knox, which accorded so ill with the legalistic internationalist aspirations of the President, was confined for the most part to two main areas, China and Latin America. In the former this policy of encouraging American investment for politico-economic reasons was singularly ineffective, and had little impact upon Anglo-American relations, except the not very serious disgruntlement of cer-

[1] Q. Bemis, p. 741.

tain British business interests; in the latter, where penetration was much more successful, it was welcomed in Britain in the same way and for the same reasons as the Roosevelt Corollary had been. Thus Taft's on the whole unsuccessful Presidency, which had in some ways fallen between the two stools of Wilsonism and Rooseveltism, was calmer than almost any other period in Anglo-American relations to date. Only in the case of the Panama Tolls Act passed by Congress in 1912 was there visible by the time his term of office was over, a dark little cloud on the horizon; it, and other very much weightier difficulties, were to make the rule of his successor altogether different.

CHAPTER SIXTEEN

WORLD WAR I (1912-21)

I N THE years between 1912 and 1921, for the first time we see to the full the absorption of our particular stream of history in the great and broadening river of world events, for as the cataclysm increasingly drove all other considerations out of the mind of Britain, so nothing else in Anglo-American relations came to count except the war and the issues rising out of it: once the war had begun Britain was more than ever determined to avoid any serious breach with the United States, for such a breach would have been simple national suicide. Happily, by 1914 there was no serious and unsettled diplomatic controversy between the two states. There were still some difficulties, such as the Irish question, and the war was to raise a great number more; Anglophobia could still show remarkable vigour, and the very closeness of the two peoples now created the problem that there was, as Grey wrote, "a certain intimacy, if it may be called so, of attraction and repulsion, which has made the relations between Britain and the United States at once more easy and more difficult, more cordial and more intractable, than those between any two other countries."[1] Yet it was very true that relations had never been better than they were in 1914; the popular celebration of the hundred years of peace between them in that year not only threw into high relief the distance they had travelled since they faced, in the years before 1812, so analagous a situation, but was a true index to the warmth of cordiality which the relationship had now reached.

The emotional strain to which, on the British side, it was to be subjected by the war was severe; for her, the three years of American neutrality were painful in the extreme. Seeing World War I, however, in the light of World War II, it is impossible not to regard the collapse of neutrality in America as an integral part of a remorseless process by which the United States, caught in the ever-widening whirlpool of the latest and greatest of international struggles, was sucked irresistibly into its vortex. Signs of the breakdown of her isolation had already been apparent under Roosevelt, but under Taft a reaction had set in

[1] Viscount Grey of Fallodon, *Twenty-Five Years 1892-1916* (London, 1923), II, p. 85.

which was continued in the early years of Wilson; the attraction—in the end to prove triumphant—of world affairs, had been welcomed by the Rough Rider, but was initially resented and resisted by the College President. When that resistance turned out to be futile, the President made a virtue of necessity by proposing the final and irreversible participation of the United States in a new world order. Not so his people: cleaving to traditional ways they repudiated the League of Nations and moved back into isolationism. But it is now no longer isolation, but isolationism; not a policy naturally produced by geographical circumstances and historical tradition, but one deliberately fabricated in defiance of a changing environment, in order to preserve artificially an outdated insulation of national life from the affairs of the wide world. Thus in these eight years the United States ran the whole gamut of experience from a remote isolation to a wholehearted participation in a great war, and then back to a new isolationism.

These years cover the first eight-year Democratic term of office since before the Civil War, and bear indelibly the imprint of Woodrow Wilson's personality. Virginian Presbyterian and professor turned politician, he effected in internal affairs what amounted to a mild liberal revolution; a convinced democrat, he had a natural bias against autocratic systems of government and a natural sympathy for the Britain he had often visited and for its Liberal government. Spring-Rice, the British Ambassador, recorded in 1914 a conversation in which, when he spoke of the sonnets Wordsworth had written at the time of the Napoleonic Wars, the President said, his eyes misty with tears, that he knew them by heart and "had them in his mind all the time", to which the Ambassador replied, "You and Grey are fed on the same food and I think you understand."[1] To his friend Colonel House he had stated some days earlier that "if Germany won it would change the course of our civilization and make the United States a military nation. . . . He said German philosophy was essentially selfish and lacking in spirituality. . . . He was particularly scornful of Germany's disregard of treaty obligations, and was indignant at the German Chancellor's designation of the Belgian Treaty as being 'only a scrap of paper'."[2] To Joseph Tumulty he declared, "England is fighting our fight."[3]

This underlying sympathy for Britain and the Allies never dis-

[1] Spring-Rice, II, p. 223.

[2] Q. Seymour, *The Intimate Papers of Colonel House*, I, p. 299.

[3] Q. H. C. Peterson, *Propaganda for War, The Campaign against American Neutrality, 1914-1917* (Oklahoma, 1939), p. 181.

appeared, despite his frequent irritation at the friction which occurred, but equally it never took control of the President's policy. Over his warm but suppressed emotions, his Calvinistic conscience maintained firm control, and always it insisted on judging the neutrality issue on the basis of American interests and American opinion; though he regarded himself as essentially the servant of public opinion, he tended to rely entirely on his own judgment as to what that opinion was. As Spring-Rice wrote earlier to Balfour : "I have been in Russia, Berlin, Constantinople and Persia, which are all popularly supposed to be autocratic governments. But I have never known any government so autocratic as this. This does not mean that the President acts without consulting the popular will. On the contrary. . . . But his interpretation of the oracle is his own secret."[1] As Spring-Rice again put it, "whatever happens, the decision lies with the President who seeks his inspiration from popular opinion as expressed in the mass, but takes no individual into his counsel."[2] His resultant isolation was almost as much temperamental as official, for, even while he was President-elect, Walter Page (later Ambassador in London) was tremendously impressed by his loneliness, and later recorded that he had a college professor's habit of doing "his own thinking, untouched by other men's ideas."[3] Towards the end, this hermit-like existence was to become almost pathological.

Spring-Rice was all too conscious of the practical difficulties arising from this situation, and wrote to Grey in 1916 :

> I want you to understand the rather-difficult position in which your representative here is placed. The direction of public affairs lies wholly in the hands of the President. He makes public utterances it is true, but their character is somewhat cryptic, and his language, while very elevated and convincing, does not immediately lead to any definite practical conclusions. In this respect he has been likened to Mr. Gladstone. For diplomatists, or at any rate for an English diplomatist, he is quite unapproachable.[4]

To overcome this difficulty Spring-Rice was forced to consent, rather reluctantly, to the good offices of the young head of British Military Intelligence in the United States, William Wiseman, who by degrees became accepted as an unofficial liaison officer. Not only was he intimate with Colonel House, even living in the same building in New York, but had extraordinary personal access to the President; in Reading's time he acted as Ambassador during the statesman's absences. This swift informal channel of communication was of vital

<hr>

[1] Spring-Rice, II, p. 372.   [2] Ibid, p. 357.
[3] Page, II, p. 174.   [4] Spring-Rice, II, p. 313.

importance, particularly because of the American desire for publicity-free contacts.

To this Presidential self-sufficiency was added a vein of obstinacy which made him exceedingly persistent in any course of action he undertook; as an American put it to Spring-Rice in 1913, "His friends say he is honest, of high principles, and lofty intentions, but obstinate and stubborn." Of his idealism, the worthiness of his motives and even the warmth of his political feelings there can be no doubt, but his isolation from, and consequent misreading of, the public opinion upon which he was proud to depend were to lead him to his supreme failure, the rejection by his own people of the Versailles Treaty and the League of Nations. It made, however, the few people who did have access to and influence upon, him, of unusual importance.

Into this category the members of his Cabinet did not for the most part come; on the whole, he took them as little as possible into his confidence. His first Secretary of State, William Jennings Bryan, he reluctantly appointed to that office, as the doyen of the Democratic party, and in fact he handled all important questions of foreign policy himself. Bryan was far less unhappy in this situation than might have been supposed, since he was chiefly concerned to press on the signature of his "cooling-off" treaties; as Spring-Rice wrote in February, 1914, "Bryan is as friendly as ever, and tells me what is on his mind. His profound and haunting desire is to get his treaties through. . . . They are his children and the sheep of his pasture."[1] These treaties, which were his own peculiar project, provided that, in every otherwise insoluble dispute, there should be no resort to arms until a recommendation had been made by a permanent commission of investigation, though each disputant could then reject the recommendation if it wished. They were thus conciliation rather than arbitration treaties, and Page wrote that they constituted a "sort of grape-juice arbitration—a distinct step backward from a real arbitration treaty",[2] but they were not quite as unrealistic as has sometimes been assumed. Thirty of them were negotiated in 1913 and 1914, and the refusal of Germany to sign one, on the ground, as the Kaiser told House, that "Our strength lies in being always prepared for war at a second's notice. We will not resign that advantage and give our enemies time to prepare",[3] was not without its effect upon German-American relations. Nevertheless, the diplomacy of the great Nebraskan Democrat contained an exaggerated strain of that naïve idealism in international

[1] Spring-Rice, II, pp. 186, 201.   [2] *Life and Letters*, I, p. 226.
[3] *Intimate Papers*, I, p. 262.

affairs of which American history shows a number of examples, and his persistent pacifism was to prove embarrassing when the war began; the Ambassador wrote nine months later, "Bryan spoke to me about peace as he always does. He sighs for the Nobel Prize, and besides that he is a really convinced peaceman. He has just given me a sword beaten into a plough share six inches long to serve as a paper-weight. It is adorned with quotations from Isaiah and himself. No one doubts his sincerity, but that is rather embarrassing for us at the present moment". Yet Spring-Rice's friendship with him remained cordial, and it was to him that he wrote in 1918, "whatever may be said of the relations, politically speaking, of England and America, one thing is absolutely certain—in no other country can an Englishman make such friendships."[1] Some of his own countrymen, and even fellow-Democrats, were less tolerant; Page actually declared during Bryan's period at the State Department that "Only the President's great personality saves the situation in foreign relations."[2]

Robert Lansing, who succeeded Bryan after the latter's resignation in 1915, though he was a very competent diplomat, had in some ways even less influence, for the President had by then assumed a virtually absolute control of foreign policy. It is perhaps because he was in the difficult position of serving two masters, an outward President bent resolutely on neutrality, and an inward President whose heart was warm towards Britain, that Lansing's actions as Secretary of State have been so controversial. To contemporaries he seemed a lawyer adamant for the letter of neutral rights, and this contemporary impression is borne out by his published papers; but in his Memoirs, brought out nearly two decades after the war, he appears as strongly pro-Ally, claiming that his objections to British actions were made "half-heartedly, as a matter of form", whereas his protests to Germany were terse and harsh, although such "short and emphatic notes were dangerous."[3] No doubt he was concerned in later years to put his own conduct in the most favourable light, but certainly he was never by any stretch of imagination sympathetic to the German cause.

Even more was this true of the only man who had throughout these years a strong and sometimes decisive influence over Wilson, his confidant and adviser, Colonel Edward Mandell House. Such a description of his role is inadequate: one would dub him, did it not have in some ways sinister implications, the *"éminence grise"* of the Administration, but there was in fact nothing sinister about it. To Spring-Rice, bred

[1] Spring-Rice, II, pp. 240, 243.   [2] *Life and Letters,* I, p. 235.

[3] Q. Peterson, p. 184.

in the English tradition of mistrust for secret royal advisers and favourites, it sometimes seemed that there was, but under the American system, where for his term of office so vast a personal power is in the hands of the President, and where no collective Cabinet responsibility exists, such relationships are not only permissible, particularly in times of crisis, but even desirable; the historian of Anglo-American relations, at least, cannot regret the influence either of Colonel House or Harry Hopkins. House—like Wilson a Southern liberal Democrat—had been largely instrumental in obtaining Wilson's nomination as Presidential candidate in 1912, and they had very rapidly established a close friendship; Page described him as "the 'silent partner' of President Wilson— that is to say he is the most trusted political adviser and the nearest friend of the President."[1] His papers clearly show that he was never afraid to criticize the President to his face, and that the President was prepared to accept such vigorous criticism, because he appreciated the friendship, the integrity and the great abilities of his adviser. Very skilled as a judge of American domestic politics, House acquired with great rapidity a sensible grasp of international affairs. He went on a peace mission to Europe on behalf of the President, especially to Germany and Britain, on the very eve of the war, and, though the mission failed, the impressions he carried back to America with him were of the greatest significance for the future.

Writing of the European situation in general, but from Berlin and with his eye on German armaments, he declared to the President:

> The situation is extraordinary. It is militarism run stark mad. Unless someone acting for you can bring about a different understanding, there is some day to be an awful cataclysm. . . . England does not want Germany wholly crushed . . . but if Germany insists upon an ever-increasing navy, then England will have no choice. The best chance for peace is an understanding between England and Germany in regard to naval armaments, and yet [an interesting addition] there is some disadvantage to us by these two getting too close.

He was seen by the Kaiser at the *Schrippenfest*, the great annual German military feast, amidst all the most distinguished officers in the hierarchy of the German armed forces. Inhabitants of states with minuscule armies (whatever the size of their navies) are apt to be excessively impressed by evidences of great strength in soldiers, and such was perhaps not the best of occasions for a pacific discussion, but what impressed House was "not so much a will to war based upon any definite plan, but an increasing nervousness which might at any moment

[1] *Life and Letters,* I, p. 245.

result in a reckless attack".[1] In Germany he felt that he was "living near a mighty electric dynamo. The whole of Germany is charged with electricity. Everybody's nerves are tense. It needs only a spark to set the whole thing off."[2]

This nervousness, though not its hysterical consequences, was naturally reciprocated in Britain, and Page was affirming at this time that the British would not be surprised if the Germans attacked any night; but House's reception there showed how very different was the atmosphere. He wrote: "I find everything cluttered up with social affairs, and it is impossible to work quickly. Here they have their thoughts on Ascot, garden parties, etc. etc. In Germany their one thought is to advance industrially and to glorify war."[3] Diplomatic delay might chafe the business-like American, but, when the war came a few days later, the contrast was never forgotten, for the Englishman's son from Texas was and remained pro-British; never quite as Anglophile as Page, he was more outspokenly so than the President. The clearest among much strong evidence is perhaps that constituted by Grey's words in *Twenty Five Years*: "House left me in no doubt from the first that he held German militarism responsible for the war, and that he regarded the struggle as one between democracy and something that was undemocratic and antipathetic to American ideals. It was not necessary to spend much time in putting our case to him. He had a way of saying 'I know it' in a tone and manner that carried conviction both of his sympathy with, and understanding of, what was said to him."[4] House's influence over the President was thus pro-Ally, and it was more considerable than that of any other person; indeed it was probably he who aroused Wilson to an early realization of the opportunity which the war presented of bringing about "a revolution in international organization by impressing upon the public mind the need of a new standard of international morals."[5]

But when all has been said, the President stood on a pinnacle, alone. As Page wrote, "The President dominates the whole show in a most extraordinary way. The men about him . . . are very nearly all very, very small fry".[6] When considering his course of conduct through the four long years of mankind's anguish, we should never be unconscious of the awful magnitude of the responsibility which he alone bore.

For in Britain no single man bears such a burden; it rests upon the

[1] *Intimate Papers*, I, pp. 255, 264.   [2] Q. Davis, p. 218.
[3] *Intimate Papers*, I, p. 268.   [4] Grey, II, pp. 120-1.
[5] *Intimate Papers*, I, p. 300.   [6] *Life and Letters*, II, p. 179.

Cabinet, the basis of whose constitutional existence is collective responsibility. For the British, too, the problem was a much simpler one. They were in the war, and had to fight it to a successful conclusion; American enmity would make victory impossible, American neutrality would make it possible, American participation would make it certain. These facts, combined with the now traditional and united British determination to ensure American friendship, made their decisions merely ones as to means and not as to ends. The Prime Minister from 1914 to the end of 1916, Asquith, said to Page: "At bottom we understand you. At bottom the two people surely understand one another and have unbreakable bonds of sympathy. No serious breach is conceivable. Mr. Page, after any policy or plan is thought out on its merits my next thought always is how it may affect our relations with the United States. That is always a fundamental consideration."[1] His successor, Lloyd George, had only to wait two months before America broke off diplomatic relations with Germany. Asquith's Foreign Secretary, Grey, we have long seen as a leading advocate of Anglo-American accord; his essential probity constituted a firm basis for it, and Page could write truly, "Now the relations I have established with Sir Edward Grey have been built up on frankness, fairness and friendship. I can't have relations of any other sort nor can England and the United States have relations of any other sort."[2] His successor Balfour, too, we have already seen to be pledged to Anglo-American friendship. In some ways his sceptical Conservative mind placed more emphasis on the peculiar importance of the relationship than did Liberals whose expanding view of democratic human progress embraced wider and remoter vistas of world security; walking closer to the earth, Balfour saw that "The world will more and more turn on the Great Republic as on a pivot,"[3] and Spring-Rice correctly expressed his fundamental belief (which accorded with the Ambassador's own) when, as he reported to Balfour, he said to the President,

I knew that you believed the hope and salvation of the world lay in a close and cordial understanding between the free nations, more especially between those who were of the household of our language. I said that we could almost endure with equanimity all the horrors of this terrible struggle if they led in the end to a close, sure and permanent understanding between the English-speaking peoples. If we stood together we were safe. If we did not stand together nothing was safe.[4]

[1] Q. ibid, p. 169.   [2] *Life and Letters,* I, p. 382.
[3] Q. ibid, II, p. 251.   [4] Spring-Rice, II, p. 425.

During the supremely critical years between the outbreak of the war in 1914 and America's entry into it in 1917, the Ambassadors in the two capitals were of singular importance, for in a sense this was the last day in which resident Ambassadors could play a decisive part in the destiny of nations. With the coming of the telegraph the diplomat had lost his old independence of action, but he had not yet been ousted by personal contacts between statesmen and politicians. This was to happen increasingly after this period, and did so with a rush as soon as America entered the war, for in 1917 Lord Reading was sent out to Washington and later replaced Spring-Rice, being a direct representative of the War Cabinet; because he was fully informed as to the mind of the Government of which he was a member, as well as because he was a brilliant man, he was exceedingly successful. After the Armistice he was succeeded until 1920 by Grey, a statesman rather than a diplomat, who was sent to sound out the situation regarding the possible American acceptance of the Versailles Treaty with reservations, and to discuss naval armaments, but since he was not even received by Wilson, ostensibly on account of the President's illness, he returned after only three months. By this time something approaching normality had returned and the post had lost much of its absolute, if not its relative, importance. In London much the same process went on, for Page was succeeded in 1918 by J. W. Davis, who had been a Solicitor-General in Wilson's administration; though inexperienced in diplomacy, and in charge of a now colossal embassy organization, his simplicity, his modesty and his enthusiasm for the cause made him very welcome to the British until his replacement in 1920. But from 1914-17 the two Ambassadors played personal roles of great importance. That of Page was the simplest though it was so largely because of the character and opinions of the man himself.

Walter Hines Page, a distinguished editor and influential supporter of Wilson, reached London on 24 May, 1913. From the first he was a fanatical advocate of Anglo-American co-operation; his enthusiasm for it permeated every part of his being. In dedicating a British monument to the Mayflower Pilgrims he said: "And Puritan and Pilgrim and Cavalier, though different, are yet one in that they are English still. And thus, despite the fusion of races and . . . contributions of other nations . . . the United States is yet English-led and English ruled."[1] He was soon in trouble with the Press at home for his Anglophilia, which led him to a conviction of the need for American intervention in world affairs long before the outbreak of the war. He wrote:

[1] Q. W.A.A.E., pp. 445-6.

[T]he English-speaking peoples now rule the world in all essential facts. They alone and Switzerland have permanent free government. In France there's freedom—but for how long? In Germany . . . hardly. . . . In Japan—? Only the British lands and the United States have secure liberty. They also have the most treasure, the best fighters, the most land, the most ships—the future in fact. Now, because George Washington warned us against alliances, we've gone on as if an alliance were a kind of smallpox. Suppose there were—let us say for argument's sake—the tightest sort of alliance . . . between all Britain . . . and the United States. . . . Anything we'd say would go.[1]

So obsessed was he with the notion, that he was at pains almost to apologize for the international inactivity of the great United States: "We've had no foreign policy, no continuity of plan, no matured scheme, no settled way of doing things and we seem afraid of Irishmen or Germans or some 'element' when a chance for real action comes."[2]

He saw with great vividness the way the world was going: "These English are spending their capital, and it is their capital that continues to give them their vast power. . . . The great economic tide of the century flows our way. *We* shall have the big world questions to decide presently. Then we shall need world policies."[3] Not that Page was un-American; one English literary man declared, "I didn't know there could be anything so American as Page except Mark Twain."[4] Neither was he unconscious of the good fortune of his country, even before the war began, for he wrote of the war fever in Europe, "We don't know in the United States what we owe to the Atlantic Ocean—safe separation from all these troubles."[5] Nor was he oblivious to English faults; he pressed Britain hard, as we shall see, over the Mexican issue, as soon as he arrived, and referred on one occasion, in the characteristic anti-colonial vein of a liberal American, to their " 'unctuous rectitude' in stealing continents."[6] But he fully reciprocated the warmth with which he, the representative of the American people, was welcomed in England. He noted that the American Ambassador in Britain was put in a class by himself and given liberties that European Ambassadors have never taken. There can be no doubt that this reflected the British determination to maintain Anglo-American friendship, but it was also a personal tribute to Page, whom Harold Nicolson called "perhaps the greatest gentleman I have ever known",[7] and of whom Balfour said, "I loved that man. I almost wept when he left England."[8] No

[1] *Life and Letters*, I, pp. 282-3.   [2] Ibid, p. 152.   [3] Ibid, pp. 144-5.
[4] Q. ibid, II, p. 296.   [5] Ibid, I, p. 162.   [6] Ibid, p. 142.
[7] Q. ibid, II, p. 302.   [8] Q. W.A.A.E., p. 462.

American Ambassador ever earned such warm affection in Britain, and perhaps no other American has ever done so.

Thus when the war came, Page's attitude was pre-ordained, inevitable. He soon became convinced that, as Grey wrote in his memoirs, "the United States could be brought into the war early on the side of the Allies if the issues were rightly presented to it and a great appeal made by the President."[1] This outcome he earnestly desired, for he was convinced of the danger of German intentions: "England is, after all, only a stepping stone. . . . I firmly believe that within a year Germany will have seized the new canal and proclaimed its defiance of the great Monroe Doctrine."[2] Subject, as he was, to the full force of English opinion, he no doubt accepted much in the way of propaganda that was rejected at home, but there is no evidence of any failure on his part to put what he considered America's true interests first. Naturally, he mistrusted increasingly the policy of his Government and on one occasion he burst out, "Neutral! There's nothing in the world so neutral as this Embassy. Neutrality takes up all our time." Equally naturally, his reputation for Anglophilia steadily grew in the Administration, though the extent of it does not seem to have penetrated to the American public at large, and he had to be warned by House "to please be more careful not to express any unneutral feeling, either by word of mouth, or by letter and not even to the State Department."[3] Page's reaction was that, "A government can be neutral, but no *man* can be."[4]

He had begun his term of office full of admiration for Wilson, and had adopted the habit of writing outspoken letters direct to him on all matters of consequence; to this habit he resolutely clung despite an increasing coldness between the two. Wilson became more and more mistrustful of his Anglophilia, calling him "more British than the British",[5] and he reciprocated, even coming to the view that Wilson "is not a leader, but rather a stubborn phrasemaker."[6] Despite this loss of the President's confidence, he continued to pour out warnings of remarkable bluntness to him, of which the general tenor was, "I cannot begin to express my deep anxiety and even uneasiness about the relations of these two great Governments and peoples. The friendship of the United States and Great Britain is all that now holds the world together. It is the greatest asset of civilization left."[7] Eventually, the President sent for him to come back, and 'take a bath', as he phrased it, in American opinion, but their one interview did not close

[1] Grey, II, p. 98.   [2] *Life and Letters*, I, p. 360.
[3] Q. W.A.A.E., pp. 451-2.   [4] *Life and Letters*, I, p. 361.
[5] Ibid, II, p. 23.   [6] Ibid, II, p. 223.   [7] Q. W.A.A.E., p. 457.

the gap, for at bottom they were divided by the fact that Wilson still hoped to avoid war, whereas Page confidently hoped for the opposite. He wrote after the *Lusitania* sinking: "I see no possible way for us to keep out, because I know the ignorance and falseness of the German leaders."[1]

It is in some ways remarkable that Page did not carry out one of his threats to resign, or that he was not dismissed. It is possible that the President could not face the uproar it might have caused; it is possible that, despite apparent disagreement, something in Wilson (it certainly existed in House) still saw the force of Page's arguments; it is also possible that his relations with the British counted for something. Certainly they were cordial in the extreme. Grey writes of an occasion typical of Page's attitude, when he had to present a critical message from the State Department, one of the kind to which Grey replied with a twinkle in his eye that it sounded as if it was addressed to George III instead of George V: " 'I am instructed,' [Page] said, 'to read this despatch to you.' He read and I listened. He then said: 'I have now read the despatch, but I do not agree with it; let us consider how it should be answered.' "[2] Even the most awkward of topics could be handled with a smile on both sides; on one occasion, when discussing some question of neutral rights in Grey's office, where hung on the wall the $15 million cheque in payment of the *Alabama* award, Page pointed to it and said with a grin, "If you don't stop these seizures, Sir Edward, some day you'll have your entire room papered with things like that!"[3]

This spirit was not confined to his association with Grey. Shortly after the news of the Marne victory arrived, Page said to one Englishman, "We did pretty well in that Battle of the Marne, didn't we?" To which the reply was, "Isn't that remark slightly unneutral, Mr. Ambassador?"[4] Thus when America at last entered the war, he wrote from the bottom of his heart to his son, "I cannot conceal nor can I express my gratification that we are in the war."[5] He did little actually to bring that great event about, though it is true that the arguments eventually used by Wilson to justify his action were those which Page had been drumming into his unwilling ears for two and a half years past, but he, more than any other individual, was responsible for keeping the air of Anglo-American relations sweet through the long period of waiting. He did not long survive his triumph, for he had worn himself out in the cause. He resigned in 1918 and died very soon afterwards,

[1] *Life and Letters*, II, p. 16.   [2] Q. Grey, II, p. 106.
[3] *Life and Letters*, I, p. 391.   [4] Ibid, p. 358.   [5] Q. W.A.A.E., p. 460.

as much a victim of the war as many a soldier. Of his embassy Roosevelt wrote with justice that he "has represented America in London during these trying years as no other Ambassador in London has ever represented us, with the exception of Charles Francis Adams, during the Civil War."[1] In the hearts of Englishmen and of all who care for Anglo-American friendship he should have a special place.

The case of Sir Cecil Spring-Rice in Washington is less simple. He occupied no comparable place in the esteem of the American people outside a relatively small group, but it was in the nature of things that this should be so, for his task was more difficult. He had to endure in silence the neutrality of the United States, while he saw the life blood of his own land—including that of his brother—ebb swiftly away. It would have been a miracle had he avoided giving any offence, and it is remarkable in some ways how little he did give. Yet he was not perfect for his purpose as was Page.

For one thing, his health was never robust and he was often short-tempered when under strain; to this, too, can perhaps be ascribed in part the pessimism which was so pronounced a trait in his character. In some ways this was salutary; wishful thinking about America and the war might between 1914 and 1917 have proved disastrous to Britain, and he left the Foreign Secretary under no illusions on this score. In the steady flow of his letters—matching those of Page in both quantity and quality, professional writer though the American was—his judgment remained on the whole remarkably cool and detached; usually this was excellent, just occasionally he carried it too far. He wrote, for instance, quite correctly, to Grey in 1915, "But do not count upon purchasing effective help by any concession. You would build on sand. Even if you could do so, it would be far safer to assume that you could not." Yet, particularly in the last year of waiting, he was unnecessarily gloomy; he placed too much emphasis on the purely financial interest of the Americans in the British cause, and came to find American intervention by force of arms inconceivable. Even when war was imminent, he thought that American action would be local in character, writing in February, 1917, that "It would be unpopular to send a large force abroad in case of war, and I think this would be wholly out of the question."[2] He always tended to under-estimate the residual strength of the British position; Britain could not get all she wanted from America, because what she really wanted was American participation in the war, but she consistently got a great deal more than Germany,

[1] Q. W.A.A.E., p. 461.   [2] Spring-Rice, II, pp. 306, 382.

and it was simply untrue to write, "It is, of course, notorious that if I had done one-thousandth part of what Bernstorff has done I should have been given my passports long ago."[1]

This pessimism, it is true, did Britain no direct harm, but it did not help his relations with the Americans, and particularly the Administration. His long association with Republican friends, such as Roosevelt and Lodge—though he was meticulous to avoid unnecessary contact with the former—without doubt raised Democratic suspicions, and his official relations tended to be formal rather than cordial. This was particularly so because of his emotional outbursts, arising in part from his extreme—his poet's—sensitivity to Britain's peril. House wrote in 1915, "The irrational . . . Ambassador may at any time precipitate matters,"[2] and there can be little doubt from the tone of some of his franker personal letters that he must have let embarrassing things slip from time to time. To one English friend he wrote: "It is rather hard to conduct a reasoned and pacific argument between a nation which is making war and a nation which is making money, but we must do our best", and to another he remarked, in reference to Wilson's proposals, while America was still neutral, to set up a League of Nations: "The good Samaritan did not pass by on the other side, and then propose to the authorities at Jericho a bill for the better security of the high roads."[3] Pale reflections of these remarks to the wrong persons could have given grave offence. Yet that he retained the affection of his many American friends is clearly demonstrated by the $75,000 fund which was rapidly raised in America after his death to educate his children and care for his wife. He kept his tongue for the most part under stern control, no doubt aware of the bite in his Irish wit—so much so that he earned the name, not altogether laudatory, of the "silent ambassador."

On the whole, however, his information—and providing it was perhaps his most important function—was extraordinarily balanced, sane and wise. He was intensely conscious that Britain would have acted as America did had she been in her place: "It is not so long ago that we boasted of our splendid isolation and only left it when we found it was impossible to maintain. It is not so very long ago since we left Denmark and France to their fate because we had not the means to prevent it, even if we had the will."[4] He was quite able to see the thing from the American point of view, and wrote with truth: "It cannot be wondered at that the American People are determined to keep out of the war which is frightful in itself to those that take part

[1] Ibid, p. 358.   [2] Q. ibid, p. 307.   [3] Ibid, pp. 250, 347.   [4] Ibid, p. 343.

in it and very profitable to those who do not. The President and his Cabinet undoubtedly reflect the feeling of the country which they represent."[1] He could even do justice to the President and his policy; he wrote to Grey in November, 1914: "There seems to be the impression here that you think this Government unfriendly. This is certainly not the case, although their action, which is their official action, appears to be so. They have to defend American interests and to maintain what they believe to be American rights. But they certainly do not wish to offer unnecessary difficulties or to hamper England in her measures of self-defence." He saw powerfully, too, the material service that the Americans were doing: "They are granting their help without stint, if it is help in money supplies and personal aid. We must not expect more and I do not think that under similar circumstances, we would give more ourselves." He put it most tersely in October, 1916: "If we want to borrow money here it is no good saying that the Americans are money grabbers."[2]

His advice on policy was on the whole sound and far seeing. On the one hand, he wrote to Grey in 1915:

> I should like to impress upon you that it is extremely important to be able to yield on certain questions where vital interests are not at stake. Don't forget that George III lost the United States through lawyers and by pressing a legal point. . . . For the vital points for us are that this country should serve as a base of supplies, and should not intervene by force, that is by convoy, to break the blockade.

On the other, he wrote again a little later, that:

> [T]here are certain things we cannot concede. . . . We cannot allow a claim on the part of neutrals to import goods into Germany and so break the blockade. We cannot allow a neutral to claim the right of extending the privileges of the neutral flag to ships which are in reality owned . . . by German interests. There is no good giving the impression that we can yield on these vital points.[3]

Not only was his broad view detached and judicious, but his analysis of American opinion was perceptive and vivid, if occasionally bleak. His view of Wilson's project for a League of Nations was remarkably sound, for he always prophesied its rejection by the people and put his finger on the consent of the Senate as the inherent necessity which weakened the whole fabric:

> With regard to the main proposition as to a sanction for the articles of peace.—The President desires what we all desire, that is a general

[1] Ibid, p. 300.   [2] Ibid, 246, 267, 322.   [3] Ibid, pp. 282, 305.

and effective sanction by the common consent of all the powers backed by their readiness to enforce that sanction. This is a pious wish in which we share. . . . But how can the President give us the desired pledge. He cannot pledge the action of Congress in advance. . . . But in return for his promise he asks for a fact, that is, the immediate surrender of our right to exercise pressure by sea-power.

He reiterated again and again, "I am sure we would make a mistake if we counted on the active intervention of America as one of the guardians of a world peace. Every indication points in the opposite direction." His understanding of America went really to the root of things in their national history and character. He wrote with great insight to Lord Robert Cecil: "We have no right to count on the good-will of the Americans. They could count on ours, but we cannot count on theirs."[1] Here he expressed the underlying truth about this era of Anglo-American relations.

The difficulty of his position was such that he perhaps appears to unfair disadvantage in it; already among contemporaries he was attacked from all sides, and historians have continued the habit. As he wrote to Sir Maurice de Bunsen, "I thought the Bird [Sir Eyre Crowe] would raise an angry beak against my pro-American tendencies. I have nearly been turned out of the State Department for my pro-nounced anti-American language. So perhaps I may assume that I steer the middle course." Certainly he may lay claim, like Page, to have died in the service of his country, for very soon after the entry of the United States into the war he was replaced by Lord Reading. This he fully realized to be necessary, though he would not have been human if he had not felt the abrupt, though not wilfully abrupt, manner in which it was done; he survived, like his opposite number, only a short time into his retirement, and died most unexpectedly—the result, as even such a man as Lodge could declare, of a broken heart. Let the last word lie, as in the case of Page, with Roosevelt: "Under the peculiar and exceedingly delicate conditions, his usefulness to his country was almost directly proportioned to the manner in which he effaced himself, and only a man of rare unselfishness . . . could in this crisis have rendered the literally invaluable service that his country—and my country, too—needed, and that Cecil rendered."[2]

II

WHEN Wilson was inaugurated in 1913 two questions had arisen to

[1] Ibid, pp. 334-5, 339.   [2] Ibid, pp. 317-8, 436.

vex Anglo-American relations, neither being of the first magnitude
in itself, but both pregnant with danger if they had not been settled
before the outbreak of the war. The President at once showed that he
proposed to take a new line in international affairs; Knox's policy of
Dollar Diplomacy was rejected because "It is a very perilous thing
to determine the foreign policy of a nation in terms of material
interest."[1] This declaration of what amounted to a new international
morality made a strong appeal to many Americans in the then troubled
state of the world; Page, for example, was enthusiastic, and was to
declare that the British "didn't instantly understand this new 'idealistic'
move. . . . [M]any private groups . . . see it now . . . and the British
people are enthusiastic as far as they understand it."[2] But some were
still sceptical, and detected in it an excessive idealism. Not without
relish, they were later to point out the ironical truth that, though Wilson
expressed his determination not to interfere for unworthy reasons in
Latin America, he in fact carried out more armed interventions there
than any of his predecessors. With these actions Britain was to have no
quarrel, as her original welcome to the Roosevelt Corollary had clearly
implied; rather was the reverse the case.

In February, 1913, Victoriano Huerta deposed the successful leader
of a liberal revolt against the long dictatorship of Porfirio Diaz in
Mexico, Francesco Madera, who was shortly murdered; these disturbances had caused heavy losses to American life and property in
Mexico, and many Americans felt that their interests demanded the
recognition of any régime, however distasteful it might be, which would
restore order. Lodge wrote bluntly in early March, 1913 : "The situation
in regard to Mexico is a threatening one. . . . I hope they have got a
man now of the Diaz type who will do sufficient throat-cutting to restore
peace. That seems an unpleasant thing to say, but it is apparently impossible to maintain order or any approach to decent government in
Mexico on any other terms".[3] With this view the British Government
which, Liberal though it might be, was more impressed than the
Administration with the importance of order in uncivilized lands, in
effect concurred. Concerned about British oil interests in Mexico, on
which the navy to some extent depended, Grey recognized Huerta,
despite his earlier assurance to Page that he would follow the President's
line in the matter, which had not yet been made clear. Unfortunately,
he made things worse by sending as Minister to Mexico Sir Lionel
Carden, an anti-American diplomat, who had become very unpopular

[1] Q. Bailey, p. 604.   [2] *Life and Letters*, I, p. 210.
[3] Q. Spring-Rice, II, p. 189.

with the State Department while Minister to Cuba, and who told the Press in New York en route to his post that the President "knew nothing about Mexico."[1] The latter meanwhile had made it crystal clear that he would never recognize the "unspeakable Huerta", and that his ideal was "an orderly and righteous government in Mexico", but his "passion", "the submerged eighty-five per cent of the people of that Republic who are now struggling toward liberty." This meant, as he told one Briton, that he was "going to teach the South American republics to elect good men."[2] He was as hostile to the British vested interests, whom he suspected of being behind Britain's policy, as to the American ones, such as Standard Oil, who took the same point of view.

The British Foreign Office saw the matter differently, and British opinion agreed with it in regarding the Wilsonian attitude as too idealistic for comfort; Spring-Rice wrote:

> The President is a very virtuous man and an obstinate one too, and he has given his word that he won't recognize the blood-stained Huerta. Bryan believes that a fair and free election disclosing the real will of the people will put everything to rights in Mexico. Between them the various foreign interests don't get much encouragement. The U.S. won't protect their own people nor allow anyone else to protect them. It is singular how the majority of the Americans are rather pleased than otherwise at the losses of rich Americans in Mexico. The rich Americans are trying to get us to take up a more energetic attitude to encourage their own Government.

This new Wilsonian policy was a revival, in an exaggerated form, of traditional American methods of diplomacy in Latin America, and it appeared to the British to reach a climax of sanguine absurdity when the Administration found itself supporting the brigand Villa against Huerta; as Spring-Rice put it, he was "the best general among the rebels, mainly because he is the cruellest. . . . Thus a Government pledged to be guided by the purest moral principles finds itself supporting the most unconscionable ruffian ever known."[3] But, whatever the bulk of British opinion, the President's obstinacy quite equalled his high-mindedness; there was, as the Ambassador wrote, "nothing to do with this hardened saint."[4] It soon became obvious to the British Government that a really grave situation might arise in Anglo-American relations out of the Mexican affair, whether it was due to a rash and imperialistic British Foreign Office or an unpractical and unrealistic President.

[1] Q. Davis, p. 211. [2] Q. Bailey, p. 603.
[3] Spring-Rice, II, pp. 196, 205. [4] Ibid, p. 202.

647

This was all the more serious since another issue between them—a much more direct one—looked like coming to a head at the same time. The 1912 Act of Congress, providing for the operation of the Panama Canal and signed by Taft, had specifically exempted American coastwise shipping from paying tolls; this, the British Government claimed, was in plain violation of the Hay-Pauncefote Treaty, which laid down that "The Canal shall be free and open to vessels of . . . all nations . . . on terms of entire equality, so that there shall be no discrimination against any such nation, or its citizens or subjects, in respect of the conditions or charges of traffic or otherwise."[1] Britain not only inclined to regard the American discrimination as a betrayal of mutual trust, but was apprehensive as to its economic effect upon her vast carrying trade. In the Presidential election, the Republican platform stated, "The Panama Canal, built and paid for by the American people, must be used primarily for their benefit",[2] and Wilson's platform also endorsed the Canal Act, which was pleasing to the Irish because it was displeasing to the British.

In November the Foreign Office protested strongly, and proposed arbitration, but Knox and Taft produced vigorous, if somewhat legalistic arguments against the British point of view. Thus this question was still unsettled when the Mexican imbroglio developed. To Wilson, the tolls question was a very difficult one with which to be faced so soon after his inauguration, because liberal opinion, which he especially represented, decried the Canal Act; it was voiced by Page from London in September, 1913: "And everywhere—in circles the most friendly to us, and the best informed—I receive commiseration because of the dishonourable attitude of our Government about the Panama Canal tolls. This, I confess, is hard to meet. We made a bargain—a solemn compact and we have broken it. Whether it were a good bargain or a bad one, a silly one or a wise one; that's far from the point."[3] This was the kind of language Wilson found it most difficult to answer, even when his political enemies were also using it; Roosevelt was writing at the time to Spring-Rice, for instance, "The Panama question of course should be arbitrated. I am strongly against making promises that ought not to be kept, and therefore I am utterly against agreements to arbitrate questions of vital national interest and honour. But I emphatically believe in the Nation, like the individual, keeping its

[1] Q. W. M. Malloy, *Treaties, Conventions, International Acts, Protocols and Agreements Between the United States of America and Other Powers* (Washington, 1910), I, p. 783.

[2] Q. Bailey, p. 600.   [3] *Life and Letters,* I, p. 249.

promise, and our promise to arbitrate applies to just such questions as this of the Canal tolls." Lodge was of the same opinion, though he preferred another method of settlement; he wrote—also to "Springy"—: "The true way to be rid of this thing is to repeal the clause which has made the trouble. It is the more dignified action for the United States."[1]

This was the course which the President in due time chose. He came to the conclusion that that national honour and that international morality, on which he had already taken his stand in other spheres, was at stake, and on 5 March, 1914, he made a personal appearance before Congress to request the repeal of the discriminatory clause, saying: "[W]e are too big, too powerful, too self-respecting a nation to interpret with a too strained or refined reading the words of our own promises just because we have power enough to give us leave to read them as we please. The large thing to do is the only thing we can afford to do, a voluntary withdrawal from a position everywhere questioned and misunderstood."[2] It was a brave, a noble and, because it was in his power to achieve what he desired, a statesmanlike appeal, which resulted, after a bitter debate in which the Democrats themselves were divided, in the repeal of the offending clause. Page proudly reported the words of an English lady to his wife: "The United States has set a high standard for all nations to live up to. I don't believe there is any other nation that would have done it."[3]

In the public mind the Mexican question was weighed against that of the Panama tolls, and the two remained associated. Page pointed out the embarrassment involved in preaching unselfishness in Mexico at a time when the United States was practising selfishness and dishonesty in Panama, and his opposite number in Washington also emphasized the connexion, in a letter written after Wilson's speech asking for repeal:

In spite of what she had suffered at the hands of the United States, England had acted in a perfectly friendly manner and had abstained under great provocation from taking advantage of the various opportunities for revenge which had presented themselves. In Mexico, she could have caused the greatest embarrassment, if she had headed a coalition, which was ready to her hands and had demanded intervention. She was serving the interests of the United States in her pacific policy there and in Japan [with whom American relations

[1] Spring-Rice, II, pp. 185, 189.
[2] Commager, *Documents*, II, p. 273.
[3] Q. *Life and Letters*, I, p. 268.

649

were again strained owing to anti-Japanese feeling in the Far West],
and it behoved the United States to bear this in mind and return
good for good.[1]

The two comments are illuminating, for they show that the British
Foreign Office, even under a Liberal Government, had by no means
accepted the kind of international code of conduct which Wilson
advocated; British calculations had national interests rather than international ideals in view.

Yet those interests were of the broadest kind, for it was clearly
appreciated in official quarters that no limited financial interest could
be allowed to stand in the way of Anglo-American friendship. Indeed,
it is questionable whether Britain in fact had the freedom of action
ascribed to her by Spring-Rice; her policy of the previous decade
towards America, the convictions of her leaders, and her widest interests
made it almost inconceivable that she should have headed a European
coalition against the United States. It is true that she desired the repeal
of the offending portion of the Canal Act, and it is probable that there
was a tacit bargain which reversed British policy in Mexico in return
for that repeal, but it is very likely that she would, if Wilson had pressed
the issue, have given way in Latin America, even without a *quid pro
quo*. Greater therefore is the honour due to Wilson, whose conduct in
the matter compares very favourably with that of Roosevelt over the
Alaskan dispute ten years before.

But whatever the details, the event was clear enough; Britain effected
a *volte-face*, and Carden, prior to his removal to another post, supported the American demand for Huerta's resignation. The latter did
not go into exile until July, 1914, and, even when he did, Wilson's
troubles with Latin America were by no means over, but they ceased
to disturb Anglo-American relations from the time that Britain swung
into line with American policy; to American intervention there she
objected not a whit. She was in any case, from August, 1914, onwards,
absorbed in much more desperate affairs; happily, she could face
them with a consciousness of clear and sunny skies over the Atlantic.

III

On 20 September, 1912, Henry Adams had written to Spring-Rice,
"Today's Boston newspaper, twelve pages, contained not one allusion
or item regarding the outside world."[2] In July, 1914, the isolation of the

<hr>

[1] Spring-Rice, II, p. 200.   [2] Q. ibid, p. 172.

United States which this implied was just as complete. Under Taft the European interventions of Roosevelt had been quietly but decisively discontinued; under Wilson Knox's politico-financial plans in the Far East had been swiftly disowned; Panama tolls and Mexican disorders were strictly American questions, and even in that sphere the Monroe Doctrine bade fair, in intention at least, to rid itself of the Roosevelt Corollary. Traditional isolationism had reasserted itself as European tension rose.

In July, 1914, the tension ended in hostilities, and when the Germans invaded France, violating the neutrality of Belgium in the process, Great Britain entered the war, on 4 August, 1914. Immediately, on the very same day, Wilson issued a proclamation of neutrality, and shortly afterwards offered, as head of one of the signatory states to the Hague Convention, his good offices to the belligerents at any time that they should be desired. This was the course expected, not only in America but also in Europe. Later, Roosevelt and Grey were to correspond, and the former to declare, "The bulk of our people do not understand foreign politics and have no idea about any impending military danger. When I was President, I really succeeded in educating them to a fairly good understanding of these matters, and I believe that if I had been President at the outset of this war they would have acquiesced in my taking the stand I most assuredly would have taken as head of a signatory nation of the Hague Treaties in reference to the violation of Belgium's neutrality". To this Grey was to reply, "If the United States had taken action, they might possibly have stopped the war."[1] But these were the altered views of a later day, for at the very first—though he rapidly changed his tune and became a vigorous advocate of support for the Allies—Roosevelt approved the President's policy of neutrality, and even showed some pro-German inclinations, while Grey wrote, "The line that the present United States Government have taken is, of course, the natural and expected one."[2]

But Madison had not found neutrality easy to maintain in 1812, and in 1914 Wilson—like him "a Virginian, a Princetonian, angular, conscientious and iron-willed"[3]—was to find it even harder. On 19 August he issued an appeal to his countrymen to "be impartial in thought as well as in action."[4] Already he was conscious of the passions which unrestrained sympathy for either side might arouse in America, and he was for many months to come to regard bitter internal disagreements, if not actual internecine strife, as a grave danger to the United

[1] Grey, II, pp. 139-140.   [2] Ibid, p. 140.
[3] Davis, p. 224.   [4] Commager, II, p. 276.

States. His concern was understandable; as Spring-Rice writes, "Twelve million Germans in one's belly is rather a severe weight for a nation which has to fight seventy millions outside",[1] and German acts of sabotage in America and in American ships added strongly to this impression of danger. Considerable nervousness was shown as America neared the brink of war, but in fact such fears proved exaggerated, indeed almost unfounded.

But there is not much doubt that the President's estimate of American sympathies was not so far wide of the mark. The mass of the people, excepting the German-Americans, the professional Anglophobes, and many Irishmen, tended to favour the Allies. But their sympathy was of the mind and heart only, and did not extend to any kind of wish to enter the war; when Spring-Rice and many others quoted the analogy of the Civil War, they could comfortingly recall that Britain remained neutral throughout that long struggle, sympathy notwithstanding. There were, however, some exceptions to this rule of strict neutrality.

In as much as it is possible to generalize about public opinion, it seems that, apart from racial sympathies and antipathies, the hard core of pro-Allied feeling was amongst the wealthy and educated; as Peterson puts it, "All classes were sympathetic with the Entente powers, but the upper classes including the rich, the powerful, the cultured, and the educated, were partisan to the extent that they were willing to assist in the defeat of Germany."[2] But two years after the beginning of the war, the keynote of the situation was still "the desire of the great majority of the American people to avoid war, so long as it . . . [could] possibly be avoided."[3] There was, too, a perceptible geographical pattern of feeling in the country. Spring-Rice reported that the Middle West was pro-German, but that feeling in New England and the Atlantic States, despite German activity in New York, was very different, as was that on the strongly pro-Allied West Coast; and modern research has tended to confirm this view. It seems probable that a *Literary Digest* poll for November, 1914, gives a fairly accurate picture; it shows, in the country as a whole, 105 pro-Allied to 20 pro-German newspapers, with 242 neutral. The pro-Allied were predominant in the East, the South and the West, and were almost equal in number with the pro-German in the Middle West. The same poll showed public opinion as pro-Ally in 189 cities, pro-German in 38, and neutral in 140, the cities having a geographical distribution very much the same. Except probably for a period in 1916, when American attempts at mediation failed, when the unrestricted submarine campaign had been suspended, and when the

[1] Spring-Rice, II, p. 244.   [2] Peterson, p. 175.   [3] Ibid, p. 172.

fearful prospect of becoming involved loomed larger, the general pro-Allied sentiment steadily increased throughout the war.

In this development British propaganda was certainly a vital factor, for it was singularly well conceived and well executed. Its foundation was the British censorship, which controlled not only the British Press, but also all outgoing material including, of course, the despatches of American newspapermen; so sensitive was this censorship to American opinion that in 1916 it would not allow correspondents to report to America the considerable irritation of British public opinion at one of the President's speeches. On 5 August, 1914, the British cut the cables between Germany and the United States: and, until rather unsatisfactory wireless communications were set up, there was no other rapid means of communication between the two countries, so that the British view had normally been accepted in America long before the German arrived. Because of the censorship of all mail from Britain, and her checking, in the processes of blockade, of mails passing to and from the enemy, Americans and American newspapers increasingly relied on British press accounts for their news of the war. Thus a marked slant was given from the beginning to American information by these negative means, and on them were superimposed more positive measures.

A special branch of the War Propaganda Bureau, the American Ministry of Information, was set up under Sir Gilbert Parker, and its work was supplemented by a number of voluntary organizations. The power of the system lay largely in its unobtrusiveness—indeed secrecy is not too strong a word. Of the negative controls people were hardly conscious, and the more positive steps were all designed to give an impression of impartiality, as the very words "Ministry of Information" suggest. Its methods were devised in the same spirit. It worked as far as possible through Americans, and ordered its agents in America, who were carefully chosen to be *personae gratae* there, to avoid obvious propaganda; it mailed to a list, which eventually contained 260,000 names of persons influential in the Union, copies of books, pamphlets, government publications, speeches and so forth, which put the British case without blatantly seeming to do so.

In the conduct of this vital campaign the increasing knowledge of the United States and its people, which Englishmen of importance had gained during the previous fifteen years, was invaluable; her wooing of America in the uneasy peace of the early twentieth century had taught Britain the need of great patience and circumspection. Deploring the lack of close contact among Anglo-American statesmen, Page

653

might write in 1917 "The great governments of the English-speaking folk have surely dealt with one another with mighty elongated tongs.... But personal and human neglect of one another by these two governments over so long a period is an astonishing fact in our history. The wonder is that we haven't had more than two wars. And it is no wonder that the ignorance of Englishmen about America and the American ignorance of England are monumental, stupendous, amazing, passing understanding."[1] Bryce himself might in 1915 bemoan "the utter hopelessness of the two people's ever understanding one another."[2] Both were a good deal too pessimistic; these things are always relative, and in the understanding of one people by another the basic standards of judgment are hardly high. Britain understood America in 1914 better than she had ever done before, and probably better than she had ever understood any other power; for once Spring-Rice struck a tone of hope which was nearer the truth than Page's uncharacteristically gloomy assessment: "There is more real community of feeling between men who think the same, according to their own free will and judgment, than between men who act together in obedience to another man, be he who he may. Our kingdom is within us."[3]

The measure of the success of British propaganda in strengthening anti-German feeling can be gauged by the American acceptance of the atrocity stories which had gained so firm a hold on the British mind. These stories may have been untrue; to the spate of American writers on neutrality in the critical period of the thirties, they were often to seem instrinsically absurd, which, in the very heyday of Nazi Germany, they should not have done. But many of these writers, themselves far from the most impartial of investigators, carried into this question an emotional conviction that America had been drawn into the great cataclysm by the persistent and Machiavellian wiles of an England in alliance with certain Anglophile and selfish American groups of insignificant dimensions which actively desired war. Of this formidable thesis, upon which the neutrality legislation of the interwar years was largely based, we shall see more later; suffice it here to say that, because it is a fact that public opinion has at least to accept diplomatic action in democracies, the question of British control over American opinion occupies a prominent position in it. By many of these writers—such as C. C. Tansill in his isolationist polemic, *America Goes To War*, published in 1938—the growth of pro-Allied opinion in America, and even her actual entry into the war, have been ascribed almost exclusively to the influence of British propaganda.

[1] Page, II, pp. 366-7. [2] Q. ibid, p. 39. [3] Spring-Rice, II, p. 290.

Yet such a view, powerful though that influence was, grossly over-estimates its efficacy, and equally grossly underestimates the good sense of the American people; if it does not quite amount to a claim that all of them were fooled all the time, it comes somewhere very near it. We have seen in Nazi and Communist hands something of the power of uninhibited propaganda under dictatorial systems, but the American system was not dictatorial and British propaganda was by no means uninhibited. Many Englishmen, including Spring-Rice, opposed it, and he was largely responsible for restricting its scope; he put his finger on the point when he said that it was "doubtful whether we can change the weather by rigging the barometer",[1] for the fundamental reason why Britain made out her case so well was that it was a good case, and appeared to great advantage beside that of the Germans. The latter, indeed, not only made bad psychological use of propaganda but continued throughout the war to hand propaganda weapons to the Allies by their continual errors in policy. America, as we have seen, had long suspected German militarism, and persistent manifestations of it throughout the war naturally hardened American opinion against the Central Powers.

The plain truth is that Germany was more to blame for the war than Britain, and that she conducted it more barbarously. From the first, the invasion of Belgium told heavily against her, for, despite her arguments *ad occasionem* that Britain behaved as badly later in Greece, it is not the same thing to violate neutral territory at the outset of a war, according to a plan coldly prepared in peace, as it is to do so in the heat of the struggle. Such German actions as the initiation of gas warfare and the Zeppelin air raids, even where not actually prohibited by treaties to which Germany was a party, were foolish in their political context. What proved in the end to be the stupidest of all the German actions, based as so often on purely military rather than politico-military considerations, was the inauguration of unrestricted submarine warfare, for not only did it affect Americans directly, but it was peculiarly heartless in its operation. In the *Lusitania,* which was attacked without warning and sank in eighteen minutes, 1,198 people were drowned, including 128 Americans and 94 children, 35 of them babies. This dramatic ruthlessness contrasted most unfavourably with the methods of the Allied blockade which, though irritating and frustrating, were humane by comparison, and the Allies made good use of this fact; as Asquith said, "Let the neutrals complain about our blockade and other measures taken as much as they may, the fact remains that no neutral national has

[1] Ibid, p. 367.

655

ever lost his life as the result of it."[1] Lansing was typical of many Americans in his acceptance of this fact, that Allied violations of international law, since they affected only goods and not human life, could be dealt with by some form of legal process; cases were tried in duly organized prize courts and compensation was paid, in the case of many confiscations on a scale which made possible a small profit for the merchant concerned. Lodge restored one Senate debate to a proper sense of proportion in this matter when he said that "his heart was more moved by the thought of a drowned baby than an unsold bale of cotton."[2] In the last resort there can be no question that it was the actions of Germany against the interests of the United States, and not British propaganda, which brought America into the war. Propaganda may have quickened and facilitated this development; it did no more.

IV

BRITAIN, though she never established so absolute a maritime ascendancy as she had possessed over France in the Napoleonic Wars, maintained effective supremacy on the surface of the seas throughout the whole war. A Germany held at bay on the European mainland had no weapon such as Napoleon's Continental System to employ, and, as experience in World War II was to indicate, it would have been ineffective in any case because of the world-wide nature of British trade, but she found in the submarine one which proved more deadly. She had not made sufficient preparations to allow it to be effective early in the war, but Britain's economic stranglehold went into effect immediately. It was not, in the technical sense of the term, a blockade, but can be loosely described as such; and behind it lay just the same realities of power as in the period leading up to the War of 1812, for it was in the interest of Britain to restrict trade with the Central Powers as much as possible, while it was in that of the United States to extend it.

But the financial and commercial links between America and Britain were infinitely stronger than those between America and the Central, or indeed any other, Powers; furthermore, this American economic interest was much more widely based in the Union than it had been a century earlier. This connexion grew incomparably stronger in the course of the war itself; it grew by what it fed on, so that America forewent nearly all her trade with Germany without ill effects, but would have suffered very severely from the loss of trade which a rupture

[1] Q. Morison and Commager, II, p. 457.   [2] Spring-Rice, II, p. 308.

with Britain would have entailed. This was particularly the case because the vast demand which the war had created for American goods among the Allies had rescued her from an imminent economic depression: all the signs of an incipient slump, which might perhaps have done serious damage to the domestic reforms of the Democratic administration, were visible in 1914. Instead, the war brought an unprecedented boom; as Spring-Rice wrote as late as the end of 1915: "The brutal facts are that this country has been saved by the war and by our war demand from a great economical crisis; that in normal times Great Britain and her colonies take forty per cent of the total export trade of the United States. We have therefore the claims of their best customer and at the present moment our orders here are absolutely essential to their commercial prosperity." In his bitterness at prolonged American neutrality he could put it much more acidly some months later: "Meanwhile the prosperity of the country increases, and it seems to be in a fair way of gaining the whole world, whatever other thing it may lose."[1] Economically, the scales of American neutrality were heavily weighted against Germany.

But this, which might seem to give Britain the whip hand in Anglo-American relations, only represents one side of the equation, for if Anglo-American trade was important to America, it was far more so to Britain. Its continuance might mean prosperity to the United States; to the United Kingdom it probably meant survival, for she was dependent upon the outside world, and particularly America, not only for her food and the raw materials of her industry, but for the very munitions of war which were to make victory possible. America might well have stopped the trade and taken the consequences; Britain could not stop the war.

Thus possible and contemplated American methods of breaking the blockade were a constant source of alarm to British observers. One was a plan for the American purchase of German shipping, to be used for trade with the Central Powers, which was constantly being pushed by pro-German interests, and which reached in 1916 the stage of a Ship Purchase Bill, though its effect, unless in conjunction with other measures, must have been small. Far more serious was the recurrent threat of an American embargo on exports to belligerents, for against this Britain could have done nothing; and there were ample, though admittedly not very happy, precedents for it in American history. The proposal for American convoys of their own ships protected by their own naval forces was more explosive still, for Britain would never have

[1] Spring-Rice, II, pp. 300, 309.

dared to enforce the blockade against them, but fortunately it was even farther than the embargo from being put into practice.

The fact remained, however, that Britain was essentially dependent upon the continuation of trans-Atlantic commerce. The Germans could calculate, albeit wrongly, that in 1917 they would win the war before America could bring effective strength to bear in it; the British could never have made, nor dreamed of, such a calculation. Anglo-American friendship, in war even more than peace, remained the axiom of her political existence. Grey expressed it very precisely:

> [B]lockade of Germany was essential to the victory of the Allies, but the ill-will of the United States meant their certain defeat. . . . It was better . . . to carry on the war without blockade, if need be, than to incur a break with the United States about contraband and thereby deprive the Allies of the resources necessary to carry on the war at all or with any chance of success. The object of diplomacy, therefore, was to secure the maximum of blockade that could be enforced without a rupture with the United States.[1]

Seldom has the essential twentieth-century dependence of Britain upon the United States been so clearly illustrated. British diplomacy was directed to approaching as close as humanly possible to the unknown point at which American irritation with, and economic hardship from, the blockade would overcome American goodwill towards, and economic interest in, the Allied cause. Britain was never in serious danger of overshooting that mark, despite the strain to which relations were at times subject.

The strain began immediately the blockade was inaugurated at the outset of the war. That it was not a close blockade by naval vessels in the traditional manner, but a more widely spread use of the traditional right of visit and search is significant. New conditions of warfare seemed to belligerents to demand new methods of using sea power, and Britain could not accept, in the midst of the battle, Wilson's contention that changes in international law must be preceded by an international conference. International law has always been peculiar in its flexibility and its lack of an accepted legislative authority, and if it were to be excessively tied to outworn forms it would be in peril of outright repudiation. As Asquith told the House of Commons in 1915, "We are not going to allow our efforts to be strangled in a network of juridical niceties."[2] Thus the method of British diplomacy was to avoid being

[1] Grey, II, p. 103. [2] Q. C. Seymour, *American Diplomacy During the World War* (Baltimore, 1934), p. 28.

tied down to precise commitments, which might limit the war effort, and to impose the maximum delay before making concessions to American protests; equivocation was the basic technique.

On the surface, the American object appeared very different; it was to prevent the undue belligerent restriction of American trade by a policy of enforcing the traditional rules of international law. But its underlying realities were not so very different; Page, for instance, saw the policy in a different light: "We've planted ourselves firmly on (1) we've stated our position on the international law involved; our record on that score stands; and (2) we've cleared the ground for claims for damages. As I see it, that's all we can do—unless we are prepared to break off relations with Great Britain and get ready for war, after arbitrators have failed."[1] But the Administration was under constant pressure at home to take more vigorous action against Allied curtailments of neutral rights, and the able Bernstorff, whenever his hands were free, urged on a somewhat embarrassed President the necessity of being as firm with Britain as he was with Germany, of equating the blockade and the submarine as illegal instruments of war. So, Lansing wrote in his *Memoirs*:

> I saw with apprehension the tide of resentment against Great Britain rising higher and higher in this country. . . . I did all that I could to prolong the disputes by preparing . . . long and detailed replies, and introducing technical and controversial matters in the hope that before the extended interchange of arguments came to an end something would happen to change the current of American public opinion or to make the American people perceive that German absolutism was a menace to their liberties and to democratic institutions everywhere.[2]

This pressure of American opinion on the State Department was the counterpart of that on the Foreign Office in Britain, for Grey had to wage a continuous struggle in the Cabinet and the country to prevent the taking of steps which would antagonize the United States; there was always a strong movement, led from the Admiralty, which sought to increase rather than reduce the severity of the blockade. As Page wrote, "They won't relax it; they can't. Public opinion wouldn't stand it an hour. As things are now, an Admiral has said in a public speech that it is necessary to hang Grey if they're going to win the war."[3] Under such pressures neither side was averse from using lengthy legal arguments as a cloak for their real intentions, the most important of. which was to prevent any kind of final breach, and in the end it

[1] Q. ibid, p. 75.　　[2] Q. Bailey, p. 621.　　[3] Q. Seymour, p. 75.

happened as Page had prophesied and wished, for they continued to argue but came to no conclusion.

Since an old-style blockade of the German coastline was never considered feasible by British naval opinion, the Allies began operations by extending the contraband and conditional contraband lists. Happily for Britain, the Declaration of London, which listed and thus limited both these categories, had not been ratified, and so the Government was able to rebut the American demand that the Declaration be accepted as an effective code. Instead they added to the contraband list certain articles, which changes in the nature of war rendered of vital military value, but they did so cautiously and with a never-failing eye on the reaction of the greatest neutral. Copper and rubber were the first, but, in view of its critical importance as an American export particularly in the then conditions of economic depression, cotton did not follow until August, 1915, by which time its production was booming. As the growing flood of American exports rendered effective protest by the United States less and less likely, both lists were gradually extended, and when the German Government, in January, 1915, assumed control over all foodstuffs for rationing purposes the British Navy began to seize all cargoes of food bound for Germany directly or indirectly, although they had hitherto been regarded as conditional contraband only.

As this indicates, British policy was that of rigorously enforcing the rule of continuous voyage, which had not normally been applied in the past to conditional contraband, nor to cases where the second leg of the journey was by land and not by sea, as for instance in the case of imports to Germany via Denmark. The United States had applied the rule in the Civil War, but not with these modifications; when she protested, the British Government limited itself to a paper concession, which merely restricted its operation to conditional contraband consigned in blank, for owing to Germany's lack of credit facilities almost all consignments were of this character. Yet another British tightening of the ropes, made on the ground of the vast increase in the size of ships and the difficulties of search and transfer of cargo at sea in modern conditions, empowered British naval vessels to order ships into harbour for comprehensive and prolonged examination.

Meanwhile, as this system developed, the Germans gave the British Government an excellent opportunity to employ any other new weapons they deemed necessary. On 7 August, 1914, they announced their intention of sowing mines at points of embarkation and disembarkation of British troops, and neutral ships were blown up as a result. Britain thereupon declared that Germany was violating international law by sowing mines of a prohibited class from cruisers disguised with neutral flags, which was of course denied by the German Government, and reserved the right to take retaliatory measures. In October these were announced, for the American reaction to the British threat of reprisals had not been strong; the British laid zones of mines in designated areas, which neutrals were notified that they would find it dangerous to penetrate, and which brought their shipping to some extent under Allied direction. On 3 November, 1914, Britain declared the whole of the North Sea a military area, so that neutrals, unless they were willing to risk being blown up on a minefield, had to stop at an English port for sailing directions, when, most conveniently, they could also be cleared for contraband.

On 4 February, 1915, in a fateful move, Germany carried retaliation even further by the declaration of virtually unrestricted submarine warfare in a zone surrounding the British Isles. Britain held that nothing could justify so inhumane an action as the sinking of peaceful vessels, often containing women and children, without warning, and that this in effect stopped all commerce in the area, whatever the commodity and whatever the country concerned. She therefore imposed the Reprisals Order of 11 March, the Prime Minister declaring that, in view of Germany's disregard of international law, "her opponents are ...driven to frame retaliatory measures in order, in their turn, to prevent commodities of any kind from reaching or leaving Germany."[1] So effective did this control become, that from January to July, 1915, out of 2,466 ships arriving in neutral ports of the North Sea, 2,132 had been carefully examined by the Allied authorities. Even British naval experts considered these measures of very doubtful legality, though of undoubted equity, but the reprisals claim dispensed in effect with the need for legality; as Asquith said on 1 March, 1915, "Under existing conditions there is no form of economic pressure to which we do not consider ourselves entitled to resort."

As in the Napoleonic Wars, the far-reaching retaliatory measures of the belligerents soon overshadowed the original grounds of international law on which belligerents and neutrals had taken their stand. The next British step could have come as no surprise, for it merely rationalized and made more efficient the system of economic strangulation. Despite the most rigorous application of the doctrine of continuous voyage, it was obvious that much was passing to Germany through her neutral neighbours. In 1914 United States exports to

[1] Q. Seymour, p. 39.

Denmark, Holland, Norway and Sweden were $187,667,040; in 1915 they rose to $330,100,646. A dramatic illustration of this was provided by the seizure of four Scandinavian steamers, proceeding to Copenhagen in October, 1914, with 19 million pounds of lard, for Denmark's total imports of lard in the two previous years had been only 1¼ million pounds. The British prize court decided that the lard was intended for Germany: "To hold the contrary would be to allow one's eyes to be filled by the dust of theories and technicalities and to be blind to the realities of the case."[1] As a result, in October, 1915, "rationing committees" were created to determine quotas of legitimate imports for the small neutrals, and these were henceforth enforced. As a result, in 1916 the imports of the same powers sank to $279,786,219. Except for embellishments, some of which—such as the black list of neutral firms suspected of trading with the enemy, and the control and holding of mails—were exceedingly unpopular in the United States, this remained the blockade situation until America broke off relations with Germany in February, 1917. After that, in fact if not in name, Britain returned to her full practice of a century earlier, that no trade with the enemy was permitted unless by British licence or consent. That it was three years before she reached this position, and even then only did so with the virtual termination of the neutrality of the greatest neutral, is a measure of the importance of the part now played by the United States in the life of Britain.

Yet these months did not pass without considerable and even dangerous strain between the two countries; this, to students of Anglo-American history, was to be expected. Spring-Rice wrote in November, 1914: "Here the situation is that the inevitable contraband cases are coming to the fore; we have command of the seas and this is a reason why we are likely to fall foul of all neutrals. The American conscience is on our side but the American pocket is being touched."[2] The analogy with the Civil War was frequently cited, and Roosevelt wrote to Grey quoting Bright's advice to Sumner at that time, especially the passage which read, *"At all hazards you must not let this matter grow to a war with England, even if you are right and we are wrong,"*[3] and he urged upon the British "the necessity of acting with almost unreasonable moderation in the matter of contraband."[4] The British Government was well aware of the supreme importance of the American attitude, but often found it hard to restrain the opinions of the public. After the

[1] Q. ibid, pp. 28, 42.   [2] Spring-Rice, II, p. 241.
[3] Q. Grey, II, p. 144.   [4] Q. Spring-Rice, II, p. 253.

dispatch of a formal American note of protest against the harshness of Allied methods of control, on 26 December, 1914, Grey cabled to Spring-Rice that public opinion was "becoming unfavourably and deeply impressed by the trend of action taken by the United States Government and by its attitude towards Great Britain. What is felt here is that while Germany deliberately planned a war of pure aggression . . . the only act on record on the part of the United States is a protest singling out Great Britain as the only Power whose conduct is worthy of reproach".[1]

Britain in truth firmly believed that she was fighting for the cause of freedom and democracy, and felt the same disappointment about the attitude of the United States that the North felt about hers in the Civil War. Insult seemed to be added to this injury by the fact that nearly all the American protests were on material questions; it seemed that she complained to Britain of blockade while Germany slaughtered her women and children. Spring-Rice wrote as early as November, 1914, "We are fighting, if any nation ever did, for the principles of liberty for which the American is supposed to live and die, and the moment that we take a measure essential to our safety which touches the Standard Oil or the Copper Trust, there is a cry that American honour is being sacrificed."[2] And to make it even worse, while certain interests pressed for action against the blockade on economic grounds, the wealth of the whole country grew apace. Against a total of American exports to the Central Powers of only $169,289,775 in 1914, most of which was lost in the next two years, exports to the Allies, chiefly the British Empire, grew from $824,860,237 in 1914 to $1,991,747,493 in 1915 and $3,214,480,547 in 1916.

These British sentiments were not justified. Fundamentally, this is shown by the refusal of the Administration to consent to, or even to consider, an embargo on all shipments to belligerents. The Germans claimed that this was the only really neutral course, since they were effectively deprived of war materials from American sources by the Allied blockade; the leading German propaganda organ declared in 1915, "We prattle about humanity, while we manufacture poisoned shrapnel and picric acid for profit. Ten thousand German widows, ten thousand orphans, ten thousand graves bear the legend 'Made in America.' "[3] But the right of neutrals to traffic in war materials was well established, and Wilson would not give up any such right; as House wrote to him, "If it came to the last analysis, and we placed an embargo upon munitions of war and foodstuffs to please the cotton men, our

[1] Q. Seymour, p. 58.   [2] Spring-Rice, II, p. 242.   [3] Q. Bailey, p. 623.

663

whole industrial and agricultural machinery would cry out against it."
From Page in London came the continual reminder that deeper considerations lay behind the question of Anglo-American relations and
the blockade:

> A cargo of copper, I grant you, may be important; but it can't be
> as important as our friendship. It's the big and lasting things that
> count now. I think of the unborn generations of men to whom the
> close friendship of the Kingdom and of our Republic will be the most
> important political fact in the world. . . . It's no time, then, to quarrel
> or to be bumptious about a cargo of oil or of copper, or to deal with
> these gov'ts as if things were normal.[1]

House expressed exactly the President's view in May, 1915, when he
wrote, "In regard to our shipping troubles with Great Britain, I believe
that if we press hard enough they will go to almost any limit rather than
come to the breaking point. But, in so doing, we would gain their eternal
resentment for having taken advantage of their position".[2]

After the failure of the American proposals for the acceptance of the
Declaration of London, and the note of protest of 26 December, 1914,
Wilson sent House to Europe to search for an opportunity of mediation,
or at least conciliation. Already his mind was turning towards this
course, from humane motives and also perhaps from a desire for that
supreme niche in history which House prophesied would belong to the
man who could restore peace to the world. In his Annual Message of
December, 1914, he declared: "[W]e are the champions of peace and
of concord. . . . Just now . . . it is our dearest . . . hope that this character
and reputation may presently, in God's providence, bring us an opportunity such as has seldom been vouchsafed any nation, the opportunity
to counsel and obtain peace in the world".[3] A plan by which the Allies
would give up the blockade of foodstuffs, in return for German abandonment of submarine attacks on merchant vessels, finally fell through
because Germany demanded the passage of raw materials as well, but
House's mission did something to restore Anglo-American confidence,
since it displayed his fundamental sympathies once more to the British,
who, in their turn, created a good impression by their apparent willingness to accept the foodstuffs plan if Germany would do so.

A further proposal was put forward by House in the spring of 1915,
to ease the pressure upon neutral rights, and thus to relieve tension
between America and the belligerents; it was the traditional American
one of the Freedom of the Seas. It was clear that the Germans would

[1] Q. Seymour, pp. 46, 49-50.   [2] Q. ibid, p. 51.
[3] *Messages and Papers*, p. 8021.

support the plan, since it proposed to exempt all neutral private property from capture on the high seas; the contraband list was also to be severely restricted, and only actual and effective blockades of the enemy's ports were to be recognized. House hoped to convince the British that this new and revolutionary policy was, in the changed conditions of warfare attendant upon the invention of the submarine, even more to their interest than to that of their enemies, since they would be secure from submarine attack, and easily able to maintain their maritime ascendancy. He argued that, though Germany would be better off with the food and materials passing to her through neutral ports, the nation with the widest overseas resources and commerce would inevitably gain the advantage. Though the Foreign Office saw perhaps more clearly, at this stage, than some conservative naval authorities, the menace of the submarine, they were not prepared to espouse the scheme; as hitherto, they preferred the reality of naval power to paper guarantees which they did not believe the Germans would honour. To anyone conscious of the role of sea power in British history it could not have been surprising that the British Government refused to abandon the blockade, which was yet to prove a decisive instrument of victory.

Thus ended positive American attempts to make arrangements between the belligerents which would obviate maritime friction with the United States; henceforth the Administration fell back on a negative policy of making where necessary strong public protests against Allied actions, though the importance of their basic sympathy is shown by the private and friendly warnings that accompanied them. No such telegrams as the following passed from Wilson to House when the latter was in Germany:

> There is something I think ought to be said to Sir Edward Grey ... which I ... must convey through you because I wish it to be absolutely unofficial and spoken merely in personal friendship. A very serious change is coming over public sentiment in this country because of England's delays and many arbitrary interferences in dealing with our neutral cargoes. The country is listening with more and more acquiescence, just because of this unnecessary irritation, to the suggestion of an embargo upon shipments of arms and war supplies, and if this grows much more before the next session of Congress it may be very difficult if not impossible for me to prevent action to that end.

The primary content of the President's message was that he wished to try and prevent this calamity, but it must not be forgotten that it did remain true that he might not succeed; diplomacy such as this took

665

much of the strain but it could not take it all. The President and his advisers, despite their sympathy, became increasingly impatient with the Allies, because they were disillusioned with the failure of their proposals for alleviating the bitterness of the struggle.

In some quarters the venerable suspicion that Britain was using the blockade to check the rival trade of neutrals, as well as of the enemy, made its mark. Secretary of the Interior Lane well expressed this American feeling of exasperation :

> We have been very meek and mild under their use of the ocean as a toll-road. . . . I cannot see what England means by her policy of delay and embarrassment and hampering. Her success manifestly depends upon the continuance of the strictest neutrality on our part, and yet she is not willing to let us have the rights of a neutral. . . . There isn't a man in the Cabinet who has a drop of German blood in his veins, I guess. Two of us were born under the British flag. I have two cousins in the British army, and Mrs. Lane has three. . . . Yet each day that we meet we boil over somewhat, at the foolish manner in which England acts. Can it be that she is trying to take advantage of the war to hamper our trade?[1]

Perhaps even more trying to the American people than the blockade itself was the way in which it was conducted; they resented, and tended to believe that Britons relished, the fact that their commerce was subject in any degree to British orders. As Spring-Rice perceived, "there is a strong sense that our sea power is exercised in a way, not so much to injure American commerce and trade, as to hurt American pride and dignity. Commerce and trade have never been so prosperous. . . . But the facts are that American trade is in a way under British control."[2]

V

WHY did this growing exasperation on both sides of the Atlantic not do more harm to Anglo-American relations? Partly owing to their growing community of material interests, partly to their strong ideological and sentimental ties, and partly to the actions of Germany. But these three conclusions are distilled from a very mixed and contentious brew of evidence. Let us first examine the element of material interest.

When, in the nineteen-thirties, great and natural attention was being paid in America to the circumstances of her entry into the war, many believed that this was due primarily to economic motives. In its simplest

[1] Q. Seymour, pp. 67-9.   [2] Spring-Rice, II, p. 343.

form this belief was that certain American financial interests pushed the country into war in order to protect their investments in the Allied cause; its most sinister aspect was the conviction that the profits of armament manufacturers were the cause of America's belligerency. This feeling, for it was little more than that, was typical of the irrational pacifism of the thirties, and had its counterpart in the contemporary British agitation for the abolition of the private manufacture of armaments because it constituted a prime cause of war. In its direct form, the idea is without foundation; no shred of evidence has been found that pressure was brought to bear on Wilson in the months before the outbreak of war by the financial interests, and few men in American history have been less likely to respond to such pressure. But the broader question is complex and deserves careful analysis.

It is a revealing study, for, just as we have noted how in a small way the Boer War neutrality of the United States anticipated some of the features of her policy in World War I, so there is an obvious but none the less informative parallel between the events of 1914-7 and those of 1939-41. In both the economic bonds between America and the Allies were of great significance. In both the economy of the United States was stimulated by the demands of war, "the great consumer"; in both her prosperity increased swiftly under its impetus; and in both a cessation of the demand would have had serious economic repercussions. These things played their part in making impossible the project for an embargo on exports to belligerents in World War I, and also the indefinite continuation of Cash and Carry legislation in World War II. But it is a very far cry from this to the argument that financial interests dragged America into the war.

The number of those who would gain riches by such an action was relatively small, yet there is little doubt that the American people as a whole supported Wilson's final action; all the evidence indicates it, and it was notoriously the President's custom to act only when he felt that he had powerful public support. It is absurd to argue that the mass of the people supported the belligerency of the United States because they might lose their employments if they did not; many hundreds of thousands of them were by no means unaware that war might bring them employment of a very different and more unpleasant nature. Nor is it a tenable thesis that they were mere puppets in the hands of the economic interests. If men have a natural desire for material benefits, they have an even more natural and powerful dislike of mutilation and death. The argument that America's entry into the war was for purely economic reasons cannot be direct, only indirect; it can only be asserted that because of economic interests in the Allied cause, an embargo or similar policy was not applied by America, and that it was lack of this which caused the submarine campaign which precipitated the war. But even this assertion cannot be substantiated, for there is no evidence, as Seymour makes plain, that an embargo on munitions or even an absolute embargo on trade with the belligerents, would have prevented the submarine campaign. America was not the only neutral, although she was the most important one, and the attacks of the submarines were indiscriminate. Only an absolute and unconditional severance of American contacts with Europe as a whole might have preserved American neutrality, and no great nation could or would accept such restrictions. The fear of the loss of economic prosperity cannot, therefore, be regarded as the principal factor in leading America to war.

Nor can the second and more specific accusation, that American financial stakes in an Allied victory led her to join the holocaust, be substantiated, even though some plausibility attaches to it because of the curious sequence of events which led to the growth of American investments in the Allied cause. When war broke out in Europe, inquiry was made by American bankers as to what their attitude should be in case they were asked to make loans to foreign governments, and the State Department laid down the austere doctrine that "There is no reason why loans should not be made to the governments of neutral nations, but in the judgment of this Government, loans by American bankers to any foreign nation which is at war are inconsistent with the true spirit of neutrality."[1] J. P. Morgans' accordingly refused to go ahead with a projected French loan, which they had not in any case regarded with great enthusiasm.

This policy bore strongly the imprint of Secretary Bryan's beliefs; he wrote on the subject to Wilson :

> Money is the worst of all contrabands because it commands everything else. . . . If we approved . . . our citizens would be divided into groups, each group loaning money to the country which it favors, and this money could not be furnished without expressions of sympathy. These expressions are disturbing enough when they do not rest upon pecuniary interests—they would be still more disturbing if each group was pecuniarily interested in the success of the nation to whom its members had loaned money. The powerful financial interests which would be connected with these loans would be tempted to use their influence through the newspapers to support the interests

[1] Q. C. Seymour, *American Neutrality, 1914-17* (New Haven, 1935), p. 98.

of the Government to which they had loaned because the value of the security would be directly affected by the result of the war. We would thus find our newspapers violently arrayed on one side or the other, each paper supporting a financial group and pecuniary interest. All of this influence would make it all the more difficult for us to maintain neutrality as our action on various questions that would arise would affect one side or the other, and powerful financial interests would be thrown into the balance.[1]

Here, almost full blown at the origin of the whole question, is the thesis of American involvement through financial interests, and it has an obvious *prima facie* appeal to a twentieth century steeped in the historical doctrine of the primacy of the economic motive, though Bryan, the Fundamentalist, of Dayton, Tennessee, fame, was the last person to give any shade of approval or support to a hypothesis of this kind. He saw the economic motive, not as an inevitable and integral part of an irresistible process, but merely as sin; this was only a more dramatic case of crucifixion upon a cross of gold. And with it went the peculiarly American idea that in foreign affairs sin can be avoided by a sufficiently vigorous renunciation; drawing aside his skirts, he would go his own way. An even less attractive version of Bryan's theory inspired the accusations of the thirties against the financial interests.

Thus at first Bryan's views prevailed, but the Allies had no immediate need of loans, since they could dispose of their large American holdings. Before long, however, they had swallowed up most of these and needed further resources. American trade was now booming and the drying up of Allied demand would have precipitated depression anew; as Lansing wrote later in 1915, "there is only one means of avoiding this situation which would so seriously affect economic conditions in this country, and that is the flotation of large bond issues by the belligerent governments."[2] As early as October, 1914, by-passing Bryan, who adhered officially to the original policy, Wilson authorized Lansing to intimate privately to certain bankers that the Administration would not oppose the granting of credits; as Spring-Rice wrote, "American trade depended on a credit being given to America's best customer. But the greatest efforts were taken to explain to the general public that this was not a foreign loan but a credit in furtherance of trade."[3] In March the State Department issued a non-committal statement, maintaining disapproval of loans, but saying of credits—the distinction was largely nominal—"It has neither approved these nor disapproved—it has

[1] Q. Peterson, p. 86.   [2] Seymour, *American Neutrality,* p. 101.
[3] Spring-Rice, II, p. 281.

simply taken no action in the premises and expressed no opinion."[1] In August, 1915, after the departure of Bryan, the State Department quietly agreed not to oppose outright loans.

Though the first of the "credit loans" was in fact put on sale for Germany, by the time of America's entry into the war, American bankers had advanced approximately $2,300 million to the Allies in cash and credit, and only $27 million to their opponents. It is estimated that the total ultimate cost of the war to Britain was about $41,455 million, of which some $4,325 million was advanced by the United States, and the American stake in 1917 was considerably less than this. Fear of depression, as we have seen, undoubtedly influenced America to lend, as did hope of gain, but, as we have also seen, national gain immediately became national loss when America entered the war. Only individuals stood to gain, and, furthermore, when America broke off diplomatic relations with Germany in 1917, it was by no means clear that the Allies would be beaten if America refrained from fighting and that American investments in Britain would thus be lost. Most conclusive of all, there is, as we have also seen, no evidence that any pressure from financial interests was brought to bear upon the Administration at this crucial time.

From the British standpoint the growing community of Anglo-American economic interest, however, was very obvious. Already parallels with 1939 have become plain: the British need of American money and materials; the American effort, though in a different form and for different reasons, to supply them with both; and the breakdown of artificial barriers to such action. From the British point of view, the United States was a superb, if not absolutely essential, source of supplies; she was already in effect the arsenal of democracy, and British dependence upon her increased steadily as the war proceeded.

The shape of things to come is now clear for all who read to see; this is the great climacteric which saw the supremacy in the Atlantic community, as well as the Anglo-American relationship, pass decisively into American hands. As Karl Ackermann wrote to House in the summer of 1918: "Before we entered the war England was the Great Power to whom the Allies looked. . . . Today the Allies look to Washington."[2] The colossal expenditure of Britain in the war and the new lending function of the United States expedited America's transformation from a debtor to a creditor community. Looking back, the pattern of Lend-Lease, World War II and Marshall Aid is already perceptible.

[1] Seymour, *American Neutrality*, p. 102.
[2] Q. A. Willert, *The Road to Safety* (London, 1952), p. 151.

Few things show more dramatically the way in which the United States had already begun to assume the international role that Britain had so long performed than her subsidization of those who were fighting for causes with which she sympathized, which had been a classical British policy. By July, 1917, Spring-Rice could put it in this manner: "The situation here is much as it was in London in Canning's time when the Russian Ambassador used to call at the Foreign Office, being ignorant of French, and slap his pockets and say 'aurum, aurum.' As England was the sole financial resource of the Allies in the war against Napoleon, so the United States are our sole resource from the financial point of view at the present moment."[1] Thus a growing community of economic interest drew the two countries together as the war continued, and this prevented any breach, though it was by no means decisive in bringing the United States into the war.

The second set of factors which prevented a serious crisis in Anglo-American relations during the years of neutrality was ideological and emotional. The whole theme of our story has been the marked improvement of the Anglo-American atmosphere since 1812, and since 1898 there had been a rapid betterment of relations. After the hundred years of peace since 1814 they were more warm and cordial than they had ever been. This sympathy had owed much to the growth of democracy in Britain, and when she now claimed, with great justice as it appeared to many Americans, that she was fighting for the cause of liberty and democratic institutions, it did not diminish. Page wrote approvingly to House of the new democracy in Britain: "I hear you are stroking down the Tammany tiger—an easier job than I have met with the British lion. . . . At times in English history he has dwelt in Downing Street—not so now . . . he's all over the Kingdom, for he is public opinion."[2]

The militarism of Germany, which had so impressed House in 1914, was distasteful to Americans on its own account and because it was associated with political institutions which concentrated vast power in a strong monarchy and an arrogant military aristocracy. Britain had no motives for entering the war except self-preservation and her indignation at the violation of Belgian neutrality, and increasingly she came to view it as a war for those ideals of government which—and there is something of irony in the fact—were to be most fully and eloquently expressed by Wilson when America entered it. Though British idealism never went to the extremes of Wilson's, just as her realism never went to the lengths of Clemenceau's, her belief in the justice of her cause

[1] Spring-Rice, II, p. 405.   [2] *Life and Letters*, II, p. 102.

was deep. Spring-Rice spoke from the heart when he declared, "[M]ore and more the principles of democracy are at stake, and as they are at stake, not only the principles on which this government is founded but also its political interests and its own security become more and more in danger."[1] This same conviction grew in many American minds, as the whole-hearted way in which America waged war when she entered it shows. Its very outbreak in 1914 was greeted by the New York *World* with the heading "Autocracy or Democracy."[2] House wrote to Wilson at the same time that a German victory would mean "[t]he unspeakable tyranny of militarism for generations to come."[3] As Wilson was to say in his final speech to Congress asking for the declaration of war, "[W]e shall fight for the things which we have always carried nearest our hearts—for democracy, for the right of those who submit to authority to have a voice in their own governments, for the rights and liberties of small nations, for a universal domination of right by such a concert of free peoples as shall bring peace and safety to all nations and make the world itself at last free."[4] The implication that America had assumed the crusader's armour of the Allies, albeit she wore it with a difference (wore it, indeed, to the American eye altogether more fittingly) was unmistakable. The long standing and deep rooted sympathy of the two peoples was plainly of the greatest significance in preventing Anglo-American friction of a formidable character between 1914 and 1917.

VI

BUT there can be little doubt that it was primarily the third of our preservatives of Anglo-American goodwill, the actions of Germany, which brought the United States into the war. From the welter of arguments advanced in the neutrality controversy of the nineteen-thirties this emerges as the only possible view of the impartial historian. Such a book as the astute and plausible tract for the times of Walter Millis, published in 1935, might end with the words, "America, men simply thought, was in the war; and among them all, none quite knew how it had happened, nor why, nor what precisely it might mean",[5] but the judgment of the most scholarly and impressive of the American historians of the era, Charles Seymour, was different. He wrote shortly

[1] Spring-Rice, II, p. 303.

[2] W. Millis, *Road to War, America 1914-1917* (London, 1935), p. 45.

[3] Q. ibid, p. 58.   [4] *Messages and Papers*, p. 8233.   [5] Millis, p. 460.

afterwards: "It frequently happens that the occasion for an event is mistaken for its cause. Sometimes, however, the occasion and the cause are the same. There is every evidence that the sole factor that could have driven Wilson from neutrality in the spring of 1917 was the resumption of the submarine campaign."[1] The submarine campaign was not the only example of the fact that the greatest Allied asset was the folly of Germany; her propaganda, directed to a minority racial bloc and not to the American people as a whole, and partaking rather of the nature of blackmail than of political persuasion, is another instance; her obtuse disregard of American sensibilities over the killing of non-combatants, particularly women and children, is another; the indiscreet activities of the Austrian Ambassador, Dr. Dumba, and of the German military and naval attachés, Von Papen and Boy Ed, were yet others. But the submarine campaign was the crucial issue.

Not that its influence was limited to the supreme crisis; it had a long history. On 4 February, 1915, Germany issued a declaration that as from 18 February, in a war zone around the British Isles, all enemy vessels would be destroyed, and that the safety of crews could not be guaranteed; neutral ships were warned of the danger of entering these waters, since mistakes would be difficult to avoid, particularly if enemy ships continued the *ruse de guerre* of raising neutral colours. Wilson protested, in a note of 10 February, that the United States "would be constrained to hold the Imperial German Government to a strict accountability for such acts", and the whole atmosphere of House's mission to Europe, then just beginning, was altered. On 12 February, Germany gave orders that especial care was to be taken not to sink neutral ships, but in March an American was drowned when the British liner *Falaba* was sunk, and on 1 May an American oilboat was torpedoed with two resultant deaths. On 17 May, the *Lusitania* was sunk with the loss of very many American lives, and from this blow the emotions of the American people never really recovered.

Wilson demanded disavowal, reparation and the prevention of future occurrences in a note on 13 May, and repeated the demand more emphatically in a second note on 9 June; Bryan insisted that a note be sent at the same time to Britain, protesting against her violations of neutral rights, and refused to accept Wilson's argument that there was a decided difference between damage to material interests and loss of human lives. On 8 June he resigned the Secretaryship of State; the second note was sent under the signature of Lansing. On 8 July Germany replied to Wilson's note without repudiating her methods, contrary to

[1] Seymour, *American Neutrality*, pp. 25-6.

the advice of Bernstorff, who realized from his vantage point in Washington how serious the crisis was. Wilson sent yet another note flatly rebutting that of Germany, on 21 July, and on 19 August the British liner, *Arabic,* was sunk with the loss of two lives. House wrote: "If I were in his [Wilson's] place I would send Bernstorff home and recall Gerard. I would let the matter rest there for the moment, with the intimation that the next offence would bring us actively in on the side of the Allies. In the meantime, I would begin preparations for defence and for war, just as vigorously as if war had been declared."[1]

In such an atmosphere it was not easy to press complaints against Britain. But, largely owing to the efforts of Bernstorff, the civilian element in Berlin was able to bring matters to a victorious, if temporary, conclusion with their naval authorities, and a formal disavowal of the action of the submarine commander, who sank the *Arabic,* the most flagrant of the violations of international law from the technical point of view, was made by the German Ambassador to the State Department on 2 October. Instructions had been given by the German Government not to sink passenger liners without warning, and this fact had been made public on 1 September by Bernstorff. Thus German-American relations passed into a period of relative calm in the autumn of 1915. But the damage had been done to the German cause and it had redounded enormously to the benefit of the Allies. As Churchill, who was First Lord of the Admiralty at the time, was to write later, "The first German U-boat campaign gave us our greatest assistance. It altered the whole position of our controversies with America. A great relief became immediately apparent."[2]

Wilson's state of mind at the time was clearly shown when the American Ambassador to Belgium said to him, "I ought to tell you that in my heart there is no such thing as neutrality. I am heart and soul for the Allies." To this Wilson replied, "So am I. No decent man, knowing the situation and Germany, could be anything else. But that is only my own personal opinion and there are many others in this country who do not hold that opinion."[3] Over his sympathies his sense of political duty stood strongly on guard. As Spring-Rice wrote of his message to Congress on 7 December, denouncing the "hyphenated" Americans who had "poured the poison of disloyalty into the very arteries of . . . national life",[4] "The passage in the President's speech denouncing the disloyal action of the hyphenated citizen was greeted

[1] Q. Seymour, pp. 87-8, 100.
[2] W. S. Churchill, *The World Crisis* (New York, 1923), II, p. 306.
[3] Q. Seymour, p. 108.   [4] *Messages and Papers,* p. 8114.

with great applause and is now the predominant element in the situation." But, "As I have often said, the President feels that he is not Woodrow Wilson, but President of the United States. . . . He is known to be a very determined character, not prone to yield or to forgive an injury. But he is not supposed to carry personal feelings into public affairs. His policy from the first was to maintain absolute neutrality and he certainly did his best to keep the straight line."[1]

His effort to do so was by no means at an end, for it was no coincidence that the settlement of the *Arabic* dispute was followed after three weeks by a comprehensive note of protest from the American Government to Britain concerning the blockade. It was, as Spring-Rice said, to be expected that anything said against Germany should be balanced by something said against Britain: "It is true they are drowning American citizens who travel in our ships, and killing Americans who are making munitions for us. But the drowned people are mostly millionaires and the exploded people are mostly foreign workmen. Neither have great influence in the polls, and the country at the present moment is not much inclined to sentiment."[2] The American note was described by Page as an uncourteous thing of thirty-five heads and three appendices, "not a courteous word, nor a friendly phrase, nor a kindly turn in it, not an allusion even to an old acquaintance, to say nothing of an old friendship. . . . There is nothing in its tone to show that it came from an American to an Englishman".[3] Naturally enough, it was not popular in England, and even the notes to Germany had hardly been more so; Englishmen had hoped for something much more forceful from the United States than notes, and were correspondingly disappointed. Roosevelt exactly expressed their feelings when he contemptuously referred to one of Wilson's notes as "No. 11,765, Series B."[4] Even at the height of the *Lusitania* crisis Wilson had declared in a public speech, "There is such a thing as a man being too proud to fight. There is such a thing as a nation being so right that it does not need to convince others by force that it is right."[5] This was cold comfort to a nation which regarded itself as a near friend and which was locked in mortal combat with a deadly foe. The President's stock sank rapidly and he was denounced freely in the British press, though, as Spring-Rice pointed out, he was vilified even worse in that of Germany, usually a good proof of neutrality.

Meanwhile, negotiations were still proceeding over the *Lusitania*, for Germany would not admit the illegality of the sinking, and, arising

---

[1] Spring-Rice, II, p. 302.   [2] Ibid, pp. 300-1.
[3] Page, II, p. 72.   [4] Q. Bailey, p. 629.   [5] Q. ibid, p. 628.

in a sense out of them, came a proposal from the Secretary of State to the Allies on 18 January, 1916, suggesting the disarmament of all merchantmen in return for a German undertaking that all submarines would issue proper warnings before attacking. The Allies could never have accepted such a proposal, on the broad grounds, as Balfour wrote to House, that Germany could not be trusted not to sink unarmed ships mercilessly; but once again Germany saved them from the embarrassing necessity of outright refusal by declaring, on 8 February, that armed merchant vessels would be treated as ships of war. This premature announcement was widely accepted, even in Germany, as a renewed declaration of unrestricted submarine warfare, and Wilson hastened to say that Lansing's proposals were purely tentative and that merchantmen had a well-established traditional right to the arms with which to defend themselves. He maintained this stand, strongly opposing the Gore-McLemore resolutions in Congress, prohibiting American citizens from travelling in belligerent ships in the war zone, for he was firmly of opinion that, though America should remain neutral, she should not do so at the expense of her international rights: "For myself," he wrote to Senator Stone,

> I cannot consent to any abridgement of the rights of American citizens in any respect. The honor and self-respect of the nation is involved. We covet peace and shall preserve it at any cost but the loss of honor. . . . Once accept a single abatement of right, and many other humiliations would certainly follow, and the whole fine fabric of international law might crumble under our hands piece by piece. What we are contending for in this matter is of the very essence of the things that have made America a sovereign nation. She cannot yield without conceding her own impotency as a nation, and making virtual surrender of her independent position amongst the nations of the world.

Such an abdication he would not countenance, and Congress supported him by rejecting the resolutions. Then all else was swallowed up in a new and more severe crisis.

Despite the Kaiser's decision in the first week in March—then unknown to the world—against the renewal of submarine warfare, eight vessels were sunk between 9 and 29 March, one of them, the channel steamer *Sussex,* with American citizens on board. The German Government's efforts to prove that the sinking was the work of a floating mine merely angered the President, who sent on 18 April his famous note declaring, "Unless the Imperial Government should now immediately declare and effect an abandonment of its present methods of

676

submarine warfare against passenger and freight-carrying vessels, the Government of the United States can have no choice but to sever diplomatic relations with the German Empire altogether."[1] Faced with these clear alternatives, the civilian element in Berlin was able, after a bitter contest, to get its way; and Germany, though in acrid tones, accepted the President's terms, but made the decision conditional upon the removal of allied blockade restrictions. This pretension Wilson repudiated in a blunt note, and there the matter rested: the new German orders to their submarine commanders remained in force. Wilson had gained a clear diplomatic victory, and though the future was to prove it merely temporary, it greatly strengthened his position in the election of that year. He had not only kept the peace but appeared to have kept it with honour. To the Allies the relief was very marked, and in Britain, even though American involvement would obviously have suited her better, it was welcomed.

It had, however, as on previous occasions, unfortunate repercussions on Anglo-American relations. With the virtual settlement of the German question, attention seemed bound to be turned once more to the Allied blockade; with the disappearance of the greater pain, America became again conscious of the less. But it was not in fact in this direction that the new difficulties were to lie. The American victory, as Wilson realized, had been won by an ultimatum which threatened a diplomatic rupture; any renewal of the submarine warfare must therefore lead to such a rupture. Bernstorff, who saw this too, was convinced of the likelihood of what Wilson feared—the renewal in due course of unrestricted submarine warfare, on the ground that America would not force the Allies to lift the blockade, which would continue to cripple Germany. Wilson's mind now turned, therefore, more and more to American mediation, or a peace made under American influence, as the only way of preventing war; he began to think that the only way to stop the fire before it reached his own house was to put it out. This accounts for the persistence of his efforts at mediation, which were highly irritating to the British because they resented bitterly the idea that they were on the same moral level as their enemies. Hitherto the President's efforts to obtain peace had been altruistic, and, correspondingly perhaps, lacking in determination, but now he was conscious of what the American people were later to appreciate: "People . . . now that they know that they may become involved . . . have a sudden realization of what this may mean, and they have an intense desire to free themselves from the danger."[2]

[1] Q. Seymour, pp. 116-7, 123.   [2] Spring-Rice, II, pp. 367-8.

So strong was Wilson's conviction of America's peril, that he was prepared to gamble that very peace, to which Americans still clung with such determination, upon the chance of successful mediation. Believing that it was better to enter the war for a specific object, the establishment of some international organization which would prevent its repetition, than to slide into it upon some issue of neutral rights, he came to accept a policy of armed mediation. Yet it is a tribute to the firm Anglo-American, or at least Allied-American, sympathy that, though an armed mediator must obviously assume an impartial posture, he never for a moment contemplated intervention against the Allies. House wrote from Germany in the very middle of his visit to Europe early in 1916, which was designed to prepare the way for American mediation, "If victory is theirs, the war lords will reign supreme and democratic governments will be imperilled throughout the world," and the President was to say later, though while America was still neutral, that Germany was a "madman that ought to be curbed."[1] Wilson was convinced, and House with him, that Germany would never accept peace terms which had any hope of approval, while the Allies refused them; he thought it probable that the Allies might accept certain reasonable terms, while Germany refused them; he hoped that, if America consented to enter the war to enforce reasonable terms, Germany might be constrained to accept them.

This was the basis of his throw for mediation, and he felt compelled to make it, not only by his fear for his country, but also by his historian's conviction that a negotiated peace, now, could not but be better for the belligerents and for mankind than a peace of exhaustion, with or without victory, at a later day. He was certainly right in prophesying a peace of exhaustion, a victory, as Churchill called it, "almost indistinguishable from defeat";[2] it is just possible that he was right in believing that a compromise peace might have been the best issue out of the afflictions of the world; he was certainly unjustified in his hope that the belligerents—particularly the Allies, tempted with the bait of American intervention—would accept his proposals.

House appears to have initiated the idea of armed intervention in October, 1915, and Wilson accepted, for inclusion in his proposals, a suggestion of Grey's in the previous month—the notion was much in the air on both sides of the Atlantic—that "the President propose that there should be a League of Nations binding themselves to side against any Power which broke a treaty". Lest Allied morale be disturbed by premature or abortive talk of negotiations, these were conducted in-

[1] Q. Seymour, pp. 147, 160.　　[2] *World Crisis*, II, pp. 1-2.

formally through House. He wrote to Grey suggesting that, if the Allies agreed, he would let Germany know of Wilson's intention to mediate "and stop this destructive war, provided the weight of the United States thrown on the side that accepted our proposal could do it. . . . If the Central Powers were still obdurate, it would *probably** be necessary for us to join the Allies and force the issue."[1] The one and only change made by Wilson in House's draft was the insertion of the word "probably". The first question asked by the British Government was whether the United States would give a formal assurance of its willingness to combine with Europe in a policy to preserve world peace, to which Wilson cabled a specific and affirmative reply. This assurance is of the greatest significance, for it marked a complete reversal of traditional American isolationism; Wilson, hitherto an isolationist himself, now felt compelled to make an American commitment far exceeding anything to which Roosevelt had felt able to engage himself during his term of office.

It became plain when House got to Europe that, as he had expected, the Germans would not accept any reasonable terms, while France's reception of the idea was not altogether discouraging; British Cabinet opinion seems to have been divided, but many members, including Grey, fully realized the significance of the American offer. After discussion with House, it was decided that the moment was not opportune for intervention by America, and it was left to the Allies to decide when an opportune time had arrived. But the informal agreement was incorporated in a memorandum drawn up by Grey of his conversations with House; this was taken by House back to Wilson, who approved it with one significant alteration, the insertion of another "probably". It began:

> Colonel House told me that President Wilson was ready, on hearing from France and England that the moment was opportune, to propose that a Conference should be summoned to put an end to the war. Should the Allies accept this proposal, and should Germany refuse it, the United States would probably enter the war against Germany. Colonel House expressed the opinion that, if such a Conference met, it would secure peace on terms not unfavourable to the Allies; and, if it failed to secure peace, the United States would *probably* leave the Conference as a belligerent on the side of the Allies.

Here then was an American offer of mediation, in a sense not repugnant to most Britons, backed with an apparent promise to enforce reasonable terms by joining the Allies if they were not accepted by the Ger-

* Author's italics.   [1] *Intimate Papers*, II, p. 90.

mans. Yet, despite frequent promptings by House and Wilson, Britain never notified the American Government that she considered the time "opportune", and so the offer was never taken up. In a letter to Grey of 8 June, House clearly showed that he realized it never would be, unless the Allies were faced with definite defeat; regretfully he wrote, "There is nothing to add or to do for the moment; and if the Allies are willing to take the gamble which the future may hold, we must rest content."[1]

Seymour wonders whether "the Allies were not guilty of an awful error in refusing the opportunity opened by Wilson."[2] Why did they not, in fact, take advantage of it? There can be little question, though Seymour does not see it in this light, that it was due to British disbelief in Wilson's power, even if not his willingness, to bring about America's entry into the war. Britain had learnt by painful experience in the past that effective control over American foreign policy often lies in the hands of the Senate rather than the President; Seymour accepts this fact, but does not seem to appreciate its effect upon the minds of Allied statesmen. To him Wilson's "probably" merely conformed to American constitutional procedure; to British statesmen it underlined the contingent nature of Wilson's commitment. That they were indeed wise to be cautious, was surely indicated by much of the future history of Wilson's relations with the Senate, and indeed with the American people. Though his Republican opponents, who were to gain control of the House in 1916, were in some ways more belligerent than he, they were very unlikely to support so idealistic, even quixotic, an American venture as armed mediation, while there can be no doubt that the mass of the American people still ardently desired to stay out of the war at almost any cost. Spring-Rice at least was convinced of this; perhaps because of his Republican connexions, he saw the limitations on Wilson's power very clearly. He wrote to Grey in October, 1915: "There is, of course, a very strong desire that the United States should be a mediator, but not the slightest indication that they would appear as guarantors of the peace which might result from their mediation."[3]

Without the certainty of American intervention, which she obviously did not have, Britain did well to avoid the President's offer, for if it had misfired it could have proved disastrous to Allied morale; it might have led to a breakdown of Allied understanding and a consequent victory for Germany. France, after House's initial talk with Briand, refused to consider any peace proposal, and in the midst of the

[1] Q. Seymour, pp. 152, 170.   [2] Ibid, p. 172.   [3] Spring-Rice, II, p. 297.

French sacrifices around Verdun, Britain did not feel she could in honour be the one to cry, "Enough!" It is possible, too, that the Allies not only doubted whether America would intervene, but also greatly underestimated what she could and would do if she did. This was a mistake, but Germany later was to be prepared to risk all on a course which would bring the United States into the war against her, and it is at least understandable that the Allies were not prepared to risk too much in order to gain her intervention.

Thus ended Wilson's positive policy for extricating the United States from her unhappy predicament. Fundamentally, it failed because he mistook the motives and underestimated the passions that move nations to political action and, above all, to war. Nevertheless, he had during this period nailed his internationalist colours to the mast, and he never struck them; though he entered the war because American rights were attacked, he fought it from the first for an international organization with America in it. For him isolationism was at an end.

The failure of the Allies to accept the American offer, which was, of course, unknown to the public, renewed the strain upon Anglo-American relations, which were worse in the last six months of 1916 than at any time in the war. In the Administration's disillusionment, the blockade became more irritating than ever; in July the Allied blacklist was published, and the President wrote to House, "I am, I must admit, about at the end of my patience with Great Britain and the Allies. . . . I am seriously considering asking Congress to authorize me to prohibit loans and restrict exportations to the Allies. . . . Can we any longer endure their intolerable course?"[1] House replied, advocating caution, and saying, "I am sorry that a crisis has arisen with Great Britain and the Allies. . . ."[2] He believed that British mistrust had been intensified by the fact that Wilson had now undertaken a large re-armament programme, declaring, "Let us build a navy bigger than hers [Britain's] and do what we please",[3] but British feelings are much more simply explained; they were deeply chagrined at the impartiality of the United States towards their increasingly bloody struggle. In a speech of 27 May Wilson's revolutionary advocacy of American participation in a League of Nations was, in Britain, lost sight of in indignation at a sentence about the war which ran, "With its causes and objects we are not concerned."[4] In his Peace Manifesto in December he was to declare, to the even greater exasperation of the British public, that "the objects which

[1] Q. Seymour, pp. 76-7. [2] *Intimate Papers*, II, p. 315.
[3] Q. ibid, p. 317. [4] Q. Seymour, p. 177.

the statesmen of the belligerents on both sides have in mind are virtually the same, as stated to their own people and to the world."[1]

Though the British feeling against the "cold neutrality" of the Americans was the basis of the trouble in this winter of their discontent, other irritants were not lacking. Ireland, for instance, was increasingly a cause of difficulty as the situation there worsened, and Grey wrote in August, "We are not favourably impressed by the action of the Senate in having passed a resolution about the Irish prisoners, though they have taken no notice of outrages in Belgium and massacres of Armenians."[2] British sentiments were most vividly expressed by the fact that in the trenches 'Tommies' were apt to refer to dud shells which did not go off as 'Wilsons'. The British Government continued assiduously to cultivate the good will of the United States by always returning the soft answer, by never pressing anything to a final issue, and by damping down British public indignation, but it was impossible to avoid the resentment which so passive, if so unalterable, a policy engendered in the minds of the British nation, which had to carry it out.

Intelligent Englishmen knew that it was right, but could not refrain from expressions like those of Spring-Rice in a letter to Balfour in December, 1916: "A war with Germany may have unforeseen consequences of the most serious character, and it would be the breakdown of his peace policy. On the other hand, it is not thought that there is any danger of war with the Allies. They will not resent an injury, certainly not by force of arms; to insult or wrong them is safe."[3] In the same letter to Balfour he declared that he had pointed out to Americans the danger of a popular explosion in British opinion against America, resulting in the loss of working class sympathy for the American ideal and a modification of Britain's support of the Monroe Doctrine, which was the most extreme menace that he could contemplate. But the threat plainly lacks conviction; to say that it was a weak argument torn from him by the agony of war, that it was unlikely to materialize, and that it was probably not believed by either writer or recipient, is not to overstate the case. The marked disturbance of the relationship in these months was superficial; beneath it lay the now deep wells of understanding which were very different from the raging shallows of American-German misunderstanding. This became clearly apparent at the critical moment when Wilson issued his peace message of 20 December, 1916.

After the failure of agreed mediation in the spring, and the Presidential election in the autumn, which returned Wilson to power on the

---

[1] Q. Spring-Rice, II, p. 353.   [2] Q. Seymour, p. 179.

[3] Spring-Rice, II, p. 359.

slogan "He kept us out of war", he determined on a final appeal to the belligerents. Germany would have welcomed a peace negotiated in her then favourable military position, and indicated to Wilson her desire that he should take the initiative. He drafted a note towards the end of November, but, while he was awaiting a good moment to publish it, the German Government issued one of their own, expressing their willingness to enter negotiations. Realizing that this had ruined the chances of his, Wilson nevertheless issued it hurriedly before the Allies closed all possible doors in answering the triumphant-sounding German demand. The resolute Lloyd George, who had just succeeded Asquith as Prime Minister, was known not to favour peace moves, and both initiatives were rejected, though even that from Germany with perhaps more caution than might otherwise have been the case after a warning from the King to his impulsive Prime Minister, lest he should, by rash words, antagonize the United States. Inevitably British public opinion connected the two proposals and, noting the offensive impartiality of the President's tone, wrote off the American plea as a German plot. Yet so far was this from being the case that the first draft of the note had been the result of Wilson's conviction, strengthened by the sinking of the *Marina* on 28 October, that a fresh submarine crisis was approaching, and that this could only be avoided by the making of peace; what is more, it took the form of an appeal to the belligerents to describe their war aims, a procedure which we know Wilson believed must inevitably favour the Allies.

This was the lowest point of Anglo-American relations in the whole war, a point so low that the King could not restrain his tears when expressing to Page "his surprise and dismay that Mr. Wilson should think that Englishmen were fighting for the same things in this war as the Germans",[1] but the almost automatic responses of the belligerents showed how far off a final breach was. Germany, though anxious for an American peace initiative, was not anxious for American mediation, and replied in effect that she was not willing to disclose her war aims, because a direct exchange of views between belligerents appeared to her best. Britain, while declining to enter negotiations and rebutting Wilson's claim as to the similarity of belligerent war aims, laid down her objectives much more definitely, and, in Wilson's words, "stated, in general terms, indeed, but with sufficient definiteness to imply details, the arrangements, guarantees and acts of reparation which they deem to be the indispensable conditions of a satisfactory settlement. We are that much nearer a definite discussion of the peace which shall end the

[1] Q. Davis, p. 231.

present war."[1] Despite her indignation, Britain did not lose her sense of proportion, her power to cleave to the essential and dispense with the inessential; this was precisely what, in a few days, Germany was to do.

Despite the importunities of Bernstorff, who realized the gravity of the step, the German Government, now under the domination of the military, decided, on 9 January, to reopen unrestricted submarine warfare. Wilson had not yet given up hope, and had tried in vain to get through Bernstorff some statement of aims from Germany, the absence of which had been given by the Allies as their reason for the refusal of negotiations. Even though this tenuous hope had not been fulfilled, he made to the Senate on 22 January his famous address, appealing to the belligerents for peace and an international organization to enforce it. It was optimistic to hope for the participation of the American people in the latter, and even more optimistic to hope, either that the belligerents would be content with "a peace without victory", or that the Allies would believe Germany fitted in 1917 to enjoy the only peace which "can last", a peace "the very principle of which is equality and a common participation in a common benefit."[2] There was more than a little unreal Wilsonian idealism in this, and the irony of it lay in the fact that, unbeknownst to the President, Germany had already cast the die.

Thus once more German folly swallowed up Anglo-American discontent. On 31 January Bernstorff informed Lansing that German submarines would sink on sight all ships met within a delimited zone around the British Isles and in the Mediterranean with the almost insulting exception of one American steamship, which could sail each week to and from Falmouth, provided it moved on a definite route and was furnished with very elaborate markings. The Germans believed that they could win the war before American intervention could become effective, if indeed it ever did so; Spring-Rice had prophesied this as long ago as March, 1916, when he wrote to Grey, "At the worst, if a breach comes, she seems prepared to face the worst that America can do".[3] The confidential despatch to the President, on the same day as the declaration of submarine warfare, of Germany's terms for peace, seemed, particularly in view of their unsatisfactory content, a mockery. Wilson "felt", in his own words, "as if the world had suddenly reversed itself; that after going from east to west, it had begun to go from west to east, and that he could not get his balance."[4] It was small wonder,

---

[1] *Messages and Papers*, p. 8199.   [2] Ibid, p. 8201.
[3] Spring-Rice, II, p. 329.   [4] House, II, p. 442.

for the sudden intrusion of harsh reality can be a disturbing experience.

He announced to Congress on 3 February that diplomatic relations with Germany were severed. This was inevitable, but he was not without some hope that drastic action might bring Germany to her senses, and he clung eagerly to his determination to await an overt act of hostility before taking the final step of going to war. Germany, however, did not weaken, and public opinion against her in the United States was fanned by the publication of the Zimmerman telegram, proposing a German-Mexican alliance in case of war, which was intercepted by British Intelligence and handed over to the State Department. On 26 February, the day it was handed over, the President appeared before Congress to ask for powers to arm merchant vessels; when this was not forthcoming, owing to a Senate filibuster by what the President castigated as "[a] little group of wilful men representing no opinion but their own" who "have rendered the great Government of the United States helpless and contemptible",[1] he proceeded to do so on his own authority under an Act of Congress of 1797. That this action was necessary is demonstrated by the effects of the submarine campaign.

For Britain it was serious in the extreme; shipping losses mounted rapidly, reaching 540,000 British and neutral tons in February, the first month of unrestricted sinkings. Unless the situation could be relieved, Britain was plainly destined to starvation and defeat, and when America finally entered the war, despite all the measures the Allies had taken Page could write, "We haven't more than six weeks' food supply".[2] This was exactly, of course, what Germany had intended, and she had envisaged, to a limited degree, the way in which the campaign would operate upon the shipping of the greatest neutral, which simply tended not to put to sea. President Franklin of the American Lines began to dismiss all his crews; he had asked the Government for protection, and they had told him he could arm his own vessels, but, as he declared, "You can't buy 6-inch guns in any store." Soon the Atlantic ports were filled with American and neutral ships which would not risk their property or their crews; the blockade of Britain was in effect a blockade of America as well, and she began to feel many of the effects she would have felt from a self-imposed embargo. This had consequences which the German Government had not foreseen with sufficient clarity, for it threatened to bring about the collapse of the whole American economy. Spring-Rice reported the "stoppage of trade, congestion in the ports, the widespread discomfort and even misery on the coast . . . even bread riots and coal famine."[3] Effects

[1] Ibid, II, p. 461.   [2] *Life and Letters*, II, p. 241.   [3] Q. Davis, p. 237.

were felt as far west as Pittsburgh and Buffalo, in the form of an acute shortage of railroad cars, and there can be no doubt that in time it would have had grave effects on American industry and commerce.

Meanwhile, the spirit of the American people awoke; Spring-Rice, always a pessimist, could write to Balfour on 23 February, "The spirit of the country is rising. This does not mean that the desire for peace is less, but that the sense that something must be done to unify the nation and to prepare for war is growing."[1] To liberal Americans the coming of a democratic revolution in Russia on 12 March gave an added sympathy for the Allied cause, which now seemed wholly respectable politically; as the President declared, "If our entering the war would hasten and fix the movements in Russia and Germany it would be a marked gain to the world and would tend to give additional justification for the whole struggle."[2] (Later, but before the American people had come to consider Bolshevism a dark menace, the Allied projects for intervention in Russia were to be a minor source of Anglo-American friction for a short period, since Wilson regarded them as the work of British "reactionaries.")

The overt acts on the part of Germany for which the President waited were not long in coming. The British *Laconia* was sunk on 5 March with the loss of two American women, the American *Algonquin* on 12 March without warning, and, in the space of twenty-four hours ending on 19 March, three more American ships. Yet still the President wrestled in his soul, determined to make a rational and not an emotional decision. British opinion held its breath in painful suspense as Page wrote, "Delay is taken to mean the submission of our Government to the German blockade. . . . So friendly a man as Viscount Grey of Fallodon writes me . . . :'I do not see how the United States can sit still while neutral shipping is swept off the sea. If no action is taken, it will be like a great blot in history or a failure that must grievously depress the future history of America.' "[3] In America opinion mounted steadily, and on 20 March the Cabinet unanimously advised the President in favour of war with Germany and recommended the early recall of Congress. There seems little doubt that he made his decision on that day, though he did not cease to regret the necessity for it. On 2 April he drove down to Congress and asked them to recognize the fact that Germany was now waging war upon the United States. His speech was greeted with great enthusiasm, but he remarked later to his secretary, "My message today was a message of death for our young men. How

[1] Spring-Rice, II, p. 382.   [2] Bemis, p. 608.   [3] Q. Seymour, p. 206.

strange it seems to applaud that."[1] On 4 April the Senate passed the war resolution by 82 votes to 6, and the House, on 6 April, by 373 to 50. The country was not wildly enthusiastic, but there is no doubt that it strongly supported the President's action; as Spring-Rice had prophesied, when he moved he carried an irresistible weight of public opinion with him.

Why did the President lead America into the war? Or rather, why did he lead it to "accept the status of belligerent which has thus been thrust upon it"?[2] The distinction is an important one, for it correctly implies that the initiative lay with Germany. In the mind of Wilson America was forced—and few Americans more reluctantly than he—into war, not by her own economic needs, still less by the financial interests of any particular economic group; not by British propaganda nor by her sympathy for the Allied cause; not by any action of her own, but by an attack upon her by the Imperial German Government. This was no mere play upon words but an expression of Wilson's belief that the unrestricted submarine campaign was a direct attack upon America, and that he could not accept any limitation of American rights at the behest of a foreign power: "There is one choice we cannot make, we are incapable of making—we will not choose the path of submission and suffer the most sacred rights of our nation and our people to be ignored or violated." The submarine campaign was the direct cause of America's entry into the war. Yet it was an attack upon "all nations" and "a warfare against mankind", and this elevated the struggle to a higher plane. Its motive should be "the vindication of right . . . of which we are only a single champion," and it should be waged, not against the German people, with whom America has no quarrel, but against the autocratic German Government, from whom, and their like, "The world must be made safe for democracy." America's object, he claimed, was unchanged from the days of neutrality; it was to "set up among the really free and self-governed peoples of the world such a concert of purpose and of action as will henceforth insure the observance" of the "principles of peace and justice . . . against selfish and autocratic power". These could become the motives and objects of war; its cause was Germany's attack. To such a task America "can dedicate" the "lives and . . . fortunes" of her people, but as to entry into war, she has no choice,—"God helping her, she can do no other."[3]

The United States, then, entered the war because of Germany's attack upon her by the submarine campaign. To Wilson this appeared chiefly as an attack upon her rights; it was his nature always to clothe

[1] Q. Bailey, p. 644.   [2] *Messages and Papers*, p. 8228.   [3] Ibid, pp. 8227-8233.

the realities of power in the garments of moral light. Yet behind this situation the historian cannot but see, particularly in view of the events of 1940-1, that at bottom it was also an attack upon America's interests and even security; the rights of a nation are very hard to distinguish from her power and safety. There were those in America in 1917, disciples conscious or unconscious of the great Mahan, who saw this fact; the editors of the *New Republic* were among them. One article of 17 February, 1917, in the preparation of which Walter Lippman played a part, declared:

> [I]f the Allied fleet were in danger of destruction, if Germany had a chance of securing command of the seas, our navy ought to be joined to the British in order to prevent it. The safety of the Atlantic highway is something for which America should fight. Why? Because on the two shores of the Atlantic Ocean there has grown up a profound web of interest which joins together the western world. . . . [I]f that community were destroyed we should know what we had lost. We should understand then the meaning of the unfortified Canadian frontier, of the common protection given Latin-America by the British and American fleets. . . . When she carried the war to the Atlantic by violating Belgium, by invading France, by striking against Britain, and by attempting to disrupt us, neutrality of spirit or action was out of the question. And now that she is seeking to cut the vital highways of our world we can no longer stand by. . . . The passing of the power of England would be calamitous to the American national interest. . . . [America would] be morally and politically isolated.

Almost unbelievably the words, and even the voice, are those of 1917 and not of 1941. As Davis puts it, "The command of the Atlantic was America's safety line, just as with the British the fate of the Low Countries brought their vital interests into question."[1]

Others saw this fundamental fact, for Page wrote in 1914, "If Germany should win, our Monroe Doctrine would be at once shot in two, and we should have to get 'out of the sun.' "[2] Roosevelt had seen it clearly in 1911 when he wrote, "If Great Britain failed . . . the United States would have to step in, at least temporarily, in order to re-establish the balance of power in Europe, never mind against which country, or group of countries, our efforts may have to be directed. . . . In fact, we are ourselves becoming, owing to our strength and geographical situation, more and more the balance of power of the whole globe."[3] Great point is added to it by the extent to which the Allies, after America's entry into the war, revealed their dependence upon her in man-power

---

[1] Q. Davis, pp. 241-2, 249.   [2] Page, I, p. 334.   [3] Q. Davis, p. 246.

and, even more, in economic and financial resources. If, on the German side, there were no specific plans for her conquest, there was contempt for and anger at America; the Kaiser announced to Ambassador Gerard after the *Lusitania* notes, "America had better look out after this war. . . . I shall stand no nonsense from America after the war."[1]

Though many Americans saw these things, many did not, and among them was the President; as Spring-Rice wrote on 1 December, 1916, "It does not seem to be suspected that the sanction of the Monroe Doctrine has been more the fleet of Great Britain and France than the military force of the United States."[2] Had America not gone to war in early 1917, it is probable that the basic facts of America's position would have become increasingly clear as the Allies failed to make headway, or even began to lose ground. But as things were, this lack of perception in some quarters mattered little; if Wilson gave no evidence of seeing the strategic realities, but only what he considered moral truths, it had no immediate effect upon the event. This same tendency in him was to lead to his nemesis over the League of Nations, but for the moment it was of small consequence. War aims must wait upon victory in war and this seemed to the Allies now a great deal closer, one might even say more likely; whatever the reasons, whatever her motives, America was in the war.

VII

To the British people, needless to say, this was an event of incalculable importance, and they welcomed it in as vociferous a manner as was possible to them. Some were doubtful whether it was vociferous enough, and Page recorded, "The Archbishop last night asked me in an apprehensive tone whether the American government and public felt that the British did not sufficiently show their gratitude."[3] The spontaneous enthusiasm with which the first American troops to reach England were greeted was matched by the warmth—very natural in the circumstances—with which the once hostile upper classes acclaimed America's action. Kipling was expressing the general view when he wrote to Page, "I'll tell you, your coming into the war made a new earth for me."[4] This feeling was more than the mere welcoming of another ally, it went deeper even than relief at being rescued from an awkward predicament by the most powerful nation in the world—it was

[1] Q. ibid, p. 227.   [2] Spring-Rice, II, p. 357.
[3] *Life and Letters*, II, p. 245.   [4] Q. ibid, p. 421.

thought to be the consummation, at long last, of a very special relationship. This was what Page implied when he quoted, in triumphant tones, Jefferson's letter to Monroe at the time of the inauguration of the Monroe Doctrine: "With her, then, we should most sedulously cherish a cordial friendship; and nothing would tend more to knit our affections than to be fighting once more, side by side, in the same cause."[1] On 4 July, for the first time in history, a foreign flag floated beside the Union Jack on the Houses of Parliament.

President Wilson did not reciprocate these sentiments in all their fulness; Spring-Rice observed that, "He is not a belligerent among other belligerents, but something apart."[2] His erstwhile feeling for England had evaporated, or been consumed in the now burning flame of his desire to save, not merely a chosen people, but the whole human race from perdition. He was perhaps disillusioned with Britain; some taint of his recent mistrust of British policy over such things as the blockade may have remained; or it may be that, though he had violated the precepts of the Founding Fathers, and entered the European arena, he instinctively felt on his guard against the sinful temptations of the Old World.

Certainly he gave a number of examples of his desire to be drawn no closer to Britain. He had brought considerable pressure on her to settle the Irish question. He discouraged—in effect prevented—a proposed lecture tour in Britain suggested by Lloyd George, on the part of former President Taft and A. Russell Lowell, saying, "I think we have already been too close to England, and I hope to see the relationship less close after the war."[3] When eventually he went to England, his reaction to his enthusiastic reception was unbending, and produced in Lloyd George a "chill of disappointment",[4] which was not entirely dispelled by a special statement from the President to *The Times*, even though this was actually drafted by an Englishman, William Wiseman. In truth, the President believed that America's motives in the war were altruistic, whereas those of Great Britain seemed to him of a less unselfish character, so that Winston Churchill was later to declare that he came to Versailles "to chasten the Allies and chastise the Germans."[5] It was not that he was anti-British, but that he believed he should not sully his hands by special connexions. His heart was set on his intellectual vision of an international society, in which all nations, great and small, were to be equal before the law, and he could not accept inferior affiliations. This was the pure milk of Wilsonianism.

[1] Q. Morison and Commager, I, p. 458.   [2] Spring-Rice, II, p. 409.
[3] Q. Davis, p. 253.   [4] Ibid, p. 252.   [5] Ibid, p. 251.

Just as he was to refuse the suggestion, put forward by many Americans such as Lansing, for a League based on areas, to which the liability of powers should be limited; just as his disciple Cordell Hull was to reject flatly the idea of regional pacts, in the negotiations leading to the establishment of the United Nations; so now, he was anxious to avoid closer political relations with Britain than with other peoples.

But, great as was the President's influence at the pinnacle of his power, he could not altogether transform the pattern of Anglo-American relations. As Davis writes, "Henry Adams, a paralyzed invalid but still able to pluck harmoniously at the strings of history, penetrated again to first causes, writing a friend in England his gratification because 'I find the great object of my life thus accomplished in the building up of the great community of the Atlantic Powers, which I hope will at last make a precedent that can never be forgotten.' " Spring-Rice could reciprocate by writing to Adams—and with truth—in April, 1917, that "it is, of course, impossible now to separate the interests of England and the United States, so far as regards the Atlantic."[1]

Nor did all this interfere with America's forceful prosecution of the war, contrary to the expectations of European pessimists, who underestimated the vigour, quality and quantity of the American effort; they had not, as Churchill was to remark of a later generation, read the history of the American Civil War. Wilson had said in his war message, which contained a great quantity of practical military planning, that America would, "if necessary, spend the whole force of the nation"[2] to end the power of the German Government, for he had few military, if he had many diplomatic, reservations. Now, in fact, the United States gave a first and convincing demonstration of her capacity to forget everything in war, except her desire for total victory. The President did not absolutely fit into this category, but most of his countrymen did, and House even advised against premature discussion of peace terms on the grounds that, "If the Allies begin to discuss terms among themselves, they will soon hate one another worse than they do Germany. . . . It seems to me that the only thing to be considered at present is how to beat Germany in the quickest way."[3] It is probable that there was in 1918 more discontent in America that Germany was not utterly overwhelmed than in Britain; certainly Pershing was the only one of the commanders on the Western Front who was against an armistice in November. America threw herself wholeheartedly into the war; as Page wrote, "To save my life I don't see how the Washing-

[1] Q. ibid, pp. 242-3.   [2] *Messages and Papers*, p. 8231.   [3] Bemis, p. 153.

ton crowd can . . . keep their faces straight. . . . Yesterday it must be a peace without victory. Now it must be a complete victory."[1]

Having fought, like the British in 1914, no major war for over half a century, and never having taken part on a full scale in a great international conflict, the Americans did not at first grasp the intensity of the immediate effort required if the Allies were to be sustained; but very soon, with that ruthless practical logic and genius for organization which is their hall-mark, they were primarily responsible for forcing upon the Associated Powers a rational, efficient and centralized system for control of the war effort. In naval affairs, for example, Page could at first complain, "We have about forty destroyers, we are sending over six!"[2] But very shortly all this was changed, for the United States insisted on sending over a division of battle-ships at once, a welcome reinforcement to the Grand Fleet after Jutland; they pressed on active offensive operations against the submarine, and persuaded the British to co-operate in closing the North Sea to submarines by a vast mine barrage. Bailey has cast doubt upon the story that F. L. Polk of the State Department on one occasion declared, "Mr Balfour, it took Great Britain three years to reach a point where it was prepared to violate all the laws of blockade. You will find that it will take us only two months to become as great criminals as you are",[3] but his detailed study of America's belligerent policy towards neutrals does not substantially invalidate the moral of the tale.

He shows, it is true, that the Washington Government "did not violate international law in a sweeping and ruthless fashion",[4] and that it proceeded largely by the methods of embargo, bunker-control and the blacklist, all of which were legal; but it should be noted that the United States had formerly protested bitterly against the use of the blacklist, and that she later employed the embargo to impose rationing upon the small neutrals adjacent to Germany. Also, he admits that the United States forewent no substantial advantage by such renunciation, and agrees, though belittling its importance, that the Allies, who were more practised in the art, were perfectly able to carry out the blockade without American aid. In fact, the extent of American naval aid in other spheres undoubtedly enabled the Allies to continue the blockade more efficiently, and it is not unduly cynical to suppose that, if the paraphernalia of American captures and prize courts, on whose absence Bemis congratulates the administration, had been needed to win the

---

[1] *Life and Letters,* II, p. 291.　　[2] Ibid, p. 241.　　[3] Q. ibid, p. 265.

[4] T. A. Bailey, *The Policy of the U.S. Towards the Neutrals* (Baltimore, 1942), p. 492.

war, they would have been forthcoming. Certainly the Civil War and the Spanish War give credence to the notion, as, even more strongly, did the making of the War Claims Agreement with Britain in 1927; this agreed, retrospectively and reciprocally, not to claim any damages arising out of the war measures of the other power, and it left most American claimants to sue in Britain's prize courts. This followed the elimination, by a State Department examiner with a British colleague, of all but 95 of 2,658 American claims against Britain. As the American declared, "We are one of the principal naval forces of the world, and should we become involved in another war it would be to our interest to have our naval forces free to operate in any way which would make them most effective against the enemy."[1] During the war, indeed, Anglo-American naval and military co-operation was intimate enough to have delighted the heart of Mahan. The relations of the American and British forces at sea, under the command of the British Admiral Bayley, might serve as a model. He flew his flag indifferently in the ships of either nation, the chain of command was strictly according to seniority, and the same courts of inquiry were shared. The military relationship could not in the nature of things be so close, for America very understandably refused a natural British suggestion that, in view of the urgent need of troops, the common language, and their own practical experience, American forces should be brigaded with theirs. But the Americans not only achieved the remarkable total of one million men in France by June, 1918, and two million by October; they were also consistent advocates of a unified command in France. Efforts were made to encourage Anglo-American military good feeling, and, whatever its effect, the receipt by every American soldier who came direct to Britain from the United States of a letter of welcome from King George V was a gesture of the right kind. He had actually welcomed General Pershing's staff with the words: "It has always been my dream that the two English-speaking nations should some day be united in a great cause, and today my dream is realized. Together we are fighting for the greatest cause that peoples can fight. The Anglo-Saxon race must save civilization."[2]

But the crux of Anglo-American co-ordination necessarily lay in the political and economic sphere. Wilson was meticulously careful to make no Alliance with the other belligerents, both because it would

[1] Bemis, p. 195.

[2] Q. Harold Nicolson, *King George The Fifth, His Life and Reign* (London, 1952), p. 317.

693

have been contrary to American traditions and because he desired to keep his own hands free; the United States became only an "Associated" Power, a term which Wilson himself appears to have originated. Neither the difficulties nor the importance of Anglo-American relations were underestimated by the British, whose Foreign Office sent out instructions to their diplomats, even before the actual entry of America into the war, stating that "full and frank co-operation between British and United States diplomatists and agents is one of the most important factors in the war."[1] Immediately war was declared, they suggested the sending of a special commission to Washington, headed by Balfour, the Foreign Secretary. The President had doubts about the procedure in view of American mistrust of anything approaching British control, but in fact, Spring-Rice wrote, "It is impossible to exaggerate the good effect of Mr. Balfour's mission here which has been a most unqualified success, a success which I think is likely to be lasting as it has created what is in my experience an entirely new atmosphere in Anglo-American relations."[2] House added a more specific tribute: "Mr. Balfour possessed an extraordinary understanding of the mind of the American people and his public utterances all evoked a desire for cordial Anglo-American co-operation. President Wilson immediately was caught by his charm of conversation and his intellectual interests."[3] Balfour's was the first official visit of a British Cabinet Minister to the United States during his term of office, as was that of Secretary of War Baker, somewhat later, that of an American Cabinet Minister to Britain. Page prophesied with some truth at the time, "I have no doubt that Mr. Balfour's visit will cause visits of many first-class British statesmen during the war or soon afterward. That's all we need to bring about a perfect understanding."[4]

The departure of the mission was followed by the despatch of Lord Northcliffe to co-ordinate British activities in America, particularly on the industrial side, but at the beginning of July a serious financial crisis threatened unless Britain could obtain more of the already bountiful American financial support; she had been the banker of the Allies—her traditional role—for three years already, and could no longer support the burden. But the United States properly demanded that some kind of authority be set up by the Allies to co-ordinate their large and often competing needs, and, though it was for a considerable time opposed on the ground that the financial autonomy of the Associated Powers would be threatened, it eventually came into existence as the Interallied

[1] Q. Seymour, p. 217. [2] Spring-Rice, II, p. 400.
[3] Q. Seymour, p. 218. [4] *Life and Letters*, II, p. 253.

Council on War Purchases and Finance. Before this occurred, still further efforts had been made to get the direct machinery to work (notably at the urging of Northcliffe) by the despatch of Lord Reading to Washington. He was very successful in getting increased help, particularly by obtaining, for the first time, credits for expenditure outside the United States, but his visit bore most fruit through his conversion to the necessity of more permanent co-ordinating machinery; as he wrote to the Government, "The growing lack of co-ordination between the programme of the Administration here and the programme of the Allies is probably, on every ground, the biggest question in front of us."[1]

As a result of this warning and the obvious gravity of the situation, the Cabinet requested the sending of an American mission to concert plans, and Wilson consented to send one headed by House, which arrived in London on 7 November, just after the Italian collapse at Caporetto and just before the Bolshevik Revolution in Russia made it plain that the Allies could no longer count on the continued existence of an eastern front. Caporetto precipitated the creation, by the agreement at Rapallo, of a Supreme War Council of the nations which had armies on the western front. While they were in London, the Americans agreed to launch 6 million tons of shipping that year and to increase their supplies of money and food, but were discontented with the progress made in the organization of interallied war machinery. In Paris, later, they got their way by the creation of the War Purchases and Finance Council, the Maritime Transport Council, the Interallied Naval Council, the Food Council, the Interallied Petroleum Conference and, in the following summer, the Interallied Munitions Council. House wrote as he set out for the United States: "The good the Conference has done in the way of co-ordinating the Allied resources, particularly the economic resources, can hardly be estimated. Heretofore, everything has been going pretty much at sixes and sevens. From now there will be less duplication of effort." The Supreme War Council was still a political body, and not military as the French wished (so that the Supreme Command of Foch in the field arose independently out of the highly dangerous German offensive of March, 1918), but it gradually began to play an important role, and eventually became merged in the Supreme Council of the Peace Conference. This purely political role was the one Lloyd George, in his mistrust of professional soldiers, wished for it, and Wilson's support for the institution probably saved the Lloyd George government at the end of 1917, although

[1] Q. ibid, p. 229.

America never had direct representatives on it, only "listeners". As André Tardieu wrote, "control reached something in the nature of perfection towards the end of 1918. Had the war lasted another year, the machinery would have been running with incredible smoothness."[1]

VIII

UNHAPPILY, a similar smoothness was not apparent when America and the Allies began to consider the peace which should follow the war. That there was a similar rift between Wilson's views and those of what was at least a powerful minority in his own country makes his initial success all the more remarkable; it was essentially a personal achievement. He had begun the war as an isolationist, convinced that America could stay out of it, but when he finally realized that the defeat of the German Government was a necessary pre-requisite of the revolution in international morality for which he yearned, he flung all America's resources into the battle. He even used his moral zeal as a potent weapon of war, and there is no doubt of the importance of his personal propaganda as a solvent of the German system. He used his unique position to drive a wedge between the German people and the German Government, and when in the end that Government wanted peace, it not only turned to him for it, but was forced to accept the terms he offered by that pressure upon it of its own people which he had done so much to arouse. Though America fought the war with all the strength she could bring to bear, Wilson determined that his war aims should remain unpolluted by a too close association with those of the European Allies. Thus a marked cleavage appeared during the last eighteen months of the war between the Allied and the American war aims, of which both were well aware, the Allies uneasily, the President with a determination to use all the strength at his command to get his way when the time came. That he would be able to do so, he did not doubt, and he proved substantially correct.

The pinnacle of power which he occupied in 1918 was, indeed, dizzy beyond even that of Roosevelt in 1944, for to the latter there was the counterweight—already vastly formidable—of Russia. The Allied and Associated Powers were more absolutely triumphant than any previous alliance in the history of Europe; into the vacuum of Eastern Europe, created by the collapse of Russia, their influence surged like a flood.

[1] Q. ibid, pp. 240, 244.

Yet among them, only the United States was still unimpaired in strength; on her the Allies depended not only for decisive military victory, for financial resources, for food and raw materials, but for reconstruction when the war was at an end. Over the destinies of the United States, whose governmental system gives far-reaching, if temporary, power to a great man in the executive office, presided Wilson; and he, by his passionate conviction and compelling powers of oratory, had become a household word in Europe.

Yet, by the end of 1920, a mere two years after the armistice, he had become a stricken man, bitter and disillusioned with all his friends and associates, and—worst of all—repudiated, with all he stood for, by his own countrymen. Verily, as Seymour declares, there is all the air of classical tragedy in his triumph and his disaster. The essence of Wilson's failure was his repudiation by his own people; its irony that he, the proud instrument of the people's will, failed because he had not their support. But this is in the future; in 1918 he occupied a position of unrivalled power, and played, therefore, a unique part in the coming and framing of the peace.

When America entered the war, the Allies were bound, by a number of secret treaties made during its course, to certain conditions of peace. Of this fact and of the general tenor of these agreements the President was made aware by Balfour on his mission to the United States, and between them and the general objectives Wilson had formulated in his mind there were a number of contradictions. As 1917 wore on, and as the leaders of the Bolshevik Revolution in November challenged the moral basis of the Allied and Associated cause, Wilson became convinced of the necessity of a statement of war aims, and approached the Allied Governments accordingly, only to find that even the most innocuous and generalized of liberal resolutions could not be agreed. He thereupon came to the conclusion that he must make independent and public statement of American war aims.

This he did initially in the famous Fourteen Points speech of 8 January, 1918, though he supplemented these on three later occasions. The speech, like most of his later diplomacy, was based on the work of a body of experts, the so-called Inquiry, assembled to prepare the American case against the coming of peace negotiations. This very liberal programme called for the abolition of secret diplomacy, the Freedom of the Seas, removal of economic barriers between nations, reduction of armaments, an adjustment of colonial claims which gave attention to the wishes of the peoples as well as the governments concerned, a number of specific peace terms in general accord with the idea of self-determination of peoples, restoration of German conquests, and "A general association of nations" to secure "mutual guarantees of political independence and territorial integrity to great and small states alike."[1] It was greeted enthusiastically in America. Except as a propaganda weapon, the Allies were less pleased with it; all had misgivings, many of them different and distinct. They were never at this stage asked to make the Points the basis of their war aims and they did not do so.

This was no doubt in the minds of the Germans when it was to Wilson that they applied, on 3 October, for an armistice on the basis of the Fourteen Points, for they might have got much shorter shrift from the Allies; thus Wilson's power was increased by the fact that he was the conduit pipe through which negotiations were carried on. The part which he played, however, was technically very correct and not unskilful, for he made it clear to the Germans that he could do nothing except to put the position before the Allies for their consideration. By playing upon the internal situation in Germany, he not only forced them to accept far worse military terms than they had ever envisaged, but was also largely responsible for the democratic revolution and the abdication of the Kaiser. When agreement had been reached between the President and the German Government, subject to Allied willingness to make peace and to do so upon the basis of the Fourteen Points, the whole matter was placed before the Allies, with House putting Wilson's case; the technical drafting of the armistice terms was carried out in the same way, by the Allied leaders and House, with the advice of their military and naval chiefs. Yet in both these proceedings the influence of the absent President was decisive because the whole foundation of the discussion was laid by him.

With the large questions of Allied-American disagreement which were thrashed out in these meetings we are not concerned, but one fact is clear, that it is impossible to generalize too freely about "the Allies" as a whole. While it is true that there was common ground between them in their opposition to certain aspects of the American case, it is even more true that Britain stood apart from them, and nearer to the United States—that she was a kind of half-way house between Europe and America. Yet even this degree of generalization is dangerous, for attitudes to the League of Nations to a great degree overran national boundaries. Wilson counted very much for support on liberal elements all over Europe, and these were particularly strong in Britain, where he

[1] Q. Bailey, p. 650.

was for the most part idolized by Labour leaders and left-wing Liberals, who would certainly have precipitated a revolt against Lloyd George if the President's programme had been seriously endangered.[1] On the other hand, Lloyd George was the head of a coalition government, and the Tories were mistrustful of an idealism which almost appeared "to assume that the reign of righteousness upon earth is already within our reach."[2] Those who thought in this way in Britain tended to stretch out their hands to Republican opponents of Wilson in America, and the tone of the *Morning Post* could rival in its comments upon Wilson anything that the opposition press in America could show. But it is clear that Britain was in a special position over the American proposals. Not only was she, as distinct from France and Italy, desirous of very little for herself at the peace conference, and hardly affected, as far as her own interests were concerned, by the provisions of the secret treaties, but her liberal opinion—and the Liberals were still powerful in the coalition—strongly supported the League of Nations and most of the principles for which Wilson stood.

Indeed, Lloyd George himself had made a statement of war aims three days before the Fourteen Points speech of Wilson, which was so similiar in content that the President actually contemplated giving up his own statement; critics have even suspected—mistakenly—that the two were concerted. The Prime Minister mentioned virtually all the Fourteen Points except open diplomacy, Freedom of the Seas, and lowering of trade barriers; with regard to the first he did at least repudiate, in the new circumstances, the secret treaty which gave Constantinople to Russia, while the third was one which might have been expected to appeal to what was still a Free Trade country. Freedom of the Seas was naturally not mentioned, and he laid considerable emphasis, as was also natural, on reparation for damages. He began by insisting on the necessity of a really democratic system in Germany, he emphasized even more strongly than the President the importance of the wishes of colonial peoples, and he laid down the necessity of a territorial settlement based on the right of self-determination, or consent of the governed. Above all, he appealed for some form of international organization to limit the burden of armaments and diminish the probability of war.

This speech was the first comprehensive statement of British war aims, and it was made prior to that of the President and without his knowledge. There were two points of serious disagreement with the

[1] Carl F. Brand, "British Labor and President Wilson" (in *Am. H.R.* XLII, 1937.   [2] *The Times*: q. Seymour, p. 291.

objects of Wilson, of which a great deal has been made and of which we shall hear shortly, but the remarkable fact, which seems so seldom to have been noticed, but which is by far the most obvious and important, is the extraordinary degree and extent of agreement between the two statements. It may be that a longer experience of the harsh realities of international affairs than that of a party which had had a Bryan before it had a Wilson, led even the Liberals among the British to be more cautious in their optimism about the League of Nations than the Democrats, but they advocated and supported it, and one of the British delegates to the Peace Conference, Lord Robert Cecil, who was a Conservative, was its devoted adherent.

These facts may be held to cast grave doubt on the thesis that Wilson went to Versailles to fight for a right conceived in America against a wrong conceived in Europe, and it certainly disposes of the idea that there were serious grounds for, or any likelihood of, a breach between Britain and the United States at this time. Even if the British had repudiated the Fourteen Points and the League, they would have done no more than they were told to do by a number of influential Americans, led by Roosevelt, who urged the Allies to pay no attention to the President and to divide the spoils: "Mr. Wilson and his fourteen points and his four supplementary points and his five complementary points and all his utterances every which way have ceased to have any shadow of right to be accepted as expressive of the will of the American people. . . . Let them [the Allies] impose their common will on the nations responsible for the hideous disaster which has almost wrecked mankind."[1] But there was no danger of the British, now more than ever conscious of the necessity of American friendship, taking so rash a step, particularly under a coalition government with a strong Liberal membership. They might disagree with the President on some points with great vigour; they might mistrust the Messianic idealism which led him, as Clemenceau is reputed to have put it, to talk like Our Lord but behave like Lloyd George; and they might resent his lack of cordiality and warmth, but in the last resort they would—they could—have done nothing fundamentally to endanger Anglo-American friendship.

This does not mean that Anglo-American feeling at this time was not sharp, indeed bitter, but even this tension arose on insubstantial almost unreal, foundations. The only fundamental issue between the two governments concerned sea power. Though the British Cabinet

[1] Q. Seymour, p. 371.

felt initial resentment at the President's unique position and also a desire not to tie the hands of negotiators by the acceptance of the Fourteen Points as the basis for an armistice, when, at the first conference of the Allied leaders with House on 29 October, the question was considered in detail, it became clear that Britain had strenuous objections only to two of the Points. The hope of France and Italy (which was not shared by Britain), that they might postpone consideration of all except the purely military terms of the armistice, thus entering the peace negotiations proper with free hands, was completely crushed by the well-timed threat of House, which showed vividly how utterly determined was Wilson to make his will prevail at this crucial juncture, that the United States might in such a case feel compelled to make a separate peace. Of the two British points of disagreement one was a desire to specify more clearly what was meant by restoration of invaded territories, in order to allow a claim for reparations for damages; this was natural in a power which had been longer at war and was in a much more serious economic condition than the United States, but it was felt, which was also natural, much more strongly still by the French. It was subsidiary in British minds to their second point of disagreement, a rooted objection to the idea of the Freedom of the Seas.

As we shall see, they carried to great lengths their opposition to what they considered this attack by America on their traditional maritime supremacy, which had been so decisive a factor in winning the war; yet within three years they were to accept virtual naval parity with the United States at the Washington Conference. Thus their first blustering resentment of American naval pretensions was very soon replaced by a now familiar acquiescence in the realities of American power, including sea power. On the other hand, we find the American Administration threatening, both now and a little later, to outbuild the British Navy decisively, a feat of which it was quite capable, but which, in its implication that the British were possible foes, ran clean counter to the whole Mahan naval doctrine on which the great American Navy had been reared. It is true that the Administration had the support of influential sections of American naval opinion in this proposal, and that the General Board of the Navy, apprehensive of Britain's power now that the counterbalance of Germany was removed, itself supported at least parity, but the Navy was by no means united in this, and the teachings of Mahan were not forgotten. The curious fact that the President, after insisting so strongly on the Freedom of the Seas in the preliminary stages of negotiation, never raised the question again later,

701

may well be significant of the disinclination of American naval authorities to discuss any such topic at a time when America was moving into the position of one of the two supreme naval powers. Thus it is hard to escape the conclusion that the tension on the American side was, equally with that on the British, based on false premises, and this should not be forgotten in assessing the seriousness of the Anglo-American discord.

At the very first meeting to discuss armistice terms Lloyd George had attacked the idea of making any mention of the Freedom of the Seas. "This point we cannot accept under any conditions, it means the power of blockade goes; Germany has been broken almost as much by the blockade as by military methods. . . . Therefore my view is that I should like to see this League of Nations established first before I let this power go." At the next meeting he agreed, given the elucidation on reparations, to accept all the other Fourteen Points except this, to which he maintained his opposition. The President then telegraphed to House: "I feel it my solemn duty to authorize you to say that I cannot consent to take part in the negotiation of a peace which does not include Freedom of the Seas because we are pledged to fight not only to do away with Prussian militarism but with militarism everywhere." But House, always more realistic than Wilson, believed that an agreement could be reached; he reiterated arguments, with which we have already become familiar in the war, to the effect that the Freedom of the Seas was now the true interest of Britain.

These arguments did, even in some naval quarters in Britain, begin to have some support; two expert British publicists, Kenworthy and Young, were later to write:

> If, then, the British now frankly and fully accepted the application of the Wilsonian principle, how would they stand? They would lose the arbitrary power they have enjoyed of initiating and imposing an economic blockade for slowly starving and strangling their enemy. . . . But this power they have in fact already lost. . . . It only became really effective when exercised in conjunction with America after its entry into war. The future exercise of it except in association with America or with American approval, will be impossible.[1]

It may be doubted whether the best way of ensuring American acquiescence in future blockades would have been to allow their own President to emasculate the weapon, against the naval interests, and probably the naval will, of his own country. (That in this matter the two navies saw eye to eye is clearly indicated by their combined demand,

[1] Q. Seymour, pp. 375, 381, 384.

in the formulation of the armistice terms, for the surrender of the whole German Navy, and not merely the internment of some and the surrender of other parts of it. House was prepared to follow the advice of the American Admiral Benson and his British colleagues in this, but ironically enough it was Lloyd George who suggested and carried a compromise, which met with Wilson's approval, agreeing to demand no more than was necessary to prevent the renewal of hostilities by Germany.) But it was in any case to remain an academic question, for the "blue-water" school of British admirals was too strong, in the full flush of victory, to allow any weakening in the attitude of the British Government.

In the first days of November the diplomatic struggle reached its height. House declared, for the benefit of Lloyd George, that unless some reasonable concessions could be made

> in his attitude upon the "Freedom of the Seas", all hope of Anglo-Saxon unity would be at an end; the United States went to war with England in 1812 on the question of her rights at sea, and that she had gone to war with Germany in 1917 upon the same question. . . . Our people would not consent to allow the British Government or any other Government to determine upon what terms our ships should sail the seas, either in time of peace or time of war.

The Prime Minister merely outstripped him in emphasis by announcing later: "Great Britain would spend her last guinea to keep a navy superior to that of the United States or any other Power, and that no Cabinet official could continue in the Government in England who took a different position."[1] The truth is that, for political and emotional reasons, both sides were adopting postures which were equally outmoded; the term 'Freedom of the Seas' produced in both conditioned reflexes, as automatic and as useless, in the new conditions, as was the saliva in the mouths of Pavlov's dogs when the bell rang but there was no longer a meal for them. What, in any case, did the term mean? The historian can sympathize with Clemenceau when he remarked, "I cannot understand the meaning of the doctrine".[2]

It was, in the end, on this long standing ambiguity, much enhanced by the alteration in conditions of warfare which had also cast increasing doubt on the exact meaning of cognate terms like "blockade", that in a kind of a way the conflict came to rest, for Wilson, under pressure from House, agreed that it was "a question upon which there should be the freest discussion and the most liberal exchange of views,"[3] and Lloyd George accepted the compromise that the subject should be open for

[1] Q. ibid, p. 385.   [2] Q. ibid, p. 375.   [3] Q. ibid, p. 386.

discussion at a later stage with the formula, "We are quite willing to discuss the Freedom of the Seas and its application."[1] The later stage was never reached. Almost the last that was heard of the question was the clause in the Allied memorandum, which was accepted by both Wilson and Germany as part of the basis for the armistice: "The freedom of the seas is open to various interpretations, some of which they could not accept. They must therefore reserve to themselves complete freedom on this subject when they enter the peace conference."[2]

But the last had not been heard of Anglo-American naval rivalry, for it came to a head during the Versailles negotiations proper. During the first stage of these, between December, 1918, and February, 1919, British opinion was very much disturbed by the proposal in Congress, with Administration approval, of a bill for naval increases which, with those of 1916, would have given America a total of forty-four post-Jutland capital ships, a force much more formidable than the British fleet. Secretary of the Navy Daniels urged upon the House Naval Committee "incomparably the greatest navy in the world", and a statement of Wilson to *The Times*—that he considered it "essential to the future peace of the world that there should be the frankest possible co-operation, and the most generous understanding between the two English-speaking democracies. . . . We fully understand the special international questions which arise from the fact of your peculiar position as an island empire"[3]—did not go far enough to quiet British alarm. Behind the scenes at the Conference, the British and American sailors were to be found in outspoken disagreement. The Americans demanded parity for their fleet: the British demanded why a country with such very limited strategic commitments required so large a force, and feared that it might presage a period of American expansion. The American demand was a reasonable one, if only on grounds of prestige, as the British were shortly to realize, and the British fears were quite groundless; soon enough the British Admiralty would come back to Mahan's truth, that the naval interests of the two powers were essentially similar, and would finally and irrevocably throw over its traditional claim to a Royal Navy large enough to rule the waves unquestioned.

But this policy did sit curiously on the shoulders of Wilson, alongside the disarmament which he desired, and his private argument, that there had to be American naval strength in the League in order to control Britain in case of need, did give more than a little point to Lloyd George's gibe that the League would be a "mere piece of rhetoric

[1] Q. Davis, p. 258.   [2] Q. Seymour, p. 393.   [3] Q. Davis, p. 261.

if we continue to build dreadnoughts."[1] Wilson probably maintained the naval armaments policy as a useful threat to hold over the heads of his opponents; his external opponents in the way it was now affecting the British, and his domestic opponents in order that he might threaten the taxpayer with vast expenditure on armaments as the only alternative to the League.

But diplomatic bluff can be called, or answered with counter-bluff, and Lloyd George seized on the opportunity presented by Wilson's desire, at the behest of politicians at home, to incorporate the Monroe Doctrine in the League Covenant, to strike a diplomatic bargain. House and Cecil arranged that, in return for British acceptance of the Monroe Doctrine amendment, the President would recommend Congress to shelve the 1918 bill, which it was inclined to do in any case from motives of economy, and would agree that future American naval plans should be talked over with Britain. The situation, which Wilson had largely created, had been in many ways an artificial one, but even after it had been ended, it left a certain emotional legacy. Anglophobe elements, for instance, revelled in continuing the demand for a big navy, lest Great Britain remain "the bully of the world",[2] and in denunciation of the Presidential 'sell-out' to the British Admiralty, while there was natural chagrin in Britain. Since almost the beginning of the century, British opinion had accepted as axiomatic in naval planning that the British Navy would never fight that of the United States; in the broader field of policy she had pursued her friendship with the United States without restraint and had accepted the growing power of America with increasing goodwill. It was, perhaps, inevitable that there should be occasional heart-burnings, and that the most serious ones should be over her surrender of the maritime supremacy which alone in the past had guaranteed her greatness. That she should surrender this to the United States was certainly inevitable; the wonder is, not that it was the occasion of so much British feeling but that it was the cause of so very little.

IX

IN the negotiations for the Treaty proper, also, as in the preliminaries, the agreements of Britain and the United States are far more remarkable than their disagreements. Apart from the naval question just discussed, there were only two really substantial differences between them; one that of indemnity and reparations whose shadow had already been

[1] Q. ibid, p. 264.   [2] Q. ibid, p. 266.

cast before it; the other that of the erstwhile German colonies. There were other minor disagreements, of course, but none was of vital importance.

In the disputes between the British and American delegations, it must be confessed that it was largely the personal determination of Wilson which made the trouble; some members of his own delegation, particularly House, were much readier to compromise than he was, and indeed it was this reasonableness, or diplomatic ability as Harold Nicolson called it, in House, which was responsible for the ultimate breakdown of his remarkable friendship with the President. The *reductio ad absurdum* of this situation, as far as Anglo-American relations are concerned, is to be found when Lord Robert Cecil strongly supported House in urging certain modifications of the Covenant on the reluctant President, lest it be rejected by the Senate. That lack of the *"tact des choses possibles"* which Wilson had already shown in his handling of the opposition at home, and which he was to continue to show in ever more marked degree in his fight with the Senate, until illness made it almost pathological, he also displayed during the Peace Conference. It was ominous for the future when House, taking his final farewell of the President in Paris, said that if Wilson were as conciliatory in dealing with the Senate as he had been with his foreign colleagues in Paris all would be well, and the President replied, "House, I have found one can never get anything in this life that is worth while without fighting for it." House's response, if less flattering than his original premise, contained more truth, "Anglo-Saxon civilization was built up on compromise".[1] Wilson's tone was the same, and was as fatal, as that in which he had declared to the American delegation on its original voyage to France that "the men whom we are about to deal with *did not represent their own people*",[2] an astounding comment for the leader of the party that had just lost the election of 1918 to make about British and French Prime Ministers powerfully sustained by their constituents.

Thus the Anglo-American disagreements, such as they were, tended to be made worse by the dogmatism of the President. But it is not alone in the paucity of disagreements that we can find proof of the fundamental Anglo-American solidarity. Over and over again, *vis à vis* the French, we find Lloyd George and Wilson in substantial agreement; we find it over Poland and Danzig, we find it over the French demand for the

[1] Q. P. Birdsall, *Versailles Twenty Years After* (London, 1941), p. 287.
[2] Q. T. A. Bailey, *Woodrow Wilson and the Lost Peace* (New York, 1944), p. 109.

Rhineland, we find it over the extent of German disarmament. We find it, very obviously, in the eventual solution of the problem created by the insatiable and understandable French thirst for military security. It was eventually slaked, or as nearly so as the Anglo-American bloc would allow, by the tripartite security treaty, which amounted to an Anglo-American guarantee of French territorial integrity. This mutual pledge to go to the aid of their ally if she were subjected to unprovoked aggression, which was, in theory at least, revolutionary for Britain, and in both theory and practice revolutionary for America, was originally suggested by Lloyd George. In Britain the step was strongly supported, but it is doubtful if it had a serious chance of acceptance by the Senate, even without the League; in fact, it was pigeonholed in Committee and was never even formally rejected. Its operation, however, had been made conditional in its effect on ratification by both Britain and the United States, so that it lapsed altogether.

But unquestionably the strongest evidence of Anglo-American accord during the negotiations is to be found in their attitude to the League of Nations. There was broad support for it, in some form or other, in both countries, though it received its chief impetus from the Liberal and Democratic parties respectively, and was strongly opposed by die-hard Tory and Republican minorities. The close connexions and voluminous correspondence between the leaders of the movement in both countries during the war continued a nineteenth-century tradition of long standing, and exemplified a considerable similarity of approach to the problem, which contrasted strongly with that of the French, who conceived of the League as a virtual continuation of the Allied military supremacy under the guise of an international police force. "Anglo-Saxon moralism," as Birdsall calls it, relied on far broader concepts, such as that of the Reign of Law, and mistrusted militaristic coercive ideas, though retaining a kind of respect for their logicality; as Harold Nicolson pungently exclaimed, "I quite admit that the French cannot see beyond their noses; but after all they are *their* noses: and, my word, what they *do* see, they see damned clearly."[1] On the other hand, "The same community of ideas and experience and the same relative immunity from constant military danger have led Great Britain and the United States to develop the practice of judicial arbitration of their international disputes with each other, which is the projection of the reign of law . . . from the national to the international sphere."

In the same sort of way, both Britain and America, though they had

[1] Q. ibid, p. 227.

applied conscription in the war, mistrusted it and thought of it as closely associated with German militarism, whereas the French regarded it as an essential basis of democracy. The British, too, strongly supported Wilson's insistence that the League must be an integral part of the treaty, and agreed that it should be discussed first; they had prepared the ground for it by drawing up preliminary drafts as thorough, if not more thorough, than those of the Americans, which is the principal reason why the Covenant was drafted in so short a time. As Birdsall puts it,

> So completely did the Anglo-American delegations intend to dominate the League Commission . . . President Wilson was its Chairman—that they presented a joint draft, named the "Hurst-Miller Draft" from the British and American legal experts who concocted it, and by sheer weight of numbers and prestige got the Commission to adopt it as the basis of discussion. To complete the humiliation of [the French] . . . , they had not even prepared a French text of this peculiarly Anglo-Saxon document.[1]

This very extensive field of agreement must not be forgotten in discussing the disagreements.

The first of these was over the disposal of the former German colonies. All were agreed that they should not return to Germany; Wilson wished to hand them over to small power trustees under what came to be known as the Mandate system, although his Fourteen Points had merely laid down that "the interests of the populations concerned must have equal weight with the equitable claims of the government"[2] concerned. The difficulty here was that the whole colonial and imperial question was one in which Anglo-American differences went very deep. It was natural enough, for Britain still had an empire, though one which had vastly altered in character during the previous century and a half, while the spirit of 1776 had left an indelible imprint upon the American character; even, as we shall see, at the height of the cordial co-operation of World War II, this became a serious cause of difference between Roosevelt and Churchill.

Yet the problem was by no means insoluble, for the British had in fact sold the Colonial pass long ago; Lloyd George was speaking in the true spirit of British Liberalism when he insisted in his war aims speech on the rights of colonial peoples. The British contention was that the British imperial system was now dedicated to the development of self-government in the colonies, which was just what the mandate system

---

[1] Birdsall, pp. 119-20, 124.   [2] Bemis, p. 156.

demanded; and as proof positive of this the home government pointed to the virtually self-governing Dominions, whose Prime Ministers themselves sat at the Peace Conference, as living witnesses to this truth. Yet so far-reaching were the ramifications of American suspicion that this very fact was used by opponents of the Treaty to beat the Administration with, for they denounced Wilson as the gullible victim of a British plot to give the British Empire six votes to America's one in the League Assembly; it was hard for them, as it has remained for many Americans since, to appreciate—even to credit—the fact of Dominion independence. Nor could they be expected easily to understand the nature of the British Commonwealth of Nations, the most paradoxical, perhaps, of political institutions in history, for its very members can hardly explain it, and its most obvious characteristic is that it combines ،community with diversity and unity with independence. Furthermore, American mistrust was natural, for Britain had only very recently—hardly fifteen years earlier—emerged from another severe bout of imperialism, and her progress towards the ideal she set before her colonies seemed maddeningly slow; she might argue that, as the Americans were finding in the Philippines, caution was necessary in giving peoples self-government before they were educated for it, but she might also—and perhaps did—use this as an excuse for delay, which might be very profitable to her.

The specific problem in 1919 was made more intractable by the fact that the Empire did not speak with a united voice. The government of the United Kingdom was early willing to accept the trusteeship principle, because the mother country had no desire for further colonies, Lloyd George declaring that it exactly described the British colonial system as it then existed. But the Dominions, and in particular Australia and New Zealand, held very different views, which were not easy to reconcile with those of Wilson. These two Dominions were adamant in their demand for certain Pacific Islands, such as Samoa and New Guinea, on grounds of military security; South Africa was desirous of acquiring German South-west Africa; none of the three was prepared to accept any restrictions on its sovereignty. Canada, like Britain, was primarily interested in seeing that the question did not disrupt Anglo-American friendship. It is interesting to note that the issue was in reality one between the Pacific Dominions and the President, rather than between Britain and the United States, but Lloyd George was impelled to raise the matter at the very beginning of the negotiations in order to make sure that the Dominions got what they wanted before a League of Nations could restrict their colonial rights. The question would have

709

been difficult in any case, but was rendered much more so by the strong personal antipathy between Wilson and the Australian Premier, Hughes, who was in his caustic realism the absolute antithesis of the President; needless to say he got on famously with Clemenceau. Wilson inquired on one occasion, "Mr. Hughes, am I to understand that if the whole civilized world asks Australia to agree to a mandate in respect of these islands, Australia is prepared to defy the appeal?" to which Hughes replied, "That's about the size of it, President Wilson." On another, Hughes said, to the face of a number of American delegates, "Some people in this war have not been so near the fire as we British have and, therefore, being unburned, they have a cold, detached view of the situation."[1] He constantly attacked the President's "intolerable" claim "to dictate to us how the world should be governed", for he "had no claim to speak even for his own country."[2] Hughes went so far that he rendered himself by no means popular with some members of the British delegation.

In the end, largely owing to the work of Smuts—South Africa played a moderating part throughout, despite her interest in South-west Africa —a compromise was reached. It classified all the former German colonies as Mandates, but divided them into three categories. Class A Mandates, those of the Arab countries, confined the role of the mandatory power to "administrative advice and assistance"[3]; Class B Mandates were the ones, like those in Central Africa, where the mandatory state was to govern the territory, subject to certain safeguards protecting the subject people; Class C Mandates were those in areas "such as *South-west Africa and certain islands of the South Pacific, which owing to the sparseness of their population, or their small size, or their remoteness from the centres of civilizations, or their geographical contiguity to the mandatory State, and other circumstances, can best be administered under the laws of the mandatory State as integral portions thereof, subject to the safeguards above mentioned in the interests of the indigenous population."[4] All mandatory powers were to report annually to the League. On this basis the colonies were distributed as the British wished, and the Mandate principle was accepted in a modified form; the solution was a compromise between abstract right and actual possession, and as such was accepted reluctantly by the President, but House wrote that "the British had come a long way, and had I been in his place I should have congratulated them over their willingness to meet us half-way."[5]

[1] Q. Birdsall, pp. 72, 242.   [2] Q. ibid, p. 52.   [3] Q. ibid, p. 66.
[4] Memorandum of Smuts: q. ibid, p. 67.   [5] Q. ibid, p. 76.

But the last had not been heard either of Pacific Islands or of Hughes, for the Japanese problem still remained. It had two aspects. The first was the fact that Japan had conquered, and now occupied, the former German islands in the Pacific north of the Equator, and that Britain was bound by treaty to support her claim to them, equally with Japanese support for the claims of the Dominions to the others; furthermore, Japan had claims, which Britain had to support as well, to extensive rights in the Shantung province of China, many of which, though not all, had been formerly exercised by the Germans. Acceptance of the first Japanese claim was implied in the arrangements already made, and Japan got the islands as Class C Mandates.

The second was more complicated, for Wilson, with a traditionally American feeling for Chinese integrity and an intense distaste for further sequestration of her rights, was strongly opposed to the Shantung demands. The Japanese were well aware of this, and utilized to the utmost the lever provided by a second aspect of the whole question, their demand for racial equality. They proposed to insert in the Covenant of the League an article guaranteeing equality of racial treatment among member states; in an extreme form this might, though it is doubtful if they hoped for so much, prevent racial discrimination in immigration—hence the desire of the Senate for an amendment excluding from the purview of the League the domestic concerns of states—but even in a milder version it would be an important matter of prestige or 'face'. They brought pressure to bear at the psychological moment, when the Italian delegates had walked out of the Conference, and Wilson thought that "They are not bluffers, and they will go home unless we give them what they should not have."[1] Personally he was sympathetic towards the plea for racial equality but he—along with the Japanese—was aware of the extent of opposition to the Treaty which acceptance of any such proposition could create in the American West, which felt so strongly on the immigration question.

But the burden of rejection was not in any case to fall on him, for Hughes, a passionate advocate of the "White Australia" policy, was prepared to oppose anything, however tentative, which would endanger it, and announced his intention, if the Japanese demand was accepted, to give the whole matter the fullest publicity at the plenary session of the Conference. This Wilson could not face, both because of the damage it might do to the Treaty as a whole, and because of the storm which it might arouse in California and elsewhere in the United States. But this rebuttal of the Japanese was made easier by the fact that

[1] Q. Bailey, *The Lost Peace*, p. 271.

Britain was forced, by Hughes's attitude as well as by that of Conservative elements at home, to oppose the suggestion, and few things show more clearly how much Britain and America tended to look at things from the same point of view than did the uneasy way in which Cecil and Wilson, the two strongest advocates of the League, between them suppressed the Japanese motion for national equality at the final meeting of the League of Nations Commission on 11 April. Cecil, his eyes fixed on the table in front of him, "regretted that he was not in a position to vote for this amendment";[1] the vote was eleven in favour of the amendment, whereupon Wilson did not ask for the negative vote, but, as Chairman, ruled—quite correctly on technical precedents—that the motion had failed because it did not command unanimous support. Between this meeting and the plenary session of the Conference, however, the Japanese, by threatening to raise the issue there, gained their desires in Shantung. They had used their diplomatic advantage to the full, but at the Washington Naval Conference three years later they were not to be so successful, for the implicit Anglo-American agreement of this time was then to become a positive British abandonment of the Anglo-Japanese alliance, at the behest of the United States. Though in 1919 Japan gained her concrete objectives in the war and emerged from it a dominant Pacific power, on the broad racial issue the pattern of future developments was already visible.

One serious cause of Anglo-American tension at Versailles remains yet to be discussed—it, too, was pregnant with consequences for the future—that of German indemnity and reparations. Here the basic difference was one both of circumstance and personality. Believing, as they did, in German responsibility for the war, a belief shared by most Americans, though by some of them, such as Wilson, with considerably less fervour, the British people held that Germany should be made to pay compensation for losses inflicted, a conviction held even more intensely by the French; indeed, the common people in the Allied countries were for the most part quite prepared to demand that Germany pay the full cost of the war.

Lloyd George, therefore, proposed on 22 January, 1919, that an expert commission be appointed to study "reparation and indemnity", but Wilson was determined to confine the payments to reparation for damages, and obtained the deletion of the wider term "indemnity". He was moved by two motives; one his belief, expressed publicly as one of the supplementary points, that there should be no punitive

[1] Q. Birdsall, p. 98.

damages, or, in other words, indemnity; the other his strong sense of what in fact Germany could pay, without plunging the world into economic disaster. He was, as an American, in a much better position to be impartial than Lloyd George, whose nation had suffered more; already in discussing the indemnity question the latter had aired an argument of which much more will be heard later: "unless President Wilson was prepared to pool the whole cost of the war, and for the United States to take its share of the whole, he was not in a position to reject our claims for indemnity."[1] But Lloyd George was not really prepared to fight for indemnities, because he realized as vividly as Wilson the strict practical limits imposed by what Germany could afford to pay. His sense of the economically possible, however, was not his only motive; he was even more keenly alive to what was politically possible in the then state of British public opinion. In this he was the antithesis of Wilson; his fault was to bow too much to the pressure of mass opinion, Wilson's—for all his protestations—to bow too little.

There is no doubt that the Prime Minister had gone into his recent election campaign impressed with the limits of Germany's capacity to pay; and that he had not lost this impression, but had allowed it to be overwhelmed by the desire to cash in on the popular demand for immense reparations. Was not the very slogan of the campaign, "Hang the Kaiser"? To have expected him to risk his political prospects by damping down popular ardour with douches of cold economics, which was the only completely honest course and the one Wilson might have followed in his place, would have been to expect too much of a man of his character and background; but he must certainly be criticized for "instinctively" raising "the pitch" of his campaign when he saw which way the wind was blowing, and for failing to check the more extreme of his followers. Even on this score, however, he is not without defence, for he covered himself in every case by quiet provisos; as Bailey writes, he said in effect: "They shall pay to the utmost farthing—*if they can do so without delaying the economic revival of the world. They shall pay the maximum possible—but what is the maximum possible must be ascertained by financial experts.*"[2] The measure of his blame is the extent to which his provisos were quiet and unnoticed, which he knew they would be, and the extent to which he whipped up the popular clamour; the extent of both was considerable. His own view was expressed light-heartedly in his remark on arrival in Paris: "Heaven only knows what I would have had to promise them if the campaign had lasted a week longer."[3] Thus he accepted without much of a

[1] Q. ibid, p. 239. [2] *The Lost Peace*, p. 244. [3] Q. ibid.

713

struggle the deletion of the word "indemnity", and later of the phrase "war costs", on which Wilson insisted.

But this was to prove merely a verbal victory for the President, since there yet remained the task of determining the nature and extent of "reparation". Here Lloyd George, under powerful and specific pressure from his supporters at home during the course of the negotiations, demanded that war pensions and separation allowances should be accepted as part of the civilian damages for which Germany was to be liable. This demand was a powerful one emotionally and lost nothing in the telling, particularly on the silver tongue of the liberal Smuts, whom Wilson admired, and it made a powerful appeal to the humane sentiments which the President concealed beneath his cold exterior; he brushed aside the objections of his experts and advisers, and accepted the suggestion. This was, given his desire to restrict the total claims, a serious error, for it greatly raised their potential ceiling, but there was still hope of a reasonable settlement, for the Americans were pressing for an expert evaluation of what Germany could pay over a fixed number of years, and the acceptance of this as the limit of what would be exacted. Estimates of this total sum were wildly divergent, ranging from $200,000 million by some French calculators, to $120,000 million by some Englishmen, and $30,000 million by the Americans. Even the last figure proved far too high, but no such ceiling was in the end imposed, and the question was left to a Reparations Commission to decide; America would have had a powerful voice on this body, and might well have kept the sum lower than it eventually was, but, in the supreme irony of events, she did not even participate. Who is to apportion the degree of blame in these circumstances between President and Prime Minister?

America refrained from using the one means at her disposal for lowering the total sum, because she believed it to be against her interest, just as the Allies did not cease to press for vast reparations, because they believed that course to be in their interest. As the American historian Bailey writes:

> There was one possible way by which the negotiators could save face, and in some measure justify a manageable sum. If the Americans would renounce all claims to the approximately $10,000 million which the Allies had borrowed from them, then the Allies could reduce by that much the amount that Germany could reasonably be expected to pay. This proposal was made repeatedly at the Conference, and repeatedly after the Conference. Wilson opposed it, his economic advisers opposed it, the United States Treasury opposed it, the United

States Congress opposed it, and the American taxpayer opposed it. Our perfectly understandable attitude on the debt problem had a great deal to do with the reparations muddle.[1]

The reparations question ended on a queer but illuminating note, which at bottom emphasizes Anglo-American agreement, but on the surface had the appearance of yet another Anglo-American disagreement, exaggerated by the divergent characters of the two leaders. Lloyd George, sensitive as always to political pressures, even of the international variety, became towards the end of the negotiations apprehensive that Germany would not sign the Treaty and began to consider certain amendments to it, including a lowering of reparations. This was not simply fear on his part of the outcome if Germany were obdurate, but the first sign of that sympathy towards Germany which was to haunt Britain for more than fifteen years to come. Wilson's attitude to this change in Lloyd George's attitude was typical:

> Well, I don't want to seem to be unreasonable, but my feeling is this: that we ought not, with the object of getting it signed, make changes in the treaty, if we think it embodies what we were contending for. . . . [T]hat makes me very sick. . . . These people that overrode our judgment and wrote things into the treaty that are now the stumbling blocks, are now falling over themselves to remove the stumbling blocks. Now, if they ought not to have been there, I say, remove them, but I say do not remove them merely for the sake of having the treaty signed.[2]

His whole character lies revealed in those words; the strength of his moral convictions; his determination, not to say resentful obstinacy; and his indifference to means in his concentration on ends. Yet the divergence, which came to nothing since the voice of his electorate still spoke louder to Lloyd George than that of Germany, should not blind us to the fact that beneath it there lies a common Anglo-American ability, naturally unshared by France, to stand back a little from the catastrophic events of Europe and see them in some sort of perspective.

X

THE last chapter of the Wilsonian tragedy in Anglo-American relations alone remains, the repudiation of the Treaty of Versailles and the withdrawal of the United States into isolationism. Responsibility for this cannot be precisely apportioned, but it must be borne both by Wilson

[1] Ibid, p. 246-7.   [2] Q. Birdsall, p. 261.

and by his opponents. These fell into two main groups, both predominantly Republican; the "irreconcilables", led by men like William E. Borah of Idaho, who were convinced isolationists with no use for the Treaty or the entry into world affairs which it involved; and the strict "reservationists", led by Henry Cabot Lodge of Massachusetts, who favoured entry into the League subject to a number of specific reservations. Personal feeling undoubtedly had something to do with the bitterness of the dispute, particularly between Wilson and Lodge, but it went much deeper than that. Party loyalty, for instance, played a very important part because of the imminence of the 1920 election, and because the Republicans controlled both the House and the Senate. This was of particular consequence because the legislature had resented what seemed to it the arrogant way in which Wilson had wielded the executive power, particularly during the war.

These things should have warned Wilson now, as they should have warned him at Paris, but the obstinate streak in him, exaggerated by the illness which fell upon him in the midst of his campaign of appeal to the people, and the isolation it involved, made him resist all suggestions of compromise. Convinced of his rectitude, and not believing that the Senate would dare to refuse the Treaty in its entirety if he offered them nothing else, he rejected all the reservations proposed by his enemies, while those proposed by his supporters, though they covered much of the important ground of Republican objection, were rejected by his opponents in their turn. Neither could a majority be obtained for the Treaty without any reservations.

On 19 November, 1919, the Senate twice refused to ratify the Treaty with Lodge's reservations (39 to 55 and 41 to 51), once refused the proposal for reconsideration with Democratic reservations (41 to 50), and finally failed to pass the Treaty without reservations (38 to 53). The crux of the disagreement was, and remained, Lodge's reservation to Article 10, which disavowed the obligations of the United States to act under the League except with the consent of Congress; all efforts to concert bi-partisan reservations came to grief on Wilson's refusal to accept this reservation, and on the refusal of Lodge and his followers to accept the article without the reservation. Though all these votes were taken after 5.30 p.m. one evening, they were preceded by four months, and followed by a further four months, of exhaustive discussion. In this way a great deal of time was consumed, and this was precisely what the Republicans wished, for they, far better than Wilson, had gauged the tenor of public opinion; they realized that the longer the delay, the more completely the traditional habits of peace-time American foreign policy would re-assert themselves. It has been said that the most formidable of Wilson's opponents were dead statesmen, and it is true also that the farther men got from the passions of the war the more they saw all that it had cost them, and the more they harkened to the voices of the Founding Fathers warning them against entangling alliances. The real answer to the question, "Did Americans want the League?", seems to be that they would have accepted it, possibly with certain reservations, had they been called upon to decide soon after the war; it is vital to realize that the whole Treaty of Versailles had been negotiated and signed within six short months of the Armistice, whereas it was two years after it that the Democrats were decisively defeated in the election of 1920. Wisely from their point of view, the opponents of the League foresaw the inevitable slump in idealism, an occurrence which Wilson temperamentally could neither envisage nor admit.

He never wavered in his belief that the people would support him to the hilt; he therefore instructed his supporters, at every turn, not merely to reject the reservations proposed by the Republicans, but to oppose the Treaty itself as long as the reservations were attached, in the expectation that the whole Treaty and nothing but the Treaty could then be passed. Whether by his will, or the efforts of his entourage to protect him from influences which would disturb him or which they mistrusted, all appeals, intended to bring home the realities of the situation to him and to persuade him to yield a little in order to gain much, were rejected; already, long before his illness, the influence of Lansing and, even more important, of House had been spurned, and now House's three letters of moderate counsel went unanswered.

His obstinacy made it almost impossible for his supporters to act well or unitedly. They eventually fell, like his opponents, into two main groups; those Democrats, mostly from the South, who never wavered in party loyalty to Wilson, but rejected both reservations and Treaty with reservations; and those who, known as mild reservationists, disobeyed their party leader, in what they believed to be the true interests of the country, by voting finally for the Treaty with reservations, as the best solution possible. Thus in a final vote on 17 March, 1920, on the Treaty with the reservations, the reservationists, strict and mild, Republican and dissident Democrat, mustered 49 yeas to 35 nays from Democratic loyalists and Republican Irreconcilables, so that the Treaty failed to obtain the necessary two-thirds majority. Efforts at reconsideration came to nothing because there was no doubt in anyone's mind that the Democrat loyalists would not waver from the commands of the President; thus the decision was virtually Wilson's own. It was what he wished, for he had talked of taking the issue to the people in "a great and solemn referendum"[1] in the election of 1920. This was not what the election was, for, though the Democratic candidate, Cox, came out for the League, he was not a Wilsonian, and Harding, his opponent, was neither clearly for nor clearly against it. Furthermore, there were other issues, as opponents of the League foresaw, which were perhaps of equal if not greater significance to the people, who were tired of the long drawn-out wrangle over the Treaty.

Harding may not have used the best of English, but he expressed the feeling of the electorate exactly when he said, "America's present need is not heroics but healing; not nostrums but normalcy; not revolutions but restorations. . . ."[2] The result was a landslide in which he carried the country by a plurality of six million votes. It has been claimed with some justice that this was not a vote against the League; this may be true, but there can be no doubt that by this time the people did not want it. Isolation was a part of normalcy, and they wanted normalcy. They were content to slide back swiftly into the old ways; they were no longer, even if they had ever been, in the mood for experiments, and least of all for a great revolution in foreign policy. It can be no surprise to the student of their history that it was so; men seldom learn at the first attempt from their experience in politics. A still more decisive lesson in the realities of America's position in the world of the twentieth century was necessary before the moral could be finally absorbed.

In these great events Anglo-American relations played a not inconsiderable part. In the first place, much of the opposition to the Treaty came from professional Anglophobes, led by the newspapers of William Randolph Hearst, the ill feeling of which was nourished by the bickering that went on between the Press of the two countries. In the unrestrained state of public emotion left by the war, there developed what Bailey calls "an utterly senseless debate as to who had won"[3] it; for this the British must bear the chief blame, since individuals, from Sir Douglas Haig down to Horatio Bottomley, were stupid or unscrupulous enough to give free rein to their tongues on the issue, and might have done immense harm had things in America taken a different course. As it was, events were controlled by much more powerful forces.

One of these was the Irish. It seemed that only the outbreak of

[1] Q. Bailey, p. 678. [2] Q. ibid.
[3] T. A. Bailey, *Woodrow Wilson and the Great Betrayal* (New York, 1945), p. 29.

hostilities in 1914 had prevented a revolt in Ulster against the Liberal Home Rule Bill, but in the end came the Southern Irish rebellion of 1916, and two years later the outbreaks of terrorism, which soon became mutual, known as the "Anglo-Irish War". At its height, negotiation for the Peace began at Paris, and strong pressure was brought to bear on Wilson—who tended to resent it—by Irish-Americans, who wished him to obtain self-determination for Ireland; in 1919 De Valera toured the United States stirring up feeling, and the House of Representatives passed, by 261 votes to 41, a resolution declaring that, "It is the earnest hope of the Congress of the United States of America that the Peace Conference now sitting at Paris . . . will favourably consider the claims of Ireland to self-determination."[1] Though Wilson had earlier pressed the British to settle the Irish question, even he did not attempt so quixotic a task as this at Versailles, but his refusal aroused Irish hate at home. On 18 March, 1920, apparently in an effort to discredit the whole idea of reservations to the Versailles Treaty, a Democratic Senator, Gerry of Rhode Island, moved an astounding reservation to the Treaty, with which it had nothing whatever to do, putting the Senate on record as favouring self-determination and independence for Ireland. To his credit, Lodge, though Massachusetts had a very influential Irish vote, fought the reservation vehemently, but it was passed by 38 votes to 36. Apart from its political irresponsibility, it accorded ill with the earlier reservation, already accepted, which excluded domestic questions from the consideration of the League, but it gives the full measure of the lengths to which Irish Anglophobia would still go. In 1921 a treaty was signed between Great Britain and Ireland which gave her dominion status, but allowed Ulster to opt out, a course which she followed. Anglo-Irish disagreements were not over, but the real sting had gone out of them. From this time forward there was little to keep the worst Anglophobia of Irish-Americans alive.

The only other reservation that was directly aimed at Britain was the fourteenth, which asserted that the United States was not bound by any action of the League in which any member cast more than one vote, a provision directed against the votes of the five British Dominions in the Assembly. Behind this reservation were mustered all the anti-British forces, which denounced the League unceasingly as a mere instrument of British policy, as a means by which, in their usual underhand diplomatic manner, the English sought to re-establish the control over America which they had lost in 1776. Even this reservation was a good deal milder than many which were suggested, such as the one

[1] Mowat, *American Entente*, p. 197.

which proposed that the United States should have forty-eight votes. The incident is characteristic of the methods of the anti-British bloc in America. Seldom is an outright attack on British influence made; rather, on the plea that British diplomacy is always the most subtle and devious in the world in its efforts to assert Britain's dominance over the United States, some technical question of this nature is mooted and on it a passionate appeal is made to the deep traditional wells of anti-British feeling among Americans. It is characteristic that Lodge, though he had often attacked Britain violently in the past for reasons seldom unconnected with the number of Irish votes in his state, was not himself anti-British, but just the reverse; Henry Adams wrote of him—to his chagrin it is true—that he was "Boston incarnate . . . English to the last fibre of his thought—saturated with English literature, English tradition, English taste".[1] It is characteristic, too, that the supporters of the motion were hardly amenable to reason. Their opponents pointed out in vain that the British Dominions were now virtually independent; that Canada would strongly resent being deprived of a vote; that America had satellites of her own, less worthy and less independent, such as Cuba, Panama and Liberia, some of which could hardly be enfranchised when Australia was not; and finally, that while Britain had six votes in the Assembly she did not have more than one in the all-important Council. In the final vote the reservation was carried by 57 to 20.

What was the effect of all this upon Britain? In the first place, it should be noted that her disillusionment came by easy stages, at each of which it was permissible to hope that things might yet turn out well: after the first Senate votes in November, and again after the second vote in March, it was still possible not to despair, and only after the Republican victory in November of the next year was the die known to be irrevocably cast. By then men had become accustomed to the idea. In the second place, Englishmen found many things on which they could cast the blame for the catastrophe, which differed according to their point of view; supporters of Wilson blamed the Republicans, those who mistrusted him blamed his own obstinacy, students of America blamed the isolationist tradition and the two-thirds rule. Many there were, strong among the Tories, who actually rejoiced at the failure of a League which they regarded as idealistic and impractical, and in which they in any case proposed to put no faith. In the third place, over all there did brood a certain understanding of America's desire to keep her hands free—to preserve her isolation. Such a policy might be regretted

[1] *Education of Henry Adams*, pp. 419-20.

by Britons from their own practical point of view, but it was too akin to much of their own experience to be regarded in quite the same spirit of untrammelled hatred as that of the French, who saw it simply as a betrayal. After all, were not voices, like that of Beaverbrook, still being raised in their own midst to advocate a policy of imperial isolation? They looked upon it, as Bailey writes, "With sorrow rather than with anger."[1]

This does not mean that the attitude they adopted was a purely passive one. There was, certainly, little that they could do, but what little was possible they did. There can be little doubt, not only that they would have accepted America's participation in the League subject to the Lodge reservations and that they indicated this pretty clearly, but also that they made some efforts to influence the American situation for the better. These attempts hinge on the mysterious mission of the now ailing Grey as a Special Ambassador to the United States in 1919. Ostensibly he was sent to discuss Ireland and naval armaments as causes of Anglo-American tension, but without question he aimed to deal with the more fundamental matter of the Treaty.

The difficulties arising out of the reservations were threefold; the general reservations against American participation, the Irish question and the six vote question. On the first, there can be little doubt that the mass of British opinion, including that of the Government, would have favoured any rather than no American participation; indeed, such was the dictate of common sense, for an acorn is better than no oak at all, and it might be hoped that growth would occur. As to the Irish reservation, offensive though it was, it had no practical effect, and could be written off as a twisting of the lion's tail with which the British were already thoroughly familiar. Even the six vote question, if it could not be overcome by negotiation, could in the opinion of many be ignored, for it merely stated that America would not be bound by any action involving the six British votes. On the reservations as a whole, Lloyd George in February, 1920, declared explicitly that as long as the other powers were not expressly required to agree to American conditions, the United States might make them what she pleased; and on 19 March just before the final vote, the Senate adopted a Lodge proposal that provided for silent acquiescence in, rather than written acceptance of, the reservations by the Allies. Thus it can hardly be doubted that Britain would have accepted the Treaty as ratified, almost whatever its form, and that both Wilson and his opponents knew this.

Grey proceeded on his mission with great caution, remarking that

[1] *The Great Betrayal*, p. 205.

721

he was well aware of the fate of one of his predecessors, Sackville-West. Grey was a figure to whom Wilson had once been sympathetic; yet the President refused even to see him to receive his credentials, although he was having public visitors. As a result of this treatment, Grey retired quietly after three months without having accomplished anything. It is hard to escape the conclusion that in pursuance of his policy of forcing the Senate to take their medicine, in the form of the treaty, the whole treaty and nothing but the treaty, Wilson deliberately refrained from seeing Grey because he knew he might urge compromise.

Some time after his return to England, when the act could hardly be construed as improper, even though he was still technically Ambassador, Grey wrote a letter to *The Times*, which, he emphasized, expressed only his personal opinion, but which he would hardly have published if it had conflicted strongly with the views of the Government. He said in effect that the League needed the moral force of American participation, and that a willing partner with limited obligations was much better than an unwilling partner with unlimited obligations; he emphasized that in practice the reservations might never be invoked. Thus far it was plainly an appeal to Britain to accept the reservations, knowledge of which intention on her part might help to break the deadlock in America. But he went farther than that, and stated that the actions of the opposition to the Treaty were largely due to the long tradition of isolationism in America, and to her fear of foreign entanglements; if, however, he continued, America stayed out of the League it would become merely an alliance of victors, the old order would return, and America would again be sucked into the inevitable war. This was plainly addressed to the American people; it was an appeal to them over the heads of their leader, of just the kind that Wilson had so unsuccessfully made to the Italians over Fiume. It was equally unsuccessful, for Wilson was not only strengthened in his obstinate resolution, but exceedingly enraged, and it was on his shoulders that the decision lay. The Irreconcilables found ample food for their fears in Grey's assertion that in practice all would be well, and the Anglophobes cried out against British interference, but the reservationists were jubilant, for it destroyed a large portion of their opponent's case. Lloyd George denied all knowledge of the Grey letter, and the incident was soon forgotten in the catastrophe it had sought to avert. It places, however, a yet greater burden of blame upon Wilson for the failure of the League, and it is interesting in Anglo-American relations because it shows how wisely cautious the British had become in their handling of affairs between the two countries.

Thus did America refuse the Treaty and abandon Europe to its fate. For peoples who had just emerged from four years of gruelling war and who had come to expect, many of them, a new earth with a new order in it under American auspices, it could be a shattering blow. For France and for others it was so, but in a way it is remarkable how little it affected Britain in any direct sense, and how little it altered the pattern of Anglo-American relations. It was certainly a disillusionment which bit deep into British experience, but it was one which they had more than half expected. Any bitterness, which was felt at the state of the world and the ultimate failure of the League, tended to be directed against wider and more obvious targets than the American defection, the reasons for which were clear enough to the British. Besides, Britain had learned well the lesson that she should not expect too much from America, and she was not surprised when she did not get it. She had, after all, received a good deal; she had received invaluable and whole-hearted aid at a supreme crisis, and her national enemies, Germany and Russia, were both, for the moment at any rate, laid low. Her own economic and moral condition, though seriously weakened, was infinitely better than that of France, and she could face the future without undue misgivings. The withdrawal of the United States from participation in the League, when all was said and done, merely created one of the great "might have beens" of history; it marked the first failure of an ideal which would doubtless suffer many more before ever it became reality. And Britain slipped back with ease into the familiar pattern of Anglo-American relations which had developed in the previous two decades. Her acceptance of American economic superiority and naval equality became explicit; to seek American friendship remained the prime motive of her policy. The American self-denying ordinance was accepted at its face value, and blinded Britons, excessively perhaps, to the realities of American interests and power, which would re-emerge in time of war; but for the present it was still clear that the friendly neutrality of the United States was infinitely preferable to her enmity, and this Britain sought without overmuch concern about ultimate problems. All this no doubt was a second best: it implied a certain disillusion. But is not disillusion the common lot of twentieth-century man? In any case, American friendship was before long to be proved a good deal less disillusioning than the actions of a resurgent and fanatical Germany.

CHAPTER SEVENTEEN

ISOLATIONISM (1921-39)

THE policy of the United States between 1921 and 1937 may be described as one of deliberate withdrawal from the affairs of the world. If President Wilson had succeeded in one thing, it was in convincing the American people that they had entered the war for moral reasons, so that when they repudiated him and all his works they naturally reverted with great fervour to their traditional belief that Europe, and European politics in particular, constituted a hopeless sink of iniquity which Americans were very fortunate to be clear of. They shook its dust from their feet with gladness and vowed never to become embroiled in its affairs again. That America, whether she willed or no, was an integral part of Western civilization, and that her great and increasing strength would impel her, if she was to go her own accustomed or chosen way, to participate in its affairs even if she did not desire to do so, was not realized by any except a very small, though sometimes vocal, minority. George Kennan writes, "I see the most serious fault of our past policy formulation to lie in something that I might call the legalistic-moralistic approach to international problems. This approach runs like a red skein through our foreign policy of the last fifty years."[1] This attitude of mind blinded the mass of Americans to the remorseless realities of power and to the responsibilities which theirs carried with it. In retrospect, these years of withdrawal seem to be years in which America was meticulously concerned to create for herself an artificial isolation from international affairs, and one which we can see was destined inevitably to collapse before the invading pressures of the real world; just as surely as the United States was drawn into the vortex of World War I by the logic of events, so was her protective shell of isolation to be ruthlessly crushed by the sequence of happenings which ended in Pearl Harbour. As Mahan would have told his countrymen, this attempt to put back the clock and to rebuild in the modern world the conditions of independent action which America had enjoyed in the nineteenth century was necessarily doomed to failure; this dream-world was to prove just as visionary as the material

[1] G. F. Kennan, *American Diplomacy, 1900-1950* (London, 1952), p. 95.

Utopia which haunted the imagination of these same Americans in the dizzy era of prosperity which preceded the Great Depression.

But the hollowness of this structure was not apparent to most Americans; as Churchill pungently puts it, "Nor can the United States escape the censure of history. Absorbed in their own affairs and all the abounding interests, activities and accidents of a free community, they simply gaped at the vast changes which were taking place in Europe, and imagined they were no concern of theirs."[1] It is not perhaps surprising that, by persistent repetition of their intention to isolate themselves, they could come to believe so desirable a dispensation possible; it is more remarkable that they were able to convince most people in Britain that it was so. Here perhaps is an example of the opposite of wishful thinking, for the British people could have had no wish more dear than that the United States should once again exert its full influence in world affairs; for them in the end such an occurrence could have meant little but good. As the shadows in the world deepened it would have been comforting to think that the power which had saved them once would, and for the same reasons, save them again. Churchill has admitted that this hope was one of the most powerful which bore him up in the first period of World War II, and no doubt he was conscious of it even before that, but for the most part men put it aside. America had so repeatedly and loudly avowed her determination to remain aloof, that it was accepted almost without question that she could do so. Indeed, it was hard for Englishmen, and public men in particular, to express any other view; it would have been awkward for them to predict American intervention in the face of such blunt and reiterated assertions, and would merely have provided fresh fuel for the fires of Anglophobia. Furthermore, of course, this American auto-suggestion did unquestionably slow down the process of American participation when war came; it made the President's task of bringing home the realities of the situation to his people a great deal more difficult. The results of the process in the history of the period are interesting, for the causes of World War II, given the situation in 1921, can be set out almost without reference to the power which was to emerge its chief victor. Of the resulting lack of diplomatic experience she—and the world—still occasionally feels the results.

Though unquestionably correct in its broad outline, this analysis of the years 1921 to 1937 as years of isolationism in the United States cannot be made without modification. It must not be forgotten that in some international matters American administrations took the lead;

---

[1] W. S. Churchill, *The Second World War*, I, pp. 60-1.

they did so in naval disarmament and in Far Eastern policy, both at the time of the Washington Conference and later. Thus isolationism was more pronounced towards Europe than towards China and Japan, and though it was, under the Democrats, the European theatre of war which first began to break down American neutrality in 1940-1, it was the outbreak of hostilities in the Pacific which brought the United States irrevocably into World War II.

But of the overall truth of the thesis of American withdrawal there can be no doubt. If proof were needed of the popular nature of America's rejection of the League, it is amply to be found in her first ostentatious refusal of contact with it. In July, 1921, Congress ended the war by a unilateral resolution, and the Administration of Harding declared that America would have nothing to do with the League. This policy was continued by his successors with only minor alterations. These took the form of a gradual and cautious participation in some of the strictly non-political activities centred in Geneva; in 1924 American "observers" took part in the Opium Conference, and by 1930 had been associated with more than forty meetings of the same kind. After that time the "observer" policy, which Clemenceau described as being represented by an ear but not a mouth, was occasionally and gingerly extended to political matters, but there was never any question of America joining the League. Even movements towards participation in the World Court, though in accordance with American traditions and supported by every inter-war President, were always foiled in one way or another by the die-hard isolationists, because, though autonomous, the Court smacked of association with the League.

The strength of public feeling which developed against the League is also clearly evinced in the general policies of the inter-war administrations. To the anti-League policy of Harding even so strong a personality as Charles Evans Hughes had to conform; he had himself been one of the Republicans who signed a manifesto during the election declaring that a vote for Harding was a vote for the League, but in his four years as Secretary of State his international initiatives were not only independent of Geneva, but made with his gaze for the most part fixed upon the Pacific. Coolidge was no less resolved than his predecessor to refrain from European entanglements, particularly in view of his strong views on the War Debts question, and his Secretary of State, Frank Kellogg, did not swim against the stream, though he was sufficient of an internationalist to sponsor many arbitration and conciliation treaties, and to serve later, like Hughes, on the World Court. But the most striking evidence is furnished by Hoover's Presidency. A man of very cosmopolitan experience—in contrast to his predecessors—he had achieved an international reputation in the semi-diplomatic tasks of European relief during and after the war, while he had also been a declared supporter of the League in the campaign of 1920. But he announced in his inaugural address that the United States would not join the League, and there seems no doubt that he had himself become convinced of its inadvisability. Certainly the public was stronger than ever in its determination, for Stimson, Hoover's Secretary of State, himself records how much his hands were tied during the Manchurian crisis by the "violent party feeling" aroused in the previous decade by the League; he went even farther and wrote in retrospect, "Even the most normal and rational steps which might be taken by an American Secretary of State in such a situation were certain to be the subject of critical scrutiny and possible attack from some of his countrymen."[1] Public demand went much farther than mere dislike of the League, and insisted upon the most scrupulous isolationism on the part of its government.

This became abundantly clear on the accession of Roosevelt to office. Not only were he and his Secretary of State, Cordell Hull, Democrats and disciples of Wilson, but he had been Vice-Presidential candidate in the election of 1920 on a League of Nations platform. But, even had he not been overwhelmed with domestic problems, there is little doubt that he could have made no serious attempt to join the League, and in fact, an articulate public opinion, dominated by isolationists like the venerated Borah, forced through during his first two terms the neutrality legislation which marked the high tide of American isolationism. Roosevelt did not attempt to veto it, but, as the world crisis deepened, made increasingly strenuous efforts to evade or modify it, and to educate American opinion in the dangers of its blind adherence to an outworn dogma. All his efforts to halt the flood of events towards war were grievously weakened, stultified almost, by the knowledge which his opponents had of an American pacifism so strong that, on the outbreak of war in 1939, no less than 99 per cent of the people of the United States favoured the maintenance of neutrality. There can be no doubt that this period can properly be characterized as one dominated by American isolationism.

Not that pacifism was by any means confined to America in these years; the British people were just as willing, if they could, to avoid looking reality in the face. Very many of the 11 million votes cast for

[1] H. L. Stimson, *The Far Eastern Crisis* (London, 1936), p. 39.

the Peace Ballot—the name itself is significant—of 1935, held under the auspices of the League of Nations Union in Britain, were cast in despite of or in ignorance of, and not because of, the clause in it which supported military sanctions. If public opinion rejected the Hoare-Laval compromise peace in Abyssinia, it went very far in fervent support of a subsequent policy which was as ostrich-like as isolationism—the appeasement programme of Neville Chamberlain. Unfortunately for Britain, the English Channel, which had enabled her in 1815 to withdraw herself from entangling European alliances, as surely if not as dramatically as the United States did in 1919, was no longer an effective barrier in time of war; air raids and food rationing had made that British isolationism, for which some still called, an obvious anachronism. Even Stanley Baldwin was forced to admit—despite the lapse of the Anglo-American guarantee to France—that Britain's frontier was on the Rhine; of this fact the Locarno pact with France and Germany, as well as Italy and Belgium, was the visible manifestation. The pact reflected, too, as did the increasingly parochial League, the way in which the attention of British policy was focused, as far as was possible for an imperial power, upon the European scene.

Her statesmen succumbed to the hypnotic effect of repeated American assertions that they were no longer interested in or concerned with the affairs of the Old World. The result in Anglo-American relations was intriguing. Though American friendship remained the fundamental basis of British policy; though her very existence at sea was bound up with that friendship; and though the social and economic impact of America upon her was far greater than it had ever been—in the political sense that friendship was accepted as purely and absolutely passive. Gone from the conscious mind of Britons was any hope, such as had blossomed in the early years of the century and even borne fruit in 1917, of American alliance or association; neutrality, benevolent neutrality perhaps, was all that could be expected. Hostility remained unthinkable, but active co-operation in the international sphere was almost equally so. This encouraged a curious and myopic absorption in European affairs, which even led British policy to fall behind that of America in the Far East; the British Government were not prepared to react vigorously to distant threats, when they could expect no corresponding American assistance in their mounting troubles nearer home. This curious duality, by which America remained an essential prop of our national life but was ignored in everyday matters of policy, was not altogether distasteful to many Englishmen, including some of their leaders. The very intensity of American social, cultural, and economic pressures upon the sister democracy, through the manifold technological developments of the day, produced a natural reaction; though American individuals were usually welcomed and though outright British political animosity to America was hardly to be thought of, there was still a strong streak of anti-Americanism among Britain's upper and middle classes.

Baldwin, the first dominating figure of the period, was remarkable for his capacity to absorb and express the sentiments of the majority of his countrymen, and his cast of mind was as English as it could be; his attitude to the United States, as to so much in foreign affairs, was curiously negative. Austen Chamberlain, his Foreign Secretary at the time of Locarno, however, is described by Baldwin's biographer as "far too friendly to France: too little friendly to the United States."[1] Neville Chamberlain, his half-brother, who was inclined to shallow and rigid, but self-confident, judgements in world affairs, took America at its own international valuation and expected nothing from her— indeed appeared to desire nothing. There were good hopes for Anglo-American relations, too, during his premiership, for it fell within the early years of Roosevelt's presidency, and his Foreign Secretary, Anthony Eden, worked hard to improve them. Indeed, it was as a result of an incredible rebuff by Chamberlain to an offer by Roosevelt —made at considerable political risk in view of the American domestic mistrust of such a project—to sponsor an international conference with the dictators at Washington in January, 1938, that Eden first contemplated the resignation which he later carried through. It is hard to acquit Chamberlain either of wearing two faces, or of fantastic short-sightedness at this time, for exactly three days after his reply to Roosevelt's offer, he wrote to an American cousin of his stepmother:

> I am just now in closer relations with the American Government than has been the case within my recollection. I have made more than one attempt, while I have been Prime Minister, to draw them even closer still and I have had more than one disappointment. But I fully recognize that goodwill on the part of the U.S. Government is not wanting, the trouble is that public opinion in a good part of the States still believes it possible for America to stand outside Europe and watch it disintegrate, without being materially affected herself. I can well understand that frame of mind. . . . Indeed, we have a similar school of thought here. . . . Yet . . . we are too close to . . . remain safe in isolation. In spite of my disappointment, I intend to keep on doing everything I can to promote Anglo-American understanding and

[1] G. M. Young, *Stanley Baldwin* (London, 1952), p. 139.

co-operation. Not because I want or expect America to pull our chestnuts out of the fire for us; in any co-operation we shall always do our part, and perhaps more than our share. But I believe that Americans and British want the same fundamental things in the world, peace, liberty, order. . . . U.S.A. and U.K. in combination represent a force so overwhelming that the mere hint of the possibility of its use is sufficient to make the most powerful of dictators pause, and that is why I believe that co-operation between our two countries is the greatest instrument in the world for the preservation of peace.

It would be impossible to find an expression more typical of the attitude of the average Englishman to America in these years: all the essential elements in the friendly Anglo-American relationship are present, but any hope of practical assistance from America has been abandoned. As Chamberlain wrote in 1937, "it is always best and safest to count on nothing from the Americans but words."[1]

It is difficult to blame the Briton in the street for this view, for it was the result of America's own words and actions, but for the British Prime Minister it was a different matter. Very different from this staggering refusal of Roosevelt's offer was Churchill's approach to American opinion in 1940 and 1941, very different his intervention at Fulton, Missouri, in 1946. Let him, with dramatic justice, pen the epitaph on this incident:

That Mr. Chamberlain, with his limited outlook and inexperience of the European scene, should have possessed the self-sufficiency to wave away the proffered hand stretched out across the Atlantic leaves one, even at this date, breathless with amazement. The lack of all sense of proportion, and even of self-preservation, which this episode reveals in an upright, competent, well-meaning man, charged with the destinies of our country and all who depended upon it, is appalling. One cannot to-day even reconstruct the state of mind which would render such gestures possible.[2]

The redeeming interlude of the inter-war period in Anglo-American relations is, interestingly enough, that of Ramsay Macdonald's premiership, for he had all that respect for the American democracy which was often to be found in radicals bred in the nineteenth century. His visit to the United States in 1929 was a popular triumph, and laid the foundation for the London Naval Conference which was, even if only a limited general success, a distinct Anglo-American one. Thus at the governmental level the tone of Anglo-American relations, though by

[1] Keith Feiling, *The Life of Neville Chamberlain* (London, 1946), pp. 322-3, 325.   [2] *Second World War*, I, p. 199.

no means really cold, was less warm between the wars than before or after them.

Nor did routine diplomatic representation do very much to better that tone, though it did little to render it worse. Both countries reverted to the practice of sending ambassadors of the normal type, career diplomats from Britain and political appointees from America. After a brief and in some ways stormy tenure by a politician, Sir Auckland Geddes, the Washington post was held by two professionals; from 1924-1930 by Sir Esmé Howard, and from 1930-1939 by Sir Ronald Lindsay. Both performed their necessary functions with quiet efficiency.

The same could not be said of the first American Ambassador in London, George Harvey, a journalist who was very full of patriotic rodomontade and who aroused such mistrust even among members of his own party that he was hastily recalled on Harding's death; like his opposite number, Geddes, he was perhaps unfortunate to encounter the first blast of post-war Anglo-American disillusionment, but he did little to temper it. Frank B. Kellogg, his successor, had hardly arrived before he was appointed Secretary of State and was succeeded in his turn by Alanson Bigelow Houghton, who came from a very successful embassy in Berlin and was as great a success as Kellogg had promised to be. His demand there for fair play for the Germans had struck a by-now sympathetic chord in Britain, and his lighter vein was appealing too. In his first public speech he declared:

> If I must say something about Anglo-American relations, let me, following the conventions of a wide-open diplomacy, confide to you that . . . I find after diligent search only one important issue now dividing our peoples, and that concerns the status in your markets of the American potato. There, apparently, certain doubts remain to be resolved. It would obviously be improper in me to speak in greater detail. But I may perhaps say this, that I begin my work in the high hope that justice, substantial justice, British justice, will ultimately be done to that really excellent American tuber.[1]

He was succeeded in 1929 by General Charles Gates Dawes, lawyer and financier, who had been chief of supply procurement for the American army in the war and the chairman of the first committee of experts of the Reparations Commission, and was thus, like Houghton, thoroughly familiar with certain aspects of Europe's affairs; he came straight from the Vice-Presidency and was a vigorous character already familiar to the public for "his underslung pipe and picturesque profanity".[2] After

[1] Q. W.A.A.E., p. 482.   [2] Bailey, p. 703.

him, from 1933-7, came a more subdued figure, R. W. Bingham, publisher, lawyer, politician and financier.

These men on both sides of the Atlantic played less part, perhaps, in forming Anglo-American relations than many of their predecessors had done, or than some of their successors were to do in the renewed emotional tension of war. But one of them, Houghton, gave expression to that underlying sympathy which we have seen was the result of the long development of Anglo-American relations over the previous century; despite any lack of active co-operation, it, and the absence of serious disputes, had come, as he said, to be accepted as a matter of course:

> I believe, as a matter of course, that the future of the world—its peace, its happiness, its general well-being—depends largely upon the existence of a sound and cordial understanding between the British and American peoples. In fact . . . I believe that, fundamentally, the basis of such an understanding already exists—not because of any marked regard or liking we may feel for one another's excellent qualities, not because of a common language, not because of ties of blood, but because, being what we are, it is inevitable that we should look out on the world and its affairs from much the same point of view. . . . We certainly think in much the same terms. We have much the same scale of values. We want the same kind of world. Consciously or unconsciously, we are seeking the same kind of future.[1]

II

THE ending of the war did not alter the fact that there were now very few direct disputes between the two countries, and that the story of their relationship more and more arises directly from the broad history of world events. It is characteristic of this lack of bilateral issues that, in a toast to King George VI during the 1939 visit, Roosevelt could say:

> The King and I are aware of a recent episode. Two small uninhabited Islands in the center of the Pacific became of sudden interest to the British Empire and to the United States as stepping stones for commercial airplanes between America and Australasia. Both nations claimed sovereignty. Both nations had good cases. To have entered into a long drawn out argument could have meant ill-will between us and delay in the use of the Islands by either nation. It was suggested that the problem be solved by the joint use of both Islands by both nations, and by a gentleman's agreement, to defer the question of sovereignty until the year 1989.[2]

[1] Q. W.A.A.E., p. 484.   [2] Roosevelt, *Personal Letters*, pp. 894-5.

The history of Anglo-American relations in these years is singularly uneventful compared with those which preceded and followed them. Two questions only are of major importance, that of war debts, which did not concern Britain alone, and that of naval rivalry, with which is associated the Japanese problem.

The truce on naval armaments made between Lloyd George and Wilson in Paris was no more than a temporary *modus vivendi*, and it did not scotch the incipient Anglo-American naval rivalry. There was vocal support in the United States for the ardent desire of some of her naval authorities to gain at least parity with Britain, and this did not serve to allay British fears. Advocates of a vast American navy gained great strength from traditional Anglophobia, which took pains to remind the country that "Great Britain has threatened our interests oftener and more seriously than all the other nations of the earth combined",[1] and the disclosure at this time that the British had cornered most of the then known petroleum reserves in Europe and Asia added oil to the flames. As early as July, 1919, House had gone so far as to remark that "the relations between the two countries are beginning to assume the same character as that of England and Germany before the war",[2] but this was, of course, greatly exaggerated, and American big-navy advocates by no means had it all their own way. Theodore Roosevelt had declared before his death, good disciple of Mahan that he was, that the British Navy was "probably the most potent instrumentality for peace in the world" and that America should "not . . . try to build a navy in rivalry to it," but should be satisfied to "have the second navy in the world."[3] Admiral Sims, Page's naval coadjutor in London in 1917 and a lifelong advocate of Anglo-American solidarity, brutally reminded Members of Congress that "A navy is built for only one purpose, and that is to fight an enemy"; unless the United States was "in more or less imminent danger of getting into armed conflict with Great Britain, or with Great Britain and Japan combined,"[4] he could not see why the world's greatest navy was needed. He did, however, put his finger on the valid theoretical point which could be made in favour of the supreme American Navy, the existence of the Anglo-Japanese Alliance. He was right that armaments are built for fighting, and that behind a naval rivalry must lie a diplomatic tension; that tension was between the United States and Japan, Britain's ally.

[1] Q. H. H. and M. Sprout, *Toward a New Order of Sea Power* (London, 1940), p. 74.
[2] *Intimate Papers*, IV, p. 510.   [3] Q. Sprout, p. 102.   [4] Q. Sprout, p. 80.

Even in 1917 only an ambiguous convention between Lansing and a visiting Japanese diplomat, Viscount Ishii, had been able to paper over the cracks of American-Japanese disagreement, and after the diplomatic contest at Paris, tension rose very high over obvious Japanese designs in Siberia and Manchuria, and over the Pacific island of Yap. The Anglo-Japanese Alliance had been originally directed against Russia and Germany, and these powers were for the moment off the international stage, but it had not after its first few years been very pleasing to the Americans. War with the United States was unthinkable for Britain and this had been made clear in many ways; we have seen, for instance, its effect upon the revision of the Anglo-Japanese treaty in 1911. When the Anglo-American treaty of arbitration failed to materialize, it appears that Britain made to the Japanese in 1914 a secret statement—whose validity they do not seem to have acknowledged—that they regarded their Bryan conciliation treaty as a treaty of arbitration, which rendered the Anglo-Japanese Alliance inoperative against America. In July, 1920, Britain persuaded Japan to make a joint statement that, if renewed, the Alliance must be put in a form compatible with the Covenant of the League, and a year later a further joint statement, issued just before the expiry of the treaty and pending further action upon it, laid down that in case of difficulty League procedures should be followed. In December, 1920, the existence of the letter of 1914 about the Bryan agreement had been made known. Thus Britain had strained every nerve to emphasize her exclusion of the United States from the operation of the Alliance, but, though this had its effect in America, Washington was still not entirely happy at the existence of even the purely theoretical threat which the combination of British and Japanese naval power represented.

This feeling found strong and vocal support in an influential quarter, Canada, and at the Imperial Conference which opened in London in June, 1920, her Prime Minister, Arthur Meighen, renewed very strongly the pressure his government had already brought to bear for the termination of the alliance. He was strongly opposed by Hughes of Australia, who clung, curiously but understandably, to this connexion between White Australia and Yellow Japan, and by Massey of New Zealand; and the feeling of the rest of the Conference was against him. His success in winning his colleagues to his point of view owed something to the vigour of his personality, more perhaps to the simultaneous pressure of the State Department and Canada, but most of all to the rule, which had by now become almost a reflex in the British mind, that the good will of the United States was the beginning of political

734

wisdom for Britain. It was agreed to seek the replacement of the Alliance by a general understanding with the other powers concerned in the Pacific area. So decisive was Meighen's victory that it is doubtful if the alliance could have been renewed under any circumstances.

Churchill is inclined to be critical of this decision, writing, "The United States made it clear to Britain that the continuance of her alliance with Japan, to which the Japanese had punctiliously conformed, would constitute a barrier in Anglo-American relations. Accordingly this alliance was brought to an end. The annulment caused a profound impression in Japan, and was viewed as the spurning of an Asiatic Power by the Western World. Many links were sundered which might afterwards have proved of decisive value to peace."[1] It does not, however, seem likely that Japan, in view of her history in the previous quarter century, could have been restrained from actions in the Pacific area such as we could not have countenanced, by the maintenance of any treaty obligation, nor does it seem probable that avoidance of this particular rebuff would have prevented the embittering of the racial problem. It is hard to believe that the refusal to renew the alliance could have done more than accelerate a process which was already far advanced. But in any case the decision was America's to make. If she was determined to make it, Britain had still to follow on, for already there are signs of that inevitable domination of the Anglo-American partnership by the greater power which was to become so obvious after World War II. Britain could influence American decisions, but she was bound to accept and follow them in the long run.

That she could influence them was shown by the outcome on this issue. The ideas of the Four Power and Nine Power Treaties, which emerged from the Washington Conference, were originally conceived by British diplomacy, "But, as in the case of the Monroe Doctrine, the Open Door notes, and the calling of the Washington Conference, the United States took the initiative in carrying the proposal through."[2] It was one of the prices that Britain had to learn to pay for American friendship, that she could seldom afford to initiate diplomatic moves involving the United States, for fear of the cries of American Anglophobes that America was again being made subservient to British interests. But powerful factors had already appeared in both countries to check the progress of the naval dispute. The first of these was financial, for neither public opinion would contemplate the indefinite payment of a vast bill for armaments, let alone armaments directed

[1] *Second World War*, I, p. 11.　　[2] Bailey, pp. 696-7.

against one another, while Britain was hardly in a position to meet such a bill even if she had wished to do so. The second factor was a public revulsion from the idea of further war. In America, where it was led by Republicans like Borah, it took the form of a radical disarmament programme, which was strongly pressed despite the opposition of the new Republican administration; from December, 1920, onwards, Borah demanded the opening of negotiations with Britain and Japan. The Administration continued to espouse the large building programme, because of continued pressure from its advocates, and because they wished to enter any conference there might be with the bargaining power it would give them, but the disarmament sentiment steadily gained strength. On 30 June, 1921, the House ratified a resolution calling for a conference with only four dissenting votes.

In Britain events followed a similar course. Public alarm grew at the threat of a naval armaments race which Britain would almost certainly lose, and great emphasis was laid on the special importance of Anglo-American friendship, which seemed to most Britons "the only firm foundation upon which to rebuild a shattered world order."[1] When Britain's capital ship "replacement" programme, involving the resumption of construction, was under discussion in the winter of 1920-1 the *New Statesman* expressed the fears of the public when it declared, "the problem of naval construction today is simply and exclusively a problem of preparation for a hypothetical war against America."[2] In January the British Ambassador was called home from Washington to discuss the problem, and in February Lord Lee of Fareham, a noted advocate of close Anglo-American relations, was made First Lord of the Admiralty.

Direct approaches would have been fatal, but immediately after the new Administration had settled in, Lee, in a speech urging naval limitation, welcomed the "hint . . . thrown out" in President Harding's inaugural address, and made, through Adolph Ochs, the sympathetic publisher of the *New York Times*, an informal, but to the journalist startling, proposal for fleet parity. The Administration still moved with caution, but the announcement of an Anglo-Irish truce on 8 July happily removed one of the major obstacles to agreement at a most convenient moment. The very day before, Lord Curzon, the British Foreign Secretary, had been forced, by great pressure for a full statement on the question, to request the American Ambassador to expedite, if he could, his Government's reply to Curzon's proposal, made two days earlier, that the President invite the Powers to a Conference on Pacific

[1]Sprout, p. 123. [2] Q. ibid, pp. 123-4, note.

and naval affairs. Lloyd George, the Prime Minister, had felt impelled on the same day, 7 July, to reveal that he was waiting for views from the United States and others, and to promise a full statement on the eleventh. The American Ambassador, with an eye more on American domestic than on international reactions, advised Harding to act quickly, in order not to let the Prime Minister steal his thunder, but this was unnecessary, for his cable crossed one from the State Department making substantially the same proposal as that put forward by Curzon, except that Hughes was at first reluctant to include the discussion of Far Eastern questions. Such a discussion was essential to the British, and was in due course accepted by the Americans, who in their turn insisted that the conference must take place on American soil. On 11 July, 1921, Harding's invitation to Britain, Japan, and certain other powers to attend the Washington Conference was made public. Britain accepted with alacrity: Japan unwillingly and after considerable delay, for though anxious for naval parleys she was suspicious of what might come out of a discussion of Far Eastern Affairs.

The British delegation was headed by Balfour, and Hughes's hand was strengthened by the inclusion in the American delegation of Lodge and Underwood, the Chairman and the senior Democratic member of the Senate Foreign Affairs Committee. In both delegations naval chiefs acted in a purely advisory capacity. Hughes, in a dramatic opening address, startled his auditors by proposing a specific programme of disarmament which included a ten-year holiday in the construction of capital ships and the scrapping of such ships as would leave the navies of the three principal naval powers, the United States, Britain and Japan, at a ratio of 5-5-3. He then proceeded with a detailed elaboration of his proposals, suggesting the destruction, first of 845,740 tons of American capital shipping, and then 583,375 tons of British; this cool inclusion of actual items of foreign, as well as American, shipping to be destroyed was sensational. Admiral Beatty, First Sea Lord of the British Admiralty, was seen to come forward in his chair, as Mark Sullivan wrote, a "slightly staggered and deeply disturbed expression" on his face, reminding one of a "bulldog, sleeping on a sunny doorstep, who has been poked in the stomach by the impudent foot of an itinerant soap-canvasser seriously lacking in any sense of the most ordinary proprieties".[1] Balfour alone of the British delegation appeared unmoved at the continuation of these proposals, which sank more British battleships "than all the admirals of the world had destroyed in a cycle of centuries."[2]

[1] Q. Sprout, p. 151. [2] Colonel Repington; q. ibid, p. 151.

After a three-day adjournment Balfour, "a white-haired man, his shoulders bowed as if weighted down by the responsibility he bore, stood with folded arms . . . and declared in the name of Great Britain the abandonment of her traditional policy of supremacy on the sea and her willingness to accept . . . naval equality with . . . the United States."[1] This "great historical" proposal by Hughes was, Balfour declared, of far-reaching significance for the British Empire and every British subject, for "without sea communication he and the Empire to which he belongs would perish." From this the case of the "solid, impregnable, self-sufficient" United States was different, for she was "wholly immune from the particular perils to which, from the nature of the case, the British Empire is subject." Nevertheless with Hughes's great and admirable scheme, "We agree . . . in spirit and in principle."[2]

An elaboration of practical difficulties then followed, but, though they, and the many others put forward by the remaining powers, slowed down proceedings and forced the acceptance of a number of compromises, the initial impetus imparted by the drastic American proposals was not altogether lost. On the purely naval side agreement was reached on the 5-5-3 ratio in capital ships, but, in return for acceptance of this ratio by the Japanese, the three powers agreed to maintain the *status quo* in the fortification of a number of their insular possessions in the Pacific area, particularly Hong Kong, the Philippines, Guam, Samoa and the Aleutians, as well as some Japanese islands. A British proposal to abolish the submarine was not acceptable to the other powers, particularly France, and there was failure to agree on any limitation of submarine tonnage; in the end, under strong Anglo-American pressure, the best that could be obtained was an agreement to use submarines only in accordance with certain specified humanitarian principles. The submarine failure resulted in a similar failure to limit auxiliary surface craft, because Britain refused to relinquish her claims to them unless the submarine was effectively controlled. She likewise refused to accept limitation of cruisers in the form suggested by the United States because the latter thought of them primarily in terms of fleet requirements, whereas in the scattered sea lanes of British world commerce they served a totally different purpose and might be required in great numbers. She did, however, accept a qualitative limitation of cruisers to a displacement of 10,000 tons and a gun calibre not exceeding 8 inches, which was designed to prevent the development of a race in heavy cruisers that would be capital ships in all but name. Though there was no limitation upon aircraft, one upon

[1] *New York Times*: q. Sprout, p. 157.　　[2] Q. Sprout, p. 158.

aircraft carriers kept roughly to the 5-5-3 ratio. Without great difficulty, Italy and, with immense difficulty, France were induced to accept a 1·7 ratio. Thus the naval provisions did achieve the remarkable triumph of the 5-5-3-1·7-1·7 ratio in capital ships and carriers, as well as the fortifications agreement in the Pacific.

The political outcome of the Conference, embodied in the Four and Nine Power Treaties, was less concrete but almost as significant in Anglo-American relations, for it provided a graceful, if obvious, means by which Britain could finally escape the bilateral Anglo-Japanese Alliance and the mistrust in America which it now aroused. The problem was to find some formula for a tripartite agreement, which would be strong enough to satisfy a highly sensitive Japan and weak enough to satisfy an American opinion deeply suspicious of any suggestion of an entangling Alliance. In the original British and Japanese drafts for the Four Power pact, the United States succeeded in making substantial changes, including one calling for the participation of France, and another confining the operation of the pact to the Pacific, instead of including Eastern Asia. Hughes took a much less lenient view of Japanese interests in the latter area than Balfour, so that in effect the agreement was cleverly transformed from an American recognition of Japan's conquests in Asia, into a Japanese pledge to respect United States possessions in the Pacific. Yet another change took out even the vague hint of teeth which had existed in the Balfour draft, and substituted a mere promise that in case they were threatened by another power the signatories would "communicate with one another fully and frankly in order to arrive at an understanding as to the most efficient measures to be taken, jointly or separately, to meet the exigencies of the particular situation." Even then the Senate added a reservation to the effect that there was "no commitment to armed force, no alliance, no obligation to join in any defense."[1]

Nevertheless, the treaty specifically terminated the Anglo-Japanese Alliance, so that it could from every point of view be regarded as an American victory, and it was one with which Britain was well pleased, since it rid her of the embarrassing Japanese entanglement and gave her hope that the new American naval power might possibly reinforce and ensure the Japanese Navy's protection of British interests in the Pacific; this was important because Britain's hopes, in view of the collapse of German sea power, of strongly reinforcing her own Pacific fleet came to naught. In fact, the net effect of the new disposition of naval and political forces was to give undisputed practical control over

[1] Q. Sprout, pp. 309-310.

the North-western Pacific to Japan, which hardly altered the existing position. Britain retained control of the Narrow Seas, the Mediterranean, and the Australian route, and America that of all the approaches to the Western hemisphere. This practical situation was obviously clear to the Japanese, and no doubt they equally appreciated that, in the then state of British and, above all, American opinion, it amounted to a free hand for them in both the Western Pacific and Eastern Asia.

This appreciation was probably enhanced by the innocuous nature of the Nine Power Pact, which, like the Four Power Pact, had no teeth of any kind in it. On paper it was both sweeping and specific, so that Bailey can write that it gave the Open Door policy "as strong a foundation as paper and ink could give it."[1] How strong that was, the future would show all too clearly. As it was, the treaty was a triumphant and logical conclusion of the policy inaugurated by Hay just over twenty years earlier; for the first time it specifically pledged the good faith of the nine powers to respect "the sovereignty, the independence, and the territorial integrity of China";[2] to give her the opportunity of self-development; and to apply to her the full Open Door policy. Like its companion the treaty was proposed by the British delegates, but its final radical form was an American achievement, and, like it again, it was probably accepted by Japan because it would almost certainly be nothing but a paper obstacle to her own development. That this would be the case was fairly clear from the refusal of the American delegates to contemplate any form of actual military commitment.

It was not absolutely certain, however, and the measure of that uncertainty is the success of the Americans in forcing upon Japan the very practical steps constituted by her complete withdrawal from Siberia, her limited withdrawal from Shantung, and her grant of American cable rights on Yap. America, when the treaties were being negotiated, had on foot a building programme for her fleet which would make her without question the paramount naval power, and even a nation as peace-inclined as the Americans then seemed does not build a navy for nothing; besides, if American renunciation of the League was in everyone's mind as a sign of the times, few had yet forgotten the display of American might in the war which had ended only three years before. It was in the shadow of American Imperialism that Hay had been able to initiate the Open Door policy; it was in the shadow of World War I that Hughes was able to consummate it; it was to be in the shadow of American isolationism that Japan would challenge

[1] Bailey, p. 697.   [2] Q. Sprout, p. 311.

it. Similarly, there is no doubt that Japan accepted the naval limitations because she could not possibly afford to compete financially with the United States. In all these aspects of the Washington Conference Japan accepted much that could not have been agreeable to her, and bided her time. She reaped the rewards of her patience between 1931 and 1943, and of her failure to honour her word, or recognize the realities of American power, between 1943 and 1945.

In Anglo-American relations the Washington Treaty was a landmark of the greatest significance. In the first place, it removed the danger of discord between the two countries over armaments and over Japan, for its reception by both peoples was, on the whole and in the end, very cordial. Naval opinion in both showed some strong elements of distaste for it, but the publics welcomed it, parts of them lyrically. In America Anglophobe elements strove to rally opinion behind the Hearst cry that the United States was "tied hand and foot to the war machine of foreign imperialism," but, though its proceedings were lengthy, it was symptomatic that the Senate accepted all the treaties. The New York *Tribune* gave characteristic expression to the widespread public approval when it wrote that the treaty was "a monumental contribution to international understanding and human progress."[1] In Britain there was even stronger civilian support, and *The Times* spoke for journals as different as the *Telegraph* on the Right and the *Chronicle* on the Left, when it wrote of "a great day for all time in the history of the world." As is always the case, more emphasis was laid there than in America on the fact that it was a great triumph for Anglo-American relations; that it had, in the words of the *Manchester Guardian*, "made a unique contribution to world peace . . . drawn close the English-speaking peoples and . . . given America more confidence in Europe."[2]

In assessing its place in our history it is hard not to agree with Paul D. Cravath, an eminent American lawyer, in his alleged words to the Council on Foreign Relations in New York, despite the fact that he later denied them under isolationist pressure. He was reported to have defended the treaty on the ground that it substituted an Anglo-American *entente* for the Anglo-Japanese Alliance. This was "not recorded at all in black and white", but he had been "told by every member of the American delegation" that the conference had established "such a degree of understanding and such a basis of sympathy" between the two countries "that both assume that in all future emergencies they

[1] Q. ibid, p. 268.   [2] Q. ibid, p. 259.

can both count on having the very closest co-operation." Cravath knew "definitely"[1] that Balfour shared this view and understood that the rest of the British delegation did so. Certainly Hughes denied pointedly that there was any secret understanding with Britain; certainly the *entente* was confined in area; certainly it was passive on the American side—much more passive than Britain would have wished —but that it in fact existed, even if in an unspoken form, there can be no doubt. It had come into existence in the time of Hay and Roosevelt, had been obscured in the early years after 1914, had reached a kind of fulfilment in the war itself, had been obscured once more in the first post-war years, and had now re-emerged in the new pattern of international naval power. In pre-war years British naval policy had acted on the fundamental assumption that England would never go to war with America; the equality now recognized between British and American sea power reverted to and reinforced that assumption, which, with the death of the Anglo-Japanese Alliance, was mutual and reciprocal. It would be hard to find a better example of an *entente*.

In the second place, the Washington treaty was a vital landmark because it formally and irrevocably recognized Anglo-American naval parity and the surrender of Britannia's solitary rule over the waves. In the history of Britain, and indeed of the world, this was truly an epoch-making event, but it was almost as remarkable a feature of American development, in that the idea of naval equality with Britain had hardly even been seriously considered for much more than a decade. In Britain Archibald Hurd, co-editor of *Brassey's Naval Annual*, wrote that, "After hundreds of years, we have dipped our flag as the one supreme sea Power, having supplied [in the late War] a vindication of the benevolent purpose of the British fleet, which formed a fitting end to a glorious chapter of our history." As a result of the Washington Conference, "the trident of Neptune passes into the joint guardianship of the English-speaking peoples". One school of British naval thinkers, reckoning in narrow and exclusively naval terms, looked aghast at this development. Typical of it was a former First Sea Lord, who had done much to render Anglo-American naval rivalry worse during the Paris negotiations, Sir Rosslyn Wester-Wemyss; he recorded that it filled him with "regret and even dismay", that Britain had won the war at sea only to lose it at the conference table, and that the Americans alone had emerged from Washington with "the substance of all they desire." Others lamented in similar vein "the bloodless surrender of

[1] Q. ibid. p. 272.

the world's greatest Empire, and its deletion as an effective voice at other than parochial conferences."[1]

But the fault was in her stars, not in herself; it was written plainly in the pages of history and the facts of the political world. Some naval men, even, who were capable of taking the broad political view accepted the inevitability, the desirability, of the naval equality; that this was so was not merely a recognition of the extent to which the lessons of Anglo-American relations in the previous quarter-century had been learnt, but also in some degree a tribute to the political wisdom of the British people and their leaders. There is indeed something quite remarkable in the calmness with which they accepted the inevitable surrender of three centuries of maritime supremacy to another power. Wemyss was right at least in this; it was, as he called it, "an act of renunciation unparalleled . . . in history."[2] "Renunciation" is perhaps too heroic a word to describe a resigned acceptance of the inevitable, but "unparalleled" it certainly was. It is safe to say that any power but America might have had to fight for its supremacy, and that the fight might have been long and grievous.

For, and it is the third reason for the importance of the Washington Treaty in Anglo-American relations, it was in fact supremacy which was being handed over to the Americans. It was implicit in the whole situation that America could seize that, as well as parity, if ever she desired it. She entered the Conference in the position, not of an equal, but of potentially by far the greatest naval power, and that position, which she renounced, was one with which no other power could hope to compete. The best evidence of her renunciation is the widespread dislike of the treaty terms by American naval authorities, who judged, like some of their equally misguided professional counterparts in Britain, on strictly and narrowly naval premises: America gained without question from the treaty as a whole. More important still, the United States retained —and continued to increase—that economic pre-eminence upon which alone modern naval supremacy can rest; the way to naval dominion was at any time open to her.

This, too, is the kernel of the Treaty's importance to our story: it symbolized the irrevocable passing of the primacy in the Anglo-American relationship to the United States. The war had not only seriously weakened Britain: it had strengthened America. From a debtor she had become a creditor nation, from the second she had become the potentially greatest naval power; she had shown herself capable of raising vast and efficient armies, her President had dominated

[1] Q. Sprout, pp. 260-1.   [2] Q. ibid, p. 260.

the political world at the Peace Conference. Not merely the naval, but the whole, leadership of the English-speaking peoples passed into the hands of the United States. She was, for two decades, to refuse the political responsibilities of that leadership, but in the end she was forced to shoulder them by the irresistible onrush of events. To this outcome the signs clearly pointed in 1921; it was the tragedy of the inter-war period that they then became lost to sight until 1941.

III

WE have been assuming, which is broadly correct, that naval parity between Britain and America was accepted in 1921. More precisely, this was only true of aircraft carriers and capital ships, and the extension of the formula to subsidiary categories not only encountered formidable practical difficulties, but also brought to light mental reservations on the whole issue which were still being harboured in some quarters in Britain. The United States participated in the work of the League Preparatory Commission for the Disarmament Conference, which dragged on from 1926 to the opening of the Conference itself in 1932; and though the participation was at first limited, its extent steadily increased, until in 1933, after the lesson of Japan's action in China, Norman Davis, the head of the American delegation, could utter the revolutionary words, "We are ready not only to do our part toward the substantive reduction of armaments but, if this is effected by general international agreement . . . to consult the other states in case of a threat to peace, with a view to averting conflict."[1] "Further than that, in the event that the states, in conference, determine that a state has been guilty of a breach of the peace in violation of its international obligations and take measures against the violator, then, if we concur in the judgement . . . we will refrain from any action tending to defeat such collective effort which these states may thus make to restore peace."[2]

Unhappily, the time for the condition, which he laid down as essential, to be fulfilled was now passed, and the proceedings of the Conference finally petered out amidst increasing international anarchy. It had achieved nothing except to reveal a certain broad kinship in the Anglo-American approach to disarmament, which should not be for-

[1] Q. M. Tate, *The United States and Armaments* (Cambridge, Mass., 1948), p. 110.

[2] Q. A. W. Griswold, *The Far Eastern Policy of the United States* (New York, 1938), p. 440.

gotten in the discussion of their few particular differences. It is indicated by such things as their common rejection of any idea of opposing the limitation of war potential, which was pressed by the industrially weaker powers, such as France. But the years were not wholly barren of achievements in the field of disarmament, though they were effected on parallel lines with, rather than through the proceedings of, the League, partly because they were confined almost exclusively to the naval aspect of the problem, since France blocked any effective discussion of other forms of disarmament. In the relations of Britain with the United States, because they were the dominant maritime powers, these achievements were very important, for they virtually terminated British jealousy of American naval strength.

The first auguries, however, were not very favourable, for the Geneva three-power naval conference of 1927, summoned by Coolidge as an answer to domestic pressure groups demanding increases in the number of American auxiliary vessels, adjourned without reaching any agreement. This was the result of Anglo-American differences, for Japan was largely content to observe, no doubt with relish, these disagreements between the two friends. The fundamental question at issue was a very real one, but it was rendered more intractable by the lack of publicity at the meetings, which was made particularly harmful by the fact that naval men were actual delegates and not merely advisers, and that they naturally tended to view "the world through a porthole."[1] The triumph at Washington had essentially been one of statesmen who overrode technicians when necessary; at Geneva this was not possible, nor, owing to the secrecy of proceedings, was the salutary pressure of public feeling, which, as we have seen on a number of occasions, was by now a formidable instrument for good in Anglo-American affairs.

The crux of the matter was the cruiser question, which arose from the essentially different strategic situations of the two powers. The United States, relatively compact and lacking distant naval bases or a widespread commercial empire, needed chiefly large long-range cruisers of heavy armament, those of 10,000 tons displacement and 8-inch guns. Britain needed fewer of these, but many more of a smaller size and lighter armament, for the protection of her commercial lifelines in time of war. This was recognized by both sides, but the difficulty came in the arrangement of practical details. In the first place, the question was complicated, particularly for Britain, by the refusal of France and Italy to enter upon any fixed ratio agreement. In the second place, it was almost impossible to reach any exact relative

[1] Tate, p. 143.

assessment of strength based purely on tonnage figures, when so many other factors, such as calibre of gun, age, unit displacement and so on, entered in. In the third place, agreement could not be reached on total tonnages, particularly of cruisers, because the British naval experts did not feel able to reduce them beyond a certain point, in view of their peculiar strategic position; and since this point was well above that desired by America, she would, by conforming, have had actually to build vessels. Thus such a ceiling would have had, in effect, the most undesirable result of sanctioning increased armaments by international agreement. The British would not go below seventy cruisers, which seemed excessive to the Americans; over other craft there was less difference. Though it was not raised openly as a problem, there can be little doubt that the traditional attitudes of the two navies to the ancient problem of the Freedom of the Seas still coloured their thinking, despite the vocal elements in the naval thought of both countries which were putting the other's point of view. Britain thought of the protection of her world-wide commerce and of blockade; the United States of freeing the seas for the passage of all merchant ships. But both attitudes had in fact little relevance to present or future reality.

But the complications did not end here, for the Conservative British Cabinet, when the deadlock was referred to London and Washington, raised a complication which amounted to a reconsideration of the whole parity question. Viscount Cecil in his autobiography states that he and the other delegates were instructed at the outset to concede mathematical parity to the United States, but, as practical difficulties arose and they began to see clearly the implications of this, the British naval experts commenced to argue for something different—what they called strategic equality. The majority of the Cabinet supported them in this, and refused to accept the American demand for mathematical equality. It was pointed out that at Washington Balfour's acceptance of parity had been confined to the battle fleet and its auxiliaries only, to equality "in strength, in offensive power"; and there is little doubt that any effort at that time to reach a wider agreement would have found the same obstacle in its path, for Balfour wrote in 1927 that it was not possible to "maintain that equality of tonnage means equality of naval strength unless you know among what kind of cruisers that tonnage is to be distributed." Churchill, in explaining the breakdown of the Conference in August, 1927, put the case clearly:

> We hold, on the contrary, that the principle of naval equality must be based, not on mere numbers or tonnage, but must take into consideration the quite different conditions of the two communities.

We feel that our island Empire is dependent for its inherent and integral existence, and, indeed, for its daily bread, upon our power to keep open the paths across the ocean. . . . We contend that our position is entirely different from that of a vast self-contained community dwelling in a continent and free from all our European preoccupations.[1]

Although, in view of the complications arising from the fact that the discussions at Geneva were trilateral and not universal, the resolution of the British Government to stand firm on an irreducible minimum of cruisers is comprehensible, and although they were not publicly committed to a specific arithmetical equality, there was plainly a development in their ideas subsequent to their first instructions to Cecil. When the Cabinet refused to compromise on this broad issue, he resigned, and it is doubtful whether he would have done so, indeed whether he would have undertaken the mission at all, had his original instructions not allowed of what he understood as numerical parity. This development was due to a failure at the beginning of negotiations to see what parity meant and to a lack of proper political preparation, rather than to disingenuousness, but to the eye of the man in the street, particularly in America, the final claim of the British that they were willing to grant equality, but not numerical equality, did sound rather like an Orwellish insistence that the two navies should be equal but one more equal than the other.

The British case seemed all the more peculiar because of the sneaking suspicion that it was in fact the last fling of Tory anti-Americanism against American naval power. Churchill, who was unquestionably influential in the decision, can certainly be acquitted of this motive; he based himself on underlying military realities, though it is by no means so certain in 1927 that they were the only realities, as it was to be five years later. One cannot be quite so sure of his colleagues, and it is the opinion of the historian of the subject that "statesmanship should have found a basis for agreement."[2] It is true on the one hand that if the United States had been willing to commit herself to an Anglo-American military alliance, the discontented British elements might well have accepted America's terms; it is true on the other that they would not accept them for the reason Cecil advanced, that in view of the amicable relations between the two countries, their two navies should be considered as "two divisions of a great Peace Fleet, and if the Americans liked to provide the larger part of it, so much the better."[3] British Conservatives would not accept, as a basis of agreement, a mythical inter-

[1] Q. Tate, pp. 157-9. [2] Ibid, p. 150. [3] Q. ibid.

national fleet, the only conceivable master of which—the League—America regarded with profound suspicion.

But Cecil sounded also a more powerful argument, though it did not necessarily appeal to him as such, when he pointed out that before the war Britain, when she was comparing her naval strength with that of other powers, simply never brought America into the calculation at all. This was in fact the only real basis for understanding; it was the one which was shortly to be accepted without demur. The point was made powerfully by Grey in a letter to *The Times* six days after the close of the Geneva Conference:

> The rock on which the Conference was wrecked at Geneva is the theory of "parity" between the British and American navies; this theory is working badly, and there is every sign that it will cause friction and not harmony between the two countries. . . . "Parity", which is designed to avoid competition, does in fact imply rivalry. It means, it is true, that neither country is to have a bigger navy than the other; but it also means that each country must have as large a navy as the other. It is in fact a state of rivalry between the fleets of the two great English-speaking nations—a condition which is not edifying. . . .
>
> Is it not possible to get back to the axiom on which the British Government tacitly acted before the war—that of not taking account of the American Navy in calculating the requirements of the British Empire?[1]

The suggestion in the first part of his letter proved to be the solution of the problem three years later, and one may be entitled to the view that—in the circumstances of 1927—Britain could have accepted America's terms without doing herself irreparable harm.

Grey had ended his letter by urging "arbitration and other agreements which rule out between conferring nations the possibility of war", but it was unnecessary to urge arbitration in Anglo-American relations where the habit of settling disputes peacefully was so firmly established. It was, however, as a result of widespread popular feeling in the world in favour of peaceful agreements that the Kellogg Pact, renouncing war as an instrument of policy, was signed by many nations, beginning in 1928. The British Government signed it, subject to a far-reaching reservation concerning the defence of the Empire, which did little to harm Anglo-American relations, for Kellogg himself had begun by being suspicious of so idealistic a convention, while the Senate, on the same day as they

[1] Q. ibid, p. 160.

ratified it by 81 votes to 1, took up consideration of the construction of fifteen cruisers. There is no doubt that a vocal pacifist opinion was chiefly responsible for the pact and, though it was strongest in the country of W. J. Bryan, it was also vociferous in Britain; the people in both countries, unrealistic and sentimental though they might be, were at one in their desire for peace.

A more practical step in this direction (though a changing international scene soon rendered its work abortive) was the London Naval Treaty of 1930. The conference which prepared it avoided the mistakes of its predecessor at Geneva by ensuring that it was a political agreement which was not dictated by naval opinion, and by seeing that there were solid preliminary Anglo-American discussions. The Anglo-American understanding which resulted was so cordial as to arouse the suspicions of other powers. It was facilitated by changes in the governments of both countries, for, rather curiously, the Labour government in Britain got on much better with the Republican administration in the United States than had its right-wing predecessor. To some extent this was a personal matter, for the Quaker-influenced, waste-hating engineer in the White House was in deep agreement with the pacifist sympathies of Ramsay MacDonald, but it was also due to the formidable agitation in both countries for the settlement of these Anglo-American differences.

The admission of the validity of other than purely tonnage measurements by America—the so-called yardstick formula—and the ultimate reduction of the British demand to fifteen large and thirty-five small cruisers, totalling 339,000 tons (as opposed to fifteen large and fifty-five small, totalling 572,000 tons at Geneva), were the essential pre-conditions of agreement and their effect was enhanced by such conciliatory gestures as the checking of actual building on both sides of the Atlantic and MacDonald's successful visit to Washington, undertaken against the advice of Ambassador Dawes, who believed it would merely provide a stick for the Anglophobes. When the Conference met, Anglo-American agreement was soon reached on a basis which gave Britain an advantage in cruiser tonnage of 12,000 tons, in a total of 339,000 tons, in return for an American advantage in the heavier type of cruiser. The two delegations agreed easily on the destroyer and submarine categories, both favouring the outlawry of the latter.

It was a different matter to get the agreement of the other powers. Japan eventually agreed to most of the provisions suggested by Britain and America, which followed the pattern of an overall fleet ratio of 100 for the United States, 102.4 for Britain (owing to weaker gun power in her smaller vessels), and 63·6 for Japan: France and Italy only accepted a few of the provisions, and finally failed to ratify the treaty altogether. Most ominous of all for the future, particularly when taken in conjunction with the fact that the Japanese statesman who had negotiated the treaty was shortly assassinated, Japan indicated that, at the naval conference planned for 1935, she would probably demand parity with the other two powers. The treaty was opposed by Churchill, on the ground that it reduced British strength below the basic safety level, and it is true that Britain and the United States were eventually to suffer at the hands of Japan from the naval restrictions consented to in 1922 and 1930, but not without long warning, for in 1934 Japan renounced the treaty, while the changed circumstances in which the London Naval Conference of 1935 met resulted in the sweeping away of virtually all practical limitations upon armaments.

But in the history of Anglo-American relations the London Conference of 1930 was an absolute, not merely a relative and passing, success, for it ended for ever British mistrust of American naval equality. More than that, it virtually terminated British jealousy of American naval power, so that by 1938 Britain had come to agree with Cecil that America should be free to build as big a navy as she pleased "and more power to it."[1] This was the fruition of a tree planted at the beginning of the century, and it was by now a sturdy growth. After World War II the appointment of an American Admiral in the Atlantic area by NATO might rouse an emotional storm-in-a-teacup in Britain, but she accepted with equanimity a vast and dominating American Navy. In the war, indeed, she was not able to welcome it warmly enough.

IV

THE next serious problem in inter-war Anglo-American relations was of a very different character, that which can be discussed under the general heading of War Debts. It was without doubt the issue that aroused most feeling among ordinary men on both sides of the ocean, because they thought it a simple one which they understood, and because, like all honest individuals, they regarded any problem concerning debts as primarily moral in its nature. In fact, international debts, by their very magnitude, lose much of their moral character, and the common people were singularly ill fitted to comprehend the exceedingly complex nature of the war-debts problem.

[1] Q. Tate, p. 194.

The debts fell into three main groups; those made prior to America's entry into the war in 1917, those made while she was at war, and those made for relief and reconstruction after the Armistice. During the first period, Great Britain took up to the best of her ability the financial part to which she had been accustomed in past Continental wars, and became the primary source or agent of Allied finance. By 1917 all of the Allied powers were debtors to Great Britain, and she had raised a great deal of money in the American market; her need for foreign exchange, particularly dollars, had by this time become so pressing that the Treasury was given the power to compel private owners of foreign securities to sell them. This was a sign of the increasing Allied, and hence British, dependence upon the material resources of the United States for the conduct of the war. As a result of this, very soon after her entry into the war, she assumed in effect the role of banker to the Allies. The reason for this was succinctly put by Northcliffe when he cabled home that "If loans stop, war stops",[1] and America had entered the war determined to win it. That point is of considerable importance, for it should be remembered when criticizing America later for her attitude to the war debts, that at the time of her entry into the war many well-informed persons believed that she would enter it on a strictly limited liability basis, but in the event she threw in all her resources.

Nevertheless, she remained only an Associated Power, and she never wavered in her view that the money she lent was lent on a strictly commercial basis; here was the beginning of the trouble, for the Allies had agreed in February, 1915, to unite their financial resources, equally with their military resources, for the purpose of carrying the war to a successful conclusion, and always regarded loans as subject to post-war adjustment. America, partly from lack of this sort of diplomatic tradition, and partly because she never fully identified herself with the common European cause, at no time accepted the Allied point of view that expenditure should be broadly adjusted in accordance with ability to pay. Though she regarded all her loans as commercial in character, it was plain that in the later negotiations the question would acquire a strongly political flavour because all loans to Britain and the Allies after 1917 were made by the American Government through the United States Treasury, and not by the American public directly as heretofore. The third class of loans, those made after the Armistice for relief and reconstruction, were recognized by Britain as being of a different type, and were dealt with by her for the most part as

[1] Q. Willert, p. 111.

ordinary loans of the kind that America claimed all the debts were.

The net position of the United States Government was that it had by 1920 lent approximately $10,000 million in all; the British Government had lent approximately $8,000 million to others, and had borrowed approximately $4,000 million from the United States. Britain had also received a certain amount of money, chiefly in the form of gold, from her Allies. Thus America was in this respect a creditor nation, owing nothing; Britain was a net creditor nation, being owed larger sums than she owed.

During the heat of the war the fundamental difference of attitude between the European powers and America concerning the debts remained unobtrusive, but it very soon moved to the forefront when peace descended on the world. During the Versailles Conference the Allies endeavoured to promote a general discussion of the position, but this was refused by the Americans, who in 1919 made a proposal for funding the debts owed to her. Negotiations, however, made little progress and in 1920 Britain raised in a formal manner the question of a general cancellation of the war debts, which was also refused by the United States. Shortly afterwards a further bone of contention was added when the British and French Governments decided to link together the debts of the Allies and the payment of reparations by Germany. Their agreement in effect recognized the right of the Allies to pay only such of their debts as could be met out of payments made to them by their war-time enemies. The two governments agreed to try and induce the United States to accept the extension of this arrangement to the monies owed to her.

This was a faint hope, for Wilson had flatly refused to recognize any such connexion at Paris; there he had endeavoured to keep reparations on a scale which Germany could afford to pay, but had not admitted the applicability of any remotely similar criterion to the debts of the Allies to the United States. Lloyd George, however, wrote to Wilson on 5 August, 1920, pointing out that France had only expressed her willingness to keep down German reparations payments to a reasonable level on the condition that her debts to the Allies were treated in the same way:

> This declaration appeared to the British Government eminently fair. But after careful consideration they came to the conclusion that it was impossible to remit any part of what was owed to them by France except as part and parcel of all round settlement of inter-Allied indebtedness. . . . British public opinion would never support a one-sided arrangement at its sole expense, and . . . if such a one-sided

arrangement were made it could not fail to estrange and eventually embitter the relations between the American and British people with calamitous results to the future of the world.

From the standpoint of Anglo-American relations it is probable that he was right, that any other course than that actually followed would have produced even more bitterness. He certainly showed how great British consideration for American feelings was, by making it clear that Great Britain would be perfectly prepared to go on with funding negotiations provided they did not prejudice any possible broader arrangement.

Wilson's reply however was blunt:

> It is highly improbable that either the Congress or popular opinion in this country will ever permit a cancellation of any part of the debt of the British Government to the United States in order to induce the British Government to remit, in whole or in part, the debt to Great Britain or France or any of the Allied Governments, or that it would consent to a cancellation or reduction in the debts of any of the Allied Governments as an inducement towards a practical settlement of the reparation claims. . . .This Government . . . cannot consent to connect the reparation question with that of inter-governmental indebtedness.

He urged the rapid despatch of an accredited British representative to arrange the funding of the debt to America which, "It is felt . . . will do more to strengthen the friendly relations between America and Great Britain than would any other course of dealing with the same."[1]

What were the essentials of the Anglo-American position which was thus made clear? First, the British case. As the nation in the world most dependent upon abundant international commerce and prosperity, she soon began to realize, what Keynes pointed out in *The Economic Consequences of the Peace*, that the economic results of the Versailles Treaty in Central Europe were likely to prove disastrous. She also realized with increasing force that the whole structure of international debt was bound to prove unworkable, and that the only solution was to cut the Gordian knot by a general all-round cancellation of debts. On the face of it she would herself lose by this arrangement, since she had lent more than she had borrowed; it was true that the United States would lose more, but it was felt that she had also suffered least and could best afford to lose. In the British view, furthermore, it ought to be possible to link the indebtedness of some countries to German

[1] Q. H. G. Moulton and L. Pasvolsky, *War Debts and World Prosperity* (Washington, 1932), pp. 66, 68-9.

reparations in such a way that the defeated aggressor power would bear the burden, although this should be reduced to reasonable dimensions. This point of view essentially regarded all the costs of the war as something to be shared by all its participants whenever they entered it. It seemed not unreasonable that America should make some retrospective contribution to the cost of the years prior to 1917, and it is probable that this is the only successful way in which to run a coalition of this kind in war. The powers that can afford more must contribute more to the common cause; such is the inevitable burden of responsibility which international greatness brings with it. Britain had for very many years accepted the need of subsidizing her poor political Allies to fight for her; in almost exactly similar circumstances, as it seemed to her, she had, from 1793 to 1816, furnished approximately £61 million of aid to her allies in the French wars, and of this total she received only £2,600,000 in repayment. In fact, at least £53 million had been advanced purely as subsidies without any expectation of repayment; Great Britain in 1816 virtually wiped the slate clean, despite her serious economic condition in that year. It did not seem to be asking too much of the great and prosperous United States that she should do the same a century later.

But to the United States things looked very different. She had no tradition of, and no longer any apparent desire for, international leadership; many of her people did not really believe that her interests had been deeply threatened by Germany and were resolved never to be entangled in a European war again. And, in any case, what would be for her the effect of a general cancellation of war debts? She might receive some money from the prostrate Germany, but the rest of the sums which her Treasury had lent to the Allies during the war she would herself have to repay. This money had had to be raised in the United States, mostly through government loans subscribed by the public; if no one else met the principal and interest payments upon these loans, the American Treasury would have to do it. Thus the American people, by taxation, would be paying back their own loans to themselves; in other words, America's external credits would become internal debts. Now these are not unusual things, and she had of course acquired quite substantial ones on her own account during the war. What was unusual was that America should be expected *in time of peace* to assume the burden of debts which she had confidently expected would be paid by her associates. It is possible that, if the Administration had thought it proper, the American people would have paid the full bill without undue despondency, if they had been called upon to make outright subsidies instead of loans during the war; men will accept in the heat of battle sacrifices they boggle at making in time of peace. But even this is doubtful, and Wilson, who would not accept even the status of an Ally, never contemplated any such arrangement, while the Allies, wisely refusing to look a gift-horse in the mouth whilst engaged in the mortal struggle, made no concrete proposals of this kind. It is not to be wondered at that America refused a general cancellation after the war was over, and it is hard to imagine that the war debts question could in fact have pursued any very different course; the attitudes of the two nations, as well as their actions, arose too directly from their differing circumstances.

What was a pity was that emotional and moral judgments were allowed to play so large a part in its settlement, for this not only made for much bitterness, but also obscured the economic and political realities which were in the end to assert undisputed control over the progress of the dispute. Americans saw the question as a moral one, and were incensed at the efforts of the Allies to wriggle out of their plain commitments. Britons—because it was their interest to do so—saw it primarily as political and economic; they were, perhaps, less impressed by the moral argument owing to their knowledge of the vast sums which their fathers had lost in the middle of the previous century, from the repudiation of their just debts by American railroads, and, even worse, American states. Thus came the bitterness which transformed Uncle Sam into Uncle Shylock—until he was once more transformed, this time into the Santa Claus of Lend-Lease and Marshall Aid. The feelings of the protagonists should never have been allowed to blind them to the economic facts. There were only two practical ways in which the debts could be paid: by gold, or by goods and services. The former was impossible, not only because of the lack of gold in Europe —one of the worst symptoms of the coming Great Depression was the uncontrolled flood of gold into the United States—but also because large-scale transfers of this kind play havoc with international exchange. Payment by goods and services was made, as American economists almost unanimously pointed out at the time, next to impossible by the American protectionist system. For America to demand payment of the debts was one thing; for her to fail to make payment possible was another, for, as Moulton and Pasvolsky write, "One thing is certain—that a country which is unwilling to receive payments cannot be paid."[1] The truth is that America, which had entered the war a debtor, emerged from it the greatest international creditor, a change

[1] Moulton and Pasvolsky, p. 402.

for which she was not prepared. Her demand for war debt payments, her desire for increased external markets for her exports, and her continued export of capital, which further augmented her overseas credits, all dictated an increase in imports and the liberalizing of trade. Continued, indeed increased, protection added to the world's difficulties, exercised a magnetic attraction upon the world's gold supplies, and contributed to the world's—and America's—economic collapse.

The reparations question, which was linked with that of war debts in a way which America refused to recognize (not merely by desire of the Allies, but by cold, hard facts) was handled very badly. Britain was early apprehensive of pressing excessively on Germany, and broke with France on this issue at the time of the occupation of the Ruhr. In the event the reparations originally imposed had to be steadily whittled down under pressure of events, first in the London settlement of 1921, and then by two commissions of experts presided over by Americans, Dawes in 1924 and Young in 1928. But even so, Germany was only able to make payments owing to the flow of American—and on a much smaller scale British—capital into the country in the twenties. Thus the Allies paid to the United States what they received from Germany, and Germany paid these sums largely out of borrowings from America; such were the effects of insistence on the payment of war debts. In the end the reparations payments helped to touch off in 1931 the European phase of the Economic Blizzard.

But what meanwhile had been the course of Anglo-American relations in the matter of the debts? When it became clear to the British that the Americans were adamant against cancellation, the British Government sent to the European countries concerned the so-called Balfour Note of 1 August, 1922. It invited Britain's war debtors to inaugurate funding negotiations, though with "the greatest reluctance",[1] since the Government favoured general cancellation. The note ran:

> With the most perfect courtesy, and in the exercise of their undoubted rights, the American Government have required this country to pay the interest accrued since 1919 on the Anglo-American debt, to convert it from an unfunded debt, and to repay it by a sinking fund in twenty-five years. Such a procedure is clearly in accordance with the original contract. His Majesty's Government make no complaint of it; they recognize their obligations and are prepared to fulfil them. But evidently they cannot do so without profoundly modifying the course which, in different circumstances, they

[1] Q. Moulton and Pasvolsky, p. 111.

would have wished to pursue. They cannot treat the repayment of the Anglo-American loan as if it were an isolated incident in which only the United States of America and Great Britain had any concern. It is but one of a connected series of transactions, in which this country appears sometimes as debtor, sometimes as creditor, and, if our undoubted obligations as a debtor are to be enforced, our not less undoubted rights as a creditor cannot be left wholly in abeyance.

It went on to point out that "Great Britain is owed more than it owes"; according to the note, exclusive of reparations, Great Britain's loans to her Allies were more than double her borrowings from America, and, including reparations, the debts to her were four times her own debts. She would have suffered a paper loss of about £750 million by a general cancellation, but still advocated it. Failing that, however, she would collect from her debtors only sums sufficient to make her debt payments to the United States: "we do not in any event desire to make a profit out of any less satisfactory arrangement" than general cancellation. "And, while we do not ask for more, all will admit that we can hardly be content with less."[1] To the British, who regarded the whole debt complex as a unity, it seemed just to place the responsibility for a refusal to accept all-round cancellation pointedly where it actually lay, on the United States.

To Americans who did not, and who would be the greatest losers by cancellation, it appeared in a very different light. Churchill writes, "I was in full accord with the . . . Balfour Note. . . . I thought that if Great Britain were thus made not only the debtor, but the debt-collector of the United States, the unwisdom of the debt collection would become apparent at Washington. However, no such reaction followed. Indeed the argument was resented."[2] So, first among the important powers, Great Britain acceded to a funding arrangement made by Stanley Baldwin in Washington early in 1923. This provided for full repayment, though over sixty-two years instead of twenty-five, and at a rate of interest which represented a reduction of approximately one third in the original terms, which was a concession to the British contention that 3·3 per cent was a fair rate for a long-term government loan. The arrangement, which was eventually accepted by the Cabinet, was unconditional, a testimonial to the power of the American Government in British life and to Britain's desire as a great financial power to retain her reputation for integrity. The terms were regarded with satisfaction in America, but with great misgivings in Britain, where many people believed that they would soon prove unworkable. The settlements with

[1] Q. ibid, pp. 111-3.   [2] *Second World War*, I, p. 20.

757

most of the other powers made by the United States followed the pattern of that with Britain, although, presumably on the basis of capacity to pay, their terms were more generous. All the agreements contained certain escape or postponement provisions, but stipulated for the most part, like that with Britain, for payment in gold or in bonds of the United States.

The effects of the relative severity of the British agreement and of its unconditional nature soon became apparent in the years which followed. In the first place, she began her American payments before her own funding agreements were made. In the second, whereas the rest of the European powers were able almost to cover their American payments out of other debts and reparations, Great Britain's payments to the United States between 1924 and 1931 exceeded, by something of the order of $200 million, her receipts from German reparations and from her own debtors. The absurdity of the reparations situation was shown by the fact that Germany paid 11,000 million marks between 1924 and 1931, but borrowed abroad in the same period approximately 18,000 million marks, of which about half came from the United States and another substantial proportion from Britain.

Prior to 1931 Great Britain paid America a sum totalling $1,911,798,300, which was not only about four times as much as that paid by the next biggest debtor, France, but approximately three-quarters of all the payments made to the United States in that period. Put more precisely and in another way, Britain, which received 41 per cent of all the loans made by the United States Treasury to fifteen foreign governments, furnished 74 per cent of all the payments received by the Treasury from those governments; the shares of all the other countries in the total payments to the United States were smaller than their shares in the original loans. Although there was no legal connexion between reparations and war debts, and though the United States had continually refused to recognize a moral one, President Hoover very promptly recognized the practical connexion when he met the collapse of the European economy in 1931, following on that of the American economy, by the proposal, on 20 June, of an all-round one-year moratorium on the payment of both reparations and debts. He had originally intended a two-year period, but even that was thought of purely as a temporary measure to enable the nations to recuperate, after which payments would be resumed. The President emphatically stated that he did not "approve in any remote sense of the cancellation of the debts to us",[1] but Congress added a specific rider to that effect.

[1] Q. Moulton and Pasvolsky, p. 324.

Hoover had seen that the dominant economic position of the United States in the world forced her to take the initiative, but neither he nor Congress realized that economic forces beyond their control were rapidly bringing about the collapse of the whole international debt structure. At Lausanne in 1932 the European powers wrote off 90 per cent of German reparations, but made the action contingent upon their reaching a satisfactory settlement with "their own creditors",[1] that is to say the United States. This action was greeted with rage in America and the President reaffirmed his position, but nothing could be done in the throes of a Presidential election. The London Economic Conference of 1933 achieved very little, largely because of the refusal of Roosevelt to agree to any arrangement which would "peg" the dollar in international exchange owing to his recent devaluation of it, and because of the refusal of the other powers to heed his demand that they concentrate on the broader questions of bettering "fundamental economic ills."[2] Efforts to bring up the debts question at the Conference were frustrated by his continuation of the refusal to link it with the general European debt situation. In the previous December, Britain and France had asked for a suspension of payments pending a general discussion, and when this had been refused, France and five others defaulted outright on the 15 December payment. Britain paid in full in gold, but gave notice that she would regard it as a capital payment in any final settlement.

MacDonald had, however, visited Roosevelt just before the Conference, and, through the haze of cordial generalities issued to the public, it appeared that the President took as broad a view of the problem as the domestic scene allowed. He had been prepared for individual discussions with the nations concerned and had recommended a part payment of $10 million (approximately 10 per cent of the sum due) by Britain in June. Chamberlain, who was Chancellor of the Exchequer, favoured a $5 million token payment, but $10 million was eventually paid three days after the London Conference opened, in the expectation that "we could get a satisfactory statement from Roosevelt that he did not consider we were defaulting".[3] If Roosevelt had made such a statement, American public opinion would have repudiated it, for after another token payment in December, the Congress passed the Johnson Act of 13 April, 1934, which provided that no person or corporation under American jurisdiction could lend money to a government that was in default on a debt to the United

---

[1] S. F. Bemis, *The United States as a World Power* (New York, 1950), p. 246.
[2] Q. Bailey, p. 733.   [3] Q. Feiling, p. 222.

States. The Attorney General then ruled that payments must be made in full if the debtors were not to be in default, whereupon Britain, along with all the other debtors except Finland, which alone had a large favourable trade balance with America, defaulted altogether in June, 1934. Payments were never resumed, and Britain set forth the final outcome in a note to the State Department; she had paid $2,205 million out of a total original debt of $4,277 million, whereas other nations had paid only $679 million out of $4,714 million. *The Economist* pointed out that in 1923 the British annuity was equivalent to six months' exports from Britain to America, whereas that due in 1932 was equivalent, owing to the shrinkage of world trade, to four years' exports. It would be hard to find a stronger argument for the inevitability of the stoppage, as long as the United States refused to contemplate a radical revision of terms.

Thus did the war debts pass from the international scene, except for the continuation of disgruntled cries from the American public in the wings. This American chagrin was, given the background of the dispute, natural and almost inevitable; the true irony of it was that within seven short years of the passage of the Johnson Act, Congress was to pour out her wealth to her Allies, and particularly to Britain, in quantities unheard of in World War I and with virtually no expectation of repayment. Few if any Americans would have credited a prophecy of this in 1934, for the immediate American reaction to British and European default was an intensification of the already potent trend towards isolationism. The war debts issue had undoubtedly caused a great deal of bad feeling between the British and American people. This was not lessened by the fact that Britain's record in the matter was better, from beginning to end, than that of any other important state; rather, because of the Balfour Note policy, did she encounter greater American animosity than her Allies. The British proposal for cancellation, which would in theory have hit the United States harder than Britain, primarily arose from the latter's paramount interest in international trade and from her saner, because more experienced, attitude to problems of international finance, but it appeared to many Americans, if not as a characteristic piece of English trickery, at least as offensively smug. Even the historians of today, writing after World War II when the worst of these problems were avoided by the generosity and wide comprehension of American statesmanship, betray their national origins all too clearly in the attitude they take towards the old war debts question. But, despite the ill-feeling, there was no lasting damage to the Anglo-American relationship; the settlement of the

760

Irish problem alone outweighed it in importance. One has only to imagine what harm such a dispute would have done in the heyday of American Anglophobia to see how firmly the foundations of common interest and common feeling had by now been laid.

V

OTHER issues in this period are of singularly little importance. There were, of course, minor rumblings such as a protest from the Administration, under pressure of American oil interests, that Britain was taking unfair advantage of its Mandates by monopolizing the world's oil resources, but they were soon settled.

Prohibition was a source of considerable friction it is true. It was looked upon by the British—according to their very pronounced domestic viewpoints—either as an appalling or commendable experiment, but was generally considered by the end of the twenties to have been impracticable and a failure. The diplomatic difficulty arose from the fact that Britain was the greatest international exporter of hard liquor, and therefore the nation with most to gain financially by the failure of prohibition. The British Government was, in fact, deeply concerned about British smuggling adventures in contravention of American law, and even consented to the extension of the long-established three-mile limit to twelve miles, in an effort to assist the American authorities to control bootlegging, a notable concession. Perhaps it was salutary that the worst friction was with the now independent Canada, one of whose vessels was, for instance, sunk by the American coastguard well outside territorial waters, for Canadian-American relations could by now stand the strain without difficulty. Except for Canadian mistrust of American neutrality during the early years of the war, of her abandonment of the League, and of her insistence on her pound of flesh in the form of war debts, they became increasingly cordial, despite a severe tariff rivalry in the twenties; American annexationism was dead, and economic and political bonds, such as those constituted by the common waterways and their joint administration, grew steadily closer. This seemed of considerable consequence when Roosevelt said to a Canadian audience in August, 1938: "The Dominion of Canada is part of the sisterhood of the British Empire. I give to you assurances that the peoples of the United States will not stand idly by if domination of Canadian soil is threatened by any other Empire."[1]

[1] Q. *United States as a World Power*, p. 328.

761

Not that Canada constituted the only important Anglo-American link; far from it, for the multiplication of ties between Britain and the United States had never been swifter. The very unreality of American political isolationism is demonstrated by this fact. To the steamship and the electric telegraph were added the trans-Atlantic telephone, the radio, and in due course the aircraft. The flood of printed matter and of mail of every kind grew beyond all recognition, particularly that passing from west to east. The cinema, which Hollywood had come to dominate in the war, was an instrument of American influence upon Britain probably surpassed by no other in the history of relationships between great nations. Naturally enough this produced some reaction in Englishmen, just as British cultural dominance had irked Americans in the early nineteenth century, but this did little if anything to check the irresistible process.

Nothing, however, more clearly showed the closeness of American ties with a world she wished to renounce than the coming of the depression in 1929 and 1931. Here was proof positive that America could not live of her own and sufficient unto herself in the economic sphere, proof as convincing as was to follow in 1940 and 1941 in the political sphere.

In the contraction of international trade at the time of the depression, which reduced the total external trade volume of the two countries by a half, few branches suffered so severely as Anglo-American commerce. American exports to Britain were reduced to less than a third of their earlier quantity and British exports to the United States to only just a little over a third. The closeness of the relationship in the financial sphere is dramatically illustrated by the British Cabinet crisis which came to a head on 23 August, 1931, when the whole British problem revolved around the restoration of confidence in the pound. What this meant in practice was—what national measures by the British Government would appear sufficient to encourage New York bankers to offer further credits or loans? MacDonald's course of action in the crisis was virtually determined by a cable on this subject from J. P. Morgan and Co., which said that there was "little prospect of the American public being willing to take up a public loan, unless and until Parliament . . . passed the necessary economic legislation."[1] When this message was read to the Cabinet, pandemonium broke loose—or so it appeared to a listener in the next room—but it convinced MacDonald that the measures must be passed in the national interest. On this

[1] Q. Nicolson, p. 463.

762

occasion at any rate—and the Labour party did not easily forget it—the policies of Britain had the appearance of being veritably dictated by Wall Street.

It has been said that no democratic government can survive in office the effects of a great world depression, and it certainly seems true to say that no policy can, for in each country the post-depression government reacted against the commercial policy its predecessor had pursued. This had paradoxical results in Anglo-American economic life. In the United States the Democrats endeavoured in traditional fashion to reduce the size of the enormous tariff wall built by the Republicans in the twenties; the Trade Agreements Act of 1934 gave the President power to raise or lower tariffs by up to fifty per cent for those nations making reciprocal concessions, though the usual American insistence on the unconditional most favoured nation clause extended these reductions automatically to many other nations which had signed similar trade agreements with the United States. By 1939 Secretary of State Hull had signed twenty-one such agreements. In a Britain which entered the slump as a free trade country, the element in the Conservative party which believed in a protective tariff and Imperial Preference gained control, and it was decided to adopt a policy of protection on a large scale for the first time for three-quarters of a century. As a result, a number of trade agreements were negotiated in the following years and tariffs were imposed; the most important of the agreements resulted from the Ottawa Conference of the members of the British Commonwealth. But the common run of the British treaties was quite different from that of the American; the effect of the latter was to reduce tariff barriers and open up international trade. The former were mostly concluded to exploit Britain's balance of trade with certain countries, and made few tariff concessions, but extracted a considerable number, by means of a British Government threat to raise tariffs yet further.

Thus English and American trade policies were moving in diametrically opposite directions, yet they were able in 1938 to sign a very far-reaching trade agreement. (The treaty showed the length of its ancestry in Article 6, which agreed on the unconditional most favoured nation clause, for the Treaty of Commerce of 1815, reaffirmed in Article 23, had probably only implied conditional most favoured nation treatment.) It is significant that most of the concessions were on the British side, for the agreement followed very much the fixed pattern of other American treaties, whereas it stood out as a solitary exception to the usual British type; in its lowering of duties it was a reversal of the whole trend of British trade policy, and necessitated considerable revision of the Ottawa Treaties. Canada, which had negotiated a separate treaty with America in 1935, was the Dominion most affected, and she negotiated a new one with the United States in 1937-8, along with Britain, which is significant of her vital role in the Anglo-American relationship.

Nevertheless, the Anglo-American Treaty is a tribute to the economic power of the United States, for reductions of duty were made on a large scale, affecting 149 different commodities in the case of Britain, and 468 in the case of the United States. More than that, it is a tribute to her political power, for there seems little doubt that the major British motive for reversing its current practice in the case of the United States was political. The historian of the agreement goes so far as to write, though admitting that motives must remain a matter of surmise:

> It is extremely improbable that the British Government regarded the agreement as an opportunity to increase the standard of living of the British people. . . . It is difficult to believe that the British Government was so naïve as to think that an Anglo-American trade agreement, however sweeping in scope, would be interpreted in Germany and Italy as a demonstration of Anglo-American solidarity. On the other hand, the British Government could hardly have been oblivious to the attitude of the dictator states if the democracies had failed in their attempt to reach an agreement. The most plausible explanation of the agreement . . . is that the initiative . . . came from the United States . . . to round out its program, and that the British Government thought it unwise to refuse the American request.[1]

The initiation of these negotiations at the very height of American isolationism in 1937 is convincing proof of the readiness of Britain to catch at any straw of American support, and of the unlikelihood of the United States being able to remain permanently aloof from the international society in which she lived, moved and had her being. Of the latter, the great maelstrom, which virtually swept this elaborate economic treaty away, along with so much else, was to be the ultimate proof.

VI

THE story of how that maelstrom came is all that remains for us to tell of the history of Anglo-American relations to 1939; it falls into two parts, the Far East, and Europe.

---

[1] C. Kreider, *The Anglo-American Trade Agreement* (London, 1943), p. 241.

The calm which fell on American-Japanese relations after the Washington Conference was short-lived, for in 1924 the old immigration question came once more to a head, and racial and naval equality began to be thought of by Japanese leaders as essential to her nationhood. The rise of nationalism in China led not only to an undeclared Chinese-Russian war in 1929, but to increased friction with Japan, particularly over her Manchurian interests. In the Chinese-Russian incident Stimson showed himself more active in the Far East than any American diplomat since Theodore Roosevelt, and, acting as a signatory of the Kellogg Pact, with some difficulty persuaded Great Britain, along with France and Italy, to issue an appeal to the disputants identical with one from the United States. His intention probably was to try and pursue a policy of collective security in the Far East, even though he dared not go farther than to promise parallel, though independent, American action to that of League members. Soon, however, a much graver problem was created by the friction between Japan and China, for on 18 September, 1931, the former launched what was in effect a carefully prepared attack on Manchuria, whereupon China appealed to the League for its good offices, as also, independently, to the United States for hers.

Stimson from the first showed readiness for action to the limit of what was politically possible for him, though he curbed his public expressions of condemnation of Japan in order to strengthen the relatively liberal hands of Japan's Government against the military clique that was gaining control there. He regarded the League as the proper agency for action, and the American Minister at Berne was instructed to attend meetings of the Council; later, Stimson even acceded to a formal request from the League to appoint a representative at meetings affecting the enforcement of the Kellogg Pact. On 23 September he agreed to a request from the League to despatch identical notes to the two powers asking them to withdraw their troops. On 5 October he urged the League to bring the heaviest pressure to bear in the matter, and promised that the American Government would "endeavor to reinforce what the League does."[1] Shortly thereafter he began to talk of "some form of collective economic sanctions against Japan,"[2] but was only able to get the League to invoke the Kellogg Pact, which the United States did at the same time. Dawes was sent to maintain contact with the Council at its November meeting in Paris, and Stimson issued a very serious warning to the Japanese Ambassador on 19 November. All that the League would consent to do was to appoint

[1] Q. Nevins, *The U.S. in a Chaotic World* (London, 1950), p. 179.

[2] Q. Griswold, p. 417.

the Lytton investigating commission, which it decided to do on 10 December with the approval of the Japanese, who hoped to profit by the fact that their case was a good deal more complex and in some respects better than is often recognized. Stimson warmly endorsed the action, but the Japanese assent resulted in the final end of liberal governments in Tokyo, and the undisputed reign of militarism. The Japanese pressed on their military campaign, and conciliation had plainly failed.

Looking in his diplomatic armoury for further weapons, the Secretary of State brought forth on 7 January, 1932, a traditional American procedure in the Far East, a note to Japan and China informing them that the United States would not recognize any agreement or treaty effected by means contrary to the Kellogg Pact, and reaffirming her faith in the Open Door and the territorial integrity of China; this was the so-called Hoover-Stimson doctrine of non-recognition. On 5 January Stimson had revealed his design to the British Ambassador, but, once more in the American tradition, did not wait for British agreement, probably lest public opinion denounce him for Anglophilia. Britain and the other European powers which were approached did not agree with the American initiative. The British response, in fact, was, as Griswold writes, "one of studied casualness—a Foreign Office *communiqué* (9 January) which credited at face value Japan's frequently professed intention of maintaining the open door in Manchuria and deprecated the necessity of addressing 'any formal note to the Japanese Government on the lines of the American Government's note.' The *communiqué* was accompanied by an editorial in the London *Times* characterizing China's administrative integrity as an ideal rather than an existing fact and endorsing the Foreign Office's wisdom in refusing to associate itself with Stimson's action."[1]

On 28 January, encouraged by this inaction, the Japanese attacked Shanghai, but were checked by the Chinese and even more by the fact that this threat to their own national property and citizens stung both the British and the Americans into sending actual reinforcements into the area, though the initiative appears once more to have come from the State Department. China had again appealed to the League, while Stimson drew up terms of peace in reply to a Japanese request for good offices at Shanghai, gained British consent to them by transAtlantic telephone (used for such a purpose for the first time), and presented them to Japan. They were refused by her. He went further and invited Sir John Simon, the British Foreign Secretary, in the most

[1] Ibid, p. 425.

pressing and repeated fashion, to join him in a formal invocation of the Nine Power Treaty, but was rebutted on the ground that Britain must act with the League, or as Griswold puts it, that Simon "would not step out from behind the constitutional shield that English membership in the League afforded him."[1] On 22 February Stimson made an effort to mobilize public opinion by a long letter to Senator Borah, which took the form of an appeal to the Nine Power Treaty and which was probably not without effect, for, under further pressure, Britain proposed and carried in the League Assembly a non-recognition resolution. Japan established and recognized a puppet Manchurian state in September, 1932, but strong pressure by the powers did obtain the withdrawal of Japanese troops from Shanghai on 31 May of that year; this pressure was forthcoming largely because it was the only point where their interests were directly at stake. Upon the adoption by the League in 1933 of the Lytton report, condemning Japanese action, albeit with reservations, Japan resigned from the League. The first step on the path to World War II had been taken.

But not only had the whole fabric of collective security suffered a severe blow: Anglo-American relations had, on the face of it, been considerably endangered. A British Foreign Secretary had violated a fundamental axiom of his country's policy in repeatedly refusing co-operation in international affairs offered to him by an American Secretary of State. As it appeared, a hand had been stretched once more across the Atlantic—this time, remarkably, from west to east—and, as it appeared, it had not been seized. The situation, however, was not quite as simple as that, and, because it was not, little harm in the end was done to Anglo-American friendship. One thing was harmful and inexcusable, the manner in which co-operation had been refused in January, 1932. It is true that Stimson acted without waiting for British consent, or a British reply to his notification of action, but the reason for caution in these matters was well known in the Foreign Office; it is true that unofficial explanations in *The Times* later admitted that the official in the Foreign Office who issued the *communiqué* did not appreciate that it would read like a rebuff to the United States. But these excuses do not remove the offence. For the risk he ran of alienating the greatest power in the world by his methods, if not his objectives, Simon must bear full responsibility.

In defence of his ends, there is more to be said. He may be accused of hiding behind the League, but he may also be excused for treating

[1] Ibid, p. 431.

American advances with caution, even scepticism. Stimson was an idealist and a forceful figure in international affairs; as a Republican, and one who had recently been High Commissioner in the Philippines, he was acutely conscious of the importance of the Far East. He was, therefore, anxious to co-operate with the League in this matter, but it was in this matter only. Britain, still smarting from the rebuff of America's original repudiation of the League, and observing that there was no proposal to go wholeheartedly back on this decision, might be pardoned for treating the offers of the American Executive with reserve. More than this, there was every sign that Stimson was far ahead of most of his countrymen, and there were even indications that Hoover himself was not behind him. Certainly the President, who originated the Hoover-Stimson proposal, was not prepared to use force; he wrote in October, 1931, in a memorandum to his Cabinet, "These acts [of Japan] do not impair the freedom of the American people, the economic or moral future of the people. I do not propose ever to sacrifice American life for anything short of this . . . [W]e will not go along on war or any of the sanctions either military or economic, for these are the roads to war."[1] The fact that the whole United States fleet was assembled at Hawaii did not convince the British, any more than the Japanese, that America really meant business unless her own interests were directly attacked, especially since, through underbuilding, her navy was now only about the equal of Japan's. This impression was enhanced by the economic condition of the country and by the vociferous opposition in the American Press and elsewhere to what Hearst's New York *American* dubbed "Stimson's Folly".[2] The real reaction of the American people was a further retreat into isolationism, and Simon was at least wise in being doubtful as to whether Stimson could have carried American opinion with him. Had Britain accepted his offers and had he then been repudiated, her position would have been most unenviable.

But this salutary caution was probably not Simon's primary motive, for he unquestionably reflected British public opinion, which was almost as reluctant as that of the United States to risk trouble in the cause of a far-off China. Some Britons looked back with lingering regret to the Anglo-Japanese Alliance; others, particularly in the Yangtze area and the Antipodes, were not sorry to see Japan turn north, where she might clash perhaps with a revivified Russia; nearly all, in a deep mood of pacifism, were unable to bring themselves to face the idea of war. Simon's fault as a leader was that he did not lead; as Burke might

[1] Q. Nevins, *The U.S. in a Chaotic World*, pp. 182-3.   [2] Bailey, p. 725.

have said of Charles Townshend, he conformed exactly to the temper of public opinion, and he seemed to guide, because he was always sure to follow it. Public opinion in Britain, as in America, must bear the ultimate responsibility. If Simon had taken a strong line in the League, it is just possible that Stimson would have been able to swing America behind him, but it is doubtful. Even Churchill, who never fails to face up to unpopular truths, implies doubt as to the success of such a course of action when he writes, "His Majesty's Government could hardly be blamed if in their grave financial, and growing European embarrassments, they did not seek a prominent role at the side of the United States in the Far East without any hope of corresponding American support in Europe."[1] Convinced believers in the vision of the great League may see in this period its first gross betrayal: the hard fact remains, as Stimson wrote, that everyone concerned "wanted Japan checked, but wanted somebody else to do it."[2]

In the end, because of the basic similarity of public opinion in both countries, the new developments did little positive harm to Anglo-American relations, and both governments ended up in the same posture when, at the instance of Sir John Simon, the League Assembly on 11 March, 1932, re-enunciated the Hoover-Stimson doctrine in emphatic terms. The same course of theoretical condemnation was followed by both states when full scale war between Japanese and Chinese began in 1937; the courses were similar but still independent. As Nevins writes, "Washington co-operated broadly with London, but on parallel lines, avoiding that joint action which might unduly incense Tokyo."[3] Roosevelt had continued Stimson's policy in form, but had been very much less active in Far Eastern affairs, partly owing to the pressure of internal events, partly owing to the Democratic reluctance to remain heavily involved in that area, which was shown clearly by the Philippine independence legislation of 1934, and partly because of intense isolationist feeling. Because of this attitude on the part of both the British and American Governments, the Brussels Conference of 1937, called to discuss the Far Eastern war, which was attended by both powers, was a fiasco. Only when their interests were immediately threatened did either react vigorously, as in the case of the Japanese attack on the American gunboat *Panay* in December, 1937, when Japan, correctly estimating the situation, hastily made the fullest apology and reparation for the action. Almost at the same time, a Japanese battery

[1] *Second World War*, I, p. 68.
[2] Q. Nevins, *The U.S. in a Chaotic World*, p. 186.
[3] A. Nevins, *The New Deal and World Affairs* (London, 1950), pp. 124-5.

shelled the two British gunboats *Bee* and *Ladybird*. Meanwhile, a virtual economic war was going on between Britain and Japan over the huge Japanese exports of cheap textiles to Empire markets. Two things did, however, emerge from the continued tension with Japan. First, it accelerated the re-armament of both Britain and America, particularly the latter, for in 1936 and successive years Roosevelt obtained the greatest peace-time naval appropriations in American history. Second, it broke finally any tenuous connexions between Britain and her one-time ally, and aligned the former irrevocably with the United States, even though neither the British nor American peoples were yet willing to realize that what were being drawn up were lines of battle.

VII

IN 1933, soon after the first phase of the Far Eastern conflict, it became apparent that even more serious threats to world peace were coming into existence in Europe. American sensitivity to the European and Asiatic threats respectively tended to vary from section to section; inhabitants of the Atlantic states were naturally more concerned over the one, and inhabitants of the Pacific Coast over the other, while in the Mississippi Valley and the great central plains was the vast body of opinion which inclined to care for none of these things. The centre of gravity of American population was still in the east rather than the west and the hereditary associations of most of the American people were with Europe, so that it is possible that the country as a whole was more concerned with European than Far Eastern dangers; on the other hand the inhibitions against intervention in European affairs were probably a good deal stronger. It was the chain of events in Europe which was to drag America to the brink of war, even if it was the Japanese attack which was actually to push her into it. In Britain, naturally, European dangers dominated all others. Certainly the influence of Australia and New Zealand, and the possession of India and the Eastern Empire, kept the menace of Japan always in the minds of British Governments, as the great expenditure on the naval base at Singapore shows, but it was with the rise of Nazi Germany, and, to a less degree, Fascist Italy that Britain was chiefly concerned.

With the manifold happenings which led to war in 1939 we cannot deal here; we can but examine the attitude of the two countries to one another during the developing crisis. In their relationship, as we have seen, the dominating fact in these years was the apparent lack of American influence over European events. At perhaps one point only did the United States exert a perceptible and positive effect, although her negative influence, exercised through the vacuum created by her withdrawal into isolationism, was of incalculable significance.

This American impotence was not in accordance with the wishes of her President, nor indeed of her Secretary of State, Cordell Hull; Roosevelt's motives are obscure, but it seems probable that, after an initial period of revulsion from European affairs (as a result partly of the "bungling" of the London Economic Conference) and after the pressure of domestic issues had abated sufficiently, he came to appreciate more clearly perhaps than many statesmen then in power, the realities of the European situation. He seems to have been somewhat slower to come to this conclusion even than the cautious Hull, but when he was convinced he never wavered, as far as one can judge, in his intentions. Certainly by 1937 he had decided to take the plunge, as we shall see when we discuss the famous "quarantine" speech at Chicago in October of that year.[1] The fact that he had access to information which had, in the nature of things, to be denied to the American public at large exaggerated the pronounced split in the American mind, the President becoming the focus of liberal and realistic policies, Congress that of myopic isolationism. Roosevelt, who had been deeply impressed by the tragedy of Wilson's career, was always acutely conscious of the necessity of keeping reasonably in step with public and Congressional opinion, and the extent to which he could restrain its isolationist tendencies, or lead it into paths of greater practicality and wisdom, was limited. The whole aspect of American foreign policy after 1937 is that of an executive trying to drag a most reluctant legislature towards a realization of some of the basic facts of international life, and in this struggle the President seemed often to be fighting on the losing side. All this handicapped him immensely in the conduct of foreign policy, for both friends and enemies abroad were very well aware of this limitation upon his effective power, and both thought of America's intervention as a matter essentially of words and not of deeds. The dictators repeated the error of the German High Command in World War I and discounted American intervention; the democracies were forced to do likewise, and this explains the almost total lack of Anglo-American history in these years. Britain continued to rely on the negative friendliness of America, but was sceptical, and usually rightly, of anything else, for the decade before America's entry into the war had

[1] W. L. Langer and S. E. Gleason, *The Challenge to Isolation* (London, 1952), pp. 16-24.

marked, if that be possible, an intensification of American isolationism.

What had happened was that it had ceased to be merely a powerful sentiment, and had found its place in the law of the land. Isolationist ideas, it is true, represented a kind of inverted nationalism and sought encouragement in the concept of hemispheric solidarity, but the American resolution to stay out of any future war found most of its justification in the increasingly ominous trend of world events.

The new wave of isolationism was perhaps given an initial impetus by the proceedings of the Nye Committee of the Senate, appointed in 1934 to investigate the munitions industry. Like the more restrained Royal Commission on the same subject in Britain, it revealed considerable evidence of unfortunate links between arms manufacture and politics, and of gross profits made in the first war, but its isolationist conclusions were so extreme as to result in diplomatic protests from Britain and other powers, for they asserted that the United States had been dragged into World War I through the pressure of financial interests and the Administration's "complete lack of neutrality".[1] Totally unwarranted though the conclusions were, they led to a strong demand for neutrality legislation and to a public belief that Congress could better be trusted to keep the peace than the President. By early 1935 nearly twenty bills designed to keep the nation out of war had appeared in Congress.

Despite the opposition of the State Department and the President, who desired a discretionary Executive power, which might strengthen the diplomatic hand of the United States and might be a means of supporting right against wrong, as well as of preventing war, a joint resolution framed by the isolationist forces—sometimes called the Neutrality Act—was passed almost unanimously by Congress, and accepted by the Administration. It was a hasty document, intended to deal with the danger arising from the Abyssinian war and to last only six months from its passage in August, 1935. It laid down that, in case of war between foreign states, the President should proclaim the existence of the war, after which the export to a belligerent, or to a neutral for a belligerent, of "arms, ammunition, or implements of war"[2] would be illegal. The President could forbid submarines to enter American ports, and had discretionary power to forbid American citizens to travel on belligerents' vessels. Before he reluctantly signed the bill, the President warned the country of the dangers of inflexible legislation for hypothetical conditions, but he put it into operation in October, partly because it had the effect of working against the Italians,

[1] Q. Nevins, *New Deal,* p. 60.   [2] Q. ibid, p. 93.

since Abyssinia had no ports, while the State Department supplemented it by a "moral embargo" on certain other war materials. Instead of giving further thought to the matter, as Roosevelt suggested, Congress in 1936 re-enacted the law with very few alterations, the most important being one prohibiting bankers from lending money to belligerent governments. The act was to remain in operation until 1 May, 1937, and was greeted with every sign of popular approval. In the Spanish Civil War the legislation did not go into legal operation, but efforts were made to give it moral effect; this all parties supported, since Roosevelt and Hull were anxious to keep national policy in line with the Non-Intervention programme of Britain and France. In January, 1937, Congress imposed a legal embargo against both sides.

But the ground swell of American opinion against the aggressive dictator powers was growing swiftly, and when the Administration in the spring of 1937 put forward a more flexible scheme to replace the expiring neutrality legislation it was only just defeated in the House. It was defeated, however, and the isolationists once more got their way, carrying legislation which even exceeded earlier measures in severity. This prohibited the carriage in American ships, not only of arms, but also of certain raw materials useful in war, if the President thought fit to impose an embargo on them. These materials were understood to include such things as oil, cotton, some metals, and rubber, and further clauses laid down that they could only be sold to belligerents at all if they were paid for in cash and if title to them passed before they left America—the famous Cash and Carry provisions. As desired by the House the Act gave the President some latitude in defining the materials, even though the Senate wished to make the list mandatory, but no discretion was allowed him to favour one belligerent rather than another. In addition, American travel upon belligerent ships was absolutely prohibited, and it was made unlawful to arm any American merchant vessel.

The United States had thus in effect renounced her international rights and surrendered her international influence; so plain had her determination to remain at peace been made, that neither friend nor foe took much account of her wishes. The object of the Kellogg Pact had been to mobilize the moral opinion of mankind against war; now Congress had served notice that they would rely upon moral forces alone to bring pressure to bear in the affairs of the outside world. This was in a not unknown vein of unrealistic American idealism, such as had produced the fatal Jefferson-Madison embargo policy well over a century before. The Act of 1937 was the high-water mark of isolationist

773

neutrality legislation, but signs of the ebb were already visible, for, despite all the legislation in the world, events were to prove that America, overwhelming in strength, capable of great military resolution and valour, and imbued with a deep faith in liberty and democratic processes, could not long remain absolutely aloof in an international community in which the three authoritarian states of Germany, Japan and Italy were running amok.

But until the coming of the war in Europe the isolationists, led by such politicians as Burton K. Wheeler, Hamilton Fish and Robert M. La Follette, Jr., such newspaper publishers as William Randolph Hearst and Colonel Robert R. McCormick, and such national figures as Charles A. Lindbergh, retained a strong grip on the public mind and prevented any effective international action by the Administration. President Roosevelt and Secretary Hull had never concealed their antipathy towards the ideology and actions of the dictators, but they dared not make formal approaches of any kind to the sister democracies in Europe.

Public feeling towards Britain was not improved by the enforced abdication of Edward VIII in 1936, when he resolved to marry Mrs. Simpson, an American citizen. The British people as a whole, as well as the Dominions, were behind their Prime Minister, Baldwin, in his determination that the King should not marry a divorcée, but inevitably many Americans, who were more accustomed to divorce than the British, ascribed the difficulty to her nationality rather than to her personal history. The fact that the crisis became public knowledge in England when it did was, interestingly enough, largely due to the wide publicity it naturally received in the American Press, for the voluntary British censorship was ultimately powerless against this spate of information in a common tongue. The damage to Anglo-American feeling was not negligible, and was only repaired—though more than repaired in the event—by the highly successful visit of the new King, George VI, and his Queen to Canada and the United States in June, 1939. As a result of it Roosevelt came to know the King well enough to maintain a regular correspondence with him.

Before the abdication crisis, Roosevelt had, in a speech at Chautauqua, New York, in August, 1936, issued a warning to his countrymen that neutrality laws were not enough to keep the peace; but the difficulty of his position was patent when he had to disavow foreign entanglements and political connexions with the League which might involve the country in war, and when, to his statement that

Americans were not isolationists, he was forced to add the words "except in so far as we seek to isolate ourselves completely from war." No foreign power could be expected to take such a statement very seriously. But the President refused to apply the Neutrality Act to the Sino-Japanese War, which broke out in 1937, on the perfectly valid technical ground that the Japanese persistently refused to declare war, but continued to talk of the Chinese "incident". This refusal favoured the Chinese and met with considerable support in the country. Probably Roosevelt over-estimated the strength of this support, although it was unquestionably growing, for on 5 October, 1937, he delivered his dramatic "quarantine speech" in Chicago, declaring that in the new era of lawlessness the foundations of the liberal world were threatened and that nobody should delude himself that America could escape the menace. The peaceful nations should quarantine war so effectively that any power planning aggression would desist. "America hates war. America hopes for peace. Therefore, America actively engages in the search for peace."[1] This was a clarion call for collective action, but it so far outran American opinion that it retarded rather than advanced the process of educating the American people in the realities of international affairs. In January, 1938, according to a Gallup poll, 70 per cent of the American people believed that the United States should make a total withdrawal of all its interests and citizens from the Orient. It was not perhaps surprising that Chamberlain wrote of the Chicago speech: "I read Roosevelt's speech with mixed feelings . . . seeing that patients suffering from epidemic diseases do not usually go about fully armed. . . . When I asked U.S.A. to make a joint *démarche* at the very beginning of the dispute, they refused."[2]

The Prime Minister, however, was in no position to cast the first stone, for on 11 January, 1938, Roosevelt sent his secret message to him offering to take the initiative in calling a conference in Washington to discuss the international situation; this was a remarkably bold proposal in view of public reaction in America to the Chicago address. As we have seen, the Prime Minister, to the consternation of his Foreign Secretary, refused the offer on the ground that he did not wish to disrupt his appeasement policy, and particularly his negotiations with Italy, whose conquest of Abyssinia he thought might be recognized as the price of Italian friendship. The President had made it clear that he would take no action without "the cordial approval and wholehearted support of His Majesty's Government",[3] and he held his hand, though

[1] Q. Nevins, *New Deal*, pp. 114, 126. [2] Q. Feiling, p. 325.
[3] Q. *Second World War*, I, p. 196.

775

expressing to Chamberlain his grave concern at the suggestion of a *de jure* recognition of Italy's position in Abyssinia. Cordell Hull delivered himself even more strongly to the British Ambassador in Washington, saying that such a recognition would "rouse a feeling of disgust, would revive and multiply all fears of pulling the chestnuts out of the fire; it would be represented as a corrupt bargain completed in Europe at the expense of interests in the Far East in which America was intimately concerned."[1] On 16 April, however, the Anglo-Italian Treaty bound Britain, in return for certain Italian promises, to raise the question of recognition of Italian Ethiopia at Geneva. Thus Chamberlain, in an egregious blunder, rebuffed Roosevelt; it is possible, though not proven, that he even more rashly rebuffed Soviet Russia later in the year at Munich. But even if the first indictment alone stands, it is appalling enough, for without the aid of one or the other powers Britain could never have won the war.

It would have been small wonder if the President, his words rejected by his own people and his offers refused by the nations they were intended to aid, had been discouraged, but he persisted in his efforts. He not only pushed on American rearmament, but was, through Secretary of the Treasury Morgenthau, actively assisting Britain and France to obtain certain types of weapons, particularly aircraft, and strategic materials, from the United States. In 1938 Admiral Leahy admitted to a Congressional Naval Committee that there had been recent conversations in London between United States and British naval staff officers; he refused to divulge their character, which was probably technical.

Humanitarian feeling in the United States continued to mount against the ruthlessness of the Germans and the Japanese in their bombing of Spanish and Chinese cities, and Secretary Hull declared after the invasion of Austria that the vital question was whether the doctrine of brute force would again prevail, or whether the peace-loving nations could maintain international order by joint action. This sentiment showed itself in growing support for the programme of American rearmament, and the President felt strong enough to take a diplomatic initiative, possibly the only effective pre-war action he was able to take, at the height of the Czechoslovak crisis. In its early stages "he had held cautiously aloof, suspecting that Chamberlain might try to maneuver America into a position where partial responsibility for the choice between war and appeasement would rest upon her shoulders. The President was determined to keep this responsibility squarely upon the

[1] Q. ibid, p. 197.

British and French Governments."[1] But after Chamberlain's unsatisfactory second meeting with Hitler at Godesberg, Roosevelt on 26 September sent an appeal to Hitler and Benes to continue negotiations; the other powers approved with alacrity, but Hitler next day replied that the decision lay solely with Prague. Immediately, Roosevelt sent a further plea to Hitler, and at the same time cabled a message to Italy appealing to Mussolini to intervene, which arrived almost simultaneously with a similar message from Chamberlain to the Italian dictator. The result was the Munich Conference. How far Roosevelt's actions were responsible is very doubtful, but, despite the mistrust between Prime Minister and President and despite sweeping criticism of appeasement by American liberals, the policies of the two countries ran on the same lines in the crisis and the feelings of relief among both peoples at the passing of the shadow of war were equally deep and sincere.

Furthermore, the reaction of both nations to the next steps of Axis aggression was the same, for though in greatly different degrees, both began to appreciate the reality of the threat to their own interests and, indeed, existence. Whereas just before Munich a Gallup poll had shown 57 per cent of the American people as willing in case of war to sell food to Britain and France, and 34 per cent to sell war materials, one taken soon after it showed corresponding figures of 82 per cent and 57 per cent; what is more, no less than 62 per cent thought the totalitarian powers would be an immediate menace to the United States if they won. These feelings grew with the worsening of the persecution of the Jews in Germany in the last months of 1938, and boycotts of German goods spread throughout the United States. When the German Chargé d'Affaires—the Ambassador had gone when Roosevelt recalled the American Ambassador from Berlin after the November pogrom—protested against a speech in which Secretary Ickes attacked Ford and Lindbergh for accepting German decorations, the protest was roundly rejected by Sumner Welles, Acting Secretary of State, and much of the public applauded.

But the last had by no means been heard of the isolationists, who opposed the gigantic budget for defence asked by Roosevelt in 1938 on the ground that it might be used to prepare for offensive operations. Senator Hiram Johnson asked Hull, among other questions, whether "any alliance, agreement, or understanding exists or is contemplated with Great Britain relating to war or the possibility of war",[2] to which the reply was a blunt, "No". The appropriations passed, but when in

[1] Nevins, *New Deal*, pp. 153-4.   [2] Q. ibid, p. 173.

his Annual Message, early in 1939, the President warned his country-men that "God-fearing democracies . . . cannot safely be indifferent to international lawlessness anywhere . . . cannot forever let pass, without effective protest, acts of aggression against sister-nations—acts which automatically undermine all of us",[1] and recommended a modification of the neutrality laws which might make participation in some form of economic embargo possible for the United States, he was not sanguine of success. He was, indeed, so gloomy about the chances of the proposal, that when a storm broke over the action of Morgenthau, which he had authorized, in allowing a French observer to see some of the latest types of military aircraft, he even went so far as to allow the suppression of the fact that he had signed the authorization, because of the effect he feared it might have in harming his main objectives. He offered explanations to a meeting of the Senate Military Affairs Committee, but minced no words, in its supposed secrecy, as to the dangers which faced America as well as the rest of the world. A rumour then leaked out that he had said in effect, "America's first line of defense is in France", and this home truth aroused such an uproar among his oppon-ents that he was forced to defend himself by declaring that some "boob" had invented this "deliberate lie."[2] He also declared that his policy included these planks—no entangling alliances, expansion of world trade, disarmament, sympathy with the peaceful maintenance of the independence of all nations—and that it had not and would not change. There is little doubt that if his hands had been free his policy would have been distinctly different, but he was always alive to the danger of defeating his own ends by pursuing them too swiftly for public opinion.

Lord Lothian, the British Ambassador in Washington from 1939, was, if he expected immediate action, being over-sanguine when he wrote, in the spring of that year, that in the nineteenth century Britain had supported the freedom of other peoples in order to secure her own, and that he thought that was "going to be the policy of the United States".[3] In the end, the President's policy would prevail over that of Congress, but only under the extreme pressure of world events. As well as being a great statesman, Roosevelt was a consummate politician, and, unlike Wilson, very prepared to make the twists, turns and retrac-tions necessary to achieve his international aims. That he was a master of the technique *reculer pour mieux sauter* is shown by his return to the charge in April, 1939, as soon as the furore had died down; he was leaving for Warm Springs, Georgia, for a rest and remarked, in an almost

[1] Q. ibid, p. 176.   [2] Bailey, p. 752.
[3] Q. Mowat, *American Entente*, p. 281.

flippant manner, "I'll be back in the fall if we don't have a war."[1] But it is a sad commentary on "government by the people" that the head of a great nation should have been reduced to such subterfuges. Prime Minister Baldwin had confessed to much the same thing when, some years earlier, he had admitted that he had not espoused rearmament as soon as he might have done because he knew the people would not stand for it, necessary as it was. Churchill alone always and fearlessly gave expression to the truth as he saw it, and he obtained his ultimate reward, but the price he paid at the time was inability to hasten re-armament by executive action. Roosevelt moved as swiftly as he dared, but it is not altogether surprising that men like Chamberlain expected only words from him and from the United States. Nevertheless, their error was grave; they should have strengthened the President's arm by framing their policies, words, and actions with one eye at least upon their effect in America. Happily, at the hour of Britain's greatest need, one ruled who was more fitted for and far more adept at this task.

Roosevelt certainly did not relax his efforts to keep under way, despite his frequent tacks, for only three days after his Warm Springs statement he issued a dramatic personal appeal to Hitler and Mussolini to pledge themselves not to attack any of a specific list of twenty-one states which he named. The dictators evaded the issue and made no written reply, and on 28 April, Hitler abrogated the Non-Aggression Pact between Germany and Poland. It was not surprising that they treated the words of the President in such a cavalier fashion for they were well aware of the temper of Congress. During these months he brought heavy but unavailing pressure to bear on Senators and Con-gressmen to accept modifications of the Neutrality legislation, which he considered more and more vital, as a support for the democracies, in proportion as war seemed more imminent. On 11 June, the Senate committee voted 12 to 11 against even reporting the bill incorporating such changes. Thus when Congress adjourned in 1939, the Neutrality Act of 1937 remained the law, except that the Cash and Carry provisions had expired on 1 May, 1939. The export of munitions directly or in-directly to belligerents remained totally forbidden, and this, as Roose-velt later declared, "played right into the hands of the aggressor nations."[2] Nor was he being wise only after the event, for, on the final failure of the Administration's effort to modify the law, he promised to call Congress into special session to revise the Neutrality Act if war came before the next regular session, and, when asked if war was pos-sible before then, replied in the affirmative.

[1] Q. Nevins, *New Deal*, p. 184.   [2] Q. Morison and Commager, II, p. 653.

CHAPTER EIGHTEEN

WORLD WAR II (1939-45)

T HE Second World War constitutes in a sense the culmination of our story, for it formed an altogether fitting climax in the long drama of Anglo-American friendship. It saw, in the words of General Marshall, "the most complete unification of military effort ever achieved by two allied nations."[1] It saw a co-ordination between the political authorities of two sovereign states possibly unsurpassed in history. It saw a maturing of the cordiality between the two peoples more swift and complete than all but the most optimistic prophets of Anglo-American comity had hoped.*

The cataclysmic events of 1940 singled out the Anglo-American relationship as the sole bastion of Western civilization against the onslaughts of Nazi might. Russia seemed still, at least on the surface, something approaching a co-belligerent of Germany, and for a year every eye was on the West, where virtually all the Allies were engulfed in three short months. Britain, sustaining the exiled governments of Europe in London, became their only effective representative. She stood alone. It is questionable whether she could have survived without the aid of America; it is certain that she could not have conquered. The fate of mankind did perhaps in literal truth depend upon what American interventionists called "the Atlantic life-line." For a year of extraordinary, dramatic intensity Anglo-American relations alone held the international stage: "Never before," wrote William Allen White, "has a nation been so beautifully dramatized as Great Britain was dramatized fighting alone."[2]

This was naturally influential in the development of these relations, for now there was an unavoidable direct conflict between the interests

---

[1] Chester Wilmot, *The Struggle for Europe* (London, 1952), p. 99.

*Unhappily, Mr. W. H. McNeill's excellent and comprehensive *America, Britain and Russia, Their Co-operation and Conflict, 1941-1946* (Oxford, 1953) was only published while I was in the last stages of reading galley proofs. Similarly, Sir Winston Churchill's final volume, *Triumph and Tragedy,* I was only able to read in the form of excerpts in the *New York Times.*

[2] Q. W. Johnson, *The Battle Against Isolation* (Chicago, 1944), p. 88.

of the United States and the sympathies of very many of her people on the one hand, and the traditional forces of isolationism and Anglo-phobia on the other. Steadily, and by any other standard but the incredible swiftness of contemporary events, speedily, America chose to sustain Britain by every means, even including in the end the open use of armed force; and though ultimately her actual, all-out participation in the war was precipitated by the Japanese attack on Pearl Harbour, the firm decision then made by Roosevelt and his advisers, to win the European war first, showed unmistakably the significance now accorded to Anglo-American relations.

The revolution which had been effected in American sentiment by the events of 1940 was proved as early as 4 June of that year by Churchill's famous words on that occasion, which are quoted below. Not only was it inconceivable that a British Prime Minister should ever have said such things before, but it was equally beyond possibility that the words could previously have been accepted with equanimity—indeed in some cases with enthusiasm—in the United States, for the allusion to America, though veiled, was unmistakable. And Britain's hour of need not only produced the man, but the man most capable of suiting the word to the action: for the history of Anglo-American relations it was a major good fortune that the great American audience, through the common tongue, could savour the full relish and feel the full impact of that word.

Even though large tracts of Europe and many old and famous states have fallen or may fall into the grip of the Gestapo and all the odious apparatus of Nazi rule, we shall not flag or fail. We shall go on to the end. We shall fight in France, we shall fight in the seas and oceans, we shall fight with growing confidence and growing strength in the air; we shall defend our Island, whatever the cost may be. We shall fight on the beaches, we shall fight on the landing-grounds, we shall fight in the fields and in the streets, we shall fight in the hills; we shall never surrender; and even if, which I do not for a moment believe, this Island or a large part of it were subjugated and starving, then our Empire beyond the seas, armed and guarded by the British Fleet, would carry on the struggle, until, in God's good time, the New World, with all its power and might, steps forth to the rescue and liberation of the Old.[1]

One might write much in detailed commentary upon this passage; its illustration of the very great importance of political oratory in the life of the English-speaking democracies; its foreshadowing of such

[1] *Second World War*, II, pp. 103-4.

terms as the "liberation" of Europe in 1944; even its mastery of linguistic effect in the substitution of the present tense, "steps", for the more usual past tense, "stepped", which gives such added reality to the word-picture of American intervention. But this same mastery is apparent in his whole handling of Anglo-American relations, and particularly during these months of American neutrality, when the hope of American participation was always in his mind. This should give us pause in any false assumption of the ease or even inevitability of Anglo-American co-operation. It is without doubt true that some form of mutual assistance would almost certainly have followed the fall of France, but the scale and rapidity of American aid might have been altogether different, and, indeed, quite inadequate, under another leader, for the democracies were already familiar enough in the recent years with the dismal story of "too little and too late." Churchill fought the long battle of diplomacy and publicity, planned to achieve American intervention, with quite as much skill as he fought the military Battle of Britain, and he did so not only because he realized its overwhelming importance but because he was also master of the problem. He never wavered from a policy which brought him rich dividends and which is perhaps a universal truth for British statesmen in their treatment of America: "No people respond more spontaneously to fair play. If you treat Americans well they always want to treat you better."[1]

Though the happy dénouement of American belligerency was not directly due to his efforts, it may be that it was merely a more rapid fulfilment of them, for he seldom uttered a paragraph without one eye at least on his American listeners. Boldly or subtly, as might best serve his cause, he continually impressed their danger and its remedy upon them. On 18 June, 1940, he said to Parliament:

What General Weygand called the Battle of France is over. I expect that the Battle of Britain is about to begin. Upon this battle depends the survival of Christian civilization. . . . Hitler knows that he will have to break us in this Island or lose the war. If we can stand up to him, all Europe may be free and the life of the world may move forward into broad, sunlit uplands. But if we fail, then the whole world, including the United States, including all that we have known or cared for, will sink into the abyss of a new Dark Age, made more sinister, and perhaps more protracted, by the lights of perverted science. Let us therefore brace ourselves to our duties, and so bear ourselves that, if the British Empire and its Commonwealth last for a thousand years, men will still say: "This was their finest hour."[2]

[1] Ibid, IV, p. 730.   [2] Ibid, II, pp. 198-9.

The appeal not only stirred the British to whom it was addressed, but convinced Americans of the two things needful at the time, the reality of the danger to the United States and Britain's determination, if vouchsafed the means, to emerge triumphant. On 20 August, after the destroyer-bases deal, he welcomed the mixing up of the affairs of the two great democracies in the words quoted at the beginning of this book; it was an extraordinary statement by a belligerent Prime Minister about a neutral nation in time of war.

But, though he was forthright when he thought it wise, he showed almost as much mastery of the subtle art of leading American opinion as Roosevelt himself. He wrote to General Smuts on 9 November, 1941:

> I do not think it would be any use for me to make a personal appeal to Roosevelt at this juncture to enter the war. At the Atlantic meeting I told his circle that I would rather have an American declaration of war now and no supplies for six months than double the supplies and no declaration. When this was repeated to him he thought it a hard saying. We must not underrate his constitutional difficulties. He may take action as Chief Executive, but only Congress can declare war. He went so far as to say to me, "I may never declare war; I may make war. If I were to ask Congress to declare war they might argue about it for three months." The Draft Bill without which the American Army would have gone to pieces passed by only one vote. He has now carried through the Senate by a small majority the virtual repeal of the Neutrality Act. This must mean, if endorsed by the other House, constant fighting in the Atlantic between German and American ships. Public opinion in the United States has advanced lately, but with Congress it is all a matter of counting heads. Naturally, if I saw any way of helping to lift this situation on to a higher plane I would do so. In the meanwhile we must have patience and trust to the tide which is flowing our way and to events.[1]

His understanding of American opinion extended to the brilliant use of humour, a weapon of which he had in his long political career at home made himself a consummate master. Nowhere is this better illustrated than by the uproariously received words contained in his first address to Congress: "I cannot help reflecting that if my father had been American and my mother British, instead of the other way around, I might have got here on my own."[2] Even more successful was his comment in Ottawa on Weygand's prophecy in 1940 that Hitler

[1] Ibid, III, pp. 527-8.

[2] Q. R. E. Sherwood, *The White House Papers of Harry L. Hopkins* (London, 1948), p. 448.

would in three weeks wring England's neck like a chicken. "Some Chicken! Some neck!"[1]

After Pearl Harbour he reaped the harvest of his skilful blend of sagacity and temerity, but he still maintained his vigilance. On 10 December, 1942, for example, at the time of the Darlan episode, which threw some temporary strain on Anglo-American relations, he said to a Secret Session of Parliament: "It is because it would be highly detrimental to have a debate upon American policy or Anglo-American relations in public that His Majesty's Government have invited the House to come into Secret Session. In Secret Session alone can the matter be discussed without the risk of giving offence to our great Ally".[2] So deep was his affection for America that he more than once proposed a common Anglo-American citizenship. He said at Harvard in 1944: "This gift of a common tongue is a priceless inheritance, and it may well some day become the foundation of a common citizenship. I like to think of British and Americans moving about freely over each other's wide estates with hardly a sense of being foreigners to one another."[3]

The triumphant vindication of Anglo-American friendship probably owed more to him than to any other man, but it was in fact the work of a multitude of hands, great and small; in varying degrees millions of Americans and Britons accelerated the understanding. But the dramatic fitness of the friendship must not lead us to over-estimate its intensity or permanence: even personal love between individuals only finds perfection in the pages of romance, and affection between vast bodies of persons, whom we lump together under the crude generalization "peoples", is a great deal more fickle and variable. During the war there were serious Anglo-American differences over strategy, there were strong disagreements between Churchill and Roosevelt with regard to the British Empire and India, and there was unfortunate emotional feeling between military leaders of the two countries; after it was over, there were to be divergences of an even more serious nature. But, given these reservations, the *entente* was amazingly close and cordial, and so weak did Anglophobia and isolationism become that by 1945 some 60 per cent of Americans favoured a permanent military alliance with Britain.

How much this Anglo-American intimacy was due to the personalities of Churchill and Roosevelt is indicated by the contrasting relationship

[1] *Second World War*, II, p. 602.   [2] *Second World War*, IV, p. 574.
[3] Q. Sherwood, p. 745.

of the President with Neville Chamberlain, for though the principal cause of the increasing warmth of the friendship in 1940 was the collapse of France, the supersession in that year of the great appeaser was also very significant, for the President could never bring himself to feel cordial towards him, and he himself was sceptical about America, ignorant of her history, and unperceptive of her overwhelming importance. It is interesting to compare the tone and content of two letters written by Roosevelt on 11 September, 1939, to the two British statesmen. That to Chamberlain read: "I need not tell you that you have been much in my thoughts during these difficult days and further that I hope you will at all times feel free to write to me personally and outside of diplomatic procedure about any problems as they arise. I hope and believe that we shall repeal the embargo within the next month and this is definitely a part of the Administration policy."[1] That to Churchill ran:

> It is because you and I occupied similar positions in the World War that I want you to know how glad I am that you are back again in the Admiralty. Your problems are, I realize, complicated by new factors, but the essential is not very different. What I want you and the Prime Minister to know is that I shall at all times welcome it, if you will keep me in touch personally with anything you want me to know about. You can always send sealed letters through your pouch or my pouch. I am glad you did the Marlborough volumes before this thing started—and I much enjoyed reading them.[2]

It is even more interesting to compare the barrenness of the first proposal with the rich fruits of the second, for Churchill "responded with alacrity, using the signature of 'Naval Person', and thus began that long and memorable correspondence—covering perhaps a thousand communications on each side",[3] and lasting till Roosevelt's death more than five years later. Churchill's swift development in stature during the first months of the war meant that his increasing closeness to Roosevelt counteracted the lingering coldness between Prime Minister and President.

The Secretary of State, Cordell Hull, though far from a figurehead, was to some extent overshadowed by Roosevelt, with whose policies he was, however, in close agreement; he strove always to preserve good, if not effusive, relations with Britain. As he wrote later in his *Memoirs*: "Throughout my career at the State Department, I felt that good relations with Great Britain were more important to us than good relations with any other country. I never varied from this view, and made every

[1] *Roosevelt Letters*, p. 919. [2] Q. *Second World War*, I, p. 345. [3] Ibid.

possible effort to achieve this end. Though we often differed we never really quarreled. We talked out our differences in calm and friendly fashion, and, if we did not always reach agreement, at least we did not descend to recrimination."[1]

Perhaps the most active figure during 1939-40 in promoting good Anglo-American relations was the British Ambassador, Philip Kerr, Marquess of Lothian, who assumed office immediately before the outbreak of hostilities in September, 1939. He had had a distinguished career on the fringes of politics, including five years as Secretary to the Prime Minister from 1916 to 1921, and had been Secretary of the Rhodes Trust since 1925; he had even visited the United States informally in 1934 to see what could be done to improve Anglo-American relations, and he now strove tirelessly to do so in his official capacity, until his death in December, 1940. Hull wrote of him, "Lothian to my mind was unexcelled as an ambassador by anyone of my acquaintance. His great abilities, intensity of purpose, and strong though charming personality made him virtually a perfect diplomatic representative."[2]

His opposite number in London, Joseph P. Kennedy, who had been Ambassador since 1937, did not prove so beneficent an influence in this critical period. A wealthy Boston financier of Irish extraction, who had served on the Securities Exchange Commission and the Maritime Commission, his appointment had coincided with the inauguration of the appeasement policy, and he had developed almost too much sympathy with its executors. As a result he was happy as long as they remained in power but, "The advent of Churchill disturbed his relations with the Government, Churchill making no bones about his aversion to the American defeatist. In his turn, Kennedy did not mask his distrust of Churchill."[3] Kennedy, in fact, "vehemently advised the President against 'holding the bag in a war in which the Allies expect to be beaten' ",[4] but, despite his own requests, was not withdrawn until after the Presidential election in 1940.

The mission of John G. Winant, his successor, was a quiet triumph. It was not spectacular because he was a very modest and unassuming man and because the increasing closeness of the governments at all levels diverted the limelight from him, particularly after America's entry into the war, but this shy, rumpled figure found a special place in the affections of the British public in the days of the "Blitz". Of good

[1] Cordell Hull, *The Memoirs of Cordell Hull* (New York, 1948), p. 385.

[2] Ibid, p. 674.

[3] F. Davis and K. Lindley, *How War Came to America* (London, 1943), p. 84.

[4] Sherwood, pp. 151-2.

New York family, he had been Governor of New Hampshire, and had gained invaluable European experience during two terms of service in the International Labour Office at Geneva. On arrival in London in 1941 he struck a genuine note from the first; someone "handed me a microphone and asked that I say a few words to the British people. I said what was really in my heart—that I was very glad to be there and that there was no place I would rather be at that time than England."[1] He held office until 1946, so that Churchill, with whom he got on very well, spoke truly when he said on the occasion of Winant's first public speech in Britain: "Mr. Ambassador, you share our purpose, you will share our dangers, you will share our anxieties, you shall share our secrets, and the day will come when the British Empire and the United States will share together the solemn but splendid duties which are the crown of victory."[2] With Eden he worked even more closely: "We had an odd informal relationship, based not only on personal friendship but also on our regard for each other's country and for our own. . . . We used to go down occasionally on a Sunday to his country house in Sussex. . . . We used to get our fun weeding the garden. We would put our despatch boxes at either end, and when we had completed a row we would do penance by reading messages and writing the necessary replies. Then we would start again. . . . I liked Eden."[3]

The Foreign Secretary himself had resigned from the Chamberlain government, largely on an issue affecting Anglo-American goodwill, and he naturally pursued a cordial understanding with the United States through his years at the Foreign Office. His public words, quoted by Winant, are characteristic: "Quite early in our work together, Mr. Winant and I understood that we just could not get through our business if each interview between us—and sometimes there were two or more in a day—was to be the subject of a detailed record; and so we decided that normally there would be no record, unless we agreed that for the information of our respective governments it was necessary to make one and repeat it to them. Such a practice and such a measure of confidence are unique in my diplomatic experience."[4]

Eden's predecessor at the Foreign Office, the Earl of Halifax, was also Lothian's successor and Winant's opposite number. A Fellow of All Souls' College, Oxford, and a former Viceroy of India, he had succeeded Eden as Foreign Secretary in 1938, and held the office in both the Chamberlain and Churchill governments, until he accepted the Ambassadorship on Lothian's death. As Churchill remarks, "For a

[1] Winant, *A Letter from Grosvenor Square*, pp. 18-19.
[2] Q. ibid, p. 28.   [3] Ibid, pp. 67-8.   [4] Q. ibid, p. 68.

Foreign Secretary to become an Ambassador marks in a unique manner the importance of the mission. His high character was everywhere respected, yet at the same time his record in the years before the war ... left him exposed to much disapprobation and even hostility from the Labour side of our National Coalition."[1] Such doubts were also felt by many in America, but they were dispelled by his high character and achievements, for even so bitter a political opponent as Harold Laski could write an article in the Washington *Post* containing considerable praise of the new Ambassador. Every effort was made to emphasize the importance of his mission, which had been offered to Lloyd George but refused reluctantly on grounds of age; he retained his membership of the War Cabinet and travelled in Britain's newest battleship, *King George V*. He received an unprecedented welcome at Annapolis from the President in person, an honour that was shortly reciprocated by the King when he met Winant. Hull wrote: "I saw at once that I could work on the same effective, cordial terms with his [Lothian's] . . . successor. Halifax, who possessed unusual ability, engaged in prodigious, fruitful labors while serving in Washington, and the extent and importance of his accomplishments were unexcelled by any other foreign representative during my tenure in office."[2] His association with the appeasement of earlier years was soon forgotten in his pursuit of victory and of Anglo-American understanding. His views on this he clearly expressed shortly after his return to Britain in 1946:

> But overriding all is something deeper, derived from the way of thought that we share and from a history that we have made and lived together. That is why, whenever any vital issue has arisen in the world, you have generally found our two countries not only thinking but acting alike; not always at once, not always simultaneously, but nearly always ultimately. If a Briton were to sit down and try to analyse the needs and purposes of British policy, and an American were to do the same service for his country, the results, I venture to think, would be very similar and would never be incompatible. . . . I can see no large or necessary divergence between the American and British interest. . . . This conviction is immensely strengthened by the experience of my years in Washington; for I can recall no occasion when British and American representatives sat round a table to discuss some matter between us and—no matter how difficult and contentious that matter had been judged to be—did not succeed in getting nearer to a solution broadly acceptable to both sides. The truth is, of course, that the differences are superficial,

[1] *Second World War*, II, p. 504.   [2] *Memoirs*, p. 926.

compared with the material for agreement, which is fundamental. . . .
Whether we wish to co-operate or not, or whether at any particular
moment we are moved by feelings of friendship or not, makes on the
whole little material difference. We shall regret, and try to avert,
those incidents which are likely to occur from time to time and create
transient alienation of sentiment; but forces are at work stronger than
any event or any human opinion; forces invisible but irresistible,
holding the two peoples together both to their own advantage and to
that of a world in anxious search of conditions, which may fairly claim
the name of peace.[1]

But the key personalities in the war remained Roosevelt and
Churchill, President and Commander-in-Chief, Prime Minister and
Minister of Defence, each exercising as nearly complete control of their
nations' war efforts as democratic institutions permitted. With the views
of the President, who remained many steps ahead of the mass of his
countrymen in his desire to aid democratic Britain, we are already
aware; in this desire he never wavered. Winant records that he was
instructed before his departure to London "to keep Winston Churchill
and the British Government patient while the American people assessed
the issues which faced them. He further instructed me to make plain
to the people of Great Britain that we believed in their cause, that
Nazism and Fascism were incompatible with the American way of
life".[2] He wrote to Churchill on 19 January, 1941, "I think this verse
applies to your people as it does to us:

> *Sail on, O ship of State!*
> *Sail on, O union, strong and great!*
> *Humanity with all its fears,*
> *With all the hopes of future years,*
> *Is hanging breathless on thy fate."*[3]

His relations with many British leaders were cordial. This was not
only true of members of the United Kingdom Government, like Eden
and Beaverbrook, but of many important figures in the Commonwealth.
He wrote to John Curtin, the Prime Minister of Australia, in early
1944: "Now that I am back from the Conferences with Mr. Churchill
and the Generalissimo and Marshal Stalin, I feel even more strongly
that you and I should meet. As you know, I have been close to
Mackenzie King almost since we were boys; Marshal Smuts and I first
met in 1918, and I had a grand reunion with him in Cairo last month,

---

[1] Halifax, p. 12.   [2] Winant, p. 15.

[3] Q. *Second World War,* III, p. 24.

and Peter Fraser has stopped off here in Washington several times".[1]
But, fundamentally, everything came to hinge on the personal relationship of Roosevelt and Churchill, and it was strong enough to bear the
immense burden; it proved, indeed, one of the most significant political
and international friendships of history. The President wrote to the
King after the Casablanca meeting in 1943: "I wish much that you could
have been with us during the past ten days—a truly mighty meeting
in its thoroughness and in the true spirit of comradeship between each
officer and his 'opposite number'. As for Mr. Churchill and myself I
need not tell you that we made a perfectly matched team in harness
and out—and incidentally we had lots of fun together as we always
do."[2]

Modern technology made possible an intimacy of contact inconceivable in an earlier age; in addition to a voluminous correspondence,
the two men met nine times in four years and held numerous transatlantic telephone conversations. These closer contacts were immensely
beneficial because the two liked one another and saw broadly eye to
eye; they do not always make for better relations. As Sir Arthur Willert
writes, "One shudders to think what would have happened had Lloyd
George been in a position to take up the telephone and talk to the
President [Wilson] under the impulse of the moment, and if he and
the President had had frequent meetings."[3] This is not to imply that
serious differences of view did not exist between Roosevelt and
Churchill. The creator of the New Deal by no means agreed on every
matter with the Tory leader, who, though he had once been a Liberal
and was never a typical Conservative, had in the inter-war years been
an orthodox financier and an imperialist of imperialists: the man who
had first instituted American diplomatic relations with the Soviet
Union was inclined to be more sanguine of Russian co-operation than
the Briton steeped in the hard realities of European politics. But these
differences were insignificant compared with the vast areas of agreement between them, not merely as representatives of the two great
democracies bound together by such manifold ties, but as men of
kindred experience and outlook. Both students of history and capable
in strategic judgment, both with political experience in, and affection
for, naval matters, both statesmen of wide vision conscious of the
great part they played in deciding the destiny of mankind, they became,
considering their positions, remarkably close.

Winant records that "when Churchill returned from the Atlantic
Charter meeting in August, 1941 . . . he stepped out of the car . . . and

[1] *Roosevelt Letters*, pp. 477-8.   [2] Ibid, p. 1394.   [3] Willert, p. 141.

came across to shake hands, with the simple statement, 'I like your President.' He never changed—he liked him to the end. Whenever I talked with the President I felt the same sense of caring on his part."[1] The degree of informality and the extent of personal feeling was very marked. On one occasion Roosevelt wrote to Churchill when the latter was ill to plead with him not to justify his popular reputation as the world's worst patient, and on another, when Churchill replied to a letter from Roosevelt saying that, contrary to the President's information, he was too big for any baby carriage on his first visit to America in 1895, F.D.R. responded:

For Former Naval Person

SOME BABY!

The White House,
March 30, 1943.

Roosevelt.[2]

Sherwood writes, however: "It would be an exaggeration to say that Roosevelt and Churchill became chums. . . . They established an easy intimacy, a joking informality and a moratorium on pomposity and cant—and also a degree of frankness in intercourse which, if not quite complete, was remarkably close to it. But neither of them ever forgot for one instant what he was and represented or what the other was and represented. Actually, their relationship was maintained to the end on the highest professional level."[3] Absolute intimacy was in any case precluded by Churchill's insistence on the fact that the President as a Head of State was the superior in rank of a Prime Minister, and the equal only of his Sovereign, so that, though in public he became "Winston" to Roosevelt,* the latter always remained Mr. President to him. Churchill had, too, a very great respect for the achievements of Roosevelt; it was later his considered judgement "that in Roosevelt's life and by his actions he changed, he altered decisively and permanently, the social axis, the moral axis, of mankind by involving the New World inexorably and irrevocably in the fortunes of the Old. His life must therefore be regarded as one of the commanding events in human destiny."[4] The two men rapidly learned, as experienced politicians, how to deal with one another, but the process was immensely facilitated by the fascinating part in their relationship played by Harry Hopkins.

[1] Winant, p. 83.   [2] *Roosevelt Letters,* p. 1416.   [3] Sherwood, p. 364.

*The obverse of the President's beneficent geniality and informality was the carelessness, almost casualness, with which he was on occasion capable of treating affairs of state, and the way in which he would sometimes let matters drift, in the hope that time would ease his difficulties.   [4] Q. ibid, p. 923.

He served not only as interpreter but as intermediary between them, for, despite all the modern techniques of communication, the personal contact still proved important; the transatlantic telephone, for instance, though speedy, was often an unsuitable medium of contact over important matters. Hopkins was Roosevelt's *alter ego,* so close to him in knowledge of his intentions that, by sending him, the President came near to going himself on vital missions that he could not in fact undertake. He inevitably challenges comparison with Colonel House. Both had the unquestioning confidence of their masters, and established invaluable relations with British leaders, but House was more of a statesman in his own right, and in the end saw the realities of the world situation more accurately than Wilson, and lost his confidence as a result; Hopkins did drift away from Roosevelt towards the end, but for personal reasons only, and he never trespassed on uncharted ground, nor ventured beyond what he knew to be the President's own intentions. With many British leaders, but above all with Churchill, he established a remarkable intimacy. For Hopkins's abilities the Prime Minister developed the greatest respect, and for his self-sacrifice in view of his precarious health came to feel the deepest admiration. The measure of his contribution to Anglo-American co-operation is, that it was he who was chosen by Roosevelt to go to Churchill in January, 1941, to deliver a message, or, more properly, to acquaint him with the President's thoughts. As Churchill tells it, "With gleaming eye and quiet, constrained passion he said: 'The President is determined that we shall win the war together. Make no mistake about it. He has sent me here to tell you that at all costs and by all means he will carry you through, no matter what happens to him—there is nothing that he will not do so far as he has human power.' "[1] Hopkins had gone to London with some mental reservations, but he was rapidly convinced of the absurdity of the persistent American belief—which Churchill ascribed largely to Ambassador Kennedy—that the British leader "dislikes either you or America—it just doesn't make sense." Whereas he had originally thought of his task as that of a "catalytic agent between two prima donnas", he now advocated strongly that they make personal contact, because he was convinced that a full meeting of minds would result.

This was the crucial thing. Hopkins was an invaluable go-between, but he was no more; at bottom the relations of Churchill and Roosevelt were what mattered. That they were, despite all that may be said, remarkably warm, was of incalculable importance not only to the future

[1] Q. *Second World War,* III, p. 21.

793

of Anglo-American relations, but to the destiny of mankind. Roosevelt once ended a cable to Churchill with the words, "It is fun to be in the same decade with you",[1] and on another occasion publicly called him "a brilliant and great leader";[2] the Prime Minister's admiration for the President we have already noted and it was put on record on many occasions. On the most solemn of these he called him, "the greatest American friend we have ever known, and the greatest champion of freedom who has ever brought help and comfort from the new world to the old."[3] It was a happy dispensation for Anglo-American relations that these two men, capable of such a relationship, held sway over the hearts and future of the two peoples at this great crisis in their history.

II

ON 5 September, 1939, two days after Great Britain formally entered the war, the President issued a Proclamation of Neutrality, putting into effect the obligations of the United States under international law and under the domestic neutrality legislation; it declared, "The laws and treaties of the United States, *without interfering with the free expression of opinion and sympathy*, nevertheless impose upon all persons who may be within their territory and jurisdiction the duty of an impartial neutrality during the existence of the contest."[4] Shortly afterwards he made the implication of this explicit when he said in a radio address: "This nation will remain a neutral nation, but I cannot ask that every American remain neutral in thought as well. Even a neutral has a right to take account of facts. Even a neutral cannot be asked to close his mind or his conscience".[5] In this unmistakable allusion to, and rejection of, the Wilsonian concept of neutrality, the President made plain the first major difference in America's attitude to the second war; in October, 1939, though 99 per cent of Americans wanted neutrality, only 2 per cent favoured Germany, whereas 84 per cent wanted the Allies to win. This overwhelmingly pro-Allied sentiment increased rather than shrank in the months which followed, and in due time it took effect in the alteration of the Neutrality Law. The clause of the Act of 1937, which forbade the export of such war materials as the President should designate except on a Cash and Carry

[1] Q. Sherwood, pp. 244, 365.

[2] S. I. Rosenmann (Editor), *The Public Papers and Addresses of F. D. Roosevelt, 1941* (New York, 1950), p. 68.   [3] Q. Wilmot, p. 635.

[4] Q. S. F. Bemis, *The United States as a World Power*, p. 365. Author's italics.   [5] Q. Sherwood, p. 127.

basis, had expired in May, 1939, so that, though the mandatory embargo on arms, ammunition and implements of war was imposed by Roosevelt, American ships were free to carry war materials of other kinds into the war zone.

The President appeared before Congress, which he had summoned into special session, on 21 September, to call upon it to amend the neutrality legislation. He based his appeal on an analysis of American history, which pointed out that the only previous occasion on which American neutrality deviated from the general principles of international law was during Jefferson's administration, when the results had been disastrous. He therefore urged "a return to international law."[1] His concrete proposals were hardly that, for though one proposition (and doubtless the one nearest his heart) was the repeal of the arms embargo, which repeal was in accordance with traditional international law, the other was the grant of power to the President to define combat zones from which all American ships were debarred, which was a further step in the opposite direction; the Cash and Carry provisions were to be applied to all forms of war material, including arms and munitions. In effect, therefore, the legislation offered a *quid pro quo* to the isolationists for the repeal of the embargo on arms, in the form of the war zone prohibition; it also maintained much of the existing legislation, such as the prohibition of loans to belligerents and of travel by Americans on belligerent ships. After a six weeks battle the legislation was finally passed by majorities which reflected a public opinion, between 50 and 60 per cent of which favoured the arms embargo repeal and over 80 per cent of which favoured the creation of the danger zone. This zone was defined by the President, and subsequently enlarged to accord with the swift spreading of the war, but, though American ships were thus altogether excluded from British ports, the repeal of the arms embargo did on balance constitute a great victory for the friends of Britain. Though she had to buy them for cash and to come and fetch them in her own ships, she could get all the war materials that she could pay for from America. Furthermore, owing to Allied control of the sea, the legislation effectively debarred Germany from gaining supplies in the same quarter and avoided much potential friction over neutral rights. In the first year of the conflict, as a result, 44·3 per cent of the total exports of the United States went to the British Empire. This represented, it is true, a colossal strain on the dollar resources of Britain, but for the moment it gave her the aid she needed.

Even the prohibition of American travel in belligerent ships, which

[1] Q. Bailey, p. 760.

had been on the statute book for some years, could not come into operation quickly enough to keep pace with the new lightning speed of war, for the British liner, *Athenia*, was sunk on the very first day of hostilities, before a Presidential Proclamation could be issued, let alone take effect, and it resulted in the loss of twenty-eight American lives. In the same way, the belligerents took only a few days to adopt the stance in matters of blockade which it had taken them years to reach in World War I. Thus on 8 September the Allies established a far-reaching "contraband control" in retaliation for submarine attacks, and in November ordered the detention of all goods whatsoever of German origin in retaliation for the indiscriminate German use of mines. Both sides ignored the hemispheric "safety belt" established, but not enforced, by the Panama Conference of American Republics. The United States could not protest the British definition of contraband, since it was almost identical with that of America in 1917, nor the British blacklist, which it had also used as a belligerent. The State Department did formally reserve its rights under the export embargo on German goods; it also protested against the forcing of American ships into British control stations and their prolonged detention there. When American opinion was aroused over the searching of mails, a formal protest was made almost exactly in the terms used in 1916 and was rejected by the Foreign Office in almost the same terms as their rejection of it in the same year, although American participation in the process themselves after 1917 was tactfully not mentioned. Quite obviously "the State Department was merely going through motions for the sake of the record."[1] All this had an air of considerable unreality at a time when a Gallup poll showed 62 per cent of those questioned in favour of doing everything possible to help Britain and France short of war. America was not only far from neutral in thought, she was not prepared to do anything about Allied actions which violated her concept of neutrality in such practical matters as these.

The contrast with Wilsonian neutrality is marked, and it existed primarily because of the hatred of the American democracy for Fascism and Nazism; the course of action was essentially political in motivation. Allied orders did, no doubt, stimulate the American economy, though possibly less than America's own rearmament programme, which was accelerated in the fall of 1939, but they do not seem to have had to save it from near-disaster as in 1914. Furthermore, isolationist opinion was all too swift to point out any examples of economic interest promoting aid to the Allies, and had succeeded in erecting formidable

[1] Bailey, p. 765.

barriers against the internationalist influence of finance and business. In fact, the prohibitions of the entry of American ships into the war zones and of the arming of merchantmen constituted, as had the Jeffersonian embargo more than a century before, a great national self-denying ordinance; it differed from the earlier one, however, in its object, since it was not conceived as an economic sanction to bring pressure upon belligerents to observe America's neutral rights, but as a means of avoiding friction with them. It was an American withdrawal from all commercial enterprises in belligerent areas and was designed to prevent her from becoming involved in the war. It was to all intents and purposes an embodiment of the policies advocated by Bryan in the first war; it endeavoured, and to a great degree successfully, to eliminate the economic motive for participation.

Though this was done by means which were not pleasing to interventionists, it was in the end not without advantage to their cause, for it made crystal clear in the supreme crisis of 1940 that the fundamental motive for American aid to Britain was political self-interest, that the defeat of Britain would have been highly dangerous, perhaps fatal, to America and her way of life. It destroyed the legend that America's only interest in the first war had been financial, and it weakened American isolationism, probably wounding it mortally. This was emphasized by the fact that the war zone prohibition did largely achieve its object, for virtually no serious maritime incident disturbed the relations of Germany with America before American intervention had begun, despite the existence of an all-out submarine and air war campaign by the Germans against shipping proceeding to Britain. The German Navy in fact went out of its way to avoid such clashes with the great neutral, but it availed Hitler little when the American hour of decision came, for that decision was very plainly one involving the whole future of the United States. In 1917 Wilson's view of America's rights had led him to war on the submarine issue, and the underlying threat by Germany to the American democracy was never fully revealed; in 1940 there could be no such doubt as to the central nature of the problem, if only because the American self-denying ordinance had avoided all lesser irritations and inducements to war. Though Pearl Harbour brought America fully to battle, what amounted to her commitment to try and sustain Britain was already made. The neutrality legislation was the Munich of the American people, in the sense that it convinced all reasonable men that the United States had gone up to, and even perhaps beyond, the bounds of national honour and safety, in order to avoid war. When the war came there was no alternative to victory.

797

But the domestic battle against isolationism had yet to be fought, and during the winter of 1939-40 its lines were steadily drawn. The Administration pressed on the policy of aid to the Allies; Secretary of the Treasury Morgenthau was particularly active, which was important in view of the isolationist leanings of Secretary of War Woodring, and there was a steady flow of war supplies to Europe. In the autumn a Non-Partisan Committee for Peace through Revision of the Neutrality Law, which was frankly pro-Ally, was set up to oppose the very vocal isolationists, who were abetted by a small but vigorous pro-German group, one at least of whose members, it was later revealed, was a subsidized Nazi agent.

Isolationism was still very strong; indeed, in the opinion of Under-Secretary Sumner Welles "public opinion had at this moment, except in one or two sections of the country, reached another climax of out-and-out isolationism. Popular feeling demanded that this government refrain from any action, and even from any gesture, which might conceivably involve the United States with the warring powers."[1] This is perhaps over-emphasized by Welles in his natural regret at the failure of his special mission to Europe in 1940 to reveal any hope of peace; it is true that by February, 1940, there was a marked decline in the number of Americans who expected the United States to be drawn into the war, but this by no means betokened a decline in the amount of aid given to the Allies, for many of its advocates genuinely believed that it would keep America at peace. William Allen White himself—President of the Committee to Defend America by Aiding the Allies, which was set up in April, 1940—was one of these. He was no slavish admirer of Britain, as his words of March, 1940, show: "What an avalanche of blunders Great Britain has let loose upon the democracies of the world! The old British lion looks mangy, sore-eyed."[2] But this did not prevent his forthright promotion of further aid to her, and, despite Welles, it is probable that sentiment in favour of aid lost no ground in the battle of words which went on throughout the winter.

But, as Nevins writes, "events, not words, are the greatest educator", and in the same way that in Britain the rapid fall of Denmark, Norway, Holland, Belgium and France in the spring of 1940 was needed to bring home to the people the full reality of war, so in the United States this catastrophe was essential to the full development of American aid. Under its impetus the movement in favour of aid swiftly acquired active and notable recruits, such as Clark Eichelberger, Nicholas Murray

[1] S. Wells, *The Time for Decision* (London, 1944), p. 63.
[2] Q. Johnson, p. 63.   [3] *New Deal*, p. 204.

Butler, Frank Knox and Henry L. Stimson, and there was a great hastening of the purchasing programme. The latest model planes were released, in return for an Allied contribution to the expenses of development; contracts were signed calling for delivery of more than 2,000 fighters and 2,000 bombers; and in April and the first half of May new commitments of $400 million brought the total projected expenditure of the Allies to about a billion dollars.

The American reaction was not swift enough to have any effect on the progress of events upon the European mainland, any more than was the installation of Winston Churchill. Welles had been of the opinion, when he returned from America at the end of March, that, "There was only one power on earth which could give Hitler and his associates pause. That would be their conviction that, in a war of devastation forced upon Europe by Germany, the United States, in its own interest, would come to the support of the Western democracies. Equally clearly, however, there was at that moment not the remotest chance that our government could tell the Nazi government that this would prove to be the case."[1] Possibly even this would not have sufficed, for those whom the gods wish to destroy they first make mad—but possibly it might, and in that possibility lay the real tragedy of American isolationism. Welles's prophecy, however, was quite accurate, and when, just after Mussolini had stabbed the Allies in the back, Prime Minister Reynaud appealed to Roosevelt for "aid and material support by all means 'short of an expeditionary force' ", and again for "clouds of planes", he could only reply that America sent her "utmost sympathy" and would send all the arms she could spare, but that "these statements carry with them no implication of military commitments. Only the Congress can make such commitments."[2]

But as the fall of France began to appear inevitable, and eventually became a fact, America's eyes were focused more and more exclusively on Britain. Could she, would she survive alone? On the answer to this question the fate of America herself might depend, and that answer might be powerfully affected by America's own actions. Yet those actions depended upon the intuitive or calculated answer which Americans themselves gave to the question. If they believed, as a decreasing number of pessimistic isolationists did, that Britain would go under, it was folly to pour vital American arms into the hands of Hitler, or at best into a useless internment, like that of one hundred and fifty American planes which were hurriedly despatched to France on the aircraft carrier *Béarn*, only to languish throughout the war in

[1] Welles, p. 97. [2] Bailey, p. 765.

the Caribbean colony of Martinique. If on the other hand they believed, as more and more Americans did, that with American aid Britain would ride out the storm, no amount of assistance was too great, for it was quite clear now that the island fortress was the main bastion of America's defence.

The President and the influential members of the Administration were wholeheartedly of the latter school; their acceleration of aid was indeed what Churchill called it, an act of faith. As well as freezing the assets and protecting the colonies of the conquered nations in the Western hemisphere and making an unprecedented appeal to Congress for defence appropriations of more than a billion dollars and an annual output of 50,000 planes, the authorities did all they could to expedite arms and war materials for Britain. On 10 June Roosevelt gave expression to this at Charlottesville, Virginia, in these words, "[W]e will extend to the opponents of force the material resources of this nation; and, at the same time, we will harness and speed up the use of those resources"[1] for our own needs. Three days before, a number of restrictions on the sale of obsolete military equipment to Britain had been swept away, and a trade-in scheme under an old law of 1917 was then inaugurated, by which the Government turned over planes to manufacturers in return for new models, so that the former could be transferred to Britain and her Allies; about 150 warplanes were made available by this means in the course of June. In the same way, through the swift action of General Marshall, something of the order of 600,000 Lee-Enfield rifles, 800 French and British 75s, 80,000 machine guns and very considerable quantities of ammunition were released by the American Army for resale to the British. Soon, a hundred obsolete American tanks were sent to Canada for training purposes, British pilots were permitted to train in Florida, and damaged British warships were allowed to undergo extensive repairs in American dockyards.

But most attention was concentrated on the naval aspect of affairs, for it is in this realm of war that, under modern conditions, forces-in-being or the lack of them, are most decisive. Men may endure air attack for considerable periods, armies of a kind may be created rapidly with a minimum of equipment, but no one can build or rebuild a navy speedily, and without a navy all power of survival at sea is lost. In his first telegram to the President after he became Prime Minister, Churchill had appealed to the President for American non-belligerency, that is to say all aid short of engaging armed forces; he had also asked the loan of forty or fifty old American destroyers. In another

[1] Q. Sherwood, p. 145.

on 20 May, five days later, he harped American fears aright, and with great skill, in an effort to hasten aid:

[O]ur intention is, whatever happens, to fight on to the end in this Island, and, provided we can get the help for which we ask, we hope to run them very close in the air battles in view of individual superiority. Members of the present Administration would (be) likely (to) go down during this process should it result adversely, but in no conceivable circumstances will we consent to surrender. If members of the present Administration were finished and others came in to parley amid the ruins, you must not be blind to the fact that the sole remaining bargaining counter with Germany would be the Fleet, and if this country was left by the United States to its fate no one would have the right to blame those then responsible if they made the best terms they could for the surviving inhabitants. Excuse me, Mr. President, putting this nightmare bluntly. Evidently I could not answer for my successors, who in utter despair and helplessness might well have to accommodate themselves to the German will. However, there is happily no need at present to dwell upon such ideas.[1]

But the American people and their leaders inevitably dwelt upon them, and all the more after the collapse of France on 22 June. However, through vigorous, if distasteful British initiatives, including military action, the French fleet was prevented from falling intact into Nazi hands or under Nazi influence; and these violent measures reinforced the effect which verbal expressions of determination had upon the Americans. And Churchill had not, as is well known, confined himself to private assurances of resolution; with his eye partly upon the American people he had given magnificent public expression to Britain's "inflexible resolve to continue the war."[2] As he wrote later, "After the collapse of France the question . . . arose in the minds of all our friends . . . 'Will Britain surrender, too?' . . . I had repeatedly declared our resolve to fight on alone. After Dunkirk . . . I had used the expression 'if necessary for years, *if necessary alone.*' This was not inserted without design."

One vital aspect of the design is shown in a highly characteristic letter to Lothian on 28 June: "No doubt I shall make some broadcast presently, but I don't think words count for much now. Too much attention should not be paid to eddies of United States opinion. Only force of events can govern them. Up till April they were so sure the Allies would win that they did not think help necessary. Now they are so sure we shall lose that they do not think it possible." Never cease to

[1] *Second World War*, II, p. 51.   [2] Ibid, p. 198.

impress on the President, he instructed the Ambassador, that if a Quisling government surrendered the Fleet to Germany.

> Feeling in England against United States would be similar to French bitterness against us now. We have really not had any help worth speaking of from the United States so far. [The rifles and field-guns did not arrive till the end of July. The destroyers had been refused.] We know President is our best friend, but it is no use trying to dance attendance upon Republican and Democratic Conventions. What really matters is whether Hitler is master of Britain in three months or not.[1]

His American aims were slowly achieved, for, to the President at once, and to the mass of the American people increasingly as time went on, it was apparent that the British Fleet must never fall into German hands and that Britain could, with American aid, fight on in the war. The problem of the next eighteen months was, how much aid was to be given, and how quickly and how was it to be got through?

Upon the fall of France Britain took over French commitments in America, and at British suggestion the new American defence legislation included power to control the export of vital raw materials from America; in addition, emergency measures were taken by the United States to break the machine-tool bottleneck which had developed, particularly in the aircraft industry. In his acceptance of the unprecedented Third Term nomination of the Democratic Convention in July the President boldly pressed his advocacy of aid for Britain and China, and three weeks earlier the Republican Convention had turned its back decisively on isolationism by the unexpected nomination of a thorough-going internationalist, Wendell Willkie, which in effect took the issue of support for Britain out of the Presidential election. On 20 June two influential Republicans, Knox and Stimson, accepted office in the Administration as Secretary of the Navy and of War respectively. These things were important, but, as Churchill declared, all still hung upon the outcome of the Battle of Britain, for on it depended whether Hitler would launch the invasion of Britain which had been recently prepared under the code name "Sea Lion". This decisive air battle, which began in earnest on 5 August, resulted in the defeat of Germany by 15 September and in the indefinite postponement of "Sea Lion" two days later.

While the contest was at its height, protracted negotiations (protracted at least by the standards of the hour) were going on over the

[1] Ibid, pp. 197, 201.

loan of the over-age American destroyers, on which subject Churchill had returned to the charge on the last day of July, being aware of the more favourable attitude towards such an idea which had developed amongst the American public. Early in August a suggestion came from Washington of trading the destroyers for American bases in the British islands of the Caribbean; it seemed to the British Government that there was a basis for agreement here:

> Believing, as I have always done, that the survival of Britain is bound up with the survival of the United States, it seemed to me and to my colleagues that it was an actual advantage to have these bases in American hands . . . and . . . [t]he transfer to Great Britain of fifty American warships was a decidedly unneutral act by the United States. It would, according to all the standards of history, have justified the German Government in declaring war upon them. The President judged that there was no danger, and I felt there was no hope, of this simple solution of many difficulties. . . . Nevertheless the transfer . . . brought the United States definitely nearer to us and to the war, and it was the first of a long succession of increasingly unneutral acts in the Atlantic which were of the utmost service to us. It marked the passage of the United States from being neutral to being non-belligerent.

Churchill's desire to lease rather than give the bases caused no difficulty, but he raised two more serious objections. Washington were anxious—naturally enough, particularly since the Prime Minister had himself put the problem forcibly to them—for re-assurance that the Fleet would never be handed over to the Germans. Churchill was anxious to avoid, as he wrote to the Foreign Secretary,

> any discussion of what we should do if our Island were overrun. Such a discussion, perhaps on the eve of an invasion, would be injurious to public morale, now so high. Moreover, we must never get into a position where the United States Government might say: "We think the time has come for you to send your Fleet across the Atlantic in accordance with our understanding or agreement when we gave you the destroyers." We must refuse any declaration such as is suggested, and confine the deal solely to the Colonial leases.[1]

To Lothian he was equally frank in a passage which illuminates distinctly his conception of the Anglo-American relationship at this time. Of American fears for the future of the Fleet he wrote that,

> We have no intention of relieving United States from any well-

[1] *Second World War*, II, pp. 357-9.

grounded anxieties on this point. Moreover, our position is not such as to bring the collapse of Britain into the arena of political discussion. I have already . . . told you that there is no warrant for discussing any question of the transference of the Fleet to American or Canadian shores. . . . Pray make it clear at once that we could never agree to the slightest compromising of our full liberty of action, nor tolerate any such defeatist announcement, the effect of which would be disastrous. . . . Of course if the United States entered the war and became an ally we should conduct the war with them in common, and make of our own initiative and in agreement with them whatever were the best dispositions at any period in the struggle for the final effectual defeat of the enemy.[1]

In all this he was quite right; any blunting of so fine a weapon as British morale at this time might have been calamitous. One must admire the superb skill and clarity of mind with which he walked the narrow path between failure to get the needed aid on the one hand and loss of British freedom of action to America on the other. In the end this aspect of the matter was settled by a compromise which he himself drafted for the President, who sent him a cable which ran:

> The Prime Minister of Great Britain is reported to have stated on 4 June, 1940, to Parliament, in effect, that if during the course of the present war . . . the waters surrounding the British Isles should become untenable for British ships of war, a British Fleet would in no event be surrendered or sunk, but would be sent overseas for the defence of other parts of the Empire. The Government of the United States would respectfully inquire whether the foregoing statement represents the settled policy of the British Government.

To this, his own draft, he replied: "It certainly does. I must however observe that these hypothetical contingencies seem more likely to concern the German Fleet, or what is left of it, than our own."[2]

His other objection to the Administration's proposal was that he was most reluctant to barter or exchange the bases for the destroyers; he would have preferred the generous gesture of outright gift on both sides. Further, he was worried at the "deep feelings" aroused by a "naked trading away of British possessions,"[3] and was reluctant to arouse opposition to the project. In so far as judgment is yet possible, it would seem that he exaggerated this difficulty. Public opinion saw clearly enough the facts of the case, and it welcomed the bargain; it would have done so whether it was dressed up or not. And the President's reasons for insistence on a direct exchange were solid and neces-

[1] Ibid, pp. 359-360.   [2] Ibid, pp. 366-7.   [3] Ibid, p. 361.

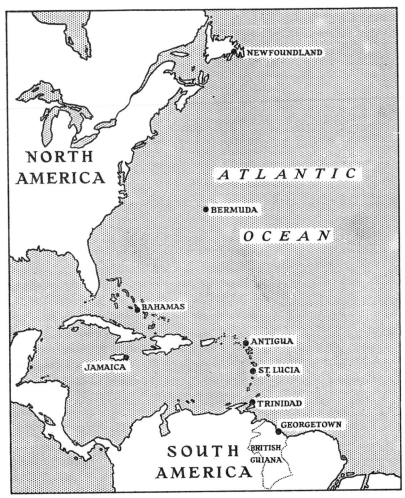

Map 7. *British Bases Leased to the United States, 1940.*

sary. Churchill himself wrote to him, "I am sure you will not misunder-
stand me if I say that our willingness . . . must be conditional on our
being assured that there will be no delay",[1] and Roosevelt was
determined to avoid the inevitable cunctation and possible miscarriage
involved in submission of the arrangement to Congress. Yet only a
month or so previously, an amendment had been inserted in a Naval
Appropriations Bill by Congress which prevented the despatch of the

[1] Ibid, p. 360.

805

destroyers unless the Navy could certify that they were useless for United States defence purposes: the only way out of the dilemma was to demand bases as a *quid pro quo*, so that Admiral Stark could "certify that the total measure would strengthen rather than weaken America's defence".[1] In the end a compromise was reached, by which the leases of the two most important bases, in Bermuda and Newfoundland, remained free gifts, separate from the rest of the deal. The agreement was notified to Congress on 3 September. It arranged the exchange of fifty over-age American destroyers for ninety-nine year leases on bases in the Bahamas, Jamaica, Antigua, St. Lucia, Trinidad, and British Guiana. Though in fact the vessels did not arrive before the Battle of Britain, they proved invaluable in the long Battle of the Atlantic in the coming winter. From the American angle Roosevelt said that it was "the most important action in the reinforcement of our national defense that has taken place since the Louisiana Purchase."[2] Both nations, and indeed Western civilization, had good reason to be pleased with the bargain.

III

MEANWHILE, public opinion in the United States, under the impact of such things as the dramatic autumn "Blitz" on Britain, and the signature of a German-Italian-Japanese treaty of alliance on 27 September, continued gradually to rally behind the Administration. The Committee to Defend America by Aiding the Allies became more and more interventionist, so that it cast off its non-interventionist members, including its President, and gained increasing public support. The isolationists, too, were now better organized under the leadership of such bodies as the America First Committee, and they could still feel intensely, as a lunatic fringe letter to White, before his split with the C.D.A.A.A. illustrates:

> Dear Mr. Warmonger: If you and the rest of your kind of lice are so anxious to help England, why don't you go to Canada and join the army. They have a lot of nice rifles up there and I am sure they would be glad to let you and Professor Conant have one. . . . If we just had some legal means of hanging such war-mongers as you and Conant, America would be a lot better place to live.[3]

But steady headway was made. On 18 August Roosevelt and

[1] Sherwood, p. 176.   [2] Q. Bemis, *The U.S. as a World Power*, p. 384.
[3] Q. Johnson, p. 149.

Mackenzie King announced the establishment of a Permanent Joint Board of Defense to consider the defence of the northern half of the Western hemisphere, and this action was followed by an increasingly close co-ordination of the production programmes of the two neighbours. On 16 September the President signed an epoch-making bill, which he had requested but which had been bi-partisan in support, the first peace-time conscription act in American history. It only passed after long debate, for, like the British (with whose law of 1939, which was also unprecedented in peace time, it is analogous), the American people mistrusted compulsory military service—but it did pass. Despite the necessity of giving some assurances, which later proved an embarrassment to him, such as that which ran, "Your boys are not going to be sent into any foreign wars",[1] Roosevelt's re-election in November by a large majority was, and was taken to be in America and elsewhere, an endorsement of his policy of aid to the Allies.

Despite the fears of some British officials, when the President went off on a fishing trip early in December, that he was resting on his oars in the matter of aid to Britain, he was in fact about to give birth to the most important conception for her support yet envisaged, one which was of incalculable significance in the winning of the war. In his very first communication to the President, on 15 May, the Prime Minister had said, "We shall go on paying dollars for as long as we can, but I should like to feel reasonably sure that when we can pay no more you will give us the stuff all the same." Though the problem had been for a few weeks swallowed up in the onrush of events, it soon began to dominate all others. Britain had, at the beginning of the war, assumed control of the dollar assets of all her citizens and, by compulsorily converting individual holdings into sterling, had thrown more and more of them into the struggle. With the assumption of French commitments and the loss of French assets the pace of expenditure had enormously increased, and the British Government would very soon be scraping the bottom of the barrel. History was repeating itself with a vengeance, and indeed with greater severity, for British dollar resources were more nearly exhausted than in 1917, when America had had to undertake the main financial burden of the struggle.

When one reflects on the difficulty Britain has had since 1945 in gaining sufficient dollars for her peacetime needs, and on the fact that in 1940 her requirements were almost infinite, while her means of earning by exports were narrowly restricted, one gains some imagina-

[1] Q. Bailey, p. 772.

tive realization of the desperate urgency of the situation. In Churchill's words, past caution in the conservation of dollar assets had to be thrown to the winds; we ordered "everything we possibly could" and left "future financial problems on the lap of the Eternal Gods"[1]—on that, one might say, of Franklin Roosevelt, who was the only possible *deus ex machina*. When Lothian visited Britain for consultations in November, the hour of reckoning was nigh, for of the $4,500 million Britain had possessed at the opening of war and the $2,000 million she had earned since, only $2,000 million were left, mostly in investments that were not very readily marketable. After the American election the Prime Minister, in a long letter to the President on 8 December, made what was primarily an appeal on the financial question; but it was more than that, for it was a masterly review of the strategic situation, and outlined "the various ways in which the United States could give supreme and decisive help to what is, in certain aspects, the common cause." It is necessary to dwell further upon this important document, if only because of the impressive manner in which it forecast much of America's future action and of the "profound effect" it had upon Roosevelt, whom it reached in the middle of his trip in the Caribbean.

It began by assuming the common interest of the two democracies and the duty of Britain to hold the front for the two years or so, until the rearmament of the United States should be complete. It pointed out the improved position of Britain provided that the Battle of the Atlantic could be won, and showed that this was quite possible if she received the necessary assistance, despite the fact that the naval situation was worse than it had been since the beginning of the war. The primary needs of Britain, therefore, the letter went on were (1) reassertion of the freedom of the seas (i.e. repeal of restrictions on American shipping); (2) protection of the lawful trading of the United States by her warships and air forces, which would "constitute a decisive act of constructive non-belligerency by the United States, and, more than any other measure, would make it certain that British resistance could be effectively prolonged for the desired period and victory gained."[2] If, however, these steps were not possible, then what was needed was (3) the transfer of many American vessels of war to British ownership; (4) American pressure on Eire for British use of Irish ports and facilities such as those surrendered in the Anglo-Irish Treaty of 1938; (5) vast supplementation of Britain's merchant fleet; (6) reinforcement of Britain's ability to manufacture combat aircraft; (7) the supply of

[1] *Second World War*, II, pp. 23, 492.   [2] Ibid, pp. 497-8.

machine tools and other munitions; (8) "Last of all, I come to the question of Finance. The more rapid and abundant the flow of munitions and ships which you are able to send us, the sooner will our dollar credits be exhausted. . . . The moment approaches when we shall no longer be able to pay cash for shipping and other supplies." Then, in a prophetic passage,

> While we will . . . shrink from no proper sacrifice to make payments across the Exchange, I believe you will agree that it would be wrong in principle and mutually disadvantageous in effect if at the height of this struggle Great Britain were to be divested of all saleable assets, so that after the victory was won with our blood, civilization saved, and the time gained for the United States to be fully armed against all eventualities, we should stand stripped to the bone. . . . We . . . should be unable, after the war, to purchase the large balance of imports from the United States over and above the volume of our exports which is agreeable to your tariffs and industrial economy. . . . You may be certain that we shall prove ourselves ready to suffer and sacrifice to the utmost for the Cause, and that we glory in being its champions. The rest we leave with confidence to you and to your people, being sure that ways and means will be found which future generations on both sides of the Atlantic will approve and admire.

His confidence was well justified, for the response to his letter was Lend-Lease, which Churchill approved and admired as "the most unsordid act in the history of any nation."[1]

On the very day after his return to Washington from his trip the President said in a Press Conference (17 December): "[T]here is absolutely no doubt in the mind of a very overwhelming number of Americans that the best immediate defence of the United States is the success of Britain in defending itself."[2] Then he went to the heart of the matter, in a way which justified Churchill's assertion that "It was never a question of the President not knowing what he wanted to do. His problem was how to carry his country with him and to persuade Congress to follow his guidance."[3] He asserted that "in all history, no major war has ever been . . . lost through lack of money", yet he knew very well that the war loan experience of the last war made such a solution unstatesmanlike, even if it were politically possible to get Congress to repeal the Johnson Act in order to make loans to Britain; recriminations of the kind that went on in the twenties would be as disastrous politically as the debts would be economically.

[1] Ibid, pp. 500-1, 503.   [2] Q. Sherwood, p. 223.
[3] *Second World War*, II, pp. 501-2.

Now, what I am trying to do is to eliminate the dollar sign. That is something brand new in the thoughts of practically everybody in this room, I think—get rid of the silly, foolish old dollar sign. Well, let me give you an illustration: Suppose my neighbor's home catches fire, and I have a length of garden hose four or five hundred feet away. If he can take my garden hose and connect it up with his hydrant, I may help him to put out his fire. Now, what do I do? I don't say to him before that operation, "Neighbor, my garden hose cost me $15; you have to pay me $15 for it!" What is the transaction that goes on? I don't want $15—I want my garden hose back after the fire is over. . . . But suppose it gets smashed up . . . during the fire. . . . He says, "All right, I will replace it!" Now, if I get a nice garden hose back, I am in pretty good shape.[1]

Though, in the event, things did not quite work out this way; though the return of goods to the United States was replaced by the concept of mutual aid—Reverse Lend-Lease—and then by unreserved American participation in the war with all her resources; and though America did not get back much hose compared with what she lent, Sherwood may be justified in writing, "I believe it may accurately be said that with that neighborly analogy Roosevelt won the fight for Lend-Lease."[2]

This aspect of the matter was "lending": the more formal "leasing" seems to have come from the Treasury discovery of a Statute of 1892, which had been implemented in the past, authorizing the Secretary of War to lease Army property "when in his discretion it will be for the public good."[3] The idea was not new (Brebner points out that "It promised to be remarkably like a British discovery of the eighteenth century which Canada had recently rediscovered, that is, that it is better to give outright to one's allies than to lend and hold them strictly to account.")[4] but it was revolutionary in its sweeping vision and vast scope. On the basis of the President's Annual Message of 6 January, 1941, the historic bill—entitled "An Act Further to Promote the Defense of the United States" and bearing the significant number H.R.1776—was introduced later in the month; it was a wide and comprehensive measure, for this time Congress must be consulted, and since a battle was inevitable it was better to make the victory worth while.

It gave power to the President to arrange the manufacture of any defence article for the government of any country whose defence he deemed vital to the defence of the United States; to lend or lease any defence article to such government; to carry out repairs for it, or com-

[1] Roosevelt, *Public Papers, 1940*, pp. 605-7.   [2] Sherwood, p. 224.
[3] Q. *Second World War*, II, p. 502.   [4] Brebner, p. 325.

municate defence information to it. It further empowered the President to arrange terms, conditions and benefits, direct or indirect, to be rendered by governments receiving such aid. Under this clause reciprocal arrangements for Lend-Lease were later made, and by an executive agreement of 25 February, 1942, after some understanding had been reached by the two governments as to the principles of the peace, the colossal aid to Great Britain was written off as subsidies. Two stipulations of the Act were significant, and showed the President's necessity, for the moment at any rate, to refuse, or hold back on, Churchill's most optimistic requests. One laid down that nothing in its provisions should be construed to authorize or permit convoying of vessels by the naval forces of the United States; this was not, as we shall see, to be very effective, partly because the President could assume this power anyway as Commander-in-Chief, and partly because other methods of protection, almost as satisfactory as convoy, could be devised. The other stipulated that nothing in the Act should authorize or permit the entry of an American vessel into a combat area in violation of the Neutrality Act of 1939. This proved a more effective clause, since, though the President could and did alter details of the war zone specifications, it prevented, for the present, the direct passage of American ships to Britain.

The struggle for the bill was stiff; it was on this occasion that Senator Burton K. Wheeler declared that the policy would mean "ploughing under every fourth American boy", which Roosevelt described as "the most untruthful, the most dastardly, unpatriotic thing that has been said in public life in my generation", adding, "Quote me on that."[1] While it was going on, the Administration was forced into many strange expedients—not always reluctantly since they made excellent propaganda—in order to keep the flow of supplies moving to a Britain suffering from an ever more acute stringency of dollars, but by ingenuity and resolution it succeeded. In March the Bill passed Congress by 60 to 31, and 317 to 71; a half an hour after the action of the legislative body was complete, the President signed it; five minutes later he approved a list of articles for immediate shipment.

Already, in January, he had sent Hopkins on a highly successful visit to London to confer with Churchill on its implementation. Though it became the universal means by which America supplied the needs of all her Allies, including Russia, it was a bill, in fact, for the support of Britain, and she obtained the lion's share of material aid. Between her and the United States, it worked on the whole with wonderful

[1] Sherwood, p. 228.

smoothness. Later, in 1941, the British, in response to very natural anxieties on the part of American business interests, issued an assurance that Lend-Lease materials had not been, and would not be, used for export, or in such a way as to enable their exporters to enter new markets or to extend their export trade at the expense of United States exporters. The legislation miraculously achieved the President's object of dispensing with the dollar sign, and it cut off at birth any likelihood that war debts would disturb the later relations of the two countries. Yet if America had insisted on the mistaken policy of lending Britain money in 1940-1, the British Government could not have refused to borrow, despite all its sense of the calamitous nature of such a course. The action was, therefore, one of great generosity and wise statesmanship, for, though, in fact, Hitler had decided that the conquest of Britain must wait on the defeat of Russia long before Lend-Lease became effective in the summer of 1941, this could not be known at the time, while in any case American pre-Lend-Lease aid had possibly been decisive in Britain's successful defence against the U-boat. Most important of all, in the later stages of the conflict, Lend-Lease was the supreme economic instrument of victory.

The new relationship of the two peoples, what Sherwood calls their "common law alliance", was proclaimed by Roosevelt in his bold and comprehensive review of the war situation on 29 December, which was a kind of public counterpart to Churchill's private letter to him. He called it a fireside chat "on national security."[1]

He showed at once how far he had moved from his attitude at the time of the Welles mission of 1940, let alone from Wilson's position in 1916, by saying, "[T]he axis . . . *proclaims* that there can be no ultimate peace between their philosophy of government and our philosophy of government. In view of the nature of this undeniable threat . . . the United States has no right or reason to encourage talk of peace, until the day shall come when there is a clear intention on the part of the aggressor nations to abandon all thought of dominating or conquering the world." After pointing out the role played in the protection of the Americas in the past by Britain's sea power and by her innocent use of that power in so far as aggression in the Western hemisphere was concerned, he pointed to the dangers if Britain went down. As Wilson had once felt before him, he feared that to survive in such a world "we would have to convert ourselves permanently into a militaristic power on the basis of war economy. . . . The British people and their

[1] Roosevelt, *Public Papers, 1940*, p. 633, *et. seq.*

812

Allies today are conducting an active war against this unholy alliance. Our own future security is greatly dependent on the outcome of that fight. . . . Great Britain and the British Empire are today the spearhead of resistance to world conquest. They are putting up a fight which will live for ever in the story of human gallantry." They

do not ask us to do their fighting. They ask us for the implements of war. . . . Emphatically we must get these weapons to them in sufficient volume and quickly enough, so that we and our children will be saved the agony and suffering of war which others have had to endure. Let not the defeatists tell us that it is too late. It will never be earlier. To-morrow will be later than today. . . . We must be the great arsenal of democracy. For us this is an emergency as serious as war itself. . . . There will be no 'bottlenecks' in our determination to aid Great Britain. . . . I have the profound conviction that the American people are now determined to put forth a mightier effort than they have ever yet made to increase our production of all the implements of defense, to meet the threat to our democratic faith.

Thus did the United States declare its intention to be the arsenal of democracy. But she by no means confined herself to the production of weapons; this was valueless unless she made sure that they arrived at their destination, which meant using every means in her power to ensure that the Battle of the Atlantic was won. In fact, it is fascinating to see how, step by step, almost every one of the suggestions made by Churchill in his letter of 8 December was put into effect. The conclusion seems inescapable that this great document, laying down Britain's requirements in order to wage victorious war, became the basis of an overall plan, formulated by the President and his advisers, for the defence of the Western world. This envisaged American participation in the work of war, in so far as ensuring the flow of supplies to Britain was concerned; it did not necessarily envisage the all-out participation of the United States, particularly if her hand was not forced by her opponents. It will be remembered that many observers had believed in 1917 that it was in just such a limited form that the United States might wage war. This was precisely what the Americans were doing in 1941, and they recognized as much; a *Fortune* poll of June, 1941, showed that 79·5 per cent of them believed that America was in the war for all practical purposes. Like Britain before her, she had become reluctantly convinced that there was no alternative to the use of force, but she still hoped that the amount of force might be limited. There were some grounds for this hope, which was the basis of Roosevelt's assertions that his course might avoid the necessity of sending vast armies overseas; and his attitude was an honest one, for he had warned his people that there was risk in any policy. But of the existence and comprehensiveness of the American plan of campaign in 1941 there can be no doubt.

Already, the extent of Anglo-American co-operation behind the scenes was very remarkable. The exchange of scientific information on all manner of subjects, including radar and atomic energy, had started with Sir Henry Tizard's mission to Washington in September, 1940; the pooling of military intelligence had begun largely through the efforts of General Marshall, as had security service liaison; numbers of American specialists had set off for England in search of the latest technical information; and plans had already been drawn up, not only for the strengthening of the American Atlantic Fleet, but for the occupation by U.S. forces of Greenland, Iceland, the Azores and Martinique. Most significant of all, the first American-British staff talks had been instituted. There had been exploratory discussions in Britain as early as August, 1940, but, partly as a result of the Tripartite Axis Pact of 27 September, these were extended into full-scale talks in Washington in January, 1941, the Britons attending in civilian clothes and disguised as technical advisers to the British Purchasing Commission. The conference lasted two months. It resolved that if the war spread to the Pacific, the European theatre should be given priority, a most important decision for Britain, and plans were formulated on this assumption. In March, 1941, American officers visited Britain to select American bases for their naval and air forces, and the development of similar bases in the western Atlantic was pressed on apace. Preparations were made for joint ocean convoy in the Atlantic. These measures extended to the diplomatic as well as the military and economic spheres. Not only was heavy American pressure brought to bear on the Vichy Government through the American Ambassador, Admiral Leahy, to prevent further concessions to Hitler, but in May Roosevelt made an unprecedented appeal direct to the French people.

But nothing illustrates more clearly the closeness of British and American objectives than Churchill's successful efforts to induce a Democratic President of the United States to bring pressure to bear upon Eire to open her ports to British naval vessels. The Prime Minister used to the full the threat of refusing any longer to convoy ships with feeding stuffs to Ireland, and diplomatic pressure was applied by Roosevelt to De Valera, but little headway was made. Though this was a cause of great chagrin to the Prime Minister, he might, in more leisured times, have reflected that the virtual independence of Ireland had at least removed the sting of the Irish in Anglo-American relations, despite the insistence of many of them on the inequity of Partition. This Irish argument made little appeal to Americans, whose connexions with Ireland were becoming steadily more remote, and did so even less after the arrival of large numbers of American troops in Northern Ireland and their continued exclusion from Eire, which remained neutral to the end, despite the great numbers of her young men who volunteered for the British forces.

After the passage of the Lend-Lease Bill on 11 March, the public steps in the implementation of what must—at least in the mind of the President—have been this controlling overall plan commenced. On 15 March he said, "We have just now engaged in a great debate . . . and it was finally settled and decided by the American people themselves. . . . Today, at last . . . ours is not a partial effort. It is a total effort. . . . Our country is going to play its full part."[1] Large appropriations were soon made by Congress. Then the President announced that the Government would maintain what he called a bridge of ships to Britain, and some of his supporters came out openly for convoys. On 30 March the Government seized sixty-five Axis-controlled ships in American ports, and gaoled nearly a thousand of the seamen for attempted sabotage. On 9 April an agreement was signed with the Danish Minister in Washington for the occupation of Greenland, and when the puppet government in Copenhagen repudiated it, Secretary Hull announced that he would continue to regard the Minister, who had been recalled, as the accredited representative of his country. On 10 April, in recognition of the British victories in Libya, and perhaps in a desire to facilitate aid to the heroic Greeks in their resistance to Mussolini's invasion, a Presidential Proclamation made the mouth of the Red Sea no longer a combat area, so that American ships could carry supplies to Britain's great base in Egypt.

Behind the scenes, a constant correspondence went on with Churchill, and early in April the United States Navy drew up Hemispheric Defence Plan No. 1, which provided for aggressive action by American warships against U-boats and surface raiders in the Atlantic. On 19 April, however, the news of the neutrality pact between Japan and Russia caused it to be replaced by Plan No. 2, which merely ordered American ships to report on the movements of German vessels west of Iceland. It was put into effect on 24 April. At a Press Conference on 25 April the President said that neutrality patrols, such as had existed since the

[1] Roosevelt, 1941, pp. 63-8.

hemispheric belt was inaugurated at the beginning of the war, would extend "[a]s far on the waters of the seven seas as may be necessary for the defense of the American hemisphere."[1] It had previously been decided, and Britain had been informed, that they would operate as far east as longitude 25 deg. though the line was turned east at the top so as to include Iceland. On 27 May, while the news was reaching the nation, not only of the attack on Crete, but also of the very dramatic sinking of the *Bismarck* by British forces in the Atlantic, Roosevelt made an eagerly awaited radio address, in which he revealed the enormous rate of Nazi sinkings of merchantmen, which had reached a climax in April. He pledged, "from the point of view of strict naval and military necessity . . . every possible assistance to Britain. . . . Our patrols are helping now to insure delivery of the needed supplies to Britain. All additional measures necessary to deliver the goods will be taken."[2] In a final dramatic passage he announced the issue of a Proclamation of Unlimited National Emergency.

He had brought the country very far from Cash and Carry, and now, almost for the first time, public opinion had the appearance of beginning to outrun him. Many of his supporters and advisers, such as Stimson, now thought that he was hanging back; while they demanded that he follow up this step with further positive action, particularly in view of the widespread approval of the proclamation, "the very day after the speech . . . at a Press Conference . . . [h]e dismissed airily any suggestion that he contemplated using the U.S. Navy for convoy duty or asking Congress for any changes in the Neutrality Law."[3] Even Hopkins, who thought he knew the President's mind, was taken aback by this. The truth no doubt is that he was being exceedingly careful—and who will back their judgment of the popular mind against his?—not to outstrip public opinion. The burden of decision on him was enormous, unique; and even his broad shoulders would sometimes bend under the weight. One has the curious impression that he occasionally welcomed even petty subterfuges arranged by himself which would appear to throw part of the responsibility for decision on others. One instance is the odd story recounted by Sherwood, of how Hopkins told him the President desired that he should draft a passage proclaiming the Emergency, for insertion in the speech already mentioned; how, in the presence of Welles, who knew nothing of it, Roosevelt, when reading through the speech, came to the passage and declared " '[W]hat's this?' He looked up from the typescript with the expression of artless innocence that he frequently put on, and asked very politely: 'Hasn't

[1] Ibid, p. 133.   [2] Ibid, p. 190.   [3] Sherwood, p. 299.

somebody been taking some liberties?'...But there was not another word about the proclamation; it remained in the speech." One must accept Sherwood's judgment; "whatever the peril, he was not going to lead the country into war—he was going to wait to be pushed in."[1] One's mind is carried back irresistibly, as no doubt his often was, to his predecessor of 1917; to Wilson's great success in eventually leading a united country into an ultimately victorious war, and to his great failure in dividing it over the peace. Roosevelt was not only determined to avoid the second mistake, he was determined to better the first example; in this he was singularly successful.

But the pause at this juncture was only temporary, for public opinion was rising steadily under renewed pressure of events, while the effect of the measures already taken to aid Britain was becoming noticeable. During the spring, for instance, Washington had transferred ten armed corvettes and twenty mosquito boats to the British flag, and allocated, as a beginning, fifty oil-tankers for use by her in American waters. Most important of all, American war production was increasing swiftly.

Events kept pace with these developments; on the very day of the Unlimited Emergency speech, the survivors of the American merchant vessel, *Robin Moor*, who had been turned loose in open boats in the South Atlantic without proper provision for their safety by the U-boat that sank them, were coming ashore. This was the first deliberate sinking of an American ship by Germany in the war, and the day before it occurred over one hundred American lives were lost in the sinking of the Egyptian steamer *Zam Zam*, also in the South Atlantic. On 6 June Congress passed a bill to take over and employ all foreign merchant ships immobilized in American ports, and both Houses threw out amendments prohibiting the transfer of any of the vessels to the British. On 14 June the President froze all German and Italian assets in the United States, and, on 16 and 20 June respectively, the Administration demanded the closing of all the consulates of Germany and Italy in the United States. On the latter day Roosevelt described the German sinkings as "piracy."[2] American warships, with secret channels of communication with British vessels, were already, in the words of Churchill, cruising "along our convoy routes" west of Iceland, to "shadow—or, as they call it, 'trail'—all raiders or U-boats observed, and broadcast their positions in plain language to the world".[3] Arrangements had already been made in the greatest secrecy for the relief of the British garrison, which had occupied Iceland, by American troops; these actually landed and the announcement was made on 7 July. American

[1] Ibid, pp. 297, 299.   [2] Bailey, p. 780.   [3] *Second World War*, III, p. 216.

convoys thereafter ran regularly to Reykjavik, and admitted foreign ships to their protection; this act by an officially neutral power enormously relieved the burden on British naval resources. On 17 July Washington announced a black list of about 1,800 firms in Latin America, having Axis connexions, with which Americans were not to do business.

Any of these acts might have justified a German declaration of war, and the German naval authorities pressed to be allowed to operate more freely against American shipping, but Hitler, wishing to avoid open hostilities with the United States, refused to give them a free hand; in the words of Alan Bullock he showed "considerable patience"[1] at American aid to Britain. In the same way, throughout these months the German Government endeavoured to persuade the Japanese to attack the British Empire, simply ignoring the American forces on their flank in the hope that they would provide too little help too late. Hitler's restraint prevented overt war between Germany and America before 7 December despite still further American acts of war, and Roosevelt and Churchill were proved right in their assessment of his intentions; his efforts to restrain his Japanese Allies were, happily perhaps for Britain and unhappily for the Japanese, much less successful.

But "restraint" in the case of Adolf Hitler must always be a relative term, for he held back here only in order to free his hands for the gigantic onslaught which he launched on Russia on 22 June. Upon the causes and effects of this act of monumental folly, fascinating though they are, this is no place to dwell; suffice it to point out the obvious fact that it transformed the whole character of the war. Churchill immediately, and Roosevelt soon afterwards, proclaimed full support for Russia, despite the gloomy and false predictions of their military experts as to the capacity of the Soviet Union for resistance. Upon Anglo-American relations the effect of the action was very considerable, as also upon the development of the Far Eastern situation. With Hitler's legions giving Russia a deep interest in honouring the Soviet-Japanese neutrality pact of April, 1941, Japan began to move decisively forward in Asia in July. This meant that the war was in the end to be a global affair; it removed the last possibility of a long struggle between Germany and Britain, with the latter sustained by a co-belligerent United States. The attack on Russia thus helped to make the crushing defeat of the Axis certain, and to make the European war a world conflict.

But it made strange bedfellows, for, great and genuine as was the sentiment in many sections of America and Britain during the

[1] A. Bullock, *Hitler, A Study in Tyranny* (London, 1952), p. 608.

remainder of the war for their Soviet partners, the Anglo-American combination, as subsequent events proved, was never able to effect a lasting *rapprochement* with Russia. The efforts of Roosevelt to do so at the end of the war did in fact throw some strain upon Anglo-American relations, but it was quite ephemeral in character, for there was far too much in favour of Anglo-American friendship and far too much against close co-operation with the Soviet Union for it to endure. But during the second half of 1941, except that it made it reasonably clear that no immediate German invasion of Britain was possible, the Russian campaign had little effect upon the development of the vital Battle of the Atlantic, where German efforts did not slacken, for it was not until the halting of the December German offensive against Russia, and the success of the limited Russian offensives in January, February and March, 1942, that it became quite clear that the dismal prophecies of the professionals were wrong, and that the war on the Eastern front would be protracted. Thus German-American relations continued to deteriorate throughout the autumn as American strength grew, and it was against this background that Anglo-American friendship was given dramatic illustration by the publication of the Atlantic Charter.

IV

HOPKINS had paid a second visit to London in July, 1941, to discuss the operation of Lend-Lease. The Americans had expressed in conference their fear that Britain was attaching too much importance, and sending too large a proportion of her military resources, to the Middle East theatre, though Hopkins asserted that this view was held more strongly by the President's military advisers than by the President himself, while it must be admitted that it was one to which even the Chief of the Imperial General Staff had at one time inclined. This idea was resisted by Churchill, but he naturally jumped at Hopkins's intimation that the President would welcome a personal meeting. Accordingly, the Prime Minister on the battleship *Prince of Wales,* and the President on the cruiser *Augusta,* met in Placentia Bay, Newfoundland, on 9 August. The secrecy in which the meeting was necessarily held, its dramatic nature, and the belief, cherished by the British public, and nursed by American isolationists, that dynamic action would result—many in Britain fondly hoped that the United States would shortly enter the war—all tended to produce over-optimism, wild rumours and a certain sense of anti-climax when the only tangible result was the publication of the Charter.

This must not be allowed to conceal or disguise the fundamental importance of the occasion. Apart from producing the Charter itself, which signified in even more unmistakable fashion than heretofore American support for Britain—particularly by referring to "the final destruction of Nazi tyranny",[1]—it brought into personal contact for the first time a number of the principal actors in the great drama. Among these, of course, Roosevelt and Churchill were supremely important, but the liking which sprang up between General Marshall and Sir John Dill deserves particular mention. The mere fact that the President of neutral America had met the British Prime Minister, both with military as well as diplomatic advisers in full force, was in itself of vast significance, even though the discussions of the officers in question were confined to narrower limits than those of the civilians; and it necessarily had a considerable effect upon world opinion. Upon those participating it had a strong emotional impact, which loses nothing in Churchill's account of the joint Sunday service on the deck of the *Prince of Wales*.

> This service was felt by us all to be a deeply moving expression of the unity of faith of our two peoples, and none who took part in it will forget the spectacle presented that sunlit morning on the crowded quarterdeck—the symbolism of the Union Jack and the Stars and Stripes draped side by side on the pulpit; the American and British chaplains sharing in the reading of the prayers; the highest naval, military, and air officers of Britain and the United States grouped in one body behind the President and me; the close-packed ranks of British and American sailors, completely intermingled, sharing the same books and joining fervently together in the prayers and hymns familiar to both.[2]

The discussions at all levels ranged over the Atlantic Battle, the threat through Spain to Gibraltar, aid to Russia and the whole Far Eastern problem. The last question might have been much the most important, though it is questionable whether any American commitment would have stopped the Japanese from their attack, for opinion in Tokyo was already virtually determined on war. Despite all the efforts of the British, however, the President and his advisers would make no "hard and fast" resolution, no irrevocable promise to go to war with Japan if she attacked British or Dutch possessions in the Far East. Churchill believed that the only hope of checking Japan was an overt American guarantee of action in case of Japanese aggression, and was very ready to give a corresponding British undertaking. Indeed, he

---

[1] Welles, pp. 140-1.   [2] *Second World War*, III, p. 384.

was more than once to give a unilateral British promise to join America
if she was attacked, but he could extract nothing definite in return. For
nearly four months longer he was to remain suspended in the unpleasant
uncertainty which Winant so graphically describes, in telling of a conversation with the Prime Minister on the very morning of the day when
Pearl Harbour was to be attacked:

> He asked me if I thought there was going to be war with Japan.
> I answered "Yes." With unusual vehemence he turned to me and said:
> "If they declare war on you, we shall declare war on them within the
> hour." "I understand, Prime Minister. You have stated that publicly."
> "If they declare war on us, will you declare war on them?" "I can't
> answer that, Prime Minister. Only the Congress has the right to declare
> war under the United States Constitution." He did not say anything
> for a minute, but I knew what was in his mind. He must have realized
> that if Japan attacked Siam or British territory it would force Great
> Britain into an Asiatic war, and leave us out of the war. He knew in
> that moment that his country might be "hanging on one turn of pitch
> and toss."[1]

Actually he had been uncomfortably aware of it since the Atlantic meeting; only, his anxiety deepened as Japan's attitude became increasingly
ominous. It always remained possible that America would enter the war
anyway in case of attack in the East, but the meeting with Roosevelt
removed Churchill's hope that a prior statement to that effect might
render its implementation unnecessary. He was, on a minor point,
successful in getting the President to drop his project of terminating
the Conference with a statement containing the explicit announcement
that the "naval and military conversations had in no way been concerned with future commitments other than as authorized by Act of
Congress."[2] This demand of Churchill's was understandable, but it
certainly contributed to the false hopes built up in Britain as a result
of the meeting, possibly without any real compensating advantage.
Though the American military officials confined themselves more
largely to the problems arising out of Lend-Lease supplies and their
delivery, their British counterparts acquainted them with their own
plans for the immediate and the distant future.

But the central work of the Conference was the drafting of the
Atlantic Charter. The origin of the idea is obscure, for Churchill
ascribes it to action taken by him on a suggestion of the President at one
of their first meetings, while Sherwood states that Hopkins and the

[1] Winant, p. 197.　　[2] *Second World War*, III, p. 387.

Prime Minister had discussed it during their voyage on the *Prince of Wales* to the rendezvous. Its nature, however, is not in doubt; it was not a treaty—for obvious reasons the President wished something more informal, while Sherwood says that the British regarded it as "not much more than a publicity hand-out"[1]—but the solemn term, Charter, which later came to be applied to it, showed the deep significance which certain sections of Anglo-American opinion attached to it. It was a necessarily vague World War II version of Wilson's Fourteen Points, issued before the United States had even entered the war. Nor is there any question that the first draft was a British one. As Churchill writes: "Considering all the tales of my reactionary, Old World outlook, and the pain this is said to have caused the President, I am glad it should be on record that the substance and spirit of what came to be called the 'Atlantic Charter' was in its first draft a British production cast in my own words."[2] It made its strongest appeal to liberal internationalists everywhere, but to those more enamoured of political realism it had the hollow ring of sanguine propaganda about it.

It contained eight clauses, which laid down a very general set of war aims for the two peoples. They renounced aggrandizement by the war; sought only such territorial changes as accorded with the wishes of the peoples concerned; respected the right of peoples to choose their own form of government; wished to ensure to the nations free access to raw materials, social security and the right freely to traverse the seas; and desired to establish peace, which could best be achieved by disarming the aggressors pending other arrangements. The President had merely wished, in the paragraph concerning disarmament of the aggressors, to make this realistic proposition without any addition, but it was Churchill who pointed out that the lack of reference to any international organization for keeping the peace would "create a great deal of opposition from the extreme internationalists." He and Welles actually favoured the insertion at an appropriate point of the words "*by effective international organization*",[3] but the President, haunted again by the ghost of Wilson, rejected them. With the aid of Hopkins, however, he was persuaded to accept the final formula: "pending the establishment of a wider and permanent system of general security".[4] One is struck forcibly by the sight of Hopkins pressing upon Roosevelt the willingness of the American people to accept a system of international organization at the termination of a war in which they were not yet full participants, but, from the angle of America's relations with Britain,

[1] Sherwood, p. 363.   [2] *Second World War*, III, p. 386.
[3] Sherwood, p. 360.   [4] Welles, p. 141.

it is much more reassuring than the spectacle of Wilson's efforts at mediation from a stance of strict neutrality in 1916.

By far the greatest interest of the Atlantic Charter to the historian of Anglo-American relations, apart from its powerful overall demonstration of the basic similarity of outlook of the two peoples (particularly, for instance, in the President's welcome to the British Cabinet's suggestion of an article on social security) lies in the two marked, and, in some respects, connected, differences, which it revealed between their two governments and to a large extent the two nations they represented. The first of these differences was less significant than the second, but it was an overt one, which in fact came to a test during this conference.

The liberalizing of international trade had always been a cardinal article in the New Deal, and the particular concern of Secretary Hull. As he was to say later, when stressing the "indispensable necessity for a broader and more liberal commercial policy after the war", it would require

> Herculean efforts such as Britain had put forth during the years following the British-French commercial treaty in the eighteen-sixties. Unless the business people in our two countries recognize that we have to turn over a new page in economic affairs and go forward as resolutely as Britain did at that time, there will simply be no foundation for any stable peace structure in the future. On the contrary, there will be the inevitable seeds of future wars in the form of vast unemployment and hunger throughout the world.[1]

Accordingly, to Churchill's draft of the fourth article, "they will strive to bring about a fair and equitable distribution of essential produce, not only within their territorial boundaries, but between the nations of the world", Roosevelt proposed to add the words "without discrimination and on equal terms."[2] According to Churchill this produced the "only serious difference" of the discussion, for he "at once" objected that this might call the Ottawa agreements into question and that he had no authority to accept such a formula without elaborate prior consultation with the Dominions, who would in any case be unlikely to accept it. "Mr. Sumner Welles indicated that this was the core of the matter, and that this paragraph embodied the ideal for which the State Department had striven for the past nine years. I could not help mentioning the British experience in adhering to Free Trade for eighty years in the face of ever-mounting American tariffs. . . . All we got in reciprocation was successive doses of American Protection. Mr. Welles seemed to be a little taken aback." This was no more than the truth,

---

[1] *Memoirs*, p. 1477.   [2] Q. *Second World War*, III, p. 386.

though the State Department, as Hull's words above demonstrate, were aware of the historical background; but, as we have seen, at the time that the Anglo-American trade agreement was being negotiated in the thirties, the trade policies of the two countries were moving in opposite directions, and the aftermath of that situation remained. Churchill then, as his account runs, suggested the elimination of the phrase "without discrimination" and the additional insertion of the phrase "with due respect for their existing obligations." "The President was obviously impressed. He never pressed the point again."[1]

Sherwood states positively that Lord Beaverbrook was, at bottom, responsible for raising the British objection; he had been to a considerable extent the moving spirit of imperial preference, and he did happen to arrive at the Newfoundland conference at the crucial moment. Sherwood seems to imply that the negotiations were less simple, and less telescoped in time, on this issue than Churchill appears to make them; Welles's account gives some slight colour to this view. Churchill does not mention Beaverbrook in this connexion, and puts his arrival twenty-four hours later than does Sherwood. But, whatever the course of diplomacy preceding the Charter, the outcome was the same—an article which read, "Fourth, they will endeavour with due respect for their existing obligations, to further the enjoyment by all states, great or small, victor or vanquished, of access on equal terms to the trade and to the raw materials of the world which are needed for their economic prosperity."[2] This was, in fact, an expression of pious hope: to the Americans it seemed more. Welles wrote, "It was fully understood, however, that this reservation was inserted solely to take care of what it was hoped would be merely temporary impediments to the more far-reaching commitment originally envisaged in that article,"[3] but the United States has not in fact felt able since the war dramatically to liberalize her own trade practices. Even less has Britain, in her peculiar and precarious economic situation, contemplated a swift return to unrestricted free trade.

The only other difference arising out of the Charter did not come fully to the surface until much later in the war, but, like the iceberg, it went very deep and had a strong, if often concealed, influence upon Anglo-American relations. Some mention has been made of it already, but it is necessary to deal with it at greater length now. (It is interesting, incidentally, to note that the article which was suggested by Roosevelt and eventually read, "Seventh, such a peace should enable all men to

[1] Ibid, pp. 386-8.　　[2] Q. Welles, pp. 140-1.　　[3] Ibid, p. 140.

traverse the high seas and oceans without hindrance",[1] was an innocent version of the old doctrine of the Freedom of the Seas, which had caused considerable difficulties even as late as Versailles; now it was rendered so innocuous by the common maritime interests of the two powers, which Mahan had long ago pointed out, that it was apparently hardly even discussed.)

The article beneath which lay the partly concealed gulf between the President and the Prime Minister was: "Third, they respect the right of all peoples to choose the form of government under which they will live and they wish to see sovereign rights and self-government restored to those who have been forcibly deprived of them".[2] Reporting to the House of Commons on 9 September, Churchill said, "At the Atlantic meeting we had in mind the restoration of the sovereignty . . . of the states . . . now under the Nazi yoke . . . quite a separate problem from the progressive evolution of self-governing institutions in the regions and peoples that owe allegiance to the British Crown." There seems little doubt that Roosevelt took a different view of the article, though the extent to which this was apparent at Placentia Bay is very dubious, since it depends, as Chester Wilmot points out, primarily upon Elliott Roosevelt's subsequent verbatim accounts of conversations of which he apparently had no verbatim record—evidence which any historian must suspect. According to him, the President said to Churchill, "I can't believe that we can fight a war against fascist slavery, and at the same time not work to free people all over the world from a backward colonial policy." He went on to show how the colonial question was in his view intimately linked with the trade question. "The peace cannot include any continued despotism. The structure of peace demands and will get equality of peoples. Equality of peoples involves the utmost freedom of competitive trade."[3]

But even if it is doubtful how much of this was actually said at the time, there is, as Wilmot says, ample evidence that the President felt very strongly on the colonial issue, as had Wilson before him. Hull wrote later: "We had definite ideas with respect to the future of the British colonial empire, on which we differed with the British. It might be said that the future of that Empire was no business of ours; but we felt that unless dependent peoples were assisted toward ultimate self-government and were given it when, as we said, they were 'worthy of it and ready for it,' they would provide kernels of conflict."[4] The American Administration would not be satisfied with the British answer

[1] Q. ibid, p. 141.   [2] Q. ibid, p. 140.
[3] Q. Wilmot, p. 633.   [4] *Memoirs*, pp. 1477-8.

that self-government could be obtained within the fabric of the British Commonwealth; no doubt Elliott was expressing one of his father's deep convictions, though perhaps with a brashness of which he was incapable even in his family circle, when he recorded him as saying: "I've tried to make it clear to Winston—and the others—that, while we're their allies and in it to victory by their side, they must never get the idea that we're in it just to help them to hang on to the archaic, medieval Empire ideas. . . . Great Britain signed the Atlantic Charter. I hope they realize the United States Government means to make them live up to it."[1] This difference was accentuated by the personalities and careers of the two leaders, for whereas Roosevelt, the Democratic New Dealer, was, naturally, entirely out of sympathy with anything smacking of the imperialism which had commended itself to his cousin and predecessor, Churchill had in the past been—on the subject of the Indian Empire at least—far to the right of most of his Tory colleagues.

But it was not a personal divergence; when the Republican, though liberal, Wendell Willkie, asked British colonial administrators in the Middle East during his world tour about the future of the British Empire, he got in reply, according to his story, "Rudyard Kipling, untainted even with the liberalism of Cecil Rhodes."[2] The United States would not allow American Civil Affairs Officers to serve under South-east Asia Command, in order not to associate itself with British colonial policy. Anti-colonialism went very deep in the American consciousness, for when general Anglophobia faded, profound mistrust of the Empire as such remained in American souls. This produced a dichotomy in American judgment in the war years, for, while they admired Britain in Europe as the last bastion of freedom, they still felt that her colonial empire, even if it was increasingly enlightened, was an evil relic of the past. This found succinct expression in the reputed remark of Roosevelt about Churchill, to the effect that "no one could have been a better ally than that old Tory."

The difficulties arising from this dilemma are still with us, but it cannot be solved on any general plan; only each specific case can provide its own answer. Churchill declared that the giving of independence to India and Burma after World War II was premature. In the case of India, despite the partition and the severe loss of life, there seems a good probability that he was wrong, for the Indian and Pakistani Governments have achieved wonders; in the case of Burma there can be little doubt that he was right.

But the complexities do not end here, for "colonialism", let alone

[1] Q. Wilmot, p. 634.   [2] W. L. Willkie, *One World* (London, 1943), p. 14.

"imperialism", is a complex phenomenon, and the word can cover a multitude of sins and even virtues, as America herself has discovered, in her march from the conquest of the Philippines to a mid-twentieth century intervention in world affairs which is loudly branded by Marxists as "imperialistic". Even if, however, we allow ourselves the luxury of ignoring the economic determinists, imperialism has still two main aspects, politico-economic and strategic. The end of the former must be self-government, independence; to this, Western liberal man is unquestionably committed. The end of the latter is not so simple; in Utopia strategic outposts no doubt should not exist, but the world in 1952 is far from Utopia. The retention of Malta and Gibraltar by Britain can hardly be justified on any obvious ethical ground, any more than can the retention of certain Pacific Islands by the United States. Such possessions are the product of an imperialism of a different kind, and one in which the United States must increasingly, as far as the eye can see, participate; it is of great importance to the future of Anglo-American relations that mental confusion on this score should be dispersed. Britain for her part must make it quite clear and certain, for example, that she is* in the Sudan concerned solely with the welfare and self-determination of the Sudanese; the United States must bring home to her people the fact that the presence of British troops in the Suez Canal zone is in no wise different from the presence of American troops in the Panama Canal zone, except that they are a good deal closer to the enemy. Few questions that remain in Anglo-American relations are of more urgency.

Churchill's stand on these issues at the Atlantic meeting gained him only a temporary respite, for Hull and the President brought very heavy pressure to bear on the British Government during the negotiations for the master Lend-Lease agreement, which was eventually signed in February, 1942, to renounce imperial preference. As Hull wrote, "Our discussions had dragged on largely because a few Tory members of the British Cabinet objected to any provision that would interfere with Empire preference. They regarded the Lend-Lease agreement I had in mind as an attempt to infringe on British Imperial sovereignty",[1] which, as Wilmot remarks, it was. But the President was determined, and, as was inevitable, got his way. Article 7 of the master agreement contained a promise of conversations for "the elimination of all forms of discriminatory treatment in international commerce, and . . . the reduction of tariffs and other trade barriers; and . . . the attainment of all the economic objectives set forth"[2] in the Atlantic Charter.

* In 1952.   [1] *Memoirs*, p. 1151.   [2] Q. Winant, p. 112.

Nor did pressure stop there. In Washington in March, 1943, Roosevelt intimated to Eden, according to a note of Hopkins, that he did not want "a commitment made in advance that all those colonies in the Far East should go back to the countries which owned or controlled them prior to the war", and even suggested that Britain should give up Hong Kong "as a gesture of 'good will'." In fact, the President had suggested a number of similar gestures on the part of the British, and Eden dryly remarked that he had not heard the President suggest any similar gestures"[1] on the part of America. According to Wilmot, the question was raised at almost all the major meetings of the two leaders, for Roosevelt would not take 'No' for an answer willingly, for he saw the whole colonial issue, if his son is to be believed, in terms that were "simple, almost naïve; and not always true."[2] "The colonial system means war. Exploit the resources of an India, a Burma, a Java; take all the wealth out of those countries, but never put anything back into them, things like education, decent standards of living, minimum health requirements—all you're doing is storing up the kind of trouble that leads to war. All you're doing is negating the value of any kind of organizational structure for peace before it begins."[3]

Churchill, however, records that at the December, 1941, meeting he reacted so strongly and at such length to the President's mention of India that it was never raised verbally again. A year later, in the confident after-glow of the Alamein victory and two days after the beginning of the North African landings, he felt able in the Mansion House Speech to express publicly and forcibly his determination not to give an inch on this issue, though few indeed of his hearers realized that the passage was directed at his great and powerful friend over the water: "Let me, however, make this clear, in case there should be any mistake about it in any quarter. We mean to hold our own. I have not become the King's First Minister in order to preside over the liquidation of the British Empire."[4] This attitude was maintained till the end.

At the Yalta conference, when the question of trusteeship, which meant so much to Roosevelt, was raised, Churchill, according to Sherwood, "exploded" at a resolution on the subject, framed by the Foreign Ministers, of which he had not been informed, saying that "he would never consent under any circumstances to the United Nations thrusting interfering fingers into the very life of the British Empire. . . . [W]hen Stettinius explained that the trusteeship principle was intended to apply to such areas as the Japanese-mandated islands in the Pacific,

[1] Q. Sherwood, pp. 716-7.   [2] Wilmot, p. 635.
[3] Roosevelt to Elliott: q. ibid.   [4] Q. Sherwood, p. 653.

but not to any part of the British Empire, Churchill accepted the explanation, but stated positively that this important distinction must be made quite clear."[1]

But it certainly was over the Indian problem that feeling was to run highest between the two war-time leaders, for India was the greatest of the British colonies and the nearest to independence. Sherwood does not much overstate the case when he writes that on this subject "the normal, broad-minded, good-humoured, give-and-take attitude which prevailed between the two statesmen was stopped cold."[2] It is true that Churchill had always had extreme views about India, but it is also true that he was able to carry the coalition Cabinet as a whole with him on the terms that were offered to the Indians, and, though some of his conclusions may be suspect, much that he says is irrefutable. He opens his discussion of the subject with the words: "The United States had shown an increasingly direct interest in Indian affairs as the Japanese advance into Asia spread westwards. The concern of the Americans with the strategy of a world war was bringing them into touch with political issues on which they had strong opinions and little experience." He goes on with a familiar British argument that the Negro question is America's Indian problem: "In countries where there is only one race broad and lofty views are taken of the colour question. Similarly, States which have no overseas colonies or possessions are capable of rising to moods of great elevation and detachment about the affairs of those who have."[3] During the early part of 1942, in response to Presidential enquiries about India, he subjected the President to an education on the complexity of the Indian question by sending him a number of documents giving other points of view than that of the Hindus, particularly that of the Moslems.

Nevertheless, on 11 March, the President sent him a long letter, which began with an expression of Roosevelt's diffidence in making any suggestions and stated "it is a subject which of course all of you good people know far more about than I do."[4] He then went on to say that he thought perhaps the historical parallel of 1776 might encourage the British Government to set up a temporary Indian government in India until permanent constitutional arrangements could be made after the war. He ended once more by saying, "For the love of Heaven don't bring me into this, though I do want to be of help. It is, strictly speaking, none of my business, except in so far as it is a part and parcel of the successful fight that you and I are making".[5] That this is not yet a dead question in

[1] Ibid, p. 854.   [2] Ibid, p. 516.   [3] *Second World War*, IV, p. 185.
[4] Q. ibid, p. 188.   [5] Q. ibid, p. 189.

Anglo-American relations is shown by comparing the comments of Churchill and Sherwood. The former writes, "This document is of high interest because it illustrates the difficulties of comparing situations in various centuries and scenes where almost every material fact is totally different".[1] The latter writes, "It may be added that, four years later, the Labour Government in Britain made a proposal to the Indian leaders which, Sumner Welles has written, was 'almost identical in principle with the suggestions made by President Roosevelt in 1942'."[2] It must, however, be noted, that victory had by then been won and that the Japanese were no longer hammering on the gates; that this victory could not have been gained without dire risk, if Britain had lost control, was the whole basis of Churchill's argument, for he was pledged already to Indian self-government at some time in the future.

American concern over India, however, did not cease, and, indeed, rose to a peak at the time of the Cripps mission in 1942. Hopkins, who was in London at the time, had some difficulty in explaining away what looked like the interference of Louis Johnson, a special Presidential representative in India, in the negotiations, but this was necessary, for if proposals framed by him with Cripps were to be rejected by Downing Street, the President would be in a very awkward position. This difficulty was met, but when Cripps had failed and was about to return home, Roosevelt felt bound to intervene again with a message for Churchill through Hopkins. In this he stated that American public opinion was very much concerned, and made an appeal for a final effort to reach agreement before Cripps departed, on some such basis as that he had suggested in his letter of 11 March. The Prime Minister's reaction was conclusive:

> I was thankful that events had already made such an act of madness impossible. The human race cannot make progress without idealism, but idealism at other people's expense and without regard to the consequences of ruin and slaughter which fall upon millions of humble homes cannot be considered as its highest or noblest form. . . . Without the integrity of executive military control and the power to govern in the war area hope and chance alike would perish. This was no time for a constitutional experiment. . . . Nor was the issue one upon which the satisfying of public opinion in the United States could be a determining factor.

But even now he, and in his turn Roosevelt, kept their feelings under control; he replied to the President's message that Cripps had already left and that in any case he did not feel he "could take responsibility

[1] Ibid, p. 190. [2] Sherwood, p. 517.

for the defence of India if everything had again to be thrown into the melting-pot at this critical juncture." He later stated that he would not have hesitated to resign on this issue, but such was not necessary; the last sentence of his letter too plainly bore the marks of sincerity: "Anything like a serious difference between you and me would break my heart, and would surely deeply injure both our countries at the height of this terrible struggle."[1] Though the President's opinion did not alter, and though the last had by no means been heard of the colonial question, the settlement of India's future was left in British hands.

But in August, 1941, in Newfoundland, all this was in the future. Japan was not yet in the war, India was not yet menaced, the United States was not yet even Britain's ally, but only her friend; in such circumstances disagreements on imperial matters could merely be in embryo. Only in the sphere of Lend-Lease could the Administration as yet bring effective pressure to bear. In any event, this difference, acute though it might be, was never to disrupt the Anglo-American harmony, which the Atlantic meeting served to make more sure and sweet. As Churchill said of his return voyage via Iceland, where he held a joint review of the British and American forces: "And so we came back across the ocean waves, uplifted in spirit, fortified in resolve. Some American destroyers which were carrying mail to the United States Marines in Iceland happened to be going the same way, too, so we made a goodly company at sea together."

Very soon new incidents and actions reminded the British people of this good companionship. An American-owned merchant ship, the *Sessa,* was sunk on 17 August, and one flying the American flag, the *Steel Seafarer,* on 5 September. The day before, an American destroyer, the *Greer,* which had been shadowing a U-boat for several hours and broadcasting its position, was attacked by two torpedoes, which missed. On 6 September Roosevelt promised Churchill sea transportation to move twenty thousand men to the Middle East to assist offensive operations there. Such things as these were the breath of life to the British public, who had been very worried by the fact that the vital extension of Selective Service, to keep the American Army in being, had, on the last day of the Atlantic Conference, passed the House of Representatives by the narrowest possible margin of 1 vote. The importance of the incidents as sustainers of morale is illustrated by the fact that even Churchill wrote a gloomy letter to Hopkins towards the end of August, painting a picture of Cabinet depression arising from Roosevelt's

[1] *Second World War,* IV, pp. 194-5.

repeated assurances to his countrymen that America was no closer to war, and going so far as to say, "I don't know what will happen if England is fighting alone when 1942 comes."[1]

His natural optimism soon re-asserted itself, however, and British opinion was somewhat uplifted by a powerful speech of Roosevelt on 1 September, in which he said: "We have not yet declared or taken a direct part in a shooting war. But we have taken a position which must force us ultimately to take such a direct part if our present policy does not prove sufficient to defeat Hitler."[2] It was even more fortified by another speech only ten days later, in which, with reference to the *Greer,* he announced:

> This was piracy. . . . To be ultimately successful in world mastery, Hitler . . . must first destroy the bridge of ships we are building across the Atlantic. . . . I think it must be explained over and over again to people who like to think of the United States Navy as an invincible protection, that this can be true only if the British Navy survives. And that, my friends, is simple arithmetic. . . . We have sought no shooting war with Hitler. . . . But when you see a rattlesnake poised to strike, you do not wait until he has struck before you crush him. These Nazi submarines and raiders are the rattlesnakes of the Atlantic. . . . From now on, if German or Italian vessels of war enter the waters, the protection of which is necessary for American defense, they do so at their own peril.

Five days after this "shoot on sight" speech, American escorts for the first time gave direct protection to the British Halifax convoys. The next day the American destroyer *Kearny* was hit by a torpedo, which killed eleven sailors and wounded ten others.

Meanwhile, a Congressional battle was being fought over the legislation requested by the President, amending the Neutrality Law to allow the arming of American merchant vessels and their entry into the war zone. Even though, on 27 October, the President spoke again, this time upon Navy Day, declaring that "the shooting has started",[3] and though, on 31 October, the American destroyer, *Reuben James,* was sunk off western Iceland with the loss of about a hundred of her crew, it was only by 50 votes to 37 that the Senate on 7 November, and by 212 votes to 194 that the House on 13 November, completed the necessary revision of the neutrality legislation.

There followed nearly a month of suspense, in which symptoms of British depression might have been seen once more; there seemed

[1] Q. Sherwood, pp. 365, 374.   [2] Q. ibid, p. 370.
[3] Roosevelt, *Public Paper* (1941), pp. 385-91, 438.

nothing else left that the President could do to help. In the words of Sherwood:

> The truth was that as the world situation became more desperately critical, and as the limitless peril came closer and closer to the United States, isolationist sentiment became ever more strident . . . and Roosevelt was relatively powerless to combat it. He had said everything "short of war" that could be said. He had no more tricks left. The hat from which he had pulled so many rabbits was empty. The President of the United States was now the creature of circumstance which must be shaped not by his own will or his own ingenuity but by the unpredictable determination of his enemies.[1]

Though unpredictable, their determination had in fact been already made.

The development of the Far Eastern crisis cannot be followed here in its full complexity. The American Government, since the application of virtual economic sanctions against Japan on 26 July—in which it was shortly joined by the British and Dutch Governments—had followed a policy of firmness, combined with readiness to negotiate on terms satisfactory to itself. It walked a thin line between appeasement, on the one hand, and an outright guarantee to the British and Dutch that America would fight if they were attacked, on the other. Despite his natural apprehensions, Churchill did not allow himself to be obsessed by the Japanese threat; he wrote later, "I confess that in my mind the whole Japanese menace lay in a sinister twilight, compared with our other needs. My feeling was that if Japan attacked us the United States would come in."[2] Whether his optimism was justified can never be known, for, though Roosevelt could not give the desired guarantee for constitutional reasons and felt that Congress would not give it, it proved in fact unnecessary. Obviously, the Japanese authorities shared fully Churchill's belief that America would not stand idly by while they gobbled up the Far Eastern portions of the British Empire; indeed, they were acutely aware of the fact that she had already taken effective action, for her oil embargo had forced them to consume four out of their total of eighteen months' reserve supplies by the time the Pacific war actually began. With the replacement of Prince Konoye by General Tojo as Prime Minister on 18 October, it was decided that, unless Washington accepted Tokyo's terms by 25 November, the attack would take place on 7 December. These terms were totally unacceptable to the United States, whose people largely shared Churchill's conviction that the

[1] Sherwood, p. 384.   [2] *Second World War*, III, p. 522.

Japanese would not have the temerity and folly wantonly to provoke their ultimately overwhelming might—that such would be "an act of suicide."[1] Yet this was the action which Japan took. It made the German nemesis more swift than it might otherwise have been: for the Japanese a special and terrible retribution was reserved at Hiroshima and Nagasaki.

The effect of Pearl Harbour upon Anglo-American relations is perhaps nowhere better illustrated than by Winant's arresting account of the first reception of the news by the man to whom it meant so much. The Ambassador was at Chequers. Just before nine o'clock Churchill, who had sat looking very grim and in complete silence, had the radio put on the table:

> It was a small fifteen-dollar portable set that Harry Hopkins had sent him after his return to the United States. The Prime Minister reached out his hand and raised the lid that set it going. For a moment there was a jangle of music, and then, suddenly, from the little black box, a voice announced that Japan had attacked our fleet at Pearl Harbour. . . . We looked at one another incredulously. Then Churchill jumped to his feet and started for the door with the announcement, "We shall declare war on Japan." There is nothing half-hearted or unpositive about Churchill—certainly not when he is on the move. Without ceremony I too left the table and followed him out of the room. "Good God," I said, "you can't declare war on a radio announcement." He stopped and looked at me half-seriously, half-quizzically, and then said quietly, "What shall I do?" The question was asked not because he needed me to tell him what to do, but as a courtesy to the representative of the country attacked. I said, "I will call up the President by telephone and ask him what the facts are." And he added, "And I shall talk with him too. . . ." It was later that night, that we got the report that the Japanese had also attacked the British in Malaya.[2]

Churchill's own considered account of what the event meant to him is as follows: "No American will think it wrong of me if I proclaim that to have the United States at our side was to me the greatest joy. . . . We had won the war. England would live; Britain would live; the Commonwealth of Nations and the Empire would live. . . . Silly people, and there were many, not only in enemy countries, might discount the force of the United States. Some said . . . [n]ow we should see the weakness of this numerous but remote, wealthy, and talkative people. But . . . American blood flowed in my veins. I thought of a remark which

[1] Ibid, p. 536.   [2] Winant, pp. 198-9.

Edward Grey had made to me more than thirty years before—that the United States is like 'a gigantic boiler. Once the fire is lighted under it there is no limit to the power it can generate'. Being saturated and satiated with emotion and sensation, I went to bed and slept the sleep of the saved and thankful."[1]

V

THE shock of Pearl Harbour not only united the American people in their determination to wage the war with all their might until final victory, but it welded the United States and Britain into one vast war machine of unprecedented power. Normal diplomatic questions at issue between them, such as a long standing one over American claims to the ownership of a number of Pacific islands useful in transoceanic aviation, were hastily dropped, and plans for joint use were made, pending the termination of hostilities. Bound together now by ties far stronger than any alliance, and by agencies for common action unprecedented in the history of war, their association was extraordinarily close. Not merely did their leaders enjoy an increasing frequency of contact, but the two peoples as a whole were mingled together in intimate association on a scale hardly before approached between two sovereign nations.

The residence of many hundreds of thousands of American soldiers, airmen and sailors for a long period in the United Kingdom, as well as in Australia and other parts of the British Commonwealth, had a profound effect on both peoples. Of course, the effect was not always happy; this is not surprising. Vast numbers of men, uprooted from their homes, turned into soldiers, and cast in celibacy for prolonged periods of relative inaction into a foreign land might, far from being good ambassadors, be expected permanently to pervert the opinions of the peoples concerned about one another, if not to wreck their relationship altogether. Yet this American invasion of Britain may have done good rather than harm; at least it gave the average Englishman some other view of Americans than that which he had so long been absorbing from Hollywood. The American army left, as armies always do, a number of illegitimate offspring behind it, but the considerable numbers of war brides it eventually took with it were perhaps something new under the sun. That the gravest practical problem of this social relationship was the insoluble one of the greater pay and the higher standard of living of the American forces, compared with that enjoyed by the British, is in

[1] *Second World War*, III, pp. 539-40.

itself a tribute to the remarkable smoothness with which this great intermingling of peoples was conducted. The hospitality offered to Americans in English homes—a thing less easily given in Britain than in America—was, of course, much more than matched by that of the American people to the relatively few Britons who visited the United States in the course of the war. This intimacy was pronounced and important at all levels of society, and it had a compulsive influence upon co-operation in government. The "turkey" dinner—"Let us make it a family affair,"[1] said the President—to which Roosevelt entertained Churchill and his daughter Sarah, on Thanksgiving Day, 1943, in Cairo, was but one of the most notable of many similar occasions.

Friendships thus joined produced spontaneous political reactions, as when Churchill was handed by Roosevelt during one of his visits to Washington a telegram giving the news of the fall of Tobruk, the second disastrous British surrender to be announced within four months: "He passed it to me without a word. . . . I did not attempt to hide from the President the shock I had received. It was a bitter moment. Defeat is one thing; disgrace is another. Nothing could exceed the sympathy and chivalry of my two friends. There were no reproaches; not an unkind word was spoken. 'What can we do to help?' said Roosevelt."[2] Three hundred Sherman tanks and one hundred self-propelled guns were withdrawn from American divisions and sent by the fastest ships to the Suez Canal. These personal relations did but give expression to a deep unity of purpose and a fundamental sympathy of outlook. To these Churchill gave full and inimitable expression on 6 September, 1943, when receiving an honorary degree at Harvard:

> Throughout all this ordeal and struggle which is characteristic of our age you will find in the British Commonwealth and Empire, good comrades to whom you are united by other ties besides those of State policy and public need. To a large extent they are the ties of blood and history. Naturally I, a child of both worlds, am conscious of these.
>
> Law, language, literature—these are considerable factors. Common conceptions of what is right and decent, a marked regard for fair play, especially to the weak and poor, a stern sentiment of impartial justice, and above all the love of personal freedom, or, as Kipling put it, "Leave to live by no man's leave underneath the law"—these are common conceptions on both sides of the ocean among the English-speaking peoples. We hold to these conceptions as strongly as you do.
>
> We do not war primarily with races as such. Tyranny is our foe. Whatever trappings or disguise it wears, whatever language it speaks, be it external or internal, we must for ever be on our guard, ever

[1] Q. *Second World War*, V, p. 300.   [2] Ibid, IV, pp. 343-4.

mobilized, ever vigilant, always ready to spring at its throat. In all this we march together. Not only do we march and strive shoulder to shoulder at this moment under the fire of the enemy on the fields of war or in the air, but also in those realms of thought which are consecrated to the rights and dignity of man.[1]

This unity of purpose found immediate expression in the establishment of a unique common machinery for conducting the war. This was made simpler by the German and Italian declarations of war on the United States, exactly four days after the Japanese attack. According to Alan Bullock, this act of folly was due to "the force of the resentment accumulating under the restraint he had so far practised in his relations with America", to "his disastrous under-estimate of American strength" and to his Wagnerian fascination at the grandiose prospect of "a war embracing the whole world" which "stimulated that sense of historic destiny which was the drug on which he fed."[2] Roosevelt had waited for these declarations which, by an intercepted message, it was known would shortly come, and they were followed by the resolute application of the staff decision already made in principle, that, in case of global war, priority should be given to the defeat of the main enemy, Germany. On the very day after the declarations, 12 December, Churchill was on his way to Washington for the first of his many war meetings with the President.

At this meeting the firm foundation of all future co-operation was laid, by the establishment of the Combined Chiefs of Staff Committee. After dealing with the urgent need for organization in the Far East by the appointment of General Wavell as Supreme Commander, Southwestern Pacific, which included virtually the whole area of active Japanese operations, and with other matters affecting only the Japanese war, the President and the Prime Minister turned their attention to the overall direction of the world war. It had been decided that Wavell should be subject to an appropriate joint body, responsible to the President as Commander-in-Chief and to the Prime Minister as Minister of Defence, for, though virtually any problem could be settled by a meeting of these two men and their advisers, it was obvious that such meetings must be intermittent.

Roosevelt realistically rejected a State Department plan for an Inter-Allied Supreme War Council, on the grounds that only Britain and the United States could really frame the strategy of the war and execute it, a contention with which Churchill strongly agreed. Furthermore, the

[1] Ibid, V, pp. 110-11.   [2] Bullock, p. 608.

President radically altered a scheme proposed by the Chiefs of Staff, by which the procedure of command would be that the Supreme Commander would telegraph any proposals to London and Washington, and that the Chiefs of Staff Committee in London would immediately telegraph to the British Mission in Washington to say whether they would be offering any opinions—a scheme in fact of liaison. His own inclinations, fortified by the insistence of General Marshall that unity of command was indispensable, led him to suggest a special, half-British, half-American body, set up for the purpose in Washington, which would receive any proposals from the Supreme Commander and immediately telegraph to London asking for opinions. This was the Combined Chiefs of Staff Committee, and its establishment for a trial period was readily agreed to; it at once became the permanent day-to-day controlling body of the whole war effort, not merely that in the Pacific. The most important decisions were always taken at the political level, very often at the periodic plenary meetings, which were later attended by Stalin and the Russians and with them virtually all liaison remained on the political plane. It is highly significant that the British, though with some natural reluctance, accepted almost at once the American contention that, because they were to provide the bulk of manpower and material, and because Washington was geographically placed between the two wars, it should be the permanent seat of the Committee. This is evidence of the relative position that the two nations had come to occupy; it conformed naturally to the realities of power.

But the system worked so well that there was by no means a constant alignment of British against Americans in the Committee; the demands of American commanders in different theatres often conflicted, while inter-service disputes in which the two navies, for instance, might face the rest, were frequently the most violent. But in the end, "However sharp the conflict of views at the Combined Chiefs of Staff meeting, however frank and even heated the argument, sincere loyalty to the common cause prevailed over national or personal interests."[1] The establishment of this Committee, upon which Sir John Dill served so magnificently until his premature death, was followed by that of a Munitions Assignment Board, though the discussion of this arrangement caused some Anglo-American feeling, since it emphasized even more clearly the supremacy of Washington. The British military authorities had suggested that London and Washington should each be responsible for allocations within their own sphere of influence, which obviously would divide the diplomatic influence exerted by such substantial sub-

[1] *Second World War*, III, p. 609.

sidies. This was not well received by the Americans who were naturally conscious of the fact that they would be providing the bulk of the munitions, but the question was never cleared up because it became lost to view in a bigger one. Roosevelt and Churchill agreed to a Board in co-equal parts in Washington and London, headed by Hopkins and Beaverbrook respectively, and responsible to the heads of governments, but General Marshall very wisely insisted that, though he had no objection to the system of parallel allocation, the Board must be subject to the Combined Chiefs of Staff, in order to maintain the principle of unity of command. He even made it clear that he could not remain Chief of Staff unless this were done, and he was supported by Hopkins and Roosevelt. Churchill and Beaverbrook therefore agreed, and the Board became in effect a sub-committee of the Chiefs of Staff, but the spheres of influence question was not settled, and continued to be a cause of minor Anglo-American friction, for the British assumed that they existed, the Americans that they did not. But since on any important issue the final decision lay with the Chiefs of Staff, this was not the cause of any serious discord. In any case the United States, because it paid most of the bills, had the whip hand in the last resort. The Munitions Assignment Board was rapidly supplemented by a Combined Raw Materials Board, a Combined Shipping Adjustment Board, a Combined Production and Resources Board, and a Combined Food Board. One has only to compare this wartime unison, established within a few days of Pearl Harbour, with the final arrangements reached in 1918, to observe how far Anglo-American relations had travelled in the previous eighteen months.

In this economic sphere the interlocking process became so complete, and Britain's consequent dependence upon America so great, that McNeill can write:

> By rationalizing production not only within but between the two national economies, the dependence on the United States, which Britain had already been compelled to accept, was increased still further; and American officials came to exercise a potential stranglehold on the whole British economy. Yet . . . [t]he pooling of industrial and raw material resources between the United States and Great Britain raised the war potential of the two nations far above what could have been achieved by each working alone; and the reality of economic interdependence facilitated and indeed required the continuance of close strategic co-operation. After 1942 it would have been almost beyond the power of either nation to disentangle itself from the alliance with the other, even had anyone considered such a step desirable.[1]

[1] McNeil, p. 17.

This close co-operation extended to every aspect of the war effort. As early as October, 1941, Roosevelt had suggested that British and American research efforts in the field of nuclear physics should be joined, and this was promptly done; on this joint foundation was raised the awesome edifice of the atomic bomb. The scientists of the two countries, indeed, developed a remarkable intimacy in all spheres of what Churchill calls "the wizard war", and the interchange of information was constant and highly beneficial. The proximity fuse, originally investigated in Britain, and rapidly perfected in the United States on the basis of the British data, provides an excellent example of this wide exchange. The American utilization of British radar experience provides another. The vast co-operative production of all forms of war material had already taken shape in Lend-Lease, which was subsequently supplemented by Reverse Lend-Lease. Strictly military co-operation was as highly developed. Interchange of information and material between the air forces, and eventual co-ordination of bombing effort in "round the clock" bombing, had a notable effect upon the progress of the war. Naval co-ordination, particularly in the Atlantic area, was even closer. Joint convoy work had already been developed; in March, 1942, the President sent his latest battleship and several other important vessels to join the British Home Fleet, rather than basing a separate American squadron on Gibraltar; and in the experiment of Combined Operations co-operation was intimate.

But it was among the soldiers that unity reached its most complete fulfilment.* In this process General Dwight D. Eisenhower was the supreme figure. Wilmot writes that North Africa was the proving ground, and Europe the culminating point, of "Eisenhower's conviction that it would be possible to create a closely knit Anglo-American command, inspired by a spirit of unity and common purpose, which would override international prejudices and inter-service rivalries. This welding together of the Allied armies in the field was Eisenhower's unique contribution to victory."[1] This was to a remarkable extent a personal achievement, arising from his own passionate conviction. As his naval Aide wrote, "To Ike, the principle of Unity of Command is almost holy",[2] and it dominated all his judgments, in great things as well

---

* It is not always realized how revolutionary this effective unity of command in the field, originally insisted on by General Marshall, was. It did not operate fully except in the Mediterranean–West European theatre, for in the Far East there was, in effect, a division into national spheres of responsibility.

[1] Wilmot, p. 115.

[2] H. C. Butcher, *Three Years With Eisenhower* (London, 1946), p. 115.

as small, from the appointment of his staff to his condemnation of an American officer whom he observed in a British restaurant at the height of food rationing ostentatiously juggling with an American grapefruit and then swamping it with American sugar. Theoretically, he stood for Allied unity, but in practice this meant Anglo-American unity. His enthusiasm, a religion almost, "contagious as fever",[1] thoroughly infected his headquarters: "The men of A.F.H.Q. were . . . so filled with Allied *esprit* they often apologised for their own government's action."[2] It penetrated throughout all his armies. It went still further, so that even "the press and radio of both countries . . . bend over backwards, as far as fairness is concerned, to hold together the two great freedom-loving (and free-speaking) publics."[3] His compelling frankness and charm captivated even the most difficult of men, and it was characteristic that after VE-Day, when he and Montgomery were each offered an important Russian decoration, the Englishman spontaneously requested that he be given it at Eisenhower's headquarters in company with the Supreme Commander under whom he had so long fought. This unity of purpose was unquestionably of the first importance in the winning of the war, and it also marked an epoch in Anglo-American relations.

VI

BUT if the Japanese had effectively turned the common law marriage of 1941 into a full matrimonial relationship in 1942, Anglo-American life together naturally had its difficulties and disagreements. Questions, some of them serious, some of them harmful, some of them insoluble, inevitably arose to mar an otherwise remarkably harmonious association. Seen against the background of almost continual reverses in 1942, and of almost continuous progress towards victory after the "Hinge of Fate" at Alamein, these Anglo-American differences constitute the main history of Anglo-American relations in the war years. We must not, however, lose sight of the fundamental rule of agreement to which they form the exception, for that remained solid, at least until the capitulation of the Germans in May, 1945. After that date, with the death of one of the giants and the virtual disappearance of another from the scene, and with one great set of war stresses removed, the closeness and cordiality does begin to fade. Signs are not lacking, even before the surrender of Japan in August, 1945, of that falling-apart of the Anglo-

[1] K. Summersby, *Eisenhower Was My Boss* (London, 1949), p. 259.
[2] Ibid, p. 75.   [3] Butcher, pp. 521-2.

American alliance, which seems to be the almost inevitable fate of war-time associations when peace comes, though signs were also visible of that force—the intransigence of Russia—which was before long to serve as a powerful stimulus to the retention or revival of much of the war-time co-operation of the United States and Britain. But the dis-agreements of the war years proper were still only minor variations on the dominating theme of Anglo-American unity. This remains true although some of them arose from fundamental differences of national situation, outlook and character; others were less deep rooted and more personal in their nature.

In this latter category must be placed the unhappy "Battle of the Generals" in Europe after D-Day, of which there was some public knowledge at the time, but which has only been revealed in its full acerbity—and in many ways pettiness—in subsequent years. Blame for the most serious of these storms must be shared by British and American participants, but it is unfortunately true that most of it must be borne by the latter. Traditional Anglophobia in Americans was stronger than anti-American sentiment among Britons, and Americans were not only less accustomed to the difficulties of war coalitions, but were on the whole less inhibited in the free expression of their sentiments than the representatives of a nation with a reputation for stiffness and reserve. The faults of those concerned, whether British or American, however, certainly appear much darker than they otherwise might by contrast with the brightness of Eisenhower's example. His wonderful record in this matter makes the mistakes of his inferiors seem remarkable to the historian, although comparable disagreements in previous wars would have appeared positively trifling as instances of discord between in-dependent Allies. It must be remembered that there was never an open breach while the war lasted, and not much public scandal. Clashes of personalities in war are bound to appear; they do so within the borders of a single nation, let alone between members of different states.

That the trouble was not confined to the European theatre is shown by the violent anti-British feelings of General "Vinegar Joe" Stilwell in the Far East, though, as his nickname suggests, he did not confine his animosity to Britain, but inveighed with equal vehemence against the Chinese Government to which he was accredited. That it was not con-fined to the ground·forces, and that it found plenty of expression in Washington itself, is suggested by what often amounted to the Anglo-phobia of Admiral King, Commander-in-Chief of the U.S. Fleet, who, Wilmot goes so far as to remark, was "never a man to miss an opportunity of embarrassing his country's principal ally."[1] His reluctance to disgorge landing craft for other theatres than the Japanese probably slowed down the European campaign significantly, and his jealousy was apparent from his view that "what operations are or are not conducted in the Pacific is no affair of the Combined Chiefs of Staff since this theater is exclusively American."[2] He showed his true colours in his first instinctive, indignant rejection of Britain's offer in September, 1944, of substantial naval and bomber forces for the central Pacific, though he was rapidly overruled in this by his colleagues, and the forces were welcomed by the American Navy in the Pacific itself with open arms. Happily, his colleagues, Marshall and Arnold, were able for the most part to control these tendencies. It was, therefore, in the disagreements in Europe that Anglo-American military ill-feeling reached its nadir.

In the Mediterranean, things had been kept under control, largely by the good relations of Eisenhower with General Alexander, whom the American described as "a friendly and agreeable type (whom) Americans instinctively liked."[3] Bradley wrote later, "Although some American subordinates thought him too ready a compromiser, especially in Anglo-American disputes, Eisenhower had demonstrated in the Mediterranean war that compromise is essential to amity in an Allied struggle. I confess that at times I thought Eisenhower too eager to appease the British command, but I admit to having been a prejudiced judge."[4] Very soon after D-Day in France, however, American ill-feeling began to show itself clearly. It centred in the first place around Montgomery's overall command of Anglo-American forces in the initial stages of the invasion, which some Americans resented. Of the bloody British battle at Caen, which alone made possible the swift American break-out on the right wing, the impatient Patton quotes one of his sergeants as saying at the time, "Fore God, General, if General Montgomery don't get a move on himself, those British soldiers are going to have grass and limpets growing on their left foot from standing in the water",[5] but it is reasonable to suppose that this reflected, not so much the ideas of the ordinary American soldier as those of General Patton, whose dominating personality was not only liable to colour the views of those around him, but even to make him unpopular with his own men. Bradley gives a juster idea of the situation when he writes: "It would be foolhardy for us to deny that tense national differences sometimes

[1] Wilmot, p. 638.   [2] Q. ibid, p. 177.   [3] Q. ibid, p. 462.

[4] Omar Bradley, *A Soldier's Story of the Allied Campaigns from Tunis to the Elbe* (London, 1951), p. 206.

[5] George S. Patton, *War as I Knew It* (London, 1949), pp. 194-5.

split the British and American commands. . . . The suspicions and jealousies that split us centred largely in the headquarters commands. The nearer one went to the front the more comradely were our relations."[1]

The actual dispute centred for the most part around the suggestion that Montgomery should retain, or later be granted again, overall tactical control of the Anglo-American armies. Bradley wrote:

> That unfortunate August split never completely healed. It persisted throughout the winter in a subtle whispering campaign that favoured Monty's restoration to over-all ground command. . . . Monty lent substance to the canard that Eisenhower functioned in Europe primarily as a political commander, unfamiliar with the every day problems of our tactical war. The inference was grossly unfair, for Eisenhower showed himself to be a superb tactician with a sensitive and intimate feel of the front.[2]

Patton was blunter: "At this time Montgomery had the nerve to get someone in America to suggest that General Eisenhower was overworked and needed a Deputy Ground Force Commander for all troops in Europe and that he, Montgomery, was God's gift to war in this respect."[3] During the autumn months, when Allied progress was slow and Montgomery favoured putting all the Allied strength into a thrust on the left wing, Bradley, urged on by Patton, apparently planned his operations so as to make it impossible for Eisenhower to adopt such a plan and to shift their troops to Montgomery's command, which if so was a grave betrayal of their commander's confidence. Emotion reached its height in the middle of the desperate German offensive in the Ardennes, for enemy spear heads split the American army in two, and Eisenhower very properly gave overall command of the Anglo-American forces north of the break to Montgomery. Even at this crisis, Bradley rebelled against the idea of Montgomery again commanding American troops, and was confirmed in his intention to protest by the reflection that it would "discredit the American command," and that, "if it were inferred that we were bailed out by the British, the damage could be irreparable to our future role in the war." There could hardly be a clearer instance of limited national self-interest interfering with the efficient conduct of Allied operations.

But, badly though Patton and Bradley behaved, it would be quite wrong to absolve Montgomery altogether from blame, and Bradley is possibly justified in claiming, "Had the senior British field commander been any one else but Monty, the switch in command could probably

[1] Bradley, pp. 58-9.   [2] Ibid, pp. 353-4.   [3] Patton, pp. 212-3.

have been made without incident, strain, or tension."[1] The personal
animosity was marked; it is nowhere better shown than in Bradley's
reaction to Montgomery's earlier bold and imaginative plan for the
Arnhem break-through: "Had the pious, teetotaling Montgomery
wobbled into SHAEF with a hangover, I could not have been more
astonished than I was by the daring adventure he proposed."[2] Kay
Summersby, then a British subject, though she later took out American
citizenship papers, wrote, "[A]s a SHAEF staff member . . . I grew to
dislike the very name of Montgomery. In my personal opinion, he gave
the Supreme Commander more worry than any one other individual in
the entire Allied command."[3] This feeling was understandable. When,
for instance, Montgomery took over command of the American First
Army at the height of the confusion engendered by the Ardennes
offensive, one of his officers recorded that he "strode into Hodges's
H.Q. like Christ come to cleanse the temple." He made things worse
by holding a Press Conference when the victory had been won, in which
he made certain tactless references and omissions; these Bradley interpreted as a slur upon himself and the American Army, and he felt
bound publicly to recognize them in a statement which defended his
conduct of operations in a firm and dignified manner.

Montgomery was certainly tactless, but he was by no means as impossible as Bradley and Patton pretended. He was passionately concerned for a rapid Allied victory, which led him into some disagreement
with Eisenhower as to means, but he was always responsive to generous
treatment. On one occasion when his professional vanity got the better
of him, and led him to be unnecessarily rude in a talk with Eisenhower,
the Supreme Commander simply leant forward and put his hand on his
knee, saying, "Steady, Monty! You can't speak to me like that. I'm your
boss," to which Montgomery at once replied, "I'm sorry, Ike."[4] Montgomery was well aware of his own failing and did his best to overcome
it. He often deliberately sent his Chief of Staff, De Guingand, to Allied
meetings, because he knew that he got on much better with the Americans. Eisenhower fully appreciated that, in the last resort, the Field
Marshal loyally executed orders, and Montgomery for his part was
expressing his genuine feelings when he wrote to the Supreme Allied
Commander in his letter of farewell: "I owe much to your wise guidance
and kindly forbearance. I know my own faults very well and I do not
suppose I am an easy subordinate; I like to go my own way. But you
have kept me on the rails in difficult and stormy times and have taught

[1] Bradley, pp. 477-8.   [2] Ibid, p. 416.
[3] Summersby, p. 153.   [4] Wilmot, p. 489.

me much. For all this I am very grateful. And I thank you for all you have done for me. Your very devoted friend, Monty."[1]

But among the principals in this distasteful episode in Anglo-American relations, Eisenhower alone emerges without blemish. He had so schooled himself, that even his instinctive reactions became, for the period of the war, Anglo-American rather than American. He performed in the military sphere for Anglo-American relations a service almost as important as, if different from, that performed by Churchill in the political. It was, characteristically, the latter, who finally poured oil upon the troubled waters after the Ardennes battle, by saying publicly: "Care must be taken in telling our proud tale not to claim for the British armies undue share of what is undoubtedly the greatest American battle of the war. . . . Let no one lend themselves to the shouting of mischief makers when issues of such momentous consequence are being successfully decided by the sword!"[2] Though most blame appears to attach to the American generals, it does not behove us to be too critical, for on no other subject are national passions more easily aroused. Nor would it be right to exaggerate the seriousness of the ill-feeling, for Bradley is probably justified in writing, "Although my fondness for Monty often ran thin during the European campaign, this attitude never impaired the personal and working relationship that existed between us. So scrupulously did we conceal our irritation with Monty that I doubt he was even aware of it."[3]*

Nor were the only causes of disagreement the national and personal emotions of the military commanders, for there were genuine differences of principle and practice arising from the diversity of background and interest of the two peoples. One factor making for misunderstanding in the field was the different approach of the two armies to the mechanics of command. This had many aspects, and of one of them Bradley wrote: "Unlike the U.S. army where an order calls for instant compliance, the British viewed an order as a basis for discussion between commanders. . . . In contrast, we in the American army sought to work out our differences before issuing an order."[4] Though some might dispute the premise, it is interesting that Churchill wrote to Alexander at the Anzio period to urge him to give *orders* to his American subordinates, declaring, "the highest American authorities

---

[1] Q. ibid, p. 573, note.   [2] Q. Bradley, pp. 488-9.   [3] Ibid, p. 299.

*Montgomery told Churchill at the time that the situation would have been "most serious . . . but for the solidarity of the Anglo-American Army." (*Second World War*, VI, *New York Times*, 3 November, 1953).

[4] Bradley, p. 138.

. . . say their Army has been framed more on Prussian lines than on the more smooth British lines, and that American commanders expect to receive positive orders, which they will immediately obey."[1]

Another and perhaps more serious aspect was the different type of command envisaged by each, for the Americans tend to give a theatre commander a mission and leave him to conduct it in his own way, whereas the British maintain a very close control over their generals in the field. This found expression at the highest level in the American project for a supreme generalissimo over the whole European, Mediterranean, and even Middle Eastern theatres, which was opposed by the British, who wished to retain control through the Combined Chiefs of Staff, but it also underlay some of the American opposition to Montgomery's command, for they were aware that, following the British custom, he would control their tactical operations far more than their own superiors in the field ever did.

Yet another difference of outlook concerned tactical maneouvre, for the Americans, as we shall see at the strategical level, instinctively favour the direct approach, almost the frontal assault, carried through by overwhelming material superiority. In 1944-5, at the height of the Ardennes assault, the American commanders were for the most part very unwilling to effect a strategical withdrawal, which Montgomery thought of as the essential foundation for subsequent victory; they wished to fight it out where they stood, and the Field Marshal had the greatest difficulty in imposing his plan. Yet tactical withdrawals are, on occasion, necessary to the swift winning of battles; Bradley wrote at the time, "Any hint of withdrawal by Army Group . . . might easily alarm the command,"[2] and this, if true, is a serious reflection on the efficiency of the command as a military machine.

The most important tactical disagreement of the European war was over Montgomery's plan for swift and final victory in the autumn of 1944. He believed very strongly that all Allied efforts should be concentrated in a single narrow thrust which would finish the war at a blow, and he was prepared to serve under Bradley if that was necessary to the accomplishment of the plan. Whether he was right or not can never be known. He did not believe that the Arnhem offensive had been a full and fair trial of the project, though some of the Americans thought it had been, and suspected that his continued insistence was due to a desire to bring the final glory of winning the war to himself and to British arms. It is undeniable that he normally erred on the side of caution, but it is also, perhaps, significant that on this one issue his

[1] *Second World War*, V. p. 432.   [2] Bradley, p. 466.

Chief of Staff did not agree with him and advised care.* Yet it is very hard not to accept the powerful contention of Chester Wilmot, after his exhaustive study of the German as well as the Allied evidence, that Montgomery's plan had a very good chance of success, if it had been put into effect at once before the German army could revive.

But whatever the verdict on its probable outcome, the causes of the American rejection of the plan are interesting. Eisenhower himself opposed it and was at one with his fellow American commanders in doing so. He believed, as did most of his country's military men, in the relentless application of strength against the enemy all along the line, and mistrusted Montgomery's well-grounded argument that overwhelming force must be concentrated at one point. The American method included the full use of their immense material superiority, the temporary lack of which Bradley lamented when he wrote: "Indeed of all the might-have-beens in the European campaign, none was more agonizing than this failure of Monty to open Antwerp. For had sufficient supply been sluiced quickly to our stalemated front through the port of Antwerp, we could have resumed an earlier autumn offensive."[1] It also included the constant use of all human material, and mistrust of the accumulation of a decisive reserve, which Montgomery considered the key to victory. Once again Bradley puts the American case at the period just before the Ardennes offensive: "Against an enemy as badly beaten as we imagined the German to be, I could not conscientiously withhold in reserve divisions better utilized on the offensive. At no time did my Group 'reserve' consist of anything more than a few divisions assigned to one or another of the Armies where they could be employed only with Group's consent."[2] But it is in the contrast between Patton and Montgomery that the national differences are perhaps brought into the clearest focus. The story is told that, in response to the pleas of one American commander that he had, in the battle after the relief of Bastogne, only two battalions left in reserve, Patton's Deputy Chief of Staff replied: "You'd better not let General Patton know you have two battalions. They are not only your reserve, but that's all the Army has in reserve. If the General hears you've got them, he'll commit them, sure as hell." When Montgomery was asked by Chester Wilmot, "When did you know that the battle of Normandy was won?" he replied, "When I was able to withdraw three armoured divisions into reserve."[3] These and other differences in military approach, arising from

---

*Churchill and the Government, however, inclined to support Montgomery on the general question of the concentration of strength.

[1] Ibid, p. 425.   [2] Ibid, p. 464.   [3] Q. Wilmot, p. 605.

the distinct traditions and capacities of the two nations, were of considerable consequence in the history of World War II.

VII

B UT it is time to turn our attention from the Battle of the Generals to an even more important and fateful series of Anglo-American differences, those which arose on the highest political level.

The first of these differences, potentially one of the gravest, never in fact materialized fully: it was whether America should give priority to the Japanese war. Happily, the planning decision, made before Pearl Harbour, to beat Hitler first, was never altered. At the first Washington meeting, to the great relief of the British, General Marshall presented a memorandum which stated: "Notwithstanding the entry of Japan into the war, our view is that Germany is still the prime enemy and her defeat is the key to victory. Once Germany is defeated, the collapse of Italy and the defeat of Japan must follow."[1] Accordingly the Staffs were able to agree that "only the minimum of forces necessary for the safeguarding of vital interests in other theatres should be diverted from operations against Germany."[2]

The only occasion on which there was a serious danger of this being reconsidered was in July, 1942, when its chief supporter, General Marshall, was out of patience with "the off-again-on-again" status of the Second Front planning, but the solemn British acceptance of the plan for invading Western Europe, which he pressed for during a hastily arranged visit to Britain with Admiral King and Hopkins, laid the ghost fairly effectively. Naturally, the decision was not pleasing to everybody, and Stilwell later wrote that "Churchill has Roosevelt in his pocket. That they are looking for any easy way, a short-cut for England, and no attention must be diverted from the Continent at any cost. The Limeys are not interested in the war in the Pacific, and with the President hypnotized they are sitting pretty."[3] This last jibe did Churchill very much less than justice. He certainly believed that the President "took an exaggerated view of the Indian-Chinese sphere," and that the Chinese story was "lengthy, complicated and minor",[4] but he was always adamant that in due time Britain should participate to the limit of her capacity in the Far Eastern war. One of his first actions after Pearl Harbour was to reject out of hand the desire of his

[1] Q. ibid, p. 100.　[2] *Second World War*, III, p. 624.
[3] Q. Sherwood, p. 726.　[4] *Second World War*, V, p. 289.

849

military advisers to decline Wavell's appointment as Supreme Commander in the Far East, lest it should be an American trick to shift the ugly responsibility to British shoulders, and he never faltered in his determination to pursue the Japanese war to final victory. Furthermore, largely in order to combat possible American criticism, he made his military advisers demand vociferously at their level that Britain should be allowed to play her full part. By the time he went out of office his country was irrevocably committed. Had he been less firm, had General Marshall not possessed so clear a perception of the military needs of the Allies, as well as the support of Roosevelt, or had a Republican administration, with its tendency to look westward, been in power in 1941, the story of Anglo-American relations, as well as of the war itself, might have been very different.

The second high-level Anglo-American difference, that over relations with France, never quite came to the boil, but bubbled steadily and vexatiously throughout the whole war. It was not a primary Anglo-American issue, but it had a persistently irritating effect upon their relations, and must have some mention. The President was imbued with all the traditional American good feeling towards France, and Churchill had a very powerful affection for her, but the trouble between the two leaders had deep roots in the events of 1940-1. General De Gaulle and the Free French movement had established firm bonds with the British when the latter stood alone, whereas the United States, in an effort to retain some influence over the actions of the Vichy Government, had retained diplomatic relations of a fairly close nature with Pétain through their Ambassador, Admiral Leahy. These contacts were rendered the more valuable by the fact that Britain had lost hers through her attack on the French Fleet in 1940, and for this reason the Foreign Office was glad of their existence.

A crisis, however, was precipitated by a seemingly trivial affair only just over two weeks after America entered the war, when Free French forces, on De Gaulle's sole responsibility, seized the little islands of St. Pierre and Miquelon off the Newfoundland Coast; certainly the powerful radio transmitter there might have been dangerous had it remained under Vichy control, but the seizure was hasty and premature. The State Department had been anxious that it should be effected in such a way as not to disrupt relations with Vichy, and feared that this abrupt action would give the Germans an excuse to extend their grip over the French colonies in Africa, but this point of view did not do full justice to the facts of life in the all-engulfing war which had so recently swept down on America. De Gaulle's act had all that arrogance and apparently calculated tactlessness which characterized his attitude throughout the war—an attitude which Churchill, in his love of France, could understand and perhaps admire, even while resenting it—for the French leader had given his word to the British Government that, in deference to the wishes of the United States, he would postpone action. On the other hand, the seizure was necessary, he gained over 90 per cent of the votes in an immediate plebiscite, and no serious repercussions followed in Vichy, so that the matter might well have sunk out of sight, as Roosevelt, amid the vast events going on elsewhere which absorbed his energies, expected that it would.

But he reckoned without his Secretary of State, who felt that his Department, representing the great United States, had been affronted, and swiftly issued a wrathful statement, in which he unwisely referred to the "so-called Free French" ships. This brought down upon his head such a torrent of outraged liberal invective about the "so-called" State Department and the "so-called" Secretary of State, that the sound arguments for retaining contacts with Vichy were practically swamped. This situation was not improved by what Hull called a "blunt"[1] conversation between himself and Churchill, for not only the Foreign Office's but the Prime Minister's own inclinations were to support De Gaulle. In a speech in Ottawa he lauded the Fighting French and did not disguise his long-held contempt for the despicable Vichy régime. American public opinion strongly supported this point of view, and even the State Department's own Ambassador in Vichy was at this time disquieted with Pétain and his advisers, but this did not assuage the feelings of Hull, whose sense of dignity had suffered. It is important to realize that he had established for himself in the previous eight years a unique position as an elder statesman; he alone among prominent Democrats had never until this time been subjected to the abuse and ridicule to which his colleagues had long become inured. So seriously was he affected that he almost resigned on the pretext of ill health, but, happily for his reputation, did not carry out his intention.

The affair, however, left its mark, and during his remaining three and a half years as Secretary of State he certainly bore a powerful grudge against De Gaulle, which did not help the Allies in their handling of that already difficult man. But the repercussions did not stop here, and affected the President's feelings towards the Free French. Though Churchill got at the time the probably correct impression that Hull did not "have full access"[2] to the President, and though the latter

[1] *Memoirs*, p. 1132.   [2] *Second World War*, III, p. 590.

probably derived some little relish from the spectacle of the hitherto sacrosanct Secretary of State receiving press punishment of a kind to which he was all too accustomed, Roosevelt depended upon the reputation of his venerable political friend. He always disliked the storms which changes in the Administration involved, and could not easily face the resignation of the Secretary of State at such a moment. He therefore resented the continuance of this problem amidst all his worries, and his resentment naturally tended to accumulate against the initiator of the uproar, De Gaulle. When the Frenchman continued to be a cause of trouble his resentment grew. Furthermore, however little Hull might be intimate with him, the President could not fail to be influenced by the anti-Free French views of the Secretary of State. Thus a compromise was patched up on the immediate issue, but the seeds of future Anglo-American difficulty over France had been scattered broadcast.

Their growth cannot be followed in detail, but it must to a great extent be ascribed to the continued arrogance of De Gaulle, whose conception of the dignity of France, though it might command respect, did not accord with the realities of the situation. Nor did it accord with the fact that the Vichy Government still existed after its fashion, and that its autonomy did have some reality in French North Africa, a vital strategic area whose political complexion was as much pro-Vichy as pro-De Gaulle. But it must also be remembered that dislike of Vichy had not sunk so deep into the American consciousness as it had into that of Britain during her embattled year of solitude. Thus when, during the invasion of North Africa in 1942, Eisenhower had to do a deal with Admiral Darlan, very strong feeling was aroused in Britain.

Nevertheless, it would be wrong to exaggerate the divergence. Churchill strongly supported Eisenhower's actions, and the President issued a very salutary statement in which he declared that he thoroughly understood and approved the feeling against any permanent arrangement with Darlan, with whom the agreement had been merely a "temporary expedient." The policies of the two countries were in fact very close, if not identical, and there was almost as much criticism of the deal in America as in Britain. Fortunately, it must be said, the Darlan chapter was closed with his assassination, and the invasion of unoccupied France by the Germans made the situation appear simpler. This was something of an illusion, for the elements in North Africa which had supported Vichy were still powerful and were still at odds with De Gaulle. The Americans, whose dominance in the North African venture had been recognized by the British, because

852

of the strong anti-British feeling which was thought to exist there, had wished to appeal to these elements, even before Darlan appeared on the scene, and had excluded De Gaulle from all information about the operation. They had endeavoured to build up General Giraud as the leader of the French in North Africa, and Roosevelt and Churchill had, after very heavy diplomatic pressure by the latter, induced De Gaulle to effect at least a superficial union of forces with Giraud during the Casablanca Conference.

Though the Administration had, in the course of 1942, extended Lend-Lease to De Gaulle's London National Committee, and recognized their control over certain French outposts in Africa and the Pacific, it would go no further. Churchill writes that in the summer months of 1943, "A very stern mood developed in Washington about De Gaulle. Not a day passed that the President did not mention the subject to me. Although this was done in a most friendly and often jocular manner, I saw he felt very strongly indeed upon it. Almost every day he handed me one or more accusing documents against De Gaulle from the State Department or the American Secret Service."[1] Churchill in his turn was angry with De Gaulle lest he should cause an actual estrangement between the British and United States Governments, but the difficulties were tided over.

The ostensible reason for the President's irritation was his belief "that no single French authority could be set up by the Allies, and recognized by them, without eventually incurring the bitter resentment of the people of metropolitan France itself."[2] He believed that the sovereignty of France resided in the French people, and that they alone had the right of choosing their government when France was liberated; their decision must not be prejudiced by granting the recognition De Gaulle demanded. An Englishman might be inclined to assume that the real reason for this attitude was the dislike of Hull and the President for De Gaulle, but this was certainly not the only or, necessarily, most important one. The belief in popular sovereignty, which is counterbalanced to some extent in the British mind by practical considerations, such as diplomatic recognition and prescriptive right, goes very deep in the American consciousness, and the lack of universal support for De Gaulle troubled Roosevelt more seriously than Churchill. British government is based upon popular consent, but, unlike that of America, it is not the only thing upon which it is based, and there is a genuine difference of national outlook behind this difficulty over France. There was an echo of the same thing in an exchange between

[1] *Second World War*, IV, pp. 569, 716.   [2] Sherwood, p. 719.

853

Montgomery and Eisenhower on the proposal to stop Patton's advance in France in order to concentrate everything in a single northern thrust. "The American public would never stand for it," said Eisenhower, "and public opinion wins war." To which Montgomery replied, "Victories win wars. Give people victory and they won't care who won it."[1]

But whether personal motives or political beliefs were paramount in determining the President's actions, there can be little doubt that his feeling against De Gaulle made him more tolerant than Churchill of Vichy, and the Prime Minister had felt compelled to protest against the excessively kind tone of the letter which Roosevelt originally proposed to address to Pétain when the invasion of North Africa began. The President obligingly toughened it up by certain deletions, such as that of the opening words "My dear old friend",[2] and, since Vichy was immediately occupied by the Germans, nothing was lost by the action.

But Giraud's failure in North Africa to withstand the pressure of the Gaullists was becoming apparent just at the moment when French unity seemed to be assured by the establishment of the Committee of National Liberation in French Algiers in June, 1943, under the joint presidency of De Gaulle and Giraud, for the latter was very soon elbowed out. When it was clear that their support of Giraud had been of no avail, the United States and Britain, in August, 1943, extended a limited recognition to De Gaulle. Notwithstanding mounting pressure to go further before the invasion of France, the President would not move, for he feared that the General harboured Napoleonic ambitions. As D-day approached, however, it became obvious that the Free French following in France was substantial, and on 2 June the Committee of Liberation declared itself the Provisional Government of the French Republic. In July, Roosevelt invited the French leader to Washington, and as a result of the better relations established it was announced on the 11th of that month that the United States would recognize the Committee as the *de facto* authority in the civil administration of France; on 23 October it was recognized by the Big Three as the Provisional Government.

Thus the Anglo-American friction over France dissolved, for in subsequent negotiations as to her future the United States and Britain saw, on the whole, eye to eye. There were differences in degree of enthusiasm, for Churchill and Eden, ever conscious of the necessity of a strong France as a counterbalance to Russia if not to Germany, "fought [for

[1] Q. Wilmot, p. 468.   [2] Sherwood, p. 643.

her] like tigers"[1] against the scepticism of Stalin. Roosevelt's feelings were similar but not so powerful; America was farther away, and, even more important, he was at this time resolute in his desire to win over the Russians to post-war co-operation, and was more ready to make concessions than Churchill. But in the end his view was very close to the British. The discussion of France's position in post-war Germany, which took place at Yalta, is characteristic. Stalin opposed any French participation at first, but subsequently agreed that they might have a zone of occupation, provided it was carved out of the British and American zones and did not affect his. He opposed French membership of the control machinery, and on this Roosevelt agreed with him; Churchill then pressed for their inclusion, though stating that he did not wish France to be numbered among the Big Three at the moment. By the seventh formal meeting, Roosevelt had changed his mind and come over to the British point of view; meanwhile Stalin had gained points of greater importance to him, and he accepted the decision. In this manner did the last wartime Anglo-American divergence over France end.

VIII

THE French case had raised the difficult question of the future of liberated states, but it was not the first, nor the last, nor yet the most damaging of its kind to Anglo-American relations. The future of Italy had already, by the end of 1943, caused considerable dissension, while that of Greece was, a year or so later, to cause even more; and the two cases, though one concerned an enemy and the other an ally, were very alike. They were analogous to one another and different from that of France in that the pre-war governments of both, and the governments claiming to rule them immediately after the retreat of the Germans, were monarchies. Americans have a comprehensible prejudice against even constitutional monarchies: Churchill had a marked predilection for them, which was a cause of suspicion to the United States.

The surrender of Italy had been made by the King of Italy and Marshal Badoglio, and Washington had agreed to co-operate with them if they would wage war against the Germans. Roosevelt, however, made it clear that this was on the definite understanding "that it is not in any way to prejudice the untrammelled right of the people of Italy

[1] Hopkins: q. Sherwood, p. 849.

to decide on the form of government they will eventually have".[1] Very soon, however, discontent was rife among what Churchill describes, in terms not altogether pleasing to American republicans, let alone New Dealers, as "the six or seven Leftish parties"[2] in Italy. The leading figure in this opposition was Carlo Sforza, as he was known to Secretary Hull, or Count Sforza, as Churchill calls him. He had spent a long exile in America and was a leading figure there, but the Prime Minister later described him in Parliament as a man "that we do not trust".[3] When in November, 1943, the King refused to abdicate under pressure from Sforza who declined to enter the government,* it was decided, largely owing to British insistence, to make no changes while the military situation was critical, but to await the fall of Rome, which was thought to be imminent. Churchill resisted further State Department pressure for a change in the first two months of 1944 on military grounds, but early in March the clamour reached a new intensity.

Rome had not fallen, the Executive Junta of the six opposition parties in Italy demanded Allied support, and the Supreme Allied Commander in the Mediterranean—the British General Wilson—recommended that it be given. The State Department proposed action, and Roosevelt wrote accordingly to Churchill, who replied that he did not agree but favoured continued support of the King and Badoglio "at this stage."[4] He ended one letter as follows: "I readily admit that the course you recommend would be the more popular and would have at least a transitory success. But I am sure that for the victorious conquerors to have their hands forced in this way by sections of the defeated population would be unfortunate. So also would be the obvious open division between you and me and between our two Governments."[5] Roosevelt felt bound to give way and replied the same day, "It is my strongest wish that you and I should continue to work in complete harmony in this matter as in all others. We may differ on timing, but things like that can be worked out, and on the big objectives like self-determination we are as one."[6] Thus did harmony seem to be restored.

But not for long. The suspicion was becoming lodged more firmly in American minds that it was not merely a matter of timing, but that Churchill was determined to support the Italian monarchy against what they could not but believe would be the wishes of the Italian people. The President's remarks on 8 March had been accompanied

---

[1] Q. ibid, V, p. 169.   [2] Ibid, p. 167.   [3] Q. Sherwood, p. 831.

* Sforza had told Churchill before his return to Italy in 1943 that he would support the King.   [4] *Second World War*, V, p. 445.

[5] Ibid, V, p. 444.   [6] Q. ibid, V, p. 445.

by a request for British suggestions as to an acceptable solution, and Churchill answered on 13 March, "My idea remains that we should construct a broadly based Government",[1] after the fall of Rome or the passage of several months. The President at once replied, in perhaps the most brusque message he had yet sent to Churchill in the course of the war. It concluded:

> The capture of Rome is still remote and major political decisions must be taken. . . . In the present situation the Commander-in-Chief and his political advisers, both British and American, have recommended that we give immediate support to the programme of the six Opposition parties. Thus we have, happily, for once, our political and military considerations entirely in harmony. We do not need to intervene beyond informing the executive junta of our support of their programme and confirming this to the King if necessary. The Italians can present the solution to the King and work out the programme among themselves. I cannot for the life of me understand why we should hesitate any longer in supporting a policy so admirably suited to our common military and political aims. American public opinion would never understand our continued tolerance and apparent support of Victor Emmanuel.[2]

Though Churchill did not share Roosevelt's conviction that things in Europe could safely be left to local groups to work out for themselves, in view of the existence there of so much naked and sometimes sinister political and military force, and though one can appreciate his caution, it is hard not to conclude that his personal predilections in fact influenced his policy, and that he did little good by pressing the retention of constitutional monarchies in areas where the national demand for them was not strong.

He obtained, however, the support of the War Cabinet for his contention that the self-determination of the Italian people should await a more suitable military situation, and in his plea that no public divergence between British and American policies should be allowed. His letter to the President on 14 March matched in tone that of Roosevelt on the previous day:

> I do not think it would be wise, without further consideration, to accept the programme of the so-called Six Parties and demand forthwith the abdication of the King and installation of Signor Croce as Lieutenant of the Realm. I will however consult the War Cabinet upon what you justly call a "major political decision." Our war with Italy has lasted since June, 1940, and the British Empire has suffered

---

[1] Ibid, p. 445.   [2] Q. ibid, V, pp. 445-6.

232,000 casualties in men, as well as our losses in ships. I feel sure that in this matter our view will receive consideration from you. We ought to make every effort to act together. Pray remember that I have committed myself in public, and that any divergence will certainly become known.

This Churchill writes, "was the end of the matter for the moment."[1]

But, once again, not for long. Having failed at the highest level, the State Department had the matter taken up again by the Inter-Allied Advisory Council for Italy, whose British members were more amenable than Churchill, although they probably prevented an outright republican solution. On 12 April the King was induced to announce that he would withdraw in favour of Crown Prince Umberto after the occupation of Rome, and on 21 April a new government under Badoglio was formed including representatives of the six anti-Fascist parties. After the capture of Rome on 4 June another government was formed under Bonomi, who wished to make Sforza Foreign Minister. Though there was British objection to Sforza, Churchill took an even broader ground of protest; in a letter to the President he objected to the formation of the Bonomi government itself, and stated his belief that the replacement of Badoglio by "this group of aged and hungry politicians"[2] was a disaster. Nevertheless, after a handsomely mild reply from the President, who certainly had the right to be incensed at Churchill's obduracy now that Rome had fallen at last, the British Government agreed to the installation of the Bonomi Cabinet.

As always, once the decision had been taken, Churchill backed the new régime strongly, and agreement was reached with the President for the progressive reinstatement of the Italian Government in full power. Britain, however, was reluctant to accept any programme of Italian economic rehabilitation which was not strictly military in object, or to re-open full diplomatic relations with Italy. Hull points out in his memoirs that this was understandable in view of their losses at Italian hands and their lack of a vociferous Italian vote, which in America reinforced the desire of the Administration to see a fully operative democratic system established in Italy; but though the British gained the substance of their desires on the first point, they gave way on the second, and accorded full recognition to the Italian Government at the same time as the United States, in October, 1944. Allied unity had so far been preserved, at least on the surface, but very soon there was to be a rift which all could see.

Diplomatic recognition did not, and could not while the war was

[1] Ibid, pp. 446-7. [2] Q. Hull, p. 1564.

still being fought on Italian soil, restore full control of its domestic affairs to the Italian Government, and there were naturally bitter tensions among Italians themselves, particularly on the future of the monarchy. In November inter-party strife came to a head, and on the 26th Signor Bonomi resigned. During the ensuing crisis, the British Government let it be known that it could not endorse any government of which Sforza was either Prime Minister or Foreign Secretary—and the fat was in the fire. The liberal hue and cry in Washington, against what was believed to be the State Department's endorsement of Churchill's "reactionary" determination to restore what Sherwood calls "the unsavoury *status quo ante*", became really intense, and the relatively inexperienced Stettinius, who had recently succeeded Secretary of State Hull, was stung into a public statement on 5 December that,

> The position of this Government has consistently been that the composition of the Italian Government is purely an Italian affair except in the case of appointments where important military factors are concerned. This Government has not in any way intimated to the Italian Government that there would be any opposition on its part to Count Sforza. Since Italy is an area of combined responsibility, we have reaffirmed to both the British and Italian Governments that we expected the Italians to work out their problems of government along democratic lines without influence from outside.[1]

The overt breach with America over Greece, which the Prime Minister had so long feared, also occurred at this unfortunate moment, though happily through the action of the Secretary of State, and not the President, who was away at Warm Springs, Georgia, but it is hard not to conclude that Churchill to a great extent brought the crisis on himself.

As events were soon to show, party political tensions in Britain had begun to reassert themselves strongly as victory hove in sight, and it is difficult to believe that the Prime Minister's Labour colleagues were enthusiastic about his Italian policy, while some of his own party's younger members must have had their doubts. It seems probable, on such evidence as is available, that on this issue, as even more on that of Greece, there began to appear that revulsion of public opinion against its war-time leader which was to be so dramatically illustrated in the General Election of the next year. Winant wrote to Hopkins after Churchill's vindication by 279 votes to 30 in the ensuing debate in Parliament: "The Parliament is definitely to the Right of the country,

[1] Q. Sherwood, pp. 829-30.

859

and did not reflect, in my opinion, the extent of a troubled public opinion. Protest resolutions passed by big trade-union groups were an indication of this fact. . . . This is the first time I have felt the Government weakened following a Vote of Confidence by the Parliament. The man most hurt, in my judgment, was the Prime Minister."[1]

His reaction to the Stettinius statement was hardly helpful, for it took the form of the most violent cable to Roosevelt that he ever sent; it stated that he would have to make a statement in the Commons, though he would try to keep his remarks free from the "acerbity" displayed in his public language by the new Secretary of State. He certainly did not succeed in this endeavour, for, compared with his formidable and ironical barrage in Parliament, the Stettinius statement reads like mere shots from a pop gun. He not only defended his Italian policy, but included—certainly an innovation for him—a number of thinly veiled gibes against American opinion:

> "Poor old England!" he said, "(Perhaps I ought to say, 'Poor old Britain!') We have to assume the burden of the most thankless tasks, and in undertaking them to be scoffed at, criticized and opposed from every quarter. . . . We have not attempted to put our veto on the appointment of Count Sforza. If tomorrow the Italians were to make him Prime Minister or Foreign Secretary, we have no power to stop it, except with the agreement of the Allies. All that we should have to say about it is that we do not trust the man, we do not think he is a true and trustworthy man, nor do we put the slightest confidence in any Government of which he is a dominating member. I think we should have to put a great deal of responsibility for what might happen on those who called him to power."[2]

The subsequent newspaper discussion of the Anglo-American disagreement was assuaged by a number of statements, including one from the Secretary of State, affirming that the two were "in substantial agreement"[3] on Italian policy, and another from the British Acting-President of the Allied Commission for Italy which was also of a soothing character; and the fissure in Anglo-American policy was hastily papered over for the rest of the war. These, however, were obvious face-saving devices: the unhappy fact remained that "relations between the White House and Downing Street were more strained than they had ever been before."[4] This was not to be without its effect upon the Yalta Conference, as we shall see.

Churchill's violence was not solely due to differences over Italy, but

[1] Q. ibid, pp. 831-2.   [2] Q. ibid, p. 831.
[3] Q. R. Dennett and R. K. Turner (Editors), *Documents on American Foreign Relations* (Princeton), VII, p. 163.   [4] Sherwood, p. 831.

may be partly explained by the almost simultaneous eruption of the Greek volcano. Though the situation in that state was similar, with a monarchical régime (in this case the King was still out of the country) awaiting the ultimate verdict of a popular plebiscite, and with an even greater wealth of political parties, which were seriously split between Right and Left and struggling for power, there were certain marked differences. For one thing, the Greeks were gallant Allies—the words had more than a formal meaning—so that public opinion in the democracies was even more sensitive to any attempt, or apparent attempt, to foist an unwelcome régime upon them. The Greeks themselves, because they were highly and properly proud of their national independence, and because they had a long and incorrigible tradition of political individualism, were very ready to resent any form of Allied pressure. This sensitivity was perhaps increased by the fact that the British had, earlier in the war, suppressed a radical mutiny among Greek troops in the Middle East by force of arms, and it certainly made things more difficult.

On the other hand, the British had almost exclusive military responsibility for the re-occupation of Greece, so that there was less excuse for American intervention and hence for Anglo-American disagreement here than in Italy, but the American mistrust of Churchill's pro-monarchial tendencies remained. Finally, and it was in the long run to be the really important fact, Greece was the neighbour of Jugoslavia and Bulgaria, both of which were or were to be, Communist and Russian controlled; the Greek parties of the Left were dominated by the Communists, and it appeared to many people exceedingly important that they should be denied control of the country. This fact was one of which Churchill was well aware, but it made very little appeal to the powerful liberal elements on both sides of the Atlantic, who were desperately anxious to work closely with Russia, and among whom the President must be numbered. The situation was eased by the fact that Stalin had reached an agreement with Britain that Greece should be a ninety per cent British sphere of interest during the war, an agreement which he observed, apparently with some care, during the crisis of December, 1944, by permitting no agitation. But to American mistrust of Churchill's monarchism was added mistrust in both Britain and the United States of his anti-Communism, and he came under the heaviest criticism of the war on the Greek question. Yet here, in contrast to the Italian scene, he was unquestionably right, and his critics wrong; the monarchical question in Italy was relatively unimportant, but that of Communist control of Greece, with the Russian domination which would follow, was vital. To be convinced of this one has only to ponder its implications for United Nations control of the Mediterranean, for the role of Turkey in the Near East, and for the position of Tito in Yugoslavia; Truman and Marshall recognized it when they sent American aid to Greece in 1947, but it was not apparent to Roosevelt at Yalta. Nor was Churchill himself in a position at this time to press his fears strongly upon the President, for he, too, though in a much more realistic manner, was still pledged to the idea of Three Power unity.

The liberation of Greece in the autumn of 1944 was accompanied by widespread political disorder, which threatened to end in civil war. The Government of National Unity was disrupted by Leftist resistance to an agreed order that all guerilla troops should hand in their arms to the British occupying authorities by 10 December. On 2 December all the Communist-sympathizing ministers resigned, and a general strike in Athens, which was reported in the world press on the morning of 5 December, dissolved into rioting and bloodshed. This was the very day on which Stettinius issued his Italian statement, and he ended it with a sentence, which was clearly a reference to Greece (and probably to Belgium where similar difficulties of a milder kind prevailed) and which added fuel to the flames of the Prime Minister's wrath. It ran: "This policy [of allowing the Italians to work out their own problems without outside interference] would apply in an even more pronounced degree with regard to Governments of the United Nations in their liberated territories."[1] Though this was much the most damaging part of the statement, since it applied to the highly critical situation in Greece, it is doubtful if it had much effect upon developments there. But Churchill's anger is understandable when it is borne in mind that, beginning on the very next day, 6 December, British troops were engaged for two months in intermittent fighting with Greek guerilla forces. It is small wonder that his speech in the Commons was full of suppressed fury, for, as he reminded the world, Britain, having entered Greece "with American and Russian consent (and) at the invitation of the Government of all parties", could not "leave Athens to anarchy and misery, followed by tyranny established on murder."[2] On 7 December Stettinius issued a conciliatory statement, approving Churchill's intention, expressed publicly on 5 December, of giving the Greeks every opportunity for self-determination, but, even if it had undone the harm his original words had done in Churchill's estimation, it was at once rendered useless by a new development.

[1] Q. Sherwood, p. 830.   [2] Q. Wilmot, p. 637.

Though the Americans had no troops in Greece, they had naval vessels operating under British command in the transport service to Greece. Feeling about the use of British troops there ran so high in Washington that Admiral King issued orders to Admiral Hewitt, the commander of the American naval forces in the Mediterranean, "not to permit any American LSTs to be used to transfer supplies to Greece."[1] On 9 December Churchill got to hear of it and had a furious and—because of a bad telephone connexion—unintelligible conversation with Hopkins, who did, however, catch the word 'Greece'. He then investigated, discovered King's order, and pointed out that Hewitt was under command of General Wilson; this meant that no such order should have been given without reference to the Combined Chiefs of Staff. King thereupon withdrew the order, which Hopkins likened to "walking out on a member of your family who is in trouble." How close a serious scandal was is shown by the fact that the British Chiefs of Staff, declaring that they had never heard of such an order, had already instructed Wilson to continue to use the ships. Hopkins and Halifax prevailed on Churchill not to send the full-blown protest he had prepared for delivery to Stettinius, and Roosevelt despatched a soothing message to the Prime Minister. Tension was thus eased, but it was all too likely to be renewed.

Even an unfortunate mistatement by Churchill, in a debate on Polish affairs in the next week, though subsequently put right by Eden, served to start American criticism again. He said, "All territorial changes must await the conference at the peace table . . . but to that principle there is one exception . . . changes mutually agreed."[2] This was taken to be a reference to secret agreements, made contrary to the principles of open diplomacy, and these were highly suspect to liberals in America. As Hopkins wrote to Churchill: "Due to the Greek situation and your statement in Parliament about Poland public opinion has rapidly deteriorated here. I must confess I am greatly disturbed. . . . Although I do not know what the President or Stettinius may be compelled to say publicly, it is quite possible that one or both of them will have to proclaim their determination in unequivocal terms to do everything we can to seek a free world and a secure one."[3] There was, as Sherwood writes, considerable "indignation in Whitehall at the somewhat sanctimonious, holier-than-thou attitude" of the United States, who seemed to be behaving, as one Briton remarked, "like an inverted Micawber, waiting for something to turn down."[4]

But the immediate tension on Greece was further allayed, largely

[1] Q. ibid, p. 638.   [2] Sherwood, pp. 833-4.   [3] Q. ibid, p. 834.   [4] Ibid.

by a typically Churchillian gesture of gallantry: the Prime Minister flew to Greece with Eden on Christmas Day, at considerable personal risk, not only while *en route* but even more after arrival. As a result, he was able to arrange for the appointment of Archbishop Damaskinos as Regent, pending a subsequent plebiscite prior to the return of King George. On this basis a start was made in the slow process of restoring order in Greece, a process only completed in the end five years later by means of substantial American military assistance. Churchill afterwards told Stettinius that if Britain had not been been prepared to use force in Greece, the Greek Communists would have seized control, but some Americans remained convinced that the Prime Minister "had interfered in the internal affairs of Greece in order to gain some selfish postwar advantage for the British Empire."[1] These misgivings, beneath the calm surface of Anglo-American relations, were to be all too apparent in the attitude with which the American delegation approached the Yalta Conference.

IX

THE Greek episode was probably exacerbated by the fact that it touched upon the tender flesh of the deepest fissure between the British and American Governments on the question of how the war should be won. The issue can broadly be described as that of the Second Front. As we have seen, the decision to win the war in Europe first was never seriously reconsidered by the President, though constant political pressure was brought to bear on him to do so, as for instance by the friends of the Republican MacArthur, who was a serious possibility as a Presidential candidate in 1944 and who was rather naturally anxious to get all the force he could for his use in the Pacific. This cleavage in the Alliance was spared largely through the resolution of General Marshall, for Admiral King tended to favour the Pacific theatre. But, deep though this difference went, it was never fully exposed, as were the divergences over Greece and Italy: it was simply a constant theme of discussion, and often disagreement, in the course of planning, for an agreed policy was always reached in the end. Churchill indeed claims —and it is possible—that the difference was never as serious as was maintained because his intentions were misunderstood; certain it is that many Americans harboured deep suspicion of the Prime Minister's

[1] Wilmot, p. 638.

strategic ideas, although there was never a grave open breach. This was perhaps made more natural by the fact that the British military authorities themselves often felt it necessary to apply the rein of facts to the galloping enthusiasms of their Minister of Defence. So the results of the disagreement were never as serious in Anglo-American relations as they might have been.

The broad question as to where the military might of the Anglo-American democracies was to be applied in the European war has two aspects, naturally interlocked but susceptible of separate treatment, the military and the political, and both have received masterly treatment in Chester Wilmot's book, *The Struggle for Europe.*

Let us deal first with its military aspect. The American Chiefs of Staff and most of the President's advisers from the very beginning believed passionately in a decisive military invasion of North-west Europe, probably in France. From this view they never wavered. But Churchill had always regarded the prospect of putting so vast a number of eggs into such a basket with some misgivings. He wrote after the war: "I knew that it would be a very heavy and hazardous adventure. . . . Memories of the Somme and Passchendaele . . . were not to be blotted out by time or reflection."[1] These are the words of calm subsequent consideration; amidst the actual stress of events, when he was concerned to impress his arguments indelibly upon the minds of his hearers, his language was more lurid; he did not hesitate to predict that the Channel would be a "river of blood."[2] When this bold master of language set out to make his misgivings clear, he succeeded in no uncertain fashion. What his American hearers often forgot was that the man who braved all to save mankind in 1940 was not likely to be restrained by apprehensions without due cause. In discussion with him, because they were liable to be outwitted in debate, the American chiefs of staff tended to follow the precept, "Don't argue, just say No."[3] Tending to believe that Churchill, in his heart of hearts, never wanted a full Second Front, they remained adamant. They suggested some limited operation such as the seizure of the Brest peninsula in 1942; when this proved impossible they demanded that the great invasion take place in 1943; when they had reluctantly to accept May, 1944, as the date, they absolutely refused to consent to Churchill's request for a six weeks postponement. Though Roosevelt, as the other man on whom ultimate responsibility must fall, was sensitive to Churchill's dire

[1] *Second World War,* V, p. 514.
[2] Q. Sherwood, p. 594. [3] Wilmot, p. 131.

prophecies, he hardened as time went on in support of his military advisers.

But—and here is the first serious difference—Churchill claims that no such reservations were ever in his mind about the European operation, Overlord, to which he had pledged himself in April, 1942. Indeed, as he wrote afterwards, he welcomed it "with relief and joy. . . . We might so easily . . . have been confronted with American plans to assign the major priority to helping China and crushing Japan."[1] The only connexion, according to his later account, between his memories of Passchendaele and the prospect of the Second Front was his very proper desire to make sure that there were sufficient means to ensure its success. This, in his view, involved delay; it also involved the need to inflict as much damage as possible on the enemy elsewhere, for by this means the forces available in France to oppose the invasion could best be weakened. Therefore, his argument runs, since the mounting of Overlord required a vast build-up of non-belligerent fighting troops in Britain, to weaken the enemy elsewhere involved maximum use all the time of all the troops in all the other theatres, particularly the Mediterranean. As events marched onwards, and the dissolution of Germany's empire in that area began, "gleaming" opportunities seemed to him to present themselves, which could be exploited with great advantage to the Allies and bitter loss to the enemy. Such was the chance of winning Turkey to a full and active, instead of suspended, implementation of her alliance with Britain, but it, like others, was lost, partly because the inflexible rigidity of American plans did not permit small and temporary detractions from the forces of Overlord and minor delays in the launching of it.

Here then is the Prime Minister's case: "[W]hile I was always willing to join the United States in a direct assault across the Channel on the German sea-front in France, I was not convinced that this was the only way of winning the war. . . ."[2] "It has become a legend in America that I strove to prevent the cross-Channel enterprise called 'Overlord,' and that I tried vainly to lure the Allies into some mass invasion of the Balkans, or a large-scale campaign in the Eastern Mediterranean, which would effectively kill it."[3] "Never had such a wish entered my mind." "I regard the failure to use otherwise unemployable forces to bring Turkey into the war and dominate the Aegean as an error in war direction which cannot be excused by the fact that in spite of it victory was won."[4]

[1] Q. *Second World War*, IV, p. 290.   [2] Churchill, V, p. 514.
[3] Ibid, p. 304.   [4] Ibid, pp. 226, 306.

For this contention, that he was always a firm supporter of Overlord, and that he merely pointed to facts which made delay till 1944 essential, and argued unavailingly for a short delay in that year in order to exploit success in the Mediterranean, there seems some justification. But there must remain an element of doubt in the mind of the historian as to whether occasional qualms, swiftly and characteristically suppressed no doubt, did not assail him and make him think of caution. If this is the reaction of the historian, even one too close to the event, it is all too easy to understand that of the American leaders at the time. In the first place, Churchill, the ebullient optimist, appeared in this one matter in the constant role of Cassandra. In the second, he was always the one who contended for delay, shifting from the argument that the Allied forces in Britain were not strong enough to attack, to the argument that just a little delay or just a little weakening of them would make their strength less necessary. Thirdly, he was the persistent advocate of expeditions which, however small, were in theatres remote from the main one, and every one is aware how easily tiny commitments can grow, and slide, by necessity of protecting investments, into big ones. In the fourth place, he was well known to be—and very properly—desirous of as swift and brilliant a victory as possible over the enemy; he believed—quite rightly—that truly great military victories are won by superior generalship, with relatively very light losses, but to many others the partition between the brilliance of Marlborough's piercing of the *Ne Plus Ultra* lines and the tragedy of the Dardanelles seemed alarmingly thin.

Finally, he was universally known as the exponent of—the term is in this case in no sense derogatory—'eccentric' operations. Had he not invented the phrase, "the soft underbelly" of Europe? Had he not proudly drawn his famous crocodile for Stalin to illustrate the point? The suspicion suggested itself to a number of people that he was sometimes trapped by the persistence of his own powerful metaphors. On one occasion he wrote, "It would be better to lay our right claw on French North Africa, tear with our left at the North Cape, and wait a year without risking our teeth upon the German fortified front across the Channel."[1] To soldiers who seldom think in dramatic word-pictures, such expressions are not always convincing. With this was linked an even deeper suspicion—that this emphasis on the Mediterranean was an echo of that other war when soldier had been so divided from statesman. When men heard him talk of controlling the Aegean and opening the Dardanelles for communication with Russia, a bell was apt to ring

[1] Ibid, IV, p. 289.

867

in their ears. To those who had not been convinced by the inter-war argument—much of it from Churchill's own pen—that the Dardanelles expedition had only failed for lack of swiftness and strength, it sounded like an alarm bell clanging a note of warning. There were even those who wondered whether it might not be, in the mysterious and inscrutable processes of the human mind and heart, that this great statesman of two wars, albeit unconsciously, sought upon a second occasion to suggest how right he had been on the first. Even if this be fantastic, it is not absurd to wonder whether he did not occasionally hope against hope that something might turn up to render Overlord unnecessary, or at least much easier. After all, among the earliest of his plans, made when Britain stood alone, had been one for the swift occupation of a demoralized Europe by small forces, in the days when bombing and blockade should have done their work. Though he is a man remarkably immune from ignoble thoughts, the fact remained that the Russians were fighting furiously and ferociously on the vast eastern front; the bombing offensive mounted in intensity; there were plots against Hitler's life. Who could be positive that Germany would not collapse before the fatal day? Certainly the misapprehensions or suspicions of the Americans are not difficult to understand.

But too much must not be placed upon Churchill's shoulders, broad though they are, for this difference was one going deep into national character, and he was but the supreme and dazzling exponent of a characteristic British trait, just as the American leaders sprang directly from the roots of their own land. Why did the latter insist on the massive Second Front, which was in the event so triumphantly successful? They were, in Wilmot's words,

> militarily unsophisticated and blunt,* Germany was the major enemy; therefore strike at her first by the most direct means—across the Channel. If the Germans were too strong in France, they argued, then the Allies should keep on building up their forces in Britain until they amassed the necessary margin of power. They proceeded on the theory that, if they made their military machine big enough, they could drive it where they willed. Only a people with a surplus, actual or potential, and with vast resources and vast self-confidence could afford to pursue such a course.[1]

American military theory had been fundamentally conditioned by the

*In rejecting Churchill's suggestion of an Adriatic military venture, Roosevelt wrote in July, 1944: "I always think of my early geometry—'a straight line is the shortest distance between two points'." (*Second World War*, VI, *New York Times*, 26 October, 1953). [1] Wilmot, p. 128.

thinking of the victors in her first great war, the Civil War; the North had won by economic and numerical power, and swiftly, since that victory, the United States had followed the lead of the North until she was pre-eminently the greatest industrial power on earth. There was little incentive for her to change her modes of military thought, though if ever a hostile Eurasian bloc develops an industrial power comparable with its population strength she may be forced to do so. Thus it was that the Americans adhered adamantly to what Hopkins called the "frontal assault upon the enemy in Northern France".[1] Though the brilliant generalship of MacArthur—on the principle, as Sherwood remarks, of "Hit 'em where they ain't"[2]—even if accompanied by a great material superiority, must give us pause before we accept this theory in its entirety. Wilmot is substantially correct when he writes that, "They preferred to out-produce Hitler rather than to out-manoeuvre him, and they were sure they could do so."[3] In this they were certainly right.

The British attitude, on the other hand, was quite different. They had never, even in their prime, had a greater population in their homeland than had their principal enemy. Their greatest soldier, Marlborough, had won his dazzling victories with an army relatively small proportions of which were British. Their long and powerful naval tradition—in America Mahan had only been dead a mere quarter of a century—had taught them that they must use the great mobility of sea power in order to overcome the enemy's advantage of interior lines. They were prepared to wait longer for victory and unwilling to risk so much on one decisive throw, in the same way that they had endured the long years that Wellington had campaigned in the Iberian Peninsula. They, too, had suffered much more severely than the United States in World War I, and these enormous casualties had been kept before the eyes of soldiers by wrathful civilian criticism between the wars. Yet the 1914 war had been the first occasion on which Britain had departed from her traditional policy of not sending vast land armies to Europe, and her leaders were reluctant to incur similar risks unnecessarily a second time. The justification of their misgivings was that during 1944 they were "scraping the bottom of the barrel" of their manpower in order to keep the ranks of their armies filled, while the United States was pouring vast masses of men and materials into Europe.

With the British attitude the Americans tended to be impatient, regarding it with some reason as over-cautious, and with less justice as

---

[1] Q. *Second World War*, IV, p. 288.
[2] Sherwood, p. 594.   [3] Wilmot, p. 129.

unimaginative. Partly owing to their natural impatience, and partly to their political situation (with a Presidential election coming up in 1944), they pressed always for the great enterprise which would end the war at a blow. Britain, who had fought Revolutionary and Napoleonic France for nearly twenty years, and had in the end beaten her by her staying power and her economic strength, was less impatient. Though the British accepted the invasion project, they were anxious to explore any avenue which might lead to a general weakening of the enemy, before they actually launched it.

It is easy to see how these habits of military thought helped to produce Anglo-American differences over the Second Front, which were further exaggerated by political misgivings. Americans as a whole, and particularly American liberals, have always been suspicious of what they regard as the artificial barriers of the Old World, the barriers of class and nation. Having, it might be said, made a continental nation out of a wilderness, they find it difficult to appreciate the depth of European divisions. General Bradley talks in his memoirs of "the artificial division of nation states in Europe",[1] and at the political level this same sentiment is apparent, though in a more sophisticated form.

Roosevelt and his advisers not only mistrusted British colonialism, they mistrusted all local international political arrangements, which they regarded as spheres of influence and regional balances of power. Though determined to be 'realistic' and avoid the errors of Wilson, they could not entirely rid themselves of one of his most powerful preconceptions—the indivisibility of peace and the community of all nations—because it went deep into the American nature. With the United States it tends to be curiously all or nothing, isolationism or a universal world system; as Churchill writes, "Their national psychology is such that the bigger the Idea the more wholeheartedly and obstinately do they throw themselves into making it a success." He cannot refrain from adding, "It is an admirable characteristic provided the Idea is good."[2] In his opposition to 'outmoded' European diplomatic ideas Secretary Hull—an undisguised disciple of Wilson—was outstanding. He writes in his memoirs: "I was not, and am not, a believer in the idea of balance of power or spheres of influence as a means of keeping the peace. During the First World War I had made an intensive study of the system of spheres of influence and balance of power, and I was grounded to the taproots in their iniquitous consequences. The conclusions I then formed in total opposition to this system stayed with

[1] Bradley, p. 454.   [2] *Second World War*, p. 494.

me."[1] These conclusions, when presented in so absolute a form, were not likely to be accepted by the man who could in the twentieth century quote—and use—an alliance made by his country with Portugal in the fourteenth century. Churchill knew, in Wilmot's words, "from long experience of European history that nations are less likely to succumb to the temptation of aggrandisement if their ambitions are restrained by a reasonable balance of power".[2]

The American Administration was strongly opposed to special political arrangements during the course of the war; and whenever they were made, out of necessity, as over Poland, they resulted in an outcry among the American public. Indeed Americans carried this phobia so far that they tended to think of victory in purely military terms; they were so concerned to win the war, that they thought little about what they would do when they had won it. They forgot, as Kennan has pointed out, in their psychological need for total victory, that war is waged for economic and political objectives. It is highly significant, not only that the State Department were in reality hardly consulted at all on military matters during the war, but that this was accepted by Hull, perhaps a little because he felt that such connexions might sully the postwar aims which he, the "Father of the United Nations,"[3] was seeking. The American leaders were thus peculiarly sensitive to the charge that they were bolstering up British political objectives in Europe. This difficulty did not attain serious proportions in Western Europe—though there was some trouble in Belgium—because there national democratic institutions were on a solid basis and capable of independent resurrection. In Eastern Europe, however, it was different. There, as the history of the Versailles era had shown, there was, despite the violence of local feelings of rivalry and independence, a certain malleability, a kind of vacuum of power. With the situation in North-eastern Europe, which was largely dominated by the Polish question, we shall be concerned later; it was one where the power of the West in practice was very weak. In the Balkans, however, the application of Western strength was very possible.

It was, therefore, here that Americans' suspicions of British intentions were gravest. They were already sceptical as to Britain's military arguments, which seemed, though Churchill persisted in denying it, to point to a large-scale Balkan campaign. This, they felt increasingly sure, was due primarily to her desire for postwar influence there, and hardly at all to simple military conviction. This confidence felt like

[1] *Memoirs,* pp. 1452-3.   [2] Wilmot, pp. 635-6.
[3] Roosevelt: q. Hull, pp. 1718.

certainty when the Prime Minister began to insist on making political arrangements for the Balkan peninsula. To the United States it seemed improper that any outside power or powers should exercise paramount influence there; the future of the Balkan peoples must be decided by those peoples in accordance with their own wishes. This theory flew in the face both of the unfortunate fact that they might in some cases be incapable of establishing stable popular governments (as were so many of the nations of Latin America), and also of the realities of Russian power, but it remained embedded in many American minds.

The dispute came nearest to breaking the surface of Anglo-American relations in the spring of 1944, when the Russian armies began to press into Rumania. Forbidden by his American allies to bring even a little military pressure to bear upon the area, Churchill became increasingly alarmed at the prospect of Russian dominance there, and sought to make political arrangements which might serve a similar purpose. At this time Britain made to the Soviet Union a proposal, unbeknownst to the United States, that the "controlling influence" in Rumania should be Russian and in Greece British. The Russians accepted, but wished the United States to be consulted. Halifax presented the British arguments for it to Hull, being careful to emphasize that this was purely a war-time arrangement and that the Foreign Office was fully alive to the "importance of avoiding even the appearance of carving up the Balkans into spheres of influence". The Secretary of State's reception of the idea was distinctly cool, and when Churchill accordingly took it up direct with the President, the latter's reply, drafted by the State Department, was equally unfavourable, particularly because the Prime Minister had by now added the suggestion of a similar arrangement for Bulgaria and Yugoslavia respectively. The reply stated that military decisions would naturally be taken by the power concerned, but that "the natural tendency for such decisions to extend into the political and economic fields would be strengthened by the agreement proposed by the British. The President stated . . . that this would surely lead to the persistence of differences between Britain and Russia and to the division of the Balkans into spheres of influence, regardless of Mr. Churchill's statement that the agreement would be limited to military matters."[1]

Very forceful expositions of the realities of the situation were thereupon received from London. These emphasized that the swiftness of actual events in the Balkans rendered rapid decisions by a single power essential and—the basic fact—that in the post-operational chaos of that area someone must "play the hand."[2] The President eventually

[1] Hull, pp. 1451-2, 1454   [2] Churchill: q. ibid, p. 1453.

agreed to a three months trial of the arrangement, though he failed to notify the State Department of his decision. He did, however, express his sense of disturbance "that the British took the matter up with us only after they had presented it to the Russians. . . . He . . . hoped matters of this importance could be prevented from developing in this way." Churchill replied that triangular information was not always possible and cited an important case—over Poland—where the President had communicated with Stalin without informing him. He expressed the hope that he might have the President's confidence and help in those spheres of action in which Britain had been assigned the initiative. "Mr. Roosevelt replied . . . that it would seem to him that each of them had inadvertently taken independent steps in a direction which they both now agreed was for the time being expedient. He emphasized that it was essential that they should always be in accord on questions bearing on the Allied war effort."

These exchanges and their formal tone, if this is accurately reproduced by Hull, give some indication of the cooling-off which had occurred in the once white heat of Anglo-American friendship as the disintegrating effects of the approach of peace were felt. The Americans were fortified in their suspicions when in October, 1944, during conversations in Moscow at which the American Ambassador was present as an observer only, Churchill made with Stalin an agreement extending "the arrangement still further, even reducing to percentages the relative degree of influence which Britain and Russia individually should have in specified Balkan countries."[1]* There the matter rested.

[1] Hull, pp. 1457-8.

* Churchill gives a vivid description of how swiftly his suggested percentages of Anglo-Russian influence, scribbled on a piece of paper, were accepted, by Stalin putting a large tick on it. On Churchill's suggestion that this note should be burned lest others think it cynical, Stalin told Churchill to keep it, which he did. The exact form of the note is interesting, particularly in the antithesis between Russia on the one hand, and "the others," or Britain "in accord with" America on the other.
"Roumania
  Russia 90%
  The others 10%
Greece
  Great Britain 90%
  (in accord with U.S.A.)
  Russia 10%
Yugoslavia 50–50%
Hungary 50–50%
Bulgaria
  Russia 75%
  The others ... ... 25%"
(*Second World War*, VI, *New York Times*, 2 November, 1953.)

Churchill felt that he had rescued something from the wreck and from the Communism which would follow it; the Americans still felt that this "Churchiavellian"[1] scheme was a sinister violation of the Atlantic Charter; Russia was well content with what she regarded as a formal recognition of her domination in the Danube basin.

X

As was rapidly becoming apparent, the pre-eminent factor in the last year of the war in Anglo-American diplomacy, as in almost everything else, was Russia. In the nature and intentions of the Soviet Government there had been, there was, and there is, a considerable element of the mysterious and unknown; Roosevelt once said that the Russians do not use words for the same purpose that we do, and Churchill called her on 1 October, 1939, "a riddle wrapped in a mystery inside an enigma. . . ."[2]

But the Soviet Union and its actions called forth violent emotional reactions among many Britons and Americans, whether for or against. Roosevelt always inclined to a favourable view; the liberal in him and in Hull encouraged this. Once Russia was attacked by Hitler, Churchill, Tory though he was, backed her to the hilt in the war, on the principle that "If Hitler invaded Hell I would make at least a favourable reference to the Devil in the House of Commons,"[3] but it made abundantly clear that he would take back nothing that he had said about the Communist system. On this basis a loose form of co-operation was established between Britain and Russia, though it was never as intimate as the Anglo-American association, even before Pearl Harbour. After 1941 the relationship became genuinely tripartite, though there was no such swift blossoming of unity, co-ordination and cordiality with Russia, as there was between Britain and America in 1942. Contrary to the wishes of conservative element in both countries, but particularly America, aid was sent to Russia in quantity, and closer contacts were established at the highest level; on both sides of the Atlantic, by contrast, liberal enthusiasm for the Soviets rose to considerable heights, and there was a general surge of warm feeling for the heroic Russian people.

Gradually, however, towards the opening of 1943, a difference in emphasis between Churchill's and Roosevelt's approach to Stalin and the Russian problem became visible. This was by no means entirely

[1] Wilmot, p. 637.   [2] Q. Bailey, p. 810.
[3] *Second World War*, III, p. 331.

personal. Britain was a good deal closer to Russia's heartland than America, and much more familiar with the realities of European power politics; Russia had, because of British imperial interests in the East, long been a rival of whom she had been apprehensive, and the two powers had fought one major war on that account. Between Russia and the United States there had, however, long been a distant sympathy, a sort of fellow-feeling between two great continental powers. But personalities added to this difference, for Churchill was essentially realistic in his diplomatic judgments and stood firm against the Soviet Union on what he considered the rights that he could maintain. (He was equally realistic, at the other extreme, in his treatment of Spain.) Roosevelt, though he saw some of the obstacles, was prepared to adopt a policy of greater *naïveté*, and to stake much on his conviction that Russia was not an imperialist but an anti-colonial and satisfied power; he believed, or at least wished to believe, that, if he could win Stalin's confidence, Russia would "play ball" after the war, and that in this way world peace could be preserved by the retention of Big Three unity. He was confident that the crux of the problem was American-Russian friendship, being sure that if this could be established on firm and reasonable foundations, Britain would inevitably, if perhaps reluctantly, fall into step. It is perhaps overstating the case to say, as does Sir James Grigg, that he was obsessed with an idea derived "from de Tocqueville by way of Henry Adams . . . to the effect that the only two nations or groups who would count after the war were Russia and America",[1] but he was certainly fully aware of the great part which the two countries must increasingly play in world affairs. He was, therefore, prepared to go to great lengths to appease Stalin and the Soviet Government.

Churchill was by no means prepared to go so far. It is true that this reluctance does not seem greatly to have influenced his strategical ideas until May, 1944—at that time he told Eden that the brutal issue was whether they were to acquiesce in the Communisation of the Balkans or not—but he had set down the view as early as October, 1942, that "it would be a measureless disaster if Russian barbarism were to overlay the culture and independence of the ancient states of Europe."[2] Never oblivious to, or even unconscious of, the risks of the Russian alliance, he had done his best to co-operate for the good of the common cause and in genuine admiration for Russian gallantry, but he became increasingly aware of the very real difficulties of such a course as the advances of the Russian armies brought them farther and farther west.

[1] *The Daily Telegraph,* 3 September, 1952.   [2] Q. Wilmot, p. 636.

By the end of 1944 and the approach of the Yalta Conference, he was fully alive to the Russian danger.

With the development of the tension between Russia and the West as such, we are not concerned here, but we are concerned with the different rates of development of the awareness of that problem in Britain and America, and particularly in Churchill and Roosevelt. It is important, however, to remember that it *was* merely a matter of timing. Roosevelt's hope of co-operation with the Russians was shared by many in Britain; the Labour Party, when it came to power in 1945, was to think gaily in terms of "Left talking to Left" in Anglo-Russian co-operation, but, though some were slow to abandon the idea, Ernest Bevin was swift to do so when he grasped the realities of the situation. In the same way, Truman was forced by the remorseless logic of Russia's actions to the firm stand he eventually took. In all these developments Russia's was the initiating hand; upon her depended, almost absolutely, the actions of Britain and America. Though Roosevelt was slower to realize the true facts of the situation than Churchill, he must not be unduly blamed for it. Churchill himself consented, though perhaps with more misgivings than the President, to the arrangements made at Yalta,* and it was not until nearly two years later that he issued to the free world at Fulton, Missouri, his first clarion call warning it in plain terms of the Russian menace. It is, perhaps, Churchill's supreme political gift to see and to proclaim the unpleasant realities behind any political situation involving mortal danger to the West, and he did not finally and openly do so until Roosevelt had been twelve months in his grave. That the President, had he lived, would in due time have seen those realities as others did, is not to be doubted. In the last messages that came from his hand before he died, he gave clear indications of this; one to Churchill read, "I would minimize the general Soviet problem as much as possible because these problems, in one form or another, seem to arise every day and most of them straighten out. . . . We must be firm, however, and our course thus far is correct."[1]

In fact, an Anglo-American disagreement about Russia never materialized, and the significance of their divergence of opinion must

*It should be remembered that Roosevelt and Churchill were both, and very rightly, prepared to pay a high price for Russian intervention in the Japanese war in the days before the successful explosion of the first atomic bomb. Roosevelt was also very anxious to secure Stalin's aid in the smooth inauguration of the United Nations.

[1] Q. ibid, p. 695.

not be overrated, but for a brief spell an ominous split seemed to threaten; had it developed, it would have become a fatal yawning gulf into which the civilization of the West could have plunged. Its first signs could be seen by the clear-sighted Churchill as the first triple meeting at Teheran drew near. As he later wrote, "There was emerging a strong current of opinion in American Government circles which seemed to wish to win Russian confidence even at the expense of co-ordinating the Anglo-American war effort", for the President was reluctant to precede the Stalin meeting by full-scale, exclusively Anglo-American talks, despite Churchill's protest that "The Russians ought not to be vexed if the Americans and British closely concert the very great operations they have in hand". The Prime Minister was "filled . . . with alarm" at the prospect of Roosevelt inviting a Russian military representative to Anglo-American military meetings, on both practical and political grounds, and repeatedly reiterated that he regarded "our right to sit together on the movements of our own two forces as fundamental and vital."[1]

At Teheran itself Roosevelt made clear his determination to offer a powerful bid for Russian confidence. In his opening remarks he said "that he was glad to welcome the Russians as 'new members of the family circle' and to assure them that these conferences were always conducted as gatherings of friends with complete frankness on all sides. He believed that the three nations represented would work together in close co-operation not only for the duration of the war, but for generations to come."[2] Churchill's speech contained less *bonhomie* and more sense of the underlying realities, though it pointed in the same direction; he said that, "here was represented the greatest concentration of power that the world had ever seen and that in the hands of those present was the happy future of mankind; he prayed that they might be worthy of this God-given opportunity."[3] It was symptomatic that, when Churchill invited Roosevelt to lunch, knowing that he and Stalin had already had a private conversation in the Russian Embassy where they were both housed, the President declined, explaining "that he did not want Stalin to know that he and I were meeting privately. I was surprised at this, for I thought we all three should treat each other with equal confidence."[4] Here spoke not only the aggrieved Briton, but the representative of a great power very slightly apprehensive lest it be shouldered out by two greater ones. But Roosevelt continued resolutely with his course of action, and even in banter he seemed to side

[1] *Second World War*, V, pp. 276-7, 279, 280.   [2] Sherwood, pp. 772-3.
[3] Ibid, p. 773.   [4] *Second World War*, V, p. 320.

877

with Stalin; he was determined to cleave to the dictum of Emerson which he quoted in his Fourth Inaugural, "the only way to have a friend is to be one."[1] He was trying to apply to the Russians the policy that Churchill had so long employed towards the Americans, that of treating them well because they always want, then, to treat you better; unfortunately Russians are not Americans.

Nevertheless, the President pressed on, even at some slight risk to Anglo-American relations, which, as we have seen, grew increasingly strained in the autumn of 1944. A number of signs of Anglo-American disagreement were plainly visible by the time of the Yalta Conference in February, 1945. Roosevelt told Stalin at his first informal meeting with him there, that he had certain differences with the British over France and the occupation of Germany. Churchill strongly supported Stalin's demand for two additional Russian votes in the United Nations Assembly, for the Ukraine and Byelo Russia, largely no doubt, as the Americans suspected, for imperial reasons. Roosevelt interposed, in a discussion between Churchill and Stalin about the effect of the veto on Britain's position in Hong Kong and the Suez Canal zone, the reminder that in the Teheran Declaration they had said, "We recognize fully the supreme responsibility resting upon us and all the nations to make a peace which will command good will from the overwhelming masses of the peoples of the world." Later, he told Stalin privately that he thought that Hong Kong should be given back to the Chinese, or internationalized as a free port. On the reparations question Roosevelt conceded a great deal more to Stalin than Churchill wished; symptomatic was a note passed by Hopkins to the President at the height of the argument which ran, "The Russians have given in so much at this conference that I don't think we should let them down. Let the British disagree if they want to—and continue their disagreement at Moscow. Simply say it is all referred to the Reparations Commission with the minutes to show the British disagree about any mention of the 10 billion."[2] Of other concessions made by Roosevelt to Stalin, such as those in the Far East, this is not the place to speak. Their price was a firm commitment that Russia would enter the war shortly after the defeat of Germany: they did not ensure that Russian post-war amenability and co-operation which was their other main object.

But that they would not do so was not clear at the time, except probably to the Russians. It was not altogether apparent to Churchill, who was, when the talking was over, a party to the decisions, and it

[1] Sherwood, p. 838.   [2] Q. Sherwood, pp. 849, 851.

would, therefore, be wrong to over-emphasize Anglo-American differences. Roosevelt was determined to make the strongest bid for Russian friendship, but he did not wish to lose British friendship as a result. Nor would he have done so, for behind all lay the fundamental realities of Russian Communist rivalry with the West. The Russian problem was increasingly to dominate the world scene in the years to come; the leading figures upon that scene were many of them changed, and in some cases lesser men succeeded, but the course of history would have been substantially the same in any case.

The Anglo-American differences at Yalta were heavily outweighed by the questions on which they were in agreement and opposed to Russia. On the main reparations question, on Poland, on Iran, there was Anglo-American concord and Russian discord; already the shape of things to come is there for the historian to see. But it was not visible to the participants; the desire for Russian co-operation threw out of focus the strength of Anglo-American bonds. This was a pity, but it was soon to be swept away by the onrush of post-war events and the beginnings of the cold war. In any case, it was overshadowed by the far more grotesque distortion of faith in the survival of Big Three unity. Hopkins said later to Sherwood, "We really believed in our hearts that this was the dawn of the new day we had all been praying for and talking about for so many years. We were absolutely certain that we had won the first great victory of the peace—and, by 'we' I mean *all* of us, the whole civilized human race."[1] In this feeling the British, including Churchill, also shared, though with more reservations and less wholehearted optimism. In his final speech after a cordial dinner at Yalta the Prime Minister said, "he felt we were standing on the crest of a hill with the glories of future possibilities stretching before us. He said that in the modern world the function of leadership was to lead the people out from the forests into the broad sunlit plains of peace and happiness. He felt this prize was nearer our grasp than any time before in history". The President had earlier said that "he felt the atmosphere at this dinner was that of a family", and that "their objectives here were to give every man, woman and child on this earth the possibility of security and well-being." Marshal Stalin "remarked that it was not so difficult to keep unity in time of war. . . . He said the difficult task came after the war. . . ."[2] This was a more realistic, a graver, perhaps a more ominous note, which he alone struck. Well might he do so.

[1] Q. Sherwood, p. 859.   [2] Ibid, p. 858.

XI

THESE, then, were the major Anglo-American disagreements during the three years of war, for after Yalta there remains only the epilogue of the drama. Colonialism, the Battle of the Generals, the future of the liberated peoples, the Second Front and the Balkans, friendship for the Soviet Union, these were real and important differences. But it would be altogether erroneous to retain the impression that the disagreements were as important as, or even comparable with, the agreements. We must restore our sense of proportion by returning our gaze for a moment to the unique closeness of the two countries in the war. Though, inevitably, divergences increased as the war neared its end, we must never forget the unity which was maintained throughout most of its course.

We must remind ourselves, in the words of Cordell Hull, that "On the military side, the efforts of the two countries were integrated to a degree probably never previously reached by any two great Allies in history."[1] We must remind ourselves of the intimate political relationship which made this possible; of the elaborate but flexible machinery of co-ordination; of the British Prime Minister presiding, in the absence of the President, over a plenary conference of the Combined Chiefs of Staff and of American and British authorities in the Council Room of the White House, which was indeed "an event in Anglo-American history";[2]* and of Roosevelt's letter to Churchill at the "dark moment" of the fall of Singapore:

> I realize how the fall of Singapore has affected you and the British people. It gives the well-known back-seat driver a field day, but no matter how serious our set-backs have been—and I do not for a moment underrate them—we must constantly look forward to the next moves that need to be made to hit the enemy. I hope you will be of good heart in these trying weeks, because I am very sure that you have the great confidence of the masses of the British people. I want you to know that I think of you often, and I know you will not hesitate to ask me if there is anything you think I can do. . . . Do let me hear from you.[3]

[1] Hull, p. 1472.   [2] *Second World War*, V, p. 123.

*This interpretation is, I think, justified, even if, as McNeill suggests, Roosevelt left Washington on this occasion in order to avoid hearing more of Churchill's arguments about the Mediterranean campaign.

[3] Q. ibid, IV, p. 94.

We must remind ourselves of the even more remarkable accomplishment of attuning the sentiments of the two great peoples to one another and to the outer world; of the fact that "On the diplomatic side, it is probably true that never before in history have two great powers tried to co-ordinate so closely their policies toward all other countries";[1] of the incident of the Congressman who complained, after one of Churchill's addresses to Congress, that they had to wait for news of the war until the British Prime Minister came and told them about it; and finally, of the spirit embodied in the peroration of the first of those addresses:

> Prodigious hammer-strokes have been needed to bring us together again, or, if you will allow me to use other language, I will say that he must indeed have a blind soul who cannot see that some great purpose and design is being worked out here below, of which we have the honour to be the faithful servants. It is not given to us to peer into the mysteries of the future. Still, I avow my hope and faith, sure and inviolate, that in the days to come the British and American peoples will for their own safety and for the good of all walk together side by side in majesty, in justice, and in peace.[2]

It was, however, inevitable that some loosening of the bonds that held them together should follow the coming of victory and the loss of the common aim that its pursuit provides, and we have seen that signs of this loosening were already visible before the beginning of 1945. By then, indeed, though few had sensed the fact, there was not far to go to final victory, and in those few months the onrush of events was so swift that the broad outlines of Anglo-American relations are somewhat obscured in the confusion. Within two months of the President's return from the Yalta Conference, he had died of a cerebral haemorrhage, and had been succeeded by the inexperienced Harry Truman. Within three months, Germany had surrendered. Within five and a half months, the British electorate had, in the middle of the Potsdam Conference, ejected the Tories, and Churchill and Eden had been succeeded by Attlee and Bevin. Within six months the atomic bomb had caused the Japanese to sue for peace and World War II had come at last to an end.

This six-month epilogue did little but give freer play to the tendencies already apparent by February, 1945. It saw a further weakening of Anglo-American ties, though the process was soon overshadowed by incipient but unmistakable symptoms of Russian intransigence and ambition. Russian actions in Poland and Rumania, and the so-called

[1] Hull, p. 1472.　　[2] *Second World War*, III, p. 596.

Berne incident, dispersed the hopes of Russian co-operation which had been once more raised by the successful termination of the San Francisco Conference, and its inauguration of the new world organization, which were so much facilitated by Hopkins's last mission to Moscow. It was, nevertheless, characteristic of the altered personal relationships that Hopkins was not permitted by President Truman to accept a pressing invitation to visit Churchill on his way back from Moscow, despite a personal appeal from the Prime Minister to the President, who sent instead the very pro-Russian Joseph E. Davies, bearing a most unwelcome proposal that Truman should meet Stalin alone before Churchill's arrival at Potsdam.

It was characteristic, also, that Churchill was reacting swiftly to the Russian attitude; not only that he pressed his fears upon the Americans, even before Roosevelt's death, but that he strongly desired to alter the strategy of the Allied Armies in Germany accordingly. He urged, in the first place, that every effort should be made to reach Berlin before the Russians, a feat which could easily have been achieved since it was now the Germans' dearest wish, but General Eisenhower, impressed with the possibility of Nazi resistance in the mountain redoubt of the south, planned to concentrate all his strength on the right wing. This Churchill strongly contested and bitterly attacked the sending by Eisenhower of a personal message on the subject direct to Stalin, on the ground that it constituted much more than the tactical co-ordination which the Supreme Commander was permitted. Since it seemed to him a strategical question involving a change of plan, he pointed out energetically that it should have been referred to the Combined Chiefs of Staff. Eisenhower's American superiors, however, supported their commander in the field; Marshall's words to the British Chiefs of Staff are revealing: "The battle of Germany is now at a point when it is up to the Field Commander to judge the measures which should be taken. . . . *The single objective should be quick and complete victory.*"[1] The American belief in victory for victory's sake, and in giving the maximum latitude to field commanders, has seldom been so clearly demonstrated, and it clashed vigorously with the views of the British, who believed that the only decisions now of importance were political and not such as to be taken by any soldier on his own responsibility.

Bradley, who had at the time supported his chief if only because it retained the initiative in his rather than Montgomery's hands, remarks rather ruefully in his book, which saw the light after he had had, as American Chief of Staff, to bear the brunt of the cold war: "We were

[1] Q. Wilmot, p. 693.

less concerned with postwar political alignments than destruction of what remained of the German Army. . . . As soldiers we looked naïvely on this British inclination to complicate the war with political foresight and non-military objectives."[1] Churchill's efforts to get a reversal of the decision on the political level, which were unlikely to have succeeded in any case owing to Roosevelt's reluctance to overrule his military advisers and to his continued hope of conciliating the Russians, were ended by Roosevelt's death, since the new President could hardly be expected to effect it.

The Prime Minister, therefore, tried a new line, and suggested to President Truman that Eisenhower's armies, even if they did not take Berlin, should advance as deeply as possible into the Soviet zone and should not withdraw unless the Russians agreed to pool German food resources, which were greatest in the east. Though no political or military agreement not to advance beyond zonal frontiers existed, the President replied that he did "not believe that the matter of retirement of our respective troops to our zonal frontiers should be used for such bargaining purposes." He reaffirmed the American principle, which was supported by his Chiefs of Staff, that "The question of tactical deployment of American troops in Germany is a military one. It is my belief that General Eisenhower should be given certain latitude and discretion."[2] The General himself was increasingly impressed with the dangers of an accidental head-on collision with the Russian armies, and so the opportunity was lost. With the advantage of hindsight, we can appreciate the irony of his plea in the Presidential campaign of 1952 for the liberation of the peoples behind the Iron Curtain: in 1945 there were but few who showed Churchill's percipience.

His departure from the scene after the election of 1945 did not appear, to American eyes, to have any effect upon Britain's policy, for Bevin was almost as stout an opponent of Russia as he had been. Despite Truman's liking for Stalin, the course of the Potsdam Conference was very different from that of Yalta. Though, on occasions, the President was able to make a proposal—usually to refer the question to the Council of Foreign Ministers—which eased the sometimes severe tension between the British and the Russians, almost all signs of Anglo-American disagreement had disappeared, or were so overlaid by common difficulties with the Soviet Union that they can scarcely be discerned. On all major issues over which there was dispute with the Russians, and this covered almost all the issues, there was substantial Anglo-American agreement—free elections in Eastern Europe,

[1] Q. Wilmot, p. 693.   [2] Q. ibid, p. 696.

the Dardanelles, reparations, Poland, all were common ground. Even the Russian tactic of evading any difficulty raised about Eastern Europe by a violent attack on British policy in Greece failed to achieve— what was no doubt one of its purposes—an Anglo-American division. The Soviet demand for one of the former Italian colonies on the Mediterranean in trusteeship, which was likely to be strongly opposed by Britain, might have had this effect but for the fact that its principal result was to banish from American minds all hope that the Soviet Union was a genuinely anti-imperialist power. The result was that the American delegation, as Byrnes says, headed home "less sanguine than the one that had departed from Yalta."[1] This marked a *rapprochement* of Anglo-American policies, which were perhaps closer than they had been for twelve months. This was so despite the loosening of personal ties, for nothing like the Churchill-Roosevelt relationship was ever established between Attlee and Truman. Very preoccupied with effecting Britain's social revolution, the Prime Minister left foreign affairs largely to his Foreign Secretary, for whom he had enormous respect. Britain was fully committed to the Japanese war, and began to deploy her forces to the satisfaction, on the whole, of her American partner, whose fear that she would be left to beat Japan almost alone was proved quite unjustified.

Russia had pledged her word to attack Japan, and, as long as that pledge was fulfilled, the Anglo-American bloc was likely to go on humouring her as far as possible until the war was won. But by now it was becoming clear that Russia was going to be the main post-war problem, and this fact alone was sufficient to cement the Anglo-American relationship, despite all the disruptive tendencies of the years which followed the war. The factors, which we have seen at work in their long history, operating to bring and keep Britain and America together, were still operative, and would probably have prevented any serious disagreement. When to them was added the supreme fact of Soviet antagonism, the tendency to drift apart was for some time to be scarcely perceptible or at any rate scarcely noticed, and when it did become marked, in 1949, it took the form, as we shall see, of a difference as to means only, and not as to ends, and was more of a cleavage between extremes in the two countries than between the moderate views of the two governments.

When this divergence occurred, it was no little owing to the intense stresses placed upon the people in the awful era of atomic power, which brought the Japanese war to a blessedly swift end, but made the hazards

[1] James F. Byrnes, *Speaking Frankly,* p. 86.

of future conflict perilous in the extreme. In terms of human power, whether for good or evil, it is perhaps true that the supreme Anglo-American achievement of the whole war was the joint production of the atomic bomb. Though effected in America and owing much to American wealth and technical skill, it was also deeply indebted to British scientists both before and during the war. It was in any event the work of "an Anglo-American army of specialists." It was essentially a joint project and it is possible that only by such co-operation could it have been achieved so soon. It may even be that only a restoration of at least this limited measure of free dissemination of nuclear physics data will ensure the permanent lead of the West in atomic science. If this is so, the importance of Anglo-American relations is increased yet again; this Dr. Conant certainly seems to believe, for he writes, "[I]f the foundations of Anglo-American relations remain secure, mankind can walk safely, I believe, even the tight rope of the atomic age."[1]

[1] J. B. Conant, *Anglo-American Relations in the Atomic Age* (London, 1952), pp. 20, 42.

CHAPTER NINETEEN

WORLD LEADERSHIP (1945-52)

D ESPITE fear of Russia and the existence of strong residual Anglo-American bonds, a number of differences arose between the two countries in the aftermath of war, and, although mutual diplomatic representation remained at a high level, it could not prevent them from making their appearance.

The American Ambassador in London from 1947 to 1950, Lewis Douglas, was a business man with political experience, who had, among other things, been for a short period Principal of a great Canadian University, McGill. He was succeeded in 1950 by a man of perhaps more orthodox type for an important American Embassy, Walter S. Gifford, a business executive whose main achievements had been in the great American Telephone and Telegraph Company. The appointment of a man of similar calibre to succeed Gifford was announced by General Eisenhower in November, 1952, Winthrop Aldrich, Chairman of the Chase National Bank, but it is significant that he had always been, and particularly since 1940, an ardent advocate of close co-operation with Britain.

Britain reverted to her pre-war habit, by sending a distinguished professional diplomat to Washington in 1946, Archibald Clark Kerr, Lord Inverchapel. He had been Ambassador to the U.S.S.R. for the previous four years, and so had a very valuable knowledge of the situation on the other side of the Iron Curtain. In 1948, however, in the midst of the complexities of planning for Marshall Aid, the British Government sent to succeed him, on his retirement, Sir Oliver Franks, no career diplomat but Provost of Queen's College, Oxford, who had spent much time in the previous nine years upon Government business, particularly in the economic sphere. In 1952 he was succeeded once more by a professional, Sir Roger Makins.

If anything more emotional than normal diplomatic contacts was needed to maintain the links between the two peoples, it was perhaps provided by a visit to the United States in 1951 of Princess Elizabeth, accompanied by the Duke of Edinburgh, which rivalled in success that of her father and mother in 1939. Once again it demonstrated that the people of the great Republic are capable of an extraordinary interest in, and indeed enthusiasm for, the British Royal Family. But if all was smooth at this height, there were possibilities of serious difficulty at the governmental level, for the election of a Labour, commonly known as a Socialist, government in Britain in 1945 was not generally popular with Americans, except those of very radical views. In some spheres this led rapidly to friction.

One of these was the British Zone of Germany. We find Secretary Forrestal complaining in May, 1947, of the British desire "to impose a socialized economy and government in their Zone," which might, had it been pressed to doctrinaire lengths, have proved a serious obstacle to the union of the American and British Zones, which eventually formed the foundation of the West German Federal Republic. Point was added by the fact that, as Forrestal wrote, the British "were operating their economy on three and a quarter billion capital obtained from this country, and that they would probably need additional working capital, and that we did not propose to have our money used to implement a German system contrary to our own ideas".[1] Here, indeed, was the rub, for Americans holding strong views against Socialism were not easily to be persuaded to subsidize a government which was putting it into effect. Thus Representative Knutson of Minnesota declared in 1946, "We are being called upon to finance the socialization of the British Empire."[2] In such circumstances it is remarkable that the lavish American aid to Britain was in fact forthcoming, and great credit is due to the American people for their ability to distinguish successfully between the permanent value to them of a strong Britain and their mistrust of a particular political party.

That they were able to do so, however, was also due to the moderation of the controlling elements in the Labour Party, while it would be wrong to suppose that all aspects of Socialist policy were displeasing to America. The acceleration of political and social equality which it implied, could not but make some appeal to Americans, who had long professed distaste for even the surviving remnants of aristocracy in Britain; still more was American opinion pleased by the now swift progress to self-government of the colonial empire. The liberation, unconditionally and rapidly, of India and Pakistan was the supreme example of this Labour policy, but there were many others, including that of the African colonies, where progress was so spectacular as to arouse serious difficulties with the permanent white populations of

[1] W. Millis (Editor), *The Forrestal Diaries* (New York, 1951), p. 273.

[2] Q. Bailey, p. 873.

887

the continent, especially in the Union of South Africa. Indeed, the
events which followed the granting of independence to Burma, and
the outburst of terrorism in Malaya, inflamed and often originated by
Communism, even inspired doubts in some American minds as to
the wisdom of such rapid emancipation. It is a measure of this change
that we find American approval of forceful British policies in Malaya,
subject to their being accompanied by political and economic reform.*
This new role was not too easily assumed by the American people;
the first American reaction to outbursts of native terrorism in Kenya
in 1952, for instance, was a curious mixture of criticism of British
economic and social policies and approval for vigorous action against
what might be called a Communist-inspired conspiracy. As *Time* put
it on another and different occasion, the United States was "divided
between its desire to please an ally and its sentimental aversion to
the old fighting word 'colonialism'."[1] But the effect upon American
opinion of Britain's great colonial reforms was unquestionably salutary,
as the fact that France in 1952 had almost become, with her North
African troubles, the main butt of American anti-colonial feeling,
clearly shows. This was principally due to the Labour party.

Even towards the domestic social security policies of the Socialists,
there were radical elements in the Democratic party which were not
altogether unsympathetic. But none the less the more extreme members
of the Labour Party were inclined to be very critical of Britain's close
co-operation with the United States. These radicals were to become
more vociferous, if no more influential, under the leadership of Aneurin
Bevan after the outbreak of the Korean War. They were in some
respects matched in America by Henry Wallace and his followers,
who, after breaking with the Truman Administration on the policy
of a firm stand against Russia, not only declared in their own land
in favour of further co-operation with the Soviets, but toured Europe
making speeches which denounced the "imperialist," "Wall-Street
dominated" policy of the United States Government. Happily for the
future of the West, neither of these factions had any chance of gaining
control of the destinies of their respective countries. Equally happy
was the fact that a Republican administration, which might have been
dominated by its extreme right wing, never attained power during these
years, for later events suggested that it might have proved very difficult
to find common ground between a British Labour—or even Conservative—government and an American administration reflecting the views

*To many Americans post-war disturbances in the Philippines seemed
an object lesson.   [1] *Time*, 20 October, 1952, p. 21.

of a General MacArthur. It was thus on a moderate policy that the governments were able to base their continuing co-operation. The British Government resisted tenaciously and effectively the pressure of their left wing for a continuation of the conciliation policy hitherto pursued towards Russia: the American Administration pursued a sturdy course between the extremes represented by Henry Wallace on the one hand and Robert Taft on the other.

Great credit must go for this to the heads of the Foreign Office and the State Department respectively. Particular praise is due to Ernest Bevin, who was Foreign Secretary throughout almost the whole period of Labour rule, for his remarkable combination of courage, common sense and imagination enabled him to make a great contribution to the maintenance of a common policy. His successor in 1951—after a brief and not very happy interregnum under Herbert Morrison—was the highly experienced Anthony Eden, a Conservative with whose strong feeling for Anglo-American friendship we are already familiar, and, as when Bevin had taken over from him six years before, the alteration produced no really perceptible change in policy.

Even more to be praised was the conduct of successive Secretaries of State, James Byrnes, George Marshall and Dean Acheson. The first, until he resigned "in a huff"[1] at the beginning of 1947, bore the brunt of the awkward transition from the Yalta to the Fulton policies; under his direction America ceased to be conciliatory towards the Russians and became increasingly adamant. General Marshall, his successor, not only controlled the State Department during the enunciation and implementation of the Truman Doctrine, whose keynote was the strengthening and supporting of those peoples who were prepared to resist Communist aggression, but was himself, as the popular name records, the originator of the much wider European Recovery Programme, or Marshall Plan. When he resigned early in 1949, he was succeeded by the one-time Under Secretary of State, Dean Acheson, to whom British sympathies went out perhaps more than to any previous Secretary of State except John Hay. Not only was he of a type congenial to Englishmen, but he maintained a policy which was, in view of the Communist conquest of China and the long-drawn-out Korean War, one of remarkable moderation, despite a torrent of political abuse which can hardly have been surpassed, even in the long history of American public outspokenness. Foreign observers were left wondering that he was able to survive at all, and he did so largely through the unflinching support of President Truman.

[1] McNeill, p. 659, footnote 2.

889

The President, indeed, was by no means the cipher in foreign affairs that it had once been thought he would be; he was personally responsible for the momentous decisions of the period, for the dropping of the atomic bomb, for the Truman Doctrine and the Marshall Plan, for the Berlin air-lift, and, above all, for the entry of the United States into the Korean War. The influence of Prime Minister Attlee was not in all probability so considerable, though he grew surprisingly in stature during his Premiership. The two men were not unlike in many ways. Compared with their predecessors, they were cut on a small scale. Personally modest, they were excellent party leaders, and advocates of policies which were, in the circumstances of their countries, radical without being extreme. They were simple and direct in their speech-making, both from inclination and from a desire to talk primarily to the plain people. There might appear to have been here the basis of a close political friendship, but after the Potsdam Conference, when they got on well enough, Truman never saw Attlee outside America because he did not visit Europe, while the Prime Minister only went to the United States twice in these five years, once in 1945 and once in 1950.

This was characteristic of the way in which the two peoples drifted insensibly apart, and allowed those close personal ties which had existed between the governments during the war to become weak from disuse. Indeed Truman's relations with Churchill, who did not cease either to visit or to woo the United States, even now that he was in Opposition, have the appearance of greater cordiality than those with Attlee, and one of the Tory Prime Minister's first actions after his return to power in the autumn of 1951 was to pay an official visit to the President in Washington. This same coolness was, though to a less degree, apparent also elsewhere. Byrnes, it is true, had the greatest confidence in and admiration for Bevin, and Marshall also got on well with him, as did Acheson with Eden, but the ardent fires of friendship had burned low. This must be deplored, for it made the strain which was to be thrown on the relationship by the Korean War seem much more severe than it actually was. But for all these mild symptoms of decay, the fundamental relationship remained sound and solid; there was too great a depth to it for transient difficulties to make much impression.

II

THIS was especially so now that it seemed certain that America was irretrievably committed to participation in world affairs. The increasing feebleness of isolationist tendencies, the virtual disappearance of outright isolationism, the acceptance of the British connexion even by Senator Taft, and, if further proof were needed, the nomination of General Eisenhower as its candidate by the Republican Convention of 1952, all removed the greatest danger that had in the past threatened Anglo-American co-operation. This change was a response to the fundamental alteration in America's position in the world. As Brooks Adams had written a half a century before, "It is in vain that men talk of keeping free from entanglements. Nature is omnipotent; and nations must float with the tide."[1]

The centrifugal forces which might, with the coming of peace, have dissipated the relationship were not allowed free play, for supreme among the causes of continued Anglo-American co-operation was the fact which dominated every branch and aspect of international affairs, the menace of Soviet Russia. It had indeed the effect of rapidly replacing the war with the Axis by a cold war between the Soviet bloc and the Western world, which forced the United States and Britain to unite and to form the heart of a powerful defensive system against Russian aggression. The great gulf between the East and the West looks like dominating the destiny of mankind for the foreseeable future, and as long as that remains so, the unity of America and Britain must remain the basis of their existence.

It was not the Government in either country, but the Leader of His Majesty's Opposition, who did most to arouse the free world to a sense of its peril. It is by no means odd that Churchill should have been the first to awaken British opinion, but it is a most extraordinary witness to his unique position in the history of Anglo-American relations that he should have been the first seriously to bring home to the American people the extent of the Russian danger. He did it on the occasion of a visit to the United States, in the very presence of President Truman, his host, at Fulton, Missouri, on 5 March, 1946. At first his outspokenness was greeted with a public outcry from some Americans, in a vein reminiscent of Harry Hopkins's view expressed in May of the previous year that "he was sceptical about Churchill, at least in the particular of Anglo-American-Russian relationship; that he thought it was of vital importance that we not be manoeuvred into a position where Great Britain had us lined up with them as a bloc against Russia to implement England's European policy." The criticism was directed particularly against the seeming endorsement of his sentiments by the President, but many American leaders were already in agreement with him, including probably the President himself. Secretary of the Navy

[1] Brooks Adams, *America's Economic Supremacy*, p. 23.

Forrestal, for instance, wrote after a conversation with Churchill four days later: "He agreed with my analysis that we are dealing not only with Russia as a national entity but with the expanding power of Russia under Peter the Great plus the additional missionary force of a religion."[1]

He set the whole course of American as well as British policy from that day forward. He said:

> From Stettin in the Baltic to Trieste in the Adriatic an iron curtain has descended across the continent. . . . The Communist parties, which are very small in all these eastern states of Europe, have been raised to pre-eminence and power far beyond their numbers and are seeking everywhere to obtain totalitarian control. Police governments are prevailing in nearly every case. . . . Whatever conclusions may be drawn from these facts . . . and facts they are . . . this is certainly not the liberated Europe we fought to build up. Nor is it one which contains the essentials of permanent peace. . . . The outlook is also anxious in the Far East and especially in Manchuria.

Yet with that coolness of judgment in adversity which is perhaps his greatest quality, he did not admit the inevitability of war:

> I do not believe that Soviet Russia desires war. What they desire is the fruits of war and the indefinite expansion of their power and doctrines. . . . Our difficulties and dangers will not be removed by closing our eyes to them; they will not be removed by mere waiting to see what happens; nor will they be relieved by a policy of appeasement. What is needed is a settlement, and the longer this is delayed, the more difficult it will be and the greater our dangers will become. From what I have seen of our Russian friends and Allies during the war, I am convinced there is nothing they admire so much as strength, and there is nothing for which they have less respect than for military weakness.

He not only called attention to the problem, but proposed a remedy, military collaboration between England and the United States, embracing common studies, similar weapons, interchange of officers, joint use of forces and bases. Mutual defence "should be extended to all the British Commonwealths with full reciprocity", and until these arrangements could be effected reliance must be had on the atomic bomb, which "It would be criminal madness to cast . . . adrift in this still agitated and ununited world." But the core of any and every measure of defence must be Anglo-American unity: "If the population of the English-speaking Commonwealth be added to that of the United

[1] Forrestal, pp. 58, 144.

States, with all that such co-operation implies in the air, on the sea, and in science and industry . . . there will be an overwhelming assurance of security."[1]

Although it does not appear that the fulness of military co-operation which he desired in fact took place, in almost every other particular his prophecies have been fulfilled and his advice has been followed to the letter. It is true that he did but speak the words which some Americans wanted, and which others were being rapidly driven, to hear, but there can be little doubt of the decisive effect of his utterance. It was five months later, in September, that Byrnes demanded, and Truman enforced, the resignation of Henry Wallace from the Cabinet, and a year later that the President first enunciated the Truman Doctrine. Churchill's influence in the United States at this time, out of power though he was in his own country, was perhaps greater than it had been even in 1940-1: certainly he has been the greatest Anglo-American since Chatham.

But if—in so far as any one man can be said to have done it—it was Churchill who first pointed to the necessity for a new Anglo-American policy, it was the United States Administration which gave it effective force and shape. The American people shouldered with remarkable good grace the burden of world leadership, a feat made easier by the paradoxical fact that the strongest isolationists among them were also, on the whole, the most violently opposed to Communism. So much was this the case that the first serious attack on the new policies—those of Wallace may be discounted—came from the right wing, and took the form of asserting that the Democratic administration was too weak rather than too forceful in the face of the Russian threat. This onslaught was to be so severe as to cause alarm in Britain on a scale sufficient to constitute during the Korean War the most serious post-war threat to Anglo-American unity. But the Democratic administration weathered the storm, and continued as steadily as possible on its course, steering between the shoals of appeasement and the rocks of war.

The formulation of the new policy owed much to an able member of the State Department, George Kennan, who was at that time Chargé d'Affaires in Moscow; some days before Churchill's speech, he had outlined in a long cable to the State Department, not of course then known to the public, all the main features of what came to be called

[1] Q. F. McNaughton and W. Hehmeyer, *Harry Truman President* (New York, 1948), pp. 47-9.

the containment policy. First, he analysed the basis of Soviet policy, which he believed arose fundamentally from "the traditional and instinctive Russian sense of insecurity"; it was "no coincidence that Marxism which 'had smoldered ineffectively for half a century in Western Europe' " should have blazed up "for the first time . . . in this land, which had 'never known a friendly neighbor' or any balanced equilibrium of social forces. . . . [N]o one should underrate the importance of the Marxist doctrine in practical Russian policy", for it gave wonderfully effective expression to the age-old and " 'uneasy Russian nationalism' in which 'conceptions of offense and defense are inextricably confused.' " Added to this was "the atmosphere of Oriental secretiveness" which pervaded the government and almost certainly distorted the picture which its leaders received of the outside world. Next he described Russian policy as that of

> a political force committed fanatically to the belief that with the U.S. there can be no permanent *modus vivendi*, that it is desirable and necessary that the internal harmony of our society be disrupted, our traditional way of life destroyed, the international authority of our state be broken, if Soviet power is to be secure. This political force has complete power of disposition over the energies of one of the world's greatest peoples and the resources of the world's richest national territory. . . . In addition, it has an elaborate and far-flung apparatus for the exertion of its influence in other countries. . . . Finally, it is seemingly inaccessible to considerations of reality in its basic reactions. For it, the vast fund of objective fact about human society is not, as with us, the measure against which outlook is constantly being tested and reformed, but a great grab bag from which individual items are selected arbitrarily and tendentiously to bolster an outlook already preconceived.[1]

Later, in a masterly passage, he pointed out the vital difference in practice between the strategy of Soviet Communism and its tactics; its objectives altered little, if at all, but the methods employed to achieve them did. In this fact, to his mind, lay the hope of the West, for it offered at least the possibility of a series of temporary accommodations. He brilliantly pictured Soviet expansionism as

> a fluid stream which moves constantly, wherever it is permitted to move, toward a given goal. Its main concern is to make sure that it has filled every nook and cranny available to it in the basin of world power. But if it finds unassailable barriers in its path, it accepts these philosophically and accommodates itself to them. The main thing is

[1] Q. Forrestal, pp. 136-9.

894

that there should always be pressure, unceasing constant pressure, toward the desired goal. There is no trace of any feeling in Soviet psychology that the goal must be reached at any given time.[1]

It was upon such an analysis as this that the Truman administration, with great wisdom and penetrating judgment, came to base American policy. For the framing and maintenance of this policy there was ample justification in the actions of Russia, and of her satellites and allies; step by step they made the rift between East and West more difficult to bridge. Furthermore, they rendered any fundamental cleavage between the United States and Britain impossible. If, on occasion, Britain was restive under what her lunatic left-wing fringe were inclined to consider as the American yoke, she had only to shift her eyes from the West to the East to be at once reconciled to her lot. This feeling was expressed, with the brilliance of which only he is capable, by the cartoonist Low, in one of his most famous drawings. In one corner of the picture the Englishman sees a vision of a stout American business man, garbed in an Indian headdress of feathers and armed with a tomahawk, performing a violent war dance. In the other corner stands an enigmatic and sinister Stalin. Underneath runs a caption which points out that, awkward as it sometimes is to be tied to the Americans, it is infinitely better than the alternative.

Yet in fact the policy of the Administration throughout these years continued to be surprisingly reasonable, considering the spate of criticism to which it was subjected. It planned to counter Communist infiltration with both military and economic weapons; military strength to repel open attacks, and economic aid to assist in the elimination of Communism's most potent ally, poverty. Firmness was not to mean truculence, and the greatest care was to be taken to avoid provocative and aggressive acts; it was hoped that, when the rearmament of the West was completed, there would be an equilibrium of power with the East, and that from this position of strength negotiation would be possible. The longer peace was preserved, the greater the chance that Russia's rulers would come to see the falseness of their dogmatic faith in the inevitability of war with a capitalist system. In any case, who could tell what changes of Russian heart time and the death of Stalin might produce? Even if cordiality never appeared, an uneasy *modus vivendi,* a willingness to live and let live, might. This policy of containment Kennan defended in historical terms: "Our interest has lain . . . in the maintenance of some sort of stable balance among the powers of

[1] Q. R. H. Rovere and A. M. Schlesinger, *The General and the President and the Future of American Foreign Policy* (New York, 1951), p. 235.

the interior [of Eurasia], in order that none of them should effect the subjugation of the others, conquer the seafaring fringes of the land mass, become a great seapower as well as a land power, shatter the position of England, and enter—as in these circumstances it certainly would—on an overseas expansion hostile to ourselves and supported by the immense resources of the interior of Europe and Asia."[1] (Here, indeed, is an example of the way in which the United States has, in the twentieth century, been compelled to take up the role in international affairs that Britain had so long played.)* But "[W]e now face the fact that it is very questionable whether in a new global conflict there could ever be any such thing as a total *military* victory",[2] and, therefore, scrupulous care not to provoke must accompany determination to contain. The Administration's policy exactly fulfilled the precept of a somewhat unlikely soothsayer: "Speak softly and carry a big stick, you will go far."

The policy first took shape in the Truman Doctrine, originally expounded by the President in his address to Congress on 12 March, 1947, asking for aid to Greece and Turkey; this was its military aspect.

> The peoples of a number of countries of the world have recently had totalitarian régimes forced upon them against their will. . . . At the present moment in world history nearly every nation must choose between alternative ways of life. The choice is too often not a free one. One way of life is based upon the will of the majority, and is distinguished by free institutions, representative government, free elections, guarantees of individual liberty, freedom of speech and religion, and freedom from political oppression. The second way of life is based upon the will of a minority forcibly imposed upon the majority. It relies upon terror and oppression, a controlled press and radio, fixed elections, and the suppression of personal freedoms. I believe that it must be the policy of the United States to support free peoples who are resisting attempted subjugation by armed minorities or by outside pressures.[3]

From this beginning, armed American help for those who wished to help themselves, spread out until it produced the North Atlantic Alliance of 1949 and the Pacific Security Pact of 1951.

In its economic aspect, the American policy took the even more remarkable, indeed the noble, shape of the European Recovery Pro-

[1] Kennan, p. 5.

*McNeill writes that during the war "the United States became heir to Britain's world position" (pp. 754-5).

[2] Ibid, p. 101.　　[3] *Documents on American Foreign Relations*, IX, pp. 6-7.

gramme, which had the twofold object of defeating Communism in Europe and of raising the world's (and thus America's) standards of living, by restoring the shattered European economy. This was first given expression by Secretary of State Marshall in a speech at Harvard on 5 June, 1947:

> The truth of the matter is that Europe's requirements for the next three or four years of foreign food and other essential products— principally from America—are so much greater than her present ability to pay that she must have substantial additional help, or face economic, social and political deterioration of a very grave character. . . . Aside from . . . the possibilities of disturbances arising as a result of the desperation of the people concerned, the consequences to the economy of the United States should be apparent to all. It is logical that the United States should do whatever it is able to do to assist in the return of normal economic health in the world. . . . Any government that is willing to assist in the task of recovery will find full co-operation, I am sure, on the part of the United States Government.

From this seed sprang the vast programme of American expenditure to rehabilitate Europe.

Meanwhile, force was given to these actions by a steady programme of rearmament, but it was repeatedly accompanied by reminders that no aggression was intended. As President Truman declared on 2 September, 1947: "In carrying out our policy we are determined to remain strong. This is in no way a threat. The record of the past speaks for us. No great nation has been more reluctant than ours to use armed force. We do not believe that the present international difficulties will have to be resolved by armed conflict. The world may depend upon it that we shall continue to go far out of our way to avoid anything that would increase the tensions of international life."[1] But the supreme proof of the determination behind America's new policy came with American military support to South Korea against the aggression of the North Koreans, and of its moderation with her dismissal of General MacArthur and with her superhuman patience at the protracted peace negotiations which began in 1951.

It was not, however, always easy to get that policy accepted by all the American people; many were never reconciled to it. Wallace liberals, though their power was very small, denounced it so fervently, as grossly unjust to Russia, that their view was indistinguishable from the Communist Party line. Far more formidable were the attacks upon

[1] Ibid, pp. 10, 18.

it as much too soft which came from the right wing. These Republican critics, however, spoke with many tongues. Some, such as Herbert Hoover, seemed to advocate a return to isolationism; others, like Robert Taft, demanded a curious amalgam of toughness and thrift; yet others, like General MacArthur, appeared to desire an outright war with China, if not Russia. Of these three voices, that of MacArthur was perhaps the most grating and frightening. Praise is due to President Truman and to his Secretaries of State, particularly Dean Acheson, for resisting the brassy clamour of public opinion, which has always been a disturbing factor in the formation of American foreign policy. As Kennan put it, ". . . a good deal of our trouble seems to have stemmed from the extent to which the executive has felt itself beholden to short-term trends of public opinion in the country and from what we might call the erratic and subjective nature of public reaction to foreign-policy questions. I would like to emphasize that I do not consider public reaction to foreign policy questions to be erratic and undependable over the long term".[1]

But with their increasing political maturity, the American people were better equipped to distinguish the permanent from the ephemeral in foreign affairs, and a substantial majority of them seem, according to the public opinion polls, to have supported the policy of the Administration. Great credit is due to them for this, particularly after the Korean casualty lists began to pour steadily in, since a policy of containment stretching over years, and perhaps even decades, is one singularly unsuited to the character or traditions of the American people. Impatient in their zeal for accomplishment, they have, in the words of General Marshall, a "tendency to rush from pessimism to jubilant optimism", and he felt it necessary to caution his countrymen in 1950 "that this is a time for calm determination, a strong resolution to do what seems wise to protect the future security of the free world. It is no time for violent emotions."[2] Their habit, as Kennan points out, of taking "legalistic-moralistic" views of foreign problems and of expecting sweeping and absolute victories in their wars makes moderation doubly hard for them. "Behind all this, of course, lies the American assumption that the things for which other peoples in this world are apt to contend are for the most part neither creditable nor important and might justly be expected to take second place behind the desirability of an orderly world, untroubled by international violence."[3] In the case of Russia this assumption was justified, and this made it all

[1] Kennan, p. 93.

[2] Q. R. Payne, *General Marshall* (London, 1952), p. 311.   [3] Kennan, p. 96.

the more difficult for the Americans to restrain their instinct to adopt a policy of "Thorough". Yet most of them did so, and there can be no doubt that a large part of the Republican Party must be included in their number. Despite a few disquieting pronouncements by General Eisenhower during the course of the Presidential campaign of 1952, there is solid ground for the belief that they will continue so to do.

That they should do so is of the greatest importance to the future of Anglo-American relations, for it is a most interesting fact that the foreign policy of the Administration very probably met with more whole-hearted and widespread approval in Britain than in the United States. It was subjected to very much the same criticism by the British left wing as by the followers of Wallace, but, though the Bevanites are perhaps stronger relatively than their American counterparts, this is easily outweighed by the almost entire absence in Britain of a right wing belligerence to match that of the Chicago *Tribune*. This is perhaps partly to be explained by the enlightenment of the Conservative Party, and partly by the twentieth century distaste of most Britons for political extremes, but most of all it was the result of a great maturity in foreign affairs and a realization of the extreme vulnerability of Britain in another war. General Marshall told Secretary Forrestal in 1948 that Foreign Secretary Bevin, a by no means pusillanimous character, kept referring constantly to the fact that the British "were in the front line";[1] and later, expressing British alarm lest they should be dragged into a world war by extremists in the United States, Arnold Toynbee was credited with coining the phrase, "No annihilation without representation."

It was, indeed, only of aberrations from Administration policy that Britain was afraid; with that actual policy they were in very substantial agreement. Their haunting fear was that an extreme tide of opinion from the Right would sweep America into provocative acts which might produce war. This seemed more likely to them than in fact it was, because they forgot, or never knew, that overstatement is as much an American characteristic as understatement is a British, and that a moderate policy in the great Republic can only be reached by the tension of vociferous and violent-seeming opposites. But in the event, as *The Economist* wrote in June, 1951, "the American foreign policy of the last four years seems to have been intelligent, consistent, courageous and in a high degree successful. . . . Can anybody reasonably doubt that, if similar courage had been shown in the years between

[1] Q. Forrestal, p. 489.

899

1933 and 1939, Hitler's war would never have happened?" The whole free world has played its part in this policy, "but the ideas, the money and the resolution have come from the Americans, and if the chances of avoiding war are greater today than they were in, say, 1938, it is to the American Administration that the major credit belongs."[1]

To such a foreign policy Great Britain found it on the whole easy to conform, but there was in fact virtually no alternative to British conformity. Nothing shows more clearly the complete reversal of the relationship between the two powers since 1783 than this necessity of British compliance, which arose from the fundamental realities of American power; there are, indeed, few clearer illustrations in history of the fact that he who pays the piper calls the tune. So much had this become the case during the war itself that McNeill can write:

> The Anglo-American success depended at bottom on the fact that the British Government *had* to agree with the Americans, and, realizing their position, yielded gracefully before the dispute had gone so far as to disturb day-to-day administrative co-ordination between the two Governments. The British voice was heard on all critical occasions, and sometimes it modified the Americans' decisions; but there was always an ultimate authority whose decision was binding. When the leaders of the American Government . . . said yes or no, action was undertaken accordingly; but the British yes and no was always subject to review.
>
> This did not result from a voluntary abdication on Churchill's part. He simply recognized that, if he insisted upon a course of action distasteful to the United States Government, the Americans could always afford, however reluctantly, to quarrel openly with him, and then bring economic pressure to bear against which no British Government could stand.[2]

The post-war situation is not exactly similar, because the facts of international power are in some respects less obvious, but fundamentally the moral is the same.

What is more, ideas of a neutral Third Force led by Britain are not only visionary but highly dangerous; serious divergence from American policy would necessarily imply the possibility of antagonism and hence of war, and in the face of American sea and air power such a contingency would mean inevitable, rapid and utter defeat for the island people of Britain. The theme of Western policy must now be principally of American formulation and execution. It is the welcome fruit of long years of co-operation that Britain is on the whole and in broad outline remark-

[1] Q. Rovere and Schlesinger, pp. 245-6.   [2] McNeill, p. 756.

ably ready to accept this fact; as Churchill declared in October, 1952, "the foundation of [British] foreign policy is a true and honourable comradeship with the United States."[1] Nevertheless, it was not always easy upon every particular occasion for the British people to accept this subordinate role, and there were from time to time gusts of popular passion, which were usually treated with sympathy by Americans. As General Eisenhower, with his experience of Britain as well as with his intuitive understanding of such issues, said, in the Presidential campaign of 1952, "With Britain, we must remember that it has demanded both great dignity and great wisdom for a proud nation to adjust so swiftly to its recent loss of financial and imperial strength".[2]

Such a popular squall blew up in Britain in 1951 over the appointment of an American as Supreme Commander of the naval forces of NATO in the Atlantic, and it provides an excellent illustration of the state of the Anglo-American relationship. There can be no doubt that the reason for the popular outcry was the injury to the maritime pride of the British people, bred as they still had been on the doctrine that Britannia rules the waves. We have seen how reluctant were many of them to accept American naval equality in the Treaty of Washington after World War I, but how in the end they accepted it with a good grace. In World War II the British Navy was hugely outstripped by the American, and the British Government halted its programme of capital ship construction in the interests of unity and economy of effort; when peace came, the disparity between the two forces was very considerable, and, in her dire economic straits, there was no longer any hope of Britain rivalling America as a naval power. Indeed, the U.S. Navy is now not only the largest peacetime fleet ever maintained by any power but also as large as all the other navies of the world put together. Yet, as was the case after the first war, British public opinion had hardly become aware of it, and when the appointment of an American Admiral to command the seas almost to Britain's very coastline brought it dramatically home, it was a severe shock. The agreement was made by the Labour Government and was heavily criticized by the Opposition, but, just after the appointment was announced, the Conservatives returned to power. Churchill then announced his intention of taking up the matter with Washington, and though he declared, "It is not a question of national pride but of a good working arrangement . . .",[3] this was not in fact the way it affected the people at large.

[1] *Time*, 20 October, 1952, p. 23.   [2] *Time*, 27 October, 1952, p. 10.
[3] *Current Developments in United States Foreign Policy*, December, 1951, p. 21.

With the passage of time, however, passions cooled, and English public opinion was ready to accept the arrangements made during Churchill's visit to the United States in January, 1952. The terms of the communiqué were highly enlightening:

> The President and the Prime Minister with their advisors have had several discussions relating to the arrangements about the Atlantic command. . . . As a result . . . they agreed that His Majesty's Government and the United States Government would recommend to NATO certain alterations in the arrangements. . . . These changes, however, do not go the full way to meet the Prime Minister's objections to the original arrangements. Nevertheless the Prime Minister, while not withdrawing his objections, expressed his readiness to allow the appointment of . . . [an American] Supreme Commander to go forward.[1]

An American was then appointed, with a British Deputy and with a Briton as Commander-in-Chief of the Eastern Atlantic. Churchill reported to the House of Commons that he had agreed to the appointment only in the interests of unity. He was very deeply concerned that "the British Admiralty should have complete control and direction of the reception area of transatlantic convoys and shipping. This . . . is . . . the foundation of the process by which 50 million people in the British Isles have been kept alive in the teeth of the U-boat menace,"[2] and, in view of this fact, the arrangements made are a singular proof of the extent to which Britain's destiny lies in the palm of America's hand. They also show that, though British influence in Washington is considerable, the United States has inevitably and finally assumed the leadership, and that, when she is irrevocably determined to advance, Britain must follow.

Yet such is the nature of the relationship that the British contribution to the common policy is by no means negligible. Both peoples display a readiness to compromise which has roots deep in their own democratic experience, as well as in the long history of Anglo-American arbitrations and agreements. To the credit of the British people, they accept the role of junior partner with as little chagrin as possible: to the credit of the American people, they are ready to accept British suggestions and take heed of British opinions, despite their inherent mistrust of anything that looks like following a British lead. One irate American, for instance, cabled a member of Congress after the President's dismissal of General MacArthur: "This is another sellout of our country

---

[1] Q. *Current Developments*, January, 1952, p. 26.

[2] *Current Developments*, December, 1951, p. 21.

to those dirty Britons who run the Far East while our sons give up their lives for British domination and dirty dollars."[1] Despite such residual Anglophobia as this, the Administration was never unwilling to consider British ideas, and, indeed, it is an interesting feature of the period that a number of its major developments were based upon notions first put forward by the British. One instance was the North Atlantic Pact, which seems to have originated, along with a similar idea for the Mediterranean, in proposals made by Ernest Bevin in March, 1948. Churchill could say on 6 November, 1951, of the warm relationship with the United States:

> I am anxious that Britain should also play her full part, and, gathering all her Commonwealth around her, present a revival of her former influence and initiative among the Allied Powers, and indeed among all Powers. It must not be forgotten that under the late Government we took peculiar risks in providing the principal atomic base for the United States in East Anglia, and that, in consequence, we placed ourselves in the very forefront of Soviet antagonism. We have therefore every need and every right to seek and receive the fullest consideration from Americans for our point of view and I feel sure this will not be denied us.[2]

Nor did the United States flinch from the difficulties which she found to be inherent in a position of world leadership; as Britain was well aware in the nineteenth century, the paramount power automatically becomes the target for the jibes of all the rest. One American journal put it, "Twisting the lion's tail used to be diplomacy's favourite parlor game. The same rules still apply, but now it is known as plucking the eagle's feathers."[3] But in major matters as well as minor, and above all in the supreme test of the Korean War, America played on the whole a part worthy of respect and admiration, a fact to which British opinion was not insensitive. In the words, once more, of Churchill, in November, 1951:

> Britain and the Commonwealth and Empire, still centring upon our island, are woven by ever-growing ties of strength and comprehension of common need and self-preservation to the great republic across the Atlantic Ocean. The sacrifices and exertions which the United States is making to deter, and if possible prevent, Communist aggression from making further inroads upon the free world are the main foundations

[1] Q. Rovere and Schlesinger, p. 8.
[2] *Current Developments,* November, 1951, p. 7.
[3] *Time,* 20 October, 1952, p. 20.

of peace. . . . I feel deep gratitude towards our great American ally. They have risen to the leadership of the world without any other ambition but to serve its highest causes faithfully.[1]

III

BUT despite the bed-rock soundness of the friendship, there were a goodly number of Anglo-American troubles in the years between the war and the end of 1952. The first of these was thrust suddenly before the eye of the public within seven days of the Japanese surrender, when a White House press release of 21 August, 1945, announced that all Lend-Lease operations would be immediately discontinued; they did in fact terminate on America's official VJ-Day, 2 September. That some such abrupt action was possible might perhaps have been guessed from the similar way in which Lend-Lease aid to Russia had been promptly terminated at the end of the European war, as well as by the proviso inserted, in April, 1945, by Congress, into the renewed Lend-Lease Act, that it should not be construed to authorize any post-war relief or reconstruction agreement. But when it was now suddenly and universally applied, there was surprise almost everywhere except the United States. The first, and very natural, American reaction was approval of President Truman's hard-headed determination to cease the lavish subsidies of war now that peace had returned, but it seems probable that this precipitate course was a fundamental error, arising from lack of forethought and of understanding of the international scene. In an immediate sense any such abrupt stoppage of so vast a flow of goods in the channels of trade was bound to cause dislocation and involve suffering, but in long terms also it was a mistake which had to be painfully rectified later. To this fact the history of the Anglo-American loan and the Marshall Plan bear eloquent witness.

To Britain the shock of sudden foreclosure was particularly sharp, since the peculiar circumstances of her economic situation rendered her extremely vulnerable to any abrupt change in the pattern of international trade, let alone one in which she had a very direct and immediate interest. The extent of this interest was that the British Commonwealth had received during the war two-thirds of all Lend-Lease, while the United Kingdom was directly dependent upon Lend-Lease supplies of food and essential materials, when the war ended, to the approximate annual value of $2,000 million. But this

[1] *Current Developments*, November, 1951, p. 7.

gives only a superficial idea of the economic difficulties of Britain at this time, for they had roots deep in her economic history and in the effects of two world wars.

For most of the nineteenth century the United States had remained within the orbit of the British economy, but inevitably and progressively during the twentieth their roles had become reversed and there had been an increasing tendency for Britain to fall, in common with many other powers, within the gravitational field of the vast American economy. Britain's position, however, was peculiar, just because she had herself once been the dominant national economic force; as the undisputed leader of the world industrial revolution during its dramatic acceleration in the early nineteenth century, she had become the greatest trader and industrialist in the world, as well as the foremost banker. In this unique position she had expanded rapidly in population and in wealth—all the more rapidly because she had, after the first quarter of the century, pursued an ever more unrestricted policy of free trade. She became the workshop of the world, by taking singular advantage of her industrial lead and of her corresponding economic specialization, though by lavish exports of capital she assisted those economic developments in other lands, particularly the United States, which were in the end to undermine her unique position.

For not only was there natural competition arising elsewhere in Britain's special fields of industrial activity, but, in addition, other nations were by no means content to accept British industrial pre-eminence indefinitely, for political if not for economic reasons, and, by the twentieth century, industrial protection by high tariffs, directed primarily at British goods, had become the rule rather than the exception among the economically advanced nations. This meant for Britain increasing difficulty in exporting sufficient goods to meet the bill for her essential imports, a bill which was inevitably large in view of the size to which her population had swollen and the standard of living to which they were accustomed. The problem was made more acute by the fact that, through a blend of geographical and political circumstances, the rival nations were far richer in resources and far larger in numbers than the United Kingdom—Germany and, above all, the United States are the outstanding examples. This disadvantage was, however, to a considerable degree offset by the existence of the British Empire and Commonwealth, and goes far to account for the revival of imperialism in the late nineteenth century and for the retention of the British colonial system. Though these developments had been foreshadowed for some time, they were kept in check in the early

905

years of the twentieth century, and only became of compelling urgency in the inter-war years.

Yet, even after 1918 Britain was able to counter them without any decline, indeed with a slight rise, in her standard of life, partly by living upon the income derived from her overseas investments, and partly by ingenious, skilful and industrious services to other nations in such fields as shipping and insurance. For a nation to be outclassed in size is by no means necessarily for it to be poor, as the brilliant example of Switzerland shows, while in an ordered world with an expanding flow of trade Britain might with relative ease have kept her place, even if she did not continue to grow as markedly in greatness and prestige. But she was, probably to an extent unprecedented in human history, dependent upon the free flow of international trade, not merely for her prosperity but for her very life. The nineteenth century was, all things considered, an extraordinarily peaceful age, partly due to Britain's interest in the preservation of peace and her power to do something to ensure it; but, through causes largely beyond her control, the twentieth century was not. In the terrible wars by which it was convulsed, Britain, though she emerged a victor, stood to lose far more economically than any other power. It became clear, for instance, that her navy was by itself no longer adequate to keep her vital sea lines open, though by a combination of supreme good fortune and great good management, which we have watched at work, it was reinforced by the overwhelming strength of the United States. In the two world wars she was engaged as an active belligerent almost exactly twice as long as her great partner, and in some respects she emerged with her economy dramatically weakened. But she had no alternative save to fight. Not for her, even suppose she had desired it, the neutrality of a Switzerland or a Sweden; her traditions as a great power, her crucial position as the fortress of the free world, her sense of her duty to herself and to mankind, all made it unthinkable. Thus she alone of all the victorious powers remained in both wars and unconquered from beginning to end. From the first one she emerged shaken, but able to rebuild something like her old way of life in the years from 1919 to 1939. In 1945 she had shed far less of her blood, but expended much more of her wealth, and her position as far as international trade was concerned was very grave.

Apart from the war on and over the seas, she had sustained great physical losses at home by air raids, and was faced with formidable reconstruction costs. She had by June, 1945, sold a very substantial portion of her foreign investments; exact estimates of the quantity differ widely. It had been commonly accepted since the war that $4½ billion* were sold, most of them in the United States and Canada, but A. R. Conan in his book published in 1952, *The Sterling Area,* takes a much more conservative view.† He estimates that $726 million of Canadian investments were sold between 1939 and 1945, leaving $1¾ billion in the latter year. His American estimates are more complicated. About $2 billion of American securities were held by Britain in 1939. He believes that $600 million of these had actually been liquidated by 1942, and that a much larger quantity had been pledged, but that it had probably not been necessary actually to sell the latter once Lend-Lease had begun to operate. It is not possible to be certain of this, since later figures have not been published in detail, but strong evidence exists in support of it, including the total figure of £203 million known to have been sold during the whole war. With the rise of prices in America the value of such holdings would have increased substantially, but even so it is somewhat surprising to find that in 1949 the Administration valued the long term investments of the United Kingdom in the United States at $2 billion, and that the Bank of England estimate of interest for them in 1948 was actually higher than that of 1938.

According to his calculations, therefore, the total sold in North America might be approximately $1½ billion, most of which loss had been made up by 1949-50. Conan in fact estimates that our investments in the United States in 1949-50 were the same, £500 million, as in 1939, and those in Canada £500 million instead of £600 million. Even more startling is his conclusion that our total investments overseas in all areas amounted to about £4,000 million as opposed to only £4,500 million before the war. Indeed, his figures lead him to the conclusion that for the years 1946-50, "the United Kingdom remained a creditor in the sense that it possessed a net income on investment account." But "[o]n capital account . . . the United Kingdom (notwithstanding its creditor position on investment income account) appears to be a net debtor", for, whereas before the war she was a creditor to the extent of £5,300 million and a debtor to the extent of only £1,300 million, in 1950 the figures were £6,000 million and £6,800 million respectively. This tallies with other estimates of an increased indebtedness of $14 billion, and is obviously of the greatest importance, despite

*The term *billion* is used throughout in the American meaning of *one thousand million.*

†I am much indebted to him, for I have followed his figures closely, although I have also quoted some American official figures for comparative purposes. For approximate exchange conversion rates see p. 44 note.

the fact, which Conan emphasizes, that the net indebtedness is only £800 million, a sum less than the current net indebtedness of Canada. The debts were mostly in the form of the blocked sterling balances, held in London, of the so-called Sterling Area.

Conan's study alters the balance of economic analysis of Britain's difficulties since the war. It does not make clear how much the situation in 1950 was the result of improvements since 1945, when the British condition was obviously exceedingly poor; but it does seem to indicate that Britain's long term balance of payments problem owes more to an unfavourable movement in the terms of trade, chiefly a rise in the price of primary products (which was bad for a nation like Britain, and which was the very reverse of the trend in the thirties which had "masked" the "deterioration in the international economic position of the United Kingdom[1]) than to inflationary pressures at home or to the costs of the war. It also indicates that loss of overseas investments has been less important than has been thought since the war, and that services like shipping have not declined as much as was believed, shipping income being greater in 1950 than in 1938. It indicates, too, that the dollar problem has become increasingly a problem for the Sterling Area as a whole, and one which is not caused by, nor can be solved by, Britain alone. In other words, it reduces, but by no means destroys, the importance of certain factors which can be directly ascribed to the war. It should, though, be noted that what appears to Conan the most serious factor in the situation, the vast increase in our Government expenditure overseas, can in a sense be called a legacy of the war. The book does not, however, give any grounds for complacency, since Britain's balance of payments has only been maintained in the post-war years by the prodigious effort represented by a huge increase in exports and an import total which has never risen above 90 per cent of the pre-war level in terms of volume. Furthermore, certain fundamental factors in Britain's situation remain of undiminished importance, the loss of her industrial pre-eminence, her dependence on a steady flow of international trade, and the great growth of her foreign indebtedness.

And in 1945 Britain's position was peculiarly serious; her recovery since then has been greatly facilitated by that American aid which was intended for just such a purpose. Britain's shipping income in 1950 may have been bigger·than in 1938, but in 1945 she had lost one-third of her merchant fleet. The sudden impact of a world where the cost of imports had risen by 50 per cent, hitherto kept at arm's length by

[1] A. R. Conan, *The Sterling Area* (London, 1952), pp. 6, 142, 168.

Lend-Lease, was shaking. These problems were of vital concern to the United States because, as President Roosevelt had said in 1944, "The real hub of the situation is to keep Britain from going into complete bankruptcy at the end of the war",[1] and because of the peculiar effect which Lend-Lease had had on the British economy during the war. With, on the whole, little thought for her economic future, Britain had unstintingly made what seemed the most efficient economic contribution to the common cause; equally unstintingly, the United States had poured forth abundant Lend-Lease aid. This was well enough in the war, but it did so happen that, as Britain was the island-base of the continental invasion, a very high proportion of her resources were consumed at home by her Allies as well as herself; the result was that her exports fell 31 per cent by volume and 55 per cent by value after 1938. A very substantial drop must have occurred under any circumstances, but it did also happen that American export trade—as was necessary and proper—did not suffer any corresponding diminution. Britain was, therefore, in 1945, in a very weak position, particularly relative to the United States, in international trade; exactly how weak is shown by her annual trade deficit of £918 million for 1942-4. Yet of all powers in the world she was the most dependent upon that trade for her livelihood, and she was faced with the necessity for something like a 175 per cent increase in her total exports, merely in order to continue to exist without a serious drop in her standard of living. This desperate, though insufficiently dramatic, situation was thrust suddenly to the forefront of affairs by the abrupt end of Lend-Lease, but it was to remain a fundamental fact in Anglo-American relations from that day forward.

The unexpected ending of the Japanese war had forced upon the British, as Lord Keynes said, "the prospect of just that interregnum which we had hoped to avoid",[2] for they had initiated discussions which envisaged the orderly tapering-off of Lend-Lease, and had actually arranged for a British mission, headed by Lord Halifax and Lord Keynes, to go to Washington in September. The termination of Lend-Lease, which forestalled them, was greeted with dismay in London; Prime Minister Attlee said that it placed Britain in a "very serious financial position", and Churchill called it "very grave and disquieting news."[3] Attlee's speech to the Commons explained that, while Britain

[1] Q. Byrnes, p. 185.
[2] Q. J. C. Campbell (Editor), *The United States in World Affairs 1945-7* (Council on Foreign Relations), (London, 1947), p. 359.
[3] *The World Almanac, 1946*, pp. 95-6.

had not expected it to "continue for any length of time after the defeat of Japan", she had hoped for "consultation and prior discussion of the difficult problems involved in the disappearance of a system of so great a range and complication."[1]

The shock to British public opinion, which felt that it deserved more considerate treatment from its ally, was alleviated by President Truman's subsequent suggestion of a long-term, low interest credit. Support for this suggestion in America grew as the effects of the President's sudden action were more widely appreciated, but it is doubtful whether it ever had the support of a substantial majority. Many Americans felt that the offer of goods already "in the pipe line" on reasonable terms, as well as of a low-interest loan, more than fulfilled their moral obligations, while the actual abruptness of the action was more in conformity with American economic practice and habit than with the cautious proclivity towards planning which was increasingly in the ascendent in British economic life. Discussions began on all aspects of the economic relationship on 14 September and were protracted for three long months. Eventually, on 6 December, three separate conventions were announced. The first agreed on the general terms for a final settlement of Lend-Lease; the second was a financial and trade agreement, granting a loan to Britain and containing a number of commercial provisions; the third was a statement, jointly sponsoring an American document, which set forth certain proposals for consideration by an international conference on trade and employment.

The first agreement aroused the least interest, being overshadowed by the others, but it did contain a decision of markedly beneficial effect upon Anglo-American relations. Had it stood by itself, without the complications arising from Britain's economic difficulties, it would have formed a fitting conclusion to the "most unsordid act in history." It laid down $650 million as the maximum British indebtedness for Lend-Lease property, which it had received and had not yet consumed, or which it was still to receive; the United States could use $50 million of this in sterling for mutually agreed projects. There was a full balancing off of Reverse Lend-Lease in the implementing agreements, which completed the transactions and were signed in March, 1946. The settlement of the whole Lend-Lease question was to be "complete and final",[2] and was based on the writing-off of all goods used up or destroyed in the war. This banished any possibility that the old war debt spectre might once more haunt the international scene. Britain had always

[1] Q. U.S.W.A., 1945-7, p. 344.

[2] *Documents on American Foreign Relations*, VIII, p. 132.

thought of the debts of the first war fundamentally in terms of equity, as a contribution that America might freely have made to what was in the end the common cause. America had never accepted this view, but had thought of them as a matter of business; and signs of the same attitude were not altogether lacking in 1945. As Keynes put it, "Our American friends were interested not in our wounds . . . but in our convalescence."[1] The final settlement abolished, at a blow and irrevocably, the sum of approximately $25 billion of Lend-Lease granted to Britain during the war. When one reflects how seldom international affairs lend themselves to solutions morally and emotionally satisfying to all parties, one must account this a blessing. When one considers how loose was much of the original thinking about Lend-Lease, with its talk of removing the dollar sign and of borrowing the hoses of neighbours until the fire should be extinguished—there was even chat about getting back a new hose if the old one was destroyed or damaged—one must, even taking account of America's subsequent entry into the war, express mild surprise that this much of an advance had been made since 1919.

But public attention, particularly in Britain, was too exclusively focused on the loan agreement to notice the negative benefits of the Lend-Lease settlement, and it was on this question that most of the protracted negotiations were spent. On the one hand, the British would have liked an outright gift, but really hoped for an interest-free loan; on the other hand, some sections of American opinion desired a substantial *quid pro quo*, in the form of such things as defence bases and special treatment for American enterprises in the British Commonwealth, and regretted that a loan was finally made below the rate charged on Export-Import Bank loans. From these contrasted and extreme attitudes a compromise emerged, by which the United States granted Britain a line of credit of $3¾ billion, drawable to the end of 1951, and repayable in fifty equal annual instalments beginning in that year, with interest at 2 per cent on the credit outstanding. The $650 million Lend-Lease sum was added to this on the same terms. The British had hoped for $5 billion, at which they estimated their balance of payments deficit over the next few years, and Keynes declared that he would never cease to regret that it was not an interest-free loan. (With the addition of a subsequent Canadian loan of $1¼ billion, the total received by Britain began to approach this figure.) The Administration pointed out, however, that it was currently granting loans to other needy nations at the usual interest rate of 2⅜ per cent. Special arrange-

[1] Q. U.S.W.A., 1945-7, p. 365.

ments were made for the waiving of interest by the United States in any year when Britain was in serious balance of payments difficulties, though there was no waiver on principal. These were the terms of the loan itself, but the agreement by no means stopped here, for from the beginning of negotiations the Americans had made it clear that they were determined to insist in return on important British pledges to move in the direction of free exchanges and freer trade, particularly with regard to imperial preference and the sterling bloc. At this point a glance backwards is necessary.

We have observed that the Anglo-American trade agreement of 1938 was in conformity with the New Deal policy of opening up the channels of international trade, but that it ran counter to the British trend towards special, often bilateral, trade arrangements. Nevertheless, as we have also seen, it was finally signed by Britain, largely for political reasons. We have taken note, too, of the continued American determination to persist in their policy at the time of the Atlantic Charter, and the Lend-Lease agreement of 1942, which pledged Britain to conversations designed for the elimination of all forms of discriminatory treatment in international commerce. Considerable pressure had been brought to bear by the State Department at the time to get the British Government to consent, and they were equally determined now.

Yet it would be wrong to infer that the British were reluctant converts to the promotion of multilateral trade; it appears more true to say that at some time during the war British official opinion reversed its pre-war trend towards restrictive practices, and embraced once more the doctrine of increasingly free trade, on the ground that Britain's need to export on an unprecedented scale could most easily be fulfilled in an expanding international commerce. The reasons for American advocacy of the doctrine of freeing trade were even simpler to comprehend, for, as the dominant industrial power, her interest, like that of Britain a century before, lay patently in the opening up of world markets to her exports. But, though there was thus apparently general agreement in principle, there were a number of practical misgivings on both sides.

As Ambassador Harriman said in 1946, "through the British Government there run these two main notes: a passionate desire for military and diplomatic co-operation with the U.S. coupled with the fear of our economic power. The British are desperately afraid of another U.S. depression, which they think might lead to world disaster."[1] American practices with regard to her own tariffs made the British incline to

---

[1] Q. Forrestal, p. 185.

scepticism when the United States pressed for a freeing of international trade. The Americans, for their part, regarded the system of imperial preference as a hindrance to multilateral trade, and when the British replied by pointing to American tariffs, were irritated at this British habit of claiming that their Empire was a single unit for these economic purposes, while insisting that its members were politically quite independent and entitled, for example, to separate representation in the United Nations; certainly this had the appearance of both eating and having one's cake.

The general Anglo-American agreement in principle found expression in the third document, the joint statement approving the American proposals for a conference to effect the freeing of international trade, but the differences over practical measures are clearly indicated by the clauses of the loan agreement dealing with broad financial and commercial questions, and, even more clearly, by the negotiations which led up to them.

The first point of attack by the Americans had been the blocked sterling balances in London, which were three times the size of the American loan and which constituted an obstacle to multilateral trade. The Administration felt that these countries should contribute to British recovery by accepting sharp reductions, as some compensation for the wiping off of Lend-Lease, but Britain, though naturally enough she did not object to this idea, pointed out that most of the sterling area countries had advanced almost all of their external resources and could not trade freely until the British Government felt strong enough to release some of these resources in the form of purchasing power. A clause in the agreement expressed the British intention to reach an early settlement of the whole question with the governments concerned, and pledged her to make freely convertible any blocked balances she released after the agreement had been in effect a year. After even sharper bargaining, the British accepted some strict limitations on her use of exchange controls, including an immediate renunciation of them in current transactions with America, and a renunciation of them within one year on all current transactions. The implementation of these American demands was not in practice to prove possible. The British Government also accepted some restrictions on import arrangements of a discriminatory character directed against American goods. All these provisions were regarded as "advance instalments on the liberal world trade policy advocated by the United States"[1] and were accepted by Britain in the hope that they would "put

[1] U.S.W.A., 1945-7, p. 362.

913

an end to the fear of an economically divided world" and make possible "throughout the world, the expansion of employment and of the production, exchange, and consumption of goods".[1]

Despite this hope there were serious doubts in the minds of some British leaders; a number of Tories, aroused by L. S. Amery, opposed acceptance of what they considered a hard and dangerous bargain, and many in both parties were lukewarm. Churchill felt strongly that a government under Conservative leadership could have got much better terms than the Socialists, whose economic ideas were mistrusted in Washington. Nevertheless, the agreement was accepted by the Commons, within two weeks of its signature on 6 December by 345 votes to 98, there being a large number of Tory abstentions; people felt for the most part that there was no reasonable alternative. The pace of American acceptance was a great deal more leisurely, so that by the time the President signed the bill on 15 July, 1946, Britain's difficulties had grown, while the American inflation had substantially reduced the value of the loan. This unprecedented peace-time loan to a foreign power was opposed on many grounds, including the unpopularity of Britain's Palestine policy, the burden on the American economy, and the lack of a satisfactory *quid pro quo*. The Administration argued for it on the ground that America's future economic development would be aided by it; it "is not," said Dean Acheson, "a reward for an ally. . . . It is not a pension, gift, or handout of any description whatever. It is an investment in the future."[2] In due course it passed both the Senate and the House, in its entirety, by reasonable margins.

It is not without significance that, though the Administration avoided using the argument, many supporters of the bill pointed out the need to strengthen Britain against Russia. All the main votes were taken after Churchill's Fulton speech, and tension in Europe was growing fast. Senator Barkley said, "I do not desire, for myself or for my country, to take a position that will drive our ally into arms into which we do not want her to be folded." Speaker Rayburn said, "I do not want . . . England . . . pushed further into and toward an ideology that I despise. I fear if we do not co-operate with this great natural ally of ours, that is what will happen. If we are not allied with the great British democracy, I fear somebody will be and God pity us when we have no ally across the Atlantic Ocean, and God pity them, too."[3] In this action of tendering a loan, which, for all the feeling in Britain that it was a tight-fisted gesture, contrasted very favourably with that of the Congress twenty-

[1] *Documents on American Foreign Relations*, VIII, p. 650.
[2] Q. U.S.W.A., 1945-7, p. 365.   [3] Q. ibid, pp. 368-9.

five years earlier, the American motive was, in the first instance, economic; some Americans were anxious to repay what they considered a great moral debt to Britain for her stand in 1940, but the Administration's appeal to self-interest was its most powerful argument. By the time the debate drew to its close, the fear of Russia was becoming increasingly important as a factor in the decision of the people. In due time it was to dominate all other considerations and to surpass even Britain's economic plight as the controlling force in Anglo-American relations.

IV

BUT for the moment another problem, inherently much less important to the relationship, was proving the most intractable one between the two peoples, that of Palestine. Its importance lay in the vital strategic and political significance of the whole Middle East, which was in a ferment of newly awakened nationalism, that of the Jews being the most forceful; its difficulty lay, from the point of view of Anglo-American relations, in the very powerful part played by Zionist interests in American politics, and in President Truman's extreme susceptibility to pressure from such interests. These things, combined with the reluctance of the United States to become involved in the practical settlement of the question, and with the absolute determination of the British not to be left holding this most obstreperous and expensive baby any longer, served to obscure the fundamental Anglo-American identity of interest in the Middle East. The disagreements did not cease with the subsidence of the Palestine question, and signs of them can still be discerned. They arose essentially from sharp disagreements between the two nations as to how to achieve their common object, which must be the denial of the Middle East to unfriendly powers, and most particularly to Russia, for whom any direct access to the Mediterranean, or the Persian Gulf and Indian Ocean, would be an immense strategic gain. The attainment of its corollary, the establishment of stable and friendly governments in the area, gave grounds, however, for serious divergences of Anglo-American opinion, though none was so grave as that over Palestine.

With that characteristic and peculiar tragedy which has pursued, or been drawn to, the Jewish people since the Diaspora, the Palestine problem had been a cause of international strife from the moment of its creation by the founding of the movement for a Jewish National Home in the Holy Land. In one of the most troublesome decisions ever made

915

by a British Government, the Balfour Declaration of World War I had sponsored this cause, though at the same time this same Government had become responsible for virtually contradictory promises to the Arab peoples as to the destiny of the land which they had helped to wrest from the Turks. The immigration of Jews between the wars had resulted in increasing and fanatical Arab hatred of what they regarded as a new Western imperialism, and in 1936 there broke out what was virtually a rebellion against the Mandatory Power. But Britain's position was not disinterested, for she was vitally concerned (and very wisely as World War II proved) in the military security of the Middle East. Cyprus was British and she had very special military and political relationships with Egypt and the Sudan, as well as other Middle Eastern powers, such as Iraq and Transjordan, all of which were of great importance as lying upon her main imperial life-line. Added to this was the fact that the vast bulk of the oil upon which her navy and air force increasingly depended was drawn from the great oilfields in this area, which were chiefly exploited and owned by British companies. As the second war approached Britain became increasingly conscious of the need to conciliate the Arabs, and abandoned a plan for the partition of Palestine into Jewish and Arab states, which she had put forward in 1937, because it was unpopular with them. In 1939 a new proposal was published, which limited Jewish immigration, and which envisaged the stabilisation of the situation in five years and the independence of a Palestine still predominantly Arab in ten years. This was a staggering blow to the hopes of certain sections of World Zionism for an independent Jewish state.

The war aggravated the situation by underlining Britain's need of Arab friendship and by awakening an Arab nationalism which showed some signs of a desire for Arab unity in the Middle East; Britain decided, probably wisely, to encourage this Arab League in order to ensure its friendliness. On the other hand, the appalling fate of the Jews in Hitler's Europe aroused Jewish determination to attain an independent Israel to fresh intensity, and greatly strengthened the hand of the World Zionist Organization. Partly owing to Jewish disillusion with British policy and partly to the natural shift of world power, the chief centre of Zionism moved during the war from London to New York. At the same time America became increasingly conscious of the whole problem. Feeling for Zionism was very marked in the United States, not merely because of its many Jews, but also because it appealed to the humanitarian and liberal beliefs of the American people at large. On the other hand, the State and Defence Departments were increasingly conscious of the need for friendly and stable powers in the Middle East, not only because of the potential Russian threat, which became steadily greater after the war, but also because of America's need for Middle Eastern oil. So enormous is American oil consumption that her needs are outstripping even her own vast supplies; Secretary Forrestal said early in 1948 "that unless we had access to Middle Eastern oil, American motor-car companies would have to design a four-cylinder motor-car sometime within the next five years."[1] Forrestal was indeed acutely conscious of the importance of the Middle East to the United States, and fought a long and unsuccessful battle with his colleagues to induce them to keep the Palestine question "out of politics." He failed, and it seems fair to assume that he did so chiefly because of President Truman's instinctive reaction to the arguments of professional politicians, though the problem was rendered more difficult by popular American ignorance of the international issues involved. Truman's predecessor had, with characteristic caution, avoided any clearcut promises and decisions, but had shown himself aware of both the pro-Arab and pro-Jewish currents in American thought and feeling.

This was the situation at the end of the war, and it found Britain in a strong cross fire between the Arab League and the Zionist movement. She restricted immigration of Jews in accordance, broadly speaking, with the 1939 plan, which involved the forcible prevention of illegal immigration and the internment of the captured immigrants in Cyprus. This policy resulted in harrowing scenes in ships tightly packed with "illegal," but intensely pathetic, Jewish refugees from the Nazi holocaust, which made the worst possible reading in the newspapers of the United States. On the other hand, sympathy for them in Britain was heavily dampened, if not extinguished, by a growing Jewish campaign of terrorism in Palestine itself. At this juncture the British Labour party, which had, while in opposition, declared in favour of opening Palestine to the Jews, came to power, and President Truman took the opportunity of advocating in a letter to Prime Minister Attlee on 31 August, 1945, Britain's acceptance of a Jewish Agency petition, recently endorsed by the U.S. Representative on the Inter-governmental Committee on Refugees, for a hundred thousand additional permits for immigration. The Labour Government, however, sobered by power and exposed to the views of Britain's Arab allies, replied that the situation in Palestine made it impossible to comply, but invited the United States to co-operate in a joint inquiry into the whole question.

[1] Forrestal, p. 357.

This was a statesmanlike effort to arrive at a common Anglo-American attitude; it was also a deliberate attempt to get the United States to accompany her free criticism of British policy by some positive assumption of responsibility in Palestine. American acceptance of the proposal seemed to imply joint action in the future.

It is characteristic of the uncertainty of purpose common to both peoples, and illustrative of the fact that the question should never have placed the strain it did upon Anglo-American relations, that the committee of inquiry did not divide on national lines. Though accepting the majority view, one Englishman and one American, Richard Crossman and Bartley Crum, strongly favoured partition and not the federal or mixed state which the Committee actually recommended. The Committee also put forward certain concrete proposals, such as the admission of a hundred thousand Jews "as soon as possible."[1] The recommendations were moderate and sensible, but pleased neither Jews nor Arabs. They might, however, have had some chance of success if wholeheartedly backed by the United States as well as Britain, but, on the day the report was released, President Truman made a statement which in effect endorsed only those parts of it which were agreeable to the Zionists, and pointedly made no mention of American co-operation to put the plan into effect. This action vitiated the prospect of Anglo-American unity, which alone offered any real hope of a peaceful settlement. On the next day Attlee stated that Britain would not consider the report except as a whole, and warned that she would not take on single-handed the heavy commitments involved; Foreign Secretary Bevin, who felt very bitter about what he considered a mere domestic political manoeuvre, heightened feeling by declaring that the American insistence on a hundred thousand Jewish permits derived from the fact that "they did not want too many of them in New York."[2]

It was unfortunate that the known cleavage in the Committee should have given the President an opportunity for his action, but there seems little doubt that he would have rejected the sections unpleasing to the Zionists anyway. James Byrnes later said to Secretary Forrestal that the decision was chiefly due to two presidential advisers who "told the President that Dewey was about to come out with a statement favoring the Zionist position in Palestine, and that they had insisted that unless the President anticipated this movement New York State would be lost to the Democrats"[3] in the forthcoming elections. Such unfortunate intrusions of American racial or economic issues into American foreign policy are, happily, becoming increasingly rare, partly because their

---

[1] U.S.W.A., 1947-8, p. 314.   [2] Q. ibid, p. 316.   [3] Forrestal, p. 347.

political necessity and even wisdom are decreasingly certain; as one American writes, it was "never demonstrated that the votes of Jewish Americans could be delivered to one party or the other as a result of declarations on Palestine".[1] For this particular intrusion, Anglo-American relations would pay a high price in continued lack of harmony, and, it is perhaps fair to say, the Middle East an even higher one in blood. From the Committee's Report emerged only Britain's determination to wash her hands of the problem as soon as possible, and America's resolution not to be dragged into participation in an imbroglio, which she did not fully comprehend and which she was inclined to regard as deriving largely from Britain's imperialistic machinations in the area in earlier days.

The work of an Anglo-American committee, which sat in July, was rendered useless by the continued insistence of Britain that the findings of the joint inquiry must be implemented as a whole, and of the United States that the hundred thousand Jews should be admitted at once. The so-called Morrison Plan, for a federal Palestine with a large degree of Arab and Jewish autonomy, which was made public during the summer, was rejected outright by the Jews, even though it contained promise of admission of the hundred thousand immediately and of more later; neither the Jewish Agency nor the Palestine Arabs consented to send representatives to a conference in London in September, whose meetings made it clear that the other Arab states were also opposed to the Plan. They demanded a unitary state with no more than one-third of the total representation Jewish, whereas the Jews had already demanded an independent state in a part of Palestine sufficiently large and well sited to be viable.

Just at the opening of new British conversations with the Jewish Agency in October, President Truman issued a statement reiterating his demand for the hundred thousand permits and supporting the Jewish demand for a separate state. The British Government was not impressed by the President's accompanying offer to recommend to Congress the admission of a number of Jews, above the normal quota, to the United States, and to send economic aid to Palestine. The Arab states protested bitterly in Washington, but could not prevail against the competitive bidding between Truman and Dewey for the Jewish vote. Bevin had appealed that the President's statement be not made, and, when it was, directly accused the Administration of responsibility for the failure of the Anglo-Jewish conference. There is no doubt that this action of the President produced a swift deterioration of the

[1] U.S.W.A., 1947-8, p. 311.

Palestine situation, and that it was very influential in promoting the later unco-operativeness of the British Government with the United Nations.

After the rejection of a final British compromise plan by both Arabs and Jews in February, 1947, Britain in effect announced her intention of washing her hands of the problem by submitting it to the United Nations for a final solution. In this the Government had the full support of the Opposition, whose leader very significantly declared that it was essential, if the United States would not share in "all the blood-shed, odium, trouble and expense."[1] If joint Anglo-American action in Palestine be accepted as a desirable object, the blame for its failure up to this time must be borne primarily by President Truman.

After this date, however, the British Government must share the responsibility for its failure, for in what had all the appearance of a prolonged fit of "the sulks" they showed themselves needlessly unco-operative towards the United Nations in its efforts to solve the problem which they had placed before it. A special session of the General Assembly met in April, and a special committee was set up to consider the question. This committee in due course produced a plan for the partition of Palestine and the rapid termination of the Mandate. Britain supported the plan in the Assembly, and declared that she was only too willing to withdraw her troops and officials. She also declared, however, that she was only prepared to enforce a solution if it were acceptable to both Arabs and Jews, which was a very remote contingency, and that she was not prepared to "impose by force of arms" any other settlement "either alone or in a major role."[2]

It is quite understandable, and perhaps justifiable, that Britain should refuse any longer to accept sole responsibility; in her difficult economic position she could not continue to bear such a thankless burden alone. It was by no means so reasonable to refuse to play any but a very minor role; this was not sufficient to fulfil her obligations as a Great Power, which had once accepted the Mandate and which still claimed its privileges as a Great Power in the United Nations. More than that, to refuse to assist in the imposition of any solution by force was a confession of political bankruptcy; it left, in effect, no alternative but a war in Palestine, in which a great deal more blood might be shed. Her motive here unquestionably was that of not angering the Arabs, which was comprehensible, but it did carry, as the *Manchester Guardian* said,

[1] Q. ibid, pp. 319-20.

[2] *Documents on American Foreign Relations*, IX, p. 720.

920

caution to the point of cowardice: "The scruples of the British Government would be more impressive if it had not, during the past two years, been trying to impose on the Jews by force of arms a situation acceptable to the Arabs."[1]

The correctness of this analysis is rendered more likely by the Arab rejection and the Jewish acceptance, even though with reservations, of the committee's recommendations. The difficulty of the question, however, is shown by the fact that the American Government was well known to be divided on the desirability of accepting partition; the President favoured it, but the State and Defence Departments had very grave doubts of the wisdom of alienating the Arabs in this fashion. Eventually, the Administration came out for partition, offering economic aid but making no mention of contributing troops to enforce this solution of the problem.

At this juncture Britain made further announcements as to her intentions. First, she set her own time-table for evacuation of her officials and troops, which would be completed by 1 August, 1948. This was perhaps necessary as a guide to the Assembly and as a practical affirmation of her intention to put a definite term to her exclusive responsibility in the area; furthermore, it complied with the very first resolution of the Committee, that the mandate should be "terminated at the earliest practicable date."[2] Second, she declared that she would hand over to a U.N. Commission on that date, but would not transfer authority to Jewish or Arab Provisional Governments, and that British troops would maintain order in the areas they occupied, but would not be available to enforce the settlement on either party. Later she was to go much further, and to refuse even to hand over authority progressively to the Commission, thus setting it an impossible task, while making the whole process of effecting a peaceful settlement more difficult by subsequent changes in her own plans for evacuation. Britain was, in other words, determined, though accepting the Assembly's decision, to do nothing to assist in the enforcement of a plan so displeasing to the Arabs, even at the price of opening the way for a war between the Jews and the Arab League.

This decision it is hardly possible to defend in a power whose colonial empire rests largely on the justification that it prevents local disorder and makes possible orderly progress towards self-government. One can argue that war now and freedom now are better than peace now and freedom later, and such must be the justification of the perhaps

[1] Q. U.S.W.A., 1947-8, p. 326.

[2] *Documents on American Foreign Relations,* IX, p. 724.

half a million lives lost in the establishment of free India and Pakistan, but it is not an argument that comes well from the lips of those ruling what is still the greatest colonial empire in the world. The American delegate was justified in complaining that the declaration of the mandatory power created "almost unsurmountable difficulties"[1] in the implementation of the plan, but from the point of view of Anglo-American relations it must also be borne in mind that this situation might never have developed had it not been for the actions of President Truman, and the unwillingness of the United States to co-operate at an earlier stage.

The partition plan was at length accepted by the Assembly on 29 November, Russia—an unusual event—voting on the same side as the United States, probably on the principle of dividing the Middle East and ensuring the departure of British forces from Palestine. It was a day of great rejoicing for the Jews, who owed their success largely to American support, but it was a remarkable indication of the schizophrenia of the Administration that when, after five months of increasing disorder in Palestine which made it clear that war must follow the withdrawal of British troops, a second special Assembly of the United Nations came together on 16 April, 1948, American policy underwent a dramatic change. Because no nation was willing to send troops to enforce the partition plan, the American delegate proposed the temporary abandonment of partition and the establishment of a United Nations Trusteeship over Palestine. This change was partly, at least, due to an increasingly influential State and Defense Department belief that America was endangering her vital strategic interests in the Middle East by allowing the outbreak of a serious war over Palestine. The underlying motives for the new American approach, even though they afford only a partial explanation of it—there was also genuine concern at the prospect of a war between Jews and Arabs—did not escape the attention of the Russians, who attacked this American subservience to the pressure of imperialist oil interests.

But the new American policy, though it brought the fundamental attitudes of Britain and the United States once more closer together, did not render possible any closer co-operation between them, for things had gone too far for that; nor did it prevent the final reference of the whole issue to the only arbitrament left—war. Even a belated American offer to send troops, if other nations would do the same, had no effect except to arouse the bitter opposition of the Jews. A final American vacillation, however, restored Zionist good humour, even if

[1] Q. U.S.W.A., 1947-8, p. 329.

it finally interred the American proposal of temporary trusteeship. President Truman had declared at a Cabinet meeting on 8 August, 1947, that he had "stuck his neck out on this delicate question [Palestine] once, and he did not propose to do it again",[1] but by this time he had apparently thought better of his good resolution, for, being dissatisfied with the results of the new American policy, to which he had given public approval, he once more reversed his position, without giving any preliminary notification even to his own delegates to the United Nations. Being informed by the representative of the Jewish Agency in Washington that the new state of Israel would come into existence at one minute after 6 p.m. on 14 May, with the termination of the Mandate, he announced, a few minutes after that hour, American *de facto* recognition of its government. Thus the United States precipitately reverted to support for partition, and there was not on this occasion an imminent election to account for the President's unpredictable step.

This was unfortunately no longer the case when, after more than four months of sporadic fighting, interspersed with periods of truce, which were all the United Nations could gain, the United Nations Mediator in Palestine, Count Bernadotte, made certain proposals for a settlement which "seemed to offer a solution on which for the first time the United States and Great Britain might be able to agree, thus removing what had been for the past few years the greatest obstacle to a settlement."[2] The British Government at last began to see reason, and to make real concessions, in an effort to reach agreement with the United States, "in the realization that continuing Anglo-American agreement was a firmer foundation for the British position in the Middle East than a series of shaky alliances with Arab governments",[3] whose weaknesses were increasingly exposed by the successes of Israel. The particular British concessions were a modification of her refusal up to this time to recognize the existence of Israel or to contemplate any solution not welcome to both parties. She now accepted the Bernadotte Plan in principle, and General Marshall, at the Assembly in Paris, also endorsed it. But in Washington President Truman had once more fallen under the spell of the guardians of the Jewish vote, and in a statement on 24 October in effect refused to accept the Bernadotte proposals, by declining to agree to changes in the original U.N. partition resolution's proposed boundaries, unless they were fully acceptable to Israel. A later statement that any changes in Israel's favour must be matched by

[1] Forrestal, p. 304.　　[2] U.S.W.A., 1948-9, pp. 392-3.　　[3] Ibid, p. 398.

equivalent changes in favour of the Arabs, made by the United States delegate in the United Nations, did not alter the fact that the hope of Anglo-American agreement, and hence of a settlement, was frustrated at least until after the Presidential election.

During this period, remarkable Israeli military successes, and equally remarkable Arab defeats and divisions, demonstrated clearly that the state of Israel had come to stay, and, despite sharp Anglo-Jewish tensions arising from the presence of British forces in the territories of her Arab allies upon the borders of Israel, the British Government continued to move in the direction of a recognition of this *fait accompli*. This was paralleled by the Egyptian and Israeli acceptance, on 6 January, 1949, of a cease-fire, which eventually led, after prolonged negotiations, to a final armistice, if not to a peace settlement, in the Middle East. The truce recognized the existence of an independent state of Israel, with much more extensive territories than had been envisaged in the original plan of partition. On 29 January Britain accorded *de facto* recognition to it, and the policies of the United States and Britain appeared once more to be approaching an accord, albeit after the issue in question had already been settled by the forceful efforts of the Jews themselves.

That this accord was very far from an identity of views is clearly demonstrated by the fact that, only two days later, the United States replaced her eight-month old *de facto* recognition by recognition *de jure*. Bitter feeling in the Arab world against the new imperialism of the Jews, who were rightly seen to have enjoyed their main support from the United States, was to remain, but so was the new Israeli state. President Truman's support of Israel in the later stages of the struggle could thus be justified on realistic grounds by her victory, but it must not blind us to the fact that it was also responsible for the legacy of anti-Americanism in much of the Arab world. And now that the aims of Zionism had been accomplished, the basic American problem of acquiring the friendship of that world, as a source of oil and as a barrier to Russian expansion, remained. This necessity was made all the greater by the weakened position of Britain, and the justification for so lengthy a consideration of the Palestine problem lies not only in its inherent importance and in the ill-feeling it caused between the American and the British peoples, but because it is so characteristic of the mid-century Anglo-American relationship.

Britain had emerged from the war with her prestige in the Middle East very much reduced; her efforts to solve the Palestine problem alone had aroused the ire of the Jews without retaining the affection of the Arabs, and rising nationalisms in the whole area had steadily weakened her influence. Egypt had become very restive under Allied military occupation during the war, and had been demanding revision of the Anglo-Egyptian Treaty of 1936 at least since 1945; Iraq had refused to enter into a new alliance with Britain in January, 1948. England had by no means lost her interest in the Eastern Mediterranean, but the dissolution of areas of her colonial empire in the East weakened it to some extent, while, more important, she had neither the economic nor political power to maintain her position alone. This was characteristic of her status everywhere, and in other theatres the United States had already stepped forward to take her place. In Europe she was doing so to an increasing degree, and in the Far East she was shortly to do so without any apparent initial hesitation. In the Middle East her hesitation was, and to a great extent still was to be in 1952, very marked; nowhere else had she shown such reluctance to assume the part that her ally could no longer play. This was in some degree due to the Palestine issue itself, and to the split in the American mind, which paralysed effective action; this paralysis was all that the Zionists needed, but it rendered America as unpopular as Britain in many parts of the Middle East. As is increasingly the case with the troublesome issues in Anglo-American relations—and it is a measure of their solidarity that it should be so—that of Palestine was merely one of reconciling British and American points of view towards a third party; it was not in any way a direct dispute between the two themselves. This being so, in an age when for the first time world affairs are truly indivisible, it is quite extraordinary that there has not been more divergence between Britain and America than there has; it is certainly in no sense remarkable that there should be differences of opinion over problems as remote and diverse as those of Palestine and Korea.

Yet the American reluctance to assume a leading role in the Middle East is very interesting, for here the Russian threat is strategically perhaps most serious, and its gospel-technique of Communism, among the poverty stricken masses of the area, perhaps most effective. In some ways there is no Soviet threat more grave nor one more likely than a push through Iran to the warm waters of the Persian Gulf. Indeed, it was here that, in 1946, the free world had first found it necessary to check the Russian advance, but since that date her resolution had apparently weakened. This requires explanation.

It is partly, of course, to be explained by the lack of overt Russian action there; the containment policy must to some extent seem in its initial stages to be one of filling holes as they appear, and America could not be strong everywhere, so that she took no more action in this area when Russian pressure relaxed. Partly, also, it is to be explained by her suspicion that Britain's interest in the Middle East is still that of a "colonial" power.* But it is also important that America is not so alive to the strategic significance of the Middle East as Britain, for whom this lesson has been taught by her whole imperial history; many Americans, including General MacArthur, had regarded the Allied Mediterranean campaigns in the Second World War as an aberration. It is natural that this should be so; there is a dichotomy in American policy between the eastern and western oceans, Europe and the Far East, but the Middle East is more remote than either. It can be no immediate threat to the United States, like the fall of Britain or the loss of Japan. But if in truth the struggle against Russian-based Communism is world wide, and if American victory in it needs allies and strategic footholds throughout the earth, the Middle East, if only as the vital bridge to Africa, is of supreme importance. This is made even more true by her growing and necessary interest in Middle Eastern oil.

Though it left a bitter legacy of Arab mistrust, the settlement of the Palestine question should have opened the way for a joint Anglo-American policy in the Middle East, designed to assuage its internecine rivalries, raise its standard of life, and strengthen its powers of resistance to Russia. Yet by 1952 joint action was still the exception rather than the rule, and in the face of the extreme difficulty of the problems, this was not sufficient to achieve their common objects. American policy was torn between its desire to retain what it regarded as its freedom from "that air of superiority in dealing with 'subject races' that so exasperated the relations of Asian peoples with representatives of some of the European colonial powers",[1] and its need for that right to maintain military forces there, which Britain possessed, but which was the chief object of suspicion and hatred on the part of the local populations. To this must be added the rivalry of British and American oil companies, which was sharp, and which occasionally forced itself on to the governmental plane. These two aspects are exemplified in the long British disputes which developed in these years with Egypt and Iran; on neither of the two was Anglo-American co-operation ever really close. Yet it was in these relations of the West with the Arab world that the chief Middle Eastern difficulty now lay, for after 1949 a British *rapprochement* with Israel began.

*This suspicion has, as McNeill points out, become steadily less important since 1946.

[1] U.S.W.A., 1949, pp. 383-4.

V

In November, 1950, the Egyptian Government opened a new offensive against the Anglo-Egyptian Treaty of 1936, which gave Britain the right to station troops in the Suez Canal zone, and demanded the immediate withdrawal of these forces. This problem was made more difficult by the Egyptian refusal to consider it separately from the claim of King Farouk to sovereignty over the Sudan, a claim made in order to ensure the unity of the Nile valley, which Egypt greatly desired; the Sudan was technically under an Anglo-Egyptian condominium, but was in effect controlled by Britain. She had for some time promised self-determination to the Sudanese as soon as they were ready for it; that is to say, they were to have the right to choose independence, association with Egypt, or membership of the British Commonwealth. This freedom of choice the Egyptians would not allow, claiming sovereignty as of right.

In the dispute over the Canal Britain stood upon her treaty rights, and in that over the Sudan upon the right of the Sudanese to self-government. It was plainly in America's vital interest that British, or some other more reliable troops than Egypt could yet produce, should be in a position to defend the supremely important area of the great waterway, but Americans were still somewhat suspicious of British intentions in the Sudan. Characteristic is the judgment of one American writer, Richard P. Stebbings, that in the way of Egyptian "aspirations stood only the determination of Great Britain not to be ousted from a position which it occupied by virtue of long-standing treaty rights",[1] for he writes as if the question of the self-determination of the Sudan did not exist.

The failure of Britain and the United States to take firm joint action made it much more difficult for them to prevent the rapid deterioration of the situation. On 8 October, 1951, the Wafd government carried out its long-standing threat and abrogated the Anglo-Egyptian Treaty, proclaiming the Egyptian monarch as "King of Egypt and the Sudan". It is significant that in the next month a meeting between the Persian and Egyptian Prime Ministers resulted in a mutual declaration of solidarity. Meanwhile, the United States had belatedly taken up a suggestion of the late British Foreign Minister, Ernest Bevin, for a joint Middle East Command, including the troops of the various Arab states as well as Britain; this suggestion was not formally made to Egypt till

[1] U.S.W.A., 1951, p. 283.

six days after the abrogation of the Treaty, and it therefore met with a very frigid reception. Disorder in the Canal Zone increased, and by November the British forces there were coping with what was, in effect, a guerilla war. On 10 October the American Secretary of State had declared that "proper respect for international obligations requires that they be altered by mutual agreement rather than by unilateral action of one of the parties",[1] and the Administration stood firm on this position, but its efforts to assuage the situation and to secure Egyptian acceptance of the Middle East Command were fatally handicapped by the tardy and incomplete nature of Anglo-American understanding. However, a strong British stand and the reinforcement of her troops began to have its effect, and, after an intensification of guerilla activity culminating in wholesale rioting in Cairo on 26 January, King Farouk dismissed Wafdist Premier Nahas Pasha, and gradually the situation began to return to normal, though the basic issues remained as yet unresolved.

In Washington some days earlier Prime Minister Churchill had, with his customary insight, put his finger on the vital factor, and had also, with his customary boldness, proposed its remedy in his address to the Congress. He declared that

> it is no longer for . . . [Great Britain] alone to bear the whole burden of maintaining the freedom of . . . the Suez Canal. . . . It would enormously aid us in our task if even token forces of the other partners in the Four Powers proposal were stationed in the Canal Zone as a symbol of the unity of purpose which inspires us. And I believe it no exaggeration to state that such token forces would probably bring into harmony all that movement by which the Four Power policy may be made to play a decisive part by peaceful measures, and bring to an.end the wide disorders of the Middle East in which, let me assure you, there lurk dangers not less great than those which the United Nations have stemmed in Korea.[2]

Conscious of the extent of the American effort in Korea, he called for no more than symbolic forces to aid Britain, but he realized the essential truth, that what was really needed was positive Anglo-American co-operation: an active joint policy alone afforded any sound prospects of success. But still it was not forthcoming, and his suggestion of direct American intervention was coolly received in Washington; joint Anglo-American utterances did not go beyond the statement that it was essen-tional "for the furtherance of our common purposes that an Allied Middle East Command should be set up as soon as possible."[3]

[1] Q. ibid, p. 286.
[2] *Current Developments,* January, 1952, p. 35.   [3] Q. ibid, p. 2.

In Egypt, though on the surface things became calmer, negotiations between Britain and Egypt, which were begun in March, dragged ominously and seemed likely to end once more in deadlock over the Sudan question. But the bitterness in Egyptian Army circles at the country's ignominious defeat in the Palestine war, ascribed to royal and political corruption, still rankled deeply, and, more deeply still, there festered the sores of Egypt's appalling poverty. This explosive mixture of nationalist spirit and economic discontent produced an irresistible revolution, under the leadership of General Neguib, which on 23 July forced the abdication of King Farouk in six bloodless hours. This turn of events appeared at least to give Anglo-American policy a welcome reprieve, by removing the technical side of the Sudanese difficulty—Farouk's claim to sovereignty over the whole Nile valley. During the autumn of 1952 it seemed possible that Britain might take advantage of this opportunity, and negotiations were pressed on between Sudanese representatives—a term had now been set to British control in the Sudan—and Egypt, as well as between Britain and Egypt.

America hoped that these might succeed, and that a strong Middle East defence bloc, integrated with the North Atlantic Treaty Organization, might soon emerge. But still the Democratic administration lagged in the necessary process of effecting a close Anglo-American understanding on the Middle East; still the old suspicions of British imperialism and all its trappings persisted. *Time* was expressing the views of many Americans when it wrote on 4 August, 1952, that "revolution nourished by nationalism and by the slow wrath of miserable peasants, threatened to whisk away all forms and institutions that lack roots in the Middle East's history. Most in danger were the quasi-constitutional monarchies . . . cultivated . . . by British imperialism. . . . [W]hile Britain was strong, the monarchies were safe. Now . . . European nations no longer pay the piper in the Middle East."[1] In this analysis there is a good deal of truth, of which Britain must take full heed, but also a good deal of half-truth dangerous to Anglo-American unity; and only if a united Anglo-American power is able to bend a growing and developing Middle East to its cause will there be any security against Russia in that area, which is so vital to the future of the free world.

It is significant that the two "quasi-constitutional monarchies" *Time* had particularly in mind were Egypt and Iran, for it was in Iran that the second Middle Eastern problem which vexed Anglo-American relations

[1] *Time*, 4 August, 1952, p. 22.

centred. The Iranian question was more dangerous than the Egyptian, both to the fabric of peace and to the cordiality of Anglo-American relations. To the former it was more perilous, not only because of the perhaps greater fanaticism of its national extremists under their leader Dr. Mosaddeq, but even more because of its immediate proximity to Soviet Russia, which actually had, by a treaty signed in 1921, the right to send troops into Iran if the country were turned into a base for anti-Soviet military operations. In 1946 world opinion had forced Russia to withdraw her war-time troops from Iran, and the quiescence of Russia during the long Anglo-Iranian dispute seems evidence of her great reluctance to precipitate a world war, but the efforts of Iran to pursue a neutral policy between the Soviets and the West inevitably rendered the situation tense. When she was under heavy Soviet pressure, particularly in 1949, she tended to lean towards the West; the Shah, for instance, visited the United States in the autumn of that year, but relatively little economic or military aid was forthcoming, since the Administration had more urgent purposes for which to provide. The disappointment resulting from this contributed to a growing Persian coolness towards the West during the following year, but it was Persian feeling against Britain which was the real source of anti-Western feeling, and—because it centred on the oil question—which was the real danger to Anglo-American relations in this area.

The fact that Middle East oil resources constituted perhaps a half of the known reserves of a world with an increasingly insatiable demand for petroleum products, and that these were being exploited by Western capital, provided largely by rival British and American companies, is explanation enough of the difficulty. Britain predominated in Iran and Iraq, the United States in Saudi Arabia and Bahrein, and they were equals in Kuwayt. To ordinary business rivalry was added the fact that the United States was by far the world's greatest consumer of oil, while oil played a very important part in Britain's vital balance of payments problem. Efforts to solve the oil dilemma jointly resulted in the negotiation of an Anglo-American Petroleum Agreement in 1947, but it did not find favour with the Senate.*

Since the question bore all the hall-marks of an authentic specimen of Marxian imperialist exploitation of colonial lands, it provided excellent fuel for the engine of Communist propaganda. This made American accusations of British "colonial" methods in the oil industry more than usually anomalous, for she herself participated in the exploitation on an equal footing. Her case against Britain depended almost ex-

* Even in 1944 a similar agreement had met the same Senatorial response.

clusively upon controversial, and not very well substantiated, charges that Britain's commercial outlook was, compared with the American, "somewhat unprogressive and unimaginative."[1] The extent of the Anglo-American discord was shown by the criticisms of Dr. Grady, the American Ambassador in Teheran until late 1951, immediately after his retirement. He declared that, "Though Iran is the softest spot in the line around Russia, we have done little to block it up and the British have more than neutralized our feeble efforts." British policy had, in his view, been "based largely on the colonial approach", and their "financial and economic measures to prevent control from slipping away" were "obsolete", "ineffectual", and "disastrous to our common position in these countries."[2] But with one assertion of Dr. Grady there can be no disagreement on either side of the Atlantic—that the difficulty lay in a lack of co-ordination between Washington and London. This potentially disastrous situation was to some extent remedied during 1952, after the departure of Dr. Grady from Teheran and the return of Churchill to office, but it is questionable whether it was not too late to win Iran fully to the cause of the West, and virtually certain that it was too late to do much for the Anglo-Iranian Oil Company in Persia.

The Company had been for many years the symbol of Western domination of Iran and the scapegoat for Persian poverty and corruption. It had negotiated early in 1951 a new oil agreement with Premier Ali Razmara, which increased substantially the Persian share of profits; the treaty was opposed by extreme elements, and, after the assassination of Razmara in March, their leader Dr. Mosaddeq came to power. On 2 May legislation effecting the immediate nationalization of the oil industry was agreed to by the Shah. Britain took her stand upon legal treaty rights, which had been negotiated under the aegis of the League of Nations, but reserved the right to take whatever action might be necessary to safeguard British lives in the strikes and riots which took place in Abadan. Britain first proposed arbitration, in accordance with the 1933 treaty, which was rejected by Iran. She then appealed to the International Court of Justice, whose jurisdiction was shortly repudiated by Iran, while the Court itself eventually decided that it had none.

Hitherto, the United States had contented herself with counsels of moderation to the Persian Government, the "State Department's mournful comments" recalling to one writer "the helpless solicitude of a Greek chorus",[3] but early in July President Truman overtly accepted the role

[1] U.S.W.A., 1951, p. 268.   [2] Q. ibid, pp. 271-2.   [3] Ibid, p. 273.

931

of mediator, by sending Averell Harriman to Teheran to help find a solution. It was a measure of the distance between Britain and America and of public knowledge of it, that the latter could thus step into the position of arbiter; it was a fundamental error to show this weakness to the Persians whose attitude hardened even more, in the hope of extracting, not merely British submission, but American aid in larger quantities. Tripartite negotiations, between a British Minister, Richard Stokes, and Mosaddeq and Harriman, broke down after three weeks, and the British Labour Government thereupon appealed to the Security Council of the United Nations.

Here they were unable to get any assistance, partly because of the lukewarm attitude of the United States, and on 19 October the Council merely decided to postpone debate until the International Court had ruled on its own competence in the matter. By the beginning of that month, the last British employees had, under threat of expulsion, been evacuated from Abadan in ships of the Royal Navy, which had for some time been standing off shore in the Persian Gulf. A blockade of Iran's oil industry was inaugurated, which was as effective as in time of war, for Iran had neither the technicians nor the tankers to get the oil flowing again herself, and Anglo-Iranian, supported by the British Government, which owned—because of the Navy's need for oil—a commanding amount of the company's stock, had great influence with other oil companies (which were by now alarmed at the precedent of expropriation), as well as a number of legal weapons that it could use. As a result, Iran's financial position grew steadily more serious.

American and British estimates of the situation differed considerably, though their long-term interests were identical. Washington feared to press Mosaddeq too hard lest the door be opened to the Communists, and was inclined to try and help him out of his "self-incurred difficulties"[1] by financial aid. Britain clung to economic and financial pressures to bring the Persians to reason, and was very reluctant to concede anything further in view of the importance of Abadan to the solution of her dollar problem. Either policy would have stood a better chance of success than the combination of both which was attempted and which failed completely, but it is probable that any solution which thought of the problem as primarily economic was doomed to failure; as Mosaddeq once remarked, "It is better to be independent and produce only one ton of oil a year than to produce 32 million tons and be a slave of Britain."[2] What is more probable is that there was still inherent American sympathy for such a statement, which was the basic reason

[1] Ibid, p. 281.   [2] Q. ibid, p. 275.

for lack of Anglo-American co-operation; certainly it was a fantastic distortion of the position occupied by the Anglo-Iranian Oil Company in Iran. As long as Britain and America were divided, the Russian menace was unchecked in this area, and American oil interests were threatened, equally with British, everywhere in the Middle East.

When in March, 1952, the International Bank's efforts to work out an agreement between Britain and Iran broke down; when, four months later, the International Court decided that it had no jurisdiction; when, at the same time, a moderate Premier, Ahmed Quavam, pledged to try and solve the oil crisis by negotiations with Britain, was forced by Nationalist riots to resign after only four days in office; and when he was succeeded by his predecessor Mosaddeq, whose hands were immensely strengthened, it became clear that something had to be done. At long last, on 30 August, the action was taken which ought to have been taken in the beginning, and a joint message was sent to Mosaddeq from the President and the British Prime Minister. It proposed the submission of the dispute as to the amount of compensation for nationalization to the International Court, negotiations to restore the flow of Iranian oil to world markets, and, in the event of acceptance of these two provisions, immediate British payment for oil sold and an immediate American grant of $10 million. Thus Britain accepted the fact of nationalization, and a serious attempt was made to offer Iran a way out of its economic impasse. Such diplomatic unity at an early stage in the dispute might have solved it, but now it was too late; Premier Mosaddeq rejected the proposals outright.

Unhappily, there were some signs that the failure weakened rather than strengthened Anglo-American unity; such were rumours of a plan for an American company to market oil and pay British compensation out of the proceeds, but there is little doubt that it would have been unacceptable both to Britain and Iran. The announcement of the State Department on 6 December, 1952, that it could not prevent American companies from making private arrangements to market Iranian oil, although camouflaged by the accompanying warning of the legal actions which might be taken by the Anglo-Iranian Oil Company, and softened by prior consultation with the British Government, was an ominous sign; since such action could hardly have been taken without the acquiescence of the incoming Republicans, it did not augur as well for Anglo-American understanding in the Middle East under the new régime as did some other things. This was particularly true in view of the fact that in November Iran ended diplomatic relations with Britain.

Thus towards the end of 1952 there was no solution to the Iranian question in sight, and an increasingly grave situation economically and strategically in that country: there was hope, but no certainty, of a way out of the Egyptian deadlock. In the Middle East generally there were still great turbulence and many unsettled problems. The new state of Israel, grafted, as it were, by a major surgical operation upon the body politic of the Eastern Mediterranean, and the hatred with which it was regarded by an Arab world still smarting from the humiliation of their defeat—a defeat of which the thousands of destitute Palestine Arab refugees were a perpetual reminder—both remained to constitute the basic internal problem of the area. Added to it was the residual anti-British feeling, which led such a country as Iraq to continue to demand revision of her defence treaty with Britain, and also the new anti-Americanism, which support for Israel and desire for oil rights had provoked. This ferment unquestionably encouraged the establishment of strong military dictatorships, such as that of Neguib in Egypt, that in Syria, and, as seemed likely in mid-November, one in Iraq also; and the Arab revival, which these perhaps presaged, boded ill for future co-operation between Jew and Arab.

Yet over all else loomed the cloud of Soviet power; the problem for the West was how to avoid that internecine strife in the Middle East which would be a standing temptation to Russia, and how to replace it by a strong defence bloc linked with NATO. For this, the expedient of relying on peripheral British bases, like Cyprus and East Africa, would not be an effective substitute. This was perhaps a matter of life and death to the nations of the Middle East themselves, but they clung still to the hope of neutrality, partly from fear of Russia and partly from mistrust of the West. In a strong Middle East league, led or supported by Turkey which was wholeheartedly in the NATO camp, they might rid themselves of both, but the creation of such a league would challenge all the joint skill and influence of Britain and the United States. Even together they might fail to effect it; separately they stood no chance of doing so. To ensure unity, both peoples must make the necessary sacrifices; Britain must appreciate her changed position, America that she cannot evade the unpopular responsibility of decisive action. In the riots in Iraq in November, 1952, as elsewhere in the Middle East, feeling was as passionate against America as against Britain; Americans must reconcile themselves to that, while Britons reconcile themselves to their need for American support, and hence to the inevitability of American influence upon their policy. Only through Anglo-American unity can the Middle East become an asset rather than a burden to the free world.

VI

But it is not merely over the Middle East that the shadow of Soviet Russia lies; it dominates the whole international scene. The history of Anglo-American relations since 1946 has been increasingly shaped and guided by the Communist threat, and cannot be understood apart from it. Thus we have seen that the passage of the loan to Britain through Congress in the summer of 1946 owed much to the growing American appreciation of it. Towards the end of that year it became apparent that no comprehensive peace settlement in Europe would be allowed by the Soviet Government on any terms that the West could contemplate, and the acceptance of this situation in Germany was marked by an economic merger of the American and British zones of occupation which formed the basis of the West German Federal Republic; Britain was anxious for some arrangement which would lessen the financial burden of occupation costs, and so she accepted this American proposal. The combination of fear of Russia with consciousness of Britain's economic difficulties was now to become a familiar pattern in Anglo-American relations. It was, for example, an economic crisis in Britain, whose effects were made more pronounced by the very severe winter of 1946-7, which caused her to inform the State Department on 24 February, 1947, that she could no longer continue, after the end of March, to give economic aid and support to Greece.

Insufficient emphasis has perhaps been placed on this financial factor, for the great increase in overseas governmental expenditure, approximately £100 million of it being military, was perhaps the most important specific change in Britain's balance of payments situation arising out of the war. Reluctant to alter any of its plans for domestic legislation, and faced with the choice between saving dollars by cutting living standards in Britain or by cutting foreign commitments, the Labour government chose the latter course with what appeared almost unseemly haste. Yet there is little doubt that they were confident in their own minds that this would not mean an extension of Soviet power, because they certainly believed that the United States would take up the task. Here is another compelling example of the manner in which America has assumed, and must assume, in the world the role which Britain has in the past played.

For British confidence in America's readiness to assume the burden there were solid grounds. American public feeling against Russia had been mounting for many months, and it was clearly in her interest, as it was her desire, to prevent the collapse of democracy and the triumph of Communism in Greece. Yet the decision was still a difficult and momentous one; President Truman, in the relative privacy of a Cabinet meeting, called it more serious than any that "had ever confronted any President." Hitherto, the United States had proclaimed her abandonment of isolationism and her leadership of the free world, only, as it were, in general terms. She had been the chief architect of the United Nations, and she had contributed vast sums for the relief and rehabilitation of a weary world, but the one was a theoretical commitment, not yet tested in practice, and the other a humanitarian gesture, albeit a gesture of great political significance. Though she had offered to do so, she had not yet signed any special military alliances or treaties, and what was needed now in the Eastern Mediterranean was more than that, it was an immediate commitment to send military and economic aid to combat the dire threat of Communist guerillas, based in the Soviet satellite states upon the borders of Greece.

There is little doubt that the decision to do so was made primarily on military grounds, for it was in such terms that General Marshall, the Secretary of State, at first conceived of the policy of containment. This was why there was so little hesitation in the Administration, for the habits and personalities of the war were still powerful, and though there were, in private discussions, signs of a normal American reluctance to undertake so significant a series of obligations, they were submerged in the predominant fear of Russia. Under-Secretary Acheson might say that "the Greek Government was not a satisfactory one to us; that it contained many elements that were reactionary",[1] and Secretary Marshall might express "sharp resentment of the British action in precipitating *now* their decision for troop withdrawal from Greece", which was, he asserted, "conditioned by political considerations at home"[2]—with some members of the Labour Party, British intervention in Greece had always been unpopular—but the compelling voice was that of Secretary of the Navy Forrestal, declaring "that what was occurring was simply the manifestation of what had been in process of development in the last four years . . . a fundamental struggle between our kind of society and the Russians' and that the Russians would not respond to anything except power."[3]

It was, too, a logical development in American foreign policy. On 25 October, 1945, President Truman had said: "We shall refuse to recognize any government imposed upon any nation by the force of any foreign power. In some cases it may be impossible to prevent force-

[1] Q. Forrestal, pp. 250-1.　　[2] Q. ibid, pp. 302-3.　　[3] Forrestal, p. 251.

ful imposition of such a government. But the United States will not recognize any such government."[1] This was merely the old Hoover-Stimson doctrine. Now, in March, 1947, he went further, and declared:

> One of the primary objectives of the foreign policy of the United States is the creation of conditions in which we and other nations will be able to work out a way of life free from coercion. . . . We shall not realize our objectives, however, unless we are willing to help free peoples to maintain their free institutions and their national integrity against aggressive movements that seek to impose upon them totalitarian régimes. This is no more than a frank recognition that totalitarian régimes imposed on free peoples, by direct or indirect aggression, undermine the foundations of international peace and hence the security of the United States.[2]

Though a logical development in United States peace-time policy, this, particularly when he also stated, "I am fully aware of the broad implications involved if the United States extends assistance to Greece and Turkey", was a radical one. That it was forced on her by the decline in Britain's powers was made amply clear by the reiteration in the case both of Turkey and Greece that "There is no other country to which" they "can turn. . . . The British Government, which has been helping . . . can give no further financial or economic aid".[3] With misgivings, but by substantial votes, Congress appropriated $400 million for initial aid in May, 1947. It was the first step in a positive American policy to resist the encroachments of Soviet Communism.

But once the first step had been taken, it was very soon realized that, though it was the one which counted, it went only a small distance towards attaining its object; many of those "broad implications" of which the President had spoken became pressing realities. In the first place, it was realized that there were numerous other places, even in Europe, which were in the long run of much greater importance to the victory over Communism than Greece and Turkey. In the second place, it was appreciated by the Fair Deal Administration that this enemy could not be fought by arms alone; since Communism thrives on poverty, that condition had to be alleviated in the areas of greatest strategic importance. This was brought strongly home to them by the fierce opposition of left wing elements at home and abroad to what they regarded as a flagrant example of American imperialism; Henry Wallace in America and the extreme elements in the Labour Party in

[1] Q. McNaughton and Hehmeyer, p. 38.
[2] *Documents on American Foreign Relations*, IX, p. 648.   [3] Ibid, p. 647.

Britain joined the Soviet chorus in denunciation of the Truman Doctrine. The British public as a whole accepted it with quiet approval, or, in the case of the Conservative Opposition, with enthusiasm. American opinion for the most part accepted it as an unpleasant necessity. But, partly because the possibility of a triumph of Communism in Western Europe was increased by the economic crisis in the spring of 1947, a crisis "above all . . . of food and dollars,"[1] and partly, no doubt, because the Administration desired to re-emphasize the humanitarian and economic, as opposed to the military, aspect of the American plan to make the West safe for democracy, the United States swiftly followed up her formulation of the Truman Doctrine by a move towards the Marshall Plan.

What Lend-Lease had been to the American military effort in World War II, the Marshall Plan was to the Truman Doctrine in the years which followed it, and, though it is impossible altogether to disentangle or distinguish the threads of the one from the threads of the other, this new move went far to convince the free world of the integrity and sanity, to say nothing of the generosity, of American policy. On 12 March the President had opened his speech by declaring that "the national security of this country"[2] was involved: on 5 June, when General Marshall, in his famous speech at Harvard, first mooted the European Recovery Programme, the emphasis was different, and quite plainly it was deliberately so. He said, "Our policy is directed not against any country or doctrine but against hunger, poverty, desperation and chaos." And this was more than verbiage, for Russia and her satellites were not excluded from the offer of assistance, and when, after some seeming hesitation, they refused to accept it, the decision was theirs alone. Let this fact never be forgotten.

In his offer of carefully planned, large-scale economic aid, Marshall had laid it down that "The initiative . . . must come from Europe";[3] that it must be a joint European programme. And more and more was to be heard in the future of the necessity for common measures among the European nations and for ultimate European unity. As the Americans poured vast sums of money into Europe, they very naturally wished to have some say as to the kind of European structure it was to help to build; they were remarkably restrained in the use they made of their economic influence, but they did press continually for a hastening

[1] U.S.W.A., 1947-8, p. 52.
[2] *Documents on American Foreign Relations*, IX, p. 646.
[3] Ibid, pp. 10-11.

of the development of economic and political unity. With a large measure of justice, they saw their own huge free trade area, united in a single political body, as one of the principal causes of their economic prosperity, and urged this panacea upon Europe; with less justice, they under-estimated the depths of Europe's traditional barriers of feeling, race and language. In this controversy, as indeed in the whole economic and political relationship of the United States with Europe, Great Britain played a unique and peculiar part. By virtue of the British loan from America in the previous year, Britain's economic relationship had been put on a special footing with the United States, but it was still Britain's Foreign Secretary, Ernest Bevin, who, realizing the enormous possibilities of the offer, took the European initiative suggested by the Secretary of State, and "grabbed the Marshall offer with both hands."[1] This implied the association of Britain with Europe, but it was soon to become clear that the degree of that association was a matter on which there could be wide differences of opinion.

There was, indeed, considerable confusion of thought on this subject, on both sides of the Atlantic as well as on both sides of the English Channel, especially among those not sobered by the realities of power or participation. It became increasingly clear to all, particularly because of Russian pressure, that some closer European organization to facilitate common action was essential, and Churchill in Opposition lent deliberate weight to the movement towards it. The British Government was, however, reluctant to tie Britain integrally and permanently to the mainland of Europe; they were accused of feeling this reluctance because Socialism appeared to be a waning force on the Continent, but, though there was no doubt something of this in it, their real motive was an awareness of the complexity of Britain's true interests. Britain, however, was strongly denounced in some American circles for "dragging her feet", and thus delaying European unity, but it was confidently expected by Americans that the return of Churchill to power would mean an acceleration towards unity. This was a natural assumption in view of his statements in Opposition, but, whether because he never intended that Britain should play a close part in the formation of a European Union, for which on the part of the Continental nations he was sincerely anxious, or because a return to power impressed on him the difficulties and dangers of such a course, the Conservative government in 1951 showed itself no more ready to participate in exclusively European organizations, such as that brought into

[1] Q. U.S.W.A., 1947-8, p. 418.

939

being under the Schuman Plan, than had the Labour Party been.

British opinion, as a whole, seemed, when faced with practical decisions in this matter, to appreciate more and more the singularity of Britain's interests; and American opinion (which was, naturally, even more ill-informed than the British) although it was very loath to abandon its infallible prescription for European progress, was forced, in its turn and by degrees, to accept these same facts. Gradually, American pressure for European unity began to be directed at the Continent alone, and tacitly to exclude Britain. Probably the turning point in this development was the ultimate recognition by General Eisenhower, as Commander-in-Chief of the European forces of NATO, who was himself a leading and ardent advocate of European unity, that for good and sufficient reasons Britain must, for the present, be counted out of any unitary European organization, and should not be expected to give it more than strong and friendly encouragement.

The truth is that Britain's interests are by no means exclusively, or even primarily, European. She has been historically, and still is, subject to three main political, social and economic attractions, that of the British Empire and Commonwealth, that of the United States, and that of Europe. Geographically she is closer to Europe; politically and emotionally she is much closer to the Commonwealth, and, in some respects, to America; economically, she is closest to the Commonwealth, next closest to Europe, and least close to the United States. In 1949-50, for example, the percentage of her exports was as follows: to the Overseas Sterling Area, most of it in the Empire and Commonwealth, 48 per cent; to Canada, 5 per cent; to O.E.E.C. countries, 24 per cent; to the United States, 4 per cent. That of her imports was as follows: from the Sterling Area, 37 per cent; from Canada, 9 per cent; from O.E.E.C. countries, 21 per cent; from the United States, 9 per cent. Politically and emotionally, her primary bonds are those with her kinsfolk, who recognize the Crown as, at the very least, the symbol of Commonwealth unity, but her relations with the United States have become, as we have seen, increasingly close and intimate over the last half century.

Furthermore, her Commonwealth and American ties are far from incompatible, but rather give mutual aid and strength. Canada lives by good Anglo-American relations, and is, in her increasing strength, a powerful bond of amity; the signature in 1951 of a Tripartite Security Treaty between the United States, Australia and New Zealand opened up ultimate prospects of even wider co-operation, although this was not its initial effect. There is, too, a growing appreciation in the United

States of the true nature of the British Commonwealth, and of its importance to America. This found expression in the words of an ex-American Ambassador to London inaugurating the appeal for a United States Memorial Fund for King George VI:

> The irresistible force of the events of the last twenty years has, it seems to me, established a very special relationship between the Commonwealth of Nations and our own country. It [the Commonwealth] is not a group of far-flung territories governed from a remote and distant London. Its members are not held together by formal legal ties. Respect for a common Crown is the only element which binds them to each other. The Commonwealth of Nations is unique because it is the most striking example in history of a voluntary association of wholly free and sovereign nations. It is with this peculiar political institution that our relationship has become of such great significance to the world.[1]

There are, it is true, still difficulties in this sphere. Though accepting the Commonwealth as a political organism, there was still a certain reluctance in post-war Democratic administrations to admit its undoubted right to frame a common economic policy, and a mistrust of agreements of the Ottawa type. However, alterations may result from a change to Republican rule, while the British sensitivity to American opinion in economic matters is shown by the fact that the Commonwealth Economic Conference of 1952 was designed merely as a prelude to a wider series of discussions with the United States.

It is true, also, that the Pacific Pact itself showed, at first, some signs of becoming a source of discord rather than harmony. The British Government has put forward very strongly the view that it should be admitted to this organization, on the ground that it is intimately concerned on both the political and strategic levels, and the three powers appear so far to have rebutted this claim. The main reason given for the rebuttal is that this would open the way to similar demands by the Dutch, the French, and perhaps others, which would widen the scope of the treaty far beyond what was envisaged, but it is possible that an additional reason is the old and familiar American reluctance to put itself in the position of seeming to endorse the governments and policies of "colonial" powers. But, as in the Middle East, this is an outmoded and strategically dangerous sentiment, and there is solid reason to hope that a Republican government, with John Foster Dulles, author of the Japanese Treaty of 1951, as Secretary of State, and with a normal Republican sensitivity to Pacific developments, will extend rather than

[1] Lewis Douglas: q. *Daily Telegraph,* 25 November, 1952.

limit Pacific security arrangements. In such an extensive organization, complementary to NATO, Britain might find her rightful place, as she must do in a Middle Eastern Command.

This unity of the British Commonwealth, and particularly Britain, with the United States is the primary interest of all parties. For America she is the best, the most reliable, the most powerful of allies; for her, American amity is a matter of life and death. Not to recognize the unique nature of this Anglo-American relationship would be a gross distortion of the long-standing realities which underly Anglo-American history.

But this does not mean that British co-operation with a United Europe must be abandoned, or confined to the rarefied and debilitating atmospheric level of the United Nations. Far from it. Despite the strength of American and Commonwealth ties, Britain must necessarily maintain a close connexion with the European mainland, for the twenty-two miles of the Straits of Dover are more like a bridge than a barrier in the atomic age. But that connexion must be fitted within a larger framework, that of the North Atlantic basin, which, although broad, is less than universal. The North Atlantic Triangle of America, Canada and Britain forms the hard core of what must be a world structure built for the protection and promotion of liberalism and democracy, but this core needs great accretions of strength throughout the world if it is to endure. We have envisaged the outposts of this system in the Pacific and the Middle East, but the co-operation of Europe is no less essential. America and Britain are bound to Europe, not merely strategically and economically, but also culturally, because it is the cradle of Western civilization, whose best values the free world must defend. Peace-loving members of the United Nations should combine in regional pacts, covering the surface of the globe, in most of which the United States and Britain must participate as major and interested partners. On the two northerly shores of the Atlantic, which links the United States with United Europe, the heart of the British Commonwealth—Canada and Britain—must remain, beating strongly, helping to invigorate not only Europe and America, but also the rest of the Commonwealth. She must be, in so far as this is possible, an equal, and it may well be that from the Commonwealth Conference of 1952 will emerge economic arrangements which will forward, if not ensure, her solvency, and that her political unity with her Empire and Commonwealth will also be strengthened, and will thus strengthen her. Only within such a broad organization as is the North Atlantic Treaty Organization can Britain find a full and happy life for her people. This must remain her level of co-operation; nothing less will satisfy her needs, anything more will not fulfil the purposes of democracy.

But in 1947 these developments were still in the future, and Britain's pressing need was, like that of the rest of Europe, for further economic aid; the loan of 1946, which had been intended to last between three and five years, was melting swiftly away in the face of Britain's heavy adverse trade balance and the continued rise in American prices. Despite the fact that her exports and total industrial production were well above pre-war level, the loss of her visible and invisible assets and the adverse movement in the terms of trade made it impossible for her to close the dollar gap without a severe and cumulative lowering of what appeared to her people their already austere standard of living. When, in accordance with the 1946 agreement, the British Government made sterling freely convertible on 15 July, 1947, a tremendous drain on Britain's dollars began, and by the time that convertibility was hurriedly ended on 20 August, a further $1·3 billion of the loan had been spent. This was well over three-quarters of the total, and the remaining $400 million was spent by 1 March, 1948, only nineteen and a half months after Congress had appropriated the money. Already, in the summer of 1947, the writing was on the wall; Britain was going to need more dollars, and her best chance of getting them was obviously, in view of the terms of the Marshall offer, to co-operate with the Continental nations. It was, indeed, under British leadership, in the persons of Ernest Bevin and Sir Oliver Franks, that a comprehensive plan was drafted for the utilization of American aid and that the Organization for European Economic Recovery was instituted, to promote the common European effort to achieve economic stability. On 3 April, 1948, the President signed an Act appropriating $5·3 billion for the European Recovery Programme; this had passed Congress partly because it was a measure of economic humanitarianism, and partly because it was a measure to prevent any more of Europe from falling, through poverty, into the arms of Russian Communism. Of this sum Britain was to acquire a large share, which began to arrive in the nick of time, soon after the final exhaustion of the original loan and of certain other credits made available in the course of 1948, such as a sum totalling $300 million from the International Monetary Fund. By the end of 1949, of a total of just under $6 billion of Marshall Aid disbursed, Britain had received $1,822 million.

In so far as the United States came more and more to insist upon European integration as the only long-term answer to the endemic dollar shortage (which was only alleviated and not permanently cured by the activities of the Economic Co-operation Administration), and in view of the fact that the hesitance, which Britain had shown from the very beginning about entering a European *Zollverein*, soon developed into a refusal to co-operate in any organic way with the budding European Economic Union, it might perhaps, with some justice, have been considered by the American people that a Britain which had rushed into the initial stages of economic co-operation in Europe with both hands open for a lion's share of Marshall Aid was not fulfilling its implied obligations; and indeed, during the course of 1949, the tone of mutual criticism in the press of both countries had an acerbity not so far matched since World War II. American criticism centred on the failings of the Labour government, and in particular on its refusal to modify its domestic programme to meet external needs and to co-operate more wholeheartedly with Europe; that Government's reaction was not moderated by the fact that the British Opposition was levelling just the same criticisms against it. A temperate speech by President Truman on 29 August, 1949, was needed to allay the strong feelings; in it he wisely pointed out that "each nation has its own political problems. . . . In the same way, nations have different business practices and different government devices for achieving the same economic ends. A community of democratic nations cannot insist on uniformity in matters of politics or business". "Mutual concessions and co-operation"[1] are essential.

But, as we have seen, Americans gradually became reconciled to Britain's continued economic and political independence of Europe, and, with the same sense of political realities, they did not pedantically complain at her oblique extension of her American loan by participation in the European Recovery Programme, for her achievement in the economic field was in some ways remarkable; her index of industrial production kept well ahead of that of Europe as a whole and her exports in 1949 were 156 per cent of the 1938 level. Despite this, however, the problem of her dollar gap remained acute, and was made more difficult to remedy through direct exports to North America by the obsolescence of much of her industrial plant and many of her production and merchandising methods. Though the resources of the Sterling Area as a whole, including such things as the rubber of Malaya, in some respects eased the difficulty, her obligations as its banker sometimes, as in the crisis of 1949, did just the reverse. The slight recession in the United

[1] Q. U.S.W.A., 1949, pp. 126-7.

944

States in the first half of 1949 resulted in a drop in American imports, and this had a disastrous effect upon Britain's gold and dollar reserves, because the dollar earning capacity of both the United Kingdom and the Sterling Area was seriously reduced; if the process had continued, all the reserves would have been used up in less than a year. One of the obstacles in the path of recovery was the large wartime sterling balances, which Britain released periodically, and for which British exports brought no tangible returns, and the United States continued to press for the "scaling-down" of these as a counterpart to American aid. But such an action involved long and laborious negotiations, and some immediate action was required. Britain took steps, therefore, to reduce her dollar imports by 25 per cent, and her example was followed in the Commonwealth, while plans for a conference with Canada and the United States in Washington in September were announced.

Despite the continued run on sterling and the pressure exercised by unofficial American publicists for a devaluation of the pound, Sir Stafford Cripps emphatically denied that such a measure was contemplated. Immediately, however, upon returning from America, he announced a drastic devaluation, from $4·03 to $2·80 to the pound; his denials had been economically necessary, but the resulting precipitancy of the action, which gave less than forty-eight hours' notice to the members of the Commonwealth and which was taken without any real consultation with the European powers, gave great offence to the latter. It was a clear illustration of the vital importance of the North Atlantic Triangle and of the true direction of British interests. Even more dramatic was the evidence of Britain's dependence upon the United States, for, though the British Government announced that the step had been decided upon before the Washington Conference, the Administration had plainly urged it strongly upon them, and it was not announced until after the Conference was over. Furthermore, the American and Canadian agreement, to do all they could to reduce their tariffs and simplify their Customs procedures, had the air of a *quid pro quo*. The fundamental economic relationship between the United Kingdom and the United States had plainly not altered much since the days in 1931 when the British Cabinet's actions hung upon a cablegram from Pierpont Morgan.

But the solution to their problems envisaged by British economists and statesmen was not the same now as it had been then. In the nineteen-thirties Americans had been disinterested in Britain's future and she had fallen back upon imperial preference and bilateral trade agreements, which alone were left to her. With the pressure of the Democratic administration for multilateral trade, and the increased interest of the United States in the fate of Europe after 1940, Britain chose during the war, as we have seen, to veer towards freer world trade, which, in an ideal or even a stable world, certainly offered better hopes of prosperity. But, because her interests were less obviously served by the policy than those of the United States, and because her nearness to economic disaster made her less sanguine than her great neighbour, she remained somewhat more sceptical about the elasticity of the dollar market and the value to her of participation in European economic integration. Nevertheless, Britain put her hand to the plough, though good fortune, hard work and constant American encouragement would be necessary to keep it there, for the footsteps of multilateral trade were dogged by the figure of the balance of payments. In December, 1949, for example, there was the first of a series of minor explosions in America, when Britain made a drastic cut in dollar oil imports. Earlier in the year, United States officials had protested strongly against certain features which they regarded as discriminatory in a preliminary draft of the five-year Anglo-Argentine trade agreement; indeed, though Britain had no love for the Peron régime, her need for Argentine meat made her more ready than the United States at this period to pursue the hard task of retaining its friendship. Nor were all the obstacles to the Administration's programme raised on the British side of the water, for, at the height of the Geneva Conference on tariff reduction, Congress, dominated by the Republicans, passed a bill virtually raising the American tariff on wool, which might, through the vigorous Australian reaction, have wrecked the proceedings which the State Department had laboured so hard to make a success; happily, President Truman's veto was effective and the Conference continued with its work.

However, the outcome of it, and of the plenary conference which followed at Havana in the winter of 1947-8—the General Agreement on Tariffs and Trade and the Charter of the International Trade Organization—bore the hall-marks of Anglo-American compromise. As the loan agreement of 1946 had contained escape clauses in the case of balance of payments difficulties, so there were now convenient hatches through which signatories might leave the vessels in case of trouble. There were very considerable and important reductions in tariffs on the part of many nations, which carried on between them four-fifths of the world's trade, but the barriers still remained formidable and, in the case of dollar countries, even dangerous, obstacles to commerce. The I.T.O. Charter, too, did not go by any means all the way to its goal of reciprocity; its principles were bold, but its reservations were numerous. Important preferential systems already in existence, such as that under the Ottawa agreements, and that between the United States and Cuba, were protected; member states, although they agreed not to increase existing preferences or create new ones, could get permission to do so from a majority of members present in conference; most important of all, though in theory they abandoned the quota system as a protective device, quantitative restrictions of this kind were allowed in special circumstances, and these immensely reduced the importance of the other measures agreed upon. As if to illustrate this, in June, 1949, the United States Senate ratified an international wheat agreement, which fixed export quotas and prices for the next four years, and certain of the measures agreed to at the Washington Conference in September ran counter to the free trade current. But, despite occasional difficulties, the liberal policies of the Administration and the sincere efforts of Britain to comply with her agreements with the United States made it possible for Anglo-American relations to remain remarkably undisturbed by the continual reappearance of the yawning chasm of the dollar gap.

That this was so can once more be partly explained by the lengthening shadow which Russia cast, not only over Europe, but also over the Atlantic. In March, 1948, Britain, France, Belgium, the Netherlands and Luxemburg signed at Brussels a mutual defence treaty plainly aimed at the Soviet Union, and in June of that year the Russian blockade of Berlin and the ensuing air lift by the United States and Britain began, while the Senate passed the Vandenberg Resolution, affirming American support for such regional arrangements as the Brussels pact, by 64 votes to 4. Already, some days before the Brussels Treaty was actually signed, Bevin had proposed to Marshall that they build on this basis plans for comprehensive Atlantic and Mediterranean security, beginning with immediate conversations in Washington—yet another example of a British initiative which was to be rapidly developed in American hands. Canada was most anxious for such a development, and there were conversations between British and United States military staffs on the subject as early as April. In July formal conversations began in Washington, by which time there was very little doubt in American minds as to the necessity of some such arrangement, for the present parallel with the events leading up to 1939 was too plain to be missed. Yet so revolutionary a step as a European military alliance in peace time still appeared to present technical and constitutional difficulties to the agencies of American government, and, in deference to the exclusive power of the Congress to declare war, the formula of the treaty ran as follows: "The Parties agree that an armed attack against one or more of them in Europe or North America shall be considered an attack against them all; and . . . each of them . . . will assist the Party or Parties so attacked by taking forthwith, individually and in concert with the other Parties, such action as it deems necessary, including the use of armed force, to restore and maintain the security of the North Atlantic area."[1] Its evolution required some ingenuity, and it was by no means as unambiguous as the agreement of the Brussels powers to render to the victim of attack "all military and other aid and assistance in their power".[2] It was a measure of the change in America's political climate of opinion that the twelve powers (the Brussels five *plus* the United States, Canada, Italy, Norway, Denmark, Iceland and Portugal) were content with so seemingly loose an obligation on the part of the United States, whose Senate had, only a quarter of a century before, refused to ratify her guarantee of French territorial integrity.

VII

INDEED, it was not to be long before European sentiments were of a quite different kind. No sooner had their fear of Russia been alleviated by the assurance of American support, than they began to be almost more fearful of war with the Communist powers than they were of those powers themselves. An outward show of caution and moderation is not usually reckoned an American characteristic, and, as we shall see, the American tendency not to do things by halves, when applied in the international sphere to the defeat of Communism, began to give the other signatories of the North Atlantic Treaty many uneasy moments. This was to become one of the most insistent notes in Anglo-American relations during the period of the Korean War. Thus, once the Allies obtained a guarantee from the United States, they began to regret the loss of freedom of action which such arrangements inevitably entail; but they did not fear American actions so much in Europe as in the Far East, where their interests were less closely involved: the bonds of NATO continued to be drawn even tighter. Its organization was set up, and thereafter rendered increasingly efficient; in 1950 the rearmament of the member powers began, the primary burden being borne by the United States and, to a lesser degree, by Britain; there began also the first tentative steps towards the ultimate re-armament of Western

[1] *Documents on American Foreign Relations*, XI, p. 613.
[2] Q. U.S.W.A., 1948-9, p. 532.

Germany, over which Britain and the United States came to agree much more closely than did either of them with the French; early in 1951, at the unanimous request of the North Atlantic Council, General Eisenhower took up his remarkably successful task as Supreme Allied Commander, Europe; in September the admission of Greece and Turkey into NATO was agreed to, in principle, by all the member states; during 1952 the question of German re-armament was pressed on, and tentative moves were made in the direction of co-operation with Spain and Yugoslavia. Thus the European members of NATO continued to show by their actions their fear of Russian Communism in Europe. But to America, Korea, Japan and China seemed almost as important as France, Germany and Italy, and the European fear of precipitate American action tended to concentrate in that—to them—far off area. Thus to some extent, the nervousness of Europe as to the possibility of a war precipitated by rash American actions was merely a reflection of their readiness to abandon the cause of the free world in the Far East from motives akin to and as fatal as those which had motivated their actions in the days of Munich. There were, however, as we shall see later, other and better motives lying behind their attitude.

But that the unity of Britain and the United States was the core or heart of the Atlantic Community was evidenced, not merely by the plain underlying realities of power, but by the continuous and obvious intimacy of their affairs. The economic link between the two countries was not only still strong, but even more impossible than before to distinguish fully from the political. America was concerned not to overstrain her economy by excessive re-armament; this was, and is, a wise concern, for in the past the democracies have profited markedly in war from the fact that their economies were basically stronger and less stretched than those of their enemies when actual hostilities broke out. This preoccupation was much more serious in the case of a Britain still pursued by a balance of payments problem. In 1950 her economic position was better than it had been since the war; her industrial production in the first quarter of the year was 149 per cent of the 1938 level, and, in the year following devaluation, her gold and dollar reserves rose by more than $1·4 billion to $2·8 billion, so that it was found possible on 13 December, 1950, to announce the suspension of Marshall Aid payments to Britain from the end of the year. This was largely due to the rise in the prices of the main exports of the sterling to the dollar area, which resulted from the Korean War. But already the war, which broke out in June, had shown the necessity for a great re-armament programme, and this made it clear that aid which was ceasing to flow in one channel would have to be turned on in another, for the British, like the French, re-armament plans were based on the assumption that large-scale American aid would be available to implement them; indeed, the British explicitly stated that their "upper limit"[1] would be determined by the extent of that aid. To Britain this re-armament was an unenviable necessity, for without it and the circumstances which made it necessary, she might very possibly have climbed to a secure economic situation, but a necessity it remained in the eyes of a majority of her people.*

Yet it was not undisputed, for the most serious split which the British Labour Party had suffered since 1931 occurred when Aneurin Bevan and a group of followers denounced the scale of British re-armament as more than the economy of the country could bear. The Bevanites remained no more than a splinter group, and, ironically enough, were only anticipating by a year or so the attitude of the new Conservative government, which in 1952 instituted considerable cuts in arms expenditure, though it must be added that by then the threat of Russian aggression appeared to have receded somewhat, no doubt largely owing to the fact that Bevan's advice was not prematurely accepted. Bevan was in fact anti-Communist, and opposed re-armament because he feared that it was the quickest way to wreck the economy of the country and precipitate the sort of economic disaster on which Communism thrives, but, because he came from the extreme Socialist wing of the Labour Party and because the Marxist-flavoured views of that wing led them to dislike what they believed to be the capitalist imperialism of the United States, there was considerable American mistrust of him and his followers, as the men representing in their fullest form the doctrinaire economic dogmas which many Americans believed to be responsible for the seeming-slowness of Britain's economic recovery. It was, therefore, happy for Anglo-American relations that his voice remained obviously unrepresentative.

Some of the dire consequences of re-armament that he had predicted came to pass though not so disastrously as to wreck the British economy, to produce an increase in Communism or even to augment

[1] U.S.W.A., 1950, p. 261

*Britain had, from 1946 until 1949, consistently spent a larger proportion of her national income on armaments than the United States; in 1949 the former spent $6\frac{3}{4}$ per cent of gross national product, the latter $6\frac{1}{2}$ per cent. By 1951 the figures were 11 per cent and $11\frac{1}{2}$ per cent respectively, and were expected (in 1952) to reach 14 per cent and 20 per cent by 1954. (H. A. Roberts and P. A. Wilson, *Britain and the United States*, London, 1953, p. 89.) Because of her greater wealth, America had spent far more per head of the population ever since the war.

his support in the country. There was a marked inflationary tendency in the prices of manufactures and in those raw materials, such as rubber, which were in great demand; though the latter was not without its advantages to the Sterling Area, the ultimate overall effects on the balance of payments was distinctly adverse, for it became clear that Britain's curve of industrial production had begun to flatten out. As 1951 wore on, her newly acquired dollar reserves began once more to melt rapidly away, and the Labour government seemed incapable of dealing resolutely with the situation, largely because they could only do so by abandoning some of the planks in their domestic platform. They were naturally, therefore, very averse from American proposals further to curtail East-West trade—trade with the Communist world—as a measure of political warfare; nor could any British Government act otherwise in view of the fact that well over one third of all Britain's essential grain imports in 1950 had come from behind the Iron Curtain, while America could not offer direct alternatives in the way of assistance or markets, for Marshall Aid had ceased and tariffs remained. But the rose she did offer, though not as sweet, was as necessary, and, in its way, as salutary; christened the Mutual Security Bill, it provided for nearly $6 billion of military aid, almost $5 billion of it for Europe, and of this Britain received a large portion. As Churchill picturesquely put it to Congress in 1952; he came here to ask "not for gold but for steel, not for favours but equipment."[1]

The Tory government, which came to power in October, 1951, then proceeded to demonstrate that, even in the midst of continuing (if reduced) rearmament, Britain had still the power to pick a path between the devil of bankruptcy and unemployment, and the deep blue sea of military weakness. Beginning with drastic cuts in imports and continuing with severe restrictions on credit, Chancellor of the Exchequer Butler staunched the flow of dollars and led the country to an economic position which, at the close of 1952, looked much healthier than it had since mid-1950. He had been aided by the lessening of international tension, particularly in Europe, and though Britain was very far from economically safe yet, she had moved decisively forward. A virtue was even made of necessity, by turning to good account Britain's role as a manufacturer of arms of all kinds, and endeavouring to persuade dollar countries to spend as much as possible in this way in Britain. After the Commonwealth Economic Conference at the end of the year, which showed itself determined to pursue a policy of co-operation with the United States, and to approach her with proposals for a World

[1] *Current Developments,* January, 1952, p. 1.

Economic Conference to discuss long-term means of bringing the obstinate dollar balance into equilibrium, there were once again hopes of ending the threat to Britain's solvency without direct American aid. Much depended upon the attitude of a Republican party, whose traditions made any process facilitating the spending of American dollars on British industrial products very difficult to inaugurate, or, perhaps, upon the extent to which the new President could impose his will upon the Congress.

In mutual defence, the bond between the two countries was correspondingly close. Though, as we have seen, much of the machinery of war-time co-operation had been dismantled, and though in the new NATO structure there was no formal place for a peculiarly or uniquely close relationship between the two powers, it plainly existed none the less. Already, before the beginning of formal discussions about a North Atlantic Treaty, within a matter of hours of the Berlin blockade crisis, the British Government had been asked, and had agreed, to accept two Groups of American B-29 bombers, presumably carrying atomic bombs, for permanent stationing in Britain; this prompt British compliance, which had come "somewhat to the surprise of the Americans"[1] and which the latter did not definitely decide to clinch for over a fortnight, shows as nothing else could, the extraordinary nature of the Anglo-American relationship, of the strength of which the treaty of 1949 was but a pale formal reflection. Meantime, the prompt British co-operation in the Berlin air-lift had shown how easily the old wartime spirit of common action could be renewed when occasion arose. In November, 1948, during a visit to England, Secretary of Defence Forrestal had long, frank and searching conversations with the British Minister of Defence and the three Chiefs of Staff. In December, 1949, it was revealed that, as a result of conversations inaugurated as long ago as 1947, the United States, Britain and Canada had joined in arrangements to move in the direction of a standardization of arms and equipment as well as training methods; these remained the practical basis of later and more formal agreements made under the auspices of NATO. There were naturally difficulties, small and large, in carrying out so far-reaching a proposal in time of peace, arising from traditional differences of national outlook and real differences of national interest; typical of the small problems was that of Britain's reluctance, partly through conviction and partly through pride, to abandon her proposed new ·280 rifle in deference to American demands for the acceptance of their ·300 as the standardized weapon of the alliance. For the most

[1] Forrestal, p. 455.

part these problems were settled without undue trouble, but one, the largest and most important of all, remained for a long time intractable, and was still under consideration at the end of 1952—that of atomic co-operation.

This is worth some discussion, not only because of its immense and singular intrinsic significance, but also because its development is very characteristic of the course of Anglo-American relations in the post-war years. It is interesting that in the defence discussions with Forrestal in November, 1948, there occurred in immediate proximity British criticisms of the "very sticky attitude" of the United States in releasing defence information to the members of the Western Union, and British comment on the fact that plans for the strategy of future war were rendered "utterly unrealistic because they do not include in sufficient detail the planning for atomic warfare."[1] This struck a deep chord in Anglo-American relations, and it reverberated far more in the minds of the leaders of Britain than appears in the record, which is the case partly because the whole question has from its birth been, and still is, shrouded in secrecy. This secrecy, which makes the task of the historian of these years difficult, was maintained after the war from fear of Russia, and was intensified by the Russian explosion of an atomic bomb in September, 1949. The extent of the security veil became a cause of great concern to scientists on both sides of the Atlantic, but was not argued upon national lines; scientists everywhere in the free world were acutely aware that the free dissemination of scientific data is the life blood of science. Some were inclined to believe that excessive secrecy might defeat its own object of maintaining the West's lead in scientific weapons, but to the majority it appeared that such arguments would be even more applicable to science behind the Iron Curtain, where other and additional barriers to the flow of information existed. By the end of 1952, voices were being raised to argue that a restoration of the war-time Anglo-American co-operation in this sphere would at least be preferable to the continued work of their independent scientists in water-tight compartments, particularly now that they were once more allies in name as well as in fact. Pressure to achieve this had been intensified on the British side after the Conservative government's announcement, on coming into office, that the secret construction of a British atomic weapon, which had been begun by its predecessor without even Parliament being aware of it, was well advanced; and reached a crescendo after the successful detonation of the bomb in the Monte-

[1] Q. ibid, p. 525.

bello Islands off the Australian coast at the beginning of October, 1952. This made Britain the third power in the world to produce atomic bombs and added great point to her renewed approaches to the United States, which, Churchill went so far as to say, he did not doubt would lead to much closer American interchange of information than had taken place in the last few years.

But the difficulty of restoring the war-time partnership was rendered formidable by the actions which had been taken since its termination. The original atomic bomb had been the joint work of American, British and Canadian scientists, although much of the technical skill and most of the money had been provided by the United States. It had been necessary for Churchill to insist on one occasion during the war, in 1943, on the adequate American fulfilment of the mutual obligation to exchange information, to which Roosevelt agreed;* and, after it was over, a misleading and precipitate statement by President Truman, in October, 1945, to the effect that the United States would retain her monopoly of the processes for the construction of atomic bombs, alarmed British opinion, though the American Cabinet had in fact decided earlier to attempt to set up some system of international control under the auspices of the United Nations. Conversations between Truman, Attlee and Mackenzie King in Washington in November resulted in agreement on the need for international action to control atomic energy and to outlaw weapons of mass destruction, with effective safeguards through inspection.

But these hopes foundered, like so many others in the post-war world, on the rock of Russian opposition. The United States, in the successive stages of the Lilienthal-Acheson Report, the Baruch Plan, and majority approval of it in the United Nations, gained wide support for a system of control by a United Nations Authority, armed with the power of inspection; "dangerous" activities would be permitted only to the Authority, and there was to be no veto on its actions in the sphere of inspection. It envisaged a transition period during which

---

*In 1954 it was revealed that the terms of the actual agreement had forbidden the use of the bomb against third parties without each other's consent. On atomic power it agreed: "In view of the heavy burden of production falling on the United States as a result of the wise division of the war effort, the British Government recognize that any post-war advantages of an industrial or commercial character shall be dealt with as between the United States and Great Britain on terms to be specified by the President . . . to the Prime Minister . . . (who) expressly disclaims any interest . . . beyond what might be considered by the President . . . to be fair and just. . . ." (*Sydney Morning Herald*, 7 April, 1954.)

American information would be disclosed to the Authority by agreed stages, to be followed by the outlawry of atomic bombs, and, finally, the destruction of stocks already in existence once the system of control was firmly established. This was certainly as enlightened a series of proposals as any nation in control—for the moment exclusively— of such a gigantic force could have been expected to put forward, but, whether because she could never have consented to international inspection under any circumstances, as seems probable, or whether because she would not do so during the transitional period when America would be at such a distinct advantage, as some Russian supporters claimed, the Soviet Union rejected the American proposals. Their own plan called for the virtually immediate prohibition and destruction of atomic weapons, but provided no adequate inspection safeguards; it was plainly an unsatisfactory plan for the free world and was rejected in its turn. This deadlock was never resolved, despite bouts of fruitless discussion, which diminished steadily in frequency.

Meanwhile, the United States had gone her own way. The McMahon Act, which was approved on 2 August, 1946, set up a governmental agency, the United States Atomic Energy Commission, with vast monopoly powers over the production of all forms of atomic energy. The Act also contained a number of restrictions on the dissemination of information, though these were couched in very general terms; this generality, combined with the curtain of secrecy which now descended, make it difficult to assess exactly the effect of the legislation and of the actions taken subsequently by the Commission, but there is no doubt that they severely curtailed, if they did not stop completely, the exchange of information with Britain and Canada. British scientists like Dr. (later Sir) W. G. Penney had participated in American tests as late as that at Bikini on 1 July, 1946, but thenceforward appear to have done so no longer. The situation is perhaps best described in the words of Attlee in Parliament in 1951: "The position of the United States administration in many of these matters was now regulated by legislation enacted in the United States since the end of the war, and the wartime arrangements had been modified accordingly, but partnership between the three countries for certain purposes in the atomic energy field continued." When further pressed by the Opposition he replied that, "It was a rather complicated and delicate matter which he would like to discuss with Mr. Churchill." Modification of the war-time agreements, particularly one made at Quebec, apparently took place by mutual consent of the three powers, but it appears likely that the arrangements made were in reality only satisfactory to the United

955

States; the negotiations, which are still on the secret list, seem to have taken place in December, 1947, and to have been embodied in a "paper stating the position of the United States and the United Kingdom",[1] in January, 1948. By this time it was becoming quite clear that no international agreement on atomic energy was likely, and the United States determined to keep control as far as possible in her own hands, so that something much less than the old war-time co-operation went into effect. But during the next two years, though the United States "military authorities" considered that "[c]ontinuance of the American monopoly . . . was entirely consistent with the principle of national specialization on which the North Atlantic defence organization was founded",[2] they felt that advantage might be taken of British scientific contributions, while they were not allowed to remain unaware of the fact that Britain and Canada controlled the sources of a number of raw materials used in atomic manufacture. New ultra-secret conferences, therefore, took place in Washington in the summer of 1949, "looking toward a partnership in the field of atomic energy based upon the most rational and economical joint utilization of materials, techniques, and knowledge available to the three countries".[3]

It is possible, though one cannot know, that these steps might, under pressure of Russian competition, which was responsible for America's decision to press on with the production of the hydrogen bomb, have led gradually to the restoration of a full interchange of atomic information, but there intervened a series of happenings which made this less rather than more likely. In practice, the past effects of the security restrictions had sometimes seemed almost comic, as in the chase led the frantic American authorities by one of their own scientists (who was sent on a visit to Britain to exchange information in July, 1948, carrying a list which inadvertently contained one forbidden subject) before he was eventually tracked down "touring Scotland".[4] The precautions seemed, at first, excessive, particularly in view of the fact that Britain was, within four years, to have produced her own atomic bomb; but they no longer seemed so after the arrest in England of Dr. Klaus Fuchs, a British, German-born scientist, in February, 1950, and his confession that he had passed vital atomic secrets to the U.S.S.R. This was not the first of the dramatic atomic espionage revelations, which was that of Dr. Alan Nunn May, a British scientist arrested in Canada in 1946, while, more recently, a Department of Justice analyst and a Soviet employee of the United Nations had been found guilty of

[1] Ibid, pp. 336-8.   [2] U.S.W.A., 1949, p. 494.
[3] Under-Secretary Webb: q. ibid, p. 495.   [4] Forrestal, p. 472.

espionage during the course of 1949. But it was almost certainly the most serious of them, and it is probable that the actions of this one man advanced by months, if not years, the first Soviet bomb. His case dramatically illustrated the difficulties of this question, for his very remarkable—indeed nearly unique—technical abilities made him almost indispensable to atomic research, and this no doubt had persuaded the authorities to take the risk of employing him. But, though he, a stateless person, possessed of great intellectual power and thus of frightening knowledge, exemplified in its highest degree that craving for emotional satisfaction which, in this era of religious decay, Communism seems so often to satisfy, Britons could not console themselves with the thought that the foreign-born alone were susceptible. May was British, and in other spheres than that of nuclear physics, Englishmen under the influence of Communism behaved in a most unpredictable manner, like the two British diplomats Burgess and Maclean, who disappeared suddenly in mysterious circumstances some months later.

Thus, though neither Canada nor the United States could boast of clean hands in the matter, Britain provided in the case of Fuchs the most terrible example of loose security, and it was of little avail to plead the strange and unreal atmosphere of atomic research, which places so great a strain even upon the most normal of men; nor was it of much value to point to similar cases in the United States, which was all too conscious of these things. These developments led to grave American mistrust of Britain's security arrangements, and to a sharpened emphasis on the secrecy surrounding America's own atomic processes. Only the passage of time and the demonstration that Britain, too, had the ability to construct atomic weapons could make possible a reopening of the old co-operation. Moves in this direction were being urged by the close of 1952, but it was not known if they were actually being taken, nor was it likely that it would be known for some time, for the veil of secrecy would remain. Only—and it was much to be desired —behind the veil there would be more seminal minds more efficiently at work for the common benefit of the three powers and of the free world.

But unfortunately the matter did not end here, for the question of atomic espionage linked up with the broader question of the internal threat of Communism to the nations of the free world, and that in its turn with the threat of Communist states to the liberty of mankind. Because of the awful power of atomic energy, Communist spies in this field were the most notorious, but they were not necessarily, in the long run, the most dangerous. The arrest of Fuchs came at a period when American fear of Communism as a menace to the democratic way of life had spread from the international arena to that of domestic politics. The two trials of Alger Hiss for perjury, culminating, in January, 1950, in a conviction which implied clearly his guilt as a Soviet spy in 1937-8, brought it home dramatically to the American people how high in their government traitors could be, and gave added strength to the arm of Senator Joseph R. McCarthy of Wisconsin, who began in February, 1950, a virulent, extravagant and largely unsubstantiated farrago of charges and insinuations against the loyalty of U.S. officials, particularly in the State Department. There is no doubt that there were a number of cases of persons in or on the fringes of public life who were secret Communists, and this aroused suspicion in the minds of many Americans. Unfortunately, the campaign against them, at some points, exceeded all bounds of decency and even common sense. The method of unproven 'smears', or slurs, convicted innocent as well as guilty; such devices proved a convenient way of destroying personal or political enemies; no distinction was made in many cases between Communism in the very different environment of the thirties and Communism in the present; and methods adopted, even by universities, such as loyalty oaths, besides their patent stupidity, constituted a real danger to freedom of thought and speech. Particular animus was displayed against all those who were associated with the particular Far Eastern policy of the United States, which had prevailed during the collapse of Nationalist China, such as Philip C. Jessup and Owen Lattimore. A furious campaign was waged for the removal of Secretary of State Acheson, as a scapegoat for the China policy and a public figure who had, in Christian charity, refused to "turn [his] back on Alger Hiss,"[1] who had once been his friend. Fortunately, he stuck to his post, and the main substance of the moderate American policy remained unchanged. Inevitably, however, in a democracy, public opinion affects policy, and the hardening of the State Department's heart towards Communist China in the vital period just before her intervention in the Korean War owed much to the domestic campaign against Communism.

All this did not pass unnoticed by the British. The excesses of the campaign, dubbed a 'witch-hunt', were deplored, particularly by intellectuals and those towards the left wing, whose counterparts were the chief sufferers across the Atlantic. This was merely disembodied criticism at first, for it did not affect Englishmen directly, but

[1] Q. U.S.W.A., 1950, p. 55.

when, under the McCarran Act—President Truman's veto of which was over-ridden by Congress—the United States began, late in 1952, to examine all foreign seamen who wished to go ashore in American ports as to their political opinions, and to refuse admission to some, the matter became more than a domestic one. Indeed, most of the British alarm arose from a fear that what was widely characterized as this 'hysteria' might sweep away all barriers and invade the international stage. Particularly after the Korean War began, this was the nightmare of many thoughtful Englishmen, and one rendered peculiarly alarming by the giant djinn of atomic energy which America commanded.

In truth, Britain seemed more concerned at this time with obtaining some say in the initial use of the atomic bomb than with its possible leakage into the hands of the enemy. It is symptomatic that in September, 1948, before the wave of fear had begun to get out of hand, Secretary Forrestal had been told by Prime Minister Attlee that "there is no division in the British public mind about the use of the atomic bomb—they were for its use. Even the Church in recent days had publicly taken this position",[1] whereas in December, 1950, when he flew to Washington at an hour's notice, one of the main objects of the Prime Minister's visit was to obtain an assurance from the President that the atomic bomb would not be used without prior consultation with Britain; he was not able to obtain this assurance, for Truman was adamant that its use lay entirely within American discretion,* though he agreed "to keep the Prime Minister at all times informed of developments which might bring about a change in the situation."[2]

It was at about this time that people in Europe began first to be fully conscious of those isolated and fanatical American voices—they had in fact existed ever since 1945—which were raised in favour of a swift and overwhelming atomic attack upon Russia, before the American technical ascendancy was lost. Churchill did not cease to point out that the American bases in Britain placed her in the forefront of any atomic war, and that, desirable though it was to have the bases, this fact gave her the right to be heard in their joint counsels; always a leading proponent of Anglo-American co-operation, he is never slow to make clear that this must take the form of a genuine partnership. It was on this subject that he obtained from the President a fuller agreement, during his visit to Washington as Prime Minister in January, 1952, when the

---

[1] Q. Forrestal, p. 491.

*It is not clear how this squares with the Churchill–Roosevelt agreement of 1943 (see p. 954, note).   [2] Q. U.S.W.A., 1950, p. 427.

joint communiqué stated, "We reaffirm the understanding that the use of these bases in an emergency would be a matter for joint decision by His Majesty's Government and the United States Government in the light of the circumstances prevailing at the time."[1] Thus British fear of American domestic anti-Communist violence owed a good deal to their greater fear of American forces making for extremism in international affairs.

But their fears in any case were a good illustration of the long distance there is yet to tread to a full and popular Anglo-American understanding. The wide differences between Britain and America had clear effects in their divergent attitudes to this problem. Britain's closely packed, homogeneous population, which is of overwhelmingly native origin; the tight bonds of her traditional unitary system of government; the British respect for authority and order; the English tendency to moderation and understatement; the strictness of Britain's law of libel and slander; and the British instinct of unity, which has been perhaps the most remarkable product of her many centuries of free government—all these things made the British people underestimate rather than over-estimate the Communist danger as it existed in America. (Indeed, they were over-confident at times about its extent at home, and this seeming casualness was not lost on Americans.) Where they chiefly failed was in an imaginative understanding of the very different situation in America. There, with no aristocratic tradition to instil an instinct of obedience, but the very reverse; with a tendency to over-statement and a political habit of reaching moderate solutions by resolving two opposite and extreme forces of opinion; with a population, vast multitudes of whom were still foreign born; with sections of that population, such as the negroes of the South or the Mexicans of the South-west, who were, despite all the wealth of America, economically depressed to an extent almost unimaginable in Britain; and with a consciousness that American patriotism had been of necessity an artificial, if marvellous, creation of recent date in many of her people—there, the problem of Communist infiltration not only seemed to be, but was, a much graver matter. For this reason many Englishmen seriously misjudged the nature and influence of the American domestic anti-Communist campaign.

VIII

BUT their fears of American extremism in foreign policy, though similarly exaggerated, had more justification, for the material of inter-

[1] *Current Developments,* January, 1952, p. 9.

national affairs is very explosive and the international experience, as well as the character, of the United States did not fit her particularly well to pursue a course of sustained moderation. But experience is the great teacher, and the Americans are from one point of view a very pragmatic people, who have learnt fast. To date there has been no collapse in the moderation of American official policy, and—contrary to the belief of some of the English pundits, who once more mistook the talk of an American election campaign for reality—there is little sign that it is likely in the history, advisers or prospects of President-Elect Eisenhower, who has already declared that he sees no swift panacea for the bloodshed of the Korean War. And it is in the Far East that the most dangerous of the discords between Britain and the United States during the post-war years has sounded.

Since the advent of the Open Door policy in China, efforts have not been lacking to reconcile British and American aims in that region, and, after the British abandonment of her Japanese alliance at America's behest and the coming of the Japanese war, a great measure of agreement was reached. One new development should, however, be noted. In 1900, with the Indian and Far Eastern Empire of Britain at its height, and with America only newly conscious of her Pacific power, the interest and influence of the two nations was not far from equal, if indeed that of Britain was not much greater; by 1950, with the independence of Burma and the self-government of India and Pakistan, and with the relative decline in Britain's economic as well as political strength, as well as with the increased power and political awareness of the United States in the Pacific (which will probably be further increased under a Republican administration), this balance was entirely upset in America's favour. The American preponderance was only to a very limited extent counteracted by the growing importance and the growing independence of Australia and New Zealand, and with Malaya on the road to independence, Britons must perforce recognize the diminution of the United Kingdom's interest and influence in the area.

During the war the chief Anglo-American difference over the Far East was that Churchill believed that Roosevelt consistently overrated the importance and power of China. In the post-war period there was some British uneasiness as to the American treatment of Japan, some scepticism as to the effect of the democratization movement, and some fear, particularly in Australia and New Zealand, of the policy of making an ally of Japan, which was embodied in the Japanese peace treaty of 1951. But it was not, in reality, until the Communist conquest of China and the retreat of Generalissimo Chiang Kai-shek to the island of

Formosa that a real rift began to appear. It was quite clear after the war was over that a new day was dawning in the Far East, symbolized by the white man's surrender of extra-territorial rights in Shanghai, and that in it the Open Door policy could have no place. If China was to be exploited, it would not be in the old fashion, though it did seem that Russian control might well have been established from her old base of Manchuria, in which her position after her brief entry into the Japanese war was stronger than it had ever been before. But she in fact left it in 1946, taking with her most of its considerable quantities of industrial machinery. What then was to replace the Open Door, in a China still, as often of old, locked in civil strife, but in this case between two great groups, the Nationalists and the Communists, either of which would be likely, if victorious, to make China's weight felt for the first time in the councils of the world? In the war, American support had gone to the Nationalists, but the idea had become prevalent in the later stages of it, that the Communists, who had also opposed the Japanese, could perhaps be induced to make an agreement with Chiang Kai-shek, in order to avoid bloodshed and in order to effect a peaceful union of their country; it was, after all, the period of Yalta and the Western hope of Soviet co-operation. But during the year which General Marshall spent in China during 1945-6, in an effort to reconcile the two factions, the suspicion grew in the West that the Communists were not mere agricultural reformers, as was claimed by some of the advocates of their cause, but ideological Communists in increasingly close contact with a Moscow whose retiring troops in Manchuria made the initial Communist offensives suspiciously easy. In any case Marshall's mission failed, and by the beginning of October, 1949, when the new Chinese Government was recognized by the U.S.S.R., the defeat of Chiang Kai-shek on the Chinese mainland was complete.

The announcement on 15 February, 1950, of a revised Sino-Soviet Treaty plainly marked a disastrous disturbance in the world's balance of power, in favour of Russia and against the free world; Russia had for the first time a major ally, a Communist power, and an apparently firm grip on the vast Eurasian land mass. The bitter Republican criticism, that had long been endemic, of the Administration's China policy now reached a new pitch of intensity. After the return of General Marshall, the United States had ceased to give any but ineffective financial and military aid to the Nationalists, and after he had become Secretary of State in January, 1947, had firmly refused to renew it on a large scale, even after a personal visit to Washington by Madame Chiang Kai-shek in November, 1948. It thus appeared that it was in default of American aid that the Communists had won their stupendous victory.

But on 5 August, 1949, the State Department issued a White Paper making its justification of its whole Chinese policy; this took the form of a scorching denunciation of the Nationalist régime which was "so inept, selfish, purblind, and faithless as to be lost beyond hope of resurrection."[1] Though there was no incentive, in the face of the catastrophe which had happened, for the State Department to understate the case, there seems little doubt that the Nationalist Government collapsed through its own corruption and inefficiency, combined with the profound and overwhelming war-weariness of the Chinese people, among whom the Communists alone still retained their zeal and the will to fight. It is virtually certain that only full-scale American political and military intervention could have saved it after 1946, even if that would have succeeded; it is perfectly certain that no American, including later critics, seriously hoped for such a policy at the time, when the demobilization cry was at its most piercing. As Marshall said in February, 1948, in reference to universal military training, "We were playing with fire while we had nothing with which to put it out." This exactly describes the activities desired in China by pro-Nationalist Republicans, for in truth, without full-scale American intervention, which was inconceivable, the Chinese problem from the American point of view was, as he said "unsolvable".[2] To Republicans who were not sobered by the realities of responsibility, it was hard, as it was later to be over Korea, to realize that there are very strict, if not necessarily clearly defined, limits to the power in international affairs, even of a country as strong as the United States. Those limits are few if she is prepared to exercise her full power, but they are much more cramping if she is not. So far, her official policy has recognized those limits with admirable clarity, but the voices of its critics are so strident that other nations in the free world are always apprehensive lest they should one day gain control of affairs, and, by reverting to the traditional American instinct for grand and thoroughgoing solutions to international problems, precipitate the third, and atomic, world war. Britons are apt to exaggerate this possibility beyond reason, but there was certainly some fire behind the smoke, and those acquainted with America's history could not but uneasily "Remember the *Maine*".

It was at this critical point, and on this topic so highly charged with emotion, that the first Anglo-American divergence appeared, for on

[1] Bailey, p. 866.   [2] Forrestal, p. 373.

6 January, 1950, Great Britain accorded *de jure* recognition to Communist China, and offered to establish diplomatic relations with Peking. Her reasons for taking this swift, perhaps precipitate action, despite the difficulties she had already encountered with the Communists, who had, for instance, fired upon British warships on the Yangtze River, were complex. She was certainly not unaware of her great commercial investments in China, and of the hostage-like character of her island colony of Hong Kong; furthermore, she was convinced that the Communist régime in China had come to stay unless it were to be defeated in war, which she emphatically would not contemplate. Having, for many centuries, lived in diplomatic relations with countries of whose forms of government she disapproved, it was her fixed policy not to let ideological considerations sway her in this matter; she was uncertain, as yet, of the fundamental character of the Chinese Communist movement, with its apparent emphasis on the redistribution of agricultural land to the peasants. She was, too, by a strange paradox, more aware than the United States, for all its anti-colonialism, of the extent to which Chinese passions were simply anti-Western in character; and her recent experience in India, which had already recognized Peking, seemed to her to indicate that a swift generosity was the only course with any hope in it for the future friendship of China.* She was also far from convinced of the reality of Chinese-Russian cordiality; Russia had long been at least as unpopular in China as the rest of the West, and the early relationship between the Chinese Communists and Moscow had given distinct evidences of difficulty. With these things in her mind, and observing the breach in 1948 between Marshal Tito of Yugoslavia and Stalin, it seemed to her wise, if distasteful, to make a virtue of necessity in China, and, by recognizing her and preparing for her entry into the United Nations, to endeavour in the long run to woo her away from her Russian partner. In many of these assumptions she was no doubt sanguine, but to her mind there was no other policy.

It seemed, in fact, to her the logical conclusion to be drawn from the State Department's emphatic views on the inevitability of the Nationalist defeat in China, and it is possible that the British Foreign Office had some grounds for supposing that the Administration would before long follow her in her course. Indeed, but for the coming of the Korean War, it is hard to see what other outcome there could have been, for the only practicable alternative was the indefinite continuance of the refusal to recognize the Communists, on the lines of the Hoover-Stimson doctrine, a prospect which cannot be described as either

* Indian influence on the British decision was probably considerable.

engaging or realistic. Still, *de jure* recognition of Communist governments who come to power against the wishes of the American people is for them a hard pill to swallow—it took the United States, after all, more than fifteen years to establish diplomatic relations with Communist Russia—and it would take a little time. But American administrations were now more realistic in their approach to international affairs, and in due course no doubt, the British felt, the recognition would be accorded. Thus Britain was, perhaps, a little hasty; America, maybe, a little dilatory.

But that haste and that delay were to sow the seeds of a vast amount of future difficulty, for it was only a month after the British recognition of Communist China that Senator McCarthy began that onslaught upon pro-Communists in the State Department which was to centre particularly upon its Far Eastern policy and the advisers responsible for it. This, while it did not force the Administration to beat a retreat or go back upon its previous declarations of policy, made any further development in the direction of a realistic recognition of the existing situation in China very difficult, if not impossible. This deadlock persisted until the attack on South Korea made it quite out of the question, and yet this broader issue was to make more intractable the whole problem of a Korean truce.

Thus, step by step, even before June, 1950, events led the nations into the impasse which was to become complete at Panmunjon, and it is hard to see how any way out to a more stable Far Eastern situation can be found which does not include an American recognition of Communist China. When in November, 1949, the question of the seating of the Communists, instead of the Nationalists, in the United Nations had first been raised in the Assembly, the United States had proposed and carried a compromise resolution which specifically left the question of diplomatic recognition to individual governments, and did no more than affirm a number of platitudes about respect for China's independence and the denial of spheres of influence, which were strangely reminiscent of the outworn Open Door policy. This had merely marked time in a world where the tide of events was waiting for no man, and when the Chinese intensified their pressures against American officials in China, the United States recalled all of them from the country, thus washing her hands of the affair, as it were, just at the time that Britain was according recognition. During the same month, the U.S.S.R. intensified its campaign to oust the Nationalist delegation from the United Nations, and on 13 January began a boycott of that organization, which was intended to last until Communist China was seated; in fact it lasted until the Soviet Union was forced back, on 1 August, by the developments in Korea. During the ensuing months the United States let it be known that she would not absolutely veto the admission of Communist China, but that she would continue to oppose it; Great Britain supported the Soviet contention that the Nationalists should be unseated. While the hunt for Acheson's head was up in the United States, the Administration no doubt felt it could do no more, and thus Britain and the United States slipped into a position of direct, if not diametrical, opposition. Once more, inaction waited upon events; if the Communists invaded Formosa and defeated Chiang Kai-shek, there could hardly be any further demand that he be supported, which might in due time create a favourable situation for the recognition of the Peking Government. But, as is the way of the world, as statesmen should know, it was not Formosa that was attacked.

IX

ON Sunday 25 June, 1950, at 4 a.m., troops of the Communist North Korean Government crossed the 38th Parallel, which had divided the Russian from the American zones of occupation and had solidified into a political frontier, in a large-scale, surprise invasion of the under-armed South Korean Republic, which had recently been evacuated by American troops. Immediately upon receipt of the news the State Department had the Secretary-General of the United Nations telephoned (in the middle of the night) to arrange an emergency meeting of the Security Council for that afternoon. Because of the continued absence of the Soviet Union delegate, the Council adopted by nine votes to none, with Yugoslavia abstaining, a resolution proposed by the United States, which declared the invasion "a breach of the peace", demanded the immediate cessation of hostilities accompanied by the withdrawal forthwith of the North Korean forces, and called upon "all Members [of the United Nations] to render every assistance to the United Nations in the execution of this resolution and to refrain from giving assistance to the North Korean authorities."[1] When, next day, the North Korean forces pushed on, President Truman announced that the United States would not only support the Council, but would assist South Korea by the "co-operative action of American personnel in Korea, [and] steps taken to expedite and augment assistance of the type being furnished under the Mutual Defense Assistance Pro-

[1] *Documents on American Foreign Relations,* XII, pp. 443-4.

gram".[1] At noon on 27 June President Truman declared, "I have ordered United States air and sea forces to give the Korean Government troops cover and support".[2]

For this bold action President Truman deserves very great credit. He was strongly supported in it by Britain, whose representative applauded this reaction to what he called an "unparalleled affront"[3] to the United Nations. In a brief spell of enthusiasm, many Englishmen compared America's action with their own in 1935 against Italy, and when, on 30 June, the President, on the advice of General MacArthur, authorized the use of "certain supporting ground units" in Korea, they compared it very favourably; they had visions, perhaps, of the coming of an era of effective collective security, and certainly any lingering fears of a recurrence of American isolationism were banished.

In future their fears were to be of a precisely opposite course of American international action. In his statement of 27 June the President had ordered the American Seventh Fleet to neutralize Formosa, and, though its implications were not at first fully realized, this meant the perpetuation, as long as the edict lasted and there was no general war, of the Nationalist régime, and the indefinite postponement of a comprehensive Far Eastern settlement. This was, in effect, an intervention in the Chinese Civil War, and gave some semblance of reality to the charges of anti-Americans that it was an overt example of reckless American 'imperialism', concerned only that Formosa should not pass into the hands of a power unfriendly to the United States because it constituted a military threat to American bases in Japan and the Pacific. But, more than that, the President's statement included the words, "The attack upon Korea makes it plain beyond all doubt that Communism had passed beyond the use of subversion to conquer independent nations and will now use armed invasion and war", which was an over-simplification of the Far Eastern problem with which many Englishmen could not agree, particularly since it implied a degree of unity in the Communist camp, which did not seem to them proven and which might, in any event, be disastrously strengthened by such an American attitude. These things did not much affect the resolution passed by the Security Council at a meeting in the afternoon of 27 June, recommending "that the Members of the United Nations furnish such assistance to the Republic of Korea as may be

[1] Q. U.S.W.A., 1950, p. 206.
[2] *Documents on American Foreign Relations*, XII, p. 444.
[3] U.S.W.A., 1950, p. 210.

necessary to repel the armed attack and to restore international peace and security in the area",[1] (though India and Egypt abstained from voting) but it certainly added to the reluctance of the fifty-three non-Communist nations, who assented, to give very practical form to their support of United Nations action.

The British Commonwealth alone made any immediate and substantial contribution, and by the end of the year only Turkey had added any considerable force. The older nations of the Commonwealth provided, first naval and air, and later ground, forces; in due course the British army contribution was stabilized at one division, a small contribution compared with that of the United States, and her naval and air effort was on the same sort of scale. In 1951 it was estimated that the British had 12,000, the United States between 160,000 and 200,000, troops in Korea, although the white population of the Commonwealth numbered as much as half of the total population of the United States. (India and Pakistan must be excluded from these calculations, particularly in view of the former's marked desire to retain the good will of Communist China, which remained one of the chief factors keeping British and American policy apart on the Korean issue. India was acutely conscious of the racial and anti-Western feeling behind the actions of the Chinese people.) This proportion is certainly a very small one, although allowance must be made for Britain's economic plight, and for the vital British military commitments elsewhere, such as the Middle East and, particularly, Malaya, where probably more than 20,000 troops were engaged in a bitter guerilla war. Casualties in Korea to the end of 1951 bring out even more clearly the extent of America's burden relative to the British, for she had suffered 103,739 to the United Kingdom's 3,033. This great discrepancy was one of which Churchill never ceased to remind the British people when they were inclined to criticize America's policy, and they were not unconscious of it. It did seem, however, to add point to their fears of American belligerence; Great Britain was, as France had been in 1919, a weary nation, conscious of her new weakness. In war, and in policy of which it is the continuation, confidence in one's moral and physical strength is a vital factor, and Britain was aware of the need for a prolonged period of recuperation if she was to rebuild her stamina. This made her cautious, whereas the United States, more conscious, in her giant strength, of her power in a world conflict, had some of that self-confidence, and occasional ebullience, which had characterized John Bull's actions in an earlier age. When the British reflected that the

[1] *Documents on American Foreign Relations*, XII, pp. 444-5.

968

total American casualties suffered in Korea by the end of 1952, a period of two and a half years, were hardly more than double what the British Armies had suffered on the very first day of the Battle of the Somme in 1916, their efforts in the Far East did not strike them as altogether unworthy.

But, though the British contributed more in Korea than anyone else, except America, this discrepancy did not make easier the solution of the political problems facing the two countries, for while American opinion hardened against allowing Communist China to enter the United Nations, which her satellite had so gravely affronted, that of Britain remained unaltered on this question, though she would not condone North Korea's action. On 11 September, for the first time, there occurred a straight vote in the United Nations Security Council as to whether Peking's representatives should be heard, on their claim that their territory had been violated by American planes; the Soviet proposal was supported by the United Kingdom, but failed to obtain the required votes to carry, although only Nationalist China and Cuba joined the United States in opposing it. To such a pass had the Anglo-American divergence of view now brought the two countries on the political plane. On the military plane, however, things looked much better, for the masterly delaying action directed by General MacArthur had turned the tide in Korea, and was succeeded on 15 September by the even more masterly and successful Inchon landings, which brought United Nations troops within striking distance of the 38th Parallel. It was in this atmosphere that the General Assembly met on 19 September. On an immediate proposal by India, that Communist China be seated, sixteen powers, including the United Kingdom, Pakistan and the U.S.S.R., voted in favour, and thirty-three, including the United States, against, while ten, including Canada, abstained. Once again no political decision was made, and once again events would not wait, though on this occasion the events were to some extent of American and also British making.

On 1 October the United Nations Commander-in-Chief in Korea, General MacArthur, appealed to the North Koreans to lay down their arms, and sent South Korean troops in *sorties* over the Parallel. He held the remainder of his forces, however, below the line, until on 7 October the General Assembly, by 47 votes to 5 with 7 abstentions, passed a comprehensive resolution proposed by Great Britain, which recommended, "All appropriate steps . . . to ensure conditions of stability throughout Korea", "All constituent acts . . . for the establishment of a unified, independent and democratic Government in the sovereign state of Korea", and that "All sections . . . of the population of Korea, South and North, be invited to co-operate . . . in the restoration of peace . . . and in the establishment of a unified Government".[1] In the enthusiasm of swift success, almost in a fit of absence of mind, nearly all the powers ignored the violent warnings of Peking, forgot the fears that may have been aroused there by such instances of American 'imperialism' as General MacArthur's recent visit to Chiang Kai-shek in Formosa, and regarded with optimism, which was later to prove no less fatuous, the United Nations offensive across the Parallel two days later. Only India sounded a note of, what was for her, mild caution, when Sir Benegal Rau expressed his country's fear "that the result may be to prolong North Korean resistance, and even to extend the area of conflict. Our fears may turn out to be wrong, but each government has to judge the situation upon the best information at its disposal and to act accordingly. Thus we view [the recommendation to cross the Parallel] with the greatest misgivings".[2] India's information turned out to be a great deal better than any other power's.

Thus General MacArthur might have been excused for misreading the political signs, although he ought to have had better military intelligence, but, as his forces advanced rapidly, he began to display an overweening confidence. This hardly seemed to be seriously disturbed by the realization towards the end of October that the Chinese had begun to commit organized units, even if they were claimed to be volunteers, in Korea—they had in fact begun to do so on 16 October—or by the consequent and sudden stiffening of North Korean resistance early in November, about fifty miles from the Yalu River border of Manchuria. It is true that, in a report to the United Nations on 6 November, he talked of the appearance of "a new, fresh army now" facing his forces, "backed up by a possibility of large alien reserves and adequate supply within easy reach to the enemy but beyond the limits of our present spere of military action"; but he added that there was not at the time "any possibility of a great military reverse." On 24 November, the day after Thanksgiving, he arrived in Korea to see the "general offensive" to "win the war" which had just started; his soldiers, he said, "will eat Christmas dinner at home".[3] This was indeed tempting Providence, and it proved a classic example of *hubris*. Within two days the United Nations were reeling back under the onslaught of two hundred thousand Chinese, and not until about

[1] Ibid, p. 459.   [2] Q. U.S.W.A., 1950, p. 361.
[3] Q. Rovere and Schlesinger, pp. 137, 143.

10 January, on the banks of the Han River some two hundred miles to the south, were they able to hold a firm line once again. For this unmitigated disaster all active United Nations parties in the Korean War must bear some of the blame. It is conceivable, but not likely, that the Chinese had always intended intervention; it is probable that they had made their dispositions in case of need and that the crossing of the Parallel convinced them of the reality of the American 'imperialist' threat, in which, it must be remembered, all Marxists necessarily believe. There was still no proof, as many asserted, that all these events, from the initial North Korean aggression to the Chinese intervention, had been engineered, or even necessarily approved, by Moscow.

In the United Nations early in December it became clear that Britain's view in favour of the admission of Communist China had not changed materially, while that of the United States against it had hardened. On a great array of other matters Anglo-American solidarity was as complete as usual, but here Britain, pressed by India, thought it indispensable to prevent the irrevocable splitting of the world into two great armed camps with no common ground between them, while the United States was adamant in its rejection of any Chinese attempt to "shoot their way" into the United Nations. General opinion in the United Nations began to shift its emphasis "from the repelling of aggression to the idea of mediation and conciliation between equals."[1] This trend America resisted, for, after agreeing on 8 November to the presence of Peking representatives at a discussion of their government's intervention in Korea, and after finding them bitterly hostile and unrepentant when they appeared on 28 November, the day on which General MacArthur signalized the catastrophe on the Yalu River by the statement that, "We face an entirely new war",[2] the United States Government reacted strongly to its Korean military defeat. On 30 November President Truman answered press questions on the subject in such a manner as to make it possible to believe that he meant that "if military action against China was authorized by the United Nations, the United States might authorize General MacArthur to use the atomic bomb at his own discretion."[3] This rash statement, although it was declared not to presage any change in American policy in this respect, almost certainly marked the lowest point in the graph of Anglo-American good relations since Pearl Harbour. So seriously was it viewed in London that the Prime Minister, amidst universal approval, decided at very short notice to fly to see President Truman

[1] U.S.W.A., 1950, p. 414.   [2] Q. ibid, p. 417.   [3] Ibid, p. 418.

in Washington. On the same day, however, the Russians had vetoed a resolution in the Security Coucil, sponsored by both the United States and the United Kingdom, which combined an assurance to China concerning its "legitimate interests" with "an urgent appeal to desist from its intervention in Korea".[1] In view of this joint action the gravity of the Anglo-American breach must not be overestimated.

But it was serious enough. The Prime Minister could get little satisfaction in the matter of the atomic bomb, and in Far Eastern policy the two men could only agree on such abstractions as support of the United Nations and avoidance of appeasement, while remaining divided on the questions of Formosa and the recognition of Communist China. The British were utterly opposed to the idea of a limited war against China, which was being openly canvassed in the United States, and it was clear that they had a majority of the United Nations behind them. Outside the Far East, happily, they remained at one, and were, in the words of the White House communiqué which closed the four-day conference on 8 December, "in complete agreement on the need for all the North Atlantic Treaty Countries to intensify their efforts to build up their defenses and strengthen the Atlantic community",[2] while even the Far Eastern disagreement was kept in its proper perspective by the discussion of European affairs. Indeed, it was not so much the policy of the Administration which frightened the British, for this, if it no longer differed from that of the Foreign Office merely on timing as it once had, was fairly clear and restrained, but the violent trends in American opinion, which were not only alarming in themselves, but made doubly so because they seemed to find strong support in the words and actions of the man who appeared for a time to be the most powerful American official in Far Eastern affairs, the United Nations Supreme Commander, General MacArthur. In fact, he became in a sense the embodiment, during these months, of all that Englishmen (and, for the matter of that, Canadians, who had known something in the past of America's belligerence of language and posture) had come most to fear in American foreign policy. The American opposition to the Administration's Far Eastern policy was a curious mixture of an old isolationism and a new universalism. The first was best embodied in men like Senator Taft and ex-President Hoover, the latter of whom gave striking expression to these sentiments in a speech on 20 December, 1950, the very day after the appointment of General Eisenhower as Supreme Commander of the Allied Forces in Europe; he called for defence of the Atlantic and Pacific Oceans, based on Japan, Formosa,

[1] Ibid, p. 419.　　[2] Q. ibid, p. 427.

and the Philippines in the West, and Great Britain in the East, and "not another man or another dollar" for Western Europe until they had "organized and equipped combat divisions of such huge numbers as would erect a sure dam against the red flood."[1] This approach did not, as time was to show, command the deliberate allegiance of many Americans; it was the swan-song of a departed era. It represented the very nightmare which had become a reality to France at the repudiation of the Versailles Treaty. But for Britain, be it noted, there had been a distinct change since the nineteen twenties, for she was now included within the pale of the projected American fortress. In one sense this was very satisfying, for it recognized the existence of a peculiar Anglo-American relationship, though in another it was not desirable, since the experience of 1940-1 had shown how difficult Britain could be to defend with the whole coastline of Europe in enemy hands.

But now Britain's chief fear was of the policy advocated in certain Republican circles of all-out action against Communist China. Mistrust of this policy in Britain was so pronounced that she, along with others, refused to authorize in November, 1950, when it was requested by the Administration, "hot pursuit of attacking enemy aircraft up to 2 or 3 minutes' flying time in Manchurian airspace".[2] The policy never did get control of the Democratic United States Government, but advocates of it seemed very strong during 1951. In the actual course of the Truman-Attlee conversations in December, 1950, a group of Republican Senators tried unsuccessfully to gain acceptance of a resolution, which would have required Senate ratification of any understanding made by the two leaders. Peculiar point was given to the British apprehensions in these months by the fact that such a policy was more and more openly advocated by General MacArthur, and that he seemed, so great was his self-confidence and prestige, largely beyond the control of the White House, let alone the State Department. These views might not be supported by the civilian Administration, but there seemed a distinct possibility that they might in fact gain control of American policy in the Far East through the action of the United Nations Supreme Commander, who had even more than the usual autonomy enjoyed by American commanders in the field.

Already, in August, 1950, MacArthur had sent a message to a Veterans' Convention in Chicago, declaring among other things that "Nothing could be more fallacious than the threadbare argument . . .

[1] Q. ibid, p. 440.   [2] Q. ibid, 1951, p. 83.

that if we defend Formosa we alienate continental Asia. Those who speak thus do not understand the Orient. They do not grasp that it is the pattern of Oriental psychology to respect and follow aggressive, resolute, and dynamic leadership."' (Indians thought that they knew a good deal more about oriental psychology than any American expatriate who had spent his life in Asia.) When the President heard of this interference of a military commander in the field of policy, he ordered the statement to be withdrawn, but not before it had made its way into many newspapers. Despite the President's firm action, increasing numbers of people wondered how much harm the General might do in his own command, if he could cause this much trouble back in America. In October, the President had journeyed half-way across the Pacific to meet the proconsul on Wake Island, and had tried, with some temporary success, to impose his will upon that of his recalcitrant commander. In November MacArthur disregarded the advice of the Joint Chiefs of Staff, based on the apprehensions of many members of the Allied Nations, to hold his forces, particularly the non-Korean ones, back from the actual Yalu frontier; and though this particular fact was not known at the time, there was a widespread uneasiness in Britain and elsewhere (amounting to panic on the left wing), at the possibility of an irrevocable act on the part of the Supreme Commander.

What exactly was it in MacArthur's policy that Britons feared? His beliefs were, from one point of view, the very reverse of those of President Hoover, for, he declared, "I believe we should defend every place from Communism. I believe we can. . . . I don't admit that we can't hold Communism wherever it shows its head". In American capacity to do this he had immense faith: "There are those who claim our strength is inadequate to protect us on two fronts. I can think of no greater expression of defeatism". So great was it, that he was quite prepared to dispense with allies if necessary: "If the other nations of the world haven't got enough sense to see where appeasement leads after the appeasement which led to the Second World War in Europe . . . why then we had better protect ourselves and go it alone". The other nation with which we are concerned bethought itself rather of the advice of Arnold Toynbee, that the trouble about learning from history is that one tends to remember only the most recent lesson, and was anxious to draw a distinction between conciliation and appeasement.

This contempt of General MacArthur for allies showed itself clearly in his later evidence before the Senate Foreign Relations Committee. Much chagrin was being caused in America by the continued trade of

' Q. Rovere and Schlesinger, p. 130.

Hong Kong with Red China at this time, despite the analogous trade which Japan had carried on in 1950 while it was under MacArthur's control, and during the course of the hearing, he read implacably through a lengthy list of strategic materials once thought to be passing through Hong Kong to China, without, however, noting aloud that opposite many of the items occurred the entries *"nil"* or "virtually *nil"*. "This omission", as Rovere and Schlesinger write, "was not calculated to reassure the British about MacArthur's attitude toward them; his action, said the ordinarily restrained *Economist,* was 'the extreme of ignorance or unscrupulousness' ".[1] Thus the basic British fear was that MacArthur might, by some rash and arrogant action, wantonly bring down upon their heads the most dreadful of world wars. They could not blame the Chinese intervention on him, though they suspected, probably without any real justice, that he had edged the United Nations gradually in the direction of that catastrophe; they were certain, particularly after the ignominious defeat on the Yalu, that the General's wounded pride and desire to re-establish his damaged reputation would make him even more prone to precipitate acts which could extend the war. Of the America represented by this particular American, it did now seem to the majority of the British people that "restraint of Communist China" was "less important than restraint of the United States."[2]

But British fears did not stop here. They were not merely apprehensive that he might strike a spark and detonate the powder-barrel, but that, when it came to the point and America found she had not enough resources to fight the battle against Communism on every front, she would, under the influence of the General and men of his persuasion, fight it on the wrong one, for he assigned a clear priority to Asia. He wrote that "here in Asia . . . the Communist conspirators have elected to make their play for global conquest . . . that here we fight Europe's war with arms while the diplomats there still fight it with words; that if we lose the war to Communism in Asia, the fall of Europe is inevitable."[3] This did not make pleasant reading in the United Kingdom, and it can hardly have been welcomed enthusiastically even in Australia and New Zealand. From the practical point of view, the British, from Churchill down, believed that a war against China would be, as General Bradley called it, "the wrong war at the wrong place at the wrong time and with the wrong enemy."[4] Had they known the fullness of it, they would have been even more alarmed than they were, for

[1] Ibid, pp. 220-22.   [2] U.S.W.A., 1950, p. 415.
[3] Q. ibid, p. 220.   [4] Q. ibid, p. 164.

MacArthur's views were founded on a deep, albeit mistaken, view of history. As would soon be known (with the publication of the Forrestal Diaries) he had declared as early as 1944 that "the history of the world will be written in the Pacific for the next ten thousand years. He said we made the same old mistake of intervening in European quarrels which we can't hope to solve because they are insoluble. He said that Europe is a dying system. It is worn out and run down, and will become an economic and industrial hegemony of Soviet Russia. . . . The lands touching the Pacific with their billions of inhabitants will determine the course of history (repeating) for the next ten thousand years".[1]

This notion would not have found a warm welcome in London; nor was it wise. Hitler was rash to talk of a thousand years of Nazism, and soldiers, however well-read, are foolish to predict the course of ten times that span of human history. They are especially unwise to do so when their whole career gives bias to their speculations, and when their feelings of personal betrayal (he declared that Washington was guilty of treason and sabotage in not adequately supporting the Pacific theatre in World War II) add yet further to it. Like little Johnny-Head-in-Air, he fell into the trap at his feet through keeping his head in the clouds; by gazing at the far horizons of history he allowed the middle ground to get out of focus. It may well be that Asia will dominate the distant history of mankind, but it is also highly probable that, if Soviet Communism captures the industrial and technological power of Europe, it will be within striking distance of the conquest of the Americas long before that far-off day. And Britain feared with justification that Republican concentration upon Asia might imperil not merely her own existence, but that of the whole Western world.

X

BUT happily for Anglo-American relations, it was not MacArthur's but Eisenhower's Republicanism, which was to make any shift that was to be made in the balance of American effort between Asia and Europe. After the retreat from the Yalu, MacArthur began to release "a bewildering barrage of special messages, exclusive interviews, and replies to editorial inquiries" directed in effect against "his being ordered to limit the war to Korea."[2] On 6 December President Truman pointedly ordered officials overseas "to clear all but routine statements with their departments,"[3] and all foreign policy statements with the State Department. But, with the stabilization of the front in Korea and the coming

[1] Q. Forrestal, p. 18.   [2] Rovere and Schlesinger, pp. 152-3.   [3] Ibid, p. 155.

of a deliberate war of attrition designed to avoid further entanglement with China, the General's impatience burst forth once more. As he said later, and in this he spoke for many Americans, who "in general are poorly equipped for campaigns of attrition"[1]: "In war there is no substitute for victory . . . war's very object is victory, not prolonged indecision."[2] On 7 March he made a very provocative statement to the Press, and on 25 March he deliberately frustrated a Presidential move advocated by many of the United Nations, to make a "further diplomatic effort . . . before any advance with major forces north of 38th Parallel", by taking the diplomatic initiative in his own fashion. He issued a statement pointing out that the Chinese could not conquer Korea, and that their lack of industrial power made them extremely vulnerable in case the United Nations departed from its "tolerant effort to contain the war to Korea";[3] it ended with an appeal, if such it could be called, to the Chinese, to negotiate their withdrawal from Korea. On 5 April Congressman Martin of Massachusetts read out in the House a letter from MacArthur, challenging the whole Administration policy, and it was clear that he had determined to appeal over the head of the President to the American people. "Here", as Rovere and Schlesinger write, "was pressure exerted simultaneously on Washington, Lake Success and Peiping".[4] His offer was, as he no doubt expected and perhaps wished, rejected by the Chinese with contumely. At 1 a.m. on the morning of 11 April, 1951, reporters, summoned for a special announcement from the White House, learned of the dismissal of General MacArthur from his command. With the President's decision the American people, despite the initial uproar with which it was greeted and the welcome accorded to the General on his first return to his homeland for many years, came in due time to agree; the British people acclaimed it at once. In this spectacular manner was ended the most acute manifestation of the Anglo-American disagreement over Far Eastern policy, and after it the fissure slowly began to close, or at least to seem less gaping.

For one thing, it became increasingly apparent that if General MacArthur was obstinate and rash, the Chinese were obdurate and bellicose. An Indian resolution, sponsored by the Arab-Asian bloc in the United Nations, calling for a cease-fire and a Far Eastern conference, was passed in the Assembly on 14 December, 1950, by 52 votes to 5, but was rejected outright by the Chinese because it contained no binding political commitments, the very reason why the United States had been willing to accept it. On 19 December the Chinese delegation to the

[1] Ibid, p. 164.   [2] Q. ibid.   [3] Q. ibid, pp. 166-7.   [4] Ibid, p. 168.

United Nations returned to Peking, and on 23 December their government made it plain that "We firmly insist that, as a basis for negotiating a peaceful settlement of the Korean problem, all foreign troops must be withdrawn from Korea".[1] Further proposals on the line of those of 19 December, which the Administration was sharply criticised in America for supporting, met the same fate, and, as a result, on 1 February a resolution declaring Communist China an aggressor, supported by the United States and the United Kingdom, was carried by 44 votes to 7; it was opposed by India. It is significant that, though the United Kingdom voted for it, she had declined to be associated with the United States in moving it. But this was better than voting on opposite sides: the gap was narrowing.

The chief agent of this improvement was Communist policy; as we have seen before, and shall see again, whenever the Anglo-American front loosens, Soviet or Chinese intransigence cements it together again. By the time that the removal of MacArthur had cleared the air over a battlefield where United Nations forces were advancing steadily in the area of the 38th Parallel, inflicting the while exceedingly heavy losses on an enemy rich in numbers but poor in fire and air power, the feeling in Britain and the United Nations that this might be a moment for a settlement began even to find signs of support in the Administration, and among the American people. A Korean compromise might, in view of the aspirations of late 1950, appear as a political defeat for the West, but it would follow on the heels of a decisive military victory. Secretary Acheson declared during the Congressional investigation in May that neither the United Nations nor the United States had ever undertaken the obligation to unify Korea; though this was, strictly speaking, true, in practice it represented a change of American policy, indeed a retreat from that of November, 1950. The Labour government in Britain also changed its apparent policy to conform more closely with that of the United States. Churchill revealed later that in May they had " 'replied to an enquiry . . . that in the event of heavy air attacks from bases in China [fighters were already operating from such bases] upon United Nations forces in Korea they would associate themselves with action not confined to Korea.' He emphasized that the discussion referred only to the possibility of attacks 'from certain airfields' and stated that the British had insisted on 'the right of prior consultation . . . in the specific instance,' a view to which the United States 'did not give an unqualified agreement . . . because they did not think that their views provided sufficiently for cases of extreme military urgency.' "[2]

[1] Q. U.S.W.A., 1950, p. 424.   [2] U.S.W.A., 1951, p. 111.

The *rapprochement* was thus left somewhat incomplete, and this aspect of it was kept secret at the time, but it was a *rapprochement* none the less. It was aided by the drawing of what appeared to be irreconcilable lines in American political life between an unrepentant minority of die-hards and a more moderate majority. Nevertheless, the die-hards gained some concessions, for there was a distinct hardening of the Administration's policy on Formosa and Chiang during the summer, while it asserted anew that it would never consent to Chinese admission to the United Nations while the war lasted and would continue to oppose it after its termination. Meanwhile, the United States pressed economic sanctions on the member nations with great vigour.

But when, on 23 June, probably because of the heavy Chinese losses in the now stalemated war in Korea, Russia proposed discussions on a cease-fire, providing for the mutual withdrawal of forces from the 38th Parallel, the British and American views were close enough for the United States cautiously to agree to negotiations between military representatives on the spot. On 10 July they began at Kaisong. With the tale of the dismal dragging on of these armistice negotiations; with their rupture for two months in August, 1951; with their resumption at Panmunjom in October; and with their languishing and spasmodic course, until they appeared to peter out in all but a formal sense almost a year later, in October, 1952, we cannot here concern ourselves. Whether the Communists were genuinely concerned with the many and vexatious objections that they saw to any United Nations proposals, or whether, as seems more probable, they started the negotiations when they were hard-pressed, continued them when they found that they brought a relief from American pressure, and declined to bring them to an end when they were, through their great build-up of forces, once more in a favourable position, is uncertain, but equally not of direct concern to us. Their remarkable and long continued obstinacy served in the long run to effect a very slight development of the Anglo-American *rapprochement*, despite the strong flurries of mutual criticism during the course of 1951, but it did not alter the fundamental position. Britain was brought with reluctance to agree to a Japanese peace treaty which side-stepped the question of Chinese approval and which was rejected by Russia. She emphasized her mistrust of the extreme nature of American strategic fears by opposing closer relations on military matters with General Franco; the left wing of the Labour Party broke with their government on the issue of British rearmament, in support of what were claimed to be extreme American demands. Even Churchill, though little more was heard of the proposal after he had come to power; declared himself in favour of "a supreme effort to bridge the gulf between the two worlds",[1] probably by some form of personal meeting of the heads of states. All these things were manifestations of the same fundamental uneasiness lest America recklessly or inadvertently fire the shot that would begin the atomic war. It was perhaps best expressed by Ralph J. Bunche, "The fear I often hear expressed is that once we have achieved superior military strength we may be inclined to become impatient and impulsive and thereby provoke unnecessarily the third world war."[2]

Yet at bottom the Anglo-American relationship probably grew closer again during 1951. NATO was greatly strengthened under the popular leadership of General Eisenhower. In September the Labour government, continuing the negotiations about action "not confined to Korea" agreed that, "in the event of a breakdown in the armistice talks and the resumption of large-scale fighting in Korea, certain action should be taken of a more limited character"[3] than that envisaged in May, without the necessity for prior consultation, although they kept their consent secret. As Secretary Acheson said, the nations of Europe were "quite willing, if war is forced upon all of us, despite the very best efforts of all of us to prevent it, to take all the suffering that that brings on them", but they did not "want that terrible catastrophe to fall on them unnecessarily or by reason of some provocation on our part."[4] There was maintained in Britain throughout all these happenings, "the universal sense of closer kinship with the United-States, which retained its vitality even when specific United States actions and policies were most harshly criticized."[5]

This underlying reality came once more into prominence with the return to power of Churchill at the close of 1951, for he was determined to try and repair what he believed to be the damage done to Anglo-American relations by the process of drifting apart which had been allowed since his defeat at the polls six years before. He visited Washington, almost at once, in January, 1952. The joint communiqué issued at the close of his visit stated that "each of our Governments has thereby gained a better understanding of the thoughts and aims of the other". As to the Far East, "a broad harmony of view has emerged from these discussions; for we recognize that the overriding need to counter the Communist threat in that area transcends such divergencies as there are in our policies toward China". This exactly stated the position. There followed a promise by both parties to "continue to give full support for

---

[1] Q, ibid, p. 380. [2] Q. ibid, p. 158. [3] Ibid, p. 163, note.
[4] Ibid, p. 159. [5] Ibid, p. 166.

United Nations measures against aggression in Korea until peace and security are restored there"*, and there was also a reaffirmation of mutual determination to build up NATO: "The free countries of the world are resolved to unite their strength and purpose to ensure peace and security."[1] In an address to Congress Churchill still further closed the gap between the policies of the two countries by making publicly the agreement that his predecessors had made privately: "if the truce we seek is reached only to be broken our response will be prompt, resolute and effective". In return the United States consented to the insertion of a pacific clause: "We share the hope and the determination that war, with all its modern weapons, shall not again be visited on mankind. . . . We do not believe that war is inevitable. This is the basis of our policies. We are willing at any time to explore all reasonable means of resolving the issues which now threaten the peace of the world".

In the building of the future, whatever it might hold, the Anglo-American partnership would plainly be of decisive importance: "The strong ties which unite our two countries are a massive contribution to the building of the strength of the free world".[2] They were still further strengthened during 1952, despite the persistence of the basic agreement to disagree over China. There might still be gusts of discontent in Britain. In June the Minister of Defence, Lord Alexander, headed what was described generally as a "fact-finding" mission to Korea, and expressed himself well satisfied with what he found, in a press conference on 16 June; but hardly had he delivered his judgment, when the biggest bombing raid of the whole war was unexpectedly launched on certain Yalu River power plants only 3,000 feet from Manchurian soil. There was an immediate outburst of criticism from the left wing in Britain, which was echoed in other sections of the community; it was not the nearness to Manchuria that worried those who protested, so much as the fact that the bombings might upset the truce negotiations at Panmunjom, while feeling was heightened by the fact that the Allies were not consulted, although the United States was under no specific obligation to do so. But upon reflection it became clear that it was exceedingly difficult to decide whether harsh action would have a beneficial or an adverse effect upon negotiations, since the lull which

---

*The authors of *Britain and the United States* detect at this time an incipient difference of attitude towards the United Nations, Britain wishing to retain its almost universal membership, so that it can continue as a forum for possible compromise, and America inclining to make it an exclusive agency of the free world.

[1] *Current Developments*, January, 1952, p. 9.   [2] Q. ibid, pp. 1, 9.

was popularly supposed to be in existence on the battlefield was in fact, as the casualty figures of the Americans clearly showed, no lull at all, but a gruelling and indecisive fight. In a very short while this, like other flurries of the storm, has ceased to darken Anglo-American relations.

Even when the basic divergence was once more exposed for all to see, and threatened to grow wider, deterioration was happily forestalled by Communist action. On 17 November India proposed a plan aimed at solving the problem of repatriation of prisoners, which had for many weeks been holding up the truce negotiations; this was not in accord with a twenty-one nation resolution sponsored by the United States on the prisoner of war issue, although the Indian Government maintained that it did not violate the principle of "no forcible repatriation" for which America stood. Britain supported the Indian move strongly, as did Canada, but the United States wished to propose certain amendments to "plug loopholes" in the plan. Britain did not feel able to support the amendments, whereupon the United States announced that it would not support the plan without them, and in America a spokesman declared that Britain had "abruptly abandoned" the twenty-one-power resolutions, an announcement described by the British in their turn as "premature".[1] This was what the *Daily Telegraph* called "the sharpest diplomatic cleavage between Britain and the United States in the history of the United Nations."[2] But even now, the firm grip of the basic importance of Anglo-American unity was never really relaxed; the original American spokesman declared, "We are still warm friends. We understand the great need for solidarity. We understand each other's position. But the United States feels that a great matter of principle is involved".[3] Britain's delegation was somewhat startled at the sudden and public nature of the American reaction, and almost at once the wheels went into reverse. India hastened to produce a modified plan, which the Americans as well as the British were to accept. But the powers might have spared themselves the effort, for, before the new compromise arrangements were even fully formulated, Russia had denounced the Indian plan and insisted on one of her own, unacceptable to all other parties, which not only dimmed hopes of peace but quite restored Anglo-American amity. Thus once more did Russia, despite her obvious desire to divide the "Anglo-American bloc", make it seem certain beyond a peradventure that the unity of the British and American peoples would endure.

[1] *New York Times*, 23 November, 1952.　　[2] 24 November, 1952.
[3] *New York Times*, 23 November, 1952.

This did indeed appear to be the prospect for Anglo-American relations as one peered into the future from the last days of 1952. Behind the two peoples lay the long years of their peaceful negotiation, of progressive settlement of their outstanding disputes, of their increasing friendship, and of their ultimate co-operation—a tale of closeness and intimacy unparalleled in history. Beneath them lay a finely woven and immensely strong and resilient mesh of common social affections, economic interests and political beliefs. In their minds was a full realization, as Sir Oliver Franks expressed it in his final speech as Ambassador, that Anglo-American partnership and interdependence were the core of freedom, and that all relationships with other countries should be approached from that standpoint. The defeat of Senator Taft by General Eisenhower for the Republican Presidential nomination in July made it certain that America would not turn her back upon Britain; the return of Churchill to power in Britain late in 1951 had weakened the hold there of radical elements mistrustful of the United States. With the election of Eisenhower and the prospect of possibly four years or more of power or influence wielded by these two men, who above all others were responsible for and symbolized the supreme achievement of Anglo-American unity in World War II, it is hard to believe that all will not be well. As Churchill declared after the election of Eisenhower: we pledge "our assurance that, to the utmost limits of our strength, we will work with him for those great causes which we have guarded and cherished in ever greater unity as the generations have rolled by."[1] As "Ike" replied to "Winston's" cable of congratulations: "I, too, look forward to a renewal of our co-operative work in the interests of a free world."[2] Churchill, historian-soldier-statesman, has in the past proven not the least accurate of prophets nor the least wise of guides for the American and British peoples. Let his be the last word:

If the population of the English-speaking Commonwealths be added to that of the United States with all that such co-operation implies . . . there will be no quivering precarious balance of power to offer its temptation to ambition or adventure. . . . Britain and the United States are working together, and working for the same high cause. Bismarck once said that the supreme fact of the nineteenth century was that Britain and the United States spoke the same language. Let us make sure that the supreme fact of the twentieth century is that they tread the same path.[3]

[1] *Daily Telegraph*, 11 November, 1952.   [2] Ibid, 8 November, 1952.
[3] *Current Developments*, January, 1952, pp. 10-11.

BIBLIOGRAPHY

THE main object of this bibliography is to guide the reader to the secondary authorities on which the work is based; from these, more detailed guidance can be obtained. It does, however, include a number of primary sources which were used in the writing of the book. It also includes a list of articles which proved of value. These three categories are listed separately in each section of the bibliography; each category is listed alphabetically, by author, editor or title.

There are five sections, a first or general section, for works covering a large proportion of the period, and four other sections, one for each Part of the book. Where books have been used very little, they have been footnoted but not mentioned in the bibliography.

A. GENERAL

(i) SECONDARY AUTHORITIES:

J. T. Adams, *Atlas of American History*. Charles Scribner's Sons, New York, 1943.

T. A. Bailey, *A Diplomatic History of the American People* (Fourth Edition). Appleton-Century-Crofts, New York, 1950.

H. H. Bellot, *American History and American Historians*. University of London, The Athlone Press, 1952.

S. F. Bemis, *A Diplomatic History of the United States*. Henry Holt, New York, 1936.

J. B. Brebner, *North Atlantic Triangle, The Interplay of Canada, the United States and Great Britain*. Yale University Press, New Haven, 1945.

C. Brinton, *The United States and Britain*. Harvard University Press, Cambridge, Massachusetts, 1945.

J. M. Callahan, *American Foreign Policy in Canadian Relations*. Macmillan, New York, 1937.

The Cambridge History of the British Empire. Cambridge University Press, 1929.

The Cambridge History of British Foreign Policy. Cambridge University Press, 1923.

W. A. Dunning, *The British Empire and the United States.* Scribner's, New York, 1914.

R. C. K. Ensor, *England 1870-1914.* Clarendon Press, Oxford, 1936.

G. P. de T. Glazebrook, *A Short History of Canada.* Clarendon Press, Oxford, 1950.

E. Halévy, *A History of the English People.* Ernest Benn, London.

J. B. McMaster, *A History of the People of the United States from the Revolution to the Civil War.* D. Appleton, New York, 1903.

A. T. Mahan, *The Interest of America in Sea Power, Present and Future.* Sampson Low, Marston, London, 1898.

S. E. Morison and H. S. Commager, *The Growth of the American Republic.* Oxford University Press, New York, 1942.

R. B. Mowat, *The American Entente.* Edward Arnold, London, 1939.

R. B. Mowat, *The Diplomatic Relations of Great Britain and the United States.* Edward Arnold, London, 1925.

C. O. Paullin, *Atlas of the Historical Geography of the United States.* Carnegie Institution of Washington and American Geographical Society of New York, 1932.

R. W. Seton-Watson, *Britain in Europe 1789-1914.* Cambridge University Press, 1945.

R. W. Seton-Watson, *Britain and the Dictators.* Cambridge University Press, 1938.

Edward Smith, *England and America after Independence.* Constable, Westminster, 1900.

B. Willson, *Friendly Relations, A Narrative of Britain's Ministers and Ambassadors to America (1791-1930).* Lovat Dickson and Thompson, London, 1934.

B. Wilson, *America's Ambassadors to England (1785-1928).* John Murray, London, 1928.

E. L. Woodward, *The Age of Reform 1815-1870.* Clarendon Press, Oxford, 1938.

(ii) PRIMARY SOURCES:

American State Papers, Foreign Relations. Washington, 1832 *et seq.*
The Annual Register. London.

R. J. Bartlett (Editor), *The Record of American Diplomacy.* Alfred A. Knopf, New York, 1947.

H. S. Commager, *Documents of American History.* Appleton-Century-Crofts, New York and London, 1948.

A. T. Mahan, *Lessons of the War With Spain and Other Articles*. Sampson Low, Marston, London, 1900.

A Compilation of the Messages and Papers of the Presidents. Bureau of National Literature, New York, 1897.

Treaties and Agreements in Force Affecting Canada Between His Majesty and the United States of America, with subsidiary Documents, 1814-1925. Department of External Affairs, Ottawa, 1927.

Treaties, Conventions, International Acts, Protocols and Agreements Between the United States of America and Other Powers (Editor, William M. Malloy). Washington, 1910 *et seq.*

Treaties and other International Acts of the United States of America (Editor, Hunter Miller). Washington, 1931 *et seq.*

B. PART I

(i) SECONDARY AUTHORITIES:

A. H. Abel and F. J. Klingberg, *A Side-light on Anglo-American Relations, 1839-1858*. The Association for the Study of Negro Life and History Incorporated, Lancaster Press, Lancaster, Pa., 1927.

D. Abel, *A History of British Tariffs, 1923-1942*. Heath Crapton, London, 1945.

A. Achinstein, *Introduction to Business Cycles*. Thomas Y. Crowell, New York, 1950.

C. F. Bastable, *The Commerce of the Nations* (Ninth Edition revised by T. E. Gregory). Methuen, London, 1923.

W. S. Bernard, *American Immigration Policy—A Reappraisal*. Harpers, New York, 1950.

C. A. Brooke-Cunningham, *Anglo-Saxon Unity and Other Essays*. Selwyn and Blount, London, 1925.

N. S. Buck, *The Development of the Organisation of Anglo-American Trade, 1800-1850*. Yale University Press, New Haven, 1925.

W. B. Cairns, *British Criticisms of American Writings, 1783-1833*, Parts I and II. University of Wisconsin Studies in Language and Literature, Madison, 1918.

Chambers Encyclopedia. New Edition, 1950.

J. H. Clapham, *An Economic History of Modern Britain*. Cambridge University Press, 1930.

J. R. Commons, *Races and Immigrants in America*. Macmillan, New York, 1907.

R. Coupland, *The British Anti-Slavery Movement*. Thornton Butterworth, London, 1933.

W. Cunningham, *English Influence on the United States*. Cambridge University Press, 1916.

M. E. Curti, *The Growth of American Thought*. Harpers, New York, 1943.

M. Davie, *World Immigration: with special reference to the United States*. Macmillan, New York, 1936.

The Encyclopedia Britannica. 1936.

H. P. Fairchild, *Immigration, A World Movement and its American Significance*. Macmillan, New York, 1928.

H. U. Faulkner, *American Economic History*. Harpers, New York, 1924.

A. B. Faust, *The German Element in the United States*. Steuben Society of America, New York, 1927.

A. E. Feaveryear, *The Pound Sterling*. Clarendon Press, Oxford, 1931.

J. M. Frankland, *The Influence of International Trade Upon British-American Relations*. Yale University Press, New Haven, 1928.

G. S. Gordon, *Anglo-American Literary Relations*. Oxford University Press, 1942.

G. Gorer, *The Americans*. Cresset Press, London, 1948.

L. M. Hacker, *England and America, The Ties that Bind*. Clarendon Press, Oxford, 1948.

L. M. Hacker, *The Triumph of American Capitalism*. Columbia University Press, New York, 1946.

The Right Hon. The Earl of Halifax, *Anglo-American Relations, Fifth Montague Burton Lecture*. University of Leeds, 1947.

R. W. Hidy, *The House of Baring in American Trade and Finance, English Merchant Bankers at Work, 1763-1861*. Harvard University Press, 1949.

C. K. Hobson, *The Export of Capital*. Constable, London, 1914.

L. H. Jenks, *The Migration of British Capital*. Alfred A. Knopf, New York and London, 1927.

S. C. Johnson, *Emigration from the United Kingdom to North America, 1763-1912*. George Routledge, London, 1913.

W. G. Kendrew, *The Climates of the Continents*. Oxford University Press, London, 1948.

F. J. Klingberg, *The Anti-slavery Movement in England*. Humphrey Milford, London, 1926.

S. Lubell, *The Future of American Politics*. Hamish Hamilton, London, 1952.

S. F. Markham, *Climate and the Energy of Nations*. Oxford University Press, New York, 1947.

987

H. L. Mencken, *The American Language, An Inquiry into the Development of English in the United States,* Fourth Edition (also Supplement One). Alfred A. Knopf, New York, 1946.

R. B. Mowat, *Americans in England.* Harrap, London, 1935.

A. Nevins, *American Social History as Recorded by British Travellers.* Henry Holt, New York, 1923.

A. Nevins, *America Through British Eyes.* Oxford University Press, New York, 1948.

V. L. Parrington, *Main Currents in American Thought.* Harcourt, Brace, New York, 1927.

C. Phelps, *The Anglo-American Peace Movement in the Nineteenth Century.* Columbia University Press, New York, 1930.

G. R. Porter, *The Progress of the Nation.* Revised Edition. Methuen, London, 1912.

W. D. Puleston, *The Life and Work of Captain Alfred Thayer Mahan U.S.N.* London, Jonathan Cape, 1939.

E. F. Roberts, *Ireland in America.* Putnam's, New York and London, 1931.

N. Roosevelt, *America and England?* Jonathan Cape, London, 1930.

The Statesman's Year Book. London.

J. A. Todd, *The Mechanism of Exchange.* Geoffrey Cumberlege, Oxford University Press, London, 1949.

J. D. Whelpley, *British-American Relations.* Grant Richards, London, 1924.

Whitaker's Almanack. London.

H. F. Williamson (Editor), *The Growth of the American Economy.* Prentice-Hall, New York, 1944.

C. W. Wright, *Economic History of the United States.* McGraw-Hill, New York, 1949.

R. A. Young, *The International Financial Position of the United States.* National Industrial Conference Board Inc., Philadelphia, 1929.

(ii) PRIMARY SOURCES:

Brooks Adams, *America's Economic Supremacy.* Macmillan, New York, 1900.

The Education of Henry Adams, An Autobiography. Constable, London, 1919.

Henry Adams and His Friends (Editor, H. D. Cater). Houghton Mifflin, Boston, 1947.

Sir Norman Angell, *American Policies Abroad: The United States and*

Great Britain. An Englishman's Point of View. University of Chicago, 1932.

C. H. Bretherton, *Midas or the Future of the United States.* Kegan Paul, Trench, Trubner, London, 1926.

Rupert Brooke, *Letters from America.* Sidgwick & Jackson, London, 1916.

The Autobiography of Andrew Carnegie (Editor, J. C. Van Dyk). Constable, London, 1920.

Census of England and Wales, 1911. H.M.S.O., London, 1912.

Census of England and Wales, 1931, Preliminary Report and General Tables. H.M.S.O., London, 1931 and 1935.

Census of England and Wales, 1931, General Report. H.M.S.O., London, 1950.

Census of England and Wales, 1951, Preliminary Report. H.M.S.O., London, 1951.

Census of Scotland, 1931, vol. I Preliminary Report, vol. II Report. H.M.S.O., Edinburgh, 1931 and 1933.

Census of Scotland, 1951, Preliminary Report. H.M.S.O., Edinburgh, 1951.

A Report of the Seventeenth Decennial Census of the United States: Census of Population, 1950, Volume I. U.S. Government Printing Office, Washington, 1952.

G. K. Chesterton, *What I Saw in America.* Dodd, Mead and Co., New York, Copyright 1922.

A. Cooke, *Letters from America.* Rupert Hart-Davis, London, 1951.

C. Dickens, *American Notes.* Chapman and Hall, London, 1842.

J. R. Dos Passos, *The Anglo-Saxon Century.* Putnam's, New York, 1903.

The Works of Ralph Waldo Emerson. Bohn's Standard Library. Bell, London, 1888.

M. Halsey, *With Malice Towards Some.* Hamish Hamilton, London, 1938.

Historical Statistics of the United States, 1789-1945. United States Department of Commerce, Bureau of Census, Washington, 1949.

The Letters of Henry James, Selected and Edited by Percy Lubbock. Macmillan, London, 1920.

C. E. M. Joad, *The Babbitt Warren.* Kegan Paul, Trench, Trubner, London, 1926.

R. Kipling, *From Sea to Sea and Other Sketches.* Macmillan, London, 1900.

League of Nations Memoranda on International Trade (1912-1926 and 1926-1938). Geneva.

J. MacGregor, *Commercial Statistics: a digest of the productive resources, commercial legislation, customs, tariffs, etc. of all nations* (vols. I-V). London, 1844-50.

D. MacPherson, *Annals of Commerce* (vols. I-IV). London, 1805.

J. L. Mesick, *The English Traveller in America 1785-1835.* Columbia University Press, New York, 1922.

National Register, United Kingdom and Isle of Man, Statistics of Population on 29th September, 1939. H.M.S.O., London, 1944.

G. H. Payne, *England: Her Treatment of America.* Sears Publishing Co., New York, Copyright 1931, by George Henry Payne.

T. Pitkin, *A Statistical View of the Commerce of the United States of America.* New Haven, 1835.

J. B. Priestley, *Midnight on the Desert. A Chapter of Autobiography.* Heinemann, London, 1937.

G. Santayana, *Soliloquies in England and Later Soliloquies.* Constable, London, 1922.

Statistical Tables and Charts relating to British and Foreign Trade and Industry (1854-1908) (Cd. 4954). Printed for H.M.S.O. by Eyre and Spottiswoode, London, 1909.

Transatlantic Exchanges, Cross-Currents of Anglo-American Opinion in the Nineteenth Century (Editor, Yvonne ffrench). Sidgwick and Jackson, London, 1951.

F. Trollope, *Domestic Manners of the Americans.* Routledge, London, 1927.

(iii) ARTICLES:

M. Beloff, "Is there an Anglo-American Political Tradition?" History, 1951.

M. H. Cannon, "Migration of English Mormons to America." Am. H.R., 1947.

F. J. Klingberg, "Harriet Beecher Stowe and Social Reform in England." Am. H.R., 1938.

I. T. Naamani, "The 'Anglo-Saxon Idea' and British Public Opinion." Can. H.R., 1951.

C. PART II

(i) SECONDARY AUTHORITIES:

R. G. Adams, *Political Ideas of the American Revolution.* Trinity College Press, Durham, N.C., 1922.

C. M. Andrews, *The Colonial Background of the American Revolution.* Yale University Press, 1924.

Sir Ernest Barker, *Traditions of Civility.* Cambridge University Press, 1948.

Carl Becker, *The Declaration of Independence.* Harcourt Brace, New York, 1922.

S. F. Bemis, *Jay's Treaty, A Study in Commerce and Diplomacy.* Macmillan, New York, 1923.

A. L. Burt, *The United States, Great Britain and British North America From the Revolution to the Establishment of Peace after the War of 1812.* Humphrey Milford, Oxford University Press, 1940.

D. G. Creighton, *The Commercial Empire of the St. Lawrence, 1760-1850.* Ryerson, Toronto, 1937.

V. H. H. Green, *The Hanoverians.* Arnold, London, 1948.

V. T. Harlow, *The Founding of the Second British Empire, 1763-1793.* Longmans, London, 1952.

L. W. Labaree, *Royal Government in America.* Yale University Press, 1930.

J. C. Miller, *Origins of the American Revolution.* Faber, London, 1945.

J. C. Miller, *The Triumph of Freedom, 1775-1783.* Little, Brown, Boston, 1948.

J. W. Pratt, *Expansionists of 1812.* Macmillan, New York, 1925.

C. H. Van Tyne, *Causes of the War of Independence.* Constable, London, 1928.

B. Williams, *William Pitt.* Longmans, London, 1913.

(ii) PRIMARY SOURCES:

S. V. Benet, *Western Star.* Farrar and Rinehart, New York, 1943.
The Works of The Right Honourable Edmund Burke. London, 1864.
Samuel Johnson, *Taxation No Tyranny.* London, 1775.
S. E. Morison, *Sources and Documents Illustrating The American Revolution, 1764-1788.* Clarendon Press, Oxford, 1923.

(iii) ARTICLES:

W. P. Goodman, "The Origins of the War of 1812: A Survey of Changing Interpretations." Mississippi Valley H.R., 1941.

A. B. Keith, "Relaxations in the British Restrictions on the American Trade with the British West Indies, 1783-1802." Journal of Modern History, 1948.

R. Robinson, "Retaliation for the Treatment of Prisoners in the War of 1812." Am. H.R., 1943.

991

A. Steel, "Anthony Merry and the Anglo-American Dispute About Impressment, 1803-6." Cambridge Historical Journal, 1949.

A. Steel, "Impressment in the Monroe-Pinckney Negotiations, 1806-7." Am. H.R., 1952.

D. PART III

(i) SECONDARY AUTHORITIES:

E. D. Adams, *Great Britain and the American Civil War*. Longmans, London, 1925.

H. C. F. Bell, *Lord Palmerston*. Longmans, London, 1936.

S. F. Bemis, *John Quincy Adams and the Foundations of American Foreign Policy*. Alfred A. Knopf, New York, 1949.

M. L. Bonham, *The British Consuls in the Confederacy*. Columbia University, New York, 1911.

A. B. Corey, *The Crisis of 1830-1842 In Canadian-American Relations*. Humphrey Milford, London, 1941.

P. Guedalla, *Palmerston*. Benn, London, 1926.

H. G. Hodges, *Diplomatic Relations Between the United States and Great Britain*. Gorham Press, Boston, 1930.

E. John, *Atlantic Impact, 1861*. Heinemann, London, 1952.

R. McElroy, *Grover Cleveland, The Man and the Statesman*. Harpers, New York, 1923.

R. D. Meade, *Judah P. Benjamin*. Oxford University Press, New York, 1943.

F. Merk, *Albert Gallatin and the Oregon Problem*. Harvard University Press, Cambridge, Massachusetts, 1950.

J. Morley, *The Life of William Ewart Gladstone*. Edward Lloyd, London, 1908.

F. L. Owsley, *King Cotton Diplomacy*. University of Chicago Press, 1931.

D. Perkins, *The Monroe Doctrine, 1823-1826*. Harvard University Press, 1927.

J. G. Randall, *Lincoln the Liberal Statesman*. Eyre and Spottiswoode, London, 1947.

J. F. Rippy, *The Rivalry of the United States and Great Britain over Latin America, 1808-1830*. Humphrey Milford, London, 1929.

L. B. Shippee, *Canadian American Relations, 1849-1874*. Yale University Press, New Haven, 1939.

J. F. Stanwood, *James Gillespie Blaine*, Houghton Mifflin, New York, 1905.

C. C. Tansill, *Canadian-American Relations, 1875-1911*. Ryerson, Toronto, 1943.

H. Temperley, *The Foreign Policy of Canning*. Bell, London, 1925.

G. M. Trevelyan, *The Life of John Bright*. Constable, London, 1925.

F. J. Turner, *The Frontier in American History*. Henry Holt and Co., New York, 1937.

C. K. Webster, *Britain and the Independence of Latin America, 1812-1830*. Published for Ibero-American Institute by Oxford University Press, 1938.

M. W. Williams, *Anglo-American Isthmian Diplomacy, 1815-1915*. Humphrey Milford, London, 1916.

(ii) PRIMARY SOURCES:

S. V. Benet, *John Brown's Body*. Doubleday, New York, 1928.

A. Lincoln, *Complete Works, Comprising His Speeches, Letters, State Papers and Miscellaneous Writings* (Editors, John G. Nicolay and John Hay). The Century Co., New York, 1920.

(iii) ARTICLES:

E. D. Adams, "English Interest in the Annexation of California." Am. H.R., 1909.

J. P. Baxter, "The British Government and Neutral Rights." Am. H.R., 1928.

M. Beloff, "Great Britain and the American Civil War." History, 1952.

N. M. Blake, "The Background of Cleveland's Venezuelan Policy." Am. H.R., 1942.

N. M. Blake, "The Olney-Pauncefote Treaty of 1897." Am. H.R., 1945.

D. L. Burn, "Canada and the Repeal of the Corn Laws." Cambridge Historical Journal, 1928.

M. P. Clausun, "Peace Factors in Anglo-American Relations, 1861-5." Mississippi Valley H.R., 1940.

R. N. Current, "Webster's Propaganda and the Ashburton Treaty." Mississippi Valley H.R., 1947.

F. A. Golder, "Russian-American Relations During the Crimean War." Am. H.R., 1926.

N. A. Graebner, "Maritime Factors in the Oregon Compromise." Pacific Historical Review, 1951.

G. F. Hickson, "Palmerston and the Clayton-Bulwer Treaty." Cambridge Historical Journal, 1931.

G. F. Howe, "The Clayton-Bulwer Treaty." Am. H.R., 1937.

P. Knaplund, "The Armaments on the Great Lakes, 1844." Am. H.R., 1935.

G. W. McGee, "The Monroe Doctrine—A Stopgap Measure." Mississippi Valley H.R., 1951.

T. Le Duc, "The Maine Frontier and the Northeastern Boundary Controversy." Am. H.R., 1947.

D. Lowenthal, "The Maine Press and the Aroostook War." Can. H.R., 1951.

F. Merk, "British Government Propaganda and the Oregon Treaty." Am. H.R., 1934.

F. Merk, "British Party Politics and the Oregon Treaty." Am. H.R., 1932.

F. Merk, "The Genesis of the Oregon Question." Mississippi Valley H.R., 1950.

F. Merk, "The Ghost River Caledonia in the Oregon Negotiation of 1818." Am. H.R., 1950.

F. Merk, "The Oregon Pioneers and the Boundary." Am. H.R., 1924.

A. T. Milne, "The Lyons-Seward Treaty of 1862." Am. H.R., 1933.

R. L. Morrow, "The Negotiation of the Anglo-American Treaty of 1870." Am. H.R., 1934.

W. N. Sage, "The Oregon Treaty of 1846." Can. H.R., 1946.

C. P. Stacey, "An American Plan for a Canadian Campaign." Am. H.R., 1941.

A. R. Stewart, "The State of Maine and Canadian Confederation." Can. H.R., 1952.

R. W. Van Alstyne, "Anglo-American Relations, 1853-57." Am. H.R., 1937.

R. W. Van Alstyne, "John F. Crampton, Conspirator or Dupe?" Am. H.R., 1936.

J. D. Ward, "Sir Henry Bulwer and the United States Archives." Cambridge Historical Journal, 1931.

C. K. Webster, "British Mediation Between France and the United States, 1834-36." Eng. H.R., 1927.

E. PART IV

(i) SECONDARY AUTHORITIES:

T. A. Bailey, *The Policy of the United States Towards the Neutrals.* Johns Hopkins, Baltimore, 1942.

T. A. Bailey, *Woodrow Wilson and the Great Betrayal.* Macmillan, New York, 1945.

T. A. Bailey, *Woodrow Wilson and the Lost Peace*. Macmillan, New York, 1944.

S. F. Bemis, *The United States as a World Power*. Henry Holt, New York, 1950.

P. Birdsall, *Versailles Twenty Years After*. Allen and Unwin, London, 1941.

C. G. Bowers, *Beveridge and the Progressive Era*. Houghton Mifflin, Riverside Press, Cambridge, Massachusetts, 1932.

A. Bullock, *Hitler, A Study in Tyranny*. Odhams, London, 1952.

W. S. Churchill, *The Second World War*. Cassell, London, 1949 *et seq.*

W. S. Churchill, *The World Crisis, 1911-1918*. Scribner's, New York, 1923-7.

A. R. Conan, *The Sterling Area*. Macmillan, London, 1952.

Current Developments in United States Foreign Policy (1950-1952), Published Monthly by the Brookings Institution, Washington.

F. Davis, *The Atlantic System*. Reynal and Hitchcock, New York, 1941.

F. Davis and E. K. Lindley, *How War Came to America*. Allen and Unwin, London, 1943.

H. S. Ellis, *The Economics of Freedom, The Progress and Future of Aid to Europe* (with an Introduction by Dwight D. Eisenhower). Harpers, New York, 1950.

L. E. Ellis, *Reciprocity, 1911*. Ryerson, Toronto, 1939.

K. G. Feiling, *The Life of Neville Chamberlain*. Macmillan, London, 1946.

J. H. Ferguson, *American Diplomacy and the Boer War*. University of Pennsylvania, Philadelphia, 1939.

D. F. Fleming, *The United States and the League of Nations, 1918-20*. Putnam's, New York, 1932.

L. M. Gelber, *The Rise of Anglo-American Friendship*. Oxford University Press, London, 1938.

A. W. Griswold, *The Far Eastern Policy of the United States*. Harcourt, Brace, New York, 1938.

R. H. Heindel, *The American Impact on Great Britain, 1898-1914*. Humphrey Milford, Oxford University Press, London, 1940.

W. Johnson, *The Battle Against Isolation*. University of Chicago Press, 1944.

G. F. Kennan, *American Diplomacy, 1900-1950*. Secker and Warburg, London, 1952.

C. Kreider, *The Anglo-American Trade Agreement*. Princeton University Press, 1943.

W. L. Langer and S. E. Gleason, *The Challenge to Isolation, 1937-40*. Royal Institute of International Affairs, London, 1952.

F. McNaughton and W. Hehmeyer, *Harry Truman, President*. McGraw-Hill, New York, 1948.

W. H. McNeill, *America, Britain and Russia*. Oxford University Press, London, 1953.

W. Millis, *Road to War, America 1914-1917*. Faber, London, 1935.

H. G. Moulton and L. Pasvolsky, *War Debts and World Prosperity*. The Brookings Institute, Washington, 1932.

R. B. Mowat, *The Life of Lord Pauncefote*. Constable, London, 1929.

A. Nevins, *The New Deal and World Affairs*. Geoffrey Cumberlege, Oxford University Press, London, 1950.

A. Nevins, *The United States in a Chaotic World*. Geoffrey Cumberlege, Oxford University Press, London, 1950 (Vol. 56, *The Chronicles of America*, Copyright Yale University Press).

H. Nicolson, *King George The Fifth*. Constable, London, 1952.

R. Payne, *General Marshall*. Heinemann, London, 1952.

H. C. Peterson, *Propaganda for War, The Campaign against American Neutrality, 1914-1917*. University of Oklahoma Press, Norman, 1939.

B. A. Reuter, *Anglo-American Relations During the Spanish American War*. Macmillan, New York, 1924.

H. L. Roberts and P. A. Wilson, *Britain and the United States, Problems in Co-operation*. Royal Institute of International Affairs, London, 1953.

R. H. Rovere and A. M. Schlesinger, *The General and the President and the Future of American Foreign Policy*. Farrar, Straus and Young, New York, 1952.

C. Seymour, *American Diplomacy During the World War*. Johns Hopkins Press, Baltimore, 1934.

C. Seymour, *American Neutrality, 1914-17*. Yale University Press, 1935.

R. E. Sherwood, *The White House Papers of Harry L. Hopkins*. Eyre and Spottiswoode, London, 1948.

H. H. and M. Sprout, *Toward a New Order of Sea Power*. Princeton University Press, 1940.

The Sterling Area, An American Analysis (Editor, John M. Cassels). Economic Co-operation Administration Special Mission to the United Kingdom, London, 1951.

M. Tate, *The United States and Armaments*. Harvard University Press, Cambridge, Massachusetts, 1948.

The United States in World Affairs (1945-9, John C. Campbell; 1949-

1951, Richard P. Stebbins). Published for Council on Foreign Relations by Harpers, New York.

C. Wilmot, *The Struggle for Europe*. Collins, London, 1952.

G. M. Young, *Stanley Baldwin*. Rupert Hart-Davis, London, 1952.

(ii) PRIMARY SOURCES:

O. N. Bradley, *A Soldier's Story of the Allied Campaigns from Tunis to the Elbe*. Eyre and Spottiswoode, London, 1951.

H. C. Butcher, *Three Years with Eisenhower*. Heinemann, London, 1946.

J. F. Byrnes, *Speaking Frankly*. Harpers, London, 1947.

W. S. Churchill, *War Speeches, 1940-1945*. Cassell, London, 1946.

J. B. Conant, *Anglo-American Relations in the Atomic Age*. Geoffrey Cumberlege, Oxford University Press, 1952.

Documents on American Foreign Relations (Vols. I-XII). For World Peace Foundation, by Princeton University Press.

The Forrestal Diaries (Editor, Walter Millis). The Viking Press, New York, 1951.

Viscount Grey of Fallodon, *Twenty-Five Years 1892-1916*. Hodder and Stoughton, London, 1923-5.

Sir Francis de Guingand, *Operation Victory*. Hodder and Stoughton, London, 1947.

The Intimate Papers of Colonel House, arranged by C. Seymour. Benn, London, 1926.

The Memoirs of Cordell Hull. Macmillan, New York, 1948.

Henry Cabot Lodge, *The Senate and the League of Nations*. Scribner's, New York, 1925.

The Life and Letters of Walter H. Page by Burton J. Hendrick. Heinemann, London, 1923.

G. S. Patton, *War as I Knew It*. W. H. Allen, London, 1949.

F.D.R., His Personal Letters (Editor, Elliott Roosevelt). Duell, Sloan and Pearce, New York, 1950.

The Public Papers and Addresses of Franklin D. Roosevelt (Editor, S. I. Rosenman). Harpers, New York, 1950.

Letters and Friendships of Sir Cecil Spring-Rice (Editor, Stephen Gwynn). Constable, London, 1929.

H. L. Stimson, *The Far Eastern Crisis*. Harpers, London, 1936.

K. Summersby, *Eisenhower was my Boss*. Werner Laurie, London, 1949.

C. C. Tansill, *America Goes to War*. Little, Brown, Boston, 1938.

Mr. President, Personal Diaries, Papers and Letters of Harry S. Truman (Editor, W. Hillman). Hutchinson, London, 1952.

Sumner Welles, *The Time for Decision.* Hamish Hamilton, London, 1944.

Sir Arthur Willert, *The Road to Safety, A Study in Anglo-American Relations.* Verschoyle, London, 1952.

W. L. Willkie, *One World.* Cassell, London, 1943.

J. G. Winant, *A Letter From Grosvenor Square.* Hodder and Stoughton, London, 1947.

(iii) ARTICLES:

C. F. Brand, "British Labor and President Wilson." Am. H.R., 1937.

C. F. Brand, "The Reaction of Labor to the Policies of President Wilson During the World War." Am. H.R., 1933.

J. L. Godfrey, "Anglo-American Naval Conversations Preliminary to the London Naval Conference of 1930." South Atlantic Quarterly, 1950.

S. W. Livermore, "Theodore Roosevelt, The American Navy, and the Venezuelan Crisis of 1902-3." Am. H.R., 1946.

F. C. Pogue, "SHAEF—A Retrospect on Coalition Command." Journal of Modern History, 1951.

M. C. Siney, "British Negotiations with American Meat Packers, 1915-1917: A Study of Belligerent Trade Controls." Journal of Modern History, 1951.

ADDITIONAL BIBLIOGRAPHY (1968)

A. GENERAL

H. C. Allen, *The Anglo-American Predicament*. St. Martin's Press, New York, 1960.

R. H. Ferrell, *American Diplomacy, A History*. Norton, New York, 1959.

B. PART I

R. T. Berthoff, *British Immigrants in Industrial America*, 1790-1950. Harvard University Press, Cambridge, Massachusetts, 1953.

R. A. Billington, *The Historian's Contribution to Anglo-American Misunderstanding, Report of a Committee on National Bias in Anglo-American History Textbooks* (with the Collaboration of C. P. Hill *et al*). Hobbs, Dorman and Company, New York, 1966.

C. Erickson, *American Industry and the European Immigrant, 1860-1885*. Harvard University Press, Cambridge, Massachusetts, 1957.

G. H. Knoles, *The Jazz Age Revisited, British Criticism of American Civilisation During the 1920s*. Stanford University Press, 1955.

G. D. Lillibridge, *Beacon of Freedom, The Impact of American Democracy Upon Great Britain, 1830-1870*. University of Pennsylvania Press, Philadelphia, 1954.

H. Pelling, *America and the British Left, From Bright to Bevan*. New York University Press, 1957.

W. S. Shepperson, *British Emigration to North America, Projects and Opinions in the Early Victorian Period*. University of Minnesota Press, Minneapolis, 1957.

W. S. Shepperson, *The Promotion of British Emigration by Agents for American Lands, 1840-1860*. University of Nevada Press, Reno, 1954.

C. K. Yearley, *Britons in American Labor, A History of the Influence of the United Kingdom Immigrants on American Labor, 1820-1914*. Johns Hopkins Press, Baltimore, 1957.

C. PART II

K. Bourne, *Britain and the Balance of Power in North America, 1815-1908*. Longmans, London, 1967.

H. L. Coles, *The War of 1812*. University of Chicago Press, 1965.

R. Horseman, *The Causes of the War of 1812*. University of Pennsylvania Press, Philadelphia, 1962.

B. Perkins, *Castlereagh and Adams, England and the United States, 1812-1823*. University of California Press, Berkeley, 1964.

B. Perkins, *Prologue to War, England and the United States, 1805-1812*. University of California Press, Berkeley, 1961.

B. Perkins, *The First Rapprochement, England and the United States, 1795-1805*. Published for American Historical Association by University of Pennsylvania Press, Philadelphia, 1955.

F. Thistlethwaite, *The Anglo-American Connection in the Early Nineteenth Century*. University of Pennsylvania Press, Philadelphia, 1959.

P. C. T. White, *A Nation on Trial, America and the War of 1812*. John Wiley and Sons, New York, 1965.

D. PART III

W. D. Jones, *Lord Aberdeen and the Americans*. University of Georgia Press, Athens, 1958.

F. Merk, *The Monroe Doctrine and American Expansionism, 1843-1849* (with the Collaboration of L. B. Merk). Alfred A. Knopf, New York, 1966.

F. Merk, *The Oregon Question, Essays in Anglo-American Diplomacy and Politics*. Belknap Press of Harvard University Press, Cambridge, Massachusetts, 1967.

W. C. Spence, *British Investments and the American Mining Frontier, 1860-1901*. Cornell University Press, Ithaca, 1958.

E. PART IV

C. Bell, *The Debatable Alliance*. Oxford University Press, London, 1964.

A. E. Campbell, *Great Britain and the United States, 1895-1903*. Longmans, London, 1960.

C. S. Campbell, *Anglo-American Understanding, 1898-1903*. Johns Hopkins Press, Baltimore, 1957.

L. D. Epstein, *Britain, Uneasy Ally*. University of Chicago Press, 1954.

H. Feis, *Churchill, Roosevelt, Stalin, the War They Waged and the Peace They Sought*. Princeton University Press, 1957.

H. Finer, *Dulles Over Suez, The Theory and Practice of his Diplomacy*. Quadrangle Books, Chicago, 1964.

L. M. Gelber, *America in Britain's Place, The Leadership of the West and Anglo-American Unity*. Frederick A. Praeger, New York, 1961.

L. M. Gelber, *The Rise of Anglo-American Friendship*. Reprint, with a new preface by the Author. Archon Books, Hamden, 1966.

P. Goodhart, *Fifty Ships That Saved the World, The Foundation of the Anglo-American Alliance*. Doubleday and Company, Garden City, 1965.

E. McInnis, *The Atlantic Triangle and the Cold War*. University of Toronto Press, 1959.

R. G. Neale, *Great Britain and United States Expansion, 1898-1900*. Michigan State University Press, East Lansing, 1966.

H. Nicholas, *Britain and the U.S.A.* Johns Hopkins Press, Baltimore, 1963.

B. M. Russett, *Community and Contention, Britain and America in the Twentieth Century*. The M.I.T. Press, Cambridge, Massachusetts, 1963.

S. P. Tillman, *Anglo-American Relations at the Paris Peace Conference of 1919*. Princeton University Press, 1961.

ARTICLES

R. N. Berkes, "The Anglo-American Alliance." Current History, 1964.

M. F. Brightfield, "America and the Americans, 1840-1860, as Depicted in English Novels of the Period." American Literature, 1959.

D. W. Brogan, "Anglo-American Relations, Retrospect and Prospect." Yale Review, 1961.

A. E. Campbell, "Great Britain and the United States in the Far East, 1895-1903." The Historical Journal, 1958.

C. S. Campbell, "The Anglo-American Crisis in the Bering Sea, 1890-91" Mississippi Valley H.R., 1961.

G. Clarfield, "Postcript to the Jay Treaty, Timothy Pickering and Anglo-American Relations 1795-1797." William and Mary Quarterly, 1966.

R. C. Cramer, "British Magazines and the Oregon Question." Pacific H.R., 1963.

J. S. Galbraith, "British-American Competition in the Border Fur Trade of the 1820s." Minnesota Hist., 1959.

R. Horsman, "British Indian Policy in the Northwest, 1807-1812." Mississippi Valley H.R., 1958.

R. H. Jones, "Anglo-American Relations, 1861-1865, Reconsidered." Mid-America, 1963.

W. D. Jones, "The Origins and Passage of Lord Aberdeen's Act." Hispanic American H.R., 1962.

W. LaFeber, "The Background of Cleveland's Venezuelan Policy, A Reinterpretation." Am.H.R., 1961.

W. D. McIntyre, "Anglo-American Rivalry in the Pacific, the British Annexation of the Fiji Islands in 1874." Pacific H.R., 1960.

F. Merk, "The Oregon Question in the Webster-Ashburton Negotiations." Mississippi Valley H.R., 1956.

N. K. Risjord, "1812, Conservatives, War Hawks, and the Nation's Honor." William and Mary Quarterly, 1961.

C. R. Ritcheson, "Anglo-American Relations, 1783-1794." South Atlantic Quarterly, 1959.

M. M. Robson, "The Alabama Claims and the Anglo-American Reconciliation, 1865-71." Can. H.R., 1961.

L. M. Sears, "John Hay in London, 1897-1898." Ohio Historical Quarterly, 1956.

G. Seed, "British Reactions to American Imperialism Reflected in Journals of Opinion, 1889-1900." Political Science Quarterly, 1958.

F. Thistlethwaite, "The Atlantic Migration of the Pottery Industry." Economic History Review, 1958.

G. A. Wheeler, "Isolated Japan, Anglo-American Diplomatic Cooperation, 1927-1936." Pacific Historical Review, 1961.

J. G. Williamson, "The Long Swing, Comparisons and Interactions Between British and American Balance of Payments, 1820-1913." Journal of Economic History, 1962.

INDEX

The following abbreviations are used: GB, Great Britain; US, United States; A/A, Anglo-American. Analytical index headings will be found, under their titles, for Chapters 3, 4, 5, 6, 7 and 8. Bold type is used for chapter titles and pages on which there is primary treatment.

1005

Cultural Tie, The: most important of A/A bonds, 129-30; difficulty of evaluating, 130-3; 'materialism' of US, 133-4; education, 134; *Language*, 134-40; *Literary Relations*, 140-52; English cultural dominance in 19th century, 140-4; "Battle of the Quarterlies", 144-50; increase in American maturity, 150-2.
Cunard shipping line: 60.
Cunynghame, Colonel Arthur: 161.
Curtin, John: 790-1.
Curzon, George Nathaniel, Marquess: 736-7.
Cushing, Caleb: 552-3.
Cyane incident: 435.
Cyprus: 916, 917, 934.
Czechoslovakia: 776-7.

Daily Mail: 47, 110, 569.
Dallas, George Mifflin: **417**, 439, 442, 462-3.
Damaskinos, Archbishop: 864.
Daniels, Josephus: 704.
Danzig: 706.
Dardanelles, the: 867-8, 884.
Darlan, Admiral: 852-3.
Davies, Joseph E.: **882**.
Davis, J. W.: 638.
Davis, Jefferson: 463, 473, 480, 486, 494-5.
Davis, Norman: 744.
Dawes, General Gates: **731**, 749, 756, 765.
Day, W. R.: 574.
Dean Inge: 25.
Death, American attitude to: 170.
Debs, Eugene: 569.
Declaration of Independence, 1776: 72, 247.
Declaration of London: **624-5**, 660, 664.
Declaration of Paris, 1856: **466-8**, 622.
Declaratory Act: 242, 247.
De Gaulle, General: 850-5.
De Grasse, Admiral: 256.
Delagoa Bay: **593**.
Delane, J. T.: **493, 506**.
De Lesseps, Vicomte Ferdinand: 525, 596.
Democracy: Civil War for, 494; growth in GB, 494-9; in GB and US, 523-4; in GB pro-American, 525; GB fighting for in World War I, 663, 672-3; also US, 688; in World War II, 796.
Democratic Party: 101, 422, 428, 568-9, 590, 700, 717-8, 726, 763, 769, 802, 888-9, 893, 941.
Denmark: 661, 662, 798, 948.

Derby, 14th Earl of: 415, 436, 481.
Destroyer–Bases deal: 800, **802-6**.
Detroit: 272.
De Valera, Eamon: 719, 814.
Devaluation of Sterling, 1949: 945.
De Wet, C. R.: 594.
Dewey, Admiral: 556, 560, 577-8, 601, 606.
Dewey, John: 152.
Dewey, Thomas E.: 918, 919.
Diaz, Porfirio: 646-7.
Dicey, A. V.: 126, 243.
Dicey, Edward: 161.
Dickens, Charles: 17, 88, 138, 145, 151, 156, 159-60, 169, 506, 572.
Dickinson, John: 236.
Dictionary of American English: 136.
"Die Wacht an Rhein": 538.
Diederichs, Vice-Admiral von: 578.
Dilke, Sir Charles: 564
Dill, Sir John: 820, 838.
Diplomatic Relationship, The: *General Character*, 174; family nature, 177-9; US assumption of British role, 179-81; British consistency, 1783-1952, 181-2; American changes in policy, 182-3; *British Foreign Policy*, traditions established by 1783, 184-5; fundamental objectives, 185-91; isolationism, 191-4; consistency, 194-5; *American Foreign Policy*, general outline, 195-6; emancipation to 1814, 197-8; isolation in 19th century, 198-9; world power after 1900, 199-201; *A/A Similarities*, 202-7; summary, 207; book follows pattern of US policy, 207.
Disraeli, Benjamin, Earl of Beaconsfield: 193, 199, 391, 445, 497, 500, 503, 515-6, 522-3.
Dissent: 111, 486.
Divorce: 113.
Dollar Diplomacy: 628-9, 646.
Dollar Gap, the: 64, 66, 87-8, 795, 806-7, **904-15**, 935, 939, 943-7, 949-52.
Dollars, conversion of into Pounds: 44, note.
Domestic Manners of the Americans: 160.
Dooley, Mr.: 101-2, 550.
Dorchester, Lord: 284-5, 286.
Dos Passos, John R.: 127.
Douglas, Lewis: 886, 941.
Drake, Sir Francis: 426.
Drugs: 172.
Dulaney, Daniel: 235.
Dulles, John Foster: 941.
Dumba, Dr.: 673.

1014

INDEX

1024